BRAHMA-SŪTRA-BHĀṢYA

of

ŚRĪ ŚAṄKARĀCĀRYA

Translated by

SWAMI GAMBHIRANANDA

Foreword by

DR. T. M. P. MAHADEVAN

Advaita Ashrama
(Publication Department)
5 Dehi Entally Road
Kolkata 700 014

Published by
Swami Bodhasarananda
President, Advaita Ashrama
Mayavati, Champawat, Uttaranchal
from its Publication Department, Kolkata
Email: mail@advaitaashrama.org
Website: www.advaitaashrama.org

Nineth Impression, October 2006
2M2C

ISBN 81-7505-105-1

Printed in India at
Trio Process
Kolkata 700 014

PREFACE TO THE FIRST EDITION

Śrī Śaṅkarācārya's great commentary on the *Brahma-Sūtras* had been translated into English twice. But the non-availability of these translations or their high price raised the need for a fresh dependable translation at a moderate price. The present publication admirably meets this demand.

The translator, Swami Gambhirananda, has to his credit a number of publications of the Ramakrishna Order. His latest work, a translation of Śaṅkara's commentary on eight principal Upaniṣads, published by us five years back, was well received and has been in constant demand ever since. He completed the translation of the *Sūtra-Bhāṣya* three years ago, but owing to various difficulties we had to postpone its publication.

The present publication has its own special features. The translator has given the word-for-word meaning of each aphorism under its Sanskrit text, followed by a running translation, with additional words in brackets for clarification. In the translation of the commentary, the texts setting forth doubts, the opponent's views, objections on the latter, and the Vedāntin's answers have been shown separately, to facilitate easy comprehension. The translation is generally based on the *Ratnaprabhā*, though the *Nyāya-nirṇaya* and the *Bhāmatī* have been consulted occasionally. Sanskrit words have been printed with diacritical marks. In quoting from the Upaniṣads, the translator has used Swami Madhavananda's translation of the *Bṛhadāraṇyaka Upaniṣad* and his own translation of the *Eight Upaniṣads* referred to above. The other texts are translated afresh. He has also added notes to elucidate difficult passages. The contents have been divided topic-wise, and an index of *sūtras* in Sanskrit has been added

We have made every effort to make the publication an attractive one, and hope that it would be welcome to all lovers of Vedānta philosophy. A part of its sale proceeds will be spent for the public library run by us in Calcutta.

Swami Vivekananda's Birthday, — PUBLISHER
January 23, 1965

PREFACE TO THE SECOND EDITION

This work is being reprinted after seven years. Our thanks go to the eminent Vedantin Dr. T. M. P. Mahadevan, Director, Centre of Advanced Study in Philosophy, University of Madras for writing a valuable foreword.

January 26, 1972 PUBLISHER

FOREWORD

The three basic texts of Vedānta are the Upaniṣads, the Bhagavad-gītā, and the Brahma-sūtra. Together they are referred to as the *prāsthāna-traya*, triple canon of Vedānta. The Upaniṣads constitute the revealed texts (*Śruti-prasthāna*); they mark the summits of the Veda which is *Śruti* (the heard, the revealed). They are the pristine springs of Vedāntic metaphysics; Vedānta is the name given to them because they are the *end* (aim as well as concluding parts) of the Veda (Veda + *anta*). The Bhagavad-gītā comes next only to the Upaniṣads. It is given a status which is almost equal to that of the Upaniṣads. As embodying the teachings of Śrī Kṛṣṇa, and as constituting the cream of the Epic *Mahābhārata*, the Bhagavad-gītā occupies a unique place in the Vedāntic tradition. A popular verse compares the Upaniṣads to the cows, the Bhagavad-gītā to the milk, Śrī Kṛṣṇa to the milkman, Arjuna, the Pāṇḍava hero, to the calf, and the wise people to the partakers of the milk. Śrī Śaṅkara describes the Bhagavad-gītā as the quintessence of the teaching of the entire Veda (*samasta-vedārtha-sārasaṅgraha-bhūtam*). As this text forms a part of the *Mahābhārata* which is a *Smṛti* (the remembered, i.e. a secondary text based on the Veda), it is called *Smṛti-prasthāna*. The third of the canonical texts is the *Brahma-sūtra* which is regarded as *Nyāya-prasthāna*, because it sets forth the teachings of Vedānta in a logical order. This work is known by other names also: *Vedānta-sūtra*, since it is the aphoristic text on Vedānta; *Śārīraka-sūtra*, since it is concerned with the nature and destiny of the embodied soul; *Bhikṣu-sūtra*, since those who are most competent to study it are the *sannyāsins*; *Uttara-mīmāṁsā-sūtra*, since it is an inquiry into the final sections of the Veda.

The author of the Brahma-sūtra is Bādarāyaṇa whom Indian tradition identifies with Vyāsa, the arranger or compiler of the Veda. A verse in the *Bhāmatī* which is Vācaspati Miśra's commentary on Śrī Śaṅkara's commentary on the Brahma-sūtra, describes Vyāsa as the incarnation of Viṣṇu's cognitive energy

(*Jñānaśakti-avatāra*). In the Brahma-sūtra, Bādarāyaṇa-Vyāsa strings together the leading concepts of Vedānta in an ordered manner. The *Sūtra* is an exquisite garland made out of Upaniṣad-blossoms. It is divided into four chapters (*adhyāyas*); each chapter consists of four parts (*pādas*); each part has a number of sections (*adhikaraṇas*); and each section has one or more aphorisms (*sūtras*). According to Śaṅkara, the number of sections is 192. The total number of aphorisms is 555.

In the first chapter which is on 'harmony' (*Samanvaya*), Bādarāyaṇa teaches that the Vedāntic texts, taken as a whole, have for their purport Brahman, the non-dual Reality. Those passages of the Upaniṣads where express mention is made of Brahman or Ātman do not present any difficulty. But there are other passages in which other terms are used—terms which do not normaly mean Brahman-Ātman. In such cases, the meaning should be construed from the context For instance, *ākāśa* means 'ether'. But in a text where it is stated that all things come out of *ākāśa* and get resolved into it, the expression *ākāśa* obviously means Brahman, which is the ground of the universe (B.S. I. i. 22). Similarly, in the Chāndogya text, "Which is that deity? He said: *Prāṇa*" (I. xi. 4-5), the term *prāṇa* means not the vital air, but Brahman, because all beings are said to merge in It (B.S. I. i. 23). The same is true in regard to other terms such as *manas* or *manomaya*. In the Chāndogya text where this term occurs, there is the commencing statement "All this, indeed, is Brahman" (III. xiv. 1-2), and also the *manomaya* is taught as the object of meditation. This can only be Brahman, and not the individual mind or soul (B.S. I. ii. 1). In all such cases, what determines the meaning of a term is not the ordinary usage, but the context, (*Prakaraṇāc-ca* : B.S. I. ii. 10), and the construed meaning of the related texts (*Vākyānvayāt* : B.S. I. iv. 19). Thus Bādarāyaṇa shows that the Vedāntic texts harmoniously teach Brahman as the plenary reality, the world-ground which is of the nature of existence-consciousness-bliss, which is the supreme object of meditation, and which is the final end to be realized.

In the second chapter which is entitled 'non-conflict' (*Avirodha*), Bādarāyaṇa discusses the objections that may be raised against the metaphysics of Vedānta. The principal objector is the follower of the Sāṁkhya system. Great attention is paid to the Sāṁkhya because it comes very close to Vedānta. If the Sāṁkhya view is shown to be untenable, it follows that the other views which are more remote are unacceptable. For instance, it is declared (B.S. II. i. 3) that the view of the Yoga of Patañjali stands refuted when it has been shown that the Sāṁkhya view is unsound. Taking its stand on logic, the Sāṁkhya argues that Pradhāna or Prakṛti is the cause of evolution. Employing the same logic, the Vedāntin shows that Pradhāna cannot account for the world-evolution. There is observed design in the world. This would be inexplicable if Pradhāna were to be the cause. How can the inert Pradhāna have a sense of design, or even the will to create? Also, why and how it begins to evolve, and why and how it ceases from evolving, it is not possible to say; for, since Pradhāna is not-intelligent, there should be either perpetual evolution or dissolution. And, any intelligent purpose is out of place; there would be only a blind process or movement without an end (B.S. II. ii. 1-6). The Vaiśeṣika system traces the world to primary atoms, posits *adṛṣṭa* as the unseen power responsible for bringing the atoms together or for separating them. This view fares even worse than the Sāṁkhya theory. Whether as located in the atoms or in the souls, the unseen potency cannot move the atoms because it is unintelligent even as the atoms are. There are other attendant defects in the system which cannot be remedied. The most serious of these difficulties is that the Vaiśeṣika believes that from the partless atoms, the things of the world with parts arise (B.S. II. ii. 11-17). There are realistic as well as idealistic schools in Buddhism. All things are aggregates, according to Buddhism: there is nothing like substantiality. For the realistic schools, there are two kinds of aggregates, the internal and the external. But, consistent with the other Buddhist doctrine of momentariness, how aggregation can take place at all passes one's understanding. There is a processor of successive moments: but how are the moments related? What connection is there between what precedes and what succeeds? These questions remain unsolved (B.S. II. ii. 18 ff). For the Buddhist idealist, there is no extra-mental reality; ideas are things; what is real is a series of momentary ideas. This view also is untenable. The appearance of ideas is sought to be explained as brought about by residual impression. But, how can there be residual impression if there are no external things. So, says Bādarāyaṇa, the Buddhist view is totally unintelligible (*Sarvathā-anupapattiḥ* : B.S. II. ii. 32). The Jaina philosophy seeks to combine opposites such as permanence and change, identity and difference. The obvious criticism of such a view would be: how could one and the same thing possess contradictory attributes? There are other doctrines, too, of Jainism which are unacceptable, e.g. that the soul has variable size. And so, the Jaina position has to be rejected (B.S. II. ii. 33 ff).

According to Vedānta, as we have seen, Brahman is the world-ground, the sole and whole cause of the world. Some theistic schools do not subscribe to this view. They hold that God is only the efficient cause who fashions the world out of extraneous matter which is co-eternal with him. This view is not sound, because God would then become limited and finite (B.S. II. ii. 37); and a limited God is no God at all. The world appears from Brahman, stays in it, and gets resolved into it. This does not involve any effort on the part of Brahman. The so-called creative activity is like sport (B.S. II. i. 33). The milk-turning-into-curds example (B.S. II. i. 24) is useful for realizing that there is no need for an external agency for world-appearance, that creation is not production *de novo*. A better analogy would be to compare the non-evolution and evolution of the world to the folded and spread out states, respectively, of a piece of cloth (B.S. II. i. 19). The truth is that the world is not separate from Brahman; it has no independent existence. The effect is non-different from the cause. In other words, the effect is appearance, the cause alone is real (B.S. II. i. 14).

What is the status of the individual soul? Is it a product of Brahman? The view of the Pāñcarātra school that the soul is produced from God is rejected by Bādarāyaṇa. The soul which is eternal cannot be what is originated (B.S. II. ii. 42). The soul is to Brahman as reflection is to prototype (B.S. II. iii. 50). It is the soul that is the subject of transmigration, the agent of action, the enjoyer of the fruit of action, the being that strives for release and eventually gains it.

In the third chapter of the Brahma-sūtra, Bādarāyaṇa discusses the means to release, *sādhana.* The Cārvāka view that there is no soul apart from the body is unsound. If consciousness is an attribute of the body, why is it that a dead body is not conscious (B.S. III. iii. 53-54). So, one must admit that the soul is non-material, non-physical, which does not perish with the decease of the body. After physical death, the soul may go along either the path of the gods (*devayāna*) or the path of the fathers (*pitṛyāna*), carrying along with it the subtle parts of the elements and the sense-organs, etc., that had formed the ingredients of its constitution. If the soul had performed the appropriate meditations, it goes along the path of the gods and reaches Brahma-loka. If it had done the necessary sacrificial rites, it goes along the path of the fathers. There is also a third place mentioned in the *Śāstras*: the souls that are not fit to pursue either of the two paths referred to attain the status of tiny, continually revolving creatures which are born and which die (B.S. III. i. 17). The souls that are bound for the other two paths also except in the case of those which have realized *Saguṇa* (Qualified) Brahman, have to return to the world of mortals, as soon as their merit is exhausted. Similarly, the souls which go to the nether worlds have to come back after their evil deeds have been accounted for. The texts describe the process by which all this happens. They give details regarding the re-entry of the soul into the mother's womb and its re-embodiment. The various states through which the embodied soul passes are also explained: states such as waking, dream, and deep sleep. The migration of the soul goes on until it gets released through the realization of the non-dual Brahman.

Brahman in itself is devoid of attributes, devoid of any form (*Arūpavad-eva hi tat-pradhānatvāt*: B.S. III. ii. 14). In some passages of the Upaniṣads, it is true, attributes are ascribed to Brahman. But this ascription is for the sake of meditation (*upāsanā*). Just as light which has no form appears to be endowed with different forms because of the objects which it illumines, Brahman which has no attributes appears as if endowed with attributes on account of the limiting adjuncts (B.S. III. ii. 15). Brahman is the non-dual pure consciousness. It appears as if many, even as the one sun gets reflected diversely in the different vessels containing water (B.S. III. ii. 18). When the adventitious conditions fall off, it will be realized that Brahman is the non-dual Absolute. In itself it is unconditioned and unsullied. In order to convey this truth, the Upaniṣads adopt the negative mode of instruction (B.S. III. ii. 22-23): Brahman is "not thus; not thus" (Bṛ. II. iii. 6).

The soul is non-different from Brahman. Because of nescience, it imagines that it is different. When nescience is removed through knowledge, the soul realizes the truth of non-difference (B.S. III. ii. 26). Scripture also denies difference (*Pratiṣedhāc-ca*: B.S. III. ii. 30). And it prescribes meditation known as *vidyās* for enabling the soul to realize its non-difference from Brahman. The meditations, although many, have one and the same purpose (B.S. III. iii. 1). What the nature and content of a particular meditation are should be determined carefully with reference to the context in which it is taught. In two different Upaniṣads, for instance, the name may be the same, but the meditations may be different. In some other cases, the names may be different, but the meditation may be the same. In regard to some meditations, the details may be given in bits in different places. The *sādhaka* must piece them all together in order to be guided in his practice. And it is not necessary that one should practise all the *Vidyās*. Any one of them will be enough for gaining the goal (B.S. III. iii. 59). The *vidyās* are meditations on the *Saguṇa* Brahman. Therefore, the one who practises them goes, after death, along the path of the gods, and eventually secures release (B.S. III. iii. 29). It is only the knower of *Nirguṇa* (Non-qualified) Brahman that does not go along any eschatological path; he attains Brahman here.

Sannyāsa is a recognized *āśrama*; it is prescribed even as the other three are. The *sannyāsins* have no need to perform ritual; they are eligible to pursue the path of knowledge. They have no other obligation such as tending the sacred fires (B.S. III. iv. 25). The sacrificial rites are intended only for those who have studied the Veda and are instructed in the ritual techniques, and who have not yet gained eligibility for knowledge. Works, when performed with some end in view, bring in their respective results. These results may pertain to this world and to the next. But, when duties are done without any motive for fruits, they serve to purify the mind and make it fit for pursuing the path of knowledge. The seeker after knowledge must endeavour to possess such virtues as calmness, equanimity, self-control, etc. (B.S. III. iv. 27). These virtues are necessary for turning the mind inward in search of the true Self. Endowed with the cardinal virtues, one follows the path of knowledge and gains the goal which is release, *mokṣa* (B.S. III. iv. 1). *Mokṣa* is not a *post mortem* state. It is the eternal nature of the Self, and is realized the very moment the veil of ignorance is lifted. So, what is required is the removal of the obstacle that bars the way (B.S. III. iv. 51). In *mokṣa* itself there are no differences of grade or kind. What is referred to as the state of release is nothing but Brahman (B.S. III. iv. 52).

The last chapter of the Brahma-sūtra is on 'the fruit', *Phala*. The one who meditates on *Saguṇa* Brahman, as was mentioned earlier, goes along the path of the gods, after physical death, carrying along with him the subtle body which lasts till release is gained (B.S. IV. ii. 8). The soul of the one who has realized *Saguṇa* Brahman reaches the region of the heart, and then departs through the *suṣumnā-nāḍī* (B.S. IV. ii. 17). Leaving the body, the soul travels along the rays of the sun, and goes to Brahma-loka (B.S. IV. ii. 18). During this journey, various deities take charge of the soul, and conduct it along the path of the gods. After reaching Brahma-loka, the soul gets identified with *Saguṇa* Brahman. And, when that *loka* is destroyed at the end of the *kalpa*, the soul realizes *Nirguṇa* Brahman, which is release (B.S. IV. iii. 10). As we have already seen, the one who follows the path of knowledge gains release in this very life. His *prāṇas* do not depart; they get resolved even here (B.S. IV. ii. 12). On Brahman-realization, one is freed from all sin (B.S. IV. i. 13). The one who is released in this life is called a *Jīvan-mukta*. His body continues till the *Prārabdha* lasts. *Prārabdha* is the *karma* which has begun to fructify and is responsible for the present body. That the body of the *Jīvan-mukta* continues till *Prārabdha* lasts is stated only from the standpoint of those who are yet unreleased. The truth is that for the *mukta* there is no body at all.

The knower of Brahman realizes the absolute non-difference from Brahman (*Avibhāgaḥ* : B.S. IV. ii. 16). When one has gained release, there is no more involvement in *saṁsāra*, no more return to the cycle of birth and death (*Anāvṛttiḥ* : B.S. IV. iv. 22).

We have now had a conspectus of the teaching of the Brahma-sūtra in the light of Śaṅkara's commentary thereon. Śaṅkara's *bhāṣya* is the earliest extant commentary on Bādarāyaṇa's text. It is celebrated for its lucidity and depth (*prasanna-gaṁbhīra*). There must have been commentaries before Śaṅkara; but none of them has come down to us. Several commentators came after Śaṅkara. Among them are Bhāskara, Yādavaprakāśa, Rāmānuja, Keśava, Nīlakaṇṭha, Madhva, Baladeva, Vallabha, and Vijñana Bhikṣu. They differ from Śaṅkara on certain moot points. But all of them have been influenced, knowingly or unknowingly, by Śaṅkara's commentary which has served as *the* model. In the Śaṅkara tradition itself there have appeared several commentarial works. On Śaṅkara's *bhāṣya,* Vācaspati wrote the *Bhāmatī,* which was followed by the *Kalpataru,* and the *Parimala.* Similarly, Padmapāda wrote the *Pañcapādikā* on Śaṅkara's *bhāṣya*; and this was followed by the *Vivaraṇa,* and the *Tattvadīpana.* These are but a few of the annotations and glosses on Śaṅkara's great *bhāṣya.*

Padmapāda, one of the direct disciples of Śaṅkara offers this obeisance to his master and the *bhāṣya*:

yadvaktramānasasaraḥ-pratilabdhajanma
bhāṣyāravindamakarandarasaṁ pibanti,
pratyāśamunmukha-vinītavineyabhṛṅgā
tān bhāṣyavittakagurūn praṇato'smi mūrdhnā.

"I bow my head before Śrī Śaṅkara, the preceptor of the humble disciples who are renowned for their knowledge of the *bhāṣya* and who drink the nectar flowing from the *bhāṣya*-lotus which owes its origin to the *mānasa*-lake of Śrī Śaṅkara's mouth and who, like the bees, are eagerly lifting up their faces from all quarters."

Appayya Dīkṣita sings the praise of the great teaching thus:

adhigatabhidā pūrvācāryānupetya sahasradhā
saridiva mahībhedān samprāpya śauripadodgatā,
jayati bhagavatpāda-śrīmanmukhāmbuja-nirgatā
jananaharaṇī sūktiḥ brahmādvayaikaparāyaṇā.

"The great teaching which issues from the lotus-face of the Bhagavatpāda, which has the non-dual Brahman as its primary import, which destroys phenomenal existence and which, while admitting of several interpretations by the (numerous) ancient preceptors, exists in all its grandeur, in the same way as the river Ganga which, issuing from the foot of Viṣṇu, assumes different courses on reaching different lands."

There are a few English translations available of the Brahma-sūtra with Śaṅkara's commentary. The earliest to appear was the one by George Thibaut. The merits of the present translation have been pointed out in the Publisher's Preface to the first edition. That a second edition has been called for itself shows how useful Swami Gambhiranandaji's translation has been. This is a faithful and helpful rendering of a work which is of perennial and profound interest. The second edition will be welcomed, like the first, by the students of Vedānta in the English-speaking world.

T. M. P. Mahadevan

Director, Centre of Advanced Study in Philosophy, University of Madras

January 5, 1972

CONTENTS

Preface iii
Foreword v
List of Abbreviations xiii
Key to Transliteration and Pronunciation

CHAPTER I

SAMANVAYA—RECONCILIATION THROUGH PROPER INTERPRETATION

SECTION I

Preamble 1

Topic

1. Deliberation on Brahman 6
2. Origin etc. of the Universe 13
3. Scripture as Source of Knowledge of Brahman 18
4. Upaniṣads Reveal Brahman 20
5. The First Cause Possessed of Consciousness 45
6. The Blissful One 61
7. The Being Inside 78
8. Space 82
9. Prāṇa 85
10. Light 88
11. Pratardana 98

SECTION II

Topic

1. The Entity Known Everywhere .. 108
2. The Eater 118
3. The Two in the Cavity of the Heart .. 120
4. The Person in the Eye 126
5. The Internal Ruler 133
6. The One That Is Unseen etc. .. 138
7. Vaiśvānara 146

Section III

Topic
1. The Abode of Heaven, Earth, etc. 159
2. Bhūman (Infinite, Plenitude) .. 167
3. Immutable 174
4. The Object of Seeing 177
5. Dahara (The Small Space) 180
6. Acting in Accordance 198
7. The Measured One 202
8. Gods 204
9. Pseudo-Śūdra 229
10. Vibration 234
11. Light as Declared in the Upaniṣad .. 236
12. Space Is Brahman, Being Different from Name and Form 238
13. Sleep and Death 239

Section IV

Topic
1. The Inferred Entity 243
2. The Bowl 259
3. Statement of Number 263
4. Causality 270
5. Bālāki 276
6. Correlation of Passages 282
7. Brahman as Material Cause 291
8. Explanation of Everything 296

CHAPTER II

AVIRODHA—NON-CONTRADICTION

Section I

Topic
1. Conflict with Smṛti 299

Topic

2. Refutation of Yoga 305
3. Difference in Nature 307
4. Non-acceptance by the Wise .. 323
5. Brahman Becoming an Experiencer .. 324
6. Origin 326
7. Non-performance of Good 346
8. Creation without Materials 350
9. Wholesale Transformation 353
10. Possession of All Powers 358
11. Need of Motive 360
12. Partiality and Cruelty 362
13. Propriety of All the Characteristics .. 366

Section II

Topic

1. Sāṁkhya View Refuted 367
2. Vaiśeṣika Objection Refuted .. 383
3. Atoms Not the Cause of Universe .. 387
4. Refutation of Buddhist Realists .. 402
5. Buddhist Idealism Refuted 416
6. Jaina View Refuted 426
7. God Is Not a Mere Superintendent .. 433
8. Bhāgavata View Refuted 439

Section III

Topic

1. Origin of Space 444
2. Origin of Air 459
3. Origin of Brahman Denied 460
4. Origin of Fire 461
5. Origin of Water 464
6. Origin of Earth 464
7. Creation from God's Deliberation .. 466
8. Reverse Order of Dissolution .. 467
9. The Origin of Mind and Intellect .. 468

Topic
10. Birth and Death 470
11. Origin of the Soul 472
12. Eternally Conscious Soul 476
13. Soul's Dimensions 478
14. Soul as Agent 494
15. The Soul under Two Conditions 497
16. Soul's Agentship Derived from God .. 503
17. Relation of Soul and God 506

SECTION IV

Topic
1. Origin of the Prāṇas 521
2. Number of Prāṇas 527
3. Atomic Prāṇas 533
4. Chief Prāṇa: Its Creation 533
5. Nature of Prāṇa 535
6. Prāṇa Is Atomic 540
7. Presiding Deities 541
8. Prāṇa and Prāṇas 544
9. Creation of Gross Objects 547

CHAPTER III

SĀDHANĀ—SPIRITUAL PRACTICE

SECTION I

Introduction 553

Topic
1. Departure from the Body 554
2. Return of the Souls 565
3. Fate of Evil-doers 574
4. Similarity with Space etc. during Descent 580
5. Intervening Period of Descent .. 582
6. The Souls in Plants and Thereafter .. 583

Section II

Topic
1. Dream State 588
2. The Soul in Deep Sleep 597
3. The Same Soul Returns from Sleep .. 603
4. Soul in Swoon 606
5. The Nature of Brahman 608
6. Unconditioned Brahman and Soul .. 623
7. Brahman One without a Second .. 633
8. Fruits of Action 640

Section III

Topic
1. Sameness of Meditation 644
2. Combination of Traits 651
3. Difference of Meditations 652
4. Specification of Om 657
5. Sameness of the Meditation on Prāṇa .. 660
6. Combination and Non-combination of Attributes of Brahman 662
7. Puruṣa as the Highest in Kaṭha .. 665
8. The Supreme Self in Aitareya .. 667
9. Ācamana and Meditation on Prāṇa .. 673
10. Same Meditation in the Same Branch .. 677
11. No Combination in Meditation on Satya-Brahman 679
12. Attributes of Brahman in Rāṇayanīya Not to be Combined Elsewhere 682
13. Puruṣa-Vidyā in Chāndogya and Taittirīya 684
14. Non-combination of Disparate Traits .. 687
15. Rejection and Reception of Merit .. 690
16. Discarding Virtue and Vice at Death .. 695
17. Paths of Those Who Know Or Do Not Know the Qualified Brahman 697
18. The Path of Gods Is for All Worshippers of Qualified Brahman 699
19. People with a Mission 701

Topic

20. Conceptions of the Immutable .. 705
21. Same Conception in Muṇḍaka and Kaṭha 707
22. The Inmost Self in Bṛhadāraṇyaka .. 709
23. Reciprocity of Conceptions 711
24. Satya-Brahman in Bṛhadāraṇyaka .. 713
25. Combination of Traits in Bṛhadāraṇyaka and Chāndogya 715
26. Agnihotra to Prāṇa .. 717
27. Meditations Connected with Rites Are Not Obligatory 721
28. Meditations on Prāṇa and Vāyu .. 725
29. Fires in Agni-Rahasya Not Parts of Sacrifice 730
30. The Self Distinct from Body .. 739
31. Meditations Connected with Accessories of Rites 743
32. Meditation on Vaiśvānara as a Whole .. 746
33. When Meditations Differ 749
34. Alternative Meditations 751
35. Meditations Yielding Worldly Results .. 753
36. Meditations Based on Subsidiaries .. 754

Section IV

Topic

1. Knowledge not a Subsidiary of Rites .. 758
2. Sannyāsa Prescribed by Scriptures .. 770
3. Injunctions for Meditation Not Eulogistic 778
4. Upaniṣadic Stories 780
5. Sannyāsins Free from Rituals .. 782
6. Rituals etc. Needed for Knowledge .. 782
7. Restrictions about Food 786
8. Duties of Orders of Life should be Fulfilled 789
9. Knowledge for People outside Orders .. 793
10. Defection from Monasticism .. 795
11. Expiation for Transgression of Celibacy .. 796
12. They are to be Excommunicated .. 799
13. Meditations Connected with Rites .. 799
14. Injunction about Meditativeness .. 801

Topic
15. The Childlike State 806
16. Time of Fruition of Knowledge .. 807
17. Liberation is Uniform Everywhere .. 809

CHAPTER IV

PHALA—RESULT

Section I

Topic
1. Repetition of Meditations etc. .. 812
2. Identity of the Self with Brahman .. 818
3. No Self-identity with Symbols .. 821
4. Superimposition of the Higher on the Lower 823
5. Subordinate parts of Rites As the Sun etc. 826
6. Meditation in a Sitting Posture .. 830
7. No Restriction of Place 832
8. Meditation till Death 833
9. Knowledge Destroys all Results of Actions 834
10. No Remnant of Virtue Even .. 837
11. Past Accumulated Results are Destroyed 839
12. Agnihotra etc. 841
13. Rites Unaccompanied by Meditation .. 843
14. Experience of the Active Merit and Demerit 845

Section II

Topic
1. At Death the Organs Merge in Mind .. 847
2. Mind Merges in Prāṇa 849
3. Prāṇa Merges into the Soul 851
4. Departure of the Enlightened and the Unenlightened 854
5. Relative Merger of Fire etc. .. 856
6. No Departure for a Knower of Brahman .. 859
7. The Organs of the Knower Merge in Brahman 862

Topic

8. Absolute Absorption of the Constituents .. 863
9. Departure of one who knows the Qualified Brahman 864
10. The Soul follows the Rays of the Sun .. 866
11. Soul's Journey during the Sun's Southern Course 868

SECTION III

Topic

1. Only One Path to the World of Brahman .. 870
2. The Departing Soul Reaches Air after Year 872
3. The Soul proceeds from Lightning to Varuṇa 874
4. Guiding Deities 875
5. The Path Leads to the Conditioned Brahman 878
6. Worship with and without Symbols .. 892

SECTION IV

Topic

1. Nature of Freedom 895
2. Liberated Soul Inseparable from Brahman 897
3. Characteristics of the Liberated Soul .. 899
4. Fulfilment of Desire through Will .. 901
5. Body after Reaching Brahma-loka .. 903
6. Entry into many Bodies 905
7. Acquisition of Divine Powers .. 907

LIST OF ABBREVIATIONS

Ai.	..	..	Aitareya Upaniṣad
Ai. Ā.	..	..	Aitareya Āraṇyaka
Ai. Br.	..	..	Aitareya Brāhmaṇa
Āp.	..	..	Āpastamba Dharma-Sūtra
B.S.	..	..	Brahma-Sūtra
Bṛ.	..	..	Bṛhadāraṇyaka Upaniṣad
Ch.	..	..	Chāndogya Upaniṣad
Īś.	..	..	Īśā (vāsya) Upaniṣad
Jā.	..	..	Jābāla Upaniṣad
Jai. Sū.	..	..	Jaimini-Sūtra
Ka.	..	..	Kaṭha Upaniṣad
Kau.	..	..	Kauṣītaki Upaniṣad
Ke.	..	..	Kena Upaniṣad
Mā.	..	..	Māṇḍūkya Upaniṣad
Mbh.	..	..	Mahābhārata
Mu.	..	..	Muṇḍaka Upaniṣad
N.S.	..	..	Nyāya-Sūtra
Pā. Sū.	..	..	Pāṇini-Sūtra
Pr.	..	..	Praśna Upaniṣad
Ṛ.V.	..	..	Ṛg-Veda
Ś.B.	..	..	Śatapatha Brāhmaṇa
Śv.	..	..	Śvetāśvatara Upaniṣad
Tai.	..	..	Taittirīya Upaniṣad
Tai. Ā.	..	..	Taittirīya Āraṇyaka
Tai. Br.	..	..	Taittirīya Brāhmaṇa
Tai. S.	..	..	Taittirīya Saṁhitā
Vai. Sū.	..	..	Vaiśeṣika-Sūtra

KEY TO TRANSLITERATION AND PRONUNCIATION

		Sounds like
अ	a	o in *son*
आ	ā	a in *master*
इ	i	i in *if*
ई	i	ee in *feel*
उ	u	u in *full*
ऊ	ū	oo in *boot*
ऋ	ṛ	somewhat between r and ri
ए	e	a in *evade*
ए	ai	y in *my*
ओ	o	o in *oh*
औ	au	ow in *now*
क	k	k
ख	kh	ckh in *blockhead*
ग	g	g (hard)
घ	gh	gh in *log-hut*
ङ	ṅ	ng
च	c	ch (not k)
छ	ch	chh in *catch him*
ज	j	j
झ	jh	dgeh in *hedgehog*
ञ	ñ	n (somewhat)
ट	ṭ	t
ठ	ṭh	th in *ant-hill*

		Sounds like
ड	ḍ	d
ढ	ḍh	dh in *godhood*
ण	ṇ	n in *under*
त	t	French t
थ	th	th in *thumb*
द	d	th in *then*
ध	dh	theh in *breathe here*
न	n	n
प	p	p
फ	ph	ph in *loop-hole*
ब	b	b
भ	bh	bh in *abhor*
म	m	m
य	y	y
र	r	r
ल	l	l
व	v	v in *avert*
श	ś	sh
ष	ṣ	sh in *show*
स	s	s
ह	h	h
ं	ṁ	ng
:	h	half h

CHAPTER I

SAMANVAYA—RECONCILIATION THROUGH PROPER INTERPRETATION

SECTION I

Preamble: It being an established fact that the object and the subject,[1] that are fit to be the contents of the concepts "you" and "we" (respectively), and are by nature as contradictory as light and darkness, cannot logically have any identity, it follows that their attributes can have it still less.[2] Accordingly, the superimposition of the object, referable through the concept "you", and its attributes on the subject that is conscious by nature[3] and is referable through the concept "we" (should be impossible), and contrariwise the superimposition of the subject and its attributes on the object should be impossible. Nevertheless, owing to an absence of discrimination between these attributes, as also between substances, which are absolutely disparate, there continues a natural human behaviour based on self-identification in the form of "I am this"[4] or "This is mine".[5] This behaviour has for its material cause an unreal nescience and man resorts to it by mixing up reality with unreality as a result of superimposing[6] the things themselves or their attributes on each other.

[1] Non-Self or matter, and Self or Consciousness, respectively.

[2] The attribute of matter is insentience, and of the Self, Consciousness. These attributes cannot have any relation of identity or non-difference.

[3] Which witnesses the intellect etc.

[4] For instance, "I am this body", where the body as such is superimposed on the Self, conceived of as "I". Or "This body is I", where a relationship with the Self is superimposed on the body.

[5] For instance, "This is my body", where the attributes of the body are superimposed on the Self. In the first case (previous f. n.) the separateness of the body and Self is forgotten; in the latter they are kept apart, but the attributes get mixed up.

[6] The phrases "by mixing up" and "as a result of superimposing" mean

If it be asked, "What is it that is called superimposition?"—the answer is: It is an awareness, similar in nature to memory, that arises on a different (foreign) basis as a result of some past experience.[7] With regard to this, some say that it consists in the superimposition of the attributes of one thing on another.[8] But others assert that wherever a superimposition on anything occurs, there is in evidence only a confusion arising from the absence of discrimination between them.[9] Others say that the superimposi-

the same thing. The implied sequence points out the chain constituted by superimposition, its impression on the mind, and subsequent superimposition, which succeed one another eternally like the seed and its sprout.

[7] Or the interpretation is: "It is somewhat like a recollected thing emerging from the impression of some past experience." The two interpretations are from the points of view of subjective and objective awareness.

[8] Four alternative theories follow successively. Of these the first two —*Anyathākhyāti* and *Ātmakhyāti*—are comprised within the present view. According to *Anyathākhyāti*, subscribed to by the Nyāya-Vaiśeṣika schools, we have at first a vague awareness of "this" with regard to the rope in front. As the mind is not satisfied with this alone, it craves for a distinct perception. But some defect in the cognizer, his instruments of perception, or environment debars this, at the same time that the similarity of the rope and the snake calls up the memory of the latter. This memory conjures up the visual perception of the snake, and so the "this" is apprehended as "This is a snake". According to some Buddhists who hold the *Anyathākhyāti* theory of error, the "this" of the externally perceivable rope is superimposed on the mentally present snake to form the erroneous judgment, "This is a snake". Their psychological explanation is this: It may so happen that owing to the past impression inhering in consciousness, there may be a simultaneous flow of the consciousness of the external "this" and the internal snake, in which case the two get mixed up. The Buddhists call this *Ātmakhyāti*.

[9] This view of *Akhyāti* is held by the followers of Prabhākara, who assert that there is no such thing as erroneous knowledge, for a contrary supposition will paralyse human action by raising doubt at every turn as to whether a particular cognition is valid or not. In a case of so-called error, we do not really have a single cognition, but two, though we err by failing to recognize the difference between the two. On the one side we have the knowledge of the "this" in its absoluteness, occurring in the judgment "This is nacre". The nacre fails to come within the range of cognition owing to some defect in the factors concerned and some similarity between nacre and silver, because of which latter fact, the

tion of anything on any other substratum consists in fancying some opposite attributes on that very basis.[10] From every point of view, however, there is no difference as regards the appearance of one thing as something else. And in accord with this, we find in common experience that the nacre appears as silver, and a single moon appears as two.

Opponent: How, again, can there be any superimposition of any object or its attributes on the (inmost) Self that is opposed to the non-Self[11] and is never an object (of the senses and mind)? For everybody superimposes something else on what is perceived by him in front;[12] and you assert that the Self is opposed to the non-Self and is not referable (objectively) by the concept "you".

The answer (of the *Vedāntin*) is: The Self is not absolutely beyond apprehension, because It is apprehended as the content of the concept "I"; and because the Self, opposed to the non-Self, is well known in the world[13] as an immediately perceived (i.e. self-revealing) entity. Nor is there any rule that something has to be superimposed on something else that is directly perceived through the senses; for boys superimpose the ideas of surface (i.e. concavity) and dirt on space (i.e. sky) that is not an object of sense-perception. Hence there is nothing impossible in superimposing the non-Self on the Self that is opposed to it.

This superimposition, that is of this nature, is considered by the learned to be *avidyā*, nescience.[14] And the ascertainment of

contact between the eyes and the nacre calls up to memory the silver seen in a shop. But the silver is remembered not in association with its time and locality, but simply as silver. So the two cognitions of "this" and silver synchronize, at the same time that their difference is not apprehended. This non-perception of difference prompts certain reactions in the perceiver.

[10] This view of *Asatkhyāti* is held by the Buddhist Nihilist, according to whom, the non-existing silver appears on the non-existing nacre.

[11] *Pratyak-ātmā* is interpreted by *Ratnaprabhā* as that (Existence-Knowledge-Bliss Brahman) which stands opposed to non-existence, insentience, and sorrow (i.e. sorrowful ego etc.).

[12] As an object, directly perceived through the senses.

[13] The Self is known as "I" to all people, learned or ignorant, and nobody has any doubt as to this.

[14] Since it is a product of nescience and is sublated by *vidyā* (illumina-

the nature of the real entity by separating the superimposed thing from it is called *vidyā* (illumination). This being so,[15] whenever there is a superimposition of one thing on another, the locus is not affected in any way either by the merits or demerits of the thing superimposed. All forms of worldly and Vedic behaviour that are connected with valid means of knowledge and objects of knowledge start by taking for granted this mutual superimposition of the Self and non-Self, known as nescience; and so do all the scriptures dealing with injunction, prohibition, or emancipation.

Opponent: How, again, can the means of valid knowledge, such as direct perception as well as the scriptures, have as their locus a cognizer who is subject to nescience?[16]

The (*Vedāntin's*) answer is: Since a man without self-identification with the body, mind, senses, etc., cannot become a cognizer, and as such, the means of knowledge cannot function for him; since perception and other activities (of a man) are not possible without accepting the senses etc. (as his own); since the senses cannot function without (the body as) a basis; since nobody engages in any activity with a body that has not the idea of the Self superimposed on it; since the unrelated Self cannot become a cognizer unless there are all these (mutual superimposition of the Self and the body and their attributes on each other); and since the means of knowledge cannot function unless there is a cognizership; therefore it follows that the means of knowledge, such as direct perception as well as the scriptures, must have a man as their locus who is subject to nescience.

Moreover, there is no difference (of the learned) from the animals (in regard to empirical behaviour). Just as animals and

tion). The commentary refers to superimposition, which is a product of Māyā, rather than to Māyā itself, because the latter is a source of evil in its derived forms and not in its unevolved states, e.g. sleep, whereas superimposition is directly so.

[15] Since superimposition is a product of nescience.

[16] If the Self, with the superimposition of "I" on It, be subject to ignorance, then the instruments of knowledge and scriptures, depending on It, become vitiated and lose their validity.

others turn away from sound etc. when these appear to be unfavourable after their ears etc. come in contact with them, and they move towards these when they are favourable; and just as by noticing a man approaching them with a raised stick, they begin to run away thinking, "This one wants to hurt me", and they approach another carrying green grass in his hands, similarly even the wise are repelled by the presence of strong, uproarious people with evil looks and upraised swords, and are attracted by men of opposite nature. Therefore the behaviour of men with regard to the means and objects of knowledge is similar to that of animals. And it is a familiar fact that the animals use their means of perception etc. without discrimination (between the body and the Self). From this fact of similarity, the conclusion can be drawn that so far as empirical behaviour is concerned, the use of the means of perception by the wise is similar to that of lower animals, (it being a result of superimposition). Of course, it is a fact that a man acting intelligently does not acquire the competence for scriptural duties unless he has a knowledge of the relationship of his soul with the next world. Still (a knowledge of) the absolute Reality, that is the Self, is not a prerequisite for such a competence; for It (i.e. Reality) has no relevance here, and It is opposed to such competence,[17] inasmuch as It is beyond hunger and thirst, free from such differentiation as Brāhmaṇa, Kṣatriya, etc., and is not subject to birth and death. And the scriptures, which are operative before the dawn of the real knowledge of the Self, cannot transgress the limits of their dependence on people groping in ignorance. To illustrate the point: Such scriptural injunction as "A Brāhmaṇa shall perform a sacrifice" can become effective only by taking for granted various kinds of superimposition of caste, stage of life, age, condition, etc. And we said that superimposition means the cognition of something as some other thing. Thus in accordance as one's wife, children, or other relatives are hale and hearty with all their limbs intact,

[17] For empirical activities, a vague idea about one's soul is quite enough, and no knowledge of the absolute Self is needed. On the contrary, when one knows the absolute Self, one loses all kinds of self-identification, and therefore actions become impossible.

or as they suffer from the loss of those limbs, one thinks, "I myself am hale and hearty" or "I myself am injured"; thus one superimposes external characteristics on the Self. Similarly one superimposes the characteristics of the body when one has such ideas as "I am fat", "I am thin", "I am fair", "I stay", "I go", or "I scale". So also one superimposes the attributes of the senses and organs when one thinks, "I am dumb", "I have lost one eye", "I am a eunuch", "I am deaf", or "I am blind". Similarly one superimposes the attributes of the internal organ, such as desire, will, doubt, perseverance, etc. In the same way, one first superimposes the internal organ, possessed of the idea of ego, on the Self, the witness of all the manifestations of that organ; then by an opposite process, one superimposes on the internal organ etc. that Self which is opposed to the non-Self and which is the witness of everything. Thus occurs this superimposition that has neither beginning nor end but flows on eternally, that appears as the manifested universe and its apprehension, that conjures up agentship and enjoyership, and that is perceived by all persons. In order to eradicate this source of evil and in order to acquire the knowledge of the unity of the Self, is begun a discussion (after the study) of all the Upaniṣads. We shall show in this discussion about the nature of the embodied soul, that this is the purport of all the Upaniṣads.

Topic 1 : Deliberation on Brahman

This is the first aphorism in the scripture which deals with the ascertainment of the meaning of the Upaniṣads and which is sought to be explained by us.

अथातो ब्रह्मजिज्ञासा ॥ १ ॥

अथ Thereafter अत: hence ब्रह्म-जिज्ञासा a deliberation on Brahman.

1. *Hence (is to be undertaken) thereafter a deliberation on Brahman.*

The word *atha* (thereafter) is used in the sense of "sequence", and not "commencement"; for *brahma-jijñāsā* is not a thing that can be commenced.[18] And the meaning "auspiciousness" cannot enter syntactically into the purport of a sentence. Besides, the word *atha*, even when used in some other sense, serves the purpose of auspiciousness from the very fact of its being heard.[19] If it implies the anticipation of something coming later by something broached earlier, then this does not differ in effect from causality[20] (i.e. sequence).

The meaning of "sequence" being taken for granted, one has to mention that earlier thing which is a prerequisite for a deliberation on Brahman, just as much as a deliberation on religious rites (or deeds) depends invariably on an earlier study of the Vedas. The mere fact of the study of the Vedas cannot be the prerequisite sought for here, since this is a common factor (in both the cases of deliberation on Brahman and religious rites).

Opponent : A previous understanding of the religious rites can be accepted here as the special factor (leading to the deliberation on Brahman).

Vedāntin : Not so, since it is logically possible for a man who has studied the Upaniṣads to undertake a deliberation on Brahman even without deliberation on the religious rites. And no sequence is meant here between these two like the procedural arrangement in the matter of taking up the heart etc., where an order is sought to be enjoined;[21] for there is no proof either

[18] *Brahma-jijñāsā* literally means a wish to know Brahman. A wish follows spontaneously from the knowledge that something is achievable by effort, and that when achieved, it will lead to desirable results. Thus a wish cannot be begun like a pot, for instance. So by implication the phrase means "a deliberation on (the nature of) Brahman"; and to complete the sentence, we have to supply "is to be undertaken". According to this interpretation also, *atha* cannot mean commencement, that idea being implied in the verb itself that has to be supplied (f. n. 26).

[19] Like the auspicious sound of a conch.

[20] *Pūrva-prakṛta-apekṣā* may mean the broaching of a later topic by presupposing something broached earlier, as for instance in enumeration. But this meaning is inadmissible, since nothing is broached before this aphorism. Or it may mean the anticipation of a later factor by the former. But in that case we come to causality.

[21] The word *avadāna* means the cutting off of a limb of the sacrificial

establishing any relation between these two like that between the whole and its parts, or showing any derivative competence (i.e. competence in one thing derived from the competence in something else).[22] Moreover, the deliberations on virtuous deeds[23] and Brahman differ as regards results and objects of inquiry. Virtuous deeds have secular prosperity as their results; and these depend on the performance (of some rites etc.). But the knowledge of Brahman has emancipation as its result, and it does not depend on any other performance. Besides, a virtuous deed that has to be inquired into is a thing still to be accomplished, and it is not present at the time of its acquaintance (from scriptures etc.), for it has to depend on human effort for its emergence. On the other hand, the Brahman to be inquired into here is a pre-existing entity; and It is not dependent on human effort, since It is eternally present. Besides, there is a difference in the mental reactions aroused by the Vedic texts (in both the cases). The Vedic texts imparting knowledge about virtuous deeds make their purport clear to people while engaging their attention to the deeds enjoined,[24] whereas the

animal for offering as an oblation. Annotators interpret it as "taking up". The text is: *Hṛdayasya agre avadyati atha jihvāyāḥ atha vakṣasaḥ*. Now these limbs cannot be taken up simultaneously; and so an order has to be followed, which is made clear by the text by using the word *atha* in the sense of "then".

[22] *Śeṣin* is the whole (or principle) and *śeṣa* a part (or subsidiary). The two deliberations are not related that way; nor is there any derivative competence, as when a man becomes competent to perform the Soma sacrifice by virtue of his having performed the Darśa-Pūrṇamāsa sacrifice. The performer of the sacrifice is the same person where either of these two relations is in evidence. But as both these are ruled out here, the persons undertaking the two kinds of deliberation can well be different.

[23] "A deed is held to be *dharma* that has no association with undesirable consequence even from the standpoint of its result, it being the cause of bliss alone" (*Śloka-vārtika*, I. i. 2, 268-269).

[24] An injunction gives rise to its meaning in the mind of a hearer, which leads the hearer to think first, "This text wants me to act in a certain way", and then, "I should act in a certain way in accordance with this injunction", the second thought being prompted by a desire for the result (e.g. heaven). Then he learns about the form of the rites leading to the result, as also their instruments, accessories, subsidiary acts, etc. Thus

Vedic texts speaking of Brahman give rise only to Its knowledge. Since knowledge is not a product of injunctions, a man is not impelled to know, just as for instance, he is not in his acquisition of knowledge through a contact of the eye with some object.[25]

Therefore something has to be pointed out as the prerequisite after which it is taught that the deliberation on Brahman can proceed.

The answer is: They are discrimination between the eternal and the non-eternal; dispassion for the enjoyment of the fruits (of work) here and hereafter; a perfection of such practices as control of the mind, control of the senses and organs, etc.; and a hankering for liberation. Granted the existence of these, Brahman can be deliberated on or known even before or after an inquiry into virtuous deeds, but not otherwise. Therefore by the word *atha* is enjoined the succession to a perfection of the practices mentioned here.

The word *ataḥ* (hence) implies causality. Since in such texts as, "To illustrate the point, just as the enjoyable things earned through work get exhausted in this world, so also do the enjoyable things in the other world that are earned through merit" (Ch. VIII. i. 6), the Vedas reveal that the Agnihotra sacrifice etc., which are the means for the achievement of higher things, have evanescent results; and since in such texts as, "The knower of Brahman attains the Highest" (Tai. II. i), the Vedas show in a similar way that from the realization of Brahman follows the highest human objective (viz liberation), therefore one should undertake a deliberation on Brahman after a perfection of the practices mentioned earlier.

Brahma-jijñāsā means a deliberation on Brahman.[26] And Brahman is that which will be defined hereafter as "That from

from the two kinds of thought follows the knowledge about the virtuous deeds, and then action.

[25] Just as we see through our eyes, so also we know Brahman through such Vedic texts as, "This Self is Brahman" (Mā. 2). Vedic texts are thus valid means of knowledge just like direct perception.

[26] The literal meaning is "wish to know Brahman"; but by implication, the meaning is, "for getting a direct knowledge of Brahman one should undertake a deliberation on the Upaniṣadic texts". "Wish" figuratively

which the universe has its birth etc." (B. S. I. i. 2). Hence there should be no misinterpretation of the word in the sense of the Brāhmaṇa caste etc. The sixth case-ending occurring after Brahman (when the compound is split up) is used in the accusative sense, and not in the sense of mere relation; for a wish to know presupposes a thing wanted to be known,[27] and no other thing to be inquired into has been indicated.

Opponent: Even if the sixth case-ending be taken in the sense of relation, it does not rule out the fact of Brahman's being the object of deliberation, for a general relation includes all special relations (e.g. of an object to its verb).

Vedāntin: Even then it involves a useless effort to give up Brahman as a direct object and fancy It to be so through a general relationship.

Opponent: Not useless, because it is sought to imply thereby that a deliberation on everything associated with Brahman is kept in view.

Vedāntin: Not so, because when the chief factor is taken in hand, the subsidiaries present themselves by implication.[28] Since Brahman is the object most desired to be comprehended through knowledge,[29] It must be the chief factor. When that chief factor is taken up as the object of deliberation, all other factors, without an inquiry into which the deliberation on Brahman remains unaccomplished, become implied *pari passu*; and hence

means "the deliberation resulting from the wish"; "knowledge" means "the special kind of direct knowledge"; and the verb "is to be undertaken" has to be supplied.

[27] Both the verbs "wish (or want)" and "know" are transitive and must have objects. Wish has knowledge for its object, and knowledge has Brahman. A man must first know something in order that he may wish for it so that knowledge becomes both a cause and an effect of wish. The difficulty is obviated by saying that the causal knowledge is an unripe and indirect apprehension, whereas the resulting knowledge is a mature one culminating in the revelation of Brahman (f. n. 30).

[28] *Arthāpatti*, a means of valid knowledge, as for instance, "Plump Devadatta does not eat in the day-time", where by implication we know that he eats at night.

[29] An object is "that which is the most desired (in a sentence) by the subject of the verb".

they need not be mentioned separately as the import of this aphorism. This is just like saying, "There goes the king", where from that very statement it follows that the king is going with his retinue. And this has to be accepted in order that it may accord with the Vedic texts. The Vedic text starting with, "That from which these beings take birth, (that by which they are sustained after birth, and that towards which they proceed and into which they get merged)", directly reveals Brahman as an object (of deliberation) by saying, "Wish to know that, that is Brahman" (Tai. III. i). And that Upaniṣadic text will be in line with the aphorism if the sixth case-ending is interpreted in the accusative sense. Accordingly, the sixth case-ending is used in the accusative sense.

Jijñāsā means "a wish to know". And the knowledge culminating in direct realization[30] (of Brahman) is the object of "wish" implied by the suffix *san* (in *jijñāsā*); for a desire aims at its result, the desire being that Brahman be realized (i.e. uncovered) by that knowledge[31] which is a valid means of apprehension. And the realization of Brahman is the highest human objective; for it completely eradicates all such evils as ignorance etc. that constitute the seed of transmigration. Therefore Brahman should be deliberated on.

Opponent : Is that Brahman, again, familiar or unfamiliar? If It be familiar, It need not be deliberated on for the sake of knowledge. Again, if It be unfamiliar, It cannot be deliberated on.

The answer (of the *Vedāntin*) is: As to that, Brahman does exist as a well-known entity—eternal, pure, intelligent, free by nature, and all-knowing and all-powerful. For from the very derivation of the word Brahman, the ideas of eternality, purity,

[30] An apparent knowledge of Brahman, that one gathers from the scriptures etc. and entertains as a common-sense point of view, is the cause of the deliberation on Brahman; and the resulting realization of the form "I am Brahman" is the effect or aim of that deliberation. Thus mediate and immediate knowledge can be the cause and effect of the deliberation.

[31] An unanalysable mental modification that expresses itself as a direct awareness of the form, "I am Brahman"

etc. become obvious, this being in accord with the root *bṛṁh*.[32] Besides, the existence of Brahman is well known from the fact of Its being the Self of all; for everyone feels that his Self exists, and he never feels, "I do not exist". Had there been no general recognition of the existence of the Self, everyone would have felt, "I do not exist". And that Self is Brahman.[33]

Opponent: If Brahman be well known in the world as the Self, then It being already known, there arises the difficulty again that It is not to be deliberated on.

Vedantin: No, for there is a conflict about Its distinctive nature. Ordinary people as well as the materialists of the Lokāyata school recognize the body alone to be the Self possessed of sentience. Others hold that the mind is the Self. Some say that it is merely momentary consciousness. Others say that it is a void. Still others believe that there is a soul, separate from the body, which transmigrates and is the agent (of work) and the experiencer (of results). Some say that the soul is a mere experiencer[34] and not an agent. Some say that there is a God who is different from this soul and is all-knowing and all-powerful; others say that He is the Self of the experiencing individual. Thus there are many who follow opposite views by depending on logic, texts and their semblances. If one accepts any one of these views without examination, one is liable to be deflected from emancipation and come to grief. Therefore[35]

[32] The root *bṛṁh* means growth, and the suffix *man*, added to it, signifies an absence of limitation (in expanse). So Brahman derivatively means that which is absolutely the greatest. And eternality etc. follow as a matter of course from this limitlessness.

[33] As is known from the text, "This Self is Brahman" (Bṛ. II. v. 19).

[34] *Bhoga* and *Bhoktā* are generally translated as enjoyment and enjoyer. But the terms are meant to include both enjoyment and suffering of happiness and sorrow; hence experience and experiencer are nearer the mark.

[35] The deliberation based on the Upaniṣads can be commenced (a) since from the fact of the universality of bondage it follows that there can be such a result as freedom, as also such a subject-matter as the unity of the individual Self and Brahman; (b) since the subject-matter of this book is not included in a deliberation on *Dharma*; (c) since a class of specially qualified persons can exist; (d) and since the general familiarity with Brahman supplies a subject-matter etc. for the book.

starting with the presentation of a deliberation on Brahman, here is commenced an ascertainment of the meaning of the texts of the Upaniṣads with the help of reasoning not opposed to the Upaniṣads themselves, for the purpose of leading to emancipation (through knowledge).

Topic 2 : Origin etc. of the universe

Opponent : It has been said that Brahman is to be deliberated on. What, again, can be the definition of that Brahman?[36]

Vedāntin : Hence the venerable aphorist says:

जन्माद्यस्य यतः ॥ २ ॥

(That) यतः from which (are derived) जन्मादि birth etc. अस्य of this (universe).

2. That (is Brahman) from which (are derived) the birth etc. of this (universe).

Janmādi can be split up thus: That of which *janma*, birth, is the *ādi*, first. In the phrase *janmādi* we have that class of *Bahuvrihi* compound where the subject presented is apprehended along with its attributes.[37] The compound implies birth, continuance, and dissolution. The mention of birth first is in accord with the statements in the Vedic texts and the nature of things. The Vedic assertion is this: "That from which these beings take birth" (Tai. III. i) where origin, continuance, and dissolution are revealed in an order. As for the nature of things, a thing that has come to exist through birth can have continuance and disintegration. By the word *idam* (this), occurring as a constituent of the word *asya* (of this), is indicated the entity (viz the universe) that is presented immediately by perception etc. And the sixth case-ending (i.e. "of") in it is meant for indicating the relation of that entity with birth etc. By the

[36] Brahman has no definition and hence cannot be deliberated on.

[37] In "*pītāmbaraṁ paśya*—see the man with a yellow cloth", the man is known along with his yellow cloth. But in "*dṛṣṭasamudram ānaya*—bring the man who saw the sea", the man alone can be brought, but not the qualifying clause.

word *yataḥ* (from which) is indicated a cause; and the clause "that is Brahman" has to be added at the end to complete the sentence. (So the meaning of the whole aphorism is): That ominiscient and omnipotent source must be Brahman from which occur the birth, continuance, and dissolution of this universe that is manifested through name and form, that is associated with diverse agents and experiences, that provides the support for actions and results, having well-regulated space, time, and causation, and that defies all thoughts about the real nature of its creation.

Birth, continuance, and dissolution only are mentioned here, since the other modifications that things are heir to are included in them.[38] Had the six modifications listed by Yāska in the words, "It originates, exists, grows," etc. been accepted (here), it might lead to the doubt that the origin, existence, and destruction of the universe from the primary source (Brahman) are not referred to, these modifications being possible only during the continuance of the universe.[39] In order that this doubt may not arise, the origin that takes place from Brahman, and the continuance and merger that occur in That Itself are referred to.

Apart from God, possessed of the qualifications already mentioned, the universe, as described, cannot possibly be thought of as having its origin etc. from any other factor, e.g. Pradhāna (primordial Nature) which is insentient, or from atoms, or nonexistence, or some soul under worldly conditions (viz Hiraṇyagarbha). Nor can it originate spontaneously; for in this universe, people (desirous of products) have to depend on specific space, time, and causation.[40] Those who stand by God as the cause

[38] The other modifications are: Growth, transformation, and decay. Growth and transformation are really forms of new birth (or evolution), while decay is a form of death.

[39] Yāska's *Nirukta* mentions six kinds of modification—birth, continuance, growth, transformation, decay, death. The aphorism, however, enumerates the three mentioned in the Upaniṣads, so as not to get involved in any other philosophy.

[40] The naturalists cannot argue that a thing originates by itself, for that is a fallacious use of the term "originate". A thing cannot originate causelessly, for that contradicts experience.

(e.g. the Naiyāyikas) rely on this very inference alone[41] for establishing the existence etc.[42] of God as distinguished from a transmigrating soul.

Opponent: Is not this very inference presented here by the aphorism starting with, "That from which" etc.?

Vedāntin: No; for the aphorisms are meant for stringing together the flowers of the sentences of the Upaniṣads; for it is precisely the sentences of the Upaniṣads that are referred to and discussed in these aphorisms. The realization of Brahman results from the firm conviction[43] arising from the deliberation on the (Vedic) texts and their meanings,[44] but not from other means of knowledge like inference etc. When, however, there are Upaniṣadic texts speaking of the origin etc. of the world, then even inference, not running counter to the Upaniṣadic texts, is not ruled out in so far as it is adopted as a valid means of knowledge reinforcing these texts; for the Upaniṣads themselves accept reasoning as a help. For instance, there is the text, "(The Self is) to be heard of, to be reflected on"[45] (Bṛ. II. iv. 5). And the text, "A man, well-informed and intelligent, can reach the country of the Gāndhāras; similarly in this world, a man who has a teacher attains knowledge"[46] (Ch. VI. xiv. 2), shows that the Vedic texts rely on the intelligence of man.

So far as the deliberation on Brahman is concerned, the direct

[41] The inference presented in the earlier sentence—"Apart from ... any other factor."

[42] Omniscience, omnipotence, etc.

[43] Ascertainment of the true meaning and the possibility of the thing to be known.

[44] When properly considered, the Upaniṣadic texts are seen to point to Brahman.

[45] Its possibility is to be established through reasoning.

[46] A man, led away from the Gāndhāra country by robbers, with his eyes covered, is left in a forest, bound hands and feet. Some passerby then takes pity on him, frees him, and tells him of the road to Gāndhāra. If he is intelligent enough (*paṇḍita*) to understand that instruction, and if he can use his deliberative faculty to guard against false steps, he can reach Gāndhāra. Similar is the case of a man under ignorance in this world that is like a forest. A teacher tells him, "You are Brahman." If he is intelligent enough to understand that and uses his reasoning faculty adequately, he reaches Brahman.

texts, indicatory marks, etc. are not the sole means of the valid knowledge of Brahman, as they are when religious duties are deliberated on. But in the former case, the Vedic texts, personal experience,[47] etc. are the valid means as far as possible; for the knowledge of Brahman culminates in experience,[48] and it relates to an existing entity. Since in the case of rites etc. that have to be undertaken, there is no dependence on direct experience (the rite etc. being still in the womb of futurity), the direct texts etc. alone are authoritative here. Besides, an act to be performed becomes what it is through human effort. Worldly or Vedic activities may or may not be undertaken, or they may be dealt with otherwise; as for instance, a man can walk, ride, proceed otherwise, or need not move at all. Similarly (there are the passages): "In the sacrifice (with Soma juice) called Atirātra, the vessel (containing the Soma juice) called Ṣoḍaśī is taken up" and "In the Atirātra sacrifice the Ṣoḍaśī is not taken up" (Tai.S. VI. vi. 2.4). "(In the Agnihotra sacrifice) the oblation is offered before sunrise", and "The oblation is offered after sunrise". These injunctions and prohibitions are meaningful here (in a context of rites), as also are the alternatives, general rules, and exceptions. But a thing cannot be judged diversely to be of such a kind and not to be of such a kind, to be existent and non-existent (simultaneously). Options depend on human notions, whereas the valid knowledge of the true nature of a thing is not dependent on human notions. On what does it depend then? It is dependent on the thing itself. For an awareness of the form, "This is a stump, or a man, or something else", with regard to the same stump cannot be valid knowledge. In such a case the awareness of the form, "This is a man or something else" is erroneous, but

[47] The meaning of a particular passage has to be determined with the help of direct assertion, indicatory mark, syntactical connection, context, position, and designation. The above six means, as also reasoning, etc., determine the meanings of Vedic passages about Brahman, and through the individual competence of each test, they give rise to a particular mental state that is of the nature of the knowledge of Brahman. That state again destroys ignorance and culminates in the revelation of Brahman.

[48] The mental modification having the form, "I am Brahman", culminates in the revelation of the real nature of Brahman.

"This is a stump to be sure" is valid knowledge; for it corresponds to the thing itself. Thus the validity of the knowledge of an existing thing is determined by the thing itself. This being the position, the knowledge of Brahman also must be determined by the thing itself, since it is concerned with an existing reality.

Opponent: If Brahman be an existing reality, It must be the object of other means of valid knowledge, so that any deliberation on the Upaniṣadic texts (for the knowledge of Brahman) becomes meaningless.

Vedāntin: Not so; for Brahman's relation with anything cannot be grasped, It being outside the range of sense-perception. The senses naturally comprehend objects, and not Brahman. Had Brahman been an object of sense-perception, knowledge would have been of the form, "This product is related to (i.e. produced by) Brahman."[49] Again, even when the mere effect (i.e. universe) is cognized, one cannot ascertain whether it is related to Brahman (as its cause) or to something else. Therefore the aphorism, "That from which" etc., is not meant to present an inference.

For what is it then?

For presenting an Upaniṣadic text.

Which, again, is that Upaniṣadic text that is sought to be referred to by the aphorism?

(It is this): Starting with, "Bhṛgu, the well-known son of Varuṇa approached his father Varuṇa with the request, 'O revered sir, teach me Brahman'," the Taittirīya Upaniṣad states, "Seek to know that from which all these beings take birth, that by which they live after being born, that towards which they proceed and into which they merge; that is Brahman" (Tai. III. i). And the answer settling the question is: "From Bliss certainly all these beings originate; they live by Bliss after being born; and towards Bliss they proceed, and into Bliss they

[49] The inference of the opponent may be either, "Whatever is an effect is a product of Brahman" or "Whatever is an effect has a cause", from either of which he may try to arrive at the existence of Brahman. But no such general idea, as implied in the first statement, is possible with regard to Brahman, since Brahman is imperceptible.

get merged" (Tai. III. vi). Other texts[50] too of the same class are to be quoted (in this connection), which speak of a cause that is by nature eternal, pure, and free, and intrinsically omniscient.

Topic 3 : Scripture as Source of Knowledge of Brahman

In the course of showing that Brahman is the source of the universe, it was implied in passing that Brahman is omniscient. By way of confirming this, the aphorist says:

शास्त्रयोनित्वात् ॥ ३ ॥

शास्त्र-योनित्वात् Because of being the source of the scriptures.

3. (Brahman is omniscient) because of (Its) being the source of the scriptures.

Brahman is the *yoni* (i.e. the material and efficient cause) of great scriptures (*śāstras*) like the Ṛg-Veda etc. which are supplemented by other scriptures[51] that are themselves sources (of various kinds) of knowledge, which reveal all things like a lamp, and which are almost omniscient.[52] For scriptures like the Ṛg-Veda, possessed of all good qualities as they are, cannot possibly emerge from any source other than an all-knowing One. For it is a well-recognized fact in the world that the person from whom

[50] For instance, Mu. I. i. 10, Bṛ. III. ix. 28, etc.

The first aphorism presents the deliberation on Brahman as a task to be undertaken by a competent person; and for him the second aphorism presents the definition of Brahman. That this is the purpose of the aphorism becomes obvious from the order followed in the Taittirīya Upaniṣad, where Bhṛgu comes as an inquirer and to him Brahman is presented as the cause of the origin etc. of the universe. This is a *taṭastha* definition of Brahman, where the characteristics mentioned are not an intrinsic part of the thing defined, though they distinguish it from others for the time being. The *svarūpa* definition is presented in such sentences as, "Brahman is Truth, Knowledge, Infinite" (Tai. II. i), where the words Truth etc., though generally meaning empirical truth etc., imply here by a figure of speech a transcendental entity which is Truth Itself.

[51] Works on mythology, logic, discussion on religious and social duties, *śikṣā, kalpa, vyākaraṇa, nirukta, chandaḥ, jyotis.*

[52] Not fully omniscient, being within Māyā.

the scriptures dealing with multifarious subjects emerge is more well informed than the scriptures themselves; for instance, grammar etc., emanating from Pāṇini and others, represent merely a part of the subject known to them. It goes without saying that, that great Being has absolute omniscience and omnipotence, since from Him emerge the Ṛg-Veda etc.—divided into many branches and constituting the source of classification into gods, animals, men, castes, stages of life, etc., and the source of all kinds of knowledge—and since the emergence of these Vedas from that Being occurs as though in sport and without any effort like the breath of a man, as is stated in the Vedic text, "Those that are called the Ṛg-Veda, (Yajur-Veda, etc.) are but the exhalation of this great Being (Bṛ. II. iv. 10).

Or the aphorism means:

शास्त्र-योनित्वात् Since the scriptures are Its valid means (of knowledge).

3. (Brahman is not known from any other source), since the scriptures are the valid means of Its knowledge.

The scriptures, viz the Ṛg-Veda etc., just enumerated, are the valid means of knowing (*yoni*) the real nature of this Brahman. The idea implied is that Brahman is known as the source of birth etc. of this universe from the scriptures alone that are a valid means of knowledge. The scriptural text, "That from which all these beings take birth" etc. (Tai. III. i) was quoted under the previous aphorism.

Opponent: What need is there again of this aphorism, since by quoting such scriptural texts under the previous aphorism itself, it was shown that Brahman is to be known from the scriptures?

The answer (of the *Vedāntin*) is: Since the scriptures were not explicitly alluded to by the previous aphorism, it might be suspected that an inference alone had been presented (as the means of knowing Brahman) by the previous aphorism, "That from which" etc. (B. S. I. i. 1). In order to eliminate that doubt, this aphorism says, "(Brahman is not known through any other means), since the scriptures are the valid means of Its knowledge."

Topic 4: Upaniṣads Reveal Brahman

Opponent: How is it again asserted that Brahman has the scriptures alone as Its valid means of knowledge? For in (the aphorism of Jaimini), "Since the Vedas are meant to enjoin action, those portions of them which have not this purpose in view are useless" (I. ii. 1), it has been shown that the scriptures are concerned with action. Therefore the Upaniṣads are useless, as they do not enjoin action. Or they may form part of an injunction about action by way of revealing the agent, the deity, etc. of that action; or they may be meant for enjoining some other kind of action such as meditation (on gods and others). For there is no possibility of the Upaniṣads being the valid means of knowing a thing already in existence, since an existing thing is known through direct perception etc.[53] And just because no human objective is gained through the revelation of something that is neither acceptable nor rejectable, it has been said, "Since the corroborative statements (*Arthavāda*)[54] can be combined with some injunction to form a single idea, they become a valid means of knowledge (of virtuous deeds) by way of eulogizing the (duties enjoined by the) injunctions" (Jai. Sū. I. ii. 7). This has been stated thus, so that such sentences as "He wept"(Tai.S.

[53] The validity of a means of knowledge consists in its revealing something that is not known through other means and is not sublated later. If a thing known through perception etc. is again revealed by the Upaniṣads, the latter lose their validity. "A thing already in existence" means some positive thing which is an established reality, and as such, it has no connection with any fresh effort for production. An action is needed for producing something, but not after it is already there.

[54] This is of three kinds—(a) *Guṇavāda*, attributive corroborative statement, e.g. "The sun becomes the sacrificial stake" Ta B. II. i. 5.2), where the statement contradicts experience and is taken to mean "a stake shining like the sun"; (b) *Anuvāda*, reassertive corroborative statement, e.g. "Fire is the remedy for cold", which is a mere restatement of a known fact; (c) *Bhūtārthavāda*, factual corroborative statement, e.g. "Indra raised his thunder-bolt against Vṛtra", which fact is known from the Vedas only. *Arthavāda* is also classified as expressing eulogy, condemnation, heroic performance, and past incident.

II. v. 11) may not become meaningless, but may serve some purpose by way of eulogizing. As for the *mantras* such as "*Iṣe tvā*" (T. S. I. i. 1) etc. they have been shown to be connected with action by virtue of their speaking about some duty or its means. Nowhere is a Vedic sentence seen to serve any purpose without some connection with an injunction, nor can it reasonably do so. Moreover, an injunction is not possible with regard to something already accomplished, for an injunction is concerned with action. Therefore the Upaniṣads become supplementary to injunctions by revealing the nature of the agents and the deities needed in some action.[55] Or if this be not accepted out of fear of ignoring the context,[56] still the Upaniṣads may relate to the meditations expressed by their own texts. Hence Brahman is not (validly) presented (as an object of knowledge) by the scriptures.

This contingency having arisen, the *answer* is being given:

तत्तु समन्वयात् ॥ ४ ॥

तु But तत् that Brahman समन्वयात् being the object of full import.

4. But that Brahman (is known from the Upaniṣads), (It) being the object of their fullest import.

The word *tu* (but) is meant to rule out the opponent's point of view. *Tat* (That) means Brahman, which is omniscient and omnipotent, which is the cause of the origin, existence, and dissolution of the universe, and which is known as such from the Upaniṣads alone.

How?

Samanvayāt, because of being the object of their fullest import; for in all the Upaniṣads the texts become fully reconciled when they are accepted as establishing this very fact in their fullest import. (As for instance): "O amiable

[55] This is the view of Kumārila Bhaṭṭa.

[56] The portion of the Vedas, presenting the unity of the Self and Brahman, is different from the portion presenting rites etc.

one, this universe, before its creation, was but Existence, one without a second" (Ch. VI. ii. 1), "Before creation this universe was but the Self that is one" (Ai. I. i. 1), "That Brahman is without prior or posterior, without interior or exterior (i.e. homogeneous and without a second). This Self, the perceiver of everything, is Brahman" (Bṛ. II. v. 19), "All that is in front is Brahman, the immortal" (Mu, II. ii. 11), etc. Besides, when the words in the Upaniṣadic sentences become fully ascertained as but revealing the nature of Brahman, it is not proper to fancy some other meaning; for that will result in rejecting something established by the Vedas and accepting some other thing not intended by them. And it cannot be held that those words have for their ultimate purpose only a delineation of the nature of the agent (viz the performer of the rites), for there are such Vedic texts as "(But when to the knower of Brahman everything has become the Self) then . . . what should one see and through what?" (Bṛ. II. iv. 14), which deny action, instrument, and result. Nor is Brahman an object of perception, even though It stands as an established, positive entity, for the unity of the Self and Brahman, as stated in "That thou art" (Ch. VI. viii. 7), cannot be known otherwise than from the scriptural texts. As for the objection that instruction about Brahman is useless inasmuch as It is neither acceptable nor rejectable, that is nothing damaging; for the attainment of the highest human goal (of freedom) becomes an accomplished fact only when the total eradication of all sorrows comes about as a result of the realization of the Self as Brahman beyond acceptance and rejection. As for the presentation of the deities etc. for the sake of meditation contained in the Upaniṣadic texts themselves, that raises no difficulty.[57] (The absolute) Brahman cannot even in that way become a factor in any injunction about meditation; for when

[57] For the purification and concentration of mind, for emancipation by stages, and for the attainment of the respective results, the Upaniṣads speak in some contexts of such deities as Prāṇa, qualified Brahman, as well as of the subsidiary factors and the results of such meditations. But that does not mean that the Upaniṣads are concerned with these alone. As a matter of fact, their main concern is to reveal the unity of the Self and Brahman.

unity is achieved, it is but reasonable that all ideas of duality, involving action, accessories, etc., should be eradicated, because (the absolute) Brahman is neither acceptable nor rejectable. Not that the perception of duality can crop up again (from past impressions) even after being (wholly) uprooted by the realization of non-duality. If that were a possibility, then alone could it be shown that Brahman becomes involved in any injunction about meditation. Although Vedic texts are not seen elsewhere to have any validity without being construed with injunction, still in the face of the fact that the knowledge of Brahman does culminate in its result (viz emancipation), the validity of the scriptures dealing with the means of that emancipation cannot be set aside.[58] Nor is the validity of the Upaniṣads to be established by inference, in which case alone it would have been necessary to cite analogous cases.[59] Therefore it is proved that Brahman is known from the scriptures alone.

Others (e.g. Vṛttikāra) stand up here in *opposition* (and say): Though Brahman is known from scriptures alone, still It is presented as a factor involved in the injunction about meditation, just like the sacrificial stake and the Āhavanīya fire, which though unknown in ordinary life, are presented by the scriptures as factors in injunctions. How can this be so?[60] (This can be so) because the scriptures have in view either persuasion for or dissuasion from activities, as is declared by those who know the import of the scriptures: "The obvious purport of the Vedas is to generate knowledge about duties" (*Śabara-Bhāṣya*, I. i. 1); "By injunction is meant a sentence impelling one to duty (ibid. I. i. 2); "An instruction (i.e. an injunctive sentence like 'He shall sacrifice') is that which imparts the knowledge of these (virtuous deeds)" (Jai. Sū. I. i. 5); "There (in the Vedas) words standing for established realities should be uttered with

[58] So far as their own purport, viz Brahman, is concerned.

[59] In illustration of a universal proposition from which the inference follows. The Vedas, perception, inference, etc. are valid means of knowledge, each within its own domain; none of these need depend on another for proving its validity within that domain.

[60] How can Brahman become a factor in an injunction about meditation?

verbal terminations etc." (ibid. I. i. 25); "Since the Vedas are meant for enjoining duties, all (the sentences) that do not have that purport are meaningless" (ibid. I. ii. 1). Therefore the scriptures become meaningful by either persuading a person to act for a particular object or dissuading him from action for some other; other sentences (e.g. *Arthavāda*) have their usefulness as forming parts of these. And since the Upaniṣadic texts have a similarity with those Vedic texts, they should be purposeful in that way alone. It being granted that the Upaniṣadic sentences have injunctions in view, it stands to reason that just as such means as the Agnihotra sacrifice are enjoined for one who desires heaven, so also the knowledge of Brahman is enjoined for one who hankers after immortality.

Objection: Has it not been pointed out that here (in the *Pūrva* and *Uttara Mīmāṁsās*) there is a difference of the objects inquired into? In the section dealing with rites etc., the things to be inquired into are the religious acts that have still to emerge into being, but here (in the section on knowledge) the object inquired into is Brahman that is an established reality, existing for ever. As between these two, the result of the knowledge of Brahman should be different from the result (heaven etc.) of the knowledge of virtuous deeds depending on performance.

Opponent (i.e. Vṛttikāra): It cannot be so, for Brahman is presented here as a factor in an injunction about some action. For there are such injunctions (about meditation) as, "The Self, my dear, is to be seen" (Bṛ. II. iv. 5), "That Self that is free from sin, . . . is to be sought for, is to be inquired into" (Ch. VIII. vii. 1), "The Self alone is to be (profoundly) meditated on" (Bṛ I. iv. 7), "One should meditate only on the world of the Self" (Bṛ. I. iv. 15), "One who wants to become Brahman shall meditate on Brahman"[61] (Mu. III. ii. 9). As a result of such texts the question arises, "What is that Self? What is that Brahman?" And all such Upaniṣadic terms as, "Eternal, omniscient" (G. II. 24), "ever satisfied" (G. IV. 20), "even pure, intelligent, and free by nature" (Nṛ. U. 9), "Brahman is con-

[61] This is the opponent's interpretation. The Vedāntic interpretation is: "One who knows Brahman becomes Brahman."

sciousness and bliss" (Bṛ. III. ix. 28), and so on, serve a purpose by presenting the characteristics of the Self and Brahman. From Its worship will accrue the result, viz liberation, which is revealed in the scriptures, but is not known from any other source. But if the Upaniṣadic sentences do not form parts of injunctions about actions and they refer merely to an entity, there will be no possibility of acceptance or rejection, so that they will become certainly useless like such sentences as, "The earth consists of seven islands", "There goes that king", and so on.

Objection : Even a simple statement about an entity as in such sentences, "This is not a snake, it is a rope", is seen to serve some purpose by removing the fear occasioned by the error. Similarly here also the Upaniṣadic sentences will, by virtue of their imparting instruction about the transcendental Self, serve the purpose of removing the error of thinking oneself as a transmigrating soul.

Opponent : This can be so if, like the removal of the error of the snake (on a rope) on hearing the nature of the rope, the error about transmigration is removed as soon as one hears of the nature of Brahman. But as a matter of fact, it is not removed, for it is seen that even in the case of one who has heard of Brahman, such characteristics of a soul in bondage as happiness, sorrow, etc. persist just as before. Besides, it is seen that reflection and meditation, occurring after hearing, are enjoined in, "The Self is to be heard of, reflected on and (profoundly) meditated upon"[62] (Bṛ. II. iv. 5). Therefore Brahman is to be accepted as having been presented by the scriptures (for meditation) in a context of injunction about meditation.

[62] *Śravaṇa, manana, and nididhyāsana,* according to the Vedāntins, are not merely acts of hearing, reflection, and profound meditation as ordinarily understood. *Śravaṇa* means a mental activity conducive to the apprehension of all Upaniṣadic texts as leading to their only import, Brahman. And this is achieved by an examination of the texts through six tests (*upakrama-upasaṁhāra* etc.—see f. n. 69). *Manana* is also a mental activity consisting in the employment of favourable arguments for the removal of the apparent contradictions that such a purport may raise against other means of valid knowledge. And *nididhyāsana* is a mental activity consisting in withdrawing the mind from other things and concentrating it on Brahman.

Vedāntin: With regard to this we say: Not so; for the results of action and the knowledge of Brahman are different. By virtuous deeds are meant those physical, vocal, and mental actions which are well known in the Vedas and Smṛtis, and an inquiry about which has been set forth in the aphorism, "Hence thereafter (should be commenced) an inquiry about virtuous deeds"[63] (Jai. Sū. I. i. 1). Even vices like injury are to be inquired into with a view to shunning them, for they too are revealed in the Vedic sentences expressing prohibition. Happiness and sorrow are the results of these two—of virtue and vice, consisting of good and evil—with regard to which the Vedic texts (of injunction and prohibition) are authoritative; and these results, arising from the contact of senses and objects, are familiarly experienced by all creatures ranging from Brahmā to the motionless (trees etc.). The gradation of happiness among embodied beings starting from men and ending with Brahmā is known from the Upaniṣads (Tai. II. viii, Bṛ. IV. iii. 33). From that again is known a gradation in its cause which is virtue. From a gradation of virtues is known a gradation among the persons qualified (for them). It is a familiar fact that competence is evaluated in terms of aspiration and ability. As for instance, the performers of sacrifices etc. proceed along the Northern Course (after death) in accordance with the excellence in their meditation and concentration of mind, whereas they move along the Southern Course, starting from smoke, as a result of performing *iṣṭa*, *pūrta*, and *datta*.[64] There again (in the world of the Moon), a gradation of happiness and the means of its attainment is known from the text, "Residing there as long as the result of action, producing the enjoyment, lasts (they come back)" (Ch. V. x. 5). Similarly the

[63] Since the Vedas convey some meaning leading to some results, therefore, after the study of the Vedas, should be commenced an inquiry about the meaning of the Vedic texts, that is conducive to the ascertainment of the virtuous deeds.

[64] Northern Course—also known as the Path of Gods; and Southern Course or the Path of Manes. *Iṣṭa*—Agnihotra and Viśvedeva sacrifices, austerity, truthfulness, study, hospitality, etc. *Pūrta*—Digging of wells, construction of rest-houses, temples, etc. *Datta*—Charity, protection of the weak, non-injury, etc.

little happiness, existing in a graded order among creatures ranging from men to the immobile and hellish ones, is known to be the product of virtuous deeds themselves about which the Vedic texts are authoritative. So also from a perception of a gradation of sorrow among higher and lower embodied beings, it becomes clear that there is a gradation in their causes which are the vicious deeds prohibited by the authoritative Vedic texts, and that there is also a gradation among the performers of those deeds. Thus it is well known from the Vedic texts, Smṛtis, and reasoning that this transient world is constituted by a gradation of happiness and sorrow, that this gradation occurs to persons who are subject to such defects as ignorance, and that it comes to them after their birth and in accordance with the gradation of their virtuous and vicious deeds (in earlier lives). In support of this there is the Vedic text, "For an embodied being there can be no eradication of happiness and sorrow to be sure" (Ch. VIII. xii. 1), which is a corroborative restatement (*anuvāda*, f.n. 54) of the nature of the world described earlier. And from the denial of any contact with happiness and sorrow as contained in the text, "Happiness and sorrow do not touch one who is definitely bodiless" (ibid.), it follows that it is with regard to emancipation, which is the same as bodilessness, that the denial is made of its ever being the result of virtuous deeds of which the Vedic texts are the only means of knowledge. For if it be a product of virtuous deeds (e.g. meditation), there can be no denial of its contact with happiness and sorrow.

Opponent : Unembodiedness (i.e. the state of not being identified with the body) can itself be the product of virtuous deeds.

Vedāntin : Not so; for unembodiedness is inherent in the Self in accordance with such Vedic texts as, "Having meditated on the Self as bodiless in the midst of bodies, as permanent in the midst of the impermanent, and as great and pervasive, the wise man ceases to grieve" (Ka. I. ii. 22), "For that Puruṣa (infinite Being) is without vital force (i.e. organs of action) and mind (i.e. organs of perception)" (Mu. II. i. 2), "For this infinite Being is unattached" (Bṛ. IV. iii. 15). Hence it is proved that the unembodiedness, called liberation, is eternal and different from the results of works that have to be performed. Among things permanent, some are changefully permanent, with regard to which the idea, "That very thing is this one", does not get sublated even though the thing goes on changing, as for instance the earth according to those who say that the world is permanent, or the three constituents of matter (*sattva*, *rajas*, and *tamas*) according to the Sāṁkhyas. But this one is unchangingly permanent in an absolute sense; It is all-pervasive like space, devoid of all modifications, ever content, partless, and self-effulgent by nature. This is that unembodiedness, called liberation, where the idea of the three periods of time does not exist and virtuous and vicious deeds cease along with their effects (happiness and sorrow), as stated in the Vedic text, "Speak of that thing which you see as different from virtue and vice, different from cause and effect, and different from the past and the future" (Ka. I. ii. 14). (Since liberation is different from the result of work, it being unrelated to virtue and vice), therefore liberation is the same as Brahman about which this deliberation is started. Had liberation been spoken of (in the scriptures) as being supplementary to action and had it been asserted as a thing to be achieved, it would become impermanent. In that case liberation would become some sort of an excellent product amidst a horde of above-mentioned products of work standing in a graded order. But all who believe in liberation admit it to be eternal. Thus (since liberation is the same as Brahman), it is not proper to talk of Brahman as though it formed a factor in some action. Besides, the (following) texts show liberation as coming immediately after the knowledge of Brahman; and thereby they deny any activity in the interval: "Anyone who knows Brahman becomes Brahman" (Mu. III. ii. 19), "When that Brahman, the basis of all causes and effects, becomes known, all the results of his (i.e. aspirant's) actions become exhausted" (Mu. II. ii. 8), "One who knows the Bliss (that is the very nature) of Brahman, ceases to have any fear from anything" (Tai. II. ix), "O Janaka, you have certainly attained (Brahman that is) fearlessness" (Bṛ. IV. ii. 4), "It knew only Itself as, 'I am Brahman', thereby It became All" (Bṛ. I. iv. 10), "Then what delusion and what sorrow can there be for that seer of unity?" (Iś. 7), and so on. So also one should refer to the following text for the denial of any duty in between the realization of Brahman and becoming All: "While realizing this (Self) as that Brahman, the seer Vāmadeva knew, 'I was Manu and I was the sun'" (Bṛ. I. iv. 10). This is just like the sentence, "Standing there he sings", where it can be understood that the man has no other activity in between his standing and singing. And the following and similar other texts show that the result of the knowledge of Brahman is nothing but the removal of the obstacles to liberation: "You indeed are our father who have ferried us across nescience to the other shore" (Pr. VI. 8), "For it has been heard from the adorable ones like yourself that the knower of the Self goes beyond sorrow. Sir, such as I am, I am sorrowful. May you, O venerable sir, ferry me across nescience" (Ch. VII. i. 3), "The adorable Sanatkumāra showed the other shore of nescience to him (i.e. to Nārada) who had become free from defects" (Ch. VII. xxvi. 2). There is also in evidence the aphorism of the great teacher Gautama, supported by reasoning: "Liberation is possible since the earlier ones in the series of sorrow, birth, impulsion (to virtue and vice), defects (e.g. attachment, repulsion, delusion, etc.), and false knowledge, get destroyed (in the reverse order) on the destruction of the immediately succeeding ones" (N. S. I. i. 2). And the removal of false ignorance follows from the knowledge of the unity of the individual Self and Brahman.

But this knowledge of the unity of the Self and Brahman is not a kind of meditation, called *Sampad*,[65] as in "The mind is certainly infinite, and the Viśvedevas are infinite. Through this meditation one wins an infinite world" (Bṛ. III. i. 9). Nor is it a form of meditation called *Adhyāsa*,[66] as in "One should meditate thus: 'The mind is Brahman'" (Ch. III. xviii. 1) and "The instruction is: 'The sun is Brahman'" (Ch. III. xix. 1), where the idea of Brahman is superimposed on the mind, the

[65] Where an inferior factor is thought of as a superior factor on account of some similarity. The superior predominates, and the inferior is almost ignored, e.g. the Viśvedevas occupy the mind for the time being.

[66] Where the factor superimposed (say, Brahman) occupies a subsidiary position, while the locus (say, the mind or sun) predominates.

sun, etc. Nor is it a meditation based on some special activity, as in, "Air is certainly the place of merger", "The vital force is certainly the place of merger" (Ch. IV. iii. 1-4).[67] Nor is it a kind of purification of some factor in some (Vedic) rite, as for instance the act of looking at the oblation (by the sacrificer's wife for its purification).[68] If the Knowledge of the unity of the Self and Brahman is accepted as a kind of *Sampad* etc., then it will flout the ascertainable meaning[69] of all the words occurring in such sentences and establishing the unity of the Self and Brahman as, "That thou art" (Ch. VI. viii. 7), "I am Brahman" (Bṛ. I. iv. 10), "This Self is Brahman" (Bṛ. II. v. 19). Besides, thereby will be set at nought such sentences as, "The knots of the heart are untied and all doubts are resolved" (Mu. II. ii. 8), in which one hears of the result (of knowledge) consisting in the cessation of nescience. Furthermore, from the point of view of *Sampad* etc., such sentences as, "One who knows Brahman becomes Brahman" (Mu. III. ii. 9), which speak of unity with Brahman, cannot be fully justified. Therefore the knowledge of the unity of the Self and Brahman is not a kind of *Sampad* or anything of that sort. Hence the knowledge of Brahman is not dependent on human action.

On what does it depend then?

It is dependent on the thing itself, as in the case of the knowledge of a thing got through such valid means as direct perception. By no stretch of imagination can such a Brahman or Its knowledge be brought into contact with work. Nor can it be held that Brahman has some association with work by virtue of Its being the object of the act of knowing; for in the text, "It is different from the known and also different from the unknown"[70] (Ke. I. 4), as also in the text, "Through what should

[67] Where the two factors, air and vital force, remain distinct, though thought of as one owing to similarity of action, viz merger of all things into air during dissolution and into the vital force during sleep.

[68] The knowledge "I am Brahman" is not meant for the mere purification of the individual being, viz the sacrificer.

[69] Meaning ascertained through the six tests—commencement-ending, repetition, uniqueness, result, eulogy, reason.

[70] Known, i.e. effect; unknown, i.e. cause.

one know that owing to which all this is known?" (Bṛ. II. iv. 14), Brahman is denied to be an object of the act of knowing. So also there is the denial of Its being the object of the act of meditation. For in the text, "That which is not uttered by speech, that by which speech is revealed", it is first declared that Brahman is not an object, and then it is said, "Know that alone to be Brahman and not what people worship as an object" (Ke. I. 5).

Opponent: If Brahman be not an object (of knowledge), It cannot logically be presented by the scriptures (as stated in B. S. I. i. 3).

Vedāntin: Not so, for the scriptures aim at the removal of the differences fancied through ignorance. Not that the scriptures seek to establish Brahman as an entity referable objectively by the word "this".

What do they do then?

By presenting Brahman as not an object on account of Its being the inmost Self (of the knower), they remove the differences of the "known", the "knower", and the "knowledge" that are fancied through ignorance.[71] In support of this are the texts,

[71] The idea is expressed thus in the Bṛhadāraṇyaka commentary (IV. iv. 20): "The scriptures too describe the Self merely by the negation of the activities of the subject, the evidences of knowledge, and so on;... and not by resorting to the usual function of a sentence in which something is described by means of names. Therefore even in scriptures, the Self is not presented like heaven or Mount Meru for instance....The knowledge of Brahman too means only the cessation of the identification with extraneous things (such as the body)." Thus since Brahman is not presentable positively by saying, "This is so", It cannot be the object of scriptural knowledge in this sense. But It can be presented negatively as "Not this, not this", and thus It can be known from the scriptures, which are a valid means of knowledge. This is technically explained thus:

Brahman is comprehended in the unanalysable mentation (*vṛtti*) of the form, "I am Brahman", that arises from hearing the great Upaniṣadic saying, "That thou art". And yet Brahman is said to be inexpressible by words, because It is not comprehended by the "resulting consciousness" or "apprehending consciousness" (*phala*), which is defined as the mentation with the reflection of Consciousness on it. In common experience, the mentation of the form of a pot, with the reflection of Consciousness on it, goes out of a person to envelop the pot. Then that mentation destroys the ignorance about the pot; still the witnessing Consciousness is needed

"Brahman is known to him to whom It is unknown, while It is unknown to him to whom It is known. It is unknown to those who know and known to those who do not know" (Ke. II. 3), "You cannot see that which is the witness of vision,...you cannot know that which is the knower of knowledge" (Bṛ. III. iv. 2), and so on. Therefore there can be no question of liberation becoming impermanent, for in it is revealed the reality of the eternally free Self, after eliminating from the Self the idea of Its being under the bondage (of birth and death), fancied on It through ignorance. But from the standpoint of one who believes that liberation is a product, it is but logical that there should be a dependence on activity—mental, vocal, and physical. The position becomes the same if liberation be a transformation of something. From either point of view, liberation must of necessity be impermanent; for neither curd that is a modification, nor a jar that is a product is seen to be permanent in this world. And no dependence on work can be proved by assuming liberation to be a thing to be acquired; for it being essentially one with one's very Self, there can be no acquisition. Even if Brahman be different from oneself, there can be no acquisition, for Brahman being all-pervasive like space, It remains ever attained by everybody. Liberation cannot also be had through purification, so as to be dependent on action. Purification is achieved either through the addition of some quality or removal of some defect. As to that, purification is not possible here through the addition of any quality, since liberation is of the very nature of Brahman on which no excellence (or deterioration) can be effected. Nor is that possible through the removal of any defect, for liberation is of the very nature of Brahman that is ever pure.

Opponent: May it not be, that though liberation is inherent

to reveal the pot through a manifestation of the identity of the Consciousness underlying the pot and the apprehending Consciousness. The mentation about Brahman destroys the ignorance about and the ignorance subsisting on It. But the apprehending Consciousness cannot reveal Brahman, the (*phala*) mentation being included in ignorance itself as the latter's product, so that it gets destroyed along with that ignorance and can have no further action.

in oneself, it remains covered and it becomes manifest when the Self is purified by action, as the brilliance of a mirror does when cleaned by the act of rubbing?

Vedāntin: No, since the Self cannot reasonably be the sphere of any action, for no action can take place without bringing about some change in its locus. But if the Self changes through action, It will be subject to impermanence, and that will militate against such texts as, "It is said to be immutable" (Gītā, II. 25). And that is undesirable. Hence the Self can have no action occurring on Itself. And action, taking place on something else, cannot purify the Self, which is not an object thereof.

Opponent: Is it not a matter of experience that the embodied soul is purified by such activities occurring on the body as bath, rinsing of the mouth, wearing the sacrificial thread, etc.?

Vedāntin: Not so. It is the soul, cognized through ignorance,[72] as constituting a factor in the assemblage of body etc., that can be purified; for bath, rinsing of the mouth, etc. are directly perceived as associated with the body. It is reasonable that something associated with the body and cognized as the Self through ignorance should be purified by the actions taking place on the body. Just as that very entity gets the result of being cured, which is conjoined with the body, which identifies itself with the body, and on which arises the idea, "I am cured", consequent on the establishment of the balance of the constituents of the body (phlegm, bile, and wind), through a treatment of the body, so also that entity is purified to which occurs the idea, "I am purified", as a result of such actions as bathing, rinsing the mouth, or wearing the sacrificial thread; and that entity certainly remains bound up with the body. For all actions are surely performed and the fruits thereof enjoyed by that entity which has the idea, "I am the doer", stemming out of the idea of "I", and which cognizes everything, as stated in the *mantra*, "One of the two enjoys the fruits having (various) tastes, while the other looks on without enjoying" (Mu. III. i. 1), as also the text, "The wise people call that the enjoyer which is associated with body, organs, and mind" (Ka. I. iii. 4). So also there are the

[72] The individual Self reflected on nescience.

texts: "The one deity remains hidden in all beings. He is all-pervasive, the indwelling Self of all, the regulator of all actions, the support of all beings, the witness, consciousness, non-dual, and without qualities" (Śv. VI. 11), and "He is omnipresent, effulgent, without body, wound, and sinews, pure and untouched by sin" (Īś. 8). These two *mantras* show that Brahman is beyond the imputation of all kinds of excellence (or inferiority), and It is ever pure. Liberation is the state of identity with Brahman, and hence it is not to be achieved through purification. Besides, apart from these,[73] nobody can show any other mode whereby liberation can be associated with action. Accordingly, apart from knowledge alone, there cannot be the slightest touch of action here.

Opponent : Is not knowledge a kind of mental action?

Vedāntin : Not so, because there is a difference. An action is in evidence where the injunction about it occurs independently of the nature of the thing concerned, and where it is subject to the activities of the human mind, as for instance in such sentences as, "When the priest (called Hotā) is about to utter (the *mantra*) *vauṣat*, he shall meditate mentally on the deity for whom the libation is taken up (by the Adhvaryu)" (Ai. Br. XI. viii. 1), "One should mentally meditate on (the deity identified with) evening" (ibid). Though meditation, that is but thinking, is a mental action, yet it can be done, not done, or done otherwise by a man; for it is dependent on man. But knowledge arises from its valid means (e.g. perception, inference, etc.); and the valid means apprehend the things just as they are. Hence (valid) knowledge is not something to be done, not done, or done otherwise, for it is entirely determined by things, and neither by injunctions nor by man. Hence though knowledge is a mental act, it has a great difference. For instance, the thinking of a man or a woman as fire in, "O Gautama, a man is surely a fire" (Ch. V. vii. 1), "O Gautama, a woman is surely a fire" (Ch. V. viii. 1), is certainly an act, since it arises from injunction alone and it is dependent on man. But the idea of fire with regard to the familiar fire is neither dependent on injunction nor on man.

[73] Production, acquisition, transformation, and purification.

What is it then?

Since it is determined by a thing coming within the range of perception, it is surely knowledge and not action. Thus also it is to be understood in the case of all objects coming within the range of valid means of knowledge. That being so, the realization of the unity of Brahman and the Self (that is never sublated) is also a kind of knowledge and it is not determined by injunction. Though verbs in the imperative mood etc. are seen (in the Upaniṣad) to be used with regard to this knowledge, they become infructuous like the sharpness of razor etc. striking against stone etc., for they are aimed at something beyond the range of human effort inasmuch as that knowledge has for its object something (i.e. Brahman) that is neither acceptable nor rejectable.

Opponent: Why are there then texts like "The Self, my dear Maitreyī, should be realized, should be heard of" etc. (Bṛ. II. iv. 5), which have a semblance of injunction?

Vedāntin: We say that they are meant for weaning one back from objects towards which one inclines naturally. For a man hankering after the highest human goal and engaging in outward objects under the idea, "May good come to me, may not evil befall me", but failing to achieve thereby the highest human goal, there are such texts as, "The Self, my dear Maitreyi, should be realized". These turn him back from the objects, naturally attracting his body and senses etc. towards them, and then they lead him along the current of the indwelling Self.[74] And for him, when he engages in the search of the Self, is presented in the following texts the reality of the Self, that is beyond all acceptance and rejection: "All these are but that Self" (Bṛ. II. iv. 6), "But when to the knower of Brahman everything has

[74] It is not an injunction but a sort of eulogy, the apparent injunction being meant for inducing the hearer to the knowledge of Brahman. By producing in his mind a current of thoughts directed towards the indwelling Self, this inspires the man to "hear, reflect, and meditate" about the Self, these processes being the means of generating the knowledge of Brahman. The *Vivaraṇa* school does not admit any injunction in the case of knowledge; but a *Niyama-vidhi*, in the primary sense, is admitted in the case of "hearing"; in the case of reflection and meditation, this is admitted in a secondary sense.

become the Self, . . . what should one know and through what? . . . Through what, O Maitreyi, should one know the knower?" (Bṛ. IV. v. 15), "The Self is Brahman" (Bṛ. II. v. 19), and so on. As for the criticism that a knowledge of the Self that does not combine with some action as its part cannot be meant either for acceptance or rejection, we admit it to be so indeed. It redounds to our credit that, on the realization of Brahman, there follow the attainment of full satisfaction and stoppage of all duties. In support of this is the Vedic text: "If a man knows the Self as 'I am this', then desiring what and for whose sake will he suffer in the wake of the body?" (Bṛ. IV iv. 12); and there is the Smṛti text: "O Arjuna, knowing this, one attains the highest intelligence and will have accomplished all one's duties" (Gītā, XV. 20). Therefore Brahman is not presented as a factor in any injunction about knowledge.

As for the assertion of some people (viz followers of Prabhākara) that apart from injunctions and prohibitions and factors connected with them as subsidiaries, no section of the Vedas speaks of mere things as such, we say that this is wrong. For the all-pervasive entity, presented in the Upaniṣads alone, cannot be a subsidiary of anything else. It cannot be said that Brahman does not exist, nor can It be realized even though It is known from the Upaniṣads as the all-pervasive entity beyond worldly qualities, as different from all things belonging to the four classes, viz those that can be produced, (purified, transformed, and achieved), and as occurring in Its own context (in the Upaniṣads) and hence not forming a part of anything else; because that Brahman is called the Self in the text, "This is the Self which has been described as 'Not this, not this' " (Bṛ. III. ix. 26) and because the Self cannot be denied inasmuch as It is the Self even of one who would deny It.

Opponent: It is not proved that the Self is known from the Upaniṣads alone inasmuch as It is contained in the idea of "I".

Vedāntin: Not so, for this has been refuted by saying that the Self is the witness of that idea. Leaving aside the (erroneous) knowledge of the Self as the agent (of actions), as contained in the idea of "I", the (real) Self—which is the witness of the idea of "I", which exists in all creatures, which is without any difference of degrees, and which is one, unchanging, eternal, and all-pervasive consciousness—(such a Self) is not known as the Self of all by anyone in the section of the Vedas dealing with virtuous deeds, or in the scriptures of the logicians. Hence this Self cannot be denied by anyone, nor can It be taken as forming a part of any injunction. And because It is the Self of all, It is beyond all rejection and acceptance; for all mutable and impermanent things culminate in Puruṣa (the all-pervasive Entity) as their ultimate limit.[75] Since Puruṣa has no cause of destruction, He is indestructible; and since there is no cause for change, He is changelessly eternal; and hence He is by nature ever pure, intelligent, and free. Thus the text, "There is nothing higher than Puruṣa; He is the culmination, He is the highest goal" (Ka. I. iii. 11) stands justified. Accordingly, the distinctive reference to Puruṣa as being known only from the Upaniṣads, as stated in the text, "I ask you of that Puruṣa who is to be known only from the Upaniṣads" (Bṛ. III. ix. 26), becomes justifiable if Puruṣa is the primary object to be revealed by the Upaniṣads. Hence it is mere bravado to say that there is no section of the Vedas dealing with things as such.

As for the statements of the people versed in scriptures that "The perceptible result of these (Vedas) is the production of the knowledge of virtuous deeds", and so on, since these relate to an inquiry about virtuous deeds, they are to be understood as referring to the scriptures dealing with injunction and prohibition. Besides, for those who accept in any absolute sense the aphorism, "Since the Vedas reveal action, those texts that do not have that purport are meaningless", all instructions about things as such become useless. If, however, it is held that, as distinct from impulsion for or repulsion from action, things are taught in the scriptures as accessories of actions, what reason can there be to assert that the unchangingly eternal entity (Brahman) is not spoken of (in the scriptures)? Not that a thing about which any instruction is imparted, becomes an action thereby.

[75] As the ultimate reality into which all things can be reduced, this Puruṣa remains unchanged, and into Him all things enter like the false snake etc. entering into the rope etc.

Opponent : Though a thing is not an action, still the instruction about a thing is meant for being acted on, it being a means for the action.

Vedantin : That is no valid objection; for even when a thing is presented for the sake of some action, there is no denying the fact that the instruction relates to something having the capacity to aid some action. It may serve that purpose by becoming a factor in some action; but this does not amount to saying that a thing as such is not taught in the scriptures.

Opponent : Granted that instruction is imparted about things, what do you gain thereby?

The answer (of the *Vedāntin*) is: The instruction about the unknown thing called the Self is possible like those very things (e.g. curd, Soma, etc.). Its knowledge serves the purpose of eradicating the unreal nescience that is the cause of the worldly state. Thus in this way its purposefulness is quite on a par with that of the instruction about things that are the accessories of work.[76] Moreover, there is the instruction about cessation from work in such texts as, "As Brāhmaṇa should not be killed". And that is neither an action nor an accessory of action. If the instruction of things not meant for action be useless, then the injunction about withholding from action in such texts as, "A Brāhmaṇa should not be killed", becomes useless. But that is undesirable. From the connection of the negative (*na*) with the meaning of the root *han* (to kill), the meaning derived is an inactivity consisting in not undertaking the act of killing that might have been resorted to out of natural proclivity. Apart from this holding aloof from killing, no other new activity, that is not guaranteed by the negative, can be fancied here. For it is the very nature of the negative to convey the idea of the non-existence of the action with which it gets connected. The idea of non-existence causes inactivity, and that idea ceases to exist automatically like

[76] *Objection* : Curd as such may have no purpose; but when used in a sacrifice, it helps in the production of the result set forth in the Vedas. But Brahman has no such connection with action, and is therefore absolutely useless.

Answer : Not so, for the instruction about Brahman serves its own purpose, viz removal of ignorance.

fire that has exhausted its fuel.[77] Therefore we think that except in such cases as the "Vow of Prajāpati",[78] the meaning of prohibition in sentences like "A Brāhmaṇa should not be killed" is mere inaction consisting in not undertaking an act for which an impulse had arisen. Therefore it is to be noted that the statement of the uselessness (occurring in the aphorism), "Since scriptures are meant for enjoining action, those words that are not meant for action are useless" (Jai Sū. I. ii. 1), relates to the corroborative statements (*Arthavāda*) like mythological stories that do not serve any human purpose. Although it was argued that a reference to any object as such, without its being connected with an injunction about work, will be useless like the statements, "The earth has seven islands", etc., that argument is demolished on the evidence of the usefulness of such statements of facts as, "This is a rope and not a snake".[79]

Opponent: Did we not say that a statement about Brahman cannot be useful like the statement about the nature of the rope, since it is a patent fact that even a man who has heard of Brahman continues to have his mundane life just as before?

Vedāntin: To this the answer is being given: For one who has realized the state of the unity of the Self and Brahman, it cannot be proved that his mundane life continues just as before;

[77] From the prohibition the hearer gets the idea, "It dissuades me from the act of killing a Brāhmaṇa. This leads to inactivity, which is the very nature of the Self. The prohibition removes the idea that he entertained of gaining something from the murder, so that when the idea of non-existence of gain dies away, the proclivity does not recur.

[78] In the "Vow of Prajāpati" a young man, about to enter the householder's life after finishing his studies, is asked not to look at the rising sun, the sun under an eclipse, the sun reflected in water, and the sun at the zenith, and not to cross over the tether of a calf. Here the meaning of the negative is not mere withdrawal from activity; for in the text, the prohibitions are preceded by a positive injunction for undertaking a vow. Hence such instances are exceptions to the general meaning of the negative as non-existence. This is the Vedāntic standpoint, whereas the opponent will say that in all cases of prohibition, the meaning is not a mere negation of some act, but the injunction of its opposite. Thus "A Brāhmaṇa should not be killed" means, "Non-killing of a Brāhmaṇa is to be resorted to".

[79] Which statement removes the fear of the snake.

for this contradicts the knowledge of the unity of Brahman and the Self arising from the Vedas which are a valid means of knowledge. From noticing the fact that a man can have sorrow, fear, etc. as a result of his identifying himself with the body etc., it does not follow that this very man will have sorrow etc. contingent on false ignorance, even when his self-identification with the body etc. ceases after the realization of the unity of Brahman and the Self, arising from the Vedas which are a valid means of knowledge. Just because a householder, who had been rich and prided himself on that account, had been seen to be sorrowing for the theft of his wealth, it does not follow that this very man will be miserable for any loss of that wealth even after he has become a monk and given up the idea of being wealthy. From the fact that a man wearing an ear-ring had been seen to be happy by thinking of himself as the possessor of that ear-ring, it does not follow that he will have that very happiness arising from the possession of an ear-ring even after he dissociates himself from that ear-ring and gives up the idea of his being its possessor. Thus it is stated in the Vedic text, "Happiness and sorrow do not touch one who has become definitely unembodied"[80] (Ch. VIII. xii. 1).

Opponent: Suppose we argue that this unembodiedness comes when the body falls, but it cannot be so for a living man.

Vedāntin: Not so, for the idea of embodiedness is a result of false nescience. Unless it be through the false ignorance of identifying the Self with the body, there can be no embodiedness for the Self. And we said that the unembodiedness of the Self is eternal, since it is not a product of action.

Opponent: May it not be that embodiedness is the result of the virtuous and vicious deeds done by the Self?

Vedāntin: No. There can be no performance of virtuous and vicious deeds by the Self, since it cannot be proved that It has any relation with the body. Since the assertion of the relation of the Self with the body (as the cause of virtue and vice) and

[80] Sorrow is destroyed not by mediate but by immediate knowledge. If one does not get immediate knowledge from the Upaniṣads, nothing is wrong with them, but it is caused by the imperfect state of the hearer's mind.

the creation of that relation by virtue and vice leads to an argument in a circle, therefore it is but blind tradition that makes one stand by such an eternal chain. Besides, the Self can have no agentship (of virtue and vice), since It is unrelated to work.[81]

Opponent: Have not kings and others an agentship by their mere proximity?

Vedāntin: No, for their agentship can be explained as resulting from the relation established with the servants through payment of wealth etc. But no such cause for any relationship of either self-identity with or ownership of (the body) can be imagined for the Self, that can compare with the relationship between the master and servant achieved through payment of money etc., while false self-identity is directly perceived as a cause (for the Self's relation with body and action). Hereby is explained how the Self can become a sacrificer (through false self-identification).

Opponent: With regard to this, they (i.e. followers of Prabhākara) say: It may be argued that the Self, though in fact different from the body etc. has self-identification with the body etc. in a secondary sense (owing to some common property); but this is not false.

Vedāntin: Not so, for it is well known that words and ideas can have primary and secondary senses only to a man to whom the differences of the things etc. are evident. To a person to whom the differences of things are obvious—as for instance, when he knows it well enough through the methods of agreement and difference that there exists a distinct animal possessing manes and distinctive features denoted by the word lion in the primary sense, and that there is a man known to be possessed abundantly of such qualities of a lion as cruelty and bravery—then to such a person the application of the word lion and its idea become possible in a secondary sense, but not so to one to

[81] The argument in a circle can be avoided on the analogy of the seed and the sprout—the merits of a previous birth can produce the experiences of the next birth and vice versa. But this leads to an unjustifiable infinite regress; for the relation of the seed and sprout is a perceived reality, whereas the relation of merit etc. with the Self, which is unattached, is fanciful.

whom the differences of the two beings are not apparent. In the latter case, the application of words and ideas to things other than those implied by them is not figurative; rather it must be the result of ignorance. In light darkness, the word man and its idea are applied to the stump of a tree when it is not distinctly cognized as "This is a stump", or the word silver and its idea are applied all of a sudden to nacre. Similarly when the word "I" and its idea are suddenly applied in a literal sense to the aggregate of body and senses owing to a non-discrimination between the Self and non-Self, how can this be said to be figurative? It is seen that even the learned, who know the distinction between the Self and the non-Self, use words and have ideas implying a non-distinction (between Self and non-Self), just like the (ignorant) shepherds and goat-herds. Therefore the idea of "I" with regard to the body etc., entertained by those who believe (from mediate knowledge) in a Self, distinct from the body etc., must be false and not figurative. Thus since embodiedness is the result of a false perception, it is established that the enlightened man has no embodiedness even while living. Thus about the knower of Brahman occurs this Vedic text, "Just as the lifeless slough of a snake is cast off and it lies in the ant-hill, so does this body lie. Then the Self becomes disembodied and immortal, becomes the Prāṇa (i.e. living), Brahman, the (self-effulgent) Light" (Bṛ. IV. iv. 7), as also, "Though without eyes, he appears as if possessed of eyes; though without ears, he appears as if possessed of ears; though without speech, he appears as if possessed of speech; though without mind, he appears as though possessed of mind; though without vital force, he appears as though possessed of vital force."[82] There is also the Smṛti text starting with, "What is the description of the man of steady knowledge, merged in *Samādhi*?" (Gītā, II. 54), which while setting forth the characteristic of a man of steady (well-poised) wisdom, reveals that in the case of an enlightened man there is a total absence of any

[82] Through a reappearance of what is sublated by the knowledge of Brahman, like the repetition of a mirage after being known to be false or the continuance of the semblance of a cloth produced by the burnt yarns still in position.

connection with any impulsion to work. Hence a man who has realized his own identity with Brahman cannot continue to have the worldly state just as before, whereas the man who continues to have the worldly state just as before has not realized his identity with Brahman. Thus[83] it is all beyond criticism.

And it was stated that from the mention of reflection and profound meditation (*nididhyāsana*) after hearing (i.e. understanding of Upaniṣadic texts—Bṛ. II. iv. 5), it follows that Brahman is complementary to some injunction, and Its knowledge is not meant for culminating in a realization of Its own nature. That is no valid objection, for reflection and profound meditation (just like hearing) are meant for giving rise to immediate knowledge. If Brahman had been known through some other source of knowledge and then used in some other act or meditation, then It could have become a part of an injunction. But that is not the case. For just like hearing, reflection and meditation are also meant for knowledge.[84] Hence it cannot be that Brahman is known from the scriptures as a factor included in any injunction about worshipful meditation (*upāsanā*). Accordingly, it stands established that Brahman is presented as an independent entity in the scriptures; for as a result of the proper determination of the Upaniṣadic texts, they are seen to speak of It. And from this point of view, the commencement of a separate scriptural text about that Brahman with the aphorism, "Hence (is to be undertaken) thereafter a deliberation on Brahman" (B. S. I. i. 1) is justified. If, however, Brahman

[83] Since the knowledge of Brahman is useful like the useful knowledge, "This is a rope and not a snake".

[84] Reflection and profound meditation are enjoined for one who does not realize from the first hearing. This is owing to his own mental defects. The illumination dawns when there is no defect. By hearing is removed the doubt from an unprepared mind that the Upaniṣads cannot impart the knowledge of Brahman. Reflection removes the doubt that the Self and Brahman cannot be one. Through meditation the mind is withdrawn from distraction and all things other than Brahman, and then Brahman stands revealed. Thus hearing etc. generate knowledge, and knowledge brings liberation. Reflection and meditation deal with the thing known from hearing. They are not meant for a fresh knowledge.

were to be presented as complementary to an injunction about worshipful meditation (*upāsanā*), then since this had been already started with in the aphorism, "Hence thereafter is commenced an inquiry into virtuous deeds" (Jai. Sū. I. i. 1), a separate scripture should not have been begun. Or even if it were commenced, it should have been begun with, "Hence thereafter is commenced a deliberation on virtuous deeds (i.e. worshipful meditation on Brahman) that had been left over (by Jaimini)", like the aphorism, "Hence thereafter (i.e. after determining what are the primary and subsidiary factors) is commenced a deliberation on things conducive to the performance of sacrifices and attainment of human objectives"[85] (Jai. Sū. IV. i. 1). But as a matter of fact the knowledge of the unity of Brahman and the Self was not premised (in Jaimini's book); therefore the commencement of this book for that purpose with the aphorism, "Hence thereafter is undertaken a deliberation on Brahman", is justifiable. Accordingly, all these injunctions as well as all the other means of knowledge have their validity till the realization, "I am Brahman". For once the non-dual Self, that is neither acceptable nor rejectable, is realized, there can be no possibility of the persistence of the means of knowledge that become bereft of their objects and subjects.[86] Moreover, they (the knowers of Brahman) say, "When on the realization of the Existence-Brahman as I, the body, son, etc. become sublated and consequently the secondary and false selves cease to exist, how can there be any action (prompted by injunction and prohibition)? The Self can be a knowing agent earlier than the rise of the complete knowledge of Brahman that has to be sought for; but (when that search has been finished), the knower, freed from the defect of sin, becomes one with the entity arrived at through the search. Just as the ideas of the body as the Self are accepted by the wise as valid postulates (for empirical dealings), similarly these

[85] Since such a determination clears the way for an inquiry about things conducive to sacrifices and human objectives, therefore the second inquiry starts after the first.

[86] The means of knowledge are valid so long as the final illumination does not occur.

empirical means of knowledge are accepted as valid till the direct knowledge of the Self dawns" (*Sundarapāṇḍya-kārikā*).

Topic 5: The First Cause Possessed of Consciousness

Thus it has been said that the Upaniṣadic texts are meant for imparting the knowledge of Brahman; that when their meaning is fully ascertained, they have the Self, which is Brahman, as their fullest import; and that they culminate in (the knowledge of) Brahman even without any connection with an action. It has also been said that the omniscient and omnipotent Brahman is the cause of the origin, continuance, and dissolution of the universe. But the Sāṁkhyas and others hold the view that a pre-existing entity can be known through other means (apart from the Upaniṣads). Inferring Pradhāna (primordial Nature) and other entities as the source of the universe, they construe the texts of the Upaniṣads as pointing to these only. They also think that in all the Upaniṣads, dealing with creation, the cause is sought to be presented through the effect with the help of inference.[87] They further hold that the contacts between the sentient souls (Puruṣas) and Pradhāna can always be inferred.[88] Again from these very texts, the followers of Kaṇāda infer God as the efficient cause and the atoms as the material cause. Similarly there are other logicians (viz Buddhists and others) who stand up here in opposition with garbled quotations[89] and sophistry as their mainstay. That being the case, the teacher (Vyāsa), who is versed in the valid imports of words and sentences, refutes the diverse ideas based on garbled quotations and sophistry by placing these in opposition, so as to prove that the texts of the Upaniṣads aim at imparting the knowledge of Brahman.

Now among these, the Sāṁkhayas think that the insentient

[87] For instance, "O amiable one, try to find out Existence as the root (of all) with the help of Its product fire" (Ch. VI. viii. 4).

[88] From the common experience that all things are the products of insentient Nature, and that insentient things remain associated with sentient beings, as for instance, a chariot.

[89] "In the beginning there was non-existence only" (Ch. VI. ii. 1), and so on.

Pradhāna, comprising its three constituents (*guṇas—Sattva, Rajas,* and *Tamas*), is the cause of the universe. They say, "The Upaniṣadic texts, which according to you (Vedāntin) reveal an omnipotent and omniscient Brahman as the cause of the universe, can be understood equally well to imply that Pradhāna is the cause of the universe. As for omnipotence, Pradhāna can also have it well enough in respect of its own modifications; similarly omniscience also is logical."

How?

Sāṁkhya: That which you consider to be knowledge is a characteristic of *Sattva,* as is proved from the Smṛti, "Knowledge springs from *Sattva*" (Gītā, XIV. 17). And the Yogins, possessed of body and senses, are well known to be omniscient by virtue of their knowledge that is a characteristic of *Sattva,* it being a familiar fact that omniscience follows from the highest perfection of *Sattva.* For it cannot be imagined that the attributeless, all-pervasive entity (Puruṣa), that is mere consciousness without a body and senses, can have any knowledge of either all things or a few. But Pradhāna, comprising its three constituents, has *Sattva,* the source of all knowledge, even in its (own primordial) state of Pradhāna (i.e. balance of the three constituents); and therefore omniscience in a secondary sense is declared in the Upaniṣadic texts for this Pradhāna even though it is insentient. In postulating omniscience for Brahman, it has to be admitted even by you that Brahman becomes omniscient by Its potentiality to know everything. Not that Brahman stands there actually knowing all things for all times. For on the assumption that Brahman's knowledge is eternal, Its independence with regard to the act of knowing will be compromised. On the contrary, if the act of knowing be impermanent, Brahman will cease to exist when the act of knowing ceases (or "may cease from the act of knowing"—according to another reading). That being the case, the conclusion that emerges is that omniscience follows from the potentiality to know everything. But your standpoint is that Brahman is devoid of any accessory before creation. It is not, however, logical that anyone should have any knowledge even in the absence of body, senses, etc. Moreover, modifications are possible for Pradhāna that is composite by nature, so that it can reasonably become a material cause like earth etc., whereas Brahman, which is uniform by nature and non-composite, can have no modification.

Vedāntin: As against such a contention, this aphorism is advanced:

ईक्षतेर्नाशब्दम् ॥ ५ ॥

(The Pradhāna of the Sāṁkhyas is) न not (the cause of the universe), (because it is) अशब्दम् not mentioned in the Upaniṣads, (which fact is clear) ईक्षतेः from the fact of seeing (or deliberation).

5. *The Pradhānā of the Sāṁkhyas is not the cause of the universe, because it is not mentioned in the Upaniṣads, which fact is clear from the fact of seeing (or thinking).*

In the Upaniṣadic texts one cannot take one's stand on the insentient Pradhāna imagined by the Sāṁkhyas as the cause of the universe; for it is not presented in the Upaniṣads.

How is it not presented in the Upaniṣads?

On account of the fact of seeing.[90]

How?

The Upaniṣads teach thus: Starting with the text, "O amiable one, before its creation, the universe was but Existence (Brahman), one without a second" (Ch. VI. ii. 1), it is stated, "That (Brahman) visualized, 'I shall become many, I shall be born.' That (Brahman) created fire" (Ch. VI. ii. 3). In that text, the universe, manifested as names and forms and referable by the word "it", is first ascertained to be identified with Existence "before its creation"; then the text shows that the creatorship of fire etc., that follows the visualization of future creation, belongs to that very entity, called Existence, which is under consideration. So also elsewhere: "In the beginning this universe was but the one Self alone; there was nothing else whatsoever that winked. He visualized, 'Let me create the worlds' " (Ai. I.

[90] Also translated as "thinking", "knowledge", "vision", "wish" (see I. iii. 13).

i. 1-2), the text speaks of creation after visualization. At some place the text declares thus after introducing the Puruṣa with sixteen limbs:[91] "He visualized, he created the vital force" (Pr. VI. 3-4). By the word *īkṣati* the (cognate) noun implied by the verb (i.e. seeing) is sought to be indicated, as is the case with the word *yajati*,[92] and not the root itself (i.e. to see). As a result, one can refer to the following texts and such others which have for their import the omniscient God as the cause (of the universe): "From Him who is omniscient in general and in detail, whose austerity (i.e. creative effort) is constituted by knowledge, emerged this Brahman (viz Hiraṇyagarbha) as well as name, form, and food" (Mu. I. i. 9).

As for the statement that Pradhāna can become omniscient through the characteristic of knowledge belonging to its constituent *Sattva*, that is not justifiable; for in that state (of Pradhāna as such, when it has not changed through a loss of balance) there can be no possibility of knowledge as a characteristic of *Sattva*, because the constituents of Pradhāna are then in balance.

Sāṁkhya: Was it not stated that Pradhāna can become omniscient by virtue of its potentiality for knowing all?

Vedāntin: That too cannot be proved. If during the state of equilibrium of the constituents, Pradhāna is said to be all-knowing by virtue of having the power to know that actually belongs to *Sattva*, then it can equally be said to have little knowledge on account of having the power of obstruction to knowledge that belongs to *Rajas* and *Tamas*. Besides, so long as *Sattva* is not illumined by the consciousness (of the witnessing soul), no change in *Sattva* can be called knowledge; and insentient Pradhāna has no power to illumine. Therefore the omniscience of Pradhāna is not justifiable. The all-knowingness of the Yogins cannot be quoted as an example, for they are conscious beings, so that they can become all-knowing through a perfection of their *Sattva*. If on the analogy of a heated lump of iron,

[91] Vital force, faith, space, air, fire, water, earth, organs and senses, mind, food, vigour, austerity, *mantras*, works, worlds, name.

[92] Used by Jaimini in his aphorism VII. iv. 1, where *yajati* figuratively means a sacrifice and not the mere root "to sacrifice".

burning something because of the fire in it, it be argued that Pradhāna has the power of seeing owing to the presence of a witnessing entity, then it is but logical to hold that the entity, owing to which Pradhāna has the power to visualize, is none other than the omniscient Brahman, and That is the cause of the universe.

Again, it has been argued that even Brahman cannot have omniscience in the primary sense, for if It is an eternal knower, It cannot have any independence as regards the act of knowing. The answer to this is: Now then, you have to be asked, sir, "How can one lose one's omniscience owing to one's possession of the act of knowing for ever?"[93] It is a contradiction to assert that one has eternally the knowledge that is capable of revealing everything, and yet one is not omniscient. For should knowledge be non-eternal, one may know sometimes and sometimes not, so that one may as well become non-omniscient. But this defect does not arise if knowledge is eternal.[94]

Sāṁkhya: If knowledge be eternal, any mention of independence about knowing becomes illogical.

Vedāntin: No, for even in the case of the sun, possessed of continuous heat and light, independence of action is seen to be asserted by saying, "The sun burns", "The sun shines".

Sāṁkhya: It is only when the sun comes into contact with things to be burnt or illumined that one says, "It burns, it lights up". But Brahman has no contact with any object of knowledge before creation; hence the illustration is inapt.

Vedāntin: No, for even in the absence of any object, it is said, "The sun shines", thereby ascribing agency to the sun. Similarly, even though Brahman had no object of knowledge, it is reasonable to ascribe agentship to It by saying, "It saw" Hence there is no inaptitude. If, however, the need of supplying an object (for the transitive verb "to know") arises, the Vedic

[93] The objection may mean either, (i) Brahman has no eternal consciousness, or (ii) Brahman does not know eternally. The next two sentences give the answers.

[94] Omniscience and knowing do not conflict, since omniscience can express itself through the acts of knowing.

texts speaking of "seeing" by Brahman become all the more logical.

Sāṁkhya : What are those objects which form the content of God's knowledge before creation?

Vedāntin : We say that they are the unmanifested name and form which cannot be referred to either as different or non-different from Brahman, and which are about to become manifested.[95] It goes without saying that the eternally pure God is ever possessed of the knowledge of creation, continuance, and dissolution; for it is held by the adepts in the Yoga scriptures that the Yogins get their direct knowledge about the past and the future out of His grace.

The further objection was raised that, since Brahman has no body etc. before creation, no seeing is possible for It. That objection can hardly be raised; for like the effulgence of the sun, Brahman has eternal consciousness by Its very nature, so that It has no dependence on the means of knowledge. Moreover, in the case of a transmigrating soul, subject to ignorance, the rise of knowledge depends on body etc., but not so in the case of God whose knowledge is free from obstacles. And thus it is that the following two *mantras* show how God is not dependent on body etc., and how His knowledge has no covering: "He has no body and no organ; none is seen to be either equal or superior to Him. The Vedas speak of His diverse supreme powers as also of His spontaneous action that is accomplished by His vigour arising from knowledge"[96] (Śv. VI. 8); "Without hands and feet He grasps and moves quickly; he sees without eyes, hears without ears. He knows (all) that is to be known, but none can know Him. Him they call the first, the great, and the all-pervasive Entity" (Śv. III. 19).

[95] In the beginning, Brahman's limiting adjunct Māyā undergoes a change conducive to creation. The causes that had brought about the dissolution become exhausted then, thus clearing the way for the creative tendency inherent in Māyā. And Brahman then visualizes all the future objects that lie buried in Māyā in a subtle form. That being an act and the objects of vision being present, God is an agent in the primary sense.

[96] The vigour of knowledge—the clear reflection of Consciousness on the transformation of Māyā.

Sāṁkhya: From your point of view there can be no soul, distinct from God, which can transmigrate and whose knowledge can have limitations, for the Vedic text says, "There is no other witness but Him, . . . no other knower but Him" (Bṛ. III. vii. 23). So what do you mean by asserting that for a soul under bondage, the rise of knowledge depends on body etc., but not so in the case of God?

Vedāntin: As to that, our answer is: Really speaking, there is no soul under bondage and different from God. Still just like the association of space with such conditioning factors as pots, jars, caves of mountains, etc., it is assumed that God has association with such limiting adjuncts as body etc. And people are seen to use words and ideas based on that association, as for instance, "The space in a pot", "The space in a jar", and so on, though these are non-different from space. And it is seen that by that association are created in space such false notions of difference as "The space within a pot". Similarly in the case under consideration, the idea of difference between God and a transmigrating soul is false, it having been created by non-discrimination (i.e. ignorance) which causes the ascription of the limiting adjuncts—body and the rest. And though the Self (as a distinct entity) continues as before, It is seen to remain falsely identified with the body and the rest, the identification having arisen from a series of errors preceding each other. Granted such a state of bondage, it stands to reason that the transmigrating soul should depend on body etc. for its acts of seeing.

And the argument was advanced that Pradhāna can be the (material) cause like clay etc., since it is a composite thing, but not so the non-composite Brahman; that was demolished by the fact that Pradhāna is outside the Vedic pale. How even logic establishes the causality of Brahman, and not that of Pradhāna etc., will be elaborated under the aphorisms starting with, "It is not so, for its characteristics are different"[97] (II. i. 4).

(The *Sāṁkhyas*) enter a protest here: As for the assertion

[97] Brahman is not the material cause of the universe, since the characteristics of the universe are different from those of Brahman.

that the insentient Pradhāna cannot be the cause of the universe in the face of the Vedic reference to the fact of visualizing, that can be explained from another point of view; for in common parlance even an insentient thing is referred to figuratively as sentient. As for instance, it is a matter of experience that on noticing the bank of a river on the point of collapsing, they say, "The bank is about (lit. "wishes") to fall", where sentience is ascribed to the insentient bank. Similarly with regard to Pradhāna, from which creation is imminent, there may be a figurative ascription of sentience by saying, "It saw". Just as somebody in ordinary life first plans thus, "I shall bathe, and then eat, and go to the village in the afternoon by riding on a chariot", and having planned thus, he acts in that order, so also Pradhāna transforms itself as Mahat and the rest in a regular order, so as to be referred to figuratively as a sentient entity.

Objection: Why, again, should the seeing in the primary sense be discarded in favour of a secondary one?

Sāṁkhya: Because the figurative use of sentience is noticed in the cases of insentient things like water and fire in such sentences as, "That fire saw (or thought)" (Ch. VI. ii. 3), "These waters saw" (Ch. VI. ii. 4). Therefore from the fact of occurring in a context of secondary uses (in Ch. VI. ii. 2-4), it is to be understood that the "seeing" by Existence (which is but another name for Pradhāna) is spoken of in a secondary sense.

Vedāntin: This contingency having arisen, an aphorism is presented here:

गौणश्चेन्नात्मशब्दात् ॥ ६ ॥

चेत् If it be argued, (that the "seeing" is) गौण: in a secondary sense, then न it is not so, आत्म-शब्दात् owing to the use of the word Self.

6. If it be argued that the seeing is in a secondary sense, we say, not so, owing to the use of the word Self.

The assertion is wrong that the insentient Pradhāna is referred to by the word Existence and that "seeing is ascribed to it in a secondary sense just as in the cases of water and fire".

Why?

"Owing to the use of the word Self." After the introductory sentence, "O amiable one, this universe, before its creation, was but Existence" (Ch. VI. ii. 1), the creation of fire, water, and earth is stated in, "It saw. . . . It created fire" (Ch. VI. ii. 3). And then the text refers to that very seeing Existence as well as those fire, earth, and water by the word "deity", and the text says, "That Deity, that is such, saw (or thought), 'Now then let me manifest name and form by Myself entering into these three deities as the *jīva* (individual soul) that is but (My) Self' " (Ch. VI. iii. 2). Now, if insentient Pradhāna had been imagined to be the seer in some secondary sense, then Pradhāna being the entity under discussion, it should have been alluded to by the text, "That Deity that is such". But in that case the Deity would not call the individual soul His own Self. For from usage and derivation the word *jīva* (the individual soul) means that which lives (i.e. has sentience), controls the body, and holds together the organs and senses. How can that soul be the Self of the insentient Pradhāna? For the Self is the same as one's very essence. The insentient Pradhāna cannot certainly have the sentient soul as its very essence. On the contrary, if Brahman, that is Consciousness, is accepted as the seer in the primary sense, Its use of the word Self with reference to the individual soul becomes justifiable. So also is the case with the text, "That (Existence) which is this (extremely) subtle thing, is the Self of all this (universe). That is Reality; That is the Self. That thou art, O Śvetaketu" (Ch. VI. vii. 8). By saying, "That is the Self", that text presents that Reality, that subtle Self, as the Self under consideration, and then in the text, "That thou art, O Śvetaketu", occurs the instruction about It as the Self of the conscious being Śvetaketu. But the "seeing" in the case of water and fire is secondary, since they are insentient inasmuch as they are objects of perception. Besides, they are mentioned as factors employed in the manifestation of name and form. Moreover, there is nothing like the word Self in their case to make their "seeing" a possibility in the primary sense. Hence it is reasonable that the "seeing" by them should be secondary as in the case of (the falling) of the bank of a river. Or the "seeing" by them too may be in the primary sense, this being possible from the point of view of the Reality forming their basis. But we pointed out that the "seeing" by Reality is not secondary because of the use of the word Self.

Sāṁkhya: It may, however, be held that the word Self can be applied even to the insentient Pradhāna, for it performs everything for the Self. This is just like using the word Self in such an expression as, "Bhadrasena is my Self", by a king in respect of a servant doing everything for him. As an officer serves a king by engaging himself in making peace, waging war, etc., so Pradhāna serves the Self, the all-pervasive conscious Entity, by arranging emancipation and enjoyment for It. Or the same word Self can mean both sentient and insentient things, for such expressions are used in common parlance as, "The elements themselves", "The organs themselves", ("The supreme Self"), etc., just as much as the same word "*jyotis*" (fire) is used for a sacrifice as well as fire. So how can it be inferred from the use of the word "Self" that "seeing" is not applied in a secondary sense?

Vedāntin: Therefore the answer is being given:

तन्निष्ठस्य मोक्षोपदेशात् ॥ ७ ॥

मोक्ष-उपदेशात् Because liberation is taught तन्निष्ठस्य for one devoted to That.

7. *(Pradhāna is not the meaning of the word "Self"), because liberation is promised for one who holds on to That.*

The insentient Pradhāna cannot be implied by the word "Self"; for the super-sensuous Existence, forming the topic under discussion, is referred to in the text, "That is the Self" (Ch. VI. vii. 8), and then by saying, "That thou art" (ibid.), the need of devotedness to It[98] is advised for a sentient being who has to be liberated. Still later, liberation itself is taught in

[98] Thinking of Existence-Brahman as identified with oneself.

the words, "One who has a teacher knows. For him there is but that much delay as is needed for freedom (from the present body); then He becomes identified with Reality" (Ch. VI. xiv. 2). If by saying "That thou art", the scripture should make one understand the insentient Pradhāna to be the meaning of the word Reality, that is to say, impart the instruction, "Thou art insentient", to a sentient being desirous of liberation, then the scripture, speaking contrariwise, will bring evil for a man and lose its validity. But the scripture being free from defects, should not be fancied to be invalid. If, however the scripture, authoritative as it is, should tell an ignorant man, aspiring for liberation, that the insentient non-Self is his Self, he will not give up that outlook about the Self, owing to his faith (in the scripture) like the blind man holding on to the tail of an ox.[99] As a result, he will not know the Self that is different from that non-Self. And in that case he will be deflected from liberation and get into trouble. Hence it is reasonable to hold that, even as the scriptures advise about such true means as the Agnihotra sacrifice for one desirous of heaven etc., so also they teach the aspirant for liberation about the real Self in such texts as, "That is the Self" (Ch. VI. vii. 8), "That thou art, O Śvetaketu" (ibid.). On this view the instruction about liberation to one sticking on to truth becomes justifiable on the analogy of one getting freed by taking hold of a heated axe.[100] On the contrary, if instruction is imparted about something as the real Self that is but indirectly so, this will only amount to a form

[99] A blind man lost his way in a forest. A wicked man accosted him courteously and, thus gaining confidence, brought a heifer and asked the blind man to take hold of its tail, assuring him that it would lead him out of the forest. In good faith the blind man followed the advice, holding on to the tail tenaciously. As a result he was dragged over rough ground and brambles, getting cuts all the time.

[100] The Chāndogya Upaniṣad cites this example (VI. xiv). When somebody, accused of theft, denied the charge, a red-hot axe was brought for testing him. If he was truthful, the truth protected him, and he was not harmed by taking hold of it. So he was released. But if he lied, the lie did not protect him; the axe burnt him, and he was punished. The point is that truth saves a man. So also one holding on to Brahman, that is Truth, becomes liberated.

of meditation called *Sampad*,[101] as contained in the instruction, "One should meditate thus, 'I am the vital force'" (Ai. Ā. II. i. 2.6), and its result will be impermanent. But to speak of it in that sense as an instruction about liberation becomes inconsistent. Accordingly, the word "Self" is not used in a secondary sense with regard to the inscrutable Reality. The use of the word "Self" in a secondary sense, in the case of a servant, in the sentence, "Bhadrasena is my Self", is justifiable since the difference between the master and the servant is obvious. Moreover, from the fact that something is referred to in a figurative sense somewhere, it is illogical to give a figurative meaning to something else when the only source of getting knowledge about it is verbal communication; for that will result in losing faith everywhere. And the statement is false that, on the analogy of the use of the same word "*jyotis*" (fire) for both sacrifice and fire, the word "Self" can be used for both sentient and insentient things; for it is wrong to assume different meanings for the same word (in the same context). Therefore (the real position is that) the word "Self", implying a conscious entity in its primary sense, is used in a figurative sense in such sentences as, "The elements themselves", "The organs themselves", by ascribing sentience to these. Even if the word "Self" be common to different things, it cannot be pronounced to imply either of the two (sentience or insentience) unless there be some determining factor like the context or a word prefixed. Not that any such factor can definitely decide here in favour of the insentient (Pradhāna). As a matter of fact, the subject under consideration is Existence that visualizes. Besides, Śvetaketu, a conscious being, is near at hand. And we said that it is not possible that the insentient should be the Self of the sentient Śvetaketu. Hence the conclusion arrived at is that the word "Self" here refers to the sentient. Even the word "*jyotis*" implies by common usage that (fire) which illumines; but from the similarity of illuminating, arrived at by some eulogistic fancy (*Arthavāda*), it is applied to a sacrifice: thus the illustration has no cogency.

[101] Where something inferior is thought of as some other superior thing owing to some similarity and not identity (see f.n. 65).

Or the aphorism can be interpreted differently. The explanation will be that, in the previous aphorism itself, the un-Vedic Pradhāna was explained away as beyond the possibility of being meant by the word "Self" in any secondary or generic sense. And so in the present aphorism, "... because liberation is promised for one who holds on to That", an independent reason is offered for refuting Pradhāna as the cause of the universe. Thus the insentient Pradhāna is not the meaning of the word "Existence" (*Sat*).

For what additional reason is Pradhāna not meant by "Existence"?

हेयत्वावचनाच्च ॥ ८ ॥

हेयत्व-अवचनात् Because of the absence of any mention of rejection, च as also (another reason).

8. (Pradhāna has not been spoken of even indirectly), because there is no subsequent mention of its rejection, and (because that militates against the assertion at the beginning).

Supposing that Pradhāna, though it is not the Self, is meant here by the word "Existence" and is taught in the texts, "That is the Self" (Ch. VI. vii. 8) and "That thou art" (ibid.), the Upaniṣad (or teacher), seeking to teach the primary Self, should have spoken later on that Pradhāna is to be rejected, so that after hearing that (earlier) instruction the aspirant may not cling on to that Pradhāna as the Self, owing to his not having been enlightened about the (true) Self. This can be illustrated thus: A man desirous of pointing out the (tiny star) Arundhatī, first shows a nearby big star indirectly as the Arundhatī itself. And then he discards it and shows subsequently the Arundhatī itself. Similarly (here also) the text should have said, "This is not the Self." But it has not been done so. Rather it is seen that the Sixth Chapter (of the Chāndogya Upaniṣad) terminates by clinging on to the knowledge of Existence.

The word "and" (in the aphorism) is used to point to an additional reason, viz that the assumption of Pradhāna runs counter to the assertion started with. Granted even that there is a subsequent denial, there arises thereby the contingency of contradicting the initial premise. The premise started with is that everything becomes known on knowing the cause; for at the start of the conversation we hear: "(Gautama says), 'Did you, O Śvetaketu, ask about that (entity which is known from) instruction (alone, and) through which the unheard becomes heard, the unthought becomes thought (*manana*), and the unmeditated becomes meditated (*nididhyāsana*)?' (Śvetaketu): 'How can that entity be possibly known from instruction alone?' 'As after knowing a lump of clay, O amiable one, everything made of clay is known, since all modifications have speech as their origin and exist in name only, clay alone being the reality (Ch. VI. i. 3), . . . thus, O amiable one, is this Reality known from instruction' " (Ch. VI. i. 2-6). Besides, even if Pradhāna, the so-called Existence which is the cause of all objects of experience (i.e. enjoyment and suffering), be known either as an acceptable or rejectable thing, those entities coming under the category of experiencers (i.e. subjects) will still remain unknown,[102] for the experiencing subjects as a class are not modifications of Pradhāna. Therefore Pradhāna is not referred to by the word "Existence".

What further reason is there to show that Pradhāna is not referred to by the word "Existence"?

स्वाप्ययात् ॥ ९ ॥

स्व-अप्ययात् Because of the merger into one's Self.

9. Because of the merger of the individual into his own Self.

With regard to the very cause, called "Existence", it is heard from the Vedic text: "O amiable one, when in the state of sleeping thus, the individual gets the epithet of *svapiti* (he sleeps), then he becomes unified with Existence, he becomes *apīta* (merged) *svam* (into his own Self). Therefore they call him *svapiti* (he sleeps), for he becomes unified in his own Self"

[102] So that the premise, "All is known by knowing one", will be falsified.

(Ch. VI. viii. 1). This text gives the derivative meaning of the name *svapiti* of the individual, as it is well known in the world. The Self is meant here by the word *sva*. The meaning is that he finds himself arrived at, that is to say, he becomes absorbed into that which is being considered here under the name "Existence". The root *i* (meaning "to go"), when preceded by the prefix *api*, is familiarly known to mean merger, for it is seen that origin and dissolution are referred to by the phrase *prabhava-apyayau*. The individual soul keeps awake so long as it is under the influence of the characteristics of those objects of sense-perception which it apprehends as a result of its contact with the conditioning factors constituted by the diverse manifestations of the mind.[103] It assumes the name of mind while seeing dreams under the influence of the impressions of the experiences of the waking state. And when these two conditioning factors become inactive in the state of sleep, it appears to be merged, as it were, in the Self, owing to the absence of particularization created by limiting adjuncts; and hence it is said to have become merged in its own Self.[104] This is like the Upaniṣadic derivation of the word *hṛdaya* (lit. heart) shown in, "That Self exists verily 'in the heart' (*hṛdi*). This indeed is its etymological meaning, '*Hṛdi ayam* (in the heart it is)'. Therefore it is called *hṛdayam*" (Ch. VIII. iii. 3). Or this is like the showing of the root meaning underlying the use of the words *aśanāya* and *udanya* in, "It is *āpaḥ* (waters) indeed that *nayante* (digest) the *aśita* (eaten food)", (and hence water is called *aśanāya* (Ch. VI. viii. 3), "It is fire indeed that *nayate* (dries up) what is drunk (i.e. *udaka*)", (therefore fire is called *udanya*) (ibid.). Similarly with the help of derivation, the text shows the meaning of the term *svapiti*, viz that the individual gets merged in his own Self called Exist-

[103] The changes occurring in the mind in relation to sense-objects are the limiting adjuncts of the Self. Through them It comes into contact with gross objects like pot etc. Through that relationship It perceives those objects, including the body, and mistakes the body as Itself. This is Its waking state.

[104] Thus merger really means freedom from limiting adjuncts and not becoming something else.

ence.[105] Furthermore, the sentient soul cannot attain the insentient Pradhāna as its very reality. Even if it be argued that Pradhāna itself is referred to by the word *sva* (its own Self), because it belongs to the soul, still it will amount to a contradiction to say that the sentient merges in the insentient. And there is this other Upaniṣadic text which reveals the merger of the individual into a conscious entity in the state of sleep: "Being completely embraced by the conscious Self, it does not know anything external or anything internal" (Bṛ. IV. iii. 21). Accordingly, that in which all sentient creatures merge is a conscious entity called "Existence", which is the cause of the universe. But Pradhāna is not so.

How, again is Pradhāna not the cause of the universe?

गतिसामान्यात् ॥ १० ॥

गति-सामान्यात् Because the knowledge is the same.

10. Because the knowledge (gathered from the various Upaniṣads) is the same (as regards Consciousness being the cause).

If the cause were diversely apprehended even in the Upaniṣads, just as it is in the schools of the logicians—if Brahman were the cause somewhere, while somewhere else it were the insentient Pradhāna, and still at other places something else—then the Vedic mention of "hearing" etc. could have been interpreted at times in a way to conform to the theory of Pradhāna as the cause. But no such difference of apprehension occurs. In all the Upaniṣads, Consciousness is apprehended uniformly as the cause, as for instance in the texts: "As from a burning fire, the sparks fly diversely in different directions, similarly from this Self all the senses and organs originate in their respective loci. After the senses originate their presiding deities, and after the deities emerge the sense-objects" (Kau. III. 8), "From that very Self, that is such, originated space" (Tai. II. i), "From the Self indeed came all this" (Ch. VII.

[105] The derivation here is not a mere figure of speech, but it points to a fact, even as the Upaniṣadic derivations do in other places.

xxvi. 1), "From the Self emerges this vital force" (Pr. III. 3), etc., where all the Upaniṣads reveal the Self as the cause. And we said that the word "Self" implies a conscious entity. This also is a great proof of the validity of the Upaniṣads, that just like the eyes etc., imparting the same kind of knowledge about colour etc., the Upaniṣads also impart the same kind of knowledge about the Self's being the cause of the universe. Hence it follows from the uniformity in the trend (of the meaning imparted) that omniscient Brahman is the cause of the universe.

What more reason is there to prove that Brahman is the cause of the universe?

श्रुतत्वाच्च ॥ ११ ॥

च श्रुतत्वात् And because revealed in the Upaniṣads.

11. And because (Brahman is) revealed (as such) in the Upaniṣads.

In the very words of the Śvetāśvatara Upaniṣad, Brahman is presented as the cause of the universe. Having introduced the all-knowing God, the Śvetāśvatara Upaniṣad says, "In this universe He has no master, no ruler; nor has He any distinguishing sign. He is the cause and the ordainer of the masters of the organs. He has no originator and no ordainer" (Śv. VI. 9). Therefore it is proved that omniscient God is the cause of the universe, and not Pradhāna or anything else.

Topic 6: The Blissful One

Opponent: It has been established with the help of logic that the Upaniṣadic texts, referred to by the aphorisms starting with, "That from which the birth etc. of this are derived" (I. i. 2) and ending with, "Because revealed in the Upaniṣads" (I. i. 11), aim at proving that omniscient and omnipotent God is the cause of the origin, continuance, and dissolution of the universe. And by asserting that the same kind of knowledge is gathered from all the Upaniṣads, it has been explained that all the Upaniṣads speak of a conscious entity as the cause. What then is the idea of proceeding with the remaining portion of the book?

The answer (of the *Vedāntin*) is: Brahman is known in two aspects—one as possessed of the limiting adjunct constituted by the diversities of the universe which is a modification of name and form, and the other devoid of all conditioning factors and opposed to the earlier. There are many texts like the following which, by making a division between the subject-matters of knowledge and ignorance, show in a thousand ways these two aspects of Brahman: "Because when there is duality, as it were, then one sees something.... But when to the knower of Brahman everything has become the Self, then what should one see and through what?" (Bṛ. IV. v. 15), "That is the infinite (absolute Brahman) where (the illumined) one does not see anything else, does not hear anything else, does not know anything else; while that is the finite (qualified Brahman) where one sees something else, hears something else, knows something else. That which is infinite is verily immortal, while that which is finite is mortal" (Ch. VII. xxiv. 1), "The supreme Self, which after creating all forms and then giving them names, (enters into them as individual souls and) continues to utter those names" (Tai. Ā. III. xii. 7), "It is without parts, action, change, defect, and virtue and vice; It is the supreme bridge leading to immortality, and It is like fire that has burnt out its fuel" (Śv. VI. 19), "Not this, not this" (Bṛ. II. iii. 6), "It is neither gross nor minute, neither short nor long" (Bṛ. III. viii. 8), "That which is different from the Absolute is finite; that which is different from the Qualified is the Absolute". That being the case, it is in the state of ignorance that Brahman can come within the range of empirical dealings, comprising the object of (worshipful or notional) meditation, the meditator, and so on. Of such meditations, some are conducive to the attainment of higher states and some to liberation by stages, and some to the greater efficacy of actions.[106] These differ in

[106] For instance, worship of symbols, meditation on Brahman as confined in the heart, meditation on *Udgītha* respectively.

accordance with the qualities or conditioning factors involved.[107] Although the one God, the supreme Self, is to be meditated on as possessed of those qualities, still the results differ in accordance with the quality meditated on, as is stated in the Vedic texts: "One becomes just what one meditates Him to be", "After departure from this world, a man becomes what he had willed to be (i.e. meditated on)" (Ch. III. xiv. 1). This is also borne out by the Smṛti, "Remembering whatever object, at the end, he leaves the body, that alone is reached by him, O son of Kuntī" (Gītā, VIII. 6). Although it is the same Self that remains hidden in all beings—moving or stationary—still in the text, "He who meditates on the Self, manifested in a more pronounced way, attains It" (Ai. Ā. II. iii. 2.1), one hears about the Self—unchanging and ever homogeneous though It is —that there is a difference in the degrees of Its manifestation of glory and power, that being caused by the gradation of the minds by which It becomes conditioned. In the Smṛti also there is the text: "Whatever being there is great, prosperous, or powerful, that know thou to be a product of a part of my splendour" (Gītā, X. 41), where it is enjoined that wherever there is an excess of greatness etc. it is to be worshipped as God. Similarly here also it will be stated that the effulgent all-pervasive entity, residing in the solar orb, must be the supreme Self, for (the mention of) the transcendence by Him of all sins is an indication to that effect (B. S. I. i. 20). This also is the line of interpretation that is noticeable in the aphorism, "The word *ākāśa* (lit. space) is used in the sense of Brahman, for Brahman's indicatory mark is in evidence" (I. i. 22), etc. Thus also it is a fact that, although the knowledge of the Self results in instantaneous liberation, yet its instruction is imparted with the help of some relationship with some conditioning factor. Accordingly, although the relationship with the conditioning factor is not the idea sought to be imparted, still from the reference to the superior and inferior Brahman the doubt may arise that the knowledge refers to either of the two; and

[107] Quality—e.g. Brahman as possessed of true resolve, etc. Conditioning factors—e.g. Brahman as existing in the heart.

this has to be decided upon by taking into consideration the trend of the sentences. The present aphorism itself, "He who is full of Bliss (i.e. the Blissful One) is Brahman, because there is a repetition (of Bliss)" may be quoted as an illustration. The remaining portion of the book is proceeded with in order to show that although Brahman is one, It is spoken of in the Upaniṣad as either to be meditated on or known (respectively) with or without the help of Its relation with the limiting adjuncts. Moreover, the refutation of any other insentient thing as the cause (of the universe) that was made by the aphorism, "Because the knowledge (gathered from the various Upaniṣads) is the same" (I. i. 10), is being elaborated in the remaining text, which, while explaining other sentences as speaking of Brahman, refutes any other cause opposed to Brahman.

Doubt: After presenting successively the selves made of food (Tai. II. i. 2), vital force (Tai. II. ii. 2), mind (Tai. II. iii. 2), intelligence (Tai. II. iv. 1), it is stated, "As compared with this self made of intelligence, there is another inner self full of Bliss" (Tai II. v. 2). Here the doubt arises: Is the supreme Brahman, presented in "Brahman is Truth, Knowledge, Infinite" (Tai. II. i), spoken of here by the word "Blissful One" (*Ānandamaya*), or is it some entity like the selfs constituted by food etc., which is other than Brahman? What should be the conclusion here?

Opponent (i.e. *Vṛttikāra*): The Blissful One must be a secondary self other than Brahman.

Why?

Because He is included in the series of the secondary selfs constituted by food etc.

Objection: Even so, the Blissful One must be the primary Self, He being the inmost of all.

Opponent: It cannot be so, for He possesses such limbs as joy etc. and because the Upaniṣad refers to His embodiedness. If the Blissful Self were the primary Self, It could not have possessed (the limbs) happiness etc. But in this context the Upaniṣad says, "Of Him, joy is verily the head" (Tai. II. v), and so on. Embodiedness is also mentioned in, "Of that preceding (intelligent) Self, this One (i.e. the Blissful One) is the embodied self" (Tai. II. iii). The meaning of this is: "Of the preceding one", i.e. of the intelligent self, "this One is the embodied Self", "which" is this One full of Bliss. And it is not possible to deny the touch of joy and sorrow so long as one has a body. Therefore by the term "full of Bliss (or Blissful)" is meant the transmigrating soul.

Vedāntin : This being the position, it is said:

आनन्दमयोऽभ्यासात् ॥ १२ ॥

आनन्दमयः The Blissful One अभ्यासात् on account of repetition.

12. The Blissful One is the supreme Self on account of repetition.

The supreme Self alone can be the "One full of Bliss" (Blissful One).

Why?

Because of repetition; for it is in reference to the supreme Self alone that the word "Bliss" is repeated many times. After introducing the Blissful One, and speaking of Him as Bliss in the text, "He is Bliss to be sure" (Tai. II. vii. 1), it is stated, "For one (i.e. the individual) becomes happy by coming in contact with Bliss. Who indeed would inhale or exhale if this Bliss were not there in the supreme space (within the heart)? For this One indeed delights people" (Tai. II. vii), "This is an evaluation of Bliss" (Tai. II. viii. 1), "He attains this self full of Bliss" (Tai. II. viii. 5), "The enlightened man is not afraid of anything after realizing the Bliss of Brahman" (Tai. II. ix. 1), and "He knew Bliss as Brahman" (Tai. III. vi). In another Upaniṣad also the word Bliss is seen to be used for Brahman Itself in the sentence, "Knowledge, Bliss, Brahman" (Bṛ. III. ix. 28.7). Thus from the repeated use of the word Bliss for Brahman, it is understood that the Blissful (*Ānandamaya*) Self is Brahman.

As for the criticism that the Blissful One is also a secondary self because of His occurrence in the chain of secondary selfs, counting from the one constituted by food, that creates no difficulty, the Blissful One being the innermost of all. Being desirous of instructing about the primary Self, the scripture follows the line of understanding of common people. Thus it (first) adopts as the Self the body constituted by food and known as the Self to the extremely dull people. And then the scripture lets the successive ones, which are really non-Selves, to be grasped as the selfs of the earlier ones, being successively inner than and similar to the earlier ones, like the images formed by pouring molten copper etc. into moulds. By following such a process for easy comprehension, the scripture teaches about the Blissful One, who is the Self in the real sense. This is the more logical interpretation. As in the case of showing the star called Arundhatī (B. S. I. i. 8), the real Arundhatī happens to be the one mentioned last after the indication of many stars which are assumed to be Arundhatī, similarly here also the Blissful One must be the primary Self, He being the inmost of all.

And the objection was raised that for the primary Self it is illogical to fancy joy etc. as Its head etc. But that fanciful ascription of limbs occurs not because of the nature of the Blissful Self, but because of the presence of the penultimate limiting adjunct (intellect) immediately before. Therefore the objection is groundless. The embodiedness of the Blissful One too is spoken of in a context of the successive embodiedness of the food-self and the rest; and hence, unlike the individual soul, the Blissful Self has no real embodiedness. Accordingly, the Blissful One is the supreme Self.

विकारशब्दान्नेति चेन्न प्राचुर्यात् ॥ १३ ॥

विकार-शब्दात् Owing to the use of a word denoting modification **न** not so, **इति चेत्** if it be argued thus, (then) **न** not (so); **प्राचुर्यात्** because of abundance.

13. If it be argued that (the Blissful One) is not Brahman, owing to the use of a word (suffix) denoting modification, we say no, for the word is used in the sense of abundance.

Here the *opponent* says: The Blissful One cannot be the supreme Self.

Why?

Because of the use of the word *mayaṭ* (as a suffix) denoting modification. The phrase "Blissful One" (*Ānandamaya*, formed from a combination of *ānanda*, Bliss, and *mayaṭ*, made of) is to be understood as denoting a modification, as distinguished from the original word (Bliss) itself;[108] for *mayaṭ* conveys the idea of modification here. Therefore the word *Ānandamaya* (made of Bliss), like the words *annamaya* (made of food) etc., conveys the sense of modification.

Vedāntin: No, for in the Smṛti (i.e. Pāṇini's grammar V. iv. 21) it is mentioned that (the suffix) *mayaṭ* has also the sense of abundance. Thus in the aphorism, "Hence *mayaṭ* is used when the intention is to convey an abundance of the basic idea (contained in the word prefixed)", it is shown that *mayaṭ* is used to indicate abundance. As in the illustration, "*Annamayo yajño bhavati*—The sacrifice must have an abundance of food", *annamaya* means an abundance of food, so also Brahman, having an abundance of Bliss, is called *ānandamaya* (full of Bliss). And the plenitude of the Bliss of Brahman follows from the fact that (in the course of a graded evaluation of Bliss in the Taittirīya Upaniṣad), the start is made from the human plane, and then it is shown that the Bliss in each subsequent plane is a hundredfold of the preceding one, the Bliss of Brahman being unsurpassable (II. viii). Hence *mayaṭ* has the sense of abundance.

तद्धेतुव्यपदेशाच्च ॥ १४ ॥

च And तत्-हेतु-व्यपदेशात् Owing to the indication as the source of that.

14. For the further reason that Brahman is indicated as the source of Bliss.

The suffix *mayaṭ* is used in the sense of abundance for the

[108] In "He eats wheat with vegetables" what is meant is that the modification of wheat (e.g. bread) is being eaten with curries. Thus the original words may denote their modifications. So by a reverse process *Ānandamaya* denotes *ānanda* itself. The opponent denies this position.

further reason that the Upaniṣadic text, "For this One indeed enlivens people" (Tai. II. vii. 1), declares Brahman as the source of Bliss. The word *ānandayāti* (in this text) means the same as *ānandayati*. One who delights others is known to be possessed of an abundance of Bliss, just as in the world a man who makes others rich is known to be abundantly rich. Thus since *mayaṭ* can be used in the sense of plenitude as well, the Blissful One must be the supreme Self.

मान्त्रवर्णिकमेव च गीयते ॥ १५ ॥

च And मान्त्रवर्णिकम् एव the very one spoken of in the *mantra* गीयते is declared.

15. And the very Brahman spoken of in the mantra is declared in the brāhmaṇa (portion explaining the mantra).

The Blissful One must be the supreme Self for this additional reason: After commencing with the sentence, "A knower of Brahman attains the Highest" (Tai. II. i. 1), the very Brahman that was introduced in the *mantra* text, "Brahman is Truth, Knowledge, Infinite" (ibid.), as distinguished by such characteristics as "truth, knowledge, infinity", is spoken of in the *brāhmaṇa* portion. That very Brahman from which the elements, counting from space, emanate, that Brahman which creates the beings and then entering into them dwells in their hearts as the inmost Self of all, that Brahman for the sake of whose knowledge a topic has been pursued by saying "another internal self", "another internal self", and so on (Tai. II. ii–v)—that very Brahman is declared in that *mantra* portion, and that very Brahman is spoken of in the *brāhmaṇa* portion by the text, "There is another self called the Blissful One who is inside this" (Tai. II. v. 2). It is proper that the *mantra* and *brāhmaṇa* (portions) should bear the same meaning, for they are never contradictory. Otherwise it will lead to the fault of abandoning the topic under discussion and starting with something not under consideration. Not that any self is mentioned as dwelling inside the Blissful One as is done in the case of the food-self etc. And "that knowledge gathered by Bhṛgu and imparted by

Varuṇa" (Tai. III. vi) relates to this only. Therefore the Blissful One must be the supreme Self.

नेतरोऽनुपपत्तेः ॥ १६ ॥

न Not इतरः the other one अनुपपत्तः because of illogicality.

16. The other is not the supreme Self, because that is illogical.

For this additional reason, the Blissful One, and not the other, must be the supreme Self. "The other" is the transmigrating being which is different from God, that is to say, the individual soul. The individual soul is not meant by the term Blissful One. Why?

Because of illogicality. Relating to the Blissful One, it is stated in the Upaniṣad, "He wished, 'Let me become many, let me be born'. He undertook a deliberation. Having deliberated, He created all this that exists" (Tai. II. vi. 1). The deliberation before the creation of body etc., the non-difference of the things created from the creator, and the creation of all the modifications mentioned in that text cannot be justifiable for any one other than the supreme Self.

भेदव्यपदेशाच्च ॥ १७ ॥

च And भेद-व्यपदेशात् because of the assertion of difference.

17. And because of the assertion of the difference (between the individual soul and the supreme Self).

For this further reason the Blissful One is not a transmigrating soul. In the context dealing with the Blissful One, the individual soul and the Blissful One are mentioned separately in the text: "He is Bliss (*rasa*) indeed. For one (i.e. the individual) becomes happy by getting that Bliss" (Tai. II. vii. 1). Not that the acquirer can be the thing acquired.

Opponent: In that case how can there be these Vedic and Smṛti texts, "The Self is to be sought for", "There is nothing higher than the attainment of the Self"? For it has been said that there can be no attainer (of one's own Self) as such.

Vedāntin: Quite so. Still in the case of ordinary people, it is seen that, though the Self ever retains Its true nature of being the Self, there is a false self-identification with the body etc. which are non-Self. Accordingly, for the Self that has become the body etc., such assertions are possible as: "The Self remains undiscovered and has to be sought for"; "It is unattained and has to be attained"; "It is unheard of and has to be heard of"; "It is unthought of and has to be thought of"; "It is unknown and has to be known"; and so on. But from the highest point of view, any witness or hearer other than God is denied in such texts as, "There is no other witness but Him" (Bṛ. III. vii. 23). God is different to be sure from the one imagined through ignorance to be embodied, the agent, the experiencer, and called the Self conditioned by the intellect, the difference being made in the same sense that the magician standing on the ground is fancied to be different from the magician holding sword and shield in hands and climbing up by a rope to the sky, though in reality the first is the very essence of the latter; or it is so in the sense that the space, unlimited by any conditioning factor, is different from the space delimited by such conditioning factors as a pot etc. Taking for granted such a difference between the supreme Self and the Self identified with the intellect, it has been said, "The other is not the supreme Self, because that is illogical", and "And because of the assertion of difference".

कामाच्च नानुमानापेक्षा ॥ १८ ॥

च And **कामात्** owing to wish **न** no **अनुमान-अपेक्षा** reliance on inference.

18. There can be no reliance on inference (for arriving at Pradhāna) owing to (the mention of) desire.

Besides, in the context of the Blissful One there is a mention of wishfulness in the text, "He wished, 'Let me become many, let me be born' " (Tai. II. vi. 1). Therefore the insentient Pradhāna, fancied by the Sāṁkhyas through inference, is not to be relied on as representing either the Blissful One or the cause of the universe. Although Pradhāna was refuted under the aphorism, "Because of the attribution of thinking, the one not taught in the Upaniṣads is not the cause of the universe" (I. i. 5), still with a view to elaborating how the texts concur in imparting the same kind of knowledge, it is being refuted over again as a side issue in connection with the wishfulness (Tai. II. vi. 3) mentioned in the text referred to by an earlier aphorism (I. i. 16).

अस्मिन्नस्य च तद्योगं शास्ति ॥ १९ ॥

च And शास्ति the scripture teaches तद्-योगं the absolute identity अस्य of this one अस्मिन् with this One.

19. Moreover, the scripture teaches the absolute identity of this one with this (One).

The phrase Blissful One is not used to mean either Pradhāna or the individual being, because the scripture enjoins the identity of this one, i.e. the enlightened individual being, with this, i.e. the Blissful One, the Self under consideration. *Tadyoga* means union in absolute identification, becoming one with that, that is to say, liberation. That union is taught by the scripture in, "Whenever the aspirant gets fearlessly established in this unseen (i.e. changeless), bodiless, inexpressible, and unsupporting One, he reaches the state of fearlessness. Whenever the aspirant creates the slightest difference in this One, he is smitten with fear" (Tai. II. vii). The idea implied is this: He does not become free from the fear of transmigration so long as he sees in this (Blissful) One the slightest difference consisting in non-identity (with the Self). But he becomes freed from the fear of transmigration as soon as he gets established in absolute identity with this Blissful One. This is possible if the supreme Self be the same as the Blissful One, but not so if either the individual being or Pradhāna be meant. Therefore it is proved that the Blissful One is the supreme Self.

Saṁkara's Correction: But we have to say this in this connection. There is a series of uses of the suffix *mayaṭ* in the sense of modification in the following passages: "That man, such as he is, is a product of the essence of food" (Tai. II. i. 1); "As compared with this self, made of the essence of food (*annamaya*), there is another inner self which is made of air (*prāṇamaya*—made of vital force)" (Tai. II. ii); "As compared with this self, there is another internal self constituted by mind (*manomaya*)" (Tai. II. iii. 1); "As compared with this, there is another internal self constituted by valid knowledge (*vijñānamaya*)" (Tai. II. iv). That being so, how can one suddenly jump to the conclusion that *mayaṭ*, occurring in *ānandamaya* (Blissful One) alone implies abundance or that the Blissful One is Brahman? For this would be like fancying an old hag as having her one half young.

Opponent : Because it is the topic of Brahman as presented by the *mantra* ("Brahman is Truth, Knowledge, Infinite").

Śaṁkara : Not so, for in that case the food-self etc. would also become Brahman.

Here the *Opponent* (Vṛttikāra) says: It is but proper that the selfs made of food etc. should not be Brahman, since other selfs are mentioned for them which are successively more internal. But in the case of the Blissful One, no internal self is mentioned. Thereby the Blissful One becomes Brahman. A contrary supposition will lead to the fault of giving up something under consideration and adopting some other thing not under discussion.

Śaṁkara : To this we say: Although unlike in the cases of the food-body etc., the Upaniṣad does not mention here any inner self for the Blissful One, still the Blissful One cannot be Brahman, inasmuch as this text occurs in regard to the Blissful One: "Of Him joy is verily the head, enjoyment is the right side, hilarity is the left side, bliss is the self (i.e. the trunk of the body), Brahman is the tail that stabilizes (or is the pedestal)" (Tai. II. v. 2). That being the case, the Brahman spoken of in the words of the *mantra* is here presented in the words, "Brahman is the tail that supports". It is in order to make that known that the five sheaths, counting from the food-self and ending with the Bliss-self are imagined. So how can there be the fault of giving up something relevant and taking up something besides the point?

Opponent : Is it not a fact that in the text, "Brahman is the tail that supports" (Tai. II. v. 2), Brahman is spoken of as a limb of the Blissful One just as it is said in, "This is the tail that supports" in the cases of the food-self and the rest? That being so, how can it be known that Brahman appears here as an independent entity in Its own right?

Śaṁkara : We say that this is known since Brahman forms the topic of discussion.

Opponent : No harm accrues by way of Brahman ceasing to be the topic even if Brahman is known as a limb of the Blissful One; for the Blissful One is Brahman.

Śaṁkara : To this we say: That will involve an illogicality inasmuch as the very same Brahman will become the whole Self, viz the Blissful One, and again It will become a part, viz the supporting tail. If either of the two has to be accepted, then it is reasonable to uphold the view that Brahman is referred to in this very text: "Brahman is the tail that supports", for the word Brahman is present there; but it is not to be sought for in the sentence presenting the Blissful One, for we miss the word Brahman there. Besides, after the statement, "Brahman is the supporting tail", it is said, "Apropos of this, here is a verse: 'If anyone knows that Brahman is non-existent, then he himself becomes non-existent. If anyone knows that Brahman does exist, then they consider him to be existing by virtue of that knowledge' " (Tai. II. vi). Since in this verse the merit and demerit of believing in the existence and non-existence of Brahman alone is mentioned without bringing in the Blissful One, it can be understood that Brahman appears in Its own right in the text, "Brahman is the supporting tail". And it is not logical to entertain any doubt about the existence or non-existence of the Blissful One; for as characterized by joy, enjoyment, etc., he is well known in the world.

Opponent : An independent entity as that Brahman is, why should It be presented as a limb of the Blissful One in the text, "Brahman is the supporting tail"?

Śaṁkara : That is no defect. The purpose is not to imply that Brahman is a limb, but to show that the Bliss, that Brahman is, is like a tail; It serves the purpose of a stabilizing (or supporting) tail. What is sought to be taught is that the Bliss, that Brahman is, is the acme and sole repository of all human joys, as is shown in another Upaniṣad, "On a particle of this very Bliss other beings live" (Bṛ. IV. iii. 32). Besides, if the Blissful One be Brahman, then a qualified Brahman, conditioned by such limbs as happiness etc., has to be accepted. But at the end of the text the absolute Brahman is heard of, It being spoken of as beyond speech and mind (in the verse): "The enlightened man is not afraid of anything after realizing that Bliss of Brahman, failing to reach which, words turn back along with the mind" (Tai. II. ix). Furthermore, the assertion of an abundance of Bliss implies the existence of sorrow as well; for in the world, abundance is dependent on the presence of a little of its opposite. And if that be admitted, then it will contradict the denial of anything except Itself in the infinite Brahman, as is stated in the text, "That is the Infinite where one sees nothing else, hears nothing else, and knows nothing else" (Ch. VII. xxiv. 1). Besides, from the difference among the various degrees of happiness in each body, it follows that the Blissful One (inside those bodies) is also different. But Brahman does not differ in different bodies, since the Upaniṣad declares Its infinitude in, "Brahman is Truth, Knowledge, Infinite" (Tai. II. i. 1); another Upaniṣad also says, "The same Deity, that is all-pervasive and the soul of all, remains hidden within all beings" (Śv. VI. 11).

Again, in the Upaniṣads it is not the repetition of the Blissful One that is met with, but rather the various synonyms of the substantive portion of the phrase (viz Bliss): "He is verily the *rasa* (source of joy); for one becomes happy by coming in contact with that source of joy. Who indeed will inhale or who will exhale, if this Bliss be not there in the supreme space (within the heart)? This One indeed enlivens people" (Tai. II. vii), "This then is an evaluation of Bliss" (Tai. II. viii), "The enlightened man is not afraid of anything after realizing that Bliss of Brahman"[109] (Tai. II. ix), "He knew Bliss as Brahman" (Tai.

[109] The Bliss that is Brahman, the "of" being used by fancying a difference, as in "The body of a building".

III. vi). Had the phrase "Blissful One" been definitely ascertained to mean Brahman, then one could fancy the repetition of the "Blissful One" even in the subsequent uses of the word Bliss alone. But the Blissful One, as pointed out by us, is not Brahman, because He has joy etc. as His head etc., and there are other reasons. Accordingly, from the use in another Upaniṣad of the substantive portion Bliss as a synonym for Brahman in the text, "Knowledge, Bliss, Brahman" (Bṛ. III. ix. 28.7), it follows that the word Bliss in such texts as, "if this Bliss be not there in the supreme space" (Tai. II. vii), refers to Brahman. But it is to be understood that the word Bliss is not a repetition of the phrase "Blissful One".

It was argued that the word *ānanda* (Bliss) is repeated together with the suffix *mayaṭ* in, "He attains the Blissful self" (Tai. II. viii). But this Blissful self does not refer to Brahman; for it occurs in a context of a succession of attainable selfs which are constituted by food etc.

Opponent: If the Blissful self to be attained be not Brahman, then the result accruing from the attainment of Brahman[110] will remain unspecified for the enlightened man.

Śaṁkara: That is no defect; for from the mention of the attainment of the Blissful One, the result achievable by the enlightened man, viz the attainment of the Brahman described as the stabilizing tail, becomes stated *ipso facto*. Besides, this result is elaborated by such texts as, "Expressive of this, there occurs this verse" (Tai. II. ix). And the text, "He wished, 'Let me become many, let me be born' " (Tai. II. vi. 2), occurring in the proximity of the Blissful One, was quoted by you. But this does not lead to the comprehension of the Brahmanhood of the Blissful One; for that text gets connected with the more proximate word Brahman, present in "Brahman is the supporting tail". And since the subsequent texts, as for instance, "That is verily the *rasa* (source of joy)" (Tai. II. vii),

[110] Stated in that context of attainment (Tai. II). In reality, *upasaṁkramaṇa* means transcendence or sublation according to Śaṁkara, and not attainment.

stem out of this text, they do not have the Blissful One as their purport.

Opponent: It is unjustifiable that "He" (*saḥ*, used in the masculine gender) in the text, "He wished" (Tai. II. vi. 2), should stand for Brahman (which is neuter).

Śaṁkara: That is not damaging; for in the text, "From that Self was born space" (Tai. II. i. 2), Brahman is referred to by the word Self (*ātmā*) which has the masculine gender. On the contrary, in the section of the Taittirīya called "The knowledge received by Bhṛgu and imparted by Varuṇa" (III. vi), it is stated, "He knew Bliss as Brahman" (ibid.), where the suffix *mayaṭ* is not used, and joy etc. are not mentioned as the head etc. Hence it is but proper that Bliss should be Brahman. Accordingly, Brahman in Itself cannot reasonably have joy etc. as Its head etc. without assuming some conditioning factor, however tenuous it be. Nor is it the intention here to reveal the conditioned Brahman, for there is the text showing the transcendence of speech and mind (Tai. II. ix. 1), Accordingly, the *mayaṭ* in *ānandamaya* is used to imply modification just as much as in *annamaya* etc., but it is not used to imply plenitude.

So the aphorisms are to be explained thus:

12. (Brahman is referred to in) आनन्दमयः the Blissful One (etc.), अभ्यासात् owing to the repetition (of the word Bliss).

Doubt: Is it the intention of the text, "Brahman is the tail that stabilizes" (Tai. II. v), to present Brahman as a limb of the Blissful One or as an independent entity?

Opponent: The use of the word tail leads to the conclusion that It is intended as a limb.

Śaṁkara: This being the position, it is said, *Ānandamayo'bhyāsāt*. (This means that) in the text, "The Blissful Self" etc., Brahman is referred to as an independent entity by saying, "Brahman is the tail that stabilizes". This is gathered from the repetition; for the absolute Brahman alone is referred to in the verse: "He becomes non-existing" etc. (Tai. II. vi. 1), which is a concluding reaffirmation (of what was started with).

13. The interpretation of *Vikāraśabdānneticenna prācuryāt* is this:

न विकारशब्दात् Not so owing to the use of a word denoting limb इति-चेत् if this be the objection, (then) न not so, प्राचुर्यात् (that word) having been used owing to continuous presence.

Your argument was that "Brahman is not an independent entity, because a limb is meant by the word *vikāra*.[111] Because the word tail, implying a limb, is used, Brahman cannot be an independent entity." That position has to be refuted. With regard to this we say: That is nothing damaging; for a word implying a limb can be justified from the standpoint of *prācurya*, which means the continuous presence (of an idea in the mind), that is to say, the persistent occurrence of the word in a context in which the limbs are predominantly in evidence. After describing the food-self etc., from the head to the tail, the turn came for the enumeration of the head and other limbs of the Blissful One; and the idea of limbs being predominant in the mind, the text said, "Brahman is the tail that stabilizes". This was not done from any motive of showing Brahman as a limb (but as a matter of habit), which fact becomes obvious from the affirmation of Brahman as an independent entity on the ground of repetition.

14. The aphorism, *Taddhetuvyapadeśācca*, is to be explained thus:

च And तत्-हेतु-व्यपदेशात् owing to the presentation (of Brahman) as the cause of all that (creation, including the Blissful One).

In the text, "He created all this that there is" (Tai. II. vi), Brahman is shown as the cause of all modifications inclusive of the Blissful One. Not that Brahman, which is the cause of Its own modification, viz the Blissful One, can be the latter's limb in any primary sense.

The other aphorisms are also to be understood, as far as

[111] Lit. "modification", but here "modified form" in the derivative sense of "that form through which anything evolves".

possible, as speaking of Brahman present in the sentence about the tail.[112]

Topic 7: The Being Inside

Doubt: It is stated in the Upaniṣad: "Now, again, He, the Puruṣa that is seen in the sun is golden in colour; His beard is golden, hair is golden, everything up to the tip of the nails is golden. His eyes are like the pink lotus that is itself as pink as the seat of a monkey. His name is *ut* (uprisen). This Puruṣa, that is such, remains lifted above all sins. Anyone meditating thus does certainly rise above sins" (Ch. I. vi. 6-8); "This is the meditation on the divine plane" (ibid.); "Then follows the meditation on the bodily plane. He, the Puruṣa, that is seen in the eye" etc. (Ch. I. vii. 5-8). Here arises a doubt: Is the Puruṣa (lit. person), who is to be worshipped in the sun and the eyes, a human being who had attained a high eminence on account of the perfection of his meditation and action, or is He the ever existing God? What is the conclusion to be arrived at?

Opponent: He must be a transmigrating soul.

Why?

Because the Upaniṣad mentions his form. For instance, such a form as possession of golden beard is mentioned for the person in the sun. For the person in the eye also we get that very form by a process of extension shown in, "Of this One that is such, the form is the same as of that One" (Ch. I. vii. 5). Not that the supreme Lord can reasonably have any form, for the

112 The remaining *sūtras* are to be explained thus:

15. च And मान्त्रवर्णिकम् एव the very Brahman mentioned in the *mantra* गीयते is declared (in the portion about the tail).

16. न इतरः The other (Blissful One) is not meant, अनुपपत्तः owing to impropriety.

17. च And भेदव्यपदेशात् owing to the teaching of difference between the two (viz that the Blissful One becomes joyous by getting the Bliss that is Brahman).

18. च And कामात् owing to the use of *kāma* (i.e. Bliss) in the sense of Brahman न no अनुमान-अपेक्षा need of inferring the Blissful One to be Brahman.

Upaniṣad says, "Soundless, touchless, formless, undiminishing" (Ka. I. iii. 15). This conclusion is supported by the mention of a place of residence in the texts: "He that is in the sun" (Ch. I. vi. 6), "He that is in the eye" (Ch. I. vii.). No residence can be asserted for the supreme Lord who is without any support, exists in His own glory, and is all-pervasive. There are also these Vedic texts in support: "On what, O venerable sir, is He seated? On His own glory" (Ch. VII. xxiv. 1), "He is all-pervasive like space and is eternal". There is this additional reason, that a limit to His glory is specified in the texts, "(He the Puruṣa in the sun) rules over the worlds that are above the sun and also over the things enjoyable to the gods" (Ch. I. vi. 8), where a limit is set to the majesty of the person in the sun; and "He, who is such, rules over the worlds below the eyes as also over the things enjoyable to men" (Ch. I. vii. 6), where a limit is set to the majesty of the person in the eye. But it is not reasonable that God's majesty should have any limitation, since it is spoken of without any reservation in the text, "This One is the lord of all, this One is the ruler (i.e. Death) of all beings, this One is the protector (i.e. Indra and other gods) of all beings; this One is like a dam that impounds so that these worlds (i.e. castes and stages of life etc.) may not get mixed up and destroyed" (Bṛ. IV. iv. 22). Therefore it is not the supreme Lord that resides in the sun and the eyes.

Vedāntin: Such being the position, we say:

अन्तस्तद्धर्मोपदेशात् ॥ २० ॥

अन्तः The One inside (is God), तत्-धर्म-उपदेशात् for His qualities are taught.

20. The Being inside is God, His qualities having been taught.

The Puruṣa[113] of whom the Upaniṣad speaks thus, "He who is in the sun, He who is in the eye" (Ch. I. vi, I. vii), must be God Himself, and not any transmigratory soul.

[113] Puruṣa is the all-pervasive entity, seen as a Person by the worshippers. Golden in that context means, made of light, i.e. self-effulgent.

Why?

Because His qualities are taught. For it is God's qualities that are taught here. Thus having revealed the name of the Person in the sun by saying, "His name is *ut* (the uprisen)" (Ch. I. vi. 7), the derivation of that name is shown as arising from the fact of remaining free from sin, in the text, "This Puruṣa that is such, remains lifted above all sins". And that name, of which the derivation has been shown, is extended to the Person in the eye by saying. "He has the same name as the other One has" (Ch. I. vii. 5). Freedom from all sins is declared about the supreme Self alone in, "That which is the Self beyond all sins" (Ch. VIII. vii), and such sentences. Similarly in the text, "He (the Person in the eye) is the *Ṛk-mantra*, the *Sāma-mantra*, the *uktha* (a kind of hymn), the *Yajur-mantra*, the three Vedas" (Ch. I. vii. 5), the Upaniṣad points out the identity of the Person in the eye with *Ṛk*, *Sāma*, etc.; and that is possible only in the case of the supreme Lord, it being reasonable that He should be everything by virtue of His being the source of all. Again, commencing with the *Ṛk* and *Sāma mantras* that are the same as the earth, fire, and so on, in the divine context, and speech, vital force, and so on, in the physical context, it is said, "Of Him the *Ṛk* and *Sāma mantras* are two bodily joints. This is in the divine context" (Ch. I. vi. 8). Similarly in the bodily context, "He (the Person in the eye) has the same two joints as the Person in the sun" (Ch. I. vii. 5). This becomes proper only if He is the Self of all. And the text, "Therefore when these people play on the *Viṇā* (lute), they sing of Him; and hence they become prosperous" (Ch. I. vii. 6), shows how He is present as music even in the human songs. This can be so if God is accepted as that Person, as is shown in the Bhagavad-Gītā, "Whatever being there is great, prosperous, or powerful, that know thou to be a product of a part of My splendour" (X. 41). Besides, the absolute power of ruling over the worlds and desires that is mentioned in the Upaniṣad, points to God. In answer to the objection that the reference in the Upaniṣad to such forms as the possession of golden beard etc. does not befit God, we say: Even for God there may be forms created at His will out of Māyā for the sake of favouring the aspirants, as is declared in the Smṛti, "O Nārada, it is a Māyā, created by Me, that you see Me in this form possessed of all the substances and qualities. You must not understand Me thus". On the contrary, when the divine aspect bereft of all qualities is spoken of, then the relevant text runs thus: "Soundless, touchless, formless, and undiminishing" (Ka. I. iii. 15), and so on. But since God is the cause of everything, He is sometimes spoken of, for the sake of adoration, as possessed of certain mundane qualities, as in, "He is possessed of all (good) action, all (good) desires, all (good) smell, all (good) tastes" (Ch. III. xiv. 2), and so on. In the same way there can be the mention of His golden beard. As for the criticism that He cannot be God, since a residence is mentioned, we say, even for the One who is established in His own glory, there can be an instruction about some seat for the sake of adoration; for being all-pervasive like space, He can very well dwell inside everything. The mention of the limitation to His majesty also occurs with reference to the bodily and divine contexts for the sake of worship. Therefore God Himself is spoken of as residing within the eye and the sun.

भेदव्यपदेशाच्चान्यः ॥ २१ ॥

च And भेद-व्यपदेशात् owing to the mention of difference अन्यः different.

21. And God is different (from the individual being) owing to the mention of difference.

God, the internal Ruler, does exist as an entity different from the individual souls identifying themselves with the bodies of the sun etc.; for their dissimilarity is stated in another Upaniṣad, in these words: "He who inhabits the sun, but is within it, whom the sun does not know, whose body is the sun, and who controls the sun from within, is the internal Ruler, your own immortal Self" (Bṛ III. vii. 9). By saying, "within the sun" and "whom the sun does not know", it is clearly shown that the internal Ruler is different from the sun which is the knower and which is an individual soul identifying itself with the intellect.[114] It is but reasonable from the similarity of the Upaniṣads that this very entity (of Bṛ. III. vii. 9) should be the Person mentioned here (in Ch. I. vi. 6-7) as inside the sun. Therefore it is proved that God Himself is spoken of here.

Topic 8: Space

Doubt : The Chāndogya Upaniṣad states thus: "(Śālāvatya asked): 'What is the goal of this world?' He (Pravāhaṇa Jaivali) answered, 'Space. For all things certainly originate from Space; and they merge by moving towards Space. For Space is certainly greater than all these, Space is their supreme goal' " (Ch. I. ix. 1). With regard to this the doubt arises: Does the word space mean the supreme Brahman or the material space?

Why does the doubt arise?

Because the word is used in both senses. The word space is well known to be used in the sense of natural space in the Vedas and common parlance; and at times it is found to be used for Brahman also, as for instance in such places as the following, where Brahman stands out as the well determined meaning from the text that follows or from the mention of some distinguishing characteristics: "If this Space that is Bliss (i.e. Brahman) had not been there" (or "If this Bliss were not there in Space") (Tai. II. vii), "Space indeed is the accomplisher (of the origin and continuance) of name and form. That in which they exist is Brahman" (Ch. VIII. xiv). Hence this doubt. What is the reasonable conclusion here?

Opponent : It must be the material space.

Why?

For that occurs to the mind instantaneously, owing to more familiar use; and this word space cannot be understood to imply both these equally, for that will lead to its having many meanings. Therefore the word space must have a secondary meaning when it is applied to Brahman, Brahman being similar

[114] The instrument of cognition, owing to identity with which the soul thinks, "I know".

to space as regards many such qualities as pervasiveness. Moreover, when a primary meaning is admissible, any secondary meaning is not to be accepted; and here it is possible to accept space in the primary sense.

Objection : If the material space be the meaning, the complementary portion of the passage becomes illogical, which runs as follows: "All things certainly originate from Space" etc. (Ch. I. ix. 1).

Opponent : That is no fault; for even material space can become the cause (of all) by evolving into air etc. in succession; for it is known (from the Upaniṣad), "From the Self, that is such, originated space, from space arose air, from air fire" (Tai. II. i), and so on. As for being greater and the ultimate goal, that is possible even for the material space with relation to the other elements. By the word space, therefore, the material space is meant.

Vedāntin : Such being the position, we say:

आकाशस्तल्लिंगात् ॥ २२ ॥

आकाशः Space (is Brahman), तत्-लिंगात् owing to the indicatory mark of that.

22. *Space (ākāśa) is Brahman, for Brahman's indicatory mark is in evidence.*

By the word Space here we should understand Brahman. Why?

Because a mark indicating Brahman is in evidence in, "For all things originate from Space to be sure" etc. (Ch. I. ix. 1). For it is an established fact in the Upaniṣads that all things originate from the supreme Brahman.

Opponent : Space, the element, has also been shown as becoming the cause by evolving through a succession of air etc.

Vedāntin : Yes, it has been shown. Yet if Brahman be not taken into account as the origin, the emphasis in the phrase "certainly from Space" and the word "all" as a qualification of "things" cannot be reconciled. So also "They merge by moving towards Space" is an indicator of Brahman. And the fact of being greater and the ultimate goal is stated in, "For Space is certainly greater than these, and Space is their ultimate goal" (ibid.). For absolute greatness is declared about the supreme Self alone in, "Greater than the earth, greater than the sky, greater than heaven, greater than all these worlds" (Ch. III. xiv. 3). Similarly the fact of being the supreme goal is more in accord with the supreme Self, It being the ultimate cause. In support of this is the Upaniṣadic text: "Knowledge, Bliss, Brahman, the supreme goal of the distributor of wealth as well as of him who has realized Brahman and lives in It" (Bṛ. III. ix. 28.7). Moreover, Jaivali, who condemns Śālāvatya's position by pointing out the defect of limitation, resorts to Space with a view to speaking of something unlimited. And then attributing the similarity of Space to *Udgītha*, he says, "This *Udgītha* (i.e. its part *Om*) is this Space, and it is great and higher than all that is high.[115] This One that is such is infinite" (Ch. I. ix. 2). That infinity is also an indication of Brahman. As for the argument that the material space occurs to the mind because of familiar use, we say that though it may occur to the mind first, it cannot be accepted after noticing the characteristics of Brahman evident in the complementary portion. We showed that the word space occurs to signify Brahman as well, as for instance in, "Space indeed is the accomplisher (revealer) of name and form" (Ch. VIII. xiv. 1). Similarly it is seen that the synonyms of space are also used for Brahman in such places as, "The Vedas are the authoritative revealers of the absolutely immutable *Vyoman* (Sky, Brahman) on which all the gods subsist" (Ṛ. V. I. clxiv. 39), "This is that knowledge received by Bhṛgu, which is established in the supreme *Vyoman*" (Tai. III. vi), "*Om Kam* (i.e. Bliss) is Brahman, *Kham* (Space) is Brahman" (Ch. IV. x. 5), "*Om* is that *Kham* (Space)—the eternal Space" (Bṛ. V. i). Even the word space occurring at the beginning of the sentence should be understood to signify Brahman, owing to the trend of the complementary portion of the text. For such a word as fire

[115] Because *Om*, a part of *Udgītha*, is great, it being the essence etc. of all and superior to all other letters.

occurring in the statement, "The fire reads the hymn", at the beginning of a text, is seen to mean a brilliant boy reading the hymn. Hence it is concluded that the word Space means Brahman.

Topic 9: Prana

In the course of discussing the meditation on *Udgītha*, it is noticed in the Upaniṣad that, after starting with, "O chanter of *Prastāva* (i.e. an introductory part of Sāma song), should you chant it in my presence without knowing the deity thereof, your head will fall"[116] (Ch. I. x. 9), the question (by Cākrāyaṇa) occurs, "Which is that deity?" And "He (Uṣasti) replies, 'It is *Prāṇa* (lit. vital force), for all these things proceed towards and merge in *Prāṇa* and from *Prāṇa* they emerge. This is that deity that is intimately associated with *Prastāva*' ", (Ch. I. xi. 4-5). The doubt arising from this and its solution are to be understood in accordance with the earlier pattern.

Doubt: The word *Prāṇa* is found to be used in the sense of Brahman in such texts as, "O amiable one, the mind is tethered to *Prāṇa*"[117] (Ch. VI. viii. 2), "*Prāṇa* of *Prāṇa*"[118] (Bṛ. IV. iv. 18). But the more familiar use in the world as well as in the Vedas is in the sense of the vital force that is a form of air (i.e. energy). Therefore the doubt arises here as to which of the two should be reasonably accepted here.

Opponent: It is proper to accept the modification of air called the vital force having a fivefold function, for it was pointed out that the word *Prāṇa* is more familiarly known to imply that.

Objection: Here also it is proper to accept Brahman, for Its characteristics are in evidence just as before. Here also the entry and emergence of all the elements, noticeable in the complementary portion, bear witness to God's activity.

Opponent: Not so, for even in case of the chief vital force

[116] This is Uṣasti's warning to Cākrāyaṇa.

[117] In deep sleep, the soul, having the mind as its limiting adjunct, becomes unified with *Prāṇa* or Brahman.

[118] *Prāṇa* or Brahman imparts existence and expression to the vital force.

(in the mouth), the entry and emergence of all the elements are noticeable in, "When a man is in deep sleep, then speech enters into *Prāṇa*, the eye enters into *Prāṇa*, the ear enters into *Prāṇa*, the mind enters into *Prāṇa*. When he wakes up again, they re-emerge from *Prāṇa* itself"[119] (Ś. B. X. iii. 3.6). It is a fact of common experience that the functions of the senses and organs get merged in the vital function that does not get lost in sleep; and at the time of waking, they rise out of *Prāṇa*. And because the senses and organs are the quintessence of the elements, it is nothing contradictory that the trend of the complementary portion of the text should point to the entry and emergence of the elements into and out of the vital force. Moreover, the Sun and Food, who are the deities of *Udgītha* and *Pratihāra* (portions of the Sāma song) respectively, are mentioned after *Prāṇa*. Not that they have Brahmanhood. Because of this similarity with them, *Prāṇa* also is not Brahman.

Vedāntin : This being the position, the aphorist says:

अत एव प्राणः ॥ २३ ॥

अतः एव On that very ground प्राणः *Prāṇa*.

23. On that very ground, Prāṇa (is Brahman).

The reason "Because Brahman's indicatory mark is in evidence" was advanced under the earlier aphorism. "On that very ground" of the presence of the indicatory mark of Brahman, the word *Prāṇa* also should mean the supreme Brahman. For the association of *Prāṇa* with the characteristics of Brahman is met with in the text, "All the things proceed towards and merge in *Prāṇa* and from It they emerge" (Ch. I. xi. 5), where the mention of the origin and dissolution of all things, stated to be proceeding from *Prāṇa*, proves that *Prāṇa* is Brahman.

Opponent : Did we not say that the mention of the entry and emergence is reconcilable even if the chief *Prāṇa* be accepted, this being a matter of experience during sleep and waking.

[119] Eye etc. stand for the corresponding organs which are the products of the elements.

To this we (*Vedāntins*) say: During sleep and waking we notice only the entry and the emergence of the senses and organs into and out of *Prāṇa,* but not of all the elements, whereas the entry and the emergence of all the things, presided over by the individual souls, along with the bodies and senses, are spoken of here, as is seen in the text, "All these things certainly" etc. (Ch. I. xi. 5). Even if this text, mentioning all things, signifies the elements, the characteristics of Brahman are found to be fully in accord.

Opponent: Is it not a fact that in the following text we come across the entry and emergence, during sleep and waking, of the senses together with their objects into and out of *Prāṇa*?—"When a sleeping man has no dream whatsoever, and he becomes one with this *Prāṇa*, then into that *Prāṇa* enters speech together with all the names" (Kau. III. 3).

Vedāntin: Even there the word *Prāṇa* means Brahman, for the characteristic of Brahman is in evidence.[120]

And the argument is baseless that *Prāṇa* is not Brahman owing to the use of the word in association (or in the proximity of) Food and the Sun; for mere proximity counts for nothing when the obvious meaning of *Prāṇa* is known to be Brahman from the trend of the complementary text. And the argument was advanced that the more usual meaning of *Prāṇa* is the vital force having a fivefold function; that has to be met in the same way as in the case of the word Space.[121] Therefore it is concluded that the Deity of *Prastāva* is Brahman.

Some people think that this aphorism alludes to the texts, "*Prāṇa* of *Prāṇa*" (Vital force of vital force) (Bṛ. IV. iv. 18), and "O amiable one, the mind is tethered to *Prāṇa* (Ch. VI. viii. 2). That too is unjustifiable, since there is no reasonable scope for doubt (in these two texts) in the face of the differ-

[120] Because *Prāṇa* is shown to be non-different from the individual soul, at the same time that It is the place of merger of all things. Again, *Prāṇa*, considered as a transformation of elements, cannot have the elements merged in itself.

[121] Since emphasis is placed on *Prāṇa* by saying, "*Prāṇa only*", and since it is declared to be the material source of all things, therefore it is Brahman.

ence in words and the force of the context. Just as in the use, "The father of the father", it is clear that the grandfather who is indicated by the nominative case is different from the one indicated by the sixth case (with of); so also in "the Vital force of the vital force" it becomes apparent from the difference in words, that some Vital force, different from the familiar one, is referred to; for the very same thing cannot be indicated to be different from itself by saying: "He is his". Moreover, it is to be understood (from the context) that if something is referred to by a different word in its own context, it must be itself alone that is thus spoken of. For instance, when under the topic of the Jyotiṣṭoma sacrifice it is stated: "In every spring one should perform the *Jyotis* sacrifice", the word *Jyotis* must mean Jyotiṣṭoma. Similarly in a context in which the supreme Brahman comes under discussion, it is stated: "O amiable one, the mind is tethered to *Prāṇa*". This being the case, how can this *Prāṇa* mean a mere modification of air? Accordingly, since there is no scope for doubt, the above passages are not to be alluded to (in this connection). But the doubt does arise about the *Prāṇa* which is the deity of *Prastāva;* and the relevant doubt and its solution have been shown above.

TOPIC 10: LIGHT

ज्योतिश्चरणाभिधानात् ॥ २४ ॥

ज्योतिः Light (is Brahman) **चरण-अभिधानात्** owing to the mention of feet.

24. Light is Brahman because of the mention of feet.

Doubt: The Upaniṣad says: "Then that (Light) that shines in the excellent unsurpassable worlds above this heaven, above all beings, and above all the worlds, is this same Light that is within a human being" (Ch. III. xiii. 7). With regard to this the doubt arises: Does the Light here refer to the Light of the sun etc. or does it mean the supreme Self? It has been said that though the connotation of a word be different, it may refer to Brahman if Brahman's characteristics are in evidence. This discussion relates to whether those characteristics themselves exist here or not. What should be the conclusion?

Opponent: The conclusion is that the light of the sun etc. is meant by the word light.

Why?

Because of familiar use. It is well known that the two words light and darkness refer to opposite things. Nocturnal gloom etc., hindering the functioning of the eye, are known as darkness; and the solar rays etc. that help vision are called light. Similarly the word "shines" in the text is in vogue with regard to the sun etc. Brahman, devoid of colour etc., cannot answer to the text "shines" in the primary sense. And an additional argument is the reference in the text to heaven as a limit. For Brahman, the source of all that moves and does not move, and the Self of all (i.e. the all-pervasive entity), cannot have heaven as a limit, whereas any light that is a product (of Brahman) can have heaven as its limit. And the text in the *brāhmaṇa* (explanatory) portion in the Upaniṣad says, "the light above this heaven".

Objection: Heaven as a limitation is irreconcilable even with the created light, for it is experienced everywhere. So let this mean the first-born unmixed fire.

Opponent: No, for the unmixed light serves no purpose.[122]

Objection: The mere fact of becoming an object of (notional) meditation is the purpose that it serves.

Opponent: No, for the sun etc. are enjoined as objects of meditation only when they serve some other purpose (apart from being an object of meditation). Besides, the Upaniṣad speaks (of all the elements) without any reservation in the text: "Let me make a threefold mixture of each one of them (i.e. light, water, and earth)"[123] (Ch. VI. iii. 3). And it is not a familiar fact that even the unmixed fire has heaven as its

[122] Pure light cannot be seen. Gross light is a mixture of the three elements—light, water, and earth—though light predominates. So also with other gross elements.

[123] That is to say, there can be no unmixed light after creation takes place.

limitation. So let the mixed fire itself be the meaning of the word light.

Objection: Did we not point out that the (mixed) light of fire etc. is met with even below heaven?

Opponent: That creates no difficulty, for though the (gross) light spreads everywhere, it is nothing contradictory to accept for meditation a certain portion of it spreading above heaven. But it is not proper to imagine any specific place for the partless Brahman. Besides, the mention of many places of residence in the text, "that which shines in the excellent, unsurpassable worlds, above all the worlds" (Ch. III. xiii. 7), is more in keeping with the created light. Moreover, in the text, "This is the same light that is within a human being" (ibid.), it is seen that the supreme light is superimposed on the fire in the stomach; and superimpositions are possible in cases of similarity, as for instance in, "Of this Being who is in the solar orb, the syllable *bhūr* is the head, for the head is one, and this syllable is one" (Bṛ. V. v. 3). It is a well-known fact that the fire in the stomach is not Brahman, for it is mentioned as possessed of heat and sound in the Upaniṣadic texts, "Of this Being, this is the perceptual evidence (that one feels this bodily heat by touch)", "Of this Being this is the audible evidence (that one hears a sound like bellowing inside, by plugging the ears)" (Ch. III. xiii. 7). Furthermore, there is the Upaniṣadic text, "This entity, that is such, should be meditated on as seen and heard" (ibid.). Again, this is not Brahman, because the result stated in, "He who meditates thus becomes a cynosure and a famous man" (ibid.), is insignificant, whereas the meditation on Brahman is intended for some great result. Unlike what is found in the case of *Prāṇa* and Space, there is nothing here in the context of light itself that can be a characteristic of Brahman. Nor is Brahman pointed out in the previous text, "Gāyatrī is surely all these beings" (Ch. III. xii. 1), the metre Gāyatrī being mentioned there by name. Even if it be conceded somehow that Brahman is presented in the previous text, still the identity is not recognizable here; for heaven occurs as a habitation in the earlier sentence, "His three feet are in heaven" (Ch. III. xii. 6), whereas it occurs as a limitation in, "the light shining above heaven" (Ch. III. xiii. 7). Accordingly, the natural light has to be accepted here.

Vedāntin: This contingency having arisen, we say, Brahman is to be understood here by the word Light.

Why?

"Because of the mention of feet."[124] For in the previous text, Brahman was shown as possessed of four feet in the *mantra*, "That much (i.e. the whole creation) is His glory; but Puruṣa is greater than that. All things constitute only one of His feet. His three feet that are immortal are in heaven" (Ch. III. xii. 6). Those very three feet of that four-footed Brahman, that are immortal and were shown in the *mantra* as constituting that aspect of Brahman associated with heaven, can be recognized here also as spoken of in association with heaven. Should any one give that up and resort to natural light, one will be open to the charge of rejecting something under discussion and taking up something extraneous. Not only is the topic of Brahman continued in the passage about Light, it will be pursued even in the succeeding meditation called the *Śāṇḍilya-vidyā* (Ch. III. xiv). Therefore Brahman is to be understood here from the word Light.

As for the contention that the words light and shine are more in vogue in connection with the created light, that is nothing damaging. For once we arrive at Brahman with the help of the context, those two words, used here without any specific exclusion of Brahman, can refer to Brahman indicated figuratively by the shining, created light. Besides, there is the *mantra* text, "Lighted up by whose effulgence the sun shines" (Tai. Br. III. xii. 9.7). Or it may be said that this word Light is not used to mean the light favouring the act of seeing, for it is found to be used in other senses as well as in, "It is through the light of speech (i.e. words of mouth) that he sits, (goes out, works, and returns)" (in deep darkness) (Bṛ. IV. iii. 5), "The mind becomes a light to those who drink ghee" (Tai. Br. I. vi. 3.3). Accordingly, whatever reveals other

[124] Because of the mention of *caraṇa* in the sense of "foot" and not "conduct".

things is referred to by the word light. Hence Brahman, which is consciousness by nature, can also be referred to by the word Light in that sense, inasmuch as It reveals the whole universe. This is also borne out by the Upaniṣadic text: "He shining, everything shines accordingly; by His effulgence all this shines diversely" (Mu. II. ii. 10), "Upon that immortal Light of all lights the gods meditate as longevity" (Bṛ. IV. iv. 16).

There was the objection that it is improper for Brahman to have heaven as a limitation. To this we say: Even in the case of the omnipotent Brahman, it is nothing incongruous to assume a certain location for the sake of worship.

Opponent : Did we not say it is impossible to fancy any locus for Brahman that has no parts?

Vedāntin : That defect does not arise; for it is reasonable to assume a locus for Brahman owing to association with limiting adjuncts. Accordingly, we find in the Upaniṣads certain meditations on Brahman in association with certain places as in, "in the sun" (Ch. I. vi. 6), "in the eye" (Ch. I. vii. 5), "in the heart" (Ch. III. xiii. 7). Hereby is explained the plurality of abodes as in "above all beings" (ibid.).

Again, it was argued: The light above heaven must also be this natural light, because it is superimposed on the natural fire that can be inferred to be existing in the stomach on the ground of the perception of its heat and sound. That too is unreasonable, since even for the supreme Brahman, the fire in the stomach can be as good a symbol as name etc. As for the facts of being seen and heard of (i.e. famous) mentioned in, "It is to be meditated on as the seen and the heard of", that too is from the point of view of symbolic worship.[125] And the argument was advanced that the Light is not Brahman, because the result (of meditation as stated above) is meagre. That too is baseless, for there is no reason for any such hard and fast rule that Brahman is to be resorted to for certain definite results and not for others.[126] Only one kind of result (viz liberation) is to be understood where the supreme Brahman, devoid of contact

[125] Hence the attributes do not really belong to Brahman.

[126] The Upaniṣads declare that people get whatever results they want from the worship of Brahman.

with all kinds of distinctions, is taught as the Self. But where Brahman is taught as having certain qualities or certain symbols, then are mentioned many results, high and low, which are included within this world as is shown in such texts as "(The great birthless Self is) the eater of food and the giver of wealth (i.e. fruits of work). He who knows It as such, receives wealth" (Bṛ. IV. iv. 24). Although the Light in the sentence under consideration has nothing specifically characteristic of Brahman, still the characteristic, as seen in the previous text, has to be accepted. That is why the aphorist says, "Light is Brahman, because of the mention of feet".

Opponent: How, again, can it be proper that the passage about Light should be torn out of its own context and misapplied just because it occurs in the proximity of Brahman mentioned in another sentence?

Vedāntin: That fault does not arise; for the pronoun "that" has the force of calling up to the mind something which preceded it. So the word "that" occurring at the very beginning in "That (Light) that shines above this heaven" (Ch. III. xiii. 7) becomes connected with Brahman in the previous text (Ch. III. xii. 6) on account of a common reference to heaven. When Brahman becomes known thus, the word Light also comes logically to refer to Brahman by implication. So Brahman is to be understood here by Light.

छन्दोऽभिधानान्नेति चेन्न तथा चेतोऽर्पणनिगदात्तथा हि दर्शनम् ॥ २५ ॥

न Not (Brahman) छन्दः-अभिधानात् because a metre is mentioned इति चेत् if this be said, न not so, चेतः-अर्पण-निगदात् for the dedication of mind is taught तथा in that way; हि for तथा दर्शनम् similar instances are found.

25. If it be objected that Brahman is not spoken of, because the mention is about a metre, we say, no, for the dedication of the mind is taught in that way; for similar instances are found elsewhere.

Opponent: It was asserted that Brahman is not spoken of even in the earlier text, for the metre Gāyatrī is mentioned there in "Gāyatrī is indeed all these things that there are" (Ch. III. xii. 1).

Vedāntin: That objection has to be met. How, again, can it be maintained that just because a metre is mentioned, Brahman is not spoken of here, when Brahman with four feet is presented in the Ṛk *mantra*, "That much is His glory" (Ch. III. xii. 6)?

Opponent: That cannot be so. The metre Gāyatrī is introduced in the text, "Gāyatrī is verily all this" (Ch. III. xii. 1), and that very Gāyatrī is explained as identical with all things, earth, body, heart, speech, and vital force. And then with regard to that very Gāyatrī, as explained, it is said, "That Gāyatrī that is such, has four feet and it is sixfold. This fact is revealed in the Ṛk *mantra*, 'That much is His glory' " etc. Having thus been quoted about that very Gāyatrī, how can this *mantra* suddenly speak of Brahman with four feet? Even the word Brahman, used there in the text, "That which is this Brahman" (Ch. III. xii. 7), refers to the metre only, for the metre is under consideration. In the text, "He who knows this secret teaching of Brahman (i.e. Veda)" (Ch. III xi. 3), it is explained that the secret teaching of the Vedas is under reference. Accordingly, may it not be argued that inasmuch as the metre is spoken of, Brahman is not under discussion?

Vedāntin: That is not valid, for "the dedication of the mind is taught in that way". "The dedication of the mind"—the concentration of the mind in Brahman; "in that way"—with the help of the metre Gāyatrī, in which Brahman inheres,—is taught by this text of the *brāhmaṇa* portion, "Gāyatrī is verily all this" (Ch. III. xii. 1). Gāyatrī as a mere assemblage of letters cannot possibly be the Self of everything. Therefore Brahman, which is the cause of the universe and inheres in Its effect, the Gāyatrī, is spoken of here as "all this", just as it is done in, "All this is verily Brahman" (Ch. III. xiv. 1). And under the aphorism, "It has non-difference from that Brahman, since terms like origin etc. are met with" (II. i. 14), we shall point out that the effect is non-different from its material cause. Similarly, meditation on Brahman with the help of natural mediums is met with elsewhere also, as in, "The followers of the Ṛg-Veda meditate on this very supreme Self as inhering in the hymn called the great Uktha; on this the followers of the Yajur-Veda meditate as inhering in fire; and on this the followers of the Sāma-Veda meditate as inhering in the sacrifice called Mahāvrata" (Ai. Ā. III. ii. 3.12). Hence, even though a metre be mentioned (by the word Gāyatrī) in the earlier text, still Brahman with four feet is spoken of there. And that very Brahman is alluded to in the text about Light, this being done with a view to enjoining a fresh meditation.

Others say that Brahman is directly referred to by the word Gāyatrī through a similarity of numbers. Gāyatrī is possessed of four feet, each consisting of six letters. So also Brahman has four feet.[127] Similarly it is found elsewhere that words denoting metres are used to signify something else through a similarity of number. This can be illustrated thus: The start is made with the statement, "These (air, fire, etc.) that are five in one context (viz divine) and these (vital force, speech, etc.) that are five in another context (viz bodily) combine to form ten and thus become that (dice called) *Kṛta*", and then it is said, "And this is the same as *Virāṭ* (the metre) which is the eater of food" (Ch. IV. iii. 8).[128] From this point of view, Brahman Itself is spoken of (directly) and not the metre (Gāyatrī). From either point of view, the Brahman under discussion is present in the previous text as well.

[127] According to the previous explanation, the word Gāyatrī in the earlier text means a metre in the primary sense, and also Brahman by a figure of speech called *Ajahallakṣaṇā*, where something more in addition to the original meaning of the word is meant. According to the present interpretation, no such figure of speech is implied. Gāyatrī does not refer to the metre at all, but to Brahman directly. The aphorism, accordingly means: The metre Gāyatrī is not meant, *cetorpaṇanigadāt*—because Brahman is spoken of by the word Gāyatrī standing as a medium for the dedication of the mind to Brahman, *tathā*—on the strength of the similarity of both having four feet.

[128] In playing with dice, when one wins with the dice called *Kṛta* having four figures, the other figures of the other dice, viz three, two, and one of *Tretā*, *Dvāpara*, and *Kali* respectively enter into it; so that the figure of *Kṛta* is converted to ten. The metre *Virāṭ* has ten letters to a foot. So *Virāṭ* and *Kṛta* are the same. Also the Vedas declare that *Virāṭ* is food; and *Kṛta* is the eater of all figures. So *Virāṭ* is both eater and eaten.

भूतादिपादव्यपदेशोपपत्तेश्चैवम् ॥ २६ ॥

च And भूत-आदि-पाद-व्यपदेश-उपपत्तेः because the representation of all the things etc. as a foot becomes possible, एवम् this must be so.

26. And this must be so, because this makes possible the representation of all the things etc. as a foot.

This has to be admitted to be so for this further reason: Brahman is the subject-matter of the earlier text, since all things etc. are mentioned as a foot. Thus after mentioning the things, the earth, body, and heart, it is said, "That Gāyatrī of this description has six aspects and four feet" (Ch. III. xii. 5). For unless Brahman is taken into account, a mere metre cannot have all the things etc. as its foot. Besides, without reference to Brahman, this Ṛk *mantra*, "That much is His glory" etc. (Ch. III. xii. 6), becomes incongruous. Brahman becomes the subject-matter of this *mantra* when it is taken in its literal sense, for Brahman alone can have the omnipresence spoken of in, "All these things are but one of His feet. His three other feet, which are immortal, are in heaven" (ibid.). In the *Puruṣa-Sūkta* also, this Ṛk *mantra* occurs by way of presenting Brahman. And the Smṛti presents such a form of Brahman in, "I exist supporting this whole universe by a portion of Myself" (Gītā, X. 42). Moreover, the reference (to Brahman) made in the words, "That which is that Brahman"[129] (Ch. III. xii. 7), can be possible in the primary sense, only if this point of view be accepted. Furthermore, the use of the phrase, "The men (i.e. the gatekeepers) of Brahman", with reference to the five openings of the heart, as found in the text, "These five, described thus, are the men of Brahman" (Ch. III. xiii. 6), can be justified only if a relationship with Brahman is the meaning implied.[130] Therefore it follows that Brahman is the subject-

[129] This sentence, occurring just after, "That much is His glory", shows that the *mantra* speaks of Brahman.

[130] At the openings of the heart are posted the five vital forces as gatekeepers of Brahman to whom this city of the body belongs. Brahman, called Gāyatrī, has to be meditated on in the heart in this way.

matter of the earlier text; and hence the conclusion is this: That very Brahman, called up to the mind by Its relationship with heaven, is referred to in the text about Light.

उपदेशभेदान्नेति चेन्नोभयस्मिन्नप्यविरोधात् ॥ २७ ॥

उपदेश-भेदात् On account of the difference in instruction न not so, इति चेत् if this be the contention, then न not so अविरोधात् because of absence of contradiction उभयस्मिन् अपि in either case.

27. *If it be argued that Brahman (of the earlier text) is not referred to here on account of the difference in the instruction, we say : No, because there is no contradiction in either case.*

And the *criticism* was advanced that in the earlier text, viz "His three feet which are immortal are in heaven" (Ch. III. xii. 6), the word heaven, used in the locative case, indicates a habitation, whereas in the text here, "That (Light) which shines above this heaven", the word used in the ablative case ("above heaven"), indicates a limitation. Hence owing to the difference in the (form of the) instruction, the Brahman of the previous text is not called to mind here. That criticism has to be met.

To this we (*Vedāntins*) say: That is no valid objection. For there is no contradiction in either case. In both the places, irrespective of whether the instruction is through an ending in the locative case or the ablative case (after heaven), the identification suffers nothing. As in common usage we find that a hawk associated with the top of a tree, is referred to either as, "The hawk on the tree top" or "The hawk above the top of the tree", similarly Brahman, though existing in heaven, is taught as existing above it. Others say: Just as a hawk, not in actual contact with the top of a tree (but hovering over it), is referred to either as "The hawk on the tree top" or "The hawk above the top of the tree", similarly Brahman, though above heaven, is taught as existing in heaven. So it can be well recognized that the Brahman, mentioned in the earlier text, is alluded to here (in the latter text). Hence it is proved that the supreme Brahman Itself is referred to by Light.

Topic 11: Pratardana

प्राणस्तथाऽनुगमात् ॥ २८ ॥

प्राण: *Prāṇa is Brahman* तथा अनुगमात् owing to such comprehension.

28. Prāṇa is Brahman, because it is comprehended thus.

Doubt : In the Kauṣītakī Upaniṣad occurs the story of Indra and Pratardana, which starts with, "The well-known Pratardana, son of Divodāsa, went to Indra's beloved palace through war and valour." There we read, "I (i.e. Indra) am *Prāṇa*, identified with Consciousness. You meditate on me, who am of such stature, as life and immortality" (III. 2). Similarly, there occurs this text at a later stage, "Now then, it is *Prāṇa* Itself, identified with Consciousness, that takes hold of the body and raises (i.e. animates) it up" (III. 3), as well as, "One should not inquire about speech, one should know the speaker" (III. 8), and so on. At the end again it is said, "That one is surely this *Prāṇa*, identified with Consciousness, which is bliss, ageless, and deathless" (III. 8), and so on. With regard to this, the doubt arises: Is the mere vital force signified here by the word *Prāṇa*, or is it some divine soul, or an individual being, or the supreme Brahman?

Objection : Was it not shown under the aphorism, "*Prāṇa* is Brahman for that very reason" (I. i. 23), that the word *Prāṇa* is used in the sense of Brahman? Here also the characteristics of Brahman are in evidence, viz "Bliss, ageless, deathless" etc. How can there be any possibility of doubt here?

Doubter : We say that the doubt arises from noticing the characteristics of many. Not that the indicatory marks of Brahman alone are present here; there are marks indicating others also. Indra's words, "Know me alone", are indicative of a divine soul. "Taking hold of this body, it raises it up" points to *Prāṇa* (i.e. vital force). "One should not inquire about speech, one should know the speaker" etc. presents the individual being. Hence the doubt is justifiable.

Opponent: In that passage, the well-known vital force is referred to by *Prāṇa*.

Vedāntin: Such being the case, it is said: The word *Prāṇa* is to be understood in the sense of Brahman.

Why?

Because it is comprehended thus. To explain: When the text is discussed in the context of what precedes and what succeeds, the words are seen to lead to an understanding of Brahman. Turning to the commencement, we find that, when told by Indra, "Ask for a boon", Pratardana thus spoke of the highest objective that a man may aspire to: "You yourself choose for me that boon which you think to be the most beneficent for men" (III. 1). When *Prāṇa* is taught to him as the most beneficent, how can It be other than the supreme Self? For a man can attain the most beneficent thing from nothing but the knowledge of the supreme Self, as declared in the Vedic text, "Knowing Him alone one goes beyond death; there is no other path to go by" (Śv. III. 8), and others. Moreover, the text "The world (viz liberation) achieved by the man who knows me is not certainly injured by any act—neither by theft nor the killing of a foetus" (Kau. III. 1), becomes justifiable only if Brahman is accepted, for it is well known from such Vedic texts as the following that all the results of works are eradicated on the dawn of the knowledge of Brahman: "When He that exists as the superior and inferior Brahman is known, all the results of one's actions get eradicated" (Mu. II. ii. 8). And the fact of *Prāṇa* being one with Consciousness becomes proper only if Brahman is the meaning. For the insentient vital force cannot be one with Consciousness. Similarly such words as, "Bliss, ageless, deathless" (III. 8), occurring at the end, cannot fully apply to anything but Brahman. There are also the texts, "He does not become greater by virtuous deeds, nor any the less by vicious deeds. It is He who makes one do good deeds whom He would raise above these worlds, and He again makes one do evil deeds whom He would cast below these worlds", "This One is the ruler over the worlds, this One is the protector of the worlds, this One is the lord of the worlds" (Kau. III. 8), which all can be understood only if the supreme Brahman is resorted to, and not the chief vital force. Therefore *Prāṇa* is Brahman.

न वक्तुरात्मोपदेशादिति चेदध्यात्मसम्बन्धभूमा ह्यस्मिन् ॥ २९ ॥

न Not so आत्म-उपदेशात् the teaching being about own self वक्तुः of the teacher इति चेत् if this be the objection, (then not so) हि for अस्मिन् here occurs अध्यात्म-सम्बन्ध-भूमा an abundance of reference to the inmost Self.

29. If it be argued that Prāṇa is not Brahman, since the instruction is about the speaker's own self, (then we say, no), for here is an abundance of reference to the inmost Self.

Opponent: The assertion that *Prāṇa* is Brahman is being refuted. The supreme Brahman is not the meaning of the word *Prāṇa*.

Why?

Because the instruction is about the speaker himself. For some embodied deity, called Indra, is the teacher, who speaks of himself to Pratardana in the first person in the introductory sentence, "Know me alone" (Kau. III. 1) and in the sentence, "I am *Prāṇa*, identified with Consciousness" (Kau. III. 2). How can this *Prāṇa*, taught as the speaker himself, be Brahman? For Brahman cannot be a speaker, as it is denied in the Vedic texts, "without the vocal organ or mind" (Bṛ. III. viii. 8), etc. Similarly in such sentences as, "I killed (Viśvarūpa) the three-headed son of Tvaṣṭā; I threw to the wild dogs the hermits averse to the Vedas" (Kau. III. 1), Indra praises himself through qualities that fit in with a body, but not with Brahman. And it is logical that Indra should be one with *Prāṇa* by virtue of his possession of strength; for we come across such a text as, "The vital force is strength" (Bṛ. V. xiv. 4). It is also well known that Indra is the presiding deity of strength, for even ordinary people assert, "Whatever vigorous effort there may be, it is the work of Indra". Oneness with Consciousness too is possible for a divine being by virtue of his unobstructed knowledge; for they say, "The deities have unobstructed knowledge". Once it is thus established that the teaching is about some divine being, such facts as the instruction about the most beneficent thing etc. have to be interpreted in the best possible way as referring to that being.

Vedāntin: Thus on the strength of the fact that Indra, the speaker, talks of himself, it is first denied that *Prāṇa* can be Brahman; then the refutation of that is stated in, "for here is an abundance of reference to the inmost Self". "Here", in this chapter, we find "an abundance of reference to the inmost Self". The text, "Life lasts so long as *Prāṇa* lives in this body" (Kau. III. 2), shows that it is *Prāṇa* alone, one with Consciousness and existing as the indwelling Self, and not any external deity (coming to exist after It), that has independence in the matter of granting life and ending it. Similarly the text, "When *Prāṇa* exists, the senses and organs exist" (ibid.), shows that *Prāṇa*, as the indwelling Self, is the support of the senses and organs. So also the text, "It is *Prāṇa*, identified with Consciousness, that takes hold of the body and lifts it up" (Kau. III. 3), (shows that *Prāṇa*, as the indwelling Self, supports the body). And starting with, "One should not inquire about speech, but should know the speaker (i.e. *Prāṇa*)" (Kau. III. 8), it is said, "To illustrate the point: As the rim of a wheel is fixed on the spokes of a chariot and the spokes are fixed on the nave, so are these (five) elements and (five) sense-objects fixed on the (five) sense-perceptions and (five) senses, and these latter are fixed on *Prāṇa*" (ibid.); "That very *Prāṇa*, as described, is one with Consciousness" (Kau. III. 8); "Bliss, ageless, deathless" (Kau. III. 8). All these texts present the inmost Self as their only object which remains unaffected by the contacts between sense-objects and senses. And the conclusion with the words, "One should know, 'He is my Self' ", becomes justifiable if the inmost Self is accepted, but not if any external being (e.g. a god born later on) is taken up. In support of this, there occurs a sentence in another Upaniṣad, "This Self, the perceiver of everything, is Brahman" (Bṛ. II. v. 19). Therefore, from the abundance of reference to the inmost Self, it follows that this *Prāṇa* is Brahman.

Why then does the speaker teach about himself?

शास्त्रदृष्टया तूपदेशो वामदेववत् ॥ ३० ॥

तु But उपदेशः the instruction शास्त्रदृष्टया proceeds from a seer's vision agreeing with scriptures वामदेववत् as in the case of Vāmadeva.

30. But the instruction proceeds from a seer's vision agreeing with scriptures, as in the case of Vāmadeva.

Indra, a divine being, who had through a seer's (natural) vision, agreeing with the scriptures, realized his own Self as the supreme Self thus, "I am surely the supreme Brahman", imparted the instruction, "Know me alone" (Kau. III. 1). This is just like what is read in, "The sage Vāmadeva, while realizing this (Self) as That (Brahman), knew, 'I was Manu and the sun'" (Bṛ. I. iv. 10); for the Upaniṣad declares, "And whoever among the gods knew this became That" (ibid.). The criticism also has to be met that after declaring, "Know me alone", Indra praises himself with such characteristics, suggestive of embodiedness, as the killing of the son of Tvaṣṭā. In answer it is said: It is not by way of eulogizing Indra, who is to be known, that such facts as the killing of the son of Tvaṣṭā and so on are presented, conveying thereby this idea, "Since I am a performer of such deeds, therefore you worship me". Why are they spoken of then? It is for the sake of eulogizing the knowledge of Brahman. This being the end in view, the daring acts like the killing of the son of Tvaṣṭā are first introduced and then these are connected with the praise of knowledge thus: "For me, while engaged in such (cruel) deeds, not a hair was lost. Of one who knows me, no acquired merit is adversely affected by any act whatsoever" (Kau. III. 1). The idea expressed is this: As I have become identified with Brahman, and hence I do not lose so much as a hair, even though engaged in such cruel deeds, therefore for anyone else, too, who knows me, there can be no injury to his acquired merit by any act whatsoever. The real entity to be known, however, is Brahman which will be presented later in, "I am *Prāṇa*, one with Consciousness" (Kau. III. 2). Therefore this is a statement about Brahman.

जीवमुख्यप्राणलिंगान्नेति चेन्नोपासात्रैविध्यादाश्रितत्वादिह तद्योगात् ॥ ३१ ॥

जीव-मुख्यप्राण-लिंगात् On account of the indicatory marks of the individual soul and chief *Prāṇa* न not so, इति चेत् if such be the objection, (then) न not so उपासा-त्रैविध्यात् because this will lead to a threefold meditation; आश्रितत्वात् because of acceptance; इह here तद्-योगात् because of the presence of those characteristics (of Brahman).

31. If it be argued that Brahman is not spoken of here on account of the indications of the individual soul and the chief vital force, then that cannot be so, since this will lead to a threefold meditation. (Besides, Prāṇa) is accepted (elsewhere) as meaning Brahman (because of the presence of Brahman's characteristics), (and these are) in evidence here.

Opponent: Although it follows from the frequency of reference to the inmost Self that the instruction is not about any (subsequently born) external divine being, still this text does not relate to Brahman.

Why?

Because there are the characteristic marks of the individual soul and the chief *Prāṇa*. As for the characteristic mark of the individual soul, it is clearly in evidence in this sentence: "One should not inquire about speech, but should know the speaker" (Kau. II. 8), and so on. For the individual soul, engaged in the use of the vocal and other organs and presiding over the assemblage of body and senses, is spoken of here as an entity to be known. So also there is the indication of the chief vital force: "Now, then, it is *Prāṇa*, one with Consciousness, that takes hold of the body and lifts it up" (Kau. III. 3); and the keeping up of the body together is the function of the vital force. For in the anecdote of *Prāṇa* it is heard about the other *prāṇas*, viz the organs of speech etc.: "To them the chief *Prāṇa* said, 'Do not be deluded; for it is I who hold this body together by dividing myself in five ways'" (Pr. II. 3). The meaning (of the Kauṣītakī text quoted above), according to those who read "*imaṁ śarīraṁ parigṛhya*", (*imaṁ* "this" being used in the masculine in place of *idam* in the neuter), the explanation will be this: "Taking hold of this individual soul or this assemblage of body and senses, it lifts up the body." Identity with Consciousness too is justifiable in the case of the individual soul on the ground of its intelligence. And this is justifiable in the case of the chief vital force also, since it supports the other organs (called *prāṇas*) which are the instruments of perception. Even if both the individual soul and the vital force be meant, still it is reasonable to mention them as one from the standpoint of the coexistence of the conscious soul and *Prāṇa;* and yet they can be mentioned separately from their own individual standpoints, as in, "That which is *Prāṇa* is intelligence, and that which is intelligence is *Prāṇa*" (Kau. III 3), "These two reside together in the body, and they leave this body together" (Kau. III. 3). If Brahman be accepted as the meaning (of *Prāṇa*), then which one will differ from the other? Therefore let either the individual soul or *Prāṇa*, or even both be the meaning, but not Brahman.

Vedāntin : Not so, for that involves a threefold meditation. On that supposition we shall be faced with three kinds of meditation—meditation on the individual soul, meditation on the chief *Prāṇa*, and meditation on Brahman. But such a meaning is inadmissible for a single sentence. For from a consideration of the beginning and complementary portion of the passage, a unity of idea becomes obvious. After starting with, "Know me alone" (Kau. III. 1), and declaring, "I am *Prāṇa*, one with Consciousness. Worship me as life and immortality" (Kau. III. 2), it is said at the end, "That very entity that is *Prāṇa* is one with Consciousness" (Kau. III. 8), "Bliss, ageless, deathless" (III. 8), where we find that the start and the finish are of the same pattern. That being so, it is reasonable to understand a unity of purport. Besides, it is not possible to apply the characteristics of Brahman to anything else, for the ten forms of elements and the ten forms of intelligence (i.e. five elements and their qualities, and five senses and five forms of sensation) cannot be merged in anything but Brahman. "Moreover, it is admitted". Since from the presence of the characteristics of Brahman, the word *Prāṇa* is admitted elsewhere to mean

Brahman (B.S. I. i. 23), and since here also is in evidence the presence of such characteristics as being the most beneficent and so on, it is understood that this is an instruction about Brahman.

And it was argued that the text, "Taking hold of this body, lifts it up" (Kau. III. 3), is an indication of the chief vital force. But that is wrong. For even the functions of the vital force are dependent on Brahman, and can thus be ascribed (figuratively) to the supreme Self, as is done in the Upaniṣadic text, "No mortal being lives through exhaling and inhaling, but through some other entity on which these two rest" (Ka. II. v. 5). Even the interpretation of the text, "One should not inquire about speech, but should know the speaker" (Kau. III. 8), as presenting a sign of the individual soul (that is shown by the opponent) cannot rule out the acceptance of Brahman. For what is known as the individual soul is not entirely different from Brahman; for the texts, "That thou art" (Ch. VI. viii-xvi), "I am Brahman" (Bṛ. I. iv. 10), and so on demolish this view. Though the individual soul is Brahman in reality, it is called an agent or an experiencer on account of the distinctions created by such limiting adjuncts as the intellect. In order to make one turn towards the inmost Self, it involves no contradiction to say, "One should not inquire about speech, but should know the speaker" (Kau. III. 8), which is meant to divest the individual soul of the distinctions created by conditioning factors and to show it as Brahman, which is its true nature. And another Upaniṣadic text, "That which is not uttered by speech, that by which speech is uttered—know that to be Brahman, and not this thing that they worship objectively" (Ke. I. 5), shows that the soul, engaged in such activities as speaking, is but Brahman.

Another objection was that the perception of difference between *Prāṇa* and the Self identified with Consciousness, as stated in, "for they both reside in this body together and they leave the body together" (Kau. III. 4), cannot be maintained by one who sticks to Brahman. That is not a valid objection. For it is possible to indicate a difference between the intellect and *Prāṇa*, as constituting the two limiting adjuncts of the indwelling Self and forming the bases of the power of knowing and acting. But the indwelling Self, that is conditioned by the two, has no difference in Itself. Hence the identification stated in "*Prāṇa* is one with Consciousness" involves no contradiction.

Or the portion of the aphorism, "*Nopāsātraividhyāt āśritatvāt iha tadyogāt*", has this other meaning (according to *Vṛttikāra*): There is no contradiction even if we meet with the characteristics of the individual soul and the chief vital force in this context dealing with Brahman.

Why?

For there is a threefold meditation. Three kinds of meditation on Brahman are meant here—with the help of the qualities of *Prāṇa*, intelligence, and Brahman Itself. Of these the qualities of *Prāṇa* are mentioned in: "Meditate as life and immortality; life is *Prāṇa*" (Kau. III. 2); "Taking hold of this body, lifts it up" (Kau. III. 3); and therefore "One should meditate on it as Uktha"[131] (Kau. III. 3). The qualities of the intellect (i.e. soul) are stated thus: Starting with, "Now we shall explain how all these things become unified in that intellect"[132] (Kau. III. 4), it is stated, "The vocal organ itself fills up one half of its (i.e. intellect's) body, names, expressed (through eye etc.) as the objects perceived, become its other half"[133] (Kau. III. 5), "Riding on the vocal organ through the intellect, it (i.e. the conscious soul) reaches all the names"[134] (ibid.). Here the qualities of the intellect are indicated. And the qualities of Brahman are shown in, "These ten elements and their enjoyable qualities are dependent on the ten senses and sense-perceptions; and the senses and sense-perceptions are dependent on

[131] That which lifts up (*utthāpayati*) the body is Uktha, i.e. *Prāṇa*.

[132] By the word "*Prajñā*" is meant here the intellect bearing on it the reflection of the Self. All things perceived through that intellect become unified in the Self which is the basis of the intellect.

[133] The Self's reflection on intellect, called the soul, is the real subject perceiving the universe of names. And this constitutes half of its body. It is also the subject perceiving the forms constituting the universe of forms. This is the other half of its body. The intellect, with the reflection of the Self on it, acts in relation to the universe of names through the vocal organ.

[134] Similarly it becomes a seer etc.

the elements and their qualities. Had not the elements and qualities been there, the senses and sensations would not have been there; and had not the senses and sensations been there, the elements and their qualities would not have been there. From neither of them is any *rūpa*, appearance, possible; nor are they different. To illustrate this point: As the rim of a chariot wheel is fixed on the spokes and the spokes are fixed on the nave, so are these elements and their enjoyable qualities fixed on the senses and sensations, and the senses and sensations are fixed on the elements and their enjoyable qualities. This *Prāṇa*, that is such, is surely one with Consciousness" (Kau. III. 8). Accordingly, this is a single meditation on Brahman, spoken of as threefold by basing it on Brahman's own qualities and the qualities of Its two conditioning factors. Elsewhere also meditation on Brahman is resorted to, as for instance, with the help of such identification with the qualities of the conditioning factors as "having identity with the mind", as "having *Prāṇa* as the body" (Ch. III. xiv. 2), and so on. That applies here also, for the unity of purport is understood from the beginning and the end of the text and because we get here the marks indicative of *Prāṇa*, the intellect, and Brahman.[135] Hence it is proved that this text propounds Brahman.

[135] *Ratnaprabhā* rejects this view and states that this is the *Vṛttikāra's* interpretation, Śaṅkara's own having been given earlier.

Section II

Introduction: In the first section, it was stated under the aphorism, "That from which are derived the birth etc. of this", that Brahman is the cause of the birth of the whole universe starting with space (B. S. I. i. 2). Thereby it was stated *ipso facto* that Brahman, as the cause of the universe, is possessed of such characteristics as omnipresence, eternality, omniscience, omnipotence, identity with all, and so on. And it was shown with the help of reason, that certain words, familiarly meaning other things, are used in the Upaniṣads in the sense of Brahman; it was thereby ascertained that though the meanings of certain sentences, bearing clear indications of Brahman, were under doubt, yet they meant Brahman. With regard to some other sentences, having indistinct indication of Brahman, the doubt again arises as to whether they establish the supreme Brahman or some other entity. The second and third sections are started for ascertaining this:

Topic 1: The Entity Known Everywhere

सर्वत्र प्रसिद्धोपदेशात् ॥ १

सर्वत्र Everywhere (in all the Upaniṣads) प्रसिद्ध-उपदेशात् the well-known entity having been taught.

1. (Brahman is the object to be meditated on), since that which is well known everywhere is taught (here in this Chāndogya Upaniṣad—III. xiv. 1-2).

Doubt: This is stated in the Upaniṣad: "All this is but Brahman, because it originates from that (Brahman), merges in that, and is sustained by that. One should meditate by becoming calm. Now then, a man is a product of his resolves. After departing from this world, a man becomes just as he wills (i.e. according to what he meditates on) here. He should have resolution. He who is identified with the mind, whose body is

Prāṇa (subtle body), and whose nature consists of light (i.e. intelligence)" (Ch. III. xiv. 1-2). With regard to this the doubt arises: Is the embodied soul, possessed of such characteristics as identification with the mind, set forth here for meditation, or is it the supreme Brahman? What would be the conclusion arrived at?

Opponent: It must be the embodied soul.

Why?

Because in its case, the relation with the mind etc. is a well-known fact, whereas it is not so in the case of the supreme Brahman, as stated in, "Because He is pure and without vital force and mind" (Mu. II. i. 2), and other texts.

Objection: Such statements as "bigger than the earth" (ibid. xiv. 1), Brahman is presented by name. So how can the doubt arise that the entity to be meditated on here is the embodied soul?

Opponent: That raises no difficulty. This sentence is not an injunction about Brahman.

About what is it then?

It is meant for enjoining calmness, as is evident from the statement, "All this is but Brahman, because it originates from that, merges in that, and is sustained by that. One should meditate by becoming calm" (Ch. III. xiv. 1-2). The idea implied is this: Since all this creation is but Brahman, because it originates there, merges there, and subsists there, and because attachment etc. are not possible when all things are the same, therefore one should meditate by becoming calm. And if this sentence is meant to enjoin calmness, it cannot at the same time be construed to enjoin a meditation on Brahman.[1] The meditation itself is enjoined in the sentence, "He should have a *kratu*", where *kratu* means resolution, that is to say, meditation. And for stating an object of that meditation, the text says, "identified with the mind and having the vital force as his body" (ibid.). Now, this is a sign of the individual soul. Therefore we say that this meditation relates to the individual soul. And the text, "performer of all actions, possessor of all desires" etc. (Ch.

[1] For that would undermine the unity of purport of a sentence.

III. xiv. 2), that we come across, becomes applicable to the individual being from the standpoint of its progressive realization (of these in different births). Again, for the individual soul, of the size of the tip of a goading stick (Śv. V. 8), and not for the infinite Brahman, can be thought of such residence in the heart and minuteness, as stated in, "Within the heart is this Self of mine which is smaller than a grain of paddy or barley" (Ch. III. xiv. 3).

Objection: Such statements as "bigger than the earth" (ibid.) cannot be thought of in connection with the limited soul.

Opponent: As to that, we say: Both minuteness and vastness cannot be applied to the same entity, for that is contradictory. And if one of the two has to be accepted, it is more reasonable to take up minuteness, mentioned earlier. But vastness can be mentioned from the standpoint of the soul's becoming Brahman. The definite meaning being the individual soul, the mention of Brahman at the end in the words, "This Brahman" (Ch. III. xiv. 4), relates to the individual soul itself, for that text is meant as a reference to a subject already being discussed. Therefore the individual being is to be meditated on as possessed of the qualities of being identified with the mind etc.

Vedāntin: This being the position, we say: The supreme Brahman Itself is to be meditated on as possessed of the characteristics of identification with the mind etc.

Why?

Because it is but reasonable that the source of the universe, connoted by the word Brahman, well known in all the Upaniṣads, and declared in the words, "All this is but Brahman", in the present text at the very start, should be taught as possessed of the characteristics of being identified with the mind, and so on. On this interpretation we avoid the fault of giving up the topic under discussion and turning to something extraneous.

Opponent: Did we not say that Brahman is presented at the beginning for the purpose of enjoining calmness, but not for Its own sake?

Vedāntin: With regard to this, we say that, although Brahman be presented in connection with the injunction for calmness, still when such qualities as identity with the mind etc. are taught, Brahman happens to be nearer to them (than the individual soul), whereas the individual soul is neither near at hand[2] nor is it presented through any of its own synonyms.[3] Here lies the difference.

विवक्षितगुणोपपत्तेश्च ॥ २ ॥

च And विवक्षित-गुण-उपपत्तेः because the intended qualities fit in.

2. *And this follows from the fact that the intended qualities are justifiable (in the case of Brahman).*

The *vivakṣitāḥ* are those that are intended to be expressed. Although the Vedas have no author, and hence in the absence of a speaker (i.e. author) the idea of intention is inadmissible, still the word intention can be used figuratively in the sense of "resulting in being accepted".[4] In common experience also, any sense expressed of a word, that is acceptable, is said to be its intended meaning, and what is not acceptable is said to be unintended. Similarly in the case of the Vedas, the intended meaning is known from the fact of its being presented as acceptable and the unintended meaning is that which is unacceptable. Acceptability or unacceptability, again, is determined from what is or is not the meaning of a Vedic text. Therefore those intended qualities that are enjoined here for being taken up during the meditation, viz true resolve and so forth, fit in with the supreme Brahman; for true resolve can be thought of only in the case of the supreme Brahman, It being possessed of absolute power in the matter of creation, continuance, and dissolution. And the phrases, "possessing true desire and true resolve", are found in

[2] When we split up the compounds, *prāṇaśarīraḥ* and *manomayaḥ* thus —This one which has *Prāṇa* as the body and this one which has mind as Its adjunct—the pronoun "This one which" readily brings Brahman to our mind, since that pronoun refers to something near at hand.

[3] Any indication of the individual found here is ruled out, since an entity subject to grief cannot be an object of meditation, such an act being illogical.

[4] The result of intending a meaning is its comprehension as such. That possibility of comprehension being present in the case of the attributes under discussion, they are "intended".

association with the qualities of the supreme Self, mentioned in the text starting with, "The Self that is free from sin" etc. (Ch. VIII. vii. 1). By the phrase, *ākāśātmā* (Ch. III. xiv. 2), which is derived in the sense of "that which has its Self (i.e. nature) like space", it is shown that Brahman has similarity with space owing to Its qualities of all-pervasiveness etc.; and this is also shown in the text, "Greater than the earth" (Ch. III. xiv. 3). Even if the earlier phrase (*ākāśātmā*) be explained in the sense of "that which has space as its Self (i.e. body)", still it is possible for Brahman, the source of the whole universe and the Self of all as It is, to have space as Its body. For the very same reason, It can be the performer of all actions. Thus here also, the qualities intended for meditation fit in with Brahman.

It was argued that "identified with the mind and having the vital force as the body" presents an indicatory mark of the individual being, and hence this text cannot apply to Brahman. We say that even this is applicable to Brahman; for Brahman is the Self of all, so that the quality of being identified with the mind, which belongs to the individual, comes to be related to Brahman. Thus it is that there are such Vedic and Smṛti passages about Brahman as: "You are a man; you are a young man; or again a young woman. You are the old man tottering along on his stick. It is you who become multi-faced after being born" (Śv. IV. 3); and "He has His hands and feet everywhere, His eyes, heads, and mouths everywhere and He has His ears everywhere in this world. He exists pervading everything" (Śv. III. 16, Gita, XIII. 13). But the distinction is that, the text, "He is without vital force and mind, and He is pure" (Mu. II. i. 2), relates to the unconditioned Brahman, while the present text, "identified with the mind and having the vital force as His body", relates to the qualified Brahman. Accordingly, it can be understood that since the intended qualities are justifiable, it is the supreme Brahman that is taught here.

अनुपपत्तेस्तु न शारीरः ॥ ३ ॥

अनुपपत्तेः Because (the qualities) do not fit in, therefore तु शारीरः surely the embodied soul न is not (meant).

3. And the embodied individual soul is not surely meant, because the qualities do not fit in with it.

The preceding aphorism spoke of the aptness of the intended qualities in Brahman. This one speaks of their inapplicability to the embodied soul. The word *tu* is used to signify emphasis. According to the reasons adduced, it is Brahman alone that is possessed of the qualities of being identified with the mind, and so on. The individual soul cannot have those qualities, the reason being this: "Having true resolve, having space as the body" (Ch. III. xiv. 2), "without speech, without any attachment" (ibid.), "greater than the earth" (Ch. III. xix. 3), and such other qualities do not properly fit in with the individual being. The word *śārīra* means existing in the body.

Opponent: Does not God also exist in the body?

Vedāntin: True, He exists in the body, but not in the body alone; for the Upaniṣad declares His pervasiveness in, "Greater than the earth, greater than the interspace" (ibid.), and "He is all-pervasive like space and eternal". But the individual being exists in the body alone; for it does not exist anywhere else apart from the body, which is the seat for its experiences.

कर्मकर्तृव्यपदेशाच्च ॥ ४ ॥

च कर्म-कर्तृ-व्यपदेशात् And because there is mention of the object and the subject.

4. And because there is reference to the object and subject.

The embodied being is not the one possessed of such qualities as being "identified with the mind" for this further reason that there is an assertion of an object and a subject (i.e. something attained and somebody attaining it) in the sentence, "Departing from here I shall attain this one" (Ch. III. xiv. 4). By the term "this one", the Self to be meditated on, as possessed of the qualities of being identified with the mind, is referred to as an object to be attained. *Abhisambhavitāsmi*, meaning "I shall attain", refers to the embodied being, the meditator, as the agent of the attainment. When a more reasonable standpoint is possible, it is not proper to refer to the same entity as both the subject and object. Similarly the relationship between the object meditated on and the agent meditating is based on difference. For this reason also, the embodied being is not the one possessed of such qualities as "being identified with the mind".

शब्दविशेषात् ॥ ५ ॥

5. Owing to the difference in the (case-endings of the two) words.

The one possessed of such characteristics as identity with the mind and so on must be different from the embodied being for this additional reason that a difference in the case-endings of the words occurs in a similar context[5] in another Vedic text: "Just as a grain of paddy or barley or *śyāmāka* (canary) or a seed of *śyāmāka is* (very small), so is the effulgent Puruṣa (i.e. the conscious all-pervasive Entity) inside the (individual) soul (*antarātman*)" (Ś. B. X. vi. 3. 2.). Here the word Puruṣa, used in the singular number, nominative case, means the Self endowed with the qualities of being identified with the mind and so on; and this word is different from the term *antarātman*[6] which is used with a seventh case-ending and refers to the embodied soul. Therefore their difference becomes obvious (so that the one identified with the mind is not the individual soul).

स्मृतेश्च ॥ ६ ॥

6. (This follows) from the Smṛti also.

The embodied soul and the supreme Self are shown differently in the Smṛti also: "The Lord, O Arjuna, dwells in the hearts of all beings, causing all beings by His Māyā to revolve, (as if) mounted on a machine" (Gītā, XVIII. 61).

Here the *opponent* puts in: What is this entity, called the embodied soul different from the supreme Self, which is denied

[5] Where the same meditation occurs.

[6] Meaning *antarātmani*, within the embodied soul, the dropping of the seventh case-ending being a Vedic licence.

by the aphorism, "The individual soul is not certainly referred to, because the qualities do not fit in with it" (I. ii. 3) etc.? As a matter of fact, the Vedic texts, as for instance, "There is no other witness but Him" (Bṛ. III. vii. 23), deny any Self other than the supreme Self. So also do the Smṛti texts, as for instance, "Me do thou also know, O descendant of Bharata, to be the knower of the *kṣetra* (i.e. body) in all the *kṣetras*" (Gītā, XIII. 2).

Vedāntin: To this we say: It is quite true that the supreme Self Itself, as delimited by the conditioning factors—body, senses, mind, intellect, etc.—is spoken of in a roundabout way as the embodied soul by the ignorant. The case is similar to the appearance of space, undivided though it is, as if divided owing to such conditioning factors as a pot, a jar, etc. And before obtaining the instruction about the unity of the Self as in, "That thou art" (Ch. VI. viii. 7), it is nothing incongruous to talk from that point of view in terms of such differences as are implied by subjects and objects. But once the unity of the Self is accepted, there will surely be an end to all empirical dealings, involving notions of bondage, liberation, etc.

अर्भकौकस्त्वात्तद्व्यपदेशाच्च नेति चेन्न निचाय्यत्वादेवं व्योमवच्च ॥ ७ ॥

अर्भक-ओकस्त्वात् On account of the smallness of the abode च and तत्-व्यपदेशात् on account of its being designated as such न not so इति चेत् if this be the objection, न not so; एवं निचाय्यत्वात् for this is so for the sake of contemplation च and व्योमवत् (this is) analogous to space.

7. *If it be objected that the supreme Self is not taught here, because of the smallness of the abode and because of its being referred to as such, then we say: No, for this is done for the sake of contemplation, as is seen in the case of space.*

Arbhaka means small (tiny), and *okas* means nest (abode). It was argued that because the inmost Self has a limited abode, as stated in, "This is my Self within the heart" (Ch. III. xiv. 3), and because the Upaniṣad mentions its subtleness in clear words in "subtler than a grain of paddy or barley" (ibid.), the embodied soul of the size of the tip of a goading rod (Śv. V. 8), must have been taught here, and not the all-pervasive supreme Self. That criticism has to be refuted. With regard to this we say: That is no defect. While it is impossible from every point of view to assert all-pervasiveness for something that is spatially limited, it is possible in the case of the omnipresent One to speak of limited presence in some sense because of existence everywhere, just as a king ruling over the whole earth can be referred to as the king of Ayodhyā.

Opponent : From what standpoint, again, is omnipresent God, spoken of as having a tiny abode and minuteness?

Vedāntin : We say that this is declared thus for the sake of being contemplated on. That God, possessed of a set of such qualities as subtleness, is taught to be meditated on there in the lotus of the heart, just as (the Lord) Hari is taught to be worshipped on a *Śālagrāma* (stone symbol). A certain state of the intellect, (brought about by the Upaniṣadic instruction), catches a glimpse of Him there. God, though omnipresent, becomes gracious when worshipped there. And this is to be understood on the analogy of space. Just as space, though all-pervasive, is referred to as having a limited habitation and minuteness from the point of view of its association with the eye of a needle, so also is the case with Brahman. Thus the limited habitation and subtleness being declared for the sake of meditation, these do not belong to Brahman in any real sense. Hereby is set at rest the doubt that might arise in this matter that, since Brahman has the heart as Its habitation, since the hearts differ in different bodies, and since parrots and others, having different habitations, suffer from the defects of being many in number, limited by bodies, and impermanent, therefore Brahman too will incur those faults.

सम्भोगप्राप्तिरिति चेन्न वैशेष्यात् ॥ ८ ॥

सम्भोगप्राप्तिः Experience (of happiness and sorrow) will be His lot इति चेत् if such be the objection, न not so, वैशेष्यात् because of difference.

8. If it be objected that God will be subject to the experience (of happiness and sorrow as a result of unity), we say, not so, for there is a difference.

Opponent: Since Brahman is connected with the hearts of all beings on account of Its all-pervasiveness like space, and since It is non-different from the embodied soul owing to Its nature of Consciousness, therefore the conclusion may be drawn that Brahman will experience happiness and sorrow just like others. And this must be so because of oneness. For apart from the supreme Self, there is no transmigrating soul, as is denied in such Vedic texts as, "There is no other witness but Him" (Bṛ. III. vii. 23). Hence It is the supreme Self Itself that undergoes transmigration.

Vedāntin: No, "since there is a difference". To explain: Just because Brahman has some relationship with the hearts of all beings, it does not follow that Brahman experiences happiness and sorrow like the embodied souls; for there is a difference. There is forsooth a difference between the embodied soul and the supreme God. The one is an agent, an experiencer (of happiness and sorrow), a source of merit, demerit, etc., and possessed of happiness and sorrow, while the other is just the opposite, being possessed of such qualities as freedom from sin, and so on. Because of this distinction between the two, the one has experiences, but not the other. If from the mere fact of proximity, and without any reference to the intrinsic nature of things, a causal relation with some effect is postulated, then space, for instance, can as well become burnt, (it being connected with fire). And this objection has to be met and refuted equally by all those who hold the view that the souls are many and all-pervasive.

There was the argument, that since Brahman is non-dual, no other Self can exist; and hence there is the possibility that when one Self has any experience, Brahman too must have it. In refutation of this we say: Apropos of this, you have to be asked, "a favourite of the gods" (i.e. a fool) that you are, how do you cling to the view that there is no other soul?

Opponent: On the authority of such texts as, "That thou art" (Ch. VI. viii. 7), "I am Brahman" (Bṛ. I. iv. 10), "There is no other witness but Him" (Bṛ. III. vii. 23).

Vedāntin: In that case, the meaning of the scripture should be interpreted in the way it should be, and you cannot resort to anything here analogous to an old hag with her one half young (and the other old).[7] Now while the scriptural text, "That thou art", teaches that the Brahman possessed of the qualities like freedom from sin, and so on, is the Self of the embodied being, it also denies thereby any experience for the embodied Self Itself. So how can there be any talk of any experience accruing to Brahman from that of the embodied Self? On the contrary, so long as the aspirant has not understood the oneness of the embodied Self with Brahman, the experience of happiness and sorrow by the embodied being is a result of false ignorance, and Brahman, the highest Reality, cannot be touched by it. For the sky does not really become possessed of a surface (i.e. concavity) or tainted by dirt etc. which the ignorant fancy on it. That fact is stated in, "Not so, for there is a difference". Not even, owing to the fact of unity, is Brahman affected by any experience undergone by the embodied soul; for there is a difference, inasmuch as true knowledge differs from false ignorance etc. The experience of happiness etc. is cooked up by false ignorance, while unity is seen through real knowledge. And it is never a fact that a thing perceived through real knowledge is affected by any experience under false ignorance. Accordingly, it is not possible to fancy the slightest touch of the experience of happiness and sorrow in God.

Topic 2: The Eater

अत्ता चराचरग्रहणात् ॥ ९ ॥

अत्ता The eater चर-अचर-ग्रहणात् on account of the appropriation of the movable and immovable.

9. The eater (is God), on account of the appropriation of all that moves and does not move.

Doubt: We read in the Kaṭhopaniṣad: "How can one know

[7] If you stand by the Vedic text, then follow it to the bitter end, and there can be no half-way house.

thus as to where It (the Self) is, for which both the Brāhmaṇa and the Kṣatriya become rice (food) and for whom death takes the place of a curry (or ghee etc. poured on rice)?" (I. ii. 25). Here we are apprised of some eater indicated by the mention of rice and its adjunct (curry). Now who can this eater be? Is it fire or the individual soul, or is it the supreme Self? This is the doubt, for no conclusive distinction is in evidence, and it is seen in this book that questions are put (to Death by Naciketas) with regard to three entities—Fire, individual soul, and the supreme Self. What should be the conclusion then?

Opponent : The eater is Fire.

Why?

Because this is gathered from the familiar use in such texts as, "Fire is the eater of food" (Bṛ. I. iv. 6), as well as common parlance. Or the individual soul may be the eater, for there is the text, "One of them eats the fruits of divergent tastes (sweet or sour)" (Mu. III. i. 1). But it cannot be the supreme Self, for there is the text, "The other looks on without eating" (ibid.).

Vedāntin : This being the position, we say: The eater here should be the supreme Self.

Why?

Because of his appropriation of all that moves and does not move. For all movable and immovable things appear here as the eatable thing with death as its (pouring) adjunct. None but the supreme Self can consume such a food fully. As for the supreme Self, it is quite possible to assert that He devours all, inasmuch as He withdraws everything into Himself during dissolution.

Opponent : But the appropriation of all that moves and does not move is not stated here. How can then the appropriation of all movable and unmovable things be accepted as an established fact to be advanced as a ground (for inferring God)?

Vedāntin : That creates no difficulty, because when Death is mentioned as the curry, all beings present themselves along with it,[8] and because the Brāhmaṇas and Kṣatriyas are cited by way

[8] The word "food" is used figuratively for destructible things; and this figurative meaning becomes obvious from the use of the word death in its vicinity. Food is destructible, and so are all beings subject to death.

of suggesting (all beings), they being the chief among them.

As for the argument that even the supreme Self cannot be the eater in the face of the Upaniṣadic revelation, "The other looks on without eating" (Mu. III. i. 1), we say: This revelation is meant to deny the enjoyment of the fruits of action, for that is near at hand (to the text). That is not a denial of the dissolution of all things (figuratively denoted by eating), inasmuch as Brahman is well known in all the Upaniṣads as the cause of creation, sustenance, and dissolution. Therefore the supreme Self alone can be the devourer here.

प्रकरणाच्च ॥ १० ॥

10. And (this follows) from the context.

For this additional reason it is the supreme Self alone that can be the eater here; for this topic, starting with, "The enlightened (or knowing) One is neither born nor does He die" (Ka. I. ii. 18), is of the supreme Self. And it is proper that the entity constituting the subject of the context should be accepted as the eater. The difficulty about "knowing" (the Self) as stated in, "How can one know thus?" (Ka. I. ii. 28), is also a pointer to the supreme Self.

TOPIC 3: THE TWO IN THE CAVITY OF THE HEART

गुहां प्रविष्टावात्मानौ हि तद्दर्शनात् ॥ ११ ॥

प्रविष्टौ The two that have entered गुहां into the cavity आत्मानौ (are) the two Selfs हि because तत्-दर्शनात् that is what is seen.

11. The two who have entered into the cavity (of the heart) are the individual Self and the supreme Self, for that is what is seen (in other texts).

Doubt : In the Kaṭha Upaniṣad itself we read: "The knowers of Brahman, the worshippers of the five fires, and those who perform the *Nāciketa* sacrifice thrice, compare to shade and light, the two drinkers of *ṛta* (inevitable results) of one's work, who have entered into the body, into the cavity (of the heart) which is the supreme abode of the Most High" (I. iii. 1). With regard to this the doubt arises: Are the intellect and the individual soul mentioned here, or the individual soul and the supreme Self? If the intellect and the soul be referred to, then the text establishes that the soul is different from the assemblage of body and organs in which the intellect predominates. That soul also has to be presented here, for it has been sought for in the question, "The doubt that arises, consequent on the death of a man, some saying that he exists and others that he does not—I would know this under your instruction. This is the third of the three boons" (Ka. I. i. 20). If, however, the soul and the supreme Self be referred to, then it is the supreme Self, distinct from the individual soul, that is propounded here. And that too has to be expounded, It having been inquired into through the question, "Tell me of that which you see as different from virtue, different from vice, different from these cause and effect, different from the past and the future" (Ka. I. ii. 14).

With regard to this the *opponent* says: Neither of these two alternatives is admissible.

Why?

The phrase "drinking of *ṛta*" (Ka. I. iii. 1) implies the experiencing of the fruit of works, for there is an indicatory mark of this in "the result of one's own work in this body" (ibid.); and that is possible for a sentient being aware of the body, but not for the insentient intellect. Besides, by the word *pibantau*, in the dual number, the Upaniṣad points to the drinking by both. Accordingly, it is not possible to side with the soul and the intellect; and for this very reason it is not possible to side with the individual soul and the supreme Self, for it is impossible even for the conscious supreme Self to enjoy the fruits of work, this having been denied in the *mantra* text, "The other looks on without eating" (Mu. III. i. 1).

In answer the *doubter* says: That raises no difficulty. It is seen that in the statement, "The people with umbrella are going", a single possessor of an umbrella (viz a king) gives the figurative epithet of "people with umbrella" to a whole group. Similarly, from the fact that one experiences, both may be said to be experiencing. Or it may be thus: The individual being alone experiences and God makes him experience. And because He causes the experience, He is said to be experiencing on the analogy of the familiar fact that one who makes others cook is said to be cooking. It is also possible to accept the intellect and the individual soul, there being a figurative use of agentship in the case of the instrument (viz intellect), for such an expression as, "The fuel cooks", is possible. And in a context of the body, no other pair of experiencers of the fruit of works is possible. Hence this doubt. Should they be either the intellect and the individual soul or the individual soul and the supreme Self? What should be the conclusion here?

Opponent: They must be the intellect and the individual soul.

Why?

Because there is the qualification, "have entered into the cavity". Whether the word cavity means the body or the heart, in either case it stands to reason that the intellect and the individual soul have entered into that cavity. Besides, if an alternative explanation is possible, it is not proper to fancy any particular location for the omnipresent Brahman. Moreover, the expression, "of the result of one's own work in the body", shows the non-transcendence of the limits of the results of work. The supreme Self is not confined within the limits of merit and demerit, as shown in, "it neither increases nor decreases through work" (Bṛ. IV. iv. 23). And the terms light and shade point to the sentient and insentient, they being opposed to each other like light and shade (Ka. I. iii. 1). Therefore the intellect and the individual soul are to be accepted as spoken of here.

Vedāntin: This being the position, we say: The individual Self, identified with the intellect, and the supreme Self have been spoken of here.

Why so?

Because both these are Selfs as well as conscious and have the same nature. For it is a matter of experience, that in a case of enumeration, people take it for granted that units of the same class are being told off. When somebody says, "A second one to (i.e. a companion for) this cow has to be sought for", a cow alone is sought out, but neither a horse nor a man. Similarly in the present case, when, after the individual Self, identified with the intellect, has been ascertained with the help of the indicatory mark of experiencing the fruits of work, a search for a second entity starts, the supreme Self which is of the same nature comes within our ken.

Opponent: Did we not say that after noticing the fact of remaining in the cavity, the supreme Self cannot be cognized?

Vedāntin: We say: The supreme Self is to be cognized from the very fact of remaining in the cavity; for the fact of remaining within the cavity is very often declared in the Vedas and the Smṛtis with regard to the supreme Self Itself, as in, "The enlightened one gives up happiness and sorrow by developing concentration of mind on the old Deity who is inscrutable, lodged inaccessibly, located in the cavity (of the heart), and seated in the midst of misery" (Ka. I. ii. 12), "He who knows the supreme One, seated in the supreme space within the cavity (of the heart)" (Tai. II. i), "Seek for the Self that has entered into the cavity", and so on. And we stated earlier that it involves no contradiction to teach about any place as suitable for the realization of Brahman, omnipresent though It is. As for the existence amidst the well earned results of work, although this is possible for one only, it can be asserted for both on the analogy of the "people with umbrella". The expression "light and shade" is also reconcilable; for the transmigrating Self and the transcendental Self are poles asunder like shade and light, for transmigration is a result of ignorance, while transcendence of transmigration is the supreme reality. Therefore the soul identified with the intellect and the supreme Self are to be recognized as the two who have entered into the cavity.

For what additional reason are the soul identified with the intellect and the supreme Self to be accepted?

विशेषणाच्च ॥ १२ ॥

12. And because there is a specification.

And the specification (made in the Upaniṣad) applies to the soul identified with the intellect and the supreme Self alone. In the subsequent text commencing with, "Know the Self to be the rider of the chariot, but the body to be the chariot" etc. (Ka. I. iii. 3), which calls up the imagery of the chariot and the rider of the chariot, the Self identified with the intellect is imagined as the rider of the chariot who has to reach either the worldly state or liberation. And the supreme Self is imagined as the goal to be reached in, "He attains the end of the road, and that is the supreme state of Viṣṇu" (Ka. I. iii. 9). In the preceding text also these two are specified as the thinker and the object of thought in the verse, "The intelligent man gives up happiness and sorrow by developing concentration of mind on the Self and thereby meditating on the old Deity who is inscrutable, lodged inaccessibly in Māyā, located in the intellect, and seated in the midst of misery" (Ka. I. ii. 12). Besides, this is the topic of the supreme Self. And the expression, "The knowers of Brahman say" (Ka. I. iii. 1), which posits a special class of speakers, becomes justifiable if the supreme Self is accepted. Therefore it is to be admitted that the individual Self and the supreme Self are spoken of here.

This line of approach has to be adopted with regard to "Two birds, ever associated and having similar names (cling to the same tree)" (Mu. III. i. 1, Śv. IV. 6), and such other texts. There also the ordinary birds are not spoken of, since the topic centres round the soul. In the text, "Of these two, the one eats the fruits of divergent tastes" (ibid.), the individual Self is to be understood on the strength of the indicatory marks of eating. And in, "The other looks on without eating" (ibid.), the supreme Self is to be understood on the strength of non-eating and consciousness. In the succeeding *mantra* also these two are specified as the seer and object seen: "On the same tree, the individual soul remains drowned (i.e. stuck), as it were; and so it moans, being worried by its impotence. When it sees thus the other, the adored Lord, and His glory, then it becomes liberated from sorrow" (Mu. III. i. 2).

Others say: The *mantra* "Two birds" etc. (Mu. III. i. 1) does not agree with the conclusion arrived at under the present topic. For in the *Paiṅgi-rahasya-brāhmaṇa* it is explained thus —"The expression, 'Of these two, the one eats the fruits of divergent tastes', refers to the *sattva*, and 'the other looks on without eating' means the *jña* (lit. knower) who witnesses without eating. So the *sattva* and *kṣetrajña* (lit. knower of the field or body) are meant." It may be argued that the word *sattva* means the individual soul and *kṣetrajña* means the supreme Self; but that is wrong, because the words *sattva* and *kṣetrajña* are well known as meaning the internal organ (mind) and the embodied soul, and because the explanation is given in that very text thus: "That thing is *sattva* by which one sees dreams, and that which is the embodied witness is the *kṣetrajña*; these two are the *sattva* and *kṣetrajña*."

Vedāntin: And yet this cannot be said to be opposed to the present topic, for the embodied Self, called the *kṣetrajña*, is not presented here (in the *Paiṅgi-Brāhmaṇa*) as endowed with such worldly qualities as agentship and enjoyership.

How is it presented then?

It is presented as free from all worldly qualities and identical in nature with Brahman Itself—with pure Consciousness—as stated in, " 'The other looks on without eating' means, 'the knower who witnesses without eating'." And this is supported by such Vedic and Smṛti texts as, "That thou art" (Ch. VI. viii. 7), "Me do thou also know to be the *kṣetrajña*" (Gītā, XIII. 2). The conclusion made thus with that much (i.e. the explanation of the *mantra*) only, in the words, "The two are the *sattva* and *kṣetrajña*. Ignorance has no effect on a man of such knowledge" etc., becomes justifiable only on this assumption (that the individual soul is spoken of as Brahman).

Opponent: From such a point of view, how can enjoyership be ascribed to the insentient mind by saying, " 'One of them eats the fruits of divergent tastes' means the *sattva* (i.e. the internal organ)"?

The *answer* is: This Vedic text does not start with the idea, "I shall speak of the enjoyership of the insentient."

What is the idea then?

The idea is: "I shall show that the sentient individual is not the experiencer, but it is Brahman by nature." It is for this purpose that enjoyership is attributed to the mind which is subject to worldly moods like happiness and sorrow etc. For these states of being an agent and experiencer are fancied on the soul and the mind, owing to a non-discrimination between their natures. In reality these are possible in neither of them; for the mind is insentient and the soul is changeless. This is all the more impossible in the mind, it being a creation of ignorance. In support of this here is a Vedic text: "Because when there is difference, as it were, then one sees another" (Bṛ. IV. v. 15), where it is shown that dealings based on agentship etc. can be possible only within the range of ignorance in the same sense as it is possible to deal with elephants etc. present in a dream. And by the text, "But when to the knower of Brahman everything has become the Self, then what should one see and through what?" (ibid.), are denied for the discriminating man such dealings based on agentship etc.

Topic 4: The Person in the Eye

अन्तर उपपत्तेः ॥ १३ ॥

अन्तरः The one inside उपपत्तेः for that is logical.

13. The One inside (is God), for that is logical.

Doubt: We read in the Upaniṣad: "He (viz Satyakāma Jābāla) said (to Upakosala) 'The One, the Person (Puruṣa) seen in the eye, is the Self. This One is immortal, fearless; this One is Brahman. Accordingly, if clarified butter or water be poured on it (i.e. the eye), it flows down to the eyelids" etc. (Ch. IV. xv. 1). Now the doubt arises here: Is a shadowy being, reflected on the eye, indicated here? Or is it the individual soul identified with the intellect? Or is it some divine being presiding over the eye? Or is it God? What should be the conclusion?

Opponent: It is a shadowy being, a reflection of some person (on the eye); for that is well known as an object of perception, and because it is taught as a familiar thing in, "The being that is seen in the eye" (ibid.). Or this may properly be an instruction about the soul identified with the intellect. For it is this being that comes nearest to the eye when perceiving colour through it, and the word Self becomes apposite in this case. Or the being in the sun that helps the eye is to be cognized here, because the Upaniṣadic text states, "He (i.e. the being in the sun) rests on the latter (i.e. the right eye) through the rays" (Bṛ. V. v. 2), and because immortality etc. can somehow be averred of the divine being (in the sun) as well. But that being is not God, since a particular locality is indicated.

Vedāntin: This being the position, we say, God Himself is taught here as the being in the eye.

Why?

Because that stands to reason; for the number of qualities taught here can logically belong to God. Of these, the fact of being the Self applies to Brahman in the primary sense, for the Upaniṣad says, "He is the Self. That thou art" (Ch. VI. viii. 7). And immortality and fearlessness are frequently declared about Brahman in the Upaniṣads. Similarly, this eye as a seat is appropriate for God. Just as God is untouched by all blemishes, His freedom from sin etc. having been spoken of in the Upaniṣads, so is the eye presented as a place untarnished by any blemish in the text, "Accordingly, if clarified butter or water be poured on it, it flows down to the eyelids" (Ch. IV. xv. 1). And the instruction about such qualities as being the "resort of all blessings", (as stated in the following text), fits in with Him: "They call Him the 'goal of the results of actions', for all the results of actions proceed towards Him" (Ch. IV. xv. 2); "This One is certainly the carrier of all good results, for it is this One that carries all good results of works (to their recipients)" (Ch. IV. xv. 3); "This One is certainly the 'ordainer of all effulgence', for it is this One that shines in all the worlds" (Ch. IV. xv. 4). Therefore the One inside is God, for that is logical.

स्थानादिव्यपदेशाच्च ॥ १४ ॥

च And स्थान-आदि-व्यपदेशात् from the mention of the place etc.

14. And (this follows) from the mention of place etc.

How again can it be logical for Brahman, omnipresent as It is like space, to have a tiny seat like the eye?

With regard to this it is said: This illogicality would have been there if it had been the only place indicated for Brahman. But as a matter of fact, there are other places like the earth, which are indicated for It by the text, "He who inhabits the earth, but is within it" etc. (Bṛ. III. vii. 3). Among these places, the eye too is counted: "He who inhabits the eye, but is within it" etc. (Bṛ. III. vii. 18). What is implied in the aphorism by the use of "etc." in "the mention of place etc." is this: The mention of location alone for Brahman is not the only irreconcilability.

What else is irreconcilable?

Name and form etc. Though Brahman is without name and form, such things are seen to be ascribed to It in, "His name is *Ut*" (Ch. I. vi. 7), "His beard is golden" (Ch. I. vi. 6), and so on. And it has been already said that though Brahman is without qualities, still for the sake of meditation, It is presented in those respective places as a qualified entity, possessed of the characteristics associated with name and form. It has also been stated that even for the omnipresent Brahman it is nothing incongruous to have certain special places for meditation like the *Śālagrāma* (stone symbol) for Viṣṇu.

सुखविशिष्टाभिधानादेव च ॥ १५ ॥

सुख-विशिष्ट-अभिधानात् एव च ।

15. And this is so for the further reason that the One possessed of bliss is referred to (in the Text, "The One that").

Moreover, there should certainly be no quarrel here as to whether Brahman is spoken of here in this sentence or not. For from the very fact that the one possessed of bliss is mentioned by the text, "The One that" etc. (Ch. IV. xv. 1-4), it follows that Brahman is meant; for Brahman is possessed of bliss. The very entity introduced at the commencement of the text, viz "*Prāṇa* is Brahman, bliss is Brahman, space is Brahman" (Ch. IV. x. 4), is spoken of here (in "The One that"); for it is reasonable to accept that which is under discussion. Besides, this must be the conclusion, because the instruction about the course (followed after death) was alone promised to be spoken of in, "But the teacher will tell you of the course"[9] (Ch. IV. xiv. 1).

Opponent: How again is it known that Brahman, possessed of bliss, is spoken of at the commencement of the text?

Vedāntin: The answer is: Hearing these words of the Fires, "*Prāṇa* is Brahman, bliss (*kam*) is Brahman, space (*kham*) is Brahman" (Ch. IV. x. 5), Upakosala said, "I know that *Prāṇa* is Brahman; but I do not know bliss (*kam*) or space (*kham*)" (ibid.). To that, this is the reply (of the Fires): "That which is bliss (*kam*) is space (*kham*), and that which is space (*kham*) is bliss (*kam*)" (ibid.). Of these the word space (*kham*) is familiar as a synonym of the material space. Had not the word *kam*, meaning bliss, been used to qualify *kham*, it would have seemed that the word Brahman is applied to the mere material space in order to present space as a symbol like name etc. Similarly, the word *kam* is familiarly in use with regard to the defective (worldly) happiness, arising from the contact of objects and senses. If it had not been qualified by *kham* (space), the idea gathered would have been that the empirical happiness is Brahman. But the words bliss and space, having qualified each other, lead us to the comprehension of Brahman which is Bliss Itself. Then again, if a second word Brahman had not been used, that is to say, if (instead of "*kam Brahma kham brahma*") the sentence ran thus, "*kam kham brahma*—bliss space is Brahman", then having been used merely as an adjective (of *kham*), bliss (as an aspect of Brahman) would not have become an object of meditation. To avert that possibility, both the

[9] Upakosala stayed with his teacher Satyakāma Jābāla for twelve years. But the teacher went out on a sojourn without instructing Upakosala about Brahman. This upset the boy. But the four sacrificial fires, tended so long with care by him, revealed their individual secrets to him, instructed him saying, "*Prāṇa* is Brahman" and so on, and concluded by saying that the teacher would tell him of the course. Then the teacher returned, and starting with, "The One that is the Puruṣa seen in the eye", told him of the course (see text below).

words bliss and space precede the word Brahman (separately) in (bliss is Brahman, space is Brahman). For the intention is that the aspect of bliss should be as much an object of meditation as the entity qualified by it. Thus it is that at the commencement of the text, Brahman possessed of bliss is spoken of. And each of the Fires—Gārhapatya and others—first speaks of his personal glory; and then they all conclude with the words, "O amiable one, thus is imparted to you the knowledge about us as also about the Self" (Ch. IV. xiv. 1), thereby suggesting that Brahman (Self) had been referred to earlier. The statement, "The teacher will tell you of the course" (ibid.), holds out a promise of the instruction about the course only, and thus precludes the intention of speaking on an additional topic. Moreover, the statement, "As water does not stick to a lotus leaf, so also sin does not cling to one who knows thus" (Ch. IV. xiv. 3), while speaking of the ineffectiveness of sin against one who knows the Puruṣa residing in the eye, shows that the Puruṣa in the eye is Brahman. It is thus that the Upaniṣad first speaks of the residence of Brahman in the eye and Its possession of such virtues as being the resort of all blessings and so on. Then with a view to speaking of the course, starting with light, that a man with that kind of knowledge has to follow, the Upaniṣad goes on: "He said, 'The One, the Person that is seen in the eye, is the Self' " etc. (Ch. IV. xv. 1).

श्रुतोपनिषत्कगत्यभिधानाच्च ॥ १६ ॥

च श्रुत-उपनिषत्क-गति-अभिधानात् ।

16. And because the course to be followed by one who has heard the secret teaching is spoken of.

For this additional reason, the Person in the eye is God: The course known as the Path of the Gods is followed by one who has heard the Upaniṣad, the knower of Brahman who has received the secret knowledge that is well known in the Vedic text, "Again, by searching for the Self through the control of the senses, *brahmacarya* (continence), faith, and meditation, they conquer the sun by proceeding along the Northern

Course. This Brahman is the resort of all that lives; this is indescribable; this is fearless, this is the highest goal;[10] for from this they do not come back" (Pr. I. 10). This is well known in the Smṛti also: "(The deities of fire, light, day-time, the bright fortnight, the six months of the northern course of sun—taking this path, the knowers of Brahman go to Brahman" (Gītā, VIII. 24). That very Path is seen to be declared for one who knows the Person in the eye. Starting with, "Whether they perform his funeral rites or not, he (the meditator on the Self) attains (the deity of) fire, (and then proceeds along day-time etc.)", it is said, "He proceeds from the sun to the moon, from the moon to lightning. Some superhuman being, coming from the world of Hiraṇyagarbha, leads those who arrive there (i.e. lightning) to Brahman. This is the Path of the Gods, this is the Path to Brahman. Those who attain (the conditioned Brahman) by proceeding along this Path, do not return to this cycle of birth and death, to this creation of Manu" (Ch. IV. xv. 5). From all this (talk about the) well-known Course followed by the knower of Brahman, it becomes established that the Person in the eye is Brahman.

अनवस्थितेरसम्भवाच्च नेतरः ॥ १७ ॥

अनवस्थितेः On account of impermanence च and असम्भवात् on account of impossibility, न इतरः none other can be (the Person).

17. *None other can be the Person in the eye on account of impermanence and impossibility.*

It was argued that the Person in the eye may be a shadowy being, or the individual Self, or some divine being. With regard to this, we say: None among the shadowy being and the rest can be accepted here.

Why?

Since it is transitory. To take up the shadowy self first, it is

[10] This is initially the state of Hiranyagarbha, identified with the cosmic and microcosmic subtle bodies. This, again, is in essence, the immortal, fearless, all-sustaining absolute Brahman. So they first realize the conditioned and then the absolute Brahman.

not possible for it to reside permanently in the eye. When a man is right in front of an eye, the image of the man is seen in it; but when he moves away, it cannot be seen. The text, "The One, the Person, that is there in the eye" (Ch. IV. xv. 1), teaches the worship of the Person present in the eye just because He is near at hand; and it is not proper to fancy that at the time of meditation, the meditator places some person near him to produce an image in the eye, and then he meditates on it. For the text, "This one gets destroyed in accordance with the death of this body" (Ch. VIII. ix. 1), shows the impermanence of the shadowy being. Besides, this is impossible; for such qualities as immortality cannot be found in that shadowy being. So also for the individual soul. Inasmuch as this soul is in general contact with the body and senses as a whole, it is not possible to speak of its existence in the eye alone. But for Brahman, all-pervasive though It is, Its association with special places like the heart for the sake of meditation is met with in the Upaniṣads. Equally impossible is the presence of such qualities as immortality in the soul identified with the intellect. Though as a matter of fact, the individual Self is the same as the supreme Self, still mortality and fear are superimposed on the former through ignorance, desire, and action; and hence immortality and fearlessness do not fit in with it. And such qualities as being the repository of all good attributes are also inappropriate for it, since it has no divine majesty. As for any divine being, though such a god exists in the eye in accordance with the Vedic text, "The former (the being in the sun) rests on the latter (the being in the right eye) through the rays" (Bṛ. V. v. 2), still that god cannot be the Self, since he exists externally. Immortality etc. are also out of place, since the Vedas mention the birth and death of gods, the immortality of the gods being spoken of only from the standpoint of their long life. Their majesty too is dependent on God and is not intrinsic, for the *mantra* says, "Out of His fear the wind blows; out of fear the sun rises; out of His fear Fire and Indra remain active, and Death, the fifth, hurries on (to the dying)" (Tai. II. viii. 1). Therefore it is to be understood that God is the Being in the eye. From this point of view, the use of the word "seen (in the eye)" (Ch. IV. xv. 1) in a familiar sense, is to be explained as arising out of the scriptural outlook, and as referring to the vision of the enlightened man, the whole thing being meant as a praise for inducing the aspirants (to this meditation).

Topic 5 : The Internal Ruler

अन्तर्याम्यधिदैवादिषु तद्धर्मव्यपदेशात् ॥ १८ ॥

अन्तर्यामी The internal Ruler अधिदैव-आदिषु in the divine and other contexts तत्-धर्म-व्यपदेशात् because the characteristics of that are spoken of.

18. The internal Ruler in the divine and other contexts (is the supreme Self), since the characteristics of that (supreme Self) are spoken of.

Doubt: Starting with, "the One who controls this and the next life and all beings from within" (Bṛ. III. vii. 1), it is stated in the Upaniṣad, "(He) who inhabits the earth but is within it, whom the earth does not know, whose body is the earth, and who controls the earth from within, is the internal Ruler, your own immortal Self" (Bṛ. III. vii. 3). Here—in the contexts of the gods, the worlds, the Vedas, the sacrifices, the creatures, and the bodies—we hear of an internal Ruler who resides inside and exercises control. Is he some divine being, identifying himself with things in the divine and other contexts; or some Yogin who has acquired the mystic power of becoming subtle and so on; or the supreme Self; or some other entity? This doubt arises from noticing this peculiar term (*antaryāmin*). What is then the true meaning acceptable to us?

Opponent: Since the term is uncommon, the entity named should be something uncommon and indeterminate. Or since it is not possible to assert the existence of any other indeterminate thing and since the term internal Ruler, conveying the (etymological) sense of controlling from inside, is not altogether unfamiliar, therefore some deity identifying himself with the earth etc. must be the internal Ruler. For in accord with this is the text, "(He knows truly who knows that being) whose abode is the earth, whose instrument of vision is fire, whose light is *manas* (mind), (and who is the ultimate resort of the entire body and organs)" (Bṛ. III. ix. 10). Since by being possessed of body and organs, he rules by residing inside the earth etc., this rulership can justifiably belong to a divine being. Or this rulership can belong to some perfected Yogin who rules by entering into all. But the supreme Self does not come within our purview, since It is not possessed of body and organs.

Vedāntin: This being the position, it is said: The internal Ruler, heard of in the divine and other contexts, is the supreme Self and none else.

Why?

"Because Its characteristics are spoken of—the characteristics of the supreme Self Itself are found mentioned here. It is the characteristic rulership of the supreme Self that becomes obvious from the fact of ruling all created things by entering into the earth and other things differentiated into the divine, (worldly, Vedic), and so on; for It can reasonably have omnipotence by virtue of Its being the source of all creation. And the Selfhood and immortality mentioned in, "this is the internal Ruler, your own immortal Self" (Bṛ. III. vii. 3), are justifiable in the case of the supreme Self understood in the primary sense. By referring to the internal Ruler as being unknown to the deity of the earth in the text, "whom the earth does not know" (ibid.), it is shown that the internal Ruler is different from the divine being. For the deity of the earth can know himself as "I am the earth". Similarly, the use of the words, "unseen", "unheard" (Bṛ. III. vii. 23), fits in with the supreme Self, It being devoid of form etc. The objection is not valid that the supreme Self cannot possibly have any rulership owing to Its lack of body and organs. For It can very well come to own bodies and organs owing to the presence of these in those whom It controls. On this view we do not land into an infinite regress by having to assume a separate ruler for that ruler of that individual being; for there is no difference (between the two). Infinite regress is possible only if there be a difference.[11]

[11] The question of rulership arises from the point of view of empirical difference. In reality Brahman is not different from the individual, and

न च स्मार्तमतद्धर्माभिलापात् ॥ १९ ॥

च And न not स्मार्तम् the one mentioned in the Smṛti अतद्धर्माभिलापात् qualities not belonging to it having been spoken of.

19. Neither Pradhāna, known from the (Sāṁkhya) Smṛti, is the internal Ruler, for qualities that do not belong to Pradhāna are spoken of.

Opponent: Perchance the qualities of being unseen etc. may fit in with Pradhāna (primordial Nature) as conceived of in the Smṛti of the Sāṁkhyas, for by them that Pradhāna is postulated to be without form etc. They mention in their Smṛti, "Beyond reason, inscrutable, and as if in deep sleep everywhere" (Manu I. 5). That Pradhāna can even be the ruler, since it is the source of all modifications. Accordingly, the term internal Ruler denotes Pradhāna. Although Pradhāna was refuted under the aphorism, "Because of the attribution of seeing, the one (i.e. Pradhāna of the Sāṁkhyas) which is not taught in the Upaniṣad is not the cause of the universe" (B. S. I. i. 5), still it forms the subject-matter of the doubt here, since the qualities of not being seen etc. can be imputed to it.

Vedāntin: Therefore the answer is being given: The Pradhāna of the Smṛti cannot be meant by the term internal Ruler. Why?

"Because the qualities that do not belong to Pradhāna are spoken of." Although the qualities of being unseen and so on are ascribable to Pradhāna, not so are the qualities of being the witness and so on; for Pradhāna is admitted by them to be insentient, while the complementary portion of the text here runs thus: "He is never seen, but is the witness; He is never heard, but is the hearer; He is never thought, but is the thinker; He is never known, but is the knower" (Bṛ. III. vii. 23). Besides, Pradhāna can never be the Self (as stated in, "your own immortal Self"—ibid.).

hence no question of rulership and infinite regress arises. Again, empirically, God is recognized as the absolute ruler. To assume another ruler over Him is to ignore the Vedas.

Opponent: If Pradhāna cannot be the internal Ruler owing to the impossibility of its being the Self and the witness, then let the individual soul be so; because the embodied soul is a conscious entity, and as such, it becomes the witness, hearer, thinker, and knower. And it is also the Self, being the inmost. It must be immortal, too, to make the reaping of the fruits of good and bad works possible. It is also a well-known fact that the embodied soul is possessed of the characteristics of not being seen and so on. For it is opposed to facts that the acts of witnessing etc. should have as their object the agent itself (of witnessing etc.), as shown in, "You cannot see that which is the witness of vision" (Bṛ. III. iv. 2), and other texts. And that soul has the capacity of controlling the assemblage of body and senses from within; for it is the experiencer (of the fruits of its own actions). Thus the embodied soul is the internal Ruler.

Vedāntin: The answer to this is:

शारीरश्चोभयेऽपि हि भेदेनैनमधीयते ॥ २० ॥

(Not) शारीरः the embodied soul च also; हि for उभये अपि both अधीयते read एनम् of this one भेदेन as different.

20. The embodied soul also (is not the internal Ruler); for the followers of both the recensions read of this one as different.

The word "not" has to be supplied from the previous aphorism. The embodied soul is not intended as the internal Ruler. Why?

Although it is possible for the embodied soul to be the witness and so on, still, being limited by conditioning factors, like space in pot, it cannot, in the fullest sense, exist within the earth etc. and rule them from inside. Besides, the followers of both the Kāṇva and Mādhyandina recensions (of the *Śatapatha Brāhmaṇa*) read of the embodied soul as being an entity different from the internal Ruler, and as being a habitation for and an object of control, like the earth, under the internal Ruler. The Kāṇvas read: "He who inhabits the intellect" (Bṛ. III. vii. 22); and the Mādhyandinas have: "He who inhabits the *ātmā*" the word *ātmā* standing as a synonym for the embodied soul. And even in the reading, "He who inhabits the intellect (*vijñāna*)", the word intellect means the embodied soul, which is but the entity identifying itself with the intellect. Therefore it stands established that God, the internal Ruler, is distinct from the emobodied soul.

Opponent : How, again, can there be two witnesses in the same body—the one that is this God, the internal Ruler, and the other that is the embodied soul?

Vedāntin : What incongruity is there?

Opponent : Since the Upaniṣadic text, "There is no other witness but Him" (Bṛ. III. vii. 23), will stand contradicted; for in that text it is denied that any Self, other than the internal Ruler under discussion, can be the witness, hearer, thinker, or knower.

Objection : May this not be meant for the denial of other rulers?

Opponent : No, for no other ruler is under consideration, and the Upaniṣadic denial is made without any reservation.

Vedāntin : With regard to this, it is said: This mention of the distinction between the embodied soul and the internal Ruler is based on the limiting adjunct of body and senses, conjured up by ignorance, but this is not so in any real sense. For the indwelling Self can be but one, and not two. The same one, however, is mentioned as two owing to conditioning factors, as for instance it is said, "the pot-space", "the cosmic space". From this standpoint, the Vedic texts about the difference between the knower and things known, the means of valid knowledge like perception, the experience of transmigration, and scriptures dealing with injunctions and prohibitions—all become justifiable. Thus it is that the text, "Because when there is duality, as it were, then one sees something" (Bṛ. II. iv. 14), shows that all dealings are possible within the range of ignorance; and the text, "But when to the knower of Brahman everything has become the Self, then what should one smell and through what, what should one see and through what?" (ibid.), precludes all dealings within the sphere of illumination.

Topic 6: The One that is Unseen etc.

अदृश्यत्वादिगुणको धर्मोक्तेः ॥ २१ ॥

अदृश्यत्व-आदि-गुणकः The possessor of the attributes of invisibility etc. (is Brahman); धर्म-उक्तेः on account of the characteristics having been stated.

21. The entity, possessed of the qualities of not being seen etc., is Brahman, for Its characteristics are spoken of.

Doubt: We read in the Upaniṣad: "Then there is the higher knowledge by which is realized that Immutable" (Mu. I. i. 5), and "(By the higher knowledge) the wise realize everywhere that which cannot be perceived and grasped; which is without source, features, eyes, and ears; which has neither hands nor feet; which is eternal, multiformed, all-pervasive, extremely subtle, and undiminishing; and which is the source of all" (Mu. I. i. 6). With regard to this, the doubt arises: Is it Pradhāna, or the embodied soul, or God that is spoken of as the material cause of all things and as endowed with the qualities of not being perceived etc.?

Opponent: Among these alternatives, the insentient Pradhāna should properly be the material source of everything, for the insentient things alone are cited there by way of illustration: "As a spider spreads out and withdraws (its thread), as on the earth grow herbs (and trees), and as from a living man issues out hair on the head and the body, so out of the Immutable does the universe emerge here (in this phenomenal creation)" (Mu. I. i. 7).

Objection: Are not the sentient spider and the human being taken here as examples?

Opponent: We say, no; for a sentient being, by itself, can neither be the material source of thread nor of hair. It is rather well known that under the control of the sentient, the insentient body of the spider becomes the source of thread and the human body of the hair on the head and other parts. The argument for the non-acceptance of Pradhāna, adduced earlier, was that, although Pradhāna could be described as not subject to visual perception etc., still it could not be spoken of as a witness etc. (B. S. I. ii. 19). But here (in this context), the qualities of not being perceived etc. are seen to be possible in Pradhāna at the same time that no incompatible quality is in evidence.

Objection: Is it not a fact that the expression, "He who is omniscient in general and all-knowing in detail" (Mu. I. i. 9), heard in the complementary text, is not applicable to the insentient Pradhāna? So how is it asserted that Pradhāna is the source of all things?

Opponent: With regard to this, it is said: It has been shown by the text, "That by which is realized that Immutable" (Mu. I. i. 5), and "That which cannot be perceived" etc. (Mu. I. i. 6), that the word immutable means the source of all things, and it is possessed of the quality of not being perceived etc. Then at the end it will be said again, "Superior to the superior immutable" (Mu. II. i. 2). Now then, the entity that is heard of as superior to the immutable, should be omniscient in general and particular; and it is Pradhāna, the material source of all things, that is mentioned by the word immutable. If, however, the word *yoni* (source) means an efficient, and not material cause, then the embodied soul also can be the source of all things, since it brings into existence all the things through its merit and demerit.

Vedāntin: This being the position, it is said: The entity that is the source of all things and is possessed of such qualities as not being perceived and so on must be God and none else.

How is this known?

From the mention of the characteristics. For the characteristics of God are obviously mentioned here in, "He who is omniscient in general and all-knowing in detail" etc. (Mu. I. i. 9). Neither Pradhāna which is insentient, nor the embodied soul which is circumscribed in its vision by limiting adjuncts, can possibly be omniscient in general and all-knowing in detail.

Opponent: Did we not say that this omniscience in general and particular belongs to the one who is higher than the source of all things (i.e. Pradhāna), called the immutable; but that omniscience does not belong to this source of all?

With regard to this the answer (of the *Vedāntin*) is: This is not possible, since the source of all things that is under discussion is mentioned as the material cause of all that is born, in the text, "Out of the Immutable does the universe emerge here" (Mu. I. i. 7); and then the omniscient Being is mentioned immediately after as the material cause of all that is born, in the text, "From Him who is omniscient in general and all-knowing in particular and whose austerity is constituted by knowledge, evolves thus this (derivative) Brahman, as well as name, colour, and food" (Mu. I. i. 9). Accordingly, since the Immutable under discussion, which is the source of all things, is called up to memory by a similarity of reference (in the second passage), it follows that the characteristics of omniscience in general and detail are declared about the Immutable Itself. And even in the text, "Superior to the superior immutable" (Mu. II. i. 2), none higher than the Immutable that is relevant and is the source of all things is referred to.

How is that gathered?

Because from the text, "That man of enlightenment should adequately impart that knowledge of Brahman by which one realizes the true and immutable Puruṣa" (Mu. I. ii. 13), it can be understood that it is but the Immutable under discussion, the source of all things and possessed of the qualities of not being perceived and so on, that is promised to be presented.

Why is it then declared to be "superior to the superior immutable"?

That we shall answer in the succeeding aphorism. Moreover, it is said here that two kinds of knowledge have to be acquired, which are the "higher and the lower" (Mu. I. i. 4). Of these, the first is mentioned as comprising the Ṛg-Veda etc., and then it is said, "Then there is the higher knowledge by which is realized the Immutable" etc. (Mu. I. i. 5). There the Immutable is heard of as the subject-matter of the higher knowledge. If, therefore, it be fancied that the Immutable, possessed of the qualities of not being perceived etc., is different from the supreme Lord, then this will not be the higher knowledge.

This division of knowledge into higher and lower is made according to the two results, viz liberation and prosperity. Not that any one can admit that the knowledge of Pradhāna leads to liberation. In that case three kinds of knowledge should have been postulated; for from your point of view, the supreme Self is presented as something different from the immutable that is the source of all things. As a matter of fact, however, it is mentioned here that two kinds of knowledge have to be acquired. Moreover, the fact that it is taken for granted that the knowledge of all becomes included in the knowledge of one, as implied in, "O adorable sir, which is that thing, which having been known, all this becomes known?" (Mu. I. i. 3), can be justifiable only if the all-inclusive Brahman be the subject-matter of the talk; but this cannot be so if the subject-matter be either Pradhāna which comprises merely the insentient, or the experiencing soul that is different from the things experienced. Further, the knowledge of Brahman is introduced as the highest in the text, "To his eldest son, Atharvā, he imparted that knowledge of Brahman that is the basis of all knowledge" (Mu. I. i. 1), then making a division between the higher and lower knowledge, it is shown that the higher knowledge leads to the realization of the Immutable; and from this it becomes revealed that this higher knowledge is the knowledge of Brahman. This knowledge that is called the knowledge of Brahman will be wrongly called so if the Immutable to be attained through it becomes different from Brahman. And since there are such declamations as, "Since these eighteen constituents of a sacrifice,[12] on whom the inferior *karma* has been said to rest, are perishable because of their fragility, therefore those ignorant people who get elated with the idea, 'This is the cause of bliss', undergo old age and death over and over again" (Mu. I. ii. 7), it follows that the knowledge of *karma*, comprised in the Ṛg-Veda etc., is presented at the commencement of the knowledge of Brahman for the sake of eulogizing the latter. And after decrying the lower knowledge it is said that those alone have the competence for the higher

[12] Sixteen priests, the sacrificer, and his wife.

knowledge who turn back from the former: "A Brāhmaṇa should resort to renunciation after examining the acquired worlds with the help of the idea, 'There is nothing here that is not a result of *karma*; so what is the need of *karma*?' For knowing the Reality he should go with sacrificial fagot in hand to a teacher versed in the Vedas and absorbed in Brahman" (Mu. I. ii. 12).

It was also argued that since the insentient earth and other things were cited as examples, therefore the source of all things, for whose sake these illustrations are presented, must be insentient as well. But that is wrong, for there is no such rule that the illustration and the thing illustrated must be absolutely similar. Moreover, just because the gross earth and other things are cited by way of example, it does not follow, even according to you, that the source of all things, that is exemplified, is postulated to be gross. Therefore the source of all things, that is possessed of the qualities of not being perceived and so on, must be God.

विशेषणभेदव्यपदेशाभ्यां च नेतरौ ॥ २२ ॥

च And विशेषण-भेद-व्यपदेशाभ्याम् on account of the mention of distinctive characteristics and difference इतरौ the other two न are not.

22. *And the other two (viz the individual soul and Pradhāna) are not meant, for there is the mention of the distinctive characteristics (of Brahman) and (Its) difference (from the two).*

For this further reason, God alone is the source of all things; and neither Pradhāna nor the individual soul is so.

Why?

"Because of the mention of distinctive characteristics and difference." For on the strength of dissimilar characteristics, the source of all things, which is relevant to the context, has been distinguished from the embodied soul in the text, "Puruṣa is transcendental, since He is formless; and since He is coextensive with all that is external and internal, and since He is birthless, therefore He is without vital force and without mind. He is pure and superior to the (other) superior immutable" (Mu. II. i. 2). These characteristics of transcendence etc. cannot logically apply to the embodied soul which identifies itself with the limitations imposed by name and form, conjured up by ignorance, and which imagines their attributes as its own. Hence Puruṣa (the conscious all-pervasive entity), met with in the Upaniṣads alone, is directly mentioned here. Similarly the source of all things, which is relevant to the context, is mentioned as different from Pradhāna in the text, "Superior to the superior immutable" ((ibid.). The immutable is the unmanifested (i.e. beginningless Māyā) that is a kind of power belonging to the source of name and form (viz God), that is the latent state of all the elements, that has God as its support, that is a limiting adjunct to God Himself,[13] and that is higher than all its own modifications, but is itself unmodified. By declaring a difference through the statement, "superior to that superior (immutable) Māyā", the text shows that what is intended here to be spoken of is the supreme Self. It is not a fact that any independent principle, called Pradhāna, is admitted, and then a difference from it is shown here (in the aphorism).

What is admitted then?

(It is held that) if a principle, called Pradhāna (meaning Māyā or nescience), be imagined, and it be asserted without any violence to the Upaniṣads that this Pradhāna is called by such terms as the "unmanifested" and the "latent state of all the elements", then you may as well follow that imagination.[14] The Upaniṣad mentions a difference (of Immutable) from that. And so it is established here that God is the source of all things.

For what further reason is God the source of all things?

[13] Making a difference between God and the creatures.

[14] For thereby you speak of Māyā only, though under another name, Pradhāna, which term may bear the etymological sense of "that which is perceived as the products". Even if the opponent should say that the aphorist refutes this very Pradhāna, and not the Pradhāna of the Sāṁkhyas, still there is nothing to quarrel about, for the Sāṁkhya view stands negated along with that.

रूपोपन्यासाच्च ॥ २३ ॥

च And रूप-उपन्यासात् owing to a presentation of form.

23. And because there is a presentation of form.

Moreover, immediately after the text, "Superior to the superior immutable", the creation of the entities, counting from the vital force to the earth, is spoken of in the verse, "From Him originates the vital force" etc. (Mu. II. i. 3). And after that we notice that the form of that very source of all things, comprising within it all creation, is presented in the verse, "The indwelling Self of all is surely He of whom heaven is the head, the moon and the sun are the two eyes, the directions are the two ears, the revealed Vedas are speech, air is the vital force, the universe is the heart, and it is He from whose two feet emerged the earth" (Mu. II. i. 4). All that is appropriate for God alone, He being the source of all creation. Such a presentation of form is incompatible with the embodied soul for its greatness is limited; and this is incompatible with Pradhāna which cannot be the indwelling Self of all beings. Therefore it is understood that God alone is the source of all things but not so are the other two.

How is it again known that this is a presentation of the form of the source of all things?

Because of the context, and because the words "it is He" (ibid.) allude to something under consideration. When after broaching the topic of the source of all things, statements such as these are made, "From Him originates the vital force" etc. (Mu. II. i. 3), "The indwelling Self of all is surely He" (Mu. II. i. 4), these must relate to the source of all things. For instance, if after starting a talk about a teacher, some one should say, "Read under him. He is versed in the Vedas and the ancillary subjects", then that statement relates to that teacher. The case is similar here.

Opponent: How can the source of all things, that is possessed of the qualities of not being seen etc., have a physical form?

Vedantin: That creates no difficulty; for the statement has in view the revelation of all-pervasiveness and not any physical form, just as it is the case in, "I am food, I am the eater of food" (Tai. III. x. 6).

Others (viz the *Vṛttikāra*), again, think: This is not a presentation of the source of all things, for the presentation is made through the fact of getting born. In the earlier verse, "From this One originates the vital force, as well as the mind and all the senses, space, air, fire, water, and the earth that supports everything"[15] (Mu. II. i. 3), all the entities, counting from the vital force to the earth, were presented from the standpoint of being born. Later on, too, the verses starting with, "From Him emerges the fire (i.e. heaven) of which the sun is the fuel" (Mu. II. i. 5), and ending with, "From Him issue all the corns as well as the juices" etc. (Mu. II. i. 9), speak only of things being born. In the midst of all this, how can the form of the source of all things be presented here alone all of a sudden? The all-pervasiveness too will be taught, after finishing with creation, in the verse, "Puruṣa alone is all this—comprising the *karma* and knowledge" (Mu. II. i. 10). In the Vedas and the Smṛtis too we notice statements about the birth etc. of the Being who has the three worlds as His body; "Hiraṇyagarbha was born first, and having been born, He became the only Lord of all beings. He held the earth and this heaven. That single Deity we propitiate with oblation" (R. V. X. cxxi. 1). The word *samavartata* in that text means "was born". So also in the text, "He is the first embodied Being, He is called Puruṣa, He is the first ordainer of all beings. Thus was Brahmā born in the beginning". Even a created person (viz Hiraṇyagarbha) can be all-pervasive, for in His aspect as the vital force, He dwells within the bodies of all beings.

If this point of view be accepted, then the explanation (of the aphorism) will be this: All the presentations of form in such texts as, "Puruṣa is all this" (Mu. II. i. 10), lead to the understanding of the supreme Lord.[16]

[15] The text implies that the all-comprehensive Hiraṇyagarbha, mentioned in, "The indwelling Self of all" (Mu. II. i. 4), emerges from Him who is the source of all things (Mu. II. i. 3). So Hiraṇyagarbha has birth just like any other thing.

[16] The assertion, "all *karma* and knowledge (i.e. meditation) are but

Topic 7: Vaisvanara

वैश्वानरः साधारणशब्दविशेषात् ॥ २४ ॥

वैश्वानरः Vaiśvānara साधारण-शब्द-विशेषात् for the words denoting many things are used specifically.

24. Vaiśvānara (the Cosmic Person) is the supreme Lord, for though the (two) words (Self and Vaiśvānara) denote many things, they are used specifically.

Doubt: (In the Chāndogya Upaniṣad) the start is made thus: "Which is our Self and what is Brahman?"[17] (V. xi. 1) and "At present you remember this Self, the Vaiśvānara. Tell us of that very entity"[18] (V. xi. 6). Then after the denunciation (by Aśvapati) of the separate meditation on heaven, sun, air, space, water, earth, as possessed of the qualities of bright light, (multiform, identity with divergent paths, vastness, wealth, support), and after the teaching (by Aśvapati) that these constitute the head, (eye, life, middle part of the body, bladder, and feet) of Vaiśvānara, the text runs thus: "He who meditates on this Vaiśvānara Self, knowing It directly as *prādeśamātra* (spatially limited, or realized in limited places) and *abhivimāna* (identified with oneself), eats food in all the worlds, through all the beings and through all the selfs. Of this Vaiśvānara Self, the head is heaven, the eye is the sun, the vital force is air, the middle part of the body is space, the bladder is water, the earth is the two feet, the chest is the sacrificial altar, the heart is the Gārhapatya fire, the mind is the Anvāhāryapacana fire, and the mouth is the Āhavanīya fire" (Ch. V. xviii. 1-2). The doubt

Puruṣa" amounts to presenting an entity inherent in everything. And so the text leads to the comprehension of the supreme Lord as the source of all things.

[17] Five Brāhmaṇas—Prācīnaśāla, Satyayajña, Indradyumna, Jana, Buḍila—discussed this problem among themselves. As they found no adequate answer, they went to Uddālaka, who also did not know the full answer.

[18] The six Brāhmaṇas went to king Aśvapati and said this to him. In answer to the king's question, the Brāhmaṇas related their own conceptions of Vaiśvānara, as stated below *seriatim*.

arises here as to what is indicated by the word Vaiśvānara. Is it the heat in the stomach, or the element fire, or the deity identifying himself with it, or the embodied soul, or the supreme Lord?

What, again, causes the doubt here?

The cause is the use of the word Vaiśvānara, which is a common term for the heat in the stomach, the element called fire, and the deity of fire, as also the use of the word Self denoting both the embodied Self and the supreme Lord. So the doubt arises as to which of these meanings should be accepted and which rejected. What should be the conclusion here?

Opponent: It is the fire in the stomach.

Why?

Because the word is seen to be used sometimes specifically to signify this fire, as in, "This fire that is within a man and digests the food is Vaiśvānara" (Bṛ. V. ix), and such other places. Or it may mean simply the ordinary fire, for it is seen to be used in a general way also, as in, "For the sake of the whole universe the gods created that Vaiśvānara (fire, i.e. the sun)" (R. V. X. lxxxviii. 12). Or it may mean the deity having fire as his body, the word being in use in that sense also: "Because Vaiśvānara, the king of the worlds, ordains happiness, and because all glories belong to him, therefore may we remain within his favour" (R. V. I. iic. 1); for according to this and other texts of this kind, the word can apply to some deity possessed of glory etc. If, however, it is held that the word Vaiśvānara is to be interpreted in consonance with the word Self, as the word Self alone is used in the beginning in the text, "Which is our Self, what is Brahman?" (Ch. V. xi. 1), still it must be merely the embodied soul, because it approximates to Vaiśvānara by reason of being an experiencer, and because the attribute of spatial limitation is possible in its case, it being limited by conditioning factors. Therefore Vaiśvānara is not God.

Vedāntin: This being the position, it is said: Vaiśvānara should properly mean God.

Why?

Because even though the two words (Vaiśvānara and Self)

denote many things, they are used specifically. *Sādhāraṇa-śabda-viśeṣa* means specification about the two common words. Although both these words—Self, Vaiśvānara—are common to many things—Vaiśvānara implying three things and Self two—yet a specification is noticed, because of which their meaning is understood to be the supreme Lord, as is seen in: "Of this Vaiśvānara Self, the head is heaven" etc. (Ch. V. xviii. 2). Here we understand that the supreme Self Itself, which has assumed a special form with heaven etc. as the head and so on, is presented as the indwelling Self, for the sake of meditation. And this can be so, for It is the cause. From the fact that all the states of an effect belong to the cause, it follows that the supreme Lord can have heaven etc. as His limbs. And the result, viz subsisting in all the worlds etc. as heard of in the text, "He (the knower of Vaiśvānara) eats food in all the worlds, among all beings, and through all the selfs" (Ch. V. xviii. 1), is possible if the ultimate cause is meant. And the indication of Brahman, contained in the text, "Thus indeed are all his sins burnt away" (Ch. V. xxiv. 3), which speaks of the burning away of all the sins of the knower of Vaiśvānara, and the indication in the commencement, as contained in the words Self and Brahman in the text, "Which is our Self, what is Brahman?" (Ch. V. xi. 1), lead us to the comprehension of the supreme Lord alone. Hence the supreme Lord alone is meant by Vaiśvānara.

स्मर्यमाणमनुमानं स्यादिति ॥ २५ ॥

स्मर्यमाणम् that (form) mentioned in the Smṛti स्यात् should be अनुमानम् an indicatory mark; इति hence.

25. The form referred to in the Smṛti is an indicatory mark (that Vaiśvānara means the supreme Lord). Hence Vaiśvānara is God.

Another reason why God is meant by Vaiśvānara is that the Smṛti mentions that the form, comprising the three worlds and having fire as the mouth, heaven as the head, and so on, belongs to God Himself: "Salutation to Him who is embodied in the three worlds with fire as His mouth, heaven as His head, sky as the navel, the earth as the two feet, the sun as the eye, and the directions as the ears" (Mbh. XII. 47. 68). This form, mentioned in the Smṛti, bears witness to the Vedic text forming its basis; and thus it becomes a ground for inferring that the (Vedic) word Vaiśvānara stands for the supreme Lord. The word *iti* is used in the sense of "hence", implying thereby, "Since this is a ground of inference leading to that conclusion, therefore Vaiśvānara means the supreme Self Itself". Though "salutation to Him who is embodied in the three worlds" is a eulogy, still a eulogy, involving the presentation of such a form, is not quite possible unless there is some Vedic text forming its basis. Other Smṛti texts like the following can also be quoted here: "His nature is inscrutable and He is the creator of all beings, of whom, the Brāhmaṇas say, that heaven is the head, sky is the navel, the sun and moon are the eyes, the directions are to be known as the ears, and the earth constitutes the two feet."

शब्दादिभ्योऽन्तःप्रतिष्ठानाच्च नेति चेन्न तथा
दृष्टयुपदेशादसम्भवात्पुरुषमपि चैनमधीयते ॥ २६ ॥

शब्द-आदिभ्यः Because of the word and other factors च प्रतिष्ठानात् and because of residence अन्तः inside, न not so, इति चेत् if this be the objection, then न not so, दृष्टि-उपदेशात् because the instruction is to conceive तथा in that way असम्भवात् because it is inapplicable (elsewhere) च and अधीयते they mention एनम् this one अपि पुरुषम् even as a Puruṣa (lit. person).

26. If it be objected that Vaiśvānara is not the supreme Self because of the word used as well as other factors, and because of residence inside, then we say : not so, because the instruction is to conceive of Brahman as such, because the specification is inapplicable to others, and because they mention Him even as a person (Puruṣa).

The *opponent* says here that the supreme Lord cannot be Vaiśvānara.

Why?

Because of the word used as well as other factors, and because of residence inside. To take up the "word" first: The term Vaiśvānara cannot possibly be used for the supreme Lord, for its conventional meaning is something else. So also the word fire, as in "This fire that is such is Vaiśvānara" (Ś. B. X. vi. 1.12), is not applicable to the supreme Self. By the term "other factors" is to be understood the conception with regard to the three fires contained in, "The heart is the Gārhapatya fire" etc. (Ch. V. xviii. 2), as well as the mention of fire as the place for the oblation to *Prāṇa*, (conceived of as the fire in Agnihotra), in the text, "Now then the food that comes first is to be offered as an oblation" (Ch. V. xix. 1). For these reasons, the meaning of the word Vaiśvānara is to be understood as the fire in the stomach. So also we hear of residence inside, "He who knows this (this fire called Vaiśvānara) as Puruṣa (Person), as having the likeness of Puruṣa, and as residing inside Puruṣa (eats food everywhere)" (Ś. B. X. vi. 1.11). That is possible for the fire in the stomach. As for the argument that because of the specification mentioned in "Heaven is the head" etc. (Ch. V. xviii 2), Vaiśvānara[19] must be the supreme Self, we ask, "In the face of the specifications supporting either point of view, how do you arrive at the decision that the specification about the supreme Lord alone is to be accepted and not the other about the fire in the stomach?" Or it may be that there is a reference to the element fire, existing inside and outside. For from the *mantra* texts, such as the following, we can gather that it too has a relationship with heaven etc.: "(That is to be meditated on) which, in the form of the sun, pervades this earth and heaven and the inter-space between heaven and earth" (R. V. X. lxxxviii. 3). Or the deity, having fire as his body can have heaven etc. as his limbs by virtue of the divinity he is dowered with. Therefore Vaiśvānara does not mean the supreme Lord here.

Vedāntin: To this we say: No, for the instruction is about conceiving in that way. From such reasons as the "use of the word" and so on, the supreme Lord should not be denied.

[19] Meaning "the entity filling up everything, present everywhere, and Consciousness by nature".

Why?

Because the instruction is about imagining (Vaiśvānara) in that way without abandoning (its meaning as) the fire in the stomach, inasmuch as the superimposition of the idea of the supreme Self on the Vaiśvānara fire in the stomach is taught here just as in, "Meditate on the mind as Brahman" (Ch. III. xviii. 1). Or the supreme Self is taught here to be meditated on as conditioned by the limiting adjunct of the Vaiśvānara fire in the stomach, just as it is done in such texts as, "identified with the mind, having the vital force as His body, having effulgence as His form" etc.[20] (Ch. III. xiv. 2). If the supreme Self be not implied here and the mere fire in the stomach be meant, then the specification in the text, "Heaven is the head" etc. will surely be impossible. We shall explain under the succeeding aphorism how this specification cannot be justified even by resorting to a deity or the element fire. If the mere fire in the stomach be meant, it can only have its residence within Puruṣa, but it cannot be Puruṣa himself. The followers of the Vājasaneya recension, however, read of this Vaiśvānara as Puruṣa himself in, "He who is Puruṣa is this fire called Vaiśvānara. He who knows this fire called Vaiśvānara as Puruṣa, having the likeness of Puruṣa, and residing inside Puruṣa' (Ś. B. X. vi. 1.11). But since the supreme Self is the Self of all, It can very well be both Puruṣa and have residence within Puruṣa.

For those who read this portion of the aphorism thus, "*puruṣavidhamapi ca enamadhīyate*—for they read of Him as having the likeness of *Puruṣa* as well", the meaning is this: On the assumption that the mere fire in the stomach is meant, it can simply have residence within Puruṣa, but it cannot have the likeness of Puruṣa. But the followers of the Vājasaneya recesion read of this One as having the likeness of Puruṣa as well, in the text, 'Know Him as having the likeness of Puruṣa and residing inside Puruṣa' ". And by the term "the likeness of Puruṣa" is to be understood, in accordance with the topic under discussion, all the limbs counting from heaven as the head to the earth as the feet in His divine aspect, and the

[20] In the first case, fire is a symbol, in the second it is a limiting adjunct.

well-known human limbs counting from the head to the chin in His corporeal aspect.

अत एव न देवता भूतं च ॥ २७ ॥

अतः एव For these very reasons न देवता not a deity च and भूतम् not any element.

27. *For these very reasons (Vaiśvānara is) neither the deity nor the element.*

And it was asserted that from the presentation of the element fire in association with heaven and the rest in the text of the *mantra*, it follows that the conception of the limbs, as contained in, "The head itself is fire" etc. (Ch. V. xviii. 1) must be made about that very element fire; or the conception of limbs has to be made about the deity that has fire as his body, for the deity is dowered with divinity. That has to be repudiated. So it is said here: For these very reasons, the deity (of fire) is not Vaiśvānara. The element fire is also not so, for the element fire that has the nature of mere heat and light cannot be fancied to have heaven as its head and so on, for a thing that is itself a product cannot be the Self of another product. So also the deity, possessed though he is of divinity, cannot be fancied to have heaven etc. as his head etc., for the deity is not their source, and his divinity depends on the supreme Lord. Besides, the inapplicability of the word Self is there to be sure in all the alternatives.

साक्षादप्यविरोधं जैमिनिः ॥ २८ ॥

जैमिनिः Jaimini (thinks) अविरोधम् non-contradiction साक्षात् अपि even if directly (meditated).

28. *According to Jaimini, there is no contradiction even in case of direct meditation.*

In conformity with the mention of residence inside and so on, it was stated earlier that the supreme Lord is to be meditated upon with the help of fire in the stomach as His symbol or He is to be meditated upon as conditioned by the fire in the stomach. But now the teacher Jaimini thinks that even if the supreme Lord (in His cosmic form of Virāṭ be understood by the word Vaiśvānara and) be accepted directly for meditation[21] without thinking of fire as a symbol or limiting adjunct, still there will be no contradiction.

Opponent : Will not the statement about residence inside and "the use of the word" and other reasons mentioned in the earlier aphorism (26) be contradicted if the fire in the stomach be not accepted as the meaning of the word Vaiśvānara?

Vedāntin : As to this, it is said: Of these, the statement about residence inside is not contradicted. For it is not a fact that the statement, "He who knows this (Vaiśvānara) as Puruṣa, having the likeness of Puruṣa, and residing inside Puruṣa" (Ś. B. X. vi. 1.11), is made with reference to the fire in the stomach; for that fire is neither under consideration nor is it mentioned by name.

What is the meaning then?

The subject under discussion is the conception of the likeness of Puruṣa, so far as the limbs counting from the head to the chin are concerned. And the statement, "He who knows this One having the likeness of Puruṣa", is made with reference to that conception. This is just like the statement, "He sees the branch fixed on the tree".[22] Or the statement, "He who knows the One having the likeness of Puruṣa and residing in Puruṣa", is made with a view to presenting the nature of the pure witness that belongs to the supreme Self under consideration. This Self has the likeness of Puruṣa since Puruṣa is Its limiting adjunct in the bodily and divine contexts.[23] Once the supreme Lord is

[21] The word Vaiśvānara stands for Brahman, and does not mean the ordinary fire at all (see f.n. 19).

[22] The limbs of Puruṣa are said to be in Puruṣa, though the limbs constitute His body and are not separate from it. Since God is superimposed on the limbs of Puruṣa, His conformity to Puruṣa's limbs amounts to His residence inside Puruṣa.

[23] Divine—counting from heaven to the earth; bodily—counting from the crown of the head to the chin. God is inside all, in the sense of being their witness.

accepted as the meaning of the text after a consideration of it in a logical order from beginning to end, the word Vaiśvānara must signify Him alone through some derivative (and not conventional) sense. Vaiśvānara is the supreme Self in accordance with these derivations: He who is the cosmos (*viśva*) as well as a person (*nara*); or He who is the ordainer (*nara*) of the universe (*viśva*); or He to whom belong all (*viśva*) beings (*nara*). He is the supreme Self, for He is the Self of all. Vaiśvānara is the same as Viśvānara, the suffix (bringing about the transformation) signifies nothing but the original word itself, as in the words *rākṣasa* and *vāyasa*.[24] Even the word *agni* (usually meaning fire), should mean the supreme Self from the derivative sense of leading to the attainment of the results of work.[25] And since the supreme Self is the Self of all, it is quite reasonable to think of It as the Gārhapatya fire (Ch. V. xviii. 2), or as the place (i.e. fire) for offering the oblations to the vital force (Ch. V. xix. 1).

Opponent: On the supposition that Vaiśvānara stands for the supreme Self, how can the text about spatial limitation (*prādeśamātratva*) (Ch. V. xviii. 1) be justified?

Vedāntin: The next aphorism proceeds to explain this:

अभिव्यक्तेरित्याश्मरथ्यः ॥ २९ ॥

अभिव्यक्तः From the point of view of manifestation इति this is (what) आश्मरथ्यः Āśmarathya (says).

29. According to Āśmarathya, it is from the point of view of manifestation (that God is referred to as spatially limited).

Even though the supreme Lord transcends all limitation, still there can be a spatial limitation for the sake of (His) manifestation. For the supreme Lord does become manifest (in His majesty) out of favour for His worshippers. Or because He becomes specially manifest in particular spots like the heart,

[24] *Rakṣas* and *Rākṣasa* both mean demon; *vayas* and *vāyasa* both mean crow.

[25] Or that which makes the world attain birth; or that which goes everywhere, or knows everything.

which are the places (*pradeśa*) for His revelation, therefore from the point of view of manifestation, the text about spatial limitation is justifiable even in the case of the supreme Lord. This is how the teacher Āśmarathya thinks.

अनुस्मृतेर्बादरिः ॥ ३० ॥

अनुस्मृतेः On account of being meditated on, (says) बादरिः Bādari.

30. According to Bādari (God is spoken of as spatially limited) on account of being meditated on.

Or He is said to be spatially determined because He is meditated on by the mind inhabiting the heart which is spatially limited,[26] just as the barley measured by a (vessel called) *prastha* is said to be a *prastha* in quantity. Although it is a fact that barley itself has some intrinsic quantity, which becomes obvious from its contact with the *prastha*, whereas the supreme Lord has no measurement to be revealed by His contact with the heart, still it is asserted that the text about spatial manifestation can somehow be explained on the basis of remembrance (of God).[27] Or to make the text about the revelation in space fruitful, the meaning is that the supreme Self, which has no spatial limitation, is to be meditated on as though spatially determined. Thus the teacher Bādari thinks that the text about spatial limitation occurs from the standpoint of meditation.

सम्पत्तेरिति जैमिनिस्तथा हि दर्शयति ॥ ३१ ॥

सम्पत्तेः Because of meditation based on superimposition इति so says जैमिनिः Jaimini, हि because तथा so दर्शयति (another text) shows.

31. According to Jaimini, the spatial limitation is (justifiable) because of the meditation based on superimposition; for this is shown (in another text).

[26] That which is measured (*mita*) by the mind, existing in the space (*pradeśa*) in the heart, is *prādeśamātra*.

[27] The spatial limitation of the heart becomes superimposed on the remembrance by the mind. And since God too is present in the same remembrance (or meditation), this limitation becomes superimposed on Him as well.

Or the text about spatial limitation may be there because of the meditation through superimposition (i.e. imagining a small thing to be great).

How?

For so in a similar context in the *Vājasaneya brāhmaṇa*, the limbs counting from heaven to the earth, of the Vaiśvānara Self, embodied in the three worlds, are superimposed on the physical limbs counting from the top of the head to the chin; and thus this *brāhmaṇa* shows how the supreme Lord becomes spatially limited in a meditation based on superimposition (Ś. B. X. vi. 1.11): (King Aśvapati said to the Brāhmaṇas, Prācīnaśāla and others)—"The gods knew Him fully as though spatially limited; they knew Him as the inmost Self. Therefore I shall speak of those limbs to you in that very way. I shall superimpose them just according to their spatial limitation. While teaching about the crop of the head, he (the king) said, 'This (crop of my head) is Vaiśvānara as the all-surpassing (heaven).' Teaching about the two eyes, he said, 'This (the two eyes of mine) is Vaiśvānara as the sun (which is His eye).' Teaching about the nostrils, he said, 'This is Vaiśvānara as air (which is His breath).' Teaching about the space in the mouth, he said, 'This is Vaiśvānara as the vast space (which is His trunk).' Teaching about the saliva in the mouth, he said, 'This is Vaiśvānara as water (which is His bladder).' Teaching about the chin, he said, 'This is Vaiśvānara as the earth (which constitutes His feet)'." By the word *cubuka* (chin) is to be understood the lower (jaw) bone of the face. Although the *Vājasaneya brāhmaṇa* speaks of heaven as all-surpassing and the sun as brilliant, while in the Chāndogya, heaven is spoken of as brilliant and the sun as possessed of many forms, still this difference is nothing damaging;[28] for the Vedic statement about spatial limitation is the same. And (it will be shown that) the same kind of meditation (on Vaiśvānara and others) is in evidence in all the branches (of the Vedas). The teacher Jaimini thinks that

[28] It will be shown later that the texts have to be reconciled by adding to one the qualities mentioned in the other. Thus both the texts have to accept heaven as both brilliant and all-surpassing. Or it may be said that, though the attributes differ, the meditation is the same.

it is more logical to say that the text about spatial limitation occurs for the sake of meditation based on superimposition.

आमनन्ति चैनमस्मिन् ॥ ३२ ॥

च And आमनन्ति they remember एतम् this One अस्मिन् in this place.

32. And they (the followers of the Jābāla branch) remember (i.e. read of) this One (i.e. God) in this place (i.e. in between the head and the chin).

And the followers of the Jābāla branch remember this One, i.e. the supreme Lord, in this place, i.e. in between the top of the head and the chin: "(Yājñavalkya)—'That which is this infinite and inscrutable Self is seated (that is to say, has to be meditated upon) on this one that is under bondage (i.e. the individual being.' (Atri)—'Where is the one under bondage seated?' 'He is established in between *Varaṇā* and *Nāsī*.' 'Which is *Varaṇā* and which is *Nāsī*?'" (Jābāla 2). In that text, again, it is ascertained that this one (i.e. the eyebrows) and the nose are *Varaṇā* and *Nāsī* from the derivation of *Varaṇā* as that which wards off (*vārayati*) all the sins committed by the senses, and of *Nāsī* as that which destroys (*nāśayati*) all the sins committed by the senses. The Jābālas read furthermore, "'Which becomes the seat for this one (i.e. the individual being)?' 'That which constitutes the link between the eyebrows and the nose becomes the link between heaven and the supreme place (of Brahman)' [29]" (ibid.). Therefore the text about spatial limitation is appropriate with regard to the supreme Self.

And the term *abhivimāna* in the text is used to indicate the innermost Self, in the derivative sense of that which is known directly (*abhivimīyate*) as the inmost Self by all beings; or in the sense of that which is directly attained (*abhigata*) as the innermost at the same time that it is free from any measurement

[29] This place is to be meditated on as the link between the two. Some read *bhruvoḥ prāṇasya ca* in place of *bhruvorghrāṇasya ca*, where *prāṇa* means *ghrāṇa* (nose).

(*vimāna*); or in the sense of that which creates diversely (*abhivimimīte*) the whole universe, It being the source of all.

Therefore it is proved that Vaiśvānara must be the supreme Self.

SECTION III

TOPIC 1: THE ABODE OF HEAVEN, EARTH, ETC.

द्युभ्वाद्यायतनं स्वशब्दात् ॥१॥

द्यु-भू-आदि-आयतनम् The repository of heaven, earth, etc. स्व-शब्दात् on account of the word denoting Itself.

1. The repository of heaven, earth, etc. (is the supreme Self) on account of the word denoting Itself.

Doubt: This is met with in the Upaniṣad: "Know that Self alone which is one without a second, on which are strung heaven, the earth, and inter-space, the mind and the vital forces together with all the other organs;[1] and give up all other talks. This is the dam (or bridge) leading to immortality" (Mu. II. ii. 5). Here from the mention of the subsistence of heaven etc., it becomes obvious that something exists as the repository. The doubt arises as to whether this container (or abode) is the supreme Brahman or something else.

Opponent: As to that, the obvious meaning is that something other than Brahman must be this repository.

Why?

Because we hear from the Upaniṣad, "This is the dam leading to immortality." A dam (or bridge) is known in this world to be connected with two banks, whereas no bank can be admitted for Brahman in the face of the Upaniṣadic declaration: "Infinite, shoreless" (Bṛ. II. iv. 12). If some other thing has to be admitted as the repository, then the Pradhāna, well known in the Smṛti, should be accepted, for it is logical for it to be the repository, it being the material cause. Or it can be the air well known in the Upaniṣad, for air is also heard of as something holding

[1] On Brahman is transfixed Virāṭ, embodied in the three worlds; and on It, again, is transfixed Hiraṇyagarbha, embodied in all the subtle minds. These two are meant by the references to the gross heaven etc., and the subtle mind etc., respectively.

together, in the text, "*Vāyu* (air), O Gautama, is that *Sūtra* (lit. thread). Through this *Sūtra* or *Vāyu* this and the next life and all beings are held together" (Bṛ. III. vii. 2). Or it can be the embodied soul; for by virtue of its being the experiencer, it can justifiably be a repository in relation to the manifold world of enjoyment.

Vedāntin : This being the position, it is said: "The repository of heaven, earth, etc." The compound word *Dyubhuvau* is formed by *dyu* (heaven) and *bhū* (earth); *dyu-bhū-ādi* means those that have heaven and earth at the beginning. Since in this sentence the universe, consisting of heaven, earth, inter-space, mind, organs, etc. have been mentioned as transfixed on some entity (Mu. II. ii. 5), hence the repository of this must logically be Brahman.

Why?

"On account of the word denoting Itself", that is to say, because of the word "Self"; for the word "Self" does occur here in, "know that Self alone that is one without a second" (Mu. II. ii. 5). And the word "Self" fits in quite aptly if the supreme Self is understood by it, but not so if the meaning be something else. Moreover, in some places, Brahman is spoken of as the repository by Its very name, as in, "O amiable one, all these beings have Existence as their source, Existence as their repository, and Existence as their culmination" (Ch. VI. viii. 4). Besides, Brahman is mentioned by Its very name earlier as well as later in this very context: "Puruṣa alone is all this—comprising the *karma* and knowledge. He who knows this supreme immortal Brahman" (Mu. II. i. 10), "All that is in front is but Brahman, the immortal. Brahman is on the right, as well as on the left. Above and below too is extended Brahman alone" (Mu. II. ii. 11). From hearing in that context of the relation, existing between a container and the thing contained, and from the appositional use (asserting Brahman's identity with all) in, "All is Brahman" (Ch. III. xiv. 1), the doubt may arise that just as a tree is a composite entity, comprising as it does the branches, trunk, and roots, so also the Self is variegated and possessed of diverse tastes. In order to obviate that doubt, the text declares with emphasis: "Know that Self alone that is one without a second" (Mu. II. ii. 5). The idea expressed is this: The Self is not to be cognized as a heterogeneous thing comprising the manifold created universe.

How is It then to be cognized?

The meaning is that, after eliminating, through knowledge, the universe conjured up by ignorance, you should know that one and homogeneous Self alone that appears as the repository. Just as when somebody is told, "Bring that on which Devadatta sits", one brings the seat alone, but not Devadatta; similarly the homogeneous Self, appearing as the repository, is taught here as the object to be known. Furthermore, we hear of the condemnation of one who clings to the unreal created things: "He goes from death to death who sees as though there is difference here (in Brahman)" (Ka. II. i. 11). As for the use of "all" and "Brahman" in apposition in the text, "All this is (but) Brahman" (Ch. III. xiv. 1), it is meant for the elimination of the universe,[2] and not for proving heterogeneity (in Brahman). For we hear of homogeneity in, "As a lump of salt is without interior and exterior, entire and purely saline in taste, even so is the Self without interior and exterior, entire, and pure Intelligence alone" (Bṛ IV. v. 13). Hence the supreme Brahman is the repository of heaven, earth, etc.

As for the objection, that from the mention of the dam in the Upaniṣad and from the fact that a dam is associated with banks, something other than Brahman should be the respository of heaven and earth, the reply is this: By the text about the dam, the only point sought to be illustrated is the fact of holding together (or impounding) and not the possession of banks. It does not follow that, since a dam in this world is made of earth and timber, the dam mentioned here is also assumed to be similarly constructed. The word dam itself (etymologically) implies mere holding together, but not possession of banks etc., for the word *setu* (dam) is derived from

[2] To remove the false conception of a stump as a thief, somebody may say, "Your thief is a stump", which statement denies the existence of the thief, and is not meant to establish the identity of the thief and the stump. So in the present case, the apposition does not imply that Brahman and creation are equally true.

the root *ṣiñ* in the sense of impounding (the water from flowing out).

Somebody else says: The knowledge of the Self met with in the text, "Know that Self alone" (Mu. II. ii. 5), and the discarding of speech met with in the text, "give up all other talks" (ibid.), are also declared here by the text, "this is the dam leading to immortality", for these two constitute the means (the bridge) leading to immortality. But Brahman as the repository of heaven and earth is not spoken of.

Vedāntin: The objection raised on that supposition, to the effect that the text about the dam reveals something other than Brahman as the repository of heaven and earth, is illogical.

मुक्तोपसृप्यव्यपदेशात् ॥२॥

मुक्त-उपसृप्य-व्यपदेशात् ।

2. *Because there is the instruction about (Its) attainment by the free.*

From this additional reason that this repository of heaven, earth, etc. is taught as the goal to be reached by the liberated, it follows that this repository is the supreme Brahman. *Muktopasṛpya* means attainable by those freed from bondage. Nescience consists in the idea of Selfhood entertained about the body etc., which are not the Self. As a result of this self-identification, follow love for those who adore that body and hatred for those who dishonour it, and fear and confusion from noticing its death. In this way, this multitude of evils, with infinite differences, that flows on for ever, is obvious to all of us. In contradiction to this, it is stated with regard to this repository of heaven and earth that It is to be reached by those who are free from such defects as ignorance, love, hatred, etc.

How is it stated?

Having declared, "When that Self, which is both high and low (i.e. cause and effect), is realized, the knots of the heart get untied, all the doubts become solved, and all actions become dissipated" (Mu. II. ii. 8), it is stated, "As the rivers, flowing down, become indistinguishable on reaching the sea by giving up their names and forms, so also the illumined soul, having become freed from name and form, reaches the self-effulgent Puruṣa that is higher than the higher Māyā (unmanifested Nature)" (Mu. III. ii. 8). And it is well known from such texts as the following that Brahman is attainable by the liberated: "When all the desires that dwell in his heart are gone, then he, having been mortal, becomes immortal and attains Brahman even in this body" (Bṛ. IV. iv. 7). But Pradhāna and the rest are nowhere known to be attainable by the liberated. Again, with regard to the entity that is the repository of heaven and earth it is stated here in the text, "Know that Self alone and give up all other talks" (Mu. II. ii. 5), that this entity is realizable after the giving up of speech (that is to say, the activities of all organs). And this very fact is found to be declared in another Upaniṣad in connection with Brahman: "The intelligent aspirant after Brahman, knowing about this alone, should attain intuitive knowledge. He should not think of too many words, for it is particularly fatiguing to the organ of speech" (Bṛ. IV. iv. 21). For this reason also the abode of heaven and earth is Brahman.

नानुमानमतच्छब्दात् ॥३॥

न Not अनुमानम् any inferential entity अ-तत्-शब्दात् on account of absence of any word indicating it.

3. No inferential entity (is the repository), for there is no word of that import.

It is being stated that there is no uncommon ground of inference establishing anything else, in the same sense that there is an uncommon ground of inference (viz the word) to prove Brahman. "The inferential entity", viz Pradhāna fancied in the Smṛti of the Sāṁkhyas, "is not" to be understood here as the abode of heaven and earth etc.

Why?

"For there is no word of that import." "A word of that import" means some word establishing that insentient Pradhāna.

An absence of such a word is meant. There is no word here to prove Pradhāna, on the strength of which the insentient Pradhāna could have been understood either as the cause or the abode. (Or the meaning of *atacchabdāt* is): There are words of contrary import in evidence here, which establish a sentient entity opposed to it (Pradhāna), as for instance, "He who is omniscient in general and all-knowing in detail" (Mu. I. i. 9). For this very reason, air too is not accepted here as the abode of heaven, earth, etc.

प्राणभृच्च ॥४॥

प्राणभृत् A living creature च also (is not so).

4. A living creature also is not so.

It is true that a living being, identifying itself with intelligence, can be the Self and can have sentience; but there can be no omniscience for one whose knowledge is circumscribed by limiting adjuncts. And hence on the very ground of the presence of words of a contrary import,[3] a living being is not to be accepted as the repository of heaven and earth. Moreover, it is impossible for a living creature, circumscribed as it is by conditioning factors, to be the repository of heaven, earth, etc. in the fullest sense. The present aphorism is framed separately (from the earlier one) in order to connect it with the succeeding ones.[4]

For what further reason is the living being not to be accepted as the repository of heaven, earth etc.?

भेदव्यपदेशात् ॥५॥

5. (And) because there is a mention of difference.

[3] Viz that "Self", used in apposition with omniscience (in Mu. II. ii. 7), can mean God alone.

[4] Although the "not" borrowed from the earlier aphorism connects these together, still the fourth one is independent, since the individual soul is dealt with here as well as in the succeeding ones, and not Pradhāna as in the third one.

Moreover, there is a mention of difference as between the knowable object and the knower, in the text, "Know that Self alone that is one without a second" (Mu. II. ii. 5). In that text the knower is a living creature, since it hankers for freedom. And by the method of residue, Brahman, mentioned by the word Self, is the object to be known and is the respository of heaven, earth, etc., but not so is a living creature.

What additional reason is there for not accepting a living being as the abode of heaven, earth etc.?

प्रकरणात् ॥६॥

6. On account of the context.

And because this is a context of the supreme Self. This is evident from the text, "O adorable sir, (which is that thing) which having been known, all this becomes known?" (Mu. I. i. 3), where the knowledge of all is made to depend on the knowledge of one. For it is only by knowing the supreme Self, that is the Self of all, that all this becomes known; but not so by knowing merely a living creature.

For what more reason a living being is not to be accepted as the abode of heaven, earth, etc.?

स्थित्यदनाभ्यां च ॥७॥

स्थिति-अदनाभ्याम् च ।

7. *And on account of the facts of staying on and eating.*

While presenting the abode of heaven, earth, etc., the facts of staying on and eating (i.e. experiencing) are stated in the text, "Two birds that are ever associated and have similar names" etc. (Mu. III. i. 1), the experience of the results of work being mentioned in, "Of these the one eats the fruits of divergent tastes" (ibid.), and staying on indifferently being mentioned in, "The other looks on without eating" (ibid.). By these two facts of staying on and eating, God and the individual soul are understood in that context. Provided God had been sought to be presented as the abode of heaven, earth, etc. (in Mu. II. ii. 5), then only it becomes proper to speak of Him, who is already the subject under discussion, as separate from the individual soul. Otherwise it will amount to speaking suddenly about something out of context and unrelated.

Opponent: Is not the mention of the individual soul as different from God equally out of context even in your case?

Vedāntin: No, for the soul (as such) is not presented as the subject-matter of the topic. The individual soul, present in every body as the agent and experiencer in association with such limiting adjuncts as the intellect, is known from common experience itself, and so it is not mentioned in the Upaniṣads for its own sake. But as God is not thus familiarly known from common experience, He is intended to be declared in the Upaniṣad for His own sake. Hence it is not proper to say that any mention of Him is uncalled for. It was also shown under the aphorism, "The two who have entered into the cavity are the individual Self and the supreme Self" (B. S. I. ii. 11), that God and the individual soul are spoken of in the verse, "Two birds" etc. (Mu. III. i. 1). Even though it is said in the explanation offered by the Paiṅgi Upaniṣad that the *sattva* (intellect) and the individual soul are spoken of in this verse, still there is no contradiction.

How?

For what is repudiated here is that any living creature can be the repository of heaven, earth, etc., the reason being that, just like the space within a pot, this creature is perceived separately in every body as identified with such limiting adjuncts as the *sattva*. But He who is cognized in all bodies as free from all limiting adjuncts must necessarily be the supreme Self. Just as much as the spaces within pots etc., when perceived as free from the limitations of the pots etc., are but the cosmic space, similarly since the living creatures (freed from their adjuncts) are not logically different from the supreme Self, therefore it is not possible to deny them (as the repository of heaven etc.). Hence what is really denied is that the soul identifying itself with the *sattva* etc. can be the repository of heaven, earth, etc. Accordingly the supreme Brahman is alone the repository of heaven, earth, etc.; and this was established by the earlier aphorism, "The entity possessed of the qualities of not being seen and so on is Brahman, for Its characteristics are spoken of" (I. ii. 21). For in connection with that very text about the source of all beings, we read, "on which are strung heaven, the earth, and inter-space" etc. (Mu. II. ii. 5). That subject is revived here for the sake of elaboration.[5]

Topic 2: Bhuman (Infinite, Plenitude)

भूमा सम्प्रसादादध्युपदेशात् ॥८॥

भूमा Bhūman (is Brahman), उपदेशात् the teaching having been imparted सम्प्रसादाद् अधि as superior to *samprasāda.*

8. Bhūman is the supreme Self, since He is taught as superior to samprasāda (i.e. Prāṇa or vital force).

Doubt: This is stated in the Upaniṣad: "(Sanatkumāra said), 'But Bhūman (the Infinite) has surely to be inquired into.' (Nārada said), 'O venerable sir, I hanker to understand the Infinite.' (Sanatkumāra said), 'That is the Infinite in which one does not see anything else, does not hear anything else, does not know anything else. And that is limited where one sees something else'" etc. (Ch. VII. xxiii-xxiv). Here the doubt arises: Is *Prāṇa* the Bhūman (Infinite) or is the supreme Self so?

Why does the doubt arise?

By the word *Bhūman* is meant plenitude, for it is mentioned in the Smṛti (i.e. Pāṇini's grammar), "The word *bhūman* is derived from the word *bahu* (much, many) with the suffix *iman* added after it, and then the *i* of the suffix is dropped and *bhū* is substituted for *bahu* (to give rise to the abstract counterpart of *bahu*)" (VI. iv. 158). The Smṛti speaks of the word *bhūman* as having a suffix added to it to impart the sense of the abstract noun. When the curiosity about the nature of that plenitude arises, it becomes obvious from the text, "*Prāṇa* is certainly greater than hope" (Ch. VII. xv. 1), that *Prāṇa is Bhūman* because of proximity. Similarly from the way the

[5] Showing that the source of all is also the inmost Self of all.

topic is introduced in, "For it has surely been heard by me from persons of your standing that the knower of the Self crosses over sorrow. Here am I such a sorrowing man, O venerable sir, ferry me across this sorrow, sorrowful as I am" (Ch. VII. i. 3), it appears equally that *Bhūman* is the supreme Self. Of these two, it becomes a matter of doubt as to which is to be accepted and which rejected. What would be the conclusion here?

Opponent : The conclusion is that *Prāṇa* is *Bhūman*.

Why?

Because it is noticed that the (series of) questions and answers are concerned with something greater (*bhūyān*), for instance, (it is asked by Nārada), "O venerable sir, is there anything greater than name?" (Ch. VII. i. 5), and the answer (by Sanatkumāra) is, "The organ of speech is surely greater than name" (Ch. VII. ii. 1). Similar are (the question), "O venerable sir, is there anything greater than the vocal organ?" (Ch. VII. ii. 2), and (the answer), "The mind is surely greater than the vocal organ" (Ch. VII. iii. 1). Here a chain of questions and answers extends from name etc. to *Prāṇa*. But after *Prāṇa* no such question and answer are found in the shape of "O venerable sir, is there anything greater than *Prāṇa*?" and "Such a thing is surely greater than *Prāṇa*." But in the text, starting with, "*Prāṇa* is surely greater than hope" (Ch. VII. xv. 1), *Prāṇa* is spoken of in detail as the greatest of all things counting from name etc. and ending with hope. Then in the text, "(Should he be told), 'You are transcending all in your speech', he should say, 'Yes, I do transcend', he should not deny" (Ch. VII. xv. 4), it is acknowledged that for one who realizes *Prāṇa*, there accrues the power of transcending all others in speech (i.e. establishing his assertion as the final one). Lastly it is said, "But this person verily transcends all others in his speech, who transcends them with the help of truth" (Ch. VII. xvi. 1), where the vow of *Prāṇa*, consisting in transcending all other things is alluded to. And without discarding *Prāṇa*, the *Bhūman* is introduced through a chain of truth and the rest. From all this it becomes clear that the text regards *Prāṇa* itself as *Bhūman*.

Objection: How, again, after explaining *Prāṇa* as *Bhūman* would you explain the text, "That in which one does not see anything else" etc. (Ch. VII. xxiv. 2), which sets forth the characteristics of *Bhūman*?

Opponent: The answer is: That definition, viz "That in which one does not see anything else", is applicable to *Prāṇa* also, since it is a matter of experience that all such activities as seeing cease in deep sleep when all the organs merge in *Prāṇa*. Thus the (Praśna) Upaniṣad also speaks of the state of sleep as a state of the merger of all the activities of the organs, in the text, "This person does not then hear, does not see" (IV. 2), and then in that very state it shows the sleeplessness of *Prāṇa* with its fivefold functions, in the text, "It is the fires of *Prāṇa*[6] that really keep awake in this city (of the body)" (Pr. IV. 3), thereby showing that the state of sleep is dominated over by *Prāṇa*. The mention of happiness in relation to *Bhūman* in, "That which is *Bhūman* is bliss" (Ch. VII. xxiii) is also not irreconcilable (with *Prāṇa*); for we hear of bliss in the state of sleep in, "Then in that state the deity does not see dreams. Then at that time there occurs this kind of happiness in the body" (Pr. IV. 6). The text, "That which is *Bhūman* is immortal" (Ch. VII. xxiv. 1) is also not irreconcilable with *Prāṇa*; for the Upaniṣadic text says "*Prāṇa* is surely immortal" (Kau. III. 2).

Objection: On the assumption that *Prāṇa* is *Bhūman*, how would you justify the introduction of the topic from the point of view of a desire for the realization of the Self, as is evident from the text, "The knower of the Self crosses over sorrow" (Ch. VII. i. 3)?

Opponent: We say that *Prāṇa* itself is here intended to stand for the Self; and that is why *Prāṇa* is shown as identified with all in, "*Prāṇa* is father, *Prāṇa* is mother, *Prāṇa* is brother, *Prāṇa* is sister, *Prāṇa* is teacher, *Prāṇa* is Brahman" (Ch. VII. xv. 1). The identity of *Prāṇa* with *Bhūman* in the sense of vastness is also possible from the mention of *Prāṇa's* identity with all

[6] Gārhapatya fire as *Apāna*, Anvāhāryapacana as *Vyāna*, Āhavanīya as *Prāṇa* (Pr. IV. 3).

and the illustration of the spokes and nave in the text, "As the spokes are fixed on a nave, so also are all these fixed on *Prāṇa*" (Ch. VII. xv. 1.). Therefore the conclusion arrived at is this that *Prāṇa* is *Bhūman*.

Vedāntin: Hence it is stated: The supreme Self alone can be the *Bhūman* here, and not *Prāṇa*.

Why?

Because of the instruction about His superiority to *samprasāda*. *Samprasāda* means deep sleep from the derivative sense of the state in which one becomes fully serene. This is confirmed by the Bṛhadāraṇyaka also because it is stated there along with the waking and dream states (IV. iii. 15-17). And since *Prāṇa* keeps awake in that state of full serenity, therefore in this aphorism, *Prāṇa* is accepted as the meaning of *samprasāda*. So the idea implied (by the aphorism) is this: "Since *Bhūman* is taught to be superior to *Prāṇa*, therefore if *Prāṇa* itself be *Bhūman*, then the teaching about its own superiority to itself will be incongruous. For instance, when the instruction is given that something is superior to name, it is not implied that name itself is superior to name."

What then is taught to be superior?

Something different from name and called vocal organ is taught in, "The vocal organ is surely superior to name" (Ch. VII. ii. 1). Similarly in all the (succeeding) stages, some things different from those respective (earlier) things themselves, counting from the vocal organ to *Prāṇa*, are taught as being superior. In the same way, the *Bhūman*, that is taught to be superior to *Prāṇa*, must be something other than *Prāṇa*.

Opponent: But there is no question here like "O venerable sir, is there anything higher than *Prāṇa*?" Nor is there an answer of the form, "Such a thing is surely greater than *Prāṇa*." So how can it be said that *Bhūman* is taught to be higher than *Prāṇa*? Moreover, in the subsequent passage we find a reference to transcendence in speech (i.e. establishing his own conclusion exclusively) by relying on *Prāṇa*: "But he really transcends all others in his speech, who transcends by relying on truth" (Ch. VII. xvi. 1). Hence nothing is taught as higher than *Prāṇa*.

Vedāntin: With regard to this we say: It cannot be asserted that the reference is to the transcendence in speech by relying on *Prāṇa* itself; for there is a specific mention (of truth) in, "He who transcends in speech by relying on truth" (ibid.).

Opponent: Should not that specific mention too refer to *Prāṇa*?

How?

Just as in the sentence, "He indeed is a true performer of Agnihotra who speaks the truth", a man does not become a performer of Agnihotra because of his truthfulness.

By what then?

By the performance of the Agnihotra itself. But truthfulness is mentioned as a special qualification of a performer of Agnihotra. Similarly in the sentence, "But he really transcends in speech who transcends by relying on truth', the transcendence in speech does not result from truthfulness.

From what then?

From the knowledge of *Prāṇa* that is under consideration. But truthfulness is intended as a special qualification of the knower of *Prāṇa*.

Vedāntin: We say, no; for that will lead to the abandonment of the meaning of the Upaniṣad. From the direct text of the Upaniṣad it is obvious that the transcendence in speech results from the reliance on truth, the meaning being, "But he really transcends in speech who transcends by relying on truth." There is no declaration of the knowledge of *Prāṇa* here. The knowledge of *Prāṇa* can perchance be brought into play with the help of the context only. But if that be done, the direct text will be overruled by the context.[7] And on this interpretation, the use of the word *tu* (but) as in, "But he really transcends in speech" (ibid.), meant to distinguish something going to be discussed from something that preceded, cannot be justified. And the text, "But truth must be inquired into" (Ch. VII. xvi. 1), which implies an additional effort, suggests that a fresh subject (other than *Prāṇa*) is intended to be introduced (by the word "truth"). Accordingly, just as when the mastery

[7] Which is inadmissible. The direct text is "*satyena*—by relying on truth". A direct statement is more authoritative than inference through context.

of a single Veda is under discussion, and some one says, "But he is really a great *Brāhmaṇa* who reads the four Vedas", the praise relates to the knower of the four Vedas who is different from the knowers of a single Veda, so also are we to understand here. Besides, there is no such rule that the intention to speak about a new thing can be gathered merely from a freshness of questions and answers.[8] For the intention of a new subject can be understood when it becomes impossible to keep within the range already attained. In the context under discussion (Ch. VII. xv-xvi), Nārada becomes silent after hearing the teaching up to *Prāṇa*. Then Sanatkumāra voluntarily expounds to him thus: The transcendence in speech by relying on the knowledge of *Prāṇa*, which is mutable and unreal, is really no transcendence, "but he really transcends all others in his speech who transcends by relying on truth". In that text the supreme Brahman is meant by the term truth (*satya*) because that is the highest reality, and because another Upaniṣad says, "Brahman is Truth, Knowledge, Infinite" (Tai. II. i. 1). To Nārada who has thus been enlightened, and who has reacted by saying, "O venerable sir, I want to transcend all things in my speech by relying on truth" (Ch. VII. xvi.), Sanatkumāra teaches *Bhūman* through a succession of practices like deep meditation etc.[9] That being the case, it is understood that the very truth which is promised to be spoken of as higher than *Prāṇa* (in Ch. VII. xvi) is mentioned here (in Ch. VII. xxiii) as *Bhūman*. Hence there does occur an instruction about *Bhūman* as superior to *Prāṇa*. And in this way the starting of the topic with the purpose of the knowledge of the Self stands justified. Moreover, it is not reasonable to say that *Prāṇa* itself is intended here as the Self, for *Prāṇa* cannot be the Self in the primary sense. Furthermore, there can be no cessation of

[8] For in the Bṛhadāraṇyaka, Maitreyī is seen to question Yājñavalkya repeatedly about the very same Self. And in the illustration of the knowers of the Vedas, the subject-matter is changed even without the help of question and answer.

[9] *Ratnaprabhā* interprets "vijñana" as *nididhyāsana* (deep concentration) and "etc." as *manana* (reflection), faith, *śravaṇa* (hearing), purity of mind, steadfastness, and efforts for attaining these.

sorrow from anything but the knowledge of the Self, for another Upaniṣad declares, "(Knowing Him alone one goes beyond death). There is no other path to reach the goal" (Śv. VI. 15). And starting with, "Take me across sorrow, such as I am, O venerable sir," (Ch. VII. i. 3), the conclusion is made with, "The venerable Sanatkumāra shows the other shore of darkness to him from whom has been rubbed away all attachment" (Ch. VII. xxvi. 2). By the word darkness (*tamas*) is meant ignorance, the source of sorrow etc. And if the instruction were really to end with *Prāṇa* as the highest, this *Prāṇa* would not have been declared to be subject to something else; and yet the *brāhmaṇa* text runs thus: "From the Self proceeds *Prāṇa*" (Ch. VII. xxvi. 1).

Opponent: It may well be that the supreme Self is intended to be dealt with at the end of the context (Ch. VII. xxvi); but *Bhūman* here is nothing but *Prāṇa*.

Vedāntin: No, for by such texts as, "On what is He (i.e. *Bhūman*) seated, O venerable sir? 'On His own glory'" (Ch. VII. xxiv. 1), *Bhūman* is carried forward right up to the end of the topic. And the characteristic of Infinity, expressed as plenitude (or vastness), fits in all the better in the case of the supreme Self, since It is the source of all.

धर्मोपपत्तेश्च ॥९॥

च And धर्म-उपपत्तेः because the characteristics are appropriate.

9. And the characteristics of Bhūman are appropriate (for the supreme Self).

Moreover, the characteristics of *Bhūman*, mentioned in the Upaniṣad, are appropriate for the supreme Self. For instance, the Upaniṣad informs us of the absence in the *Bhūman* of such acts as seeing, in the passage, "That is *Bhūman* where one does not see anything else, does not know anything else" (Ch. VII. xxiv. 1); and this absence of such acts as seeing is known to pertain to the supreme Self from the other Upaniṣadic passage, "But when to the knower of Brahman everything has become the Self, then what should one see and through what?" (Bṛ.

IV. v. 15). Even the absence of such acts as seeing in the state of sleep, mentioned earlier (Pr. IV. 3), was done so with a view to declaring the absence of any relationship in the case of the Self Itself, and not for revealing the nature of *Prāṇa*, for the topic there was of the supreme Self. Again, the happiness that was spoken of in that state (Pr. IV. 6) was stated with a view to revealing the nature of the Self as Bliss Itself; for it is said, "This is its supreme Bliss. On a particle of this very Bliss other beings live" (Bṛ. IV. iii. 32); and here (in the Chāndogya) also it is said, "That which is *Bhūman* is Bliss. There is no happiness in the limited; the Infinite (*Bhūman*) Itself is Bliss" (Ch. VII. xxiii), where, after rejecting the happiness mixed with sorrow, *Bhūman* is shown to be nothing but Brahman that is Bliss. The immortality that is heard of in the passage, "That which is Infinite (*Bhūman*) is immortal" (Ch. VII. xxiv. 1), leads us to understand the supreme cause; for the immortality present in the created things is only a relative reality, as is evident from another Upaniṣad, "Everything else but this is perishable" (Bṛ. III. iv. 2). Similarly also, all such characteristics as truth, establishment in His own glory, all-pervasiveness, identity with all, which are met with in the Upaniṣad, are appropriate for the supreme Self alone, and not for anything else. Therefore it is proved that *Bhūman* is the supreme Self.

Topic 3: Immutable

अक्षरमम्बरान्तधृतेः ॥१०॥

अक्षरम् The Akṣara (Immutable) अम्बर-अन्त-धृतेः on account of supporting everything up to space.

10. Akṣara is Brahman because of supporting all things up to (and including) space.

Doubt: It is heard in the Upaniṣad: "(Gārgī asked), 'On what is space woven and transfixed?' (Bṛ. III. viii. 7). (Yājñavalkya replied), 'O Gārgī, the knowers of Brahman say, this Akṣara (immutable Brahman) is that. It is neither gross nor minute'" etc. (Bṛ. III. viii. 8). With regard to this the doubt arises: Is the letter (*Om*) meant by the term Akṣara (lit. letter), or is the supreme Lord Himself meant?

Opponent: As to that, in such passages as "The enumeration of letters" (group of 14 aphorisms of Pāṇini), the word *akṣara* is familiarly used in the sense of letter, and it is not reasonable to ignore common usage. Another Upaniṣad also says, "*Om* is certainly all this" (Ch. II. xxiii. 3), where for the sake of meditation, the letter *Om* is declared to be identical with all. Therefore the word *akṣara* is used to indicate a letter.

Vedāntin: This being the position, we say, the supreme Self is meant by the term Akṣara.

Why?

"Because of holding everything up to and including space", because of supporting all created things from earth to space. For it is first stated in the text, "That remains woven and transfixed on unmanifested space" (Bṛ. III. viii. 7), that all created things counting from earth, which are comprised within the three divisions of time, are supported by space; and then this topic of Akṣara is mooted through the question, "On what is space woven and transfixed?" (ibid.). The conclusion is also made in a similar way: "On this Akṣara, O Gārgī, is the (unmanifested) space woven and transfixed" (Bṛ. III. viii. 11). This supporting of everything including space is not possible for anything else but Brahman. As for the quotation, "*Om* is surely all this" (Ch. II. xxiii. 3), that must be understood in the sense of praise, since *Om* is a means for the realization of Brahman. Therefore Akṣara must be the supreme Brahman according to its derivative sense of that which does not decay and that which pervades all, conveying thereby the ideas of eternality and omnipresence.

Opponent: It may be argued that, if by the fact of supporting all things including space be meant the dependence (i.e. inclusion) of the effect on the cause, then this holds equally good in the case of those (Sāṁkhyas) who stand by Pradhāna as the cause. So how can *akṣara* be known to be Brahman from the fact of supporting all things ending with space?

Vedāntin: Hence the answer comes:

सा च प्रशासनात् ॥११॥

च And सा that act (of supporting) प्रशासनात् owing to the mention of mighty rule.

11. And that act of supporting is possible for God only, owing to the mention of His mighty rule.

That act, viz the supporting of all things ending with space, belongs to God alone.

Why?

"Owing to the mention of the mighty rule." For we hear of the mighty rule in the text: "Under the mighty rule of this Akṣara (Immutable), O Gārgī, the sun and the moon, are held in their positions" etc. (Bṛ. III. viii. 9). And this mighty rule is a work of the supreme Lord. The insentient *Pradhāna* cannot exercise this mighty rule; for insentient things like earth etc. do not have this mighty rulership over pot etc., though they are the material causes of these.

अन्यभावव्यावृत्तेश्च ॥१२॥

12. And on account of the exclusion from being other entities.

For the further reason of exclusion from being other entities, it follows that Brahman alone is the meaning of the term Akṣara, for it is Brahman alone and nothing else to whom belongs the act of holding all things ending with space.

Opponent: What is meant by this "Exclusion from being other entities"?

Vedāntin: What is meant is this: *Anyabhāva* means the state of being something else; the exclusion from being so is *anya-bhāva-vyāvṛtti*. The text, "This Akṣara, O Gārgī, is never seen, but is the witness, It is never heard, but is the hearer; It is never thought of, but is the thinker; It is never known, but is the knower" (Bṛ. III. viii. 11), distinguishes Akṣara, supporting all things including space, from everything else that is different from Brahman and That can be presumed to be the meaning of the term Akṣara. In that text, the attributes of not being seen and so on can be ascribed to Pradhāna also, but Pradhāna cannot be said to be a witness and so on, since it is insentient. From the denial of any difference in the Self, as stated in, "There is no other witness but this" (ibid.), it follows that the embodied soul too, conditioned by limiting adjuncts as it is, cannot be the meaning of Akṣara. And this is so for the additional reason that all conditioning factors are denied by the text, "without eyes or ears, without the vocal organ or mind" (Bṛ. III. viii. 8), for there can be no embodied soul unless there be conditioning factors. Hence the definite conclusion is that the supreme Brahman alone is the Akṣara.

Topic 4: The Object of Seeing

ईक्षतिकर्मव्यपदेशात् सः ॥१३॥

ईक्षति-कर्म-व्यपदेशात् Owing to the mention as an object of seeing सः He (is meant).

13. From the mention as the object of the act of seeing (īkṣaṇa), it follows that the supreme Self is meant.

Doubt: Starting with the sentence, "O Satyakāma, this very Brahman that is (known as) the inferior and superior, is but this *Om*. Therefore the illumined soul attains either of the two through this means (or symbol) alone" (Pr. V. 2), it is stated, "Again, anyone who meditates on the supreme Puruṣa (all-pervading entity) with the help of this very syllable *Om*, as possessed of three letters, becomes unified in the sun, consisting of light. He is lifted up to the world of Brahman (Hiraṇya-garbha) by the *Sāma mantras*" (Pr. V. 5). The doubt arises whether in this sentence the meditation on the supreme Brahman or the inferior Brahman is enjoined; for the topic is started with, "attains either of the two through this means alone", and both are relevant.

Opponent: Now then, the conclusion is that it is the inferior Brahman.

Why?

Because in the text, "He enters into the sun consisting of

light, he is lifted up to the world of Brahman by the *Sāma mantras*" (ibid.), a result, limited in space, is vouched for the knower of that Brahman. It is not reasonable that the knower of the supreme Brahman should attain a spatially limited result, inasmuch as the supreme Brahman is omnipresent.

Objection: On the assumption that the inferior Brahman is meant, does not the qualification "the supreme Puruṣa" (ibid.) become inappropriate?

Opponent: This creates no difficulty, for in comparison with the gross body (of Virāt), Hiraṇyagarbha (the inferior Brahman) is justly higher.

Vedāntin: This being the position, it is said: The supreme Brahman Itself is taught here for meditation.

Why?

Because the object of *īkṣaṇa* is mentioned. *Īkṣaṇa* means seeing. And *īkṣati-karma* means the object covered by the act of seeing. The Puruṣa that is to be meditated on is presented in the complementary portion of the passage as an object of seeing: "From this total mass of creatures (i.e. Hiraṇyagarbha), he sees the supreme Puruṣa that penetrates everything and is higher than the higher (Hiraṇyagarbha)" (Pr. V. 5). Of the two acts of seeing and meditating, the object of meditation may even be an unreal thing; for a fanciful thing may as well be the content of meditation; but in this world, the content of seeing is constituted by a real thing. Therefore we understand that it is the supreme Self Itself, forming the content of full realization, that is mentioned as the object of *īkṣaṇa*. And that very Self whose identity is revealed by the Upaniṣadic terms—"the Supreme", "all-pervading Entity"—is presented here as the object of meditation.[10]

Opponent: Is not the supreme Puruṣa mentioned in connection with the meditation, whereas the "higher than higher" is mentioned in connection with the seeing? So how can the one be recognized as identified with the other in another context?

[10] So it cannot be considered that the object of meditation is Hiraṇyagarbha and the object of seeing is Puruṣa (which word means either the "All-pervasive Entity" or the "Entity residing in this city of the heart").

Vedāntin: The answer is this: As to that, the two terms, supreme (*para*) and Puruṣa are common to both the texts (about seeing and meditation). And it cannot be said that the term, "total mass of creatures (*jīvaghana*)" alludes to the supreme all-pervading entity that is relevant and is meant for meditation, in which case alone this other all-pervading entity (Puruṣa) that is to be seen can be "higher than that high one".

Opponent: Who is it then that is mentioned by the term, "total mass of creatures"?

Vedāntin: The answer is: A mass is a formation (like a lump of salt); a formation constituting an individual being is this "total mass of creatures". By the term "total mass of creatures" is meant a limited manifestation of the supreme Self in the likeness of an individual being (viz Hiraṇyagarbha) which is comparable to a lump of salt. And this is conjured up by limiting adjuncts, and it is higher than the sense-objects and the senses.

(About the meaning of "He sees the supreme Puruṣa, higher than the higher *jīvaghana*") *someone else* says: By the term *jīvaghana* (lit. a mass of creatures) is meant here the world of Brahman that is higher than the other worlds and is indicated in the immediately preceding sentence, "By the *Sāma mantras* he is lifted to the world of Brahman" (ibid.). The world of Brahman can be a mass of creatures (by a transference of epithet), because all the individual beings delimited by their senses become united in Hiraṇyagarbha, inhabiting the world of Brahman and identifying Himself with the totality of organs. Therefore it is understood that the supreme Self that is transcendental to that world and is the object of "seeing", is also the object of "meditation". The epithet "supreme all-pervading entity" becomes appropriate on the acceptance of the supreme Self alone, for the supreme Self alone can be the supreme all-pervading entity, beyond which there can be nothing else, as stated in another Upaniṣad, "There is nothing higher than Puruṣa (the all-pervading entity). He is the culmination, He is the highest goal" (Ka. I. iii. 11). When the Upaniṣad makes a distinction by saying, "This very Brahman, that is known as the inferior and the superior, is but this *Om*" (Pr. V. 2), and adds just after this that the supreme Puruṣa is to be meditated on with the help of *Om*, it makes us understand that the supreme Puruṣa is none other than the supreme Brahman. The declaration of the result, viz freedom from sin as contained in, "As a snake becomes freed from its slough, exactly in a similar way he becomes freed from sin" (Pr. V. 5), indicates that the supreme Self is the object of meditation here. As for the objection that one who meditates on the supreme Self can have no spatially limited result, our answer is this: The result vouchsafed for one meditating on Brahman with the help of *Om*, as constituted by three letters, is the attainment of the world of Brahman, and the emergence subsequently of complete realization by stages. In this way this is meant for leading to emancipation by stages, so that there is nothing faulty.

Topic 5: Dahara (The Small Space)

दहर उत्तरेभ्यः ॥१४॥

दहरः The small space (in the heart) उत्तरेभ्यः owing to subsequent reasons.

14. The small space (dahara ākāśa) is Brahman, on account of the subsequent reasons.

Doubt: In the Chāndogya Upaniṣad it is stated, "Then in the small palace of the shape of a lotus that stands in this city of Brahman, there is a small space. That which is inside that[11] is to be sought for, that is surely to be inquired into" etc. (VIII. i. 1). Now the doubt arises with regard to the small space, heard of in this sentence as existing within the small lotus of the heart, as to whether it is the material space (called subtle ether), or the individual Self identified with the intellect, or the supreme Self.

Why should the doubt arise?

[11] *Tasmin*, inside that, may mean in the heart, or in the individual soul, or in the material space; in all cases Brahman is the Entity inside. The opponent construes it thus. The Vedāntin says that the small space Itself is Brahman.

Owing to the presence of the words *ākāśa* and city of Brahman. Since this word *ākāśa* is seen to be used in the senses of both material space and the supreme Self, therefore the doubt arises as to whether the material space or the supreme Self should be the small space here. Again the doubt arises: Is some individual soul meant by the word Brahman, occurring in the phrase "city of Brahman", and is this city called the city of Brahman owing to its being owned by that individual? Or is the city called so because it belongs to the supreme Brahman? That being the case, the doubt arises as to who among the two—the individual Self and the supreme Self—is the owner of the city and is (referred to as) the small space.

Opponent: As to that, the conclusion to be arrived at is that the material space is meant here by the term small (space), for that is the conventional meaning; and that space is called small (*dahara*) in relation to the small place where it subsists. Again the relationship, as between the illustration and the thing illustrated, that is established (here) between two portions of space by dividing it into the internal and the external in the text, "The space that is within this heart is of the same magnitude as the space outside" (Ch. VIII. i. 3), is possible for the material space alone. Within that space can be "included heaven, earth, and the rest" (ibid.); for the material space, in its characteristic of providing space, is but one. Or the conclusion may be that the individual soul is the small space, for the term used is the city of Brahman. This body that is the city of the individual soul is called the city of Brahman, because it is earned by the soul's own work, the soul being called Brahman in a figurative sense. For the supreme Brahman can have neither identity with nor ownership of the body. Now the owner of a city, as for instance a king, is seen to inhabit a portion of the city. And the individual soul is limited by the mind and the mind is generally seated in the heart. Therefore this existence within the heart must be a fact in the case of the soul alone. The smallness too is appropriate for it, since it is compared (in the Upaniṣad) to the tip of a goading stick (Śv. V. 8). And the comparison with space etc. is possible when the intention is to speak of it as identical with Brahman. Besides, the small space is not spoken of in the Upaniṣad as the thing to be sought for or to be known; for in the clause, "That which is inside that" (Ch. VIII. i. 1), the little space is presented as the abode of that (supreme Self) which is inside.[12]

Vedāntin: Hence we offer this answer: The supreme Lord alone can be small Space here; and neither the material space nor the individual soul can be so.

Why?

"On account of the subsequent reasons", because of the reasons occurring in the complementary portion of the passage. Thus with regard to the small space that is to be sought for, the objection is raised: "Should anyone ask him (i.e. the teacher), 'What is it that exists here that has to be sought for and that has to be known?'" (Ch. VIII. i. 2). And then this text occurs by way of an answer: "He (i.e. the teacher) should say, 'The Space that is within the heart has the same magnitude as the space outside. Both heaven and earth are verily included within it'" etc. (Ch. VIII. i. 3). Lest the Space in the text should be understood to be small owing to the smallness of the lotus (of the heart), the teacher repudiates that smallness through a comparison with the familiar material space, which fact leads us to understand that the teacher thereby denies the small Space to be the material space. Though the word space conventionally means the material space, still the suspicion about its (i.e. the small space) being the material space is ruled out, since the material space itself cannot be adopted as a standard of comparison for itself.

Opponent: Did we not say that even the same space can be adopted as the standard of comparison and the thing compared by an assumption of internal and external difference?

Vedāntin: This cannot be so. To resort to a fanciful difference betrays a failure to discover any other way out. Besides, even for a man who would explain the relation between the thing compared and the standard of comparison by fancy-

[12] Or the meaning is: Since the object of being searched for, mentioned in "That which is inside" etc., is taken to imply the supreme Self, *dahara* cannot mean Brahman.

ing an imaginary difference between them, the internal space cannot have the vastness of the external space since the former is limited.

Opponent: Is it not impossible even for the supreme Lord to have the magnitude of material space, since another Vedic text declares, "Greater than space" (Ś.B. X. vi. 3.2)?

Vedāntin: That is no fault, for the sentence is meant to deny the smallness arising from the delimitation by the lotus (of the heart). It is not meant to affirm that much of magnitude only; for the sentence will lose its unity of purport if it should mean both (magnitude and negation of limitation). Again, a portion of space, fancied to be different and contained within the lotus, can never include heaven, earth, etc. within it. And the characteristics of being the Self and free from sin etc. that are mentioned in the text, "This is the Self free from sin, old age, death, sorrow, hunger, and thirst, and possessed of true desire and true resolve" (Ch. VIII. i. 5), are not possible for the material space. Although the word Self applies to the individual soul as well, yet this possibility for the soul is overruled by other reasons. The smallness created by the enveloping lotus cannot be denied in the case of the individual soul, for it is delimited by conditioning factors and it is compared to the tip of a goading stick (Śv. V. 8).

Opponent: All-pervasiveness can be asserted as having been intended to be spoken of for the individual soul since the real intention is to speak of it later on as non-different from Brahman.

Vedāntin: Then it is reasonable to assert all-pervasiveness etc. as having been directly intended to be spoken of for that very Brahman in identity with which the all-pervasiveness etc. are sought to be declared about the individual soul.

It was also argued that, since in the term "the city of Brahman", the city is suggestively determined by the individual soul, this soul should be accepted as the master of the city, who, just like a king, inhabits a part of that city. To this we say that this body is spoken of as the city of Brahman just because it belongs to the supreme Brahman Itself, that being the primary meaning of the term Brahman. Brahman has a relation even with this city, it being the place for Its realization as is mentioned in such Upaniṣadic passages as, "From this total mass of creatures (that Hiraṇyagarbha is) he (the aspirant) sees the supreme Puruṣa that has entered into every body and is higher than the higher (Hiraṇyagarbha)" (Pr. V. 5), "He that is this Puruṣa exists within the hearts in all the bodies" (Bṛ. II. v. 18). Or the idea may be that it is in the city of the individual soul itself that Brahman is perceived directly, just as Viṣṇu is on a *śālagrāma* (symbol). Again the text says, "Just as the results of work get exhausted here, so also the results of good works get exhausted in the other world" (Ch. VIII. i. 6), which expresses the finitude of the results of work; and then it is said, "Again those who depart after knowing here the Self and these true desires (existing in It) get freedom of movement in all the worlds" (ibid.), which reveals the infinite result accruing from the knowledge of the small Space under discussion. Thereby the text suggests that the small Space is Brahman.

It was also stated that the small Space is not heard of in the passage as an object to be sought for or to be known, it having been presented as a receptacle of that (supreme Self) which is inside. In answer to this we say: If Space be not presented as an object to be sought for, then the revelation of the nature of Space in, "The Space that is within the heart is of the same magnitude as the space outside" (Ch. VIII. i. 3), becomes inappropriate.

Opponent: Is not even this mentioned by way of revealing the existence of something inside? For the objection is first raised thus: "Should anyone ask him, 'The small palace that there is of the shape of a small lotus within this city of Brahman and the small space that there is within that lotus, what can it be that exists there and that has to be sought for and known?' " (Ch. VIII. i. 2). And then in the course of meeting the objection, the illustration of space is first resorted to and then it is shown that heaven, earth, etc. exist within it.

Vedāntin: This is not so; for if that had been the case, the purport would have been that the heaven, earth, etc., which exist within, are to be sought for and known. But the complementary portion of the passage does not conform to this interpretation. For there the Space, that is the receptacle, serving as the repository of heaven, earth, etc., is alluded to in, "Within this are included all desirable things. This is the Self free from sin" etc. (Ch. VIII. i. 5); and then in the passage, "Those who depart without realizing here the Self and these true desires" etc. (Ch. VIII. i. 6), the concluding portion of the text shows, by using *ca* in the sense of "and", that the things to be known are the Self, that is the repository of the desires, and the desirable things that are held therein (in the Self). Accordingly, it is understood that even in the beginning of the text, the small Space, seated in the lotus of the heart, is spoken of as the entity to be known together with the earth etc., as well as the true desires included within It. And in accordance with the reasons adduced, this must be the supreme Lord.

गतिशब्दाभ्यां तथा हि दृष्टं लिंगं च ॥१५॥

गति–शब्दाभ्याम् From the facts of going and the use of the word; **तथा हि** likewise **दृष्टम्** (it is) seen; **लिंगम्** indicating mark **च** as well (is present).

15. From the facts of going and the use of the word (Brahmaloka), (it follows that the small Space is Brahman); likewise it is seen in other Upaniṣads, and an indicatory mark is also present.

It has been said that the small Space is the supreme Lord, on account of the subsequent reasons. Those very subsequent reasons are being elaborated now. The small Space is the supreme Lord for this further reason that in the text, complementary to the passage relating to the small Space, occurs this sentence, "These creatures, though going everyday to this Brahmaloka (the world that is Brahman), do not know It" (Ch. VIII. iii. 2), where the act of going and the term used furnish a proof of the supreme Lord alone. In that sentence, the small Space under consideration is referred to by the phrase Brahmaloka, and then it is related that the individual souls, mentioned by the term creatures, approach towards It; thereby it is shown that the small Space is Brahman. Similarly in other Upaniṣadic texts, we come across the approach of creatures towards Brahman, as for instance in, "O amiable one, then (during sleep), the individual becomes merged in Existence (Brahman)" (Ch. VI. viii. 1). In common parlance also, it is said with regard to a man in deep sleep, "He has become Brahman, he has gone to the state of Brahman". Similarly the term Brahmaloka, used there with reference to the small Space under consideration, rules out the assumptions about the individual soul and the material space, and makes us understand the term small Space in the sense of Brahman.

Opponent : May not the term Brahmaloka mean the world of Brahmā (Prajāpati)?

Vedāntin : It may, if the compound Brahmaloka is explained as having been formed with an implied sixth case-ending (meaning the world of Brahman); but if it is explained in the sense of apposition, viz "the world that is Brahman", then it will lead us to the supreme Brahman alone. And this very fact of repairing to Brahmaloka everyday is an indication that the (compound) word Brahmaloka is to be explained in the sense of apposition; for it cannot be imagined that the creatures go everyday to the world of Brahmā otherwise called Satya-loka.

धृतेश्च महिम्नोऽस्यास्मिन्नुपलब्धेः ॥१६॥

च And धृतेः owing to holding in place; अस्य महिम्नः the glory उपलब्धेः : being noticed अस्मिन् as pertaining to this One.

16. And owing to the fact of holding (the worlds) in place, (the small Space must be God); for this glory is noticed (in other texts) as pertaining to Him.

Also from the fact of holding (the worlds) in place, it follows that the small Space is the supreme Lord.

How?

The start is made with, "within this is a small Space" (Ch. VIII. i. 1); and then after presenting the analogy of (material) space, everything is said to be included in that (small) Space. With regard to this very entity, again, the word Self is used and It is taught to be endowed with such characteristics as freedom from sin and so on. And lastly that self-same Space, which still continues to be the subject-matter of the Upaniṣadic topic, is mentioned in, "Then, again, that which is the Self is a dam, a reservoir (an impounder) to prevent the worlds from getting mixed up" (Ch. VIII. iv. 1). In that passage, the word *Vidhṛti* means an impounder (which holds in position), it being placed in apposition with the word Self (which is in the nominative case); for the suffix *ktic* is used, according to grammar, in the nominative sense. As a dam is an impounder of an expanse of water, so that the valuable cultivable fields may not lose their demarcations, so this Self is a dam, a reservoir, to prevent these worlds, divided according to the different planes, viz the bodily plane etc., and the castes, colours, etc., from getting intermixed.[13] Thus it is shown that this small Space under consideration has the glory of holding (the worlds) in position. And this glory is known from another text to pertain to the supreme Lord alone: "Under the mighty rule of this Immutable, O Gārgī, the sun and moon are held in their positions" etc. (Bṛ. III. viii. 9). Similarly in other passages, that definitely speak of the supreme Lord, it is heard, "It is the Lord of all, It is the ruler of all beings, It is the dam that serves as the boundary to keep the different worlds apart" (Bṛ. IV. iv. 22). Accordingly, on account of this fact of holding in place, this small Space must be the supreme Lord.

प्रसिद्धेश्च ॥१७॥

17. And because of familiar use.

For this additional reason, it is the supreme Lord that is spoken of by the text, "Within this is a small Space" (Ch. VIII. i. 1): The word space is well known to denote the supreme Lord, as is evident from such uses as, "That which is known as Space is the manifester of name and form" (Ch. VIII. xiv),

[13] *Vidhṛti* in the Upaniṣad means an impounder or supporter. *Dhṛti* in the aphorism, however, means holding together or supporting, the suffix here being *ktin*, imparting a cognate sense in the feminine gender to the root. Dam (*setu*) implies the idea of not allowing intermixture, while *vidhṛti* implies keeping in position.

"All these beings surely originate from Space" (Ch. I. ix. 1). But the word space is never found in use in the sense of the individual soul. And although the material space is very often meant by that word, still it was pointed out by us that it cannot be accepted because of such reasons as the impossibility of the same thing becoming the illustration and the thing illustrated.

इतरपरामर्शात् स इति चेन्नासम्भवात् ॥१८॥

इतर–परामर्शात् Owing to the allusion to the other सः he (is meant), इति चेत् if such be the argument, न not so, असम्भवात् owing to impossibility.

18. If it be argued that the other one (viz the individual soul) should be the small Space, since it is alluded to (at the end), then not so, for that is impossible.

Opponent: If on the strength of the complementary portion, the small Space is understood to mean the supreme Lord, then the other, viz the individual soul also, is alluded to in the complementary portion in, "He said, 'Now then, that is the Self which is this serene one (*samprasāda*) that raises itself up from this body, and realizing itself as the supreme Light, attains its own real nature.[14] This is the Self" (Ch. VIII. iii. 4). Since the word *samprasāda* (complete serenity) is used in another Upaniṣadic passage in the sense of deep sleep, it can call to mind the soul in that state in the text under consideration, but not anything else. Similarly, it is possible for the individual soul alone, existing in the body, to rise up from the body. Just as air etc., existing in space, can emerge from space, similar is the case here. Moreover, though the word space is not familiarly used in the world in the sense of the supreme Lord, still in such texts as, "That which is called Space, is surely the manifester of name and form" (Ch. VIII. xiv), the word is accepted as standing

[14] The Vedāntic explanation of this text is: The man of knowledge completely detaches himself from the assemblage of body and senses and realizes the detached Self as Brahman, which is his true nature. Thereby he attains that supreme Light, his knowledge and attainment being the same.

for the supreme Lord because of its association with the characteristics of God. In a similar way, it can be used for the individual soul as well. Accordingly, from the fact that the other (namely individual soul) is alluded to (at the end of the text), it follows that it is the individual soul that is referred to in the passage, "The small Space that there is within it" (Ch. VIII. i. 1).

Vedāntin: This cannot be so.

Why?

"Because this is impossible", for the individual soul, identifying itself with such limiting adjuncts as the intellect, cannot be compared with space; nor can such qualities as freedom from sin and so on be possible for something identifying itself with the limitations of conditioning factors. This was elaborated under the first aphorism (I. iii. 14). But the subject is mooted again for removing additional doubts. Another aphorism also will be advanced later: "And the allusion is meant for a different purpose"[15] (I. iii. 20).

उत्तराच्चेदाविर्भूतस्वरूपस्तु ॥१९॥

(Space is the soul) उत्तरात् owing to subsequent reference, चेत् if this be the objection, आविर्भूत-स्वरूपः that is the revealed real nature, तु rather.

19. If it be argued that the small Space is the individual soul, because of the subsequent reference to it (in the same chapter), then we say: Rather it is spoken of there in its own revealed nature.

Opponent: The assumption about the individual soul, that had arisen from the allusion to some one other than Brahman, has been dismissed on the ground of impossibility. Here again, "on the strength of the subsequent references"—on the strength of the utterance of Prajāpati—that very assumption about the individual soul is being revived like the resuscitation of the dead by the sprinkling of nectar. In that very context (Ch. VIII) the

[15] viz to draw attention to Brahman to which the soul repairs in sleep.

assertion started with is that the Self possessed of the attributes of freedom from sin and so on, as stated in, "The Self that is free from sin" (Ch. VIII. vii. 1), is to be sought for and known; and then by saying, "This Puruṣa that is seen in the eye is the Self" (Ch. VIII. vii. 4), the witnessing individual soul, seated in the eye, is pointed out as the Self. Then after alluding to that very individual soul again and again, by saying, "I shall explain this very one to you over again" (Ch. VIII. ix. 3–8), the individual soul is explained under varying conditions (by Prajāpati to Indra) in the texts, "The one that moves about in dream, adored (by objects conjured up by past tendencies), is the Self" (Ch. VIII. x. 1), and "At the time when one sleeps in such a way that one gets all one's senses withdrawn and hence becomes wholly serene, and does not see dreams,[16] then that is the Self"[17] (Ch. VIII. xi. 1). For that individual soul are shown such attributes as freedom from sin and so on. in, "This one is immortal, fearless, this one is Brahman" (ibid.). Again, after the perception of some defect (by Indra) in the state of sleep, as stated (by him) in, "Alas, this (sleeping) man does not certainly know himself now (in sleep) as 'I am this', nor does he know those beings! (But he attains annihilation, as it were. I do not find anything desirable here)" (ibid.), (in reply) Prajāpati first says, "I shall explain this very one to you over again, and not anything other than this" (Ch. VIII. xi. 3); then he denounces all association with the body; and lastly he says, "This *samprasāda* (wholly serene one) raises itself up from this body and realizing the supreme light, attains its own real nature. It is the highest Puruṣa" (Ch. VIII. xii. 3), where Prajāpati shows that the individual soul itself, that has risen up from the body, is the highest Puruṣa. Therefore the attributes of the supreme Lord are possible in the individual being. Accordingly, the individual soul is spoken of in the text, "The small Space inside that".

Vedāntin: Should anybody argue like this, then one should

[16] Reduces the universe to mere nescience.

[17] *Prājña* (individual soul) in a causal body and witnessing it through its own consciousness. It is the witness by virtue of imparting existence and sentience to others; but it is not free, since ignorance still persists.

tell him: (Even there) "the individual soul is rather spoken of in its own revealed nature". The word "rather" is used for repudiating the opponent, the idea implied being that even on the strength of the subsequent text, the assumption of the individual soul is not possible here.

Why?

Because even there the individual soul is intended to be presented in its real revealed nature. "The individual soul in its own revealed nature" means the soul of which the true nature has become manifest, the term "individual soul" being retained even after enlightenment, in continuation of the earlier (conventional) uses in the text. The sense conveyed is this: The Witness, suggested through the word "eye", is first pointed out by the text, "He that is in the eye" (Ch. VIII. vii. 4). Then in the Brāhmaṇa, presenting the analogy of the water in a plate[18] (Ch. VIII. viii), this very one is freed from the conception of identity with the body. And this very one is repeatedly alluded to for the purpose of explanation with the utterance, "I shall explain this very one to you" (Ch. VIII. ix. 3). Then after presenting the states of dream and deep sleep, it is said, "realizing the supreme Light, attains its own real nature" (Ch. VIII. xii. 3), where this individual soul is explained in its true nature, which is Brahman, but not in its nature as an individual. The supreme Light that is mentioned in the Upaniṣad as the thing to be realized is the supreme Brahman. That Brahman has such characteristics as freedom from sin and so on; and that is the real nature of the individual being, as shown in such texts as, "That thou art" (Ch. VI. viii-xvi), but not so is the other nature (as that is) conjured up by limiting adjuncts. The individuality of the individual persists so long as, like the elimination of the false idea of a man superimposed on a stump of a tree, he does not eradicate ignorance expressing itself as the

[18] Prajāpati said to Indra and Virocana, "You ask me about whatever you do not understand regarding your Self after looking at yourself in a plate full of water." After this had been done, Indra argued, that a thing, casting a reflection, is itself subject to growth and decay, as was evident from the reflection itself presenting the changes in the body. Thus the body could not be the Self. Prajāpati confirmed this.

world of duality and does not know that Self as "I am Brahman" —the Self that has no change and is eternal and a witness by nature. But when the individual is roused from the assemblage of body, senses, mind, and intellect by the Upaniṣad which makes him understand, "You are not the assemblage of body, senses, and intellect, nor are you a transmigratory being. What are you then? That which is truth—the Self of the nature of pure Consciousness—that thou art", then he realizes the Self that has no change and is eternal and a witness by nature, and then that very individual rises above its identity with the body and the rest to become the Self Itself—unchanging, eternal, and a witness by nature. This is declared in such Upaniṣadic texts as, "Anyone who knows that supreme Brahman becomes Brahman indeed" (Mu. III. ii. 9). And that is the soul's supremely real nature by virtue of which it attains its essential stature after rising above the body.

Opponent: How, again, can the attainment of its true nature by itself be possible for that entity which is unchanging and eternal? In the cases of gold and other things, whose distinct characteristics remain unmanifest owing to coverings over their real nature arising from contact with foreign matters, there may be such a thing as the attainment of their own nature by becoming purified by addition of salts. Similarly in the case of the stars whose light becomes dimmed in the daytime, there may be an attainment of their real nature at night when the dimming factor is removed. But in the case of the eternal Light that is Consciousness Itself, there can be no overpowering by anything, since just like space, It can have no contact with anything, and since this contradicts common experience. The individual soul's nature comprises seeing, hearing, thinking, and knowing. And that is ever in evidence as a patent fact even for the soul that has not risen up from the body. For all beings live and behave in this world by seeing, hearing, thinking, and knowing; otherwise life comes to a standstill. If that nature be attainable only by the soul that has risen above the body, then the behaviour noticed earlier stands contradicted. Hence what does this rising up from the body mean, and in what does the attainment of the real nature consist?

Vedāntin: In reply to this we say: Before the dawn of discriminating knowledge, the individual soul's nature of Consciousness, expressing through seeing etc., remains mixed up as it were, with the body, senses, mind, intellect, sense-objects, and sorrow and happiness. Just as before the perception of distinction, the transparent whiteness, constituting the real nature of a crystal, remains indistinguishable, as it were, from red, blue, and other conditioning factors; but after the perception of distinction through the valid means of knowledge, the crystal in its latter state is said to attain its true nature of whiteness and transparence, though it was exactly so even earlier; similarly in the case of the individual soul, remaining indistinguishably mixed up with such limiting adjuncts as the body etc., there springs up a discriminatory knowledge from the Upaniṣads constituting his rising from the body (consciousness); and the result of the discriminatory knowledge is the attainment of the real nature, its realization of its nature as the absolute Self. Thus unembodiedness or embodiedness for the Self follows respecttively from the fact of discrimination or non-discrimination, as stated by the *mantra*, "Bodiless in the midst of bodies" (Ka. I. ii. 22), and by the Smṛti, "The supreme Self, O son of Kunti, neither acts, nor is affected though existing in the body" (Gītā, XIII. 31), which mention the absence of any such distinction as embodiedness or unembodiedness. Therefore the individual soul continuing in the state of its unmanifested nature, owing to the absence of discriminatory knowledge, is said to have its real nature manifested when discriminatory knowledge dawns. For manifestation or non-manifestation of any other kind is not possible for what is one's own nature, just because it is intrinsic with one. Thus the difference between the individual soul and the supreme Lord springs from ignorance alone, but not from the things themselves, for both are equally free from attachment etc. (as well as partless and so on) like space.

Opponent: How again is this to be known thus?

Vedāntin: Because Prajāpati first teaches, "The Being that is seen in the eye" (Ch. VIII. vii. 4), and then says, "This is immortal and fearless. This is Brahman" (ibid.). If the well-known seer in the eye, who is thought of as the Witness, were different from Brahman, characterized as immortal and fearless, then that seer would not have been put in apposition with the fearless and immortal Brahman. Nor is the reflection in the eye indicated here by the word eye, for that will lead to a prevarication on the part of Prajāpati. So also at the second stage, Prajāpati told Indra, "This one that moves about in dream receiving the adoration (of women and others) is the Self" (Ch. VIII. x. 1). Here also none other than the Witness, the Being in the eye, pointed out at the first stage, is indicated; for the introduction is made with the words, "I shall explain this very one to you over again" (Ch. VIII. ix. 3). Moreover, a man after waking up speaks thus: "I saw an elephant in a dream today; I do not see it now". What he repudiates here is what he saw, whereas he cognizes the identity of that very witness thus: "I myself who saw the dream now see the things of the waking state". Similarly at the third stage, Indra says, "This one does not certainly know himself now (in sleep) as 'I am so and so', nor does he know these beings" (Ch. VIII. xi. 2), where the absence of particularized cognition is shown in the state of sleep, but the Witness is not denied. As for the statement of Indra, "There it undergoes extinction, as it were" (Ch. VIII. xi. 1), that too is made with regard to the wiping out of particularized cognition, but not in the sense of the annihilation of the knower; for another Upaniṣad declares, "For the knower's function of knowing can never be lost, because it is immortal. (But there is not that second thing separate from it which it can know)" (Bṛ. IV. iii. 30). Similarly at the fourth stage, Prajāpati starts with, "I shall explain this very one to you over again, and nothing different from it" (Ch. VIII. xi. 3), and then he adds, "O Maghavan (i.e. Indra), this body is surely mortal" etc. (VIII. xii. 1), by which elaborate statement is denied any relationship with such conditioning factors as the body. And then by saying, "It attains its own nature" (VIII. xii. 2), Prajāpati reveals the individual being, called *samprasāda* (one wholly serene in sleep) in its identity with Brahman, and thereby he does not show the individual soul to be anything other than the supreme Brahman which is immortal and fearless by nature.

Some, however, think that if the idea sought to be imparted

)e that of the supreme Self, then it is improper to drag in the ndividual soul in connection with the text, "I shall explain this very one to you over again" (Ch. VIII. ix. 3); so they consider the meaning of that sentence to be this: "I shall explain to you again, this very one, that is the Self, pointed out at the commencement of the topic (Ch. VIII. vii. 1), and that is possessed of the characteristic of freedom from sin and so on". If their interpretation be accepted, the Upaniṣadic word "this", which naturally relates to something proximate, becomes distantly related, and the phrase "over again" becomes meaningless, for what is stated at the earlier stage is no longer repeated at the later. Again, if Prajāpati starts wih the promise, "I shall explain this very one to you", and then explains a fresh entity (viz the soul in dream and sleep) at every stage, earlier than the fourth, then he will be open to the charge of prevarication. Therefore (the correct interpretation is this): After the unreal aspect of the individual being, conjured up by ignorance etc., tainted by many such defects as agentship, experiencership, love, hatred, etc., and subject to many evils, has been eliminated, the opposite aspect, viz the reality that is the supreme Lord, possessed of the characteristics of freedom from sin and so on, becomes revealed, just as the rope etc. are revealed after eliminating the snake etc. (superimposed on them through error).

There are other doctrinaires, as also some of our Vedāntins, who think that the creature aspect is real. This *Śārīraka* text (i.e. this book, discussing the embodied soul) is begun as a protest against all of them who are opposed to the complete realization of the oneness of the Self. The theme of this *Śārīraka* text is this: The supreme Lord is but one—unchanging, eternal, absolute Consciousness; but like the magician He appears diversely through Māyā, otherwise known as *Avidyā* (ignorance).[19] Apart from this there is no other Consciousness as such.

[19] *Ratnaprabhā* makes no distinction between Māyā and *Avidyā*, though it is admitted that the juxtaposition of the two terms implies a difference between the two powers of Māyā—of covering and disturbing—which fact may give rise to different terminology. But others would maintain that Māyā refers to cosmic nescience and *Avidyā* to individual ignorance.

As for the assumption of the individual soul in a text relating to the supreme Lord, and its subsequent repudiation by the aphorist under the aphorism, "Should not the other one be the small Space, since that is alluded to? No, for that is impossible" (I. iii. 18), etc., his intention there is this. When he affirms the difference between the supreme Self and the individual soul his idea is this: "Just as some surface and dirt are fancied on the sky, so the idea of the individual soul, opposed though it is to the supreme Self, is superimposed on the supreme Self which is by nature eternally pure, intelligent, free, everlasting, unchanging, one, and unattached; I shall remove that superimposition later on, and demolish all theories of duality with the help of texts that have the support of logic, and then establish the unity of the Self". But he will not establish the difference of the individual soul from the supreme Self, though he simply restates the popular notion of the difference of the individual that is fancied through ignorance; and he will show that when such a procedure is adopted, the injunctions about rites and duties, based on this reiteration of instinctive agentship and experiencership, do not become contradicted. But under the aphorism, "But the instruction follows from the point of view of the vision agreeing with the scriptures, as in the case of Vāmadeva" (I. i. 30) etc., he shows that the conclusion to be arrived at about the purport of the scriptures is only the unity of the Self. It was also shown by us how the conflict with the injunctions about the rites and duties is to be resolved by a reference to the distinction between the enlightened and unenlightened men.[20]

अन्यार्थश्च परामर्शः ॥२०॥

च And अन्य-अर्थः for a different purpose परामर्शः (is the) reference.

20. *Moreover, the reference (to the individual soul in the complementary passage) is meant for a different purpose.*

Opponent: It was pointed out earlier that in the passage,

[20] Rites etc. are meant for the unenlightened, still groping in ignorance.

'Now then that which is this *samprasāda* (wholly serene one)" etc. (Ch. VIII. iii. 4), occurring in the complementary passage of the topic of the small Space, the individual soul is referred to. That reference will become meaningless if the small Space is explained to be the supreme Lord, for then there will be no meditation on the individual soul, nor will this be an instruction about some distinct attribute of the small Space under discussion (which is different from the individual).

Vedāntin: Hence follows this answer: This reference to the individual soul has a different purport; it is not meant merely to determine the nature of the individual.

What does it determine then?

It determines merely the nature of the supreme Lord.

How?

The individual being, referred to by the term *samprasāda*, plays the role of the supervising director of this cage, made up of the body and senses, during all the wakeful dealings; and then moving in the nerves, it experiences the dreams created by the impressions of that wakeful state. Then becoming tired and desirous of having some refuge, it rises above (i.e. gets detached from) its identity with both kinds of bodies (gross and subtle), approaches in the sleep state the supreme Light, that is the supreme Brahman referred to by the term Space, and getting rid of the particularized cognition attains its true nature. The supreme Light which it has to approach as also its own nature in which it becomes established, is the Self possessed of the attributes of freedom from sin and so on; and this Self is to be meditated on. Thus this reference to the individual soul for that purpose becomes logical even for those who stand by the supreme Lord.[21]

अल्पश्रुतेरिति चेत्तदुक्तम् ॥२१॥

अल्पश्रुतेः Owing to the mention of smallness in the Upaniṣad इति चेत् if such be the objection, तत् उक्तम् that has been already answered.

[21] Even if Prajāpati refers to the individual for proving its Brahmanhood, there is no contradiction. Since the individual as such is not dealt

21. If it be argued that from the Upaniṣadic mention of smallness, (the small space must be the individual being), then this has been repudiated earlier.

And the objection was raised that the smallness of Space that is heard of in the passage, "The small Space that is within it" (Ch. VIII. i. 1), cannot properly fit in with the supreme Lord, whereas it quite befits the individual soul that is comparable to the tip of a goading stick (Śv. V. 8). A refutation of that is called for. This objection was disposed of under the aphorism, "If it be objected that the supreme Self is not taught here because of the smallness of the abode and because of its being referred to as such (by the Upaniṣad), then we say, no, for this is done for the sake of contemplation as is seen in the case of space" (I. ii. 7), where it was shown that a limitation for the supreme Lord is possible from a relative standpoint (for the sake of meditation). The aphorist here suggests that the refutation made there is to be applied here as well.

Moreover, this limitation is repudiated by the Upaniṣad itself by resorting to a comparison with the famliar space in the passage, "The Space within this heart has the same magnitude as this (material) space" (Ch. VIII. i. 3).

Topic 6: Acting in Accordance

अनुकृतेस्तस्य च ॥२२॥

अनुकृतेः Because of the fact of acting in accordance च तस्य and the word "His".

22. Because of the fact of acting (i.e. shining) in accordance, and because of the use of the word "His", (the Light mentioned in the Muṇḍaka Upaniṣad must be Brahman).

Doubt: The Upaniṣad reads thus: "There the sun does not shine, nor the moon or the stars; nor do these flashes of lightning shine there. How can this fire do so? Everything shines in

with by Prajāpati, one cannot conclude that the individual forms the subject-matter of discussion here.

accordance with His shining; by His light all this shines diversely" (Mu. II. ii. 10; Ka. II. ii. 15). Now the doubt arises with regard to this text as to whether the entity in whose wake all these shine and through whose light all this shines diversely, is some natural lustrous matter or the conscious Self.

Opponent: When in such a predicament, the conclusion is that it is some lustrous matter.

Why?

Because what is denied is the shining of lustrous entities like the sun etc., it being well known that the luminaries—moon, stars, etc.—do not shine in the daytime when the bright sun keeps shining. Similarly it can be understood that the luminous substance in whose presence all these moon, stars, and so on cease to shine together with the sun, must be by nature a luminary. And "shining in accordance with another" also fits in with the assumption of a natural luminary; for action in imitation is seen in the case of things of the same nature, as for instance, in the act of following someone going ahead. Therefore it must be some natural light.

Vedantin: Under such circumstances we say: It must be the conscious (self-luminous) Self.

Why?

Because of "acting in accordance", which phrase means imitation. This shining in imitation, as implied in, "He shining, all this shines", fits in exactly if the conscious Self is accepted; for the conscious Self is mentioned in the Upaniṣad as "luminous by nature and having true resolve" (Ch. III. xiv. 2). For it is not a matter of experience that the sun and other things shine in accordance with some other shining substance. The luminaries like the sun etc. are similar in nature, so that they do not have to depend on some other luminary, in accordance with which they have to shine. For a lamp does not shine in imitation of another lamp. As for the assertion that acting in imitation is seen in the case of things of the same nature, there is no such hard and fast rule; for action in imitation is seen in the case of dissimilar things as well. For instance, a red-hot ball of iron simulates fire and burns things in accordance with the fire's doing so. Or take another illustration: The particles of earth blow about as the wind does so. By saying, "Because of the fact of acting in accordance", the aphorist suggests "shining in accordance with". And by the words "and" "His", the aphorist refers to the fourth line of this verse, "by His light all this shines diversely", where also it is stated that the shining of the sun etc. is caused by the Lord, and thereby he points to the conscious Self. Besides, they (the followers of the Bṛhadāraṇyaka Upaniṣad) read thus of the conscious Self: "Upon that immortal Light of lights the gods meditate (as longevity)" (IV. iv. 16). It is against experience and a contradiction in terms to say that the luminaries like the sun etc. shine variously with the help of another light, for one light dims out the other. Or it may be that it is not merely the diverse shining of the sun etc., enumerated in the text, that is caused by Him.

What else is illuminated by Him?

From the text "all this" (Mu. II. ii. 10), used without any reservation, it follows that the manifestation, noticed in the cases of all these names, forms, actions, and results, is caused by the existence of the light of Brahman, just as the revelation of all kinds of colour is caused by the existence of the light of the sun etc. And by the use of the word "there" in the verse, "There the sun does not shine" etc. (ibid.), it is shown that the subject-matter already under consideration is to be accepted. The subject-matter that is being dealt with in the verses, "On which are strung heaven and the earth and interspace" (Mu. II. ii. 5) etc. is Brahman. Subsequently also, it is said, "In the supremely bright sheath[22] is Brahman, free from taints and without parts. It is pure,[23] and It is the Light of lights. It is that which the knowers of Brahman realize" (Mu. II. ii. 9). To show how Brahman is the Light of lights occurs the verse, "There the sun does not shine" etc. (Mu. II. ii. 10).

It was also argued by the opponent: Just as it can be held that no other light can shine in the presence of the sun, so also the denial of illumination by the luminaries like the sun etc. is

[22] The blissful sheath which is higher and brighter than the other sheaths—bodily, vital, mental, and intellectual.

[23] Taintless—free from adventitious defects; pure—free from natural defects.

possible if there be some other entity which is itself a luminous principle. As to that, it was shown by us even earlier that He (the Lord) alone and nothing else can be that luminous principle.[24] It is proper to deny that they can have any illumination even in respect of Brahman; for whatever is perceived is perceived through the light that is Brahman, but Brahman is not perceived through any other light, It being by nature self-effulgent.[25] On a contrary supposition alone, the sun and the rest could illumine It. Brahman reveals all others, but Brahman is not revealed by them, as is shown in the Upaniṣadic texts, "It is through the light of the Self that one sits, (goes out, works, and returns)" (Bṛ. IV. iii. 6), "It is imperceptible, for It is never perceived" (Bṛ. III. ix. 26), and so on.

अपि च स्मर्यते ॥२३॥

अपि च Moreover, स्मर्यते (it is) mentioned in the Smṛti.

23. Moreover, (this aspect) is mentioned in the Smṛti.

Moreover, in the Smṛti this aspect is mentioned as belonging to the conscious Self, as in the Gītā, "That the sun illumines not, nor the moon, nor fire; that is my supreme abode, going whither they return not" (XV. 6), and "The light which residing in the sun illumines the whole world, that which is in the moon and in the fire—know that light to be mine" (XV. 12).

[24] If there can be some light in whose presence the sun etc. can be dimmed, then the opponent can raise the question, "Is it that light or some other light that is mentioned here?" As a matter of fact, the Upaniṣad mentions only Brahman, so that the question of any other light cannot arise at all.

[25] The opponent is misled by thinking that the word *tatra* in the text —"*Na tatra sūryo bhāti*—there the sun shines not"—means, "If He be there", that is to say, "in His presence"; and so he argues, "If Brahman be there and nothing can shine in Brahman, then the sun etc. will never shine, for Brahman is eternally present". The Vedāntin says, "*Tatra* means, with regard to that as an object". So the idea is, "Brahman is not an object that can be illumined". The locative case in *tatra* is not *sati-saptamī*, but *viṣayasaptamī*.

Topic 7: The Measured One

शब्दादेव प्रमितः ॥२४॥

शब्दात् एव From the very term प्रमितः the measured One (is Brahman).

24. From the term itself it follows that the measured One is the supreme Self.

Doubt: It is mentioned in the Upaniṣad, "The Being (Puruṣa) of the size of a thumb, resides (in the heart) within the body" (Ka. II. i. 12), as also, "The Puruṣa, who is of the size of a thumb, is like a light without smoke. He is the ruler of the past and the future. He exists today and He will exist tomorrow. This is That" (Ka. II. i. 13). The doubt arises as to whether the Puruṣa of the dimensions of a thumb, that is mentioned there, is the individual soul identified with the intellect or the supreme Self.

Opponent: Now then, the conclusion to be drawn from the teaching about the dimensions is that the soul identified with the intellect is spoken of. For the Upaniṣad cannot present the supreme Self, which is infinite in length and expanse, as having the size of a thumb. But from some point of view, it is possible for the soul, which is identified with the intellect, to be of the size of a thumb since it has its limiting adjuncts. This is borne out by Smṛti also: "After that, Death dragged out forcibly from the body of Satyavān, the Puruṣa, of the size of a thumb, which was tied with a noose and was completely at his mercy" (Mbh. III. ccxcvii. 17). The supreme Lord cannot certainly be dragged out forcibly by Death. Thereby it is established in that text that the transmigratory soul has the size of a thumb. And it is that very soul that is spoken of here.

Vedāntin: This being the position, we say: The supreme Self alone can be the Puruṣa here of the size of a thumb.

How so?

From the text itself, viz "the ruler of the past and the future", inasmuch as none other than the supreme Lord can be the absolute ruler of the past and the future. And "This is That"

(Ka. II. i. 3) refers back to the subject-matter inquired into (by Naciketas). It means: "The Brahman that is asked about is this indeed." The entity enquired about in the text, "Tell (me) of that entity which you see as different from virtue, different from vice, different from cause and effect, and different from the past and future" (Ka. I. ii. 14), is Brahman. "From the term itself" (in the aphorism) means this: From the term ruler (*īśāna*) used in the Upaniṣad, it is gathered that the supreme Lord is meant. This is the idea.

How, again, is the all-pervasive supreme Self taught as possessed of size?

With regard to this we say:

हृद्यपेक्षया तु मनुष्याधिकारत्वात् ॥२५॥

तु But अपेक्षया from the point of view of हृदि existence within the heart मनुष्य-अधिकारत्वात् (the scripture) being concerned with human beings.

25. But the size is spoken of from the point of view of existence within the heart, the scripture being concerned with human beings.

Just as the space within a section of a bamboo can be spoken of as being a cubit in length, so from the point of view of existence within the heart, it can be asserted that though the supreme Self is all-pervasive, It has the size of a thumb. For the supreme Self, which as a matter of course transcends all limitations, cannot really have the size of a thumb. And it was pointed out that because of the words "ruler" etc., none other than the supreme Self can be acceptable here.

Opponent: Since the hearts have no definite size as they differ from creature to creature, the possession of a size like that of a thumb is not possible even from that point of view.

Vedāntin: Hence the answer is being given, "The scripture being concerned with human beings". Though the scripture speaks impersonally, still it postulates the competence of human beings only, because human beings are able, desirous (of results), and not debarred, and because there are texts about initiation with the sacred thread. This is elaborated under the topic of the characteristics of a competent person (Jai. Sū VI. i. 25-28). Moreover, the human body has a definitely proportionate size; and human hearts have ever the definite size of the (respective) thumbs. Accordingly, the scripture being concerned with men, it is but logical that the supreme Self should have the size of a thumb from the standpoint of Its residence within the human heart. It was argued, that from the teaching of the size and on the authority of the Smṛti, it is to be understood that the entity, that has the size of a thumb, is the transmigrating soul. That is being repudiated. It is taught here that the very soul that transmigrates and has the size of a thumb is Brahman, just as it is done in the text, "That is the Self. That thou art" (Ch. VI. viii. 7). For the texts of the Upaniṣads assume two forms: sometimes they determine the nature of the supreme Self and sometimes they teach the identity of the soul, conditioned by the intellect, with the supreme Self. That being the fact, what is taught here is the identity of the soul, conditioned by the intellect, with the supreme Self, and not that anything has the size of the thumb. This fact will be clarified later on (by the Upaniṣad) in the verse: "Puruṣa, the indwelling Self of the size of a thumb, is ever seated in the hearts of men. With a masterly control of the senses, one should separate Him from one's body like stalk from the Muñja grass. Him one should know as self-effulgent and changeless" (Ka. II. iii. 17).

Topic 8: Gods

तदुपर्यपि बादरायणस्सम्भवात् ॥२६॥

तदुपरि अपि (Beings) higher even than these बादरायणः (according to) Bādarāyaṇa सम्भवात् for that is possible.

26. Bādarāyaṇa thinks that beings higher than these (men) (are also qualified for knowledge), for that is possible.

It has been said that the Upaniṣadic text about the size of a thumb stands justified in relation to the heart, the scriptures being concerned with human beings. In connection with that it is said: It is true that the scriptures sanction the competence of human beings (for religious deeds); but with regard to the knowledge of Brahman there is no hard and fast rule that the sanction in this field (also) is for the human beings alone. The teacher Bādarāyaṇa thinks that the scriptures sanction the competence even of those divine beings and others who exist above these men.

Why?

Because that is possible; for they too have the desire etc. that confer the competence. Among those factors, even the gods can have the hankering for liberation, caused by a reflection on the impermanence etc. of divine glory, included as it is within the range of created things. Similarly they can have the ability, since it can be gathered from the Vedic verses, corroborative passages, anecdotes, mythology, and common belief, that they have bodies. Moreover, they are not debarred anywhere. Nor can it be said that they are barred out by the scriptures about the investiture with the sacred thread; for investiture is meant for the study of the Vedas, and to them the Vedas get revealed spontaneously (owing to their study in previous births). Besides, the scriptures speak of their following the vow of *brahmacharya*[26] for the mastery of knowledge as in, "Indra lived with Prajāpati for one hundred and one years under the vow of *brahmacarya*" (Ch. VIII. xi. 3), "Bhṛgu, well-known son of Varuṇa, went to his father Varuṇa with the prayer, 'Teach me Brahman, O venerable sir' " (Tai. III. i), and so on. Though the competence for rites is denied in, "There is no competence for the gods, since they have no gods (to sacrifice to)", "The *ṛṣis* have no competence for the performance of rites, since they have no *ṛṣis* (to perform to)" (Jai Sū. VI. i. 6-7), still that non-competence does not apply to knowledge (of Brahman). For when Indra and others are admitted to be qualified for knowledge, they do not have to do anything to another set of Indra and the rest, nor have Bhṛgu and other *ṛṣis* to do to another set of Bhṛgu and others belonging to the same lineage. So who can

[26] Living with a teacher for the study of the Vedas under a vow of continence.

deny the competence for knowledge even for the gods and others? And even in the case of the gods, the Upaniṣadic text about the soul of the size of a thumb is not improper when their own thumbs are kept in view.

विरोधः कर्मणीति चेन्नानेकप्रतिपत्तेर्दर्शनात् ॥२७॥

विरोधः A contradiction कर्मणि in the matter of rites, इति चेत् if such be the objection, न not so अनेक-प्रतिपत्तेः दर्शनात् since in the Vedas are seen the assumption of many bodies.

27. *If it be objected that this (corporeality of the gods) will give rise to a contradiction (in the matter of the gods being associated) in rites, then we reply: Not so, for in the Vedas are noticed the assumption of many bodies.*

Opponent: It may come to this: If by admitting bodies etc. for the gods, it is argued that they have competence for knowledge, then just because they are possessed of bodies, it has to be admitted that like the priests and others, Indra and others also take part in the rites by their physical proximity. In that case an incompatibility will crop up in the matter of rites; for Indra and others are not seen to form parts of the rites by their physical presence, nor is that possible, for Indra cannot be bodily present at many sacrifices at the same time.

Vedāntin: That incongruity does not arise.

Why?

Because of the assumption of many bodies—because even for a single god there is the possibility of assuming many bodies simultaneously.

How is this known?

"Because this is noticed in the Vedas". Starting with the (question of Śākalya), "How many gods are there?" (Bṛ. III. ix. 1), the number of gods is determined (by Yājñavalkya) to be "three hundred and three, and three thousand and three". And when the question is put, "Which are those?", the Upaniṣad states, (through Yājñavalkya), "These are but the manifestations of them; but there are only thirty-three gods" (Bṛ. III. ix. 2), by which statement the Upaniṣad shows that each god can have many forms simultaneously. Similarly the thirty-three are shown to be included in six; and so it goes on till to the question, "Which is the one God?" the answer is given, "The Vital Force (Hiraṇyagarbha)" (Bṛ. III. ix. 9). By showing here the identity of all the gods with Hiraṇyagarbha, the Upaniṣad reveals that Hiraṇyagarbha Himself has multiple forms simultaneously. Similar is the Smṛti text, "O best of the line of Bharata, the Yogin, after attaining the mystic power (of Yoga), should create many bodies for himself, and should move over the earth through them all. He should acquire (desirable) objects through some of them, and through some he should perform hard austerities. And again, he should withdraw them all like the (setting) sun withdrawing its rays". This and other Smṛtis of a similar purport show how even the Yogins, who succeed in acquiring the mystic powers of becoming subtle etc. (at will), can have association with many bodies at the same time. Therefore it goes without saying that the gods, dowered with perfection from birth, will have these multiple bodies. And since it is possible to assume many bodies, each god can divide himself into multifarious bodies to be associated simultaneously with many sacrifices. And yet they cannot be seen by others because of their power of remaining invisible. Thus it all stands justified.

Or the second part of the aphorism may be explained otherwise (to mean, "because various ways of taking part in a sacrifice are in evidence"). Even for embodied beings it is seen that in the matter of injunction for becoming associated with rites etc., there are various ways of doing so. Sometimes no single embodied being is associated simultaneously with many rites; for instance, when feasts are offered by many, no single Brāhmaṇa is fed simultaneously. But sometimes even a single embodied being becomes associated with many acts, as when a single Brāhmaṇa is greeted by many saluting him at the same time. Similarly, here also, since sacrifices consist in parting with one's things in honour of somebody, many can offer their respective things in the name of a single embodied god. Thus nothing stands in the way of the gods, so far as rites are concerned, even though they have bodies.

शब्द इति चेन्नातः प्रभवात्प्रत्यक्षानुमानाभ्याम् ॥२८॥

शब्दे In relation to the Vedic words (the contradiction will arise) इति चेत् if such be the objection, न not so, अतः प्रभवात् since from that it arises प्रत्यक्ष-अनुमानाभ्याम् as is proved by direct revelation and inference.

28. If it be objected that this contradicts the validity of Vedic words, then not so, for the universe arises from this, which fact is proved by direct revelation and inference.

Opponent: Granted even that even if bodies are assumed for gods, no contradiction will arise in the matter of their association with rites, still a contradiction will arise as regards the authority of the Vedic words.

How?

It is on the basis of the inborn relationship between words and their meanings from the very beginning that the validity of the Vedas has been established by saying, "Because of independence of other means of proof" (Jai Sū. I. i. 5). According to the present view, however, although a god, assumed to have a body, can enjoy the oblation at many sacrifices by virtue of his possession of mystic power, still owing to embodiedness, he will be subject to birth and death just like ourselves. And this will militate against the validity of the Vedic words, which is based on the perception of an eternal relation between eternally present words with their eternal meanings.

Vedāntin: This contradiction, too, does not exist.

Why?

"Since from this it arises"—because the universe, consisting of the gods and others, originates verily from the Vedic words.

Opponent: Under the aphorism, "That from which this universe has its birth etc." (I. i. 2), has it not been ascertained that the universe originates from Brahman? How can it be said here that it originated from words? Moreover, even if it be conceded that it arose from the Vedic words, how can this obviate the contradiction as regards the (eternality of) words, since such objects denoted by words as the Vasus, Rudras, Ādityas, Viśvedevas, Maruts, will be non-eternal, just because those objects had an origin? And if the gods be impermanent, who can avoid the non-eternality of Vedic words "Vasus" etc. which signify those gods? For it is a well-known fact in the world that it is only after a son is born to Devadatta that the boy is given some such name as Yajñadatta. Accordingly, this (embodiedness of the gods) is a real obstacle against the (validity of) words.

Vedāntin: No, since the relationship between such generic words and their meanings, as for instance cowhood and cows, is seen to be eternal (i.e. beginningless). Not that the distinguishing characteristics (i.e. genus) of the cows etc. are created afresh each time these cows etc. are born; for the individual forms of substances, qualities, and actions alone can have origin, but not so their distinguishing (general) characteristics (i.e. genus). And words are connected with the general characteristics and not with the individuals; for the individuals are infinite, and it is impossible to comprehend the relation of a word (with all of them). Thus, even though the individuals are born, the distinctive general characteristics (or features) remain constant, so that this creates no difficulty about the eternality of the words cow etc. Similarly it is to be understood that even though the birth and death of individual gods be admitted, still their distinctive general characteristics (or features) have no beginning. Accordingly, this does not militate in any way against (the eternality of) the words Vasus and so on. As for the distinctive general characteristics of a particular deity, they are to be gathered from what is known from the embodiedness etc. mentioned in the *mantra* and corroborative portions of the Vedas. And like the words commander etc. the words Indra etc. are used in relation to certain ranks etc. Accordingly, those who occupy the respective positions are called by the various names—Indra and so on. Thus there is nothing contradictory. And this origination from words is not spoken of in the sense of birth from a material cause, as it is done in the case of origination from Brahman.

In what sense then?

When there is first a word without a beginning and bearing a meaning with which it has an eternal connection, then only is there a possibility of an individual cropping up which can be fit to be referred to by that word. In that sense it is said to originate from a word.

How, again, is it known that the universe originates from words?

"From direct revelation and inference." By "direct revelation" is meant the Vedas, since they do not depend on any other means of knowledge for their validity. By "inference" is meant the Smṛti, for it depends on other sources for its validity. Both of them show that creation was preceded by words, as is declared in the Veda: "Brahmā created the gods by (thinking of) the word *ete*; He created men and others by the word *asṛgram;* by the word *indavaḥ* the manes; by the word *tiraḥpavitram* the planets; by the word *āśavaḥ* the hymns; by the word *viśvāni* the *śastras;* and by the word *abhisaubhagāḥ* the other beings"[27] (Ṛ. V. IX. 62). Similarly elsewhere in "He (Prajāpati) brought about the union of speech (the Vedas) with the mind"[28] (Bṛ. I. ii. 4), and other places where the Vedas speak of creation as preceded by words. The Smṛti also speaks similarly: "In the beginning was projected by Prajāpati, the eternal speech in the form of the Vedas which have no beginning and end, which are divine (i.e. run through the traditional line alone), and from which proceed all activities." And even this projection of speech is to be understood in the sense of starting of a cycle of transmission through a line of teachers and students; for no other kind of projection is possible for the Vedas which are without any beginning and end. Similar is the text: "In the beginning, He, the great Lord, created from the words of the Vedas alone, the names and forms of the creatures and promoted

[27] As Prajāpati recollects the words in the beginning of creation, the meanings of the words call up to His mind the things thus: *ete* —these, a pronoun, indirectly reminds Him of the gods; *asṛk* means blood, so *asṛgram* stands for men, since they delight in the body in which blood predominates; *indu*—moon, points to the manes living in the lunar world; *pavitra—Soma, tiraḥpavitra—the grahas* (planets) that hide this *Soma* within themselves; *Ṛk* hymns set to music are *āśavaḥ;* the *śastras* used after the hymns are *viśva;* those who are blessed everywhere are recollected through *saubhaga.*

[28] He reflected on creation as revealed in the Vedas.

religious activities" (Manu. I. 21); "In the beginning, He created from the Vedic words themselves, the names of all beings, and all actions separately, as also the separate modes of life". Besides, it is a matter of experience to us all that when one has to accomplish some desired thing, one remembers first the word denoting it and then accomplishes it. Similarly it is understood that in the case of Prajāpati also, when He was intent on creation, the Vedic words flashed in His mind before creation and then He created the things according to these. In confirmation of this occur the Vedic texts, such as, "He uttered the syllable *bhūḥ*, He created the earth" (Tai. Br. II. ii. 4.2), which show the creation of the worlds—the earth and the rest—from the words *bhūḥ* and so on, coming to His mind.

What particular nature of the words is meant when it is asserted that creation comes out of the words?

They (the grammarians) say, it is the *sphoṭa*.[29] If it be held that creation proceeds from the letters (constituting the words), then since the letters have a beginning and an end, the view that the gods spring from the eternal words will have no legs to stand on. And the letters have a beginning and an end, since at every fresh utterance they appear differently. That is why even when a person is not in sight, it can be clearly determined from the sound of the reading itself, e.g. "This is Devadatta's reading" or "This is Yajñadatta's reading". This apprehension of the difference in respect of the letters is not false inasmuch as no other apprehension emerges to contradict this. Nor is it reasonable to hold that the meaning is gathered from the letters; for the letters cannot convey the meaning individually, since this is not universally true.[30] Nor can there be a comprehension of a totality of letters, for the letters occur in sequence.[31] It may be argued that the last letter, in association with the

[29] The impression created in the mind on hearing a sound (e.g. cow) expressive of meaning and itself expressed by the letters constituting the sound (e.g. cow).

[30] For it is not a fact that the utterance of a single letter conveys the meaning; and if a single letter suffices, the others will be useless.

[31] Each letter, as it is uttered, lasts for one moment, and hence the letters cannot form a totality.

impressions of the letters uttered earlier in succession, will convey the meaning. But that cannot be, for just as it is seen in the case of smoke (that it can make the fire known when it is itself known), so a word can convey its meaning only when it is itself known in association with the impressions (as having a connection with its meaning like smoke with fire). But it is not possible to apprehend the successive letters in association with the impressions of earlier letters, since impressions are not perceived directly (by sense-organs). If it be argued that the last letter, in association with the impressions made known through the effect (viz the comprehension of meaning or memory) resulting from the impressions, will convey the meaning, that also cannot be.[32] For even memory, produced by the impressions, proceeds in a sequence.[33] Accordingly, a word is of the nature of a *sphoṭa*. The apprehension of the letters individually sows the seed in the mind in the form of impression, which attains full maturity on the apprehension of the last letter, and then becoming the object of a single apprehension, it flashes in the mind without further effort.[34] This singleness of apprehension, again, is not a form of memory (of a collection of letters), for the letters being many, they cannot form the content of a single perception. And this *sphoṭa* has no beginning, since its identity is recognizable at every utterance (of the word). The idea of difference springs from the difference of the letters. Therefore the universe of actions, agents, and results,

[32] This will be arguing in a circle, the impressions being known from the comprehension of meaning and the comprehension of meaning being dependent on the apprehension of impressions. The memory of the meaning of a word can occur after the knowledge of the word. So the knowledge of a word, defined as the knowledge of the last letter in association with the impressions of earlier letters, cannot produce the knowledge of the word.

[33] The impressions, inferred from the recollections occurring in sequence, will have a sequence, and will thus fail to form a single entity.

[34] Just as the secret of gems flashes in a mind trained through repeated observations. The *sphoṭa* emerges in the form of the apprehension, "This is a single word", without further cogitation in a mind that has been prepared thus.

standing for the meaning of word, emerges from the eternal word, conceived of as a *sphoṭa*, which indicates it.

Vedāntin: But the venerable Upavarṣa is of opinion that the letters themselves constitute the words. As for the objection raised earlier that the letters have a beginning and an end, the reply is that it is not so, for they are recognized as "Those are the same as these". If it be argued that the recognition is caused by similarity, as in the case of hair etc., the answer is that it cannot be so, since the recognition cannot be repudiated by any other means of knowledge. If it be said that the recognition arises from (the unity of) species, the answer is that it cannot be so, since the individual letters are recognized to be the same. The recognition would have been caused by the species if the letters were cognized as separate entities like the individual cows at the time of each fresh utterance. But this is not so, for it is the letters themselves that are cognized to be the same at each fresh utterance, the recognition taking the form, "The word cow is uttered twice", but not, "There are two words 'cow' ". It may be argued that it was pointed out earlier that owing to differences in pronunciation, letters also appear differently, as is obvious from a distinction that can be made between the readings of Devadatta and Yajñadatta from a mere hearing of the sound of reading. The answer will be this: Granted that there is a definite recognition of the identity (of the letters), the peculiarity about the (distinction of) letters that is perceived can be explained as arising not from their intrinsic difference (at every fresh utterance), but from the difference in the instruments of their expression. For letters are expressed by the association and dissociation of air, proceeding upward and striking against such parts of the mouth as the palate etc. Besides, to make recognition possible, species for the (individual) letters will have to be posited even by one who holds the view that individual letters differ (at different) utterances. With regard to these species, again, one will have to admit differences created by conditioning factors. That being so, it is better to say[35] in

[35] Better than to say that (1) each letter is infinite in number, (2) on those infinite letters the species inheres individually, (3) in them adventitious differences are created by pitches—high, low, medium, etc.

conformity with the law of parsimony (or brevity of imagination) that the ideas of difference arise with regard to the individual utterances of the letters owing to the presence of conditioning factors, and the recognition (of identity) arises from their intrinsic nature. This very fact of the recognition of identity is a bar against any idea of difference in relation to each utterance of any letter. When a letter, for instance "g", is the same, how can it possibly become divergent at that very same time to different people uttering it simultaneously as high-pitched, low-pitched, medium-pitched, or nasal, non-nasal, and so on?

Or the true position is this: This cognition of difference is created by the sound and not the letter itself; and hence there is no fault.

Opponent: What is this sound?

Vedāntin: This sound is that which reaches the ear of a distant hearer without apprising him of any distinction of letters, but invests the letters with such differences as high or low pitch etc. in his ears as he approaches nearer. The difference in loudness etc. is a creation of this sound and not of the letters as such; for the identity of each letter is recognized at every fresh utterance.[36] From this point of view, the highness etc. of pitch gets a basis; otherwise, from the fact that each letter, when uttered, seems to be different, though it is recognized as the same, one would have to fancy that the difference is created by the air coming in contact with or getting disconnected from the vocal apparatus. But since these conjunction and disjunction are not perceived by the ear, the distinction created by them will fail to be associated with the letters, and hence this cognition of pitches—high, low, etc.—will be baseless. Moreover, the view does not deserve consideration that though the letters are recognized to be the same, still they differ in accordance with the differences in pitch; for anything continuing to be the same does not differ simply because of the difference in something else, for instance a species is not considered to be different

[36] But the sound of the letters differs. Accordingly, letters and sound are different. Thus nobody thinks of the unuttered letters as intonated or of the music in a *viṇā* as letters.

owing to the difference in the individuals (of the species). Besides, inasmuch as the comprehension of meaning can follow from the letters, it is useless to assume a *sphoṭa.*

Opponent : I do not assume, but I directly perceive the *sphoṭa,* for it flashes suddenly in the intellect imbued with the impressions of letters occurring successively.

Vedāntin : No, for that comprehension also relates to letters. The single concept "cow", arising after the comprehension of letters individually, emerges on the basis of the letters as a whole and not any other thing (called *sphoṭa*).

How can this be known?

Even in this comprehension, the letters "c" etc. (of cow) are in evidence, but not the letters "d" etc. For if a *sphoṭa,* which is different from the letters "c" etc., had formed the content of that comprehension, then the *sphoṭa* would have ruled out "c" etc. just as it does "d" etc. But facts are otherwise. Accordingly, this idea of identity is based on the memory of letters alone.

Opponent : Did we not say that the letters being many, they cannot form the basis of a single concept?

Vedāntin : To that we say: Even many things can be the basis of a single concept as is seen in the cases of a line, a forest, an army, ten, hundred, thousand, etc. As for the idea that "cow" is a single word, that is only a secondary idea of unity applied to the letters "c o w" because of their being related to the same object "cow", as is the case with the ideas of forest, army, etc.

Here the *opponent* says: If the letters alone, as a group, form the basis of a single concept and become a word, then in such instances as *jāra* (paramour)—*rājā* (king), *kapi* (monkey)—*pika* (cuckoo), the words should not be comprehended distinctly, since the very same letters appear in different places in a different order.

Vedāntin : To this we say: Although all the letters in a word are cognized, still like the ants entering into the idea of a line in a definite order, the letters enter into the notion of a word in their definite sequence. That being the case, there is nothing illogical in understanding a particular word arising from a particular arrangement, even though the letters may be the same. At the time of apprehending the meaning of words from the use of them by older people, these letters, as uttered in a certain sequence, were understood (by a child) to be related to certain meanings; so at the time of his own dealings with them (by the child), the letters apprehended individually, appear in that very sequence in the intellect which groups them together, and thus they invariably convey those particular senses. In this way, those who hold by the letters have the law of parsimony in their favour, whereas those holding the theory of *sphoṭa* have to face the difficulties of rejecting an obvious thing and accepting something fanciful.[37] Besides that theory assumes too many things, inasmuch as these letters, apprehended in succession, reveal a *sphoṭa*, and then that *sphoṭa* reveals the meaning. Or even if it be the case that the letters are quite new at every fresh utterance, still to explain the recognition of identity, species of letters has to be admitted perforce. And thus the process of expression of meaning, that has been shown in the case of letters, has to be transferred to the species (by them).

Thus (since the letters are permanent and convey meanings, therefore) it involves no contradiction to say that the gods as individuals emerge from the eternal words.

अत एव च नित्यत्वम् ॥२९॥

च And अत एव from this very fact नित्यत्वम् (follows) eternality.

29. And from this very fact follows the eternality (of the Vedas).

The beginninglessness of the Vedas stands established (in the Pūrva-Mimāṁsā) from the fact that no independent author of the Vedas is remembered (i.e. known). That having been taken for granted, the admission of the origin of individual deities from the Vedic words, raised a doubt about the non-eternality of the words themselves. This was refuted by saying, "For the universe arises from this" (I. iii. 28). Now this fact of eternality of the Vedas, that stands unaffected, is being confirmed by

[37] The obvious fact that letters express an idea, and the fanciful fact that there is such a thing as *sphoṭa*.

saying, "And from this very fact follows eternality." "From this very fact"—from the fact that the universe of gods and others, having a definite form, emerges from the Vedic words—it is to be understood that the Vedic words also are eternal. So also the *mantra* text, "The sacrifices, having acquired the fitness to receive the Veda as a result of the earlier performance of good deeds, received it as it had already existed among the *ṛṣis*" (Ṛ. V. X. lxxi. 3), shows the acquisition of the Veda that had already existed. Veda-Vyāsa also writes in his Smṛti thus: "In days of yore, the great *ṛṣis* received through austerities, with the permission of the self-born One, the Veda, together with the anecdotes, that had remained withdrawn during dissolution".

समाननामरूपत्वाच्चावृत्तावप्यविरोधो दर्शनात् स्मृतेश्च ॥३०॥

च And समान-नाम-रूपत्वात् owing to the similarity of names and forms अपि even आवृत्तौ in the revolution of world cycles, अविरोधः there is no contradiction दर्शनात् as is known from the Vedas च and स्मृतेः from the Smṛti.

30. And there is no contradiction, since similar names and forms are repeated even in the revolution of the world cycles, as is known from the Vedas and the Smṛti.

Opponent: Now it may be granted that, if the individual gods originate continuously like individual animals and others, and they disappear in the same way, then there will be no discontinuity in the continuance of behaviour based on words, meanings of words, and pronouncers of words; and thus owing to a continuity of relationship, the defect of Vedic words becoming non-eternal can be avoided. But how can this difficulty be avoided in the face of the statements in the Vedas and the Smṛtis that the whole creation, consisting of the three worlds, loses its names and forms and gets dissolved without a trace, and it emerges again as a fresh entity?

Vedāntin: As to that this is the answer: (There is no contradiction with the beginninglessness of the Vedas), because of the similarity of names and forms. (If final dissolution and creation thereafter be believed in) even then the beginninglessness of creation has to be admitted. The teacher (Vyāsa) will establish this beginninglessness in the aphorism, "Moreover, this is logical and so it is met with" (II. i. 36). Just as it is the case that although we hear of merging and emerging in sleep and waking, still it involves no contradiction, because the behaviour in the succeeding waking state follows the pattern in the earlier one in the case of the beginningless worldly state, so also it is to be understood that the creation and dissolution in a subsequent cycle raise no difficulty. And merger and emergence of consciousness in sleep and waking states are heard of in the Upaniṣadic texts, "When a sleeping man sees no dream, then he becomes unified in this *Prāṇa* (i.e. Self) Itself. Then the organ of speech, together with all the names, merges in *Prāṇa*; the organ of sight, with all the forms, gets unified in *Prāṇa;* the organ of hearing, with all the sounds, gets united in *Prāṇa;* the mind, with all the thoughts, merges in *Prāṇa.* And when the soul wakes up, then just as sparks dart to all the quarters from a blazing fire, similarly from the Self all the organs proceed to their various seats; from the organs emerge the gods, and from the gods the sense-objects" (Kau. III. 3).

Opponent: It may be conceded that in sleep there is no contradiction, since the empirical behaviour of other individuals continues unbroken and since the man who wakes up from sleep can recollect his behaviour in the past. But since all behaviour is eradicated in final dissolution, and since the behavour in a previous cycle of creation cannot be called up to memory like the behaviour in a past life, the analogy is inapt.

Vedāntin: That defect does not arise; for although the final dissolution intervenes to obliterate all empirical behaviour, still by the grace of God, it is reasonably possible for divine beings like Hiraṇyagarbha to recollect the behaviour in an earlier cycle. From the fact that ordinary creatures are not seen to recollect their past lives, it does not follow that the fact must be the same in the case of divine beings as well. It is noticed that although as living creatures all are the same, counting from men to a clump of grass, still the obstruction to the manifestation of knowledge, glory, etc. increases successively all through the series at each stage; similarly when it is mentioned more than once in the Vedas and Smṛtis that knowledge, glory, etc. become increasingly more manifest at each successive stage counting from men themselves up to Hiraṇyagarbha, it cannot be brushed aside as non-existent. From this it logically follows, on the analogy of a man risen up from sleep, that the recollection of the behaviour in a past cycle is possible for beings like Hiraṇyagarbha, who had undertaken meditation and work in a superexcellent way in a past cycle, who have emerged at the beginning of the present cycle (as a result of past achievement), and who have been vouchsafed the grace of God. In support of this here is a Vedic text: "Hankering after liberation, I take refuge in that self-effulgent Being, revealing Himself in my intellect that is transformed in the likeness of that Being Himself, who created Hiraṇyagarbha in the beginning and transmitted the Vedas to Him" (Śv. VI. 18). And Śaunaka and others mention that the *ṛṣis*, Madhucchandas and others, were the seers of the *mantras* of the Ṛg-Veda. And in the same way (it is mentioned by) Bodhāyana and others, with regard to the (Kāṇḍas) parts of the other Vedas, that they also were seen by *ṛṣis*. Moreover, the Vedas also show that the rites are to be performed with *mantras* after knowing their seers. For instance, after starting with, "Anyone who conducts a sacrifice or teaches with a *mantra*, of which he does not know the seer, the metre, the deity, and the application, enters into motionless things or falls into hell", it is said, "Therefore one should know these in every *mantra*". Furthermore, virtuous deeds are enjoined for the acquisition of happiness by creatures, and vicious deeds are prohibited for the avoidance of sorrow. And likes and dislikes occur in respect of happiness and sorrow that are known directly or from the scriptures, but not in respect of others. Accordingly, it follows that when successive creations take place as the result of virtue and vice, they are brought into existence exactly like the previous creation. Bearing on this is a Smṛti text:[38] "Among them, the creatures that had adopted certain courses of action in a previous creation, adopt those

[38] *Viṣṇu-Purāṇa*, I. v. 59-61; Mbh. śā., 231.48-49.

very courses when created again and again, they being under the influence of those works, be they injurious or non-injurious, soft or cruel, associated with virtue or vice, and true or false. Accordingly, each has a liking for his respective work." When this universe gets dissolved, it dissolves by keeping its latent power intact, and the next creation emerges from that latent power. For otherwise it will all be a matter of chance (i.e. result occurring without cause). Now we cannot imagine diverse powers of different kinds.[39] That being the case, it is to be understood that just as the relation between the senses and the sense-objects is fixed, so also is fixed in this beginningless universe, the arrangement of the succession of masses of creatures like gods, men, and animals, and the arrangement of castes, stages of life, virtue and vice, and their results, which originate after intervening breaks. For like the impossibility of fancying objects for the sixth organ, it is not possible to fancy that the pattern of behaviour, as manifested, for instance, in the relation between the senses and the sense-objects, can be different in every fresh creation.[40] Therefore from the facts that the pattern of behaviour is the same in every cycle of creation and that the mighty divine beings can recollect the lives in the earlier cycles of creation, it follows that the particulars in each creation emerge with the same (characteristics of) names and forms. No contradiction with the validity of the Vedas arises from holding that the universe has the same kind of names and forms in its cycles (of final dissolution and fresh creation). The similarity of names and forms is shown by Vedic texts and Smṛtis: "The ordainer created the sun and moon, as also heaven, which is an abode of happiness, the earth, and interspace, just as before" (Ṛ. V. X. cxc. 3), which means that the supreme Lord created

[39] Nescience being the only power admissible.

[40] The mind is the sixth organ (Gītā, XV. 7). It has no distinct object of its own, for happiness etc. are cognized by the Witness. So "fancying objects for the sixth organ" means thinking of a nonentity. Or the meaning is that there is no sixth organ in addition to the eye etc., and so there can be no question of the existence of its objects. As for the other sense-organs and sense-objects, there is a fixity of relation; for instance colour cannot be perceived by the ear, in any cycle of creation.

the universe of sun, moon, etc. like what it was in the previous cycle. "Fire desired, 'I shall become a bestower of food to the gods.' In honour of the (gods of the stars in the) Kṛttikā constellation, he[41] performed in fire a sacrifice, in which was offered the cakes cooked in eight plates" (Tai. Br. III. i. 4.1), where the text shows that the sacrificer who offered the oblation in fire in the course of performing the sacrifice in honour of the stars, and the fire into which the offering was made, had the same name and form. Other texts of a similar purport are to be quoted here. There are Smṛti texts: "To the seers, born after the end of dissolution, the unborn One imparts those very names and those very visions of the Vedic texts as they had before. As the signs of various kinds of the different seasons are seen to revolve in order, in that very way all the things emerge at the beginning of a *yuga* (cycle), and whatever forms, peculiar to each, the beings had in the past, those exactly conform to these of the present beings—the gods being similar to the gods of the past in forms and names" (Mbh. Śā., 231.58, 210.17). Such other texts are also to be referred to.

मध्वादिष्वसम्भवादनधिकारं जैमिनिः ॥३१॥

असम्भवात् Owing to impossibility (of competence) मधु-आदिषु in the *Madhu-vidyā* etc., जैमिनिः Jaimini (asserts) अनधिकारम् incompetence.

31. Jaimini asserts (that the gods and others have) no competence (for knowledge of Brahman), owing to the impossibility of their competence for Madhu-vidyā etc.

The assertion made here that even the gods have competence for the knowledge of Brahman is being challenged. The teacher Jaimini holds that the gods are disqualified.

Why?

Because of the impossibility of their being qualified for the *Madhu-vidyā* (meditation on honey, i.e. the successive quin-

[41] The sacrificer performing the sacrifice with the idea, "I shall become fire, the eater of food", becomes the god Fire in the next cycle, and hence he is called Fire even when he is a sacrificer.

tessences of things), etc. If their competence for the knowledge of Brahman be admissible, it should be so with regard to *Madhu-Vidyā* etc. as well, for they too are equally forms of *vidyā* (knowledge). But this is not possible.

How?

According to the text, "This sun is *madhu* (honey) to the gods" (Ch. III. i. 1), human beings should meditate on the sun by superimposing the idea of honey on it. If the gods and others be accepted as (competent) adorers, then which other sun will the (god) Sun adore? Then again, after introducing the five kinds of nectar, red and the rest, that exist in the sun, it is said that the five groups of gods—Vasus, Rudras, Ādityas, Maruts, and Sādhyas—subsist on these nectars seriatim. After this instruction, it is shown in the text starting with, "He who meditates on this nectar thus, becomes one with the Vasus themselves and gets satisfied by seeing this nectar, with Fire in his leading" (Ch. III. vi. 3), that those who know the honey on which the Vasus and others subsist attain the glory belonging to Vasus and others. But whom else can the Vasus and others know as the enjoyers of the nectar? And what other glory, belonging to the Vasus and others, will they desire to get? So also in other places, as for instance in, "Fire is a quarter, Air is a quarter, the Sun is a quarter, the Directions are a quarter" (Ch. III. xviii. 2), "Air is indeed the place of merger" (Ch. IV. iii. 1), "The sun is Brahman—this is the instruction" (Ch. III. xix. 1), where meditations on the deities themselves are enjoined, and where those very gods cannot be qualified for undertaking those very meditations. So also in such texts as, "These two (ears) are Gotama and Bharadvāja: This one is Gotama, and this one Bharadvāja" (Bṛ. II. ii. 4), where meditations about the seers are enjoined, and where those very seers cannot be qualified for those very meditations.

For what more reason are the gods disqualified?

ज्योतिषि भावाच्च ॥३२॥

च And भावात् owing to the occurrence (of words) ज्योतिषि in respect of a sphere of light.

32. Because of the occurrence of the words in respect of a sphere of light.

To this sphere of light exisiting in the sky, that illumines the world by rotating throughout day and night, are applied such words as the sun etc. which are indicative of gods; because in this sense of a mere sphere they are familiar in the world and are recognized as such in the complementary portion of the text.[42] Not that we can understand any connection of this sphere of light with any human form, comprising the heart etc., or with sentience, desire etc.; for it is known to be insentient like the earth etc. Hereby are explained away fire and the rest (which are equally insentient).

Objection: No such fault arises, since the gods are known to have forms etc. from the *mantras*, corroborative statements, anecdotes, mythologies, and common experience.

Jaimini: No, for there is no such independent means of valid knowledge called common experience. Any object that is known through the well-known means of knowledge, such as perception, may be said to be known from common experience when these means are not applied with careful scrutiny. But with regard to the matter under discussion, none of the valid means of proof—perception and the rest—can be cited. As for anecdote and mythology, they too originate from human beings, and hence must be dependent on some other valid means for their authenticity. Vedic corroborative statements are also subservient to some injunctions, and hence they cannot prove the embodiedness etc. of the gods on the strength of any independent meaning. The *mantras* also, that are applied to rites according to the (six) tests of *śruti* etc. (direct assertion, indicatory mark, syntactical connection, context, position, designation), denote things intrinsically connected with ritual application; and accordingly it is said that they are not the valid means of knowledge of any object. Hence the gods have no competence.

[42] For instance, "As long as the sun will rise in the east and set in the west", occurring at the end of *Madhu-vidyā*.

भावं तु बादरायणोऽस्ति हि ॥३३॥

तु But बादरायण: Bādarāyaṇa (upholds) भावम् existence (of competence) हि for अस्ति exists.

33. But Bādarāyaṇa upholds the existence of competence (for the gods); for (the requisite for competence) exists (in them).

Vedāntin: The word "but" rules out the opposite point of view. But the teacher Bādarāyaṇa thinks that competence does exist even for the gods and others. Although the gods and others cannot have any competence for *Madhu-vidyā* etc., where the gods, as also the others, get intermingled, still they have the possibility of competence for pure knowledge of Brahman, since this competence is dependent on desire, ability, non-prohibition, etc. Not that competence can be ruled out even where it is possible, just because it is impossible somewhere else. Even in the case of men, not all of them are competent for all things; for instance, the Brāhmaṇas have no competence for the *Rājasūya* sacrifice. The logic that applies there, applies here as well. Under the topic of the knowledge of Brahman we come across a Vedic indicatory mark revealing the competence of gods and others for the knowledge of Brahman: "And whosoever among the gods knew that Brahman also became that; and the same with sages and men" (Bṛ. I. iv. 10); as also, "They said, 'Let us search for that Self, searching for which one attains all the worlds and all the desirable things.' Thinking thus, Indra, among the gods, started out (for Prajāpati's place), and so did Virocana of the devils" (Ch. VIII. vii. 2). There is a similar sign in the Smṛti also; as for instance the story of Yājñavalkya and the Gandharva (Viśvāvasu).[43]

And it was argued: "Because of the occurrence of the words in respect of a sphere of light". To this we say: Although the words sun etc. may refer to a sphere of light, still from their use in the sense of gods, they present those respective gods as

[43] Mahābhārata, Mokṣadharma, where the Gandharva Viśvāvasu inquires and learns about Brahman. So also in other places (e.g. in the story of Prahlāda and Ajagara) non-human beings get this knowledge.

possessed of sentience and divine powers; for these words are thus used in the *mantras* and corroborative statements. Being endowed with divine power, the gods certainly have the capacity to remain in identity with a sphere of light etc., and also to assume various bodies at will. Thus in the sentence, "Come Indra, thou ram of Medhātithi" etc., occurring in the corroborative statement about Subrahmaṇya (the priest singing the Sāma), it is said, "For Indra, in the form of a ram, carried Medhātithi of the line of Kaṇva" (*Ṣaḍviṁśa Brāhmaṇa*, I. 1). In the Smṛti also it is mentioned, "The sun came to Kunti by assuming a human form." In the case of the earth etc. also, sentient presiding deities are admitted as ruling over them, for there are such Vedic texts as, "Earth said", "Water said", etc. (Ś. B. I. vi. 3.2-4). We pointed out that in the case of the sun and the rest, the material substances like light etc. are held to be insentient, but in accordance with the uses in the *mantras* and the corroborative statements, their presiding deities are held to be sentient.

As for the argument that the *mantras* and corroborative statements are meant to serve some extraneous purpose, so that they have no power to reveal corporality etc. for the gods, we say that the existence or non-existence of a thing is proved from the emergence or not of some valid knowledge (from the application of some valid means), and it is not dependent on whether it is meant for some other purpose (e.g. rites) or not. For instance, a man, travelling for some purpose, certainly perceives the existence of grass and leaves that lie on the way.

To this the *opponent* says: The analogy is inapt, for there the means of perception are directly in contact with the grass, leaf, etc. so that their existence becomes known. But here the corroborative statement conveys its purport in syntactical combination with another sentence meant as an injunction: and hence it cannot be made to mean some existing thing through an independent purport of its own. For when a sentence as a whole conveys its sense, its component parts are not admitted to have their own independent purports as well. Thus from the sentence, "One should not drink wine", formed with a negative (not), a single idea, viz the prohibition of drinking, is understood from a combination of the three words (not, should drink, and wine); but from a connection between the two words "wine" and "should drink", one cannot also understand an injunction of the form, "One should drink wine".

Vedāntin : To this the answer is: The analogy is not inappropriate. It is quite proper that in the matter of prohibition of drinking wine, no other meaning can be accepted since the words combine (in a single construction) round a single idea. But in the cases of injunction and corroboration, the words in the corroborative portion do combine to denote some independent existing thing; and then when the question of the purpose to be served is raised, they become corroborative of the injunction as far as possible. Thus in the sentence, "One who wants prosperity shall sacrifice a white goat in honour of Air" (Tai. S. II. i. 1), the words Air etc. occurring in this injunctive sentence are directly strung up with the injunction itself; but not so are the words in the text, "Air is indeed a swift deity. He runs to Air himself with his own portion. It is he who brings prosperity to this (performer of sacrifice)" (Ibid.). Here the words occurring in this corroborative sentence are not to be construed with the injunction, for Air or the swift god cannot be conjoined with the injunctive verb to imply, "Air is to sacrifice", or "the swift god is to sacrifice", and so on. But they first form into a secondary combination for declaring the nature of Air, and then eulogize the injunction by conveying the idea that this rite has such a distinguished deity. Accordingly, wherever the meaning of a subsidiary sentence is known to be true from some other valid means of knowledge, the corroborative statement proceeds to serve its purpose by way of recapitulating (or recalling) that meaning.[44] But wherever such a meaning runs counter to other means of knowledge the corroborative statement proceeds by way of an interpretation in the sense of an attribute.[45] In the absence of both

[44] For instance, "Fire cures cold"—*Anuvāda*.

[45] For instance, "The sun is the sacrificial stake", where the meaning is: "The stake is bright like the sun"—*Guṇavāda*.

(contradiction and non-contradiction with other means)[46] the question arises as to whether it is to be interpreted in the attributive sense, since there is no other valid means of knowledge, or it is to be interpreted as referring to some existing thing, since there is no conflict with other means of knowledge. When under such a predicament, people who stand by knowledge, should interpret it to mean something existing, but not of an attribute. This also explains the standpoint to be adopted with regard to the *mantras*.[47]

Moreover, when the injunctions enjoin that certain oblations are meant for the gods—Indra and others—they have certainly an eye on the nature of those gods—Indra and the rest. For Indra and others cannot be conceived of by the mind without the help of their own characteristics; nor can oblations be offered to the respective gods without having some mental image of them. And the Vedic text reads thus: "When uttering the *mantra Vaṣaṭ* one shall meditate on the deity in whose honour the oblation is taken up" (Ai. Br. III. viii. 1). It cannot be said that the meaning consists in nothing but the words themselves, (the gods being nothing more than the words), for words and meanings are not identical things.[48] That being so, anyone who believes that the Vedic words are an independent source of knowledge cannot deny the nature of the gods—Indra and others—just as it is found in the *mantras* and corroborative statements. Similarly, the anecdotes and mythologies, based on the *mantras* and corroborative statements, can supply knowledge according to the process shown, and they can prove the corporality of the gods and others. Besides, it is quite possible that the anecdotes and mythologies are based on direct perception (by Vyāsa and others). For things imperceptible to us can

[46] For instance, "Indra with a thunder in hand—*Bhūtārthavāda*. (See f.n. 54, I. i. 4), where Indra's existence is admitted.

[47] A *mantra* is to be taken in its literal sense when it is not a recapitulation of something already known and it does not contradict known facts. Thus a god can have a body, since the *mantras* and corroborative statements say so.

[48] Should it be postulated that the *mantras* mention only the forms (species) but not any person, the answer is: A form cannot exist without a person.

be perceptible to immortal beings. Thus it is mentioned in the Smṛtis that Vyāsa and others deal directly with the gods. Anyone saying that like the modern beings, the ancient ones also had no capacity to deal with the gods, denies variety in the world, and may as well say that just as in the modern age, so also in the past, there was no Kṣatriya king ruling over the whole earth. He will also have to set his face against the injunction about the *Rājasūya* sacrifice etc., and he will have to assume that the rules of caste and stages of life were as unstable in other periods as at present. From that point of view, he will also set at nought the scriptures meant for establishing norms of conduct. Hence the proper position is that the immortal beings should have dealings with the gods as a result of the perfection of their virtue. Besides, the Smṛti declares: "From the repetition of the *mantra* follows the proximity to (and conversation with) one's chosen deity" (*Yoga-sūtra*, II. 44). Besides, since Yoga is spoken of in the Smṛti as leading to the attainment of such mystic powers as becoming minute, it cannot be denied by a mere bold assertion. The Vedas also declare the glory of Yoga: "When the five elements—earth, water, fire, air, space—have been conquered,[49] and when the Yogic powers (of becoming minute etc.) have started functioning, then for the aspirant, who has acquired a body constituted by the fire of Yoga, there is no disease, no decrepitude, no death" (Śv. II. 12). The power of the seers who visualize the *mantra* and *brāhmaṇa* portions of the Vedas are not to be measured in terms of our power. Therefore the anecdotes and mythologies have a true basis. Common belief too should not be dismissed as baseless so long as there is some probability. Hence it is proper to understand from the *mantras* etc. that the gods and others have bodies. And since on that account they can have aspiration etc., their competence for the knowledge of Brahman is justifiable. Moreover, such facts

[49] Thinking on the different parts of the body as the five elements (from the soles of the feet to knees—earth; knees to navel—water; navel to neck—fire; neck to where the hair of the head starts—air; from there to the crown of the head—space), and bringing them under control through such thoughts of identity.

as gradual emancipation, mentioned in the Vedas, become logical from this standpoint.

TOPIC 9: PSEUDO-ŚUDRA

शुगस्य तदनादरश्रवणात्तदाद्रवणात् सूच्यते हि ॥३४॥

अस्य To him occurred **शुक्** grief **तत्-अनादर-श्रवणात्** on hearing his disparagement **तत्-आद्रवणात्** as is evident from his approaching him **हि** for **सूच्यते** this is hinted at.

34. To him (i.e. Jānaśruti) occurred grief on hearing his (i.e. swan's) disparaging utterance, as is evident from his (Jānaśruti's) approaching him (Raikva), for this is hinted at (by Raikva by using the word Śūdra).

It may be argued that, even as any hard and fast rule about the competence of men alone is denied and the competence of the gods as well for different kinds of knowledge is upheld, similarly by denying any monopoly of qualification by the three classes of the twice-born alone, the Śūdras also may be accepted as qualified. In order to remove such an assumption is begun the present topic.

Opponent: Now then, the apparent conclusion is that a Śūdra also is qualified, for he can have the aspiration and ability. And unlike the prohibition, "Therefore the Śūdra is unfit for performing sacrifices" (Tai. S. VII. i. 1.6), no prohibition against his acquisition of illumination is met with. Even the disqualification for sacrifices that arises for the Śūdra from the fact of his not being qualified for lighting a sacrificial fire, is no sign of his being debarred from knowledge. For it is not a fact that a man who has no fire—Āhavanīya and the rest—cannot acquire knowledge. Moreover, there is an indicatory sign confirming the Śūdra's competence. In the section dealing with the knowledge of *samvarga* (merger of all things), Jānaśruti, grandson of Putra and an aspirant of knowledge, is referred to by the word Śūdra: "Fie, O Śūdra, keep to yourself the chariot and the necklace, together with the cows" (Ch. IV. ii. 3). And in the Smṛtis are mentioned Vidura and others as born in the

Śūdra caste but endowed with special knowledge. Hence Śūdras have competence for different kinds of knowledge.

Vedāntin: Faced with this, we say: The Śūdra has no competence, since he cannot study the Vedas; for one becomes competent for things spoken of in the Vedas, after one has studied the Vedas and known these things from them. But there can be no reading of the Vedas by a Śūdra, for Vedic study presupposes the investiture with the sacred thread, which ceremony is confined to the three castes. As for aspiration, it cannot qualify anyone unless one has the ability. Mere ability in the ordinary sense also cannot qualify anyone; for scriptural ability is needed in a scriptural matter. But this scriptural ability is denied by the prohibition of the right to study. As for the text, "The Śūdra is unfit for performing a sacrifice" (Tai. S. VII. i. 1.6), since it is based on a logic having common application, it suggests that the Śūdra has no right to knowledge as well, for the logic applies both ways. And what you take for an indicatory mark occurring in the section dealing with the knowledge about merger, that is no mark at all, for there is no logic behind it. An indicatory mark becomes suggestive when stated logically; but that logic is lacking here. Granted even that this mark qualifies the Śūdra for the *samvarga-vidyā* (meditation on merger) alone, because it occurs there, still it cannot qualify him for all kinds of knowledge. The fact, however, is that this word Śūdra cannot guarantee his competence anywhere, because it occurs in a corroborative statement (*Arthavāda*). On the contrary, this word Śūdra can be construed with some one already having the competence.

How?

The answer is: On hearing this utterance of the swan, "Hullo, who is this one, insignificant as he is, of whom you speak as though he were like Raikva of the chariot?" (Ch. IV. i. 3), which was a personal disparagement for him, Jānaśruti, grandson of Putra, was struck with grief (*śuk*). Raikva hinted at this grief by using the word Śūdra, thereby revealing his own power of television. This is what we can understand. For a born Śūdra has no right to knowledge.

How, again, is it suggested by the word Śūdra that he was struck with grief?

The answer is: "*Tat-ādravaṇāt*". Because the word Śūdra can be split up thus to mean that he (Raikva) approached towards (*abhidudrāva*) that (*tat*) grief (*śucam*); or he was approached (*abhidudruve*) by that (*tat*) sorrow (*śucā*); or he rushed (*abhidudrāva*) to that (*tat*) Raikva, because of sorrow (*śucā*). And this derivative meaning has to be accepted because the conventional meaning is inadmissible. Moreover, this meaning is obvious from the story itself.

क्षत्रियत्वगतेश्चोत्तरत्र चैत्ररथेन लिंगात् ॥३५॥

च And क्षत्रियत्व-गतेः owing to his Kṣatriyahood being known उत्तरत्र later on लिंगात् from the indicatory mark चैत्ररथेन of mention along with a descendant of Citraratha.

35. And because his Kṣatriyahood is known later on from the indicatory mark of his mention along with a descendant of Citraratha.

For this further reason Jānaśruti is not a Śūdra by birth, for from a consideration of the topic it transpires that he is a Kṣatriya, which fact becomes obvious from his suggestive mention later on along with the Kṣatriya Abhipratārin of the line of Citraratha. Later on in the complementary portion of the section on the knowledge about the merger (*Samvarga-vidyā*) Abhipratārin of the line of Citraratha is mentioned as a Kṣatriya in, "Now then, a Brahmacārin begged of Śaunaka of the line of Kapi, and Abhipratārin, son of Kakṣasena, when they were being served by the cook" (Ch. IV. iii. 5). That Abhipratārin belonged to the line of Citraratha is to be understood from his association with a descendant of the line of Kapi; for the association of the descendant of Citraratha with that of Kapi is known from the text, "The Kāpeyas made Citraratha perform this (*Dvirātra* sacrifice)" (*Tāṇḍya Brāhmaṇa*, XX. xii. 5). For the people of the same lineage generally have the priests of a common descent. Besides, it is known that he was a Kṣatriya from the text, "From him issued one named

Citrarathi who was a Kṣatriya king", where we find him to be a Kṣatriya king. Accordingly, the mention of Jānaśruti along with the Kṣatriya Abhipratārin, in the context of the same kind of knowledge, suggests that the former is a Kṣatriya; for equals are generally found to be mentioned together. Moreover, Jānaśruti is known to be a Kṣatriya from the fact of his despatching a Kṣattā[50] and his possession of riches. Hence a born Śūdra has no right to knowledge.

संस्कारपरामर्शात्तदभावाभिलापाच्च ॥३६॥

संस्कार-परामर्शात् On account of the mention of purificatory rites च and तत्-अभाव-अभिलापात् declaration of the absence of these.

36. Because purificatory rites are mentioned (for others) and absence of these is declared (for the Śūdra).

For the additional reason that, in the contexts where knowledge is spoken of, such actions for acquiring the right to knowledge are declared as investiture with the sacred thread etc.,[51] for instance, "Him he vested with the sacred thread" (Ś. B. XI. v. 3.13), "Uttering the sacred formula, 'Teach me venerable sir', he approached" (Ch. VII. i. 1), "They, who were adepts in the Vedas, adhered to the qualified Brahman, but were intent on an inquiry about the supreme Brahman, went to the venerable Pippalāda with sacrificial faggot in hand, under the belief, 'This one will certainly tell us about It'" (Pr. I. 1). And the text, "Even without initiating them" (Ch. V. xi. 7), only shows that those (who were exempted from initiation) had it already. The absence of purificatory rites for the Śūdra is mentioned in the Smṛti thus: "The Śudra belongs to the fourth caste and has but a single birth" (Manu, X. 4), as also in such texts as, "The Śūdra has no sins, nor is he fit for any purificatory rite" (Manu, X. 126).

[50] One born of a mixed parentage—from a Śūdra father and Kṣatriya mother or of a slave woman—whose duty was to drive chariots, wait on princes, and so on.

[51] Etc.—study, service of the teacher, and so on.

तदभावनिर्धारणे च प्रवृत्तेः ॥३७॥

च Moreover प्रवृत्तेः on account of inclination having arisen तत्-अभाव-निर्धारणे when the absence of that had been ascertained.

37. And because (Gautama's) inclination arose (to initiate and instruct Satyakāma) when the absence of that (Śūdrahood) had been ascertained.

Here is an additional reason why a Śūdra has no right. When owing to the utterance of truth (by Satyakāma Jābāla), the absence of Śūdrahood had been established, then Gautama proceeded to initiate and instruct (Satyakāma) Jābāla, which fact is gathered from an indicatory sign in the Upaniṣad: "No non-Brāhmaṇa can dare utter such a truth. O amiable one, bring sacrificial faggot, I shall initiate you because you did not depart from truth" (Ch. IV. iv. 5).

श्रवणाध्ययनार्थप्रतिषेधात् स्मृतेश्च ॥३८॥

च And श्रवण-अध्ययन-अर्थ-प्रतिषेधात् hearing, study, acquisition of meaning are prohibited स्मृतेः according to Smṛti.

38. And because the Smṛti prohibits for the Śūdra the hearing, study, and acquisition of the meaning (of the Vedas).

This is another reason why the Śūdra has no right: By the Smṛti he is debarred from hearing, studying, and acquiring the meaning of the Vedas. The Smṛti mentions that a Śūdra has no right to hear the Vedas, no right to study the Vedas, and no right to acquire the meaning of the Vedas (and perform the rites). As for prohibition of hearing, we have the text, "Then should he happen to hear the Vedas, the expiation consists in his ears being filled with lead and lac"[52], and "He who is a Śūdra is a walking crematorium. Hence one should not read in the neighbourhood of a Śūdra"[53]. From this follows the prohibition about study. How can one study the Vedas when they are not to be recited within his hearing? Then there is the chopping

[52] Gau. Dh. Sū., XII. 4 [53] Vāsiṣṭha, 18

off of his tongue if he should utter the Vedas, and the cutting of the body to pieces if he should commit it to memory[54]. From this it follows by implication that the acquisition of meaning and acting on it are also prohibited, as is stated in, "Vedic knowledge is not to be imparted to a Śūdra"[55], and "Study, sacrifice, and distribution of gifts are for the twice-born"[56]. But from those to whom knowledge dawns as a result of (good) tendencies acquired in the past lives, as for instance to Vidura, Dharmavyādha, and others, the reaping of the result of knowledge cannot be withheld, for the result of knowledge is inevitable. This position is confirmed by the Smṛti text, "One should read out to the four castes (keeping the Brāhmaṇa in front)"[57], which declares the competence for all the four castes for the acquisition of the anecdotes and mythologies. But the conclusion stands that a Śūdra has no right to knowledge through the Vedas.

Topic 10: Vibration

कम्पनात् ॥३९॥

39. (Prāṇa is Brahman) because of (the mention of) vibration.

The side issue about competence is concluded. Now we revert to the discussion of the meanings of texts we were engaged in. By following the root meaning of the verb *ejṛ* which is "to vibrate" (to move), this aphorism refers to the text, "All this universe that there is, emerges and vibrates because there is *Prāṇa* that is a great terror like an uplifted thunder. Those who know this become immortal" (Ka. II. iii. 2). In this sentence we hear of the whole creation pulsating on *Prāṇa* as its support, and of some great source of fear that is imminent and is mentioned by the word thunder, as also of the attainment of immortality from that knowledge.

Opponent: Now in this context, a deliberation is bound to arise, since it is not clear as to what that *Prāṇa* is and what that

[54] Gau. Dh. Sū., XII. 4
[55] Manu, IV. 80
[56] Gau. Dh. Sū., IX. 1
[57] Mbh. Śā., 327. 49

terrible thunder is. When such a deliberation ensues, we arrive at the conclusion that the familiar vital force, with its five functions, is the *Prāṇa*. And from familiar use, the thunder must be the thunderbolt. This is a eulogy of *Prāṇa*.

How?

All this creation pulsates by getting its support on air, called *Prāṇa*, having five functions. And it is through the energy of air that the thunderbolt is lifted up; for they say that when air moves about in the form of clouds, then there are the movements (or flashes) of lightning, roar of clouds, rain, and thunder. And this immortality ensues from the knowledge of air itself. In support of this, occurs another Upaniṣadic text, "Air is the particular (separate parts) and air is the genus (or whole). He who knows this conquers accidental death" (Bṛ. III. iii. 2). Therefore the entity here is to be understood as air.

Vedāntin: Such being the position, we say: Brahman Itself is to be understood here.

Why?

From a consideration of what precedes and succeeds; for we notice that in the earlier and following texts, it is Brahman that is dealt with. So why should we, all of a sudden, understand air in this verse alone? In an earlier verse we have, "That is bright (pure), that is Brahman; and that is called immortality. On It is fixed all the universe. It is this that nothing can transcend" (Ka. II. iii. 1), where Brahman is mentioned. That Brahman is spoken of here as well because of proximity. Besides, from the recognition of Its being the support of the universe, as stated in, "This whole universe that emerges and moves because *Prāṇa* is there" (Ka. II. iii. 2), it is understood that Brahman is referred to. Moreover, even this word *Prāṇa* is used for the supreme Self, since we find such a use in the Upaniṣad as, "*Prāṇa* of *Prāṇa* (Vital force of vital force) (Bṛ. IV. iv. 18). This power to move (the whole universe) also fits in with the supreme Self, but not with mere air (of which the vital force is a form). It has been said accordingly, "No mortal lives by *Prāṇa* or *Apāna* (exhaling or inhaling), but all live by something else on which these two depend" (Ka. II. ii. 5). Later on too, Brahman and not air is declared in, "From fear of Him fire burns, from fear shines the sun; from fear run Indra and Air, and Death, the fifth" (Ka. II. iii. 3), where Brahman is spoken of as the source of fear for the whole universe including Air. Furthermore, from the fact of proximity and from the recognition of the identity of the source of fear as indicated in, "A source of terror like an uplifted thunder" (Ka. II. iii. 3), it can be understood that the same Brahman is declared here as well. The word thunder is used on account of the similarity of striking terror. Even as the king's subjects and others continue ever under the rule of the king under the fear, "This uplifted thunder will fall on my head unless I obey his rule", similarly this universe of fire, air, sun, etc. continues in its own course out of fear of this very Brahman. So Brahman is likened to a terrifying uplifted thunder. Similar is another Upaniṣadic text about Brahman: "Out of His fear the Wind blows. Out of fear the Sun rises. Out of His fear runs Fire as also Indra, and Death, the fifth" (Tai. II. viii. 1). From the mention of immortality as the result (of knowledge), it is understood that Brahman Itself is this Entity; for it is known from the verse, "Knowing Him alone one attains immortality. There is no other path to proceed by" (Śv. VI. 15), that immortality results from the realization of Brahman. As for the immortality (referred to by the opponent and) declared in some contexts as resulting from the knowledge of Air (Hiraṇyagarbha), that is merely relative; for in that very (Bṛhadāraṇyaka) Upaniṣad, the text turns to another topic and after speaking of the supreme Self, it declares the perishableness of all else—Air and the rest—in, "Everything else is perishable" (Bṛ. III. iv. 2). From the context under discussion as well, the supreme Self stands established, for the question asked is: "Tell (me) of that thing which you see as different from virtue, different from vice, different from this cause and effect, and different from the past and the future" (Ka. I. ii. 14).

Topic 11: Light as Declared in the Upaniṣad

ज्योतिर्दर्शनात् ॥४०॥

ज्योतिः Light दर्शनात् owing to its being met with.

40. Light is Brahman, for it is met with as such (in the Upaniṣad).

Doubt: In the Upaniṣad it is heard, "This serene one (*samprasāda*), rising up from this body, and realizing the supreme Light, becomes established in his own nature" (Ch. VIII. xii. 3). The doubt arises as to whether the word light refers to the light visible to the eye and dispelling darkness, or to supreme Brahman. What should be the conclusion then?

Opponent: It must be the common light.

Why?

Because the word light conventionally means this. Under the aphorism, "Light is Brahman, because of the mention of feet" (I. i. 24), it was of course shown that from the force of the context, the word light gives up its own meaning and implies Brahman. But no cause for discarding the common meaning is noticed here. Similarly in the chapter, dealing with the nerves, the attainment of the sun by the aspirant for liberation is spoken of thus: "Now (after the loss of consciousness) when one departs from this body in this way (befitting death), then one proceeds upward along these very rays (associated with the nerves)" (Ch. VIII. vi. 5). Accordingly the familiar light is meant by the word light here.

Vedāntin: This being the position, we say: The supreme Brahman Itself is meant by the word light.

Why?

"Because it is met with in that sense in the Upaniṣad". It is obvious in this context that Brahman is repeatedly alluded to as the subject-matter. Thus in the beginning of the topic, the Self that is possessed of such characteristics as freedom from sin and so on, as mentioned in, "The Self that is free from sin" (Ch. VIII. vii. 1), is declared as the entity to be searched for and to be aspired after for realization. It is also alluded to in, "I shall explain this very one to you over again" (Ch. VIII. ix. 3). And this Self stands declared from the fact of the attainment of this Light for the sake of becoming unembodied, as mentioned in, "Happiness and sorrow do not certainly touch one who has become unembodied" (Ch. VIII. xii. 1); for unless it be by identity with Brahman, there can be no unembodiedness anywhere else.[58] Another reason for this is the use of such attributes as "supreme Light" (Ch. VIII. iii. 4), "the transcendental Being" (Ch. VIII. xii. 3). As for the criticism that the attainment of the sun by the aspirant for liberation is spoken of, that is not the absolute liberation inasmuch as it is dependent on a course to be followed, and that after departure from the body. We shall state later on that in the case of the absolute liberation, there are no such things as a course to be followed or departure from the body.

TOPIC 12: SPACE IS BRAHMAN, BEING DIFFERENT FROM NAME AND FORM

आकाशोऽर्थान्तरत्वादिव्यपदेशात् ॥४१॥

आकाशः Space अर्थ-अन्तरत्व-आदि-व्यपदेशात् since it is declared as being something else and so on.

41. Ākaśa (Space) is Brahman, because of the declaration of being something different and so on.

Doubt: In the Upaniṣad we hear: "That which is called *ākāśa* is the accomplisher of name and form. That in which they are contained is Brahman; that is immortal and that is the Self" (Ch. VIII. xiv. 1). Now the discussion arises, whether the word *ākâśa* denotes the supreme Brahman or the familiar material space.

Opponent: Under such a predicament, it is reasonable to accept the element called space (ether); for the word *ākāṣa* conventionally means that, and the fact of the accomplishment of name and form can fit in with it in the sense of providing space (for them). Besides, nothing that can be a clear indication of Brahman, as for instance, creatorship, is heard of here.

Vedāntin: This aphorism is enunciated to meet that position. The supreme Brahman alone can be the meaning of the word *ākāśa* (Space) here.

[58] The embodied Sun cannot be this goal, and establishment in one's own nature does not mean becoming something else. So the Self, and not the Sun, is the goal.

Why?

"Because of the declaration of Its being something different and so on." For by saying, "That in which they are contained is Brahman" (Ch. VIII. xiv. 1), it is declared that *ākāśa* is something different from name and form. Nothing but Brahman can be different from name and form, since the whole of creation consists of a manifestation of name and form (i.e. word and its meaning). And the manifestation of name and form in an absolute sense is not possible for anything but Brahman; for the Upaniṣad mentions that Brahman is the agent of their revelation: "Let me manifest name and form by Myself entering as the individual soul" (Ch. VI. iii. 2).

Opponent: Is it not a matter of direct experience that the individual being also has the power of manifesting name and form?

Vedāntin: True, he has; but the intention (of the text, "by Myself entering as the individual soul") is to declare the identity of the individual and Brahman (and not the agentship of the individual). From this very declaration of the manifestation of name and form, creatorship etc., as the indicatory signs of Brahman become stated *ipso facto*. The sentences, "That is Brahman; that is immortal; that is the Self" (Ch. VIII. xiv. 1) are also indications that Brahman is spoken of. This is an elaboration of the aphorism, "Space is Brahman, for Brahman's characteristic is in evidence" (I. i. 22).

Topic 13: Sleep and Death

सुषुप्त्युत्क्रान्त्योर्भेदेन ॥४२॥

(Because of the declaration) भेदेन as being different सुषुप्ति-उत्क्रान्त्योः in sleep and death.

42. Because of the declaration of being different in sleep and at the time of departure, (the supreme Lord is the subject-matter of teaching).

The portion, "Because of the declaration" follows (from the earlier aphorism) to complete the sense.

Doubt: In the sixth part of the Bṛhadāraṇyaka Upaniṣad, the start is made with, "'(Of all the entities cognized through the idea of I) which is the Self?' 'This infinite entity (*Puruṣa*) that is identified with the intellect and is in the midst of the organs, the self-effulgent light within the heart (i.e. in the intellect)'" (IV. iii. 7), and then the subject of the Self is amply elaborated. The doubt arises whether that text is concerned simply with the explanation of the true nature of the transmigrating soul, or with establishing the true nature of the transcendental Self. What should be the conclusion?

Opponent: It is concerned only with the true nature of the transmigrating soul.

How do you know?

From a consideration of the start and finish. At the start, an indicatory sign of the embodied soul is found in, "the entity that is identified with the intellect and is in the midst of the organs", and the non-rejection of that soul is found at the end in, "That which is identified with the intellect and is in the midst of the organs is this great birthless Self" (Bṛ. IV. iv. 22); that very soul is dealt with elaborately in the middle also through a presentation of the waking state etc.

Vedāntin: Under these circumstances, we say: This text is meant for speaking about the supreme Lord alone, and it is not meant for speaking further about the embodied soul.

Why?

Because in the state of deep sleep and at the time of departure from the body, the supreme Lord is mentioned separately from the embodied soul. In sleep for instance, the supreme Lord is mentioned separately from the embodied soul in, "So this Puruṣa, being fully embraced by the supremely intelligent Self—*prājña ātmā*—does not know anything at all, either external or internal" (Bṛ. IV. iii. 21). In that text the Puruṣa must be the embodied soul, since it is he who is the knower inasmuch as the knowledge of anything external or internal can be denied only when the possibility of knowing exists. And the supremely intelligent Self is the supreme Lord, for He is never separated from intelligence (*prajñā*) which is of the nature of omniscience. So also at the time of departure the supreme Lord is mentioned separately from the individual in, "So does the embodied soul, being presided over by the supremely intelligent Self, go making noises" (Bṛ. IV. iii. 35). There too the embodied soul must be the individual being, since it is the master of the body; but the supremely intelligent One must be the supreme Lord Himself. Therefore from the separate mention in sleep and at the time of departure, it is to be understood that the entity sought to be taught here is the supreme Lord. In answer to the argument that from the indicatory signs of the individual soul at the start, middle, and end, it follows that this text is meant for presenting the soul, we say: The nature of the transmigrating soul is not sought to be presented at the start in the sentence, "that is identified with the intellect and is in the midst of the organs".

What is meant then?

The intention is to show the identity of the transmigrating soul with the supreme Self after a restatement of the former's characteristics. For the succeeding text, viz "it meditates as it were, it runs as it were" etc. (Bṛ. IV. iii. 7), is seen to be devoted to the elimination of the characteristics of the transmigrating soul. Similarly at the end, as at the start, the conclusion runs thus, "That Self which is identified with the intellect and is in the midst of the organs is this great birthless Self" (Bṛ. IV. iv. 22). The idea conveyed is that the transmigrating soul, that is perceived as identified with the intellect and in the midst of the organs, is proved by us to be but this great birthless Self, the supreme Lord. But one who would infer, from the presentation of the waking state etc., in the middle, that the nature of the transmigrating soul is sought to be taught here, may as well pop up in the western direction when sent towards the east, for the presentation of the states of waking etc., is meant neither to imply the possession of any state nor of transmigration.

What is meant then?

What is meant is freedom from the states and transmigration.

How is that known?

Because at every turn Janaka requests Yājñavalkya: "Please instruct me further about liberation" (Bṛ. IV. iii. 14-16, 33), and because the answer given at every step is: "He is untouched by whatever he sees in that state, for this infinite Being is unattached" (Bṛ. IV. iii. 15–16). Further, it is stated, "(This aspect of his) is untouched by good work and untouched by bad work, for he is then beyond all the woes of his heart (intellect)" (Bṛ. IV. iii. 22). Accordingly, it is to be understood that this text is meant for establishing the nature of the supermundane Self.

पत्यादिशब्देभ्यः ॥४३॥

पति-आदि-शब्देभ्य: From such words as ruler.

43. This is confirmed by such words as ruler.

Here is an additional reason why this text is to be understood as establishing the nature of the supermundane Entity; for the words ruler etc., occurring in this text, are calculated to establish the nature of the supermundane Entity and to rule out the nature of the transmigrating soul. Of these two objectives, such sentences as, "It is the controller of all, the lord of all, the ruler of all" (Bṛ. IV. iv. 22), are meant for establishing the nature of the supermundane Entity; and such sentences as, "It does not become better through good work, nor worse through bad work" (ibid.), are meant for denying the nature of transmigration. Hence it is understood that the supreme Lord, who is not subject to transmigration, is spoken of here.

Section IV

Topic 1: The Inferred Entity

After broaching the subject of the deliberation on Brahman, the definition of Brahman was given: "That is Brahman from which the birth etc., of this are derived" (B. S. I. i. 2). Then the doubt was raised that this definition applies equally to Pradhāna (primordial Nature), and it was dismissed by saying, "Because of the attribution of seeing, the one (viz Pradhāna) which is not taught in the Upaniṣads is not the cause of the universe" (I. i. 5), the reason being that it is not mentioned in the Upaniṣads. It was also shown in the earlier portion of this book that the sameness of the knowledge imparted by the Upaniṣads is in favour of the belief in Brahman as the cause (I. i. 10), but not in favour of the theory that Pradhāna is the cause. Now are being raised some doubts not considered hitherto.

Opponent: The assertion made that Pradhāna is not mentioned in the Upaniṣads is groundless; for in some sections are heard words calculated to suggest Pradhāna. So it comes to this that when the great seers Kapila and others adopted the causality of Pradhāna, they did so on the authority of the Vedas themselves. Accordingly, as long as those words are not proved to convey some other meaning, so long the theory that Brahman is the cause will remain under doubt, even though it has been proved earlier.

Vedāntin: Hence the succeeding topic starts with a view to showing that they mean something else:

आनुमानिकमप्येकेषामिति चेन्न शरीररूपकविन्यस्तगृहीतेर्दर्शयति च ॥१॥

आनुमानिकम् The inferred entity अपि even (is revealed) एकेषाम् to the followers of some recension इति चेत् if this be the contention, (then) न not so शरीर-रूपक-विन्यस्त-गृहीतेः since it is cognized as occurring in a simile illustrating the body च and दर्शयति (the Upaniṣad) shows (this).

1. If it be said that even the inferred entity (Pradhāna) is revealed to the followers of some recension, we say, not so, for the word is cognized as occurring in a simile illustrating the body. And the Upaniṣad also shows this.

Opponent: Even the inferred entity, even Pradhāna, arrived at through inference, is met with by the followers of some recensions, as having been mentioned by name. For the Kaṭha Upaniṣad has this reading: "The unmanifest (*avyakta*) is higher than *mahat*, *puruṣa* is higher than *avyakta*" (I. iii. 11), where *mahat*, *avyakta*, and *puruṣa* are found exactly under the same epithets and in the same order as they are known from the (Sāṁkhya) Smṛtis. Of these, by the word *avyakta* is meant Pradhāna, well known in the Sāṁkhya Smṛti, for the word *avyakta* is in common use in the Sāṁkhya Smṛti, and being devoid of sound etc. (Ka. I. iii. 15), it can be derived in the sense of that which is not manifest (*na vyakta*). Having been mentioned thus in the Upaniṣad, it remains unproved that it is not mentioned. Now that very Pradhāna is the cause of the universe, it being well known to be so from the Upaniṣads, Smṛtis, and reason.

Vedāntin: This is not so. This sentence of the Kaṭha Upaniṣad is not meant for proving the existence of the *avyakta* and *mahat* of the Sāṁkhyas. For we do not come here across the very same Pradhāna, as it is taught in the Sāṁkhya Smṛtis as an independent cause constituted by its three (component) attributes. The only identical thing we come across is the mere word *avyakta*, which from its derivative sense of that which is not manifest can be applied equally to any other subtle and inscrutable thing. And this word does not conventionally mean any particular thing. As for such a conventional usage among the followers of the theory of Pradhāna, that is only a technical term for them, and as such, it cannot be adduced as a reason for ascertaining the meaning of a Vedic text. The identity of a thing cannot be established merely from the similarity of the order of treatment, unless the nature of the thing itself is recognized as identical; for unless one is a fool, one will not conclude by seeing a cow in a stable that it must be a horse. From a consideration of the context also, the Pradhāna, fancied by others, does not emerge as the meaning, "for the word is cognized as occurring in a simile illustrating the body". The body in fact, occurring in the simile of the chariot, is understood here by the word *avyakta*.

How?

On the strength of the context and the method of residue. Thus the text, immediately preceding, shows how the Self, body etc., are analogous to the master of the chariot, chariot, etc. (respectively): "Know the Self as the master of the chariot, and the body as the chariot. Know the intellect as the charioteer, and the mind as verily the bridle. They call the senses the horses; know the objects (of the senses) as the ways. The discriminating people call that Self, associated with the body, senses, and mind, as the experiencer" (Ka. I. iii. 3–4). And then it is shown that one attains the worldly state through those organs etc., when they are not under control; but that when they are under control, one "reaches the end of the road that is the highest place of Viṣṇu" (Ka. I. iii. 7–9). When after this has been shown, the desire arises to know what that highest place of Viṣṇu is, the text shows that the supreme Self is transcendental to those very senses etc., that are under discussion, and that It is at the end of the road and is the highest place of Viṣṇu: "The sense-objects are higher than the senses, and the mind is higher than the sense-objects; but the intellect is higher than the mind and the great soul (*mahān ātmā*) is higher than the intellect. *Avyakta* is higher than *mahat*, Puruṣa is higher than *avyakta*. There is nothing higher than Puruṣa. He is the culmination, He is the highest goal" (Ka. I. iii. 10–11). The very senses etc., that were spoken of as the horses etc., in the imagery of the chariot are (to be understood as) spoken of here in this text as well, so that the fault of giving up the subject-matter under discussion and taking up something else, not within purview, may not arise. Of these, the words senses, mind, and intellect occur in common in the preceding and present texts. The sense-objects, namely such things as sound and the rest, were mentioned as the road for the senses, conceived of as horses. They (the objects) are higher than the senses, in accordance with the fact well known in the Upaniṣad (Bṛ. III. ii. 1–6) that the senses are the *grahas* and the sense-objects are the *ati-grahas*.[1] The mind is superior to the sense-objects, for the interactions between the sense-organs and sense-objects are based on the mind. The intellect is superior to the mind, for the objects of experience approach the experiencer by riding on the intellect. That great soul (*mahān ātmā*) that is higher than the intellect (Ka. I. iii. 10) is presented in the words, "Know the Self (*ātmā*) as the master of the chariot" (Ka. I. iii. 3).

How?

Because the word Self (*ātmā*) is used, and because the experiencer can reasonably be superior to the objects of experience. Further Its greatness is justifiable because It is the master. Or by the phrase *mahān ātmā* (Ka. I. iii. 10) is meant here the intellect of the first-born Hiraṇyagarbha which is the highest basis of the intellects of all beings in accordance with the Smṛti, "That which is read of by the learned people as mind (i.e. the power of thinking), pervasive, presentiment (i.e. power of determining the future), soul, the refuge (of all enjoyable things), intellect (power of determining the present), (power of) fame, (power of) rulership, intuition (of things of all times), (power of) expression, consciousness, memory (of all the past)" (Mbh. XIII. x. 11), and in accordance with the Upaniṣad, "He who created Hiraṇyagarbha in the beginning and transmitted the Vedas to Him" (Śv. VI. 18). That (cosmic intellect) was mentioned there in the earlier verse by the simple word intellect; and therefore to make the idea clearer, it is mentioned here separately (in its cosmic aspect); for that intellect too is justly higher than ours. But on this interpretation, according to which the word Puruṣa in the latter text (Ka. I. iii. 11) is accepted as implying the supreme Self, the individual soul which is the master of the chariot becomes enumerated *ipso facto*, for in reality there is no difference between the supreme Self and the soul identified with the intellect. So the

[1] *Graha* is that which perceives, hence an organ. *Atigraha* is that which is greater than a *graha*, hence sense-objects determining the nature of the perception.

body alone, among those (six) factors (Ka. I. iii. 3–4) is left over. With a view to leading to the realization of the supreme state, the Upaniṣad (Ka. I. iii. 10–11) goes on enumerating seriatim those other factors themselves that were being discussed (in Ka. I. iii. 3–4). While engaged thus, the Upaniṣad (after pairing off the others), points out the remaining factor, viz body occurring in the earlier passage (Ka. I. iii. 3), by the remaining factor, viz *avyakta* in the present text (Ka. I. iii. 11). This is how we understand it. For what is sought here to be taught is the realization of the identity with Brahman, which is the inmost Self, by the experiencer (i.e. the individual soul) who is under ignorance and is associated with body, senses, mind, intellect, and experiences of sense-objects. This is done for him by chalking out the path of liberation from the worldly state with the help of the comparison of the body and the rest with a chariot etc. Thus it is that the place of Viṣṇu is spoken of as difficult of approach in the verse: "He is hidden in all beings; and hence He does not appear as the Self of all. But by the seers of subtle things, He is seen through a pointed and fine intellect" (Ka. I. iii. 12). Then Yoga meant for its realization is revealed in: "The discriminating man should merge that mind into the cognizing self; he should merge the cognizing self into the *mahān ātmā* (great soul); he should merge the great soul into the peaceful Self" (I. iii. 13). The idea implied is this: "He should merge the organ of speech into the mind" means that he should give up all the external activities of the organs of speech etc., and continue to act only through the mind; and because the mind also has a tendency to think of objects, he should discover the defect inherent in thinking of pros and cons, and then he should hold the mind confined steadfastly in the intellect that has the faculty of determination and is referred to by the term "cognizing self". That intellect, again, he should withdraw into the great soul, the experiencer, or into the acute intellect, sharpened through meditation. The great soul is, however, to be established by him in the peaceful Self, in the supreme Puruṣa under consideration, that is to say, in the "highest goal" (Ka. I. iii. 11). Thus when we run through the context, preceding and succeeding, there remains no scope for Pradhāna pointed out by others.

सूक्ष्मं तु तदर्हत्वात् ॥२॥

तु Rather सूक्ष्मं the subtle तत्-अर्हत्वात् for it deserves that.

2. *Rather the subtle (causal state) is meant (by avyakta), for it deserves that epithet.*

It has been said that on the strength of the context and the method of residue the word *avyakta* refers to the body and not Pradhāna. But the *doubt* arises now: How can the body be called *avyakta* (unmanifest)? For from the fact of its grossness, the body deserves the term manifest all the more, whereas the term unmanifest (*avyakta*) is meant for something indistinct (or undeveloped).

Hence the *answer* is being offered: But here the subtle one—the body in its causal state—is sought to be spoken of; for the subtle (cause) deserves to be mentioned by the word unmanifest. Though this body is gross and cannot in itself be called unmanifest, still the subtle elements from which it is produced can be called unmanifest. And the word denoting the material cause is seen to apply to its product also as for instance in, "The Soma juice is to be mixed with the cows (i.e. cow's milk)" (Ṛ. V. IX. xlvi. 4). The Upaniṣadic text, "This universe was then undifferentiated" (Bṛ. I. iv. 7) also shows that this very world, diversified through names and forms, was in the beginning in a state of latency, devoid of differentiation into names and forms, and hence fit to be called undifferentiated.

तदधीनत्वादर्थवत् ॥३॥

तत्-अधीनत्वात् Being dependent on that; अर्थवत् it serves some purpose.

3. *(Avyakta is not Pradhāna) because it is dependent on that (God); (but this avyakta has to be admitted as) it serves some purpose.*

The *opponent* argues here: If it be admitted that when in the beginning the world was in its causal state, and remained undifferentiated through names and forms it was fit to be called unmanifest, and if it be held that in a similar state the body also could be called unmanifest, then that amounts to an admission of the theory of Pradhāna as the cause; for the primordial (undifferentiated) state of this very universe is called Pradhāna.

Vedāntin: To this it is said: Should we admit some primal state as an independent cause of the world, we shall be opening the door for the theory of Pradhāna as the cause. But this primal state is held by us to be subject to the supreme Lord, but not as an independent thing. That state has to be admitted, because it serves a purpose. Without that latent state, the creatorship of God cannot have any meaning, inasmuch as God cannot act without His power (of Māyā), and without that latent state, the absence of birth for the freed souls cannot be explained.[2] Why?

Because liberation comes when the potential power (of Māyā) is burnt away by knowledge. That potential power, constituted by nescience, is mentioned by the word unmanifest. It rests on God, and is comparable to magic. It is a kind of deep slumber in which the transmigrating souls sleep without any consciousness of their real nature. This thing, that is *avyakta*, is sometimes referred to by the word space, as stated in the text, "By the Immutable, O Gārgī, is (the unmanifest) space pervaded" (Bṛ. III. viii. 11). Sometimes it is called the immutable as in, "Higher than the higher immutable" (Mu. II. i. 2); sometimes it is called Māyā as in, "Know Māyā to be Nature and the master of Māyā to be the great God" (Śv. IV. 10). That Māyā is surely unmanifest, for it can neither be ascertained as real nor as unreal. This is why it has been stated that "*Avyakta* is higher than *mahat*" (Ka. I. iii. 11); for if the cosmic intelligence of Hiraṇyagarbha be meant by the word *mahat*, then *avyakta* is higher than *mahat*, for *mahat* springs from the former. If, however, the individual being be the meaning of *mahat* (vide

[2] That power of Māyā has to be admitted whose presence makes birth, death etc., possible, and whose cessation brings about liberation.

end of commentary on I. iv. 1), still the statement, "*Avyakta* is higher than *mahat*", is admissible, since the state of becoming an individual creature depends on the influence of *avyakta* (Māyā) acting as a limiting adjunct. For ignorance is *avyakta*; and it is because of the possession of ignorance by the individual soul that all kinds of empirical behaviour continue for ever. This superiority to *mahat*, that *avyakta* has, is also fancied in the case of its modification, the body itself, by thinking of them as figuratively identical. Although the organs are as much the products of *avyakta* as the body, still the identity is figuratively fancied in the case of the body alone, whence it is spoken of as *avyakta*, the organs having already been referred to by their own names, and the body alone having been left over (to be paired off with *avyakta*).[3]

Pseudo-Vedāntin: Others explain that the bodies are of two kinds—gross and fine. The gross one is what is directly perceived, and the fine will be referred to later on in, "The soul goes out of the body, enveloped with the subtle parts of the elements, with a view to obtaining a fresh body; so it is known from the question and answer in the scripture" (B. S. III. i. 1). Both these bodies were equally described earlier as the chariot. But the fine body is mentioned here by the word *avyakta;* for the fine deserves that epithet. And since all behaviour, associated with bondage or freedom is "dependent on this" fine body, it is higher than the individual being. This is just like saying that the sense-objects are higher than the senses owing to the dependence of the senses on their objects.

Vedāntin: But they have to answer this question: Since in the earlier text both the bodies were described in common as the chariot, and since both are equally under discussion here in the latter text, and both remain to be enumerated (i.e. paired off), why should the fine body alone be mentioned here and not the gross?

Pseudo-Vedāntin: We can only interpret the meaning of what is stated by the scripture, but cannot question it. And the

[3] The senses etc. are mentioned in Ka. I. iii. 3-4 and I. iii. 10, and the gross body in Ka. I. iii. 3.

word used by the scripture is *avyakta,* which can mean only the fine and not the reverse, that being *vyakta* (manifest).

Vedāntin: Not so, for the meaning has to be determined by keeping the unity of purport in view. Not that these words, mentioned earlier and later, can convey any sense without getting connected through a common purport, for that will lead to the fault of giving up something under discussion and taking up something extraneous. And unity of purport cannot exist unless the subsequent portion is connected with the earlier by way of completing some idea. Now since the completion of the idea requires the consideration of both the bodies equally, the unity of purport itself will be vitiated, unless the relationship between the two (earlier and later) parts be admitted in accordance with this requirement. In that case how can the meaning of any scriptural expression be understood? Besides, it is not to be thought thus: "The fine body is mentioned here because it is difficult to be purified;[4] but the gross one is so palpably repugnant that it can be easily purified, and hence it is not mentioned." For the purification of anything is not intended to be spoken of here, inasmuch as no verb occurs here to enjoin purification. But since "the highest place of Viṣṇu" (Ka. I. iii. 9) was pointed out in the immediately preceding verse, the question arises, "What is it?" Hence the intention here (Ka. I. ii. 11) is to speak of that place. Accordingly, it is pointed out in succession that a certain thing is higher than the one preceding it; and then it is declared, "There is nothing higher than Puruṣa" (ibid.). However we lose nothing by accepting any one of these two points of view, since both are calculated to demolish the inferred entity, Pradhāna. So it may well be as you put it.

ज्ञेयत्वावचनाच्च ॥४॥

च And ज्ञेयत्व-अवचनात् owing to the non-mention of being known.

4. *And because (avyakta is) not mentioned as an entity to be known.*

[4] Ascertained that it is not the Self, that is to say eliminated.

Pradhāna is presented in the Sāṁkhya Smṛti as a thing to be known, since according to them, freedom (or the detachment of the soul from Nature) ensues from knowing the difference between the *guṇas* (that constitute Pradhāna) and *puruṣa* (soul). One cannot know the *puruṣa* to be different from the three *guṇas*, unless one has known the nature of the *guṇas*. And at places they mention Pradhāna as a thing to be known for the sake of acquiring supernatural powers. But here in the Upaniṣad, this *avyakta* is not mentioned as a thing to be known, the term *avyakta* being used as a mere epithet. There is no other text to show that *avyakta* is either to be known or adored. Moreover, it cannot be upheld that the knowledge of the term *avyakta* itself can lead to some fruitful human result even though it be not enjoined as such in any scripture; (for that alone can be understood as a thing to be known which has been enjoined as such). From this point of view also, Pradhāna is not referred to by the word *avyakta*. Our standpoint, on the contrary is beyond cavil, since according to us this word *avyakta* is used with a view to revealing the state of Viṣṇu by a process of following the comparison of the body etc., with the chariot etc.

वदतीति चेन्न प्राज्ञो हि प्रकरणात् ॥५॥

(The Upaniṣad) वदति does speak इति चेत् if this be the contention न not so; हि because प्राज्ञ: the conscious Self (stands out) प्रकरणात् from the context.

5. If it be argued that the Upaniṣad does mention Pradhāna (by the word avyakta), we say : No, for the conscious Self is understood from the context.

Here the *Sāṁkhya* says : The aphorism, "And because *avyakta* is not mentioned as an entity to be known", remains unproved. How?

For later on we hear of Pradhāna, mentioned by the word *avyakta*, as a thing to be known, in the text, "One becomes freed from the jaws of death by knowing that which is soundless, touchless, colourless, undiminishing, and also tasteless, eternal, odourless, without beginning and without end, higher than *mahat*, and ever constant" (Ka. I. iii. 15). Pradhāna, presented in this text for the sake of knowledge, conforms exactly to the Pradhāna mentioned in the Smṛti as being devoid of sound etc., and higher than *mahat*. Hence it is Pradhāna that is declared here, and that, again, is pointed out by the word *avyakta*.

Vedāntin : To this we say: Pradhāna is not presented here as a thing to be known; on the contrary we understand that the conscious Self, which is the supreme Self, is presented here for realization.

How is it so?

From the context. It is the topic of the conscious Self that spreads out elaborately; because it is declared, "There is nothing higher than Puruṣa. He is the culmination, He is the highest goal" (Ka. I. iii. 11), and so on; and because by mentioning the inscrutability of the Self, the curiosity to know that very Self is roused by the text, "He is hidden in all beings, and hence He does not appear as the Self (of all)" (Ka. I. iii. 12); and because the control of the organs of speech etc., is enjoined for the sake of the knowledge of the Self alone in, "The discriminating man should merge (the organ of) speech into the mind" (Ka. I. iii. 13); and because the result is the delivery from the mouth of death (Ka. I. iii. 15). For it is not held by the Sāṁkhyas that one becomes freed by knowing Pradhāna alone, their theory being that one becomes free by knowing the sentient soul. Besides, in all the Upaniṣads, such attributes as soundlessness etc., are vouched for the conscious Self alone. Hence it is not Pradhāna that is the thing to be known here, nor is it meant by the word *avyakta*.

त्रयाणामेव चैवमुपन्यासः प्रश्नश्च ॥६॥

च And त्रयाणाम् of the three एव only उपन्यासः is the presentation एवम् thus च and प्रश्नः the question.

6. And thus there is the presentation of three things alone, and the question also is concerned with them.

An additional reason why Pradhāna is neither meant by *avyakta*, nor is it a thing to be known is that three things alone—Fire, individual soul, and the supreme Self—are met with in this book, the Kaṭha Upaniṣad, as things presented for being spoken of in conformity with the granting of the boons; and the question also relates to them. No other thing is asked for, nor is it presented. Of these, the question about Fire is contained in, "O Death, such as you are, you know that Fire which leads to heaven. Of that you tell me who am full of faith" (Ka. I. i. 13). The question about the individual soul occurs in, "This doubt that arises consequent on the death of a man, some saying, 'It exists', and others saying, 'It does not exist'—I would know this under your instruction. Of all the boons this one is the third boon" (Ka. I. i. 20). And the question about the supreme Self is contained in, "Tell me of that thing which you see as different from virtue, different from vice, different from these cause and effect, and different from the past and future" (Ka. I. ii. 14). In the answer also, Fire is spoken of in, "Death told him of the Fire that is the source of the world, the form and number of bricks" (Ka. I. i. 15); the individual soul is spoken of in the remote passage, "Well, O Gautama, I shall tell you of this secret, eternal Brahman, and also how the soul fares after death. Some souls enter the womb for acquiring bodies, and others follow the motionless, in accordance with their works and in conformity with their knowledge" (Ka. II. ii. 6–7); and Brahman is spoken of elaborately in the text starting with, "The intelligent Self is neither born nor does It die" (Ka. I. ii. 18). But there is no such question about Pradhāna; and since it has not been asked for, it has no need to be presented.

To this the *opponent* says: Is the same Self that is inquired about in the question, "The doubt that arises consequent on the death of a man, some saying, 'It exists', others saying, 'It does not exist'" (Ka. I. i. 20), again alluded to in, "Tell me of that thing which you see as different from virtue, different from vice" etc. (Ka. I. ii. 14), or is a fresh question raised here that is different from the earlier one?

What are you driving at?

Should you say that the earlier question itself is alluded to, then there will be only two questions relating to Fire and the Self, the two questions about the Self having coalesced. Hence it cannot be said that only three questions have been put. If, however, it is maintained that a fresh question has been raised here, then just as there is no harm in fancying any question outside the boons granted, so also there can be no harm in thinking that Pradhāna is presented irrespective of any relevant question.

Vedāntin: With regard to this it is said: We do not, in that sense, imagine here (in Ka. I. ii. 14) any question outside the boons offered, for we are backed by the way the topic is started. It is noticeable that the course of the whole narration in the form of a talk between Death and Naciketas, as presented by the Kaṭha Upaniṣad, has for its starting point the offer of the boons. Death granted three boons to Naciketas who had been dismissed by his father. Naciketas on his part, asked for his father's mental composure through the first boon. Through the second boon he prayed for the knowledge of Fire. Through the third, he asked for the knowledge of the Self thus: "The doubt that arises consequent on the death of a man" etc. (Ka. I. i. 20). That this is the third boon is known from the indicative sign, "Of all the boons, this one is the third" (ibid.). Now if a fresh question is raised in, "... different from virtue" etc. (Ka. I. ii. 14), then the unity of purport (or consistency of the text) will be marred by the imagination of something outside the boons offered.

Opponent: Since the subject-matter of the question is different, the question itself must be new. The earlier question was about the individual soul, for therein was mentioned a doubt about existence and non-existence in the words, "The doubt that arises consequent on the death of a man" etc. Besides, the individual soul is within the range of virtue etc., so that it cannot be the subject of the question, "... different from virtue" etc. But the intelligent Self can be the subject-matter of the question, "... different from virtue" etc., that Self being beyond virtue etc. The modes of the questions are also noticed to be dissimilar; for the earlier question relates to existence and non-existence, whereas the latter relates to something beyond virtue etc. Hence from the absence of a recognition of identity, it follows that the questions are different, and that it is not a fact that the earlier subject-matter is reverted to in the latter.

Vedāntin: No, for it is admitted that the individual soul and the intelligent Self are one. Had the individual soul been different from the intelligent Self, then the question could have been different owing to a difference of subject-matter. But the difference is non-existent according to other Upaniṣadic texts, as for instance, "That thou art" (Ch. VI. viii. 7). And here also the answer to the question, "... different from virtue" etc., is "The intelligent Self is never born, nor does It die" (Ka. I. ii. 18), which, through a denial of birth and death, reveals the identity of the embodied soul and the supreme Lord; and this is the fact that is sought to be established. A denial is appropriate when a certain possibility is under discussion. And that possibility is the birth and death that can occur to the embodied soul owing to its association with the body, but not to the supreme Lord. Similarly the text, "Having realized that great and all-pervading Self, with the help of which a man perceives the objects in both the sleeping and waking states, a wise man does not grieve" (Ka. II. i. 4), shows that one becomes freed from sorrow by contemplating on the greatness and pervasiveness of that very individual soul which witnesses the states of sleep and wakefulness; and there it refuses to show that the individual soul is different from the conscious Self. For it is the conclusion of the Upaniṣads that sorrow ends after the realization of the conscious Self. Similarly, a little later it is said, "What indeed is here is there; what is there is here likewise. He who sees as though there is difference here goes from death to death" (Ka. II. i. 10), which repudiates the idea of difference between the individual soul and the conscious Self. Similarly, after the question regarding the existence or non-existence of the individual soul, Death goes on tempting Naciketas by offering various desirable things, as stated in the verses commencing with, "O Naciketas, ask for some other boon" (Ka. I. i. 21). But when Naciketas remains unmoved even under the temptation, Death shows to him the division between worldly prosperity and liberation as also the division between enlightenment and unenlightenment. After that he praises Naciketas by saying, "I consider Naciketas to be an aspirant for knowledge, since the covetable things, multifarious though they are, did not tempt you" (Ka. I. ii. 4). Then praising his question also, Death says, "The intelligent man gives up happiness and sorrow by developing concentration of mind on the Self and thereby meditating on the old Deity who is inscrutable, lodged inaccessibly, located in the intellect, and seated in the midst of (the body and senses which are a source of) misery" (Ka. I. ii. 12). From this also it becomes obvious that what is sought to be spoken of here is the non-difference of the individual soul and the conscious Self. If Naciketas had discarded the question for which he earned the high encomium of Death, and raised another question just after that appreciation, then all that praise would have been misplaced. Accordingly, "... different from virtue" etc. (Ka. I. ii. 14) only reiterates the question asked in, "The doubt that arises consequent on the death of a man" (Ka. I. i. 20). As for the assertion that the modes of the questions are different, that creates no difficulty; for the details about the earlier question are asked. The existence of the soul in dissociation from the body was inquired into earlier, and of that very soul the state beyond birth and death is inquired into later on. For as long as ignorance does not vanish, so long there can be no going out of the range of virtue etc. and no cessation of the individuality of the soul. When this ignorance is removed, the individual soul is revealed to be nothing but the conscious Self in the text, "That thou art" (Ch. VI. viii. 7). The thing itself is not affected in any way by the existence, continuance, or elimination of ignorance. For instance, somebody mistaking a piece of rope lying in deep darkness to be a snake may run away from it, shaking with fear, and some one else may tell him, "Do not be afraid; this is not a snake, but simply a piece of rope." Then on hearing this, the former gives up the fear of the snake as well as his shaking and retreat. But neither during the continuance of the idea of the snake, nor when it leaves, is the thing itself affected in any way. So also are we to understand here. From this it follows that the text, "The intelligent Self is neither born, nor does It die" (Ka. I. ii. 18), and the succeeding texts stand as an answer to the question about the existence and non-existence (of the soul). But the aphorism is to be construed from the standpoint of a fancied difference between the individual soul and the intelligent Self; for though the question is the same, still the earlier portion of the text can be imagined to be concerned with the individual soul, because the question about the Self during the state of departure from the body involves a doubt regarding merely the existence of the soul distinct from the body, and because its mundane aspect of being the agent of activity etc. still persists (in the questioner's mind). But the later portion of the text relates to the conscious Self, since in it are described non-association with virtue etc. From this it is quite justifiable to think of Fire, the individual soul, and the supreme Self (as the subject-matters of the questions). But on the supposition of Pradhāna, we can find no offering of boon, no question, and no answer. This is the difference.

महद्वच्च ॥७॥

7. *And like mahat (avyakta does not signify any Sāṁkhya category).*

The word *mahat* is used by the Sāṁkhyas to mean Pradhāna's first evolved effect (viz intellect), which is endowed with a predominance of the quality of *sattva* (light, transparence, pure intelligence, etc.). But that meaning is not in evidence in Vedic uses, because the word *ātmā* (Self) is seen to be used (along with it) in such texts as, "The *mahān ātmā* (great soul) is higher than the intellect" (Ka. I. iii. 10); and also because of such texts as, "Having meditated on the *ātmā* as *mahān* (great) and pervasive, the wise man does not grieve" (Ka. I. ii. 22);[5] "I know this *mahān* (great) Puruṣa beyond darkness"[6] (Śv. III. 8). Just as *mahat* does not signify the pure intellect of the Sāṁkhyas (in Vedic literature), so also the word *avyakta* cannot mean *Pradhāna* in Vedic uses. For this reason also the inferred *Pradhāna* has no Vedic authority.

[5] This freedom from grief does not fit in with thoughts on *mahat*.
[6] This transcendence of ignorance is not possible for *mahat*.

Topic 2: The Bowl

चमसवदविशेषात् ॥८॥

चमसवत् As in the case of the bowl अविशेषात् special characteristics not having been stated.

8. (The word ajā does not refer to Pradhāna), because special characteristics have not been stated as in the case of the bowl.

Opponent: The believer in Pradhāna makes the rejoinder that Pradhāna is not un-Vedic.

Why?

Because of the *mantra* text: "One *aja* (lit. birthless entity) while enjoying the *ajā* (feminine of *aja*), lies by the side of that *ajā* which has the variegated hues of red, white, and black, and which gives birth to many creatures akin to itself. But another *aja* discards her after enjoyment" (Śv. IV. 5). In this *mantra* the qualities of *rajas* (activity), *sattva* (intelligence), and *tamas* (inertia) are indicated by the words "red, white, and black". The red is *rajas*, since it attracts; the white is *sattva*, since it is of the nature of light; and the black is *tamas*, for it hides. The state of their balance (i.e. Pradhāna) is expressed through the qualities of the constituents—red, white, and black. The word *ajā* is derived in the sense of one that has no birth, for it is declared, "Primordial Nature is changeless" (Sā. Kā. 3).

Objection: Does not the word *ajā* conventionally mean a she-goat?

Opponent: True, but that conventional meaning cannot be subscribed to here, since it is a context of philosophy. That Nature does produce many creatures, endowed with the three qualities of *sattva, rajas,* and *tamas*. "One *aja*", that is to say, a *puruṣa* (conscious soul), while enjoying or while being delighted by that Nature, "lies by her side", accepts that Nature as identical with itself through ignorance, and transmigrates by becoming deluded by ideas of "I am happy, I am unhappy, I am unenlightened" etc., owing to its non-discrimination. "Another *aja*", again, that is to say, another *puruṣa* whose power of discrimination has been aroused, becomes detached, and he discards this Nature after having enjoyed her, gives her up when she has accomplished her task of furnishing experience and liberation; that is to say, he becomes free. Thus the postulation of Pradhāna etc. by the followers of Kapila has a Vedic basis to be sure.

Vedāntin: This being the position, we say: It is not possible to find out a Vedic basis for the Sāṁkhya theory by a reliance on this *mantra*; for this *mantra*, in its isolation from the context, cannot lend support to any theory. Inasmuch as primordial Nature (*ajā*) etc. can be established anywhere through some sort of manipulation, there is no special reason for emphasizing the fact that the theory of the Sāṁkhyas alone is presented here. This is just as in the case of the bowl. To explain: As in the text, "There is a bowl that opens out at the bottom and bulges at the top" (Bṛ. II. ii. 3), the bowl cannot be independently and definitely identified with any kind of bowl by name, for the fancying of an opening below etc. can be somehow applied to all kinds of things, similarly here also, this *mantra*, "one *aja*, while enjoying" etc. mentions no specific characteristic. And so it cannot be categorically asserted that Pradhāna alone is meant by the word *ajā* in this *mantra*.

Opponent: But in that text (Bṛ. II. ii. 3) a particular type of bowl is understood from the complementary portion: "The 'bowl that opens out at the bottom and bulges at the top' is this head of ours, for it is a bowl that has its opening below and bulges at the top" (ibid.). But in what sense is this *ajā* to be understood here?

Vedāntin: In answer to this we say:

ज्योतिरुपक्रमा तु तथा ह्यधीयत एके ॥९॥

तु Certainly ज्योतिः-उपक्रमा (the source consists of) those counting from fire हि for तथा so एके some अधीयते read (of them).

9. The ajā certainly consists of the elements counting from fire, for some read of them as such.

By this *ajā* is to be understood the material source of the four classes of beings.[7] It sprang from the supreme Lord, and it

[7] Born of eggs, moisture, uterus, and earth.

consists of the elements counting from fire, viz fire, water, and food (i.e. earth). The word *tu* (lit. but) is used to imply emphasis, (the meaning being), this *ajā* is to be understood as consisting of the three elements, and not as constituted by the three attributes (of *sattva*, *rajas*, and *tamas*).

Why so?

For the followers of a certain Vedic recension read of the origin of fire, water, and food from the supreme Lord and then read of their colours as red etc.: "That red colour that the (gross) fire has is the colour of the (unmixed element) light; that which is the white colour (in the gross fire) is the colour of (unmixed) water; that which is the black colour (in the gross fire) is the colour of (unmixed) food" (Ch. VI. iv. 1). Those very fire, water, and food are found identically here as well, because of the common words "red" etc., and because the words "red" etc. primarily imply particular types of colour, and only figuratively imply the constituents of Pradhāna. And they consider that an ambiguous passage should be understood with the help of something unambiguous. So also here (in the Śvetāśvatara Upaniṣad we read): "The teachers of Brahman say, 'Is Brahman the cause (of the universe)?' " Making the start with this, it is said, "They (the teachers of Brahman) entered into Brahman through the Yoga of meditation, saw the hidden power, existing identified with the Deity Himself and remaining hidden (i.e. superimposed on Brahman) together with its (three) constituents" (I. 1–3). Thus it is the power of the supreme Lord which creates this universe that we come across here in the very beginning of the text. Towards the end of the topic also that very power is met with in the text, "Know Māyā to be Nature (material cause), and the master of Māyā to be the great Lord" (Śv. IV. 10), and "He who, though one, presides over every source[8] (i.e. the power of ignorance)" (Śv. IV. 11). Hence it cannot be asserted that the *mantra* about the *ajā* presents any independent Nature (material cause), called Pradhāna. From the trend of the context it is held by us that

[8] Māyā, though one, has parts, constituting the limiting adjuncts of individuals. This Māyā is not Pradhāna, for Māyā has only one ruler, God; but the Sāṁkhyas believe in many *puruṣas* (souls).

this very divine power in which names and forms remain undifferentiated and which is the latent form of names and forms, is mentioned by this *mantra* (Śv. IV. 5) as well. But that power is spoken of as having a triple form, just because its products have a triple form.

Opponent: How again from the three characteristics of fire, water, and food can we arrive at the *ajā* (she-goat) which is different in form? For the shape of the *ajā* (she-goat) is not present in fire, water, and food. Again, since the Upaniṣad mentions the birth of fire, water, and food, the word *ajā* (in the sense of birthless) cannot apply to them just because of birthlessness.

Vedāntin: Hence the answer is being given:

कल्पनोपदेशाच्च मध्वादिवदविरोधः ॥१०॥

च And कल्पना-उपदेशात् since that is an instruction in the form of an imagery मधु-आदि-वत् as in the case of honey etc., अविरोध: there is no contradiction.

10. And since this is an instruction in the form of an imagery, just as in the case of honey etc., therefore there is no incongruity.

The word *ajā* is not used from the point of view of the form of a she-goat (*ajā*), nor is it used in the derivative sense (of that which is unborn).

How is it used then?

"This is an instruction in the form of an imagery"; the analogy to a she-goat is taught here about the (material) source of all things—moving and immobile—that consists of fire, water, and food. Thus even as in the world, there may perchance be a she-goat (*ajā*), red, white, and black in colour, with kids, many in number and of similar constitution with hers, and some he-goat (*aja*) may lie by her, while some other may discard her after enjoyment, similarly this source of all elements (i.e. Māyā), consisting of fire, water, and food, and having three colours, gives birth to many products that are similar to her. She is enjoyed by the unenlightened knower of the body (i.e. the individual soul) and discarded by the enlightened one. But it is not to be assumed that since one soul lies by her, while another discards, therefore there emerges a real difference among the souls as is upheld by the others (Sāṁkhyas). For this is not an attempt at establishing any difference among the souls; rather this is an attempt at explaining the mechanism of bondage and freedom. This process of bondage and freedom is explained by taking the help of the commonsense difference (among souls). This difference, however, is a creation of limiting adjuncts; and is conjured up by false ignorance. It is not real as is shown in such Upaniṣadic texts as: "The one single Deity lies hidden in all beings. He is all-pervasive and the inmost soul of all" (Śv. VI. 11). This is analogous to honey etc. Just as the sun, which is not honey, is thought of as honey (Ch. III. i); or as the organ of speech which is not a cow, is fancied to be a cow (Bṛ. V. viii); or as heaven and other things, which are not fire, are imagined to be fire (Ch. V. iv-viii; Bṛ. VI. ii. 9); so here also, like these and other similar instances, something (viz Māyā), that is not a she-goat, is thought of to be a she-goat. This is the idea. Therefore it is nothing incongruous to apply the word she-goat to fire, water, and food (i.e. earth).

Topic 3: Statement of Number

न संख्योपसंग्रहादपि नानाभावादतिरेकाच्च ॥११॥

न Not अपि even संख्या-उपसंग्रहात् on the strength of the mention of number, नाना-भावात् because the entities are disparate च and अतिरेकात् there is an excess.

11. Not even on the strength of the mention of number can Pradhāna have Vedic sanction, because the entities are disparate, and they involve an excess.

Though the *mantra*, having a reference to the she-goat, has thus been disposed of, still the *Sāṁkhya* comes forward with another *mantra*. In the *mantra*, "That in which the *pañca pañca-janāḥ* (five of the quintuplet) and space are placed, that very Self I regard as the immortal Brahman. Having known (Brahman),

I am immortal" (Bṛ. IV. iv. 17), we hear of *pañca pañcajanāḥ*. In this phrase one number five is heard of in connection with another number five; for the word five is used twice. So these quintuplets taken five times make up twenty-five. And the number of things that can be enumerated as twenty-five corresponds exactly to the number of the categories mentioned by the Sāṁkhyas, as in, "Primordial Nature is the undifferentiated (category); seven, counting from *mahat*, are both sources (of others) and are (themselves) modifications (of Nature); and sixteen are the evolved products.[9] But *puruṣa* is neither a source nor a modification of it" (*Sāṁkhya-Kārikā*, 3). Since the number twenty-five, known from the Upaniṣad, stands for the twenty-five categories, therefore Pradhāna and the rest come to have Vedic authority again.

Vedāntin: Therefore we say: No hope of Vedic sanction of Pradhāna and the rest should be entertained "even from the mention of number".

Why?

Because the entities are disparate. For these twenty-five (Sāṁkhya) categories are diverse indeed; they do not have five common qualities to form five groups, in which case alone one could have split up the number twenty-five afresh into five divisions of five each. For such numerals as two and the rest are not applied to divergent things that do not display some unifying common factor. If, however, it be maintained that (there is no grouping in that sense), but the mere number twenty-five is indicated here with the help of its component numbers, as for instance a drought continuing for twelve years is described thus: "Indra did not pour rain for five and seven years"; that too is unjustifiable. The weakness of such a view is that one has to resort to an indirect indication. Moreover, the second word *pañca* here combines with *jana* to form the compound word *pañcajanāḥ*, which is known to be a single word from its way

[9] Seven modifications—*mahat* (i.e. intellect), egoism, and five subtle elements (space, air, fire, water, earth); they are both modifications and sources. *Mahat* evolves from Pradhāna and evolves into egoism. The subtle elements evolve from egoism and evolve into gross elements. The sixteen evolved products are the five gross elements and the eleven organs.

of pronunciation according to *Bhāṣika* rules (about pronunciation) with (or without) accent on the last vowel alone. Besides, from another use also, "O oblation, I take you up in honour of the *pañca pañcajanas* (five deities), (so that this body of mine which is like an instrument for the gods and which is the basis of enjoyment here and hereafter may remain unimpaired)" (Tai. Sa. I. vi. 1.2), we know it to be a single word uttered in the same breath and having a single case-ending. Besides, since one five forms a compound word (with *jana*), there can be no such repetition of five (as "five fives").[10] Accordingly, we cannot have two fives (or ten). Nor can be one number five be joined to another number five, for an attributive word cannot take another adjective.[11]

Opponent: May it not be that the word *janāḥ* (entities), with the number five already construed with it, is qualified again by the number five, so that *janāḥ* can appear as twenty-five in number, just as it is in the case of *pañca pañcapūlyaḥ*, where twenty-five pieces of grass are understood.[12]

Vedāntin: We say, no. The term *pañcapūlī*, being an instance of a compound term signifying a group (i.e. a bundle of five pieces of grass), the curiosity arises about a qualifying numeral: "How many bundles?" And hence we get a phrase, "five of the bundles of five grass pieces (each)". But here, in the very use, *pañcajanāḥ* (five entities), (which is not a *samāhāra-dvigu*),[13] the qualifying numeral (five) being already present, no curiosity

[10] the *pañca* of *pañcajanāḥ* cannot be detached to be construed separately with *pañca* (five) to make twenty-five.

[11] Even if *pañcajanāḥ* be not a compound word, so that its *pañca* can be treated separately, still one *pañca* cannot qualify the other *pañca*, since both are numerals qualifying *janāḥ*. Even if the two fives are construed with *janāḥ* we get only ten *janāḥ*.

[12] *Pañcajanāḥ* is not a compound. But five is not connected with another five directly, nor are both fives construed separately with *janāḥ*. One five is first joined to *janāḥ*, and this phrase is then qualified by another five, thus making 25 *janāḥ*.

[13] In *pañcapūlī* we have the *samāhāra-dvigu* compound (with a numeral in the first part); and so *ī* is added at the end (Pā. Sū. II. i. 52, IV. i. 21). But in *pañcajanāḥ* there is no *ī* at the end, which fact clearly shows that it is not a *dvigu* compound.

about any numerical determination arises; and hence *pañca pañcajanaḥ* cannot be a numerical determination. If *pañca* be still a numeral adjective, (the first) five will qualify the second five (and not *janāḥ*).[14] The consequent defect (that one adjective cannot qualify another) has already been pointed out.

"And since they involve an excess", the twenty-five categories are not meant; for the number twenty-five is exceeded by the Self and space (which would make the number twenty-seven). Of these two, the Self is here mentioned as the receptacle holding others; for the entity indicated by the locative case in *yasmin* (in which) is referred back as the Self in, "that very Self I regard"[15] (Bṛ. IV. iv. 17). The Self is the conscious Puruṣa (all-pervasive entity). Since that Puruṣa is already included (by the Sāṁkhyas) among the twenty-five (categories), that Puruṣa cannot be both the container and thing contained. Again, if the Self be taken in some other sense, the number of categories will still be exceeded. This militates against the Sāṁkhya theory. Similarly, it is not proper to enumerate space separately by saying, "and space is placed", it having been already included in the twenty-five (categories). If some other meaning be given to it, the accruing defect has been pointed out already. Why, again, from hearing the mere number twenty-five should one jump to the twenty-five categories that are not talked of? For the word *jana* does not conventionally mean a (Sāṁkhya) category, and the number can be justified in some other sense as well.

Opponent: How would you then explain, *pañca pañcajanāḥ*?

The *answer* is: According to the special rule of grammar, "Words denoting direction (or quarter) and number are combined with nouns to form terminologies"[16] (Pā. Sū. II. i. 50), the word *pañca* is combined with *jana* to give rise to a technical term. So some beings, called *pañcajanāḥ* are meant in a conventional sense, and not the categories of the Sāṁkhyas. When the

[14] For as shown, *janāḥ* has its own numeral adjective.

[15] "That in which the five of the quintuplet and space are placed, that very Self I regard as the immortal Brahman."

[16] *Dakṣiṇāgni* (lit. the south-fire, i.e. the fire having that name), *Saptarṣis* (i.e. a group of seven well-known sages, who are also conceived of as the seven stars of the Great Bear).

curiosity arises to know how many they are, the word five is added again to it. There are some entities (conventionally) called a quintuplet (*pañcajanāḥ*), and they are five in number. This is just as one might say, "The *saptarṣis*[17] (seven-ṛṣis) are seven".

Who, again, constitute that quintuplet?

That is being answered:

प्राणादयो वाक्यशेषात् ॥१२॥

प्राण-आदय: The vital force and the rest वाक्य-शेषात् from the complementary passage.

12. The vital force and the rest (are the pañcajanāḥ), (as is known) from the complementary passage.

In the verse, following "That in which five of the quintuplet" etc. (Bṛ. IV. iv. 17), the five entities—vital force and the rest—are enumerated for the sake of ascertaining the nature of Brahman: "Those who have known the Vital Force of the vital force, the Eye of the eye, the Ear of the ear, the Food of food and the Mind of the mind, (have realized the ancient, primordial Brahman)" (Bṛ. mādhyandina recension IV. iv. 21). On account of proximity, the ones enumerated in the complementary passage are meant by the quintuplet.

Opponent: How, again, can the word *jana* (lit. person) be used with regard to the vital force and the rest?

Vedāntin: How can it either be used with regard to the Sāmkhya categories? Since either of the two interpretations involves a transgression of common usage, the vital force etc. must be accepted on the strength of the complementary passage. And the vital force etc. become fit to be referred to by the word *jana* (person) by virtue of their association with a synonym of *jana* (viz *puruṣa*). Moreover, the word *puruṣa*, which is a synonym of *jana*, is used to denote the vital force etc. in, "These are in fact the five persons of Brahman (*Brahmapuruṣāḥ*)" (Ch.

[17] Which does not mean seven times seven, or forty-nine *ṛṣis*, but simply seven *ṛṣis* constituting the group called *Saptarṣis*.

III. xiii. 6). There is also the *brāhmaṇa* text, "The vital force is the father, the vital force is the mother" (Ch. VII. xv. 1). Besides, on the strength of the formation of the compound, the whole phrase can well be a conventional term without any contradiction.

Opponent: How can a conventional sense be accepted in the absence of earlier usage?

Vedāntin: The answer is: It can be so as in the case of the words *udbhid* etc. When a word with an unfamiliar import is used in the proximity of words of familiar meaning, its meaning is determined by that association itself, as in, "One (desiring animals) should endeavour to acquire the desired result by sacrificing 'through *udbhid*'[18]", "He splits the sacrificial stake[19]", "He prepares an altar[20]". Similarly, this word *pañcajanāḥ*, being understood on the strength of the formation of the compound to stand for the name of something, raises an inquiry about the thing it names, and thereby it points to the vital force etc. occurring in the complementary passage.

Some explain that the *pañcajanas* are the gods, manes, *Gandharvas*, devils, and demons, while others accept the four castes with the *Niṣādas* (i.e. Brāhmaṇa's sons by Śūdra wives) as the fifth. In some places, again, the word *pañcajanāḥ* is found in the sense of creatures, as in, "(It is but proper) that assuming the form of a human being, born of the *pañcajanāḥ* (i.e. creatures), He created calls for the invocation of Indra" (Ṛ. V. VIII. liii. 7). No incongruity arises even if we accept any of these senses. But when the teacher Vyāsa says, "The vital force and the rest are the *pañcajanāḥ* as is known from the complementary passage", he wants to show that the twenty-five categories are not to be understood here.

[18] Though *udbhid* may mean other things in other contexts, the association, obvious in "by sacrificing", points out that it is the name of the sacrifice itself.

[19] From association with "splitting", the word "stake" here means some timber fit to be shaped into a stake.

[20] "Altar" here means not the finished altar, but some sacrificial place yet to be sanctified, which meaning follows from its association with the word "prepares".

Opponent: The vital force and the rest can be the *pañcajanāḥ* for the followers of the Mādhyandina recension who read of food along with the vital force etc. But how will the followers of the Kāṇva recension get their *pañcajanāḥ*, who do not read of food in their enumeration of the vital force etc.?

Hence the answer is being given (by the *Vedāntin*):

ज्योतिषैकेषामसत्यन्ने ॥१३॥

(The number is filled up) ज्योतिषा by light एकेषाम् for some अन्ने असति when food is not present.

13. For the followers of some recension, the number five has to be made up with light in the absence of food.

Although the followers of the Kāṇva recension miss food, their quintuplet is made up of light (fire), for in the verse, "Upon that immortal Light of all lights the gods meditate as longevity" (Bṛ. IV. iv. 16), which precedes the verse, "That in which the five *pañcajanāḥ*" etc., they read of light for the very purpose of determining the nature of Brahman.

Opponent: How, again, can this light, read of equally in both the recensions, be accepted for some but not for others as having been referred to by the number five, occurring in the same verse?

The answer (of the *Vedāntin*) is being given by saying that this is owing to a difference in necessity. In the case of the Mādhyandinas, the quintuplet consists of the vital force and the rest. They being all present in the same verse, there is no need to turn to light occurring in another verse. But since in the case of the Kāṇvas, these are not so present, the need arises for taking the help of light. And although the *mantra* about the light is the same, light is accepted or not according to the difference of need. This is just like the acceptance or non-acceptance of (the sacrificial vessel called) Ṣoḍaśin, on the basis of a difference of injunction, although the Atirātra sacrifice (in which the vessel is used) is the same.[21]

[21] The opponent may say that in Atirātra we are concerned with action, where alternatives are admissible, but not so when the knowledge of

Thus, in any case, there is no familiar mention (i.e. sanction) of Pradhāna in the Upaniṣads. As for familiarity through Smṛti and reasoning, that will be repudiated in future.

TOPIC 4: CAUSALITY

कारणत्वेन चाकाशादिषु यथाव्यपदिष्टोक्तेः ॥१४॥

च And कारणत्वेन as the cause आकाशादिषु in respect of space and the rest, यथा-व्यपदिष्ट-उक्तेः It having been spoken of in all the Upaniṣads as in any one.

14. (Brahman is presented by all the Upaniṣads); for as the cause of space and the rest, Brahman is spoken of in all the Upaniṣads just as It is in any one of them.

Opponent: The characteristics of Brahman have been shown (B. S. I. i. 2); and the uniformity of knowledge of Brahman in all the Upaniṣads has also been proved (I. i. 10). Moreover, it has been established that Pradhāna is not mentioned by the Upaniṣads (I. iv. 1). Now in that connection another objection is being raised. It cannot be proved either that Brahman is the cause of the universe or that the texts of the Upaniṣads lead to an identical knowledge of Brahman.

Why?

On account of the divergence that comes to view. The creation in every Upaniṣad seems to be divergent, owing to the difference in the order etc. (of creation). For instance, at one place creation is described as starting with space: "From the Self emerged space" (Tai. II. i). At some place it starts with light: "That Existence (Brahman) created light" (Ch. VI. ii. 3). At another place, creation has the vital force at its head: "He created the vital force; and from the vital force He created faith" (Pr. VI. 4). At still another place the emergence of the worlds is recounted irrespective of any order: "He created these worlds—heaven, interspace, the earth, the nether world" (Ai. I.

things is concerned. The answer will be that here also we are concerned with the act of meditation, in which Brahman becomes an object, thought of as the abode of five things, viz *Prāṇa* etc. and either food or light.

i. 2). Similarly at some places we read of creation starting from non-existence. "In the beginning all this was but non-existence. From that sprang existence" (Tai. II. vii), and "This was but non-existence in the beginning. That became existence. That became ready to be manifest"[22] (Ch. III. xix. 1). At some places the theory of creation from nothing is refuted, and creation from existence is asserted. For instance, starting with, "With regard to that some say that the universe was non-existence before creation", it is stated, " 'But how can this be so, O amiable one?' he said, 'How can existence emerge out of non-existence? This was but existence, to be sure, in the beginning' " (Ch. VI. ii. 1–2). The evolution of the universe is stated at some places to be spontaneous: "In the beginning this was undifferentiated. That became differentiated into name and form only" (Bṛ. I. iv. 7). Thus since there are many such opposing ideas, and since a thing in itself is not paradoxical, it is not proper to hold that the Upaniṣads are concerned with any definite ascertainment of the cause of the universe. But in consonance with the theory, well recognized by the Smṛtis and reasoning, it is proper to accept some other thing as the cause.

Vedāntin: Under such circumstances we say: Although the Upaniṣads are individually at variance in the matter of the order of creation etc. of space and other things, they have no difference as regards the Creator.

How?

Because all the other Upaniṣads declare just what any one of them does. In the very same way that the omniscient, omnipotent, omnipresent, the One without a second is declared in any one of the Upaniṣads as the cause, so in that very way is that One declared in the other Upaniṣads. Take for instance the text: "Brahman is Truth, Knowledge, Infinite" (Tai. II. i). By

[22] The Vedāntic interpretation of these two texts are: (1) This universe of name and form did not exist as such before its manifestation; it remained in a causal state without the differentiation of name and form. From that state emerged the gross universe as we see it. (2) The universe remained identified with Brahman before creation. In that causal state came a stir, as it were; and then from that emerged a sprout, as it were, the very first subtle state of creation.

the use of the term knowledge in this text and by speaking of "wishing" by It in a subsequent passage (Tai. II. vi), Brahman is ascertained as Consciousness; and God is spoken of as the cause by virtue of not being dependent on others (ibid.). By using the word Self with regard to Him subsequently, and by placing (The Self) successively inner and inner in a series of sheaths, counting from this body, He is shown to be the inmost Self of all (Tai. II. ii–v). By teaching how the Self became many, in the text, "He wished, let me be many, let me be born" (Tai. II. vi), it is stated that the mutable, created things are non-different from the Creator. Similarly by declaring the creation of the entire universe in the text, "He created all this that exists" (Tai. II. vi), the Upaniṣad asserts that a single Creator without a second existed before creation. The characteristics under which Brahman is known here as the cause, are exactly the same as those under which It is known in other Upaniṣads as well: "In the beginning, O amiable one, all this was but Existence (Brahman)—one without a second" (Ch. VI. ii. 1); "He saw (or deliberated), 'I shall become many, I shall be born'. He created light" (Ch. VI. ii. 3). Similarly, "In the beginning, all this was but the Self—one without a second. Nothing else winked. He saw (or deliberated), 'Let me create the worlds' " (Ai. I. i. 1). In this way (there is no disagreement about the creator) since the texts of this kind, which ascertain the nature of the cause, are not at variance in any one of the Upaniṣads. But difference is noticed in the case of the products —for instance, sometimes creation starts with space, sometimes with light, and so on. But just because there is a difference as regards the products, it cannot be asserted that Brahman is not the intended purport of all the Upaniṣads even though It is known as the cause from all of them without any doubt. For such an assertion will lead to unwarranted conclusions.[23] The teacher (Vyāsa) will reconcile the variations, so far as the products are concerned, under the aphorisms starting with, "Space is not created, as it is not so stated in the Upaniṣads" (II. iii. 1). Or

[23] The *opponent* argues: "The cause must be doubtful, since the effects are so." The *Vedāntin* can say: "Dreams differ and they are false; should then the dreamer also be different and false?"

divergences may well be there in the case of the effects, for they are not the things sought to be taught. Not that all these forms of manifestation, that creation is, are sought to be propounded (by the Upaniṣads); for no human goal is seen or heard of in the Upaniṣads as remaining linked up with them: nor can this be imagined to be so, for in those respective places, they are seen to combine with the texts about Brahman to convey a single unified idea. This is what the Upaniṣad also shows: "O amiable one, with the help of this sprout that food is, search out its root that is water. With the help of this sprout that water is, O amiable one, search out the root that fire is. With the help of this sprout that fire is, O amiable one, search out the root that Existence is" (Ch. VI. viii. 4). Besides, we can understand that when the Upaniṣad speaks of the forms of manifestation etc. in extenso, the intention is to declare the non-difference of the effects from the cause with the help of such illustrations as clay (Ch. VI. i. 4–6). And this is what people versed in the Vedāntic tradition say: "The creation that is taught divergently with the help of clay, iron, sparks, etc. is only a means for inculcating the knowledge of Brahman; but there is no diversity whatsoever" (Mā. Kā. III. 15). But the result associated with the realization of Brahman is heard of in, "The knower of Brahman attains the supreme (Brahman)" (Tai. II. i), "The knower of the Self transcends sorrow" (Ch. VII. i. 3), and "Knowing Him alone one goes beyond death" (Śv. III. 8). And this result is a matter of direct experience, for the transmigratory selfhood ceases on the attainment of the transcendental Selfhood as a result of the instruction, "That thou art"[24] (Ch. VI. viii. 7).

The divergence in the case of the cause that was pointed out by quoting, "In the beginning all this was but non-existence" (Tai. II. vii) etc., has to be reconciled. As to that it is said:

समाकर्षात् ॥१५॥

15. (Non-existence does not mean void), because of its allusion (to Brahman).

[24] This must be a fact realizable by the enlightened ones, for this is

In the text, "In the beginning all this was but non-existence", non-existence, conceived of as void, is not presented as the cause; for the theory of non-existence is repudiated in the verse: "If any one knows Brahman as non-existence, he himself becomes non-existent. If any one knows that Brahman does exist, then they consider him as existing by virtue of that knowledge" (Tai. II. vi. 1). And then this Brahman, which is Existence, is ascertained as the indwelling Self with the help of a succession of sheaths counting from that made of food. Again, after referring to that Brahman under consideration in the text, "He wished" (Tai. II. vi. 1), it is stated that creation in all its ramifications stemmed out of Brahman, and the conclusion is made with, "They call that Brahman Truth" (ibid.). Lastly, by saying, "Pertaining to this, there occurs this verse," (ibid.), the verse, "In the beginning all this was but non-existence" etc. (Tai. II. vii. 1), is quoted in connection with that very subject-matter that is being discussed. If something, non-existent in the sense of a void, be the purport of this (latter) verse, then the whole text will become incoherent as involving the citation of something irrelevant to what is sought to be referred to. Therefore it follows that because the word "existing" is used in common parlance to imply things manifested through names and forms, therefore Brahman which surely existed before creation is mentioned here as though non-existent before creation in a secondary sense owing to this absence of manifestation. This is how the text, "In the beginning this was but non-existence" (Ch. III. xix. 1) has also to be construed, for the same is alluded to later on with the words, "That was Existence" (ibid.). Had absolute void been asserted, what would have been referred to later on by saying, "That was Existence"? And even in the text, "With regard to that some say that this universe was but non-existence before creation" (Ch. VI. ii. 1), the view of "some" people is not presented as having the sanction of some other Upaniṣad; for unlike action, an object is not paradoxical. Accordingly, it is to be understood that the theory of non-

supported by the Upaniṣadic texts, and the result of this realization is confirmed by them.

existence, fancied by the people of dull intellect, is raised and repudiated with a view to strengthening the idea of Existence, accepted by the Upaniṣads. Even in the text, "This universe was then undifferentiated (Bṛ. I. iv. 7), the differentiation (or evolution) of the universe is not spoken of as proceeding without an ordainer; for in the text, "He (the Self) has entered into these bodies up to the tips of the nails" (ibid.), the ordainer is alluded to as having entered into the differentiated products. If the differentiation be understood as having taken place without an ordainer, who would have been alluded to as having entered into the products by the pronoun "He", occurring later on, which can advert only to something already under consideration? And this act of entry into the body is heard of (in the Upaniṣad) about the sentient Self; for in the text, "... when It sees, It is called the eye; when It hears, the ear; and when It thinks, the mind" (ibid.), the Upaniṣad speaks of the consciousness of the entity that has entered. Besides, it can be understood that at the time of the first creation, the universe required some ordainer for its differentiation into names and forms, just as much as even today it has somebody to guide it when differentiating into names and forms (as pot, cloth, etc.). For any fancy that does not agree with observation is illogical. Moreover, another text, "Let me manifest name and form by Myself entering this as this individual soul" (Ch. VI. iii. 2), shows that the universe differentiated under some guidance. And although God was there as the creator, still the use of the object (universe) as the subject of the (intransitive) verb "differentiated" (in "it differentiated into name and form only"—Bṛ. I. iv. 7), is to be understood as pointing to the ease and facility in the act of differentiation, even as one might say, "The field is harvesting well", it being possible for the crop to be harvested well only if there be some peasant to harvest. Or it is to be understood that (it is a transitive) verb used in the passive voice with relation to some subject called up to mind by the trend of the topic, as in "The village is being reached"

Topic 5: Balaki

जगद्वाचित्वात् ॥१६॥

16. Because (the word "work" is) indicative of the universe, (He of whom this is the work must be Brahman).

Doubt: In the course of the conversation between Bālāki and Ajātaśatru in the Kauṣītakī Upaniṣad, it is heard, "He indeed is to be known, O Bālāki, who is in fact the creator (or master) of these *puruṣas* (beings), or rather of whom this is surely the work (IV. 19). With regard to this, the doubt arises: Is it the individual soul that is taught to be known, or the chief vital force, or the supreme Self? What should be the conclusion to be drawn?

Opponent: It must be the vital force.

Why?

Because the Upaniṣadic text is: "He of whom this is surely the work". For work, consisting of movement, is dependent on the vital force; the vital force is met with in the complementary part of the topic: "Then it becomes unified in *Prāṇa* itself" (Kau. IV. 20); and the term *Prāṇa* is familiarly used for the chief vital force. Moreover, the vital force is also the master of the persons (*puruṣas*) referred to by Bālāki in the earlier portion of the sentences: "The being in the sun" (Kau. IV. 3), "The being in the moon" (Kau. IV. 4), and so on. For the deities of the sun etc. are merely different aspects of the vital force as is well known from another Upaniṣad, " 'Which is the one god?' 'The vital force; the vital force is Brahman which is called *Tyat* (That)' " (Bṛ. III. ix.9).

Or it may be the individual being that is taught here as the entity to be known; for his activities, too, constituting virtue and vice, are fit to be mentioned in such words as, "Of whom this is the work" (Kau. IV. 19). He, too, as being the experiencer, can justifiably be the master of all these *puruṣas* who serve as the things of his experience. And in the complementary text also we come across a sign indicative of the individual being; for it is because of this fact that, when Bālāki approached Ajātaśatru to know the creator of the *puruṣas* (in the sun etc.) who had been presented as the entity to be known, Ajātaśatru, being desirous of enlightening Bālāki, called a sleeping man by name;[25] and then from the fact that the man did not heed the call, Ajātaśatru made Bālāki understand that the vital force and the rest are not the experiencer. Lastly, from the fact of waking up as a result of being struck by a stick, he makes him understand that the individual soul, which is different from the vital force and the rest, is the experiencer. Similarly from the subsequent text also can be gathered a sign indicative of the individual soul: "To explain this point: As the head (of a guild) lives on (what is brought by) his own people or retinue, or as his own people or retinue live on him, so also this conscious soul (i.e. the individual) lives on these souls (of the sun etc.), and these souls live on this soul"[26] (Kau. IV. 20). The individual soul can well be called the vital force, for it sustains the vital force. Hence either the individual soul or the vital force is to be accepted here, but not the supreme Lord, for we do not perceive any sign to indicate Him.

Vedāntin: Faced with this, we say: The creator of these *puruṣas* must be the supreme Lord Himself.

How?

On the strength of how the topic is started with. For Bālāki started to talk with Ajātaśatru here with the words: "I shall tell you of Brahman" (Kau. IV. 1); but he became silent after asserting that some persons (*puruṣas*) residing in the sun etc. are fit to be looked upon as Brahman in the primary sense. Ajātaśatru then told him, "Falsely indeed you promised me, 'I shall tell you fully of Brahman' ", and thus he repudiated Bālāki for speaking of those that were Brahman only in a secondary sense. Then the king presented another as the creator of them all and as the entity to be known. Should Ajātaśatru also be a seer of the secondary Brahman, it will run counter to the commencement of the text. Therefore this must be the supreme Lord. And the creatorship of all these persons cannot be thought of as belonging exclusively and independently to any one other than the supreme Lord. The text, "He of whom this is surely the work" (Kau. IV. 19), does not refer either to actions in the

[25] i.e. the synonyms of the vital force—*Bṛhat*, *pāṇḍaravāsa*, *soma*, *rājan*.

[26] The sun etc. give him light etc., and he offers them oblation etc.

form of movements or those constituting virtue and vice; for neither are they under discussion nor are they mentioned by the Upaniṣad by name. Nor are the persons indicated thus (as objects of the verb by the text, "this work"), they having been already mentioned in, "the creator of these persons"[27] (Kau. IV. 19). Besides, that would involve a contradiction in gender and number.[28] Nor is it indicative of some action (i.e. creative function) or of the result of such action pertaining to the persons (undertaken by the creator); for these have already been referred to by the word "creator."[29] As the last resort, the universe that is perceived proximately (or directly) is referred to by the word "this" (occurring in "this work"); and that very universe is referred to by the word "work" in the derivative sense of "that which is accomplished" (i.e. product).

Opponent: Is it not a fact that even the universe is not under discussion, nor is it mentioned by name?

Vedāntin: Quite so. Still from the fact that when there is no specific mention, things in general that lie near at hand[30] become signified by a pronoun that stands for proximate things in general; but it does not mean anything specific, for nothing specific is near at hand. Moreover, the persons (in the sun etc.), forming a part of the universe, had been specifically mentioned earlier, so that it can be understood that the unspecified universe is taken up here. The idea expressed is this: "He who is the creator of these *puruṣas*, constituting a part of the universe, or rather, leaving aside such a specification, He of whom this whole universe, without any specification, is a work". The word "rather" is meant for rejecting the creatorship of a limited portion. But the specific mention (of the *puruṣas*—persons) is made in order to show that the persons spoken of as Brahman by Bālāki are not Brahman. In this way, through general and specific

[27] A second mention is redundant.

[28] For in *etat karma* (this work), *etat* is neuter and singular, whereas *puruṣāḥ* (persons) is plural and masculine.

[29] In the earlier half of the text, "...who is the creator of these *puruṣas*" (Kau. IV. 19), the activity of creation and the result of producing the persons are already mentioned. So "this work", occurring in the second half cannot refer to these.

[30] That occurs to the mind as the object of activity.

statements, on the analogy of "the Brāhmaṇas and mendicants",[31] the creator of the universe is taught as the entity to be known. And the supreme Lord is affirmed as the creator of the whole universe by all the Upaniṣads.

जीवमुख्यप्राणलिंगान्नेति चेत्तद् व्याख्यातम् ॥१७॥

जीव-मुख्यप्राण-लिंगात् Owing to the presence of the indicatory marks of the individual soul, and the chief *Prāṇa*, न not so, इति चेत् if this be the objection, तत् that व्याख्यातम् has been already explained.

17. If it be contended that the supreme Self is not meant, owing to the presence of the indicatory marks of the individual soul and the chief Prāṇa, then that has already been explained.

Opponent: Now then, the argument was advanced that from the indicatory marks of the individual soul and the chief *Prāṇa* (vital force) met with in the complementary portion of the text, either of the two must be accepted, but not the supreme Lord. That has to be answered.

Vedāntin: With regard to this we say: This was repudiated under the aphorism, "(If it be argued that Brahman is not spoken of here, since there are the indications of the individual soul and the chief vital force, then we say), that cannot be so, since this will lead to a threefold meditation. Besides *Prāṇa* is admitted elsewhere as meaning Brahman (owing to the presence of Brahman's characteristics) which are in evidence here" (I i. 31). For on such an assumption, a threefold meditation will crop up here—meditation on the individual soul, on the vital force, and on Brahman. But this is not justifiable; for from a consideration of how the passage starts and ends, it is seen to refer to Brahman. Of these, it has already been shown how Brahman is dealt with at the commencement. And from the mention of the highest result (at the end), the concluding

[31] On the assumption that Brāhmaṇas alone can become mendicants, when some one says, "Feed the Brāhmaṇas and the mendicants", the word Brāhmaṇas is to be understood as meaning all Brāhmaṇas who are not mendicants. So also "work" here implies the creation of all except the *Puruṣas*, they having been mentioned separately.

portion also is seen to point to Brahman thus: "He who knows thus, destroys all the sins and becomes the foremost (in attainment) among all, sovereign (over all), and independent (of all)" (Kau. IV. 20).

Objection: On such a view, the ascertainment of the meaning of this passage is anticipated by the text about the dialogue of Pratardana (under B.S. I. i. 31).

Vedāntin: Not so, for the sentence, "Or rather He of whom this surely is the work", was not ascertained there as pertaining to Brahman. Accordingly, the doubt about the individual soul and the chief vital force that arises here again is set aside over again. Moreover, the word *Prāṇa* is seen to be used in the sense of Brahman: "For, O amiable one, the mind (i.e. soul) is tethered to *Prāṇa* (Brahman)" (Ch. VI. viii. 2). As for the indicatory signs of the individual soul here, they are to be interpreted as used from the standpoint of the identity (of the soul with Brahman), for Brahman is known to be the subject-matter of discussion from the consideration of the beginning and the end.

अन्यार्थं तु जैमिनिः प्रश्नव्याख्यानाभ्यामपि चैवमेके ॥१८॥

तु But जैमिनिः Jaimini (holds): अन्य-अर्थं (the reference to be) for a different purpose, प्रश्न-व्याख्यानाभ्याम् on the strength of the question and the answer; अपि च moreover, एके some people एवम् thus.

18. But Jaimini holds the reference (to the individual soul) to be meant for a different purpose, as is known from the question and the answer. Moreover, some mention this clearly.

Moreover, there need be no dispute here as to whether this text has the individual soul primarily in view or Brahman; for the teacher Jaimini is of opinion that the allusion to the individual soul in this text is meant for a different purpose. viz the comprehension of Brahman.

How?

"On the strength of the question and the explanation." As for the question, it is seen that when it has been demonstrated by waking a sleeping man that the individual soul is distinct from the vital force etc., there occurs another question with regard to something beyond the individual soul: "O Bālāki, where did this person sleep? Or where did he stay thus, and whence did he come thus?" (Kau. IV. 19). The answer also is: "When a sleeping man dreams no more, then he becomes unified with *Prāṇa* Itself" etc., as also, "From this Self the organs move towards their own seats; from the organs issue the presiding deities; from the deities issue the sense-objects" (ibid.). Now it is a settled conclusion of the Upaniṣads that the individual soul becomes unified with the supreme Self in sleep, and that the universe, inclusive of the organs etc., issues from the supreme Self. So it is to be understood that the entity in which this individual being has an absence of particularized knowledge, in which it has its deep sleep, consisting in the absence of the defect of perturbation, in which it has its real nature of freedom from particularized knowledge caused by limiting adjuncts, from which occurs its emergence, consisting in a break in that state—that entity is the supreme Self, taught here as the thing to be known. Besides, in this very context of the conversation between Bālāki and Ajātaśatru, the followers of a certain recension, viz the Vājasaneyins, mention clearly the individual soul by the term "*vijñānamaya*" (identified with the intellect), and then read of the supreme Self, beyond it, in the question, "When this being, identified with the intellect, was thus asleep, where was it, and whence did it thus come?" (Bṛ. II. i. 16). In the answer also they recite: "... and lies in the Space (supreme Self) that is in the heart" (Bṛ. II. i. 17). The word Space is used for the supreme Self, as in "the small Space that is inside it" (Ch. VIII. i. 1). It is to be understood here in the Bṛhadāraṇyaka that when they mention the emanation of the conditioned self from some other entity in the text, "All these selfs emanate" (Bṛ. II. i. 20), they really point to the supreme Self as the source. And the instruction about (the individual soul as) an entity other than the vital force, that is imparted with the help of the act of waking up a sleeping man, is an additional reason ruling out the vital force.

Topic 6: Correlation of Passages

वाक्यान्वयात् ॥१९॥

19. (The Self to be realized, heard of, reflected on, and profoundly meditated upon is the supreme Self), because (this is the meaning gathered) from the correlation of the passages.

Doubt: Starting with: "It is not for the sake of the husband, my dear, that he is loved," it is said, in the *Maitreyī Brāhmaṇa* of the Bṛhadāraṇyaka Upaniṣad, "It is not for the sake of all, my dear, that all is loved, but for one's own sake that all is loved. The Self, my dear Maitreyī, should be realized—should be heard of, reflected on, and profoundly meditated upon. By the realization of the Self, my dear, through hearing, reflection, and profound meditation, all this is known" (II. iv. 5, IV. v. 6). About this the doubt arises: Is it the individual soul, identified with the intellect, that is taught to be realized, heard of, etc. or is it the supreme Self?

Why, again, should there be this doubt?

Since the start is made with the enjoying soul, called up by the suggestive word "loved",[32] it appears that the individual soul identified with the intellect is meant. Again, from the instruction that all is known when the Self is known, it would seem that the supreme Self is meant. What should be the conclusion then?

Opponent: This is an instruction about the individual soul.

Why?

On the strength of the commencement. It is said at the start that this whole universe of enjoyment, consisting of husband, wife, son, and others, is loved for the sake of oneself. In this passage the enjoying soul is presented through the suggestive word love; and then when the seeing (i.e. realization) etc. are taught of the Self, to what other Self (apart from the individual) can this refer? In the middle also it is taught, "... even so, my dear, this great, endless, infinite Reality is but pure intelligence.

[32] Such lovable objects suggest that they have some one, a soul, as their enjoyer.

(The Self) comes out (as a separate entity) from these elements, and (this separateness) is destroyed with them. After attaining (this oneness) it has no more (particularized) consciousness" (Bṛ. II. iv. 12, IV. v. 13), where the "great Reality", which has to be realized, is spoken of as "coming out from the elements" in the form of an individual being identified with the intellect; and thereby it is revealed that it is the individual being (identified with the intellect) that has to be realized. Similarly when the conclusion is made in the text thus: "Through what, my dear, should one know the knower?" (Bṛ. II. iv. 14, IV. v. 15), with a word (viz knower) denoting an agent of knowing, it is shown that the individual soul is taught here. Accordingly, the statement about the knowledge of everything accruing from the knowledge of the Self must be taken in a secondary sense to indicate all the enjoyable things meant for the enjoying soul.[33]

Vedāntin: This being the position, we say: This is an instruction about the supreme Self Itself.

Why?

On the strength of the correlation of this with other passages. When this passage is examined in its proper context, its parts are seen to be linked up with the supreme Self.

How?

That is being shown. Hearing from Yājñavalkya, "But there is no hope of immortality through wealth" (Bṛ. II. iv. 2, IV. v. 3), Maitreyī expresses her desire for instruction about immortality in these words: "What shall I do with that which will not make me immortal? Tell me, sir, of that alone which you know (to be the only means of immortality)" (Bṛ. II. iv. 3, IV. v. 4). Then Yājñavalkya imparts to her the knowledge of the Self. And the texts of the Upaniṣads and Smṛtis declare that there can be no immortality from anything other than the knowledge of the Self. Similarly when it is stated that the knowledge of everything results from the knowledge of the Self, it cannot bear any literal import unless the knowledge of

[33] Since the enjoyer is the master of the enjoyable things, it is said figuratively that all enjoyable things become known when the enjoying soul is known.

the supreme Cause be meant. And we cannot resort to any secondary meaning here, since the assertion is first made that everything is known by knowing the Self, and then it is expounded by saying, "The Brāhmaṇa ousts one who knows him as different from the Self" etc. (Bṛ. II. iv. 6, IV. v. 7). For a false perceiver, who perceives the universe, consisting of Brāhmaṇas, Kṣatriyas, and others, as having emerged into existence independently of the Self, is ousted by that very falsely apprehended universe of Brāhmaṇas, Kṣatriyas, and others. After repudiating the dualistic vision thus, the Upaniṣad broaches the topic of the non-difference of all things from Brahman by saying, "... and this all are this Self" (Bṛ. II. iv. 6, IV. v. 7). Again, that very non-difference is confirmed with the illustration of the drum etc. (Bṛ. II. iv. 7–9, IV. v. 8–10). Besides, when in the text, "... the Ṛg-Veda, (etc.) are like the breath of this infinite Reality" (Bṛ. IV. v. 11), the Upaniṣad states that the Self under consideration is the source of this vast expanse of name, form, and action, it only shows that this Self is nothing but the supreme Self. Again, when with the help of the process of merger in the same thing (Bṛ. IV. v. 12), the Upaniṣad speaks of the Self as the goal of the whole universe of sense-objects, senses, and internal organs, and as without interior and exterior, and wholly a mass of pure intelligence (Bṛ. IV. v. 13), it only shows that this Self is the supreme Self. Therefore it is understood that this instruction about realization etc. is concerned with the supreme Self alone.

The further objection was raised that from the way the start is made with the suggestive word love, the realization etc. that are taught here are of the individual soul. Our reply is:

प्रतिज्ञासिद्धेर्लिंगमाश्मरथ्यः ॥२०॥

प्रतिज्ञा-सिद्धे: Of the fulfilment of the declaration लिंगम् (this is) an indication आश्मरथ्यः (thinks) Āśmarathya.

20. Āśmarathya thinks this (statement of non-difference between the individual soul and supreme Self) to be a sign indicative of the fulfilment of the declaration.

A solemn declaration is made here (in the text under discussion) that all this becomes known when the Self is known (Br. IV. v. 6), as also, "...and all this are the Self" (Bṛ. IV. v. 7). The mention of the Self, called up by the suggestive word love, as an entity to be realized and so on, is a sign indicating the fulfilment of that declaration. Were the individual soul different from the supreme Self, the individual soul would remain unknown even when the supreme Self became realized, so that the promise made that everything becomes known by knowing one would be falsified. Hence the teacher Āśmarathya thinks that it is with a view to fulfilling the declaration that the start is made with the help of the non-different aspects of the supreme Self and the individual Self.[34]

उत्क्रमिष्यत एवम्भावादित्यौडुलोमिः ॥२१॥

एवम् भावात् since such becomes the state उत्क्रमिष्यत: of one who is about to die इति this is what औडुलोमि: Auḍulomi (says).

21. Auḍulomi says that (the statement about the identity of the individual soul and the supreme Self occurs in the beginning) since this state of identity comes to the soul when it departs from the body.

The teacher Auḍulomi thinks that the start is made with the individual soul in a way as though it is identified with the supreme Self, because the individual soul, remaining tainted on account of its association with the aggregate of body, senses, mind, and intellect, becomes serene (and purified) through the practice of knowledge, meditation, etc.; and as such, it can justifiably be united with the supreme Self only after it departs from this assemblage of body etc. In support of this, occurs the Upaniṣadic text, "This serene one (i.e. the individual soul) rises up from this body and realizing the supreme Light becomes established in its true nature" (Ch. VIII. xii. 3). Besides, in some

[34] Both partial difference and partial non-difference exist between the two Selves. To fulfil the declaration, the individual is made the starting point, keeping the eye only on those of its aspects that are non-different from the supreme Self—this is how Āśmarathya thinks.

texts it is shown with the help of the simile of the river, that name and form also rest on the individual soul: "As rivers, flowing down, become indistinguishable on reaching the sea, by giving up their names and forms, so also the illumined soul, having become freed from name and form, reaches the self-effulgent Puruṣa that is higher than the higher (Māyā)" (Mu. III. ii. 8). In keeping with the parallelism between the illustration and the thing illustrated, the meaning of the verse is obviously this: Just as in this world the rivers approach the sea by discarding the names and forms belonging to themselves, so also the individual being approaches the higher Puruṣa by discarding the name and form belonging to itself.

अवस्थितेरिति काशकृत्स्नः ॥२२॥

अवस्थितेः: Owing to the existence (of the supreme Self as the individual Self) इति so says काशकृत्स्नः Kāśakṛtsna.

22. *Kāśakṛtsna thinks (the statement about the identity in the beginning of the text is in order) because of the existence of the supreme Self as the individual soul.*

The teacher Kāśakṛtsna opines that inasmuch as this very supreme Self exists as the individual soul, this commencement with a statement of identity is quite in order. In conformity with this occur such *brāhmaṇa* texts as: "Let me manifest name and form by Myself entering in the form of this individual being" (Ch. VI. iii. 2), and so on, which reveal the existence of the supreme Self as the individual soul. There are *mantra* texts also such as: "(One becomes immortal by knowing) that omniscient Being, who after having created all the forms (i.e. products), and given names to them (has entered into them) and exists there by performing the acts of talking (etc.)" (Tai. Ā. III. xii. 7). While speaking of the creation of light etc. the Upaniṣad does not make any separate mention of the creation of the individual soul, in which case alone the soul could have been different from the supreme Self, it being (in that case) a product of the Self.

The view of the teacher Kāśakṛtsna is that the supreme Lord

Himself appears as the individual soul without undergoing any change. As for Āśmarathya, though the non-difference of the individual soul from the supreme Self is admitted by him, still from his conditional statement, "For the fulfilment of the declaration" etc., it becomes clear that his intention is to posit some sort of relationship as found between a cause and its effects. According to Auḍulomi, both difference and non-difference become clearly discernible as bound up with the different states (of the soul under bondage and freedom). Of these, the view of Kāśakṛtsna is understood to be in accord with the Upaniṣads, for it agrees with the instruction sought to be imparted, as stated in such texts as, "That thou art" (Ch. VI. viii. 7), and from this standpoint, (of non-difference), the attainment of immortality as a result of the knowledge of the Self is quite in order. But if the individual soul be a created thing (as Āśmarathya thinks), then since the modification of a substance loses itself on merging into its material cause, the assertion of the attainment of immortality through knowledge does not become logical.[35] (Just because immortality can result from knowledge only if the difference is imaginary), therefore (contrary to what Auḍulomi thinks) name and form cannot be the natural appendages of the individual soul. Hence also the name and form belong to the limiting adjuncts; but they are stated by way of concession (to common experience) as belonging to the soul. For this very reason, the origin of the individual being, that is sometimes mentioned in the Upaniṣads with the help of the simile of sparks darting out from fire, should be understood as spoken of from the standpoint of the limiting adjuncts alone.

Furthermore, it was argued thus: When it is shown that the "great Reality", that is to be realized and that is under discussion, "comes out from the elements in the form of the individual soul" (Bṛ. II. iv. 12), what is really presented as the entity to be realized is the individual soul. For the refutation of this

[35] An imaginary difference can be removed by knowledge; but the assertion of any real difference rules out that possibility. Besides, the acceptance of origin and annihilation for the soul will militate against the earlier assertion of birthlessness and immortality for it.

argument as well, these three aphorisms are to be interpreted thus: "Āśmarathya thinks this reference to the realization etc. of the Self to be a sign indicative of the fulfilment of the declaration"—the declaration alluded to here being, "Everything becomes known when the Self is known" (Bṛ. II. iv. 5), and "... all this are the Self" (Bṛ. IV. v. 7). This stands proved by reason of all the modes of manifestation of name and form emerging from and merging into the same single entity, and by reason of demonstrating the identity of the cause and effect through the illustration of the drum etc. And the teacher Āśmarathya is of opinion that the statement made about the "coming out of the great Reality from the great elements in the form of the individual soul" is a sign indicative of the fulfilment of the declaration; for the knowledge of one thing can lead to the knowledge of all if there is identity among them. "Auḍulomi says that since this state of identity comes to the soul when it departs from the body"—the teacher Auḍulomi thinks that this statement about identity is made just because an identity with the supreme Self is possible for the individual soul when, after becoming purified through knowledge and meditation, it departs from the body. "Kāśakṛtsna thinks (that this is so) because of the existence of the supreme Self as the individual soul"—the teacher Kāśakṛtsna is of opinion that since it is the very supreme Self that exists in the form of the individual soul, this statement of non-difference is justifiable.

Opponent: The statement—"The Self comes out from these elements and is destroyed with them. After this attainment there is no more consciousness" (Bṛ. II. iv. 12)—being a statement of annihilation, how can this be a declaration of non-difference?

Vedāntin: There is no such difficulty; for this statement about destruction relates to the eradication of particularized knowledge, but not to the annihilation of the soul. For after reverting to the topic with, "Just here you have thrown me into confusion sir," (Bṛ. II. iv. 13), the Upaniṣad itself shows a different meaning in: "Certainly I am not saying anything confusing. This Self is indeed immutable and indestructible, my dear. But there is a dissociation for it from the sense-objects" (Bṛ. IV. v. 14). The idea is this: The individual soul is verily unchanging, eternal, and a mass of homogeneous consciousness; there can be no possibility of its annihilation. But as a result of knowledge, there is a dissociation for it from the *mātrās* comprising the senses and the elements that originate from ignorance. And since from an absence of contact, particularized knowledge arising from that contact cannot exist, it has been said, "After this attainment there is no consciousness".

The further assertion was made that this realization is of the individual Self itself, for in the concluding portion, "Through what, my dear, should one know the knower?" (Bṛ. II. iv. 14), occurs a word (viz knower) suggestive of one who knows. That also is to be refuted with the help of Kāśakṛtsna's view. Moreover, in the text commencing with, "Because when there is duality, as it were, then one sees something" (Bṛ. IV. v. 15), it is stated elaborately that for that selfsame soul there is particularized knowledge when it is within the range of ignorance. And then in the text, starting with, "But when to the knower of Brahman everything has become the Self, then what should one see and through what?" (ibid.), it is shown that for that very soul there is an absence of particularized knowledge like seeing etc. when it is within the ambit of illumination. Then, again, the apprehension is raised that even though there be no other object of knowledge, still one may know the Self; and in answer to this it is said, "Through what, my dear, should one know the knower?" (ibid.). Hence from the fact that the text is devoted to the proving of the absence of particularized knowledge, it can be understood that, though the Self is Consciousness Itself and remains for ever in Its absoluteness, still by keeping in mind how It had appeared (in the state of ignorance), It is referred to by the word *vijñātā* (knower), formed with the suffix *tṛc* and conveying the sense of an agent of the act (of knowing). It was shown earlier that the view of Kāśakṛtsna accords with the Upaniṣads. So the interpretation that should be accepted by all those who follow the Upaniṣads is that the difference between the individual Self and the supreme Self is a creation of conditioning factors like body etc. constituted by name and form which are conjured up by nescience; the difference is not real; for this view is supported by such Upaniṣadic texts as: "O amiable one, in the beginning, all this was but Existence, one without a second" (Ch. VI. ii. 1), "All this is but the Self" (Ch. VII. xxv. 3), "All this is but Brahman" (Mu. II. ii. 11), "...and all this are the Self" (Bṛ. II. iv. 6), "There is no other witness but Him" (Bṛ. III. vii. 23), "There is no other witness but this" (Bṛ. III. viii.). and so on; as also by such Smṛti texts as, "...that all this is Vāsudeva" (Gītā, VII. 9), "O scion of the race of Bharata, know Me also to be the individual witness in all the bodies" (ibid. XIII. 2), "...the Lord Supreme, existng equally in all beings" (ibid. XIII. 27), and so on. Furthermore, the same conclusion follows from the rejection of the dualistic outlook in, "While he who worships another god, thinking, 'He is one and I am another', does not know. He is like an animal to the gods" (Bṛ. I. iv. 10). "He goes from death to death who sees difference, as it were, in It" (Bṛ. IV. iv. 18), and similar other passages. Besides, all changes are denied in the Self by the passage, "The great birthless Self is undecaying, immortal, undying, fearless, and Brahman (infinite)" (Bṛ. IV. iv. 25). For unless this be understood thus, the aspirants for liberation will not have any illumination that defies sublation; nor can any knowledge be gained by them that carries with itself the fullest conviction. For the knowledge about the Self that is sought here is that knowledge alone that is beyond all refutation and sets at rest all questions, as declared by the Upaniṣadic passage, "Those to whom the entity, presented by the Vedic knowledge, has become fully ascertained" (Mu. III. ii. 6), as also, "What delusion and what sorrow can persist there for one who has realized Unity?" (Īś. 7). This follows also from the Smṛti text, setting forth the characteristics of the man of steady wisdom (Gītā, II. 55–72). When the full illumination about the oneness of the Supreme Self and the Self witnessing the body becomes established, such terms as "the witness of the body", "the supreme Self" betrays a mere difference in terminology; and hence this insistence on the theory that this "witness of the body" is different from the supreme Self and the supreme Self is different from the "witness of the body", that centres round the idea of difference of the two Selves, is meaningless. For the Self is but one, though spoken of differently on the basis of difference in mere nomenclature. Not that the text, "Brahman is Truth, Knowledge, Infinite. He who knows that Brahman as existing in the cavity of the intellect" (Tai. II. i), is spoken of in relation to any particular cavity; nor does anything else but Brahman exist in the cavity (of the intellect), since we hear of the entry of the Creator Himself in the text, "Having created that, He entered into that" (Tai. II. vi). Those who insist on difference, shut the door to the understanding of the purport of the Upaniṣads and thereby shut out full illumination itself that leads to liberation. Moreover, they fancy that liberation is a product and impermanent, and they do not conform to logic.

Topic 7: Brahman as Material Cause

प्रकृतिश्च प्रतिज्ञादृष्टान्तानुपरोधात् ॥२३॥

(Brahman is) प्रकृति: the material cause च as well प्रतिज्ञा-दृष्टान्त-अनुपरोधात् so as not to contradict the proposition and the illustration.

23. Brahman must be the material cause as well, so as not to contradict the proposition and the illustration.

Doubt: It has been said that just as virtue and vice are to be deliberated on since this leads to secular well-being, so also Brahman is to be deliberated on since this leads to liberation. And Brahman was defined as "That from which the universe has its birth etc." (I. i. 2). That definition is applicable either to the material cause in the sense in which earth, gold, etc. are the causes of pots, necklaces, etc., or to the efficient cause in the sense in which a potter, a goldsmith, and others are the causes. Therefore the doubt arises: In what, again, does Brahman's causality consist?

Opponent: While under such a predicament, it would appear that It can only be the efficient cause.

Why?

For creatorship, preceded by reflection is heard of. From such Upaniṣadic texts as, "He deliberated" (Pr. VI. 3), "He created the vital force" (Pr. VI. 4), the causality of Brahman is understood to have been preceded by reflection. And creation after reflection is noticed in the cases of efficient causes like the potter and others. It is also seen in the world that success in a work depends on many accessories. That logic should be extended to the first Creator as well. Besides, this follows from the fact of His being well known as the Lord; for efficient causality is alone noticed in the cases of lordly beings like kings, Death, and others. In conformity with this it is but proper to understand efficient causality alone even in the case of the supreme Lord. Besides, this universe, which is a product, is seen to be composite, insentient, and impure; so its material cause, too, must be of the same nature, since the cause and effect are seen to be similar. But Brahman is known to be devoid of such a nature from such texts as, "Without parts, motionless, unchanging, taintless, and free from *tamas*" (Śv. VI. 19). As a last resort, some material cause, other than Brahman, that is well recognized in the Smṛtis and is possessed of the characteristics of impurity etc., has to be admitted; for the Upaniṣads speaking of Brahman as the origin, speak of nothing more than efficient causality.

Vedāntin: This being the position, we say: Brahman has to be admitted as the material cause as well as the efficient cause. It is not merely the efficient cause.

Why?

"So that the proposition and the illustration may not be contradicted." Of these the proposition is: "Now then, did you ask about that subject-matter of instruction by which the unheard becomes heard, the unthought becomes thought, and the unknown becomes known?" (Ch. VI. i. 2), where it is obvious that by knowing one thing all other things, even though unknown, become known. And that knowledge of all things can be possible only from the knowledge of their material cause, since the effect is non-different from its material, whereas the effect is not non-different from its efficient cause, as is evident from the difference noticed in the world between the architect and his architecture. The illustration cited also relates to the material cause, as in, "O amiable one, as by knowing a lump of earth, all things made of earth become known, since earth alone is true and all transformations exist only in name, having speech as their origin (or support)" (Ch. VI. i. 4). Similar also are the illustrations: "All modifications of gold become known by knowing a piece of gold", "All things made of iron become known when a nail-cutter is known" (Ch. VI. i. 5–6). So also it is seen in the other Upaniṣads that the proposition is stated thus: "O adorable sir, (which is that thing) which having been known, all this becomes known?" (Mu. I. i. 3), and the illustration is: "As herbs grow on the earth" (Mu. I. i. 7). Elsewhere, too, the proposition is: "All this, my dear, becomes known when the Self is seen, heard of, reflected on, and meditated upon" (Bṛ. IV. v. 6), and the illustration is: "As when a drum is beaten, one cannot distinguish its various particular notes, but they are included in the general note of the drum or in the general sound produced by different kinds of strokes" (Bṛ. IV. v. 8). In this way, in each Upaniṣad, the proposition and illustration are to be understood, so far as they go, as pointing to the material cause. The phrase, "that from which—*yataḥ*" occurring in, "That from which these beings emerge" (Tai. III. i.), is to be understood as pointing to the material constituting the basic substance, in accordance with the special rule of grammar, "The basic substance of anything that is being born is used in the ablative case (i.e. with the pronoun, from)" (Pā. Sū. I. iv. 30). As for the efficient causality of Brahman, it is to be understood from the absence of any other ordainer. Unlike the basic substances like earth, gold, etc., acting under the control of their moulders—the potter, goldsmith, and others—Brahman, even though It is a basic substance, does not depend on any other ordainer; for it is emphasized that before creation, all this was but one without a second. And it is to be understood that this absence of any other ordainer has to be assumed so that no conflict between the proposition and the illustration may arise. For if any ordainer be admitted apart from the material, it will become impossible again to have a knowledge of all from the knowledge of one, and so the proposition and the illustration will be at variance. Accordingly, the

Self is the ordainer since there is no other designer, and It is also the material cause since there is no other material.

What more reason is there to show that the Self is the agent as well as the material?

अभिध्योपदेशाच्च ॥२४॥

च And अभिध्या-उपदेशात् because of the teaching about the will to create.

24. This is also understood from the teaching about the will to create.

"The teaching about the will to create", also leads to the understanding of the Self as the efficient and material cause: "He wished, 'let me be many, let me be born'" (Tai. II. v. 2), and "It deliberated, 'I shall become many, I shall be born'" (Ch. VI. ii. 3). In those texts the Self is known to be the agent by virtue of independent action proceeding from deliberation. And it is understood that the Self is the material cause as well, since the will to become many as expressed in, "I shall become many", relates to Himself.

साक्षाच्चोभयाम्नानात् ॥२५॥

च And उभय-आम्नानात् both having been taught साक्षात् directly.

25. And because both (origin and dissolution) are taught directly (from Brahman).

This is again in continuation of the material causality. Brahman is the material cause for this further reason that both creation and dissolution are spoken of by accepting Brahman directly as the cause in the text: "All these beings originate from Space (Brahman) alone, and they merge by proceeding towards Space" (Ch. I. ix. 1). It is recognized that anything from which something originates and in which it merges, must be its material cause, as for instance, earth is of paddy, barley, etc. By the word "directly" the aphorist implies that the text, "Originates from Space alone", means that no other material was accepted.

And a product is not seen to be absorbed into anything other than its material cause.

आत्मकृतेः परिणामात् ॥२६॥

आत्म-कृतेः Because of action related to Itself परिणामात् by way of change of form.

26. *(Brahman is the material cause) because of action related to Itself by way of change of form.*

Brahman is the material cause for the further reason that in dealing with the topic of Brahman, it is shown in the text, "That created Itself by Itself" (Tai. II. vii), that the Self is both the object and the subject—"Itself" denoting the object, and "created by Itself" presenting the subject.

Opponent : How, again, can a pre-existing entity, standing there as the agent (of some action), be reduced to an object that is being produced?

Vedāntin : We say that this can be so by way of change of form, the idea being that the Self, pre-established though It is, changed Itself into a special form as the Self of the modifications; and particular changes into modified things are in evidence in the cases of such material causes as earth etc. The use of the qualifying phrase "by itself" indicates that there was no dependence on any other cause. (Or the second word) *pariṇāmāt* may be an independent aphorism, the meaning being this: Brahman is not the material cause for this further reason that this modification of Brahman Itself into created things is mentioned in the Upaniṣad by using the same case-ending after Brahman in, "It became the (elements)—gross (earth, water, fire) and subtle (air, space)" etc. (Tai. II. iii).

योनिश्च हि गीयते ॥२७॥

च And हि because योनिः as the source गीयते is declared.

27. *And because Brahman is declared to be the source (yoni).*

Brahman is the material cause for this additional reason:

Brahman is mentioned in the Upaniṣad as the source, as in, "...the creator, lord, indwelling soul, Brahman, the source" (Mu. III. i. 3), and "the source of all beings which the wise perceive" (Mu. I. i. 3). The word *yoni* is understood in the world as signifying the material cause, as in, "The earth is the *yoni* (source) of the herbs and trees". The female organ too (called *yoni*) is a material cause of the foetus by virtue of its constituent (materials). Sometimes the word *yoni* is used in the sense of a place, as in "O Indra, I have placed a *yoni* (seat) for you" (Ṛ. V. I. civ. 1). But in the present texts (of the Upaniṣads), *yoni* is used in the sense of the material cause, which fact becomes clear from such complementary portions as, "As a spider projects and withdraws" (Mu. I. i. 7), and so on. Thus it is a well-known fact that Brahman is the material cause. As for the argument that creation after deliberation is seen in the world only in the cases of such efficient causes as the potter and others, but not in the case of materials, that is being answered. Any argument from common sense is not applicable here; for this is not a truth to be arrived at through inference. Rather, it being known from the Vedas (alone), its meaning should conform to Vedic statements. And we said that the Vedas affirm that the deliberating God is the material cause as well. We shall expound this point again more elaborately.

Topic 8: Explanation of Everything

एतेन सर्वे व्याख्याता व्याख्याताः ॥२८॥

एतेन Hereby सर्व all (theories) व्याख्याताः are explained व्याख्याताः explained.

28. Hereby all (other theories of the cause of the universe) are explained. They are explained.

Starting with, "Because of the attribution of seeing, the one (i. e. Pradhāna of the Sāṁkhyas) which has not been taught by the Upaniṣads is not the cause of the universe" (B. S. I. i. 5), the theory of Pradhāna as the cause was raised and refuted again and again by the aphorisms themselves. This was so, because in the Upaniṣads are found some semblances of indicative signs, which appear in the eyes of the people of dull intellect as reinforcing that theory. Inasmuch as that theory admits the non-difference of the cause and the effect, it approaches very near to the Vedāntic theory, and it has been drawn upon in their own texts by some writers like Devala, who composed aphorisms on injunctions and prohibitions (religious duties etc.). For this reason, a great effort was made for repudiating it, and not so for the repudiation of the theories of the atom etc. as the cause. But they too have to be disproved, since they are opposed to the theory of Brahman as the cause. Some Vedic indications may appear in the eyes of the people of poor intellect as seemingly confirming those views. Hence the same arguments are being extended to them on the analogy of defeating the chief wrestler. "Hereby", by the arguments refuting the theory of Pradhāna as the cause, "all other theories" about the atom etc. as the causes, are also to be understood as "explained", proved to be fit for rejection; for they too are not mentioned in the Vedas, and they too are opposed to the Vedas. The repetition of "explained" is by way of showing the end of this Part.

CHAPTER II

AVIRODHA—NON-CONTRADICTION

SECTION I

TOPIC 1: CONFLICT WITH SMṚTI

In the course of showing how all the Upaniṣadic texts are in agreement in presenting Brahman (as the cause of the universe), it was proved in the First Chapter that the omniscient Lord of all is the source of the origin of the universe, just as clay, gold, etc. are of pots, necklaces, etc.; that by virtue of His being the ordainer of the created universe, like the magician of his magic, He is the cause of the continuance of the universe; that He is the cause of the withdrawal of the manifested universe into Himself, like the earth withdrawing the four kinds of creatures; and that He is the Self of us all. Moreover, the theories that Pradhāna and other things are the causes were demolished on the ground of being un-Vedic. Now the Second Chapter is begun for showing that the Smṛtis and logic are not antagonistic to our own point of view; that the theories of Pradhāna and the rest as the causes are based only on a semblance of logic; and that the processes of creation etc. are not at variance in the different Upaniṣads. Of these the contradiction with the Smṛtis is presented and refuted first.

स्मृत्यनवकाशदोषप्रसङ्ग इति चेन्नान्यस्मृत्यनवकाशदोषप्रसङ्गात् ॥१॥

स्मृति-अनवकाश-दोष-प्रसङ्गः There arises the defect of the (Sāṁkhya) Smṛtis being left without any scope इति चेत् if such be the objection, न not so, अन्य-स्मृति-अनवकाश-दोष-प्रसङ्गात् for (otherwise) arises the defect of other Smṛtis being left without any scope.

1. If it be argued (that from the acceptance of Brahman as the cause of the universe) arises the defect of the (Sāṁkhya)

Smṛtis being left without any scope, then not so, for otherwise will arise the defect of other Smṛtis losing their scope.

Opponent: The assertion made that the omniscient Brahman is the cause of the universe is untenable.

Why?

Because that is tantamount to leaving no scope for the Smṛtis. The Smṛtis are the scriptural text called *Tantra*, written by the great seer (Kapila) and accepted by the good people, and also the other Smṛtis that are in accord with them. These will lose their scope on the acceptance of this view. For in them the insentient Pradhāna is upheld as an independent cause. As for the Smṛtis of Manu and others, they retain their scope in so far as they present the accessories postulated by religious rites and ceremonies like the Agnihotra sacrifice etc., comprised within the domain of injunctions and prohibitions, as for instance, such and such a caste should have the ceremony of investiture with the sacred thread at such a time, in such a manner, and such should be the mode of conduct, such the study of the Vedas, such the returning from the teacher's house after the completion of the study, and such the marriage with a woman who will perform the religious rites conjointly. So also they enjoin many kinds of human objectives and rites and duties of the four castes and four stages of life. But the Smṛtis of Kapila and others have no such preoccupation with things to be performed; for they are composed from the standpoint of the fullest insight leading to liberation. If they are left without scope even there, they will surely become useless. Accordingly, the Upaniṣads have to be explained without contradicting them.

Objection: As it has already been established on the strength of such reasons as "seeing (or reflecting)" that the purport of the Upaniṣads is that the omniscient Brahman is the cause of the universe, why is it again called into question under the apprehension of the defect of the Smṛtis being left without any scope?

An Explanation: This kind of acceptance of Vedānta without any question may be quite possible for people of independent intellect; but people generally depend for their enlightenment on the scriptures written by others. Being unable to comprehend the meaning of the Upaniṣads independently, they will turn to the Smṛtis that have well-known authors, and they will comprehend the meaning of the Upaniṣads with their help; but they will not rely on our explanation, since the authors of the Smṛtis command great respect. Besides, the Smṛtis mention that Kapila and others had the (unobstructed prophetic) vision of seers. And there is the Upaniṣadic text, "(One should realize that God) who saw the seer Kapila emerging out in the beginning of creation and filled him with knowledge after his birth" (Śv. V. 2). Therefore it is not possible to make their view appear false. Moreover, they establish their interpretation with the help of logic. Hence from this point of view also, the Upaniṣads have to be explained with the help of the Smṛtis. Hence this objection is raised again.

Vedāntin: The solution of that difficulty is this: "No, because that will leave other Smṛtis without scope." If by arguing under the fear of some Smṛtis being left without scope, the theory of God as the cause be set at naught, then other Smṛtis speaking of God as the cause will be left without any scope. We shall quote them: After commencing about the supreme Brahman with the words, "That which is that subtle, inscrutable entity", and stating, "for He is called the indwelling Self of all beings, and the witness of the bodies", it is declared, "from that arose, O best among the Brāhmaṇas, the Unmanifested, possessed of the three *guṇas*". Similarly, it is said elsewhere, "O Brāhmaṇa, the Unmanifested gets merged in the attributeless Puruṣa", and "Therefore hear this again in brief: The eternal Nārāyaṇa is all this. At the time of creation, He projects everything, and eats it up again at the time of dissolution." These are statements in the Purāṇas. In the Gītā also occurs this: "I am the origin and dissolution of the whole universe" (VII. 6). And Āpastamba has this with regard to the supreme Self: "All things, counting from space, originate from Him; He is changeless and He is eternal" (*Dharmasūtra*. I. viii. 23.2). Thus in the Smṛtis also, God is revealed in quite a number of places as both the material and efficient cause. The reason for presenting the defect of other Smṛtis being left without scope is this: "With the help of the Smṛtis, we shall meet the arguments of those who take their stand on the Smṛtis." It was shown earlier that the Upaniṣads have for their purport God as the cause. In a case of conflict among the Smṛtis themselves, when it become incumbent to accept some and reject others, the Smṛtis agreeing with the Upaniṣads are to be accepted as valid, while the others are not to be relied on. Thus it has been said in the course of determining the validity of the means of knowledge: "When a Smṛti contradicts a Vedic text, it is not to be relied on (and ought to be rejected); for a Vedic text can be inferred to exist as the basis of a Smṛti passage only when there is no such contradiction" (Jai. Sū. I. iii. 3). And one cannot surmise the possibility of perceiving supersensuous things without the help of the Vedas, for there is no ground for this.

Opponent: It is possible for Kapila and others who have attained perfection in their practices; for their knowledge is unobstructed.

Vedāntin: No, for even perfection is dependent on other things, it being contingent on the practice of virtue etc. And virtue (and vice) are indicated by injunction (and prohibition). Hence the meaning of an injunction, existing even earlier (than anybody's perfection), cannot be overridden on the authority of somebody's words who attains perfection subsequently. Besides, even if it be fancied that we have to rely on the adepts, still in the face of the fact that perfected beings are many, in a case of conflict among their Smṛtis, there is no other means of ascertaining their meanings unless it be by an appeal to the Vedas. And even for people whose intellects are dominated by the scriptures of others, it is not proper to entertain a bias for any particular Smṛti without question. For if anybody has any bias for any point of view, then since the power of understanding differs from man to man, there will be no definiteness in the matter of the ascertainment of Reality. Accordingly, even the intellect of such a man has to be won back to the proper course through a presentation of the conflict among the Smṛtis and a consideration of their agreement or disagreement with the Vedas. As for the allusion to the Upaniṣadic text showing the excellence of the wisdom of Kapila, one cannot on that score put faith on any view of Kapila even when it contradicts the Vedas, because that conclusion has for its basis only a similarity of the name Kapila, and because another Kapila, called Vāsudeva, is mentioned in the Smṛti, who burnt away the sons of Sagara. Moreover, a passage meant for imparting knowledge of one thing cannot prove the existence of something else (mentioned casually), unless the latter has some independent basis.[1] Besides, there is a Vedic text declaring the greatness of Manu: "Whatever has been spoken by Manu is a curative medicine" (Tai. Sa. II. ii. 10.2). And Manu says, "That sacrificer to the Self, who sees his own Self equally in all beings, and all beings in his own Self, attains independent sovereignty" (XII. 91), where we understand that he eulogizes the vision of everything as the Self and thereby condemns the (dualistic) view of Kapila. For Kapila does not approve the realization of everything as the Self, since he admits a multiplicity of souls. The passage, "O Brāhmaṇa, are the souls many or one?" in the Mahābhārata, raises a discussion, the opponent's point of view being stated in "O king, the souls are many according to those who base their discussion on Sāṁkhya and Yoga". Then by way of demolishing that theory, the start is made with the passage, "Just as the same earth is spoken of as the source of many human forms, so also I shall tell you of that cosmic Person endowed with transcendental qualities". And lastly omnipresence itself is established in the passage: "He is my indwelling Self as well as yours; He is the witness of all others who are spoken of as associated with bodies; but He is not perceived by anybody anywhere. All heads are His, all hands are His; all legs, all eyes, all noses are His. He is one, but moves through all beings at His will. He is blissful and free from sorrow". There are also Vedic passages about the Self of all, as for instance, "When (at the time of realization), all beings become the Self of the

[1] The text, "(One should realize that God) who saw the seer Kapila emerging out" etc. (Śv. V. 2), enjoins the realization of the supreme Self, so that the mention of the perception of the omniscience of Kapila is only by way of restating a fact known otherwise. Now, if that fact cannot be proved on some independent ground, the present text, which is a mere reiteration (*Anuvāda*), cannot prove it either.

enlightened man, then (during that state) what sorrow can there be and what delusion to that seer of non-duality?" (Īś. 7). Hence both to the Vedas and the teachings of Manu which follow the Vedas, the scripture of Kapila is antagonistic not only so far as it assumes an independent *Prakṛti* (primordial Nature), but also because of its assumption of a multiplicity of souls. For the Vedas have an independent authority with regard to what they reveal (within their own province), just as much as the sun has with regard to its colour, whereas the authority of any human being is remote, since it depends on some other source of knowledge and since the memory of the speaker intervenes. Hence it is nothing damaging if the Smṛtis are left without any application in matters contradictory to the Vedas.

Why, again, it constitutes no defect to leave the Smṛtis without any scope?

इतरेषां चानुपलब्धेः ॥२॥

च And इतरेषाम् of the others अनुपलब्धः there being no perception.

2. *And (Pradhāna is not the cause) since the others are not met with (in the Vedas and common experience).*

Categories, other than Pradhāna, such as *mahat* and the rest, which are assumed in the Smṛtis as the derivatives of Pradhāna, are not met with either in the Vedas or in common experience. Of these the elements and the senses can have a place in the Smṛtis, since they are well known in the world and the Vedas. But since *mahat* and the rest are unfamiliar, like the objects of a sixth sense, both in the world and the Vedas, they are not fit to be mentioned in the Smṛtis. Even though words appearing to suggest them may occur occasionally in the Vedas, they do not really bear those meanings, as it was explained under the aphorism, "If it be said that even the inferred entity is revealed to the followers of some recension" (I. iv. 1). The idea implied is that, since the reference to the derivatives (*mahat* and the rest) is invalid, the Smṛti referring to the source (Pradhāna) must be equally so. From this point of view also there can be no fault arising from leaving the (Sāṁkhya) Smṛtis without scope. As for the logical validity of the Sāṁkhya view, it will be demolished under the aphorisms commencing with, "Brahman is not the cause of the universe, since the world is of a different nature" (II. i. 4).

Topic 2: Refutation of Yoga

एतेन योगः प्रत्युक्तः ॥३॥

एतेन Hereby योगः Yoga प्रत्युक्तः is refuted.

3. Hereby is refuted Yoga.

The arguments under the last topic are being extended here to another topic by saying that "hereby", by the repudiation of the Sāṁkhya Smṛti, it is to be understood that the Yoga Smṛti is also repudiated. For there also, in contradiction to the Vedas, occurs the assumption of Pradhāna as an independent cause, as also of its derivatives, *mahat* and the rest, though these have no place in common experience or the Vedas.

Opponent: If that be so, all this is already implied in the earlier aphorism. So why is this fresh extension?

Vedāntin: Because an additional doubt does crop up, Yoga having been enjoined in the Vedas as a means to the realization of full illumination, as in, "The Self is to be realized—to be heard of, reflected on, and profoundly meditated upon" (Bṛ. II. iv. 5). Moreover in the Śvetāśvatara Upaniṣad we come across an elaborate injunction about Yoga, comprising the arrangement of seat and the rest, which commences with the verse, "Holding the body in balance, with the three limbs (chest, neck, and head) erect" (II. 8). And thousands of Vedic signs indicative of Yoga are met with, as in, "The holding of the senses and organs unperturbed and under control is called Yoga by the adepts" (Ka. II. iii. 11), "Getting fully this knowledge (of Brahman) and the process of Yoga" (Ka. II. iii. 18), and so on. In the philosophy of Yoga also, it is said, "Now then, starts Yoga which is a means to the realization of Reality", where it is admitted as a means to complete illumination. So a portion of the Yoga Smṛti being acceptable to either side, it cannot be discarded just as much as the Smṛti about the *Aṣṭakā* ceremony cannot be.[2] This additional doubt is also disposed of by extending the application of the previous aphorism. Though there is an agreement in respect of a portion of the subject-matter, still since disagreement is in evidence in respect of others, as shown above, an effort is being made against the Sāṁkhya and Yoga Smṛtis alone, though many Smṛtis dealing with spiritual matters are extant. For the Sāṁkhya and Yoga are well recognized in the world as means for the achievement of the highest human goal (liberation), and they are accepted by the good people and are supported by Vedic indicatory marks, as in, "One becomes freed from all the bondages after realizing the Deity that is the source of these desires and is attained through Sāṁkhya and Yoga". Their refutation centres round only this false claim that liberation can be attained through Sāṁkhya knowledge or the path of Yoga independently of the Vedas. For the Upaniṣads reject the claim that there can be anything apart from the Vedic knowledge of the unity of the Self that can bring about liberation, as is denied in, "By knowing Him alone, one goes beyond death. There is no other path to proceed by" (Śv. III. 8). But the followers of Sāṁkhya and Yoga are dualists, and they do not perceive the unity of the Self.

As for the reference to realization in the quotation, "One becomes freed after realizing the Deity that is the source of all desires and is attained through Sāṁkhya and Yoga" (Śv. VI. 13), the Vedic knowledge and meditation are there referred to by the words Sāṁkhya and Yoga[3], for these latter have an affinity of meaning to the former. This is how it is to be understood. But it is admitted that Sāṁkhya and Yoga have their applica-

[2] *Aṣṭakā*, a kind of obsequial ceremony, is neither mentioned in the Vedas nor prohibited there. So it is inferred that since the Smṛtis are meant for the followers of the Vedas, the Smṛti enjoining the ceremony had its source in some lost Vedic text. Hence it is undertaken accordingly.

[3] Derivatively Sāṁkhya means full knowledge, and Yoga means constant meditation of "I am Brahman", and not mere "Stoppage of mental transformations", as Patañjali says.

tion so far as those features are concerned which are not antagonistic to the Vedas; for instance, the absolute (qualityless) Puruṣa (infinite conscious Entity) that is well known in such Upaniṣadic texts as, "For this infinite Being is unattached" (Bṛ. IV. iii. 15), is accepted by the Sāṁkhyas when they affirm that their *puruṣa* (individual soul) is without any quality. Similarly the followers of Yoga, when instructing about the qualifications of monks etc., subscribe to the path of detachment as it is well known from the Upaniṣadic text, "Then there is the monk with his discoloured (ochre) cloth, shaven head, and non-acceptance of all gifts" (Jābāla, 5).

Thus also are to be refuted all the Smṛtis of the Nyāya-Vaiśeṣika schools.

Opponent: Through inference and supporting reason, they too are conducive to the knowledge of Reality.

Vedāntin: Let them be so conducive. But the knowledge of Reality springs from the Upaniṣadic texts alone, as is stated in such passages as, "One who is not versed in the Vedas cannot reflect on the great Entity" (Tai. Br. III. xii. 9.7). "I ask you of that infinite Being known only from the Upaniṣads" (Bṛ. III. ix. 26).

Topic 3: Difference in Nature

न विलक्षणत्वादस्य तथात्वं च शब्दात् ॥४॥

(Brahman is) न not (the cause), विलक्षणत्वात् owing to the dissimilarity in nature अस्य of this (universe); च and तथात्वं the fact of being so शब्दात् follows from the Vedas.

4. Brahman is not the cause of the universe owing to the dissimilarity in the nature of this universe; and the fact of being so is known from the Vedas.

The objection to the view that Brahman is the material as well as efficient cause of the universe, that was raised from the standpoint of the Smṛtis, has been disposed of. Now is being met the objection raised from the standpoint of logic.

Objection: When this meaning of the Vedas has once been

ascertained, how can there be any scope for doubt from the standpoint of logic? Are not the Vedas as much an independent authority about Brahman as they are about virtue and vice?

Opponent : Such an objection could have been raised, if like religious rites etc., that have to be accomplished, the subject-matter here had to be known from the Vedas alone, and not from any other source of knowledge. But Brahman is recognized as an entity already existing (and not a thing to be accomplished). With regard to an existing reality, other means of knowledge have also an applicability, as for instance in the case of the earth etc. And just as in a case of conflict among Vedic texts, all the rest are made to conform to one, so also when the Vedic texts contradict other means to knowledge, they should be made to conform to others. Besides, inference is nearer to perception inasmuch as it presents an unknown thing in conformity with the characteristics of the known, whereas the Vedic passages are remote from perception inasmuch as they present their subject-matters on the basis of (dogmatic) tradition. It is held that the knowledge of Brahman, culminating in personal realization, has a perceived (or tangible) result in the form of removing ignorance and leading to liberation. The Upaniṣadic text, "The Self is to be heard of, reflected on" (Bṛ. II. iv. 5), which enjoins reflection over and above hearing, shows that reasoning is also to be given due consideration. Hence the doubt is again preferred from the standpoint of logic, by saying, "Brahman is not the cause of the universe owing to the dissimilarity in nature". The assertion made that conscious Brahman is the material cause of the universe has no legs to stand on.

Why?

Because this product is dissimilar to the material cause. For this universe, that is believed to be a product of Brahman, is seen to be different in nature from Brahman, it being insentient and impure, whereas Brahman is declared in the Upaniṣads to be dissimilar in nature from the universe, It being conscious and holy. It is not a matter of experience that things differing in nature can be related as the material cause and its effect. For products like gold necklace etc. cannot have clay etc. as their material cause, nor can earthen plates etc. have gold as their material. As a matter of fact, clay things are made from clay, and gold things from gold. Similarly this universe—insentient, full of happiness, misery, and delusion as it is—must be the product of something which is insentient and abounds in happiness, misery, and delusion. But it cannot be the product of Brahman which is dissimilar. That the universe is dissimilar to Brahman is to be understood from noticing the former's insentience and impurity. This universe is impure because it abounds with happiness, sorrow, and dejection, and as a result leads to enjoyment, grief, and delusion etc., and it remains diversified into such high and low states as heaven, hell, etc. And the universe is insentient, since it is admitted to be serviceable to the sentient (souls) by becoming transformed into bodies and senses. There can be no action and reaction in the form of mutual benefit when two things are absolutely equal, for two lamps do not help each other.

Objection: Though the body and organs be sentient, they can still be beneficial to the experiencing soul on the analogy of the master and the servant.

Opponent: Not so, for even in the case of the master and the servant, it is the insentient part alone that is beneficial to the sentient (master). Those things which constitute the insentient appendages of the one sentient being, viz the intellect and the rest, are alone serviceable to the other sentient being. But one conscious entity does not by itself either help or harm another conscious entity. For the Sāṁkhyas are of opinion that the conscious souls are devoid of degrees of perfection and imperfection, and hence they are not the agents of action. Therefore the bodies and organs are insentient. Not that there is any proof of consciousness residing in wood or lumps of earth. This distinction between the sentient and the insentient is quite familiar in the world. Accordingly, this universe cannot have Brahman as its material cause, for it is different from Brahman in nature.

Objection: Somebody might make such an assertion: Hearing from the Vedas that creation has Consciousness as its material cause, we can understand on the strength of this, that the whole universe is conscious, for the characteristics of the material are seen to inhere in the product. The non-perception of consciousness is caused by some peculiarity of the transformation. Just as the sentience of the souls, which is a patent fact, is not felt in states of sleep, unconsciousness, etc., similarly the sentience in wood, lumps of earth, etc. can remain unmanifest. And on account of this very peculiarity brought about by manifestation or non-manifestation of Consciousness, and on account of the presence or absence of forms etc., it involves no contradiction to have a relationship of superiority and inferiority between the soul and the assemblage of body and senses, although as Consciousness they are the same. And just as meat, soup, and rice, which are equally the products of earth, become helpful to one another (as courses of food) by virtue of their individual peculiarity, similarly it can be here as well. For that very reason (of distinction created by expression and non-expression), the well-known division between the sentient and the insentient is also not contradicted.

Opponent: In this way also the well-known division between sentience and insentience can at the most be somehow circumvented; but even so the distinction between the holy and the unholy cannot be explained away. Nor can the other dissimilarity (shown below) be really reconciled. This is stated in, "And that fact of being thus different is known from the Vedas." If sentience for everything, even though this fact is surely unknown in this world, be assumed on the strength of the Vedic declaration that Consciousness is the material cause and in accordance with people's reliance on the Vedas, then that assumption is opposed by the Vedas themselves, since "the fact of being so (different) is known from the Vedas" as well. "The fact of being so" means, "the fact of being different from the material cause". In the passage, "It became the sentient and the insentient" (Tai. II. vi.), the Vedas themselves apprise us of the insentience of some portion and thereby let us know that the insentient creation is different from Brahman.

Objection: Is not sentience also asserted sometimes by the Upaniṣads for the elements and organs which are considered to be insentient? For instance, in "Earth said", "Water said" (Ś.

B. VI. i. 3. 2-4), "That Fire deliberated", "That Water deliberated" (Ch. VI. ii. 3-4), etc., we come across Vedic texts about the sentience of the elements. There are also texts about the organs; "Those organs, disputing over their respective greatness, went to Brahman" (Bṛ. VI. i. 7), "They said to the organ of speech, 'Chant the Udgītha for us'" (Bṛ. I. iii. 2), and so on.

Opponent: Hence comes the answer:

अभिमानिव्यपदेशस्तु विशेषानुगतिभ्याम् ॥५॥

तु But अभिमानि-व्यपदेश: the reference is to the presiding deities विशेष-अनुगतिभ्याम् Owing to the mention of distinction and inherence.

5. But this is only a reference to the presiding deities, because of the mention of distinction (between the sentient deities and the insentient organs and elements) and the inherence (of these deities in them).

The word "but" discards the objection. It is not to be assumed from such Vedic passages as "Earth said", that the elements and organs have sentience, since this is only a reference to the presiding deities—the sentient deities identifying themselves with earth etc. and the organs of speech etc. being referred to as engaged in activities befitting conscious beings, such as talking and disputing (or quarrelling). But the mere organs and elements are not so referred to.

How can this be?

"Because of the mention of distinction and inherence." For the distinction, expressing itself as a division, of the experiencing souls and the elements and organs, into the sentient and the insentient, was mentioned earlier. And this becomes illogical if everything is conscious. Moreover, with a view to obviating any assumption regarding the mere organs and for accepting the presiding deities, the followers of the Kauṣītaki recension qualify them by the word deity in the course of the anecdote of *Prāṇa* thus: "In days of yore, these deities, while disputing about their respective supremacy" (Kau. II. 14), and "All these deities, coming to know that their supremacy was in the keeping of (i.e. derived from) *Prāṇa*" (Kau. II. 14). Besides, from *mantras*, corroborative statements, anecdotes, mythologies, etc. it is known that the sentient presiding deities inhere everywhere (in the elements and organs). Such texts as, "Fire entered into the mouth by becoming the organ of speech" (Ai. I. ii. 4), reveal the benevolent presiding deities inhering in the organs. In the subsequent portion of the text also, dealing with the anecdote of *Prāṇa*, occurs the passage, "Those organs approached their father Prajāpati and said" (Ch. V. i. 7), where we meet with such behaviour as going to Prajāpati in order to ascertain their supremacy, the understanding of the supremacy of *Prāṇa* by following a process of agreement and difference, according to Prajāpati's advice, by the leaving of the body successively and the carrying of presents to *Prāṇa* (Bṛ. VI. i. 13). These and other forms of behaviour of this kind, which are seen to be quite like ours, confirm the view that the reference is to the presiding deities. It is to be understood that in the text, "That Fire deliberated" also, the deliberation referred to belongs to the supreme, presiding Deity (Brahman) who inheres in all His modifications (viz the inferior deities). Hence this creation is certainly different from Brahman, and being different, it does not have Brahman as the material cause.

Vedāntin: Such being the objection raised, the aphorist refutes it:

दृश्यते तु ॥६॥

6. But it is seen.

The word "but" rules out the opponent's view. The assertion that this universe does not have Brahman as its material cause, since its characteristics are different, is not wholly true. For it is a matter of common experience that from a man, well-known as a conscious being, originate hair, nail, etc. that are different in nature (being insentient), and scorpion etc. grow in cow-dung etc. known to be insentient.

Opponent: Is it not a fact that the insentient bodies etc. of men and others are the sources of the insentient hair, nails, etc., and the insentient bodies of scorpions etc. are produced from the insentient cow-dung etc.?

The answer (of the *Vedāntin*) is: Even so, there is this difference that some insentient things constitute the basis for some sentient beings, while others do not. Besides, the departure from their own source (by hair, nails, etc.) through transformation is very great indeed, since human bodies and hair, nails, etc. differ in appearance, (size), etc. Similar is the difference between a scorpion etc. and cow-dung. Had they been quite similar, the very conception of cause and effect would have vanished. If, however, it is argued that some characteristics, inherited by man from his earthly origin, persist in the hair and nails etc., and so also those of cow-dung etc. persist in the scorpion etc., then in that case the characteristic of existence, belonging to Brahman, is seen to persist in space etc. And when somebody objects to the theory of Brahman's being the material cause of the universe by relying on the act of dissimilarity, he has to explain whether the dissimilarity is caused by the non-persistence of all the characteristics, or of some one of them, or of Consciousness. From the first standpoint the whole theory of the material cause becoming transformed into the effect will fall through, for in the absence of some distinctive feature (in the effect) there can be no such thing as the modification of a material cause. From the second standpoint, the objection has no basis, since it has been pointed out that the characteristic of existence, belonging to Brahman, is seen to inhere in all things counting from space. From the third standpoint, there is an absence of confirmatory illustration, for what can possibly be cited against the believers in Brahman by saying, "Whatever is not endowed with Consciousness is seen to be produced from something other than Brahman"? For all things are held by us to have Brahman as their material cause. And the contradiction with the scriptures is quite obvious, for it has been established that the purport of the scriptures is that Brahman is the material as well as efficient cause of the universe.

As for the argument that Brahman being an existing thing, other means of knowledge should apply to It, that too is a mere figment of the brain. For this Entity is not an object of perception, It being devoid of form etc. And It is not subject to inference, being devoid of all grounds of inference etc. But like the religious acts (producing virtue), this entity is known from the scriptures alone. In support of this occurs the Upaniṣadic text, "This idea about Brahman is not to be induced by (independent) logic. O dearest one, when imparted by some (knower of Brahman) who is other than the logician, this idea becomes conducive to realization" (Ka. I. ii. 9), and the Vedic text, "Who ever knew here that thing directly from which this diverse creation originated, and who ever spoke of this in this world? The gods were later than this creation. So how can anyone know that from which creation originated?" (Ṛ.V. I. xxx. 6). These two verses show that the origin of the universe is inscrutable even to the perfected lordly (divine) beings. There is also the Smṛti text: "Entities that are beyond thought are not to be approached through logic. The definition of the unthinkable is that which is beyond nature"; as also "The Self is said to be unmanifested, unthinkable, and unchangeable" (Gītā, II. 25), "Neither the hosts of gods, nor the great *ṛṣis* (seers) know My origin, for in every way I am the source of all the gods and the great *ṛṣis*" (Gītā, X. 2), and similar other passages.

It was also argued that by enjoining "reflection" over and above "hearing", the (Bṛhadāraṇyaka) Upaniṣad shows that logic also is to be honoured. But through such a subterfuge, empty logic cannot find any scope here; for logic, conforming to the Upaniṣads, is alone resorted to here as a subsidiary means helping realization. And this is of this kind: Since the states of sleep and wakefulness contradict each other, the Self is not identified with any one of them; since the individual soul dissociates itself from the world in the state of deep sleep to become one with the Self which is Existence, it must be the same as the transcendental Self; since creation has originated from Brahman, and since the law is that the cause and effect are non-different, creation must be non-different from Brahman; and so on. The aphorism, "Because reasoning has no conclusiveness, (it cannot upset the conclusions of Vedānta)" (II. i. 11) will show that independent reasoning is misleading.

And it was pointed out that in accordance with the Vedic declaration that the material cause of the universe is conscious, the pseudo-Vedāntist concludes that the whole of creation is conscious. Still we say that even from his standpoint, the text, "It became the sentient and insentient" (Tai. II. vi.), which speaks of the division between the conscious and the unconscious, can surely be reconciled on the basis of the manifestation or non-manifestation of Consciousness. It is rather from the standpoint of the other party (i.e. the Sāṁkhyas) alone, that even this Vedic mention of division becomes irreconcilable.

How?

Because here the Upaniṣad reveals the presence of the supreme Cause in the whole of creation by saying, "It became the sentient and the insentient". On the basis of this text, just as it can be argued on the one hand that it is impossible for the sentient to become insentient owing to dissimilarity, so also it can be argued on the other, that the insentient (Pradhāna) cannot become the sentient creatures. As, however, the dissimilarity (between Brahman and creation) has already been explained away (with the help of such illustrations as cow-dung and scorpion), therefore a conscious cause is to be accepted just as it is mentioned in the Upaniṣads.

असदिति चेन्न प्रतिषेधमात्रत्वात् ॥७॥

(The effect is) असत् non-existent इति चेत् if this be the contention, न not so; प्रतिषेध-मात्रत्वात् it being a mere negation.

7. *If it be said that the effect (in that case) is non-existent (before creation), then not so; for it is merely a negation (without any object to deny).*

Opponent : If Brahman, that is conscious, pure, and free from sound etc., be accepted as the cause of the effect that is opposed to It, being unconscious, impure, and possessed of sound etc., then it comes to this that the effect was non-existent before creation. And that conclusion is undesirable for you (Vedāntins) who believe in the pre-existence of the effect (in the cause).

Vedāntin: That creates no difficulty, for yours is a denial without any object to deny. This denial cannot amount to a rejection of the existence of the effect before creation.

How?

Because it can be understood that even as today, the effect (universe) has existence only in identity with its material cause (Existence-Brahman), so it had its existence in that very way even before creation. For even now, this creation does not exist independently of the Self that is its material source, as is shown in the Upaniṣadic text, "All ousts one who knows it as different from the Self" etc. (Bṛ. II. iv. 6). But the existence of the product as the cause before creation is in an indistinguishable form.

Opponent: Is not Brahman, the (alleged) source of the world, devoid of sound etc.?

Vedāntin: True; but the effect, possessed of sound etc., does not certainly exist separately from its Self, the material cause, either before creation or now. Thus it cannot be said that the effect is non-existent before its creation. We shall speak about this elaborately when dealing with the non-difference of the cause and effect (B.S. II. i. 14).

अपीतौ तद्वत्प्रसङ्गादसमञ्जसम् ॥८॥

अपीतौ In dissolution तत्-वत्-प्रसङ्गात् owing to the predicament of becoming just like that असमञ्जसम् it becomes incongruous.

8. Since in dissolution there is the predicament of the cause becoming just like that effect, therefore this (theory that Brahman is the material cause) becomes incongruous.

To this the *opponent* makes this rejoinder. If it be admitted that this creation, possessed of grossness, parts, insentience, limitation, impurity, etc., has Brahman as Its material cause, then during merger, i.e. dissolution, when the course of creation is reversed and the effect becomes indistinguishable from the cause, it will taint the cause with its own attributes. Thus since in this way arises the possibility of Brahman's becoming tainted during dissolution by the impurities etc. of creation, the Upaniṣadic view that the omniscient Brahman is the material cause of the universe is incongruous. There is also another absurdity. When all differences become obliterated, there will be no possibility of a re-emergence with a division between the experiencers and the objects of experience, since there can be no fixity of rules to guide the new creation. Besides, there will be this impropriety: If it be admitted that the experiencing souls can be reborn after they have become unified with supreme Brahman during dissolution when even the results of their past actions become obliterated, then there will arise the possibility of even the free souls being reborn. If on the contrary it be held that even in dissolution this world maintains its distinction from the supreme Brahman, then there will be no possibility of dissolution; and yet there can be no effect that is non-different from the cause. In this way this is all inconsistent to be sure.

न तु दृष्टान्तभावात् ॥९॥

तु But न not so दृष्टान्त-भावात् owing to the existence of supporting illustration.

9. But that cannot be so on account of the existence of supporting illustration.

Vedāntin: The answer here is: There is certainly nothing incongruous in our point of view. As for the argument that when the effect merges in the cause, it will tarnish the cause with its own drawbacks, that is unacceptable.

Why?

For there are illustrations to substantiate this; there are illustrations to show that even though the effects merge in their causes, they do not pollute the latter with their own peculiarities. For instance, such products as plates etc., fashioned out of the material earth, have the peculiarities of being high, medium, and flat during their separate existence; but when they become re-absorbed into their original substance, they do not transfer their individual features to it. Nor do such products as necklaces etc., fashioned out of gold, transfer their individual peculiarities to gold during their merger into it. The host of living creatures of four classes, emerging from earth, do not transmit their individual characteristics to the earth during their absorption into it. But there is no such illustration in support of your point of view. Resorption itself will be an impossibility if the effect should persist in the cause together with its peculiarities. And though cause and effect are non-different, the effect has the nature of that cause and not vice versa, which fact we shall state under the aphorism, "The non-difference of the effect from the cause is known from words like 'origin'" (II. i. 14). And your argument that the effect will pollute the cause during resorption does not go very far; for the position is the same even during the state of continuance (of creation), since the cause and effect are admitted to be non-different. The effect is recognized to be equally non-different from the cause during all the three periods of time according to the Upaniṣadic texts like the following: "... and this all are the Self" (Bṛ. II. iv. 6), "All this is but the Self" (Ch. VII. xxv. 2), "All this that is in front is but Brahman, the immortal" (Mu. II. ii. 11), "All this is certainly Brahman" (Ch. III. xiv. 1). The way that the objection has to be met there (during continuance) by holding that the cause is not affected by the product and its characteristics, these being superimposed on the cause by nescience, is equally to be followed in the case of dissolution as well. Moreover, there are parallel instances. As a magician himself is not affected at any time—past, present, or future—by the magic conjured up by himself, it being unreal, so also the supreme Self is not affected by this world which is a delusion. As a dreamer, remaining the same under all conditions, is not affected by the delusion of dreaming, just because that delusion does not persist in him during the states of wakefulness and sleep, so also the witness of the three states, who ever remains the same, is not touched by the three variable states. This appearance of the supreme Self in identity with the three states is a mere superimposition, as in the case of the rope appearing as a snake etc. With regard to this it is said by the teacher Gauḍapāda, versed in the traditional views of Vedānta, "When the individual sleeping under the influence of beginningless Māyā is awakened, then he realizes the birthless, sleepless, dreamless, non-dual (*turīya*)" (Mā. Kā. I. 16). Thus the objection that was raised that in resorption, the cause, like the effect will be open to the defects of grossness etc., has no validity.

And it was pointed out that if all distinctions are obliterated during resorption there will be no reasonable ground regulating the re-emergence of creation with the usual differences. That too is untenable for the very reason that there is a supporting illustration. As in natural slumber and *samādhi* (absorption in divine consciousness), though there is a natural eradication of differences, still owing to the persistence of the unreal nescience, differences occur over again when one wakes up, similarly it can also happen here. Bearing on this is the Upaniṣadic text, "All these beings, when they become one with Existence (during sleep), do not know, 'We have become one with Existence'. Whatever they might have been here—tiger, lion, wolf, pig, worm, butterfly, gnat, or mosquito—they become so over again (after returning)" (Ch. VI. ix. 3). As during the state of the continuance of the world, it is seen that like dream, there are empirical differentiations under the influence of unreal ignorance, despite the existence of the supreme Self as an undifferentiated entity, so also we can infer that even in dissolution, a power of diversification, possessed by unreal nescience, persists. Hereby is answered the objection that free souls may become subjected to rebirth. For (in their cases) unreal nescience stands eradicated by full illumination. And the other objection that was implied at the end that even in dissolution the universe will continue in the supreme Brahman with all its diversification, that too is dismissed by the non-admission of such a position. Hence this view of the Upaniṣads is quite logical.

स्वपक्षदोषाच्च ॥१०॥

च And स्व-पक्ष-दोषात् owing to (your) own point of view being open to defects.

10. And because the defects cling to your own point of view.

Besides, these defects will crop up equally from the standpoint of our opponent.

How?

The answer is: The objection advanced that this universe cannot have Brahman as its material cause on account of its dissimilarity is applicable equally against the theory of Pradhāna as the material cause; for it is admitted (by the Sāṁkhyas) that the universe of sound etc. springs out of Pradhāna which is devoid of sound etc. So from the admission of the origin of a dissimilar effect, the defect of the product having no previous existence persists equally. Similarly from the admission (by the Sāṁkhyas) of the non-difference of the effect from the cause during dissolution, the defect arising from such a position is equally applicable. Again, when during dissolution the effects are divested of all their peculiarities and they become non-differentiated, then the differences that could have been distinguished individually before dissolution, by saying that such and such a material created such and such a person, and such and such a material created that other, cannot be so determined at the time of a new creation; for there is no such regulating basis for this. And even if in the absence of any basis, a regularity in the recurrence (of difference) be maintained, then the absence of a basis being the same, such a theory may lead to the rebirth of a free soul as well. If, again, it be argued that some distinctive features become effaced during resorption while others are not, then those that do not part with their peculiarities will not be the products of Pradhāna. These defects being thus equally shared, they are not to be hurled at either point of view. Thus this merely strengthens the faultlessness of the Vedāntic standpoint, which has to be accepted in any case.

तर्काप्रतिष्ठानादप्यन्यथाऽनुमेयमिति चेदेवमप्यविमोक्षप्रसङ्गः ॥११॥

तर्क-अप्रतिष्ठानात् Owing to the inconclusiveness of reasoning अपि also अन्यथा in a different way अनुमेयम् it has to be reasoned इति चेत् if it be argued thus, एवम् अपि even so, अविमोक्ष-प्रसङ्गः there will be no getting away (from the defect).

11. If it be argued that although reasoning is inconclusive, still it has to be done in a different way, (so as to avoid this defect), then even so there will be no getting away from the defect.

For this further reason, one should not on the strength of mere logic challenge something that has to be known from the Vedas. For reasoning, that has no Vedic foundation and springs from the mere imagination of persons, lacks conclusiveness. For man's conjecture has no limits. Thus it is seen that an argument discovered by adepts with great effort is falsified by other adepts; and an argument hit upon by the latter is proved to be hollow by still others. So nobody can rely on any argument as conclusive, for human intellect differs. If, however, the reasoning of somebody having wide fame, say for instance, Kapila or someone else, be relied on under the belief that this must be conclusive, even so it surely remains inconclusive, inasmuch as people, whose greatness is well recognized and who are the initiators of scriptures (or schools of thought)—for instance, Kapila, Kaṇāda, and others—are seen to hold divergent views.

If, again, it be said (by the *opponent*): "We shall infer in some other way, so that no defect of inconclusiveness can arise. It cannot certainly be asserted that there can be no conclusive argument whatsoever; for even this inconclusiveness of reasoning is established by reasoning itself. For by noticing that some reasonings are inconclusive, it is concluded that others of the same class must be so. Moreover, on the assumption that all reasonings are inconclusive, all human dealings will be upset. It is noticed that people wishing to get happiness or avoid misery pursue future courses on the analogy of the past and present courses. And when there is any divergence as regards interpretation of Vedic passages, it is through reasoning, meant for the determination of the meaning of sentences, that false interpretations are discarded and the proper import is determined. Manu is also of the same opinion when he says, 'One who would extricate virtue from vice, should fully master three things—direct perception, inference, and scriptures that have come down through different traditions' (XII. 105), and 'He, and nobody else, knows virtue and vice who seeks to understand the teachings about virtue and vice, imparted by the sages, with the help of reasoning that does not run counter to Vedic literature' (XII. 106). This in fact constitutes a recommendation for reasoning that it is thought to be inconclusive (i.e. not dogmatic), for it is thus that one has to discard faulty reasoning and resort to the faultless one. There is no sense in being a fool just because one's forefathers were so. Hence the assertion that reasoning has no finality creates no real difficulty."

To this (we *Vedāntins* say): "Even so there is no getting away from the defect." Although reasoning may be noticed to have finality in some contexts, still in the present context it cannot possibly get any immunity from the charge of being inconclusive; for this extremely sublime subject-matter, concerned with the reality of the cause of the Universe and leading to the goal of liberation, cannot even be guessed without the help of the Vedas. And we said that It cannot be known either through perception, being devoid of form etc., or through inference etc., being devoid of the grounds of inference etc.

Besides, (taking *avimokṣa* to mean "absence of liberation"), it is the accepted view of all who stand by liberation that freedom from bondage comes from true illumination. And that true enlightenment has no diversity, since its content is the thing-in-itself. That content of knowledge is said to be the most real since it ever remains the same; and in the world, the knowledge of that kind is said to be right knowledge, as for instance, the knowledge about fire that it is hot. This being the case, people should have no divergence when they have true knowledge, whereas the difference among people whose knowledge is based on reasoning is well known from their mutual opposition. For it is a patent fact of experience, that when a logician asserts, "This indeed is the true knowledge", it is upset by somebody else. And what is established by the latter is disproved by still another. How can any knowledge, arising from reasoning, be correct, when its content has no fixity of form? Again, the follower of the theory of Pradhāna is not accepted by all logicians as the best among adepts in reasoning, in which opposite case alone could his knowledge be accepted by us as right knowledge. It is not also possible to assemble all the logicians of past, present, and future at the same place and time, whereby to arrive at a single idea, having the same form and content, so as to be the right knowledge. But since the Vedas are eternal and a source of knowledge, they can reasonably reveal as their subject-matter something which is (well established and) unchanging; and the knowledge arising from them can be true, so that no logician, past, present, or future can deny it. Hence it is proved that the knowledge arising from the Upaniṣads is alone the true knowledge. And since there can be no other source of true knowledge, (*avimokṣaprasaṅgaḥ*) "there will arise the possibility of liberation being ruled out". So the conclusion stands firm that in accordance with the Vedas and reasoning conforming to the Vedas, conscious Brahman is the material and efficient cause of the universe.

Topic 4: Non-acceptance by the Wise

एतेन शिष्टापरिग्रहा अपि व्याख्याताः ॥१२॥

एतेन Hereby शिष्ट-अपरिग्रहाः the views not accepted by the wise अपि also व्याख्याताः are explained.

12. Hereby are explained all the (other) theories that are not accepted by the wise.

As the theory of Pradhāna as the material cause of the universe approximates to the Vedāntic philosophy; as it is supported by plausible reasons; and as it is accepted by some good followers of the Vedas, therefore the objection has been demolished that could be raised against the Upaniṣadic passages on the strength of the logic based on that theory. Now, some people of dull intellect raise certain objections against the Upaniṣadic passages on the strength of logic based on the views that the atoms etc. are the material causes. Hence the arguments advanced earlier are being extended here on the analogy of defeating the chief wrestler.

Those views that are accepted are *parigrahāḥ*; those that are not accepted are *aparigrahāḥ*. Those unacceptable to the wise are *śiṣṭa-aparigrahaḥ*. "Hereby", by the reasons advanced or refuting the theory of Pradhāna as the cause; it is to be understood that the theories of atoms etc. as the causes, which are not accepted even partially by wise people like Manu, Vyāsa, and others, "are also explained" as not to be accepted; they are to be understood as having been repudiated. The reasons for the refutation being the same, there can be no room for anything else that can be doubted. The reasons in support of the refutation—viz that the supreme cause of the universe is beyond the ken of logic, that reasoning is inconclusive, that even if inference be applied otherwise, it cannot get out of the difficulty, that there is contradiction with the Vedas, and so on—are equally applicable here.

Topic 5: Brahman Becoming an Experiencer

भोक्त्रापत्तेरविभागश्चेत् स्याल्लोकवत् ॥१३॥

भोक्तृ-आपत्ते: From the fact of (objects) becoming the experiencing soul अविभाग: distinctions will cease चेत् if such be the contention स्यात् it can well exist लोकवत् as seen in common experience.

13. If it be argued that the distinction between the experiencer (of happiness and sorrow) and the things experienced will cease when the (experienced) objects turn into the experiencer, then we say that such a distinction can well exist as observed in common experience.

Opponent: The view that Brahman is the cause is being controverted again with the help of reasoning from another point of view. Although the Vedas are a valid means of knowledge within their own domain, still when they contradict some fact known through other means, they must be interpreted otherwise (in a secondary sense), as for instance, in the case of the *mantras* and corroborative statements. Even reasoning will be fallacious when it oversteps into fields that are not its own, such as the fields of virtue and vice.

What follows if it be so?

From this it follows that it is illogical that the Vedas should overrule something well ascertained through some other means of knowledge.

How again do the Vedas deny what is well established by other means of proof?

Apropos of this it is said that the division between the experiencer and the things experienced is quite familiar in this world —the experiencer (*bhoktā*) being the conscious embodied soul, and sound etc. being the objects experienced (*bhogya*). For instance, Devadatta is the experiencer (enjoyer) and food is the thing experienced (enjoyed). That division will be nullified if the experiencer should become the things experienced and vice versa. Yet this interchange of position between them will result from the assumption of their non-difference from Brahman, the supreme cause. But this well-known division should not be effaced. On the contrary, on the analogy of the division between the experiencer and things experienced, as it exists now, the inference should be that the same was and will be the case in the past and the future. Accordingly, the assertion of Brahman as the material cause is improper, for it leads to a denial of the well-known division between the experiencer and the thing experienced.

Vedāntin: Should anyone raise such an objection, the answer to him will be: Such a distinction may well exist just as it is in common experience. This division can be upheld from our point of view as well; for so it is seen in the world. Thus though foam, ripple, wave, bubble, etc. which are different modifications of the sea, consisting of water, are non-different from the sea, still amongst themselves are perceived actions and reactions in the form of separating or coalescing. And yet the foam, wave, etc., do not lose their individuality in relation to one another, even though they are modifications of the sea and non-different from it, which is but water. Again, even though they do not lose their individuality in one another, they are never different from the point of view of their being the sea. Similar is the case here. The experiencer and the things experienced never get identified with each other, nor do they differ from the supreme Brahman. Although the experiencer is not a transformation of Brahman, for in the Upaniṣadic text, "Having created that, He entered into that" (Tai. II. vi), it has been stated that the Creator Himself, without undergoing any change, has become the experiencer by entering into His product (the body), still some difference accrues to one who has entered into the product, owing to the presence of the product which serves as the limiting adjunct, just as much as space becomes divided, owing to the presence of conditioning factors like pot etc. Thus it is said that though all things are non-different from the supreme cause, Brahman, still there can be such a distinction as the experiencer and the things experienced on the analogy of the sea and its waves etc.

Topic 6: Origin

तदनन्यत्वमारम्भणशब्दादिभ्यः ॥१४॥

तत्-अनन्यत्वम् There is non-difference of those (cause and effect) आरम्भण-शब्द-आदिभ्यः on account of the texts about origin etc.

14. There is non-difference of those cause and effect on account of the texts about origin etc.

Assuming, for the sake of argument, an empirical difference between the experiencer and the things experienced, the refutation (under the previous aphorism) was advanced by holding that "the distinction can well exist as observed in common experience". But in reality, this difference does not exist, since a non-difference between those cause and effect is recognized. The effect is the universe, diversified as space etc. and the cause is the supreme Brahman. In reality it is known that the effect has non-difference from, i.e. non-existence in isolation from, that cause.

How so?

"On account of the texts about origin etc." (in the Upaniṣad). As for the word "origin", it occurs by way of citing an illustration, called for by the assertion that the knowledge of all follows from the knowledge of one: "As, O amiable one, all things made of clay are known when a lump of clay is known, since a modification has speech as its origin and exists only in name; as clay alone it is true" (Ch. VI. i. 4). The idea implied is this: When a lump of clay is known as nothing but clay in reality, all things made of clay, for instance pot, plate, jar, etc., become known, since they are non-different as clay, because of which fact it is said, "A modification has speech as its origin and exists only in name". A modification, e.g. a pot, plate, or jar, etc. originates from speech alone that makes it current by announcing, "It exists". But speaking from the standpoint of the basic substance, no modification exists as such (apart from the clay). It has existence only in name and it is unreal. As clay alone it is real. This is an illustration about Brahman cited in the Upaniṣad. From the use of the phrase, "speech as its origin", in connection with the illustration, it can be understood that even from the standpoint of the thing illustrated (viz Brahman), no modification has any existence separately from Brahman. Again, after stating that fire, water, and food (earth) are the effects of Brahman, the Upaniṣad says that the products of fire, water, and food have no existence in isolation from fire, water, and food themselves: "The firehood of the (gross) fire is gone, since a modification has speech as its origin and exists only in name. The three colours are alone true"[4] (Ch. VI. iv. 1). Because of the use of the word "etc." in "on account of texts about origin etc.", are to be cited the many texts establishing the oneness of the Self, such as, "All this has That as its essence; That is the Reality; That is the Self; That thou art" (Ch. VI. viii. 7), "... and this all are the Self" (Bṛ. II. iv. 6), "All this is but Brahman" (Mu. II. ii. 11), "All this is but the Self" (Ch. VII. xxv. 2), "There is no difference whatever in It" (Bṛ. IV. iv. 19), etc. Moreover, the knowledge of all cannot be brought about by the knowledge of one in any other way. As the spaces within pots or jars are non-different from the cosmic space or as water in a mirage

[4] The gross fire is a mixture of the subtle elements—fire, water, and earth, which are red, white, and black in colour respectively. The gross fire gets all these colours from its constituents, and when analysed back, it is seen as nothing but those subtle elements with their own characteristics. 'Food' here means earth.

is non-different from a (sandy) desert—since they sometimes appear and sometimes vanish away, and as such their nature cannot be defined, even so it is to be understood that this diverse phenomenal world of experiences, things experienced, and so on, has no existence apart from Brahman.

Opponent: But Brahman consists of many things. As a tree has many branches, so Brahman has many powers and functions. Hence both unity and diversity are necessarily true, even as a tree, considered as a tree, is one, but has diversity in its aspect of branches; or as a sea, considered as a sea, is one, but has diversity in its aspects of foam, wave etc.; or as clay, considered as clay, is one but has diversity in its aspects of a pot, a plate, etc. That being so, liberation can well be accomplished through knowledge from the standpoint of (the) unity (of Brahman), whereas social and Vedic activities can be justified from the standpoint of diversity. And in this way the analogy of clay etc. will become appropriate.

Vedāntin: This cannot be so, since in the illustration, the truth of the material cause alone is emphasized by saying "as clay alone it is true" (Ch. VI. i. 4) and the unreality of all modifications is spoken of in the words, "has speech as its origin" (ibid.). In the case of the thing illustrated also the supreme cause alone is ascertained to be real in, "All this has That as its essence; That is the Reality" (Ch. VI. viii. 7). This also follows from the teaching that the embodied soul is Brahman in essence in the passage, "That is the Self; That thou art, O Śvetaketu" (ibid.). This identity of the embodied soul, that is taught, is a self-established truth, and it has not to be accomplished through some extraneous effort. From this it follows that like the idea of the rope removing the ideas of snake etc. (superimposed on it), the acceptance of the unity of the (individual) Self with Brahman, as declared in the scripture, results in the removal of the idea of an individual soul bound up with the body, that is a creation of beginningless ignorance. When this (false) notion that the embodied soul is the real Self is removed, all those activities become sublated which are based on that assumption, which are created by ignorance, and for supplying a rationale for which a separate diversified part is imagined in Brahman. It is further shown by the Upaniṣad, with the help of such passages as, "But when to the knower of Brahman everything has become the Self, then what should one see and through what?" (Bṛ. II. iv. 13) etc., that in the case of one who has realized Brahman as the Self, all (empirical) dealings cease that are concerned with action, instruments, and results. It cannot be said that this negation of dealings (in the Self) is confined within a certain state (during liberation only), for the identity of the Self and Brahman stated in, "That thou art", is not contingent on any particular state. Besides, when with the help of the simile of the thief it is shown that one banking on lying comes under bondage and one adhering to truth becomes freed (Ch. VI. xvi), the point established in the Upaniṣad is that unity alone is the highest truth and that multiplicity is conjured up by false ignorance. If both difference and non-difference be true, why should a creature be condemned as married to unreality even though he be within the domain of empirical existence? The text, "He goes from death to death who sees difference as it were in It" (Bṛ. IV. iv. 19), while condemning the dualistic vision, reveals only this very fact. Besides, from this point of view (that both difference and non-difference are true) the attainment of liberation through knowledge cannot be justified, since (in this view) no such false ignorance is admitted as a cause of the transmigratory state that can be removed by right knowledge. For if both difference and non-difference be true, how can it be asserted that the knowledge of unity will falsify the knowledge of multiplicity?

Opponent: If absolute unity be affirmed, multiplicity will stand negated, and so direct perception and the rest which are the empirical means of valid knowledge will be nullified; for they will have no valid content like the ideas of a man etc. superimposed on a stump etc. Similarly the scriptures about injunction and prohibition, which depend on multiplicity, will be falsified when diversity is uprooted. Even the scriptures about liberation, based on such differences as between the teacher and the taught, will be contradicted. Moreover, how can the unity of the Self, propounded by the scriptures about liberation, be true when they themselves are false?

Vedāntin: As to this, the reply is: That is no defect; for earlier than the realization of the identity of the Self with Brahman, all activities can justly be true like the activities in dream before waking up. So long as the oneness of the true Self is not realized, nobody entertains the idea of unreality when dealing with the means of knowledge, objects of knowledge, and the results; rather, as a matter of fact, all creatures discard their natural oneness with Brahman to accept through ignorance the modifications themselves as "I and mine"—that is to say, as one's Self or as belonging to oneself. Hence all common human dealings or Vedic observances are logical (and valid) prior to the realization of the identity of the Self and Brahman, just as much as knowledge with the stamp of conviction, supposed to be attained through direct perception, does occur, before waking up, to an ordinary man when he is asleep and dreams of things high and low. The idea that these are semblances of perceived things does not occur to him during that dream.

Opponent: But how can the true knowledge of the identity of the Self with Brahman arise from the unreal Upaniṣadic texts? For a man does not die when bitten by a snake superimposed (by him) on a rope, nor are such needs as drinking and bathing fulfilled by the water in a mirage.

Vedāntin: That creates no difficulty, for death etc. are seen to result from the suspicion of poison etc., and in the case of a man in a state of dream even such acts as being bitten by a snake and bathing in water do happen. Should one argue that such an act too is false, we would say that though the snake-bite and bathing in water in the case of a dreamer be false, still the knowledge resulting from those acts is true, since that knowledge is not sublated even when he wakes up. For even when a man knows after waking that the acts of snake-bite and bathing in water etc., experienced by him in dream, were false, he does not surely consider the knowledge of those acts to be false as well. By this—this non-sublation of the knowledge acquired by a dreamer—it is to be understood that the doctrine of the identity of the Self with the mere body is also discarded.[5]

[5] After seeing oneself in a dream as possessed of a grotesque body, one wakes up to see oneself in another body, but even then one remembers,

In support of this (true result arising from an unreal basis) is the Vedic text: "If in the course of performing some rite with a view to obtaining results, one sees a woman in a dream, one should conclude from that dream that the rite will be successful" (Ch. V. ii. 8), which shows the true fulfilment of a desire from the seeing of a false dream. So also, after declaring that when some evil omens come within the range of one's direct perception, one should conclude, "Methinks I shall not live long", it is said, "Then again, a black man with black teeth, if seen in a dream, causes the death of the dreamer", which text shows that true death is indicated by that false dream itself. Moreover, it is a well-known fact in this world, that to people, well versed in the method of inferring from agreement and difference, a dream of a particular type prognosticates something, while a dream of another type foreshadows something else. Similarly from the false perception of the presence of letters in some lines (drawn on paper) the true letters like *a* etc. are grasped.[6] Furthermore, the Upaniṣads are the ultimate (conclusive) means of valid knowledge, establishing the truth of the oneness of the Self,[7] after which nothing else remains to be sought after for knowledge. Unlike the curiosity arising in common life to know "what, with what, and how" on hearing the injunction "one should sacrifice", there remains nothing more to be sought for after one is taught, "That thou art" (Ch. VI. viii. 7). or "I am Brahman" (Bṛ. IV. iv. 5), for that knowledge has for its content the Self which is all. A curiosity can arise only when something is left over, but nothing remains there beyond the oneness of the Self about which one may become curious. Besides, it cannot be said that such a knowledge does not arise, since there are the

"I dreamt thus". This recognition of oneself in different bodies would not have been possible if the cognizing Self did not exist as the changeless witness in all the states, and different from the bodies.

[6] The letters of the alphabet are known from the spoken languages, though they are represented by symbolical lines on paper. These scribblings are not the real letters.

[7] So unity and diversity cannot coexist. The Upaniṣads are an independent means of a unique knowledge of non-duality, which cannot be sublated by other means of knowledge, whereas this ultimate knowledge eradicates all ideas of duality.

Upaniṣadic texts like, "That reality of the Self he knew from him" (Ch. VI. xvi. 3). And this conclusion also follows from the enjoining of hearing etc., and study etc. of the Vedas as (direct and indirect) means to realization. It cannot be said that this realization is useless or erroneous, since it is seen to lead to the eradication of ignorance, and since there is no other knowledge to override it. We said earlier that before the realization of the oneness of the Self, all ideas of true and false involved in human and Vedic dealings remain intact. Hence when all the old ideas of multiplicity become uprooted after the establishment of the oneness of the Self by the ultimate means of valid knowledge, there can be no fancying of Brahman as a composite thing.

Opponent : From the citation of the analogy of clay etc., does it not follow that, according to the scriptures, Brahman is capable of transformation? For things like clay etc. are known in the world to be changeful.

Vedāntin : We say, no, since Brahman is known to be changeless from the Upaniṣadic texts denying all kinds of change, such as, "That great birthless Self is undecaying, immortal, undying, fearless, and Brahman" (Bṛ. IV. iv. 25), "This Self is that which has been described as 'Not this, not this' " (Bṛ. IV. iv. 22), "Neither gross nor minute" (Bṛ. III. viii. 8) etc. For one cannot comprehend that the same Brahman can be possessed of the attributes of change and changelessness.

Opponent : It can be like motion and motionlessness.

Vedāntin : No, for Brahman has been qualified as changeless; for the changeless Brahman cannot be possessed of diverse attributes like motion and motionlessness. And we said earlier that Brahman is changeless and eternal, it having been denied that Brahman can undergo any modification whatsoever. It cannot be argued that just as the knowledge of Brahman as the one (non-dual) Self brings about liberation, so also Its knowledge as an entity transforming Itself into the world is intended to lead to some independent result; for there is no evidence in support. The scripture reveals only the result arising from the realization of the unchanging Brahman as the Self; for instance, the commencement is made with, "This Self is that which has been described as 'Not this, not this' " (Bṛ. IV. ii. 4), and then it is said, "You have attained that which is free from fear" (ibid.); there are also other texts of this kind. That being so, the conclusion to be drawn is this: Since in a context speaking of Brahman, it stands proved that the result (i.e. liberation) accrues only from the realization of Brahman, devoid of all distinctions created by attributes, therefore when in that context some other fact is heard of that has no result, as for instance, the modification of Brahman into the world, that fact has to be interpreted as a means leading to that realization. And this has to be done on the strength of the adage, "Any act enjoined without mentioning a result, closely on the heels of some other act having a result, has to be accepted as forming a part of the latter"; but it is not imagined to bear a separate result. It is not reasonable to say that from a knowledge of Brahman as capable of transformation, one will get that capacity of transforming one's own Self;[8] for liberation is changelessly eternal.

Opponent: Since the believers in a changeless Brahman have a predilection for absolute unity, there will be no ruler and the ruled, so that the assertion that God is the cause (of the universe) will be contradicted.

Vedāntin: No, since that omniscience (of God) is contingent on the manifestation of name and form which are creations of ignorance and which constitute the seeds of the world. In accordance with the texts like, "From that Self which is such, originated space" (Tai. II. i. 2), it was asserted under the aphorism, "That from which this world has its birth etc." (B. S. I. i. 2), that the origin, continuance, and dissolution of the world result not from the insentient Pradhāna or anything else, but from God who is by nature eternal, pure, intelligent, and free, as also omniscient and omnipotent. That assertion remains intact. Nothing contradictory to that is stated here again.

Opponent: How is it not stated by one who speaks of the absolute oneness and non-duality of the Self?

Vedāntin: Listen, how it is not stated. Name and form which

[8] According to the declaration that one becomes just what one meditates Brahman to be.

constitute the seeds of the entire expanse of phenomenal existence, and which are conjured up by nescience, are, as it were, non-different from the omniscient God, and they are non-determinable either as real or unreal, and are mentioned in the Vedas and the Smṛtis as the power, called Māyā, of omniscient God, or as *prakṛti* (primordial Nature). But omniscient God is different from them, as is known from the Upaniṣadic text, "That which is Space (Brahman) is the accomplisher of name and form. That in which they subsist is Brahman" (Ch. VIII. xiv. 1). And there are also in evidence texts like, "Let me manifest name and form" (Ch. VI. iii. 2), "The omniscient Being who creates all forms, gives them names, (and entering into them) goes on uttering these" etc. (Tai. Ā. III. xii. 7), "He who diversifies the single seed" (Śv. VI. 12). Thus like space conforming to the conditioning factors like pot, jar, etc., God conforms to the limiting adjuncts—name and form—created by nescience. And within the domain of empirical existence, He rules it over the selves which identify themselves with the (individual) intellects and are called creatures, and which though identical with Himself, conform, like the spaces in pots etc., to the assemblages of bodies and senses created by name and form that are called up by nescience. Thus God's rulership, omniscience, and omnipotence are contingent on the limiting adjuncts conjured up by nescience; but not so in reality can such terms as "the ruler", "the ruled", "omniscience", etc., be used with regard to the Self shining in Its own nature after the removal of all limiting adjuncts through illumination. Hence it has been said, "That is infinity where one does not see anything else, does not hear anything else, does not know anything else" (Ch. VII. xxiv. 1), as also, "But when to the knower of Brahman everything has become the Self, then what should one see and through what?" (Bṛ. II. iv. 14, IV. v. 15), and so on. Thus all the Upaniṣads speak of the cessation of all empirical dealings in the state of the Highest Reality. So also in the *Song Divine*: "Neither agency, nor actions does the Lord create for the world, nor (does He bring about the union with the fruit of action. It is universal ignorance that does it all). The Omnipresent takes note of the merit and demerit of none. Knowledge is enveloped in ignorance, hence do beings get deluded" (Gītā, V. 14-15). In this text it is shown that in the state of the highest Reality, all transactions as between an ordainer and things ordained cease to exist. But within the state of phenomenal existence, even the Upaniṣads mention such behaviour as divine rulership, as in the text, "He is the Lord of all. He is the ruler of all beings, He is the protector of all beings. He is the embankment serving as the boundary to keep the different worlds apart" (Bṛ. IV. iv. 22). So also in the *Song Divine*: "The Lord, O Arjuna, dwells in the hearts of all beings, causing all beings by His Māyā, to revolve (as if) mounted on a machine" (Gītā, XVIII. 61). The aphorist (Vyāsa) also has the supreme Reality in mind when he writes the aphorism, "It has non-difference from That (Brahman)" etc. (II. i. 14); but when he has the empirical standpoint in view, he says, "Such distinction can exist as observed in common experience" (II. i. 13), where he speaks of Brahman as comparable to a vast ocean. Again, without denying the vast phenomenal creation, he resorts to the process of transformation, in so far as this can be made use of in the worship of the qualified Brahman.

भावे चोपलब्धेः ॥१५॥

च And उपलब्धेः because (the effect is) perceived भावे when (the cause is) present.

15. (Cause and effect are non-different) since the effect is perceived when the cause is there.

The effect is non-different from the cause for this further reason, that the effect is perceived when the cause is there, but not otherwise.[9] For instance, the pot is perceived when the clay is there, and the cloth is perceived when the yarns are there. But it is not an (usual) invariable fact that something is seen when something other than it is present, for it is not the case that a cow, which is different from a horse, is seen only where

[9] Not only is the existence of the effect dependent on the existence of the (material) cause, but its perception also is dependent on the perception of the material.

a horse is present. Nor is it a fact that a pot is perceived only when the potter is there, even though there is the relation of agentship and effect; for they are different.

Opponent: Even the presence of something is invariably perceived when something other than itself is present, as for instance smoke can exist only if fire is present.

The answer (of the *Vedāntin*) is, no; for even when the fire is extinguished, smoke, as held up in a cowherd's pot etc., is seen to persist. Should you, however, qualify the smoke as subject to certain conditions (e.g. a smoke that rises up from a place in a continuous stream), and say that a smoke of that kind cannot exist unless there be fire, still it will not vitiate our proposition; for we say that the reason for holding that the (material) cause and effect are non-different is that (not only can the effect exist only when the cause exists, but also that) the idea of the effect can exist only when the idea having the impress of the cause persists. And this coexistence we do not get in the case of fire and smoke (see f.n. 9).

Or the aphorism is: भावाच्चोपलब्धेः ॥

The meaning is this: Not only is the non-difference of the cause and effect to be accepted on the authority of scriptures, their non-difference is "also to be accepted on the strength of the existence of such a perception"; for direct perception does occur about the non-difference of the cause and effect. It is thus: In a cloth constituted by an arrangement of yarns, one does not perceive the cloth apart from the yarns; but the yarns themselves, arranged as warps and woofs, are perceived independently. Similarly with regard to the fibres forming the yarn, and the constitutents of the fibre in relation to the fibre itself. By this direct perception are known the three colours—red, white, and black (of fire, water, and earth—Ch. VI. iv)—(as constituting the minute parts of the fibre etc.). From these are to be inferred[10] (the imperceptible) subtle air and subtle space. Beyond that is the supreme Brahman—one without

[10] Where we lack perception, the cause has to be inferred thus from the effect: "The thing under consideration must be non-different from its material cause, for it is a product, just as much as a cloth."

a second. And we said that in It culminate all means of knowledge.

सत्त्वाच्चावरस्य ॥१६॥

च And सत्त्वात् owing to the existence अवरस्य of the posterior one.

16. And (cause and effect are non-different) because the posterior one has (earlier) existence (in the cause).

From this additional reason the effect is non-different from the cause: The subsequently originating effect is heard of (in the Upaniṣad) as existing in the cause in identity with it before its own origin; for in the texts, "O amiable one, this world was but Existence Itself before creation" (Ch. VI. ii. 1), and "In the beginning this was but the absolute Self alone" (Ai. I. i. 1), the effect, referred to by the word "this", occurs in apposition (having the same case-ending) with the cause (showing that they are identical). And a thing which does not exist in and in identity with something does not originate from that, as for instance oil from sand. Hence from the fact of non-difference before origin, it is understood that the effect must be non-different from the cause even after its birth. Just as Brahman, the cause is never without existence in all the three periods of time, so also the universe, which is the effect, never parts with Existence in all the three periods. But Existence is only one. And this is a further ground for the non-difference of the effect from the cause.

असद्व्यपदेशान्नेति चेन्न धर्मान्तरेण वाक्यशेषात् ॥१७॥

असत्-व्यपदेशात् Owing to the declaration of non-existence न (the effect did) not (exist) (before creation) इति चेत् if such be the objection, न (it is) not so, वाक्य-शेषात् since from the complementary portion (it is known that the word is used) धर्म-अन्तरेण from the standpoint of a difference of characteristics.

17. If it be argued that the effect did not exist before creation, since it is declared (in the Upaniṣad) as "non-existent", then we say, no, because from the complementary portion it is known that the word is used from the standpoint of a difference of characteristics.

Opponent: Is not the non-existence of the effect also declared by the Upaniṣads now and then, as in, "This was indeed non-existent in the beginning" (Ch. III. xix. 1), "This was non-existent in the beginning to be sure" (Tai. II. vii. 1). Therefore from the declaration of this non-existence, the effect did not exist before creation."

Vedāntin: We say, no, for this declaration of the non-existence of the effect before creation is not meant to imply absolute non-existence.

What is the implication then?

The condition in which name and form become evolved is different from the condition in which name and form are not so evolved. Hence although the effect exists as non-different from the cause before creation, still from the standpoint of this difference in conditions the effect is declared to be non-existent before creation.

How is this known?

From the complementary portion of the passage. A passage whose meaning is doubtful in the beginning is ascertained from its complementary portion. Here, for instance, (in the Chāndogya passage quoted above), what is referred to in the beginning by the word "non-existence" in the sentence, "This was indeed non-existent in the beginning", is again alluded to by the word "that" and specified as "Existence" in, "That was Existence" (Ch. III. xix. 1). Moreover, since non-existence has no relation with any sequence of time, preceding or succeeding, the word "was" becomes illogical. In the sentence, "This was non-existent in the beginning to be sure" (Tai. II. i. 1) also, absolute non-existence is not meant, since in the complementary portion occurs the qualifying sentence, "That created Itself by Itself"[11] (ibid.). Therefore this declaration of non-existence of the effect before creation is made from the standpoint of a

[11] Non-existence cannot be the subject or object of any action.

difference of conditions. Since in the world a thing is said to exist when it manifests itself through name and form, therefore, as a concession to common sense, the universe is said to be non-existent before being evolved through name and form.

युक्तेः शब्दान्तराच्च ॥१८॥

युक्तेः From reasoning शब्द-अन्तरात् from another passage च as well.

18. (The pre-existence and non-difference of the effect are established) from reasoning and another Upaniṣadic text.

From reasoning also, as well as another Upaniṣadic text, it is known that the effect exists before its creation and that it is non-different from the cause. Of these, the reasoning is being adduced first. In the world it is seen that people wanting curds, pots, necklaces, etc. take up their well-established respective (material) causes—milk, clay, gold, etc. Not that a man wanting curds takes up earth, or a man wanting a pot takes up milk. This fact does not fit in with the theory of the non-existence of the effect before origination. If everything be equally non-existent everywhere before creation, why should curds be produced from milk alone and not from clay; and why should a pot come out of clay and not out of milk? It may be said that although non-existence before creation is indistinguishable, still curds have some special property (of being latent) in milk alone, but not in clay, and the pot has some special property (of being latent) in clay alone, but not in milk. (Or—"Milk, but not clay, has some special potency for curds, and clay, but not milk, has some special potency for a pot"). But then as a result of this possession of potency by the state preceding origination, the theory of the non-existence of the effect before creation will fall through,[12] and the theory of the pre-existence of the effect will stand confirmed. Again, when some potency is assumed in the

[12] Is the special quality (latency or potency) an attribute of the effect or cause? In the former case, the effect, as possessed of an attribute even before creation, cannot be pronounced non-existent.

cause, to determine the effect, that potency cannot influence the effect by being different (from the cause and effect) or non-existent (like the effect), since (on either supposition) non-existence and difference will pertain to that potency as much as to the effect.[13] Therefore the potency must be the very essence of the cause, and the effect must be involved in the very core of the potency. Besides, we do not have any such idea of difference between cause and effect, substance and qualities, and such other pairs as between a horse and a buffalo; and hence their non-difference has to be admitted. Even if a relationship of inherence be postulated,[14] it will lead to an infinite regress, since if the inherence has to be related to a thing in which it is to inhere by the assumption of another relation (between the inherence and the thing), one will be forced to fancy another relation to connect this one with inherence, etc., and still another relation to connect the new relation, and so on. Or if this new relation be not admitted, the things will remain disconnected. If it be said that inherence being itself a relation, it becomes connected with entities by itself without the help of any intermediate relation, then the relationship of conjunction also, being a relation, should become so connected (with entities) without the help of inherence.[15] Moreover, since identity between substance and qualities etc. is actually apprehended, it is vain to assume a relationship of inherence. And while subsisting in the cause (i.e. the component parts), in what way will the product, constituted by parts, subsist in its cause, viz the component parts? Will it

[13] If the potentiality be different from both cause and effect or if it be non-existent, it may produce anything rather than the effect, for its features of being different and non-existent are equally present in relation to other things.

[14] To the objection that if cause and effect be (substantially) different, they should be perceived as such, the opponent may reply that the difference is not perceived owing to the relation of inherence (invariable concomitance) between them.

[15] According to Nyāya philosophy, the relation between substance and quality, genus and individuals, etc. is inherence. But two things become joined through conjunction, which becomes connected with each through inherence. Conjunction is an attribute and not a relation.

inhere in the parts as a whole or correlatively in them part by part? If it exists on the parts as a whole, then there will be no perception of the product, since it is impossible to have a (simultaneous) sense-perception of all the parts; for the whole, existing in all its bases taken together, is not apprehended by perceiving its bases separately. If, however, the effect subsists in all the (constituent) parts correlatively (part by part), still we have to postulate some (fresh) parts for that product other than those constituent parts themselves, by virtue of which the product may reside correlatively in the parts producing it; for a sword fills up a scabbard through such of its component parts as are different from the components of the scabbard. And this will lead to an infinite regress, for we shall have to imagine at every step some new components to be inserted into the earlier ones. Again, if it subsists (successively) in all the parts taken separately, then when action takes place in one part, there will be no action in others; for when Devadatta is present at Srughna, he is not present on that very day at Pāṭaliputra. If presence in various parts at the same time be meant, that will presuppose a multiplicity of (causal) entities, as in the case of Devadatta and Yajñadatta residing in Srughna and Pāṭaliputra (respectively).

Opponent: There is no fault since the inherence can be like the (single) genus "cowhood" inhering in its entirety in all the cows individually.

Vedāntin: No, since it is not perceived thus. If the whole (composite product) resided in its entirety in all the components individually like cowhood etc., then just as cowhood is directly perceived in each of the individual cows, so also the whole should have been perceived wholly in all the separate parts. But this does not occur invariably. Moreover, if the whole (composite product) abides in its totality in each part, then since the whole has competence to perform all its own functions, and since it is the same (even when existing separately on all the parts) it should perform the duties of the teats even through the horn (of the animal), and the duties of the back through the chest. But this is not our experience.

Furthermore, if the effect does not exist before origination, the creative action will be without any agent and without any reality. But creation is an act, which, like motion etc., must have an agent. It is a contradiction in terms that there can be an act but no agent.[16] When, therefore, somebody would speak of the origin of a pot (as "The pot originates"), the act of origin would not have the pot itself as the subject.

What will be the subject then?

It has to be imagined that the origin has something else as the subject (of the verb). Similarly, when the origin of the (two) parts of a pot is spoken of, it will have to be imagined that the origin has some other thing (and not the two halves) as the subject. And if that be so, then when it is asserted that a (non-existing) pot is originating, it will mean that the agents like the potter etc. are originating. But it is not a fact of common experience that when the origin of a pot is spoken of, the emergence of the potter etc. is perceived. Rather, what is perceived is that the potter etc. have already originated.

If it be argued again that the origin of a thing means but the relation in inherence that the product has with its own cause or with existence (*sattā*), and that is also what constitutes its emergence into being, then one should explain how a thing can have any relationship with others before it has any being. For a relationship can subsist between two existing things, but neither between the existing and non-existing, nor between two non-existing things. Besides, non-existence has no name and form (i.e. it is unreal), and hence it is illogical to indicate any limit for it by saying, "non-existence before its creation". For in the world we see boundaries set to fields and houses, that is to things that exist, and not to non-existing ones. About the unreal son of a barren woman it is not asserted, "The son of a barren woman became a king before the enthronement of Pūrṇavarman", whereby he can be allotted to a certain period of time in the sense that he became, is becoming, or will become

[16] When one says, "The pot moves", the pot is the agent in the sense of providing the basis for the act of moving. So when one says, "The pot originates, the pot must precede the act so that it can be the agent providing the basis for the act of origination. So also the creative action has to take place on some material. Without the material, action can have no meaning.

a king. Were it possible for the son of a barren woman to emerge into being after the accessories of production (causal agents) were activated, then could it be equally asserted that the effect, non-existing (before origin), would originate after the activity of the causal agents. But as a matter of fact what we find is that since the son of a barren woman and the non-existence of an effect (before origin) are equally non-existent, the non-existent effect cannot spring into being even after the causal agents become activated, just as much as the barren woman's son does not after the operation of the causal agents.

Opponent: In that case the activity of the causal agent will become useless. Just as nobody tries to bring into existence or cause what already exists, so also nobody will make any effort to bring about an effect which already exists (in the cause) and is non-different from it. But people do engage. Accordingly, in order to make the activity of the causal agent purposeful, we think that the effect does not exist before its production.

Vedāntin: That is not damaging since the activity of the causal agent gains a meaning by transforming the cause into the shape of the effect. For we have said already that the aspect that the effect assumes is also non-different from the cause, and that anything not existing already in the cause cannot be produced. A thing does not become different just because of the appearance of some peculiarity; for Devadatta, even though noticed in different attitudes when he has his hands and feet contracted or extended, does not differ in his personality, since the recognition of identity persists as, "It is he himself". Similarly though the positions, in which father and other relatives are placed every day, do not remain the same all along, still the father and others do not become some other persons, they being recognized as, "My father", "My brother", "My son", and so on.

Opponent: Since birth and death do not intervene, that kind of recognition is possible in those cases only, but not elsewhere.

Vedāntin: No, since even milk etc. are recognized as having assumed the form of curds etc. When (tiny) invisible things like the seeds of a banyan tree grow in size through the accretion of additional cells of the same class and become visible as sprouts etc., it is called their birth; and when they become invisible again through a decay of those very cells, it is called their death. Now then, if from the intervention of such birth and death, the non-existent should be considered to come into existence and the existent should be considered to become non-existent,[17] then there arises this predicament that the child lying in its mother's womb and lying on its back after birth must be different. Similarly the contingency arises that a person will become different in boyhood, youth, and old age, and all such conventional relationships as father etc. will cease to exist. For the same reason the (Buddhist) theory of the momentariness of everything is to be understood as repudiated. Again, in the case of one who believes that the effect does not exist before origin, the activity of a causal agent will have no purpose in view, since non-existence cannot stand for the object of any effort, and it will be tantamount to wielding various weapons with the purpose of killing space.

Opponent: The activity of the causal agent will have for its object the (material) causes that produce the effect (through inherence).

Vedāntin: No, since it will overshoot the mark if it is argued that the causal agent, concerned with one thing (viz the material) will produce something else (which is not the material).

Opponent: The effect is nothing but some sort of a peculiar disposition of the inherent cause.

Vedāntin: Then that will lead to the theory of the pre-existence of the effect (in the cause). Thus since things like milk etc., are themselves called products when they exist in the forms of curds etc., therefore nobody can establish even in a hundred years that the effect differs from its cause. Similarly it is the primary cause (Brahman) Itself that like an actor evolves into the respective products up to the last one, and thus becomes the object of all empirical dealings. From such reasoning it is known

[17] Neither the parts nor the whole has any birth or death as such; but that kind of terminology is used on account of the addition or diminution of parts. If the opponent still argues that even if this be the meaning of birth and death, still the things experiencing them are substantially different and have no identity, then this is wrong.

that the effect exists before its origin and that it is non-different from the cause.

This is also known from "another Upaniṣadic text". Since texts denoting non-existence were referred to under the previous aphorism, "another" here means a passage which is different from those and which refers to existence, for instance, "O amiable one, in the beginning all this was but Existence, one without a second" (Ch. VI. ii. 1). Again, the theory of non-existence is first alluded to in the words, "with regard to this some say, 'All this was but non-existence in the beginning'." Then this is challenged by saying, "How can existence come out of non-existence?" And lastly it is asserted, "O amiable one, in the beginning all this was Existence to be sure" (Ch. VI. ii. 1-2). In that passage we find that the word "this", meaning the product (i.e. creation), is placed in apposition with Existence, from which fact the product is established to be both existing (in) and non-different (from the cause). If the effect were non-existing before its origin, and inhered in the cause after the origin, then it would be different from the cause, and in that case the declaration, "That by (knowing) which the unheard becomes heard" (Ch. VI. i. 3), would be set at naught. But it can be upheld only by understanding that the effect exists before its birth and it is non-different from the cause.

पटवच्च ॥१९॥

पटवत् On the analogy of cloth च as well.

19. And the effect is non-different from the cause on the analogy of a piece of cloth.

A piece of rolled up cloth is not recognized as to whether it is cloth or something else; but when it is spread out, its real nature becomes revealed through that spreading and it is recognized thus: "The thing that remained rolled up is a piece of cloth to be sure". Or even though it is cognized as cloth when remaining rolled up, its length and breadth are not definitely known; but when it is spread out, it is known as possessed of a definite length and breadth. And yet it is never known to be something other than the rolled up piece of cloth. Similarly such products as the cloth etc. are unmanifest so long as they remain latent in their causes, viz yarns etc.; but they are known distinctly when they become manifest as a result of the activity of such causal agents as the shuttle, loom, weaver, etc. So on the analogy of the cloth rolled up and spread out, the effect is non-different from the cause. This is the meaning.

यथा च प्राणादि ॥२०॥

यथा As च also प्राण-आदि (are) the outgoing breath etc.

20. And this is so just as in the case of the outgoing breath etc.

In the world it is seen that when through *prāṇāyāma* (control of breath) the different forms of the vital force—outgoing and incoming breath etc.—are stopped, when these remain only in their causal form, the mere act of living is continued, but not so the other acts of expansion, contraction, etc. Again, when those very forms of the vital force become active, then expansion, contraction, etc. are performed in addition to mere sustaining of life. But the various forms of the vital force, though distinct from one another, are not different from the vital force itself, since they equally partake of the nature of air (energy). Similarly the cause is non-different from the effect. Accordingly, since the whole world is a creation from and non-different from Brahman, the Upaniṣadic assertion, "That by knowing which the unheard becomes heard, the unthought becomes thought, and the unknown becomes known" (Ch. VI. i. 1) stands vindicated.

Topic 7: Non-Performance of Good

इतरव्यपदेशाद्धिताकरणादिदोषप्रसक्तिः ॥२१॥

इतर-व्यपदेशात् On account of the mention of the other हित-अकरण-आदि-दोष-प्रसक्तिः faults like not doing what is good and so on will arise.

21. Since the other (individual soul) is mentioned (as identi-

cal with Brahman), faults like not doing what is beneficial and so on will arise.

Opponent: Consciousness as the cause is being challenged again in another way. By depending on a conscious entity as the originator of the process of creation, the door will be left open for such defects as non-performance of good.

Why?

"On account of the mention of the other"—for the Upaniṣad mentions the identity of the other, viz the embodied being, with Brahman, for the state of enlightenment is declared thus: "That is the Self; That thou art, O Śvetaketu" (Ch. VI. viii. 7). Or the meaning may be this: The Upaniṣad mentions the identity of the other, viz Brahman, with the embodied being in the text, "Having created that, He entered into that" (Tai. II. vi), where it is said that Brahman, the creator, entered into the body without undergoing any modification, thereby showing that Brahman became one with the embodied being. And in the text, "Let me manifest name and form by Myself entering as the individual soul" (Ch. VI. iii. 2), the supreme Deity alludes to the individual being as His Self, thereby showing that the embodied being is not different from Brahman. Therefore the creatorship that is declared about Brahman belongs really to the embodied being. Accordingly, being an independent agent, the soul should create such beneficial things as it likes, and not bring about death, old age, disease, and such other hosts of evil states which are harmful. For nobody creates a prison house for himself and enters into it unless it be under duress. No one who is absolutely holy would accept this extremely unholy body as himself. And even if he had done something causing pain, he would voluntarily eschew it and accept what is pleasant. Besides, he would have remembered thus: "This wonderful sphere, that the universe is, has been created by me." For all people clearly remember after accomplishing a notable act, "This has been done by me". As a juggler withdraws at will and without effort the magic spread out by himself, so the embodied being also would be able to withdraw this creation at will. But as a matter of fact, the embodied being cannot easily do away even with his own body. Thus from the fact of non-perception of the performance of beneficial works and so on, it follows that the theory of tracing the world process to some conscious entity is unjustifiable. This is how the opponent thinks.

अधिकं तु भेदनिर्देशात् ॥२२॥

तु But अधिकं greater भेद-निर्देशात् on account of the declaration of difference.

22. *But (Brahman is) greater (than the embodied being) on account of the declaration of the difference (between the two).*

Vedāntin: The word "but" rules out the opposite point of view. We speak of that entity as the creator of the universe which is by nature eternal, pure, intelligent, and which is something greater than, that is to say, different from the embodied being. With regard to that Brahman, the faults of not doing what is beneficial and the like cannot arise, for there is nothing beneficial to be achieved or harmful to be eschewed by that Brahman which is by nature eternally free. Nor is there anything to debar Its knowledge or power, since It is omniscient and omnipotent. But the embodied being is not of that kind. With regard to him can arise the fault of not doing what is beneficial and the like. But we do not call him the creator of the world.

How can it be so?

"On account of the declaration of difference" in, "The Self, my dear, is to be realized—to be heard of, reflected on, and profoundly meditated upon" (Bṛ. II. iv. 5), "He is to be searched for, He is to be inquired into" (Ch. VIII. vii. 1), "O amiable one, he then becomes unified with Existence" (Ch. VI. viii. 1), "the Self that is in the body, being presided over by the Supreme Self" (Bṛ. IV. iii. 35). Such statements, mentioning the differences of the agent, object, etc., show that Brahman is greater than the individual soul.

Opponent: Has not the declaration of non-difference also been cited as in, "That thou art" (Ch. VI. viii. 7) and similar texts? How can both difference and non-difference be possible, they being contradictory?

Vedāntin: That is no defect; for we have established the possibility of this in the relevant places on the analogy of the cosmic space and the little bits of space in pots etc. Moreover, when the idea of non-difference is generated by such declaration of identity as "That thou art", then the transmigratoriness of the individual is removed as also the creatorship of Brahman; for all dualistic dealings, brought about by unreal ignorance, get sublated by right knowledge. Then in that state where can creation come from, and from where the defects like non-accomplishment of beneficial results? We have stated more than once that the mundane existence, characterized by the non-accomplishment of beneficial results etc., is an error arising from the non-recognition of the difference (from the soul) of the limiting adjunct constituted by the assemblage of body and senses which are a creation of name and form called up by ignorance. It does not exist in reality. This (false notion) is of a piece with the notions that one has birth, death, injury, wound, etc. But so long as the dualistic dealings persist, the superiority of Brahman (to the individual) known from texts like, "He is to be sought for, He is to be inquired into" (Ch. VIII. vii. 1) rules out the presumption of such faults attaching to Brahman as the non-accomplishment of beneficial results etc.

अश्मादिवच्च तदनुपपत्तिः ॥२३॥

अश्म-आदि-वत् On the analogy of stone etc. **च** as also (for other reasons), **तत्-अनुपपत्तिः** that is untenable.

23. On the analogy of stone etc. as also for other reasons, that (opponent's view) is untenable.

Moreover, as it is found in the world that, though stones possess the common attributes of having been formed from earth, there is a great diversity among them—some are precious jewels like diamond, lapis lazuli (*vaiḍūrya*), etc., others are of medium value like crystal etc., while still others are worthless pieces of stone to be used for pelting at dogs, crows, etc. for driving them away; or as it is seen that though all the seeds grow on the same soil, there is a great variety in their leaves, flowers, fruits, odour, taste, etc., as is noticed in sandalwood, the *kimpaka*, etc.; or as from the same chyle originate different products like blood etc., hair and down etc.; so it is justifiable even for the non-dual Brahman to have such distinctions as becoming the embodied soul and God, and the different products (like earth etc.). Therefore "that is untenable", that is to say, the defects fancied by the opponent cannot be sustained. Moreover, this is untenable since the Upaniṣads are authoritative, since "the modifications have speech alone as their origin" (Ch. VI. i. 4), and since this is possible on the analogy of the variety of things seen in a dream (though the dreamer remains the same). This is the idea implied by "as also".

Topic 8: Creation without Materials

उपसंहारदर्शनान्नेति चेन्न क्षीरवद्धि ॥२४॥

उपसंहार-दर्शनात् Owing to the observation of the collection of materials (in common life) न (Brahman is) not (the cause) इति चेत् if this be the objection, न not so, हि because (it is possible) क्षीरवत् like milk.

24. If it be said that (Brahman) cannot be the cause, since one is noticed to procure materials (for the production of an object), then we say, no, for it is possible on the analogy of milk.

Opponent: The assertion made that conscious Brahman alone, without a second, is the cause of the universe cannot stand scrutiny.

Why?

"Since one is noticed to collect materials." In common experience it is seen that potters and others who make pots, cloth, etc. engage themselves in those works after they have provided themselves with the requisite causal means by collecting such materials as clay, rod, wheel, string, and so on. And you maintain that Brahman is without any help. But how can there be any creatorship for Brahman unless It has procured an assemblage of other accessories? Therefore Brahman is not the cause of the universe.

Vedāntin: That fault does not arise, since on the analogy of milk it can be reasonably maintained that this can happen on account of the peculiar nature of the thing itself. As in the world, milk or water gets transformed into curds or ice by itself without depending on any extraneous accessory, so it can be here as well.

Opponent: Even when milk etc. turn into curds etc. they have to depend on external factors like heat etc. So how can it be said, "For it is possible on the analogy of milk"?

Vedāntin: That creates no difficulty, for whichever may be the transformation and whatever its extent, it is milk itself that undergoes that modification, while heat etc. merely accelerate the process. If it had not any intrinsic capacity to turn into curds, then it could not have been forcibly transformed into curds even by heat etc.; for neither air nor space can be forced by heat etc. to become curds. An accession of paraphernalia only perfects the capacity of milk. Brahman, however, is possessed of the fullest power, and It has not to depend on anything else for imparting an excellence (to that power). In support of this is the Upaniṣadic text: "He has no work and no instrument; none is seen either as equal or superior to Him. His supreme power is heard of as of various kinds. And His knowledge, power, and action are natural" (Śv. VI. 8). Hence even though Brahman is one, it is possible for It, by virtue of the possession of diverse powers, to be transformed variously on the analogy of milk etc.

देवादिवदपि लोके ॥२५॥

देव-आदि-वत् As in the case of gods and others अपि as well लोके in this world.

25. Also (Brahman can create without extraneous help) like gods and others (as is seen) in this world.

Opponent: It may be granted that insentient things like milk etc. turn into curds etc. without the help of external means, it being a matter of experience; but conscious beings like potters and others are seen to depend on the requisite means while engaging in their respective works. So how can Brahman, conscious as It is, act without help?

Vedāntin: We say, it can be so "as in the case of gods and others". For on the authority of the *mantras* and (other) corroborative statements (in scriptures), anecdotes, and mythologies, it is a known fact "in this world" that the gods, manes, *ṛṣis*, and others, very powerful and sentient as they are, create by themselves through mere will and without any external help, many such things as bodies, palaces, chariots, etc., of various shapes, because they are possessed of special powers. The spider also creates its threads by itself; the crane conceives without mating by hearing merely the roar of clouds; and the lotus stalk moves from one lake to another without waiting for any vehicle. Similarly, Brahman, conscious though It is, may well create the universe by Itself without looking for external means.

If the *opponent* argues thus: When you take up your gods and others as illustrations for Brahman, they do not bear any similarity to Brahman which is sought to be illustrated. For the insentient bodies themselves of the gods, and not their conscious souls, furnish the material for the manifestation of their divine powers in the shape of other bodies etc. In the case of the spider, it is the saliva that becomes solidified as a result of eating smaller insects and thus turns into thread. The crane conceives by hearing the roar of clouds. And the lotus stalk moves, under the impulsion of its consciousness, from lake to lake with the help of its body like a creeper climbing up a tree; not that the insentient lotus starts moving by itself to another lake. Hence these analogies do not apply in the case of Brahman.

Vedāntin: To him one can say: That is no defect. For the point emphasized is the mere difference from the illustrations of the potters and others. Though the potters and the gods and others are equally sentient beings, the potters depend on external accessories for undertaking their work, whereas the gods and others do not. Similarly, Brahman, though conscious, will not depend on external means. It is merely this much that we imply by citing the cases of the gods and others. Therefore what is implied (by the aphorist) is that there cannot be any such invariable rule that the power of everybody must conform to that of somebody we are familiar with.

Topic 9: Wholesale Transformation

It is established that Brahman—conscious, one, and without a second—becomes the cause of the universe through a transformation that needs no extraneous help as in the case of milk etc., or of gods and others, without any external help. But an objection is being raised again with a view to placing the purport of the scriptures beyond cavil:

कृत्स्नप्रसक्तिर्निरवयवत्वशब्दकोपो वा ॥२६॥

कृत्स्न-प्रसक्तिः There will be the contingency of wholesale transformation वा or निरवयवत्व-शब्द-कोपः the violation of Upaniṣadic texts about partlessness.

26. (If Brahman changes into the world, then) there will arise the contingency of either wholesale transformation or the violation of the texts about partlessness.

Opponent: There arises the contingency of the whole of Brahman becoming transformed into creation, since It has no parts. Had Brahman been composite like the earth etc., one of Its parts could change while the other would remain intact. But Brahman is partless as is known from such Upaniṣadic texts as, "Partless, actionless, peaceful, faultless, taintless" (Śv. VI. 19), "Puruṣa is transcendental; He is coextensive with all that is external and internal and He is birthless" (Mu. II. i. 2), "This great, endless, infinite Reality is but pure Intelligence" (Bṛ. II. IV. 12), "This is that Self that is known as 'Not this, not this'" (Bṛ. III. ix. 26), "Not gross, not minute" (Bṛ. III. viii. 8), and others which deny all distinctions. Accordingly, it being impossible to change partially, there arises the question of changing wholly, in which case you cut at the very root. And the instruction about seeing (i.e. the realization) of Brahman becomes useless since the created things can be seen without any special effort, and there remains no other Brahman outside these products. Besides, the texts about the birthlessness of Brahman will be violated. If, however, Brahman be accepted to be composit just for the sake of avoiding this difficulty, then this will militat against the texts cited above about the partlessness of Brahmar Furthermore, Brahman will become non-eternal if It has part: Thus this theory cannot be substantiated from any point o view. This is the objection.

श्रुतेस्तु शब्दमूलत्वात् ॥२७॥

तु But श्रुतेः on the Upaniṣadic authority शब्द-मूलत्वात् (Brahman) being known from Upaniṣads alone.

27. *But (this has to be accepted) on the authority of the Upaniṣads, for Brahman is known from the Upaniṣads alone.*

Vedāntin : By the word "but" the objection is ruled out. No defect certainly attaches to our point of view. For instance, there is no possibility of change (of Brahman) as a whole.

Whence is it so?

"On the authority of Upaniṣadic texts." The Upaniṣads speak as much about transcendence of all modifications by Brahman, as they do about the creation of the universe from It; for the material cause and its product are mentioned separately in such texts as, "That Deity that was such, deliberated, 'Let this be so, that I manifest name and form after Myself entering into these three gods as the individual soul' " (Ch. VI. iii. 2), "That much is His glory. But Puruṣa is higher than that. All beings are but one foot of His, But His three immortal feet exist in heaven" (Ch. III. xii. 6). This also follows from the declaration of the heart as His seat, and absorption in Existence (in sleep). Had Brahman wholly evolved as this creation, it would have been unreasonable to speak of any speciality in the state of deep sleep, as is done in, "O amiable one, he then becomes absorbed in Existence" (Ch. VI. viii. 1), for in that case an individual would have been ever in union with the transmuted Brahman, so that there would have been no unchanged Brahman left over (into which to merge). This follows also from the denial of Brahman as an object of the senses, whereas all transformations are objects of perception. Hence Brahman does exist as an unchanged Entity. There is no violation of the texts about partlessness, since partlessness is accepted on account of its very "mention in the Upaniṣads", and the Upaniṣads are the only authority about It, but not so are the senses etc. Hence It has to be accepted just as It is presented by the Upaniṣads. The Upaniṣads prove both the facts for Brahman—the non-transformation of Brahman as a whole and partlessness. Even the things of this world like gems, incantations, herbs, and so on, are seen to possess many powers capable of producing incompatible effects under the influence of a variety of space (environment), time, and cause. And even these powers can be known not from mere reasoning but from such instruction as, "Such a thing has such kinds of potency with the aid of such things, on such things, and for such purposes". So what need has one to argue that the nature of Brahman, whose power is beyond all thought, cannot be ascertained unless it be through the Vedas? So also it has been said by an author of a Purāṇa, "Do not bring those things within the range of argumentation which are beyond thought. The nature of a thing beyond thought consists in its being other than the things within Nature." Hence a supersensuous thing is truly known from the Vedic source alone.

Opponent: Even the Vedas cannot make us understand a self-contradictory thing, when they say for instance, that the partless Brahman changes (into the world), but not wholly. If Brahman be partless, then either It will not change at all, or else It will change wholly. If, however, it be said that Brahman changes in some aspects, but remains intact in others, then from this imagination of aspects, Brahman will surely become heterogeneous. It is only when a contradiction appears in the context of some action, as for instance with regard to the two injunctions "One should take up the (vessel called) Ṣoḍaśin during the Atirātra sacrifice", "One should not take up the Ṣoḍaśin during the Atirātra sacrifice", that one has to resort to an optional course for resolving the contradiction; for the performance of an act is dependent on the person concerned. But the contradiction cannot be resolved here even by taking shelter under option, since a thing, as such, is not dependent on any person. Hence this (contradiction) is difficult to reconcile.

Vedāntin: That is nothing damaging, since it is admitted that this difference of aspects is created by ignorance. For a thing does not become multiformed just because aspects are imagined on it through ignorance. Not that the moon, perceived to be many by a man with blurred vision (*timira*—diplopia), becomes really so. Brahman becomes subject to all kinds of (phenomenal) actions like transformation, on account of the differences of aspects, constituted by name and form, which remain either differentiated or non-differentiated, which cannot be determined either as real or unreal, and which are imagined through ignorance. In Its real aspect Brahman remains unchanged and beyond all phenomenal actions. And since the differences of name and form, brought about by ignorance, are ushered into being through mere speech, the partlessness of Brahman is not violated. Besides, this text about transformation is not meant to establish transformation as a fact, for no fruit is seen to result from such a knowledge. But this is meant to establish the fact that all this is in essence one with Brahman that is beyond all phenomenal processes; for some fruit is seen to result from such a realization. Thus after starting with, "That which is the Self is known as 'Not this, not this'", it is said, "O Janaka, you have certainly attained that which is beyond fear" (Bṛ. IV. ii. 4). Hence there is no possibility of any defect arising from our point of view.

आत्मनि चैवं विचित्राश्च हि ॥२८॥

हि Because (it occurs) एवम् thus आत्मनि in the soul च as well; च and (creations) विचित्राः of diverse kinds (occur in the cases of gods and others).

28. Because it occurs thus in the case of the individual soul as well, and creations of diverse kinds occur in the cases of gods and others.

Moreover, there is no occasion for dispute here as to how there can be creation of various kinds in the same Brahman without changing Its nature; for we read in the Upaniṣad that a diverse creation occurs in the same soul in dream without any change of nature: "There are no chariots, nor animals to be yoked to them, nor roads there, but he creates the chariots, animals, and roads" (Bṛ. IV. iii. 10). In the world also it is seen in the case of gods, as also jugglers and others that various kinds of creation of elephants and so on take place without any destruction of their nature. Similarly even in the same Brahman there can be a diverse creation without any destruction of Its nature.

स्वपक्षदोषाच्च ॥२९॥

29. And because the opponent's own point of view is equally vitiated.

The others also have the same defect attaching to their own point of view. For the view of the believers in Pradhāna is also the same, viz that Pradhāna which is partless, limitless, attributeless (devoid of sound), and so on, becomes the cause of a product that is composite, limited, and possessed of sound etc. In that case also arises the possibility of Pradhāna changing as a whole, since Pradhāna is partless; else there arises the possibility of the theory of partlessness being contradicted.

Opponent: But they do not certainly believe in a partless Pradhāna. For there are its three constituents—*sattva*, *rajas*, and *tamas* (representing intelligence, activity, and inertia); *Pradhāna* is the state of their balance. Pradhāna has parts on account of these constituents.

Vedāntin: The defect under consideration cannot be avoided by (accepting) this kind of heterogeneity, for each one of these *sattva*, *rajas*, and *tamas* is equally partless; and each one of these individually, in co-operation with the other two, becomes the material cause of a creation (which must be) homogeneous with itself. In this way arises the predicament of their own view being equally open to these charges.[18]

[18] The three qualities acting as a whole cannot produce a heterogeneous world, so that each must have some free hand in creation. Now does each change wholly or partially? Either point of view is open to the above objection.

Opponent: In keeping with the maxim that reasoning has no conclusiveness, Pradhāna has to be accepted as heterogeneous (by discarding the inconclusive arguments about Pradhāna's partlessness).

Vedāntin: Even so there arises the contingency of such defects as impermanence etc.

Again, if it be your contention that the various powers of Pradhāna, inferable from the diversity seen in its products, are its constituents, then such powers can be equally upheld by the believers in Brahman.

Similarly also in the case of the believers in atoms, when one atom unites with another, then since an atom has no parts, it must unite as a whole, so that no magnitude will arise from that combination;[19] and hence this will end in an atom only. Or if it should unite in one part, then the theory that the atom has no part will fall through. So the fault vitiates equally their own point of view as well. And since the defect is shared equally, it should not be directed against one of the disputants (viz the Vedāntin) only. But as a matter of fact, the believer in Brahman has freed his own point of view from this defect.

TOPIC 10: POSSESSION OF ALL POWERS

सर्वोपेता च तद्दर्शनात् ॥३०॥

च And सर्व-उपेता possessed of all (powers) तत्-दर्शनात् it having been thus revealed.

30. Moreover (the Deity is) possessed of all (powers), it having been revealed thus (in the Upaniṣads).

It has been said earlier that a kaleidoscopic phenomenal creation can very well stem out from the same Brahman on account of Its being endowed with multifarious powers.

Opponent: How, again, is it known that the supreme Brahman is endowed with diverse powers?

Vedāntin: That is being answered: "The supreme Deity is

[19] The combination of the second with the first leaves the first alone, which has no dimension.

possessed of all powers, it having been revealed thus." It has to be accepted that the supreme Deity is endowed with all powers.

How does this follow?

Because so it is revealed. Thus the Upaniṣads show that the supreme Deity is possessed of all the powers in such passages as, "He is the doer of all (good) actions; He is possessed of all (good) desires, all (good) smells, all (good) tastes, and He pervades all this. He is without the organ of speech, and has no hankering" (Ch. III. xiv. 4), "His desires are true, and His will is inviolable" (Ch. VIII. vii. 1). "He who is all-knowing in general and particular" (Mu. I. i. 9), "Under the mighty rule of this Immutable, O Gārgī, the sun and the moon are held in their positions" (Bṛ. III. viii. 9).

विकरणत्वान्नेति चेत्तदुक्तम् ॥३१॥

विकरणत्वात् Owing to the non-possession of organs न (Brahman is) not (the agent) इति चेत् if such be the objection, तत् that (objection) उक्तम् was answered.

31. If it be argued that (Brahman cannot act) on account of absence of organs, that was answered earlier.

Opponent: It may be so. But the scripture teaches that the supreme Deity is without organs, as in such texts, "without eyes or ears, without the vocal organ or mind" (Bṛ. III. viii. 8). How can He be able to perform action even though omnipotent? For it is known that even though the gods are sentient and equipped with all kinds of power, still they can accomplish their respective duties only when they are in possession of bodies and organs in a physical context. Now how can the Deity from whom all distinction is ruled out by saying, "Not this, not this" (Bṛ. IV. v. 15), become associated with all kinds of powers?

Vedāntin: Whatever can be stated in this matter has already been stated earlier (B. S. II. i. 27). This supreme and sublime Brahman is to be known from the Vedas alone, but not from reasoning. Moreover, there cannot be any such rule that since somebody is seen to have some power in some way, another should also have it in the same way. Moreover, this also has already been stated that even though all distinctions are denied in Brahman, still It can have an accession of all powers owing to the presence of a variety of aspects conjured up by ignorance. In support of this is the scripture, "He moves and grasps even though He is without feet and hands, He sees without eyes, and hears without ears" (Śv. III. 19), which shows the possession of all kinds of power by Brahman, even though It is devoid of organs.

Topic 11: Need of Motive

That a conscious entity can be the creator of the universe is being challenged again in another way (by the *opponent*):

न प्रयोजनवत्त्वात् ॥३२॥

न Not (the cause) प्रयोजन-वत्त्वात् owing to the need of motive.

32. (Brahman is) not the cause, owing to the need of some motive (for creation).

The conscious supreme Self can never create this sphere of the universe.

Why?

"Owing to the need of motive" for action. It is a matter of common experience that an intelligent man whose engagement in work is preceded by forethought, does not start any activity, easy of performance though it be, unless it is conducive to his purpose. What to speak of an undertaking requiring stupendous effort? And there is an Upaniṣadic text confirming this well-known human fact: "It is not for the sake of all, my dear, that all is loved, but for one's own sake that all is loved" (Bṛ. II. iv. 5). The creation of this spherical universe, consisting of a multiple conglomeration of high and low things is a huge task. Even if this effort be imagined to be conducive to some purpose of the conscious supreme Self, then the mention in the Vedas of Its contentment will be contradicted. Alternatively if there be no purpose, then there will be no activity. It may, however, be argued that it is a matter of experience that a mad man, sentient though he is, acts on account of the derangement of his brain, even where he has nothing to gain; and on this analogy the supreme Self too can have action. But on that assumption the mention of His omniscience in the Vedas will be contradicted. Hence it is incongruous to hold that creation stems out from an intelligent being.

लोकवत्तु लीलाकैवल्यम् ॥३३॥

तु But लोक-वत् like what is seen in the world लीला-कैवल्यम् (creation is) a mere pastime.

33. But (creation for Brahman is) a mere pastime like what is seen in the world.

Vedāntin: The objection is rebutted by the word "but". As in the world it is seen that though a king or some councillor of the king who has got all his desires fulfilled, may still, without any aim in view, indulge in activities in the forms of sports and pastimes, as a sort of diversion, or as inhalation, exhalation, etc. proceed spontaneously without depending on any external motive, so also God can have activities of the nature of mere pastime out of His spontaneity without any extraneous motive. For any motive imputed to God can have neither the support of reason nor of the Vedas. Nor can one's nature be called into question. Although the creation of this sphere of the universe appears to us to be a stupendous task, yet to God it is a mere pastime, because His power is infinite. Even though people may fancy that sport also has some subtle motive behind it, still no motive can be thought of here, since the Vedas declare that He has all desires fulfilled. Again, there can be neither inactivity, nor any mad activity, since there are the Vedic texts about creation and omniscience. And yet the Vedic statement of creation does not relate to any reality, for it must not be forgotten that such a text is valid within the range of activities concerned with name and form called up by ignorance, and it is meant for propounding the fact that everything has Brahman as its Self.

Topic 12: Partiality and Cruelty

On the maxim of driving a pole deeper[20], the view that God is the cause of the origin etc. of the universe is being challenged again, in order to make the proposition all the more well established.

वैषम्यनैर्घृण्ये न सापेक्षत्वात् तथा हि दर्शयति ॥३४॥

वैषम्य-नैर्घृण्ये Partiality and cruelty न (do) not (occur) सापेक्षत्वात् owing to consideration of other factors हि for तथा so दर्शयति (the Vedas) show.

34. No partiality and cruelty (can be charged against God) because of (His) taking other factors into consideration. For so the Vedas show.

Opponent: God cannot reasonably be the cause of the world. Why?

For that would lead to the possibility of partiality and cruelty. For it can be reasonably concluded that God has passion and hatred like some ignoble persons, for He creates an unjust world by making some, e.g. gods and others, experience happiness, some, e.g. animals etc., experience extreme misery and some, e.g. human beings, experience moderate happiness and sorrow. Hence there will be a nullification of God's nature of extreme purity, (unchangeability), etc., that are declared in the Vedas and Smṛtis. And owing to infliction of misery and destruction on all creatures, God will be open to the charge of pitilessness and extreme cruelty, abhorred even by a villain. Thus on account of the possibility of partiality and cruelty, God is not an agent.

Vedāntin: To this we say, "No partiality or cruelty can be charged against God."

How can this be so?

"Because of His taking other factors into consideration." Had

[20] In soft earth a pole is first forced in and then pulled out to force it down still deeper. This process is repeated many times till the pole reaches firm ground and is held fast in position.

God created this erratic world by Himself, irrespective of other factors, He would be open to these charges of partiality and cruelty. But in His isolation (from these) He has no creatorship, for God makes this unequal creation by taking the help of other factors.

What factors does He take into consideration?

We say that these are merit and demerit. No fault attaches to God, since this unequal creation is brought about in conformity with the virtues and vices of the creatures that are about to be born. Rather, God is to be compared to rain. Just as rainfall is a common cause for the growth of paddy, barley, etc., the special reasons for the differences of paddy, barley, etc., being the individual potentiality of the respective seeds, similarly God is the common cause for the birth of gods, men, and others, while the individual fruits of works associated with the individual creatures are the uncommon causes for the creation of the differences among the gods, men, and others. Thus God is not open to the defects of partiality and cruelty, since He takes other factors into consideration.

How, again, is it known that God creates this world of high, low, and medium conditions in accordance with other factors? "For so the Vedas show" in, "It is He indeed who makes him perform virtuous deeds whom He would raise high above these worlds; and it is He indeed who makes him perform vicious deeds whom He would cast below these worlds" (Kau. III. 8), "It becomes virtuous through good acts, and vicious through evil acts" (Bṛ. III. ii. 13, IV. iv. 5). The Smṛti also shows that God's dispensation of favour and disfavour is contingent on the specific merit of the work done by each creature, e.g. "In whatever way men worship Me, in the same way do I fulfil their desires" (Gītā, IV. 11), and other texts of a similar import.

न कर्माविभागादिति चेन्नानादित्वात् ॥३५॥

न Not (so) कर्म-अविभागात् on account of *karma* remaining undifferentiated इति चेत् if this be the objection, न not so, अनादित्वात् because of the beginninglessness (of the transmigratory state).

35. If it be argued that it is not possible (to take Karma—merit and demerit—into consideration in the beginning), since the fruits of work remain still undifferentiated, then we say, no, since the transmigratory state has no beginning.

Opponent: There could have been no *karma* (result of work) before creation, in accordance with which a diverse universe could have emerged; for nondifferentiation is emphasized in the text, "O amiable one, in the beginning all this was but Existence, one without a second" (Ch. VI. ii. 1). It is only after creation that results of work, depending on the diversification into bodies etc., could be possible, and the diversification into bodies could be possible by depending on the results of work. This would lead to the fallacy of mutual dependence (logical seesaw). Thus, well may God become active by depending on the fruits of work after the creation of multiplicity. But before this emergence of diversity it would come to this that the first creation would perforce be without any variety, since the fruits of work bringing about differentiation would be absent.

Vedāntin: That is no defect, since the transmigratory state has no beginning. This defect would have arisen if transmigration had a beginning. But if that state has no beginning, there is nothing contradictory for the fruits of work and the variety in creation to act as cause and effect of each other on the analogy of the seed and the sprout.

How, again, is it known that this transmigratory state has no beginning?

To this the answer is:

उपपद्यते चाप्युपलभ्यते च ॥३६॥

च अपि Moreover उपपद्यते this is logical च and उपलभ्यते is met with.

36. Moreover, this is logical, and (so) it is met with (in the scriptures).

And it is logical for the transmigratory existence to have no beginning; for had it emerged capriciously all of a sudden, then there would have been the predicament of freed souls also being reborn here, as also the contingency of results accruing from non-existing causes, for the differences in happiness and misery would have no logical explanation. It has been pointed out already that God is not the cause of inequality, nor is ignorance by itself a source of this, it being homogeneous. Ignorance can at best become the creator of inequality in consequence of the fruits of work, which are acquired as a result of the influence of past impressions of the three infatuations—love, hatred, and delusion. The fallacy of mutual dependence does not arise from the impossibility of bodies being created without *karma* and *karma* being performed without bodies; for if creation is beginningless, all this becomes reasonable on the analogy of the seed and the sprout, and hence there will be no defect.

And we realize the beginninglessness of creation from the Vedas and the Smṛtis. In the Vedas, for instance, occurs the text, "Myself entering into this as the embodied soul (Jīva-ātmā —living being)" (Ch. VI. iii. 2). Referring to the beginning of creation, this text speaks of the embodied soul as the "living being" on account of its sustaining life, and thereby it shows that creation had no beginning; for if creation had a beginning then, since the soul had no life to sustain (at that time), why should the "living being" have been referred to in that text through the word *jīva* (living one) which comes into use from the fact of supporting the life process (*jīvana*)? It cannot be that the term *jīva* is used in anticipation that it will support life in future; for an existing relationship is stronger than a future one, inasmuch as the former is an accomplished fact. And the *mantra* text, "The Ordainer created the sun and moon like those of the previous cycles" (Ṛ. V. X. cxc. 3) shows the existence of earlier cycles of creation. In the Smṛti also the transmigratory state is noticed to be without beginning, as in, "Its form is not here perceived as such, neither its end, nor its origin, nor its continuance" (Gītā XV. 3). The conclusion made in the Purāṇas also is that the past and future cycles of creation are numberless.

Topic 13: Propriety of all the Characteristics

सर्वधर्मोपपत्तेश्च ॥३७॥

37. *And Brahman is the cause on account of the propriety of all the characteristics (of a cause in It).*

After it has been ascertained that the Vedas have for their purport the conscious Brahman as the efficient and material cause of the universe, the teacher (Vyāsa) refuted the objections raised by others on such grounds as the difference between Brahman and the world. Now he concludes the subject mainly concerned with the establishment of his own point of view, before he commences the subject mainly concerned with demolishing the opposing points of view (B. S. II. ii). This philosophy based on the Upaniṣads is not to be cavilled at; for when this Brahman is accepted as the cause, all the characteristics of a cause, namely that Brahman is omniscient, omnipotent, and a great conjurer, fit in with It in the way already indicated.

Section II

Topic 1: Samkhya View Refuted (Impossibility of Design)

रचनाऽनुपपत्तेश्च नानुमानम् ॥१॥

रचना-अनुपपत्तेः Owing to the inexplicability of design च and (other reasons) अनुमानम् the inferred one न is not.

1. The inferred one (Pradhāna) is not (the cause) owing to the impossibility of explaining the design, as also for other reasons.

Although this scripture is begun with the purpose of establishing the fact that the texts of the Upaniṣads have such a thing (viz Brahman) alone in view, but it is not begun for proving or disproving any conclusion with the help of mere reasoning, as is done in the books of logic, still for anyone explaining the texts of the Upaniṣads, it becomes incumbent to repudiate the philosophies of the Sāṁkhyas and others which run counter to the right knowledge. This is why the succeeding (i.e. the present) section begins. And because the determination of the correct meaning of the Upaniṣads is meant for right knowledge, his own point of view has been first established (by Vyāsa) in the course of determining that meaning; for that is preferable to the rejection of opposite views.

Opponent: It is proper to establish one's own point of view for the sake of determining what the right knowledge is, it being a means for the attainment of liberation by people aspiring for release; what need is there of demolishing others' points of view, which amounts to being inimical to others?

Vedāntin: Well, it is just as you say. But there are some people of dull intellect who on noticing that the great scriptures of the Sāṁkhyas and others are accepted by the honoured ones and that they proceed under the plea of bestowing the right knowledge, may conclude that these too are to be accepted as a means to right knowledge. Besides, they may have faith in these, since there is a possibility of weight of reasoning and since they are spoken by omniscient people. Hence this effort is being made to expose their hollowness.

Opponent: Have not the views of the Sāṁkhyas and others been thrown overboard even earlier with the help of the aphorisms: "Because of the attribution of seeing, the one not taught in the Upaniṣads is not the cause" (I. i. 5), "There can be no reliance on inference owing to the mention of desire" (I. i. 18), "Hereby are explained all other theories" (I. iv. 28)? What need is there of doing it all over again?

That is being answered (by the *Vedāntin*). Even the Sāṁkhyas and others cite the Upaniṣadic texts for reinforcing their own points of view, and they explain these in conformity with their own theories. What was done before was just to prove that their interpretations are mere fallacies and not the correct explanations. But here follows a refutation of their reasonings independently of the texts. This is the difference.

With regard to this the *Sāṁkhyas* argue thus: As it is seen in this world that the modifications like pots, plates, etc. which remain transfused with earth as their common substance, originate from the material cause earth, so all the different products, external or corporeal, which remain transfused with happiness, misery, and delusion, must spring from a material cause constituted by happiness, misery, and delusion. Now the material cause constituted by happiness, sorrow, and delusion is the same as Pradhāna, which is constituted by the three *guṇas (sattva, rajas*, and *tamas*—intelligence, activity, and inertia), which is insentient like earth, and which engages in activity by undergoing diverse transformation under a natural impulsion for serving a sentient soul (by providing experience or liberation). So also they arrive at that very Pradhāna on such grounds of inference as limitation, (origination from the potency of the cause, evolution from cause, merger into cause, unity as source of diversity).[1]

Vedāntin: With regard to this we say that if this has to be

[1] The inferences take such forms: "Diverse things like earth has an unmanifested cause, they being *limited* like a pot." "*Mahat* and others

decided on the strength of analogy alone, then it is not seen in this world that any independent insentient thing that is not guided by some sentient being can produce modifications to serve some special purpose of a man; for what is noticed in the world is that houses, palaces, beds, seats, recreation grounds, etc., are made by the intelligent engineers and others at the proper time and in a way suitable for ensuring or avoiding comfort or discomfort. So how can the insentient Pradhāna create this universe, which cannot even be mentally conceived of by the intelligent (i.e. skilful) and most far-famed architects, which is seen in the external context to consist of the earth etc. that are fit places for experiencing the results of various works, and in the context of the individual person, of the body and other things having different castes etc., in which the limbs are arranged according to a regular design, and which are seen as the seats for experiencing various fruits of actions? For this is not noticed in the case of a lump of earth or stone. Even in the cases of earth etc. it is noticed that special creations take place under the control of potters and others. On that analogy, the possibility arises of Pradhāna also being under the control of some conscious entity. There can be no hard and fast rule that the primal cause is to be traced through the attribute (of insentiency) that inheres in the very nature of the material causes like earth, but that it is not to be traced through the qualities inherent in the external factors like the potter. And from this latter point of view nothing is contradicted, rather the Vedas stand vindicated, since the Vedas present a conscious entity as the cause. Accordingly, by reason of the impossibility of design as well, the insentient Pradhāna should not be inferred to be the cause of the universe. By the word "and" (in the aphorism) is adduced the additional argument that the ground of inference (i.e. the middle term) is absent from the major

must have emerged from *the potency in their cause* like pot etc., from the potency of their material." "The effect is seen to *evolve from a cause*, as a pot from clay." "All things *merge* successively into finer and finer material sources." "All variety must have some *unity as its source* on account of causal relation and the principle of merger of the effect into the material cause."

term (universe) on account of the hollowness of the argument about the inherence of the qualities of happiness etc. in the universe (that was advanced by the Sāṁkhyas). For the external and corporeal modifications cannot logically remain transfused with happiness, misery, and delusion as their very substance, for happiness etc. are perceived to be internal (i.e. mental), whereas sound etc. are not perceived to be of that kind (they being external), and the latter are perceived as the cause of the former. Moreover, even when the sound etc. continue to be the same, happiness etc. (connected with them) are felt to be different in accordance with the mental attitudes towards them. Similarly if somebody infers that "since limited products like roots, sprouts, etc. are born out of a combination of many materials, therefore all external and corporeal modifications too must have been similarly formed out of the combination of many materials; for they too are limited", then one will be faced with the predicament of *sattva*, *rajas*, and *tamas* also springing out of a combination of many materials, they too being equally limited. On the contrary, as a causal relation is in evidence even in the case of beds, seats, etc., that are (seen to be) manufactured (by sentient beings) after deliberation, therefore after noticing a causal relationship in the cases of external things and personal modifications one cannot jump to the conclusion that these must also have been created by some insentient entity.[2]

प्रवृत्तेश्च ॥२॥

च And प्रवृत्तेः owing to (the impossibility) of the tendency to act.

2. *And the inferred (Pradhāna) cannot be the cause, since the tendency to create (cannot logically arise in it).*

Leave alone this design. It is not possible for the insentient

[2] The Sāṁkhya's argument was that Pradhāna is that principle where the series of division between the cause and effect terminates. But the Vedāntin holds that the series can as well end in either Brahman or Māyā. The series does not end in an insentient principle that has no

Pradhāna in its isolation, even to have the tendency—the departure from the state of balance, consisting in attainment of a condition of relative superiority and inferiority by *sattva*, *rajas*, and *tamas*, the state of imminence for the creation of some distinct product—(that is necessary for that design); for such (independent action) is not seen in the case of earth etc. or chariot etc. For neither earth etc. nor chariot etc., which are themselves insentient, are seen to have any tendency to behave in a particular way unless they are under the guidance of potters and others or horses and the like. The unseen has to be inferred from the seen. So on account of the absence of any logical ground for acquiring the tendency to act, the insentient (Pradhāna) is not to be inferred to be the cause of the universe.

Sāṁkhya: Well, even in the case of a mere sentient entity (in its isolation), no such tendency to act is in evidence.

Vedāntin: This is true. Still insentient things like chariot etc. are seen to have a tendency to act only when in association with a sentient being.

Sāṁkhya: But a sentient being is not seen to develop a tendency to act even when in contact with insentient things.[3]

A third party: So what should be the reasonable position here? Should the tendency belong to that (insentient thing) in which it is noticed or to him in association with whom it is seen to develop?

Sāṁkhya: Well, the reasonable position is that it should belong to that in which it is actually noticed, for here both (the tendency to act and the bases on which it rests) are perceived together as such, whereas a sentient being by itself is not perceived like the chariot etc. to be the seat of the tendency to act. It is only by noticing the difference of a living body from a mere insentient chariot etc. that a sentient being can be inferred to exist in association with the body etc., which serve as the seat of the tendency to act. And it is from this very fact

intelligence to guide it, for what is noticeable is that all articles are produced by intelligence.

[3] For instance, a sleeping man does not look up and begin to run just because a piece of cloth is thrown on his body. So all tendency to act is based on the insentient.

of sentience and activity being perceptible when a body exists but being imperceptible when the body does not exist, that the materialists infer that even sentience belongs to the body itself. Therefore the tendency to act belongs to the insentient alone.

Vedāntin: That is being answered: We do not say that the tendency does not belong to the insentient entity in which it is noticed. Well may it belong to it. But we say that this tendency is derived from the sentient, since it exists or does not exist in accordance as the sentient entity exists or does not exist. For instance, even though such transformations as burning and emitting light subsist in fuel etc. and though they are not in evidence in fire in its isolation (from fuel), still they originate from fire itself, for they occur as a result of contact (of fuel) with fire and do not occur when that contact is absent. The case is the same here. Even according to the materialists a sentient body is seen to be the impeller of the insentient chariots, etc., and hence the view that the sentient is the impeller of action stands undisputed.

Opponent: But from your point of view, the Self, even when in association with the body etc., cannot reasonably have any tendency to act over and above having Its intrinsic nature of pure consciousness, and hence it cannot be upheld that it can impart any tendency (to others).

Vedāntin: No, for on the analogy of the magnet and colour etc. something bereft of any tendency to act can still impart this to others. For instance, a magnet, though possessing no tendency to act by itself, still induces that tendency in iron; or objects of perception like colour etc., which by themselves have no tendency to act, still impart this to the eye etc. Similarly it is but logical that God who is all-pervasive, the Self of all, omniscient, and omnipotent, should be the impeller of all even though He is Himself free from any tendency to act.

Objection: Since God is one (without a second), and there is nothing else to be impelled, the impellership itself is a fiction.

Vedāntin: No, for it has been said again and again that God can be the impeller because of an illusory association with name and form conjured up by ignorance. Hence the existence of such tendency becomes a possibility only if omniscient God be accepted as the cause (of creation), but not so on the assumption of something insentient as the cause.

पयोऽम्बुवच्चेत् तत्रापि ॥३॥

पयः-अम्बु-वत् Like milk and water चेत् if this be the claim, then अपि even तत्र there.

3. If it be claimed (that Pradhāna acts spontaneously) like milk and water, then even there (intelligence is the guide).

Opponent: It may be like this. As insentient milk has a natural tendency to act for the nourishment of calves, or as insentient water flows spontaneously for the good of people, similarly insentient Pradhāna will also naturally act for fulfilling human needs.

Vedāntin: This is not a correct statement, since we infer that even in those cases, the milk and water develop a tendency to act when they are under the guidance of some sentient beings; for the chariot etc. which are admitted by both of us to be insentient, are not seen to have any action by themselves. The scripture also shows that all motion in this world has God as its source as in, "He who inhabits water but is within it (whom water does not know), .. . and who controls water from within (is the Internal Ruler)" (Bṛ. III. vii. 4), "Under the mighty rule of this Immutable, O Gārgī, some rivers flow eastward" (Bṛ. III. viii. 9), and such other texts. Accordingly, the illustrations of milk and water should not be cited in opposition, since they too are very much of a piece with your point of view that is being disputed (viz that insentient Pradhāna can have any independent tendency). Besides, it is logical to hold that milk is induced to flow under the affectionate desire of the cow; and it is drawn out by the sucking of the calf. Water too is not quite independent since its flow is dependent on the slope of the ground etc. And it was shown earlier that in all cases there is a dependence on sentience. But under the aphorism, "If it be said that Brahman cannot be the cause, since one is noticed to collect materials for the performance of an act, then we say no, for it is possible on the analogy of milk" (B. S. II. i. 24), the illustration was cited from the common-sense point of view to show that action can take place in a thing itself without the aid of any external means. But from the scriptural point of view it is known that all acts take place under God's bidding. Hence this does not contradict the earlier one.

व्यतिरेकानवस्थितेश्चानपेक्षत्वात् ॥४॥

च And व्यतिरेक-अनवस्थितेः owing to the absence of anything extraneous अनपेक्षत्वात् since (Pradhāna can have) nothing to rely on.

4. *And (Pradhāna is not the cause) since (nothing extraneous to it exists, so that) it has nothing to rely on (for impulsion to or stoppage from action).*

Pradhāna according to the Sāṁkhyas, consists of the three *guṇas* in a state of balance. Apart from these, nothing else exists externally to Pradhāna, on which it can depend for either impelling or stopping it. As for the (external) soul (*puruṣa*), it is a passive (witness), neither impelling nor stopping. Hence Pradhāna is without any other help, and being without help, it is wrong to maintain that it gets sometimes transformed into *mahat* etc., while at other times it does not.[4] But since God has omniscience, omnipotence, and the great power of Māyā, His engagement in or disengagement from activity presents no contradiction.

अन्यत्राभावाच्च न तृणादिवत् ॥५॥

च And अभावात् owing to non-occurrence अन्यत्र elsewhere न it cannot be तृण-आदि-वत् like grass etc.

5. *And Pradhāna cannot change (automatically) like grass etc. (into milk in a cow) for such a change does not occur elsewhere (e.g. in a bull).*

[4] For there is no adventitious ground for these changes of mood, merit and demerit also being a part and parcel of Pradhāna, and not an extraneous compelling force.

Opponent: It may happen thus: As grass, leaves, water, etc. change naturally into milk without the help of any other factor, even so Pradhāna can change itself into *mahat* and the rest.

How is it known that grass etc. are not helped by other factors?

Because no other factor is observed. If we could discover some causes, then we could have taken up grass etc. along with those causes at will and would have manufactured milk; but we cannot do so. Therefore the change in the grass etc. is spontaneous. So also it can be the case with Pradhāna.

Vedāntin: With regard to this we say: Pradhāna can change naturally like grass etc. if the change in the grass etc. be accepted as automatic. But this is not admitted, since other causes are perceived.

How is it known that there are other causes?

From the non-occurrence (of such a thing) elsewhere. For grass etc. eaten by a cow alone changes into milk; but not so when rejected or eaten by a bull etc. If this could happen without any cause, then grass etc. would have become milk even without entering into a cow's body. A thing does not become causeless just because men cannot manufacture it at will. For some effects can be produced by men, while others happen under divine dispensation. Besides, men also can produce (more) milk by adopting the requisite methods, as for instance, procuring grass etc. For people wanting plenty of milk feed the cows with plenty of grass, and thereby they procure milk abundantly. Hence the changes in Pradhāna cannot occur naturally on the analogy of grass etc.

अभ्युपगमेऽप्यर्थाभावात् ॥६॥

अपि Even अभ्युपगमे when admitted अर्थ-अभावात् on account of the absence of purpose.

6. Even if (spontaneous modification of Pradhāna be) accepted, still (Pradhāna will not be the cause) because of the absence of any purpose.

It has been established that Pradhāna has no natural tendency to act. If now as a concession to your belief we admit that Pradhāna has a spontaneous impulsion to act, still defects will persist.

Why?

Because of the absence of any purpose. If it be said that Pradhāna has a spontaneous tendency to act and that there is no need of any other auxiliary in this matter, then from this it will follow that just as Pradhāna does not require any help for its activity, so also it will not stand in need of any purpose as well; and thereby the proposition that Pradhāna acts for accomplishing the purposes of the soul will be set at naught. If, however, the opponent says that the need of any auxiliary alone is discarded, but not so any purpose, still we have to search for the purpose leading to Pradhāna's actions. This purpose may be experience (of joy and sorrow) or liberation, or both. If experience of pleasure and pain be the motive, then what kind of experience can be provided (by Pradhāna) for a soul which has no scope for its own perfection or imperfection (which such an experience can bring about)? Besides, liberation will become an impossibility.[5] If liberation be the purpose, then liberation being an accomplished fact[6] even before Pradhāna acts, its engagement in activity will be useless. Moreover, there will be the contingency of an absence of the experience of sound etc.[7] If both the purposes (experience and liberation) be admitted, still since the products of Pradhāna, which are to be experienced, are infinite, there will arise the predicament of non-release (from them, since the experience will be limitless). And the impulse to act cannot be for the sake of satisfying some desire (or curiosity), since neither the insentient Pradhāna can have any curiosity, nor can the partless and pure soul have it. If out of a fear that the powers of knowing and creating (that are present in the soul and Pradhāna respectively) will become infructuous (in the absence of objects and creation), Pradhāna be supposed to act, then just as the soul's power to know can never be eradicated, so also Pradhāna's power to create will continue inter-

[5] For Pradhāna will not be working for it.

[6] The soul being naturally free.

[7] For Pradhāna, when acting for liberation, has no such purpose in view.

minably, so that the predicament of liberation becoming impossible will be just the same. Hence it is wrong to say that Pradhāna acts for the sake of the soul.

पुरुषाश्मवदिति चेत्तथाऽपि ॥७॥

पुरुष-अश्म-वत् On the analogy of a man and a loadstone इति चेत् if such be the contention तथा अपि even so.

7. *If it be argued that like a (lame) man (riding on a blind man) or a loadstone (moving iron), (the soul can stimulate Pradhāna), even then (the defect will persist).*

Sāṁkhya: It may be like this: As a man having the power of sight but not that of movement, he being lame, acts by riding on the shoulders of somebody else who has the power of action but not the power of vision, or as a loadstone, does not move by itself and yet makes a piece of iron move, similarly the soul can impel Pradhāna.

Opposition thus raises its head by relying on analogy.

Vedāntin: To this we reply that "even so", there is no escaping the defect. For instance, the defect of discarding your proposition crops up inasmuch as your hypothesis is that Pradhāna has an independent tendency to act and the soul is not an impeller. Moreover, how can the passive soul impel Pradhāna? Even a lame man guides a blind man by his speech, but the soul has no such causal function to induce action in Pradhāna, since it is actionless and attributeless. And it cannot stimulate movement like a loadstone by mere proximity, for proximity (between soul and Pradhāna) being eternal, the possibility will arise of such movement also becoming endless. In the case of a loadstone, (the proximity being inconstant), there can be such an activity as the attraction (of the iron to itself), for the proximity is inconstant. Besides, the loadstone depends on cleaning etc. for its action. Hence the illustrations of the man and the loadstone are inapt. Again, there can be no relation between the soul and Pradhāna, since Pradhāna is insentient, the soul is indifferent, and there is no third factor to bring them into relation. If, however, the relation follows from their intrinsic fitness to be related (with each other)[8], there will arise the predicament of liberation becoming non-achievable, since that fitness cannot be uprooted. As in the previous aphorism, so here also the absence of purpose has to be taken into consideration from different points of view.[9] But in the case of the supreme Self there is the greater advantage that It has inactivity from Its own point of view, but a driving urge (for creation) from the standpoint of Māyā.

अङ्गित्वानुपपत्तेश्च ॥८॥

अङ्गित्व-अनुपपत्तेः On account of the impossibility of the relation of the Principal (and the subordinate) च as well.

8. Besides, Pradhāna cannot act on account of the impossibility of (the existence of) any relationship of the principal and its subordinates (among the guṇas constituting Pradhāna).

For this additional reason no activity for Pradhāna is possible. The state of Pradhāna is a condition of balance of the three constituents *(sattva, rajas,* and *tamas)* continuing in their absolute intrinsic nature after giving up the reciprocal relation of predominance over or subordination to one another. There cannot be any relation of predominance or subordination among them in that state of their existence in their pristine nature which is independent of their reciprocal relation; for a contrary supposition will lead to a negation of their individual nature. And since there is no external factor to excite them, there can be no origin of *mahat* and the rest that results from the disturbance of the balance of the three constituents.

अन्यथाऽनुमितौ च ज्ञशक्तिवियोगात् ॥९॥

च And अन्यथा-अनुमितौ even if the inference be pursued in another way, (still the defect will persist) ज्ञ-शक्ति-वियोगात् on account of the absence of the power of intelligence.

[8] The soul being a knower, and Pradhāna the object of knowledge. The one presupposes the other.

[9] Whether the purpose be experience, or liberation, or both?

9. And even if the inference be pursued otherwise (still the defect will persist) owing to the absence of the power of intelligence (in Pradhāna).

Sāṁkhya: Even then, we shall draw the inference in a different way, so that this last defect may not crop up. For we do not admit that the *guṇas* are by nature mutually independent or that they are changeless; for such a hypothesis lacks proof. But their nature is postulated in accordance with the modifications springing from them. Their nature must be postulated to be such as may logically lead to the production of the effects. And the accepted view is that the *guṇas* are naturally unsteady. From this it follows that even during equilibrium the *guṇas* exist in a state of potential divergence.

Vedāntin: Even so, the faults like the impossibility of sustaining design etc. rationally, as mentioned earlier, persist just as before, since Pradhāna is bereft of the power of intelligence. Should the opponent infer this power of intelligence as well (for Pradhāna), he will cease to be an opponent; for that will open the door to the belief in the theory of Brahman, that a single sentient entity is the material cause of the universe of varied appearances. Again, even if the *guṇas* possess a potentiality for imbalance,[10] still once they are in a state of equilibrium, they cannot undergo loss of balance in the absence of some cause for this; or should they become disturbed without a cause, it will lead to the predicament of their remaining in a state of disturbed equilibrium through eternity, for the absence of a cause is equal in either state. In this way the defect (of the non-emergence of the derivatives like *mahat*) stated last, will certainly crop up.

विप्रतिषेधाच्चासमञ्जसम् ॥१०॥

च And विप्रतिषेधात् owing to contradictions असमञ्जसम् incoherent.

10. And (the Sāṁkhya doctrine is) incoherent because of the contradictions involved.

[10] Consisting in reciprocal domination and subordination.

And this thesis of the Sāṁkhyas is self-contradictory. For sometimes they enumerate seven organs and sometimes eleven; similarly sometimes they teach about the origin of the subtle elements from *mahat*, and sometimes from the ego; so also sometimes they mention three internal organs, and sometimes one. And their opposition to the Upaniṣads, speaking of God as the cause, as also to the Smṛtis which follow the Upaniṣads, is a patent fact. For these reasons also the philosophy of the Sāṁkhyas is incoherent.

To this the *Sāṁkhya* says: Is not the philosophy of the followers of the Upaniṣads equally incoherent, since in this it is denied that the tormented (individual being) and the tormentor (world) belong to distinct categories? For when they postulate that the one Brahman, which is the Self of all, is the cause of the entire world-appearance, they have necessarily to admit that the afflicted and the afflicter are but two aspects of one and the same Self, and that they do not belong to different categories. If these two, the tormentor and the tormented, be but two aspects of the same Self, then that Self will never get freed from those two, so that the scripture teaching about right knowledge for the sake of getting rid of affliction will become useless. For a lamp possessed of the properties of heat and light cannot reasonably get freed from heat and light so long as it continues to be a lamp. As for the illustration of water, ripple, wave, foam, etc., even there, the same single water has the appearances of ripple etc. which merge and emerge for ever, so that in the case of the water as well, there can be no getting rid of these ripple etc. Moreover the tormentor and the tormented are well known in this world to belong to distinct categories. Thus it is that the seeker (who is afflicted by the desire) and the thing sought (which afflicts), are seen to be entirely different. If the thing sought did not differ in substance from the seeker, then the thing sought by any seeker being ever an accomplished fact for that seeker, he should have no desire for that thing, just as a lamp, that is nothing but light, has got its light ever present in itself so that it has no desire (i.e. need) for it; for a seeker desires something that is still unattained. And so also an object (of desire) will cease to be an object (unless there be a difference between the man and his object). And should it be ever coveted, the desire will be only about itself. But this does not accord with facts; for the terms seeker and the sought are relative expressions, they being mutually determined. A relation can subsist between two (mutually) related things, but not in a thing standing singly. Hence these seeker and the thing sought must be different and so also must be the detester and the thing detested. That which is favourable to the seeker is the desirable thing and that which is unfavourable is the undesirable thing. And a person becomes related to the desirable and the undesirable by turns. Since the desirable things are few, while the undesirable things are many, both the desirable and the undesirable are in effect a source of evil, and are hence called a source of torment. The tormented is the person who, though one, gets connected with each of these two by turns. If these afflicter and afflicted be identical, no liberation will be possible. But if they belong to different categories, then liberation may perchance be possible at times as a result of the removal of the cause[11] of their coming into contact.

Vedāntin: With regard to this the answer is: There is no defect, since the relation of the tormentor and tormented cannot exist in the face of this very fact of unity (of the Self). This defect would have existed if even within the unity of the Self, the tormentor and the tormented could be related by way of being the subject and the object of each other. But this cannot be so precisely because of this unity. For fire does not either burn or illuminate itself precisely because it is one even though possessed of the different attributes of heat and light and subject to transformation. Need it be said that the relation of the tormentor and the tormented cannot be possible in the changeless Brahman which is one?

Where will then this relation of the tormentor and the tormented exist?

[11] Non-discrimination between the soul and the intellect. Bondage arises from this error of identity, and liberation from a knowledge of their difference. Bondage and liberation really belong to the intellect; but just like the figurative ascription of victory and defeat of the army to the king, bondage and liberation are asserted about the soul.

The answer is: Do you not see that the living body which stands as the object (of the act of scorching) is the tormented and the sun is the tormentor?

Opponent : Torment means pain and that can affect a sentient being, but not the insentient body. Should affliction belong to the body, it will cease with the death of the body, so that no spiritual practice need be found out for the removal of that affliction.

Vedantin : The answer is: A sentient being, when unassociated with a body, is not seen to suffer. Even you do not uphold the view that a change, called affliction, comes over the sentient being in its isolation; and the body and the sentient (soul) cannot get mixed up, since that would give rise to impurity etc. (in the soul). Nor do you admit that torment can torment itself. So even from your point of view how can there be a state where one becomes the tormentor and the other the tormented?

Opponent: The attribute *sattva* is the tormented and the attribute *rajas* is the tormentor.

Vedāntin : No, since the sentient (soul) cannot enter into any combination with these two.[12]

Opponent : Since sentience conforms to (i.e. becomes reflected on) *sattva*, it seems to be afflicted.

Vedāntin : Then it comes to this that in reality it (i.e. the soul) is not afflicted at all, for you use the word "seems". And if it is not afflicted, then the word "seems" is not misplaced. For if somebody says, "A (non-poisonous) *dundubha* (snake) is like a (poisonous) snake", the *dundubha* does not thereby become poisonous; or if one says "A snake is like a *dundubha*," the snake does not thereby become non-poisonous. So it has to be understood that this state of one being the afflicted and the other the afflicter is a creation of ignorance; it does not exist in the truest sense. If such be your position, I too lose nothing. On the contrary if you understand that the sentient soul is afflicted in

[12] If *sattva* and *rajas* be the afflicted and the afflicter, the soul need not strive for liberation. And this affliction cannot pass on to the soul by reason of its non-discrimination from the afflicted *sattva*, for the soul being unattached, cannot get attached to *sattva* etc. at all.

a real sense, then since you uphold that the tormentor (*rajas*) is eternal, there will be all the less possibility of liberation from your side.

Opponent: Although the power to afflict and the capacity of being afflicted be everlasting, still affliction being dependent on the contact coexisting with the cause,[13] an absolute cessation of contact follows from the cessation of non-perception (*tamas*) which is the cause of the contact. Absolute liberation becomes a logical outcome of this.

Vedāntin: It cannot be so, since you hold that *tamas*, which is of the nature of non-perception, is eternal. And since there is no fixed rule about the appearance or disappearance of the *guṇas*, the cessation of the cause (i.e. non-perception) of the contact (between Nature and soul) is not subject to any fixed law. Thus the separation between the two (soul and Nature) being also unpredictable the absence of liberation follows as an inevitable result of the Sāṁkhya view itself. But from the Upaniṣadic point of view, one cannot doubt even in dream of there being no liberation, because here it is admitted that the Self is one, that the one cannot be both the subject and object, and that all the different modifications are mentioned in the Upaniṣad to be based on mere speech. Yet within the range of empirical experiences, the state of one being the tormentor and another the tormented is to be accepted for the time being just for what it is worth. And (since its eradication follows as a matter of course from right knowledge) it is not either an object to be questioned about or avoided (in the state of knowledge).

Topic 2: Vaisesika Objection Refuted

The theory of Pradhāna as the cause of the universe has been demolished. Now it is the turn of the theory that the atoms are the cause. While on this task, we first meet the objection that can be fancied against the believers in Brahman by the believers

[13] The "cause" is ignorance consisting in the non-perception of the distinction between Nature and soul; it is *tamas*. The "contact"—i.e. the union between Nature and soul, which means "the idea that the soul has the attributes of *sattva*, *rajas*, *tamas*"—coexists with that "non-perception" or *tamas*.

in the atoms as the cause. In this matter the postulate of the Vaiśeṣika (atomist) is that the qualities inhering in the causal substance reproduce in the substance, constituting the product, (a set of) new qualities of the same class; for a white cloth is seen to be born out of the white yarns, but the contrary is not in evidence. Hence if intelligent Brahman be posited as the (material) cause of the universe, intelligence will inhere in it. But since this is not noticeable, intelligent Brahman cannot be the (material) cause of the universe. By following this line of argument of the atomists themselves, the aphorist shows that such a postulate is not invariably true:

महद्दीर्घवद्वा ह्रस्वपरिमण्डलाभ्याम् ॥११॥

वा Rather महत्-दीर्घ-वत् like the great and long (arising) ह्रस्व-परिमण्डलाभ्याम् from the short and inextensive.

11. Rather (the universe may originate from Brahman) even as the great and long (triads etc.) originate from the short (dyad) or the inextensive (atom).

This is their (i.e. Vaiśeṣikas') process of creation. (During dissolution) the (ultimate) atoms continue for some time in their rudimentary state without producing any effect, but suitably possessed of the respective qualities of colour etc. Then under the influence of the merits and demerits (*adṛṣṭa*—unseen potential results of works) etc. of creatures aided by the conjunction (with one another) they begin creating all things starting from dyads; and the qualities of the causes produce new qualities in the effect. When two (ultimate) atoms create a dyad, the colours, viz white etc., inhering in the atoms, produce a new whiteness etc. in the dyad. But the special characteristic of the atoms, viz their inextension (i.e. atomicity) does not produce a new inextension; for it is postulated that a dyad comes to possess a new magnitude; for according to them a dyad is microscopic in size and has no length. When again two dyads produce a tetrad (combination of four atoms) the whiteness etc., inhering in the dyad, produce other whiteness etc. in a similar way. But the dyad-ness (i.e. microscopic size) and the lack of length, though inhering in the dyads, do not produce their counterparts; for their tenet is that a tetrad has an accretion of magnitude (or greatness) and length. The same line of argument is to be followed even if many atoms, or many dyads, or the atoms in combination with the dyads, produce an effect. Thus even as from the (ultimate) atoms, which are inextensive, arise dyads which are microscopic in size but have no length, and the triads which have both magnitude and length, or as from the microscopic and non-linear dyads are formed the triads having volume and length, but neither atomicity nor absence of length is reproduced, so also if the insentient universe emerges out of intelligent Brahman, what do you lose?

You (the *atomist*) may, however, think thus: The resulting substance, a dyad for instance, is beset by an opposing magnitude; hence we do not admit that the atomicity etc. inherent in the cause (atom) produce any effect (in the dyad). But the universe is not beset by any other attribute, called insentience opposed to consciousness, owing to which the consciousness present in the cause (Brahman) could not produce another consciousness in the effect (universe). For there is no such (positive) attribute called unconsciousness (residing in the world) which is opposed to consciousness, unconsciousness being only a negation of consciousness. Hence consciousness being dissimilar to atomicity etc., it (consciousness) should perforce reproduce another consciousness (in the universe).

Vedāntin: You should not think like that; for even as the atomicity etc., though present in the cause (atom), do not become the producers of atomicity etc., so also it can be in the case of consciousness. To this extent, both are on the same footing here.

And it cannot be the case that atomicity etc. do not reproduce themselves because they are opposed by adverse magnitude; for the atomicity etc. can very well reproduce themselves before being opposed by any adverse magnitude (which has still to emerge), your view being that even when a thing is being produced it remains momentarily without any quantity, before the qualities actually come into being. It cannot be said that atomicity etc. become so very preoccupied with the production of other dimensions, that they do not reproduce the dimensions of their own class, it being understood by you that some things (e.g. duality) which are entirely different from these (atomicity etc.) produce the other dimensions. For the aphorisms of the Vaiśeṣikas run as follows: "Magnitude is produced from the multiplicity of the causes, the magnitude of the cause, and the abundance (i.e. a particular combination) of the cause"[14] (Vai. Sū. VII. i. 9); "But the atom is opposed to this"[15] (Vai. Sū VII. i. 10); "Hereby are explained length and shortness" (Vai. Sū. VII. i. 17). It cannot be argued that owing to some peculiar disposition, multiplicity etc. alone of the causes are reproduced, but not so its atomicity etc., for when some other thing or quality is being produced, all the qualities of the cause are equally present (in the cause) through inherence. So it comes to this that just as atomicity does not reproduce itself in the effect, owing to its peculiar nature, so also can be the case with consciousness as well. This is how it is to be understood. And since it is noticed that entirely dissimilar things (and attributes) are produced from the combination of different things etc., there is no invariable rule that things (and attributes) of the same class alone are produced.

Vaiśeṣika: When a substance is under discussion, it is improper to cite the illustration of a quality.

Vedāntin: Not so, because the point sought to be emphasized by the illustration is merely the production of dissimilars. And there is no reason behind a rule that a substance must be illustrated by a substance alone or a quality by a quality. For even your aphorist cited a quality for illustrating a substance in the aphorism: "Since a conjunction between the perceptible and the imperceptible is imperceptible, nothing can exist that is a

[14] The magnitude of the triad follows from the multiplicity of the dyads; the magnitude of the pot follows from the magnitude of earth; and the volume of a large heap of cotton follows from the volume in the smaller heaps making it up.

[15] The imperceptible atom is opposed to magnitude which is perceptible; multiplicity and volume are also absent from the dyad. The idea of duality, present in God's mind resulting in relational judgment, is the cause of the duality in the dyad.

combination of the five elements" (Vai. Sū. IV. ii. 2). What is implied by the aphorist is this: Just as the quality, called conjunction, existing through the relation of inherence in the perceptible earth and the imperceptible space (when they combine), is not perceptible, similarly if the body inheres in (i.e. be a combination of) the perceptible and imperceptible five elements (as its material causes), it should not be perceived. But as a matter of fact the body is directly perceived. Hence it is not formed by the five elements. Here (in this illustration) conjunction is a quality and the body is a thing.

Furthermore, it was elaborated under the aphorism, "But it is seen" (B. S. II. i. 6) that the effect can be dissimilar (to the cause).

Opponent: If that be so, the present topic was anticipated there itself.

Vedāntin: We say no, for that was an argument against the Sāṁkhyas, whereas this is against the Vaiśeṣikas.

Opponent: Was not an extension of those arguments made to other systems as well under the aphorism, "Hereby are explained all the theories that are not accepted by the wise" (II. i. 12), the reasons being the same in both the cases?

Vedāntin: That is true. Still at the commencement of the scrutiny of the Vaiśeṣika system, those very reasons are elaborated here with the help of illustrations accepted by themselves.

Topic 3: Atoms not the cause of universe

उभयथाऽपि न कर्मातस्तदभावः ॥१२॥

अपि उभयथा Even from either point of view न कर्म no action (is possible) अतः hence तत्-अभावः (there is) absence of that.

12. *(Whether adṛṣta leads the atoms or conjunction helps them), in either case no action is possible, and hence there can be no creation or dissolution.*

Now the doctrine that the ultimate atoms are the causes of the universe is being demolished. That doctrine originates thus: In common experience it is seen that such things as cloth etc., which are possessed of parts, are produced from such things as yarns etc. in which they inhere and which are helped by the quality of conjunction. On the analogy of this, it is known that all things that are composed of parts are produced from those respective things in which they inhere and which are helped by the quality of conjunction. The (ultimate) atom is the culmination of minuteness where this division between the whole and its parts ceases. Again, this whole universe consisting of hills, seas, etc., is a composite thing, and being composite, it has a beginning and an end. An effect is not produced without a cause. So the ultimate atoms are the cause of the universe. This is what Kaṇāda (father of the Vaiśeṣika theory) implies. Now from noticing these four elements—earth, water, fire, and air—to have parts, the ultimate atoms are imagined to be of four kinds. Since the ultimate atoms stand at the furthest limit of minuteness, so that there can be no division beyond them, therefore earth etc. in the course of destruction reach the ultimate atoms as the culmination of their disintegration. That is the time of dissolution. After that at the time of creation, some action starts in the ultimate atoms of air under the influence of *adṛṣṭa* (unseen potential fruits of works of creatures). That action unites the atom, on which it occurs, with another atom. From that combination originates air through a gradual process starting with (the production of) dyads. Thus also originate fire, water, and earth, and thus the body together with the sense-organs. In this way, this whole universe originates from the atoms. And from the (qualities of) colour etc. inherent in the atoms, the colour etc. of the dyads etc. are produced just as it occurs in the case of the yarns and cloth. This is how the Vaiśeṣikas think.

With regard to this we say: It has to be admitted that the combination of the atoms, existing in their isolation is contingent on action, since the yarns are seen to combine when they are being acted upon (by others). And since action is an effect, some cause for it has to be assumed. If such a cause be not admitted, then in the absence of any cause, no initial action will be possible in the atoms. And even if a cause be admitted, it must be accepted in conformity with common experience to be something like effort, impact, etc. But since these are impossible (during the state of dissolution), no initial action will take place in the atoms. For in that state, no effort, which (according to the atomist) is a quality of the soul, can be possible in the absence of a body; for effort springs up as a quality of the soul when a contact between the mind and the soul takes place in the mind having the body as its seat. By the same reason, all ordinarily cognized causes like impact etc.[16] are to be rejected; for all these come after creation, and hence cannot be the causes of the initial action (in atoms).

Again, if it be maintained that *adṛṣṭa* is the cause of the initial movement, then in what does it inhere—in the soul or the atoms? In either case the first movement in the atom cannot possibly result from *adṛṣṭa*, since *adṛṣṭa* is insentient. For in the course of examining the Sāṁkhya point of view it was said that an insentient thing by itself neither acts nor makes anything else act unless it is presided over by some sentient being. As for the soul, its (quality of) consciousness does not emerge in that state (according to the Vaiśeṣika), so that it is insentient; hence even if *adṛṣṭa* be admitted to inhere in the soul, it cannot be the cause of action in the atom, for *adṛṣṭa* has no connection with the atom.

Opponent : The soul possessing the *adṛṣṭa* is in conjunction with the atoms.

Vedāntin : Then from a constancy of that conjunction, the predicament will arise of action becoming constant; for nothing else exists to put a check. Thus from the absence of any well-determined cause of action, the initial action cannot occur in the atoms. And because of the absence of any action, any conjunction that depends on such an action will be impossible. In the absence of conjunction, dyads and other products coming out of conjunction will have no existence.

Again, when an atom comes into conjunction with another, does it do so wholly or in some part? If the conjunction occurs wholly, then there will be no increase in magnitude,[17] so that the result will be a mere atom. Besides, this leads to contradic-

[16] Impulsion, weight, acceleration, elasticity, etc.

[17] The incoming atom will be wholly absorbed in the one *in situ*, so that no additional space will be covered by the two.

tion of common experience, for a thing having dimensions is seen to combine with another having them. Should (on the other hand) the ultimate atom combine through some art, it will result in making the atom a composite thing (thus demolishing the atomists' theory).

Opponent: The ultimate atoms may have imaginary parts.

Vedāntin: Since imaginary things are unreal, the conjunction will surely be unreal, and hence it will not become the non-inherent (*asamavāyin*) cause of the thing produced. In the absence of the non-inherent cause (viz conjunction), such products as the dyads etc. will not come into being. As in the first creation the atoms cannot possess any action for producing conjunction, there being no cause for that action, similarly on the eve of the cosmic dissolution the atoms will have no action for causing their separation; for even then, no well-determined cause can be noticed to make them act. As for *adṛṣṭa*, it is meant for producing experience (of happiness and sorrow) and not dissolution. Hence in the absence of any cause, the atoms can have action neither for bringing about their conjunction nor disjunction. This absence of conjunction and disjunction will lead to an absence of creation and dissolution. Therefore this theory of the atoms as the cause stands discredited.

समवायाभ्युपगमाच्च साम्यादनवस्थितेः ॥१३॥

च And समवाय-अभ्युपगमात् on account of assuming inherence (creation and dissolution become impossible), अनवस्थितेः because of infinite regress साम्यात् arising from a parity of reasoning.

13. And (there can be no creation or dissolution) by reason of assuming inherence, for this leads to an infinite regress on a parity of reasoning.

The portion "And by reason of assuming inherence" is to be connected with "there can be no creation or dissolution" (in the previous aphorism) which was meant for refuting the theory of the atoms as the cause of the universe, which is the topic under discussion. Your (Vaiśeṣika's) theory is that the dyad, originating from two atoms, becomes entirely dissimilar to these two, and it inheres in both of them. But one accepting such a view cannot substantiate the theory of the atoms as the cause.

Why?

Because "this leads to an infinite regress on a parity of reasoning". Just as the dyad, though absolutely dissimilar to the two atoms, becomes connected with them through the relationship of inherence, so also inherence itself, which is absolutely different from the inhering things, should be connected with the inhering things through a separate relationship of the nature of inherence, since the fact of similarity of absolute difference exists here as well. And from this it follows that for those successive relationships, other relationships of inherence have to be imagined. In this way the door is laid open for an infinite regress.

Opponent: Inherence is an everlasting relationship that is actually grasped through the idea of "here" along with the things inhering. It is not perceived in its isolation (apart from the related objects) or through some other relationship, hence no other relation need be sought for it; so there can be no possibility of infinite regress.

Vedāntin: The answer is, no; for in that case conjunction also can be an everlasting relationship between the things conjoined, so that no other relationship like inherence need be sought for it. If now it be said that conjunction is different (from the things conjoined), so that it has to be related through another relationship, then inherence also must need some other relationship, since it too is different (from the things inhering). And it is not reasonable to assert that conjunction has need of some other relationship, it being a quality, whereas inherence has no such need, since it is not a quality; for in either case the need determining such a relationship is the same. The technical terminology (of the Vaiśeṣikas) dubbing conjunction as a quality (and inherence as a relationship) has no bearing in the matter of determining this need.[18] So far as those who consider inherence as a separate category are concerned, an infinite

[18] Conjunction is as much dissimilar to the things conjoined as inherence is to the things inhering, hence both must be classed together.

There can be no such rule that whatever subsists on a substance

regress is inevitable. And when this infinite regress becomes a possibility, and when the whole series of successive relationship of inherence fails on the failure of any one relationship in that series being proved to be ultimate, a dyad cannot arise out of two atoms. For this reason also the theory of the atoms as the cause is untenable.

नित्यमेव च भावात् ॥१४॥

च Furthermore, भावात् owing to persistence नित्यम् एव eternally.

14. (The atomic theory is inadmissible) for the further reason of (activity etc.) persisting eternally.

Again, the atoms have to be accepted as naturally active, inactive, both active and inactive, or neither active nor inactive; for no other alternative is possible. But all the four alternatives are inadmissible. If the atoms be naturally active, it will lead to the possibility of ruling out dissolution altogether, for activity will persist eternally. If the atoms be naturally inactive, it will lead to the possibility of ruling out creation altogether, for inactivity will persist eternally. And they cannot naturally have both activity and inactivity, for that is irreconcilable owing to contradiction. If they have neither activity nor inactivity, by nature, then one will have to admit that these two originate from some cause; but then if such causes as *adṛṣṭa* be ever at hand, it will lead to constant activity; and if they are not under the guidance of *adṛṣṭa* etc., it will lead to constant inactivity. For this reason also the theory that the atoms are the cause is unjustifiable.

रूपादिमत्त्वाच्च विपर्ययो दर्शनात् ॥१५॥

च And रूप-आदि-मत्त्वात् owing to possession of colour etc. विपर्ययः a reversal will occur दर्शनात् for this accords with experience.

must be a quality like colour etc., for action etc. also exist on substances. And if, owing to the denial of inherence in the case of conjunction, the latter ceases to be a quality, the Vedāntin loses nothing thereby.

15. And on account of the possession of colour etc. there will be a reversal (of the nature of the atoms), for this accords with experience.

The Vaiśeṣika asserts that the ultimate atoms stand at the last limit of a process of breaking up of composite things till there can be no further division, that these atoms are of four kinds, possessed of colour etc., that they are the constituents of the four elements and the modifications of the elements endowed with the qualities of colour etc., and that they are eternal. That tenet of theirs is baseless. For by virtue of possessing colour etc. the atomicity and everlastingness of the atoms stand contradicted; that is to say, the atoms become grosser and less eternal than (what) the ultimate cause (should be), a position that is the opposite of what the atomists intend.

Why so?

For thus it is seen in the world. Anything that is possessed of colour etc. in this world is seen to be grosser and less permanent than its cause; for instance a cloth is grosser and less permanent than its yarns; and the yarns are grosser and less permanent than the fibres. Similarly, as these ultimate atoms are admitted by them to have colour etc., they too have some cause in comparison with which they will be grosser and less permanent. If this be the case, the grounds of eternality shown by them in (the aphorism), "Anything that has existence and is unproduced is eternal" (Vai. Sū. IV. i. 1) would not apply to the ultimate atoms, for on account of the reason shown above the atoms also should have some cause. As for the second ground of eternality stated by them in, "And (atoms are eternal, for on that assumption alone) there can be a specific denial about an effect by saying, 'It is impermanent'"[19] (Vai. Sū. IV. i. 4), that also does not prove the permanence of the atoms as a matter of necessity. For while it is true that unless there is something eternal, the negative (*na*) cannot form a compound term

[19] The denial of permanence in the product by saying, "This product is impermanent", would not be possible if the causes, the ultimate atoms, were also impermanent; for existence and non-existence are correlative terms.

with eternality (to mean non-eternality), yet on such a ground it cannot be asserted that the compound term (*anitya*—non-eternal) has to depend (for its meaning) on the eternality of the ultimate atoms alone; for as a matter of fact, the eternal Brahman is already available as the supreme cause. Moreover, it is not a fact that the existence of anything becomes established merely because a certain word signifying a certain thing is in common use.[20] Rather it is only when words and ideas become established to be true with the help of other valid means of proof (viz perception, inference, etc.) that they find vogue in common usage. The third ground of eternality is stated in, "And want of knowledge" (Vai. Sü. IV. i. 5). Now if this aphorism be explained to mean, "Eternality is also deducible from 'Want of knowledge' consisting in not knowing through direct perception any cause of those existing causes whose effects are fully in view", then the dyad also will become eternal.[21]

Now if the qualifying term "not having any substance as the cause" be added after "cause" (in the previous explanation),[22] still eternality will be determined by the absence of a cause; but then that was stated earlier (Vai. Sū. IV. i. 1) and it will involve a repetition to restate it in the aphorism, "And want of knowledge". Again, if the explanation be this, "The eternality of the cause is determined by the 'Want of knowledge', consisting in the impossibility of there being any other third cause of destruction, apart from the destruction of the non-inherent cause and the destruction of the inherent causes",[23] then we

[20] For otherwise a ghost spoken of as residing in a tree would become true.

[21] For the causes of the dyad, viz two ultimate atoms, also are imperceptible; and imperceptibility of the cause is adduced by you as a ground for the eternality of the effect.

[22] The explanation now will be, "Want of knowledge, consisting in not knowing any substance as the cause of those causes whose effects" etc. The atoms being known as the causes of the dyads, the dyads will not become eternal.

[23] A cloth is destroyed by the destruction of its non-inherent cause, viz conjunction among yarns, or by the destruction of its inherent cause, viz the yarns. Both these causes are impossible for an ultimate atom which has no parts. Hence it is eternal.

say that there is no such rule (as propounded by you) that a thing undergoing destruction must be destroyed in either of the two ways only. This could be so only on the supposition that whenever a new thing is produced, it is produced by many things helped by their conjunction. When, however, it is admitted that a common cause (e.g. earth, gold, etc.), considered in itself as devoid of the peculiarities (present in the products), becomes the originator of something else by getting transformed into another distinct state, then the destruction may follow from the cessation of the particular state as in the case of the melting away of the solidified clarified butter. Hence on account of the possession of colour etc. the ultimate atoms will stand opposed to what they are postulated to be. From this point of view also the atomic theory is inadmissible.

उभयथा च दोषात् ॥१६॥

च And दोषात् on account of defect उभयथा from either point of view.

16. And (the atomic theory is untenable) because it is defective from either point of view.

Earth is gross and is possessed of the qualities of smell, taste, colour, and touch; water is fine and possessed of the qualities of colour, taste, and touch; fire is finer and is possessed of colour and touch; and the finest is air possessed of touch. Thus it is seen in this world that these four elements have (an increasingly) greater or lesser number of the qualities and are comparatively gross, fine, finer, and finest. Should the ultimate atoms also be considered likewise to be possessed of qualities in a comparatively greater or less degree, or should they not? In either case they will inevitably be open to defects. For instance, if it be thought that they have an abundance or paucity of qualities, those atoms that have an abundance will have an augmentation of grossness, so that they will cease to be the ultimate atoms. And it cannot be said that qualities can increase even without having an augmentation of grossness, for in the gross products of the elements it is seen that an accretion of attributes is followed by an increase in grossness. If, however, no comparative abundance or paucity of qualities be thought of and for establishing a parity among the atoms it is considered that each of the atoms possesses a single quality, then there will be no perception of touch in fire, no colour and touch in water, and no taste, colour, and touch in earth, for the qualities in the products orignate from the qualities of the causes. Again, if all the ultimate atoms be assumed to be possessed of four qualities, then smell should be perceived even in water, smell and taste in fire, and smell, colour, and taste in air. But this does not conform to experience. For this reason also the atomic theory is illogical.

अपरिग्रहाच्चात्यन्तमनपेक्षा ॥१७॥

अपरिग्रहात् On account of non-acceptance **च** as well **अत्यन्तम्** absolute **अनपेक्षा** non-reliance.

17. This (theory of atom as the cause) is to be entirely ignored, since it is not accepted (by the worthy).

The theory of Pradhāna as the cause is partially incorporated in their writings even by some Vedic scholars like Manu on the ground of its being helpful in establishing such views as the pre-existence of the effect in the cause, (the non-attachment of the soul, its sentience), etc. But this atomic theory is not adopted even in the least by any worthy person. Hence it is to be wholly discarded by the followers of the Vedas. Moreover, the Vaiśeṣikas admit, as the subject-matter of their scriptures, six categories, viz substance, quality, action, class, distinction, and inherence which differ entirely from one another and which are possessed of dissimilar characteristics, like man, horse, and hare. Having defined them to be so, they admit contrary to their own theory, that the other categories are dependent on substance. But that is untenable.

How?

Just as it is seen in the world that among a hare, Kuśa grass, and a Palāśa tree, which live by maintaining their absolute distinctness, there can be no subjection of the rest to any one of them, similarly qualities and the rest, should not be dependent on substance, since substance and the rest are entirely different. Again if quality and the rest be dependent on substance, then since they exist when a substance is there, and cease to exist when the substance is not, it would amount to this that the substance alone becomes the content of various words and ideas in accordance with differences in its own forms, conditions, etc., even as the same Devadatta comes to be known through many words and ideas (like father, brother, son, kind, learned, etc.) owing to the differences in his states and circumstances. But in that case there will be the possibility of the Sāṁkhya theory cropping up and your own theory being stultified.

Atomist: Is it not a fact that smoke, though different from fire, is seen to depend on fire?

Vedāntin: True, it is seen. But precisely because a difference between them is perceived, it is concluded that smoke and fire are different. But in the case under discussion, the substance itself being known as possessed of the respective attributes in such perceptions as, "a white blanket", "a red cow", "a blue lotus", and so on, there can be no such perception of difference between a substance and a quality as between fire and smoke. Hence the quality is one with the substance. Hereby is explained how action, class, distinction, and inherence are also one with the substance.

If it be argued that the dependence of a quality on its substance follows from the fact of their inseparability, then does that inseparableness consist in not having different loci, or different times, or incompatible nature? But none of these alternatives can be justified. If their inseparableness consists in not being present in different places, then your own position will be reversed.

How?

For according to you, a piece of cloth produced from yarns exists in the yarns and not in a distinct place of its own; but the quality of the cloth, viz whiteness etc., are admitted to exist in the place occupied by the cloth and not in that occupied by the yarns. For this is what the atomists assert: "Substances produce other substances, and qualities other qualities" (Vai.

Sū. I. i. 10). The yarns which are the material substance, give birth to the cloth as their product; and the qualities of whiteness and the rest, existing in the yarns, generate similar other qualities —whiteness and the rest in the product, the cloth. This is what they postulate. That postulate will be contradicted if substance and quality have to remain in the same locus. If inseparability be held to be non-existence in different times, then inseparableness will belong even to the right and left horns of a cow.[24] Similarly if inseparableness means want of incompatibility of natures, then substance and quality can have no difference in essence; for a quality is apprehended in identity with the substance. And their theory that the relation between two things artificially combined is conjunction, but the relation between two naturally inseparable categories is inherence is false; for the cause existing even before the effect cannot logically have any inseparability from the effect. It may, however, be maintained that this proposition means that one of the two factors involved in inseparableness, viz the effect which is inseparable from the cause, becomes related to the cause through inherence. Even so, the effect which has no pre-existence and has not emerged into being, can have no relation with the cause, since a relationship is dependent on two factors.

Atomist: The effect becomes related after emerging into being.

Vedāntin: In that case, if the effect be admitted to have any existence before being related with the cause, then the statement, "The cause and effect can have neither conjunction nor disjunction, for that would lead to an absence of inseparable connection" (Vai. Sū. VIII. ii. 13), will be difficult to maintain. Moreover, just as it is held by you that a product, at the first moment of its emergence, has no action and it remains related to other all-pervasive substances like space through the relationship of conjunction, but not inherence, so also the relationship between that entity and its material cause would be conjunction itself and not inherence. Besides, there is no proof that the relationship of either conjunction or inherence has any existence apart from the related factors.

[24] They are related through inherence having been born simultaneously.

Atomist: Conjunction and inherence must have separate existence since words and ideas expressive of the relationships of conjunction and inherence exist apart from the words and ideas expressing the things so related.

Vedāntin: This cannot be so, since even when there is but a single entity, it may give rise to many words and ideas from the individual and relative points of view. As for instance, Devadatta is one; but in the world he may be the object of many words and ideas, such as a man, a Brāhmaṇa, well versed in the Vedas, generous, boyish, youthful, old, a father, a son, a grandson, a brother, a son-in-law, and so on, from his personal and relative points of view; or as a digit (or line) though one, may have different words and values to express it, such as one, ten, hundred, thousand, and so on in accordance with the position to which it is shifted. Similarly the related things themselves come to be associated with such words and ideas as conjunction and inherence, rather than with the words and ideas denoting the two related things themselves; but this does not occur because of the existence of some distinct categories (like the relationships of conjunction and inherence). Accordingly, from the fact of the non-perception of some other categories (viz such relationships as conjunction and inherence), which are inferred to exist (from a supposition of their perception apart from the related things), it follows that those other things (viz relationships) do not exist (independently).

Atomist: If words and ideas standing for relationships denote merely the things related, then those words and ideas standing for relationships will persist for ever (that is to say, words and ideas expressing relationships will be present whenever the things related exist).

Vedāntin: This objection cannot be raised, for it was explained earlier that words and ideas are used from the individual and relative points of view.

Moreover, atoms, souls, and minds cannot have any conjunction, since they are without parts; for it is seen that substances having parts come in contact with other substances having parts.

Atomist: The atoms, souls, and minds can have imaginary parts.

Vedāntin: No, for if one can resort to imagining the existence of things that do not exist, then anything can be proved to exist; and there is no restriction to the effect that such and such non-existing things alone, and nothing else, are to be imagined to exist irrespective of whether they be contradictory or not. Besides, imagination is its own master and it can well be prolific. Moreover, there is no such overriding reason that apart from the six categories imagined by the Vaiśeṣikas, other categories, greater in number—say a hundred or a thousand—are not to be imagined. Accordingly, anything that anyone likes will stand established. Some kind-hearted man may wish that creatures may never have this round of birth and death, full of misery as it is; while some hedonist may imagine that the liberated souls should be born again. Who can debar either of them? Moreover, a dyad, which has parts, cannot come into intimate contact (or cohesion) with two partless ultimate atoms, just as much as it can have no intimate contact with space. For earth etc. and space do not come into intimate contact like wood and lac.

Atomist: Since the relationship of the container and the thing contained, subsisting between the two substances, viz the effect and the cause, cannot be justified in any other way, inherence has to be posited as a matter of course.

Vedāntin: No, for that leads to the fallacy of mutual interdependence (logical seesaw), inasmuch as the relationship of the container and the thing contained (or abode and the abider subsisting between the cause and the effect as propounded by you) can be established only after the cause and effect are proved to be different, and their difference can be established on the establishment of their relationship of being the container and the thing contained, just as in the case of a basin and the jujube[25] in it (which mutually distinguish each other). Thus ensues the fallacy of mutual interdependence (involving an argument in a circle). Not that any difference or any relationship of the container and the thing contained is admitted

[25] Or "The bowl and the berry tree (near it)" where the two things determine each other's position.

between the cause and the effect by the followers of Vedānta, for their position is that the effect is a peculiar condition of the cause itself.

There is this additional argument. As the ultimate atoms are limited in size, they must have as many surfaces (or parts) as there are directions—be they six, eight, or ten; and having parts, they will be impermanent. Thus the view that they are permanent and partless will be nullified.

Atomist: The very parts, that you assume to be defined by the different directions, are exactly the so many atoms admitted by me.

Vedāntin: Not so, for all things are subject to destruction through a process of change from the gross to the fine, till they reach the ultimate cause (which must be Brahman). For instance, earth, which, though a substance, gets destroyed, it being the grossest in comparison with the dyads etc.; then the subtle substances that belong to the same class as earth, but are subtler than earth, get destroyed; then the dyad disintegrates; so also the ultimate atoms too will disintegrate, since they belong to the same class as earth.

Atomist: Even while getting destroyed, they disintegrate merely through a process of being divided into their parts; (but ultimate atoms do not disintegrate, since they are partless).

Vedāntin: That creates no difficulty, for we said that destruction may take the form of the cessation of solidity, as in the case of a lump of clarified butter (*ghee*). Just as in the cases of *ghee* or gold, though there is no destruction of their parts, still a destruction of their solidity may take place on becoming liquefied by coming in contact with fire, even so in the case of the ultimate atoms there may be a destruction of grossness etc. by their reversion to the ultimate cause. Similarly an effect is not produced merely by a conjunction of parts; for milk, water, etc. are seen to turn into curd, ice, etc. even without the addition of parts. Thus since this doctrine of the atoms as the cause is based on such comparatively hollow grounds, since it runs counter to the Vedic texts holding forth God as the cause, and since it is not accepted by such worthy persons as Manu and others who abide by the Vedas, therefore it is to be entirely ignored. "Ignored by all respectable persons aspiring for the highest good"—this much has to be supplied at the end (of the aphorism).

Topic 4: Refutation of Buddhist Realists

It has been said that the doctrine of the Vaiśeṣika is not to be relied on since it is bolstered up by bad logic, it goes against the Vedas, and it is not accepted by the worthy people. This is semi-nihilistic having an affinity with nihilism; and hence we now proceed to show that the conclusions of the full nihilist are to be ignored all the more.[26] That nihilism, again, takes various forms in accordance with the doctrinal difference (in the presentation by one who explains) or the mental calibre of those who are taught. Among them there are three schools: some are Sarvāstitvavādins (divided into the Sautrāntikas and Vaibhāsikas, believing respectively in the inferential and perceptual existence of all things); some are Vijñanavādins (or Yogācāras, believing in the existence of consciousness or ideas alone); while others are Sarvaśūnyavādins (or Mādhyamikas, denying the existence of everything), (i.e. they are realists, idealists, and nihilists respectively). Now we first refute those Sarvāstitvavādins who admit both external things, viz the elements and elementals, and the internal things, viz the *citta* and *caittas*. Of these the elements are earth and other materials. The elementals are colour etc. and organs of sight etc. The four kinds of atoms of earth etc. which have the characteristics of solidity, fluidity, heat, and motion, get massed together in the form of (gross) earth etc. This is how they think. So also there are the five *skandhas*, (groups), viz the group of colour (consisting of the sense-organs and their objects), the group of egoism (*ālaya-vijñāna*—rousing constantly the idea of "I"); the group of feelings (of happiness etc.), the group of conceptual knowledge (such as "this is a cow" and so on), and the group

[26] The Vaiśeṣika thinks some things are permanent while others get destroyed and vanish into nothing. This partial nihilism being unacceptable, full nihilism is unacceptable all the more.

of attitudes (of liking, disliking, delusion, merit, demerit).[27] These also combine to form the basis of all internal dealings. This is how they think.

With regard to this, we say:

समुदाय उभयहेतुकेऽपि तदप्राप्तिः ॥१८॥

अपि Even समुदाये in (the supposed) combination उभय-हेतुके arising from either of the causes तत्-अप्राप्तिः that (combination) will not be achieved.

18. Even if the integration be supposed to arise from either of the causes, that will not be achieved.

From either point of view "that will not be achieved", there will not emerge any combination (or integration) that is supposed by others to have these two kinds of causes and to be of those two kinds. Even if the combination be supposed to arise from either of the two sets of causes, that will not materialize, that is to say, no combination will result—be it either a combination of the elements and the elementals arising from the atoms, or a combination of the five groups of things arising from those groups.

Why?

Because the components of such a combination are insentient and because consciousness can flash (from a contact between sense-organs and objects) only if a combination of things (forming the body etc.) is already there, and because no other steady and independent entity is admitted which is sentient, an experiencer, and a ruler, and which can bring about the combination. If impulsion to activity be postulated for them independently of any agent, then there will be the possibility of such impulsion continuing interminably.[28] Again, since currents (of ego-consciousness) cannot be determined to be either different or non-different (from the individual forms of consciousness constituting the current), and since everything (including the

[27] Of these, egoism is called *citta,* and the other four groups go by the name of *caittas.*

[28] So there will be no liberation.

current) is supposed to be momentary, there can be no activity (in this momentary current), and hence no impulsion (apart from its own birth). Therefore a combination cannot emerge, and in the absence of combination, all mundane existence dependent on it will be nullified.

इतरेतरप्रत्ययत्वादिति चेन्नोत्पत्तिमात्रनिमित्तत्वात् ॥१९॥

इतर-इतर-प्रत्ययत्वात् On account of being the cause of one another, (a combination will be possible) इति चेत् if this be the position, न it cannot be उत्पत्ति-मात्र-निमित्तत्वात् for (each is merely the cause of the origin (of another just succeeding).

19. If it be argued that a combination becomes possible since (nescience and the rest) can be the causes of one another (in a successive series), then we say, no, (for nescience etc.) can each merely be the cause of origin of another just succeeding.

Buddhist : Even if no sentient and steady experiencer or ruler be admitted as the agent bringing about the combination, still the transmigratory existence will be possible, since nescience and the rest are the causes of one another; and if the transmigratory existence becomes a possibility, there remains no need for depending on anything else. Those nescience etc. are: nescience (the idea of permanence with regard to things momentary), attitudes (attachment, detachment, and delusion arising from that false knowledge), ego-consciousness, name (i.e. the four elements depending on names), form (or colour), the six sense-organs (having egoism, four elements, and form as their habitations), touch (contact among name, form, and senses), sensation, thirst (for objects), impulsion (caused by that thirst), merit etc. (which are the sources of birth), birth (of the body), maturity (of the groups coming into being), death, sorrow, wailing, pain, misery, etc. (i.e. evils like honour, dishonour, etc.) —these and others of the same class which are sometimes indicated briefly or sometimes stated elaborately in the books of the Buddhists. These categories cannot be denied by other schools as well. So may it not be that when these nescience and the rest go on revolving for ever like (the cups in) a Persian wheel, as the cause and effect of one another, a combination of things, emerging out of the force of circumstances, becomes a possibility?

Vedāntin: That cannot be so.

Why?

Because they are merely the causes of the origination (of one another). A combination may be possible if any cause for the combination can be ascertained; but as a fact, it cannot be ascertained. For although nescience etc. be the causes of one another, the earlier ones will merely give rise to the later ones. That may well be so; but nothing can possibly become the source of a combination.

Buddhist: Did we not mention earlier that nescience and the rest (revolving in order) lead to the assumption of the existence of a combination by implication?

Vedāntin: To this we say: If your idea is that since nescience etc. cannot emerge unless there is a combination (in the form of a body), therefore they, as a matter of course, imply its existence, then you have still to tell me the cause of that combination. But in the course of examining the Vaiśeṣika theory we said that this is not possible even on the assumption of permanent atoms and experiencing souls which can sustain the acquired merits; and can this be possible here, my dear friend, simply by assuming momentary atoms which have no experiencers and which are not related with everything by way of being the abider and the abode (or the benefited and the benefactor)?[29] On the other hand, if this be your idea that nescience and the rest themselves constitute the source of combination, then how can they be the source of that combination when they themselves have to emerge into being by depending on that combination? Or if you think that the combinations themselves recur constantly like a current in this beginningless world, and nescience etc. are sustained by them, even then, when one combination emerges out of another, it will be either regularly similar or irregularly similar or dissimilar. If regularity

[29] Or according to a different reading, "experiencer and accomplisher of combination".

be admitted, then a human body can have no possibility of being transformed into divine, animal, or hellish bodies. And if irregularity be admitted, then a human body may at times turn momentarily into an elephant, and then be transformed again into a godly or human form. But either point of view goes against your own position. Moreover, your theory is that there is no permanent experiencer for whose experience the combination (i.e. body) should come into being. That means that an experience occurs merely for the sake of experience, and there need be none else to desire it. Similarly liberation will occur for its own sake, and so there need be none else to want liberation. Were there somebody else who could desire these, then he would be present both during the times of experience and liberation. And if he does so, the doctrine of momentariness will be negated. So even if nescience etc. be the sources of the emergence of one another, let them be so; still no integration (into a body) will be achieved thereby, for there is none to experience. This is the idea.

उत्तरोत्पादे च पूर्वनिरोधात् ॥२०॥

च And पूर्व-निरोधात् because the earlier one gets obliterated उत्तर-उत्पादे when the succeeding one originates.

20. *And because the earlier is negated when the later emerges, (therefore nescience and the rest cannot each be the cause of the next in the series).*

It has been stated that since nescience etc. are merely the causes for the origin of one another (successively), the formation of an aggregation cannot be achieved. But now it is being shown that even this assumption of being the cause of origin is not tenable. The postulate of those who swear by momentariness is that with the emergence of the entity of the succeeding moment, the entity of the earlier moment is obliterated. But one who postulates like this cannot establish any relationship of cause and effect between the two entities of preceding and succeeding moments. For the entity of the preceding moment that is getting obliterated or is already obliterated is involved in non-existence, and as such it cannot reasonably be the cause of the entity of the next moment. If, however, the idea be that the entity of the earlier moment becomes the cause of the next when the former has actually emerged into being and is in a state of positive existence, still it cannot become the cause of the entity of the next moment; for if any operative activity be assumed for a thing that has come into existence at an earlier moment, then the contingency will arise of its becoming associated with a subsequent moment (when the activity occurs). Again, if it be held that its operative activity (i.e. causality) consists in its mere presence, still this is unjustifiable; for no effect can emerge that is not transfused with the essence of the material cause. If, however, it be assumed that the essence of the cause persists in the effect, then you will be forced to give up the theory of momentariness owing to the presence of the essence of the material cause during the (succeeding) time that the effect lasts. If causality be admitted even without any transfusion of the effect by the essence of the cause, then it can be had anywhere; and so this will lead to the predicament of an unwarrantedly wide application (i.e. this causality of anything may be assumed anywhere).

Moreover, origination and annihilation must be the very nature of things, or some states of them, or some new things. None of these alternatives can be reasonably upheld. If origination and annihilation be the same as the very nature of a thing, then the word "thing" and the terms "origination and annihilation" will become synonymous. If, however, you think that there is some distinction and that by the terms origination and annihilation are meant the first and last states of a thing which is itself in a state intermediate between the two, even then the theory of momentariness will be destroyed, since the thing will get related to three moments—the first, the intermediate, and the last. Again, if origination and annihilation be absolutely disconnected with the thing like a horse and a buffalo, then the thing will become permanent, since it will not have any connection with either origination or annihilation. Even if the origination and annihilation consist in the perception and non-perception of the thing, still these (perception and non-perception) will be merely the qualities of the perceiver and not of the thing; and so the predicament of the thing becoming permanent will be just the same. From this viewpoint also, the Buddhist doctrine is illogical.

असति प्रतिज्ञोपरोधो यौगपद्यमन्यथा ॥२१॥

असति In the absence (of cause) प्रतिज्ञा-उपरोध: the proposition will fall through अन्यथा else यौगपद्यम् simultaneity (will take place).

21. *(If it be contended that the effect arises) even when there is no cause, then your assertion (of causation) will be stultified; else (if you contend that the entity of the earlier moment continues till the entity of the later moment emerges), the cause and effect will exist simultaneously.*

It has been said that since, according to the theory of momentariness, the entity of the earlier moment is swallowed up into annihilation, it cannot be the cause of the entity of the later moment. Should the Buddhists now assert that the effect arises even in the absence of the cause, their own assertion will be nullified, that is to say, their proposition that the perception of colour etc. and happiness etc. (*citta* and *caitta*) arises as a result of acquiring the four kinds of causes[30] (objects, senses, accessories, and past tendency), will be negated. And if origination be without any cause, then anything may originate anywhere, for there is nothing to hinder this. Should they, however, assert that the entity of the earlier moment continues till the origination of the entity of the later moment, then the cause and effect will become simultaneous. Even so, their assertion will be contradicted just the same; their declaration that all entities are momentary will stand discredited.

प्रतिसंख्याऽप्रतिसंख्यानिरोधाप्राप्तिरविच्छेदात् ॥२२॥

प्रतिसंख्या-अप्रतिसंख्या-निरोध-अप्राप्ति: There can be no arrival at

[30] In the case of a perception of blueness, blue is the *ālambana-pratyaya*, eye is the *adhipati-pratyaya*, light is the *sahakāri-pratyaya*, and the impression of a similar earlier perception is the *samāntarapūrva-pratyaya*.

artificial annihilation and natural annihilation अविच्छेदात् on account of non-termination.

22. *Neither pratisaṁkhyā-nirodha (artificial annihilation) nor an apratisaṁkhyā-nirodha (natural annihilation) is possible, for there can be no cessation (either of the current or of the individuals forming the current).*

Moreover, the nihilists (i.e. Buddhists) fancy that whatever becomes an object of knowledge and is different from the three categories, has an origination and is momentary. As for the three, they say, they are these—*pratisaṁkhyā-nirodha* (artificial annihilation), *apratisaṁkhyā-nirodha* (natural annihilation), and *ākāśa*. They think that all these three are non-substantial, non-existent, and illusory. The annihilation of a thing brought about deliberately is technically called *pratisaṁkhyā-nirodha*; the opposite of that is *apratisaṁkhyā-nirodha* (natural annihilation); and *ākāśa* is the mere absence of any obstruction (or screening). The aphorist will refute their *ākāśa* later on. The two kinds of annihilation are now being refuted. "There can be no arrival at", that is to say, there can be no possibility of the two kinds of annihilation, artificial and natural.

Why?

"Because there can be no cessation." These two kinds of annihilation—artificial and natural—will be perceivable in relation to either the chain of causality or the individuals (forming the chain). But they cannot relate to the chain. Since in all the chains, the individuals forming the chain continue uninterruptedly as a succession of causes and effects, therefore the chains cannot cease. They cannot relate to the individuals, because the individuals can have no such destruction as to leave no trace of recognition or to become non-existent, for under all circumstances, the common (material) substratum is seen through a process of recognition to persist uninterruptedly.[31] Where such recognitions are not obvious, the persistence of the common substratum can be inferred from the fact of its percep-

[31] In a pot, potsherd, and dust, the same earth is recognized as the common material.

tion elsewhere.[32] Hence annihilation of either kind, fancied by others, is untenable.

उभयथा च दोषात् ॥२३॥

च And दोषात् owing to defect उभयथा from either point of view.

23. And (the Buddhist view is untenable) owing to defect arising from either point of view.

The annihilation of nescience and the rest, that is assumed by the others and is classified under the heads of artificial and natural annihilations, must be achieved either as a result of complete knowledge associated with its accessories (of self-control etc.) or (spontaneously) by itself. On the first assumption will arise the predicament of discarding the theory of destruction being an uncaused event. On the second assumption will arise the predicament of instruction about the spiritual path (as taught by Buddha) becoming useless. Thus, being subject to defects from either point of view, this philosophy is incoherent.

आकाशे चाविशेषात् ॥२४॥

च And अविशेषात् on account of absence of dissimilarity in the case of space.

24. And (non-existence cannot be asserted) in the case of ākaśa on account of the absence of (its) dissimilarity (with destruction).

As for their view that the two kinds of destruction and *ākaśa* have no reality, we have already refuted the assertion that the two kinds of destruction are nonentities. Now it is being refuted that *ākāśa* is a nonentity. It is unreasonable to assert with regard to *ākāśa* that it is a nonentity, for even in its case

[32] Doubt may arise, for instance, in the case of the seed becoming the sprout, but the process of inference with regard to persistence of earth, can be extended to this case as well.

nothing stands in the way of knowing it as an entity equally like the artificial and natural destructions. As for Vedic proof, it is established from such Vedic texts as, '*Ākāśa* originated from the Self' (Tai. II. i. 2), that *ākāśa* is a substance. But for those who are not convinced by Vedic texts, it can be inferred through its quality of sound, for qualities such as smell and the rest are seen to abide in substances like earth and the rest. Moreover, according to you, *ākaśa* is merely an absence of obstruction (or covering). So when any one bird flies in space, there is the presence of obstruction (and so absence of space); hence another bird that may try to fly will find no scope for doing so.

Opponent: It will fly where there is no obstruction.

Vedāntin: In that case, that very thing with the help of which "the absence of obstruction" is specified, will itself be the positive entity *ākāśa*,[33] and it will not be a mere absence of obstruction. Moreover, when the Buddhist asserts that *ākāśa* consists in a mere absence of obstruction, he lands himself into a self-contradiction. For according to the Buddhist view, in the chain of questions starting with, "Sir, on what does earth rest?" occurs this question after earth etc., "On what does air rest?" And the answer to that question is, "Air rests on *ākāśa*", That becomes logically consistent if *ākāśa* is a substance. For this reason also it is illogical to say *ākāśa* is a nonentity. Besides, it is contradictory to say that the two kinds of annihilation and *ākāśa*—these three are nonentities and yet they are eternal; for that which is non-existent can neither be eternal nor non-eternal, for all judgements about relationship, as between a quality and the thing possessing it, are based on the existence of something. And if such a relationship, as between a quality and the thing qualified, does exist, then this will inevitably mean that the thing itself is as much real as a pot, for instance, and it cannot be a nonentity.

अनुस्मृतेश्च ॥२५॥

च And अनुस्मृतेः on account of remembrance.

[33] For, a negation presupposes the existence of its counterpart.

25. And (a permanent soul has to be admitted) because of the fact of remembrance (i.e. memory).

Moreover, when the nihilist asserts all things to be momentary, he will have to assert the perceiver also to be momentary. But that is an absurdity because of the fact of remembrance. Remembrance means recalling to mind something after its perception, and that can happen only when the agent of perception and memory is the same; for one person is not seen to remember something perceived by another. How can there be an awareness of the form, "I who saw earlier see now", arise unless the earlier and later perceiver be the same? Moreover, it is well known to all that direct experience in the form of recognition, such as "I who saw that, see this now", occurs only when the agent of seeing and remembering is the same. Should their agents be different, then the awareness will take such a form, "I remember, but somebody else saw"; but nobody in fact experiences in this way. Where cognition takes such a form, all understand the agents of seeing and remembering to be different, as for instance in, "I remember that he saw this then". But in the present case where occurs the remembrance of the form, "I saw this then", even the nihilist understands the agent of seeing and remembering to be but he himself, and he does not deny his own past vision by saying, "I did not see that", just as much as he would not deny that fire is hot or that it emits light. That being the case, the nihilist cannot avoid a rebuttal of his theory of momentariness in the face of a single agent becoming connected with the two moments of perception and remembrance. And why should not the nihilist be ashamed of himself when he holds on to the theory of momentariness at the same time that he recognizes all his perceptions from now on to the last breath and the past ones from his very birth till now as having happened to his own very same self?

If he should maintain that this can come about through similarity, then he should be answered thus: Since similarity, which is apparent in such a judgement as "This is similar to that", is dependent on two factors, and since from the point of view of the believer in momentariness, there is no single perceiver of two similar things, it amounts to a false incoherent jargon on his part to assert that recognition results from similarity. This can only be possible if the perceiver of the similarity of the entities of the preceding and succeeding moments be the same. But then the theory of momentariness will be adversely affected on account of the presence of the same person during two moments.

Buddhist: The cognition, "This is like that", is an entirely new cognition which is not dependent on the perception of the things of the earlier and succeeding moments.

Vedāntin: No, since in the awareness, "This is like that", are involved (three) distinct factors.[34] If this experience of similarity be an independent experience (not related to the two similar factors), then the expression, "This is like that", would be meaningless, and the expression would simply be "similarity".[35] If people engaged in judging something do not take into account the facts that are universally accepted, then even after the statement of the validity of one's own point of view and the invalidity of one's opponent's view it will not appear to be convincing to the intellect of either the judges or oneself. That alone should be spoken of which has been ascertained as, "This thing is certainly so". Were one to speak of something other than this, one would simply expose one's garrulousness. Moreover, human dealings cannot be said to be dependent on mere similarity, for the experience is of the existence of the entity itself (expressing itself as, "I am that very person") and not of mere similarity with that (as would be expressed in, "I am like that person"). It may be conceded, however, that in the case of an external thing there may be the possibility of doubt of the form, "It may be either that very thing or similar to that", for in the case of an external thing there is scope for delusion. But in the case of the cognizer himself there can never be such a doubt as, "I may be either that very person or similar to him".

[34] This, that, and the similarity.

[35] True judgement requires a consideration of both points of view, and that cuts at the root of the theory of momentariness, since such a consideration spreads over several moments.

For there occurs a definite recognition of identity, as in, "I who saw yesterday, am remembering today". For this reason also, the nihilist theory cannot be reasonably sustained.

The nihilist theory is untenable for this additional reason that the nihilists do not admit any lasting and persisting cause (inhering in the effect), so that their view amounts to saying that something comes out of nothing. And they show that existence comes out of non-existence when they assert, "The effect cannot arise without destroying the cause; for the sprout comes out of a seed when the latter is destroyed and a pot out of a lump of clay when the latter is destroyed. Were a product to come out of an unchanging cause, anything could come out of anything and anywhere; for the cause is common to all". Thus since (according to them) the sprout and the rest emerge from the seed and the rest when these latter get swallowed up in non-existence, they conclude that existence comes out of non-existence. With regard to this we say:

नासतोऽदृष्टत्वात् ॥२६॥

न Not असत: from non-existence, अदृष्टत्वात् because this is not seen (thus).

26. Something does not come out of nothing, for this does not accord with experience.

Existence does not come out of non-existence. If something can come out of nothing, then it becomes useless to refer to special kinds of causes, since non-existence as such is indistinguishable everywhere. There is no distinction, as regards the nature of non-existence, between the non-existence arising from the destruction of the seed and the rest and the horn of a hare, both being equally unsubstantial (false). Had there been any distinction, then only would the assertion of such separate causality be meaningful as, "The sprout comes out of the seed alone, and the curd out of the milk alone". But when an indistinguishable non-existence is posited as the cause, the sprout and the rest may as well spring out of a hare's horn and the like. This is, however, contradicted by experience. If, again, distinctive attributes be ascribed to non-existence on the analogy of the lotus etc. having blueness etc., then on that very analogy of the lotus etc., non-existence will turn into existence by the very fact of possessing distinctive qualities. Moreover, non-existence can never be the source of anything, precisely because it is non-existent like the hare's horn etc. Were existence to arise out of non-existence, all the effects would be imbued with non-existence. But that goes against experience, for all things are perceived to exist as positive entities with their respective distinguishing features. Not that anybody will admit that such real objects as earthen plates etc., in which earth inheres, are the transformations of threads for instance. As a matter of fact, people perceive all real earthen things as the transformations of earth itself.

As for the assertion that something can come out of nothing since no immutable thing can become a cause unless it be by destroying its real nature, that is a wrong assertion; for gold and the rest that are recognized as remaining unchanged assume the roles of such cause and effect in the cases of products like a gold necklace and so on. Even in the cases of the seed and the rest where there is an appearance of destruction of substance, it is not the earlier state, undergoing destruction, that is understood to be the cause of the subsequent state; for what is admitted is that those parts (or cells) of the seed and the rest which remain undestroyed and which persist (in the sprouts and the rest) become the material causes of the sprout and the rest. Accordingly since nothing that actually exists is seen to result from nonentities like the horn of a hare etc., and since it is seen that from existing things like gold etc. originate existing things (like necklace etc.), the assertion of something coming out of nothing cannot be substantiated. Moreover, all people get deluded by the nihilists (i.e. Buddhists) who first assert that the ego-consciousness and the mental moods arise from the four causes and that the aggregates of elements and elementals arise from the atoms (see p. 405), and then again assume that something comes out of nothing and thus negate their own assertions.

उदासीनानामपि चैवं सिद्धिः ॥२७॥

च And एवम् in this way सिद्धिः success (should come) अपि even उदासीनानाम् to the indifferent.

27. *And (if something can come out of nothing, then) on the same ground, success should come even to the indifferent people.*

Moreover, if it be admitted that something can come out of nothing, then on the same ground even the indifferent people who are inactive should attain their desired results, for non-existence is clearly evident even there; and so a husbandman who does not engage in cultivation should get his crop, a potter who makes no effort for preparing the clay should get his vessels ready, and a weaver who does not make any effort for weaving the yarn should get a cloth just as much as one that weaves. And nobody need in any way strive for heaven or liberation. But such a position is neither reasonable nor is it accepted by anybody. Therefore this assertion of something coming out of nothing is unjustifiable.

Topic 5: Buddhist Idealism Refuted

Vijñānavāda: The defects, such as the impossibility of formation of aggregates that arise against the views of those Buddhists who believe in external things, having been pointed out, the Vijñānavādin (Buddhist Idealist believing in momentary consciousness) now stands up in opposition. (He asserts): This (earlier) viewpoint, based on the belief that external things exist, was taught (by Buddha) as a concession to some of those followers who were noticed to have a predilection for external things. But that was not the view of Buddha himself, whose real sanction was for the doctrine of the group constituted by consciousness (subjective cognition) alone. According to this Vijñānavāda, all dealings concerned with means of knowledge, objects of knowledge, and ends of knowledge become possible as subjective occurrences superimposed on consciousness;[36] for

[36] Consciousness itself appearing as the imaginary blue colour becomes the perceived object; as awareness it becomes knowledge; as the power

even though an external object may exist, there can be no activity of the means of knowledge etc., unless it be through a superimposition of that object on consciousness (i.e. unless the mind or intellect is aware of it). If it be asked, "How, again, can it be known that all these processes are subjective, and that nothing but subjective cognition exists"?—the answer he (the Buddhist) gives is that, this is so because no external thing can possibly exist. When external objects are assumed, they must either be the individual atoms or an aggregate of them—a pillar for instance. Of these the knowledge of the atoms cannot be acquired through a perception of the pillar etc., for the atoms are not objects of perception.[36a] And a pillar etc. cannot be a conglomeration of atoms, since the (aggregates like) pillar etc. cannot be ascertained to be either different from or identical with the atoms. Thus also are to be rejected genus, (quality, action), etc. Moreover, knowledge, as it arises, has the common feature of being a mere awareness; but it displays a selective bias for individual forms, such as the knowledge of a pillar, the knowledge of a wall, the knowledge of a pot, the knowledge of a cloth, and so on. This particularization cannot be possible unless there be some peculiarity in each individual cognition itself. And so in this way it has to be admitted that knowledge has a tendency to have the same form as its content. And once this is admitted, the objective appearances become explicable from the standpoint of consciousness alone (they being included within the knowledge itself), and it becomes useless to assume external objects. Moreover, from the fact of the simultaneous awareness of the knowledge and its object, it follows that the object and its knowledge are identical. For neither of them can be known without the other. This simultaneity would not have been possible if knowledge and its object were naturally different;[37] for there would be nothing to cause a hindrance

of that revelation it becomes the means of knowledge; and as the repository of that knowledge it becomes the knower.

[36a] Are not perceived as possessed of the qualities of a pillar, e.g. unity, solidity, etc.

[37] For momentary consciousness would not then be reasonably associated with an object that is different from it.

(to the cognition of one even when the other is not cognized) For this reason also there is no external object.

This is to be understood as analogous to dream etc. Even as the cognitions in a dream, a magic, water in a mirage, a phantom city in the sky, etc. have stamped on them the perceptions of the knowledge and the known, though there are no objects, so also it is to be understood that the perceptions of a pillar etc. in the waking state are of a similar nature, for as perceptions they do not differ. If it be asked, "Were there no external objects how could there be a diversity in knowledge?" then the Vijñānavādin says that this is possible owing to a diversity of mental impressions.[38] For it is nothing contradictory in this beginningless state of transmigration that cognitions and mental impressions should have a variety, acting as they do alternately as the causes and effects of one another like the seed and the sprout. Moreover, it is known through a process of agreement and difference (i.e. from positive and negative instances) that variety in knowledge occurs from past impressions; for by both of us it is admitted that even in the absence of objects, a variety in cognition, caused by past impressions, takes place in dream etc. But it is not admitted by me that even without such mental impression, knowledge can have a variety in conformity with external objects. Hence also external objects do not exist.

Vedāntin: This being the position we say:

नाभाव उपलब्धेः ॥२८॥

न Not अभाव: non-existent उपलब्धेः because of perception.

28. (External objects are) not non-existent, for they are perceived.

It cannot be asserted that external things do not exist.

Why?

"Because they are perceived." As a matter of fact such things

[38] The previous knowledge occurring in a beginningless chain creates the impression (or tendency). Through its force, a variety of cognitions, in the form of blueness etc., can occur even after the interval of several moments.

as a pillar, a wall, a pot, a cloth, are perceived along with each act of cognition. And it cannot be that the very thing perceived is non-existent. How can a man's words be acceptable who while himself perceiving an external object through sense-contacts still says, "I do not perceive, and that object does not exist", just as much as a man while eating and himself experiencing the satisfaction arising from that act might say, "Neither do I eat, nor do I get any satisfaction"?

Vijñānavādin: Well, I do not say that I do not perceive any object, but all that I hold is that I do not perceive anything apart from the perception.

Vedāntin: Yes, you do speak like that, since you have no curb to your mouth; but you do not speak logically, for something other than the perception has to be admitted perforce, just because it is perceived. Not that anybody cognizes a perception to be a pillar, a wall, etc., rather all people cognize a pillar, a wall, etc. as objects of perception. And it is for this reason that all people understand those others (viz the Buddhists) as really assuming the existence of an external thing even while they deny it by saying, "That which is the content of an internal awareness appears as though external". For they use the phrase "as though" in the clause "as though external" just because they too become aware of a cognition appearing externally in the same way as is well known to all people, and yet they want to deny any external object.[39] Else why should they say, "as though external"? For nobody speaks thus: "Viṣṇumitra appears like the son of a barren woman". Accordingly, those who accept truth to be just what it is actually perceived to be, should accept a thing as it actually reveals itself externally, and not "as though appearing outside".

Buddhist: Since no object can possibly exist externally, I come to the conclusion that it appears as though it is outside.

Vedāntin: This conclusion is not honest, since the possibility or impossibility of the existence of a thing is determined in accordance with the applicability or non-applicability of the

[39] What people understand from the Buddhist teaching is that to the Buddhist the internal awareness of an object appears as occurring outside. That understanding itself is a proof of their awareness of externality.

means of knowledge to it, but the applicability or non-applicability of the means of knowledge is not ascertained in accordance with the possibility or impossibility (of the thing). What is known through anyone of the means of knowledge, such as direct perception etc., is possible, and what cannot be known through any one of these means of knowledge is impossible. In the case under discussion, the external things are known individually by the respective means of knowledge; so how can they be declared to be impossible by raising such alternatives as different, non-different, etc.?[40] For external things are perceived as a matter of fact. It is wrong to say that external things do not exist merely on the ground that cognition is seen to have the likeness of an object, because the very likeness of an object is not possible unless the object itself be there, and also because the object is cognized outside. So also it has to be admitted that the regularity in the simultaneous appearance of the cognition and its object is owing to the relation of causality between them and not owing to their identity. Again, in (such forms of awareness as) "knowledge of a pot", "knowledge of a cloth", the difference is seen in the two qualifying parts, pot and cloth, but not in the substantive part knowledge, even as in the cases of "a white cow" and "a black cow" we find that whiteness and blackness alone differ, but not so the cowhood. And the difference of the one (viz cowhood) from the two (whiteness, blackness) stands out clearly, as also the difference of the two from the one. Therefore an object and its knowledge differ. Similar should be our comprehension in the cases of the seeing of a pot and the remembrance of a pot. Here also the substantives, viz seeing and remembering differ, but not so the adjectival portion, viz pot; this is just as in the cases of the cognitions, "the smell of milk", and "the taste of milk", where the substantives smell and taste alone differ, but not so the adjectival part milk.

[40] The Buddhists argue that external objects cannot logically exist because a pillar, for instance, cannot be proved to be either different or non-different from the atoms constituting it. But the Buddhist view is illogical; for according to them, consciousness alone exists, and it is not gross. So it cannot have for its content things that are many and gross; hence there can be no idea of external things according to their theory.

Moreover, as regards two cognitions occurring successively, which vanish after self-revelation, there can be no logical apprehension of the one by the other. And in that case will be nullified all the assertions made in the Buddhist scriptures themselves about the difference among cognitions, momentariness and other attributes, individual characteristics, common characteristics, bequeathing of tendency by one cognition to the other, true, false, or mixed attributes arising from contact with nescience, as also about bondage, liberation, and so on.

Again, if one admits a distinction between knowledge and knowledge, why should not one admit external objects such as a pillar, a wall, and so on?

Buddhist: A cognition is actually perceived.

Vedāntin: External things too are perceived, and so they too should be admitted.

Buddhist: Since cognition is a luminous thing it stands self-revealed like a lamp, but an external object is not like that.

Vedāntin: Then like assuming that fire burns itself, you assume that something can act on itself by itself, which is absolutely opposed to reason; yet you do not admit the well-known fact, bearing no contradiction, that an external object is known through a cognition which is different from the object. What a great display of erudition you make! It cannot be asserted that consciousness is known to itself as something apart from objects for the simple reason that there can be no action on oneself.

Buddhist: If a cognition has to be known by some entity other than itself, that second one will have to be known by another, and that one again by another. This will lead to an infinite regress. Moreover, since cognition is an illuminator like a lamp, if you should imagine a second cognition (to know it), then since both the cognitions are similar there will be no revelation of the one by the other, so that this whole assumption will fall to the ground.

Vedāntin: Both these arguments are wrong, for once an awareness of the cognition occurs, no further desire to apprehend the witness of the cognition can arise; and so there is no possibility of infinite regress.[41] And since the witness and the cognition are different by nature, there can be a relationship of the perceiver and the perceived among them. Besides, the self-evident witness cannot be denied.[42] There is another consideration. When you assert that cognition shines by itself like a lamp without requiring some other cognition, you virtually say that a cognition is not apprehended by any other means of knowledge or by anything else, which would be like saying that a thousand lamps shine (unknown) within a massive boulder.

Buddhist: Exactly so; for cognition being of the nature of an awareness (suggested by you), you have only approved the view that we hold.

Vedāntin: No, for it is seen that some other perceiver having the eye etc. as his instrument, perceives a lamp etc. So it is understood that since cognition has equally to be revealed by some one else, it can be perceived like a lamp only when a distinct perceiver is present.

Buddhist: By upholding the theory that the perceiving witness is self-effulgent, you only accept under a different garb of words my own view that cognition shines by itself.

Vedāntin: Not so, for you admit many such distinctions for cognition as origin, destruction, multiplicity, and so on. And hence it is that we establish the apprehension of that cognition by some entity outside it, as in the case of a lamp.

वैधर्म्याच्च न स्वप्नादिवत् ॥२९॥

च And वैधर्म्यात् on account of difference of nature न not स्वप्न-आदि-वत् like dream etc.

[41] As soon as a mode (*vṛtti*) occurs in the mind as a result of contact between the senses and objects, the object and this mental cognition (*vṛtti-jñāna*) become revealed by the witnessing Self. An object cannot reveal itself, it being inert; the mental apprehension also cannot reveal itself, being equally inert. But when the existence of the witness gets revealed on that mental apprehension, there can be no further question of revealing the witness. This witness is different from the mental cognition. Thus there is no infinite regress.

[42] To substantiate the difference among your momentary cognitions you have to admit the witness which stands aloof to see this difference.

29. And because of the difference of nature (the waking state is) not (false) like dream etc.

It has been said by those who deny the existence of external things that perceptions of things like a pillar etc. in the waking state occur even in the absence of external things, just as they do in a dream; for as perceptions, they are similar. That has to be refuted. With regard to this we say, the perceptions of the waking state cannot be classed with those in a dream.

Why?

Because of difference of characteristics; for waking and dream states are really different in nature.

In what does that difference consist?

We say that it consists in being subject to sublation or not. To a man, arisen from sleep, the object perceived in a dream becomes sublated, for he says, "Falsely did I imagine myself in contact with great men. In fact I never came in contact with great men; only my mind became overpowered by sleep; and thus this delusion arose." So also in the case of magic etc., adequate sublation takes place. But a thing seen in the waking state, a pillar for instance, is not thus sublated under any condition. Moreover, dream vision is a kind of memory, whereas the visions of the waking state are forms of perceptions (through valid means of knowledge). And the difference between perception and memory, consisting in the presence and absence of objects, can be understood by oneself, as for instance when one says, "I remember my beloved son, but I do not see him, though I want to see". That being so, it cannot be asserted by a man, who feels the difference of the two, that the perception of the waking state is false, merely on the ground that it is a perception like the perception in a dream. And it is not logical for those who consider themselves intelligent to deny their own experience. Moreover, one who cannot speak of the waking experiences as naturally baseless, just because this would contradict experience, wants to speak of them as such on the strength of their similarity with dream experiences. But anything that cannot be the characteristic of something in its own right, cannot certainly be so because of a similarity with another. For fire which is felt to be warm does not become cold because of some similarity[43] with water. As for the difference between dream and the waking states, this has already been shown.

न भावोऽनुपलब्धेः ॥३०॥

न Not भावः existence अनुपलब्धेः: because of non-perception.

30. (Tendencies) can have no existence since (according to you) external things are not perceived.

And the assertion has to be refuted that even in the absence of objects, the diversity of experience can be explained on the strength of the variety of tendencies (or impressions). To this we say: The tendencies cannot logically exist; for according to you, objects are not perceived externally. It is precisely owing to the perception of objects that a variety of (mental) tendencies corresponding to the diverse objects can arise. But how can a variety of tendencies arise when no object is perceived? Even if these tendencies have no beginning (on the analogy of the seed and the sprout), this infinite regress will amount to a baseless assumption leading us nowhere like the blind leading the blind,[44] and it will thus cut at the root of all human dealings, so that your aim will remain unfulfilled. And it is to be noted that the positive and negative instances that were adduced by those who would deny the existence of external objects by saying, "All these experiences are caused by tendencies and not by objects"—those instances also stand refuted from this standpoint; for no tendency can arise unless there be a perception of some object. Moreover, from the admission that apprehension of objects is possible even in the absence of past tendencies,

[43] For instance, both being "substances".

[44] The whole chain of one tendency creating another will start with the initial defect of the first tendency being created without an external object. Thus, being basically illogical, it cannot help you out of the rut. The analogy of the seed-and-sprout is illogical; for both seed and sprout are perceived as causing each other interminably, both backward and forward; but you do not admit that an object produces a perception.

and from the non-admission that tendencies are possible in the absence of perception of object, it follows that such positive and negative instances (adduced by you) also prove the existence of objects. Besides, what you call a tendency is a kind of impression (or predisposition); and from common experience it is known that a disposition cannot be imagined to exist unless it has some basis to stand on, whereas you have nothing to supply this need; for nothing can be found (by following your view) to stand as an abode for dispositions.

क्षणिकत्वाच्च ॥३१॥

च And क्षणिकत्वात् on account of momentariness.

31. And (the ego-consciousness cannot be the abode), for it is momentary.

As for the ego-consciousness that is assumed to be the abode of disposition (or tendency), that too has no stable form, since you postulate its momentariness like sense-perception. Hence it cannot be the abode of tendencies. For unless there be some principle running through everything and abiding through all the three periods of time or some unchanging witness of all, there can be no human dealing involving remembrance, recognition, etc. which are contingent on past impressions that are stored up in conformity with environment, time, and causation. If the ego-consciousness be (assumed to be) unchanging by nature, your doctrine (of momentariness) will be set at naught. Moreover, since the theory of momentariness is upheld equally in Vijñānavāda, all the defects arising from momentariness that were levelled (by us) against the theory of those (Buddhists) who believe in the existence of (momentary) external things, viz those shown under the aphorisms starting from, "And because the earlier is negated when the later emerges" (II. ii. 20), are to be remembered in this context as well. Thus are refuted both these Buddhist points of view—of both those who believe in the external things and those who believe in (subjective) consciousness. As for the view of the absolute nihilist, no attempt is made for its refutation since it is opposed to all means of valid knowledge. For human behaviour, conforming as it does to all right means of valid knowledge, cannot be denied so long as a different order of reality is not realized; for unless there be an exception, the general rule prevails.

सर्वथाऽनुपपत्तेश्च ॥३२॥

च Besides, सर्वथा from every point of view अनुपपत्तेः being untenable.

32. Besides (this view stands condemned), it being untenable from every point of view.

To be brief, from every point of view that this Buddhist doctrine may be examined for finding out some justification, it breaks down like a well sunk in sand; and we do not find any the least logic here. Hence also all behaviour based on the Buddhist scripture is unjustifiable. Moreover, Buddha exposed his own incoherence in talk when he instructed the three mutually contradictory theories of the existence of external objects, existence of consciousness, and absolute nihilism; or he showed his malevolence towards all creatures, acting under the delusion that these creatures would get confused by imbibing contradictory views. The idea is that the Buddhist view should be abjured in every way by all who desire the highest good.

Topic 6: Jaina View Refuted

नैकस्मिन्नसम्भवात् ॥३३॥

न Not एकस्मिन् in the same thing असम्भवात् owing to impossibility.

33. (The Jaina view is) not right since the presence (of contradictory attributes) in one and the same thing is impossible.

The view of Buddha has been disproved. Now is being invalidated the view of the naked ones (Jainas). The categories approved by them are seven—called (1) the soul (experiencer),

(2) non-soul (the experienced objects), (3) impulsion (of sense-organs towards objects), (4) control (of senses and organs), (5) austerities (which completely demolish merit and demerit through experience of happiness and sorrow), (6) bondage (action), (7) liberation (a continuous upward movement). In brief, there are only two categories—soul and non-soul, for the others get included, as best they can, in these two only. This is how they think. They speak of these two in another way thus: There are five categories called *asti-kāyas*—the category of soul, the category of body (combination of atoms), the category of merit, the category of demerit, and the category of space (want of hindrance). They describe many subsidiary divisions of each one of these according to the assumptions of their own doctrine. And in all cases they apply this logic of what they call the logic with seven facets: (1) somehow (may be it) exists, (2) somehow (may be it) does not exist, (3) somehow exists and does not exist, (4) somehow indescribable, (5) somehow exists and is indescribable, (6) somehow does not exist and is indescribable, (7) somehow exists, does not exist, and is indescribable. Thus they apply this logic with seven facets (*sapta-bhangi-naya*) to unity and permanence as well.[45]

With regard to this we say: This assumption is not justifiable. Why?

"Owing to the impossibility of presence in one and the same thing"; for it is not possible for such contradictory characteristics as existence, non-existence, and so on to be associated simultaneously with the same thing; just as much as cold and heat cannot be. These seven categories that are definitely ascertained to be so many in number and such in character, must either be just as they are described or they must not; for else the resulting knowledge of such an indefinite nature, which may

[45] Unity and permanence somehow may exist, may not exist, may both exist and not exist, and so on. When the intention is to speak of a thing as successively existing and non-existing, they use the third mood. But when the intention is to speak of existence and non-existence simultaneously, the two states being inexpressible at the same time, they call it indescribable.

either be as it is described or may not be so, will certainly be unauthoritative like doubts.[46]

Jaina: When knowledge of a definite nature, viz that a thing has different facets, does arise, it cannot be invalid like doubts.

Vedāntin: We say, no; for one who would unrestrictedly affirm indefiniteness for every object without exception, the definiteness of his knowledge itself being equally an object of knowledge, would come under the application of such alternatives as, "somehow it may exist, somehow it may not exist", and so on; and hence this knowledge would have an indefinite nature all the same. Similarly, the ascertainer, as also the knowledge that results from the ascertainment, would be somehow partially existent and somehow partially non-existent. This being so, how can a teacher of the Jaina school, (who has to be assumed to be) an authority, impart instruction when the means of knowledge, objects of knowledge, the knower, and knowledge remain indefinite in nature?

Also how can those who rely on his views act upon his instruction about things which remain indefinite in their nature? For all people engage without hesitation in the requisite practices for acquiring some result when that has been ascertained to be inevitable, but not otherwise. For this reason also, if anyone should write a scripture of such indefinite significance, his words will be unacceptable like those of the mad or intoxicated. So also when the doubt arises as to whether the categories mentioned as five in number (viz soul, non-soul, etc.), have really that number or not, the conclusion from one point of view will be that the number is five, and from another point of view that it is not so; and hence those things can be greater or less in number. Besides, these categories cannot be indescribable (that is to say, existing and non-existing at the same time); for if they be indescribable, they cannot be expressed in words. It involves a contradic-

[46] For the soul etc. are averred these seven alternative moods as also their own characteristics of being the soul etc. Now, are these "existence" and "non-existence" constant or are they spasmodic? In the first case, the position is untenable, since it contradicts such perceptions as, "This pot does exist". In the second case, there can be no definite knowledge of anything.

tion to utter them in words and yet to hold that they are indescribable. Again, even when they are expressed in words, they may either be understood as such or may not be understood. Similarly the perfect knowledge, arising from the comprehension of all this, may exist or may not; so also its opposite, false knowledge, may or may not exist. Anyone who would speak in that way, would be classed with the intoxicated and the mad, but not with people whose words can be trusted. Moreover, no reasonable inspiration for action to achieve liberation or heaven will follow from an indefinite knowledge that heaven and liberation exist on the one hand and do not exist on the other; or similarly that they are eternal from one point of view and impermanent from another. And the eternally free souls (Arhats) and the rest (who either become free through spiritual practices or continue in bondage), whose natures have been determined to be so in their own (Jaina) books, will tend to have an indefinite nature. Thus since it is not possible for any of the categories, counting from the souls, to have such contradictory attributes as existence and non-existence, and since in the presence of the attribute of existence there can be no possibility of the presence of the other attribute of non-existence, just as much as existence is not possible in the presence of non-existence, therefore this Jaina doctrine is illogical. Hereby it is to be understood that all such tenets of indeterminateness, to the effect that the very same thing is one and many, permanent and impermanent, different and non-different at the same time, that are assumed by them, are demolished as well. As for their imagination that the aggregation, called *pudgala* (body) can result from the combination of atoms, that stands discredited as a result of the earlier refutation of the Vaiśeṣika theory of atoms. Hence no separate attempt is made for overthrowing it.

एवञ्चात्माऽकात्स्न्यम् ॥३४॥

एवम् Similarly च also आत्म-अकात्स्न्यम् non-pervasiveness of the soul.

34. Similarly also (arises the defect of) the soul having no all-pervasiveness (or having only a medium dimension).[47]

Just as the defect consisting in the impossibility of the presence of contradictory attributes in the same substratum arises in the Jaina view, so also arises the other defect of the embodied soul becoming limited (or of a medium dimension).

How?

The Jainas think that the embodied soul has the dimension of the body. Now if it conforms to the size of the body, then the soul will be of a medium dimension—non-omnipotent and limited; and so like the pot etc. the soul will be subject to impermanence. Again, because the bodies have no fixed dimensions, the soul born as a man will assume the size of a human body. Then when as the result of the fruition of some past action it is born as an elephant, it will not pervade the whole of the elephant body, and when it is born as an ant, it will not be wholly contained in the body of the ant. This defect applies equally to the different stages of boyhood, youth, and old age during the same life.

It may be held that the soul has infinite parts; these parts get condensed in a small body and expanded in a large one. But then it has to be stated as to whether there is any obstruction to the different parts of the soul becoming concentrated at the same place or not. Should there be any impediment, the infinite parts will not be contained in the same limited space; and even if there be no impediment, then all the parts can very well be accommodated in the place occupied by a single part, so that there will be no possibility of increase in magnitude. As a result, the predicament will arise of the embodied soul becoming atomic in dimension. Besides, it cannot even be imagined that the soul that is limited by the size of the body should have infinite parts.

Again, if it be argued that whenever in due sequence the soul gets a large body, it has an accretion of some parts, and when-

[47] *Ratnaprabhā* has "*Akārtsnyam-Madhyama-parimāṇatvam*"; *Bhāmatī* has, "*Akṛtsnatvam-paricchinnatvam*". *Madhyama-parimāṇa* is a dimension changing according to the body; and *paricchinna* means limited.

ever it gets a small body it has a reduction of some parts, then the answer is:

न च पर्यायादप्यविरोधो विकारादिभ्यः ॥३५॥

च And न not अपि even पर्यायात् from (assumption of) sequence अविरोध: contradiction can be avoided, विकार-आदिभ्य: in the face of mutability etc.

35. And the contradiction cannot be avoided even by an assumption of sequence (in the increase and decrease of parts), for still there will be the defects of mutability etc.

Even by assuming the increase and decrease of parts in succession it is not possible to establish beyond any contradiction the fact that the soul conforms to the size of the body.

Why?

For this will lead to the defects of changefulness etc. for the soul. In the first instance, mutability becomes unavoidable for the soul that increases and decreases for ever through the accession and depletion of parts. And if it be mutable like a piece of leather, it will be subject to impermanence. In that case will be falsified the assumptions about bondage and liberation, which facts are expressed by saying that the soul, surrounded by eight kinds of *karma*,[48] remains sunk in the sea of this world like a bottle gourd, and it floats upward when that bond is snapped. Moreover, the parts that come and go will be other than the soul precisely because they are adventitious like the bodies etc. In that case some part that is everlasting will be the soul. But

[48] Covering knowledge, covering vision, deluding, and screening—which four are called *ghāti-karma*. These are explained thus: (1) belief that liberation does not follow from knowledge of reality, (2) belief that liberation does not follow from the hearing of the Jaina tenets (3) not finding any speciality about the path shown by the Jaina teachers, (4) hindering the progress in the path of liberation. *Aghāti-karmas* are: (1) *vedaniyam*—belief that I have to know the reality, (2) *nāmikam*—belief that I have such a name, (3) *gotrikam*—the idea that I have entered into the rank of your disciples, (4) *āyuṣkam*—work done for the maintenance of the body, or it means the body made of blood and semen. *Gotrika* may also mean—making this body fit for the realization of truth.

that cannot be pin-pointed to be so and so. Again, it has to be stated from where these incoming parts emerge and where the outgoing ones submerge. It cannot be that they come out of the elements and merge into the elements; for the soul (of which they are the parts) is not material. And nothing else can be ascertained as either the common or uncommon source of (any one or all) the parts of the (individual) soul; for that lacks evidence. Furthermore, in such a case, the nature of the soul will remain indeterminate; for the incoming and outgoing parts will have no definite measurement. Thus owing to the predicament of such defects, it is not possible to take shelter under a successive increase or decrease in the parts of the soul.

Or the explanation will be this: Under the previous aphorism the *doubt* raised was that, if the soul be of the size of the body, the soul will be subject to limitation (or incompleteness) owing to its assumption of other enlarged or attenuated bodies, and thus it will not be eternal. In reply to that doubt it may be held (by the *Jainas*) that though the size of the soul has no fixity, owing to successive changes, still the soul can have permanence on the analogy of a current of a river. Just as the russet-robed (Buddhists) hold that though cognitions have no permanence, yet a current of these cognitions can well be permanent, similar may be the position of the naked ones (Jainas) as well. This was the opposite point of view presented under the earlier aphorism. The *answer* (of the *Vedāntin*) to that is being given under the present one: As to that, if the current be false, you will land into a theory of the non-existence of the soul. Or if it be true, the soul will be subject to such defects as mutability. Hence this view is unjustifiable.

अन्त्यावस्थितेश्चोभयनित्यत्वादविशेषः ॥३६॥

च And अन्त्य-अवस्थिते: on account of the permanence of the ultimate size, उभय-नित्यत्वात् since both the (other) sizes become permanent अविशेष: distinction ceases to exist.

36. The ultimate size attainable (by the soul) being permanent, the other two sizes also must be so; and hence there will be no distinction (among the sizes).

Besides, the Jainas hold that the ultimate size attained by a soul on the eve of liberation becomes permanent. Just like that, the earlier initial size and the intervening size of the soul can also be permanent, and hence there will be similarity (among the magnitudes). Thus the soul will have the size of one single body only and it will not acquire any other inflated or deflated body.[49]

Or the explanation is this: Since the ultimate size of the soul is permanent, its sizes in the two earlier stages also must be the same. In that case the soul has to be admitted to be atomic or non-atomic at all times equally. Thus the Jaina view is as illogical as the Buddhist view; and hence it is to be ignored.

Topic 7: God is not a mere Superintendent

Now is being refuted the theory that God is a mere superintending cause (and not a material cause as well).

How can this be understood?

Because by the teacher (Vyāsa) himself God has been established as both the material and efficient causes in the aphorism, "And Brahman must be the material as well, so as not to contradict the declaration and the illustration" (I. iv. 23), as also in, "This is also understood from the teaching about the will to create" (I. iv. 24). If it be maintained now that God's causality in general is being refuted here, then from a contradiction between the earlier and later portions, the objection would be raised that the aphorist stultifies himself. Therefore, what is being diligently rebutted here is the view that "God is not the material cause, but is simply the efficient cause," because it runs counter to the Vedāntic conclusion that Brahman is one without a second. This un-Vedic conception takes various forms. Some, following the Sāṁkhya and Yoga tenets, conclude that God, who is the ruler of *Prakṛti* and *puruṣa* (Nature and soul), is merely an efficient cause, and that God, Nature, and soul are

[49] In order that there may be no incompatibility among the three sizes, the earlier bodies must have the same size as the ultimate one, for if the bodies differ in size, the soul's conformity to them will be impossible, as already shown.

totally different from one another. The Māheśvaras (Śaivas and others), however, think that the five categories—effect (i.e. *mahat*, *ahaṁkāra*, etc.), cause (i.e. Nature and God), union (*samādhi*), observances (e.g. bathing three times a day etc.), and the end of sorrow (liberation)—have been taught by the Lord Śiva for the removal of bondage (*pāśa*) of the creatures (*paśus*). Paśupati (Lord of the creatures) is God, and He is the efficient cause. This is how they propound it. Similarly there are some Vaiśeṣikas and others who speak of God as the efficient cause by somehow keeping within their own sphere of thought. Hence the answer is being given in the aphorism:

पत्युरसामञ्जस्यात् ॥३७॥

पत्युः For the Lord (there can be no creatorship) असामञ्जस्यात् on account of incongruity.

37. For the Lord there can be no creatorship, for that leads to incongruity.

"For the Lord", that is to say, for God, there can be no causality towards the universe by becoming (a mere) superintendent over Nature and souls.

Why?

"On account of incongruity."

What is that incongruity?

For a Lord who creates the various creatures by dividing them into grades of inferiority, mediocrity, and superiority will be open like ourselves to the charges of likes, dislikes, etc., so that He will cease to be God.

Opponent: That defect will not arise, for He acts in accordance with the past actions of the creatures.

Vedāntin: Not so, for if such God and actions be mutually the impeller and the impelled, it will lead to a logical seesaw (or argument in a circle, each being prompted by the other).

Opponent: This fault will not arise, since creation is without beginning.

Vedāntin: No, just as at present, so also in the past that defect f arguing in a circle is equally present;[50] so that we are faced vith the logic of the blind leading the blind (for both action nd God are impelled, there being no impeller). Moreover, it is he accepted view of the logicians that by noticing an impulsion o work it can be inferred that there are such defects (i.e. ikes, dislikes, delusion, etc.)—(*Nyāya-sūtra*, I. i. 18). For ıobody is seen to engage in any work for one's own or for omebody else's sake unless one is impelled by these defects. As ı rule, all people serve other people's purposes only when they ıre impelled by their own interest. In this way also this is ncongruous; for God will cease to be God by being selfish. The ncongruity arises even from the admission that God is a special type of *puruṣa* (soul), for that *puruṣa* is admitted to be indifferent to everything.

सम्बन्धानुपपत्तेश्च ॥३८॥

च And सम्बन्ध-अनुपपत्ते: owing to impossibility of relationship.

38. And (the incongruity arises) because of the impossibility of a relationship.

There is still another incongruity. God who is different from Nature and soul cannot rule them unless it be through some relationship. But the relationship of conjunction is not possible, since God, Nature, and souls are all omnipresent and partless. Nor can it be the relationship of inherence, because of the impossibility of determining which is the container and which the thing contained. Nor can any other relationship be inferred from the presence of the effect, since that very causal relationship has yet to be established.[51]

[50] The Vedāntins also adopt this logic of the beginninglessness of the world for escaping out of the defect of a logical seesaw (B. S. II. i. 34). But to them the world is unreal, and their argument amounts to showing that everything is indescribable. Everything is within Māyā—God, creation, creatures, and all. Others say, they are true (See p. 436 top).

[51] It has not been proved so far that the universe is a creation of *Prakṛti* (Nature) under the promptings of God. So the relationship of God with Nature cannot be proved from the existence of creation.

Opponent: How does the believer in Brahman solve thi problem?[52]

Vedāntin: He has no difficulty; for in his case an indescrib able relationship of identity (between God and Māyā) i reasonably sustainable (Śv. I. 3). Moreover, a believer ir Brahman ascertains the cause etc. in accordance with the Vedas and so for him there is no such need that he must accept al things just as they are perceived. But the opponent, who deter mines the nature of the cause etc. on the strength of illustra tions, has to accept things just as they are perceived. Here lie the excellence.

Objection: Your opponent too can have the scriptures composed by omniscient teachers; as such both of you are equally backed by scriptural authority.

Vedāntin: No, for that will lead to arguing in a circle, omniscience being proved from the knowledge of the authority of the scriptures and the (authority of the) scriptures being proved from the knowledge of the omniscience of the author. Therefore the ideas about God held by the Sāṁkhyas and Yogins are illogical. This charge of incongruity can be equally levelled in a suitable manner against all other theories that are outside the Vedic pale.

अधिष्ठानानुपपत्तेश्च ॥३९॥

च And अधिष्ठान-अनुपपत्तेः because of the impossibility of being directed.

39. And (the position is untenable) because of the impossibility of (Nature) coming under (His) direction.

For this additional reason the God imagined by the sophists has no justification. Were God just what He is imagined to be, He could impel Nature (Pradhāna) etc. by becoming their director (i.e. moulder) in the same way as a potter is in the case of clay etc. But this cannot be proved; for Nature, which is

[52] Your Māyā and Brahman also are both pervasive and partless, and you do not admit inherence as a relationship.

beyond the range of perception etc. and is devoid of form etc., cannot come under God's direction (i.e. moulding), it being different from clay etc.

करणवच्चेन्न भोगादिभ्यः ॥४०॥

करण-वत् Like (presiding over) the organs चेत् if this be the contention, न not so भोग-आदिभ्यः on account of (resulting) experiences etc.

40. Should it be argued that God will direct Nature like (a man directing) the organs, then it cannot be so, for that will result in God's having experiences (of happiness, sorrow etc.).

Opponent: It may be thus. Just as the individual soul directs the senses, counting from the eye, which cannot be perceived and which are without forms etc., so also God can direct Nature.

Vedāntin: Even thus it is not possible to maintain this. It is by noticing such facts as the experiencing (of happiness and sorrow) that one is led to infer that the set of sense-organs has a director. But in this case, such experience etc. (accruing to God from Nature) are not in evidence. And if Nature etc. be equated with the set of sense-organs, then God will have the same kind of experiences as the transmigrating souls.

Or the two aphorisms can be explained in another way:

अधिष्ठानानुपपत्तेश्च ॥३९॥

39. And (God cannot be proved), since no physical support (adhiṣṭhāna) is possible for Him.

For this further reason, God as He is conceived by the sophists has no logical justification. In this world, a king, having the support of a body, is seen to rule over a kingdom, but not so without a physical support. Therefore, if anyone wants to fancy an unseen God by drawing upon that analogy, one will have to imagine some body as the seat of the sense-organs of God. But such a conception is impossible, since a body comes into being after creation starts; it is not possible before creation. And if God has no physical support, He cannot be a director. For this is what accords with experience.

करणवच्चेन्न भोगादिभ्यः ॥४०॥

40. If a body, equipped with sense-organs, be assumed for God, (we say that) this is not possible; because of (consequent) experiences etc.

Again, if in accordance with common experience, it be fancied that God can have a body to hold His organs, even then His ordainership will not be logically sustainable; for if God has a body, He will have to undergo experiences like any transmigrating soul, so that we shall be faced with the predicament of God Himself being deprived of His Godhead.

अन्तवत्त्वमसर्वज्ञता वा ॥४१॥

अन्तवत्त्वम् Finitude वा or असर्वज्ञता absence of omniscience.

41. God will be subject to finitude or loss of omniscience.

For this additional reason, the God, as conceived by the logicians, is an impossibility. For by them He is declared to be omniscient as well as infinite. So also are admitted by them an infinite Nature and infinite souls which are different from one another. Now, that being the case, the question is: Can the limits (in number and extension) of Nature, souls, and Himself be determined by God or not? Either standpoint is open to defect. How?

According to the first view, Nature, souls, and God will inevitably come to an end, since their limits in number or extension are grasped by God. For this accords with human experience, according to which whatever in this world has any limitation in number or dimension has an end, for instance a pot. Similarly, Nature, souls, and God, all three being circumscribed in number or dimension, must have an end. As for a limitation in number, that arises from the enumeration of Nature, souls, and God as three entities. And their characteristic of dimensions, as also the vast number associated with the souls, may well be determined by God. From this the conclusion arises that the world as well as the state of transmigration will have an end for those transmigrating souls which become freed from this world from among these numerically and physically limited souls. Thus also when other souls become free in succession, the transmigratory existence itself, as also those who are in that state of existence, will come to an end. According to them, it is Nature together with her derivatives, acting under the direction of God, that constitutes the state of transmigration for providing experiences to the souls. Now in the absence of that as well, over what will God assume His directorship, and Divine power? If Nature, soul and God have an end in this way, they will have a beginning as well. When they have both beginning and end, we shall be landed into nihilism. Again, if for avoiding this defect, they stick to the other alternative that the number and extension of Nature, souls, and God are not determinable by God, then this will lead to the other defect that God will lose His omniscience. For this reason also the theory of the causality of God, as it is advocated by the sophists, is illogical.

TOPIC 8: BHAGAVATA VIEW REFUTED

उत्पत्त्यसम्भवात् ॥४२॥

उत्पत्ति-असम्भवात् Owing to the impossibility of origin.

42. *(The Bhāgavata view that Saṁkarṣaṇa and others originate successively from Vāsudeva and others is wrong), since any origin (for the soul) is impossible.*

We have refuted the view of those who hold that God is simply a directing, efficient cause without being the material cause as well. Now is being discarded the view of those who hold that God is both the material and efficient causes.

Opponent: Was not Brahman ascertained to be both the material and efficient causes exactly like this with the help of

Vedic texts (B. S. I. iv. 23)? And it is the accepted principle that a Smṛti is authoritative when it follows the Vedic texts. So what is the reason for this attempt at disproving this (Bhāgavata) view?

Vedāntin : To this we say: Although a portion of this kind is common to both of us and should not be a matter of dispute, there is another portion which leads to disagreement. Hence this endeavour at rebutting it.

With regard to this the *Bhāgavatas* think: God as Vāsudeva, who is pure consciousness by nature, is the supreme reality. He has divided Himself and set Himself up as a fourfold figure—in the form of Vāsudeva, in the form of Saṁkarṣaṇa, in the form of Pradyumna, and in the form of Aniruddha. The supreme Self is referred to by the name Vāsudeva, the embodied soul is pointed out by the term Saṁkarṣaṇa, mind has the epithet of Pradyumna, and egoism is called Aniruddha. Of them Vāsudeva is the highest material cause, while Saṁkarṣaṇa and others are His products. By adoring Him for a hundred years through such a process as visiting Him in His temples (in a proper state of body, mind, and speech), acquiring the requisites for worship, worship, *japa* (constant recital) of His *mantra*, and meditation, one becomes freed from such drawbacks (as likes and dislikes), and then one attains the Lord Himself.

Vedāntin : Now, we do not refute the view stated therein that Nārāyaṇa, who is superior to Nature and is well known to be the supreme Self and the Self of all, has divided Himself by Himself into many forms; for from such Vedic texts as, "He assumes one form, He assumes three forms" (Ch. VII. xxvi. 2) etc., it is known that the supreme Self does become multifarious. As for the predilection for His propitiation, consisting in visiting His temple etc. and so on, with exclusive devotion and for long, that also is not denied. For the contemplation of God is well in evidence in the Vedas and Smṛtis. But with regard to the view that Saṁkarṣaṇa originates from Vāsudeva, Pradyumna from Saṁkarṣaṇa, and Aniruddha from Pradyumna, we say that it is not possible for an individual soul, called Saṁkarṣaṇa, to be created from the supreme Self, called Vāsudeva; for such a view will lead to such defects as impermanence. If the individual soul has any origin, it will be subject to such defects as being impermanent and so on. Owing to this drawback, liberation, consisting in attaining God, will not be possible for the soul, for an effect gets completely destroyed on reaching back to its source. The teacher (Vyāsa) will deny any origin for the individual soul in the aphorism, "The individual soul has no origin, because the Vedic texts do not mention this and because the soul is known from them to be eternal" (II. iii. 17). Accordingly this assumption is unjustifiable.

न च कर्तुः करणम् ॥४३॥

च And न not कर्तुः from an agent (originates) करणम् an implement.

43. And (this view is wrong because) an implement cannot originate from its agent (who wields it).

That (Bhāgavata) assumption is wrong for this additional reason that in the world it is never seen that such implements as an axe etc. originate from the agent of the action (of cutting etc.), say for instance Devadatta. But the Bhāgavatas describe this thus: From the individual soul, called Saṁkarṣaṇa, who is the agent, originates the instrument mind, called Pradyumna; and from the mind, originating from the agent, emerges egoism, called Aniruddha. We cannot, however, comprehend this in the absence of any confirming parallel illustration, nor do we come across any such Vedic text.

विज्ञानादिभावे वा तदप्रतिषेधः ॥४४॥

वा Alternatively विज्ञान-आदि-भावे (even) on the (assumption of the) possession of knowledge etc. तत्-अप्रतिषेधः there is no remedy of that defect.

44. Alternatively even if (it be assumed that Vāsudeva and others are) possessed of knowledge, (majesty, etc.), still the defect cannot be remedied.

Opponent: It may rather be the case that these Saṁkarṣaṇa and others are not considered to be the individual souls and so on.

In what way are they conceived then?

They are all believed in as Gods, being endowed with all such divine attributes as the mental power of knowledge and divinity, physical strength, heroism, and boldness; they are all Vāsudevas to be sure, free from the defects (of likes, dislikes, etc.), not born of Nature, and free from destruction etc. Hence the defect alluded to, of origin being impossible, does not arise.

Vedāntin: To this our reply is that even so that defect is not remedied; the impossibility of origin persists all the same. The idea is that the defect of the impossibility of origin does crop up from another side.

How?

If the idea be this that these four Gods, counting from Vāsudeva, are entirely different from one another and are yet possessed of equal attributes, and that they do not constitute a single Self, then it is useless to imgine many Gods, since the divine functions can be accomplished by a single one. Besides, this goes against their own conclusion, inasmuch as it is admitted that God as Vāsudeva alone is the supreme Reality.

Again, if the position be this that these four forms belong to a single God, though they have equal attributes, still the impossibility of origin remains where it was. For in the absence of any distinguishing quality, Saṁkarṣaṇa cannot spring from Vāsudeva, nor can Pradyumna from Saṁkarṣaṇa, or Aniruddha from Pradyumna. As between the cause and effect, some distinction has got to be admitted as existing, as in the case of clay and a pot, for unless some peculiarity exists, it is not possible to distinguish them as cause and effect. But in any one or all of them, counting from Vāsudeva, the followers of the Pañcarātra school do not admit any distinction created by degrees of knowledge, majesty, etc.; for they believe that all the forms are but Vāsudeva without any distinction. Besides, these forms of God cannot remain confined within the number four, since they believe that the whole universe, starting from Brahmā and ending with a clump of grass, is but a form of God.

विप्रतिषेधाच्च ॥४५॥

च And विप्रतिषेधात् owing to contradiction.

45. Besides, (in this scripture) many contradictions are met with and it runs counter to the Vedas.

And in the scripture of the Bhāgavatas many kinds of contradiction are in evidence, concerning, for instance, qualities and the things qualified. Thus one comes across beliefs like this. The qualities, viz the power of knowledge and divinity, physical strength, heroism, and boldness, are nothing but so many selves and they are the same as Vāsudeva, the Lord. Moreover, this scripture contradicts the Vedas, since it is seen to cast a slur on the Vedas by declaring, "Not finding the highest good in the four Vedas, Śāṇḍilya studied this scripture". Therefore it is concluded that this assumption is illogical.

Section III

Topic 1: Origin of Space

Introduction: In various places in the Upaniṣads we come across texts dealing with creation etc. which seem to represent different schools of thought. Some mention the origin of space, while others do not; similarly some mention the origin of air, while some do not; so also with regard to the individual soul and the organs and senses. In the same way, contradiction is met with in the different Upaniṣads in the matter of the order of creation etc. The ground for ignoring the opponents' points of view was shown to be their self-contradiction. So our own point of view may run the risk of being ignored on that very ground of self-contradiction. Hence begins the succeeding amplification (in two sections) for clarifying the purport of all the Upaniṣadic texts about creation. And when that purport is clarified, the result achieved will of course be the removal of the doubt already mentioned. So to begin with, it is being considered about space as to whether it has any origin or not.

Pseudo-Vedāntin: As to that, it is being propounded:

न वियदश्रुतेः ॥१॥

न Not वियत् space अश्रुतेः because not heard of.

1. Space is not (a created thing), since this is not heard of in (some of) the Upaniṣads.

Space does not certainly originate.

Why?

"Since this is not heard of." There is no mention of it in the context dealing with creation. For in the Chāndogya Upaniṣad occurs the text, "O amiable one, all this was but Existence in the beginning—one without a second" (VI. ii. 1), where Brahman, called Existence, is presented as the topic, and then with regard to this Brahman, it is said, "That deliberated" and

"That created fire" (VI. ii. 3), where fire, (usually) occupying the middle place among the five great elements, is placed first and mention is made of the creation of (only) the three elements fire, water, and food (earth). Vedic texts are the valid means to us in the matter of generating knowledge about the supersensuous things. And no text is in evidence here proving the origin of space. Hence space has no birth.

अस्ति तु ॥२॥

तु But अस्ति there is.

2. But there is (a mention of the origin of space).

Opponent: The word "but" is used to indicate the preference for another point of view. Space might not have been mentioned as having any origin in the Chāndogya Upaniṣad, but it is (so mentioned) in another Upaniṣad. After starting with, "Truth, Knowledge, Infinity is Brahman" (Tai. II. i. 1), the followers of the Taittirīya recension recite thus, "From that Self, that is such, originated space" (II. i. 1). Thereby the two Upaniṣads come into conflict, inasmuch as creation starts in one with fire, and in another with space.

Vedāntin: Is it not proper that these two Upaniṣadic passages should be reconciled?

Opponent: They should truly be reconciled; but it is not known how to do so.

Why?

For the creator who is mentioned only once in, "That created fire" (Ch. VI. ii. 3), cannot reasonably be brought (simultaneously) into association with two created things (fire and space) by asserting, "That created fire, That created space".

Vedāntin: Is not an agent, mentioned but once, seen to have (successive) connection with two different acts, as in the statement, "He cooks rice after cooking a curry"? Similarly we can connect the creator with the two created things by saying, "That created fire after creating space."

Opponent: That is not logical. For in the Chāndogya, fire is understood as the first creation, whereas in the Taittirīya space comes first. And both cannot be the first creation. Hereby is also exposed the contradiction involved in other Vedic texts. Thus in the text, "From that Self, which is such, originated space" (Tai. II. i. 1), the ablative case (in *ātmanaḥ*—from the Self) and origination are mentioned but once; now to connect these two (ablative case and origination) with both space and fire at the same time to imply, "From that originated space, from that originated fire", will not be logical. Besides, a different process is mentioned in the text, "From air came fire" (Tai. II. i)[1].

Faced with this contradition, somebody else says:

गौण्यसम्भवात् ॥३॥

गौणी Secondary असम्भवात् because of impossibility.

3. (The Upaniṣadic passage about creation of space has) a secondary sense, for real creation is impossible.

Pseudo-Vedāntin: Space has no origin, just because there is no Vedic mention. As for the other text quoted as speaking of the origin of space, that must have "a secondary sense".

Why?

"Because of impossibility", for it is not possible to establish the origin of space so long as the followers of the views of the venerable Kaṇabhuk (i.e. Vaiśeṣikas) live. For they set aside the theory of the origin of space just because of the absence of the requisite causes. All that is seen to originate, does so from the inherent (material), non-inherent (concomitant), and efficient causes. And an inherent cause of an object is constituted by an abundance of substance of the same class. But for space there can be no such abundance of any substance of the same class, which can constitute its inherent cause; nor is there any conjunction of such substances which can be accepted as the non-inherent cause from which space can emerge. And since these two causes are absent, any efficient cause for space, which func-

[1] Just as the Chāndogya contradicts Taittirīya, so also the latter contradicts the former. First, the precedence of fire in Chāndogya is irreconcilable. Secondly, in Taittirīya, air is the source of fire; in Chāndogya, the Self is the source.

tions when these are favourable, becomes a far cry. In the case of fire, etc., however, which have origin, it is possible for them to have some peculiarity before and after creation; for instance, such phenomena (or effect) as illumination do not exist before their creation, but they come to exist after creation. But for space, no such peculiarity can be conceived of either before or after creation. For before the creation of space, what indeed can be conceived of as existing without space, interstices, or cavities? Moreover, space is proved to be without any origin on account of its being different in nature from earth etc. and owing to its characteristics of all-pervasiveness etc. Hence, just as we meet with such expressions in common usage as, "Make space (i.e. room)", "Space (room) is provided", and so on, in which the word space is used in a secondary sense (to mean room); or just as there are references to the differences in the same space in a secondary sense in such expressions as, "the space in a pot", "the space in a jar", "the space in a house"; or just as there are such expressions even in the Vedas as, "They sacrifice the forest-animals in the spaces"; similarly the Vedic texts about creation are to be understood in a secondary (or figurative) sense.

शब्दाच्च ॥४॥

च And शब्दात् from Vedic texts.

4. And (this is borne out) by Vedic texts.

Pseudo-Vedāntin: The Vedas as a matter of fact, declare the birthlessness of space, since it is stated, "Now the subtle—it is air and space. It is immortal" (Bṛ. II. iii. 3); for that which is immortal cannot have an origin. And the text "It is all-pervasive and eternal like space", while comparing Brahman with space in respect of the attributes of omnipresence and eternality, also indicates that space has those two characteristics. As such, space cannot reasonably be maintained to have an origin. There is also the statement, "This Self is to be known to be as infinite as this space", as also the texts, "Brahman has space as Its body" (Tai. I. vi. 2), "Space is the Self" (Tai. I. vii. 1). If space had an origin, it could not have been used as an attribute of Brahman, like blueness in the case of a lotus. So it is understood that Brahman is ever on a par with space.

स्याच्चैकस्य ब्रह्मशब्दवत् ॥५॥

च And स्यात् it is possible एकस्य for the same (word) ब्रह्म-शब्द-वत् like the word Brahman.

5. And it is possible for the same word ("originated") to have (primary and secondary senses) like the word Brahman.

This aphorism follows in succession the series of objections raised about the word "originated".

It may be objected thus: How can the single word "originated" occurring in the context, "From that Self, which is such, originated space" (Tai. II. i. 1), have the primary sense when used at a later stage in connection with the words fire and the rest which come subsequently, whereas it has a secondary sense when used (earlier) in connection with space?

Pseudo-Vedāntin: Therefore the reply is being given. Just as the word Brahman can have primary and secondary senses with reference to different objects, so also the same word "originated" can have primary and secondary meanings with reference to different objects. As for instance, the same word Brahman has a secondary sense with reference to food etc. (in the expressions "Food is Brahman" etc.), occurring in the context, "Try to know Brahman through concentration of mind; concentration is Brahman" (Tai. III. 2); but it has a primary sense with regard to Bliss (in "He knew Bliss to be Brahman"—Tai III. vi.) in the same context; or as the word Brahman is used by way of courtesy with regard to concentration which is a means to the knowledge of Brahman, but directly (in the primary sense) in connection with the Brahman to be known; similar is the case here.

Objection: If, again, space has no origin, how can the declaration, "(Brahman is) one only without a second" (Ch. VI. ii. 1), be supported? For does not Brahman come to have a second to Itself by the presence of space? How then can it be true that

ll becomes known when Brahman is known (for the unpro-
luced space remains still unknown)?

Pseudo-Vedāntin: That is being answered. The text, "One only" can be justified when considered with reference to (the absence of) Its own effects (before creation). Somebody, for instance, who had seen clay, turning rod, and potter's wheel at the potter's house on the previous day and then notices next day different kinds of vessels spread about, might say, "It was all but clay alone the other day". What he would imply by that declaration would be that the products of clay alone did not exist on the previous day, but not that the rod etc. also were not there. Similarly the text ("without a second") speaking about (the) non-existence of a second rules out any other ordainer: unlike the potter who is observed to be an ordainer apart from the clay which is the material cause of the earthen vessels, there is no other ordainer for the universe apart from Brahman which is its material cause. And it cannot be that Brahman becomes associated with a second entity owing merely to the presence of space. Multiplicity is created by differences in the characteristics (of entities). But it is not a fact that before creation Brahman and space have different characteristics; because like milk and water in a mixture, they both (then) possess the common properties of pervasiveness, want of features, (partlessness, formlessness), etc. At the time of creation, however, Brahman becomes active for producing the universe, while the other (viz space) remains motionless; and hence it is thought that they are different. In this way also the identity of Brahman and space in a secondary sense stands proved according to such Vedic texts as, "Brahman has space as Its body" (Tai. I. vi. 2). And thus also is proved the attainment of omniscience through the knowledge of Brahman. Moreover, whatever has origin, originates in some space and time that are non-separate from the space and time of space itself, which again is non-separate from Brahman. So when Brahman and Its effects are known, space also becomes known *ipso facto*. Just as the few drops of water thrown into a potful of milk become taken up when the milk itself is taken, for when the milk is taken up, the drops of water do not stand apart to be taken up separately, so also when

Brahman is known, space becomes known as a matter of cours for space does not stand apart from Brahman and Its effect either in space or time. Hence the Vedic text about the origi of space has a figurative sense.

Vedāntin: Such being the position, the aphorist says:

प्रतिज्ञाऽहानिरव्यतिरेकाच्छब्देभ्यः ॥६॥

प्रतिज्ञा-अहानिः The declaration stands unaffected अव्यतिरेकात् from the non-difference (of effects); शब्देभ्यः (confirmed) fron Vedic texts.

6. The (Vedic) assertion (that "all things become known when the one is known") can remain unaffected only if all the effects are non-different from Brahman; and this is confirmed by Vedic texts.

In all the Upaniṣads, individually, we come across a declaration on the following line, "That by knowing which all that is not heard becomes heard, all that is not thought becomes thought, all that is not known becomes known" (Ch. VI. i. 3), "All this becomes known, my dear, when the Self is seen through hearing, thinking, and meditation" (Bṛ. IV. v. 6), "What is that, sir, by knowing which all this becomes known?" (Mu. I. i. 3), "There is no knowledge of all outside Myself". "That declaration can remain unaffected", unhampered, "only if all things (without exception) are non-different from the Brahman" that is to be known. For if anything be different from Brahman, the declaration that "all becomes known when one is known" will be stultified. And that non-difference can be upheld justifiably only if all things without exception originate from Brahman alone. And it is in accordance with the logic of the identity of the material cause and its effects, that the justifiability of the declaration is revealed in the Vedic texts themselves. It is precisely for this reason that the declaration is first made in, "That by which the things unheard become heard", and then this declaration is confirmed with the illustrations of clay etc. which are calculated to establish the non-difference of cause and effect. It is in affirmation of this very fact that the subsequent texts, "O amiable one, all this was Existence alone in the beginning, one without a second" (Ch. VI. ii. 2), "It saw (or thought), It created fire" (Ch. VI. ii. 3) show that the effects arise from Brahman; and then non-difference is shown in the texts starting with, "All this has that alone as its Self" (Ch. VI. viii. 7), till the end of the sixth *Prapāṭhaka*. Now if space be not a product of Brahman, it will remain unknown even when Brahman is known. But that will undo the declaration. It is not proper, however, to invalidate the Vedas by hurting this declaration. So also in every Upaniṣad, the appropriate texts establish that very declaration with the help of suitable illustrations, for instance, "...and this all are the Self" (Bṛ. II. iv. 6), "All that is in front is but the immortal Brahman" (Mu. II. ii. 11), and so on. Accordingly, space also originates just like fire and the rest. The assertion is unjustifiable that space has no origin because of the absence of any such Vedic statement; for another Vedic text, speaking of the origin of space, was quoted earlier, viz "From this Self that is such, originated space" (Tai II. i. 2).

Opponent: True it was quoted, but this conflicts with this other text, "That created fire" (Ch. VI. ii. 3).

Vedāntin: No, for all the Vedic texts have a unity of purport, (that is to say, they can be reconciled).

Opponent: Let the non-contradictory texts have a unity of purport (and be reconcilable). But contradictions have been pointed out here to the effect that the creator who is heard of only once cannot be connected with two things to be created, that the two things cannot both be born first, and that there can be no possibility of alternativeness (in either of the two being the first).

Vedāntin: That is no defect, for the creation of fire is heard of third in the Taittirīya Upaniṣad in, "From that Self which is such, was born space, from space air, and from air fire" (II. i. 2). And this text cannot be construed in any other way, whereas the Chāndogya text can be interpreted thus, "Having created space and air, That (Brahman) created fire" (Ch. VI. ii. 3). This (latter) text, which has for its main purport the presentation of the birth of fire, cannot rule out the birth of space well known in other Upaniṣads, for the same single sentence cannot operate in two ways.[2] The creator, though one, can create many products in succession. And since there is a possibility of maintaining a unity of purport (among the texts by reconciling them), a Vedic text should not be abandoned by imagining some contradictory meaning. Again, it is not a fact that we want to connect the same creator, heard of only once, with the two things (space and fire) that are to be created; rather a second thing to be created is drawn upon on the authority of another (i.e. Taittirīya) Upaniṣad.[3] Besides, just as the direct mention of the creation of everything from Brahman in the text, "All this is certainly Brahman, for everything is born from, rests in, and merges in Brahman" (Ch. III. xiv. 1), does not overrule the order of creation stated elsewhere with fire as the first (Ch. VI. ii. 3), similarly the Vedic mention of creation of fire from Brahman cannot rule out the order of creation with space in the forefront as mentioned in another (i.e. Taittirīya) Upaniṣad.

Opponent: Is not the sentence, "Everything is born from, rests in, and merges in Brahman; worship with calmness" (Ch. III. xiv. 1), meant for enjoining (meditation with) tranquillity? This is not a passage about creation, so that it cannot overrule the order of creation established elsewhere (in the Chāndogya Upaniṣad). The text, "That created fire", however, speaks of creation itself, so that the order as stated there in the (Chāndogya Upaniṣad, VI. ii. 3) has to be accepted.

Vedāntin: To this the answer is, no; for the entity space, as established in another Upaniṣad, cannot be rejected just because fire has got the first place (somewhere); for an order follows the nature of things. Moreover, in the text, "That created fire", no (explicit) word indicating order is in evidence, the order being posited (merely) from the implication of the sentence. That, however, is ruled out by the order known from another Upaniṣad, viz "from air comes fire" (Tai. II. 1). As for assigning the first place to space and fire, either alternatively or

[2] If it means the creation of fire, it cannot also mean the non-creation of space.

[3] We are not open to the charge of making one sentence of Chāndogya serve two purposes; we rather rely on two sentences.

jointly, that is ruled out because of impossibility and non-acceptance (by the Upaniṣads). Hence there is no contradiction between the two texts. Moreover, the assertion, "That by knowing which things unheard become heard", is found at the commencement. For confirming this statement, one has to include space among the things created, though it is not mentioned (there in the Chāndogya). That being so, it is all the more unreasonable not to take space into account, though it is mentioned in the Taittirīya Upaniṣad.

And the statement was made that space being non-different from everything so far as the time-space relation is concerned, it becomes known, as a matter of course, along with Brahman and Its products, and that hence the declaration ("everything becomes known when one is known") is not compromised, nor is the Vedic text "one without a second" contradicted, for like milk and water (mixed together), Brahman and space can reasonably be non-different. As to this, our answer is that this fact of everything becoming known through the knowledge of one is not to be understood on the analogy of milk and water. From the presentation of the illustrations of clay etc. (in the Upaniṣad) it is to be understood that this all-knowingness is to be explained rather in conformity with the logic of the (non-difference of the) material and its products. If omniscience is understood in conformity with the illustration of milk and water, it will not be perfect knowledge, for the knowledge of water acquired through the knowledge of milk is not a complete knowledge at all. And it cannot be argued that like men, the Vedas also ascertain a thing through delusive, equivocal, or deceptive statements etc. Moreover, if the emphatic statement, "One without a second" (Ch. VI. ii. 2), be interpreted on the analogy of milk and water, it will be adversely affected. It is not also proper to assert that this all-knowingness (i.e. the knowledge of everything arising from the knowledge of one), as also the state of being one without a second, relates only to one particular feature of a substance, viz the modifications of itself; for in that case these statements will be equally valid even in the cases of clay etc.,[4] so that they have no need to be

[4] All modifications of clay are known by knowing clay. So this should

presented (in the Upaniṣad) as unique truths (not known except through the Upaniṣads), as it is actually done in the text, "O Śvetaketu, now that you appear to be so conceited, proud of your knowledge, and irreverent, did you inquire about that subject of instruction after knowing which all that is unheard becomes heard?" etc. (Ch. VI. i. 2-3). Hence it is to be understood that the all-knowingness is concerned with the knowledge of everything without exception, and that this statement is made from the point of view that everything is an effect of Brahman.

As for the statement that the Vedic text about the origin of space is to be taken in a secondary sense, since the creation of space in the primary sense is impossible, our reply is this:

यावद्विकारं तु विभागो लोकवत् ॥७॥

तु But विभाग: separateness (is present) यावत्-विकारम् wherever there is a modification (i.e. effect), लोकवत् as it is noticeable in the world.

7. *But (space is a product); for separateness persists wherever there is an effect, as it is seen in the world.*

The word "but" is used for barring out any apprehension of impossibility. In the matter of the possibility of the creation of space, no doubt should be entertained. Whatever is known as a product in this world—be it a pot, a pitcher, or a jar; a bracelet, an armlet, or an ear-drop, a needle, an arrow, or a sword—everything is seen to be a separate entity; but nothing that is not a product is seen to be separate (as for instance the Self). And space is known to be separate from earth etc., hence space also must be a product. Hereby it is also explained how directions, time, mind, and atoms are also products.

Opponent: Is not the Self also separate from space etc, and so does It not also become a product like a pot etc.?

Vedāntin: No, for there is the Vedic text, "From the Self

constitute all-knowingness. And vessels being non-different from clay, clay should be "without a second". But this is absurd, because the Vedas are not meant for such commonplace information.

rose space" (Tai. II. i. 3). Now, if even the Self be a product, hen since nothing higher than the Self is heard of (as the cause), ll the products counting from space will be without a Self (i.e. ltimate substance), just because the Self is itself a product. nd this will give rise to nihilism. Any idea of the possibility f denying the existence of the Self is illogical, just because it s the Self.[5] The Self is not an adventitious effect of any cause, t being self-established.[6] For the Self of any one does not equire to be revealed to any one with the help of any other neans.[7] For such means of knowledge as perception etc., that re taken up for proving the existence of other things that emain unknown, belong to this very Self.[8] Not that space and other things are understood by any one to be self-established, ndependently of other means of knowledge. But the Self being the basis of all such empirical dealings as the use of the means of knowledge, stands there as a postulate even prior to the use of those means. And it is not possible to deny such a Self; for it is an adventitious thing alone that can be repudiated, but not so one's own nature. The Self constitutes the very nature of the man who would deny it. The heat of fire cannot be denied by the fire itself. Thus it is that when a man says, "It is I myself who know the present object now, it is I who know the past and the remote past, and it is I who shall know the future and the remote future", it is seen that though the object to be known has different modes varying with the past, present, and future, the knower remains unchanged; for he has the nature of being ever present. Similarly even when the body is reduced to ashes, the Self is not reduced to nothing, Its nature being such

[5] Does the one who would deny the Self exist or not? If he exists, he is himself the Self; if he does not exist then the denial is not possible.

[6] Its existence and revelation are not dependent on any other cause. It could be denied if it were a dependent effect.

[7] "The all-pervading Self is self-effulgent" (Bṛ. IV. iii. 9), "By his light all this is lighted variously" (Ka. II. ii. 15).

[8] On what need one depend for proving the existence of that Self, through whose grace all such things as the knower, means of knowledge, object of knowledge, and cognition derive their substance?"—Sureśvarācārya. So the Self precedes all these means of knowledge, and they are valid by depending on It.

that It is ever present; and precisely because of this it is not possible to conceive of any change in Its nature. Thus owing to this very fact of its nature of being undeniable, the Self is not a product, whereas space etc. are products.

As for the argument that (for its own production) space has not got an abundance of material substance of the same class (which can produce it), that is being refuted. For one thing there is no such rule that things of the same class, and not of different classes, produce an effect. For the yarns and their conjunction (constituting the inherent and non-inherent causes of the cloth) do not belong to the same class; since they are classified as substance and quality. Nor do the instrumental causes, e.g. the shuttle, the loom, etc., belong invariably to the same class. It may be argued that this rule about belonging to the same class, is upheld in the case of the inherent causes only, but not in the case of other (non-inherent and instrumental) causes. But that too is not universally true. For it is seen that a single rope is made of cotton yarn and cow's hair belonging to different classes; so also they weave chequered blankets with cotton yarn and wool etc. If, however, this rule be upheld by relying on the common properties of having existence, substance, etc., then the rule itself becomes useless, for in that case anything can belong to the same class as any other. Again, there is no such rule that an effect is produced by a multiplicity of things, but not by one, single cause; for in the cases of an atom and the mind, an initial activity has to be admitted, it being upheld (by you) that an atom or a mind starts its own initial activity by itself, and not in conjunction with any other thing.[9]

Opponent: The rule about a multiplicity (of materials) producing an effect relates to the production of things (and not production as such).

Vedāntin: Not so, for what is admitted (by you) is transformation (as against emergence out of nothing, advocated by

[9] Conjunction is the non-inherent cause of a dyad (produced through the conjunction of two atoms); and it is also the cause of cognition (produced by the conjunction of mind and soul). For these conjunctions, an initial activity is admitted in the atom and the mind respectively.

the Vaiśeṣikas). The above rule can be true if it be a fact that a material cause, in association with conjunction, produces an entirely new thing; but as a matter of fact, the position upheld is that the very same material comes to be called an effect when it attains a different state with certain peculiarities. And there, again, sometimes many things get transformed into a single effect, as for instance, earth, seed, etc. into a sprout and sometimes a single thing gets transformed, as milk into curd etc. There is no divine ukase that only a multiplicity of (material) causes must produce an effect. Hence on the authority of the Vedic texts it is firmly ascertained that the universe sprang from the one Brahman alone in a regular order beginning with the origin of the great elements, space and the rest. And thus it has been stated, "If it be said that Brahman cannot be the cause, since one is seen to collect materials (for the performance of an act) then we say, no; for it is possible on the analogy of milk (turning into curd)" (B. S. II. i. 24).

And the assertion is false that no such distinction between the conditions of space before and after its creation can be conceived of as can make the creation of space a possibility. For it can be understood that the very distinctive attribute (of sound) by virtue of which space becomes distinguished from earth etc. at present and is comprehended as having an individual nature of its own, (that very distinctive attribute) did not exist before creation. And from the Vedic texts, "Brahman is without space", it can be understood that Brahman is free from the characteristics of space, just as much as it is known from such Vedic passages as, "not gross, not fine" (Bṛ. III. viii. 8), that Brahman is not possessed of such attributes as grossness etc. that belong to (Its products) earth etc. Thus it is proved that before creation Brahman was without space.

The assertion is wrong that space is birthless owing to its being dissimilar in character to earth and the rest. For the logical position is that when an inference about the impossibility of origin contradicts a Vedic text, it stands condemned as fallacious. And we showed the inference about the creation (of space). Such syllogisms also can be used as: Space is impermanent like a pot, since it is the substratum of impermanent attributes.

Opponent: This inference does not hold good in the case of the Self.[10]

Vedāntin: Not so, for the possession of any impermanent attribute is impossible for the Self according to one who holds on to the Upaniṣads. And the possession of all-pervasiveness etc. by space is impossible according to one who believes in the origin of space.

As for the assertions that space is eternal on the authority of the Vedas (B. S. II. iii. 4), we say that the Vedic mention of immortality of space in that text (Bṛ. II. iii. 3) is to be understood in the same sense as the statement, "The heavenly beings are immortal"; for origin and dissolution of space have been expounded earlier. Even when it is said, "(The Self is) all-pervasive and eternal like space", the comparison is made with the well-known vastness of space, so as to reveal the Self's unsurpassable vastness, but not to equate the Self with space. This is like the declaration, "The sun runs like an arrow", where the point of comparison is the quickness of motion, but not any equality of speed with the arrow. Hereby is explained the Vedic text expounding infinitude through illustration.[11]

Besides, from such texts as, "Greater than space", space is proved to have lesser dimensions than Brahman. And the text, "There is nothing to compare with Him" (Śv. IV. 19), shows that Brahman is incomparable. The text, "Everything else but this is perishable" (Bṛ. III. iv. 2), shows that all things—space and the rest—other than Brahman are perishable. And the argument that the birth of space is mentioned in the Vedas in a secondary sense, like the term Brahman used in a secondary sense to mean *tapas* (concentration), has been refuted with the help of Vedic texts and inference proving the origin of space. Hence it is established that space is a product of Brahman.

[10] The Self possesses such impermanent qualities as will, intelligence, endeavour; and yet your Vedāntins call the Self eternal.

[11] The reference is to such Upaniṣadic passages as, "The illustration is: just as space is infinite so also is the Self infinite", where the Self being a greater entity cannot be equated with a lesser entity like space, possessed of origin and destruction as it is.

Topic 2: Origin of Air

एतेन मातरिश्वा व्याख्यातः ॥८॥

एतेन By this मातरिश्वा air व्याख्यातः stands explained.

8. Hereby is explained air.

This aphorism extends (to air) the conclusion (about origin) already stated. "Hereby", by this explanation of space, *mātariśvan*, "air", supported by space, also stands explained." In its case also (as in that of space), the opposing viewpoints are to be suitably formulated (and answered) thus: One viewpoint is that air has no origin, since this is not stated in the context dealing with creation in the Chāndogya Upaniṣad. The other view is that this is mentioned in the context of creation in the Taittirīya Upaniṣad: "Air came out from space" (II. 1). From this it follows according to another view that since the Upaniṣads are at variance, the text about the origin of air must bear a secondary sense; for air can have no origin, since that is impossible. And the impossibility is shown with the support of the text, "This then is the deity, called air, that never sets" (i.e. ceases from action) (Bṛ. I. v. 22), where setting down is denied, and also in accordance with the Vedic statement of its immortality etc. The (Vedāntin's) conclusion is that air must have an origin, because it is thus that the declaration ("everything becomes known when one is known") is not set at naught, and because it is admitted that separateness persists wherever there is a product (B. S. II. iii. 6-7). The denial about air ever going to rest is made within the range of inferior knowledge (of Hiraṇyagarbha); it is a relative one in the sense that air is not seen to go to rest like fire and the rest. And the Vedic mention of immortality etc. as in, "Air and inter-space—these are immortal" has already been explained (as relative).

Opponent: Since in the contexts of creation, the origin or non-origin of air and space is mentioned or not mentioned equally by the Vedas, let there be a single topic (*adhikaraṇa* in the *Vedānta-sūtras*) comprising both. So why should you resort to a process of extension of application when no special point is at issue?

The (*Vedāntin's*) answer is: This is quite so. Still this extension of application is resorted to for removing the doubt from those people of poor intellect who base their misconceptions merely on words. For after hearing of the gloriousness of air as a thing to be meditated on, as stated in connection with the contemplation on merger (*saṁvarga-vidyā*—Ch. IV. iii. 1-4) etc., and from such facts as the denial of its setting down, some one might be led to believe that air is eternal.

Topic 3: Origin of Brahman Denied

असम्भवस्तु सतोऽनुपपत्तेः ॥९॥

तु But असम्भवः impossible सतः for Existence (Brahman) अनुपपत्ते: owing to illogicality.

9. But (origin) for Existence (Brahman) is impossible on account of illogicality.

Hearing that even space and air, whose birth seems to be impossible, have still an origin, somebody might be led to think that Brahman too must have some source of origin. Again, hearing that all subsequent products come out of space etc., which are themselves products, somebody might think that space also, in its turn, sprang from Brahman which is Itself a product. This aphorism, "But origin is impossible", stands for removing that misconception. It should never be conceived that Brahman which is Existence by nature can come out of, i.e. originate from, anything else.

Why?

"On account of illogicality". Brahman, being mere Existence, cannot certainly originate from that pure Existence Itself. For in the absence of some distinguishing feature a causal relationship cannot be reasonably maintained. Nor can Brahman be derived from a particular form of Existence, as that goes against common experience; for particulars are seen to emerge from the general, as pot etc. from clay, but not the general from the particulars. Nor can Brahman come out of non-existence, for non-existence is without any substance. Besides, an objection (to this) is contained in the text, "How can existence come out of non-existence?" (Ch. VI. ii. 2). And a creator of Brahman is denied in the text, "He is the cause, the ordainer of those who stand as causes,[12] He has no begetter, nor any ordainer" (Śv. VI. 9). Again, we pointed to (texts telling of) the origin of space and air; but Brahman has no (such text about Its) origin. This is the difference.

Opponent: Since it is seen that products come out from other things that are themselves products, Brahman also should be a product.

Vedāntin: No, for unless a primary material cause is admitted, it will all end in an infinite regress. And whatever is understood to be the primary cause will itself be our Brahman. Hence there is no possibility of conflict.[13]

Topic 4: Origin of Fire

तेजोऽतस्तथा ह्याह ॥१०॥

तेजः Fire अतः from this one, हि because आह (it) says तथा so.

10. Fire originates from this one (i.e. air); for the Upaniṣad says so.

Opponent: In the Chāndogya Upaniṣad, fire is spoken of as originating from Existence (VI. ii. 3), whereas in the Taittirīya Upaniṣad it is spoken of as originating from air (II. i. 2). Now then, since there is a conflict in the Upaniṣads about the source of fire, the conclusion drawn is that fire has Brahman as its source.

Why?

[12] Or "the ordainer of the ordainers of the sense-organs" according to a different reading.

[13] Unless some cause is admitted, chance will have full sway. Unless a beginningless cause is accepted the door will be opened for infinite regress. To accept a cause without a beginning will lead to our belief in Brahman, for all such causes as primordial Nature were negated earlier.

Because the introduction is made with, "In the beginning it was Existence alone" (Ch. VI. ii. 3), and then it is said, "That created fire" (ibid.); because the declaration about "everything becoming known through the knowledge of one" becomes possible if everything originates from Brahman; also because there is the general text, "Everything originates from That, rests in That, and merges in That" (Ch. III. xiv); and lastly because in another Upaniṣad the introduction is made with, "From this arises vital force" (Mu. II. i. 3), and then it is shown that everything without exception is born of Brahman.[14] In the Taittirīya (Upaniṣad) also we come across the text, "Having practised *tapas* (concentrated deliberation), He created all that there is" (III. vi. 1), where an all-comprehensive statement is made. Accordingly, the statement, "From air came fire" (Tai. II. i. 2), is made from the standpoint of subsequent occurrence, meaning thereby that fire originated (from Brahman) after air.

Vedāntin: This being the position, the answer is offered that fire comes out from this air.

How can this be so?

For that is how the Upaniṣad says, "From air came fire". If fire had directly originated from Brahman without any intermediary, and if it had not come out of air, the text, "From air came fire", would be falsified.

Opponent: Did we not say that this text would mean a subsequent occurrence?

Vedāntin: We say, not so. For in the earlier text, "From that Self, that is such, was born space" (Tai. II. i. 1), the word (*ātmanaḥ*—from the) Self, occurring as the ablative (i.e. source) of the verb "to be born" has the fifth case-ending ("from"). In the text under discussion as well that topic of "being born" holds the field. Again, in the subsequent text, "From earth were born herbs" (Tai. II. i. 3), where also origination holds sway, we come across the fifth case-ending in the ablative sense. Hence it is understood that in the text, "From air came fire", the fifth case-ending that occurs (after air, "from air") is used in the

[14] "From this is born vital force, mind, and all the senses, and space, air, fire, water, and the earth that supports all."

ablative sense (meaning "fire was born from air"). Moreover, to arrive at the meaning, "After air was born fire", you have to fancy the association (of the verb) with some word (e.g. "*ūrdhvam*—after") as prefixed to it; whereas the sense (of "origination from") conveyed by the (fifth) case-ending in, "Fire was born from air", is already a patent fact. (And a patent fact is more powerful than what can be inferentially read into a passage). Hence this text conveys the idea of the origination of fire from air.

Opponent: Does not the other text, "That created fire" (Ch. VI. ii. 3), also convey the idea of the origin of fire from Brahman?

Vedāntin: No, for it does not involve any contradiction even if that text should imply the birth (ultimately from Brahman) in an order of succession. If it is conceived that after creating space and air (successively), Brahman, who had assumed the form of air, (next) produced fire, even then it will involve no contradiction to have Brahman as its (ultimate) origin. This is just like saying, "Her (i.e. cow's) hot milk, her curd, her cheese" etc. And in the text, "He formed Himself into the world by Himself" (Tai. II. vii. 1), the Upaniṣad shows how Brahman exists in Its own modifications as their Self. Moreover, we come across this Smṛti text from the Lord (Śrī Kṛṣṇa), starting with, "Intelligence, knowledge, non-delusion" (Gītā, X. 4), and ending with, "The diverse characteristics of the creatures originate from Me alone" (Gītā, X. 5). For although it is known that intelligence etc. are born directly from their respective causes, still all these multitude of entities are derived either directly or indirectly (immediately or mediately) from God. Thus are also explained the Vedic texts that do not mention any order of creation, for they can be interpreted logically as speaking of the origin from Brahman alone in every way (be it mediately or immediately); but the texts mentioning an order cannot be interpreted in any other way (without the help of an order of creation). The declaration (of all things being known from the knowledge of one) also has reference only to the derivation of all from Existence, and not to any direct origination. Thus, there is no contradiction.

Topic 5: Origin of Water

आपः ॥११॥

11. Water (was born from this fire).

Water "was born from this fire, for the Upaniṣad says so"—this much has to be supplied at the end of "Water is born from this fire."

How is this known?

For so says the Upaniṣad, "That (Existence Brahman) created water" (Ch. VI. ii. 3). And in the face of the text, "from fire came water" (Tai. II. i. 2), there is no place for doubt. Having explained the origin of fire and being about to explain that of earth, the aphorist thinks, "I shall insert water in between the two, so that it may not be left out"; hence he frames the aphorism "water".

Topic 6: Origin of Earth

पृथिव्यधिकाररूपशब्दान्तरेभ्यः ॥१२॥

(*Anna*—food means) पृथिवी earth अधिकार-रूप-शब्द-अन्तरेभ्यः on the strength of the subject-matter, colour, and other Vedic texts.

12. (The word "food" means) earth on the strength of the topic, colour, and other Vedic texts.

Doubt: We come across the text, "That water deliberated, 'Let me be many, let me be born'. That water created food" (Ch. VI. ii. 4). With regard to this the doubt arises: "Are paddy, barley, etc. (i.e. corn) meant here by the word food, or is it some eatable (cooked) food like rice (i.e. articles of food), or is it earth?"

Opponent: Among these, the conclusion to be drawn is that the term food means either paddy, barley, etc. or cooked rice etc., for the word food is commonly used in these senses. Besides, this complementary portion of the Upaniṣadic passage confirms this view: "Therefore food grows plentifully whenever there is rainfall" (Ch. VI. ii. 4). For only paddy, barley, etc., and not earth, grow abundantly when there is a rainfall.

Vedāntin: This being the position, we reply: It is earth itself that is intended to be conveyed by the word food mentioned as growing out of water.

On what grounds?

"On the strength of the topic, the colour, and other Vedic texts." As for the topic, it is seen that the text, "That created fire, That created water" (Ch. VI. ii. 3), relates to the great elements. That being the case, it is not proper to skip over the creation of earth that follows in order, and jump suddenly to paddy, barley, etc. Similarly the colour mentioned in the complementary portion of the text also conforms to that of earth: "That which is the dark (or gray) colour, belongs to food" (Ch. VI. iv. 1-4). For articles of food like rice etc. do not invariably have the dark colour, nor do paddy etc. have it.

Opponent: Not even earth is invariably dark in colour. For fields are seen to be whitish like milk and reddish like burning charcoal.

Vedāntin: That is no defect. The colour is mentioned from the point of view of frequency (preponderance). Earth is most generally dark (grey) in colour, but not either white or red. The writers of Purāṇa (Paurāṇikas) also speak of night as the shadow of the earth. And night is darkish; therefore it is appropriately understood that the earth's colour is dark. Moreover, another Vedic text, dealing with the same topic, says, "Earth came from water" (Tai. II. i. 2). There is also the text, "What was there like scum on the water was solidified and became this earth" (Bṛ. I. ii. 2). But paddy etc. are shown as growing out of earth, as in, "From the earth grow the herbs, and from the herbs food" (Tai. II. i. 2). Thus in the face of the topic etc. which set forth earth, how can paddy etc. be understood (from *anna*—food)? Even the fact of that being the usual meaning (of the word *anna*) is ruled out by the topic etc. And it is to be understood that when the complementary portion of the passage mentions that food is produced from earth, it merely indicates thereby that it is earth that grew out of water. Accordingly, it is earth that is expressed here by the word "food".

Topic 7: Creation from God's Deliberation

तदभिध्यानादेव तु तल्लिंगात्सः ॥१३॥

तु But तत्-अभिध्यानात् from profound meditation on that सः: He एव only (created) तत्-लिंगात् (as is known) from His indicatory marks.

13. It is He only, who through profound meditation on each thing (created it), as is known from His indicatory marks.

Doubt: Do these elements, space and the rest, create their own products by themselves or is it God, existing as the Self of these elements, who produces the effects through His profound meditation?

Opponent: Faced with this doubt, the conclusion to be arrived at is that the elements themselves create.

Why?

For in such texts as "From space came air, from air fire" (Tai. II. i. 1) we hear of their independence.

Objection: Is not independent action denied in the case of the insentient things?

Opponent: That is nothing damaging. For we hear of the sentience of the elements as well, in such texts as, "That fire deliberated, that water deliberated" (Ch. VI. ii. 4).

Vedāntin: As against such a position, it is said: It is God Himself, abiding in these elements as their Self, that creates every effect through profound meditation.

How can this be so?

Because of His indicatory marks. For example, the scriptural statement, "He who inhabits the earth but is within it, whom the earth does not know, whose body is the earth, and who controls the earth from within (is the Internal Ruler, your own immortal Self)" (Bṛ. III. vii. 3), and other texts of the same class show that the elements have activity only when they are presided over by someone else. So also, starting with, "He decided, let me become many, let me be born" (Tai. II. vi. 1), it is stated in, "He became the gross and the fine. He created Himself by Himself" (ibid.), that He Himself is the Self of all. As for the mention of seeing (i.e. deliberation) by water and fire, that is to be understood as owing only to the controlling presence of God; for the text, "There is no other witness but Him" (Bṛ. III. vii. 23) denies the existence of any other seer. Moreover, in the text, "He deliberated, let me be many, let me be born" (Ch. VI. ii. 3), it is the witnessing Existence (Brahman) that forms the topic.

Topic 8: Reverse Order of Dissolution

विपर्ययेण तु क्रमोऽत उपपद्यते च ॥१४॥

तु But अतः as compared with this (order of creation) क्रमः the order (of dissolution) विपर्ययेण proceeds in the reverse way, च and उपपद्यते (this) is logical.

14. But as compared with this order of creation, the order of dissolution proceeds in a reverse way. This is logical too.

Doubt: The order of creation of the elements has been considered. After that the order of dissolution is being considered now, as to whether the dissolution comes about without any order, or it follows the order of creation, or it occurs in the reverse way. In the Upaniṣads we hear of all the three—the creation, continuance, and dissolution of the elements—as dependent on Brahman, as in, "That from which these elements emerge, that by which they are sustained after being born, and that towards which they proceed and into which they merge" (Tai. III. i. 1).

Opponent: Now then, with regard to this, the conclusion is that there is no set order, as no specification is made; or if anyone should search for an order after hearing of a sequence stated in the Upaniṣads with regard to creation, then dissolution too may have the same sequence. This is what it comes to.

Vedāntin: Hence we say: As compared with this order of creation, dissolution ought to have a reverse order. For the common experience is that the order in which a man ascends a staircase, is reversed when he comes down. Besides, it is seen that pots, plates, etc., which originate from earth, are reduced to earth again when they disintegrate; and ice, hail, etc. formed from water return to water. Hence also this is logical that earth which originates from water, should at the end of its period of continuance as earth, return to water; and water which is born out of fire, should merge in fire. It is also to be understood that the whole creation enters thus in this order successively into the finer and finer causes, and ultimately merges into Brahman which is the supreme cause and the acme of fineness. For it is not proper that a product should merge into the cause of its cause by skipping over its own cause. In the various places in the Smṛti also, dissolution is shown as occurring in the order opposite to that in which creation occurs, as for instance in such texts as, "The end of the world comes about thus, O divine saint: Earth, the basis of this world, is dissolved in water; water dissolves in fire; fire gets absorbed in air; (air dissolves in space, and space in the Unmanifested)"(Mbh. XII.339. 29). The order of creation is mentioned in connection with dissolution. Moreover, that order is not expected in the case of dissolution, it being irrelevant there; because so long as the effect persists, the cause cannot logically dissolve, for when the cause gets dissolved, the effect cannot continue; but it is quite logical that the cause can persist even after the dissolution of the effect; for this is what is observed in the case of clay etc.

Topic 9: The Origin of Mind and Intellect

अन्तरा विज्ञानमनसी क्रमेण तल्लिङ्गादिति चेन्नाविशेषात् ॥१५॥

विज्ञान-मनसी Intellect and mind (must find a place somewhere) अन्तरा in between क्रमेण in sequence तत्-लिङ्गात् owing to indicatory marks of their existence इति चेत् if such be the view, न not so अविशेषात् for that creates no difference.

15. If it be contended that the intellect and mind must find accommodation in some order in some intermediate stage, because indicatory marks of their existence are in evidence, then not so, because their presence creates no difference (i.e. does not disturb the order of creation or dissolution).

Opponent: It has been stated that the creation and dissolution occur in the direct and reverse orders respectively. It has also been stated that creation starts from the Self and dissolution ends in the Self. Now in the Smṛtis and Vedas the existence of mind together with the senses, as also of the intellect, is a well-known fact, as is evident from such indicatory marks in the texts as, "Know the intellect to be the charioteer, and the mind to be the rein. They say that the senses are the horses" (Ka. I. iii. 3). Their creation and dissolution in an orderly way must also be placed within some intermediate stage, for all things are claimed to have originated from Brahman. Moreover, in the Upaniṣad of the Atharva Veda, under the topic dealing with creation, the senses are enumerated in between the Self and the elements in, "From this (Self) are born the vital force, mind, all the senses, space, air, fire, and the earth that supports all" (Mu. II. i. 3). As a result, the order of creation and dissolution of the elements, stated earlier, will be disturbed.

Vedāntin: No, for no difference or disturbance is involved, because if the senses have come out of the elements, then their creation and dissolution follow as a matter of course from the creation and dissolution of the elements, and so no other order need be searched for these. And signs are in evidence to show that the senses are formed of the elements, as for instance in, "O amiable one, the mind is formed of food, the vital force is formed of water, and speech is formed of fire" (Ch. VI. v. 4), and so on. The separate mention of the elements and senses at some places is to be construed according to the maxim of the Brāhmaṇa and mendicant.[15] Again, even if the senses are not the products of the elements, still the order of creation of the elements is not disturbed by the senses, for the position then can be either that the senses originate first and the elements

[15] Brāhmaṇas alone can be mendicants. So when somebody says "Brāhmaṇas and mendicants", he means by the word Brāhmaṇa those that are not mendicants. So "elements" are those that have not become "senses".

later, or that the elements come out first and the senses later. What is done in the Upaniṣad of the Atharva Veda is a mere enumeration of the senses and elements one by one, but no order of creation is mentioned.[16] Similarly at another place the order of the origin of the senses is mentioned separately from (i.e. independently of) that of the elements: "In the beginning, all this (universe) was but Prajāpati (Hiraṇyagarbha). He meditated on Himself. He created the mind. Then the mind alone existed (and not all this). He thought of Himself. He created the organ of speech."[17] Hence the order of the creation of elements is not disturbed thereby.

Topic 10: Birth and Death

चराचरव्यपाश्रयस्तु स्यात्तद्व्यपदेशो भाक्तस्तद्भावभावित्वात् ॥१६॥

तु But तत्-व्यपदेश: the mention of these (birth and death) स्यात् must be चर-अचर-व्यपाश्रय: in relation to the moving and the motionless; (with regard to the soul it is) भाक्त: used in a secondary sense, तत्-भाव-भावित्वात् being applicable when that (body) exists.

16. The mention of birth and death must be in the primary sense in relation to the moving and the motionless; in relation to the soul it must be in a secondary sense, the application (of such words) being possible when a body is present.

Somebody may have the misconception that even the individual soul has origination and dissolution, since there are such references in the human world as, "Devadatta is born, Devadatta is dead", and because purificatory rites like those following on birth are enjoined.

Vedāntin: We remove that misconception. In order that the scriptural mention of the association of the individual person with the results of his work may stand justified, the individual

[16] In enumeration, things have to be told off one after the other. That sequence does not represent any definite order.

[17] The five fine elements constitute the body of Hiraṇyagarbha. So they exist earlier; the senses come later from Hiraṇyagarbha.

soul can have no origin or dissolution. Were the individual soul destroyed along with the body, the injunctions and prohibitions, meant for the acquisition of desirable results and avoidance of undesirable results in another body, would become useless. The Upaniṣad also declares, "It is this body that dies when it is left by the soul, but the soul does not die" (Ch. VI. xi. 3).

Opponent: Did we not point out that the terms birth and death are used about the soul in common talk?

Vedāntin: True it was pointed out, but this reference to the birth and death of the soul is only in a secondary sense.

Opponent: In relation to what, again, are the terms birth and death used in the primary sense, in contrast with which this can be secondary?

Vedāntin: The reply is that "the primary use of the two words is concerned with both the moving and the stationary"—the words birth and death have reference to the bodies of the moving and motionless entities. The entities—both moving and non-moving are born and they die. So while the words birth and death have those in view in the primary senses, they are used figuratively with regard to the individual souls inhabiting them, for "the application of the terms birth and death is contingent on the presence of the bodies" (which are the limiting adjuncts of the souls). The words birth and death are used when there are manifestation and disappearance of the body, but not otherwise. For no one notices the soul to be born or to be dead unless it be in association with the body. The text, "That man (individual soul), when he is born or attains a body, is connected with evils (i.e. the body and organs); and when he dies or leaves the body, (he discards these evils)" (Bṛ. IV. iii. 8), shows that the words birth and death are used from the point of view of the association with or dissociation from the body. And the rule pertaining to the performance of rites connected with birth etc. is also to be understood as related to the emergence of the body, for there can be no emergence of the soul. In the next aphorism will be discussed whether or not the soul originates like space etc. from the supreme Self. But in the present aphorism it is explained that the terms origin and dissolution (birth and death) in the (popular) gross sense apply to the body, but they do not apply to the individual soul.

Topic 11: Origin of the Soul

नात्माऽश्रुतेर्नित्यत्वाच्च ताभ्यः ॥१७॥

आत्मा The soul न is not (born) अश्रुतेः because this is not heard of (in the Upaniṣads); नित्यत्वात् because of eternality ताभ्यः as known from them; च and.

17. The individual soul has no origin; because the Upaniṣads do not mention this, because its eternality is known from them, and (because of other reasons).

Doubt: That the soul, called *jīva* (living one), presiding over this cage of the body and senses, and becoming associated with the fruits of work, does exist is without doubt. But a doubt arises, from the conflict among the Vedic texts, as to whether the soul originates from Brahman like space and the rest, or it does not originate like Brahman Itself. For in some texts the origin of the living beings from the supreme Brahman is spoken of with the help of the illustrations like sparks (flying from fire), whereas in some texts it is declared that without undergoing any modification Brahman enters the body to assume the state of a living being; but no origination is affirmed.

Opponent: As to that, the conclusion arrived at is that the soul does originate.

Why so?

So as not to override the (scriptural) declaration. The assertion that "everything becomes known when one is known" will remain unaffected if all things (including the soul) originate from Brahman, whereas this assertion will be adversely affected if the individual soul be an independent entity. And it cannot be understood that the unmodified supreme Self Itself is the individual soul, for their characteristics differ. The supreme Self has such attributes as being free from sin etc., whereas the individual soul is the opposite of that. And that the latter is an effect (of Brahman) becomes established from the fact of its delimitation. All that is delimited, counting from space downward, is a product. Besides, the origination of everything counting from space is already known. Since the individual soul undertakes pious and impious works, since it is subject to happiness and sorrow, and since it is separate in each body, therefore it too must have originated in the course of the emergence of this entire creation. Moreover, in the passage, "As from a fire tiny sparks fly in all directions, so from this Self emanate all organs" (Bṛ. II. i. 20), the scripture first gives instruction about the creation of the organs etc., constituting the set of objects to be experienced, and then imparts instruction about the separate creation of the experiencing souls in the passage, "all these souls emanate"[18] (Bṛ. II. i. 20). The origin and dissolution of the individual souls are also spoken of in, "As from a blazing fire emanate a thousand sparks of the same nature as fire, similarly from the Immutable, O amiable one, are born different classes of creatures, and they merge there itself" (Mu. II. i. 1). From the phrase "of the same nature" it follows that the individual souls are similar to the supreme Self, for they have the gift of consciousness. An omission in mentioning (something) somewhere cannot override the mention (of it) elsewhere. For everything mentioned (afresh) in other texts has to be taken as implied everywhere if it is not contradictory and if it supplies an additional idea. Under the circumstances, the texts about the entry (of God into the bodies and creation) are also to be explained as meaning such entry by assuming a modified state, as it is done in the case of the text, "He made Himself by Himself" (Tai. II. vii. 1). Therefore the individual soul has an origin.

Vedāntin : To this we say, the soul, that is to say, "an individual living being", "has no origin".

Why?

"Because the Upaniṣads do not mention this". In most of the places dealing with creation, the individual soul is not mentioned.

[18] This is the Mādhyandina reading. The Kāṇva reading is, "all gods and all beings emanate".

Opponent: Did we not say that an absence of mention somewhere cannot overrule the mention made elsewhere?

Vedāntin: True, you said so. But we say that the very origin is impossible for it.

Why?

"Because its eternality is known from them (i.e. the texts), and (because of other reasons)". By the word "and" is to be understood, "and because its birthlessness etc. (follow from those texts)". For its eternality is understood from the Vedic texts, and so also it is understood that it is birthless and changeless, that it is the unchanging Brahman Itself existing as the Self of the individual living being, and that the soul is one with Brahman. Any origination for a soul of this kind can never be logically possible.

Opponent: Which are those Vedic texts?

Vedāntin: "The individual being does not die" (Ch. VI. xi. 3), "That birthless Self is undecaying, immortal, undying, fearless, and Brahman (infinite)" (Bṛ. IV. iv. 25), "The Intelligent one is not born and does not die. This ancient one is birthless, eternal, unchanging" (Ka. I. ii. 18), "Having created that, He entered into that" (Tai. II. vi. 1), "Let me manifest name and form by Myself entering as the individual soul" (Ch. VI. iii. 2), "This Self has entered into (i.e. permeates) those bodies up to the tips of the nails" (Bṛ. I. iv. 7), "Thou art That" (Ch. VI. viii. 7), "I am Brahman" (Bṛ. I. iv. 10), "This Self, the perceiver of everything, is Brahman" (Bṛ. II. v. 19). These and such other texts which stand there to declare eternality etc. override the possibility of the origin of the individual soul.

Opponent: Was it not said that anything that is delimited is subject to change, and anything having change has origination?

Vedāntin: As to that, this is the answer: The delimitation does not belong to it naturally, for the Vedic text says, "The one deity remains hidden in all creatures; He is all-pervasive and the inmost Self of all creatures" (Śv. VI. 11). Just as space seems to be divided owing to the presence of pots etc., so also the appearance of division occurs in Brahman owing to the presence of limiting adjuncts like the intellect etc. To this effect are the texts: "The Self is indeed Brahman, as well as identified with the intellect, the *manas* (mind), and the vital force, with the eyes and ears" (Bṛ. IV. iv. 5), etc., which show that the individual soul, though always the same and one with Brahman Itself that has no change and is one without a second, still appears to be identified with diverse things like the intellect etc. The identity with the intellect etc. is to be understood to consist in appearing as though coloured by these adjuncts owing to a non-manifestation of the pure nature of the Self, as it occurs for instance in such cases as, "That voluptuous rogue is all sex".[19] As for the Vedic mention of the birth of the individual soul at some rare places, that too is to be interpreted, for this very reason, as caused by its contact with the limiting adjuncts. It originates with the origin of the limiting adjuncts and dies with their death. This is shown in, "The Self is pure intelligence alone; it comes out (as a separate entity) from these elements (forming the body) and is destroyed with them. After this death, it has no more (particular) consciousness" (Bṛ. IV. v. 13). Similarly this very fact, viz the destruction of the limiting adjunct alone and not of the Self, is proved in this very context by raising the question, "Just here you have led me into the midst of a confusion, sir; I do not at all comprehend this" (that after death the soul has no consciousness), and then offering the answer to this thus, "Certainly I am not saying anything confusing, my dear. This Self is indeed immutable and indestructible. But it becomes dissociated from objects" (Bṛ. IV. v. 14). And thus there is no overriding of the declaration, inasmuch as it is admitted that the changeless Brahman Itself appears as the individual soul. The difference in the characteristics of the two is also created by the presence of limiting adjuncts, for in the passage, "Please instruct me further about liberation" etc. (Bṛ. IV. iii. 14-16, 33), where the very soul, which remains identified with the intellect and forms the topic of the discussion, is shown to be one with the supreme Self through a process of denial of all worldly attributes. Accordingly, the soul never has any origin or dissolution.

[19] The Sanskrit word is *strīmaya*, where the suffix *mayaṭ* is used in the sense of abundance, the man being almost full of, i.e. identified with women (sex). Similarly are to be understood *vijñānamaya* etc.

Topic 12: Eternally Conscious Soul

ज्ञोऽत एव ॥१८॥

ज्ञः (The soul is an eternal) cognizer अतः एव for this very reason.

18. The soul is eternally a cognizer for this very reason (of being free from origin and dissolution).

Doubt: Schools of thought are not agreed as to whether the soul is naturally insentient but becomes endowed with an adventitious sentience as is believed by the followers of Kaṇāda, or it is eternally conscious by nature as the Sāṁkhyas believe; therefore a doubt arises. What is the conclusion to be arrived at then?

Opponent: The conclusion is that the consciousness of the soul is adventitious, arising from the conjunction of the soul and the mind, like redness etc. resulting from the contact of fire and a pot etc. For if the consciousness be eternal, it should be in evidence even in the cases of those who are asleep, have fainted, or are possessed by supernatural beings. But when questioned (afterwards), they say, "We were not conscious of anything"; and they are seen to have consciousness when brought back to normalcy. Thus since the soul is possessed of impermanent (intermittent) consciousness, its consciousness is adventitious.

Vedāntin: This being the position, it is being refuted: "This soul is a cognizer", it is endowed with eternal consciousness, exactly for the reason already adduced, viz that it has no origin, but that it is only the supreme Brahman Itself, which while remaining immutable, appears to exist as an individual soul owing to association with limiting adjuncts. That the supreme Brahman is eternal consciousness by Its very nature is mentioned in such Vedic texts as, "Knowledge, Bliss, Brahman" (Bṛ. III. ix. 28.7), "Brahman is Truth, Knowledge, Infinite" (Tai. II. i. 1), "Without interior or exterior, entire, and pure Intelligence alone" (Bṛ. IV. v. 13), etc. Now if the individual soul is but the supreme Brahman Itself, then it can be understood that like fire possessing heat and light, the soul is also possessed of eternal consciousness by its very nature. Besides, in the course of the topic dealing with the soul identified with the intellect occur such texts as the following: "Himself awake, watches those (organs of speech etc.) that are asleep" (Bṛ. IV. iii. 11), "In this (dream) state, the man himself becomes his own light (i.e. self-effulgent)" (Bṛ. IV. iii. 9, 14), "for the knower's function of knowing can never be lost" (Bṛ. IV. iii. 30), and so on. And from the fact that there is a continuity of knowledge through the medium of all the sense-organs, such as, "I know this, I know this", it can be concluded on the authority of the text, "And he who knows, 'I smell this', is the Self" (Ch. VIII. xii. 4), that the individual soul has that nature (of eternal consciousness).[20]

Opponent: If the soul be eternal consciousness by its very nature, then the senses of smell etc. become superfluous.

Vedāntin: No, for the senses are meant for perceiving the particular objects of smell etc. And this is shown by saying, "The sense of smell is meant for perceiving smell" (Ch. VIII. xii. 4) etc. As for the objection that the people in sleep etc. have no awareness, that is answered by the Upaniṣad itself when it says with regard to the sleeping man, "That (the soul) does not see in that state is because, although seeing then, it does not see; for the vision of the witness can never be lost, because it is immortal. But (then) no second thing exists there separate from it which it can see" (Bṛ. IV. iii. 23), etc. This is what is meant: This appearance of absence of awareness is owing to the absence of objects of knowledge, but not owing to the absence of consciousness. It is like the non-manifestation of light, spread over space, owing to the absence of things on which it can be reflected, but not owing to its own absence. And the arguments of the Vaiśeṣikas and others are falsified because of their opposition to Vedic texts. Hence we confirm that the soul is eternal consciousness by its very nature.

[20] The sense-organs change, but consciousness continues invariably. This cannot be so unless there is a soul which is eternally conscious.

Topic 13: Soul's Dimensions

उत्क्रान्तिगत्यागतीनाम् ॥१९॥

(There is mention) उत्क्रान्ति-गति-आगतीनाम् of departure (from) (or leaving the body), going, returning.

19. (The individual soul must be atomic in dimension owing to the mention in the Vedas) of its departure from the body, going (to the next world by following a course), and coming back (from there).

Doubt: Now is being considered the dimensions of the individual soul—whether it is atomic, or of an intermediate size, or vast (infinite).

Objection: Has it not been said that the soul has no origin and that it is eternal consciousness? From this it follows that the individual soul is none other than the supreme Self; and it is stated in the scripture that the supreme Self is infinite. So how can any question be broached about the dimensions of the soul?

Doubt: This is truly so. But the Vedic texts about the soul's leaving (the body), its movement to the other world, and return to this world lead to a limitation in dimensions. Again, the Vedic texts sometimes speak of its atomic size in clear words. So this discussion has to be started for resolving these conflicts.

Opponent: That being the position, the conclusion to be derived from the Vedic texts about leaving the body, going to, and coming from the other world is that the individual soul is limited and atomic in size. Of these the text about departure is: "When he departs from this body, he departs together with all these" (senses etc.) (Kau. III. 3); about going elsewhere: "Those people whoever depart from this world, go to the moon indeed" (Kau. I. 2); and about coming: "From that world they return to this world for (fresh) work" (Bṛ. IV. iv. 6). From the Vedic mention of their death, going (i.e. following a course), and returning, it is understood that the individual soul is limited; for no movement can be imagined for one that is infinite. And limitation being accepted, the soul must be atomic, for its correspondence to the size of the body (i.e. medium size) was discarded in the course of examining the Jaina view.

स्वात्मना चोत्तरयोः ॥२०॥

च And स्व-आत्मना (the relation) with one's own soul उत्तरयोः of the latter two.

20. (The soul's atomicity stands confirmed) owing to the relation of one's own soul with the latter two facts (viz. following of a course and coming back).

As for leaving (or giving up), it may sometimes be imagined as occurring to the unmoving soul through a cessation of its mastery over the body owing to exhaustion of results of work, just like the cessation of one's ownership over a village. But the latter two—viz going elsewhere and coming back—cannot happen to a soul that does not move; and yet their relation is with the soul itself; for the root "*gam* (to go)" indicates an action inhering in the agent. Now, since the soul is not (admitted to be) of medium dimension, its going (by following a course), and coming can be possible only if it be atomic in size. And going and coming being granted, it becomes obvious that (leaving the body or) death also is a moving away from the body, because going and coming are not possible for a soul that has not moved out of the body. Again, this is so, because particular parts of the body are mentioned as the places of departure, as in, "The soul departs through the eye, or from the head or from other parts of the body" (Bṛ. IV. iv. 2). There are also movements of the soul even inside the body, as stated in, "completely withdrawing these particles of light, he comes to the heart" (Bṛ. IV. iv. 1), "And taking the shining organs with him, he comes again to the waking state" (Bṛ. IV. iii. 11). Hence also is proved its atomicity.

नाणुरतच्छ्रुतेरिति चेन्नेतराधिकारात् ॥२१॥

न Not अणुः atomic अतत्-श्रुतेः since its size is heard of as not being so इति चेत् if this be the objection, न not so, इतर-अधिकारात् since the context relates to the other.

21. If it be objected that the soul is not atomic because its size is heard of as not being so, we reply, no, since that context relates to the other (i.e. the supreme Self).

Objection: Somebody may, however, object that the soul is not atomic.

Why?

Because it is heard of in the Vedas as not being so, that is to say, because its size is heard of to be the opposite of that of the atom. For the texts like the following will be contradicted if the soul be atomic: "That Self is verily great and birthless that remains identified with the intellect and in the midst of the organs" (Bṛ. IV. iv. 22), "And it is all-pervasive like space and eternal", "Brahman is Truth, Knowledge, Infinite" (Tai. II. i. 1).

Opponent: That creates no difficulty.

How?

Because that topic is about the other (supreme Self). For this other kind of dimension is mentioned only in a context dealing with the supreme Self, inasmuch as it is the supreme Self that is (most often) presented in the Upaniṣads as the chief reality to be known. And from such texts as, "The Self is spotless, beyond space" (Bṛ. IV. iv. 20), it is known that the supreme Self is the special subject-matter of those texts.

Objection: In the passage, "The Self that remains identified with the intellect and in the midst of the organs" (Bṛ. IV. iv. 22) etc., it is the embodied soul itself that is indicated as possessed of vast dimension (in the sentence, "That Self is great and birthless" (Bṛ. IV. iv. 22).

Opponent: But this mention is to be understood as made from the scriptural point of view as in the case Vāmadeva (B. S. I. i. 30). Accordingly, the atomic size of the soul is not contradicted, since the mention of other dimension in the Vedas relates to the conscious (supreme) Self.

स्वशब्दोन्मानाभ्यां च ॥२२॥

स्व-शब्द-उन्मानाभ्याम् owing to direct (Upaniṣadic use of the) word and (mention of) infinitesimality **च** as well.

22. And the individual soul is atomic because of the direct Upaniṣadic use of the word as well as mention of infinitesimality.

The soul is atomic for this further reason that the Upaniṣad directly uses a word implying atomicity: "The atomic Self into which the vital force has entered in five ways has to be comprehended through the intellect"[21] (Mu. III. i. 9). From the association with the vital force it is understood that it is the individual soul that is here referred to as atomic. Similarly the infinitesimally small dimension of the individual soul mentioned in, "That soul is to be known as a hundredth part of the hundredth part of the tip of a hair" (Śv. V. 9), makes us understand that it is atomic in nature. And there is another illustration of infinitesimality in, "That inferior (individual) soul is seen to be finer than the tip of the iron piece at the head of a goading stick" (Śv. V. 8).

Objection: If the soul be atomic (and consequently located in one place), will this not involve a contradiction for it to have perceptions all over the body while remaining at one place? It is a matter of common experience that people remaining immersed in the Gangā or some lake feel a coolness in every part of the body, while in summer they feel a heat all over the body.

Hence the answer is given (by the *opponent*):

अविरोधश्चन्दनवत् ॥२३॥

अविरोधः There is no contradiction चन्दनवत् as in the case of sandalwood paste.

23. (The soul's atomicity and its feeling over the whole body involve) no contradiction, just as in the case (of a drop) of sandal paste.

Just as a drop of yellow sandal paste, coming in contact with a particular part of the body, produces a delightful sensation all over the body, similarly the soul, though located at one part of the body, will have perception all over the body. And a

[21] For Śaṅkara's interpretation, see his commentary on the Upaniṣad.

31

perception (or feeling) all over the body is not opposed to the soul's nature, since it is in contact with the organ of touch for the contact of the soul with the organ of touch exists all over the skin, and the skin spreads over the whole body.

अवस्थितिवैशेष्यादिति चेन्नाभ्युपगमाद्धृदि हि ॥२४॥

अवस्थिति-वैशेष्यात् Owing to peculiarity of position (of sandal paste) इति चेत् if such be the objection, then न not so, अभ्युपगमात् for (peculiar position is) admitted (for soul also) हि because हृदि (it is) in the heart.

24. If it be objected that (the argument holds good in the case of sandal paste) owing to its peculiarity of position, (but that is not evident in the case of the soul), then we say, no, (a peculiar location) for the soul is admitted in the Upaniṣads, for it exists in the heart.

Objection: Someone may make the rejoinder that the statement, "No contradiction is involved as in the case of sandal paste", is illogical, for the illustration and the thing illustrated are not similar. The illustration of the sandal paste will apply only if it can be proved that the soul exists merely in a part of the body; but the peculiarity of the location, viz existence in one part of the body, in the case of the sandal paste, as well as its imparting delight to the whole body, is a matter of direct perception; while in the case of the soul what is perceived is only its awareness over the whole body, but not its particular location. If it be said (by the opponent) that this is inferable, then (we say that) an inference is inadmissible here, for the following doubts cannot be removed (even by such an inference): Does the awareness pertaining to the whole body arise because the soul spreads over the whole body like the sense of touch, or because it is all-pervasive like space, or because it is atomic in size and exists at one place only?

Opponent: To this we say, this creates no difficulty.

Why?

Because that is the admitted fact; for it is admitted even in the case of the soul that, like a drop of sandal paste, it exists at a particular part of the body; it has a peculiarity of location.

How?

The answer is: Because this soul is mentioned in the Upaniṣads as existing in the heart, as is evident from such instructions as, "For this Self is (i.e. resides) in the heart" (Pr. III. 6), "That Self, that is such, is in the heart" (Ch. VIII. iii. 3), "Which is the Self? This infinite entity (Puruṣa) that remains identified with the intellect and is in the midst of the organs, the (self-effulgent) light within the heart" (Bṛ. IV. iii. 7). Hence from the absence of any disparity between the illustration and the thing illustrated it is but logical to conclude that no contradiction is involved, as in the case of a drop of sandal paste.

गुणाद्वा लोकवत् ॥२५॥

वा Or गुणात् through the quality (of sentience) लोकवत् as is seen in the world.

25. Or on the analogy of what is seen in the world, (the soul may pervade the whole body) through its attribute (of sentience).

Or because the quality of sentience (or intelligence) of the soul is pervasive, therefore, though the soul is atomic, still there is no incongruity if its action (of perception) spreads over the whole body. This is just like what is observed in common life; for instance the light of a gem or a lamp, occupying only a corner of an inner apartment, spreads over the whole apartment and does its work everywhere in the apartment.

It might be objected that since the sandal paste consists of parts, it can produce delight in the whole body by scattering its minute particles; but the atomic soul has no particles through which it can spread over the entire body. Having this misconception in view, the aphorism says, "through the quality of sentience".

Objection: How again can an attribute exist elsewhere than in the substance (in which it inheres), for the whiteness of a cloth is not seen to exist somewhere other than the cloth?

Opponent: It can be possible like the light of a lamp.

Objection: No, for that too is considered to be a substance, for a luminous substance in a state of compactness (of its particles) is the lamp, and that very luminous substance in a state of diffusion is light.

Opponent: Hence the reply is being given:

व्यतिरेको गन्धवत् ॥२६॥

व्यतिरेक: Separate existence गन्धवत् like smell.

26. (The quality of sentience can have) separate existence like smell.

As smell, for instance, which is a quality, can have existence separately from the odorous substance, since the smell is perceived even when the odorous things like flower etc. are nowhere in view, similarly though the soul is atomic, its quality of sentience can remain detached from it. Hence this ground for inference that a quality cannot be detached from its substance, it being a quality like colour (or form) etc., has no invariable application, since smell, which is a quality, is seen to exist in isolation from its substance.

Objection: Even in the case of smell, the fact is that it gets detached from its substance together with a part of it (viz particles of matter).

Opponent: No, for the main source from which this detachment will occur would in that case become attenuated; but it is seen to continue undiminished from its previous state; for else it would become diminished in weight (mass) etc. as compared with its earlier state.

Objection: It may be that the detached particles on which smell rests are so few in number (and minute in size) that their detachment goes undetected. The minute atoms of smell spread all around and give rise to the perception of smell by entering into the nostrils.

Opponent: No, for the atoms are supersensuous (and so the nose cannot perceive the atoms of smell), at the same time that a distinct strong fragrance is felt in the case of such flowers as

Nāgakeśara. The experience in common life is not of the form, "A substance with aroma has been smelt", but the common people experience thus: "It is the aroma itself that has been smelt".

Objection: Since it is not a matter of experience that form (or colour) etc. can exist apart from their substances, it is also improper to think that smell can exist separately from its substance.

Opponent: No, for this being a matter of experience, inference can have no scope here. Accordingly, things are to be accepted by the seekers of truth, just as they are actually perceived, for no such rule can be (inferentially) arrived at, that because the quality of taste is felt by the tongue, therefore all the qualities starting from colour should be perceived by the tongue itself.

तथा च दर्शयति ॥२७॥

च And (the Upaniṣad) दर्शयति shows तथा this.

27. *And the Upaniṣad also shows this.*

After stating that the soul resides in the heart and that it has the size of an atom the Upaniṣad shows in the text, "up to the tip of the hair, up to the tip of the nail" (Ch. VIII. viii. 1, Bṛ. I. iv. 7, Kau. IV. 20), that through the quality of sentience, that very soul pervades the whole body.

पृथगुपदेशात् ॥२८॥

उपदेशात् Because taught पृथक् separately.

28. *(The soul and its intelligence are separate), since they are taught separately (in the Upaniṣads).*

From the text, "presiding over the body with the help of intelligence" (Kau. III. 6), where the soul and intelligence are spoken of separately as having the relationship of the agent and the instrument (respectively), it is understood that the soul pervades the body through its quality of intelligence. And in the text, "it absorbs at the time (of sleep) the power of perception of the organs through its own consciousness" (Bṛ. II. i. 17), there occurs an instruction about consciousness existing separately from the agent, the embodied soul; and this instruction only confirms this very idea. Hence the soul is atomic.

Vedāntin: This being the position, we say:

तद्गुणसारत्वात्तु तद्व्यपदेशः प्राज्ञवत् ॥२९॥

तु But तत्-व्यपदेशः such appellation (occurs) तत्-गुण-सारत्वात् owing to the dominance of the modes of that (intellect), प्राज्ञवत् as in the case of the supreme Self.

29. But the soul comes to have such appellations because of the dominance of the modes of that intellect; this is just as in the case of the supreme Self.

The word "but" overrules the opposing point of view. It is not a fact that the soul is atomic. It has been said that the soul is none other than the supreme Brahman, for there is no mention of its origin in the Vedas, while the entry of the supreme Brahman is mentioned there and the identity of the two is taught. Now if the individual soul be none other than the supreme Brahman, then the soul should have the same magnitude as the supreme Brahman; and as it is mentioned in the scripture that the supreme Brahman is omnipresent, so the soul also must be omnipresent. Thus only will those statements stand vindicated that are made in such texts of the Vedas and Smṛtis about the omnipresence of the soul as: "That Self is great and birthless which remains identified with the intellect and in the midst of the organs" (Bṛ. IV. iv. 22). Moreover, it does not stand to reason that an atomic soul should have a feeling of pain all over the body.

Opponent: This can be so owing to its contact with the organ of touch.

Vedāntin: No, for in that case, even when a thorn pricks the skin, one should feel the pain all over the body, since the contact between the thorn and the skin is a contact with the skin as a whole, which spreads over the whole body. But as a matter of fact, a man pricked by a thorn under the foot feels the pain in the sole of the foot only. It is not also possible for any quality of the atom to spread out (beyond the substratum), since the quality exists where its substance is. Unless the quality subsists in its own substance, it will cease to be a quality at all. And it was explained how the light of a lamp is but a separated substance (and not a mere quality). Smell also, which is understood to be a quality, can move out only when carried on its substance (particles), for else it may as well cease to be a quality. Thus it has been said by the adored Dvaipāyana, "After perceiving smell in water, should some inexperienced people say that it belongs to water, still one should know that smell belongs to earth, though it floats on water and air". If the intelligence of the soul spreads over the entire body, then the soul cannot be atomic; (for) intelligence must be the soul's very nature like heat and light of fire. No such distinction as between a quality and its substance can exist here. And the view was refuted that the soul is of the size of the body. As a last resort, the soul is omnipresent. To explain how in that case there can be any mention of atomicity etc., the aphorism says, "But the soul comes to have such appellations because of the dominance of the modes of that intellect". Desire, dislike, happiness, sorrow, etc. are the modes of that intellect. These modes constitute the essence or chief factors in the attainment of the state of transmigratoriness by the soul. For unless it be through the modes of the intellect there can be no transmigratory state for the absolute Self. Though the Self is not an agent and experiencer, and though It has no transmigratoriness and is ever free, still It comes to have the states of being an agent and an experiencer, this being caused by the superimposition of the modes of the intellect acting as a limiting adjunct. Hence owing to the predominance of the modes of that intellect, the soul is said to have a dimension corresponding to that of the intellect. And it is said that it departs from the body and so on, in accordance as the intellect does so; but the soul does not do so naturally. Thus it is that after speaking of the atomicity of the soul, the Upaniṣad speaks of infinitude about that very soul in, "The soul is to be known as a hundredth part of a hundredth part of a hair's end, into which it can be fancied to be divided. And that soul again is infinite" (Śv. V. 9). This can be reasonably reconciled only if the atomic size of the individual soul be owing to limiting adjuncts, but infinitude be its innate nature; for both these cannot be thought of to be true in the primary sense. Nor can it be understood that is has infinitude in a figurative sense, since it is the identity of the individual soul with Brahman that is sought to be taught in all the Upaniṣads. So also in another declaration of infinitesimality, "The soul appears to be inferior and of the size of the tip of a goading stick, owing to the appearance of the modes of the intellect as its own attributes" (Śv. V. 8), the soul is declared to have the dimension of the tip of a goading stick owing to its contact with the attributes of the intellect, but not naturally in itself. Even in the text, "This atomic (subtle) Self is to be realized through the intellect" (Mu. III. i. 9), it is not taught that the individual soul is atomic in dimension, for it is the supreme Self that has been introduced in that context as something to be known through the favourableness (i.e. purity) of the intellect, It being beyond the grasp of the eye etc.[22] Moreover, atomicity in the literal sense is inadmissible even for the individual soul. Hence it is to be understood that the mention of atomicity is intended to convey the idea that the Self is inscrutable or that this is done from the point of view of the limiting adjunct. Similarly in such texts as, "Presiding over the body through intelligence" (Kau. III. 6), where a separation (between soul and intellect) is spoken of, the sentence is to be construed to mean that the soul presides over the body through the intellect alone which is its limiting adjunct. The mere statement (of difference) here is like talking of the body of a stone pestle (where the "body" and the "stone" are non-different); for it has been already stated that there is no such division here as between quality and substance. As for the statement that the heart is the residence of the soul, that too is made from the standpoint of the intellect, for the intellect

[22] The previous verse being, "It is not comprehended through the eye, nor through speech, nor through the other senses.... Since one becomes purified in mind through the favourableness of the intellect, therefore can one see that indivisible Self through meditation" (Mu. III. i. 8).

resides in the heart. So also in the following texts it is shown that such actions as departure from the body are dependent upon limiting adjuncts: "He deliberated, 'As a result of whose departure shall I rise up (from the body)? And as a result of whose continuance shall I remain established?' He created *Prāṇa*" (i.e. energy that is non-different from intelligence) (Pr. VI. 3-4). And from the absence of its death, it is gathered that the going to and coming back from the other world are also (intrinsically) absent in the soul. For unless one has got detached from the body, there can be no following a course or returning. Thus since in the case of the individual soul, there is a predominance of the attributes of its adjuncts, it has the appellations of atomicity etc., "as in the case of *Prājña* (the supreme Self)". Even as in the case of *Prājña,* who is the supreme Self, there is a mention of atomicity etc. in connection with Its meditation as a qualified entity, where the attributes of the limiting adjuncts dominate, as for instance in, "Minuter than a grain of paddy or barley" (Ch. III. xiv. 3), "He is identified with the mind and has the vital force as His body, all (good) smells are His, all (good) tastes are His, all (good) desires are His. His resolves are true" (Ch. III. xiv. 2), and so on, so also is the case with the individual.

Opponent : It may be objected thus: If the soul be thought of as attaining the worldly state (of transmigration) under the dominance of the modes of the intellect, then a cessation of the conjunction between the soul and the intellect, which are divergent, must be inevitable. Thus when the intellect gets detached, the soul will become undiscernible, and hence there will arise the predicament of its becoming non-existent or ceasing to be a transmigratory soul.

Vedāntin : So the reply is being given:

यावदात्मभावित्वाच्च न दोषस्तद्दर्शनात् ॥३०॥

च And यावत्-आत्म-भावित्वात् since (this association of soul and intellect) persists as long as the soul continues to be a transmigratory entity न दोषः no defect arises, तत्-दर्शनात् for so it is seen (in the scriptures).

30. And because the contact between the soul and the intellect persists so long as the worldly state of the soul continues, there can be no defect, for this is what is met with in the scriptures.

There should be no such defect as mentioned just now.

Why?

Because the contact with the intellect endures all through the state of the soul's transmigratory existence. The contact of the soul with the intellect does not cease so long as the soul continues in its transmigratory state, so long as its condition of transmigratoriness is not sublated through complete realization. And this individuality and the worldly state of the soul last only as long as there is this connection with the intellect serving as a limiting adjunct. In reality there is no such thing as an individual soul apart from what it appears under the influence of the intellect acting as a conditioning factor. For when engaged in ascertaining the purport of the Upaniṣads, we do not come across any other (second) conscious entity besides God who is by nature ever free, about which fact these texts stand as evidence: "There is no other witness but Him, no other hearer but Him, no other thinker but Him, no other knower but Him" (Bṛ. III. vii. 23), "That thou art" (Ch. VI. viii-xvi), "I am Brahman" (Bṛ. I. iv. 7), and a hundred others of this kind.

Opponent: How again is it gathered that the contact with the intellect lasts as long as the state of transmigratoriness of the soul persists?

The (*Vedāntin's*) answer is given in, "For this is what is met with (in the scriptures)". Thus the scripture reveals: "This infinite entity (*puruṣa*) that remains identified with cognition (*vijñāna*) in the midst of the organs, the (self-effulgent) light within the heart. Assuming the likeness (of the intellect), it moves between the two worlds; it thinks as it were, and shakes as it were" (Bṛ. IV. iii, 7) etc. The term "identified with cognition", occurring there, means "identified with the intellect"; for elsewhere occurs the text, "identified with cognition (i.e. the intellect), identified with the mind, identified with the vital force, identified with the eye, identified with the ear" (Bṛ. IV.

iv. 5), where the one "identified with cognition" is mentioned along with the one identified with the mind etc., and the identity with the intellect is meant to imply a dominance of the modes of the intellect. It is like saying, "Devadatta is all sex" where the idea sought to be implied is that he is dominated by a passion for women. And the text, "Assuming the likeness (of the intellect), it moves between the two worlds (this and the next)" (Bṛ. IV. iii. 7), shows that even while going to another world, there is no dissociation from the intellect. Likeness of what? It can be understood that the likeness is with the intellect itself, for that is near at hand. And that very fact is pointed out in, "It thinks as it were, and shakes as it were" (ibid.), where the idea implied is this: "This one does not think by itself, nor does it move; but when the intellect thinks, it seems to think, and when the intellect moves, it seems to move." Moreover, this connection of the soul with the intellect has but false ignorance at its root, and this false ignorance cannot be removed by anything other than complete knowledge (of Brahman). Hence this connection with such limiting adjuncts as the intellect does not cease so long as the identity of the Self with Brahman is not realized. And this is shown in, "I have known this great Puruṣa (infinite entity) who shines like the sun (i.e. self-effulgent), and is beyond darkness (i.e. untouched by ignorance). Knowing Him alone one goes beyond death. There is no other path to proceed along" (Śv. III. 8).

Opponent: You cannot certainly admit any connection of the soul with the intellect during sleep and dissolution, for the Upaniṣad says, "O amiable one, he then becomes identified with Existence (Brahman), he becomes absorbed in his own Self" (Ch. VI. viii. 1). This also follows from the admission of the (final) dissolution of the entire creation. So how can there be the persistence of the contact with the intellect as long as the transmigratory state of the soul endures?

Vedāntin: The answer is thus:

पुंस्त्वादिवत्त्वस्य सतोऽभिव्यक्तियोगात् ॥३१॥

तु But अभिव्यक्ति-योगात् because of becoming manifest अस्य सत:

in the case of this which already exists पुंस्त्व-आदि-वत् like manhood etc.

31. Rather because that contact (with the intellect etc.) which remains latent (in sleep and dissolution) can become manifest (during waking and creation) like manhood etc. (from boyhood etc.).

We see in the world that manhood etc. though existing all the time in a latent state, are not perceived during boyhood etc. and are thus treated as though non-existent, but they become manifest in youth etc.; and it is not a fact that they evolve out of nothing, for in that case even a eunuch should grow those (moustaches etc.). Similarly, too, the contact with the intellect etc. remains in a state of latency during sleep and dissolution and emerges again during waking and creation. For thus alone it becomes logical. Nothing can possibly be born capriciously, for that would lead to unwarranted possibilities (of effects being produced without causes). The Upaniṣad also shows that this waking from sleep is possible because of the existence of ignorance in a seed form (remaining dormant in sleep): "Though unified with Existence (Brahman) in sleep, they do not understand, 'We have merged in Existence.' They return here as a tiger or a lion" (just as they had been here before) (Ch. VI. ix. 3) etc. Hence it is proved that the contact with the intellect etc. persists as long as the individuality of the soul lasts.

नित्योपलब्ध्यनुपलब्धिप्रसङ्गोऽन्यतरनियमो वाऽन्यथा ॥३२॥

अन्यथा Else नित्य-उपलब्धि-अनुपलब्धि-प्रसङ्गः will arise the possibility of constant perception or non-perception वा or अन्यतरनियमः either of the two (powers) becoming debarred (or delimited).

32. Else (if the existence of the internal organ be not admitted) there will be the possibility of either constant perception or non-perception or it will have to be admitted that either of the powers (of the soul or of the organs) becomes (suddenly) debarred (or delimited or lost).

This internal organ, constituting a conditioning factor for the Self is variously spoken of in different places as the *manas* (faculty of thinking—Bṛ. I. v. 3), *buddhi* (faculty of knowing—Ka. II. iii. 10), *vijñāna* (cognition or egoism—Tai. II. v. 1), *citta* (feeling or memory—Mu. III. i. 9, Pr. IV. 8). Occasionally it is called variously in accordance with its moods—it being called the mind when it functions as the doubter, (thinker), etc., the intellect when it makes specific ascertainment, and so on. And it must of necessity be admitted that an internal organ of this kind does exist, for unless that organ is admitted, there will be the contingency of either constant perception or non-perception. For when the accessories of perception, viz the soul, organs, and objects of perception, are in contiguity, perception should occur always. Or even if in the presence together of all the factors of perception no result is produced, then there will be the possibility of constant non-perception. But this does not tally with experience. Or else it will have to be admitted that the power of either of the factors (involved in perception)—viz the soul or the sense-organ—stands debarred from itself. But it is not possible for the power of the soul to be debarred from the soul, since the soul is changeless. Nor can the power of any sense-organ be debarred from the organ, for an organ that has its power intact in the earlier and succeeding moments, cannot have it denied suddenly (in the middle). Accordingly the mind must be the entity, through the alertness of which perception occurs, and through the want of alertness of which it does not occur. In support of this is the Vedic text, "I was absent-minded, I did not see it; I was absent-minded, I did not hear it" (Bṛ. I. v. 3), and "It is through the mind that one sees and hears" (ibid.). The Upaniṣadic text also shows that desire etc. are its modes, "Desire, resolve, doubt, faith, want of faith, steadiness, unsteadiness, shame, intelligence, and fear—all these are but the mind" (ibid.). Hence the aphorism stands justified that "The soul comes to have such appellations because of the dominance of the attributes of that intellect" (II. iii. 29).

Topic 14: Soul as Agent

कर्ता शास्त्रार्थवत्त्वात् ॥३३॥

कर्ता (The soul must be) an agent शास्त्र-अर्थवत्त्वात् so that the scriptures may have a purpose.

33. The individual soul must be an agent, for thus alone the scriptures become purposeful.

In continuation of the topic dealing with the qualities of the intellect as mainly influencing the soul, another attribute of the soul is being elaborated: "This individual soul must also be an agent."

Why?

"For thus only the scriptures become purposeful." In this way only, such texts about injunction as, "One should perform a sacrifice", "One should pour an oblation", "One should make gifts", etc. become purposeful. Otherwise they become meaningless. For they enjoin particular duties for an agent whose presence is a reality; and that kind of injunction can have no sense if there be no (soul with) agentship. Similarly, it is only thus that this text becomes meaningful: "And this one is the seer, feeler, hearer, thinker, ascertainer, doer—the Puruṣa that is a knower by nature" (Pr. IV. 9).

विहारोपदेशात् ॥३४॥

विहार-उपदेशात् Because of the teaching about roaming.

34. (The soul is an agent) because there are teachings about its roaming.

The individual soul is an agent for this further reason that in a context dealing with the soul, the Upaniṣad speaks of the soul's roaming about in the intermediate state (of dream): "(Himself immortal), he goes wherever he likes" (Bṛ. IV. iii. 12), and "It moves about, as it pleases, in its own body" (Bṛ. II. i. 18).

उपादानात् ॥३५॥

35. (The soul is an agent) because of its taking up (the organs).

The soul has agentship for the further reason that under the topic of the soul the Upaniṣad speaks of the taking up (or using) of the organs by the soul: "(When this being, full of consciousness, is thus asleep), it absorbs at the time the power of perception of the organs through its own intelligence" (Bṛ. II. i. 17), and also, "taking up the organs" (Bṛ. II. i. 18).

व्यपदेशाच्च क्रियायां न चेन्निदशविपर्ययः ॥३६॥

च And व्यपदेशात् because of mention (as an agent) क्रियायां in respect of work न चेत् were it not so, निर्देश-विपर्ययः there would have been a contrary indication.

36. And the soul is an agent because of the mention (as such) in respect of action; were it not so, there would have been a contrary indication.

That the individual soul has agency follows from this additional consideration that the scripture designates it as being the agent in respect of Vedic and ordinary duties, "*Vijñāna* (or Intelligence, i.e. the individual soul having it) spreads (i.e. performs) the sacrifices as well as works" (Tai. II. v. 1).

Opponent: Is not the word *vijñāna* known as a synonym for the intellect? So how can it indicate the agency of the soul?

Vedāntin: Not so, for this is in fact a designation of the soul and not of the intellect. Had it not been used for the soul, there would have been a reversal of the designation—the indication would have been made by saying "through the intellect" (by using *vijñāna* in the instrumental case, and not in the nominative case). Thus it is that at another place, where the intellect is meant, the word *vijñāna* is seen to be used with the instrumental case-ending: "It absorbs at the time the power of perception of the organs *vijñānena*—through its own intelligence" (Bṛ. II. i. 17). But here in "*Vijñāna* spreads the sacrifice", the use is with the nominative case-ending, whereby the soul, different from the intellect, is indicated. Hence it is nothing wrong.

Here somebody (an *opponent*) says: If the soul, which is quite different from the intellect, be the doer, then, being independent, it would do things that are delightful and beneficial to itself, and not act contrariwise. But as a matter of fact, it is noticed to do the opposite as well. Such irregular activity cannot be possible for the independent soul.

Vedāntin: Hence the answer is being given:

उपलब्धिवदनियमः ॥३७॥

उपलब्धिवत् As in the case of perception अनियमः there is no uniformity.

37. As in the case of perception (there is no uniformity), so also there is no uniformity (in the case of action).

Just as this soul, independent though it is as regards its own perception, yet perceives both good and bad without any invariable rule, so also it can accomplish both good and bad without any uniform rule.

Opponent: It is not independent even as regards perception, for it is dependent on the acceptance of the means of perception.

Vedāntin: No, for the means of perception serve only the purpose of presenting the objects; but in the actual perception the soul is independent, since it is endowed with consciousness. Moreover, the soul is not wholly independent in the matter of activities yielding results, for it has to depend on particular space, time, and cause. An agent does not cease to have its agentship just because it has to depend on accessories; for a cook can very well be a cook even though he has to depend on fuel, water, etc. And because of a diversity of the accessories, it is nothing contradictory for the soul to engage in an irregular way in activities yielding good, bad, and indifferent results.

शक्तिविपर्ययात् ॥३८॥

शक्तिविपर्ययात् Because of a reversal of power.

38. (The soul must be the agent), for (if the intellect be so), it will lead to a reversal of power.

For this reason also the soul, that is different from the intellect, should be the agent. On the contrary, if the intellect, understood by the word *vijñāna*, be the agent, then there will be a reversal of power—the instrumental power of the intellect will be negated and the power of the agent will accrue. Again, on the assumption that the power of the agent belongs to the intellect, it will have to be admitted that the intellect itself constitutes the subject of egoity; for all tendency to activity is seen to be preceded by the ego-consciousness, as in "I go", "I come", "I eat", "I drink", and so on. Again, for that intellect that is equipped with the power of the agent and possessed of the ability of doing everything, we have to fancy some other instrument that can be used for accomplishing everything. For despite the ability possessed by an agent, he is seen to engage in works with the help of some instruments. In that case, the fight (between us) will centre round a term, but there will be no difference as regards the thing itself, since (in either case) agentship is conceded for one who is different from the instrument.

समाध्यभावाच्च ॥३९॥

च And समाधि-अभावात् because of the negation of deep meditation.

39. And (the soul must be an agent) because (a contrary supposition will) lead to a negation of deep meditation (on God).

Samâdhi (deep meditation), taught in the Upaniṣads as a means for the realization of that Self that is known from the Upaniṣads alone, is spoken of in such texts as, "The Self, my dear, should be realized—should be heard of, reflected on, and profoundly meditated upon" (Bṛ. II. iv. 5), "That is to be searched for, that is to be realized" (Ch. VIII. vii. 1), "Meditate on the Self thus with the help of *Om*" (Mu. II. ii. 6), and so on. This meditation, too, cannot be reasonably sustained if the soul be not the agent (of meditation). From this fact also the agentship of the soul is proved.

Topic 15: The Soul under two Conditions

यथा च तक्षोभयथा ॥४०॥

च And (rather) यथा as तक्षा a carpenter उभयथा (exists) under both conditions.

40. And (rather) this is like the carpenter existing under both conditions.

Thus the agentship of the embodied soul has been shown with the help of such reasons as the purposefulness of the scriptures. Now it is being considered whether this is natural or a result of conditioning factors. When in such a *doubt,* the conclusion arrived at (by the *opponent*) may be that it follows from these very reasons of the purposefulness of the scriptures and so on that the agentship is natural, for no reason is in evidence for modifying this conclusion.

Vedāntin : This being the position, we say that it is not possible for the soul to have natural agentship, for that would lead to a negation of liberation. If agentship be the very nature of the Self, there can be no freedom from it, as fire can have no freedom from heat. Moreover, for one who has not got rid of agentship, there can be no achievement of the highest human goal (liberation), for agentship is a sort of misery.

Opponent : Even while the power of agentship continues, the highest human goal can be achieved through the giving up of activities consequent on that. And that avoidance of activity follows from the avoidance of its causes (viz merit, demerit, etc.). This is just like the absence of the act of burning by fire when the fuel is removed, even though the fire has still the power to burn.

Vedāntin : No, since the causes (of activity, viz merit, demerit, etc.) become connected with (the agent through) the activities that his power necessarily evokes, (for power without the corresponding act is inconceivable). And when they become connected in this way, it is impossible to get rid of them wholly.

Opponent : Liberation will be achieved on the strength of the Vedic injunction itself.[23]

Vedāntin : No, since anything that can be acquired through practice is impermanent. Moreover, it has been stated that liberation stands established from the fact that the soul has been expounded (in the Upaniṣads) to be eternally pure, enlightened,

[23] As the Vedic injunction (about sacrifices etc.) can change a human being into god, so it can change an agent into non-agent.

and free. But the presentation of such a soul cannot be logically justified if agentship be natural. Hence the agentship of the soul arises from the superimposition of the attributes of the limiting adjuncts; it is not innate. In support of this is the Vedic text, "It thinks as it were, and shakes as it were" (Bṛ. IV. iii. 7). The text, "The intelligent people call the soul which is associated with body, organs, and mind, as the enjoyer" (Ka. I. iii. 4), shows that the soul when in association with the limiting adjuncts, gets the special characteristic of being an enjoyer. To the discriminating people there can be no individual soul, distinct from the supreme Self, which can be the agent or experiencer, for the Upaniṣad declares, "There is no other witness but Him" (Bṛ. III. vii. 23), etc.

Opponent: If apart from the supreme Self, there be no intelligent soul which is an agent and distinct from the assemblage of body and organs, then it would come to this that the supreme Self Itself would be the entity undergoing transmigration and becoming the agent and the experiencer.

Vedāntin: No, since the states of being an agent and an experiencer are conjured up by ignorance. Thus the scripture also shows that the individual soul is an agent and an experiencer when in a state of ignorance: "Because when there is duality, as it were, . . . then one sees another" (Bṛ. II. iv. 14); and then the scripture denies those very agentship and experiencership in the state of enlightenment: "But when to the knower of Brahman everything has become the Self, then what should one see and through what?" (ibid.). Similarly, the Upaniṣad shows how like a falcon flying in the sky, the soul becomes tired in the waking and dream states owing to its association with limiting adjuncts; and then the Upaniṣad shows the absence of that fatigue in the sleep state where the soul is embraced by the intelligent (supreme) Self; for the commencement is made with, "That is his real form, in which all objects of desire have been attained and are but the Self, and which is free from desires and devoid of grief" (Bṛ. IV. iii. 21); and the conclusion is made with, "This is its supreme attainment, this is its supreme glory, this is its highest world, this is its supreme bliss" (Bṛ. IV. iii. 32). This fact is stated by the teacher (Vyāsa) in, "And (rather) this is like the carpenter existing under both conditions". The word "*ca* (and)" is used in the sense of "but" (rather). It is not to be thought thus that the agentship is natural to the soul just as heat is to fire. On the contrary, as it is seen in the world that a carpenter feels unhappy when working as an agent with instruments like an adze, and that this very man becomes happy when he reaches his own home leaving behind the instruments like the adze; then he is at nobody's beck and call, he is free from worries, and free from all activity; similarly the soul in association with the duality, brought about by nescience, becomes an agent and is unhappy in the dream and wakeful states; but when for becoming free from that fatigue, that very soul enters into its own Self, the supreme Brahman, in the state of deep sleep, and becomes free from the assemblage of body and organs, it is no more an agent, and it becomes happy. So also in the state of liberation it has the darkness of ignorance dispelled with the lamp of knowledge, and becoming the absolute Self, it attains happiness. The point in the illustration of the carpenter is to be understood as applying merely thus far that the carpenter becomes an agent only when he is in need of the pre-requisites like the adze etc. for the set works of planing etc. but he is a non-agent in his mere physical presence. So also the soul becomes an agent only when it requires the instruments like the mind etc. for all kinds of work; but considered in itself, it is surely not an agent. The soul has, however, no limb (like the hand) with which to pick up or put aside the organs (i.e. instruments of work) like the mind etc., just as the carpenter picks up or puts away the adze etc. with his hands etc.

As for the assertion that the soul must have agentship for such reasons as the need of imparting purposefulness to the scripture, that is wrong. When the scripture imparts injunction, it takes for granted the conventional agentship and then teaches about particular forms of duty; but it does not itself prove the agentship of the soul. Moreover, we stated earlier that the soul has no agentship intrinsically, for there is instruction about the identity of the individual Self and Brahman. This is our standpoint. Hence any injunctive text will find enough scope by accepting the conventional agentship created by nescience. Besides, since the texts, such as this, "The Puruṣa, a knower by nature, is a doer" (Pr. IV. 9), which are mere recapitulations of facts already known otherwise, may well be valid as merely referring to the empirical agentship as it is created by ignorance. Hereby are refuted the arguments about roaming (II. iii. 34), and taking up the organs (II. iii. 35), for they too are mere reiterations (of conventionally accepted facts).

Opponent: Since the fact of roaming about by the soul is dealt with by saying that in the dream state, when all the organs have gone asleep, the soul moves about in its own body at will (Bṛ. II. i. 18), it amounts to asserting that the absolute Self has agentship. So also in the matter of taking up the organs. Since the text, "it absorbs at the time the power of perception of the organs (*vijñānam*) through the intellect (*vijñānena*)" (Bṛ. II. i. 17), the objective and instrumental case-endings are used after the organs (in *vijñānam* and *vijñānena*), therefore we are led to the conclusion that the absolute Self has agentship.

Vedāntin: In answer it is said: As for the dream state, there is no absolute stoppage of the use of the organs by the soul; for in the text, "Entering the dream state in association with the intellect, he (the Self) goes beyond this world" (Bṛ. IV. iii. 7—Mādhyandina), we hear of the association with the intellect even in that state. So also in the Smṛti: "Know that to be the state of dream experience, where after the stoppage of the organs, the mind remains active and experiences the objects". Besides, the Upaniṣad declares that desire etc. are the modes of the mind (Bṛ. I. v. 3); and they are witnessed in dream. Therefore the soul moves about in dream in association with the mind. The roaming there also is not a reality but only a product of past impressions. Thus it is that the Upaniṣad describes the dream activities by qualifying them with the phrase "as if": "He seems as if enjoying himself in the company of women, as if laughing or even seeing frightful things" (Bṛ. IV. iii. 13). Ordinary people also describe the dream experiences in a similar way: "As if I were ascending a mountain peak", "As if I saw a forest". Similarly even with regard to the "taking up of the organs", although the objective and instrumental case-endings are used after the organs (*vijñāna*), still the soul's agentship is to be understood as occurring as a result of conjunction with them, for we showed earlier that there can be no agentship in the absolute Self. In the common world also, the speaker's modes of expression can be very various, as for instance, "The warriors are fighting", or "the king is fighting through the warriors". Moreover, in this case of "taking up" what is intended to be spoken of is the stoppage of the activity of the organs, and not the independent agentship of anyone (i.e. of the soul), for even when somebody goes to sleep without any conscious effort, the organs are seen to stop from activity.[24]

As for the allusion to the statement, "*Vijñāna* spreads the sacrifice" (Tai. II. v. 1), that only makes us understand the agentship of the intellect, since the word *vijñāna* is very often used in that sense, since it is mentioned immediately after the mind, and since in the text "faith is indeed his head" (Tai. II. iv), such limbs as faith etc. are declared for the Self identified with the intellect, and faith etc. are well known to be the modes of the intellect. Moreover, in the complementary passage occurs the sentence, "All the gods worship *vijñāna* (intellect), the eldest, as Brahman" (Tai. II. v. 1); and it is a well-known fact that the intellect (identified with Hiraṇyagarbha) is the eldest or the first born (Bṛ. V. iv. 1). Besides, this is confirmed by the assertion in another Vedic text that a sacrifice is performed by the organ of speech and the intellect: "That which is a sacrifice consists in a succession of speech and the intellect one after the other."[25]

And it cannot be argued that if the organs (including the intellect) are assumed to be the agents, then there will be a reversal of the power of the intellect (from instrumentality to agentship—B. S. II. iii. 38), for all the things (even though) appearing with different case-endings must have agentship in their own respective spheres (of actions).[26] The organs become

[24] In the earlier argument it was conceded for argument's sake that the soul takes up the organs when entering sleep. That activity too is denied here.

[25] The sacrifice emerges from mental thought followed by the utterance of *mantras* through speech. Here also the agent of the sacrifice is the intellect.

[26] We say, "Rice is cooking", "fuel is burning", "the vessel contains"

instruments when considered from the standpoint of the act of perception; but the perception itself is by the soul. Here, again, the soul has no agency, for it is eternal consciousness by its very nature. The witnessing soul cannot have any agentship even through the ego-consciousness, for egoity itself is an object of perception to the soul. Again, if this position is accepted, there will be no need for fancying some other organ; for the intellect is admitted as the instrument.

The objection that *samādhi* (profound meditation) would not be possible (B. S. II. iii. 39), stands refuted through the refutation of the assertion that the soul must be an agent so as to impart purposefulness to the scripture (B. S. II. iii. 33), for *samādhi* is enjoined by accepting the conventional agentship. Therefore the conclusion stands firm that the agentship of the soul is a creation of the limiting adjuncts.

Topic 16: Soul's Agentship Derived from God

परात्तु तच्छ्रुतेः ॥४१॥

तु But परात् (derived from) the Highest, तत्-श्रुतेः for that is declared by Vedic texts.

41. But the agentship (of the individual soul) is derived from God, for that is what is stated in the Vedic texts.

Doubt: It has been said that the agentship of the individual soul occurs owing to the limiting adjuncts during the state of ignorance. Now it has to be considered whether that agentship occurs with or without any dependence on God.

Opponent: Under the circumstances, the conclusion arrived at is that the soul does not depend on God for its agentship.

Why?

Because there is no need to depend. For this soul, impelled by likes, dislikes, etc. and endowed with all the other paraphernalia of action, can by itself have experiences of agentship. What has God to do for it? And it is not a recognized fact in the world

and so on. The fuel is an agent so far as its own action is concerned, but as regards cooking, it is an instrument.

that in such works as agriculture one has need of God, in the sense that one has of bullocks etc. Besides, a God, who creates creatures and endows them with an agentship that is essentially painful, will be open to the charge of cruelty as well as partiality owing to ordaining an agentship that leads to unequal results.

Objection : Was it not said that "No partiality and cruelty (can be charged against God) because of His taking other factors into consideration" (B. S. II. i. 34)?

Opponent : What was said would have been true if God could possibly depend on other things; and that dependence would be possible for God if the creatures could possess merit and demerit. These again would have been possible if the individual souls had agentship. Now, if that agentship be dependent on God, then on what will God have His dependence? (If again God ordains without dependence on results of action), then on that supposition the individual will get unmerited fruits. Hence the individual has his agentship independently and naturally.

Vedāntin : This contingency is ruled out by the aphorist by the word "but", and his own position is stated in "the agentship (etc.)". During the state of ignorance, when the individual soul is blinded by the darkness of ignorance and cannot understand itself to be different from the assemblage of body and organs, it derives its transmigratory state, consisting in its becoming an agent and experiencer, from the behest of the supreme Self who presides over all activities and resides in all beings, and who is the witness (of all), imparts intelligence (to all), and is the supreme Lord. Liberation, too, results from realization that is vouchsafed by Him out of His grace.

Why?

That is what is stated in the Vedic texts. Although the individual being is impelled by such defects as attachment and is endowed with the accessories of activity, and although in ordinary experience, such activities as agriculture are not recognized as caused by God, still it is ascertained from the Vedic texts that God is the directing (i.e. ultimate efficient) cause behind all activities. To this effect occurs the text: "It is He who makes him do good works whom He would raise above these worlds, and it is He who makes them do evil works whom

He would drag down" (Kau. III. 8), as also "He who dwells in the sound and controls the soul from within" (Ś. B. XIV. vi. 7.30, Bṛ. III. vii. 3-23), and other texts of this kind.

Opponent: If God has the (ultimate) power of directing in this way, He will have partiality and cruelty and the individual beings will reap unmerited results.

The (*Vedāntin's*) answer is given in the negative:

कृतप्रयत्नापेक्षस्तु विहितप्रतिषिद्धावैयर्थ्यादिभ्यः ॥४२॥

तु However कृत-प्रयत्न-अपेक्षः dependent on the efforts made, विहित-प्रतिषिद्ध-अवैयर्थ्य-आदिभ्यः on grounds of the enjoined and prohibited duties not becoming meaningless and so on.

42. (God is), however, dependent on the efforts made, so that injunctions and prohibitions may not become meaningless and other defects may not arise.

The word "however" is used for refuting the objections raised. In causing the individual to act, God takes into account the efforts—characterized either as virtuous or vicious—which the individual makes. Hence the defects, pointed out, do not arise. God acts merely as a general instrumental cause, dividing the resulting fruits of works unequally in accordance with the inequality of merit and demerit acquired by the individual beings, even as rain does. It is seen in the world that rain becomes the common instrumental cause of long and short creepers etc. or of rice and barley etc. which grow in accordance with their own seeds, and yet unless there be rainfall, they can have no differences in sap, flower, fruit, leaves, etc., nor can they have these in the absence of their own seeds; so also it stands to reason that God ordains good and bad for the individual beings in accordance with the efforts made by the beings themselves.

Opponent: If the agentship itself of the individual be dependent on God, then God can have no dependence on the effort made by the individual.

Vedāntin: That creates no difficulty. Although the individual's agentship is dependent on God, still it is the individual who really acts. God directs him just as he himself would proceed with his work. Moreover, God directs him now in accordance with what he did previously, and He directed him earlier in accordance with what he had done still earlier. Thus since the state of transmigratory existence is without beginning, all this is above cavil.

Opponent: How again is it known that God depends on the efforts made?

The (*Vedāntin's*) answer is contained in, "so that the injunctions and prohibitions may not become meaningless and other defects may not arise". For thus alone such injunctions and prohibitions as, "One desirous of heaven shall perform a sacrifice", "A Brāhmaṇa is not to be killed", will not be stultified; else (if God does not depend on the acts done, then) these will become meaningless, and God Himself will be installed (as an absolute dictator) in the place of injunction and prohibition, since the individual will be absolutely under God (and not under the scriptures). Similarly (God being without any standard), He will strike with evil one who acts according to scripture, and bestow gifts on one who acts against it. In that case the authority of the Vedas will be set aside. Moreover, if God be absolutely autocratic, even ordinary personal efforts will become useless, and so also space, time, and causation will be meaningless. Furthermore, there will be the defect stated earlier (of getting unmerited results, etc). These and such other drawbacks are indicated by the term "other defects".

TOPIC 17: RELATION OF SOUL AND GOD

अंशो नानाव्यपदेशादन्यथा चापि दाशकितवादित्वमधीयत एके ॥४३॥

अंशः A part व्यपदेशात् because mentioned नाना as different, च अपि as also अन्यथा otherwise एके some अधीयते read of दाश-कितव-आदित्वम् identity with *Dāśas* (fishermen and slaves), *Kitavas* (gamblers), and others.

43. *(The individual souls are) parts of God because of the mention that they are different, also because some read other-*

wise of (Brahman's) identity with fishermen, slaves, gamblers, and others.

Doubt: It was stated earlier that as between the individual soul and God, there exists (a relationship based on) a feeling of one being the favoured and the other the favourer. And such a relationship is seen to subsist in the world between two mutually related entities, as for instance a servant and his master, or a fire and its sparks. Thus when it is admitted that the individual and God are mutually the beneficiary and the benefactor, the question arises, whether their relationship is like that between the master and the servant, or like that between fire and its sparks.

Opponent: When this doubt arises, the conclusion may be either that the relationship is irregular, or since the feeling as between the ruler and the ruled is well known to be of the pattern subsisting between the master and the servant, it must be similar to that here as well.

Vedāntin: Hence the aphorist says, "A part" etc. The individual should be a part of God even as a spark is of fire. The individual is a part only apparently, for the partless Brahman can have no part in the literal sense.

Opponent: Why should not the individual be God Himself on this very ground of partlessness (of God)?

Vedāntin: (No), "because of the mention that they are different". Unless there is some dissimilarity, the statement of difference, as contained in, "He is to be searched for, He is to be sought to be known" (Ch. VIII. vii. 1), "Knowing It alone one becomes a sage" (Bṛ. IV. iv. 22), "He who dwells in the soul and controls the soul from within" (Ś. B. XIV. vi. 7), and similar texts, cannot be justified.

Opponent: This reference to difference fits in more aptly if it be understood to be like that between a master and his servant.

Vedāntin: Hence the aphorist says: "it is mentioned otherwise also" etc. Not that the individual is known merely to be a part from the mention of difference. What else then? The mention is made in other ways also to establish non-difference.

Thus the followers of a certain section of the Atharva Veda read in their hymn to Brahman of the identity of Brahman with the *Dāśas, Kitavas,* and others in, "The *Dāśas* are Brahman; the *Dāsas* are Brahman; even these gamblers are but Brahman" etc. The *Dāśas* are the people known as *Kaivartas* (fishermen); the *Dāsas* are those others (i.e. slaves) who surrender their bodies to a master; and (*kitavas* are) those others who are the gamblers engaged in playing dice; they are all nothing but Brahman. With the help of these illustrations of inferior beings the text shows that all individual souls are Brahman, who have entered into the aggregates of body and organs created by name and form. Similarly elsewhere also, when dealing with Brahman Itself, this very idea is elaborated: "You are woman, you are man, you are a young man or even a maid; you are old tottering about with the help of a stick; having taken birth, you have your face everywhere" (Śv. IV. 3), and "One becomes immortal by knowing that intelligent One who, after having created all the forms and names, (and after having entered there) goes on uttering (i.e. making use of) them" (Tai. Ā. III. xii. 16). This idea finds confirmation from such Vedic texts as, "There is no other witness but Him" (Bṛ. III. vii. 23). And consciousness is common to both God and the individual beings even as heat is to fire and a spark. Thus since both difference and non-difference are known (from texts), it is gathered that the individual is a part.

Why, again, should it be known to be a part?

मन्त्रवर्णाच्च ॥४४॥

च And मन्त्र-वर्णात् on the authority of the words of the *mantras.*

44. This follows from the words of the mantras also.

The *mantra* text also reveals this fact: "Thus far (i.e. the whole creation) constitutes His glory; Puruṣa (i.e. the infinite Being) is greater even than that (creation). All *bhūtas* (beings) are merely a foot (part) of His; His other three immortal feet are in heaven" (i.e. transcendental) (Ch. III. xii. 6). By *bhūtas* (beings) is (suggestively) indicated here everything that moves or does not move, the living creatures being the most prominent among them; for we come across such a use, "(One attains the world of Brahman) by practising non-injury to all the *bhūtas* on all occasions apart from where the scriptures sanction it" (Ch. VIII. xv. 1). The words *aṁśa* (part), *pāda* (foot or quarter) are synonymous with *bhāga* (a portion). From this also the individual is known to be a part.

What more is the reason for knowing it to be a part?

अपि च स्मर्यते ॥४५॥

अपि च Moreover स्मर्यते mention is made in the Smṛti.

45. And this is also stated in the Smṛti (Gītā).

In the Bhagavad-Gītā also (which is a Smṛti) it is stated that the individual is a part of God: "An eternal portion of myself having become an individual soul in the world of the creatures" (XV. 7). From this also it is known that it is a part. As for the argument that in common experience it is well recognized that the relation of the ruler and the ruled obtains only among such persons as the master and the servant, although that is the well-known fact in the world, still it is ascertained from the scriptures that the relationship here is like that between a part and a whole as also like that between the ruled and the ruler. And it involves no contradiction to hold that God, having His unsurpassable limiting adjunct, rules over the individual souls having their inferior limiting adjuncts.

Here the (*opponent*) says: If the individual be admitted to be a part of God who is the whole, then God will have to experience the pain of the transmigratory existence suffered by (all) the individuals, even as in the ordinary world, Devadatta, possessed of his own hands, feet, etc. suffers pain when it occurs to any one of the limbs. From this it will follow that those who reach Godhood will suffer greater pain; and as compared with this liberation, the earlier state of worldly existence will be preferable, so that the predicament will arise of full enlightenment becoming useless.

Vedāntin : To this comes the reply:

प्रकाशादिवन्नैवं परः ॥४६॥

परः The supreme Self न एवम् does not (suffer) thus प्रकाश-आदि-वत् like light etc.

46. The Supreme Self is not so (touched by the suffering of the individual soul), even as light etc. are not (affected by the things that condition them).

We solemnly declare that God does not suffer the woes of the world like an individual being. The individual soul, under the influence of ignorance, seems to become identified with the body etc., and it suffers the sorrows occurring to the body, owing to its belief that the sufferings created by ignorance are its own. But God has no such identity with the body etc. nor any conception of suffering in Himself. In the case of the individual soul as well, the feeling of suffering that it has, arises from an error consisting in not realizing its difference from the limiting adjunct constituted by the body, organs, etc. which are created by name and form that are the products of ignorance; but in reality it has no suffering. Just as a man, owing to his erroneous identity with the body, feels the pain caused to his body by a burn, a bruise, etc., so also he feels the pain caused to his son, friend, and others, owing to an erroneous identity with them under the idea, "I am the same as my son", "I am the same as my friend", arising from strong attachment to the son, friend, etc. caused by his love for them. From this it becomes known as a certainty that the feeling of sorrow is caused by an error of false identity. And this is understood from an observation of the opposite instances. Thus it is that when many sit together—both those who have sons, friends, etc. and have a feeling of relationship with them, and those that have no such conception—and such pieces of news are broken that a son is dead, a friend is dead, and so on, then from that news, sorrow comes only to those who have the belief of having friends and sons, but not to those, e.g. monks and others who have no such belief. Thus since complete (i.e. discriminating) knowledge is seen to serve some purpose even for a man under ordinary circumstances, what more need we speak of its purposefulness in the case of one who does not see anything apart from the Self which is never an object, and who has become one with what is by nature eternal consciousness? Hence there can be no question of complete enlightenment being useless. "As light etc." is said by way of an illustration. As the light of the sun or moon spreads over the whole sky, and yet when it comes in contact with a conditioning factor like a finger etc., it seems to become straight or bent like them as these things become so, but not so in reality; or as space seems to move when pots etc. change places, but not so in reality; or as the reflection of the sun in a plate of water etc. seems to shake with the shaking of those things, but not so the sun that is the prototype; similarly even though a part of God, which is conjured up by nescience, conditioned by the intellect etc., and called an individual soul, suffers pain, still God, the possessor of that part, has no suffering. And we said that even the suffering of the individual being is brought about by ignorance. Hence it is that the Upaniṣadic texts, as for instance, "That thou art" (Ch. VI. viii. 7), establish the soul's identity with Brahman Itself through a negation of the state of individuality caused by ignorance. Hence there can be no question of God becoming afflicted with pain owing to the individual's suffering.

स्मरन्ति च ॥४७॥

स्मरन्ति They say in the Smṛtis च and.

47. They say so in the Smṛtis, and (the Upaniṣads declare thus).

Moreover, Vyāsa and others recollect (i.e. mention) (in their Smṛtis), how the supreme Self is not afflicted by the suffering of the individual being: "Among these two, that which is the supreme Self is stated to be eternal and without attributes; and like the lotus leaf unaffected by water, It remains untouched even by the results of work. The other one that is the basis of all works, is subject to bondage and liberation, and it is he that becomes again associated with the (subtle body constituted by) the seventeen factors."[27] By the word "and" (in the aphorism) it is to be understood that "the Upaniṣads also state this", for instance, "Of these two, the one eats the fruit of divergent taste, and the other looks on without eating" (Mu. III. i. 1, Śv. iv. 6), and "Similarly the Self, that is but one in all beings, is not tainted by the sorrows of the world, It being transcendental" (Ka. II. ii. 11).

Somebody (an *opponent*) says here: If then the innermost Self of all beings be the same, then how will acquiescence and inhibition (i.e. injunction and prohibition)—both scriptural and human—fit in?

Objection: Has it not been said that the individual soul is a part of God? And because of this difference among them (i.e. God and His various parts), injunction and prohibition, which centre round this difference, can well maintain their distinction. So what is the point in your question here?

The answer (of the *Opponent*) is this: This cannot be so, for the Vedic texts, speaking of non-difference, establish the other fact also that the individual is not a part, as in, "After creating it, He entered into it" (Tai. II. vi. 1), "There is no other witness but Him" (Bṛ. III. vii. 23), "He goes from death to death, who sees difference as it were, in It" (Bṛ. IV. iv. 19), "That thou art" (Ch. VI. viii-xvi), "I am Brahman" (Bṛ. I. iv. 10), and other passages of the same class.

Vedāntin: Was it not said that from coming across both difference and non-difference (in the texts), the conclusion to be arrived at is that the individual is a part?

Opponent: This could be so if both difference and non-difference were intended as facts to be established; but it is non-difference alone that is sought to be taught here, for the highest human goal is achieved through the realization of the identity of the individual soul with Brahman. The difference, comprehended empirically, is referred to only by way of a restatement of a known fact. And it was said that the individual cannot be a part of Brahman in the literal sense, for Brahman

[27] Ten organs of perception and action, five vital forces, mind, and intellect.

is partless. Hence it is the same supreme Self, which is the innermost Self of all beings, that assumes the state of the individual souls. This being the position, the logicality of injunction and prohibition has to be explained.

Vedāntin: That is being explained by us:

अनुज्ञापरिहारौ देहसम्बन्धाज्ज्योतिरादिवत् ॥४८॥

अनुज्ञा-परिहारौ (scriptural) acquiescence and inhibition (are feasible) देह-सम्बन्धात् owing to association with the body ज्योतिः-आदि-वत् as in the case of light etc.

48. Injunction and prohibition become effective owing to physical association, just as it is in the case of light etc.

"One shall approach one's wife at the proper time" is an injunction; "One shall not approach one's teacher's wife" is a prohibition. Similarly, "One shall sacrifice an animal to Agni and Soma" is an injunction; "One shall not injure any being" is a prohibition. So also in common life, "One shall entertain one's friend" is an injunction; "One shall avoid one's enemy" is a prohibition. Even though the Self is one, this kind of injunction and prohibition are possible owing to "physical association". "Physical association" means the contact with different bodies.

What is this bodily contact?

It consists in a rise of a perverse idea to the effect, "This aggregate of body etc. is but myself". This is seen to exist in all creatures and to take such forms as: "I go", "I come", "I am blind", "I am not blind", "I am dull", "I am not dull", and so on. There is nothing else apart from full enlightenment that can eradicate this. Before the dawn of that enlightenment, this error permeates all creatures. In this way, even though the Self is admitted to be one, still injunction and prohibition can find scope owing to the distinctions created through the association with the limiting adjuncts like the body etc., conjured up by ignorance.

Opponent: In that case, injunction and prohibition are meaningless for one who is fully enlightened.

Vedāntin: No, for he is beyond the range of scriptural direction, as he has already got all that can be achieved. One who has to be directed will be directed with regard to something to be avoided or something to be accepted. But how can one be directed who does not see anything other than the Self? Not that the Self can be asked to be engaged in action on Itself.

Opponent: It is precisely one who knows that the Self is different from the body that can be directed (by the scriptures).

Vedāntin: No, for (such fitness for injunction follows when) one has still a notion that one is the aggregate of body etc.[28] Though it is true that one is directed (by the scriptures) only when one knows (intellectually) the Self to be different from the body, still only that person alone can have the idea that he is being directed (by the scriptures) who does not realize the Self to be (actually) dissociated from body etc. even as space etc. (are from jar etc.). For nobody who understands the Self to be dissociated from the body etc. is ever seen to come under the range of direction, what to speak of one who realizes the unity of the Self? And it cannot be said that if the man of enlightenment is beyond all (scriptural) obligation, he may as well behave capriciously; for it is self-identity (with body etc.) that is seen to promote action everywhere, but in the case of the enlightened one there is no such self-identity. Therefore injunction and prohibition become possible only as a result of association with the body, "as it is in the case of light". As fire from the cremation ground is avoided, but not the others, though as fire they are all the same; as sunlight falling on an unholy place is avoided, but not so the sunlight on holy ground, though as sunlight it is all the same; as diamonds, beryls, etc., which are particles of earthly matter, are accepted, but not so human corpses etc., though they are equally earthly things; as also the urine and dung of a cow are accepted, (the

[28] An intellectual conception of the difference between the body and soul cannot remove the notion of the identity with the body that one actually has. Till that notion is removed by direct, actual realization, one is well within scriptural domination.

cow being holy), but not so the excreta of other species; so also is the case here.

असन्ततेश्चाव्यतिकरः ॥४९॥

च And असन्ततेः on account of want of connection अव्यतिकरः there is no intermixture.

49. And there is no intermixture (of actions and results), since the soul has no connection with all (the bodies).

Opponent: Conceded that injunction and prohibition will be possible owing to the association with particular bodies even though the Self be the same. But as regards the association with the results of work, it will all become a jumble on the assumption of a single Self, for the possessor (of experiences) will be but one.

Vedāntin: This will not be so, because the connection is not universal. The soul, either as an agent or as an experiencer, has no connection with all the bodies. For it has been stated that the individual soul is dependent on its limiting adjunct. As this limiting adjunct does not spread everywhere, so also the soul has no universal connection. Thus there can be no intermixture of either works or their results.

आभास एव च ॥५०॥

च And आभासः a false appearance (i.e. reflection) एव certainly.

50. And (the individual soul) is only a reflection (of the supreme Self) to be sure.

And it is to be understood that this individual soul is a reflection of the supreme Self like the semblance of the sun in water. Not that the soul is the Self Itself, nor is it something else. From this also it follows that just as when any one of the reflections of the sun moves, the others do not, similarly when any one individual soul becomes associated with the result of its work, no other soul is associated with it. Thus the works and the results of works do not certainly get intermixed. And since a false appearance is a creation of ignorance, it is but logical that the transmigratory state centring round that appearance must also be a creation of ignorance; and hence the instruction is logically proper that the identity of the soul with Brahman, which is the supreme reality, is attained by eradicating that appearance. On the contrary, this intermixture (of works and results) arises in the case of those only who believe in many souls, each one of which is omnipresent.

How?

"The souls are many and omnipresent, and by nature they are consciousness, devoid of qualities, and unexcelled. For serving their purposes they have in common one primordial Nature (Pradhāna). And the experiences (of happiness and sorrow) as well as liberation accrue to these souls from that Nature"—This is what the *Sāṁkhyas* say.

(The *Vaiśeṣikas* maintain that) although the souls are many and omnipresent, still they are intrinsically unconscious, and are mere substances like pots, walls, etc. The minds which serve them are atomic and unconscious. That being so, from a contact of the substance called soul and the substance called mind, emerge nine distinct qualities of the soul, viz desire and the rest,[29] and they inhere individually in the soul without getting intermixed. This is the transmigratory state. The absolute cessation of the emergence of those nine qualities of the soul is liberation. This is the view of the followers of Kaṇāda (i.e. Vaiśeṣikas).

Of these two views, as regards that of the Sāṁkhyas, since all the souls are consciousness by nature and the proximity of Pradhāna is common to them all, when any one of them becomes associated with happiness or sorrow, all the others become equally so.

Sāṁkhya: It may be like this: Since Nature acts for the liberation of the souls, some individual differentiation (or adjustment) will be made (by her), for else the activity of Nature will amount merely to a display of her own glory, and in that case there will be no liberation.

[29] Intelligence, happiness, sorrow, desire, dislike, effort, merit, demerit, and impression.

Vedāntin: This is vain talk, for it is not possible to understand any such individual adjustment required (on utilitarian grounds) for the fulfilment of (individual) desired ends. The adjustment has, therefore, to be explained on the basis of some valid reason.[30] In the absence of any reason, however, the desired liberation of the soul may very well remain unaccomplished, while the intermixture becomes inevitable owing to the absence of any valid ground for individual adjustment.

Even from the point of view of the followers of Kaṇāda, whenever the mind becomes connected with any one of the souls, it will have connection with the other souls also without obstacle, for (the causes for that connection, viz) proximity, etc. are equally in evidence, (the souls being omnipresent). From this indistinguishability of cause, the result also will be indistinguishable, and so from the contact of one soul with happiness and sorrow all the other souls will be open to these.

The *opponents* may argue that the individual adjustment will follow from the unseen potential results of work. But the *aphorist* says, no—

अदृष्टानियमात् ॥५१॥

अदृष्ट-अनियमात् Since the unseen potential results of works cannot be allocated individually.

51. (Even the unseen potential results of works cannot regulate individual allocation), since the unseen potential results (themselves) cannot be allocated thus.

The unseen potential results of works, consisting in merit and demerit, are earned (individually) through mind, speech, and body, even though the souls continue to be many, all-pervasive like space, and equally contiguous to every body, in and out. Now then, from the Sāṁkhya standpoint, there is nothing to

[30] Inert Nature cannot study the desires of the souls; and the liberation that is still in the womb of futurity and is itself inert cannot give rise to any individual adjustment. Hence this adjustment is accepted by you not from the point of view of any valid reason, but from that of utility for serving an unproved hypothesis.

regulate the experiencing of happiness and sorrow by each soul individually, since the unseen potential results do not inhere in the soul (the soul being attributeless), but they abide in Nature, which again is common to all. The same fault arises in the case of the followers of Kaṇāda as well, since the unseen potential results are brought about by contacts between the souls and mind which (contacts) are common to all, just as much as in the earlier case, so that there is no reason to maintain any such rule that a particular result will belong to a particular soul.

The (Vaiśeṣika) *opponent* may argue thus: Such resolves etc. as, "I shall get this result", "I shall avoid this", "I shall make such effort", "I shall act thus", and so on, which spring in each soul individually will regulate the mastery of the souls over their (respective) unseen results.

But the *aphorist* says, no—

अभिसन्ध्यादिष्वपि चैवम् ॥५२॥

अपि Even अभिसन्धि-आदिषु in the case of resolution etc. च also एवम् it is the same.

52. *And the same (defect springs up) even in the case of resolves etc.*

Since resolves etc. are also made in the proximity of all the (omnipresent) souls through a contact between a soul and the mind (which contact becomes) common to all, therefore these resolves etc. cannot be logically accepted as regulating the allocation (of pleasure and pain). And hence the defect pointed out will certainly arise.

प्रदेशादिति चेन्नान्तर्भावात् ॥५३॥

प्रदेशात् On the basis of different parts इति चेत् if this be the position, न not so, अन्तः-भावात् because of getting included (in all).

53. *If it be said that this (individual allocation of pleasure and pain) can be possible in accordance with the separate part (of*

each soul in each body), then it cannot be so, because of all (the omnipresent souls) getting included in all (the bodies).

Opponent: It may now be argued that though the individual soul is omnipresent, still its contact with the mind, residing in the body, will happen in a particular part of that soul that is circumscribed by that body, and thus the allocation of resolves etc., unseen potential results of works, and happiness and sorrow will be encompassed in relation to that part.

Vedāntin: Even that is not valid.

Why?

"Because of getting included (everywhere)". Since all the individual souls are equally omnipresent, they become included in all the bodies. That being the case, it is impossible for the Vaiśeṣikas to imagine any part of a soul that becomes separated by a body. And even if this be imagined, that part of the partless soul will not be able to regulate (the allocation of) actual effects, this separation having existence merely in imagination. And the body, coming into being as it does in the vicinity of all the souls, cannot be assigned to any particular soul rather than to all the others. Even if a difference of parts (in souls) be accepted, still (such parts cannot determine the allocation of experience; for) two souls, having in store for them the same happiness and sorrow may at times have those experiences through a single body, since it is possible for the two souls to have an unseen (potential) result bound up with the same locality. Thus when Devadatta's body moves away from a locality where Devadatta had experienced happiness and sorrow, and then Yajñadatta's body moves into the same place, he is seen to have the same kind of happiness and sorrow as the former; that would not be the case unless Devadatta and Yajñadatta had an unseen potential result (in store for them) bound up with the same locality. And the possibility of not enjoying heaven etc. also arises from the standpoint of one who talks of parts in the soul; for (there must be a unity of the agent and enjoyer; but according to your theory) the unseen potential results of works may be earned in the Brāhmaṇa bodies etc., whereas the heavenly enjoyment etc. have to occur in a different locality.[31] Moreover if the souls be many, they cannot be all-pervasive, since there is no such illustration to prove this. Cite for me then those (illustrative) things that are many at the same time that they occupy the same place.

Opponent: Take for instance colour, (taste, smell), etc. (existing in the same flower).

Vedāntin: No, for they too are non-different so far as they are identical with the substance to which they belong; and in themselves they have distinct characteristics. But the many souls have no distinctive characteristics.[32]

Opponent: The difference is possible owing to the presence of an ultimate *viśeṣa* (inherent differentia) in the souls.

Vedāntin: No, since the supposition of difference in the souls (resulting from the inherent differentia) and the inference of such differentia (on the strength of the differences among the souls) would lead to a logical seesaw. Moreover, even the omnipresence of space etc. is unacceptable to the believers in Brahman, since these are understood by them to be products. Hence the conclusion is that all defects can be obviated only by those who believe in the unity of the Self.

[31] Any part of the soul, determined by the body, as also the contact between mind and soul, is common to all souls, they being omnipresent. So any particular body can determine the parts for all the souls, and any mind can be in contact with all the souls. Thus experiences cannot be kept distinct. Even an unseen potential result does not mend matters, for the part of the soul where this result arises does not move about; and if this fixity be conceded, then it has to be admitted that other souls can have the same experiences at that very locality, for that is what we see in ordinary life. Moreover, that particular part being motionless, the result acquired in a Brāhmaṇa body cannot move to heaven for fruition.

[32] Colour is nothing but its own material, viz the element "light"; smell is nothing but "earth", taste is nothing but "water"; and so on. Apart from these substances, there is no such thing as a flower. Besides, colour, taste, etc. differ among themselves, but not so the souls, which have the same characteristics. Thus the illustration falls through.

Section IV

Topic 1: Origin of the Pranas

Introduction: In the third section was resolved the conflict among the Vedic texts about (the creation of) space, etc. In the fourth section is now being resolved the conflict about *prāṇas* (organs).[1] Now then, in such contexts dealing with creation as, "That created fire" (Ch. VI. ii. 3), "From that Self that is such emerged space" (Tai. II. i. 1), and others, the origin of the *prāṇas* (organs) is not mentioned. Again in some contexts, their origin itself is denied, as in, "This was but non-existence in the beginning" (Tai. II. vii). (This is not nihilism;) for in, "With regard to that they asked, 'What is it that was non-existent?' The *ṛṣis* themselves were non-existent in the beginning. With regard to that they asked, 'Who were the *ṛṣis*?' The *prāṇas* were the *ṛṣis*" (Ś. B. VI. i. 1.1), we hear of the existence of the *prāṇas* even before creation started. In other places, however, the origin of the organs as well is stated, as in, "As from a blazing fire tiny sparks fly in all directions, so from this Self emanate all the *prāṇas* (organs)" (Bṛ. II. i. 20). "From Him originates *Prāṇa* (vital force) as well as the mind, all the senses, (space, air, fire, water, and earth that supports everything)" (Mu. II. i. 3), "From Him emerge the seven *prāṇas* (sense-organs)" (Mu. II. i. 8), "He created *Prāṇa*, from *Prāṇa* He created faith, space, air, fire, water, earth, organs, mind, food" (Pr. VI. 4), and other places. Since a textual conflict is obvious in those places, and since it is not possible to discover any reason for adopting either of the two alternatives, the result is bound to be a non-comprehension of the meaning; or since the existence of the organs before creation is mentioned by the texts, the conclusion may be that the texts speaking of the origin of

[1] The creation, nature, and number of *prāṇas* will be decided. The word *prāṇa* has several meanings, of which three will be considered in this section—organs, vital force in each individual, and *Prāṇa* in its cosmic aspect.

the organs are to be taken in a secondary sense. Hence the answer is given in the aphorism:

तथा प्राणाः ॥१॥

तथा Similarly प्राणाः the *prāṇas* (organs).

1. Similarly the organs (are produced from the supreme Self).

Opponent: How again does the word "similarly" fit in here, since nothing is presented by way of an illustration, (this being only the beginning of a section)? The topic dealt with at the end of the section just preceding was the refutation of the theory that the souls are all-pervasive and many. That, however, cannot serve the purpose of an illustration, since there is no similarity. Something can serve as an illustration when it has similarity, as for instance, "Balavarman is like a lion". It may be argued (by some one) thus: "The word 'similarly' is meant for showing the similarity with unseen potential results (occurring at the end of the last section); the meaning being that the organs originating in the vicinity of all the all-pervasive souls cannot be allocated to any particular soul, just as much as the unseen potential results originating in the vicinity of all the all-pervasive souls cannot be assigned to any one of them". But since that position has been already dealt with by saying that the bodies cannot be assigned to the souls individually, (the souls being all omnipresent), a fresh consideration will mean a mere repetition. Moreover, the organs cannot be compared with the souls, for that would be going against the accepted point of view, inasmuch as it was stated that the souls are not produced, whereas the intention here is to speak of the creation of the organs. Hence the word 'similarly' seems to be inappropriate.

Vedāntin: No, for a relation (of 'similarity') can be established even with the illustration presented in the illustrative (scriptural) sentences themselves. The illustration in the present case is contained in the texts speaking of the origin of the organs, as for instance, "From this Self emanate all the organs, all worlds, all gods, and all beings" (Bṛ. II. i. 20), and similar others. The meaning in those texts is that the organs originate from the supreme Brahman just like the worlds etc. So also in the text, "From Him originates *Prāṇa*, as well as the mind, all the organs, space, air, fire, water, and the earth that supports everything" (Mu. II. i. 3), as also in similar others, it is to be understood that the organs originate like space etc. Or it may be like this. Just as Jaimini relies on a connection with a remote example in such places as in the aphorism, "When one vomits after drinking in the course of a Vedic sacrifice, the remedy is to be undertaken in the same way as when a fault arises from giving away a defective horse in a sacrifice" (Jai. III. iv. 32), (so also Vyāsa can do likewise). Just as it is understood that space etc., spoken of in the previous and other sections are the products of Brahman, so also the organs are the products of the supreme Brahman. This is how it is to be construed.

Opponent: What again is the reason for accepting the organs as products?

Vedāntin: The very fact that the Upaniṣads mention this.

Opponent: Was it not pointed out that in some places the origin of the organs is not spoken of?

Vedāntin: That conclusion is wrong, since origin is spoken of in other places; for any omission in mentioning something somewhere cannot rule out the mention made elsewhere. Hence it is well affirmed that since there are Vedic mentions of origin, the organs originate even as space etc. do.

It was argued that since the texts mention the existence of the *prāṇas* (organs) before creation, therefore, any text that speaks of the origin of the organs, must be taken in a secondary sense. That position is refuted in:

गौण्यसम्भवात् ॥२॥

गौणी-असम्भवात् Because of the impossibility (of the text about origin) in the metaphorical sense.

2. (Origin of the organs has to be accepted) because of the impossibility of (the text about origin having) the secondary sense.

The compound in *gauṇyasambhavāt* is formed by dropping the sixth case-ending after *gauṇī* (meaning thereby: "Because of the impossibility of the secondary use"). The text speaking of the origin of the organs cannot have a secondary sense, for that would lead to an abandonment of the general assertion. The assertion of the knowledge of all through a knowledge of one is contained in, "O adorable sir, (which is that thing) which having been known all this becomes known?" (Mu. I. i. 3); and for propounding that assertion it is stated: "From Him originates *Prāṇa* etc." (Mu. II. i. 3). If the whole of this creation starting from *Prāṇa* be a product of Brahman, then only can that assertion become justified in accordance with the reasoning that a product cannot exist apart from its material cause. But if the creation of all this, starting from *Prāṇa*, be only in a secondary sense, then the assertion will be falsified.[2] And it is in keeping with this, that the assertion made (earlier) is concluded thus: "Puruṣa alone is all this—(comprising) the *karma* and knowledge. He who knows this supremely immortal Brahman, (as existing in the heart, destroys here the knot of ignorance)" (Mu. II. i. 10), and "This world is nothing but Brahman, the highest" (Mu. II. ii. 11). So also such Upaniṣadic texts as, "By the realization of the Self, my dear, through hearing, reflection, and meditation, all this is known" (Bṛ. II. iv. 5), are to be understood as making the same declaration.

Opponent: Why then does a Vedic text speak of the existence of the *praṇas* (organs) before creation?

Vedāntin: That sentence does not speak of the ultimate material cause (Brahman as existing in association with *Prāṇa*), for in the text "He is without *Prāṇa*, and without mind; He is pure and superior to the (other) superior immutable (i.e. *Māyā*)" (Mu. II. i. 2), it is asserted that the ultimate material cause is free from all such distinctive features as *Prāṇa* etc. But it is to be understood that the assertion about the existence of the *prāṇas* (organs) before creation is made from the standpoint of the (organs of the) subsequent material cause (Hiraṇyagarbha

[2] If Brahman be the material cause in a figurative sense, all things will not be known even when Brahman is known.

derived from Brahman) which is again a cause of its own derivatives. For it is well established on the strength of the Vedas and Smṛtis that the things that have become manifested (through names and forms) in several stages are themselves related by way of being the material causes and products (in a successive order). As the aphorism "*gauṇyasambhavāt*" (II. iii. 3) appearing under the topic of space stated the position of the opponent, it was explained to mean: "Any Vedic text about origin is secondary, for a primary sense is impossible". And the answer was given there by saying that such an interpretation would lead to an abandonment of the "general assertion" (or original declaration). But since the present aphorism states the conclusion of the Vedāntin, the explanation is made by saying, "Because of the impossibility of (the text about origin having) the secondary sense". Those, however, who in conformity with that earlier aphorism, would interpret this one also to mean, "Any Vedic text speaking of origin is used metaphorically, for a primary sense is inadmissible", would ignore (the consequent difficulty, viz) the abandonment of the original declaration (of all being known from one).

तत्प्राक्श्रुतेश्च ॥३॥

च Also तत्-प्राक्-श्रुतेः because that term, (*jāyate*, "is born"), is used earlier in the Upaniṣad.

3. Also because that term, ("is born"), is used earlier (in the primary sense) in the Upaniṣad (in connection with Prāṇa).[3]

For this further reason the Vedic text about the origin of the *prāṇas* is to be taken in its primary sense just as in the case of space etc., for the very same term *jāyate*, signifying origin, that is heard of earlier in connection with the *prāṇas* (organs) is applied later to space etc. as well. It was proved that the origin of space etc. is spoken of in the primary sense

[3] "From Him originate (*jāyate*) *Prāṇa* as well as the mind, all the senses, space, air, fire, water, and earth that supports everything" (Mu. II. i. 3), where the origin of *Prāṇa* is spoken of in the primary sense earlier than the origin of space etc. in the primary sense.

in the text, "From Him originates *Prāṇa*" etc. (Mu. II. i. 3). Because of the use of the same word "origin" (in connection with space, etc.) the origin spoken of in the case of the *prāṇas* also should be understood in the primary sense. For a single term, used only once in the same context in the same sentence and connected with many things, cannot be understood to have a primary sense in some places and a secondary sense at others; for that would involve a distortion. So also in the text, "He created *Prāṇa*, and faith from *Prāṇa*" (Pr. VI. 4), the term "creation" heard of in connection with *prāṇa*, becomes connected with faith and the rest that too have origin. This logic applies equally at places where a term denoting origin is met with in the latter parts of a sentence, but has to be connected with earlier words, as for instance, the term "emanate (*vyuccaranti*)" used at the end of the passage, "all the beings emanate"[4] (Bṛ. II. i. 20) is connected with the *prāṇas* and the rest occurring in the earlier part of the sentence.

तत्पूर्वकत्वाद्वाचः ॥४॥

तत्-पूर्वकत्वात् On account of their precedence वाचः over speech (etc.).

4. (Prāṇas must have originated from Brahman) since speech is preceded by them.

Although the origin of the *prāṇas* is not mentioned in the context, "That created fire" etc. (Ch. VI. ii. 3), the origin of the three elements—fire, water, and earth—alone being heard of, still from the mention of the fact that (the organ of) speech, the vital force (*Prāṇa*), and the mind emanate from fire, water, and earth (respectively), which have Brahman as their material cause, it follows that all the organs must have originated from Brahman, for the latter too are on a par with the former, (all being equally *prāṇas*—organs). To explain this: In this very context (of the Chāndogya), speech, the vital force, and the mind

[4] "All the organs, all worlds, all gods, and all beings emanate from this self."

are mentioned as proceeding (respectively) out of fire, water, and earth in the text, "For the mind is formed out of food (earth), O amiable one, the vital force is formed out of water, and speech is formed out of fire" (Ch. VI. v. 4). Now if their birth from earth etc. be spoken of in the primary sense in that text, it goes without saying that they must have originated from Brahman. Even though a secondary sense be assumed, still from the fact that their origin is mentioned in the course of (describing) the process of the manifestation of names and forms by Brahman, and from the fact that the start is made with the text, "That by knowing which the unheard becomes heard" (Ch. VI. i. 3) and the conclusion is made with the text, "All this has that (Brahman) as its self" (Ch. VI. viii. 7), and from the fact that this is a well-known fact in the other Upaniṣads, it becomes evident that when the mind etc. are spoken of as having originated from food etc., the motive is to elaborate the fact that they are produced from Brahman Itself. From this also it follows that the *prāṇas* originated from Brahman.

Topic 2: Number of Pranas

The Vedic textual conflict about the origin of the *prāṇas* has been resolved. Now is being resolved the conflict about number. While on this topic of *prāṇas*, the (chief) *Prāṇa* (vital force) will be dealt with (by the aphorist) later; now is being determined the number of the other *prāṇas* (organs).

The *doubt* (about the number) arises here owing to a conflict among the Vedic texts. At one place the *prāṇas* are declared to be seven, as in, "From Him emerge the seven *prāṇas*" (Mu. II. i. 8). At another place again eight *prāṇas* characterized as *grahas* (i.e. perceivers or sense-organs), are declared, as in, "There are eight *grahas* and eight *atigrahas* (i.e. super-*grahas*, i.e. sense-objects determining the nature of the perceptions)"—(Bṛ. III. ii. 1). At some place the number is nine: "The *prāṇas* in the head are seven indeed, and two are below" (Tai. S. V. i. 7.1). In some place the number is ten: "Nine indeed are the organs in a man, and the tenth is the navel" (Tai. S. V. iii. 2.3). In another place it is eleven: "The ten organs in the human body with the mind as the eleventh" (Bṛ. III. ix. 4). In some place it is twelve, for instance in the text (beginning with): "As the skin is the one goal of all kinds of touch" etc. (Bṛ. II. iv. 11); somewhere it is thirteen, as in the text (beginning with): "The organ of sight and the object of vision" etc. (Pr. IV. 8). Thus are the Vedic texts at variance as regards the number of the *prāṇas*. What then is the conclusion to be arrived at?

सप्त गतेर्विशेषितत्वाच्च ॥५॥

सप्त seven (in number) गतेः because of being so understood च and विशेषितत्वात् because of being specified.

5. The prāṇas are seven in number because of being so known and because of such a specification.

Opponent: The *prāṇas* are surely seven in number.

Why?

"Because of being so known", because the organs are known to be so many from such Vedic texts as, "From Him emerge the seven *prāṇas*" (Mu. II. i. 8). Moreover, they are specified as such in, "The *prāṇas* in the head are seven indeed" (Tai. S. V. i. 7.1).

Objection: We come across a repetition of the word "seven" in the text: "The *prāṇas* have been deposited (in the cavity of the heart) by seven and seven" (Mu. II. i. 8). And that repetition leads us to understand that the *prāṇas* are more than seven.

Opponent: That is no defect; for the repetition is made from the point of view of the different persons, meaning thereby that the *prāṇas* are seven in each person, but not that each group of seven *prāṇas* differs from other groups of seven *prāṇas* intrinsically.

Objection: Have not the numbers eight, etc. also been cited in regard to the *prāṇas*? So how can they be seven only?

Opponent: True, they have been cited; but since there is a conflict, only one of the numbers has to be accepted. But as it is reasonable to assume the smallest number, (according to the law of parsimony), we stick to the number seven. The other figures that are met with in the texts, are used from the point of view of the difference of functions.

Vedāntin : To this the reply is being given:

हस्तादयस्तु स्थितेऽतो नैवम् ॥६॥

तु But हस्त-आदयः hands etc. (are there); स्थिते it being established (thus) अतः therefore न एवम् not so.

6. But the hands etc. are there; since (an excess is) established thus, therefore it is not so.

But hands and other *prāṇas* are mentioned in the Upaniṣads in addition to the seven *prāṇas* in such texts as, "The hands indeed are the *grahas*; they are controlled by the *atigraha*, work, for one does work with the hands" (Bṛ. III. ii. 8). "It being established" that there is an excess over seven, it is even possible to justify the number seven by considering it to be included in the greater number. When there is a dispute about a smaller and a greater number, the greater number should be accepted, for the smaller one can be accommodated within the greater; but not so can the greater be accommodated within the smaller. Hence it is not to be thought that the *prāṇas* must be seven in number in keeping with the logic of preferring the less (in conformity with the law of parsimony). Rather those *prāṇas* should be eleven only, in accordance with the (greater) number occurring later. In support of this, the text was quoted: "The ten organs in the human body with the *ātmā*, as the eleventh" (Bṛ. III. ix. 4). By the word *ātmā*, we are to understand the internal organ (mind), for the context is of the organs (and not of the Self which is the usual meaning of *ātmā*).

Opponent : Were not numbers greater than eleven, viz twelve and thirteen cited by us?

Vedāntin : Truly they were cited; but there are no such objects (or functions) over and above eleven, for the sake of which one would have to posit more organs. The five sense-objects are sound, touch, colour, taste, and smell; and there are five sense-organs (ear, skin, eye, tongue, and nose) for their perception. The five activities are speaking, grasping, walking, ejecting, and enjoying, for which are the five motor-organs. And the mind which has to deal with all the objects and which operates over all the three periods of time is but one having various functions. According to the difference of these functions, that same internal organ is sometimes referred to by various names, viz mind, intellect, mind-stuff (memory), and egoism, as though these are quite different. Thus it is that after enumerating the different functions starting with desire, the Upaniṣad says: "(Desire, resolve, doubt, faith, want of faith, steadiness, unsteadiness, shame, intelligence, and fear)—all these are but the mind" (Bṛ. I. v. 3). Moreover, one who would consider the seven organs (two eyes, two ears, two nostrils, and tongue) in the head to be the only organs, would really accept four organs (of seeing, hearing, smelling, and talking); for though they are really four, they become manifested in different places and are then counted as seven, viz two ears, two eyes, two nostrils, and one tongue. It cannot be asserted that the other organs are but the different functions of these four, for the functions of the (motor-organs like) hands etc. belong altogether to a different class. Similarly in the text, "Nine indeed are the *prāṇas* in a man, the tenth is the navel" (Tai. S. VII. v. 1.2), the *prāṇas* are numbered as ten from the point of view of the orifices in the body, but not from the point of view of the difference in the nature of the organs, which fact becomes clear from the statement, "The navel is the tenth." For no such organ as the navel is recognized anywhere. But for the chief vital force, the navel, too, is a special place of residence, and hence it is said that the navel is the tenth. Some organs are counted somewhere for the sake of meditation (Tai. S. V. i. 7.1), whereas elsewhere they are counted by way of illustrating (some point in view) (as in Bṛ. III. ii. 1). Thus since the counting of the organs follows diverse patterns, one has to consider what point of view is involved in a particular statement. The final conclusion that stands established, however, is that the mention of the *prāṇas* as eleven is authoritative, since that conforms to the objects (or functions) of the organs.

Here is an alternative way of explaining the two aphorisms: *Opponent*: The *prāṇas* (organs) must be seven in number, since the Upaniṣad mentions the departure of seven only (at the time of death) in the text, "When it (the soul) departs, the vital force follows; when the vital force departs all the (sense-) organs follow" (Bṛ. IV. iv. 2).

Objection: Is not the word "all" also mentioned there? Why is it asserted that the seven organs alone depart?

Opponent: The answer is given in, "because there is such a specification". The relevant seven organs alone, counting from the eyes to the skin, are "specified", that is to say, dealt with here one by one by making the start with, "[When this (soul) becomes weak and senseless, as it were, the organs come to it] ...When the presiding deity of the eye turns back from all sides, the man fails to notice colour. The eye becomes united (with the subtle body); then people say, 'He does not see' " (Bṛ. IV. iv. 1-2). Besides, the word "all" refers to all that is relevant (to the context). Thus when it is said, "All the Brāhmaṇas have to be fed", the invited Brāhmaṇas, who form the subject of the speech, are alone meant by the word "all" and not the others (who are uninvited). Similarly in the present context, the seven *prāṇas* which are under discussion (viz the organs of vision, smell, speech, enjoyment, hearing, thinking, touch) are referred to by the word "all", but not the others.

Objection: Is not the intellect also counted (in Bṛ. IV. iv. 2) as the eighth? So how can it be said that the seven alone are enumerated?

Opponent: That is no defect; for although the mind and the intellect differ in their functions (of thinking and knowing), they have no substantial difference; and hence the number seven is justifiable. Therefore the *prāṇas* are seven only.

Vedāntin: This being the position, we say: "But there are in evidence other organs like the hands etc. over and above the seven", as mentioned in such texts as, "The two hands are the *graha*" etc. (Bṛ. III. ii. 8). This state of being a *graha* conveys the sense of bondage, implying that the embodied soul becomes bound down by this bondage called the *graha* (lit. one that grasps). That embodied soul is not bound down to a single body, for bondage exists equally in other bodies as well. So by implication this comes to mean that this bondage, called *graha*, moves over to other bodies as well. And in support of this is the Smṛti text: "He (the soul) becomes associated with the assemblage of eight,[5] counting from *Prāṇa*, which (eight) become its indicatory marks. One becomes bound when one is under their bondage, and free when liberated from them." This text shows that till liberation, the soul does not become dissociated from this bondage, called *graha*. And in the Praśna Upaniṣad of the Atharva Veda, where the organs and their objects are enumerated in the passage opening with, "the organ of sight, and the object of vision" (IV. 8), the organs (of action) like hands etc. are also enumerated along with their objects in a similar way in, "the hands and the objects grasped, sex and enjoyment, the organ of excretion and the excreta, the feet and the space trodden" (ibid.). Similarly, the text, "These are the ten organs in the human body, with the mind as the eleventh. When they depart from this mortal body, they make (one's relations) weep" (Bṛ. III. ix. 4), shows that the eleven organs leave the body (after death). And the word "all", being connected with the word *prāṇas*, indicates all the *prāṇas*, and hence it cannot be confined to the seven alone on the strength of the immediate topic; for a direct Vedic text is of higher authority than a topic. Even in the example, "All the Brāhmaṇas are to be fed", we should logically understand all the Brāhmaṇas on the earth, for that is the meaning of the word "all". But since the feeding of all is not possible, we understand by a figure of speech that the "all" implies all the invited Brāhmaṇas. But in the case under discussion there is no valid ground for restricting the meaning of "all". Therefore all the *prāṇas* are to be understood here by the word "all", though the seven are presented by way of illustration. Thus this is beyond criticism. Hence, the conclusion arrived at is that the *prāṇas* are eleven in number as gathered from the Vedic texts and in accordance with their function.

[5] (i) The five vital forces, (ii) the five subtle elements, (iii) the five organs of actions, (iv) the five organs of perception, (v) the mind in its four aspects, (vi) ignorance, (vii) desire, and (viii) action.

Topic 3: Atomic Pranas

अणवश्च ॥७॥

7. *And the organs are atomic (i.e. subtle and limited in size).*

Now is being added another characteristic of the organs themselves. These organs, that are being considered, are also to be known as atomic. The atomicity of the organs consists in their being fine (beyond sight and touch) and limited (of a medium size); but they are not like the ultimate atoms, for that would make their activities over the entire body impossible. These organs are subtle; for if they were gross, they would have been perceived by people near a dying man, when they come out of the body like a snake out of its hole. And these organs are limited in size; for if they be all-pervasive, it will set at naught the Vedic texts speaking of their departure from and coming back (to the body); and in that case, it will not be established that "the soul comes to have such appellations because of the dominance of the modes of the intellect"[6] (B. S. II. iii. 29).

Opponent: Even though the organs be all-pervasive, they can function only in the body.

Vedāntin: Not so, for it is reasonable to hold that every function is a *karaṇa* (i.e. an organ for the soul); for according to us, whatever (in the body) performs a function is itself a *karaṇa*, call it a function or something else (a function or a functionary).[7] That being the case, the contention would centre round a mere term. Hence it would be useless to fancy that the organs are all-pervasive. Thus we assert that these organs are subtle and limited in size.

Topic 4: Chief Prana: Its Creation

श्रेष्ठश्च ॥८॥

8. *So also the foremost (Prāṇa is a product of Brahman).*

[6] If the organs be all-pervasive, then it cannot be proved that the soul comes to be considered as atomic owing to its association with the organs.

[7] The organs are the *karaṇas*, which term is defined as a cause serving best to produce the effect. For instance the eye is a *karaṇa* of vision, and hands of grasping.

The conclusion (that the other *prāṇas* are the products of Brahman) is being extended to the chief *Prāṇa* to imply that it too is a product of Brahman like the other *prāṇas*. And this is thus: It has been said in a general way that all the *prāṇas* are the products of Brahman, for in the Upaniṣadic text, "From Him originates the vital force (*Prāṇa*) as well as the mind and all the senses" (Mu. II. i. 3), we hear of the origin of *Prāṇa* separately from the origin of the mind associated with the organs; and we also have this from such texts as, "He created *Prāṇa*" (Pr. VI. 4).

Opponent: What again is the need for this extended application?

Vedāntin: It is meant for removing another doubt. For in the *Nāsadīya Sūkta* (hymn starting with "*nāsad āsīt*") which has Brahman as its subject-matter, there is a descriptive verse (of dissolution): "Then there was neither death, nor even nectar; there was neither (moon) the symbol of night, nor (sun) the symbol of day. Only the one Brahman breathed (or vibrated, i.e. existed) together with the *Māyā* held in Itself, but without any air. Apart from it, nothing existed either as different or higher". (Ṛ V. VIII. vii. 17). Since in the word "*ānīt* (lit. vibrated or breathed)", the activity of *prāṇa* is mentioned, (it may be argued that) the text indicates as though *Prāṇa* existed before creation. From this somebody may arrive at the conclusion that *Prāṇa* is birthless. That misconception is being removed with the help of the extended application (of the previous conclusion). Even the word *ānīt* does not indicate the existence of *Prāṇa* before creation, for it is modified by the word *avātam* (without air). Moreover, in the text, "He is without *Prāṇa* and without mind; He is pure" (Mu. II. i. 2), it is shown that the ultimate material cause is free from all such attributes as the *Prāṇa*. Accordingly, the word *ānīt* (in the sense of *āsīt*) is here used only to show the existence of the cause (Brahman).[8]

The word *śreṣṭha* (foremost) denotes the chief vital force,

[8] According to the opponent, *ānīt* means "breathed or vibrated"; but the Vedantin interprets it as "*āsīt*—existed".

for this is pointed out by the Upaniṣadic text, "*Prāṇa* is indeed the first born and the foremost" (Ch. V. i. 1). *Prāṇa* is the eldest because it starts functioning from the very act of depositing the seed (in the womb). Were *Prāṇa* inactive at the time, the seed deposited in the uterus would either suppurate or fail to lead to conception. But none of the other organs—ear and the rest—is the eldest; since it can function only after its aperture, such as the ear-hole, is developed. And *Prāṇa* is the foremost, because of its superior qualities; for the Upaniṣad declares: "We cannot live without you" (said the other organs), (Bṛ. VI. i. 13).

Topic 5 : Nature of Prana

न वायुक्रिये पृथगुपदेशात् ॥९॥

न Not वायु-क्रिये air and function पृथक्–उपदेशात् on account of being taught separately.

9. Prāṇa is neither air nor a function, because it is taught separately.

Now is being considered the nature of this chief *Prāṇa*. When on this subject, the *apparent view* is that *prāṇa* is air according to the Upaniṣad: "That which is *Prāṇa* is air, and that air is of five kinds: outgoing breath, incoming breath, that which is spread over the whole body, that which moves upward, and that which digests." Or the conclusion may be that *Prāṇa* is the combined activity of all the organs, as it is believed by another school of thought (Sāṁkhyas). For the followers of that school speak thus: "The five kinds of *vāyu* (air), counting from *Prāṇa*, are merely the combined activities of the organs."

Vedāntin: With regard to this the answer is: "*Prāṇa* is neither air nor any function (of the organs)."

Why?

"Because it is taught separately." For example, *Prāṇa* is spoken of separately from air in, "*Prāṇa* indeed is a quadrant of Brahman; it shines and scatters heat[9] with air as its light" (Ch. III.

[9] Becomes manifest and active in its own sphere.

xviii. 4). Had *Prāṇa* been the same as air, it would not have been mentioned separately from air. Similarly *Prāṇa* is spoken of separately from the activities of the organs, for after enumerating the organs of speech and the rest one by one, instruction is given about *Prāṇa* separately at various places. Since one who functions and the function itself are non-different, therefore *Prāṇa* would not have been spoken of separately if it were a mere function of the organs. Besides, we should take into consideration the instructions about *Prāṇa* separately from air and the functions as contained in such texts as: "From Him originates *Prāṇa* as well as the mind and all the organs, space, and air" (Mu. II. i. 3). Moreover, it is not a possibility that all the organs should have a single combined function, for each one has its individual function, and a collection of things cannot have any such independent activity.

Opponent: This can be possible on the analogy of moving a cage. Just as eleven birds living in the same cage can have their well-determined individual activities, and yet in their combination may shake the cage, similarly, though the eleven organs contained in the same body have their well-defined individual functions, yet in their combination they perform a function which is called *Prāṇa*.

Vedāntin: The answer is, no. In the illustration, it is quite possible for the birds to shake the cage in their combination, endowed as they are with some individual subsidiary activities conducive to the shaking of the cage; for this is a matter of experience. But in the case under discussion, it is not reasonable to hold that the organs, possessed of the subsidiary (individual) functions of hearing etc., should perform in their combination the function of *Prāṇa* (viz living), because there is no proof in support of this, and because the function of living is quite different in nature from those of hearing etc.[10] Moreover, the declaration of the superiority etc. of *Prāṇa*, and the taking up of positions subordinate to it by speech etc., do not fit in with a *Prāṇa* conceived of as a mere function of the organs. Therefore

[10] There is nothing to prove that the ears etc. act in a way to produce life. Also there is no proof that all of them act simultaneously.

(the chief) *Prāṇa* is different both from air and the functions (of the organs).

Opponent: How then can there be such a text as: "That which is *Prāṇa* is air" (Bṛ. III. i. 5)?

Vedāntin: The answer is: It is the selfsame air itself that, after entering the body and assuming five aspects, and existing there with some specialized features (not present in common air), is called by the word *Prāṇa*; but it is neither a different principle nor is it mere air. Hence there is no conflict between the texts showing identity and difference.

Opponent: It may well be then that just like the soul, (the chief) *Prāṇa* also becomes independent in this body by virtue of its own predominance and the acceptance of secondary positions by the organs of speech and the rest. It is in accordance with this that many kinds of glory of *Prāṇa* are mentioned by the Vedic texts, such for instance as: "When the organs go to sleep, *Prāṇa* alone keeps awake"; "*Prāṇa* alone is not overpowered by death" (Bṛ. I. v. 21); "*Prāṇa* is the place of merger" (Ch. IV. iii. 3), for it withdraws into itself the organs of speech etc.; "*Prāṇa* protects the other organs like a mother her sons" (Pr. II. 13). Hence there arises the possibility of *Prāṇa* too having independence like the soul.

Vedāntin: That position is being refuted.

चक्षुरादिवत्तु तत्सहशिष्ट्यादिभ्यः ॥१०॥

तु But (not independent) चक्षु:-आदि-वत् just like the organs of vision etc. तत्-सह-शिष्टि-आदिभ्यः on account of having been taught along with them and other reasons.

10. But Prāṇa is not independent just like the organs of vision etc., because instruction is imparted along with them and because of other reasons.

The word "but" rules out the view that (the chief) *Prāṇa* is independent like the soul. As the eye etc. are not independent, but are subservient to the soul for making possible its agentship and experience, even as the king's subjects are to the king, so also the chief *Prāṇa* is subservient to the soul, managing everything for it like the minister of a king; but it is not independent.

Opponent: Why?

Vedāntin: "Because instruction is imparted (in the scriptures) along with them, and because of other reasons." For in such places as the story of *Prāṇa*, it is spoken of along with them, i.e. the organs of vision etc. And it is reasonable to instruct about things of the same nature together, as in the case of the hymns *Bṛhat*, *Rathantara*, etc. (which are sung together in a sacrifice). By the term "other reasons" are shown such additional grounds for eliminating *Prāṇa's* independence, as its being a composite thing, unconscious, and so on.

Opponent: It may be said that if *Prāṇa* be assumed to be an organ of the soul just like the organs of vision etc., then it should have its own distinct object like (the eye etc. having) colour etc. For the eye etc. become the organs of the soul, owing to such individual functions as the cognition of colour and so on. Moreover, the functions are counted to be eleven only, viz perception of colour and so on, in conformity with which the organs are also enumerated as eleven; but no such twelfth group of functions is met with for accommodating which this twelfth organ has to be assumed.

Vedāntin: Hence comes the answer:

अकरणत्वाच्च न दोषस्तथा हि दर्शयति ॥११॥

च And अकरणत्वात् since it is not a sense-organ, न दोषः no fault (arises); हि for तथा so दर्शयति (the Upaniṣad) shows.

11. No fault accrues, because Prāṇa is not a sense-organ. For thus it is shown in the Upaniṣads.

The defect of a fresh object being needed does not arise, for *Prāṇa* is not an organ, inasmuch as *Prāṇa*, unlike the eye etc., is not recognized to be a sense-organ from the point of view of its determining (through cognition) some object of perception. But this is not, however, tantamount to its having no function.

How?

For the (Chāndogya) Upaniṣad shows in such contexts as the story of *Prāṇa* etc. that the (chief) *Prāṇa* has a distinct function, which is not possible for the other *prāṇas* (organs). The start is made with, "Once upon a time the organs (of perception and action) began to dispute about their individual supremacy"; then the statement (of Prajāpati) is made, "That one among you is the greatest, on whose departure, the body seems to become the most impure" (Ch. V. i. 6-7), and then it is shown that after the departure of the organ of speech etc. individually, life continues as before, though without the function of the particular organ. Then the Upaniṣad shows that when the (chief) *Prāṇa* attempts to depart, the organs, of speech etc. become weakened, and there arises the possibility of the death of the body. While showing all this, the Upaniṣad demonstrates that the continuance of the body and organs is dependent on *Prāṇa*. This same fact is stated in the Upaniṣadic text, "To them the (chief) *Prāṇa* said, 'Do not be deluded; it is I who hold this body together by dividing myself in five ways and providing support for it.'" (ibid.). And in the text, "(The radiant infinite being) . . . preserves this unclean nest (of a body) with the help of *Prāṇa* (vital force), (and roams out of the nest)", the Bṛhadāraṇyaka Upaniṣad (IV. iii. 12) shows that when the organs sleep, the preservation of the body is effected by *Prāṇa*. It also shows that the nourishment of the body and organs is accomplished through *Prāṇa*, in such texts as, "From whatever member the vital force departs, right there it withers" (Bṛ. I. iii. 19), "Whatever the individual eats or drinks through *Prāṇa*, thereby he nourishes the other organs" (echo of Bṛ. I. iii. 18). The departure of the soul from the body and its continuance there are shown to be owing to *Prāṇa* in the texts, "(He deliberated), 'As a result of whose departure shall I rise up? And as a result of whose continuance shall I remain established?' He created *Prāṇa*" (Pr. VI. 3-4).

पञ्चवृत्तिर्मनोवद्व्यपदिश्यते ॥१२॥

व्यपदिश्यते It is taught (that *Prāṇa* is) पञ्चवृत्तिः possessed of five modes मनोवत् like the mind.

12. It is taught that Prāṇa has five states like the mind.

Prāṇa has its own distinct functions for this further reason that *Prāṇa* is spoken of in the Upaniṣads as possessed of five modes (or states of existence): "*Prāṇa*, *apāna*, *vyāna*, *udāna*, and *samāna*" (Bṛ. I. v. 3). And this distinction of states is derived from the different kinds of activity. *Prāṇa* is that which moves forward and performs the function of exhaling etc. *Apāna* is that which goes backward and performs the function of inhaling etc. *Vyāna* exists in between these two and performs works requiring strength. *Udāna* moves upward and is the cause of such acts as departure from the body. *Samāna* is that which carries the essence of food equally (*samāna*) to all the limbs. Thus "*Prāṇa* has five states (modes) like the mind". Just as the mind has five modes, so has *Prāṇa*. The five modes of the mind that are caused by the (five) organs, ear etc., in relation to the (five) objects, sound etc., are well known. But desire, resolve, etc., enumerated in the Upaniṣad (Bṛ. I. v. 3), are not to be accepted (here), for they exceed the number five.

Opponent: Even from this viewpoint there are other mental states comprehending the past, future, etc., which are independent of the ear etc., and so here is an excess over the number five just the same.

Vedāntin: In that case, in accordance with the dictum, "Unless an opponent's view is forbidden, it can be accepted as one's own", the five mental states well-known in the books on Yoga, can be accepted, which are, "Right knowledge, error, false knowledge, sleep, memory" (Patañjali, I. i. 6). Or it may be understood in this way, that, *Prāṇa* is compared with the mind in point of the plurality of the states only (but not their number). And the aphorism is to be construed to mean that since *Prāṇa* has five states, it is also an instrument of the soul just like the mind.

Topic 6: Prana is Atomic

अणुश्च ॥१३॥

13. And the chief Prāṇa is atomic (i.e. subtle and limited in size).

And like the other *prāṇas* (organs) the chief *Prāṇa* is also subtle (invisible) and limited in size. The atomicity is to be understood, in this connection as well, to mean subtleness and limitation in size and not any similarity to the ultimate atoms, for through its five states it pervades the whole body. *Prāṇa* is subtle since people near by do not see it at the time of its leaving the body; and it is limited in size in accordance with the Upaniṣadic texts speaking of its departure from and coming back to the body.

Opponent: Is not the all-pervasiveness also of *Prāṇa* mentioned by the scriptures in such texts as the following: "It is equal to a white ant, equal to a mosquito, equal to an elephant, equal to these three worlds, equal to this universe" (Bṛ. I. iii. 22)?

Vedāntin: The reply to this is: This all-pervasiveness is declared not from the point of view of any individual body, but from that of the universal and individual aspects of the same divine *Prāṇa* residing in Hiraṇyagarbha. Moreover, the statement, "equal to the white ant" etc., which speaks of equality (with different creatures), only points out the fact that *Prāṇa*, as it exists in such individual creatures, is limited in dimension. Hence there is no defect.

Topic 7: Presiding Deities

ज्योतिराद्यधिष्ठानं तु तदामननात् ॥१४॥

तु But ज्योतिः-आदि-अधिष्ठानम् there is (the fact of) presiding over by Fire and others, तत्-आमननात् for so it is taught in the scriptures.

14. But there is the (fact of) presiding over by (the deities) Fire and others, for so it is taught in the scriptures.

Now it is being considered whether the *prāṇas* under discussion are capable of engaging in their respective works by virtue of their own powers, or they do so under the guidance of deities.

Opponent: As to that, the conclusion drawn is that the

prāṇas engage in their respective works by virtue of the power each is equipped with for performing those works. Besides, on the assumption that the *prāṇas* act under the guidance of deities, those presiding deities themselves will become the experiencers, so that the experiencership of the embodied soul will be stultified. Hence these organs engage in work by virtue of their own power.

Vedāntin: This being the position, the aphorism is enunciated: "But there is the presiding over by Fire and others" etc. The word "but" refutes the opposite view; and the assertion is made that the organs of speech and the rest engage in their respective works when they are presided over by light etc., that is to say, by the deities identifying themselves with light (i.e. fire) etc. The reason is advanced in, "for so it is taught in the scriptures". For it is stated thus, "Fire entered into the mouth, taking the form of the organ of speech" (Ai. I. ii. 4) etc. The assumption of the form of speech by Fire and his entry into the mouth as a deity, are stated by taking it for granted that Fire presides (over speech). If this relation (of presiding) as a deity be denied, fire is not noticed to have any special relation either with the mouth or speech. In a similar way are to be interpreted the sentences starting with, "Air entered into the nostrils in the form of the organ of smell" etc. (ibid.). So also elsewhere, this very fact is confirmed by speaking of the organs of speech etc. as being illumined by Fire etc., as in, "Speech indeed, is a fourth quadrant of Brahman (eye, ear, and mind being the other three). It shines and emits heat (i.e. becomes manifest and active) through the light that is fire" (Ch. III. xviii. 3), and similar texts. This very fact is indicated by such texts as, "It (the vital force) carried the organ of speech, the foremost one, first. When the organ of speech got rid of death, it became Fire" etc. (Bṛ. I. iii. 12), where occur statements about the organs of speech etc. becoming Fire etc. And wherever an enumeration of speech etc. and Fire etc., is undertaken by dividing them into the two classes of the physical and the divine, it is made on this pattern (of some being presided over and others being their deities). In the Smṛti also, as in the following verse and others, it is shown in detail how speech etc. are presided over by Fire etc.; "The Brāhmaṇas who have realized truth, say that the organ of speech exists on the bodily plane, the objects of speech on the natural plane, and Fire on the divine plane". As for the statement that the organs can engage in their works by virtue of the powers they themselves possess, that is unreasonable; for carts etc. though capable of performing their own function, are seen to act when impelled by bullocks etc. Moreover, though activity may be possible either way—(either spontaneously or under impulsion)—still on the authority of the scriptures it is affirmed that the organs are presided over by their deities.

And the objection is being demolished that those deities themselves will become the experiencers, and not so the embodied soul:

प्राणवता शब्दात् ॥१५॥

(Connected) प्राणवता with the possessor of the organs शब्दात् as is known from the Vedic texts.

15. (The organs are) connected with the possessor of the organs, as is known from the Vedic texts.

Though there are the deities presiding over the organs, still it is understood from the Vedic texts that these organs are related with the embodied soul itself which is the master of the assemblage of body and organs, and which is the possessor of the vital force. Thus there is the text, "Then (after the entry of the vital force in the body), the organ of sight enters into the space that is within the black pupil, there exists the soul (identifying itself with the eye); and the eye is meant for the sake of seeing by the soul. Again that which knows, 'I smell this', is the soul, and the sense of smell is for the sake of smelling by it" (Ch. VIII. xii. 4). These and other texts of the same class speak of the relation of the organs with the embodied soul itself. Moreover, the deities presiding severally over the organs are many in number; and hence they cannot be considered to be the experiencers in this body; for from the possibility of co-ordinated recognition etc.[11] it is realized that the embodied soul which experiences in this body is but one.

तस्य च नित्यत्वात् ॥१६॥

च And नित्यत्वात् on account of the constancy तस्य of that one (i.e. the soul).

16. And on account of that soul's constant relation (with the body).

And the embodied soul, as the experiencer,[12] has a constant relation with the body; for it has the possibility of being affected by virtue and vice and the experiences of happiness and sorrow, but not so the deities. For they are seated in their exalted divine spheres, and cannot therefore reasonably become the experiencers in this ignoble body. To this effect occurs the text, "(Howsoever these beings may grieve, that grief of theirs remains connected with them). But only merit goes to Him (Hiraṇyagarbha). No demerit ever goes to the gods" (Bṛ. I. v. 20). Besides, the connection of the organs is ever with the embodied soul, for they are seen to accompany it at the times of death etc., as is stated in such Vedic texts: "When it (the soul) departs, the (chief) *Prāṇa* (vital force) follows; when the vital force departs, all the *Prāṇas* (organs) follow" (Bṛ. IV. iv. 2). Hence although the deities are there, presiding over the organs, yet the embodied soul does not cease to be the experiencer; for the deities are to be classed with the organs and not with the experiencing souls.[13]

TOPIC 8: PRANA AND PRANAS

त इन्द्रियाणि तद्व्यपदेशादन्यत्र श्रेष्ठात् ॥१७॥

अन्यत्र Apart श्रेष्ठात् from the chief (*Prāṇa*), ते they (the other *prāṇas*) are इन्द्रियाणि organs तत्-व्यपदेशात् on account of being designated thus.

[11] Unless the soul be one, there can be no such recognition of identity as, "I who saw the colour hear the music."

[12] In the body earned by the soul by its past actions.

[13] Just as a lamp helps the eye, so also Fire helps the organ of vision. Similarly in other cases. The lamp has no experience, neither has Fire, the deity of the eye.

17. As distinguished from the chief Prāṇa, the other prāṇas (eleven in number) are the organs, for they are so designated.

Doubt: The chief *Prāṇa* which is one and the other eleven *prāṇas* have been presented in order. Here, now, crops up another doubt whether the other *prāṇas* are only the various modes of the chief *Prāṇa* or they are independent realities. What is the conclusion to be arrived at then?

Opponent: The others are mere modes of the chief *Prāṇa* itself.

How is this known?

From the Vedic texts. Thus it is that by presenting the chief *Prāṇa* and the other *prāṇas* in close proximity, the Upaniṣad declares that the others are identical with the chief *Prāṇa*: "Well, let us all be of its form, saying this they all (the organs) assumed its form" (Bṛ. I. v. 21). Moreover, the word *prāṇa* is common; and hence the objects denoted by it are ascertained to be the same; for otherwise the word *prāṇa* will come to have various meanings; or else it will have the primary meaning at one place and a figurative meaning at another, all which is improper. Hence the eleven organs of speech etc. are as much the modes of the same *Prāṇa* as the five modes, *prāṇa*, *apāna*, etc. are.

Vedāntin: To this we say that speech etc. are really independent entities, different from *prāṇa*.

Why?

"Because they are designated separately."

In what does this difference of designation consist?

These organs (*prāṇas*) under discussion, which remain after leaving aside the (chief) *Prāṇa*, are called the eleven organs, for such a presentation is met with in the Vedic texts. In such texts as, "From Him originates *Prāṇa*, as well as the mind and all the organs" (Mu. II. i. 3), *Prāṇa* is mentioned separately, and separately are mentioned the organs.

Opponent: If such be the line of argument, then the mind like (the chief) *Prāṇa* should be taken out of the organs, for it is noticed to be separately mentioned in "the mind and all the organs" (ibid).

Vedāntin: Quite so; but in the Smṛti the organs are counted as eleven, and hence the mind also is accepted to be an organ like those of hearing etc. But *Prāṇa* is not recognized as an organ either in the Upaniṣads or the Smṛtis. And this difference in designation becomes logical if there is a substantial distinction. But, if they are the same in substance, then it amounts to a contradiction to hold that the very same *Prāṇa* sometimes gets the appellation of an organ and sometimes not. Accordingly, the other organs differ in substance from the chief *Prāṇa*.

Why, again, do they belong to a different category?

भेदश्रुतेः ॥१८॥

18. Because of the (mention of) difference in the Upaniṣads.

For everywhere in the Upaniṣads (the chief) *Prāṇa* is mentioned separately from the organs of speech etc. (In the Bṛhadāraṇyaka Upaniṣad) the commencement is made thus: "They (the organs) said to the organ of speech" (Bṛ. I. iii. 2); then the organs of speech etc. are presented as being struck with the evil of the *Asuras* (demons), and the topic of the organs of speech etc. is concluded; after that the chief *Prāṇa*, the shatterer of the *Asuras*, is presented separately in, "Then they said to this chief vital force" (Bṛ. I. iii. 7). So also are to be cited the other texts about difference, such as, "('Three He designed for Himself' means:) The mind, the organ of speech, and *Prāṇa* (vital force). These He designed for Himself" (Bṛ. I. v. 3). From this also it follows that the other *prāṇas* (organs) form a category different from the chief *Prāṇa*.

What further reason is there for their being different in category?

वैलक्षण्याच्च ॥१९॥

19. And (the organs are different from Prāṇa) because of the dissimilarity in characteristics.

Moreover, there is a dissimilarity in characteristics between the chief *Prāṇa* and the others. When the organs of speech etc. go to sleep, the chief *Prāṇa* alone keeps awake; and it alone is beyond the grasp of Death (i.e. the evil of attachment), whereas the others are within Death's reach. The continuance or death of the body is dependent on the continuance or departure of the vital force and not of the other organs. The organs are the causes for the perception of their objects, but not so is *Prāṇa*. There are many other differences of characteristics of this kind between (the chief) *Prāṇa* and the organs. From this also it is proved that they belong to different categories.

The opinion was advanced that the vital force itself has become the organs according to the text, "They all assumed its form" (Bṛ. I. v. 21); that is illogical, for difference becomes obvious even there when the sequence of thought in the topic as a whole is taken into consideration. Thus the start is made with the organs of speech etc. in the text, "The organ of speech took a vow, 'I will go on speaking' " (ibid.); and then it is stated that the organs of speech etc. were captured by Death in the form of fatigue in the text, "Death captured them in the form of fatigue. Therefore the organ of speech invariably gets tired" (ibid.). Last of all is mentioned the vital force separately as not overwhelmed by Death in the text, "But Death did not overtake this vital force in the body" (ibid.). Its superiority is affirmed in, "This one is the greatest among us" (ibid.). So in conformity with all this, it is to be understood that the assumption of the form of the vital force by the organs of speech etc. means that the acquisition of their power of activity is dependent on *Prāṇa*, but it does not mean an identity with it. From this fact also, it becomes established that the word *Prāṇa* is applied to the organs by a figure of speech. And just in line with this is the text, "They all assumed its form. Therefore they are called by this name of *Prāṇa*" (ibid.), which shows that the word *prāṇa*, denoting the chief *Prāṇa*, is applied to the organs by a figure of speech. Therefore the organs belong to a category different from *Prāṇa*.

Topic 9: Creation of gross objects

संज्ञामूर्तिक्लृप्तिस्तु त्रिवृत्कुर्वत उपदेशात् ॥२०॥

संज्ञा-मूर्ति-क्लृप्तिः The arrangement of designation and shape तु however (is) त्रिवृत्-कुर्वतः by Him who made the elements tripartite उपदेशात् for (so) it is taught.

20. The arrangement of designation and shape, however, is by Him who made the elements tripartite, for it is taught (in the Upaniṣads).

Doubt: In the course of speaking about Existence-Brahman, the creation of fire, water, and food (earth) is spoken of, and then it is taught, "That Deity, that is such, deliberated, 'Well, let me manifest names and forms by Myself entering into these three gods as their individual souls. Let Me make each of them tripartite'" (a mixture of the three) (Ch. VI. iii. 2). Here the doubt arises: Is this manifestation of names and forms an act of the individual soul or of God?

Opponent: While in this predicament, the conclusion to be arrived at is that this evolving of names and forms is an act of the individual soul.

Why?

Because of the qualifying phrase, "as the individual soul". Just as in common experience it is seen that a king ascribes to himself the act of estimating the enemy's strength by saying, "Let me enter into the enemy's ranks through scouts and estimate their strength", where he uses the first person in, "Let me estimate", because he is the directing agent of the act of counting by the scouts, even so the Deity attributes to Himself the act of evolving names and forms by saying in the first person, "Let Me manifest", because He is the directing agent of the (actual) act of manifestation by the individual soul. Moreover, it is seen that the individual soul is the agent in such manifestations as the coining of names like *ḍittha* (a wooden elephant), *ḍavittha* (a wooden deer) and so on, as also the shaping of articles like a pot or a plate. Therefore this manifestation is an act of the individual soul.

Vedāntin: This being the position, the aphorist says, "The arrangement of designation and shape, however" etc. By the word "however" is refuted the opponent's point of view. "The arrangement of designation and shape" means the manifestation of names and forms. And God is referred to in "by Him who made the elements tripartite";[14] for in the matter of

[14] Two-thirds of each of the three subtle elements—fire, water, and

creating the tripartites His agency is stated to be indubitable. This creation of names and this creation of forms such as fire, sun, moon, lightning, etc. (in the divine context), as also the creation of names and forms for every individual and every species like Kuśa grass, Kāśa grass, Palāśa tree etc. (in the material context), and animals, deer, men, and others (in the corporeal context), must be an act of God who created fire, water, and earth.

Why?

"For so it is taught." Thus by opening with the sentence, "That Deity, that was such, deliberated", and then using the first person in the statement, "Let Me manifest names and forms," it is the creatorship of the supreme Brahman Itself that is taught here.

Opponent: On the strength of the use of the qualifying phrase, "as this individual soul", it has been ascertained that the manifestation is an act of the individual soul.

Vedāntin: This is not so. The phrase "as this individual soul" is to be construed with "by Myself entering into" and not with "Let Me manifest", for the former is in immediate proximity. Should the construction be with the latter, the use of the first person, as referring to the Deity, in "Let Me manifest", will have to be imagined to be figurative. Moreover, an individual soul, bereft of divinity as it is, has no power of creatorship with regard to such diverse kinds of names and forms as mountains, rivers, seas, etc. Even in the case of those things, with regard to which the soul has any power, it is only under God's dispensation that it has this. And there is no such thing as an individual soul absolutely different from God, like a scout from the king, for the individual is described as "Myself", the state of individuality being contingent on the conditioning factors alone. From this it follows that even if this revelation of names and forms be an act of the individual, it is really an act of God. Moreover, the conclusion arrived at in all the Upaniṣads is that God alone is the revealer of names and forms, as is evident

earth—are mixed with one-sixth of each of the other two to form the three gross elements perceived by us. This process is technically called *trivṛtkaraṇa*.

from such texts as, "That which is called Space (Brahman) is surely the accomplisher of name and form" (Ch. VIII. xiv. 1). Therefore, the manifestation of names and forms is surely an act of God who brought about the intermixture of the three elements. And it is the intention here to declare that the revelation of names and forms was preceded by the making of each element tripartite, for in the very statement of the origin of fire, water, and earth is implied the manifestation of the name and form of each one of them. That fact of making tripartite is shown by the Upaniṣad in the case of fire, sun, moon, lightning, etc. in "That which is the red glow of (gross) fire is the colour of (the subtle element) fire; that which is the white glow of (gross) fire, is the colour of (the subtle element) water; that which is the dark (i.e. gray) glow of (gross) fire, is the colour of (the subtle element) earth" etc. (Ch. VI. iv. 1). In the case of fire, the form fire is first revealed. And when the form is manifested, an object comes to exist, and then the name fire is revealed for it. This is how it is to be understood in the cases of the sun, moon, lightning, etc. And through this illustration of fire is shown the process of making tripartite all the three kinds of products, earth, water, and fire; for the commencement and conclusion of the topic are common to all the three. To elaborate this: The opening is made from a common standpoint in the passage, "Each of these three deities becomes tripartite" (Ch. VI. iii. 4), and the conclusion is also made from a common standpoint in the passage commencing with, "That which appeared (in the gross product) as though red was the colour of (subtle) fire", and ending with, "And that which appeared as though non-descript was the combination of those alone" (Ch. VI. iv. 6-7).

Taking for granted that these three deities have their external state of tripartite existence, another state of tripartite existence for them in the bodily context was stated in, "These three deities undergo a triple conglomeration when they reach the state of men" (Ch. VI. iv. 7). This very fact is now being shown by the teacher (Vyāsa), in accordance with the Upaniṣad itself, with a view to removing some defect that may be suspected here:

मांसादि भौमं यथाशब्दमितरयोश्च ॥२१॥

मांस-आदि Flesh etc. (are) भौमं produced from earth यथा-शब्दम् as shown in the Upaniṣads; इतरयोः from the other two च as well.

21. Flesh etc. are produced from earth as it is shown in the Upaniṣads. From the other two as well (evolve other things).

According to the process shown in the scriptures, such products as flesh are generated from earth after it has become tripartite and is eaten by men. Thus there is the Upaniṣadic text, "Food when eaten becomes divided into three parts. That which is the grossest constituent of it becomes excreta; that which is the medium, becomes flesh; and that which is the subtlest becomes the mind" (Ch. VI. v. 1). The idea is that it is but the gross earth (made tripartite) that is eaten in the form of rice, barley, etc. Of that earth the grossest part goes out in the form of excreta. The medium portion builds up the flesh in the body; and the subtlest portion develops the mind. It is to be understood in accordance with the scriptures that the products of water and fire also develop similarly. Thus urine, blood, and *prāṇa* evolve out of water, while bone, marrow, and the organ of speech are the products of fire.

Here the *opponent* says that if in accordance with the text, "He made each of them tripartite" (Ch. VI. iii. 4), which speaks equally for all, it be the case that the elements and elementals are all tripartite, then from what do such special designations follow as "This is fire", "This is water", "This is earth", as also such references in the bodily context as "These flesh etc. are the products of the food (earth) eaten", "The blood etc. are the products of the water drunk", and "The bone etc. are the products of the fire (i.e. butter etc.) eaten?"

Vedāntin: With regard to this it is said,

वैशेष्यात्तु तद्वादस्तद्वादः ॥२२॥

तु But वैशेष्यात् owing to preponderance (occurs) तत्-वादः the (corresponding) designation of that, तत्-वादः (occurs) that corresponding designation.

22. *But owing to the preponderance (of any one) occurs the corresponding designation, occurs the corresponding designation.*

By the word "but" is refuted the objection raised. The abstract noun from *viśeṣa* is *vaiśeṣya*, which means preponderance. Although the process of making everything tripartite has taken place, still some elemental substance is found to preponderate in something, as for instance, in fire there is a preponderance of fire, in water there is a preponderance of water, and in earth there is a preponderance of earth. This process of triple combination is undertaken for the sake of making possible human dealings (i.e. phenomenal existence). Had the three elements formed into a single whole like the three strands of a rope twisted into one, no distinctive result could have been derived by human beings from the three elements separately. Hence though there is this triple intermixture, these particular designations of fire, water, and earth in the cases of both the elements and the elementals, follow from the preponderance of each. The repetition of the phrase "corresponding designation" indicates that the present Chapter is ended.

CHAPTER III

SĀDHANA—SPIRITUAL PRACTICE

Section I

Introduction: In the Second Chapter have been answered the objections that can be raised from the standpoints of the Smṛtis and logic against the realization of Brahman as propounded in the Upaniṣads. It has been explained why the views of others should be ignored. The conflict of Upaniṣadic passages has also been removed. It has further been stated therein that all entities, except the individual souls, which are the means for the souls' experiences, emanate from Brahman. Now in this Third Chapter will be considered these subjects. The mode of transmigration of the individual soul, conditioned as it is by these paraphernalia; its other states; the nature of Brahman; the difference or non-difference of meditations; the assemblage or non-assemblage of the attributes; the attainment of the highest human goal through complete knowledge; the difference among the injunctions for the methods of complete knowledge; and absence of any gradation in the state of liberation (attained during the birth in which the means of knowledge are adopted). Besides, some other topics will be discussed that crop up in connection with these. Of these subjects, the different courses of transmigration are shown in the first section by confining the attention to the meditation on the five fires; and this is done for generating dispassion,[1] for the Upaniṣad says at the end, "Therefore one should hate this"[2]

[1]The first section will deal with dispassion. Through a consideration of the states of dream etc. the second section will ascertain the nature of the individual and Brahman. The third will determine the meaning of the *mahāvākyas* and discuss the different kinds of meditation. And the fourth will discuss liberation.

[2] Since transmigration, following as a result of work, is an evil, the enlightened man should have a repulsion for the results of works. This is said at the end of the meditation on the five fires.

(Ch. V. x. 8). It has already been known that when the individual soul leaves the previous body and attains another, it is helped by the chief *Prāṇa*, it is accompanied by the senses and the mind, and it has ignorance, results of past actions, and the tendencies acquired in the previous birth as its main prop. This conclusion is arrived at from the passage starting with, "When the soul becomes weak and senseless, as it were, the organs come to it" (Bṛ. IV. iv. 1), and ending with, "So does the soul throw this body away, or make it senseless, and creates another, a newer and better, form (i.e. body)" (Bṛ. IV. iv. 4), which deals with the subject of transmigration. And this is true, because it becomes possible thus to experience the results of virtue and vice.

Topic 1: Departure from the body

Doubt : Now it has to be considered whether the transmigrating soul moves out from this body without being surrounded by the (mixed) subtle elements which are the seed of the next body, or it goes surrounded by them. What should be the conclusion to be arrived at?

Opponent : It goes without being surrounded.

How is this known?

For unlike the soul's taking up the particles of light (i.e. organs), it is not mentioned in the Upaniṣads that the elements are also taken up (at the time of departure). In the text, "completely withdrawing these particles of light it comes to the heart" (Bṛ. IV. iv. 1), the taking up of the organs is mentioned by the term "particles of light"; for in the complementary text are mentioned the sense-organs like that of vision (ibid.); but there is no such mention of the taking up of the particles of elements. Moreover, the particles of elements are easy to get, they being present wherever the new body is to be formed. And hence it is unnecessary to carry them over. Therefore the soul goes without being surrounded by them.

Vedāntin : This being the position, the teacher (Vyāsa) advances the aphorism:

तदन्तरप्रतिपत्तौ रंहति सम्परिष्वक्तः प्रश्ननिरूपणाभ्याम् ॥१॥

तत्-अन्तर-प्रतिपत्तौ In the matter of obtaining the next one, (the soul) रंहति moves out सम्परिष्वक्तः enveloped (by subtle elements), (as is known) प्रश्न-निरूपणाभ्याम् from the question and its solution.

1. In the matter of obtaining the next one (i.e. body), the individual soul moves out enveloped (by the subtle elements), for so it is known from the question and its solution.

It is to be understood that "in the matter of obtaining the next one, the individual soul moves out", that is to say, when acquiring a fresh body after leaving the present one, it sallies forth enveloped by the subtle parts of the mixed elements, which are the seed of the next body.

How is this known?

"From the question and its solution". Thus there occurs the question, "Do you know (O Śvetaketu), how the water (i.e. the liquid that is poured as oblation in the five fires), comes to be called man after the fifth oblation is poured?" (Ch. V. iii. 3). The solution of the question is in its answer (by Pravāhaṇa Jaivali). The five oblations, viz faith, moon, rain, food, and semen, are shown as poured into the five fires, viz heaven, rain-god, earth, man, and woman; and then the question is answered by saying, "Thus indeed the water comes to be called a man in the fifth oblation" (Ch. V. ix. 1). Therefore it is understood that the soul goes out enveloped by water.

Opponent: But another Upaniṣadic text shows that the soul does not leave the earlier body so long as it does not get hold of another like a leech: "Just as a leech supported on a straw goes to the end of it, takes hold of another support, and contracts itself, so does the soul throw this body aside, take hold of another support and contract itself" (Bṛ. IV. iv. 3).

Vedāntin: There is no contradiction even here; for the point brought out through the analogy of the leech is that to the soul, remaining still surrounded by the subtle elements, occur such thoughts about the future body as are called up by the accumulated results of past actions; and this expectancy becomes lengthened out to the next body like a leech.[3] This being the manner of acquiring a fresh body, as shown by the Upaniṣads, all other theories arising from the human intellect, such for instance as, (the Sāṁkhya theory) that when the all-pervasive senses and soul acquire a new body as a result of past actions, they start functioning there itself; or (the Buddhist theory) that the soul alone, by itself, acquires its function there, while the senses, just as much as the body, are born afresh in those different spheres of experience; or (the Vaiśesika view) that the mind alone proceeds to the new place of experience; or (the Jaina view) that the soul alone jumps from one body to another like a parrot from one tree to another—all these are to be ignored as running counter to the Vedic view.

Opponent: From the question and answer cited above, we gather that the soul goes out accompanied by water alone; for this conclusion is borne upon us by the Vedic mention of the word water. So how is it asserted in a general way that it goes out along with the subtle parts of all the (mixed) elements?

Vedāntin: Hence comes the reply:

त्र्यात्मकत्वात्तु भूयस्त्वात् ॥२॥

तु But (the soul is not enveloped by water alone) त्रि-आत्मकत्वात् it having three components; (water is mentioned), भूयस्त्वात् owing to preponderance.

2. *But the soul is not enveloped by water alone, since water has three components; water is mentioned because of its preponderance.*

By the word "but" is demolished the objection raised. Water consists of three components, according to the Upaniṣadic text about the elements becoming tripartite (Ch. VI. iii). So when water it admitted as the constituent (of the body), the other two elements must be admitted *pari passu*. Moreover, the body is a product of the three elements, since all the three, viz fire,

[3] Death pangs make one forget the present body etc. Past actions then create in the soul a dream-like expectancy of the future body—or a body made of thought. The soul mentally attaches itself to that body.

water, and earth, are seen to be involved in its making. In another way also it is constituted by three things; for it is constituted by the three humours, viz bile, phlegm, and wind. Such a body cannot be constituted by water alone by rejecting the other elements. Hence the word "water" found in the question and answer in, "water comes to be called man" (Ch. V. iii. 3, V. ix. 1), is used because of its predominance, and not to imply water alone; for in all the bodies, liquids such as secretions, blood, etc. abide in abundance.

Opponent: The earthly (solid) substance is seen to predominate in the bodies.

Vedāntin: That is no defect; for water is found to be in greater proportion than the rest of the elements (other than earth); moreover, in blood (i.e. ovum) and semen, forming the seed of the body, the liquid portion is seen to predominate. Again, past actions are the efficient cause for the production of the next body; and these activities in the form of such sacrifices as Agnihotra, depend on such liquid substances as Soma, clarified butter, milk, etc. Besides, it will be stated in a later text that this water (i.e. liquid), referred to by the word "faith", and invariably associated with rites, is poured as oblation in the (first) fire that is heaven.[4] For this reason also water is known to be preponderant. And because of this preponderance, all the subtle parts of the mixed elements, constituting the seed of the body, are referred to by the word water. Thus there is no defect.

प्राणगतेश्च ॥३॥

3. *And from the going out of the organs (it follows that the elements also move out).*

And the Upaniṣads speak of the departure of the organs at

[4] Water (i.e. liquids) is a means for the performance of the rites, and is thus associated with them. After being poured as oblation, it assumes a subtle (potential) form, moves about by virtue of its subsistence in the soul, and is called "faith" (potential result of rites). That faith, along with the impressions of past rites, first fire, is poured as oblation in the heaven, and thus it produces a lunar body.

the time of reincarnation, in such texts as, "When it (the soul) departs, the vital force follows, when the vital force departs, all the organs follow" (Bṛ. IV. iv. 2). But since the moving out of the organs is not possible unless they have something as their support, it becomes evident that to make the motion of the organs possible, water too, which is their material basis, moves out with them in association with the other elements. For the organs cannot either go or stay anywhere unless they have a material support, since this is not noticed in any living creature.

अग्न्यादिगतिश्रुतेरिति चेन्न भाक्तत्वात् ॥४॥

अग्नि-आदि-गति-श्रुतेः On account of the Upaniṣadic statement about repairing to Fire and others, इति चेत् if this be the objection, न not so, भाक्तत्वात् (that statement) being metaphorical.

4. *If it be objected (that the organs do not accompany the soul at the time of death) since the Upaniṣadic texts mention their entry into (the deities) Fire and others, then we say, not so, for that is said in a secondary sense.*

Opponent: It may well be that the organs do not go with the soul at the time of reincarnation, for they are shown in the Upaniṣads as going to Fire and others. Thus the text beginning with, "When the vocal organ of a man who dies is merged in Fire, the nose (i.e. sense of smell) in Air" (Bṛ. III. ii. 13), shows that the organs of speech etc. merge in such deities as Fire.

Vedāntin: Not so, for that occurs in a secondary sense. The Upaniṣadic mention of the merger of speech etc. in Fire etc. is figurative, for this is not seen in the case of the hair of the body and head, though the relevant text there is, "the hair of the body (merges) in the herbs, that of the head in the trees" (ibid.). For it is not possible for the hair of the body and head to fly away from the body and reach the herbs and trees. Besides, it is not possible to conceive of any going for the soul if it be denied that the organs follow it as its conditioning factors; nor can the soul have any experience in the next body in the absence of the organs. Moreover, in other texts it is clearly stated that the soul goes elsewhere along with the organs (Bṛ. IV. iv. 2). Accordingly, having the fact in view that Fire and other deities, presiding over speech and the rest and helping them in their activities, cease to favour them thus at the time of death, it is said in a figurative way that speech etc. enter into Fire etc.

प्रथमेऽश्रवणादिति चेन्न ता एव ह्युपपत्तेः ॥५॥

प्रथमे In the first instance अश्रवणात् not having been heard इति चेत् if this be the objection, न not so, ताः एव that (water) itself (is meant) हि because उपपत्तेः of reasonableness.

5. If it be objected (that water does not come to be known as man), since it is not heard of in the first instance, then not so, for on logical grounds, water itself is meant.

Opponent: Granted even that this is so, how can it be ascertained that "water comes to be known as man in the fifth oblation" (Ch. V. ix. 1), for water is not heard of in connection with the first fire (heaven)? In this context the five fires, heaven and the rest, are mentioned as the receivers of the five oblations. In the course of enumerating them, the introduction is made with, "O Gautama, the other world (heaven) is indeed a fire" (Ch. V. iv. 1), and then it is said, "In this fire that is such, the gods pour faith as an oblation" (Ch. V. iv. 2), where faith is presented as the thing to be offered, but water is mentioned there as an offering. If you want to imagine that water is the oblation offered in the four succeeding fires starting with the Rain-god, you may very well do so, for Soma and the other things adopted for being offered in those fires have a preponderance of water. But it is an unwarranted boldness to reject faith which is mentioned in the Upaniṣad and imagine water instead which is not mentioned as an offering in the case of the first fire. And faith means a kind of disposition (or attitude), for that is its usual purport. Hence it is unreasonable to say that water gets the name of man in the fifth oblation.

Vedāntin: This is nothing damaging, since that very "water is mentioned by the word faith" in connection with the first fire.

How so?

"On logical grounds". Because on such an interpretation alone, this whole topic reduces itself to an unequivocal single idea running consistently through the beginning, middle, and end of the topic. On a contrary supposition, again, this unity of idea (i.e. syntactical harmony) will be set at naught, since the question will relate to one thing and the answer to another, inasmuch as the question relates to how water becomes known as man in the fifth oblation, whereas during the course of the reply a thing called faith which is other than water is introduced as the offering in the first oblation. And the conclusion made with the words, "In this way indeed water comes to be known as man" (Ch. V. ix. 1), confirms this conclusion. Besides, the products of faith, viz Soma, rain, etc., are noticed, as they become gross, to have a preponderance of liquidity; that too is a pointer to faith itself being a liquid, for the effect conforms to the cause. Moreover, the attitude called faith, whether it be an attribute of the soul or the mind, cannot be separated from the possessor of the attribute like the hearts etc. from the animals to be offered as oblation; and thus water alone should be the meaning of faith (here). Moreover, the word faith becomes appropriate with regard to water, for such a Vedic use is met with in, "Faith indeed is water" (Tai. S. I. vi. 8-9). Besides, water becomes the seed of a fresh body by attaining a subtleness like that of faith; hence also it can be called faith, even as a man having the prowess of a lion is called leonine. Again, since water is associated with the rites performed with faith, it is but appropriate that the word faith should be applied to water on the analogy of a man shouting out from a platform being referred to by saying, "The platform is shouting". Furthermore, water can be called faith, since it is the cause of faith, as is evident from the Vedic text, "It is (holy) water that (by its very sight) generates faith in him for the performance of virtuous deeds (like bathing)."

अश्रुतत्वादिति चेन्नेष्टादिकारिणां प्रतीतेः ॥६॥

अश्रुतत्वात् On account of not being mentioned in the Upaniṣads इति चेत् if it be said so, (then) न not so, प्रतीतेः since it is perceived (to be so) इष्ट-आदि-कारिणाम् in the case of the performers of sacrifices etc.

6. If it be argued (that the soul does not depart enveloped by water) since it is not mentioned thus in the Upaniṣads, then not so, for it is perceived to be so in the case of those who perform sacrifices etc. (i.e. it can be verified by what happens to the sacrificers).

Opponent : Even if it be conceded from a consideration of the question and answer that water itself, being offered as faith etc. in succession, assumes a human form during the fifth oblation, still it is not ascertained that the individual souls go out enveloped by water, for this is not heard of in the Vedic texts. We do not find any word in this context to denote the souls, like the word used to denote water. Hence your statement that the "soul departs from the body, enveloped by the subtle parts of the mixed elements" (B. S. III. i. 1) is illogical.

Vedāntin : This is nothing damaging.

How?

"Because it is perceived to be so in the case of those who perform sacrifices etc." For starting with the text, "Again, those who living in villages perform sacrifices, humanitarian works and charity, etc. (and meditate on the five fires) proceed along the path of smoke" (Ch. V. x. 3), it is shown that the performers of sacrifices etc. reach the moon by proceeding along smoke etc. constituting the path of the manes: "From space they reach the moon, which is king (or the shining) Soma" (Ch. V. x. 4). Those very individuals are in evidence here as well (in the context under discussion); for there is a similarity with the text, "In this fire, that is such, the gods pour faith as an oblation. From that oblation arises king (or the shining) Soma" (Ch. V. iv. 2). And those (performers of sacrifices) are seen directly to possess water in the form of curd, milk, etc., which are the means for the accomplishment of such rites as Agnihotra, Darśa-pūrṇamāsa, etc., for curd etc. are mainly liquid. When these are offered in the Āhavanīya fire, they assume the form of the subtle unseen results of rites, and come to rest on those performers of the sacrifices etc. Their (dead) bodies are offered by the priests to the last fire (for cremation) in accordance with the rules of last rites while reciting the *mantra*, "Let such-and-such a performer of rites proceed to heaven. *Svāhā*!" Then those waters, or the liquid oblations associated with the rites performed with faith, become the unseen potency of the rites performed, and envelop the beings who had performed those sacrifices etc., and carry them to the other world for the fruition of their acts. This fact is mentioned here (Ch. V. iv. 2) by the term "pours as oblation" in the text, "He pours faith as an oblation" (Ch. V. iv. 2, Bṛ. VI. ii. 9). So also by the sentences starting with, "These oblations, when they are poured, rise up" (Ś. B. VI. ii. 6), that occur at the end of the topic of Agnihotra by way of summing up the six questions and answers (with regard to Agnihotra), it is shown that the two oblations poured in the Agnihotra sacrifice (in the morning and evening) proceed to the other world for their fruition.[5] Therefore, the individual souls depart from the body enveloped by the water that is nothing but the oblations.

Opponent: How again can this be asserted that the performers of sacrifices etc. move out for experiencing the results of their own work, since it is shown in the text that after reaching the moon through the path symbolized by smoke, they turn into food: "This is the moon, the king (or the shining one), which is the food of the gods. The gods eat it" (Ch. V. x. 4). There is also another text of the same purport: "Reaching the moon, they become food. There the gods enjoy them like the

[5] Janaka asks Yājñavalkya six questions about the Agnihotra: "Do you know how the two oblations in the morning and evening—(1) rise up, (2) move, (3) bring about establishment, and (4) satisfaction, and (5) return, and how (6) the body takes form? Yājñavalkya replies, "(1) These two oblations rise up after being offered, (2) then they go to heaven through the sky, (3) they establish the Āhavanīya as heaven, (4) they satisfy heaven, (5) then they return from there and are poured in the bodies of man and woman, and then (6) they assume human form."

priests drinking the shining Soma juice (repeatedly saying as it were), 'Be filled up, be emptied' "[6] (Bṛ. VI. ii. 16). And it is not possible for those to have any enjoyment who are being eaten up by the gods as though by tigers.

Vedāntin: Hence the answer is:

भाक्तं वाऽनात्मवित्त्वात्तथा हि दर्शयति ॥७॥

वा Or rather भाक्तं it is figurative अनात्म-वित्त्वात् on account of non-realization of the Self; हि because तथा thus दर्शयति the Upaniṣad shows.

7. *Or rather the statement (that the souls become the food of gods) is made in a metaphorical sense on account of their non-realization of the Self. For the Upaniṣad shows the same.*

The phrase "or rather" is used for obviating the defect shown. That they become food is only in a metaphorical and not primary sense. For if the literal sense be implied, then such texts as, "One desiring heaven should perform a sacrifice" which enunciate the competence for the performer, will become nullified. For if the performers of sacrifices etc. do not get any enjoyment in the lunar world, why should those who are qualified for them, undertake the rites involving great effort? Moreover, the word food is seen to be used figuratively with regard to things that are not food, simply because of the similarity of producing enjoyment, as for instance in, "The subjects are the food for kings, and the cattle are the food for the subjects". So what is meant by "the eating by the gods" is the enjoyment of the happy companionship of those who have performed sacrifices etc. and are now under their subjugation, like the people in this earth enjoying the companionship of beloved wives, sons, friends, and others who hold subordinate positions. But no such thing as munching or swallowing of sweets is meant. For mastication etc. are denied in the case of the gods in the text, "The gods do not certainly eat or drink, but they become satisfied simply by witnessing this nectar" (Ch. III. vi-x). And even as

[6] They drink cup after cup of Soma, filling it and emptying it.

the followers of a king, depending on him for their subsistence, can still have individual enjoyment, so also those performers of sacrifices etc. who become subservient to the gods, can still have their individual enjoyment. Moreover, it is reasonable that the performers of sacrifices etc. should become objects of enjoyment to the gods since they are unenlightened. Thus it is that the Upaniṣad speaks of the unenlightened men becoming objects of enjoyment to the gods: "While he who worships another god thinking, 'He is one and I am another,' does not know. He is like an animal to the gods" (Bṛ. I. iv. 10). Like animals such a man serves the gods even in this world by pleasing them with sacrifices etc.; and in the other world also he serves the gods like animals by depending on them for livelihood and enjoying the fruits of work as directed by them. This is what we understand.

The other explanation of the second portion—"on account of their non-realization of the Self, for the Upaniṣad shows the same"—(of the aphorism) is this: People "not having realized the Self" are those who are engaged in ritualistic works alone, that is to say, those who do not undertake rites and meditation as a combined process. The phrase "realization of the Self" in the aphorism is used metaphorically to mean "the meditation on the five fires". This is what is gathered from the force of the context. Because of the fact that they are devoid of the meditation on the five fires, the performers of (mere) sacrifices are here presented as the food of the gods in a secondary sense, so as to eulogize the meditation on the five fires. For what is sought to be enjoined here is the meditation on the five fires, as can be gathered from a consideration of the purport of the text. And in line with this, another text shows the existence of enjoyment in the lunar world: "Having experienced his greatness in the lunar world he turns round again" (Pṛ. V. 4). Similarly there is another text, "When the joy of those manes who have won that world (of the manes) is multiplied a hundred times it makes one unit of joy in the world of the celestial minstrels (*Gandharvas*). This joy in the world of the celestial minstrels multiplied a hundred times makes one unit of joy for the gods by action, i.e. those who attain their godhood by their actions," (Bṛ. IV. iii. 33), which shows that the performers of sacrifices etc. get enjoyment while staying with the gods. Thus since the sentence about becoming food has a secondary meaning, it becomes comprehensible that the individuals performing sacrifices etc. do go out from the body. Hence it has been said quite appropriately that "the individual soul moves out enveloped (by the subtle elements)" (B. S. III. i. 1).

Topic 2: Return of the souls

कृतात्ययेऽनुशयवान् दृष्टस्मृतिभ्यां यथेतमनेवञ्च ॥८॥

कृत-अत्यये After the actions (i.e. earned merits) are exhausted, (the soul returns) अनुशयवान् in association with (the residual) *karma* (results of action). दृष्ट-स्मृतिभ्याम् as is known from the Upaniṣads and Smṛtis, यथा-इतम् along the path followed while going च as also अनेवम् differently.

8. After the actions are exhausted, the soul returns together with (the residual) karma, as is known from the Upaniṣads and Smṛtis, along the path followed (by it) while going as also differently.

The descent of those performers of sacrifices etc. who proceed along the "path of smoke" etc. to reach the lunar world and complete the enjoyment of the fruits of their work, is stated in the text, starting with, "Having resided there (*yāvat-sampātam*) till the limit of *karma* is reached, they return by the very route by which they had gone" (Ch. V. x. 5), and ending with, "The men of virtuous deeds are born among the Brāhmaṇas and others, while those of vicious deeds are born among the dogs, etc." (ibid.).

Doubt: Here the thing to be considered is this: Do they return after enjoying all the results of action without any (residual) *karma*, or do they come with (residual) *karma*? What is the conclusion to be arrived at then?

Opponent: They return without (residual) *karma*.

Why?

Since the qualifying phrase there is "*yāvat-sampātam*—up to the limit of the totality of their actions". By the word *sampāta* is meant here the total result of actions, being derived in the sense of that by which one ascends from this world to the other for the sake of experiencing the result. And by the text, "having resided up to the limit of the totality of their actions", it is shown that the total result of one's *karma* is experienced there. By another Upaniṣadic text, "And when their past work is exhausted, (they reach this space, from space air, from air rain, and from rain the earth)" (Bṛ. VI. ii. 16), this very fact is revealed.

Objection: It may be like this: We shall imagine that a man enjoys in that world only that much of the result of his actions as is to be enjoyed there.

Opponent: You cannot imagine that way; for elsewhere the mention is made of "whatever work" in "Exhausting the results of whatever work he did in this life, he returns from that world to this for (fresh) work" (Bṛ. IV. iv. 6). Thus this other text shows by referring to "whatever work", without any reservation, that all the works done in this world get exhausted in the other world. Moreover, death is the manifester of all works that had not yielded their results, (that is to say, it makes them ready to do so); for before death such works cannot yield their results, they being obstructed by those other works which had started their results in the present body. And (since there is nothing to curb the power of death) it makes all the works that had not been fruitful (in this life) ready, without exception, to yield their results (in the next life). For when a cause is common to all, it is not logical that the results should be different. It is not proper that when the proximity of a light is the same, a vessel will be illumined but not so a cloth. Therefore the souls descend without any residual *karma*.

Vedāntin: This being the position, we say, that "After the exhaustion of (good) work a soul returns along with (the residual) *karma*". When the results of those works, for enjoying which the soul had ascended to the lunar world, get exhausted through enjoyment, then the watery body that had been produced for that soul for enjoyment in the lunar world gets evaporated by the touch of the fire of sorrow enkindled at the sight of the exhaustion of enjoyment, like snow and hail melting at the touch of the sun's rays or the solidity of clarified butter being removed by the touch of the flames of (sacrificial) fire. Hence the soul returns with (the residual) *karma* itself "after its *karma* is exhausted", that is to say, when such works as sacrifices etc. get exhausted through the enjoyment of their results.

Opponent: What is the reason for that?

Vedāntin: The aphorist says, "as is known from the Upaniṣads and the Smṛtis". Thus there is a direct Vedic text revealing the descent of souls along with their (residual) *karma*: "Among them those whose conduct has been good (*ramaṇīya-caraṇāḥ*) will quickly attain some good birth, be it among the Brāhmaṇas or among the Kṣatriyas or among the Vaiśyas. Again those whose conduct has been bad (*kapūya-caraṇāḥ*) will quickly attain bad birth, be it among dogs or among swine or among Chaṇḍālas" (Ch. V. x. 7). The aphorist will state later that (residual) *karma* is indicated here by the word *caraṇa* (lit. conduct). And it is a matter of experience that enjoyments are graded as higher and lower for each creature from the very birth; now since a theory of chance is inadmissible here, this division indicates the existence of (residual) *karma*; for the scriptures tell it in a general way that virtue and vice are the causes of happiness and sorrow. Smṛti also shows that the souls descend with (residual) *karma*: "People belonging to the different castes and stages of life, who sincerely perform their duties, experience the fruits of their works after death, and then through the residual *karma* get births amidst special environment and have special caste, family, outstanding beauty, long life, knowledge, good conduct, wealth, happiness, and intelligence."

Opponent: What is this residual *karma*?

Some (*pseudo-Vedāntin*) says that the residual *karma* is that portion of the results of work, conducive to heavenly life, which is left over after enjoying heaven, like water sticking to an emptied vessel. Just as an oil-pot does not become wholly empty even when the oil is poured out, since some oil still sticks to it, similar is the case with residual *karma*.

Opponent: It is improper to say that the result of any work persists even after its enjoyment, inasmuch as the unseen potency of work cannot co-exist with its product (viz happiness and sorrow, by producing which it gets destroyed).

Pseudo-Vedāntin: This is no defect, for we do not assert that the results of work are wholly enjoyed there (in the lunar world).

Opponent: Is it not a fact that one ascends the lunar world for the full enjoyment of one's acquired merit?

Pseudo-Vedāntin: True, and yet one cannot continue there when only a little bit of one's merit remains. Just as somebody wanting to serve a king may reside in his court with all the articles necessary for the king's pleasure; but owing to his long sojourn there, he may run through most of his possessions, being ultimately left with only his umbrella, sandals, etc., and then he cannot live in the king's court any longer; similarly a soul that is left with its residual *karma* alone cannot continue in the lunar world.

Vedāntin: This view does not appear to be correct; for it is illogical to say that any portion of the result of work conducive to heaven should persist after enjoyment. It has been pointed out that the unseen potency of work cannot outlive its result.

Pseudo-Vedāntin: Did we not also say that the results of work conducive to heaven are not wholly enjoyed there?

Vedāntin: This is unsound; for people who follow the authority of the Vedas cannot lend any credence to such a fancy that the merit leading a man to heaven does not bestow on him all the acquired heavenly results even after he has reached heaven, but that a modicum of those results fructify for him even after his fall from heaven. As for the residual oil sticking to an oil-pot, that is quite logical, since it is a matter of experience. Similarly too the king's councillor is seen to be left with only a few materials. But in the case under discussion we can neither find any remnant of the merit that had been conducive to heaven, nor conceive such a thing, for that would contradict the scriptures declaring that such a merit is conducive to heaven. And this is to be known as a certainty that unlike oil sticking to a vessel, residual *karma* does not mean the survival of some remnant of the heavenly result acquired from such acts as sacrifice etc. If, however, residual *karma* means a part of that very result of the meritorious works like sacrifice etc., owing to which the souls have already enjoyed heaven, then a residue of a good type alone must be the residual *karma*, and not its opposite; but in that case the Upaniṣadic text making the division (of residual *karma*) by saying, "Among them those whose conduct here is good", "and then those whose conduct here is bad" (Ch. V. x. 7), will be contradicted. Therefore by residual *karmas* are meant those other results of actions which are calculated to produce effects in this world and which still stand over after experiencing the results that were to fructify there (in heaven); with these former the souls descend.

As for the argument that from the mention of "whatever work" etc. (Bṛ. IV. iv. 6), without any qualification, it follows that, through the enjoyment of the results, the souls in heaven exhaust all the (results of) works done on this earth, and then descend without any residual *karma*, our reply is that it is not so; for it has been established (by us) that residual *karma* persists. It is understood that they return here after exhausting through experience "whatever work" they had done here with a view to getting the results in heaven, and after those works had fructified there. The other argument was that death induces all works without exception, that had not fructified here, to become ready for yielding results, and that it is not possible to make any such division among those works as to show that some of them produce results in heaven whereas others do so on this earth. This point of view is refuted by us by the very fact of proving the existence of residual *karma*. Moreover, the reason for asserting that death induces all unfulfilled results of works to become ready to yield fruits has to be clarified (by the opponent). Should it be argued that the unfulfilled results of works remain without any function, they being hindered by the results of works that have become effective in this life, so that at the time of death, when the active results of this life cease, the dormant ones start functioning, then we reply thus: In that case the reasonable position is that if the dormant *karma* cannot function before death, it being obstructed by the active *karma*, then since on the same ground the conflicting results of diverse works cannot fructify simultaneously at the time of death, the weaker *karma* cannot reasonably become active then, it being obstructed by the stronger one. It cannot be said that though the results of actions be many and have to be enjoyed in different births, still, owing to the fact that they constitute a single class from the comprehensive view that all of them are dormant, they become simultaneously ready for producing results on the eve of a single death, and thus they bring about a single birth. For such an assertion goes against the ordination of particular results for particular works. It cannot also be argued that some one (strong) *karma* becomes activated at the time of death, while some other (weaker one) is annihilated; for that contradicts the view that causes must have their results inevitably. It is not possible for any *karma* to be eradicated except through such causes as expiation etc. Smṛti also shows that a *karma* can remain dormant for a long time when it is obstructed by some other *karma* having a contrary result; for instance there are texts of the following class: "Sometimes it so happens that for a man sunk in this world, a virtuous work remains dormant here till he becomes free from sorrow (through suffering)." If, again, all the latent *karmas* become activated at a single death and thus lead to a single birth, then since the scriptures do not proclaim any competence for acquiring fresh *karma* in heaven or hell or among lower creatures, therefore there will be no emergence of fresh merit and demerit. Hence in the absence of any cause, no other birth after that can be possible, so that the declaration in the Smṛti that each of the sins like the killing of a Brāhmaṇa causes many births, will be set at naught. And no source other than the scriptures can be fancied to impart knowledge about the nature, result, cause, etc. of merit and demerit. Moreover, death cannot possibly induce such rites as Kārīrī (meant for rainfall) to yield their own results which are directly perceptible here (and are not to be achieved elsewhere through the medium of unseen potency). Thus this imagination about death activizing all *karmas* is out of place in those cases. The illustration of the lamp also stands nullified by the very fact that the results of actions have been shown to be either strong or weak.[7] Moreover, (even if death be a revealer), the analogy of the lamp is to be understood from the point of view of its revelation or non-revelation of gross and subtle things. Just as a lamp reveals a gross thing but not a subtle one, though they be equally at hand, similarly death induces the functioning of the stronger *karma* alone but not of the weaker, though all the dormant works get an equal opportunity then for their expression. Therefore this theory about the inducement of all *karmas* to activity by death is improper, since it offends against the Vedas, Smṛtis, and logic. And the flurry about liberation becoming impossible if residual *karma* lasts is groundless, since the Upaniṣads mention that all results of actions are eradicated on the dawn of enlightenment. Hence the conclusion remains intact that the souls descend with their residual *karmas*. And when they come down, they do so along the path followed (by them) while going up, as also differently. *Yathetam* (lit. as it had been reached) means—"just as they had gone"; and *anevam* means "in the opposite manner". Because smoke and space, included in the path of the manes, are mentioned at the time of descent, and because the phrase "as it had been reached" is used, it follows that *yathetam* means "as they had gone up by". Again, from the omission of night etc. and the addition of cloud etc. it follows that the course (of return) may be different as well.

चरणादिति चेन्नोपलक्षणार्थेति कार्ष्णाजिनिः ॥९॥

चरणात् Owing to the use of the word "conduct" इति चेत् if it be objected thus, न not so उपलक्षणार्था (the passage is) used suggestively इति this is (how) कार्ष्णाजिनिः Kārṣṇājini (thinks).

9. If it be contended that (the soul gets its rebirth) owing to conduct (and not residual karma), then according to Kārṣṇājini, it is not so, that (Upaniṣadic passage) being used suggestively (for residual karma).

[7] Unlike a lamp revealing colour, death reveals nothing; but in the absence of a stronger result, a weaker result becomes predominant at the time of death.

Opponent: Now, again, we see that the Upaniṣadic text quoted by you for proving the existence of residual *karma*, viz "Among them those who have good conduct (*ramaṇīya-caraṇāḥ*) here" (Ch. V. x. 7), only shows that rebirth occurs on account of *caraṇa* (conduct), but it does not show it as occurring on account of residual *karma*. Conduct is a different thing, and different also is residual *karma*. Conduct (*caraṇa*), character (*caritra*), good behaviour (*ācāra*). good form (*śīla*)—are all synonymous terms, whereas by residual *karma* is meant that *karma* which survives those others whose fruits have been experienced. And the Upaniṣads also show how action and conduct differ, as in, "As he acts and as he behaves, so he becomes" (Bṛ. IV. iv. 5), as also, "The works that are not blameworthy are to be resorted to, but not the others. Those behaviours of ours which are commendable are to be followed by you, but not the others" (Tai. I. xi. 2). Therefore it follows that since rebirth is mentioned in the Upaniṣad as occurring from conduct, the theory, of residual *karma* is not proved.

Kārṣṇājini: This is no defect, since the teacher Kārṣṇājini thinks that this Upaniṣadic passage about conduct is used suggestively for residual *karma*.

आनर्थक्यमिति चेन्न तदपेक्षत्वात् ॥१०॥

आनर्थक्यम् (Conduct) will cease to have any usefulness इति चेत् if it be objected thus, न not so, तत्-अपेक्षत्वात् because action (*karma*) is dependent on that conduct.

10. If it be objected that (in that case) conduct will cease to have any usefulness, then it is not so, because karma is dependent on that conduct.

Opponent: It may be so. But why again should Vedic conduct be rejected as the meaning of the word *caraṇa* (conduct), and it should be made to convey the figurative meaning of residual work? The Vedic conduct itself, resulting from both injunction and prohibition, and expressing itself as virtue and vice, can have, as its effect, birth among good and bad creatures. Moreover, one has perforce to admit some result for conduct, for else conduct will become useless.

Kārṣṇājini : That is no defect.

Why?

"Because action is dependent on conduct"; for rites such as sacrifices are dependent on good conduct, since one devoid of good conduct cannot have the requisite qualification for them, as is said in Smṛti texts like, "The Vedas do not purify one who is devoid of good conduct". And even if conduct be meant for personal purification, still it is not useless. For when rites like sacrifices start yielding their results, right conduct, though centring round a person, may still produce some excellence in the results of those very rites. The well-recognized fact in the Vedas and Smṛtis is that it is action that produces everything. Hence it is the view of Kārṣṇājini that actions themselves that are implied indirectly by the word conduct, and are reduced to residual *karma*, become the cause of rebirth. For when rebirth can be deduced from actions, it is illogical to father it on conduct. When one can save oneself by running on foot, one should not move on one's knees.

सुकृतदुष्कृते एवेति तु बादरिः ॥११॥

तु But सुकृत-दुष्कृते good and evil works एव certainly इति this is how बादरिः Bādari (thinks).

11. But (the teacher) Bādari thinks that good and bad works themselves are meant (by the word caraṇa).

Vedāntin : The teacher Bādari opines that actions, good and evil, are themselves meant (directly and not figuratively) by the word *caraṇa*. *Caraṇa*, performance, action—these are synonymous words. It is seen thus that the root *car* (to act) is used with regard to all actions in general. For when a man performs a virtuous deed like sacrifice etc., ordinary people say, "This great-souled man is acting (*carati*) religiously". Conduct (*ācāra*) too is a form of religious action (or observance). As for the reference to the difference between virtuous acts and (good) conduct, it can be reconciled on the analogy of the Brāhmaṇa and the mendicant (i.e. a Brāhmaṇa who has chosen the monastic life). Hence the conclusion is that *ramaṇīya-caraṇāḥ* (men of good conduct) are those who perform the laudable acts, and *kapūya-caraṇāḥ* (men of bad conduct) are those who perform the condemned acts.

Topic 3: Fate of evil-doers

अनिष्टादिकारिणामपि च श्रुतम् ॥१२॥

अपि च Even also अनिष्ट-आदि-कारिणाम् for the performers of evil etc. श्रुतम् it is heard of.

12. It is known from the Vedic texts that (the moon is the goal) even for the performers of unholy acts etc. as well.

Doubt: It has been said that the performers of holy works (like sacrifices) etc. go to the lunar world. But now it is being considered whether those who perform unholy works etc. also go there or not.

With regard to this the *opponent* says that it is not a fact that the performers of holy acts etc. alone go to the lunar world.

Whence is it so?

Opponent: Since the lunar world is mentioned in the Upaniṣads as a goal for the performers of unholy acts as well. Thus the followers of the Kauṣītakī recension read: "All those who depart from this world, reach the moon to be sure" (Kau. I. 2). And the acquisition of a fresh body, by those who are reborn, cannot be conceived of without their having reached the moon; for the number of oblations is fixed in the statement, "In the fifth oblation" etc. (Ch. V. ix. 1). Therefore all will reach the moon.

Objection: It is not proper that the path for both the doers of holy and unholy acts etc. should be the same.

Opponent: Not so, for the others (of unholy acts, go there but) have no experience.

संयमने त्वनुभूयेतरेषामारोहावरोहौ तद्गतिदर्शनात् ॥१३॥

तु But इतरेषाम् in the case of others (descent occurs) अनुभूय after having suffered संयमने in the abode of Death. (Thus occur their) आरोह-अवरोहौ ascent and descent; तत्-गति-दर्शनात् for their course is met with in the Upaniṣads.

13. (Vedāntin) : But as for others (they have their descent) after suffering in the abode of Death; (thus occur their) ascent and descent, for their course is met with in the Upaniṣads.

The word "but" refutes the other point of view, by implying that it is not a fact that all go to the moon.

How is this known?

The ascent to the moon is meant for experiences and not for nothing; nor is it meant for the sake of mere descent. For instance, a man verily climbs a tree for gathering flowers and fruits, but neither purposelessly nor for merely dropping down from it. And it has been stated earlier that those who do not perform holy acts etc. have no experiences in the moon. Hence only the performers of holy acts ascend to the moon, not the others. As for the others, they enter into the place of Death (i.e. hell) and suffer the torments of hell in accordance with their own misdeeds, and then ascend to this world. Thus occur their ascent and descent.

How is this known?

Because "Their course is met with in the Upaniṣads". Thus a Upaniṣadic passage, under the garb of a speech of Death concerning the departed evil-doers, shows how they come under the sway of Death: "The means of the attainment of the other world does not become revealed to the non-discriminating man who blunders, being befooled by the lure of wealth. One that constantly thinks thus, 'There is only this world, and none hereafter', comes under my (Death's) sway again and again" (Ka. I. ii. 6). There are other suggestive sentences indicating that people come under the sway of Death: "Let Death, to whom men have to go, be propitiated with oblations" (Ṛ. V. X. xiv. 1).

स्मरन्ति च ॥१४॥

14. And they mention this in the Smṛtis.

Moreover, such respected teachers as Manu, Vyāsa, and others mention in the Smṛtis, in connection with such stories as that of Naciketas, that the results of evil deeds is suffered in the abode of Death under Death's command.

अपि च सप्त ॥१५॥

15. And (they are mentioned as) seven (hells in the Purāṇas).

Moreover, seven hells, counting from Raurava are described by the followers of the Purāṇas, as the fields for reaping the results of bad deeds. There the doers of unholy acts etc. are cast. How can they then reach the moon? This is the idea.

Opponent: Is it not a contradiction to assert that the sinners suffer the pains inflicted by Death, since the Smṛtis mention many others like Citragupta, who preside over those Raurava and other hells?

Vedāntin: The answer is being given in the negative:

तत्रापि च तद्व्यापारादविरोधः ॥१६॥

अपि Even तत्र there च also तत्-व्यापारात् on account of his (Death's) control अविरोधः there is no contradiction.

16. Since Death's control extends even there, no contradiction can arise.

No contradiction is involved since it is admitted that even in those seven hells, Death exercises control as the chief dignitary; for the Smṛtis mention that Citragupta and others are officers appointed by Death.

विद्याकर्मणोरिति तु प्रकृतत्वात् ॥१७॥

तु But विद्या-कर्मणोः of knowledge (meditation) and action इति this is (what is meant by the expression "of these two paths") प्रकृतत्वात् that being the topic under discussion.

17. But (by the expression "of these two paths") what is meant is "of knowledge (i.e. meditation) and action", for that is the topic under discussion.

Under the topic of the meditation on the five fires, in the course of the answer to the question, "Do you know how the other world does not get filled up?" it is stated in the Upaniṣad, "Then there are those who go by neither of these two paths (of the gods and the manes) and who become those tiny, continually transmigrating creatures under the divine command, 'Be born and die'. This is the third state. That is why that other world (heaven) does not get filled up" (Ch. V. x. 8). In this text, the expression "these two paths" stands for "the paths of knowledge (i.e. meditation) and work".

Why so?

For that is the topic under discussion. For knowledge and action are discussed here as the means for the attainment of the paths of the gods and the manes. Knowledge is mentioned in "Among these, those who know (meditate) thus" (Ch. V. x. 1), and it is declared that through that meditation is attained the path of the gods. Work is mentioned in, "sacrifices, philanthropic works, charity (*dakṣiṇā*)" (Ch. V. x. 3), and it is declared that through that is attained the path of the manes. It is in connection with these that the Upaniṣad says, "Then there are those who go by neither of these two paths." The idea conveyed is this: For those is meant this ever rotating third path consisting in becoming tiny creatures, who are neither qualified for the path of the gods through the practice of meditation nor for the path of the manes through the performance of rites etc. From this also follows that those who do not perform holy deeds etc. do not reach the moon.

Opponent: It may be that they too ascend to the moon and then descend from there to become the tiny creatures.

Vedāntin: That also is not possible, since the ascent itself is useless. Moreover, if all who depart, reach the moon, the other world would get filled up by the departing creatures; and hence the answer would run counter to the question (viz "Why does not the other world get filled up?"). The answer is to be given in a way that can show how the other world does not get filled up.

Opponent : From the admission of descent it becomes possible for the other world not to become filled up.

Vedāntin : No, since such a thing is not mentioned by the Upaniṣad. It is true that the world may not get filled up because of the fact of descent as well; but the Upaniṣad explains the fact of not being filled up by describing the third state thus: "This is the third state. That is why the other world does not get filled up" (Ch. V. x. 8). From that it follows that the non-filling is caused by the absence of ascent in their case. For otherwise the descent being the common lot of the performers of holy deeds etc. as well, the mention of the third state would be useless. The word "but" is used for uprooting the misconception generated by the text of another branch that all the souls go to the moon. This being the case, it is to be understood that the word "all" used (in "all who depart") in the other branch (i.e. Kauṣītakī, I. 2), is meant to imply "all who have the qualification (to ascend)"; the idea being that all those who depart from this world with the requisite qualification certainly reach the moon.

And the objection was raised that all should go to the moon, so that their acquisition of fresh bodies may be possible in accordance with the number of oblations fixed in the statement, "in the fifth oblation" (Ch. V. ix. 1); that is being answered:

न तृतीये तथोपलब्धः ॥१८॥

न Not (applicable) तृतीये in the case of the third state; उपलब्धः (this) being noticeable तथा thus.

18. (The specification about the number of oblations) is not applicable in the case of the third state, this being noticeable (in the Upaniṣad).

Not much importance is to be attached to the fixity of the number of the oblations as five, so far as the acquisition of a body in the third state is concerned.

Why?

"This being (the position) noticeable (in the Upaniṣad)". For it is found in the Upaniṣad that the third course is attained in accordance with the process stated and irrespective of the specification about the number of oblations: "under the divine command, 'Be born and die'. This is the third state" (Ch. V. x. 8). Besides, in the text, "The water comes to be known as man in the fifth oblation" (Ch. V. ix. 1), the number of oblations is declared as a cause for the acquisition of a human body, but not as the cause for the bodies of insects, moth, etc., for the word man (*puruṣa*) stands for humanity as a class. Moreover, the instruction is about water becoming known as man in the fifth oblation; but it is not meant to overrule its becoming so in any oblation other than the fifth; for that would lead to a duality of meaning (equivocation) for the same sentence. That being the position, those who have the possibility of ascent and descent alone will get their bodies during the fifth oblation; for others, their bodies will be created by water, in association with the other elements, irrespective of the number of oblations.

स्मर्यतेऽपि च लोके ॥१९॥

अपि Moreover, स्मर्यते the Smṛtis record, लोके in the Mahābhārata etc. च well; (and there is popular belief).

19. Moreover, there are records in the Smṛtis (of birth without parentage) as also in the Mahābhārata etc.; and there is popular belief as well.

Moreover, the Smṛtis record how in this world Droṇa, Dhṛṣṭadyumna, and others, and Sītā, Draupadī, and others were born without parentage. Of them Droṇa and others lacked the oblation in the mother's womb, while Dhṛṣṭadyumna and others lacked the oblations in both man and woman. Just as in those cases the number of oblations is ignored, so also it can be in other cases. And it is a popular belief that female cranes conceive without contact with the males.

दर्शनाच्च ॥२०॥

20. Moreover, it is seen (that creatures are born without the five oblations).

Moreover, it being noticed that among the four kinds of life—viviparous, oviparous, life springing from moisture, and plant life—the latter two classes are born without any mating. And hence the number of oblations is overlooked. This can be the case for others as well.

Opponent: Those creatures have only three sources of life; for in the passage, "oviparous, viviparous, and plant life" (Ch. VI. iii. 1), only three classes of creatures are shown. So how is it asserted that the creatures are grouped into four classes?

Vedāntin: In answer it is said:

तृतीयशब्दावरोधः संशोकजस्य ॥२१॥

तृतीय-शब्द-अवरोधः The third term is inclusive संशोक-जस्य of the one born from moisture.

21. Life springing from moisture is included in the third term (plant life).

It is to be understood that in the text "oviparous, viviparous, and plant life", life springing from moisture is included in the third term plant life, for both plant life, and life springing from moisture have the common feature of coming out by pushing their way through earth or liquids. But since germination from motionless life is distinct from germination from motile life, a difference is drawn elsewhere between the plants and creatures born out of moisture. Hence there is no contradiction.

Topic 4: Similarity with Space etc. During Descent

साभाव्यापत्तिरुपपत्तेः ॥२२॥

साभाव्य-आपत्तिः Attainment of similarity उपपत्तेः that being reasonable.

22. (The descending soul) attains similarity (with space, air, etc.); for that is reasonable.

It has been said that the performers of holy works etc., reach the moon and stay there till the residual *karma* is reached; then they descend with their residual *karma* (III. i. 8). Now is being examined the process of descent. As to that, here is an Upaniṣadic text speaking of the descent: "Then they resort to this very path again, just as they had come. They reach space, from space air; having become air, the sacrificer becomes smoke; having become smoke, he becomes vapour; having become vapour, he becomes cloud; having become cloud, he pours down (as rain)" (Ch. V. x. 5).

Doubt: Here the doubt arises as to whether the descending souls become identified in nature with space etc., or they become similar to them.

Opponent: The conclusion that can be arrived at here is that they become identified with space etc.

How can this be so?

Opponent: For such is the Upaniṣadic text; for else we shall have to interpret the text figuratively. When a doubt arises about the literal and figurative senses, the literal one is to be accepted, and not the figurative. That being so, the texts "becoming air, he becomes vapour" etc. are to be taken in the sense of attaining identity with those things. Hence the conclusion is that the soul becomes transformed into space etc. in the literal sense.

Vedāntin: This being the position, we say that they attain a state of similarity with space etc. As the liquid body, formed in the lunar world for the sake of enjoyment, starts to melt away after the exhaustion of enjoyment, it becomes fine (and light) like space. Then it comes under the influence of air. Then it comes in contact with smoke etc. This fact is stated in, "Just as he had come. He reaches space, from space air" (Ch. V. x. 5) etc.

How do you know this?

"Because that is reasonable." For it is not logical that something should be transformed into something else in the primary sense. If it were to become space itself, its descent through air etc. in succession would not be actualized. Moreover, the soul as well as space being omnipresent, it has a constant relationship with space; and hence there can be no other relationship (e.g. conjunction) of the soul with space than the assumption of a form similar to it.[8] And when the literal sense of a text is inadmissible, it is but logical to resort to a figurative sense. Hence in this context the attainment of a state of similarity with space etc. is meant figuratively here by "becoming space" etc.

Topic 5: Intervening Period of Descent

नातिचिरेण विशेषात् ॥२३॥

(The descent takes place) न not अति-चिरेण after a long time विशेषात् on the authority of a special statement.

23. (The descent of the soul from one state to another takes place) not after long intervals, (as is known) on the authority of a specific statement (in the Upaniṣad).

Doubt: While on this topic, a doubt arises with regard to the soul's becoming space etc. before becoming paddy etc., as to whether it continues in its similarity with the earlier stages for long intervals before it attains similarity with the succeeding stages, or it continues so during small intervals.

Opponent: As to that, there is no rule, since no categorical scripture is in evidence.

Vedāntin: This being the position, the aphorist says, "not after long intervals"; the souls descend to this earth with the showers of rain after staying in the states of space etc. for short intervals.

How is this known?

"On the authority of a specific statement". Thus it is that after the attainment of similarity with paddy etc., the Upaniṣad says, "It is indeed more difficult to come out of this state" (Ch. V. x. 6). In the word *durniṣprapataram*, one *ta* is to be understood

[8] No other relationship but that of similarity is possible between two all-pervasive things—space and soul. Hence the Upaniṣad speaks of two entities—soul and space. The soul cannot be both soul and space at the same time, as milk converted into curd cannot be both milk and curd at the same time. And unless the soul and space remain distinct, the soul cannot re-emerge from space as the soul to follow its further course. The same relationship of similarity holds good in the case of air etc.

as dropped as a Vedic licence (the word being actually *durniṣprapatataram*). The meaning is that it becomes more difficult to get out of this state of similarity with paddy etc. Thus the coming out (*niṣprapatana*) being shown to be difficult in this case, the idea implied is that the coming out is easier in the earlier stages. And this difference of happiness and sorrow as shown during the coming out has reference to the shortness or length of the interval of coming out; for the body is not formed during that interval, and so no experience is possible. Hence the soul's descent up till the moment of becoming similar to paddy etc. occurs in a short time indeed.

TOPIC 6: THE SOULS IN PLANTS AND THEREAFTER

अन्याधिष्ठितेषु पूर्ववदभिलापात् ॥२४॥

पूर्व-वत् As in earlier stages (the soul stays in paddy etc.) अन्य-अधिष्ठितेषु inhabited by other souls; अभिलापात् for so it is declared.

24. As in the earlier stages, so also (in the later stages) the soul merely resides in paddy etc. that are already inhabited by other souls, for so it is declared.

Doubt: While dealing with that very course of descent, the text mentions after the fall in the form of a shower, "Those descending souls are born here (on the earth) as paddy, barley, shrubs, trees, sesamum, pulses, etc." (Ch. V. x. 6). With regard to this the doubt arises, whether the souls when descending with their residual *karmas*, enjoy and suffer the happiness and sorrow natural to the plants etc., after reaching this stage and becoming themselves motionless plants etc., or they merely come into contact with plant bodies which are possessed by other souls? What is the conclusion to be drawn then?

Opponent: The descending souls, possessed of residual *karmas* are born as plants etc.; and thus they have experience of happiness and sorrow belonging to these species.

How do you know this?

Since the verb "to be born" should be accepted in the literal sense. Besides, life as plants is well recognized in the Vedas and Smṛtis as a state for the souls' experiences. Moreover, it is reasonable that acts like sacrifices etc. should have evil results, since they are connected with animal sacrifice etc. Hence like birth as dogs etc., the descending souls having residual *karma*, are born as paddy etc. in the primary sense. Just as the descending souls have "births among dogs, swine, or Caṇḍālas" (Ch. V. x. 7) in the primary sense, and in those births they have the experiences of the respective happiness and sorrow, so also have they births as paddy etc.

Vedāntin: To this, our reply is that, as in the previous stages, similarly here also, the souls, having residual *karma*, merely come into contact with paddy etc. which are already inhabited by other souls, but they do not share in their happiness and sorrow. As the attainment of the states of air, smoke, etc. by the descending souls consists in their mere contact with these, so also the attainment of the states of paddy etc., consists merely in a contact with those that are plants etc. from birth.

How is this known?

Because the Upaniṣadic declaration here is similar to the earlier.

Opponent: What is meant by the Upaniṣadic declaration being similar to the earlier?

Vedāntin: Their similarity consists in the declaration being made without any reference to (this state being attained through) a fruition of *karma*. As in the stages starting with space and ending with rainfall, no mention of fruition of *karma* is made, so also is it with regard to the births among paddy, barley, etc. Hence the descending souls have no experience here of happiness and sorrow. But where the intention is to speak of the experience of such happiness and sorrow, the fruition of *karma* also is mentioned by such statements as, "the people of good conduct, the people of bad conduct etc." (Ch. V. x. 7). Moreover, if the birth of the souls, having residual *karma*, among paddy, barley etc. be taken in the literal sense, then when the paddy etc. are harvested, fried, cooked, or eaten, the souls identifying themselves with these will be thereby ejected from them. For it is a well-known fact that a soul that inhabits any body leaves that body when it is subjected to great torment. In that case the Upaniṣad would not have mentioned that from the state of similarity with paddy etc. the descending souls attain similarity with male creatures possessed of progenitive power. Hence the souls that have residual *karma* merely come into contact with paddy etc. that are already inhabited by other souls. As a result of this, one has to reject the primary meaning of the verb "to be born", as also the state of plant life as a place for experiencing happiness and sorrow (by those souls). At the same time we do not deny that the plant life is a state for experiencing the fruits of work. Let this be a state of experience for those souls which, owing to their lack of merit, have attained the state of plant life. But the souls descending from the moon with their residual *karmas* do not have any experience in identification with plant life. This is our standpoint.

अशुद्धमिति चेन्न शब्दात् ॥२५॥

(Sacrifices etc. are) अशुद्धम् unholy इति चेत् if such be the objection, न not so, शब्दात् owing to the sanction of scriptures.

25. If it be argued that rites (involving killing of animals) are unholy, we say, no, since they are sanctioned by scriptures.

Opponent: It was argued that sacrificial actions are impure inasmuch as they are connected with animal-killing etc. and therefore their results can be inferred to be evil, so that the birth of the souls, having residual *karma*, as paddy, barley, etc., can well be in the literal sense, and it is useless to imagine a figurative meaning there.

Vedāntin: That argument is being refuted. That is not so, for knowledge of virtue and vice is derived from the scriptures. The scriptures alone are the source for knowing that such an act is virtuous, and such another is not virtuous; for merit and demerit are supersensuous realities and they are not invariable for all space, time, and environment. Any deed that is performed as virtuous in relation to certain place, time, and circumstances, becomes non-virtuous in relation to other places, times, and circumstances, so that nobody can have any knowledge about virtue and vice, unless it be from the scriptures. And from the scriptures it is ascertained that the Jyotiṣṭoma sacrifice, involving injury, favour, etc., is virtuous. So how can that be declared to be impure?

Opponent: By saying, "One should not injure any of the creatures", the scripture itself shows that injury done to any creature is unholy.

Vedāntin: True; but that is only a general rule; and here is the exception, "One should immolate an animal for Agni and Soma". Both the general rule and the exception have their well-defined scopes. Hence Vedic rites are quite pure, since they are practised by the good people and are not condemned by them. Hence birth as plants cannot be their corresponding result. Nor can birth as paddy etc. be on an equal footing with birth as dogs etc., for the latter is spoken of in connection with the doers of evil; but no specific liability (to be born as such) is met with here (as regards plant life). Hence the mere association with paddy etc. of the souls descending from the moon with their residual *karmas* is indirectly spoken of as becoming those plants.

रेतःसिग्योगोऽथ ॥२६॥

अथ Then रेतः-सिक्-योगः (occurs) connection with an inseminator.

26. Then (the soul) gets connected with an inseminator.

This is a further reason why what is meant by becoming paddy etc. is only association with them. After the statement about becoming paddy etc., the scripture states that the descending soul becomes a progenitor, as in, "For the soul becomes one with whomsoever eats food and performs the act of generation" (Ch. V. x. 6). But identity with the progenitor is not possible here in the literal sense, for one becomes a progenitor long after birth when one attains adolescence. So how can the descending soul that remains associated with the food that is eaten become identified with the progenitor unless it be in a secondary sense? In that text then it has perforce to be admitted that the mere connection with the progenitor is spoken of as becoming himself. Therefore what is meant by becoming paddy etc. is also nothing but being connected with them. Thus there is no contradiction.

योनेः शरीरम् ॥२७॥

योनेः From the womb शरीरम् (comes) a body.

27. *From the womb (comes) a new body (for the descending soul).*

Then after being connected with a progenitor the soul with its residual *karma* enters a womb and gets a body fitted for the experience of its (residual) *karma*. This is what is said in the scripture in, "Among them, those who have good conduct on this earth" (Ch. V. x. 7). etc. From this too it is known that when during the course of a soul's descent, an occasion arises for connection with paddy etc., those very bodies do not become a source of happiness and sorrow. Hence it is concluded that the mere contact with paddy etc. is spoken of as the birth of the souls descending with their residual *karmas*.

Section II

In the previous section, the topic of the meditation on the five fires was raised and the different courses of transmigration of the individual souls were discussed. Now is being elaborated the different states of those very souls.

Topic 1: Dream State

सन्ध्ये सृष्टिराह हि ॥१॥

सन्ध्ये In the intermediate stage सृष्टिः (occurs) creation, हि since (the Upaniṣad) आह says (so).

1. In the intermediate stage (of dream) occurs (real) creation; for the Upaniṣad says so.

Opening with the passage, "When he dreams" (Bṛ. IV. iii. 9) the scripture states, "There are no chariots, nor animals to be yoked to them, nor roads there, but he creates the chariots, animals, and roads" etc. (Bṛ. IV. iii. 10).

Doubt: The doubt arises with regard to this, whether the creation in dream is as real as in the waking state, or it is only illusory.

Opponent: While on this topic, it is gathered that the creation in the intermediate stage (lit. occurring at the junction) is real. By the term "Intermediate stage" is meant dream, for such a use is met with in the Vedas, as in, "The dream state which is the third is at the junction of the two (waking and deep sleep)" (Bṛ. IV. iii. 9). It occurs at the juncture of the two worlds—(the other and this)[1], or between the two states of waking and deep sleep; therefore it is called the *sandhya* (intervening stage).

[1] When the senses are withdrawn at the time of death, the dying man has no sense-perception; yet at that time he remembers this world as a sort of mental impression, and in that mind flashes a picture of the next world which is expected as a result of his actions. This is the juncture.

The creation that occurs in that intervening period must necessarily be real.

Why?

Since the Upaniṣad, which is authoritative, says thus: "but he creates the chariots, animals, and roads" (Bṛ. IV. iii. 10). etc. And from the conclusion, "For he is the agent" (Bṛ. IV. iii. 10), this becomes confirmed.

निर्मातारं चैके पुत्रादयश्च ॥२॥

च And एके some (consider the soul) निर्मातारम् as the creator; च and पुत्रादयः sons and others (are the objects desired).

2. And some (following a particular branch) consider the Self to be a creator (of things desired); and sons and others (are the objects desired).

Moreover, the followers of one branch of the Vedas mention the Self as the creator of desires (i.e. desirable things) in this very intervening stage: "Puruṣa (the all-pervading conscious entity), who keeps awake and goes on creating desires even when the senses fall asleep, is pure" (Ka. II. ii. 8). And sons etc. are the "desires" mentioned in the text, the word being derived in the sense of "things wished for or desired".

Objection: By the word *kāma* should be denoted different kinds of desire.

Opponent: No, for the subject is broached thus: "Ask for sons and grandsons who will be centenarians" (Ka. I. i. 23), and the conclusion is made with, "I make you fit for the enjoyment of all *kāmas* (delectable things)" (ibid. 24), where the word *kāma* is used in the relevant places for sons etc. who are under consideration. From the subject-matter of the chapter and the complementary portion also we understand that the supreme conscious Self is the creator. For the subject-matter of the topic is the supreme Self, as stated in the beginning, "Tell me of that thing which you see as different from virtue, different from vice" (Ka. I. ii. 14); and the complementary passage also relates to It, "He is pure, He is Brahman, and He is called the immortal. All the worlds are fixed on Him; none can transcend Him" (Ka.

II. ii. 8). It is also known that the creation by the supreme Self within the range of wakefulness is real; so equally real must be the creation in the domain of dream. In support of this occurs the Upaniṣadic text, "Others, however, say that the dream state of a man is nothing but the waking state, because he sees in dreams only those things that he sees in the waking state" (Bṛ. IV. iii. 14), which shows the applicability of the same logic to the dream and waking states. Hence the creation in the intervening state must be real indeed.

Vedāntin: To this the aphorist makes the rejoinder:

मायामात्रं तु कात्स्न्र्यानभिव्यक्तस्वरूपत्वात् ॥३॥

तु But (the dream creation is) माया-मात्रम् mere Māyā, कात्स्न्र्य-अनभिव्यक्त-स्वरूपत्वात् because of its nature of not being a complete manifestation. (A different reading—"कात्स्न्र्येन fully").

3. But the dream creation is a mere Māyā, because of its nature of not being a complete manifestation of the totality of attributes (found in the wakeful state).

The word "but" refutes the opposite view. It is not as you asserted, that the creation in the intervening state is real, for the creation in the intervening state is a mere product of Māyā, there being not the slightest touch of reality in it.

Why?

"Because of its nature of not being a complete manifestation of the totality of attributes (found in the wakeful state)". For a dream is not such by nature as to be manifest with the totality of the attributes of a real thing.

Opponent: What, again, is meant here by totality?

Vedāntin: It means the state of being endowed with the adequate space, time, and circumstances, as well as its not being sublated. For the space, time, and causality adequate for a real thing, as well as the absence of sublation, can never be possible in the case of a dream. For instance, the space needed for a chariot etc. is not possible in dream; for within the narrow limits of the body, the chariot etc. cannot get sufficient room.

Opponent: It may well be that a dreamer dreams outside the body, since he perceives things that are far removed. Moreover, the Upaniṣad also shows that dream occurs outside the body: "The radiant infinite being who is immortal and moves alone preserves the unclean nest (of a body) with the help of the vital force, and roams out of the body. Himself immortal, he goes wherever he likes" (Bṛ. IV. iii. 12). And the difference in the ideas (or perceptions) of staying in and moving out (occurring in dream) cannot be reconciled unless the soul goes out.

Vedāntin: We say, no; for it is not possible to conceive it for a sleeping man that in a moment he can reach a place hundreds of miles away and return from there. And sometimes a man relates a dream in which there was no return, as in the statement: "Then having laid down in the country of the Kurus and fallen asleep, I went in dream to the country of the Pāñcālas, and woke up there." Had he gone out of the body, he would have awakened in the country of the Pāñcālas itself, as he is supposed to have reached there; but as a matter of fact he wakes up in the Kuru country. And the body, with which the dreamer dreams that he goes to another country, is seen by people nearby to be lying just where it was. Besides the places, as the dreamer sees them in dream, do not correspond with actuality. Were he to speed away to those places to see them, he would perceive them just as he does in the waking state. Moreover, the Upaniṣad shows that dream occurs within the body. Opening with, "When it (the soul) remains in the dream state" (Bṛ. II. i. 18), the Upaniṣad says, "it moves about, as it pleases, in its own body" (ibid.). For this reason also, that the Upaniṣad and logic become contradicted, the text about "roaming out of the nest (i.e. body)" (Bṛ. IV. iii. 12) is to be explained figuratively to mean that the immortal soul seems to go out of the body. For a soul, that derives no benefit from the body even while inhabiting it, is as good as outside it. This being so, the different ideas (or perceptions) like staying in, moving out, etc. are to be admitted to be illusory. Moreover, incongruity of time is also apparent in a dream. A man asleep at night thinks that it is daylight in India. Similarly in a dream lasting for a moment, he sometimes passes through a number of years. Again, the materials necessary for the consequent perceptions or actions are not adequately present. For instance, he has no eye etc. for the perception of chariot etc., his senses having been withdrawn (in sleep). And from where does come his power to make a chariot in a moment, and from where the timber? Besides, these chariot etc. seen in a dream are sublated in the waking state. Not only this, they are easily sublated in the dream itself, since there is contradiction between their beginning and end inasmuch as something ascertained in dream to be a chariot turns into a man the next moment, or someone ascertained to be a man changes suddenly into a tree. The scripture also tells us clearly that chariot etc. do not exist in dream: "There are no chariots, no animals to be yoked to them, nor roads there" (Bṛ. IV. iii. 10). Hence things seen in a dream are mere Māyā.

सूचकश्च हि श्रुतेराचक्षते च तद्विदः ॥४॥

(Dream is) च also सूचकः an omen; हि for (this is known) श्रुते from the Upaniṣads, च and तत्-विदः experts in dream-reading आचक्षते say (so).

4. A dream is also an omen, for so it is known from the Upaniṣads, and experts say so.

Opponent: In that case, since it is all mere Māyā, there is no touch of reality in dream.

Vedāntin: We say, no; for dream becomes the indicator also of good and evil in future. Thus it is mentioned in the Upaniṣad: "If one should see a woman in dreams while engaged in performing some rites with a view to getting results, then one should know from the occurrence of the dreams that those rites will be fruitful" (Ch. V. ii. 8). Similarly the scriptures declare that the text, "Should a man dream of a black person with black teeth, that person will cause his death" and such other texts indicate imminent death. Moreover, people conversant with the science of dream, say, "Dreams of mounting on elephants etc. are auspicious, whereas those of mounting on ass etc. are bad omens". They think that some dreams caused by *mantras*, gods, and special substances have a touch of reality in them. But even in these cases, though it may be granted that the things prognosticated are true, the indicative omens like the seeing of a woman are certainly unreal, for these get sublated. This is the idea. Hence it is proved that a dream is merely illusory.

As for the reference to the Upaniṣadic text in the aphorism, "because the Upaniṣad says so" (III. ii. 1), that should be explained in a figurative sense in the light of the conclusion arrived at thus. This is like the statement, "The plough sustains the bullocks", where the plough is said to be the cause of sustenance because it is metaphorically so. Not that the plough really sustains the bullocks etc. So also from the mere fact that a sleeping man becomes an accidental cause for creation, it is said that he creates the chariots etc. and that "he is the agent" (Bṛ. IV. iii. 9-10). And it is to be explained that the soul becomes an accidental cause for the creation of chariot etc. in the sense that happiness and fear are seen to arise from the sight of chariot etc., of which merit and demerit are the causes, and the soul is the efficient cause of those merit and demerit. Moreover, the topic of dream is introduced for revealing the self-effulgence of the witnessing Self as a distinct fact. This is done because in the waking state we have the existence of the contact between the objects and senses and an admixture of the light of the sun etc., so that the self-effulgence of the Self cannot be distinguished from them. That being the case, if the text about creation of chariot etc. be taken in the literal sense, then the self-effulgence of the Self will remain undetermined. Hence in the light of the mention of the unreality of chariot etc., it is to be explained that the text about the creation of these is figurative. Hereby is explained the text about creatorship (B. S. III. ii. 2, Ka. II. ii. 8).

And the assertion was made that the followers of a particular branch of the Vedas consider this creator to be the supreme conscious Self; that too is improper; for in another Upaniṣad this is shown to be the activity of the individual soul in the text, "Himself puts the body aside and himself creates (a dream body in its place), revealing his own lustre by his own light—and he dreams" (Bṛ. IV. iii. 9). In the text under discussion also, it is shown by a restatement of a known fact in, "He who keeps awake even when the senses fall asleep" (Ka. II. ii. 8), that this creator of desirable things is none other than the individual soul. In the complementary portion of the passage, however, the individuality of that soul is removed and it is shown to be none other than Brahman in the text, "He is pure and He is Brahman" (Ka. II. ii. 8), even as it is done in such texts as, "That thou art" (Ch. VI. viii-xvi). Thus it does not go against the topic of Brahman with which the context deals. Nor do we deny the activity of the supreme Self even during dream, for that supreme Self is the Lord of all; and as such it is He who can be reasonably upheld to be the ordainer under all circumstances. But what we want to show is only this much that in truth, this creation in dream is not of the same order of reality as the creation of space etc. And yet the creation of space etc. also has no absolute reality; for under the aphorism, "The effect is non-different from the cause since terms like 'origin' etc. are met with" (II. i. 14), we showed that the whole creation is but Māyā. But before the realization of the identity of the Self with Brahman, creation counting from space etc., continues just as it is, whereas the creation within dream is abrogated every day. Hence the statement that dream is merely Māyā has a special significance.

पराभिध्यानात्तु तिरोहितं ततो ह्यस्य बन्धविपर्ययौ ॥५॥

पर-अभिध्यानात् By meditation on the supreme Lord, तिरोहितम् that which is obscured (becomes manifest); हि for ततः from Him (are derived) अस्य its (the soul's) बन्ध-विपर्ययौ bondage and its opposite.

5. *From the meditation on the supreme Lord, however, becomes manifest that which remains obscured; because the soul's bondage and freedom are derived from Him.*

Opponent: Even so, it may be that the individual soul is a part of the supreme Self just as a spark is of a fire. That being so, just as the fire and the spark have the same power of combustion and light, so also the soul and God have the same power of knowledge, divinity, (true resolve, etc). And from this it follows that the soul can through its divinity (i.e. true resolve), create such things in dream as a chariot as an act of its will.

Vedāntin: To this it is said: Though the soul and God may be related as the part and the whole, still the soul is directly seen to be possessed of attributes opposed to those of God.

Opponent: Do you mean that the soul has no attribute similar to God's?

Vedāntin: Not that it has not; but though present, this similarity remains hidden, since it is screened off by ignorance. That similarity, remaining hidden, becomes manifest in the case of some rare person who meditates on God with diligence, for whom the darkness of ignorance gets removed, and who becomes endowed with mystic powers through the grace of God, like the regaining of the power of sight through the potency of medicine by a man who had lost it through the disease called *timira*. But it does not come naturally to all and sundry.

Why?

Vedāntin: Because "from him", i.e. owing to God, are "his", of this creature, "bondage and freedom", bondage that comes from the ignorance about the nature of God and freedom that comes from the knowledge of His reality. To this effect occurs the Upaniṣadic text, "On the realization of the Deity (i.e. Brahman with attributes), all the bondages (i.e. such evils as ignorance, desire, etc.) fall off; and on the eradication of these evils, there is complete cessation of birth and death. But (as compared with bondage and freedom) the third thing (viz mystic powers) occurs as a result of meditation on Him (with attributes), and after the death of the body comes unsurpassable divinity, and after that one becomes the Absolute with all the desires fulfilled" (Śv. I. 11). There are also other texts of this kind.

देहयोगाद्वा सोऽपि ॥६॥

वा Or rather देह-योगात् owing to connection with the body (occurs) सः that (covering) अपि also.

6. Or rather that covering occurs also on account of connection with the body.

Opponent: If the soul be a part of God, why should it have its knowledge and divinity (Lordship) under cover, the reasonable position being that knowledge and divinity should remain uncovered for a soul as much as combustion and illumination remain so for a spark?

Vedāntin: The answer is being given: What you say is truly so. But "that too", that covering up also, of knowledge and divinity, in the case of the individual soul, "occurs from the connection with the body", from the association with body, senses, mind, intelligence, perception of objects, etc., And we have an analogy on this point: As the power of combustion and illumination, though inherent in fire, remains hidden for it when it is (latent) inside the fuel, or as it remains hidden when the fire is covered with ashes, similarly there occurs a covering up of the knowledge and Lordship of the soul owing to an error of non-distinction of the soul from the body etc., arising from its association with the limiting adjunct comprising the body etc., and created by name and form, which are conjured up by nescience. The words "or rather" (in the aphorism) are meant for obviating the misconception about the difference between the soul and God.

Opponent: Why should not the soul be accepted as different from God, since its knowledge and Lordship are covered up? What is the need of fancying this as arising from association with the body?

Vedāntin: The answer is in the negative; for it does not stand to reason that the soul can be different from God. For starting with the text, "That Deity, that was such, deliberated" (Ch. VI. iii. 2), the individual soul is referred to by the word Self in the text, "I Myself having entered into it as this individual soul" (ibid.). And in the text, "That is Truth; That is the Self, That thou art, O Śvetaketu" (Ch. VI. viii-xv), the individual is taught as being identical with God. Hence the conclusion is that though the individual soul is non-different from God, its knowledge and Lordship become covered up owing to association with the body. From this also it follows that the creation of chariot etc. in dream is not an achievement of the individual soul by its will. If, on the contrary, dream creation were an act of will, one would not have an evil dream, for one does not will evil for oneself. As for the statement that the Upaniṣadic text equating dream with waking (viz Bṛ. IV. iii. 14—"others, however, say that the dream state of a man is nothing but the waking state" etc.), declares the reality of dream, that declaration of similarity does not signify reality, for that would run counter to the self-effulgence of the Self. Moreover, the Upaniṣad itself shows the absence of chariot etc. in dream. The idea implied there is that dream being a product of the impressions acquired during wakefulness, it has the verisimilitude of wakefulness. Hence it is reasonable to say that dream is mere Māyā.

Topic 2: The Soul in Deep Sleep

तदभावो नाडीषु तच्छ्रुतेरात्मनि च ॥७॥

तत्-अभाव: The absence of that (dream), (that is to say, deep sleep), (takes place) नाडीषु in the nerves च and आत्मनि in the Self, तत्-श्रुते: that being known from the Upaniṣads.

7. *The absence of that dream (i.e. dreamless sleep) takes place in the nerves and the Self, as it is known to be so from the Upaniṣads.*

The dream state has been considered: now is being considered the state of sleep. Here are some Upaniṣadic passages about sleep: "Now then, (among these states), when one sleeps in such a way, that all his organs are withdrawn and he becomes completely serene (in mind) and does not dream, then the soul remains spread over these nerves" (Ch. VIII. vi. 3). In another place, however, in connection with these very nerves it is heard, "it comes back along the seventy-two thousand nerves called *hitā*, which extend from the heart to the pericardium, and sleeps in the *purītat*" (i.e. the heart) (Bṛ. II. i. 19). Elsewhere also, while dealing with the nerves themselves, it is said, "When the sleeping individual sees no dream, he happens to be in those nerves; then he becomes united in this *Prāṇa*" (Kau. IV. 19). Similarly in another place: "And (he) lies in the *Ākaśa* (supreme Self) that is in the heart" (Bṛ. II. i. 17).

So also elsewhere: "O amiable one, then he becomes unified with Existence, he attains his own Self" (Ch. VI. viii. 1), as also, "So this infinite Being (Self), fully embraced by the Conscious Self (supreme Self), does not know anything at all, either external or internal" (Bṛ. IV. iii. 21).

Doubt: While on this subject, the doubt arises: Are these nerves and other places of sleep different from one another, or are they mutually interdependent and constitute a single place of sleep? What should be the conclusion here?

Opponent: They are different places.

Why?

Since they are meant to serve the same purpose. Things that are meant to serve the same purpose are not seen to depend on one another, as in the case of paddy, barley, etc. (optionally used for sacrificial cakes). And the nerves etc. are seen to serve the same purpose during sleep; for in "remains spread over these nerves" (Ch. VIII. vi. 3), "sleeps in the *purītat*" (Bṛ. II. ii. 19), the seventh (locative) case-ending ("in") is seen to be equally in use.

Objection: But in the case of Existence (*Sat*) the seventh case-ending is not used thus in, "O amiable one, he then becomes unified with Existence" (Ch. VI. viii. 1) (where the instrumental case is used).

Opponent: This is no defect; for there too the sense of the seventh case can be understood; for in the complementary passage it is stated that the individual soul, in search of an abode repairs to Existence: "Not getting an abode anywhere else, he resorts to *Prāṇa* Itself" (Ch. VI. viii. 2), where the Existence under discussion is referred to by the word *Prāṇa*. And the sense of the seventh case is implied in the word *āyatana* (abode). Moreover the use of the seventh case is clearly in evidence in the complementary text: "Having become merged in Existence, they do not know, 'We have become merged in Existence' " (Ch. VI. ix. 2). In all these cases, the nature of deep sleep, consisting in the cessation of particularized knowledge, does not differ. Therefore, it follows that since the nerves etc. serve the same purpose, the soul resorts optionally to some one of them some time for its sleep.

Vedāntin: This being the position, it is being explained: "The absence of that takes place in the nerves and the Self". "The absence of that" means the absence of the relevant dreaming, that is to say deep sleep. That occurs in the nerves and the Self. By the use of "and" in the sense of combination, the idea conveyed is that the soul resorts to these nerves etc. collectively for sleep and not alternatively.

Whence is it so?

Since it is seen to be so from the Upaniṣads. To explain: All these nerves and other things are mentioned in the respective contexts (in the Upaniṣads) as the places of sleep; and all these become reconciled if they are accepted collectively, whereas if they are accepted alternatively then the others become ruled out.

Opponent: Was it not pointed out that, serving as they do the same purpose like paddy, barley etc., the nerves, (*purītat*, and Self), can be accepted alternatively?

Vedāntin: The answer is, no. From the mere fact that the same case-ending is used it does not follow that they serve the same purpose or that they can be taken alternatively. For even in the case of things having divergent purposes as well as some collective purpose, the same case-ending is found to be used, as in, "He sleeps in a palace, he sleeps in a couch"[2], and such other instances. Similarly it is but reasonable here that a combination is to be accepted in the sense that he sleeps in the nerves, *Purītat*, and Brahman. In support of this is the Upaniṣadic text, "When the individual soul sees no dream, he happens to be in those nerves; then he becomes united in the *Prāṇa*" (Kau. IV. 19), where the text speaks collectively of the nerves and *Prāṇa* in deep sleep; for both are presented in the very same sentence. And it has been ascertained that *Prāṇa* is Brahman in the aphorism, "*Prāṇa* is Brahman, because it can be harmonized thus" (B. S. I. i. 28). Where the Upaniṣad speaks of the nerves as though they are independent places of sleep as in, "Then he remains asleep in these nerves" (Ch. VIII. vi. 3), there also

[2] The palace contains the couch which helps sleep. Their purposes are different; and yet both help sleep indirectly and directly and thus become associated.

Brahman, well known (to be the place of sleep) from other texts is not ruled out, and hence the idea derived is that the soul rests in Brahman by proceeding along the nerves. Even from such a viewpoint the use of the locative case after the nerves is not contradicted; for though the soul approaches Brahman through the nerves, it happens to be in the nerves, just as a man proceeding to the sea along the river Gaṅgā, remains as a matter of fact in the Gaṅgā. Moreover, the thing sought to be taught in this text (Ch. VIII. vi) is the path constituted by the nerves and the rays and leading to the world of Brahman. The declaration about the soul's remaining spread over the nerves is meant for eulogizing the nerves; for first it is said, "He remains spread over the nerves", and then it is added, "no sin touches him" (Ch. VIII. vi. 3), in which latter sentence the nerves are praised. The reason for being free from the touch of sin is also stated in, "For he then becomes enveloped by *tejas* (light)" (ibid.), which means that the organs of the soul then become enveloped by the light (of the sun in the nerves) called bile, and so it cannot perceive external things. Or by the term "by light", Brahman Itself is referred to, for in another Upaniṣad, the word *tejas* (light) is used for Brahman in the text, "Brahman, Itself, the Light" (Bṛ. IV. iv. 7). The idea implied is that since the soul then becomes unified with Brahman by proceeding along the nerves, therefore no sin can touch it; for from such Upaniṣadic text as, "All sins turn back from here, for this is the world of Brahman that is unafflicted by sin" (Ch. VIII. iv. 1), it is known that merger in Brahman is the cause for remaining untouched by sin. This being so, the conclusion arrived at is that the nerves, dependent on Brahman as they are, have to be construed as the place of sleep collectively with Brahman which is well known to be the place of sleep from other Upaniṣadic texts. So also the *purītat*, having been mentioned in connection with Brahman, is understood to become a place of sleep in subordination to Brahman, which fact is known thus: The *Ākāśa* (Brahman) in the heart, which is the place of sleep, is introduced in, "And lies in the *Ākāśa* that is in the heart" (Bṛ. II. i. 17); and in that context it is said, "sleeps in the *purītat*". (Bṛ. II. i. 19). By the word *purītat* is meant a covering of the heart. One sleeping in the *Ākāśa* within the heart, enveloped by the *purītat*, may as well be said to be sleeping in the *purītat*; for somebody living within a city surrounded by a rampart is said to be living in the rampart. Now, under the aphorism, "The small *Ākāśa* (i.e. space in the heart) is Brahman, because of the subsequent reasons" (I. iii. 14), it was ascertained earlier that the *Ākāśa* in the heart is Brahman. And from the reference to the nerves and *purītat* in the same sentence, "It comes back through the nerves called *hitā* and sleeps in the *purītat*" (Bṛ. II. i. 19), it is known that the nerves and *purītat* are to be construed collectively. Besides "Existence" (Ch. VI. viii. 1) and "Conscious Self" (Bṛ. IV. iii. 19) are well known to be terms denoting Brahman. In these Upaniṣadic texts three places only are mentioned as the places of sleep—the nerves, the *purītat*, and Brahman. Among these the nerves, as also the *purītat*, are mere entrances, Brahman alone, without a second, being the unchanging place of sleep. Moreover, the nerves as well as the *purītat* become merely the encasements for the individual soul by virtue of being its limiting adjuncts, for in them exist its organs. Without the association with the limiting adjuncts, the soul cannot have any natural encasement, since it is ever established in its own glory owing to its identity with Brahman. As for its having Brahman as its locus (or abode) during sleep, that too is not stated by way of making a distinction as between a container and the thing contained.

In what way then?

By way of showing their identity, since it is said, "O amiable one, he then becomes unified with Existence, he attains his own Self" (Ch. VI. viii. 1), where the supreme Self is referred to by the phrase "own Self (*sva*)", the idea implied being that a man while asleep remains established in his true nature. Moreover there is no time when the soul is not in union with Brahman, since one's own nature is unchangeable. But the statement, "He attains his own Self" is made, because in dream and wakefulness the soul seems to assume another's garb under the influence of the limiting adjuncts with which it remains associated, whereas in sleep that garb falls off, so that in comparison with the earlier stages, sleep is sought to be spoken of as the state of assumption of the real nature. From this it is clear that it is improper to say that in sleep the soul sometimes becomes unified with Existence and sometimes not. Besides, even if it be understood that sleep can have different alternative loci, still deep sleep, as consisting in the cessation of particularized perception, is always the same. And under such circumstances, it is but logical that a soul, merged in Existence, should not know anything just because of its non-duality, as is shown in the text, "then what should one know and through what?" (Bṛ. II. iv. 14). But should the soul sleep in the nerves or the *purītat*, no reason for its non-recognition of objects can be ascertained, since (particularized) cognition is concerned with duality (and duality is present there), as is shown in the text, "When there is something else, as it were, then one can see something". (Bṛ. IV. iii. 31).

Opponent: Even things within duality may remain unknown owing to great distance etc.

Vedāntin: This can be truly so, if the individual soul is supposed to be naturally limited, even as Viṣṇumitra (who is different from his house) does not see his own house when on a sojourn. But the soul has no limitation apart from that caused by conditioning factors. Even if you say that in the case of the soul also, non-cognition is caused by the great distance etc. inherent in the limiting adjuncts, still the reasonable position is that when the adjuncts cease in sleep, the soul does not know because of its merger in Existence Itself. But when talking of a collection of factors (in sleep), we do not suggest here that the nerves etc. combine in equal partnership (with Brahman); for nothing is gained from the knowledge that the nerves, as also the *purītat*, are the locus of sleep, since neither any result is mentioned in the Upaniṣads as attached to such a knowledge itself, nor is it construed that such a knowledge forms part of something else that has its own result. We are out to prove that Brahman is the invariable locus of sleep. Such a knowledge serves a purpose, namely that the soul is ascertained to be identical with Brahman, and it is realized to be free from the dealings consequent on the dream and wakeful states. Hence the Self is the locus of sleep.

अत: प्रबोधोऽस्मात् ॥८॥

अत: Hence प्रबोध: awakening (is) अस्मात् from this.

8. For the same reason, the soul's waking up is from this supreme Self.

Since the Self Itself is the locus of sleep, therefore, for that very reason, it is taught in the context of sleep that wakefulness occurs invariably from this Self, by the texts, "As from a fire tiny sparks fly in all directions, so from the Self emanate all organs" (Bṛ. II. i. 20), etc., said in the course of the answer to the question, "Whence did it come?" (Bṛ. II. i. 16). This is done also by the text, "Having emerged from Existence, they do not know, 'We have come from Existence'" (Ch. IV. x. 2). Had the loci of sleep been but optional, the Upaniṣad would have instructed that the soul wakes up sometimes from the nerves, sometimes from the *purītat*, and sometimes from the Self. From this also follows that the Self is the locus of sleep.

TOPIC 3: THE SAME SOUL RETURNS FROM SLEEP

स एव तु कर्मानुस्मृतिशब्दविधिभ्यः ॥९॥

तु But स: एव that (soul) itself (returns) कर्म-अनुस्मृतिशब्द-विधिभ्य: because of the reasons of action, remembrance, scriptural authority, and injunction.

9. But the very same soul returns from sleep because of the reasons of action, remembrance, scriptural authority, and injunction.

Doubt: It is being considered whether the one who awakes from that merger in Existence is the same at the time of awakening as one was at the time of merger, or whether it may either be the same entity or some one else.

Opponent: When under this doubt, the conclusion arrived at is that there is no hard and fast rule.

Why?

When a drop of water is thrown into a mass of water, it

becomes one with that mass. And when an attempt is made to take it up again from there, it is impossible to have that very same drop. Similarly when the sleeping soul has become one with the supreme Self and has attained quiescence (i.e. freedom from everything), that very soul cannot wake up again. Hence the conclusion is that the waking being may be either the original soul, or he may be God, or some other individual soul.

Vedāntin: To this the aphorist says, "But (it is) the very same soul", which had gone to sleep and attained its own Self, that rises up again; and it is none else.

What are the reasons for that?

"Because of the reasons of action, remembrance, scriptural authority, and injunction." We shall elaborate the reasons separately. To begin, the selfsame soul alone can awake, and none else, because an unfinished action is seen to be resumed. Thus one is seen to take up and finish a piece of work left incomplete on the previous day. One cannot reasonably engage oneself in some work left incomplete by another, since a contrary view will lead to unwarranted conclusions. Hence it is understood that the same person is the doer of the same work on the previous and next days. For this further reason also the selfsame person wakes up: If the person waking up be different, then there should be no memory of what was perceived earlier, which proposition is contrary to what is evident in the recollection, "I saw this on the previous day". For something seen by one cannot be remembered by another. And a recognition like, "I am that very person", in which one's own identity is recognized cannot be imagined to occur if some other soul should wake up. Again, from scriptural texts it is known that the selfsame person wakes up, as for instance, "He comes back again in the inverse order to his former condition, the waking state" (Bṛ. IV. iii. 16), "All these creatures who repair to this world of Brahman every day, do not know It" (Ch. VIII. iii. 2), and "Whatever they might have been here (in the previous waking state)—be it a tiger, a lion, a wolf, a boar, a worm, an insect, a gnat, or a mosquito, they become those very creatures then (after waking from sleep)" (Ch. VI. ix. 3). These and other texts occurring in the context of sleep and waking up cannot be reconciled if the waking soul be different. This also is the conclusion that follows from the injunctions about rites and meditations; for else the injunctions about rites and meditations become useless, since on the supposition of some other soul waking up, the conclusion will be that any one becomes free as soon as one goes to sleep. And if this be the case, then would you tell me what is the need of undertaking a rite or a meditation that will yield its fruit in future? Again, on the hypothesis that some other (bound) soul wakes up, it will either mean that some soul that had been working through a second body wakes up (in the sleeping body under consideration), in which case there will be the predicament of that (active) soul's activity ceasing in that second body. Or if it be held that the soul sleeping in the second body wakes up in the first, then that supposition is useless; for when one sleeping in any body can wake up in that very body, what do you gain by supposing that some one sleeping in one body wakes up in another? Again, if it be held that a free soul wakes up in the body (in which another had slept), then liberation will become terminable. Moreover, it is illogical that one for whom ignorance has ceased should become embodied again. Hereby is also refuted the view that God wakes up in the body, since in Him ignorance is eternally absent. Besides, the defects of deriving some unearned result and losing something earned will be inevitable on the supposition that some other soul wakes up in the body after sleep. Hence that very (sleeping) soul wakes up and none else.

And it was argued that just as a drop of water thrown into a mass of water cannot be singled out, so also a soul merging in Existence cannot spring up again. That is being refuted. In the analogy it is quite in order to say that the (selfsame) drop of water cannot be singled out, since there is nothing to mark out its individuality. But here we have *karma* and ignorance as the factors making the (individual) distinction. The two cases are thus different. Moreover, it is a matter of experience that though milk and water, when mixed together, cannot be separated by any one of the human race, still they can be separated by ducks. Besides, there is no such entity, different from the supreme

Self, which has to be distinguished from Existence like a drop of water from a mass of water. It has been shown more than once that Existence Itself comes to be called indirectly a soul, because of the intervention of limiting adjuncts. This being the case, as long as a soul continues to be bound up with a particular set of adjuncts, so long do we deal with it as the very same one; and when it comes to be bound up with another set of adjuncts, we deal with it as though it is different. That very same set of adjuncts persists in sleep and wakefulness on the maxim of the seed and seedling, so that the reasonable position is that the selfsame soul wakes up from sleep.

TOPIC 4: SOUL IN SWOON

मुग्धेऽर्धसम्पत्तिः परिशेषात् ॥१०॥

मुग्धे In the case of a person in swoon अर्ध-सम्पत्तिः occurs only partial attainment (of the state of sleep), परिशेषात् that being the last alternative.

10. In the case of one in swoon, there is only partial attainment (of the state of sleep), that being the last alternative.

Opponent: There is such a phenomenon as a man in a swoon whom people call unconscious. When the condition of such a man is under scrutiny, it is said: The soul inhabiting a body is known to have three states—wakefulness, dream, and sleep. The fourth is the departure from the body. But no fifth state is known to exist for the soul either in the Vedas or the Smṛtis. Therefore unconsciousness must be classed under one of the four conditions.

Vedāntin: This being the position, we say: Of these states, a man in a swoon cannot be in the waking state; for he does not perceive objects through his senses.

Opponent: Well, this can be so on the analogy of an arrow-maker. As an arrow-maker, being occupied with the arrow, does not perceive anything but the arrow, though he is wide awake, similarly a man in a swoon, though still awake, does not perceive anything else because his mind is fully overwhelmed by the pain arising from a blow dealt with a club etc.

Vedāntin: No, since he behaves as one having no consciousness (at the time). For the arrow-maker, whose attention had been fully engaged, says afterwards, "I was perceiving simply the arrow so long". But the unconscious man says on regaining his consciousness, "For so long I was immersed in blinding darkness, and nothing was perceived by me." Besides, a waking man, who has his mind concentrated on one object, holds his body erect, whereas the body of an unconscious man drops down to the ground. Therefore neither does he keep awake nor does he see dreams, for he has no consciousness (i.e. capacity of perception). Nor is he dead, for he has life and warmth. For when a man faints, people having doubts as to whether he is dead or alive feel his heart to ascertain if he has warmth; and to ascertain if he breathes, they examine his nostrils. Should they fail to perceive the existence of both breath and warmth, they conclude that the man is dead and so carry him to the forest for cremation. On the contrary if they feel the existence of either breath or warmth, they conclude that the man is not dead, and so they resort to treatment for bringing back his consciousness. Also from the fact that the unconscious man rises up again, it follows that he was not dead; for one who goes to the king of death, never comes back from that domain.

Opponent: Let it be then that he is in deep sleep, since he has no consciousness at the same time that he is not dead.

Vedāntin: Not so, for there is a difference. A man in a swoon may not breathe for a long time, but his body may be in tremors and his face may be distorted (with a look of terror), and the eyes may remain wide open. But a man in deep sleep has a calm face, he breathes rhythmically again and again, his eyes remain closed, and his body has no contortion. A sleeping man is awakened simply by pushing him with the hand, whereas an unconscious man cannot be brought back to consciousness even by beating with a club. Furthermore, the causes of swoon and sleep differ, for fainting results from blows from a club etc., while sleep comes as a result of fatigue. And people never acknowledge that a man under a swoon sleeps. By a process of elimination we realize that swooning away is a state of half sleep; for he is partially asleep owing to absence of consciousness, and still he is not fully asleep as his state is different from sleep.

Opponent: How again can a swoon be described as a partial sleep, since with regard to the sleeping man the Upaniṣads say, "O amiable one, he then becomes unified with Existence" (Ch. VI. viii. 1), "In this state a thief is no thief" (Bṛ. IV. iii. 22), "Night and day do not overflow this embankment (i.e. Brahman), nor old age, nor death, nor sorrow, nor merit, nor demerit" (Ch. VIII. iv. 1)? For an individual being gets the results of merit and demerit through the generation of the ideas of his being happy or sorry; but neither the idea of happiness nor of misery exists in sleep; so also they are absent in a swoon. Hence it follows that in a swoon, as in sleep, there is a complete merger in Existence owing to the cessation of the limiting adjuncts; but it is not partial merger.

Vedāntin: With regard to this the answer is, that it is not our view that in a swoon a man becomes half merged in Brahman.

What do you say then?

A swoon is partially a form of sleep, and partially of some other state. We have already shown its similarity and dissimilarity with sleep. And it is a door to death. So long as the individual's *karma* lasts, his speech and mind return from a swoon; but when the *karma* has no residue, his breathing and warmth depart. Hence the knowers of Brahman call swoon a partial sleep. As for the objection raised that no fifth state is known to exist, that is nothing damaging. On account of being a casual state, it is not so widely noted; and yet it is well recognized in this world and in the books of medicine. By admitting it to be a partial sleep, we do not reckon it to be a fifth state. In this way it is all beyond criticism.

Topic 5: The Nature of Brahman

न स्थानतोऽपि परस्योभयलिङ्गं सर्वत्र हि ॥११॥

न Not स्थानतः according to (difference of) place (i.e. limiting adjunct) अपि even (can there be) उभय-लिङ्गम् a twofold characteristic परस्य of the supreme Brahman हि for सर्वत्र everywhere (It is taught otherwise).

11. Not even according to place can Brahman have a twofold characteristic, for everywhere (It is taught to be without attributes).

With the help of Upaniṣadic texts, the nature of that Brahman is now being ascertained with which the individual soul becomes unified in sleep when its limiting adjuncts become quiescent. Vedic texts about Brahman are met with which are indicative of Brahman both with qualification and without qualification. Such texts as, "He is the doer of all (good) acts, possessed of all (good) desires, all (good) smell, all (good) tastes" (Ch. III. xiv. 2), indicate that Brahman has attributes. And the texts, "It is neither gross, nor minute, neither short nor long" (Bṛ. III. viii. 8) and others, indicate that It is devoid of attributes.

Doubt: Now should it be understood that in these texts Brahman is spoken of as possessed of a twofold characteristic, or that It is spoken of as possessed of either of the two characteristics? Again, even if one of these characteristics be true, it has to be ascertained whether the aspect with attributes is to be accepted or the aspect without attributes.

Opponent: As to that, on the authority of the texts presenting a dual aspect, Brahman must have both the aspects.

Vedāntin: This being the position, we say: As to that, the supreme Brahman, considered in Itself, cannot logically have both the characteristics; for it cannot be admitted that the very same thing is naturally possessed of attributes like form etc., and that it is also without these; for that is self-contradictory.

Opponent: Then let this be so owing to position, that is to say, on account of association with such limiting adjuncts as earth.

Vedāntin: That too is not logical. For even by association with the limiting adjuncts a substance that is different in kind cannot change its nature into another; for a transparent crystal cannot become opaque even when in contact with limiting adjuncts like red lac, the idea of opaqueness being a mere error. Moreover, adjuncts are conjured up by ignorance. Hence, even if we have to take up either of the two characteristics, it is the Brahman that is absolutely attributeless and unchangeable that has to be accepted and not the opposite. For in all texts which aim at presenting the real nature of Brahman, as for instance in, "soundless, touchless, colourless, undiminishing" (Ka. I. iii. 15), etc., Brahman is presented as devoid of all distinguishing attributes.

न भेदादिति चेन्न प्रत्येकमतद्वचनात् ॥१२॥

"न Not so भेदात् owing to differences" इति चेत् if it be argued thus, (then) न not so, अ-तत्-वचनात् because of the negation of such differences प्रत्येकम् individually.

12. If it be argued that (Brahman cannot have only one characteristic), on account of differences (met with in the scriptures), (we say that) it is not so, because the scriptures negate each of these differences individually.

Opponent: It may still be argued thus: It does not stand to reason to assert, as it has been done, that Brahman is beyond all distinctions and has but one characteristic, and that It cannot have a double characteristic either naturally or owing to the influence of position.

Why?

"On account of differences". For the aspects of Brahman are taught differently in connection with the individual meditations, as for instance, "Brahman has four feet (or quarters)" (Ch. III. xviii. 2), "Brahman has sixteen digits (parts)" (Pr. VI. 1), "Brahman is the bestower of the results of actions on those persons" (Ch. IV. xv. 3), "Brahman has the three worlds as Its body" (Bṛ. I. iii. 22), and It is called "Vaiśvānara' (Ch. V. xii-xviii), and so on. Hence Brahman has to be admitted as possessed of attributes as well.

Vedāntin: Did we not say that it is not possible for Brahman to have a dual characteristic?

Opponent: That too creates no difficulty, because a difference in aspects is created by limiting adjuncts; for otherwise the texts talking of difference will be left without any scope.

Vedāntin: We say, this is not so.

Why?

"Because the scriptures negate each of these differences individually. "For along with (the mention of) each difference created by a limiting adjunct, the scriptures affirm the non-difference alone of Brahman, as in, "The same with the shining immortal being who is in this earth, and the shining immortal corporeal being in the body. (These four) are but this Self" etc. (Bṛ. II. v. 1). Hence the difference having been spoken of for the sake of meditation, and non-difference being the real purport of the scriptures, it cannot be held that the scriptures support the view that Brahman is possessed of diverse aspects.

अपि चैवमेके ॥१३॥

अपि च Moreover, एके some (followers of some branches) एवम् thus (declare).

13. Moreover, the followers of certain branches declare thus.

Moreover, the followers of certain sections declare in favour of the realization of non-duality after condemning the dualistic outlook, as in, "This is to be attained through the mind. There is no diversity whatsoever. He who sees as though there is difference, goes from death to death" (Ka. II. i. 11). Similarly others have: "After deliberating on the experiencer, the things experienced, and the ordainer, one should know all these three to be but the Brahman I speak of" (Śv. I. 12), where the entire variety of phenomenal manifestation, consisting of the objects of experience, the experiencing souls, and (God) the ordainer, is declared by the Upaniṣad to be none other than Brahman in essence.

Opponent: Since two classes of Upaniṣadic texts, speaking of Brahman as with form and also as without form, are in existence, how can it be asserted that Brahman is formless alone?

Vedāntin: Hence comes the answer:

अरूपवदेव हि तत्प्रधानत्वात् ।१४॥

अरूपवत् Formless एव only हि to be sure, तत्-प्रधानत्वात् that being the dominant note.

14. Brahman is only formless to be sure, for that is the dominant note (of the Upaniṣadic teaching).

Brahman is surely to be known as having no form constituted by colour etc., and not as having it.

Why?

"For that is the dominant teaching", inasmuch as it has been established under the aphorism, "But that Brahman is known from the Upaniṣads, because of their being connected with Brahman as their main import" (I. i. 4), that the texts like the following have for their main purport the transcendental Brahman which is the Self, and not any other subject-matter: "It is neither gross, nor minute, neither short nor long" (Bṛ. III. viii. 8), "Soundless, touchless, colourless, undiminishing" (Ka. I. iii. 15), "That which is known as Space is the accomplisher of name and form; That in which they are included is Brahman" (Ch. VIII. xiv. 1), "Puruṣa is transcendental, since He is formless; and He is coextensive with all that is external and internal, since He is birthless" (Mu. II. i. 2), "That Brahman is without prior or posterior, without interior and exterior. The Self, the perceiver of everything, is Brahman" (Bṛ. II. v. 19), and so on. Hence in sentences of this kind, the formless Brahman alone, just as It is spoken of by the texts themselves, has to be accepted. But the other texts, speaking of Brahman with form, have the injunctions about meditations as their main objectives. So long as they do not lead to some contradiction, their apparent meanings should be accepted. But when they involve a contradiction, the principle to be followed for deciding one or the other is that, those that have the formless Brahman as their main purport are more authoritative than the others which have not that as their main purport. It is according to this that one is driven to the conclusion that Brahman is formless and not its opposite, though texts having both the purports are in evidence.

Opponent: What would then be the fate of the texts speaking of forms?

Vedāntin: Hence comes the reply:

प्रकाशवच्चावैयर्थ्यात् ॥१५॥

च And (Brahman can have appearances) प्रकाश-वत् like light अ-वैयर्थ्यात् so that scriptures may not be rendered purportless.

15. And like light, Brahman can (be assumed to) have different appearances, so that the scriptures may not become purportless.

Though the light of the sun or moon spreads over the whole space, still when it comes in contact with adjuncts like fingers etc., it seems to assume the forms, straight or bent, as those adjuncts may have; similarly Brahman, too, seems to have the forms of earth etc., when in contact with those things. And it is nothing contradictory to enjoin meditations on Brahman based on those forms. Thus the sentences presenting Brahman as having forms do not become meaningless, for it is not proper to interpret some Vedic sentences as having meaning and the others as meaningless, since they are all valid.

Opponent: Even so, does not the assertion made earlier that Brahman cannot have a dual characteristic even in association with limiting adjuncts, stand contradicted?

Vedāntin: We say, no, since whatsoever is brought about by an adjunct is not the essential characteristic of a thing, since the adjuncts themselves are conjured up by ignorance. And we said in the respective contexts that all social and Vedic behaviours crop up only when the beginningless nescience is taken for granted.

आह च तन्मात्रम् ॥१६॥

च And (scripture) आह declares (Brahman to be) तत्-मात्रम् that much (i.e. consciousness) only.

16. The Upaniṣad also declares Brahman to be Consciousness alone.

The Upaniṣad also says that Brahman is pure consciousness, devoid of other aspects contrary to this, and without any distinguishing feature, as in, "As a lump of salt is without interior or exterior, entire, and purely saline in taste, even so is the Self without interior or exterior, entire, and pure Intelligence alone" (Bṛ. IV. v. 13), which means that the Self has no internal or external aspect apart from pure consciousness, Its nature being mere impartite consciousness without any interstices. Just as a lump of salt has the saline taste alone both inside and outside, and no other taste, so also is this Self.

दर्शयति चाथो अपि स्मर्यते ॥१७॥

च Moreover दर्शयति (Vedic text) reveals अथो likewise स्मर्यते it is mentioned in the Smṛti अपि as well.

17. Moreover, the Vedas reveal this; likewise this is mentioned in the Smṛtis also.

Moreover, the Vedas reveal through a negation of other aspects that Brahman has no distinguishing feature, as for instance in, "Now therefore the description (of Brahman): 'Not this, not this'" (Bṛ. II. iii. 6), "That (Brahman) is surely different from the known; and, again, It is above the unknown" (Ke. I. 4), "That Bliss of Brahman, failing to reach which, words turn back along with the mind" (Tai. II. ix. 1), and so on. And it is also known from the Vedic texts that Bādhva being asked by Bāṣkali, replied merely by not uttering a word, as stated in, "He (Bāṣkali) said, 'Teach me Brahman, sir.' He (Bādhva) became silent. When the question was repeated a second and a third time he said, 'I have already spoken, but you cannot comprehend. That Self is Quiescence'". Similarly in the Smṛtis, the instruction is given through a negation of other things, as in, "I shall tell you of that which is to be known and by knowing which one attains immortality. The supreme Brahman is without any beginning. It can neither be called gross (visible) nor fine (invisible)" (Gītā, XIII. 12), and so on. Similarly the Smṛti mentions how Nārāyaṇa in His cosmic form said to Nārada, "O Nārada, that you see me as possessed of all the (five divine) qualities of all elements, is only because of My Māyā, called up by Myself. For else you should not understand Me thus."

अत एव चोपमा सूर्यकादिवत् ॥१८॥

अतः एव Hence च also उपमा the illustration सूर्यक-आदि-वत् like the reflection of the sun etc.

18. Hence also are the illustrations of the sun's reflection etc.

Since this Self is by nature Consciousness Itself, distinctionless, beyond speech and mind, and can be taught by way of negating other things, hence in the scriptures dealing with liberation an illustration is cited by saying that it is "like the sun reflected in water". Here the aspect kept in view is the one with attributes, which is not real and which is created by limiting adjuncts, as it is done in such texts, "As this luminous sun, though one in itself, becomes multifarious owing to its entry into water divided by different pots, similarly this Deity, the birthless self-effulgent Self, though one, seems to be diversified owing to Its entry into the different bodies, constituting Its limiting adjuncts." Similarly, "Being but one, the Universal Soul is present in all beings. Though one, It is seen as many, like the moon in water" (Amṛtabindu, 12) and other texts.

Here the *opponent* raises his head:

अम्बुवदग्रहणात्तु न तथात्वम् ॥१९॥

तु But अम्बु-वत्-अग्रहणात् as nothing is perceived to be similar to water तथात्वम् that kind of parallelism न (does) not (apply).

19. But that kind of parallelism is inapplicable as nothing is perceived to be similar to water.

The comparison with the reflection of the sun in water cannot be reasonably upheld here (in the case of the Self), since nothing like that is perceived (here). A material thing, such as water, is seen to be clearly separate from and remotely placed from the sun etc. which are themselves material entities (with forms). There it is proper that an image of the sun should be formed. But the Self is not such a material entity (having form); and since It is all-pervasive and non-different from all, It can have no limiting adjuncts either separate or remote from It. Hence this illustration is inapt.

Vedāntin: The objection is being remedied:

वृद्धिह्रासभाक्त्वमन्तर्भावादुभयसामञ्जस्यादेवम् ।।२०।।

वृद्धि-ह्रास-भाक्त्वम् There is a participation in increase and decrease अन्तः-भावात् on account of the entry (immanence): उभय-सामञ्जस्यात् on account of the propriety of both (the illustration and the thing illustrated) एवम् in this way, (there can be no contradiction).

20. Since Brahman has entered into the limiting adjuncts, It seems to participate in their increase and decrease. The illustration is apt since the illustration and thing illustrated have propriety from this point of view.

On the contrary, this illustration is quite apt, inasmuch as the point sought to be illustrated is pertinent. For as between the illustration and the thing illustrated, nobody can show equality in every respect over and above some point of similarity in some way, which is sought to be presented. For if such an all-round similarity exists, the very relation between the illustration and the thing illustrated will fall through. Moreover, this illustration of the reflection of the sun in water is not cooked up by anybody's imagination. But this illustration having been already cited in the scripture, its applicability alone is being pointed out here.

Where, again, is the intended point of similarity?

The reply is this: "A participation in increase and decrease", inasmuch as the reflection of the sun in water increases with the increase of water, and decreases with its reduction, it moves when the water moves, and it differs as the water differs. Thus the sun conforms to the characteristics of the water; but in reality the sun never has these. Thus also from the highest point of view, Brahman, while remaining unchanged and retaining Its sameness, seems to conform to such characteristics as increase and decrease of the limiting adjunct (body), owing to Its entry into such an adjunct as the body. Thus since the illustration and the thing illustrated are both compatible, there is no contradiction.

दर्शनाच्च ॥२१॥

21. And (this is also) in accordance with (the Vedic) revelation.

The Upaniṣads also show that the supreme Brahman Itself has entered into the limiting adjuncts, such as the bodies and the rest, as in, "He made bodies with two feet and bodies with four feet. That supreme Being first entered the bodies as a bird (i.e. the subtle body)" (Bṛ. II. v. 18), as also, "Myself entering as this individual Self" (Ch. VI. iii. 2). Therefore it has been aptly said, "Hence also are the illustrations like the sun's reflections etc." (III. ii. 18). Accordingly, the conclusion is that Brahman is without any distinguishing feature, and has but one aspect, and not two or an opposite one.

Some people (i.e. *pseudo-Vedāntins*) fancy here two topics. The first topic is concerned with whether Brahman has but one characteristic, devoid of all the variety of phenomenal manifestations, or It has many features just like the universe. It being established that Brahman is devoid of the variety of manifestations (B. S. III. ii. 11-14), the second topic (B. S. III. ii. 15-21) considers whether Brahman has the characteristic of existence or consciousness or both.

Vedāntin: With regard to this we say: Considered from every point of view, it is useless to start a fresh topic. If the effort made here is meant merely for refuting a multiplicity in the characteristics of Brahman, that has already been done under the topic starting with, "Not even according to place can Brahman have a twofold characteristic" (III. ii. 11), so that the succeeding topic, starting with, "And possessed of consciousness" etc. (III. ii. 15) will be uncalled for. Furthermore, it cannot be held that Brahman has merely the characteristic of existence and not consciousness; for that would set at naught such texts as "impartite Consciousness to be sure" (Bṛ. IV. v. 13). And how can a Brahman bereft of consciousness be taught (by the scripture) as the Self of a sentient individual being? It cannot also be said that Brahman is characterized by consciousness only, but not by existence; for that would nullify the Upaniṣadic texts like, "The Self is to be realized as existing" (Ka. II. iii. 13). How, again, can a consciousness that has no existence be conceived of? It cannot also be argued that the second topic proves that Brahman has a dual characteristic, since that would contradict what was accepted (by you) earlier. And if Brahman be asserted either to be characterized by consciousness devoid of existence or by existence devoid of consciousness, it will lead to Brahman's becoming dowered with a variety of manifestations, a position already refuted under the previous topic.

Opponent: That is nothing harmful inasmuch as the Vedic texts declare this.

Vedāntin: No, since the same entity cannot have many natures.

Again, even if it be contended that existence itself is the same as consciousness, as also that consciousness itself is existence, so that the one does not rule out the other, still the alternative positions taken up, viz whether Brahman is characterized by existence, or by consciousness, or by both, have no ground to stand on.

As for ourselves we have grouped the aphorisms under the very same topic.

Moreover, it was seen that if on finding that the Vedic texts, while speaking of Brahman, present It as both with and without form, and thus land themselves into self-contradiction, one understands them as revealing only the formless Brahman, then one has to provide perforce a scope for the rest of the texts. The aphorisms starting with, "And like light taking the forms of objects" (III. ii. 15), become more purposeful as finding out that scope.

As for the view that even the Vedic texts speaking of Brahman's forms are meant merely for leading to the formless Brahman through a sublation of the manifested universe, but that they have no independent purpose, it may be said that that, too, does not appear to be proper.

Why?

Some of the manifestations that are spoken of in a context of the supreme knowledge, as in, "For to Him are yoked ten organs, nay hundreds of them. He is the organs; He is ten, and thousands—many, and infinite" (Bṛ. II. v. 19), etc. may be admitted to be meant for sublation, since the conclusion is made with, "That Brahman is without prior or posterior, without interior or exterior" (ibid.). But the manifestations revealed in a context of meditation, as in "Identified with the mind, having *Prāṇa* as his body, and effulgence itself by nature" (Ch. III. xiv. 2), and so on, cannot reasonably be held to be meant for sublation; for they are connected with some injunction for meditation forming the subject-matter of the context, as for instance, "He should make a resolve" (ibid.). And when the text itself presents these attributes as meant for meditation, it is not proper to interpret them figuratively as meant for sublation. Furthermore, if all manifestations are equally meant for sublation, the statement (in the aphorism), "Brahman is only formless to be sure, because that is the dominant note of the Upaniṣads" (III. ii. 14), where the reason for accepting one of the alternatives is presented, will have no ground for its presentation. Besides, the results of these meditations are surely known from the instructions as being sometimes attenuation of sins, sometimes getting divine powers, and sometimes emancipation by stages. Hence it is proper that the texts about meditations and about Brahman should have different purposes in view, and it is not proper to reduce them to the very same idea. Moreover, (if they convey a single idea) it has to be shown how that sameness of idea can be arrived at.

Opponent: Since they appear to be connected with a single injunction,[3] they have to be combined like the injunctions about the (main) Darśa-pūrṇamāsa and (subsidiary) Prayāja sacrifices.

Vedāntin: No, for there is no injunction in texts about Brahman. It was elaborately proved under the aphorism, "But that Brahman is known from the Upaniṣads, because of their becoming connected with That as their main import" (I. i. 4), how the texts about Brahman have only the knowledge of the

[3] About the sublation of the universe by one who wants illumination.

(pre-existing) thing itself as their purport, but they are not meant for enjoining any action. Again, it has to be shown what (kind of activity) the injunction here should be concerned with; for a man, when he is being employed in some duty, is directed with the order, "Do", with regard to the duty he has to perform.

Opponent: The sublation of all the variety of manifestations within duality will be the object of the injunction. Since the realization of the reality that is Brahman is not achieved so long as the dual world of manifestations is not sublated, therefore, the world of manifestations, that is opposed to the realization of the reality that Brahman is, stands there as a thing to be sublated. As a sacrifice is enjoined as a duty for one who hankers after heaven, so the sublation of the world of manifestations is enjoined for one who wants liberation. And as darkness, standing as an obstruction to the perception of a vessel etc. covered with darkness, is removed by one who wants to know the vessel etc., so the world of manifestations standing opposed to the realization of Brahman has to be sublated by one who wants to realize Brahman; for this phenomenal universe of manifestations has Brahman as its essence and not that Brahman has the phenomenal manifestations as Its essence. Hence the reality that Brahman is has to be realized through a sublation of name and form.

Vedāntin: Here our question is: What is meant by this sublation of the universe of manifestations? Is the world to be annihilated like the destruction of the solidity of *ghee* by contact with fire; or is it that the world of name and form, created in Brahman by nescience like many moons created in the moon by the eye-disease called *timira*, has to be destroyed through knowledge? Now if it be said that this existing universe of manifestations, consisting of the body etc. on the corporeal plane and externally of the earth etc., is to be annihilated, that is a task impossible for any man, and hence the instruction about its extirpation is meaningless. Moreover, (even supposing that such a thing is possible, then) the universe, including the earth etc., having been annihilated by the first man who got liberation, the present universe should have been devoid of the earth etc.

Again, if it be said that this universe of manifestations superimposed on the one Brahman alone through ignorance has to be sublated by enlightenment, then it is Brahman Itself that has to be presented through a denial of the manifestation superimposed by ignorance by saying, "Brahman is one without a second" (Ch. VI. ii. 1), "That is Truth, That is the Self, That thou art (O Svetaketu)" (Ch. VI. viii. 7-16). When Brahman is taught thus, knowledge dawns automatically, and by that knowledge ignorance is removed. As a result of that, this whole manifestation of name and form, superimposed by ignorance, vanishes away like things seen in a dream. But unless Brahman is (first) taught (by scripture etc.), neither does the knowledge of Brahman dawn nor is the universe sublated even though the instruction, "Know Brahman, sublate the world", be imparted a hundred times.

Opponent: After Brahman has been taught, the injunction may relate either to the act of knowing Brahman or to the act of sublating the universe.

Vedāntin: No, since both these objects will be fulfilled from the very instruction that Brahman that is free from the universe of manifestations is one's Self. For from the very revelation of the nature of the rope, mistaken as a snake, follows the knowledge of its real nature, as also the removal of the manifestation of snake etc. on it brought about by superimposition through ignorance. It cannot be that a thing already achieved has to be done over again. Moreover, the individual being, that is known during the state of phenomenal manifestation as the person to be directed by the scriptures, must either belong to the world of manifestations or to Brahman. On the first supposition, when Brahman is taught as devoid of phenomenal manifestations, the individual also becomes negated along with the earth etc.; and so with regard to whom would you talk of an injunction for the sublation of the universe; and of whom would you assert that he is to achieve liberation following the injunction? On the second supposition, when Brahman is taught by saying that the real nature of the individual being is Brahman Itself which is by nature beyond all injunctions and that (the soul's) individuality is a creation of ignorance, then from that will follow a cessation of all injunctions, since there will be none towards whom injunction can be directed. As for expressions like "(The Self) is to be seen" (Bṛ. II. iv. 5), which are met with in the context of the supreme knowledge, they are meant mainly for attracting one's mind towards Reality, but do not aim mainly at enjoining any injunction about the knowledge of Reality. In ordinary parlance also, when such directive sentences as, "Look at this", "Lend ear to that", etc. are uttered, all that is meant is, "Be attentive to these", but not, "Acquire this knowledge directly". And a man, who is in the presence of an object to be known, may sometimes know it, and sometimes not. Hence a man who wants to impart the knowledge of the thing has to draw his attention to the object of knowledge itself. When that is done, the knowledge arises naturally in conformity with the object and the means of knowledge. It is not a fact that any knowledge (of a given thing), contrary to what is well known through other means of valid knowledge, can arise in a man even when acting under some direction. And should the man, under the belief, "I am directed to know this in such a way", know it otherwise, this cannot be true knowledge.

What is it then?

It is a mental act (i.e. deliberate fancy). But (apart from injunction), if it should arise otherwise by itself, it will merely be an error. Knowledge arises, however, from its valid means (like perception etc.), and it conforms to its object, just as it is. It can neither be produced by a hundred injunctions, nor debarred by a hundred prohibitions. For it is not a matter of personal option, it being dependent on the object itself. For this reason also there is no scope for injunction (about Brahman). Moreover, if it be asserted that the whole scope of the scripture consists in nothing more than its adherence to injunction alone, then the position taken up earlier that the individual soul is one with Brahman which is beyond all injunction, becomes invalidated. Again, if it be held that the scripture itself speaks of the soul's unity with the Brahman that is beyond injunction, and it also enjoins a man to know that unity, then the very same scripture about Brahman will be open to the charge of duplicity or self-contradiction. Again, on the assumption that the scriptures are concerned with injunction alone, no one can avoid such defects as the rejection of what is heard in the scriptures and imagination of what is not heard, and the defect of liberation becoming a result of the unseen potency of work and hence impermanent like the results of rites and sacrifices. Hence the texts about Brahman have enlightenment alone as their goal, and they are not concerned with injunction. Accordingly, it is wrong to argue that they impart a single idea (about Brahman), since they come within the scope of a single injunction. Even if the existence of injunction be presumed in the case of the texts speaking of Brahman, still it remains unproved that the very same injunction is present in the instructions about the conditioned Brahman and unconditioned Brahman. For when through such proofs as the use of different words, a difference of injunctions becomes palpable, it is not possible to resort to the plea that the same injunction exists everywhere. As for the texts about the Prayāja and Darśapūrṇamāsa, it is proper to accept their unity, since the portion dealing with the competence (of their performer) is the same. But here as regards the injunctions about the qualified and unqualified Brahman, no such section of the text is available that declares the sameness of the qualification of the man seeking for them. For such attributes as "effulgence itself by nature" are not conducive to the sublation of the universe of manifestation, nor is the sublation of the universe helpful to such qualities as "effulgence itself by nature"; for they are mutually contradictory. It is not logical to accommodate in one and the same substratum such attributes as the sublation of all, and the persistence of a part of the phenomenal manifestations. Therefore the division made by us of the (separate) instructions about Brahman with form and without form is more reasonable.

Topic 6: Unconditioned Brahman and Soul

प्रकृतैतावत्त्वं हि प्रतिषेधति ततो ब्रवीति च भूयः ॥२२॥

The Upaniṣad प्रतिषेधति denies प्रकृत-एतावत्त्वं the limitation that is under discussion हि certainly; च and ब्रवीति speaks भूयः something more ततः after that (negation).

22. The Upaniṣad certainly denies the limitation that is being dealt with and then speaks of something more.

The Upaniṣad starts with the text, "Brahman has but two forms—gross and subtle, mortal and immortal, limited and unlimited, and defined and undefined" (Bṛ. II. iii. 1). Then having divided the five great (subtle) elements under two heads,[4] and having revealed such aspects as the possession of the colour of the turmeric by that essence of the subtle form, called the infinite Being (Puruṣa),[5] the text again goes on, "Now therefore the description (of Brahman): Not so, not so. Because there is no other and more appropriate description than this 'Not so' " (Bṛ. II. iii. 6). Now we ask, against what is this negation directed? For nothing is perceived here as having been pointed out by saying, "This is that", which can constitute the object of negation. But the use of the word "so" seems to indicate that something has been presented here as the object of negation. For in the text, "Not so, not so", the word "so" is used after the word "not"; and "so", usually used in connection with something proximate, is seen to be applied in the same way as "this", as for instance in such expressions as, "So has the teacher said". And the things we get near at hand here from the force of the context are the two forms of Brahman together with their ramifications. And Brahman is that which has the two forms.

Doubt: That being the position, the doubt arises in us: Does this negation deny the forms as well as the possessor of forms, or only one of them? Again, if either of the two is denied, then whether Brahman is denied keeping intact the forms, or are the forms denied, retaining Brahman?

Opponent: That being so, and both being the subject-matters under discussion, we apprehend that both are negated. Besides, we have here two negations, the phrase "not so" being used twice, from which fact the idea arises that by one of them the form of Brahman consisting of the phenomenal manifestations

[4] (1) Gross—earth, water, fire; (2) fine—air, space.

[5] Hiraṇyagarbha, the Being in the sun and the right eye, and identifying Himself with the organs, i.e. the subtle body, known otherwise as *Prāṇa*.

is denied, and by the other is denied Brahman, the possessor of the form. Or it may be that Brahman Itself, of which the two forms are the two aspects, is denied; for being beyond speech and mind, the existence of that Brahman cannot be conceived of, and hence It is a fit object of denial; but the phenomenal expressions are not fit to be denied as they come within the range of perception etc. The repetition (of "not so") is meant to show earnestness (or generation of conviction).

Vedāntin: In reply to this we say that so far as these alternatives go, the denial of both cannot be reasonable, for that would lead to nihilism. Something unreal is denied on the basis of something real, as for instance a snake etc. on a rope etc. And that is possible only if some positive entity is left over (after the denial). For should everything be denied, what other positive substratum will be left over? And unless something else outlives the denial, the thing sought to be denied, cannot be negated; and hence the latter thus becomes a reality, so that the contemplated denial itself becomes impossible. Besides, the denial of Brahman is not reasonable, for that would contradict the introduction made with, "I will tell you of Brahman" (Bṛ. III. i. 1), as also the condemnation contained in such texts as, "If anyone knows Brahman as non-existent, he himself becomes non-existent" (Tai. II. vi. 1), and the affirmation made in, "The Self is to be realized as existing" (Ka. II. iii. 13). That would also lead to overriding all the Upaniṣads. As for the statement that Brahman is beyond speech and mind, that is not meant to imply that Brahman is non-existent. For it is not logical to deny that very Brahman after establishing It with a great show of girding up one's loins, in such sentences of the Upaniṣads as, "The knower of Brahman attains the highest", "Brahman is Truth, Knowledge, Infinity" (Tai. II. i. 1); for as the popular saying has it, "Rather than wash away the mud, it is much better to avoid its touch from a distance". As a matter of fact, the text "Failing to reach which, words turn back with the mind" (Tai. II. ix. 1), presents only a process of propounding Brahman. The idea expressed is this: Brahman is beyond speech and mind; It cannot be classed with objects of knowledge; It is one's inmost Self; and It is by nature eternal, pure, intelligent, and free. Hence it is to be understood that the phenomenal expression alone of Brahman is denied, and Brahman Itself is left over. That very fact is stated in the aphorism, "The Upaniṣad certainly denies the limitation that is being dealt with" etc. The word "so" (*iti*) denies only that which is the topic under consideration, viz the forms of Brahman characterized as gross and subtle, which are definable as "this much", that is to say, which are limited. For these are the things under discussion and have been elaborated in the earlier texts under the headings divine and corporeal. And there is the other form growing out of this one. It consists of desires; it is constituted by the essence of the subtle aspect; it is referred to by the word Puruṣa; it subsists in the form of the subtle body; and it is shown with the help of the illustration of turmeric etc. For the subtle body, formed of the quintessence of the fine elements, cannot have a visible form. Thus it is understood that by the word "so" (*iti*), indicative of something near at hand, these very aspects of Brahman, consisting of phenomenal expression, are placed in apposition with "not", the word of denial. As for "Brahman", It is presented in the earlier text, with the sixth (genitive) case-ending, as a word qualifying "form" (in *Brahmaṇaḥ rūpam*—Brahman's form), but It is not presented in Its own right (as the subject of the sentence). And when after the two forms of Brahman have been elaborated, the curiosity arises to know the nature of the possessor of the forms, then commences the text with "Not so, not so" (Bṛ. II. iii. 6). From this it is ascertained that the underlying assumption in this text is that the denial of the forms is tantamount to a presentation of the true nature of Brahman; for all creation, based on that Brahman, is denied to be true by saying "Not so, not so". And it is but proper that all creation should be denied by saying "Not so, not so", since from such Upaniṣadic phrases as "originating only in name" (Ch. VI. i. 4) creation is known to be unreal; but not so can Brahman be denied, since It is the basis of all phenomena. And the misconception has no scope here as to why the scripture itself should first show the two aspects of Brahman, only to deny them the next moment contrary to the popular adage, "Rather than wash away the mud, it is much better to avoid its very contact from a distance". For this scripture does not present the two aspects of Brahman as subjects fit for being expounded, but it simply refers to these aspects that are superimposed on Brahman and are popularly well recognized; and this is done for the sake of denying them and establishing the real, pure nature of Brahman. Thus it is all beyond cavil. These two negatives deny respectively the two aspects, gross and subtle, according to their numeral order. Or it may be that the first negative denies the totality of elements, and the second negative, the totality of impressions. Or the "Not so, not so" is used in a repetitive sense, implying thereby that whatever is guessed on Brahman as "this much" has no reality. For should the negation apply only to the limited things already enumerated, the question may arise, "If this is not Brahman, what else is?" But when the "repetition" is used, all objects of knowledge become denied, and it follows that one's inmost Self, that is not an object of knowledge, is Brahman; thus the curiosity to know further ceases. Hence the conclusion is that the phenomenal expressions, imagined on Brahman, are denied, and Brahman stands out as outside the negation.

This conclusion is arrived at from the further consideration that after that denial it is stated again, "There is something other than this which is beyond" (Bṛ. II. iii. 6). Were the negation to end in mere non-existence, what else could have been referred to by the text as being different and beyond? On this interpretation, the words (of the aphorism) are to be construed thus: "Having taught Brahman with the words 'Not so, not so' (ibid.), the Upaniṣad explains that instruction over again."

What is the meaning of "Not so, not so"?

The meaning is this: Since there is surely nothing besides this Brahman, therefore Brahman is called "Not so, not so". It does not mean that Brahman Itself does not exist. And that very fact is shown by asserting that a Brahman does exist which is beyond all else and which is not denied.

The words of the Upaniṣad may, however, be construed thus: "Because there is no other (and more appropriate) description than this, therefore it is called 'Not so, not so'" (ibid.), the meaning being, "Because apart from teaching by way of negating the phenomenal world of manifestations, there is no better description of Brahman". Then in that case the words of the aphorism, "(The text) speaks of something more than that" should be taken to mean "Its name"; for the text speaks about the name thus, "Now is Its name, 'The Truth of truth'. The vital force is truth, and It is the Truth of that" (ibid.). That becomes proper if the negation leads to (i.e. stops short of) Brahman. For if the negation culminates in non-existence, what could have been mentioned as the "Truth of truth"? Hence our definite conclusion is that this denial leads to Brahman and does not end in non-existence.

तदव्यक्तमाह हि ॥२३॥

तत् That (Brahman) is अव्यक्तम् unmanifest, हि for आह (the Upaniṣad) says (so).

23. *That Brahman is unmanifest, for the Upaniṣad says so.*

Opponent: If Brahman, different from and superior to the manifold world of manifestation that has been denied, does exist, why is It not perceived?

Vedāntin: The answer is: Because It is not manifest, because It is supersensuous,·It being the witness of all. For the Upaniṣads declare It thus in the texts: "It is not comprehended through the eye, nor through speech, nor through the other senses; nor is It attained through austerity or *karma*" (Mu. III. i. 3); "This Self is that which has been described as 'Not so, not so'. It is imperceptible, for It is never perceived" (Bṛ. III. ix. 26); "That which cannot be perceived and grasped" (Mu. I. i. 6); "Whenever an aspirant gets fearlessly established in this changeless, bodiless, inexpressible, and supportless Brahman" (Tai. II. vii. 1), and so on. The Smṛti also says, "He is said to be undetermined, unthinkable, immutable" (Gītā, II. 25), and so on.

अपि संराधने प्रत्यक्षानुमानाभ्याम् ॥२४॥

अपि Moreover, (Brahman is realized) संराधने in *samādhi* (perfect meditation or absorption) प्रत्यक्ष-अनुमानाभ्याम् as is known from direct revelation and inference.

24. Moreover, Brahman is realized in samādhi, as is known from direct revelation and inference.

Moreover, the Yogins realize, during *saṁrādhana*, this Self (i.e. Brahman) which is free from the entire universe of phenomenal manifestation and is supersensuous. *Saṁrādhana* means the act of devotion, contemplation, deep meditation, and such other practices (e.g. *japa* etc.).

Opponent: How, again, is it known that they experience this during such adoration?

Vedāntin: "From direct revelation and inference", that is to say, from Vedic texts and Smṛtis. To quote from the Vedic texts: "The self-existent Lord destroyed (i.e. incapacitated) the outgoing senses. Therefore one sees the outer things and not the inner Self. A rare discriminating man, desiring for immortality, turns his eyes away and then sees the indwelling Self" (Ka. II. i. 1), "Since one becomes purified in mind through the favourableness of the intellect, therefore can one see that indivisible Self through meditation" (Mu. III. i. 8), and so on. There are also Smṛti texts, "Salutation to that Effulgence, the Self, that is realizable through Yoga, and is seen by those who practise meditation, who are free from sleep (lethargy), who have controlled their senses. The Yogins realize that Lord who is eternal", and similar texts.

Opponent: On the assumption of a relationship between the entity meditated on and the meditator, the supreme Self and the individual Self become separated.

Vedāntin: The reply is, No.

प्रकाशादिवच्चावैशेष्यं प्रकाशश्च कर्मण्यभ्यासात् ॥२५॥

च And प्रकाशः the effulgent One (i.e. Self) (appears to be different) कर्मणि during activity (like meditation) प्रकाश-आदि-वत् as is the case with light etc.; च yet (naturally there is) अ-वैशेष्यम् non-difference; अभ्यासात् as is evident from repetition.

25. And the effulgent Self appears to be different during activity, as is the case with light etc.; yet (intrinsically) there is non-difference as is evident from repetition (of "That thou art").

As light, space, the sun, etc. appear to be diversified in relation to the activity taking place in such limiting adjuncts as a finger, a pail, water, etc., and yet they do not give up their natural unity, so also this difference in the Self is a creation of limiting adjuncts; but in Its own essence It is the one Self alone. And thus it is that the non-difference of the individual soul and the supreme Self is established repeatedly (in such texts as "That thou art"—Ch. VI. viii-xvi).

अतोऽनन्तेन तथा हि लिंगम् ॥२६॥

अत: Hence (unity) अनन्तेन with Infinity; हि because तथा such (is) लिंगम् the indicatory mark.

26. Hence (the individual gets) unity with the Infinite; for such is the indicatory mark (in the Upaniṣad).

"Hence", too, for this further reason that non-difference is natural whereas difference is a creation of ignorance, the individual destroys ignorance through knowledge and attains unity with the supreme, eternal, conscious Self. "For such is the indicatory mark"—contained in such texts as, "Anyone who knows that supreme Brahman becomes Brahman indeed" (Mu. III. ii. 9), "Being but Brahman, he is absorbed in Brahman" (Bṛ. IV. iv. 6), and so on.

उभयव्यपदेशात्त्वहिकुण्डलवत् ॥२७॥

तु But उभय-व्यपदेशात् since both (difference and non-difference) are mentioned, (the relationship is) अहि-कुण्डल-वत् as between a snake and its coil.

27. But since both difference and non-difference are mentioned, the relationship (between the supreme Self and the individual is) as that between the snake and its coil.

With regard to that very relationship between the entity meditated on and the meditator, another view is adduced with the idea of clearing our own. In some places a difference between the individual soul and the supreme Self is mentioned, as in, "Therefore can one see that indivisible Self through meditation" (Mu. III. i. 8), where the difference exists like that between the subject and object of meditation or between the seer and the seen; in "reaches the self-effulgent Puruṣa that is higher than the higher Māyā" (Mu. III. ii. 8), where the difference is as between the attainer and the goal to be attained; in "who controls all beings from within" (Bṛ. III. vii. 15), where exists the difference as between the ruler and the ruled. Elsewhere, again, the non-difference of those very ones is mentioned, as in, "That thou art" (Ch. VI. viii-xvi), "I am Brahman" (Bṛ. I. iv. 10), "This is your Self that is within all" (Bṛ. III. iv. 1), "This is the Internal Ruler, your own immortal Self" (Bṛ. III. vii. 3-22). Now in the face of this dual mention, if non-difference alone be accepted to the exclusion of difference, the mention of difference will be left without any substance. So from the mention of both difference and non-difference, the reality here must be like the snake and its coil. As in the illustration, the snake in itself is non-different, but it differs in its having a coil, or a hood, or an extended posture; so also is the case here (with Brahman).

प्रकाशाश्रयवद्वा तेजस्त्वात् ॥२८॥

वा Or प्रकाश-आश्रय-वत् like light and its source तेजस्त्वात् (both) being effulgence.

28. Or they are like light and its source, both being but effulgence.

Or this is to be understood on the analogy of light and its substratum. Just as the sunlight and its substratum, the sun, are luminous, and not entirely different, both being equally effulgent, and yet they are thought of as different, similar is the case here.

पूर्ववद्वा ॥२९॥

29. Or (the relationship between the individual and the supreme Self is) as already shown.

Or it may be just as it was presented earlier by saying, "And the effulgent Self appears to be different during activity, as is the case with light etc." (III. ii. 25); for on that view alone bondage is a creation of ignorance, so that the achievement of liberation through knowledge becomes justifiable. If on the other hand, it is understood that the individual soul is under bondage in a real sense, and that it is a certain state of the supreme Self on the analogy of the snake and its coil, or a part of that Self on the analogy of the light and its source, then since a bondage that is real cannot be removed, the scripture speaking of liberation will become useless. And it is not a fact that the Upaniṣads declare both difference and non-difference as equally valid in the present case; on the contrary the Upaniṣads declare non-difference alone as the view to be established, while with the idea of speaking of something else (i.e. non-difference), they merely refer to difference as a thing already conventionally recognized. Hence the real conclusion is this: There is no difference "as is the case with light etc."

प्रतिषेधाच्च ॥३०॥

30. And on account of the denial.

And this conclusion is confirmed by the fact that the scripture denies the existence of any other conscious entity apart from the supreme Self, in texts like, "There is no other witness but Him" (Bṛ. III. vii. 23), and so on, as also in, "Now therefore the description of Brahman, 'Not so, not so'," (Bṛ. II. iii. 6), "That Brahman is without prior or posterior, without interior or exterior" (Bṛ. II. v. 19). Since this variety of phenomenal manifestation is denied to exist separately from Brahman, and since Brahman alone is left over as the only ultimate reality, therefore we understand that this alone is the established conclusion.

Topic 7: Brahman One without a Second

From the fact that the Upaniṣads are at variance a *doubt* arises as to whether any reality exists or does not exist which is higher than this Brahman that is ascertained to be devoid of the entire variety of phenomenal manifestations. Certain sentences, when taken in an apparent sense, seem to prove some other entity higher even than Brahman. This is an attempt at refuting those texts.

परमतः सेतून्मानसम्बन्धभेदव्यपदेशेभ्यः ॥३१॥

परम् Superior अतः to this (Brahman) सेतु-उन्मान-सम्बन्ध-भेद-व्यपदेशेभ्यः because of the mention of embankment, measure (i.e. limitation), connection, and difference.

31. There is some entity superior to this Brahman, because of the mention of embankment, measure, connection, and difference.

Opponent: There should be an entity higher than this Brahman.

Why?

Because of the reference (in the Upaniṣad) to embankment, magnitude, connection, and difference. Of these the mention of the term embankment occurs in, "Now then, that which is the Self is an embankment, a sustainer (or impounder)" (Ch. VIII. iv. 1), where Brahman, referred to by the word Self, is declared to be an embankment. And the word embankment is in vogue in the world in the sense of a barrage of earth and timber to check the flow of a current of water. Here also the word embankment, having been used for the Self, leads us to understand that, as in the case of the ordinary embankment, something other than it exists, so also something other than the Self, called the embankment, does exist. This is confirmed by the use of the term "crossing over" in, "having crossed over the embankment" (Ch. VIII. iv. 2), from which it is gathered that just as in life somebody crosses (a stream) over the embankment to reach solid ground, which is other than the embankment, so also one crosses over this embankment, that is the Self, to reach something that is not the embankment of the Self.

There occurs also the mention of measurement (i.e. limited size) as in, "This Brahman, that is such, has four feet" (Ch. III. xviii. 2), "Brahman has eight hoofs, sixteen parts"[6] (Ch. IV. v). It is also seen in common life that whatever can be measured (or counted) to be so much, as for instance (the coins called) *kārṣāpaṇas*, presupposes the existence of something other than itself; so also as Brahman has been measured, there must be something other than Itself.

Thus also there is the mention of connection: "O amiable one, the individual soul then becomes unified with Existence" (Ch. VI. viii. 1), "the embodied soul" (Tai. II. iii. 1), "fully embraced by the supreme Self" (Bṛ. IV. iii. 21). And limited things are seen to come into contact with a limited thing, as for instance human beings with a city. The Upaniṣad mentions the connection of the individuals with Brahman in sleep. Therefore it is understood that there is something unlimited which is superior to Brahman.

The mention of difference also leads to the same idea. Thus in the text, "Now then the golden (effulgent) infinite Being that is seen in the sun" (Ch. I. vi. 6), the Lord residing in the sun is mentioned; and then the Lord residing in the eye is mentioned separately in, "And the infinite Being that is seen in the eye" (Ch. I. vii. 5). Then the forms etc. of the Being in the sun are ascribed to the Being in the eye as well: "Of this latter one the form is the same as of the former; He has the same knuckles as the former, and the same name as His" (ibid.). The text also refers to the limited Godhood of both of them: of the former it is spoken in, "And He rules over the worlds that are above the sun, and the things dear to the gods" (Ch. I. vi. 8); of the latter it is shown in, "And He rules over the worlds that are below (the earth) and the things dear to men"

[6] The first part consists of the four directions; the second of earth, sky, heaven, and sea; the third of fire, sun, moon, and lightning; the fourth of eye, ear, speech, and mind. Each foot has two hoofs; thus there are eight hoofs, and each foot has four parts, thus making up sixteen parts. The feet are called bright, unlimited, luminous, and spacious respectively.

(Ch. I. vii. 6). This is like saying, "This is the domain of the king of Magadha, and this of the king of Videha".

Vedāntin: The conclusion having been drawn from these references to embankment etc. that there is some entity superior to Brahman, it is being explained.

सामान्यात्तु ॥३२॥

32. But (the Self is referred to as an embankment) on account of similarity.

The use of the word "but" rules out the conclusion shown. Nothing whatsoever can exist separately from Brahman, for that lacks proof. As a matter of fact, we do not find any proof of the existence of anything else. For it has been ascertained that anything that has an origin derives its birth etc. from Brahman. An effect is non-different from a cause; and nothing apart from Brahman can exist that is birthless, because it is definitely stated thus: "O amiable one, before creation all this was but Brahman, one without a second" (Ch. VI. ii. 1). And because the assertion is made by the Upaniṣads that all can be known when the One is known, nothing can be conceived of as existing apart from Brahman.

Opponent: Was it not pointed out by us that the references to embankment etc. indicate the existence of some entity different from Brahman?

Vedāntin: In answer it is said, no. As for the reference to the embankment, it cannot prove the existence of anything outside Brahman; for the text simply says that the Self is an embankment, but it does not also aver that there is something beyond It. Now the ground for your assumption of something superior is that the idea of embankment cannot arise unless there is something different from it. But this is not logical. This queer assumption of something unknown is sheer dogmatism. Moreover, if on finding the Self being referred to as an embankment, one can assume something outside this embankment on the analogy of the commonly known embankment, then one may as well assume earth and timber as the constituents of this embankment (which is the Self). But this is not proper, since that would contradict the texts about birthlessness etc. So the proper position that emerges is that the word embankment is used with regard to the Self on account of Its similarity with the embankment, the point of similarity of the Self with the embankment being that the Self holds together the world (as its Inner Ruler) and maintains its boundaries (of norms, duties, etc.). In this way the Self under discussion is praised by saying that it is like an embankment. As for the expression, "having crossed over the embankment" (Ch. VIII. iv. 2), the literal sense of going beyond being impossible here, the meaning that stands out is that of "attaining", as for instance the expression, "He has crossed over grammar" means "He has mastered it", but not gone beyond.

बुद्धयर्थः पादवत् ॥३३॥

बुद्धि-अर्थः For the sake of intellectual grasp **पाद-वत्** like the feet.

33. For the sake of intellectual grasp (Brahman's magnitude is spoken of) just like the feet (of the mind or of space), (or the quarters of the kārṣāpaṇa).

As for the argument that something superior exists on account of the mention of magnitude, our answer is this: Even the reference to measure is not meant for conveying the idea of some entity other than Brahman.

What is it meant for then?

It is meant for intellectual grasp, that is to say, for the sake of meditation. How can a man ever have any steady idea that Brahman is possessed of four feet, eight hoofs, and sixteen parts? Hence it is (for the sake of meditation) that some magnitudes are merely fancied about Brahman with the help of changeful things. Not that all men can fix their minds steadily on Brahman, changeless and infinite as It is, for men's intellects may be sharp, mediocre, or dull. It is like the imagination of the four feet, as it is in the case of mind and space, which are mentioned as the two symbols of Brahman on the corporeal and divine planes. As speech (nose, eye, ear), etc. are fancied as the four feet in the case of mind, and fire, (air, sun, and direction), etc. as the four feet in the case of space, so also is the case here. Or *pādavat* means like quarters. As in the case of (the coin called) *kārṣāpaṇa*, it is fancied to be divided into four quarters in order to facilitate transaction through it, inasmuch as all cannot use a whole *kārṣāpaṇa* in all kinds of dealing everywhere, the volumes of sale and purchase being variable, similarly in the infinite Brahman (magnitude is imagined for the sake of meditation).

स्थानविशेषात्प्रकाशादिवत् ॥३४॥

स्थान-विशेषात् On account of particular environments (i.e. limiting adjuncts) प्रकाश-आदि-वत् as in the case of light etc.

34. (Connection and difference are mentioned about Brahman) from the point of view of limiting adjuncts, as in the case of light etc.

The two objections about the mention of connection and difference are met in this aphorism. The statement, too, that was made that from the references to connection and difference it follows that something superior to Brahman exists, is wrong, for these references can be possible for the very same thing from the points of view of particular situations. As for the text referring to connection, it means this: Particularized knowledge arises from the contact of the Self with particular environments consisting of such limiting adjuncts as the intellect. When that particularized knowledge ceases on the cessation of the limiting adjuncts, that cessation is metaphorically spoken of as the (individual soul's) contact with the Self; this is spoken from the point of view of the limiting adjunct, but not from any idea of limitation. So also the reference to difference is made from the point of view of the diversity of the limiting adjuncts of Brahman, but not from Its own point of view. "As in the case of light etc." is said by way of furnishing an illustration. Just as a single light, be it of the sun or the moon, undergoes diversity owing to contact with conditioning factors, but it is said to become united with its source when the conditioning factors are removed, and the same light is said to be different owing to the difference in the conditioning factors, so also is the case here. Or it is like the mention of connection and difference from the point of view of mere limiting adjuncts in such cases as the spaces within the eye of a needle, a loop etc.

उपपत्तेश्च ॥३५॥

35. And because (such a position alone is) logically justifiable.

And this kind of connection alone, and not of any other kind, is logically sustainable; for it is self-identity that is spoken of as this relation in, "He attains his own Self" (Ch. VI. viii. 1). And this is so, since one's own nature is inalienable. The relation here cannot be like that between a man and a town. But precisely because the true nature has a covering of limiting adjuncts, the text, "He attains his own Self", can be logically sustained. So also the difference cannot be of any other kind, for that would contradict the oneness of God well recognized in numerous Upaniṣadic passages. It is thus also that the Upaniṣad explains how there can be a mention of difference in the case of the very same space owing to differences of environment, in such texts as, "The space that is outside a man" (Ch. III. xii. 7), "The space that is within a man" (Ch. III. xii. 8), and "The space that is within the heart" (Ch. III. xii. 9).

तथान्यप्रतिषेधात् ॥३६॥

तथा Similarly अन्य-प्रतिषेधात् from the denial of all else.

36. Similarly from the denial of everything else (it follows that there is nothing but Brahman).

Having thus set at naught all the reasons, like the use of terms like embankment, that were advanced by the opponent, the aphorist now concludes by supporting his own position by another reason: "Similarly from the denial of everything else", too, it is understood that there is nothing else superior to Brahman. Thus there are the texts, "It is He who exists below, it is I who exist below" (Ch. VII. xxv. 1), "It is the Self that is below" (Ch. VII. xxv. 2), "All oust one who knows it as different from the Self" (Bṛ. II. iv. 6), "All this is but Brahman" (Mu. II. ii. 11), "All this is but the Self" (Ch. VII. xxv. 2), "There is no diversity whatever in It" (Bṛ. IV. iv. 19), "That beyond which there is nothing either superior or inferior (prior or posterior)" (Śv. III. 9), "That Brahman is without prior or posterior, without interior or exterior" (Bṛ. II. v. 19). These and such other texts, which occur in the contexts dealing with Brahman Itself and cannot be interpreted otherwise, rule out any thing other than Brahman. And from the text that Brahman is in all creatures (Ka. II. ii. 9-11, Bṛ. II. v. 19) it is understood that there is no other Self within the supreme Self.

अनेन सर्वगतत्वमायामशब्दादिभ्यः ॥३७॥

अनेन Hereby सर्व-गतत्वम् omnipresence आयाम-शब्द-आदिभ्यः on the strength of words like extension etc.

37. *Hereby (is established) the omnipresence (of the Self), (as is known) on the strength of (Upaniṣadic) words like extension and other sources (i.e. Smṛti and logic).*

"Hereby", that is to say, from the refutation of (the arguments based on) the mention of terms like embankment etc., and with the help of the negation of all other things, "is also established the omnipresence of the Self". For it cannot be proved otherwise, since on the assumption that the terms like embankment etc. are mentioned in a literal sense, the Self will become a limited entity, inasmuch as the embankments etc. are themselves limited in that sense. Similarly, if the denial of all other things (by the scriptures) be not a fact, the Self will become a limited entity, since one thing becomes delimited by another. And the omnipresence of the Self is known from such terms as extensiveness, the word extension being used in the sense of pervasiveness. Texts like the following, "The Space (Brahman) within the heart is as extensive as the Space outside" (Ch. VIII. i. 3), "He is omnipresent like space and eternal", "He is greater than heaven" (Ch. III. xiv. 3), "greater than space" (Ś. B. X. vi. 3.2.), "This one is eternal, omnipresent, steady, unchanging" (Gītā, II. 24), and similar Upaniṣadic and Smṛti texts, as well as logic, teach the omnipresence of the Self.

Topic 8: Fruits of Action

Of that Brahman Itself another characteristic is being described that is in evidence during phenomenal existence in which occurs a division between the ordainer and the ordained.

फलमत उपपत्तेः ॥३८॥

फलम् Fruit (of action) अतः (comes) from this one, उपपत्तेः on grounds of logic.

38. The fruit of action is from Him, this being the logical position.

Doubt: With regard to the well-known results of actions of creatures which fall under three classes—the desirable, the undesirable, and the mixed—and belong to the state of transmigration, the thought arises as to whether they spring from the *karmas* (rites etc.) or from God.

Vedāntin: While in this predicament, the reasonable position is that "the fruit (of action)" should be "from this one", from God.

Why?

"This being the logical position." Since He presides over everything, and since He is fully aware of the specific environment and time conducive to the different kinds of creation, preservation, and dissolution, it is but logical that He should ordain the fruits of works for the people according to their merit. But it does not stand to reason that fruits can come at some future time from actions which get destroyed the next moment; because something cannot come out of nothing.

Opponent: It may well be that an action, even while it is being destroyed produces a result proper to itself, during the time that it lasts, and then only it is destroyed; and that result is attained by the agent of the act at some distant time.

Vedāntin: That too does not remove the difficulty; for there can be no such thing as a result till the agent of the act comes to possess it, inasmuch as any happiness or sorrow experienced by any soul at any time is recognized in the world to be such a result relatively to that very time. And common people do not recognize any happiness or sorrow unrelated to a soul to be a result. Again, if it be maintained that though the result may not issue just after the action, it can issue (in the future) out of the unseen potency emerging out of the act, that too is unjustifiable, for potency, which is inert like stocks and stones, cannot act unless stimulated by some conscious agent. Besides, such an unseen potency lacks any valid proof.

Opponent: Presumption from the seen result (*arthāpatti*) is a proof in its support.

Vedāntin: No; for God having been proved to be the ordainer of results, any presumption is ruled out of court.

श्रुतत्वाच्च ॥३९॥

39. (God is the ordainer of results) for the further reason that the Upaniṣads say so.

It is not merely on grounds of reason that we think of God as the ordainer of results.

On what more grounds then?

We think of God as the ordainer of results, because that is how the Upaniṣads speak. For instance, there is the text, "That great birthless Self is the bestower of food all round and the giver of wealth," (Bṛ. IV. iv. 24), as also other texts of this class.

धर्मं जैमिनिरत एव ॥४०॥

अत: एव For these very reasons जैमिनि: Jaimini (thinks) धर्मं virtue (i.e. scriptural conduct), (to be the cause).

40. For these very reasons Jaimini considers virtuous deeds to be the yielder of results.

Mīmāṁsaka: "The teacher Jaimini, however, considers virtuous deeds to be the yielder of results", "for these very reasons", on the authority of the Vedas and reason. This fact is mentioned in the Vedas in "One wishing for heaven shall perform a sacrifice" (Tāṇḍya), and similar texts. That text contains an injunction, and since an injunction is understood to have an object in view, the sacrifice becomes the object. From this it becomes obvious that the sacrifice is the producer of heaven; for else this sacrifice would find no performer, so that the instruction about it would become meaningless.

Objection: Has not this viewpoint been refuted by saying that *karma* that has but a momentary existence cannot produce such a result?

Mīmāṁsaka: That is no defect, since there is the Vedic authority. If the Vedic authority is accepted, one has to think in the way that would justify the kind of relation between action and the result of action that is mentioned in the Vedas. Unless the action, while undergoing destruction, produces some unseen potency, it cannot produce its result after an interval. Hence the inference to be drawn is that there is such a thing called unseen potency which may be either some subtle state of the action itself or some previous (seed) state of the result. In this way the position stated earlier becomes logical. But the theory that God ordains the results is illogical. For one uniform cause cannot produce variegated results; that will lead to partiality and cruelty on God's part and the performance of action will be useless. Hence the conclusion is that results are produced by virtuous deeds alone.

पूर्वं तु बादरायणो हेतुव्यपदेशात् ॥४१॥

तु But बादरायण: Bādarāyaṇa (considers) पूर्वम् the earlier One हेतु-व्यपदेशात् owing to (His) mention as the cause (even of action).

41. But Bādarāyaṇa considers the earlier One (viz God) (as the bestower of results), because He is mentioned as the cause of even action.

But the teacher Bādarāyaṇa considers the earlier One, i.e. God Himself, as the bestower of results. The word "but" refutes the views that the result is obtained either from the action itself or the unseen potency of action. The accepted conclusion is that the result comes from God, be it either by taking into account the action itself or the unseen potency, as it may.

Why?

"Because He is mentioned as the cause". For God is presented as the cause both by way of making others act virtuously or viciously and of bestowing the results, in the text, "It is He Himself who makes him do a good deed whom He wishes to raise up from these worlds; and it is He Himself who makes him do a bad deed whom He wishes to throw down" (Kau. III. 8). This fact is mentioned in the Gītā as well, "Whichever divine form a devotee wants to worship with faith, I ordain for him unswerving faith in that very form. Endowed with that faith, he continues in the worship of that form, and obtains from it the results he desires, as ordained by Me" (Gītā. VII. 21-22). In all the Upaniṣads creations are declared as the acts of God. And God's bestowing of results consists precisely in His creating the creatures according to individual merits. The defects of the impossibility of the emergence of variegated results from the very same cause, and so on, do not arise since God acts by taking into account the efforts made by the creatures.

SECTION III

TOPIC 1: SAMENESS OF MEDITATION

सर्ववेदान्तप्रत्ययं चोदनाद्यविशेषात् ॥१॥

सर्व-वेदान्त-प्रत्ययम् Any (particular) conception (for meditation) imparted in all the Upaniṣads (is the same) **चोदना-आदि-अविशेषात्** on account of the sameness of injunction etc.

1. Any (particular) conception for meditation (vijñāna) imparted in all the Upaniṣads is the same on account of the sameness of the injunction etc.

The reality of Brahman, that is to be known, has been explained. Now is being considered whether the *vijñānas* differ according to the different Upaniṣads or not.

Opponent: Has it not been ascertained that the Brahman to be known is devoid of the differences of priority and posteriority (i.e. cause and effect), and It is homogeneous like a lump of salt? So how can a consideration about the difference or non-difference of *vijñānas* (conceptions about Brahman) arise? For it cannot be that like the variety of rites and rituals, the Upaniṣads seek to teach any multiplicity about Brahman as well; for Brahman is one with a uniform characteristic. It is not possible to have different kinds of *vijñāna* of the same Brahman that has a single uniform nature. To know a thing otherwise than what it is cannot be anything but erroneous. Should the different Upaniṣads, however, teach diverse conceptions about the same Brahman, one of these conceptions will be correct while the rest will be erroneous, so that this will open the gate to a loss of faith in the Upaniṣads. Hence no such misconception should be entertained that the conceptions about Brahman differ in different Upaniṣads. It is not also possible to affirm an identity of the conceptions on the basis of the uniformity of the injunctions, for the knowledge of Brahman is such that it cannot be indicated by any injunction. Under the aphorism, "But that Brahman is known from the Upaniṣads, because of their becoming connected with Brahman as their main purport" (I. i. 4), the teacher (Vyāsa) said that the knowledge of Brahman arises from (Vedic) texts about Brahman which do not convey the sense of any injunction, and which culminate in the realization of the thing itself. So how can this discussion about difference and non-difference be started?

Vedāntin: That is being stated. This discussion about difference and non-difference of *vijñānas* relates to the qualified Brahman and to *Prāṇa* etc., so that there is no defect. For in this field there is a possibility of difference and non-difference of meditations just as much as in the case of the rites etc. Like ritualistic actions, the meditations are also spoken of as having seen and unseen results. Some of them lead to liberation by stages by way of giving rise to perfect knowledge ultimately. With regard to these there is a possibility of the discussion whether a particular *vijñāna* differs from Upaniṣad to Upaniṣad or it does not.

As to that, the reasons from the *opponent's standpoint* are being adduced: To start with then, names are well known to stand for different conceptions, as in the case of such designations as *jyotir* (light, indicating the Jyotiṣṭoma sacrifice). Here also as regards the meditations, enjoined in the different Upaniṣads, we meet with such differences of names as Taittrīyaka, Vājasaneyaka, Kauthūmaka, Kauṣītaka, Śaṭyāyanaka, and so on. Similarly also the difference of form is well known to indicate a difference of rites, as in such texts, "The coagulated milk (got by mixing curd with hot milk) is for the Viśvadevas (all gods), the cheese-water is to be offered to the sun"[1]. And here, (as regards the meditations), a difference of forms is in evidence; for instance, in some recensions they read of a sixth and entirely different fire in the context of the meditation on the five fires, whereas others have only five. So also in the parable of *Prāṇa* etc., some have a fewer number of the organs such as that

[1] The assumption is that the second portion, "cheese-water" etc. is not just an appendage of the *Viśvedeva* sacrifice, but it suggests a different sacrifice.

of speech etc., while others have a greater number. So also it is argued that a special attribute is suggestive of a difference in rites as in such cases as the Kārīrī sacrifice.[2] In the context of *vijñānas* also, the mention of special attributes is met with, as for instance, the vow of holding fire on head, enjoined for the followers of the Atharva Veda (Mu. III. ii. 10). Thus also other tests like repetition, (met with in the Pūrva-Mīmāṁsā), which mark out one act from another, are to be suitably applied here as well. Hence the *vijñānas* differ from Upaniṣad to Upaniṣad.

Vedāntin: Such being the position, we say: "The *vijñānas* (conceptions for meditation) imparted in all the Upaniṣads" must be the same in the respective Upaniṣads.

Why?

"On account of the sameness of the injunction etc.", the "etc." being used for implying the reasons (viz connection, form, and name) that determine non-difference, as they are contained in the aphorism stating the accepted view in that section of the Pūrva-Mīmāṁsā that deals with the texts of other branches (of the Vedas). The meaning is that the meditations are the same because of the similarity of connection, form, injunction, and name. Even as in the case of the same Agnihotra sacrifice, though occurring in the different branches of the Vedas, the same kind of human effort is enjoined by saying "one shall sacrifice", similarly the injunction of the followers of the Vājasaneya branch is, "He who knows (i.e. meditates on) that which is the oldest and greatest" (Bṛ. VI. i. 1), and similar is the injunction of the Chandogas (Ch. V. i. 1). The connection with the result also is the same, which is, "He becomes the oldest and the greatest among his relatives" (Bṛ. VI. i. 1). And the form of the *vijñāna* in both the places is the same, viz that the principal *Prāṇa* is possessed of the special qualities of being the oldest and the greatest. Just as the materials and the deities determine the form (or nature) of the sacrifice, so also it is to be known that

[2] Students of the texts about the Kārīrī sacrifice (meant for rainfall), who belong to the Taittirīya branch, eat on the ground, but not so the others. Some, when reading of the sacrificial fire, carry the water jar of the teachers, others do not. Now such differences in conduct cannot be useless. Hence these sacrifices differ according to their attributes.

the form of the *vijñāna* (is determined by the object, viz the reality called *Prāṇa*). For the *vijñāna* is stamped according to the principle meditated on. The name too is the same in both places, namely "the meditation on *Prāṇa*". Hence the *vijñānas* are known to be the same in all the Upaniṣadic concepts of meditation. The same interpretation is to be applied to all such meditations, as the meditation on the five fires, the meditation on Vaiśvānara, the *Śāṇḍilya-Vidyā*, and so on.

As for the argument that (differences in) names, forms etc. apparently imply differences, that was refuted in the Pūrva-Mīmāṁsā under the aphorisms starting with, "Rites do not differ, just because of the occurrence of different names, for they are not used as names for enjoined rites"[3] (XI. iv. 10).

Apprehending another possible objection, the aphorist refutes that as well:

भेदान्नेति चेन्नैकस्यामपि ॥२॥

भेदात् Owing to difference (in subsidiary matters) न (the *vijñānas* are) not the same इति चेत् if such be the view न not (so) एकस्याम् अपि (for) even in the same *vijñāna* (differences in details are possible).

2. *If it be said that the vijñānas cannot be the same owing to the difference in details, then not so, for difference can occur even in the same vijñāna.*

Opponent: It may well be that the sameness of the *vijñānas* in all the Upaniṣads cannot be logically upheld on account of the differences in details. Thus it is seen that when dealing with the meditation on the five fires, the followers of the Vājasaneya branch mention a sixth fire thus, "This fire becomes his fire" etc. (Bṛ. VI. ii. 14). The Chandogas do not mention it, but they conclude with the number five: "Now then, he who knows (i.e. meditates on) these five fires thus" (Ch. V. x. 10). And how can the meditations be the same for both those who have

[3] The names Kāṭhaka, Kalāpaka, for instance, are not the names of the rites, but have reference to books. Even slight differences in form also do not make the rites different. The special characteristics mentioned there relate to study and not to any rite.

that additional factor and those who have not? It is not possible to understand that there should be a combination of the details (found in both the places for the same thing), since the number five becomes irreconcilable. Similarly in the parable of *Prāṇa*, the Chandogas read of four other *prāṇas*, viz speech, eye, ear, and mind, over and above the *Prāṇa* that is the greatest, whereas the Vājasaneyins read of a fifth as well in, "The seed is Prajāti (having the power of generation). He who knows it to be such becomes enriched with children and animals" (Bṛ. VI. i. 6). Moreover, the entity to be meditated on differs according as something is added to or dropped out[4]; and from the difference of the entity meditated on, the meditation itself differs, just as much as the sacrifices differ according to the difference in their deities and accessories.

Vedāntin: That is nothing damaging, since this kind of variation in details is admissible in the very same meditation. Although (on account of the irreconcilability of the number five) the sixth fire cannot be added (by taking it from elsewhere), still the five fires counting from heaven being in evidence in both the places, there cannot be a difference in the meditation, just as the Atirātra sacrifice does not differ in spite of taking up or not taking up the sacrificial vessel called Ṣoḍaśī[5]. Moreover, the Chandogas also read of a sixth fire: "When he departs for attaining the world earned by his merit, they carry him to the (funeral) fire itself" (Ch. V. ix. 2). The Vājasaneyins, however, in their eagerness to eliminate (from the funeral fire) the imagination of smoke, faggot, etc. that are associated with the imaginary five fires, read thus: "The (material) fire becomes his (i.e. dead man's) fire, the (material) fuel his fuel" etc. (Bṛ. VI. ii. 14). That is only by way of a restatement of a commonly known fact.[6] Or even if this (sixth) fire be meant for meditation, then

[4] *Āvāpa*—adding something from another injunction, and *udvāpa*—rejecting something enjoined somewhere.

[5] In regard to this sacrifice two contradictory injunctions about using and not using the Ṣoḍaśī are met with; still the Mīmāmsakas argue that the sacrifice is the same, the use of the Ṣoḍaśī being optional.

[6] That the common fire burns the dead meditator. This is not a fire to be meditated on, the five foregoing ones only being meant for that.

the Chandogas also can add this trait to theirs. And it should not be apprehended that the number five will stand in the way; for this number, enumerating the five imaginary fires (involved in the meditation based on superimposition), is a restatement of the fact already known (earlier that the fires are five), so that it is not a part of any injunction. Hence there is no conflict. Similarly in the anecdote of the *Prāṇa* and so on, it is nothing contradictory to add somewhere a new trait. It should not be apprehended that either the entity meditated on or the meditation differs in accordance as a detail is added to or given up; for though a certain small trait may be added or deducted from the entity meditated on, yet the meditation is recognized to be the same from the (persistence of the) greater quantum of the thing to be known. Hence the meditations are the same in the different Upaniṣads.

स्वाध्यायस्य तथात्वेन हि समाचारेऽधिकाराच्च सववच्च तन्नियमः ॥३॥

(The rite of carrying fire on the head is an appendage) स्वाध्यायस्य of Vedic study; हि because समाचारे in the *Samācāra* (it is enjoined) तथात्वेन as being so, च also अधिकारात् on account of competence, च and तत्-नियमः that regulation (is) सववत् as in the case of libations.

3. The rite of carrying fire on the head is an appendage of Vedic study, because it is stated to be so in the Samācāra, and also because of competence. And that regulation is like that about libations.

It was argued that since the followers of the Atharva Veda acknowledge the vow of holding fire on the head, (sitting amidst fires), etc. as necessary preconditions for the acquisition of knowledge, while others do not do so, therefore the knowledge (*vidyā*) differs. That is being refuted. This is a trait of the Vedic study, but not of knowledge.

How is this known?

Because the followers of the Atharva Veda read of this also as a Vedic vow "stated to be so", mentioned as a feature of the study of the Veda, in the *Samācāra*, in the book imparting instruction about Vedic vows. And from the text, "One that has not fulfilled the vow (of holding fire on the head) does not read this" (Mu. III. ii. 11), which is concerned with the competence of the person concerned, and where the word "this" is used and the study of the text is clearly mentioned, it is ascertained that this vow is a concomitant (feature) of the study of their own Upaniṣad.

Opponent: Since in the text, "To them alone should one expound this knowledge of Brahman who are engaged in the practice of disciplines, versed in the Vedas, and devoted to Brahman... and by whom has been duly performed the vow of holding the fire on the head" (Mu. III. ii. 10), the vow is connected with the knowledge of Brahman, which is the same in all the Upaniṣads, therefore it follows that this concomitant (trait) will get combined with the knowledge everywhere.

Vedāntin: No, for in that text, too, the term "This (knowledge of Brahman)" brings to notice the subject under discussion, which is the knowledge of Brahman gathered from that particular text; and hence this concomitant trait remains associated with a particular text only.

"And that regulation is like that about the (seven) libations" is said by way of citing an illustration. Just as from the fact that the seven kinds of oblation, counting from *Saurya* to *Śataudana*, have no connection with the three (sacrificial) fires mentioned in the other Vedas, but are connected with the one fire (called Ekarṣi) mentioned in the Atharva Veda, these oblations become restricted to the followers of the Atharva Veda alone, so also this concomitant feature must be restricted only to a particular kind of Vedic study, since it is connected with that. From this also it follows that the sameness of knowledge everywhere is beyond cavil.

दर्शयति च ॥४॥

4. Moreover, (the scripture) reveals (this fact).

The Vedas also show the unity of the knowledge, for in all the Upaniṣads the selfsame entity to be known is taught, as it is said in, "That goal which all the Vedas with one voice proclaim" (Ka. I. ii. 15); similarly, "The followers of the Ṛg Veda (i.e. Hotṛs) discuss this very one in the context of the great Uktha (hymn), the priests of Yajur Veda (i.e. Adhvaryus) sacrifice to this one in the fire, and the Chandogas (Udgātā priests, following the Sāma Veda) sing to this one in their great vow" (Ai. Ā. III. ii. 3.12). So also the quality of striking terror belonging to God, that is mentioned in the Kaṭha Upaniṣad in, "The supreme Brahman that is a great terror" (II. iii. 2), is seen to be referred to in the Taittirīya Upaniṣad for the sake of condemning the idea of duality, in the text, "Whenever the aspirant creates (even) a little difference in this Brahman, he is struck with fear" (II. vii. 1). So also the Vaiśvānara Self, conceived of in the Bṛhadāraṇyaka (I. i. 1) as extending from heaven to earth, is referred to in the Chāndogya Upaniṣad as something already well known: "But he who worships this Vaiśvānara Self as extending from heaven to earth and recognized as one's inmost Self" (Ch. V. xviii. 1). Again, it is seen that by way of demonstrating the unity of the purport of all the Upaniṣads, the Ukthas (collections of hymns) etc. enjoined in one Upaniṣad are adopted in other Upaniṣads for the sake of meditation; and from this it can be concluded, on the logic of frequent occurrence, that (like the unity of the knowledge of Brahman) the meditations also are the same in all the Upaniṣads.

Topic 2: Combination of Traits

उपसंहारोऽर्थाभेदाद्विधिशेषवत् समाने च ॥५॥

च And उपसंहारः A combination (is to be effected) समाने in similar meditations अर्थ-अभेदात् owing to non-difference of application विधि-शेष-वत् like the subsidiaries of an injunction.

5. And in similar meditations (all) the traits are to be combined, for there is no difference in application like the subsidiaries of an injunction.

This aphorism is meant for stating the result of the previous discussion. It having been established thus that all the Upaniṣads present the same ideas about all the meditations, the traits of any meditation mentioned in any one Upaniṣad have to be combined with the same meditation everywhere else; for their applications are not different. In whatever sense any one of these traits becomes helpful to a meditation at one place, it becomes so in the same way elsewhere as well; for the meditation is the same in either place. Hence "a combination is to be made, like the subsidiaries of an injunction". Just as the particular features of such rites as the Agnihotra, which are presented as subsidiary matters in connection with the main injunctions (of Agnihotra etc.), are combined together because of the sameness of that Agnihotra rite everywhere, so also is the case here. Had the meditations been different, the (individual) traits would remain tagged on to their separate meditations which, however, would not become inter-connected by way of one being a primary meditation and the others subsidiary, so that the traits would not become combined together. But such is not the case when the meditations are the same.

An elaboration of this very aphorism, stating the result as it does, will be made in the aphorisms starting with, "on account of the non-difference of the meditation everywhere" (III. iii. 10).

Topic 3: Difference of Meditations

अन्यथात्वं शब्दादिति चेन्नाविशेषात् ॥६॥

अन्यथात्वम् (There is) difference शब्दात् on the authority (of the difference) of texts इति चेत् if such be the contention न not so अ-विशेषात् owing to non-difference.

6. If it be said that the (Udgītha) meditations (in the Chāndogya and Bṛhadāraṇyaka Upaniṣads) are different on account of the difference of (texts), then not so, for there is no difference.

In the Bṛhadāraṇyaka Upaniṣad the start is made thus: "The gods said, 'Now let us surpass the Asuras (devils) in (this) sacrifice through the Udgītha'. They said to the organ of speech, 'Chant the Udgītha for us'" (Bṛ. I. iii. 1-2), and then the inferior *prāṇas* (organs) of speech etc. are condemned as struck with evil by the Asuras (devils), and lastly the chief *Prāṇa* (in the mouth) is mentioned thus: "Then they said to this (chief) *Prāṇa* (vital force) in the mouth, 'Chant (the Udgītha) for us.' 'All right', said the vital force and chanted for them" (Bṛ. I. iii. 7). So also in the Chāndogya Upaniṣad the commencement is made with, "Then the gods resorted to the Udgītha, under the idea, 'We shall defeat these (devils) by this' " (I. ii. 1); after that the *prāṇas* (organs) are condemned as struck with sin by the devils; and then in the very same way the preference for the chief *Prāṇa* (in the mouth) is shown thus: "Then they meditated on this vital force, that is in the mouth, as the Udgītha (*Om*)" (I. ii. 7). It can be understood from the eulogy of *Prāṇa* at both the places that what is enjoined is a meditation on *Prāṇa*.

A *doubt* arises in this matter: Do the meditations differ here, or are they the same? What should be the conclusion then?

Opponent: The meditations are the same on account of the arguments already advanced.

Objection: The sameness of the meditations is untenable because of the difference in the manner of starting. The Vājasaneyins start in one way, while the Sāmavedins do in another way. The Vājasaneyins mention *Prāṇa* as the singer of the Udgītha in their text, "(Then they said to this vital force in the mouth) 'Chant the Udgītha for us' " (Bṛ. I. iii. 7), whereas the Sāmavedins mention the vital force as Udgītha in, "They meditated on him as Udgītha" (Ch. I. ii. 7). So how can there be an identity of the meditations?

Opponent: That creates no difficulty, for the identity of the meditation is not ruled out by this (slight) variation, inasmuch as many more points of similarity are in evidence, for instance, the beginning is made with a description of the war between the gods and devils, the Udgītha is introduced for the sake of defeating the devils, the mention is made of the organs like the organ of speech, resort is made to the vital force in the mouth after decrying those organs, and the analogy of the stone and a lump of earth (smashed by being thrown at the stone) is cited by way of illustrating the destruction of the devils by the prowess of the vital force; many other points of similarity of this kind are also in evidence in both the places. Even in the Bṛhadāraṇyaka we come across an appositional use of *Prāṇa* with Udgītha: "This indeed is also Udgītha" (I. iii. 23). Hence in the Chāndogya Upaniṣad also, the agency of *Prāṇa* (in singing) is to be inferred metaphorically. From this also follows the identity of the meditations.

न वा प्रकरणभेदात् परोवरीयस्त्वादिवत् ॥७॥

न वा Rather not प्रकरण-भेदात् owing to a difference in subject-matter परः-वरीयस्त्व-आदि-वत् even as in such cases as being higher than the high.

7. *Rather not owing to a difference of subject-matter even as in such cases as (meditation on the Udgītha as) possessed of the quality of being higher than the high, (greater than the great).*

Vedāntin: The identity of the meditations is not certainly tenable; the reasonable position here is that the meditations are different.

Why?

"Owing to a difference of *prakaraṇa* (lit. subject-matter)", that is to say, "owing to a difference of *prakrama* (lit. introduction)—the way the two meditations are started with". Thus a difference in the manner of starting is obvious here. The Chāndogya begins with, "Let one meditate on the letter *Om* as Udgītha" (I. i. 1). Thus the subject introduced is the meditation on *Om*, a letter forming a part of the Udgītha. Then it is expounded as possessed of such qualities as being the quintessence. And then that very *Om*, forming a part of the Udgītha is again alluded to in, "Now then starts a proximate elaboration of that very letter" (I. i. 10), and proceeding through the narration of the war between the gods and the devils the text says, "They meditated on *Prāṇa* as the Udgītha" (I. ii. 2). Now if by the word Udgītha, occurring there, be meant the entire division of Sāma (song, that goes by that name), and the priest Udgātā be meant as the singer (identified with *Prāṇa*), then the introduction would be contradicted, and a necessity for resort to metaphorical interpretation would crop up. It is proper that in the same context, conveying a single idea, the conclusion should be in accordance with the introduction. Hence in this text what is enjoined is the superimposition of the idea of Prāṇa on *Om* forming a part of the Udgītha. But in the Bṛhadāraṇyaka Upaniṣad, there being no reason to understand a part of the Udgītha from a use of that word, it is presented as a whole (along with all its parts). And even in the text, "you chant for us" (Bṛ. I. iii. 2), the priest called Udgātā, who is the singer of that entire Udgītha is enjoined to be looked upon as *Prāṇa*. Thus the manner of presentation is different. Although there, in the Bṛhadāraṇyaka, *Prāṇa* is placed in apposition with Udgītha, yet this is meant for demonstrating the fact that *Prāṇa*, which has been sought to be shown as the priest Udgātā, is also the Self of all. So this does not lead to an identity of the two meditations. Again, there (in the Bṛhadāraṇyaka text), the term Udgītha is used to indicate the whole of it, so that there is difference between the two. It cannot be argued that the idea of *Prāṇa* being the Udgātā has to be rejected on the ground of impossibility; for *Prāṇa* is taught as the Udgātā for the sake of meditation just like its being taught as the Udgītha for the same purpose. Besides, it is with the energy of *Prāṇa* that the Udgātā sings the Udgītha, so that there is no impossibility. Thus it is stated by the Upaniṣad in that very context, "Indeed he chanted through speech and the vital force" (Bṛ. I . iii. 24). Again, when the intended meaning is understood to be different (in the two Upaniṣads), it is not proper to decide on an identity of meaning with the help of mere similarity of the language of the sentences. An illustration of this is found in the sentences (in Pūrva-Mīmāṁsā) about the rising of the moon and desire for cattle, where a similarity of injunction is found in, "The rice grains are to be divided into three parts" (which text deals with moon-rise) and "with those that form the middle part, one shall offer a cake in eight potsherds for fire, possessed of the quality of a giver" (which sentence deals with the desire for cattle). Though in the two sentences there is a similarity of injunction, still owing to a difference in the introductory sentences, it is ascertained that in the sentence dealing with moon-rise, the idea implied is a (mere) change of deities, whereas in the sentence dealing with desires, the injunction is about a sacrifice.[7] Hence here also the meditations differ owing to a difference in the introductory sentences, "just as it is in the case of Udgītha possessed of the quality of being higher than the high and greater than the great". Although the superimposition of the idea of the supreme Self is similar in "Space (Brahman) is indeed greater than these. Space is the highest goal. This is the Udgītha that is higher than the high (*Prāṇa*), and greater than the great (*Prāṇa*), and it is infinite" (Ch. I. ix. 1-2), and in the text superimposing the idea of the supreme Self on the sun and the eye, still the meditation on Udgītha as possessed of the quality of being higher and greater than the high and great is different from the meditation on Udgītha as possessed of the quality of being established in the sun and the eye and being possessed of golden beard etc. (Ch. I. vi. 7). But even as within the same branch of the Vedas, there is no combination of the features of two different meditations, so also is it the case with different meditations occurring in different branches.

संज्ञातश्चेत्तदुक्तमस्ति तु तदपि ॥८॥

(Sameness follows) संज्ञात: from (the sameness of) designation चेत् if it be said so, तत् that उक्तम् has been answered. तु However, तत्-अपि that also अस्ति exists.

8. If from the sameness of name, (the two meditations are held to be the same), that has already been answered. But that

[7] The Darśa sacrifice takes place on the new-moon night (the fifteenth day of the dark fortnight). Now if by mistake it is done on the fourteenth day, and the moon rises afterwards, the sacrificer is faced with evil consequences. To get over this, the sacrificer shall divide the rice grains into three parts. Of these the medium portion will be offered to Fire, the bigger portion with curds to Indra, and the smaller cooked into a pudding with milk to Viṣṇu. But this is not a new sacrifice, the deities alone being changed. The text dealing with desire for cattle also has a similar ending. Still it is different from the above.

(sameness of name) is met with (even with regard to things quite different).

If it be held now that the meditation is the same here on account of the sameness of the name, it being called the meditation on the Udgītha at both the places, then that too is not tenable; for it has been already said, "Rather not, owing to a difference of subject-matter (i.e. introduction) even as in such cases as meditation on the Udgītha as possessed of the quality of being higher than the high and greater than the great" (III. iii. 7). That applies here more aptly, inasmuch as it conforms to the letters of the Upaniṣad, the name being used in a secondary sense only by common people dealing with the subject, who take their cue from the mere occurrence of the word Udgītha in both the places. Moreover, this identity of name is met with even in the face of well-recognized differences underlying such meditations as that on the Udgītha (i.e. Brahman) as possessed of the qualities of being higher than the high and greater than the great, where also the single name "meditation on Udgītha" is used. Just as such sacrifices as Agnihotra, Darśapūrṇamāsa, etc., which are well known as different, are seen to be referred to by the common name Kāṭhaka, merely because they are read of in the selfsame book of the Kaṭha branch of the Vedas, so is the case here. But where no such reason for difference is met with, the meditations may well be identical as for instance the meditation on *Saṁvarga* (merger), etc.

Topic 4: Specification of Om

Doubt: In the text, "Let one meditate on the letter *Om* (as) the Udgītha" (Ch. I. i. 1), we hear of an appositional use of *Om* and Udgītha, from which fact one of the four alternatives—superimposition, ablation, identity, qualification—may be accepted as the meaning of the apposition. So the consideration arises above the appropriateness of any one of these in the present context. Of these, superimposition occurs where the idea of one of the two things is superimposed on the idea of the other even while the individual idea of the latter is not sublated; the idea of the thing on which the idea of another thing is superimposed persists even when the superimposed idea of the latter is in evidence. For instance, even when the idea of Brahman is superimposed on a name (e.g. *Om*) the idea of the name persists and it is not negated by the idea of Brahman; or it is like the superimposition of the ideas of Viṣṇu and other gods on images etc. So also it may be that either the idea of Udgītha is superimposed here on the letter *Om* or the letter *Om* is superimposed on Udgītha. Ablation occurs where a thing has got fastened on to it a deep-rooted, persistent, unreal idea, and then the true idea dawns to drive away the earlier unreal idea. For instance, the idea of Selfhood persisting with regard to the assemblage of body and senses is driven away by the subsequent true idea of Selfhood with regard to the Self Itself springing up from the (instruction), "That thou art" (Ch. VI. viii-xvi); or a confusion about directions is removed by the true idea of directions. So it may be that here also either the idea of the Udgītha is removed by the idea of the letter *Om* or the idea of the letter *Om* is removed by the idea of the Udgītha. Identity means that the connotation and denotation of *Om* and Udgītha are the same. Neither more nor less, as in the case of synonymous terms like, "the best among the twice-born", a "Brāhmaṇa", an "earthly god". The adjectival use[8] can occur in the sense that the letter *Om*, present in all the Vedas and liable to be understood as such, is presented as associated with the actions of the Udgātā. Just as somebody might say, "Bring the lotus that is blue", so here also the meaning is, "Meditate on the *Om* that is the Udgītha". Thus when we think over this sentence presenting an apposition, all these alternatives come to the surface.

Vedāntin: Since under this predicament one finds no reason for accepting anyone of the alternatives, the aphorism is enunciated:

व्याप्तेश्च समञ्जसम् ॥९॥

च And व्याप्ते: because of the pervasion (of all the Vedas), समञ्जसम् it is proper (to qualify *Om* by Udgītha).

[8] Distinguishing something from other things of the same class.

9. Since Om pervades all the Vedas, it is appropriate to qualify it by the word Udgītha.

The word "and", used in place of the word "but", is meant for ruling out the three other alternatives. The three alternatives, being defective in the present context, are rejected, while the adjectival alternative alone is accepted as it is faultless. Now, on accepting superimposition, the word denoting the idea that is to be superimposed on the other will be subject to a metaphorical interpretation,[9] and a result also for it will have to be imagined.

Opponent: But the result is stated by the Upaniṣad itself in, "It becomes indeed the gratifier of desires" etc. (Ch. I. i. 7).

Vedāntin: No, since it is the result of another thing, it being the result of the meditation on (*Om* as possessed of) the qualities of being the fulfiller of desires, and so on, and not of the superimposition of Udgītha. As regards ablation also, the absence of a result is equally in evidence.

Opponent: The result can be the removal of false ignorance.

Vedāntin: No, since that (negation of *Om* or Udgītha) is not known to lead to any desirable human goal.[10] And the idea of *Om* can never be alienated from *Om*, nor can the idea of Udgītha from Udgītha (since these ideas are true). Besides, this passage does not aim at establishing the nature of anything, it being meant for enjoining a meditation.

The other alternative, identity, too is not appropriate, for in that case the utterance of two words (*Om* and Udgītha) would be useless, since one word alone could convey the intended idea. Moreover, (the term) Udgītha is not known to imply the idea of the word *Om* as implied by the letter *Om*, that is used along with the acts of the priest Hotā (of the Ṛg Veda) or the priest Adhvaryu (of the Yajur Veda). Nor is the word *Om* well known as standing for the whole of the second part

[9] But this is inadmissible when a direct meaning is possible, that being more authoritative.

[10] Cessation of ignorance brings about a cessation of evil and attainment of bliss. But the negation of the ideas of *Om* and Udgītha by one another can bring no such result.

of a Sāma song which is indicated by the word Udgītha, in which case alone the *Om* could have been a synonym for Udgītha. As a last resort, the adjectival alternative is accepted, "on account of the pervasion of *Om*", that is to say, on account of its being common to all the Vedas. Lest the letter *Om* extending over all the Vedas be taken up here, the letter *Om* is qualified by the word Udgītha, so that the *Om*, forming a part of Udgītha, may somehow be understood.

Opponent: Is not a metaphorical interpretation necessary even from this point of view, since the word Udgītha is metaphorically made to imply a part of itself (viz *Om*)?

Vedāntin: This is quite so; but even in the case of a figure of speech, there may be an approximation to or departure from the primary meaning. In the case of superimposition, the idea of something is superimposed on something else, so that the figure of speech here involves a departure; whereas in the case of the adjectival use, a word denoting a whole is made to imply a part of itself, so that the figure of speech involves a proximity; for words indicating the whole are seen to be used with regard to the parts as well, as in the case of a cloth or a village.[11] Hence it is flawless and appropriate that *Om*, which is common to all the Vedas, should be qualified by the term "Udgītha" in the text, "the letter *Om*".

Topic 5: Sameness of the Meditation on Prana

सर्वाभेदादन्यत्रेमे ॥१०॥

सर्व-अभेदात् Owing to non-difference of all, इमे these (traits) अन्यत्र (are to be added) elsewhere.

10. All (the meditations on Prāṇa) being the same, these traits (found here in one) are to be added elsewhere.

Doubt: In the anecdote of *Prāṇa*, as related both by the Vājasaneyins and the Chandogas, it is enjoined that *Prāṇa* is to be meditated on as possessed of the quality of being the greatest.

[11] Even when a portion is burnt, people say, "The cloth is burnt", "The village is burnt".

And the organs of speech etc. are spoken of there as possessed of the attributes of being *vasiṣṭha* (most comfortably accommodated) etc.[12] These attributes are again ascribed to *Prāṇa* in the texts starting with, "The organ of speech said, 'That attribute of being the *vasiṣṭha* that I have is yours' " (Bṛ. VI. i. 14). But while in other branches of the Vedas, for instance in the Kauṣītaki and others, the pre-eminence of *Prāṇa* is mentioned in the anecdotes of *Prāṇa* in such texts as, "Now then, here is the ascertainment of greatness. These gods, such as they were, quarrelled about personal greatness" (Kau. II. 14), such attributes as being the steadiest are not mentioned. So the doubt arises here: Should these attributes of being the steadiest etc. occurring somewhere be added elsewhere as well or should they not?

Opponent: While in this doubt, the acceptable position is that they are not to be added to.

Why?

Because of the use of the word "thus", for in the respective places, the thing to be known (and meditated on) is presented by using the word "thus" as in, "Similarly, if anyone indeed, after having known (*Prāṇa*) thus (as possessed of the quality of being the greatest), (meditates on *Prāṇa*), then he, through his meditation on *Prāṇa* as the greatest, (becomes the greatest)" (Kau. II. 14). And the word "thus" has a reference to proximate things alone; so it has no capacity to present the attributes of a similar nature mentioned in other branches. Hence the curiosity (to know what is meant by "thus") has to be satisfied by the attributes found in its own context.

Vedāntin: This being the position, the refutation is being given. Some of these attributes that have been spoken of, viz that of being the *vasiṣṭha* and so on, are to be thrown in (i.e. added) elsewhere as well.

Why?

"On account of non-difference of all" (everywhere); for everywhere we recognize the meditation of *Prāṇa* as identical, the anecdote etc. of *Prāṇa* being similar. And when the medita-

[12] An attractive speaker lives happily.

tion is the same, why should not these attributes mentioned at some place be added elsewhere?

Opponent: Was it not said that the word "thus", wherever it may occur, indicates that the sets of attributes in those respective places, are to be understood separately?

Vedāntin: With regard to this the answer is: Although by the word "thus", occurring in the Kauṣītaki-Brāhmaṇa, the set of attributes mentioned in the Vājasaneyi-Brāhmaṇa are not referred to, they being far removed from it, yet by the word "thus", occurring in the Vājasaneyi-Brāhmaṇa, in the course of that very meditation (on *Prāṇa*), all these attributes are surely intimated; and so the set of attributes, even though they be restricted to the selfsame meditation in another branch (viz Vājasaneyi) cannot be distinguished from the set in one's own branch (viz Kauṣītaki). And such an interpretation will not lead to the defects of imagining something not spoken of by the Vedas and rejecting something enjoined by them; for the attributes even though they be heard of in one branch, become acceptable everywhere, since the possessor of the attributes (viz meditation on *Prāṇa*) is the same. For if Devadatta is well known in his native land for his qualities of valour etc., he does not become alienated from these qualities even when he goes to another country where the people are not cognisant of his qualities of valour etc. And as from better acquaintance, those qualities of Devadatta can come to be recognized in that country as well, so also as a result of better knowledge, the attributes to be meditated on in one branch come to be added to the meditation in another branch. Hence the attributes associated with the selfsame principal entity have to be added in every other branch as well, although they are mentioned in one place only.

Topic 6: Combination and Non-combination of Attributes of Brahman

Doubt: In the texts presenting the real nature of Brahman a few only of such characteristics of Brahman as of being naturally bliss itself, impartite consciousness, omnipresent, Self of all, and so on, are met with here and there. With regard to them the doubt arises: Are only those attributes of Brahman such as bliss etc. to be accepted in a particular place just as they are specifically mentioned there, or are all the attributes to be accepted everywhere?

Opponent: Under such circumstances, the obvious conclusion is that the attributes are to be accepted just as they appear separately under the different contexts.

Vedāntin: To this the reply is:

आनन्दादयः प्रधानस्य ॥११॥

आनन्द-आदयः Bliss and other characteristics **प्रधानस्य** of the principal entity (are to be combined).

11. Bliss and other characteristics of the principal entity (i.e. Brahman) are to be combined.

All such characteristics of Brahman as bliss etc. are to be understood as belonging to It everywhere (in all the contexts). Why?

Precisely because of non-difference in all the places; for that very principal entity, Brahman, is equally the substantive everywhere. Hence the attributes of Brahman exist (collectively) everywhere, in accordance with the illustration of the valour of Devadatta shown under the previous topic.

Opponent: In that case all such characteristics as "having joy as the head" will also get mixed up everywhere. Thus in the Taittirīya Upaniṣad, after introducing the self constituted by bliss, it is said, "of him joy is verily the head, enjoyment is the right side, hilarity is the left side, bliss is the Self (i.e. trunk), Brahman is the tail that stabilizes" (II. v. 1).

Vedāntin: Hence comes the answer:

प्रियशिरस्त्वाद्यप्राप्तिरुपचयापचयौ हि भेदे ॥१२॥

प्रिय-शिरस्त्व-आदि-अप्राप्तिः There is no addition of such attributes as having joy as the head and so on; **हि** because **उपचय-अपचयौ** augmentation and depletion **भेदे** (occur) in a context of duality.

12. Attributes such as having joy as the head and so on are not to be added everywhere, since (they have) degrees of intensity and feebleness, (which are) possible in a context of difference (i.e. duality).

The attributes of "having joy as the head" and so on, mentioned in the Taittirīya Upaniṣad, are not to be added elsewhere, since joy, enjoyment, hilarity, and bliss are perceived to be of different degrees of intensity or feebleness in relation to one another and in respect of the (different) enjoyers. Intensity or feebleness co-exist only with difference, whereas Brahman is without any difference, as is known from such texts as, "one only without a second" (Ch. VI. ii. 1). And it was taught by us under the aphorism, "He who is full of Bliss is Brahman on account of repetition" (I. i. 12), that these attributes of "having joy as head" etc. do not belong to Brahman, but to the blissful sheath. Moreover, these are imagined as means for concentrating the mind on the supreme Brahman, but they are not meant for realization (as actual characteristics). While this is their purpose, this is all the more reason why the attributes of "having joy as the head" and so on are not to be added everywhere. But admitting for the sake of argument that these are attributes of Brahman, the teacher (Vyāsa) has only shown the reason why the attributes of "having joy as head" and so on, are not to be added elsewhere. This reasoning is to be applied to other attributes also that undoubtedly belong to Brahman, and are enjoined for meditation, such for instance as, *saṁyad-vāma* (resort of all blessings—Ch. IV. xv. 2) and *satyakāma* (having inevitable desire—Ch. III. xiv. 2). Even though the Brahman to be meditated on is the same in all of them, yet the meditations differ according to the different contexts, and as such the attributes found in one are not to be transferred to another. Just as the two wives of a king may adore him in two ways—one with a chowrie (fly-whisk) and the other with an umbrella, and the behaviour of the king may differ there according to the mode of adoration, although the person adored is the same, so also is the case here. The possession of intensive or feeble attributes is possible in the case of the qualified Brahman alone, with regard to whom dualistic ideas persist, but not so in the case of the unqualified supreme Brahman. Hence the attributes of "having inevitable desires" etc. which are heard of in particular contexts are not to be added everywhere. This is the idea.

इतरे त्वर्थसामान्यात् ॥१३॥

इतरे The other (characteristics) तु however (are to be understood) अर्थ-सामान्यात् on account of identity of purport.

13. But the other characteristics are to be understood everywhere on account of identity of purport.

But all the other attributes like bliss, which are spoken of for propounding the real nature of Brahman, are to be understood everywhere, since they have an identity of purport, that is to say, the Brahman, which possesses these attributes and which they seek to establish, is the same. Hence there is a difference (between the two groups of attributes), inasmuch as these (latter) are meant simply for the attainment of knowledge (and not for meditation).

Topic 7: Puruṣa as the Highest in Kaṭha

आध्यानाय प्रयोजनाभावात् ॥१४॥

(Kaṭha verses I. iii. 10 etc. are) आ-ध्यानाय meant for deep meditation (on Puruṣa), (and not for stating the relative positions of others) प्रयोजन-अभावात् as that serves no purpose.

14. What is mentioned in the Kaṭha Upaniṣad is meant for deep meditation on Puruṣa, (and not for stating any gradation), as that serves no purpose.

Doubt : In the Kaṭha Upaniṣad, the start is made with, "The sense-objects are higher than the senses, and the mind is higher than the sense-objects" (I. iii. 10); and then it is said, "There is nothing higher than Puruṣa. He is the culmination, He is the highest goal" (I. iii. 11). Here the doubt arises whether all those things starting with sense-objects are propounded to be each higher than the preceding one, or it is propounded that Puruṣa is the highest of all.

Opponent: As to that, the idea gained is that each of these is expounded here to be higher (than its predecessor); for the Upaniṣad talks of them as "such a one is higher than such another", and "such another is higher than still another", and so on.

Objection: If many objects are propounded to be (successively) higher, it will result in splitting the unity of idea (conveyed by a single sentence).

Opponent: That is no fault, since it can well be that there are many sentences. For it is but proper that these sentences should be many, so that they may speak (separately) of many things possessed of superiority. Hence here we have a propounding of the superiority of each of these objects individually.

Vedāntin: Such being the conclusion, we say that the reasonable position is that Puruṣa is proved to be superior to all of them, but not that each one of the objects is propounded to be higher (than the earlier one).

Why?

"As that serves no purpose", inasmuch as no objective is either seen or mentioned in the Upaniṣads as being fulfilled by proving the other things to have any relative superiority, whereas, when it is established that Puruṣa (the infinite Being), who is free from all evil, is superior to the organs, the achievement of liberation stands out as a discernible fact. In support of this is the Upaniṣadic text, "one becomes free from the jaws of death by knowing that which is... ever constant" (Ka. I. iii. 15). Moreover, by denying anything higher than Puruṣa (I. iii. 11), through the use of such words as "culmination" (ibid.), the text evinces a preference for Puruṣa, and thereby it also makes it obvious that the mention of a chain of graded things is meant for explaining Puruṣa alone. "For deep meditation" means, "for the sake of complete realization through meditation", since meditation is taught here only as a means for complete enlightenment, but not as an objective by itself.

आत्मशब्दाच्च ॥१५॥

च Also आत्म-शब्दात् because of the word Self.

15. And (this must be the conclusion) on account of the use of the word Self.

That this mention of the chain of successive superiority (over things) starting from the sense-organs, is meant for realizing Puruṣa is proved from the further fact that the Puruṣa under discussion is spoken of as the Self in, "He is hidden in all beings, and hence He does not appear as the Self (of all). But by the seers of subtle things, He is seen through a fine and pointed intellect" (Ka. I. iii. 12). And from this it can be understood that the rest are not meant to be spoken of as the Self. That Puruṣa Himself is shown to be inscrutable and yet comprehensible by the fully purified mind. It is for the realization of that Puruṣa that meditation is enjoined in, "The discriminating man should merge the organ of speech into the mind" etc. (Ka. I. iii. 13). All this was explained under the aphorism, "If it be said that in some recensions even the inferred entity (Pradhāna) is also mentioned, we say no" etc. (I. iv. 1). Thus it is noticed how variously and abundantly the Upaniṣads have for their main purport Puruṣa and nothing else. Moreover, when it is declared, "The man attains the end of the road (i.e. goal of his journey), which is the highest place of Viṣṇu" (Ka. I. iii. 9), the curiosity arises as to what exactly is that "highest place of Viṣṇu" which is "at the end of the road". In response to this are enumerated the sense-organs etc. serially. So from this it is clear that this effort is made for the realization of the "highest place".

Topic 8: The Supreme Self in Aitareya

आत्मगृहीतिरितरवदुत्तरात् ॥१६॥

आत्म-गृहीतिः The supreme Self is to be understood (in the Aitareya Upaniṣad) इतर-वत् as elsewhere उत्तरात् because of what follows.

16. The supreme Self is to be understood in the Aitareya Upaniṣad, just as elsewhere (in other texts about creation), on account of the subsequent qualification.

Doubt: In the Aitareya Upaniṣad it is mentioned, "In the beginning this was but the absolute Self alone. There was nothing else whatsoever that winked. He thought, 'Let Me create the worlds'. He created these worlds, viz *ambhas* (region beyond heaven), *Marīcī* (sky) *mara* (earth) *āpaḥ* (nether regions)" etc. (I. i. 1-2). With regard to this the doubt arises, whether the supreme Self Itself is here referred to by the word Self or some one else. What should be the conclusion then?

Opponent: The supreme Self cannot be referred to here by the word Self.

Why?

On account of what is discernible from the trend of the sentence.

Objection: Is not the connected sequence of the sentence seen to be more in favour of the supreme Self, since the assertion is made about the oneness of the Self before creation and because of the mention of creation after deliberation?

Opponent: We say no, because this narration is about the creation of the worlds. If the supreme Self were to be accepted as the creator, the creation of the great fine elements should have been stated first, whereas the creation of the worlds is narrated here first. The worlds are only peculiar arrangements of the elements. So also *ambhas* etc. are merely the worlds that are spoken of in such sentences as, "That which is beyond heaven is *ambhas*" (Ai. I. i. 2). And from the Vedas and Smṛtis it is gathered that the creation of the worlds is the act of some divine being under the direction of God. Thus there occurs the Upaniṣadic text: "In the beginning this universe was but the Self (Virāṭ) of the human form" etc. (Bṛ. I. iv. 1). And there is also the Smṛti text, "He is the first embodied Being, He is called Puruṣa. He is the first creator of all beings, born first as Brahmā". The followers of the Aitareya branch also mention in an earlier context, in the text, "Then follows the creation from semen. The gods are the semen (i.e. products) of Prajāpati

(Virāṭ)" (Ai. Br. II. i. 3.1), that the diverse creation is an act of Prajāpati. The word Self is also found to be used for him, as in, "In the beginning this universe was but the Self (Virāṭ) of the human form" (Bṛ. I. iv. 1). The assertion of his unity also becomes appropriate when contrasted with the diversity which is his product. And his deliberation also is justifiable because he is admitted to be conscious. Moreover, the class of particular activities, well known in the case of the different common souls, are met with here in such sentences as, "For them he brought a cow, . . . to them he brought a horse, . . . to them he brought a man, . . . They said" (Ai. I. ii. 2-3). Hence the Self mentioned here must be some entity having some limitations.

Vedāntin: This being the position, we say: "The supreme Self is to be understood here by the word Self, as elsewhere". Just as the supreme Self is understood in other Upaniṣadic texts about creation, such as "From that Brahman, which is the Self, was produced space" (Tai. II. i. 1), or as the inmost Self Itself is meant by the use of the word Self in common parlance, so also must be the case here. But the Self with limitations must be the meaning in such texts as that beginning with, "In the beginning this universe was but the Self (Virāṭ)" (Bṛ. I. iv. 1), where occur such other qualifying terms as "of a human form" (ibid.). Here, however, the subsequent qualification that is met with, is itself conducive to the acceptance of the supreme Self, for instance, "He thought, 'Let Me create the worlds'" (Ai. I. i. 1), "He created these worlds" (Ai. I. i. 2), and so on. Hence the reasonable position is to accept the supreme Self.

अन्वयादिति चेत्स्यादवधारणात् ॥१७॥

अन्वयात् (It follows) from the trend of the sentences (that the supreme Self is not meant) इति चेत् if such be the contention, स्यात् it must be so अवधारणात् because of definite statement.

17. If it be objected that it follows from the trend of the sentences that the Supreme Self is not meant, (the reply is that) it must be so because of the definite statement (that the Self alone existed in the beginning).

It was argued that from the trend of the context it follows that the supreme Self is not meant. That has to be refuted. "It must be so because of the definite statement"—the acceptance of the supreme Self must be appropriate here.

Why?

"On account of the definite statement"; for the definite statement about the oneness of the Self before creation becomes appropriate only if the supreme Self is meant, else it will become inappropriate. As for the sentence about creation of the worlds, we shall interpret it as meaning the creation (of the worlds) after the creation of the great elements, as is well known in other Upaniṣads. As we interpreted the sentence, "That Brahman created fire" (Ch. VI. ii. 3), to mean that the creation (of fire) was after the creation of space and air well known in other Upaniṣads, so also it can be done here. For any speciality mentioned in one Upaniṣad with regard to the same subject has to be added to it in the other Upaniṣads as well. As for the ascription of a particular type of behaviour to the Self in such sentences as, "He brought a cow to them", that too has to be understood in a way that is conducive to the ascertainment of the idea sought to be imparted. For it cannot certainly be held that the mere narration of this anecdote, as a whole, is the only purport, since that does not lead to any human goal. But in fact the intended purport here is the identity of the (individual) Self with Brahman. And thus it is that after imparting instruction about the creation of the worlds and their presiding deities like Fire, and then teaching about the sense-organs and the body as their seats, the text shows how the creator Himself thought, "How indeed can it be there without Me" (Ai. I. iii. 11), and then He entered into this body: "Having split up this end (on the head where the parting of the hair occurs), He entered through this door" (Ai. I. iii. 12). Again the text says that after taking the activities of the organs into consideration thus, "If utterance is done by the organ of speech, smelling by the sense of smell" (Ai. I. iii. 11), and then having reflected, "What then am I?" (ibid.), "He entered through this door, having split up this end (at the parting of hair on the crown of the head)" (Ai. I. iii. 12), where the identity of the Self with Brahman is categorically asserted by saying "He realized this very Puruṣa as Brahman, the most pervasive" (Ai. I. iii. 13). Later on too, this very fact of the identity of the Self with Brahman is asserted by starting with, "This one is the inferior Brahman; this is Indra" etc. (Ai. III. i. 3), where all the things within the world of duality, inclusive of the great elements, are enumerated one after the other, and then the conclusion is made with, "All these have Consciousness as the giver of their reality; all these are impelled by Consciousness. The universe has Consciousness as its eye, and Consciousness as its end. Consciousness is Brahman" (Ai. III. i. 3). Hence it goes without any contradiction that the supreme Self is meant here.

The other interpretation of the aphorisms beginning with "*ātmagṛhītiritaravaduttarāt*" is this:

आत्मगृहीतिरितरवदुत्तरात् ॥१६॥

16. The Self is to be understood (in the Chāndogya Upaniṣad), just as in the other (Bṛhadāraṇyaka) Upaniṣad, because of the subsequent (instruction about identity).

Doubt: In the Bṛhadāraṇyaka Upaniṣad it is said, "Which is the Self? 'This infinite entity (Puruṣa) that is identified with the intellect and is in the midst of organs, the self-effulgent light within the heart (intellect)'" (Bṛ. IV. iii. 7), where the start is made with the word Self, and then by proving that very Self to be free from all attachments, it is definitely stated that the Self is identified with Brahman. The conclusion is also made accordingly: "That great birthless Self is undecaying, immortal, undying, fearless, and Brahman" (Bṛ. IV. iv. 25). But in the Chāndogya Upaniṣad the start is made thus, "O amiable one, in the beginning all this was but Existence, one without a second" (IV. ii. 1), where the word Self is not used, but the identity (of the individual and Brahman) is taught at the end in the words, "That thou art" (VI. viii. 7). Now the doubt arises, whether these two scriptural texts have the same meaning or not.

Opponent: The acceptable position is that they have different meanings, since the texts are dissimilar. For in a case of textual divergence, it is not proper to accept a similarity of meaning, since the meaning should be understood in accordance with the scripture. As for the Bṛhadāraṇyaka, it is obvious from the use of the word Self in the beginning that the instruction is about the reality of the Self. But since in the Chāndogya the start is made in a different way, there is a dissimilarity in the instruction.

Vedāntin: Was it not pointed out that even the Chāndogya contains instruction about the identity of the (individual) Self and Brahman at the end?

Opponent: You said so, to be sure; but since the conclusion must accord with the commencement, it can be considered that this is only a fanciful conceit of identity.

Vedāntin: That being the position, it is said: "The (supreme) Self is to be understood" even by the Chandogas in their text, "O amiable one, in the beginning all this was but Existence, one without a second" (Ch. VI. ii. 1); "Just as in the other Upaniṣad"—Just as the (supreme) Self is implied in the Bṛhadāraṇyaka text, "What is the Self?" (IV. iii. 7), so also is it here.

Why?

"Because of the subsequent instruction of identity".

अन्वयादिति चेत्स्यादवधारणात् ॥१७॥

17. If it be argued that the rule about the conformity of the commencement and the conclusion leads to the idea that the Self is not meant, then we say that it must be so because of the definite statement.

Opponent: It was pointed out that the conclusion has to conform to the beginning; and since the word Self is not used in the beginning, the Self is not meant. How would you avoid that difficulty?

Vedāntin: That is being stated: "It must be so because of the definite statement". On account of the definite statement, the reasonable position here is that the Self is meant. To explain:

It is asserted in the text, "That by knowing which the unheard becomes heard, the unthought becomes thought, and the unknown becomes known" (Ch. VI. i. 1), that everything becomes known when the One is known; and then to expound this, the Upaniṣad starts with, "O amiable one, in the beginning" etc. That assertion becomes established if the (supreme) Self is meant (in the text under discussion); for else this Self, that is the supreme entity, remains unknown, so that the knowledge of all arising from the knowledge of One remains unaccomplished. Hence it is only from the point of view of the assertion of the identity (of the Self and Existence) that one can reconcile all such facts in the Chāndogya Upaniṣad as the assertion of oneness before creation, reference to the individual being by the word Self, statement of the attainment of the state of that Self in sleep, and the definite assertion, "That thou art", made again and again in response to (repeated) inquiry; but not so if the identity be merely a fanciful conceit. Besides, the argument about the concurrence of the conclusion with the commencement should not be raised here, for neither any statement nor any non-statement of the Self is in evidence in the beginning. And a prelude in a general form cannot be contradicted by any special statement in the complementary portion, since a general statement raises expectations about the particulars. Moreover, the meaning of the word, "Existence", when fully considered, cannot be other than the supreme Self, since all other things are unreal by reasons of having their origin in speech etc. (B. S. II. i. 14). Even difference in scriptural readings (i.e. forms of sentences) cannot give rise to a difference in purport, since no such difference of meaning is in evidence in the case of such sentences as, "You fetch this vessel" and "This vessel, you fetch". Hence the conclusion is that although the process of expounding may differ in passages of this class, the thing expounded does not differ.

Topic 9: Acamana and Meditation on Prana

कार्याख्यानादपूर्वम् ॥१८॥

कार्य-आख्यानात् Since (the rinsing of the mouth, *ācamana*, is) mentioned as a duty (already known), (it occurs here) अपूर्वम् in connection with a new injunction.

18. Since ācamana is mentioned as a duty already recognized, it occurs (in the Upaniṣad) in connection with a fresh injunction (of meditation on Prāṇa).

Doubt: In the anecdote of *Prāṇa* (vital force), the Chandogas as well as the Vājasaneyins mention that all that is food to the creatures right down to the dogs is the food of the vital force (*Prāṇa*), and then they mention water as its cloth. Subsequently the Chandogas have this text, "It is for this reason indeed that people when eating cover it up with water just before and after eating"[13] (Ch. V. ii. 2). And the Vājasaneyins have this text, "Therefore wise men who are versed in the Vedas sip a little water just before and after eating. They regard it as removing the nakedness of the vital force" (Bṛ. VI. i. 14); "Hence men possessed of this knowledge shall sip a little water while sitting for a meal and sip a little water after finishing the meal. While doing so they shall think that they are removing the nakedness of this one (the vital force)" (ibid.). Here two acts are met with, viz sipping of water and thinking of the removal of *Prāṇa's* nakedness. Now it is to be considered whether both these acts are enjoined, or merely sipping or the thinking of the removal of *Prāṇa's* nakedness. What should be the conclusion then?

Opponent: The conclusion is that both the acts are enjoined. Why?

Since both these are obvious from the text, and since both these are fit to be enjoined as they are unique duties (met with here for the first time). Or it may be that the sipping alone is enjoined, since the imperative case-ending about it is clear: "Hence a man possessed of this knowledge shall sip a little water while sitting for meal, and sip a little water after finishing the meal". And the declaration of the removal of nakedness is meant only for the eulogy of that act (of sipping).

[13] "The sipping of a little water from the palm of the hand serves as a cloth for *Prāṇa*"—this is how it is to be fancied.

Vedāntin: This being the position, we say that it cannot be logically upheld that this is an injunction about sipping, since the text only alludes to this duty that is already enjoined elsewhere. This act of sipping, as it is already known from the Smṛti as an act meant for purification, is merely alluded to here.

Opponent: Should not this (very) Vedic text form the basis of that Smṛti?

Vedāntin: The reply is, no, since the subject-matters differ. The Smṛti, concerned with a general subject-matter, enjoins sipping of water for all persons, and this act is calculated to purify them. But the Vedic text occurs in a context of meditation on *Prāṇa*; if it should at all enjoin a rule about the sipping of water, it can at best do so only in connection with that alone. And as between a Vedic text and a Smṛti text, no one thinks of establishing a relationship of the source and its subsequent development, when they deal with different subject-matters. It cannot be held that this Vedic text enjoins some unique rule about the sipping of water in connection with the meditation on *Prāṇa*, for it is recognized to be the already known sipping commonly resorted to by all men. For this very reason too it is not an injunction about both. Moreover, if both are enjoined, it will lead to a splitting of the unity of idea (that each sentence has). Hence after referring to the already known fact of sipping water by people before and after partaking of their meals, the present text imparts in the sentence, "While doing so, they think that they are removing the nakedness of this one" (Bṛ. VI. i. 14), a new injunction about thinking (or fancying) in connection with the meditation on *Prāṇa* of the removal of the nakedness of *Prāṇa* with the water used for the sipping. Besides, it is not proper to hold that this statement about the removal of the nakedness is meant as a eulogy for the sipping, since the sipping is not a matter for injunction here, and since the imagination about the removal of nakedness appears on its own right as the subject-matter of the injunction. It cannot also be argued that from such a point of view the same sipping will come to serve two purposes, viz that of purification and of a garment; for these are admitted to be two different acts, inasmuch as the sipping as an act in itself is admitted to be meant for the purification of a man, while the imagination of the water, used by him for the purification, as a cloth for *Prāṇa*, is certainly a separate act which is introduced for the purpose of providing a garment for *Prāṇa*. Thus this is free from all criticism.

As for the text, "Whatever is (known as) food for all, right down to dogs, worms, insects, and moths, is your food" (Bṛ. VI. i. 14), it cannot be interpreted to mean that all kinds of food are enjoined for use, since no such word of injunction is in evidence, and since this is an impossibility. But the injunction is about looking upon everything as the food of *Prāṇa*. And owing to association with this, it is but reasonable to maintain that even in the text, "water is garment", no injunction is given for sipping water, but the injunction is about looking upon the well-known water used for sipping as the garment (of *Prāṇa*); for there can be no such thing as half murder.[14] Moreover, the predicate "(They) sip", having been used in the present tense, cannot imply an injunction.

Opponent: Is not the verb "(they) think" also equally used in the present tense?

Vedāntin: That is truly so. But if one injunction alone can be imparted, then from the mention of the act of covering by water, it follows that what is enjoined here is the unique act of thinking of water as the garment, but not so the sipping as it is the selfsame sipping already known. This is what we have propounded earlier. As for the argument that the imperative form is clearly visible in the case of sipping, that too is refuted on account of sipping being followed as a usual course. For this very reason that the sipping has not to be prescribed, the text of the Kāṇva recension stops with, "They regard it as the removal of the nakedness of the vital force" (Bṛ. VI. i. 14), and they do not have the (additional Mādhyandina) text, "Hence a man possessed of this knowledge" etc. Therefore in the Mādhyandina recension also, it is to be understood that what is referred to by "a man having such a knowledge" is a meditation

[14] "One cannot both eat the cake and have it." The sipping cannot be an injunction for physical action and "all food" an injunction for meditation.

on (or imagination about) the cloth of the vital force, which is the relevant subject-matter and which is prescribed by taking for granted the sipping as a usual practice. It is not proper to suppose that in one place the actual sipping and at another the imaginary conception about the cloth is enjoined, for the trend of such statements as "water is the garment" is the same in both the places. Hence the reasonable position is that the imaginary conception of cloth is prescribed here and not sipping.

Topic 10: Same Meditation in the Same Branch

समान एवं चाभेदात् ॥१९॥

समाने In the same (branch) च also एवम् similar (sameness of meditation and combination of traits) अभेदात् owing to non-difference (of object).

19. (The meditations) in the same branch are similarly the same (and their traits are to be combined) because of the non-difference of the object.

Doubt: In the Vājasaneyi branch, under the topic of the "secret knowledge of fire", there occurs a meditation stamped with the name of Sāṇḍilya (to whom it was revealed). In the course of this, we hear of such traits as, "He should meditate on the Self as identified with the mind, having the vital force as the body, and effulgence for appearance". In the same branch, the Bṛhadāraṇyaka, again, has this text, "This being, identified with the mind and resplendent (is realized by the Yogins) within the heart like a grain of rice or barley. He is the lord of all, the ruler of all, and He governs whatever there is" (Bṛ. V. vi. 1). The doubt arises here: Is it the same meditation and are all the traits found in the "secret knowledge of fire" and the Bṛhadāraṇyaka to be combined? Or are the meditations different and are the traits to be kept apart? What should be the conclusion?

Opponent: The conclusion is that the meditations are different and the traits are not to be combined.

Why?

So that the contingency of repetition may not arise. Having

considered the fact that the charge of repetition can be avoided by taking shelter under the plea that this repetition occurs owing to a difference among the students and the meditators in the different branches of the Vedas, it was determined that (despite this fact) the meditation is the same, and it was stated that the traits found in excess in one place are to be combined with the other traits (stated elsewhere) in connection with the anecdote of *Prāṇa* etc. But in the case of the same branch, this (kind of) avoidance of the charge of repetition becomes impossible owing to the absence of any difference among the students or meditators (of the very same branch), so that the meditations, occurring in remote contexts, cannot be the same. And it is not possible to make a division to the effect that one portion of the scripture is meant for prescribing meditation and the other for prescribing attributes; for in that case dissimilar new traits alone would have been mentioned in different places, whereas both similar and dissimilar traits, as for instance "identified with the mind", are prescribed at both the places. Hence the attributes are not to be combined reciprocally.

Vedāntin: This being the position, we say: Just as it is proper that the meditation should be the same and the traits also should be combined in the different branches, so also it should be the case in the same branch, for the entity meditated on is non-different. We recognize that the very same Brahman is to be meditated on in both the places as possessed of the attributes of being "identified with the mind" etc. The entity to be meditated on determines the nature of the meditation; and when there is no difference in nature, we cannot assert that the meditations are different or that the attributes differ (and remain restricted) in consonance with the difference of the meditations.

Opponent: Have we not to assert a difference of meditation in order to avoid the charge of repetition?

Vedāntin: The answer is in the negative, for a division of purport is reasonable, inasmuch as it involves no illogicality to maintain that one of the texts is meant for prescribing meditation and the other for attributes.

Opponent: If such be the case (i.e. if the Bṛhadāraṇyaka prescribes the attributes while the "secret teaching about fire" presents the entity to be meditated on), then what is not stated in the "secret teaching about fire" should alone have been stated in the Bṛhadāraṇyaka, as for instance, "He is the lord of all" etc. (Bṛ. V. vi. 1), and what is stated there, for instance, "identified with the mind" etc. should not have been stated here.

Vedāntin: That is no defect, since it is with the help of that (similarity) alone that we recognize the identity of the meditation occurring elsewhere. For it is precisely through the presentation of similar traits that "the meditation of Śāṇḍilya" occurring remotely (in the "secret teaching about fire") is shown to be the same as the meditation here (in the Bṛhadāraṇyaka); and after establishing this fact, the Upaniṣad adds to that (earlier) meditation this injunction about attributes (in the Bṛhadāraṇyaka). Otherwise, how can it be said that this (text in the Bṛhadāraṇyaka) is by way of prescribing the attributes with regard to that (in the other place)? Moreover, when a sentence can be held to have served a purpose by presenting something that was not known earlier, the portion therein that presents something already known can be logically held to be merely a restatement of a known fact; thus the recognition of identity cannot be refuted on that score (of repetition). Hence the logical position here is that even though the two texts occur in the same branch of the Vedas, the meditation is the same, and the attributes are to be combined.

Topic 11: No Combination in Meditation on Satya-Brahman

सम्बन्धादेवमन्यत्रापि ॥२०॥

सम्बन्धात् On account of connection एवम् (it should be) so अन्यत्र elsewhere अपि also.

20. Elsewhere also (in the case of meditation on Satya-Brahman), (the attributes have to be combined) as here (in the case of Śāṇḍilya-Vidyā), on account of the very fact of connection (with the same object of meditation).

Doubt: In the Bṛhadāraṇyaka Upaniṣad the beginning is made with "Satya[15] is Brahman" (V. v. 1); and then it is said, "That which is Satya is that sun—the Being who is in that orb and the Being who is in the right eye" (V. v. 2), where the particular abodes of that very Satya-Brahman is taught in the divine and corporeal contexts. Then after the *vyāhṛtis* (mystic syllables—*bhūḥ*, *bhuvaḥ*, and *svaḥ*) are conceived of as His body (V. v. 3), two secret (mystic) names are taught, "His secret name is Ahar." This is in the divine context (V. v. 3), "His secret name is Aham (I)."[16] This is in the corporeal context (V. v. 4). Now the doubt arises: Are these secret names to be understood jointly in both the places, or are they to be understood separately, one in the divine context and the other in the corporeal?

Opponent: With regard to this, it is thus surmised by the aphorism itself: Just as in the case of the "meditation of Śāṇḍilya", a combination of attributes has been spoken of although the meditation itself is stated separately in two places, similar must be the case elsewhere also where the subject-matter is similar; for they (the traits) are connected with the same meditation. For this meditation on Satya, recited under the divine and corporeal contexts, is but one, owing to the non-difference of the introduction and the mention of the two in an intermixed manner. Why should not an attribute mentioned therein belong to that very meditation? For any code of conduct that is enjoined in relation to a teacher, for instance in the matter of serving him, is equally applicable whether he (the teacher) be in a village or in a forest. Hence both the secret teachings (about the names) are to be understood at both the places.

Vedāntin: This being the position (of the opponent), the refutation is stated in:

[15] *Sat* means the imperceptible elements—earth, water and fire; *tyat* means air and space. So Satya means Brahman as Hiraṇyagarbha identifying Himself with the imperceptible five elements.

[16] Ahar is derived from *han* or *hā* meaning to kill or shun (evil); and Aham points to the inmost Self.

न वा विशेषात ॥२१॥

वा Rather न not, विशेषात् because of distinction.

21. Rather they are not to be combined on account of a distinction.

Rather both the secret names are not to be added to both. Why?

Because of a distinction, because they are firmly associated with (two) distinct places of meditation.

Opponent: How is there an association with distinct places?

Vedāntin: The answer is this: The Upaniṣad introduces the Person (Puruṣa) in the divine plane with the words, "Of this Being who is in the solar orb" (Bṛ. V. v. 3), and then recites, "His secret name is Ahar" (ibid.). Again, introducing the Being in the corporeal plane with the words, "Of this Being who is in the right eye" (Bṛ. V. vi. 4), the Upaniṣad recites, "His secret name is Aham" (Ibid.). Now the pronominal form "of this" refers to a proximate object. Hence these secret names are taught in connection with particular abodes alone. So how can both be added to both the places?

Opponent: Is not the infinite Being the selfsame entity on the divine and corporeal planes; for two abodes are spoken of with regard to the selfsame Satya-Brahman (Hiraṇyagarbha)?

Vedāntin: This is quite so. Yet since particular secret names have been taught for the same Being in relation to the particular modes of that Being, the names must belong to Him under those particular modes alone. We have a parallel instance of this. Although the teacher continues to be the selfsame person, the service rendered to him while he is seated cannot be the same while he keeps standing, and what is meant for him while he is standing cannot be the same when he is sitting. As for the illustration of the same conduct towards the teacher whether he be in a village or a forest, that is beside the point. Since the personality of the teacher does not differ in the village and the forest, and so no difference in the attributes associated with his personality is brought by the village or the forest, the service is the same at both the places. Hence the two secret names have to be dealt with separately (by restricting each to its own place).

दर्शयति च ॥२२॥

22. The scripture also indicates the same thing.

Moreover, signs indicative of the separate treatment of such attributes are in evidence thus: "Of this one the form is the same as of the other one, this one has the same knuckles as the other one, the same name as the other one" (Ch. I. vii. 5).

Opponent: How can this be an indicator?

Vedāntin: That is being shown: Noticing that the attributes differ according to the difference of the solar orb and the eye, and so cannot be combined with each other (naturally), the text resorts here to the process of extending (notionally) the attributes of the Being in the solar orb to the Being in the eye by saying, "Of this one the form is the same as of that one" (ibid.) etc. Hence the conclusion is that these two secret names are to be dealt with separately.

Topic 12: Attributes of Brahman in Ranayaniya Not to be Combined Elsewhere

सम्भृतिद्युव्याप्त्यपि चातः ॥२३॥

च And सम्भृति-द्यु-व्याप्ति-अपि Unchallenged power and pervasion of heaven also (are not to be combined) अतः for this very reason.

23. And (the attributes of Brahman such as) possession of unchallenged powers and pervasion of heaven are also not to be added to other meditations for the same reason (of association with special abodes).

In the supplementary text (*khila*, that contains no injunction or prohibition) of the Rāṇāyanīya branch (of the Sāma Veda) occurs this passage: "The powers (of creating space etc.) have

Brahman alone as their source, and they are held by Brahman without any challenge. That pre-existing Brahman pervaded heaven in the beginning (even before the birth of the Gods)", where mention is made of such exalted qualities of Brahman as possession of unchallenged powers, pervasion of heaven, and so on. And in their Upaniṣad itself are stated such meditations on Brahman as the "meditation of Śāṇḍilya". When the consideration arises as to whether the exalted qualities of Brahman are to be added to those meditations or not and the conclusion (of the opponent) is that they are to be combined, since they are connected with Brahman, the answer (of the Vedāntin) is given: Such exalted qualities as the possession of unchallenged powers and pervasion of heaven etc. are not to be combined with such meditations as that of Śāṇḍilya, on account of that very reason, viz association with special abodes. Thus in the "meditation of Śāṇḍilya", the heart is spoken of as the abode of Brahman: "This my Self is within the heart" (Ch. III. xiv. 3). Similarly it is so in the meditation on the small one (*Dahara-Vidyā*) as well: "A small abode of the size of a lotus; within that is the small Space (Brahman)" (Ch. VIII. i. 1). But in the "meditation of Upakosala", the abode is the eye: "The Being that is seen in the eye" (Ch. IV. xv. 1). Thus different abodes are discernible on the corporeal plane for these separate meditations, whereas the exalted qualities, such as possession of unchallenged powers and pervasion of heaven occur on the divine plane. How can these be available on the corporeal plane?

Opponent: But the exalted qualities of the divine plane are heard of in connection with these as well, as for instance in, "Greater than heaven, greater than these worlds" (Ch. III. xiv. 3), "This one is indeed the bestower of effulgence, for this One shines in all the worlds" (Ch. IV. xv. 4), "The Space within the heart is as vast as that other Space. Within this are included both heaven and earth" (Ch. VIII. i. 3), and so on. Moreover, there are also other meditations on Brahman, unassociated with any special abode, such as on Brahman having sixteen digits.

Vedāntin: This is truly so. Yet there is a special reason here for not combining the attributes like the possession of unchallenged powers. The reasonable position is that when the mention of similar attributes calls up to memory (i.e. establishes the identity of) the meditations occurring at remote places, then the attributes occurring at remote places have to be taken together. But the attributes like the possession of unchallenged powers, and the attributes mentioned in connection with the texts of such meditations as that of Śāṇḍilya are mutually incompatible, and hence they cannot call up (i.e. establish the sameness of) the meditations occurring in remote contexts. Besides, it cannot be said that by reason of a mere connection with Brahman, a meditation occurring in a remote context can be called up; for that logic can apply even in a case of actual difference of meditations. The settled conclusion is that even though Brahman is the same, It can be meditated on differently in accordance with a difference of the exalted qualities; for differences are noticeable in the cases of meditations with such qualities as "being higher than the high and greater than the great" (in the case of the same Udgītha—Vide B. S. III. iii. 7). Hence the attributes of possessing unchallenged powers etc. are not to be combined with such meditations as that of Śāṇḍilya.

Topic 13: Purusa-Vidyas in Chandogya and Taittiriya

पुरुषविद्यायामिव चेतरेषामनाम्नानात् ॥२४॥

च And (the traits of the *Puruṣa-Vidyā* are not to be added to the Taittirīyaka conception) अनाम्नानात् because of not having been recited इव as इतरेषाम् in other branches पुरुष-विद्यायाम् in the course of *Puruṣa-Vidyā* (i.e. thinking about the aspirant).

24. And the characteristics of the Puruṣa-Vidyā are not to be added to the Taittirīyaka because they have not been recited there as it is done in the course of the Puruṣa-Vidyā in other branches.

Doubt : Both in the *brāhmaṇa* portions of the Tāṇḍins and the Paiṅgins, dealing with secret teachings, occurs the meditation on *puruṣa* (lit. man, i.e. the aspirant himself). There the aspirant is imagined to be a sacrifice; the whole span of his life is divided into three parts and are conceived of as the three periods of a sacrifice (i.e. *savanas*, during which the Soma juice is extracted); his hankering for food and so on are imagined to be initiation for a sacrifice and so on; and some other characteristics, such as prayer and utterance of *mantras* are also met with there (Ch. III. xvi. 1-6). The Taittirīyakas also conceive of some sort of *puruṣa*-sacrifice in the section starting with, "Of that very man of knowledge, fancied as the sacrifice, the soul is the sacrificer, faith is the wife" etc. (Tai. Ā. VI. lii. 1., Nārā. 80). With regard to this, the doubt, arises: Are the characteristics of the *puruṣa*-sacrifice, as stated elsewhere, to be added to those met with in the Taittirīyaka, or are they not?

Vedāntin: When the possibility of combination arises from the fact of both being *puruṣa*-sacrifices, we say that the characteristics are not to be combined.

Why?

Since we fail to recognize the one to be of the same form as the other. That is why the teacher (Vyāsa) says, "As in the *puruṣa*-meditation" (in the Chāndogya Upaniṣad) etc. The text about the meditation on *puruṣa*, as it occurs in some, viz the Taittirīya branch, is not the same as found in some other branches, viz of the Paiṅgins and Tāṇḍins. For in the Taittirīya, the conception of the *puruṣa* as a sacrifice is seen to be dissimilar to that of the others, inasmuch as the latter enumerate a different series consisting of the wife, the sacrificer, Veda, the altar, a bundle of Kuśa grass, the sacrificial stake, the *ghee*, the sacrificial animal, the priests, and others.[17] As for the conception of the *savanas*, that too differs from others, inasmuch as their text is, "Those which are afternoon, morning, and noon are the *savanas*" (Nārā. 80), (whereas the Tāṇḍins conceive of the life span as such). As for the similarities of the conception of death

[17] "Of that very sacrifice of the man of knowledge, the soul is the sacrificer, faith is the wife, the body is the fuel, the chest the altar, the bundle of *Kūśa* is the tuft of hair on the head; the heart is the sacrificial stake, desire is *ghee*, anger is the animal, austerity is fire, the quietening self-control is *dakṣinā* (payment to the priests), speech is the priest called Hotā (pourer of the oblation), *Prāṇa* is the priest Udgātā, the eye is the priest Adhvaryu, the mind is the Brahmā (Tai. Ā. VI. lii. 1).

as the final bath marking the end of the sacrifice, and so on, these are so few that they are overridden by a host of differences, and as such cannot bring about a recognition of identity. Moreover, in the Taittirīyaka, the *puruṣa* is not spoken of as a sacrifice, the text there being "of this sacrifice of the man of knowledge"; and the sixth case-endings there (in *viduṣaḥ yajñasya*) are not used in apposition conveying the sense of "the man who is the sacrifice". For the *puruṣa* (aspiring man) cannot be a sacrifice in the primary sense. The sixth case-endings are used here in a non-appositional (non-co-ordinate) sense, meaning thereby "of the sacrifice of the man of knowledge". For a man can have a relation with a sacrifice in the primary sense; and when there is a possibility of the primary sense, that alone should be accepted and not any secondary sense. And in the sentence "the soul is the sacrificer" (see foot-note) the text speaks of the man as the sacrificer, thereby showing that the sacrificer is related with the sacrifice in a non-appositional sense. Moreover, in the face of the text "of the sacrifice of that very man of knowledge" (see foot-note), which restates something which is assumed to be already known, should anyone hold that the man is identified with the sacrifice and that the soul etc. are identified with the sacrificer and others, he will open himself to the charge of splitting up the same text into two. Besides, when it is noticed that in the earlier text the knowledge of the Self, in association with the renunciation of (everything), is taught and then it is stated in a regular sequence, "of this very man of knowledge" etc., we understand that this text is complementary to the earlier text and not an independent one. So also we notice that the same result is shown for both the sections, which is, "He attains the greatness of Brahman" (Tai. Ā. VI. lii. 1). But in the case of other (Chāndogya) branches, the meditation on *puruṣa* is presented independently of (and not as complementary to) any other, and it has for its result the prolongation of life, for it is said in that very connection, "He who meditates thus lives for a hundred and sixteen years". Hence the prayer, *mantras*, etc., spoken of in those other branches as the characteristics of the meditation on *puruṣa*, are not to be added to the Taittirīyaka.

Topic 14: Non-combination of Disparate Traits

वेधाद्यर्थभेदात् ॥२५॥

वेध-आदि Piercing etc. (are not to be combined) अर्थ-भेदात् since their purports are disparate.

25. *Piercing etc. are not to be applied in meditation, since (the mantras of piercing etc. are) disparate in purport.*

At the commencement of the Upaniṣad of the Atharva Veda is found the *mantra*, "O deity, destroy my enemy by piercing his body all over—specially by piercing the heart, separating the veins and arteries, breaking up his skull all around. Let my enemy be disintegrated thus in three ways" etc. The *mantra* occurring in the text of the Tāṇḍins is: "O god Sun, get the sacrifice accomplished" etc. The *mantra* of the Śātyāyanins is, "O Indra of the white horse, and having a blue hue like sapphire" etc. Of the Kaṭhas and the Taittirīyakas it is, "Let Mitra (Sun) be benign to us, let Varuṇa be benign to us" etc. (Tai. I. i. 1). But for the Vājasaneyins the Upaniṣad is preceded by the *Pravargya Brāhmaṇa* thus: "In days of yore, the gods made up their minds to perform a *satra*" (a sacrifice lasting from 13 to 100 days) etc. For the Kauṣītakins also the *Agniṣṭoma Brāhmaṇa* is read before the commencement of the Upaniṣad thus: "Brahman Itself is the Agniṣṭoma sacrifice; the day in which it is performed is also Brahman Itself. Therefore those who resort to this sacrifice every day, attain immortality" (i.e. supreme Brahman, in due course) etc. Now we have to consider whether all these *mantras*, counting from, "O deity, destroy my enemy" etc., and all the rites counting from Pravargya are to be combined with the meditations or they are not. What is then the conclusion that dawns on us?

Opponent: These are to be added to the meditations.

Why?

Because these occur in the proximity of the Upaniṣadic texts in which meditations predominate.

Objection: But we do not perceive these to have been prescribed (by any injunction) for use in meditation.

Opponent: Truly so; but though they are not perceived to be so, we infer this on the strength of proximity. For in a case where proximity gives some purpose to a sentence, it is not proper to leave it floating in the air capriciously.

Objection: But we do not notice any indication in these *mantras* suggestive of the use of these things in meditation. And how can we understand such rites as the Pravargya to be meant for use in meditation also when they are palpably enjoined for some other purpose?

Opponent: That creates no difficulty, inasmuch as we can infer on the strength of the use of the term *hṛdaya* (heart) that these *mantras* have some applicability in connection with meditations as well. For the heart, etc. are very often taught as the places etc. for meditation. In that way, the *mantras* "piercing the heart" and so on, can very justifiably become contributory factors in meditation. And as a matter of fact, such *mantras* as, "I attain the earth by this one, by this one, by this one" (Ch. III. xv. 3), and so on, are seen to be used in meditations. Hence, even though the rites like Pravargya are used in other contexts, there is nothing contradictory in their being used in meditation, just as the Bṛhaspati-sava (sacrifice) is used in course of the Vājapeya.[18]

Vedāntin: This being the position, we say that these are not to be combined with the meditations.

Why?

"Since (the *mantras* about) piercing etc. are disparate in purport." The purports, namely piercing etc. of the heart and so on, that are conveyed by such *mantras* as, "pierce the heart", are disparate, that is to say, they are disconnected with the meditations spoken of in the Upaniṣads, so that they have no capacity to combine with them.

Opponent: We surely propounded earlier that the heart etc. are connected with meditations, and through them, these also become connected with meditations.

Vedāntin: The answer is, no. All that could be imagined

[18] The Bṛhaspati-sava leads to the attainment of *Brahmavarcas*. Yet though having an independent result, it is also enjoined as a part of the Vājapeya sacrifice.

somehow in this way would be the appropriateness of the mention of the heart alone; but the *mantra* here does not mean the heart alone; for the meaning as a whole of this *mantra*, viz "piercing the heart, separating the veins", and so on, cannot be connected with the meditations; for it purports to serve as a magic spell for a malevolent purpose. Hence the *mantra*, "Piercing his body all over", and so on is connected with some malevolent rite. Similarly from the text "O god Sun, accomplish the sacrifice", which bears the imprint of the accomplishment of the sacrifice, it would appear that it is connected with a rite. As for the particular form of that connection, it is to be known from some other valid source. So also is the conclusion with regard to the other *mantras* which are known from some indication, explicit words, or some other valid means of knowledge to be applicable for other purposes. Even though they may be read of in the Upaniṣadic parts, they do not form a part of those meditations on the ground of mere proximity. For the relative unimportance of proximity in comparison with explicit text etc. has been stated in Pūrva-Mīmāṁsā in "As among explicit statement, indication (or word capacity), syntactical connection, context, order, and name, when any two of them are at variance with regard to anything, the succeeding one is weaker than the earlier, since the succeeding one is put at a disadvantage by the predecessor as regards the meaning implied."[19] (Jai. Śu. III. iii. 13). So also the rites like Pravargya, which have their application elsewhere, have no scope in the sphere of meditation; for these have nothing in common with meditation etc. As for the Bṛhaspati-sava, its application as an addendum to Vājapeya is gathered clearly from, "After performing the Vājapeya sacrifice one shall perform the Bṛhaspati-sava". Moreover, this single rite Pravargya, enjoined only once, has been assigned by a more powerful valid means of knowledge to other rites (viz Jyotiṣṭoma etc.), and hence it cannot be assigned elsewhere (to meditation) by a weaker means of knowledge (e.g. proximity, order). This would have been the

[19] For getting at the meaning, the succeeding means of knowledge depends on the earlier and not vice versa.

case if the predominance of any one of the two means of knowledge were not obvious. But as between two strong and weak means of knowledge, it is not possible to have that kind of absence of distinction as regards predominance, for strength and weakness themselves constitute that distinction. Hence from the mere fact of the proximity of the texts, it is not proper to jump to the conclusion that either *mantras* or rites of this kind form part and parcel of meditations. Rather one should remain content with the fact that the textual proximity occurs on account of some common feature of both, namely that they are recited together by people who retire to the forest.

Topic 15: Rejection and Reception of Merit

हानौ तूपायनशब्दशेषत्वात् कुशाच्छन्दस्तुत्युपगानवत्तदुक्तम् ॥२६॥

तु But हानौ when the rejection (is mentioned, acceptance also is implied) उप-अयन-शब्द-शेषत्वात् it being connected with the correlative term कुशाः-छन्दः-स्तुति-उपगान-वत् as in the case of *kuśas* (wooden sticks), metres, praise, and recitation; तत् that उक्तम् has been stated.

26. *But where only the rejection of virtue and vice is spoken of, the reception of these by others has to be inferred, on account of the term reception being a counter-correlative of rejection. And this is on the analogy of kuśas, metres, praise, and recitation, as has been explained (by Jaimini).*

Doubt: The Taṇḍins have this Upaniṣadic text: "Like a horse becoming clean by shaking away its (dead) hair (along with dust), or the moon becoming bright by freeing itself from the mouth of Rāhu (who causes an eclipse), I shall cast off (i.e. become free from identity with) the body, and becoming identified with the ever-existing Self, I shall attain the world of Brahman" (Ch. VIII. xiii. 1). So also those belonging to the Atharva-Veda have the text, "Then the illumined one completely shakes off both virtue and vice, becomes taintless, and attains absolute equality" (Mu. III. i. 3.).[20] Similarly the Śāṭyā-

[20] Some editions quote Mu. III. ii. 8.

yanins have this text: "His sons inherit his properties, the friends his virtuous deeds, and the enemies his vicious deeds". Similarly also the Kauṣītakins have, "He shakes off both virtues and vices; his beloved relatives get his virtues and his hated relatives his vices" (Kau. I. 4). Thus it is seen that in some texts virtues and vices are spoken of as being rejected; in some texts as being shared separately by the people loved and hated; and in some texts both acceptance and rejection are spoken of.

Opponent: As to that, if both the facts are clearly stated, we have nothing to say. Where the acceptance alone is spoken of, but not the rejection, there also the rejection is to be understood through "presumptive implication"; for when one's good and evil deeds are received by others, their (earlier) rejection becomes a necessity. But where rejection alone is spoken of and not acceptance, and the doubt arises whether the acceptance will take place or not, the conclusion is that it will not take place, since it is not heard of, and since what is heard of in another branch belongs to some other kind of meditation. Moreover, the rejection of the virtues and vices is by the actor himself, whereas their acceptance is by others; now how can rejection imply any acceptance where both these are not connected inevitably? Hence acceptance is not implied in a case of (mere) rejection.

Vedāntin: This being the position, the answer is given in the aphorism, "But where only the rejection of virtue and vice is spoken of" etc. Even if rejection alone be heard of in a text, acceptance should become added to it, since it forms a counterpart of rejection; and in the Kauṣītaki Upaniṣad, the word "acceptance" is heard of as a correlative of "rejection". Hence acceptance follows as a matter of course even at other places where the word "rejection" alone is heard of. As for the argument that the one does not follow the other, because it has not been mentioned by the Upaniṣad, because it is included in some other meditation, and because there is no inevitable connection, that is being answered: This pronouncement of restriction[21] would

[21] When the conceptions differ, the traits remain confined to their contexts; but when the conceptions are the same, they are combined.

be right in a case where something to be done has been spoken of at one place and then it is sought to be extended somewhere else. But neither rejection nor acceptance is here declared as something to be undertaken, they being spoken of only for the sake of praising knowledge thus: This knowledge of Brahman is so glorious that by its power are shaken off good and evil from the enlightened man, even though they are the causes of transmigration; and then they get lodgement in his friends and foes (respectively). Since this declaration is made by way of praise, and since acceptance is mentioned in some texts as occurring immediately after rejection, the aphorist thinks that in other texts also, wherever there is a mention of rejection, acceptance will also follow consequentially, so that the eulogy may be complete. It is a well-known fact that one corroborative statement (*Arthavāda*) derives its application by drawing on another, as for instance such passages as, "The yonder sun is the twenty-first counting from this earth" (Ch. II. x. 5), and others. How can it be asserted here that the sun is the twenty-first in order unless one draws upon the other corroborative statement contained in the text, "The months are twelve, the seasons are five, these worlds are three, and that sun is the twenty-first"? Similarly in the cases of the corroborative statements like, "The two *triṣṭubhs* (metres of that name) are conceived of for the sake of endowing (the sacrifice, which is thought of as a person) with organs", it is noticed that one has to draw upon such other corroborative texts as, "Then organ is indeed the *triṣṭubha*". The statement about "acceptance" being meant as a (corroborative) eulogy for knowledge, one must not worry oneself too much over the problem as to how the good and evil of one can be taken over by others. And by using the word "term" in "on account of the term reception being a counter-correlative of rejection", the aphorist indicates that the succession of acceptance after rejection is mentioned merely for the sake of eulogy; for if the combination of the characteristics had been meant, it would have been stated that the "thing itself (viz virtue) denoted by the word acceptance follows the "thing" (viz vice) denoted by the word rejection. (As a matter of fact, he speaks of "term" and not "thing"). Hence in the course of the discussion about the combination of characteristics, this aphorism occurs (as a side issue) by way of showing the process of combining the corroborative passages.

The portion, "on the analogy of *kuśas* (i.e. wooden sticks for keeping count of the hymns sung), metres, praise, and recitation" is stated by way of citing illustrations. Thus in the text of the Bhāllavins, "O *kuśas*, you have been fashioned from the great trees. Such as you are, you protect me (the sacrificer)", we hear of the origin of the *kuśas* from great trees in a general way; but according to the text of the Śāṭyāyanins, viz "The *Kuśas* are made of the Audumbara tree", where a specific mention occurs, the *kuśas* made of the Audumbara wood are resorted to. Or take another illustration: In some texts about the metres of the gods (having more than nine syllables to a quarter) and the metres of *Asuras* (with nine syllables only to a quarter), when the possibility arises of their being used indiscriminately either first or last, the decision is taken according to the text of the Paiṅgins which says, "The metres of the gods have precedence" There is still another illustration: When in some text no particular time for the chanting of the hymn meant for taking up the vessel called Ṣoḍaśin (in the course of the Atirātra sacrifice) is in evidence, the particular time is ascertained from the text, "Near about the time of the sunrise, the hymn is to be chanted", which occurs in the scriptural statement in the Ṛg-Veda. There is also this other illustration: In some texts the chanting of hymns is prescribed for the priests in general; but according to the special mention in the text of the Bhāllavins that the Adhvaryu is not to sing, he is left out. The idea conveyed (by these illustrations) is that just as in the cases of these *kuśa* etc., the special characteristic has to be borrowed from other texts, so also must "receiving" be combined with "rejection". For unless the special characteristic mentioned in one Vedic text, be accepted in another, it will lead to an option (alternativeness) everywhere; but that is improper where there is a way out. Hence it has been said in the Pūrva-Mīmāṁsā (Jai. Sū. X. viii. 15), "What is really meant is the ruling out of the other in conformity with the complementary passage, for if a simple negation be the meaning it will lead to alternativeness which is a defect".[22] (This is the first interpretation).

Or the alternative interpretation is this: With regard to these very texts about "(*vidhūnana*) shaking", the point to be considered is whether by this mention of "shaking" is conveyed the idea of rejection (i.e. shaking off) of good and evil or something else.

Opponent : As to that, the conclusion to be drawn is that the verb "to shake (*dhū*)" does not mean rejection, since grammar says that the root *dhūn* is used in the sense of fluttering, as it is seen in such expressions as, "The tips of the flags flutter", when the tips of the flags are moved by wind. Hence by *vidhūnana* is meant causing disturbance, and that disturbance means the prevention of good and evil results from their fruition, they being kept in abeyance for some time.

Vedāntin : After propounding the opponent's view thus, the answer has to be given: It is but proper that this word *vidhūnana* should mean rejection, since it has as its complementary the word acceptance. For unless the good and evil accruing to somebody be discarded by him, they cannot be received by another. Although it is not possible for the good and evil of one to be received by another in the proper sense, still in accordance with the fact that it has been declared so by the Upaniṣad, it can be ascertained that rejection itself is denoted by *vidhūnana*. And even though this reception is heard of

[22] It is enjoined that the *mantra*, "We also perform the sacrifice" is to be used in all the sacrifices; and it is also enjoined that in an Anuyāja this *mantra* is not to be used. Somebody may, however, conclude that since an Anuyāja is also a sacrifice, the *mantra* should be used there; and this will give rise to an alternativeness. The conclusion is that the injunction is not a simple negation, but a restriction—the *mantra* is to be used in all sacrifices other than an Anuyāja.

Or—In connection with the Jyotiṣṭoma sacrifice it is enjoined; "The initiated man (*dīkṣita*) shall not offer any gift, shall not perform any sacrifice, shall not cook". But this contradicts the injunction that "one has to perform the Agnihotra sacrifice as long as one lives." Hence the meaning is not a simple negation in the first sentence, but rather "A man other than a *dīkṣita* shall perform the sacrifice etc."

By this interpretation, the optional use in either case is avoided.

only in some particular context, in the proximity of *vidhūnana* (shaking off), it becomes a determining factor everywhere in the matter of ascertaining the meaning by supplying a lacuna in all those places, even as it is by the Vedic passages in the cases of the *kuśas*, metres, praise, and recitation. Moreover, it is not possible to shake virtue and vice like the tip of a flag, since they are not material substances. Again (in the case of) the horse, when it discards the dust by shaking its hair, it also "shakes off" its old hair; and the *brāhmaṇa* text is, "Shaking off sin like a horse shaking off its hair" (Ch. VIII. xiii. 1). Since a verbal root can have many meanings, there is no contradiction with grammar. The portion *taduktam* has been already explained.

Topic 16: Discarding Virtue and Vice at Death

साम्पराये तर्तव्याभावात्तथा ह्यन्ये ॥२७॥

साम्पराये While departing (from the body) तर्तव्य-अभावात् since nothing remains to be attained हि for तथा so अन्ये others (say).

27. *(A man of knowledge gets rid of virtue and vice) at the time of death, since nothing remains to be attained. For thus it is that others (i.e. the followers of the other branches) state.*

The Kauṣītakins mention in connection with the *Paryaṅka-Vidyā* that the aspirant gets rid of his virtue and vice even while going along the path of the gods to Brahman, seated on a *paryaṅka* (couch). The start is made with, "He attains this path of the gods and then arrives at the world of Fire" (Kau. I. 3), and then it is said, "He arrives at the river Virajā, which he crosses by the mind alone, thereby (i.e. as a result of crossing) shaking off virtue and vice" (Kau. I. 4). As regards this, should the text be understood in its obvious sense, implying the separation from virtue and vice on the way itself, or does this separation occur even at the beginning when one moves out of the body? When this consideration arises and when on the textual authority it appears that the obvious meaning should be accepted, the aphorist says, "A man of knowledge gets rid of virtue and vice at the time of death" etc. That is to say, the aphorist asserts that at the very time of death, at the time of moving away from the body, occurs this discarding of virtue and vice as a result of the power of knowledge. The reason is given in, "since nothing remains to be attained" inasmuch as a man, who has left for the other world, and who wants to attain Brahman through illumination, can have nothing to attain in the interregnum through the help of virtue and vice, for the sake of which it can be imagined that virtue and vice linger intact for a while. As a matter of fact, however, they get sublated by the power of knowledge, since their result is opposed to that of the latter. And that sublation should occur as soon as knowledge is ready to yield its result. Hence though this destruction of virtue and vice really occurs earlier (at the time of death), it is stated later (in the Kauṣītaki). Thus it is that others, viz the Taṇḍins and the Śātyāyanins read of this discarding of virtue and vice as occurring at the earlier state itself in, "Having shaken off sin like a horse shaking off its hair" (Ch. VIII. xiii. 1), "His sons inherit his properties, the friends his good deeds, and the foes his bad deeds".

छन्दत उभयाविरोधात् ॥२८॥

उभय-अविरोधात् Since there is no conflict between the two texts (as also between cause and effect) छन्दतः (on the admission that virtue and vice can be destroyed) by voluntary practices.

28. As there is no conflict between the two (i.e. two texts, or cause and effect) on the admission that destruction results from voluntary effort, (therefore such effort must take place before death).

If it be the case that the destruction of good and evil has to be admitted in the middle of the course for an aspirant who has departed from the body and is on his journey along the path of the gods, then since, after the death of the body, he cannot undertake at will such human efforts as *yama*, *niyama* (self-control and regulated conduct), pursuit of knowledge, etc., on which such attenuation of virtue and vice depends, the destruction of good and evil, resulting from such human effort, cannot be reasonably upheld as happening midway. Hence such means have to be practised voluntarily at an earlier period during the stage of aspiration; and it is to be noticed that the attenuation of virtue and vice results from that alone. In this way the cause and effect can be brought into logical relationship and the texts of the Tāṇḍins and Śāṭyāyanins can be reconciled.

TOPIC 17: PATHS OF THOSE WHO KNOW OR DO NOT KNOW THE QUALIFIED BRAHMAN

गतेरर्थवत्त्वमुभयथाऽन्यथा हि विरोधः ॥२९॥

अर्थवत्त्वम् Purposefulness **गतेः** of the (soul's) course (after death) **उभयथा** (is) in two (different) ways, **हि** because **अन्यथा** otherwise **विरोधः** (will arise) contradiction.

29. The soul's course after death must have purposefulness in two ways, for else it will lead to contradiction.

Doubt: In some texts the path of the gods is heard of in the proximity of the discarding of virtue and vice; but in other texts it is not. So the doubt arises as to whether the path of the gods will follow for all invariably after such destruction of good and evil or it will follow differentially (in different cases), emerging sometimes and sometimes not (for the followers of the qualified and non-qualified Brahman respectively).

Opponent: As to that, just as the reception of virtue and vice follows in all cases of their rejection, so also should the path of the gods follow everywhere.

Vedāntin: Faced with this conclusion, we say, "The soul's course after death must have purposefulness in two ways", that is to say, it should emerge differentially (in accordance with the knowledge of Brahman with or without attributes), the course being sometimes available and sometimes not; but it is not available invariably. Otherwise if the course be available uniformly for all, it will lead to a contradiction; for instance, any path leading to some region will stand opposed to the Upaniṣadic text, "shakes off both virtue and vice, becomes taintless and attains absolute equality" (Mu. III. i. 3). For how can the taintless one, who has no motion, reach a different region? His goal is absolute unity which is not contingent on reaching some other world, so that according to us any course to be followed is meaningless in this context.

उपपन्नस्तल्लक्षणार्थोपलब्धेर्लोकवत् ॥३०॥

(This is) उपपन्नः reasonable, तत्-लक्षण-अर्थ-उपलब्धे because facts, indicative of (a soul's journey), are met with, लोकवत् as is the case in common life.

30. This (differentiation) is reasonable, for facts indicative of a soul's journey are met with (in the case of meditation on the qualified Brahman alone), just as (much as such a difference is) met with in common life.

And this possibility of having two aspects, that is to say, the fact that the course is purposeful in some cases, but not so in others, is quite intelligible, since the "facts indicative of such a journey are met with". For facts implying the need of a journey are discernible in such meditations on the qualified Brahman as the *Paryaṅka-Vidyā*; for in that connection are mentioned many results such as ascending the couch, conversation with Brahman seated on the couch, and experience of special kinds of fragrance, etc., which are achievable only by going to a different region (i.e. Brahmaloka). The journey of the soul has a meaning there; but in the case of full illumination, no such fact indicative of such a journey is in evidence. For the men who realize the unity of the Self, whose desires all become fulfilled, who get all the seeds of evil burnt away even while living, have nothing else to look for except the exhaustion through experience of all the residual *karmas* that have begun to yield their results in the present bodies. In their case a journey is meaningless. And this division is to be understood in the same way as it exists in the world. "Just as in common life" one has to take the help of a road leading from one place to another when he wants to reach a village, but not so when he wants to get cured, even so is the case here. We shall deal with this more elaborately in the Fourth Chapter.

Topic 18: The Path of Gods Is for All Worshippers of Qualified Brahman

अनियमः सर्वासामविरोधः शब्दानुमानाभ्याम् ॥३१॥

अनियमः Non-restriction; सर्वासाम् (applies) equally to all (meditations); अविरोधः there is no contradiction, शब्द-अनुमानाभ्याम् as is known from Vedic and Smṛti texts.

31. (The journey of the souls along the path of the gods is) not restricted (to any particular meditation). It applies to all meditations (on the qualified Brahman). This involves no contradiction as is known from Upaniṣadic and Smṛti texts (lit. direct text and inference).

Doubt: It has been said that the soul's journey has a meaning in a context of meditations on the qualified Brahman, but not so in the realization of the absolute Brahman. As for meditations on the qualified Brahman, a journey is mentioned in connection with some, as for instance, the *Paryaṅka-Vidyā*, the meditation on the five fires (*pañcāgni*), the meditation of Upakosala, and the meditation on the small space (*dahara*), but not so in connection with others, as for instance the meditation on the essence (*madhu*), the meditation of Śāṇḍilya, the meditation on Brahman with sixteen digits (*ṣoḍaśakalā*), and the meditation on Vaiśvānara. With regard to this the doubt arises: Should the soul's journey be considered to be restricted to those meditations only where it is mentioned, or should it be accepted in connection with all the meditations of this class? What is the conclusion then?

Opponent: Restriction. The context being the determining factor, the journey should be accepted only where it is heard of. For if the journey heard of in one context be extended to another meditation, then the authority of the Upaniṣadic texts etc. will be stultified on account of everything becoming acceptable everywhere. Moreover, the selfsame course starting with light (i.e. the path of the gods) is read of equally in the meditation on the five fires and the meditation of Upakosala. Now, if it were meant for all, this repetition would have been meaningless. Hence restriction is to be accepted.

Vedāntin: This being the position, the aphorist says, "There is no restriction" etc. The path of the gods should pertain to all the meditations on the qualified Brahman, calculated as they are to lead to good fortune (i.e. Brahmaloka).

Opponent: Was it not pointed out that unless a restriction is admitted, it will lead to a contradiction of the context?

Vedāntin: "There is no such contradiction, on account of direct text and inference," that is to say, the Upaniṣads and Smṛtis. As for the Upaniṣadic texts, we have this on this point: "Among the qualified people, those who know (meditate) thus (reach the path of light)" (Ch. V. x. 1), which introduces the path of the gods for people meditating on the five fires; and then it is shown in the text, "And those who, while living in the forest, meditate thus on faith and austerity" (ibid.), that those others who practise other kinds of meditation, follow the same path as the meditators on the five fires.

Opponent: How, again, is it known that this text declares the same path for others following other kinds of meditation, that path being possible only for those who have faith and austerity, those alone having been mentioned there?

Vedāntin: That is no defect, for this path cannot be attained through mere faith and austerity, in the absence of the strength of knowledge (i.e. meditation), since another Vedic text declares, "Through knowledge (i.e. deep meditation) they ascend to that region from where all desires are turned back; the people treading the southern path do not reach there, nor do the unenlightened men of austerity". Hence meditations, other than that on the five fires, are indicated by the words "faith and austerity". The Vājasaneyins, moreover, have this in connection with the meditation on the five fires, "those who know this as such, and those others who meditate with faith upon Satya" (Bṛ. VI. ii. 15), which should be explained to mean, "those people of faith who meditate on Satya-Brahman", the word *satya* being frequently used for Brahman. Again, the people meditating on the five fires having been referred to by the clause "those who know thus" (Ch. V. x. 1), others who engage in other kinds of meditation should be the people mentioned here in the second clause (ibid.). Again, since the text, "while those others who do not know those two ways become insects and moths, and these frequently biting things (gnats and mosquitos)" (Bṛ. VI. ii. 16), shows the painful lowly state of those who deviate from these two paths (of the gods and manes), therefore it thereby includes these (meditators) within the paths of the gods and manes. There again they attain the path of the gods as an effect of excellence in meditation (and the path of the manes as a result of *karma*). The Smṛti also says, "those two paths of light and darkness are there for this world through eternity; going by the one a man never returns, while going by the other he has to come back" (Gītā, VIII. 26). As for the description of the path of the gods, starting from light, twice in the meditation of Upakosala and the meditation on the five fires, that is meant for enjoining meditation even on the path itself.[23] Hence there is no restriction (of the path of the gods to any particular meditation).

Topic 19: People with a Mission

यावदधिकारमवस्थितिराधिकारिकाणाम् ॥३२॥

आधिकारिकाणाम् For people with a mission अवस्थिति: there is (corporeal) existence यावत्-अधिकारम् as long as the mission demands it.

32. Those who have a mission to fulfil continue in the corporeal state as long as the mission demands it.

Doubt: It is being considered whether the man of knowledge does or does not get another body after the existing one dies.

Objection: When knowledge, which is the means to liberation, comes to fruition, it is out of place to consider whether

[23] It is known from the context that the meditation on the path is a part of the main meditation.

liberation is accomplished or not. For it is not possible to start cogitating whether food can be got ready when all the materials for cooking are already in hand; nor is it doubted whether a man's hunger will be appeased even when he has started eating.

Doubt : This consideration, however, is appropriate since it is seen from the histories and mythologies that some men of illumination get rebirth. Thus it is mentioned in the Smṛti that an ancient seer and Vedic teacher named Apāntaratamas was born under Viṣṇu's direction as Kṛṣṇa-dvaipāyana, at the juncture of the two ages of Kali and Dvāpara. And Vasiṣṭha, though a mind-born son of Brahmā, lost his previous body owing to a curse of Nimi, and was again born of Mitrā-Varuṇa, at the behest of Brahmā. It is also mentioned in the Smṛti that Bhṛgu and others, who were mind-born sons of Brahmā himself, were reborn from the sacrifice of Varuṇa. Sanatkumāra, who was also a mind-born son of Brahmā, was reborn as Skanda as a result of his granting a boon to Rudra. So also in the Smṛti are met with many anecdotes of the rebirth of Dakṣa, Nārada, and others owing to various reasons. In the *mantra* and corroborative portions of the Vedas also such facts are very often met with. Some had rebirth after the original bodies fell, whereas others took up other bodies in accordance with the process of entering several bodies simultaneously by virtue of their power of Yoga, even while retaining their own original bodies. And all of them are mentioned in the Smṛtis as having the realization of all the truths presented by the Vedas. Thus from noticing the rebirth of all of them the conclusion seems to be that the knowledge of Brahman sometimes produces liberation and sometimes not.

Vedāntin : That being the position, the answer is being given: It is not so, since the corporeal existence of Apāntaratamas and others, engaged in the mission of encompassing the well-being of the world through such works as the promulgation of the Vedas and so on, is regulated by the mission itself. Just as the divine Sun after fulfilling his mission in the universe for a thousand ages, will at the end attain liberation, free from rising and setting, as it is declared in the Upaniṣadic text, "then after that (when his mission is fulfilled), he (the sun) will ascend higher up (as Brahman) not to rise and set again, but he will be alone existing in his own Self" (Ch. III. xi. 1); or just as some illumined souls of the present time, who have realized Brahman, (continue to be free even while living and then) at the end of the exhaustion of the *karma*, producing their present bodies, experience liberation, in accordance with the text, "His delay is for that long only as his body does not fall; and then he becomes merged in Brahman" (Ch. VI. xiv. 2); similarly Apāntaratamas and others, though they are divine, are entrusted with their respective missions by God; and hence though they are possessed of full vision, leading to liberation, they continue in their bodies so long as their missions demand this and so long as their actions are not completed; and when that is fulfilled they become freed. Thus there is no contradiction. For the fulfilment of their missions they move on from one body to another with perfect liberty, as though from one house to another, while ridding themselves of their residual *karmas* that have started bearing their fruits once for all in those particular lives; and while retaining an unobliterated memory (of their identity etc.), they do this by creating new bodies and owning them either simultaneously or successively, for they are the masters of the materials that produce the bodies and senses. At the same time, they cannot be classed with the (unenlightened) people who (merely) remember their past lives (*jātismaras*), since it is well known from the Smṛti that "they are those very ones".[24] For instance it is stated in the Smṛti that a woman discourser on Brahman named Sulabhā, who wanted to have a discussion with Janaka, gave up her body, entered the body of Janaka, and having finished the discussion with him re-entered her own body.

If it be the case that when the *karma*, which has once started bearing fruit (by producing the present body), has been used up, some other *karma*, productive of a fresh body, can crop up, then any other *karma* whose seed has not been burnt away, may

[24] A *jātismara* is one who has perforce to leave the earlier body and enter another, and yet in the new body remembers the experiences of his past life. The enlightened man is, however, independent in his movements, and he remembers his identity under all circumstances.

spring up just like it; and in that case only can it be apprehended that the knowledge of Brahman may or may not be an inevitable cause of liberation. But such an apprehension is not reasonable, inasmuch as it is a well-recognized fact in the Vedas and Smṛtis that knowledge burns away the seed of *karma*. Thus we have the Upaniṣadic texts: "When that Self, which is both high and low (or cause and effect), is realized, the knot of the heart gets untied, all doubts become solved, and all one's actions become dissipated" (Mu. II. ii. 8), "When true memory (of 'I am Brahman') is regained, all the knots become untied" (Ch. VIII. xxvi. 2), and so on. And the Smṛti texts are, "O Arjuna, as a blazing fire reduces the fuel to ashes, similarly the fire of knowledge burns away all the *karmas*" (Gītā, IV. 37), "As seeds scorched by fire do not sprout again, so also the Self is not affected again by the 'evils' consumed by knowledge", and so on. It does not logically follow that when the "evils" like ignorance, (egoism, etc.) are burnt away, the residual *karma*, which is the seed of "evil", burns away in one part, but sprouts out through the other; for a *śāli* (rice) seed burnt by fire is not seen to sprout in one part. As for the residual *karma* that has begun to yield fruit (in the present body), that ceases from the exhaustion of its momentum like an arrow shot from the bow, because it is said, "For him the delay is only for that long as the body does not fall" (Ch. VI. xiv. 2), where the waiting lasts till the falling off of the body. Hence it is proper that the man with a spiritual mission has the corporeal existence so long as the mission demands it.

But thereby the effect of knowledge does not cease to be inevitable, inasmuch as the Upaniṣadic text shows that liberation follows from knowledge in all cases without exception, "And whoever among the gods knew it also became that, and the same with the sages and men" (Bṛ. I. iv. 10). It may well be that some great sages succumb to the lure of other kinds of meditation resulting in the acquisition of mystic powers; but later they become detached by noticing how these powers decay; and then following steadfastly the knowledge of the supreme Self, they attain liberation. This is what stands to reason; for the Smṛti says, "When the final dissolution comes at the end of the reign of Hiraṇyagarbha, the men of knowledge, with their minds purified, enter into the supreme state of liberation together with Brahmā Himself". Since knowledge produces an immediately felt direct result, there can be no fear of non-acquisition of it. With regard to heaven etc., coming (long after) as the result of (past) action, there may be such a fear as to whether it will come or not; but the result of knowledge is a matter of direct experience, because it is so stated in, "The Brahman that is immediate and direct" (Bṛ. III. iv. 1) and because the text, "That thou art" (Ch. VI. viii. 7), speaks of it as an already realized truth. For the sentence, "That thou art", cannot be construed to mean that you will become That (Brahman) after death, because the text "The sage Vāmadeva, while realizing this (Self) as That (Brahman), knew, 'I was Manu, and the sun' " (Bṛ. I. iv. 10), shows that the result of knowledge, consisting in becoming identified with all, occurs simultaneously with the rise of complete illumination. Hence liberation comes inevitably to a man of knowledge.

Topic 20: Conceptions of the Immutable

अक्षरधियां त्ववरोधः सामान्यतद्भावाभ्यामौपसदवत्तदुक्तम् ॥३३॥

अक्षर-धियाम् Of the (negative) conceptions about the Immutable, तु however, अवरोधः (should be) a combination सामान्य-तत्-भावाभ्याम् because of the similarity of defining and the sameness of object औपसद-वत् like the Upasad sacrifice; तत् that उक्तम् has been stated (by Jaimini).

33. All the (negative) conceptions of the Immutable are to be combined, since the process of presentation is similar and the object dealt with is the same. This is just as it is in the case of the Upasad sacrifice, as has been shown by Jaimini.

Doubt: In the Bṛhadāraṇyaka Upaniṣad it is said, "O Gārgī, the knowers of Brahman say, this Immutable (Brahman) is that. It is neither gross nor minute, neither short" (Bṛ. III. viii. 8) etc. Similarly it is heard of in the Muṇḍaka Upaniṣad, "then there is the higher knowledge by which is realized the Immutable" (Mu. I. i. 5), "That which cannot be perceived and grasped, which is without source, features" (Mu. I. i. 6). So also elsewhere the supreme Brahman is taught by way of eliminating distinctions. There again in some texts some fresh traits are eliminated that are not mentioned elsewhere. Now should all these ideas involving elimination of distinctions be combined together everywhere, or are they to be restricted to where they occur?

Vedāntin: When for resolving such a doubt it is concluded (by the *opponent*) that the Upaniṣadic texts being different, the ideas too are to be treated separately, our answer is: "All the conceptions of the Immutable", that is to say the conceptions involving the negation of distinctions, "are to be combined" everywhere, "since the process of presentation is the same and the object dealt with is the same". For the process of presenting Brahman, consisting in the negation of all distinctions, is similar everywhere; and that very same Brahman is sought to be explained everywhere. So what is meant by saying that the conceptions obtaining at one place should not be transferred elsewhere? And this is how it has been explained under the aphorism, "Bliss and other characteristics of the principal entity (Brahman) are to be combined" (III. iii. 11). But the positive attributes were considered there, whereas the negative ones are considered here. And so this separate discussion is undertaken here for elaborating this distinction. (Or according to a different reading, "This is the distinction. And this separate discussion is meant for elaborating this").

"As in the case of the Upasad sacrifice" is said by way of illustration. The meaning is this: It is enjoined that in connection with the *Ahīnasatra* (lasting for more than a day) of Jāmadagni, one has to perform the Upasad sacrifice in which *puroḍāśas* (cakes) have to be offered. Now, the *mantras*, "*Agnerverhotram veradhvaram*", and so on, which are enjoined to be used while offering the cakes, are found in their original form in the Veda of the Udgātā (i.e. the Sāma-Veda, Taṇḍya Br. XXI. x. 1), yet they come to be associated (that is chanted) by the Adhvaryu priests (of the Yajur-Veda), since the *puroḍāśa* has to be offered by the Adhvaryu (and not the Udgātā), and since the subsidiary sacrifices are regulated according to the main sacrifices (in which the Adhvaryu makes the offerings). Similarly here also, the attributes of the Immutable, that are dependent on the Immutable, are everywhere to be associated with the Immutable, irrespective of the place of their occurrence. "That has been said (by Jaimini) in the first part (i.e. the Pūrva-Mīmāṁsā)", in the aphorism, "In a case of disparity between the subsidiary text (revealing the *mantra* for the first time) and the principal text (revealing the application), the subsidiary text has to be associated with the main injunction, since the former is meant for the latter" (III. iii. 8).

Topic 21: Same Conception in Mundaka and Katha

इयदामननात् ॥३४॥

(The conceptions are the same) इयत्-आमननात् on account of the mention of this much (i.e. limit).

34. The conceptions (in the Muṇḍaka and Śvetāśvatara on the one hand and Kaṭha on the other) are the same, on account of the mention of a particular limit.

Doubt: They of the Atharva Veda, as also the Śvetāśvataras, recite this verse in the context of the body, "Two birds that are ever associated and have similar names, cling to the same tree. Of these, the one eats the fruit of divergent tastes and the other looks on without eating" (Mu. III. i. 1, Śv. IV. 6). The Kaṭhas also have this verse: "The knowers of Brahman, the worshippers of the five fires, and those who perform the Nāciketa sacrifice thrice, compare to shade and light, the two enjoyers of the inevitable results of work, who have entered into the cavity (of the heart) which is the supreme abode of the most High (Brahman)" (Ka. I. iii. 1). The doubt here is whether the conceptions are the same or different. What should be the conclusion?

Opponent: The conceptions are different.

Why?

Owing to obvious distinction. In the *mantra* "two birds" etc., one is noticed to be enjoying and the other abstaining, while in the *mantra* "the two enjoyers of the inevitable results of work" etc., both are seen to be enjoying. Thus the objects of the conceptions being distinct, the resulting conceptions must be distinct as well.

Vedāntin: This being the position, the aphorist says that the conceptions are the same.

How is it so?

Because in both these *mantras*, the Upaniṣads mention the nature of the entity to be known as circumscribed by a limit, and as having a second (associate), and (hence) non-different.

Opponent: Has not the difference in nature been pointed out (by me)?

Vedāntin: The answer is, no; for both these *mantras* describe God as having the individual being as a second, but they do not describe (the individual as) something different. To explain: In the *mantra* "two birds" etc., the supreme Self that transcends (all feelings of) hunger etc. is shown in the portion "the other looks on without eating". And in the complementary portion of the topic also, in the text "when he sees the other one, the worshipful God" (Śv. IV. 7), the very same God is seen to form the subject-matter. Even when the individual being enjoys, the supreme Self, though transcending (all feelings of) hunger etc., is spoken of in the text, "the two enjoyers of the inevitable results of work" etc., as (though) enjoying, on the analogy of the statement "the people with umbrella are moving"[25]; and this is so because the supreme Self is associated with the individual being. This is of course a context of the supreme Self, for the commencement was made with, "Tell (me) of that thing which you see as different from virtue and different from vice" (Ka. I. ii. 14). And even here the very same subject is presented in the complementary portion in, "that which is the undecaying supreme Brahman, beyond fear, for those who want to cross over (the world)" (Ka. I. iii. 2). This was also elaborated under

[25] When a king moves with one umbrella held over his head, his followers are referred to as "the people with umbrella", though they have none.

the aphorism, "The two who have entered into the cavity are the individual Self and the supreme Self" (I. ii. 11). Hence there is no difference as regards the entity to be known, and hence also the meditations are the same. Moreover, all that is gathered from a consideration of the trend of all these three Upaniṣads is the knowledge of the supreme Self; the individual being is introduced in order to reveal its identity (with the Self) and for nothing else. It was stated earlier that so long as a discussion is concerned with the supreme Self, there is no scope for any consideration as to whether there is any difference-cum-non-difference. Hence this (present) attempt is meant merely for elaborating that very truth. Hence also it follows that the additional attributes have to be combined.

Topic 22: The Inmost Self in Brihadaranyaka

अन्तरा भूतग्रामवत् स्वात्मनः ॥३५॥

स्व-आत्मनः About one's own Self (it has been declared that it is) अन्तरा inmost of all, भूत-ग्राम-वत् as in the case of the aggregate of elements (or as in the case of all beings).

35. (The conception of the Self is the same in Bṛhadāraṇyaka III. iv. 1 and III. v. 1, since) one's own Self is declared to be the inmost of all as in the case of the aggregate of elements. (Or —since one's own Self is declared to be the inmost of all, just as it is shown to be the Self of all in Śvetāśvatara VI. 11).

Doubt: The Vājasaneyins recite the text, "Explain to me the Brahman that is immediate and direct, the Self that is within all" (Bṛ. III. iv. 1, III. v. 1), twice, just one after the other, in course of the question of Uṣasti and Kahola. The doubt arises there whether the conceptions are the same or they are different.

Opponent: The conceptions must be different.

Why?

By reason of the repetition; for otherwise it would be meaningless to speak twice of the very same thing, neither more nor less. Hence just as rites differ in a case of repetition, so also must these conceptions differ for the very same reason of repetition.

Vedāntin: That being the position, the aphorist utters the refutation: That conception is the same on account of absence of any distinction in the presentation of one's own Self as the inmost entity. It is one's own Self, that is also the inmost Self, that is questioned about and explained without any distinction in both the places. For two Selfs cannot both be the inmost in the selfsame body. In that case (that is to say, if there be two Selfs), one of the Selfs alone can feasibly be conceived of as being the inmost, while the other cannot be the inmost, even as it is the case with the assemblage of elements. As in the body, constituted by the five elements, water is inner than earth, fire is inner than water, and so on, and thus there can be such a thing as existence inside in a relative sense, though none can be the inmost in the primary sense, so also is the case here. Or "*bhūtagrāmavat*—just as it is shown to be the Self of all" may refer to another Upaniṣadic text, "The one Deity remains hidden in all beings. He is all-pervasive and the inmost Self of all *bhūtas* (beings)" (Śv. VI. 11), in which *mantra* the selfsame Self is spoken of as existing as the inmost Self of all beings. As it is the case there, so also is it in both these *brāhmaṇas* (of the Bṛhadāraṇyaka). Hence, from the identity of the entity that is to be known, it follows that the knowledge also is the same.

अन्यथा भेदानुपपत्तिरिति चेन्नोपदेशान्तरवत् ॥३६॥

अन्यथा Otherwise (i.e. unless the conceptions be different), भेद-अनुपपत्तिः the separate (repetitive) statements cannot be justified इति चेत् if such be the objection, न not so, उपदेश-अन्तर-वत् (it being) like another instruction (of this kind).

36. If it be argued that unless difference be admitted the separate statements become illogical, the reply is that this is not so, for it can be like another instruction of this kind.

And the argument was advanced that unless the conceptions be admitted to be different, the separate (repetitive) statements cannot be explained. That objection has to be met. With regard to this it is said that it does not constitute a defect, since this can be reasonably so like some instruction elsewhere. In the sixth part of the Upaniṣad of the Tāṇḍins, it is taught nine times, "That is the Self, That thou art O Śvetaketu" (Ch. VI. viii. 7); still the knowledge does not differ. So also must be the case here.

Opponent: How again does not the knowledge differ even though imparted nine times?

Vedāntin: Since the identity of the knowledge can be understood from the introduction and the conclusion, since with a view to expounding the very same subject, over and over again, it is reopened time and again with the (very same) request, "Sir, explain this to me again" (Ch. VI. v. 4), and since a repetition of the explanation more than once can be justified on the ground of removing fresh doubts. Here also the beginning and end are seen to be concerned with the same subject since the form of the question is identical and the end is made in a similar way with the words, "everything else but this is perishable" (Bṛ. III. iv. 2, III. v. 1). And by using the word "*eva*" (very) in "the very Brahman that is immediate and direct" (Bṛ. III. v. 1), in the second question (of Kahola) as well, the Upaniṣad shows that the subject-matter of the first question is alluded to in the second. Besides, in the earlier *Brāhmaṇa* (III. iv), the existence of the Self beyond cause and effect (or body and organs) is spoken of, whereas in the latter that very Self is spoken of as having the distinction of being beyond such worldly characteristics as hunger etc. Thus the unity of purport comes out logically, and hence the knowledge is the same.

TOPIC 23: RECIPROCITY OF CONCEPTIONS

व्यतिहारो विशिंषन्ति हीतरवत् ॥३७॥

(There should be) व्यतिहार: reciprocity,[26] हि for विशिंषन्ति (the Upaniṣadic readers) distinctly recite so, इतर-वत् as in the case of other (attributes).

[26] The noun and adjective being mutually interchangeable.

37. There should be a reciprocal interchange as in the case of other traits; for so the readers (of the scriptures) recite distinctly.

Doubt: The Aitareyins have this text with regard to the Being in the solar orb, "Now, He is the same as I am, and I am the same as He is" (Ai. Ā. II. ii. 4.6), similarly the Jābālas have this, "O glorious Deity, I am what you are, and you are what I am". The doubt arises here: Should the conception have two forms involving a process of reciprocity or should it have one form alone?

The *opponent* says in this matter that the conception should have one form only; for apart from thinking of one's Self as identical with God, there is nothing else to be thought of. If, however, any such speciality about the thought is to be imagined, viz that the transmigrating soul is identical with God and God is identical with the transmigrating soul, then the transmigrating soul will get some added excellence through its identity with God, whereas God will be reduced in stature by His identity with the transmigrating soul. Hence the conception is to be thought of as having one form (i.e. one-sided) only. As for the reciprocal reading in the scripture, it is meant for emphasizing the unity.

Vedāntin: This being the position, the aphorist refutes it: This reciprocity is spoken of in the scripture for the purpose of meditation, just as in the case of other attributes. As the other attributes like "being the Self of all" are spoken of for the sake of meditation, so also is the case here as well. For thus it is that by reciting this either way, "I am what you are, you are what I am", the reciters of the passage point this out distinctly; and that becomes meaningful if the meditation is to be resorted to in a twofold way; for otherwise this specific recitation in two ways becomes useless, one alone being enough.

Opponent: Did we not point out that if the double reading be imagined to convey some special meaning, the Deity will become one with the transmigrating soul, and will thus become reduced in stature?

Vedāntin: That is nothing damaging, since it is precisely this identity that is thought of through such a process.

Opponent: In that case that very identity of the two (referred to by us) will become all the more strengthened.

Vedāntin: We do not avoid this strengthening of identity.

Object: What do you do then?

Vedāntin: What we seek to establish is that on the strength of the text, the meditation is to be resorted to reciprocally (in a double way), and not in one way only. As a result the identity also becomes virtually confirmed. The point may be illustrated thus. Although such attributes as possession of inevitable desire etc. are prescribed for meditation, still God becomes established thereby as possessed of those attributes; similar is the case here. Hence this reciprocity is meant for meditation (that way); and this process has to be applied to similar (other) contexts (where only one way is stated).

Topic 24: Satya-Brahman in Brihadaranyaka

सैव हि सत्यादयः ॥३८॥

हि Since सा एव that very same *vidyā* (conception, obtains at both places, therefore) सत्य-आदयः truth etc. (are to be combined).

38. Since the same Satya-Vidyā is taught in both the places (of the Bṛhadāraṇyaka Upaniṣad), therefore traits like Satya have to be combined.

Doubt: In the text beginning with, "He who knows this great, adorable, first-born Being (i.e. Hiraṇyagarbha) as the Satya-Brahman" (Bṛ. V. iv. 1), the Bṛhadāraṇyaka Upaniṣad prescribes a meditation called the *Satya-Vidyā*, together with the meditation on the letters of the name (Satya),[27] and there it is stated, "That which is that Satya is that sun—the Being who is in that orb and the Being who is in the right eye" etc. (Bṛ. V. v. 2).

[27] "This name Satya (lit. truth) consists of three letters (*Sa, ti, ya*). The first and last letters are truth. In the middle is untruth. The untruth is enclosed on either side by truth." (Bṛ. V. v. 1).

Now the doubt arises: Are these two different meditations on Satya, or are they one?

Opponent: As to that the conclusion is that they are two, for the emergence of result occurs separately, for the former it being "(He) conquers these worlds" (Bṛ. V. iv. 1), and for the latter, "He who knows as above destroys and shuns evil" (Bṛ. V. v. 3). As for reference to (Satya) the subject-matter of the previous context, it is done because of the sameness of the entity meditated on.

Vedāntin: This being the position, we say that this *Satya-Vidyā* is but one.

How?

On account of the bringing forward of the subject-matter of the former to the latter on the basis of the identity of the entity meditated on by saying, "That which is that Satya" (Bṛ. V. v. 2).

Opponent: But it was pointed out that even though the meditations may differ, the object of the earlier meditation may be referred to in the latter on the basis of the identity of the entity meditated on.

Vedāntin: This cannot be so; for this may be the case where the difference of the meditations becomes obvious from some other cogent reason. But since it is possible to have it either way in this connection, a reference to the matter under discussion is made in "that which is that Satya" (Bṛ. V. v. 2), whereby it is known that the Satya, connected with the earlier meditation, is alluded to in the latter. Thus the unity of the meditation becomes well established.

As for the argument that the reference to a separate result leads to the conclusion that the latter is a separate meditation, the answer is this: This is no defect since this mention of a separate result is by way of eulogizing the teaching about the other parts of the meditation stated in "His secret name is Ahar" (Bṛ. V. v. 3), "His secret name is Aham" (Bṛ. V. v. 4). Moreover, the rule is that when the meditation is the same, and the results have to be gathered from the corroborative passages, the various results heard of in connection with the subsidiaries have to be added to the main meditation itself. Accordingly, since that very same *Satya-Vidyā* is spoken of as being associated with particular special traits, therefore all the traits such as Satya, are to be combined in the same application (i.e. act of meditation).

In connection with this aphorism, however, some others cite this text about the Being in the solar orb and the eye as stated in the Bṛhadāraṇyaka Upaniṣad, along with the texts, "And then this golden (effulgent) Being that is seen in the solar orb" (Ch. I. vi. 6), and "And then the Being that is seen in the eye" (Ch. IV. xv. 1), in the Chāndogya Upaniṣad; and they say that the very same meditation on the Being in the solar orb and the eye is contained in the latter, and the meditations are the same in both the Upaniṣads. Under this impression they think that such traits as Satya mentioned in the Bṛhadāraṇyaka are to be borrowed from there by the followers of the Chāndogya. But that does not seem to be proper. For in the Chāndogya, this meditation is presented in connection with a rite (viz Jyotiṣṭoma) and is based on the Udgītha (used in that rite), inasmuch as indicatory marks connecting it with a rite are met with in the beginning, middle, and end. In the beginning occurs the text, "This (earth) is the Ṛk *mantra* and fire is the Sāma *mantra*" (Ch. I. vi. 1). In the middle is, "Of Him the Ṛk and Sāma *mantras* are the knuckles; hence it is Udgītha"[28] (Ch. I. vi. 8). And at the end is, "He who having known thus, sings the Sāma song" (Ch. I. vii. 9). But in the Bṛhadāraṇyaka there is no such sign to connect it with a rite. Since thus the meditations differ owing to a difference of the contexts, it is but proper that the traits should have separate application.

Topic 25: Combination of Traits in Brihadaranyaka and Chandogya

कामादीतरत्र तत्र चायतनादिभ्यः ॥३९॥

कामादि (True) desire etc. (are to be added) इतरत्र elsewhere; च and तत्र (those) in the other (are to be added here) आयतन-आदिभ्यः on account of abode etc.

[28] Ṛk and Sāma *mantras*, referred to by the word Udgītha, having been presented as the knuckles, we can conclude that it is the supreme Self that is referred to by the word Udgītha.

39. Traits like (true) desire etc. (mentioned in the Chāndogya) are to be added to the other (viz Bṛhadāraṇyaka), and those mentioned there are to be added here, because of the (sameness of) abode etc.

Starting with the text, "Now, the *dahara* (small) house (i.e. heart) of the shape of a lotus, that is within this city of Brahman (viz the body), within that is a small Space (i.e. Brahman)" (Ch. VIII. i. 1), it is said "this is the Self free from sins, and from dirt, death, sorrow, hunger, and thirst, which has true desire and irresistible will" (Ch. VIII. i. 5) etc. And the Vājasaneyins have this: "That great birthless Self which is identified with the intellect and is in the midst of the organs lies in the space that is within the heart. It is the controller of all, the lord of all, the ruler of all" (Bṛ. IV. iv. 22) etc. Here the doubt arises, whether the knowledge is the same or not, and the conclusion arrived at (by the *opponent*) is that the knowledge is the same.

Vedāntin: With regard to this it is said, "Traits like desires" etc. What is meant by "desire" is "(unfailing) true desire", just as one would call Devadatta simply Datta, or Satyabhāmā simply Bhāmā. The attributes like unfailing desires that are met with in the Chāndogya Upaniṣad, as applied to the space within the heart, have to be inserted elsewhere (in the Bṛhadāraṇyaka) in the text, "That great birthless Self" etc. And the attributes like "controller of all", met with in the Bṛhadāraṇyaka, have to be inserted in the Chāndogya text, "This is the Self free from sin" etc.

Why?

"Because of the sameness of the abode" etc. For in both the places, the heart is equally the abode, God is equally the entity to be realized, and God is equally the barrage (*setu*) serving to maintain the boundaries (of the things) of this world, (that is to say, to prevent promiscuity); and so also many other similarities are met with.

Opponent: Are not differences also met with? For the attributes in the Chāndogya are associated with the space within the heart, whereas (in the Bṛhadāraṇyaka) they are associated with Brahman within that space.

Vedāntin: Not so, for under the aphorism, "The small space is Brahman, on account of the subsequent reasons" (I. iii. 14) it was established that the term Space means Brahman even in the Chāndogya. Of course there is a difference here. For in the Chāndogya Upaniṣad a meditation on the qualified Brahman is taught, inasmuch as desires etc. are mentioned as things to be known along with the Self, in the text, "Then, again, those who depart from here without knowing the Self and these unfailing desires" (Ch. VIII. i. 6), whereas in the Bṛhadāraṇyaka, the entity taught is the absolutely supreme Brahman, as is evident from a co-ordinated study of such questions and answers as, "Please instruct me further about liberation itself" (IV. iii. 15), "For this infinite Being is unattached" (ibid.). As for such attributes as being "the controller of all", these are declared in the Bṛhadāraṇyaka by way of glorifying the (unqualified) Brahman. And it is in line with this (mere glorification) that the conclusion is made later on with the absolute Brahman in the text, "the Self is that which has been described as 'Not this, not this' " (Bṛ. III. ix. 26) etc. But it has to be noted that since the qualified Brahman is the same as the unqualified, a combination of the attributes is mentioned by this aphorism in order to show the exalted nature of God, but this is not (to be done in the Bṛhadāraṇyaka) for meditation.[29]

TOPIC 26: AGNIHOTRA TO PRANA

आदरादलोपः ॥४०॥

अ-लोपः There can be no omission आदरात् because of deference.

40. There can be no omission (of the performance of the

[29] The Chāndogya and Bṛhadāraṇyaka mention the attributes for meditation on and glorification of God respectively. It involves no contradiction, rather it suits these purposes to assume these attributes at both the places. But while they have to be added to the former from the latter, in the latter they are implied by the text itself.

Agnihotra to Prāṇa) on account of the respect shown (in the Upaniṣad).

Doubt: In connection with the meditation on Vaiśvānara it is heard in the Chāndogya Upaniṣad, "That morsel of food that comes first is to be offered as an oblation. And when he offers that first oblation, he should offer it with the *mantra*, 'Svāhā to *Prāṇa*'" (V. xix. 1). Offerings to the five *prāṇas* are prescribed there. And with regard to them the word Agnihotra is used later on in, "He who knowing this thus performs the Agnihotra sacrifice" (Ch. V. xxiv. 2), as also in, "As hungry boys sit waiting around their mother, so also all beings wait for the Agnihotra (i.e. eating of such a man of knowledge)" (Ch. V. xxiv. 5). With regard to this the question to be discussed is whether the Agnihotra sacrifice offered to *Prāṇa* ceases to exist on the day (of fasting) when there is no eating, or whether it does not cease.

Vedāntin: Since there is a mention of the connection of the arrival of the first morsel of food (with the Agnihotra under consideration) in "that morsel of food" etc., and since the arrival of a morsel of food is meant for eating, the Agnihotra to *Prāṇa* ceases to exist when there is no eating.

That being the conclusion, the *opponent* makes the rejoinder that it does not cease.

Why?

"On account of the respect shown". Thus it is that in connection with this very meditation on Vaiśvānara occurs this text of the Jābālas: "One (who resorts to this Agnihotra to *Prāṇa*) shall precede the guests in eating. As one might perform another's Agnihotra before performing his own, this (feeding of guests earlier) would also be like that". Here by condemning the feeding of the guests first, the eating by the master of the house is enjoined first, thereby showing a respect for the Agnihotra performed in honour of *Prāṇa*. And a text which cannot tolerate the omission of the first place for the performer of the Agnihotra can tolerate much less the omission of the Agnihotra that has such precedence over all.

Vedāntin: Since there is the mention of the coming of the

first morsel meant for eating, therefore when there is no eating, there can be no Agnihotra.

Opponent: No, since that is meant for prescribing some particular thing. Since in the common Agnihotra, milk etc. are regularly prescribed, so here also, from the use of the word Agnihotra, the possibility may arise that the milk etc. used there are to be used here as well in the Agnihotra to *Prāṇa*, on the analogy of milk etc. being used in the sacrifice of the Kauṇḍapāyins, called the Māsāgnihotra (Agnihotra for a month) and forming a part of their longer *satra*, just because the word Agnihotra is used there by way of courtesy. And hence this sentence "that morsel of food" etc. occurs in order to prescribe the subsidiary injunction about the morsel of food (by way of ruling out milk etc.). Thus in accordance with the aphorism, "Although a subsidiary may be omitted, not so the main one" (Jai. Sū. X. ii. 63), even if the subsidiary, consisting in using the morsel of food, be omitted, not so can the main act of performing Agnihotra to *Prāṇa*.[30] Thus the conclusion is that even though there may be omission of eating, the obligatory Agnihotra to *Prāṇa* is to be performed by water or some other thing in accordance with the rule of using substitutes.[31]

Vedāntin: Hence comes the aphorist's reply:

उपस्थितेऽतस्तद्वचनात् ॥४१॥

(The Agnihotra is to be performed) अतः from that itself उपस्थिते when it is present (i.e. served), तत्-वचनात् for so is the declaration.

[30] On the analogy of the Māsa-Agnihotra, milk etc. are liable to be used in the Prāṇa-Agnihotra. This would be a general application. But the prescription about the morsel of food comes as an exception to this. Hence the rule about the morsel of food being an exception, when there is omission of food, the subsidiary, viz morsel of food, also becomes omitted, and yet the primary act of Agnihotra cannot be omitted, since in the absence of an exception to the contrary, that Agnihotra can be performed with milk etc.

[31] An obligatory rite that is once commenced, must be finished. So if the prescribed things are not available the rite should be completed even with substitutes.

41. The Agnihotra is to be performed from that (food) itself when it is present, for such is the declaration (of the Upaniṣad).

"When it is present", when the food comes; "from that itself", from that very eatable thing that presents itself first, the Agnihotra to *Prāṇa* is to be accomplished.

Why?

"For such is the Upaniṣadic declaration." To explain: By using the word "that" with regard to the morsel of food occurring immediately after in the text "that morsel of food that comes first is to be offered as an oblation" (Ch. V. xix. 1), as something actually present, the Upaniṣad enjoins that the oblations to *Prāṇa* are to be made with a thing meant for some other purpose (viz eating). But how can these oblations call for a substitute when, on the omission of eating, they themselves become stripped of the circumstances that make them possible?[32]

And it cannot be said that the characteristics of the common Agnihotra have to be applied here. In the case of the *ayana* (i.e. *satra*) of the Kauṇḍapāyins, the word Agnihotra, appearing in the injunctive text, "One shall perform the Agnihotra for a month", may well be accepted as presenting an injunction about the common Agnihotra, so that the subsidiary features of Agnihotra can become applicable there; but in the present case, the word Agnihotra is used in the eulogistic portion, so that it cannot enjoin a similar Agnihotra. Again, should, however, the applicability of the characteristics of the common Agnihotra be admitted, the production of fire (by rubbing wood) also would become applicable; but that is not a possibility. The production of fire is meant to provide a place where to offer the oblations, but this oblation is not meant to be poured on fire, since that would nullify the use of the food for eating. And from the association with the things made ready for eating it follows that the oblation is to be made in the mouth itself. So also the text of the Jābālas, "one should precede the guests in eating", shows that this sacrifice has to be accomplished in the mouth. It is for

[32] There can be Agnihotra only if there is eating, but not otherwise; for the offerings are mere consequences of the main act of sitting for meal.

this very reason that here also (in the Chāndogya) the accessories of the Agnihotra are shown as got through ideas of superimposition, in the text, "His chest is the sacrificial altar, his hair the kuśa grass, his heart the Gārhapatya fire, his mind the Anvāhāryapacana fire, and his mouth the Āhavanīya fire" (Ch. V. xviii. 2). The word "altar" here is to be understood as meaning a sacrificial place (*sthaṇḍila*) in general; for the Agnihotra, in the principal sense, has no altar, and its accessories are got here only with the help of notional superimposition. Moreover, owing to the connection (of the Agnihotra to *Prāṇa*) with the time (noon and evening) fixed for eating, there is no possibility of its being performed at the times (morning and evening) fixed for the ordinary Agnihotra. Similarly some other characteristics like adoration (or saying of prayer) etc. also would be contradicted in some way or other. Hence from the association of the *mantras*, things, and the deities with eating itself, it follows that these five oblations are to be accomplished in that connection. As for the show of respect noticed (in the Jābāla text), that is meant for enjoining merely the precedence in eating, for the meaning of a sentence cannot be overstressed.[33] It is not possible on the authority of this fact of mere precedence (of the host) here that this Agnihotra has to be performed invariably. So when there is an omission of eating, the Agnihotra to *Prāṇa* is omitted *pari passu*.

TOPIC 27: MEDITATIONS CONNECTED WITH RITES ARE NOT OBLIGATORY

तन्निर्धारणानियमस्तद्दृष्टेः पृथग्ध्यप्रतिबन्धः फलम् ॥४२॥

तत्-निर्धारण-अनियमः There is no obligatory rule about that, तत् दृष्टेः for so it is seen (in the Upaniṣad), हि for पृथक् separate फलम् result (arises, which is) अप्रतिबन्धः elimination of hindrance.

[33] The Vedas and Smṛtis enjoin that a man should eat after his guests. That precedence is altered in the case of a man who performs the Agnihotra to *Prāṇa*; but this cannot become a general rule, on the strength of which the Agnihotra can become a daily act.

42. There is no obligatory rule about that (i.e. the meditations becoming connected always with rites), for that is obvious from the Upaniṣad, inasmuch as a meditation has a separate result, consisting in the elimination of hindrance to a rite.

Doubt: There are certain conceptions (or meditations) connected with the accessories of rites as for instance in "One should meditate on the letter *Om* as Udgītha" (Ch. I. i. 1), and other places. We have to consider whether these meditations are the regular features of the rites like the Juhū (the sacrificial ladle) made of Palāśa wood, or they are irregular like the milking pot (f.n. 36)? What should be the conclusion here?

Opponent: They are regular features.

Why should this be so?

On account of their occurring in the sentences enjoining application. For although these meditations are not read of in connection with the commencement of any particular rite, yet by virtue of their connection with sacrifices through Udgītha etc., they become connected with the injunctions about the performance of the rites, in the same way as the other subsidiaries become so connected with them. As for the results mentioned in their own contexts, as for instance, "He certainly becomes a fulfiller of desires" (Ch. I. i. 7), and so on, they are merely eulogistic having been used with verbs in the present indicative mood (and not imperative mood), as in such scriptural statements as, "He hears no evil", and they have no fruit as their principal objective. Hence just as in the case of such sentences as, "He whose *Juhū* (ladle) is made of Palāśa wood never hears a sinful verse", which do not occur in their proper contexts and yet get connected with the sacrifices through the medium of the Juhū etc., and thus become regularly applicable like other accessories read of in their proper contexts, so also must be the case with the meditations on the Udgītha.[34]

[34] In such cases, Palāśa, Juhū, etc. help the sacrifice and thus contribute to the origin of the remote fruit of the sacrifice, so that the mention of the proximate result has to be understood otherwise, that is to say, the result, viz "non-hearing of sinful verse" is said by way of a eulogy. So also the fulfilling of desires in the case of the Udgītha is a eulogy.

Vedāntin: That being the position, we say, "there is no obligatory rule about that (i.e. the *upāsanās*—meditations—becoming connected with rites)". These phrases that determine the meditation on the true characteristics of the accessories (like Udgītha) of the rites, viz that the Udgītha is the quintessence, the acquirer, and source of prosperity, that it is the foremost, it is *Prāṇa*, it is the sun, and so on, cannot be regularly connected with rites in the same way as their obligatory accessories.

Why?

"For that is obvious from the Upaniṣad." Thus it is that the Upaniṣad shows that meditations of this kind are not obligatory, inasmuch as, in the text, "Both those who know this *Om* thus (as forming part of the Udgītha and possessed of the attributes of being the quintessence etc.), and those who do not know thus, perform their rites with this *Om*" (Ch. I. i. 10), it is admitted that the rites can be performed by the uninformed as well. And it is seen that the priests Prastotā and others,[35] even though ignorant of the deities of the Prastāva etc., perform the duties of priests as stated in the text, "O Prastotā, should you chant the Prastāva without knowing the deity presiding over the Prastāva" (Ch. I. x. 9), "(O Udgātā), should you sing the Udgītha without knowing that deity" (Ch. I. x. 10), "O Pratihartā, should you chant the concluding portion (Pratihāra) without knowing the deity" (Ch. I. x. 11). Moreover, it is mentioned in the Upaniṣad that for meditations of this kind, which are connected with rites, results, other than those for the rites themselves, accrue, consisting either in removing some obstacle in the path of the fruition of a rite or in adding some excellence to its successful fruition; "Both those who know this *Om* thus and who do not know, perform their rites with this *Om*. But different are knowledge and ignorance (i.e. they have different results). That alone which one does with knowledge, with faith, and with meditation on the deities, becomes more powerful" (Ch. I. i. 10). From the separation of the under-

[35] The Prastotā chants the first portion, Prastāva; the Udgātā sings the middle portion, Udgītha; and the Pratihartā chants the final portion, Pratihāra.

takings of the knowers and the non-knowers by saying, "But different are" etc. and from the use of the comparative degree in "more powerful" in that text, it is understood that a rite bereft of knowledge is also powerful (effective). And that becomes possible only if the meditation is not a permanent feature of the rite. Were it invariable, how could it have been admitted that a rite bereft of meditation is powerful? For the accepted view is that a rite becomes powerful when it is performed along with all its subsidiaries. Similarly in such meditations as that involving the superimposition of the worlds on the Sāma (songs), results are spoken of as fixed for the meditations individually, as for instance, "For him are ordained the worlds (of enjoyment) both above and below (the earth)" (Ch. II. ii. 3), and so on. And it is not proper to argue that this mention of result is by way of a corroborative statement (i.e. mere eulogy), for in that case it would amount to an attributive corroboration (*Guṇavāda*), whereas in a case where the result is mentioned, one has to admit a eulogy of the main thing. As for (the eulogistic interpretation of the results stated in connection with) such subsidiary rites as the Prayāja etc., since they are necessary for the main rites (viz Darśa-Pūrṇamāsa), which depend for their proper performance on the adequate fulfilment of all the subsidiary rites, it is but reasonable that the mention of the results along with the Prayāja etc. should be taken in the sense of a eulogy (of Prayāja etc.) And this is also the case with the "Palāśa Juhū" etc. which occur in contexts other than that of any rite to be performed. For such things as a Palāśa Juhū which are not acts by themselves, cannot be imagined to produce any result unless they be based on some rite. But in the cases of the milking pot and so on, the declarations of results become justifiable since these become necessarily connected with such acts as carrying water that are needed in a rite.[36] So also in such cases

[36] The injunction is "When the water is being carried, it should be done in a milking pot for a man who desires cattle, and in a bronze (*Kāṁsya*) vessel for one who wants the holiness (or the eminence of a Brāhmaṇa)" The milking pot is not an absolute requisite in a sacrifice, a *camasa* being quite in order. So this is not a eulogy but a fresh injunction.

as the sacrificial stake being made of Bilva wood,[37] it is proper that injunctions about results should be admitted, since they are based on such things as stake etc. that are already connected with a relevant sacrifice. In the cases, however, of "being made of Palāśa" and so on, there is no supporting factor connected with a sacrifice under discussion. If in the latter case, however, the terms Juhū etc. (occurring in the text) are accepted as the ground for the Palāśa Juhū becoming connected with a relevant sacrifice, and then again on the authority of that very sentence an injunction about the result of using the Palāśa Juhū be accepted, that will lead to a break in the unity of purport (that every sentence should have). But in the case of meditations, since they are themselves acts, they can be the subjects of distinct injunctions; and hence the injunctions about the meditations based on Udgītha etc. involve no contradiction. Therefore just as the milk pail etc., even though dependent on sacrifices, are not permanently connected with them, precisely because they have their separate results, similarly also are to be judged the meditations based on Udgītha etc. And it is precisely for this reason that the authors of the *Kalpa-Sūtras* did not treat such meditations as included in the sacrifices.

Topic 28: Meditations on Prana and Vayu

प्रदानवदेव तदुक्तम् ॥४३॥

प्रदान-वत् Like the offering एव to be sure; तत् that उक्तम् has been stated.

43. *(The meditations on Prāṇa and Vāyu or Air are to be kept apart) exactly as in the case of offerings, as that has been stated by Jaimini.*

Doubt: In the text, "The organ of speech took a vow, 'I shall go on speaking' " etc. it has been ascertained in the Bṛhadā-

[37] The injunction runs thus: "The sacrificial stake of one who wants food to eat should be made of the *Bilva* wood, but of one wanting prowess, it should be made of catechu (*Khādira*) wood."

raṇyaka (I. V. 21) that in the corporeal context *Prāṇa* (vital force) is the chief among all the organs counting from that of speech, and that in the divine context Air (Hiraṇyagarbha) is the chief among all counting from Fire. So also in the text, "Air indeed is the place of merger" (Ch. IV. iii. 1), it has been ascertained that on the divine plane Air is the place of merger for all counting from fire, and in, "*Prāṇa* indeed is the place of merger" (Ch. IV. iii. 3), it has been ascertained that *Prāṇa* is the place of merger of the organs of speech etc. on the corporeal plane. Now the doubt arises here as to whether this Air and *Prāṇa* are to be approached (i.e. meditated on) separately or in combination.

Opponent: While in this predicament, the conclusion is that they are to be approached jointly, for in essential nature they are identical; and when the principle to be meditated on is the same, it is not proper to meditate on it separately. Besides, the Upaniṣad shows that the principle is essentially the same on the corporeal and divine planes in the text starting with, "Fire entered into the mouth assuming the form of the organ of speech", ("*Vāyu* entered into the nostrils assuming the form of *Prāṇa*") etc. (Ai. I. ii. 4). Similarly the text "These are all equal and all infinite" (Bṛ. I. v. 13) shows that the organs in the body have divine glory as their very Self (i.e. essence). So also in other places the essential non-difference of the divine and the corporeal is shown in various ways in the respective contexts. At one place, again, Air and *Prāṇa* are clearly identified by saying, "That which is *Prāṇa* is Air". So also in the very context of the Bṛhadāraṇyaka Upaniṣad, from which some passages have been quoted earlier, it is said in the course of the concluding verse, viz "the Gods observed the vow of that from which the sun rises and in which it sets" (Bṛ. I. v. 23), that "the sun indeed rises from *Prāṇa* and also sets in it" (ibid.), where unity is revealed by making the conclusion with *Prāṇa* itself.[38] This is also confirmed by the text, "Therefore a man should observe

[38] The previous paragraph ends with *Vāyu* (i.e. Hiraṇyagarbha) that knows no setting. The verse quoted here refers to that *Vāyu*. Hence *Vāyu* and *Prāṇa* are one.

only a single vow—do the functions of *Prāṇa* and *Apāna* (expiration and inspiration)" (ibid), inasmuch as the conclusion is made here with the single vow of *Prāṇa*. Similarly in the Chāndogya Upaniṣad, the place of merger is taught to be but one by saying, "The single deity Prajāpati (Brahmā) who is the protector of the universe, swallowed the four great ones (Fire, Sun, Water, and Moon on the divine plane and speech, eye, ear, and mind on the corporeal plane)" (Ch. IV. iii. 6); but this text does not say that the place of merger for the one group of four is one, while that for the other group is another. Hence the meditation is non-different.

Vedāntin : Faced with this conclusion, we say: Air and *Prāṇa* are to be meditated on separately.

Why?

On account of being taught separately; for this instruction about the division on the divine and corporeal plane is meant for meditation; and this will be meaningless if the meditations are not to be undertaken separately.

Opponent : It was pointed out that the meditations should be identical owing to the essential non-difference of the entities.

Vedāntin : That is no defect, since even though there is no such difference in essence, still there can be difference in instruction based on differences of modes; and hence there can be a difference in meditation according to that instruction. Even though the suggestion in the above concluding verse may be reasonably interpreted as showing the essential unity of *Prāṇa* and *Vāyu*, still this can have no power to rule out their distinction as two separate objects of meditation, as has been shown earlier.[39] Their difference as objects of meditation cannot be nullified also because *Prāṇa* and *Vāyu* are treated as an illustration and the thing illustrated in, "As is the vital force (*Prāṇa*) in the body among these organs, so is *Vāyu* (Air) among these gods" (Bṛ. I. v. 22). Hereby is explained the argument

[39] The sunrise and sunset being dependent on Air (cosmic Energy), and *Prāṇa* being non-different from Air, it is said that the sunrise and sunset occur owing to *Prāṇa*. But from this the verse can have no power to overrule the two meditations separately on the divine and corporeal planes, as stated by the Upaniṣad itself.

about the teaching of the vow.[40] The "only" used in "only a single vow" (Bṛ. I. v. 23) is meant for resorting to the vow of *Prāṇa* to the exclusion of the vows of the organs of speech etc., for speech etc. are spoken of as baffled in their vows in the text, "Death captured them in the form of fatigue" (Bṛ. I. v. 21); but that is not meant for excluding the vow of Air, since starting with the text, "Now a consideration of the vow" (Bṛ. I. v. 21), it has been ascertained that *Prāṇa* and Air both remain equally unbaffled in their vows. Again, having said, "a man should observe only a single vow" (Bṛ. I. v. 23), it is stated again, "through it he attains identity with this deity, or lives in the same world with him" (ibid.), where the result is shown to be the attainment of (the deity) Air, thereby proving that the vow of Air has not been ruled out. The word "deity" in the above quotation must mean Air, since the result sought here is the attainment of identity with the unlimited one,[41] and since it has been used so in an earlier text, "Air is the deity that never sets" (Bṛ. I. V. 22). Similarly the Chāndogya Upaniṣad mentions them separately in, "These two that are such are the two places of merger—Air among the deities, and *Prāṇa* among the organs" (Ch. IV. iii. 4), and the conclusion also is made separately in, "These then that are five in one group and five in another make up ten, and that is Kṛta"[42] (Ch. IV. iii. 8).

Hence the approach (in meditation) must be separate, as in the case of the offerings. Thus it is that in connection with the sacrifice called Tripuroḍāśinī (having the offering of three *puroḍāśas* or cakes), as prescribed in the passage, "*puroḍāśas* on eleven potsherds are to be offered to king Indra, so also it is to be offered to Indra, the super-lord of the organs, and to Indra,

[40] Just as the above verse speaks of the oneness of the entity, but not of the meditations, so also the mention of the oneness of the vow is from the standpoint of the oneness of the entity, but not of the meditations.

[41] Fire etc. are delimited by Air, since they merge in Air. But Air is not so delimited by them. So merger in the unlimited means merger in Air.

[42] The four sides of the dice are marked with 4, 3, 2, and 1, which figures, when added up, make ten, and are collectively called Kṛta.

sovereign in heaven" (Tai. S. II. iii. 6), there occurs this sentence, "They shall take up the oblations making these available for all deities, so that the uttering of the word *vaṣaṭ* may be unfailing in its result". From this sentence and from the fact that the deity Indra is the same, the opponent (of Mīmāṁsā) would conclude that the offerings are to be made simultaneously,[43] whereupon Jaimini concludes that (though Indra is one), the attributes of kingship, (super-lordship, sovereignty), etc. being different, the *yājyā* and *anuvākyā mantras* having been enjoined to be reversed,[44] and the deities being separate as they are separately enumerated, the offerings also must be separate.

Similarly here also, although in reality *Prāṇa* and *Vāyu* are the same, still owing to a difference in the aspects to be meditated on, the meditations also differ. And thus it is said in the *Devatā-Kāṇḍa* of the Pūrva-Mīmāṁsā, "The gods are certainly different, since they are cognized differently". But it is to be noted that in the Pūrva-Mīmāṁsā, the difference among sacrifices is also admitted even in accordance with the difference of things and deities; but that kind of difference of meditations does not exist here, since from the introduction and the end of the instructions on the divine and corporeal planes etc. it is obvious that the selfsame meditation is enjoined. And yet even though the meditations be the same, the meditator's function differs (with regard to them) in accordance with the difference in the divine and corporeal contexts, just as it is the case with regard to the Agnihotra sacrifice which differs as an act in accordance with the difference of morning and evening. With this idea in mind it has been said, "As in the case of the offerings (in the Puroḍāśa sacrifice)".

[43] If the offerings be made one by one for the same deity, the succeeding offerings become useless; but this is not so when simultaneous offering is made.

[44] The *mantra* read after the Adhvaryu's direction "*Yaja*" (sacrifice) is *yājyā*, and the *mantra* read after his direction, "*anubrūhi*" (utter) is *anuvākyā*. In this sacrifice, the *yājyā* in the first offering becomes the *anuvākyā* in the second, the *anuvākyā* of the first becomes the *yājyā* of the second.

Topic 29: Fires in Agni-Rahasya not Parts of Sacrifice

लिंगभूयस्त्वात् तद्धि बलीयस्तदपि ॥४४॥

(Fires in the *Agni-rahasya* are not parts of any rite), लिंगभूयस्त्वात् on account of abundance of indicatory marks हि for तत् that (mark) बलीयः is more powerful (than a context), तत् that अपि also (was said by Jaimini).

44. The fires (of the mind, speech, etc. of Agni-rahasya) do not form parts of any rite, on account of the abundance of indicatory marks; for these marks are stronger than the context. That also was said by Jaimini.

Doubt: In the *Agni-rahasya* (esoteric teaching about the fires), occurring in the *brāhmaṇa* of the Vājasaneyins, which starts with, "All this was neither existent nor non-existent before creation," it is stated with regard to the mind, "That mind saw itself as thirty-six thousand; it saw the adorable fires as belonging to itself, lighted up by the mind, and conceived of as identified with the mental modes" etc. Similarly such notional fires are read of separately as, "lighted up by (the organ of speech), lighted up by (the organ of smell), lighted up by the eye, lighted up by ear, lighted up by the hands, lighted up by (the organ of) touch".[45] With regard to these the doubt arises whether these fires, lighted up by the mind etc., are to be used in connection with rites and they form parts of them, or they are independent, existing only for meditation.

Vedāntin: Now when from the context it might appear that the fires are to be used in rites, the aphorist asserts their independence by saying, "on account of the abundance of indicatory

[45] First the creation of mind is spoken of. Then it is said, "the mind saw itself"; and then "it saw the fires". Although the mental modes are infinite, still they are delimited by the human life having a span of a hundred years, divided into 36,000 days. Hence the mental modes are also 36,000, which are thought of as the bricks of the altar, on which the fire is lighted up by the mind itself. The mind saw its own modes, conceived of as bricks. Similarly speech etc. also saw their modes as so many fires, since the fires are lighted up by those modes, thought of as bricks.

marks" etc. For in this *Brāhmaṇa* are to be met with an abundance of indicatory marks supporting the view that these are meant merely for meditation, as for instance, "That being so, whatever the beings think of through their minds, by all that are lighted up these very fires", and "Whether a man of such knowledge is awake or asleep, all beings light up these fires for him for ever".[46] Of course, these indicatory marks are more authoritative than the context. That too has been stated in the Pūrva-Mīmāṁsā: "In a case where express statement, indicatory marks (word capacity), syntactical connection, context, order, and name" are in evidence in groups, those coming later in order are ruled out by the earlier, since the meanings imparted by the succeeding ones are checkmated by the earlier" (Jai. Sū. III. iii. 14).

पूर्वविकल्पः प्रकरणात् स्यात् क्रिया मानसवत् ॥४५॥

प्रकरणात् On the strength of the context (the conceptual fires are to be used as) पूर्व-विकल्पः alternatives for the earlier (actually enjoined) fire; स्यात् क्रिया they should constitute (i.e. form parts of) some rite मानस-वत् like the imaginary (drinking).

45. On the strength of the context, the conceptual fires are to be used alternatively for the actual fire enjoined earlier. They constitute some rite like the imaginary drinking (of Soma juice).

Opponent: It is not proper to say that these fires are independent and not parts of any rite. Since these fires are read of in the context of the (actual) earlier fire associated with rites, this instruction must be about a particular alternative form of that very fire; but it is not an independent instruction.

[46] When one's meditation of the form, "My mental fires are lighted up by all the mental moods of all beings" becomes well established, then by all the thoughts of all beings are lighted up the mental fires of that meditator.

The first text indicates that the fires form parts of a meditation only and not of any rite, since "doing anything whatsoever" cannot form part of a rite, which latter act can be known only from an injunction. Similarly the second text speaks of actions by all for ever, whereas an accessory of a rite is regulated as to its time, place, and occasion by an injunction.

Objection: Is not an indicatory sign more authoritative than a context?

Opponent: That is true; but even an indicatory mark of this kind is not more authoritative than the context; for it is noticed to be meant for some other purpose, it being meant for the glorification of the conceptual fires.[47] Although anything which is indicatory of something else can logically be interpreted as presenting some subsidiary matter, when that something else is not in evidence, yet it cannot rule out a context. Hence though these fires are got through superimposition, yet by force of the context they will subserve some rite. This is like imaginary acts. As on the tenth day (actually the eleventh day), called the *avivākya* (speechless, *mantra*-less) day of the sacrifice which is known as *Daśa-rātra*, the sea, imagined to be the Soma Juice, is taken up in the earth, imagined to be a vessel, for offering to the deity Prajāpati. In connection with that, the taking up of the Soma vessel, the placing of the vessel on its proper place, the offering of the Soma as libation, the taking up of the remainder after the offering, invitation by the priests to one another to partake of the Soma, and the drinking of the Soma by them, that are mentioned in the Vedas, are all but mental acts. But though that imagination of Soma be mental, it becomes a part of the rite, since it occurs in the context of the rite. So also must be this imagination of fire in the present context.

अतिदेशाच्च ॥४६॥

46. And (this conclusion is supported) by the fact of extended application.

And the extended application of the attributes of the actual fire to these mental ones, strengthens the case for their use in rites (the extension being made owing to the similarity with the accessories of the rites), as shown in, "The adorable fires are thirty-six thousand, and each one of them is as great as the

[47] An indicatory sign occurring in an injunction can rule out a context, but not so one occurring in a eulogy. "All beings think for ever" is a eulogy after all. This sentence has to be construed with an injunction, for a eulogy cannot present a new accessory for any rite.

(sacrificial) fire mentioned earlier". For extension of application is based on similarity; and from this it follows that since this text extends the application of the fire lighted up on the brick altar to these mental fires, it thereby indicates that these latter subserve some rite.

विद्यैव तु निर्धारणात् ॥४७॥

तु Rather (they constitute) विद्या एव a meditation only निर्धारणात् for so it is determined.

47. The fires rather constitute only a meditation, for so it is determined (in the Vedas).

Vedāntin: The word "rather" sets aside the opposite point of view. These fires, lighted up by the mind etc., ought to constitute a meditation only, and be independent of rites; they are not accessories of any rite. That is how it has been ascertained in: "All these fires, as such, are lighted up by meditation alone" and "For a man of knowledge these fires become surely lighted up by meditation".

दर्शनाच्च ॥४८॥

48. And owing to the indicatory mark met with.

There is also an indicatory mark to show that these are independent of rites. This was shown earlier under the aphorism, "On account of an abundance of indicatory marks" (III. iii. 44).

Opponent: Even an indicatory mark cannot be authoritative about anything when that other thing (other than action i.e. meditation) itself is not in evidence. Hence the indicatory mark has to be rejected; and it should be concluded on the strength of the context that the fires are accessories of a rite.

Vedāntin: Hence the aphorist replies:

श्रुत्यादिबलीयस्त्वाच्च न बाधः ॥४९॥

श्रुति-आदि-बलीयस्त्वात् Owing to the greater authoritativeness of express statement etc. च also, न बाधः there is no setting aside.

49. Moreover, the view (that the fires constitute a meditation) cannot be set aside owing to the greater authority of express statement etc.

It is not proper to ascertain on the strength of the context that they form parts of some rite and thus to set aside their independence of rites, since express statement etc. (indicatory mark, syntactical connection) are more authoritative than context; for the conclusion arrived at under the aphorism about express statement, indicatory mark, etc., has been that express statement, indicatory mark, and syntactical connection are more authoritative than context (Jai. Sū. III. iii. 14). And these are found here to lead to the view about the independence (of the fires).

How?

As for express statement, it is, "All these fires, as such, are lighted up by meditation alone". Similarly the indicatory mark occurs in, "and whether a man of knowledge is awake or asleep, all beings light up those fires for ever". Similarly there is syntactical connection in, "By meditation alone are these fires lighted up for a man of knowledge". The express statement "lighted up by meditation alone" made with a restrictive particle (*eva*—alone) will become nullified if these are admitted to be connected with rites.

Opponent: This restriction should be interpreted to mean that no external accessory is to be used (in lighting the fires).

Vedāntin: The answer is in the negative. If that were the implication, then that would have been served by simply saying, "lighted up by meditation", which would amount to declaring that these fires in essence constitute a meditation which is free from external things, so that this restriction (by "alone") would be uncalled for, since by nature they would be free from external accessories. And yet even though these fires are independent of external accessories, there may arise the possibility of their becoming used in rites like the mental drinking of Soma. Thus the restriction becomes purposeful by serving to rule that possibility out. Similarly the continuity of the act noticed in the text, "whether the man of knowledge is awake or asleep, all beings light up these fires for him for ever", can be possible only if these are independent of rites. Just as in connection with the Agnihotra sacrifice performed with the organ of speech and the vital force, through an act of mental superimposition, it is first said, "Then he offers the vital force to the organ of speech, then he offers the organ of speech to the vital force" (Kau. II. 5), and then it is said, "He offers these two unending immortal oblations for ever in wakefulness and sleep" (ibid.), similar is the case here. But if the fires formed parts of rites, they would not have been thought of as being used continuously, since their application in rites would have lasted only for a short time. And it cannot be reasonably held that this is a mere eulogy. For a simple declaration (without clear injunction) of anything can properly be accepted as a eulogy only where one comes across distinct indicative marks etc. pointing out an (independent) injunction. But since no other clear injunction is discernible here, the application of these meditations has to be inferred from the mere declaration itself. And that can be inferred only in conformity with the declaration; therefore, by noticing the continuous application of the fires, they have to be inferred to be continuous. From this it follows that in keeping with this situation, these fires stand proved as independent of rites. Hereby is explained the text, "That being so, whatever the beings think of through their minds, by all that are lighted up these very fires," etc. So also the syntactical connection contained in, "for a man of knowledge", which speaks of the connection of these fires with a distinct person only, militates against any connection with a sacrifice. Hence the view about independence is more weighty.

अनुबन्धादिभ्यः प्रज्ञान्तरपृथक्त्ववद्दृष्टश्च तदुक्तम् ॥५०॥

अनुबन्ध-आदिभ्यः Owing to being linked up (with the mind) and such other reasons, (the mental fires are independent) प्रज्ञा-अन्तर-पृथक्त्व-वत् even as other meditations have their separateness. च And दृष्टः it is seen (that sacrifices are treated as separate); तत् that उक्तम् was stated (by Jaimini).

50. On account of being linked up with the mind and such

other reasons, the mental fires are independent even as other meditations are. And it is seen that the sacrifices are treated as independent (irrespective of their context), as was pointed out by Jaimini.

The context has to be waived and the independence of the fires, lighted up by the mind etc., have to be understood for this further reason that all the subsidiary acts presupposed in a rite are linked up here with the modes of the mind etc. in the text, "They (the fires) are established merely mentally, built up mentally only; mentally only is the Soma vessel taken up; the Udgātā sings the Sāma (song) mentally, the Hotā recites the hymns mentally. And whatever else has to be done in this sacrifice, that is either indirectly or directly conducive to the fulfilment of the sacrifice, all that is but mental, all that is to be done mentally (by the man of knowledge) in connection with those fires consisting of thoughts and lighted up by the mind". This linking up with the mind leads to the conclusion that it is all a case of meditation through superimposition. And it cannot be proper that anyone should hanker to get the (material) accessories of a sacrifice with the help of imaginary superimposition when these materials themselves are physically present. It should not be misconceived here that just like the meditation on the Udgītha (Ch. I. i. 1), the mental fires are connected with the accessories of a sacrifice, and so they should form parts of a sacrifice; for the Vedic texts are dissimilar. The text here does not say that a certain accessory of a rite is to be taken up and the notion of such and such a thing should be superimposed on it; but it merely selects the thirty-six thousand different mental moods and imagines them to be fires, vessels, etc., just as it is done in the case of a man thought of as a sacrifice (Ch. III. xvi.). As for this number, it is to be understood that the number as found in the case of the days in the whole span of a man's life is superimposed on the mental moods. Thus the fires lighted up by the mind etc. are independent of rites owing to their being linked up with the mind.

The portion "and such other reasons" (in the aphorism), is

to be understood to include "extended application" etc. as far as possible. For instance the text, "each one of them is as great as the former (fire used in an actual sacrifice)", extends the greatness of the fire in an ordinary sacrifice to each one of the fires in the meditation, thereby showing a disregard for rites. It cannot be argued that the latter (mental fires) can be accepted as substitutes for the former (actual fires) on the mere ground of their having some connection with rites, for the latter (conceptual fires) cannot be helpful to a rite in the very same way as the former (actual) fire is by holding the offering, and so on. As for the assertion that the argument about extension of application confirms the opponent's view as well, inasmuch as an application of the method of extension is possible where there is a similarity, that (argument) is refuted by pointing out that in our view also there is the similarity of both being fires, for even the imaginary fires are fires. The other reasons like "express statement" have already been advanced.

Thus owing to such reasons as being linked up with the mind, the fires lighted up by the mind etc. are independent of rites even as other meditations are independent. As other meditations, for instance, the "meditation of Śaṇḍilya", which being linked up with their respective related objects, are certainly different from rites and are also separate from other meditations, similar is the case here. Moreover, it is seen that the rite called Aveṣṭi, read of in the context of the Rājasūya sacrifice, has more excellence (e.g. wider use) than the context warrants, since it is linked up with the three castes, whereas the Rājasūya sacrifice has to be performed by the kings alone. This has been stated in the Pūrva-Mīmāṁsā in the aphorism, "If it be argued that the Aveṣṭi sacrifice forms a part of the Rājasūya sacrifice, then we say that it is not so, since the Aveṣṭi is associated with the three castes"[48] (XI. iv. 7).

[48] In the course of prescribing the Rājasūya sacrifice, the Aveṣṭi sacrifice, to be performed by the three castes is mentioned. The Rājasūya is to be performed by a Kṣatriya only, but the Aveṣṭi can be performed by Brāhmaṇas, Kṣatriyas, and Vaiśyas. Hence it is independent of and better than the Rājasūya.

न सामान्यादप्युपलब्धेर्मृत्युवन्न हि लोकापत्तिः ॥५१॥

न Not अपि even सामान्यात् on the ground of similarity (the mental fires become parts of rites) उपलब्धेः for it is noticed (that they are useful to a man) मृत्युवत् as it is in the case of death; हि for न लोक-आपत्तिः the (heavenly) world does not become (fire, because of similarity).

51. Not even on the ground of similarity can the mental fires become subservient to rites, since they are noticed to serve human needs, just as it is in the case of death; for the world does not become fire just because of a similarity.

It was stated (by the opponent) that like the imaginary Soma juice etc. the mental fires are but substitutes for the fire used in the actual sacrifice (III. iii. 45). That is being refuted. Not even from the similarity with the imaginary Soma etc. are the fires, lighted up by the mind etc., to be considered parts of a rite, since from the reasons like "express statement", adduced earlier, they are seen to serve merely human purposes (i.e. of the aspirant).[49] Not that something cannot be similar to something else in some respect; but its individual distinction is not obliterated thereby, as in the case of death. Thus in the texts "This very Being indeed, that is in the solar orb, is Death" (Śa. B. X. v. 2.3), and "Fire is Death" (Bṛ. III. ii. 10), the word Death is used equally for fire and the Being in the sun; yet they do not become absolutely the same. Again, just as in the text, "O Gautama, the other world is surely a fire, and of this the sun is the fuel" (Ch. V. iv. 1), the world does not become a fire just because of the analogy of fuel etc., so also is the case here.

परेण च शब्दस्य ताद्विध्यं भूयस्त्वात्त्वनुबन्धः ॥५२॥

परेण According to the subsequent (*brāhmaṇa* text) च also (is known that) शब्दस्य the scripture has ताद्विध्यम् that injunction in view; तु but अनुबन्धः the connection (with the actual fire) भूयस्त्वात् is on account of the abundance (of the attributes of the latter that are imagined).

[49] And not the purposes of a sacrifice.

52. From the subsequent brāhmaṇa text also it is known that the scripture has that (prescription of a meditation) in view; but the connection with fire occurs because of the abundance of the attributes of fire that have to be imagined here.

Even later on, in the immediately subsequent *brāhmaṇa* text starting with, "This world is surely the sacrificial fire that is lighted up", it is gathered that "the scripture has that injunction in view", that the purpose of the text is merely to enjoin a meditation, and not imparting any injunction about any purely subsidiary part of a ritual. Even there occurs the verse, "They ascend there through meditation where all desires get vanquished. People proceeding by the Southern Path do not reach there, nor even the ignorant people engaged in austerities" (Śa. B.), in which this very fact is shown by condemning mere rites and praising meditation. Similarly also even in the earlier *brāhmaṇa* text starting with, "this (solar) orb that scatters heat" (Śa. B. II. v. 2.23), the predominance of meditation is noticeable and not that of rites, since the conclusion is made with the words, "He who has Death as his Self, becomes immortal", which state the result of meditation. (In common with them) this must be the case here as well (in the middle portion) because of similarity with them. On account of the further reason, however, that quite a number of attributes of the sacrificial fire are to be imagined in this meditation, the meditation is linked up with that fire; but this is not done so owing to its being a part of any rite. Hence it is established that the fires lighted up by the mind etc. constitute nothing but a meditation.

Topic 30: The Self Distinct from Body

एक आत्मनः शरीरे भावात् ॥५३॥

एके Some (deny) आत्मनः the soul's (existence) भावात् owing to its existence शरीरे when the body is.

53. Some deny the existence of the soul, its existence being dependent on the existence of the body.

The existence of the soul, as distinct from the body, is being confirmed here in order to establish its aptitude for bondage and liberation. For if there be no soul, distinct from the body, there can be no logicality for imparting instruction about results to be attained in the other world; and in that case, for whom can it be taught that his soul is identical with Brahman?

Opponent: In the very beginning of the scripture (of Pūrva-Mīmāṁsā), in the first chapter, the existence of the soul, competent to enjoy the fruits mentioned in the scriptures and distinct from the body, was spoken of.

Vedāntin: True it has been said so by the commentator; but no aphorism occurs there about the existence of the soul, whereas here the existence of that soul is established by the aphorist himself after raising a doubt about its existence. When the teacher Śabarasvāmī discussed the existence of the soul in connection with the characteristics of valid means of proof in the Pūrva-Mīmāṁsā, he drew upon this aphorism itself. And it is for this reason that the great Upavarṣa cited this one by saying, "We shall discuss this in the Vedānta-Sūtra", when the occasion arose in the Pūrva-Mīmāṁsā to speak of the existence of the Self.[50]

Now, here, in the course of discussion of the meditations got from injunctions, this existence of the soul is being considered in order to show that this question underlies all the scriptures. Moreover, under the previous topic it was taken for granted that something could be taken apart from its context, and thereby it was shown that the fires lighted by the mind etc. are conducive to human good (by forming parts of meditation). It having become necessary now to explain who that aspirant is and for whose sake these fires lighted by the mind etc. exist, it is being stated here that the soul has its existence apart from the body. This first aphorism is presented by way of doubting that existence, the idea being that when the statement of refuta-

[50] When the truth of the text, "the sacrificer, armed with sacrifices, goes to heaven", had to be proved by showing the existence of the soul and no aphorism was in evidence in the Pūrva-Mīmāṁsā, Śabarasvāmī had to depend on the present aphorism. That he did so, is clear from what Upavarṣa says.

tion comes after raising the doubt, it produces a firm conviction about the subject-matter presented, on the analogy of driving in a peg.[51]

(*Opponent* :) With regard to this, there are some materialists who identify the soul with the body itself, and think that there is no soul distinct from the body. Under this belief they consider it possible that although sentience is not seen to belong to the external things like earth etc. taken either individually or collectively, yet it may belong to the elements transformed into bodies, and they say that sentience is but consciousness arising from them like the power of intoxication (existing imperceptibly in betels etc.), and that a man is nothing but the body dowered with sentience. They also assert that apart from the body, there is no soul able to attain either heaven or liberation, and that the body itself is both sentience and soul. They adduce this reason: "its existence being dependent on the existence of the body". Anything whose existence depends on the existence of another, and which ceases to be when that other thing is not there, is ascertained to be an attribute of the latter, as for instance, heat and light are attributes of fire. As regards such attributes as the activities of the vital force, sentience, memory, etc., which are held to belong to the soul according to the believers in the soul, they too are perceived within the body and not outside; and hence so long as any substance other than the body cannot be proved, they must be the attributes of the body itself. Hence the soul is not distinct from the body.

Vedāntin : Under such a predicament we say:

व्यतिरेकस्तद्भावाभावित्वान्न तूपलब्धिवत् ॥५४॥

तु But न not so; (there is) व्यतिरेक: distinction तत्-भाव-अभावित्वात् because of non-existence (of consciousness) even when that (body) exists, उपलब्धिवत् as in perception.

54. But this is not so; there is a distinction (between the soul and the body) because consciousness may not exist even when the body exists, as it is in the case of perception.

[51] When driving in a post into soft ground, one repeatedly pulls it out and forces it into the ground, so that it may get fixed deep and firm.

But the fact is not as it is stated, viz that the soul is not distinct from the body. For it must be distinct from the body, "since consciousness does not exist even when the body is there". If from the fact that the attributes of the soul exist when the body exists, you infer that those attributes belong to the body, then why should it not also be inferred that they are not the attributes of the body owing to their non-existence even when the body is present, they being different from the characteristics of the body? For attributes like form (or colour) etc., which belong to the body, may very well last as long as the body persists; but such characteristics as the activities of the vital force do not occur after death even though the body exists. And such attributes of the body as form (or colour) etc. are perceived by others (outside the body), but not so are such characteristics of the soul as consciousness, memory, etc. Moreover, the existence of these attributes can be conclusively determined when the body continues during a man's life, but their non-existence cannot be so determined from the non-existence of the body. For even when this body has fallen, perchance these attributes of the soul may well persist by transferring themselves to some other body. Even (if this be a doubtful theory), that doubt can well demolish the opposite point of view. And the opponent has to be asked as to what he thinks the nature of this consciousness to be that he would fain derive it from the elements. For the materialists do not accept any principle over and above the four elements (earth, water, fire, and air).

Opponent: Consciousness is nothing but the perception of the elements and the derivatives of elements.

Vedāntin: In that case these elements etc. are objects of perception, and hence sentience cannot be an attribute of these elements etc., since a thing cannot act on itself. For fire, though possessing heat, does not burn itself, nor does an actor (or acrobat), trained though he be, ride on his own shoulder. And it cannot be that consciousness which is an attribute of the elements and their derivatives, (and is hence one with them), will perceive those elements etc. For neither one's own form nor of anybody else is perceived by forms etc., whereas external elements and their derivatives are perceived by consciousness. Hence just as the existence of this perception of the elements and their derivatives is admitted, so also must its separateness from them be admitted. According to us, the soul is by nature the very essence of perception itself; and hence the soul is distinct from the body; and it is eternal, because consciousness is uniform by nature. For, although the soul comes to be associated with other states (i.e. limiting adjuncts), still in such experiences as, "It is I that saw this", its identity as the perceiver is recognized; and this identity has to be admitted so that memory etc. may be reasonably upheld.[52] As for the argument that since consciousness occurs in the body, it must be an attribute of the body, that is refuted in the way we have already shown. Moreover, though perception takes place when light and other accessories are present, but not when they are absent, it does not follow from this that perception is an attribute of the light etc. That being the case, it does not follow that consciousness should be an attribute of the body just because it occurs where the body is present and does not occur where the body is absent; for the usefulness of the body can be explained away as serving merely the purposes of an auxiliary like light etc. Furthermore, the body is not seen to be an absolutely contributory factor in perception, since even when this body lies inactive in dream, many kinds of perception are seen to take place. Hence the existence of the soul distinct from the body is beyond criticism.

Topic 31: Meditations Connected with Accessories of Rites

अंगावबद्धास्तु न शाखासु हि प्रतिवेदम् ॥५५॥

अंग-अवबद्धाः The (meditations) connected with the accessories (of rites), **तु** however, **न** (are) not (to be confined) **शाखासु**

[52] In dream, a man has no consciousness of the gross body; still self-identity persists. Even if it be argued that he is conscious of his dream body, then let us take the case of memory, wish etc., where the identity of the perceiver and the one who remembers or wishes has to be admitted perforce.

to the branches (of the Vedas where they occur); हि because प्रति-वेदम् (they are to be adopted) in all the (branches of the) Vedas.

55. But the meditations connected with the accessories of rites are not to be confined to the branches of the Vedas in which they obtain, for they are to be adopted in all the (branches of the) Vedas.

The topic of the soul that cropped up incidentally is finished. Now we follow the subject under discussion.

Doubt: Some meditations that are connected with the accessories of rites like Udgītha etc. and are enjoined in all the Vedas in their different branches, as for instance, "One shall meditate on the letter *Om* as Udgītha" (Ch. I. i. 1), "One shall meditate on the fivefold Sāma by superimposing on it the idea of the worlds" (Ch. II. ii. 1), "That which people mention as 'Uktha', ('Uktha', a hymn used as a part of a rite) is but this that is the earth" (Ai. Ā. II. i. 2), "This fire that is lighted (in the sacrifice) is but this world" (Śa. B. X. v. 4.1), and so on; are these to remain confined to the Udgītha etc. just as they obtain in the respective branches, or are they to be extended to all the branches? This is the doubt, and it arises from the fact that the Udgītha etc. differ from one branch to another owing to a difference in their intonation etc. So what should be the conclusion?

Opponent: They are enjoined in connection with the Udgītha etc. as presented in their own respective branches.

Why?

Because of proximity. For the curiosity to know the particular (Udgītha) after hearing the text, "One shall meditate on *Om* as the Udgītha" (Ch. I. i. 1), stated in a general way, is removed by the (proximately) particularized (Udgītha) contained in that very branch itself, so that there is no justification for skipping over this and borrowing any particular one from another branch. Hence the meditations remain confined to the branches where they obtain.

Vedāntin: This being the position, the aphorist says, "But the meditations, connected with the accessories" etc. The word "but" rules out the opponent's view. These will not remain confined each to the branch of its own Veda, but will extend to all the branches.

Why?

Because the Vedic text about Udgītha etc. are stated in a general way. If it be confined to its own branch, then the text "One shall meditate on the Udgītha", which is stated in a general way and is not meant for any restricted application, will remain confined to a particular context on the strength of proximity, and thus the general (express) statement will be adversely affected. But this is not proper. For an express statement is more authoritative than proximity. It cannot also be argued that no concept (and hence meditation) is possible with regard to a general factor. Hence though there is a difference in intonation etc. (in the different branches), still on account of the fact that the Udgītha is one and the same, this kind of meditation should be undertaken with regard to the Udgītha etc. in all the branches.

मन्त्रादिवद्वाऽविरोधः ॥५६॥

वा Or rather मन्त्र-आदि-वत् as in the case of *mantras* etc. अविरोधः there is no contradiction.

56. Or rather (they are to be adopted in other branches) like the mantras; (and thus) there is no contradiction.

Or there is no scope for any doubt as to how the conceptions about Udgītha etc. occurring in one branch can apply to those in other branches; because it can be shown that there is no contradiction in this even as there is none in the case of *mantras* etc. For it is seen that *mantras*, rites, and subsidiaries occurring in one branch are taken over to some other branch. Thus even for those (belonging to the Yajur-Veda) who do not have the *mantra*, "*Kuṭarurasi* (thou art the *kuṭaru*)", meant for use when taking up a stone pestle (for grinding rice), the injunction for its application is seen to be stated thus: "He shall take up the stone with the *mantra*, 'Thou art *kuṭaru*' or 'thou art *kukkuṭa*' (i.e. cock)." Similarly even for those (of the Maitrāyaṇa branch) who do not have the scriptural mention (in their own branch) of the subsidiary sacrifices, viz Samidh, (Tanūnapāta, Iḍā, Barhiḥ, Svāhākāra), still an injunction about the subsidiaries (i.e. about their number) is found there in the text, "The five Prayājas (counting from Samidh) are (equal in number to) the five seasons (autumn and winter being counted as one), and they are to be performed in one and the same place". So also for those (of the Yajur-Veda) who have no such *mantra* as, "The goat is meant to be sacrificed to Agni-Soma," stating the class of the animal to be sacrificed, (but simply have the *mantra*, "He shall sacrifice the animal to Agni-Soma"), for them also a *mantra* text suggestive of that particular animal is found in the *mantra* (recited by the Adhvaryu), "O(priest Hotṛ), chant the hymn for the offering of the fat and marrow of the goat". Thus also the *mantras*, "*Agnerverhotram veradhvaram*—O Fire, promote the Hotā and the sacrifice", originally occurring in the Sāma-Veda, is seen to be applied to the Yajur-Veda. So again the *mantra*, "He, O people, is Indra who from his birth was the greatest in virtues and possessed of discrimination", originally found in the Ṛg-Veda, is seen to be adopted in the Yajur-Veda as noted in the text, "The *mantra* starting with, 'He, O people', is to be used for application by the priest Adhvaryu". Thus as the accessories of rites on which meditations are based are seen to be adopted in all the branches, so also should be the meditations based on them. And hence there is no contradiction.

Topic 32: Meditation on Vaisvanara as a whole

भूम्नः क्रतुवज्ज्यायस्त्वं तथा हि दर्शयति ॥५७॥

(Meditation) भूम्नः on the whole has ज्यायस्त्वम् greater importance क्रतुवत् as in the case of sacrifices, हि for तथा so दर्शयति (the Upaniṣad) shows.

57. *The meditation on the whole is of greater importance just as in the case of sacrifices. For so the Upaniṣad shows.*

Doubt: The meditation on Vaiśvānara in parts, as also as a whole, is heard of in the anecdote starting with, "Prācīnaśāla, son of Upamanyu" (Ch. V. xi. 1). As for the meditation on partial aspects, it occurs in such texts as, "(Aśvapati Kekaya asked), 'O son of Upamanyu, on what do you meditate as the Self?' He said, 'O venerable king, I meditate on heaven itself (as Vaiśvānara).' 'This Self that you meditate on is (that aspect of) the Vaiśvānara Self called the effulgent one'" (Ch. V. xii. 1), and so on. Similarly also the meditation as a whole occurs in, "Of this Vaiśvānara Self, the head is the effulgent heaven, the eye is the sun, the vital force is air, the trunk of the body is space, the bladder is water, and the feet are the earth itself" (Ch. V. xviii. 2). With regard to that the doubt arises, should there be a double meditation here, both in parts and as a whole, or should it be only of the whole? What should be the conclusion?

Opponent: Owing to the use of the predicate "(you) meditate" in connection with every limb counting from heaven, and owing to the mention of separate results as in, "In your line would be extracted the Soma juice (that is to say, the Soma sacrifice will be performed) well and plentifully" (Ch. V. xii. 1), the conclusion to be drawn is that the meditations are to proceed in parts.

Vedāntin: Hence it is said: The idea intended to be imparted in this text ought to be, "a greater importance", because of the pre-eminence of the entire thing, viz of the meditation on Vaiśvānara as a whole, comprising all His parts; but the idea is not of the meditation on the limbs separately. This is "as it is in the case of sacrifices"—this is just as it is in such sacrifices as the Darśa-Pūrṇamāsa etc. where an integral act, comprising the principal sacrifice and its limbs as a whole is intended, but not so the separate performance of Prayāja etc., nor even the performance of the principal sacrifice along with a particular part alone.

Why so?

"Because of the greater importance of the whole. Thus it is that the text shows the pre-eminence of the whole inasmuch as the whole text is seen to imply a single idea; for from a consideration of the sequence of the narration it becomes clear that it imparts a single idea about the meditation on Vaiśvānara. Thus it is seen that the narration begins with the statement that six seers counting from Prācīnaśāla to Uddālaka, who were not able to arrive at any complete knowledge about the meditation on Vaiśvānara approached Aśvapati, king of the Kekayas. Then we are told one by one of heaven etc. meditated on by these sages separately. Later on the text teaches that these are but head etc. of Vaiśvānara in such sentences as, " 'But this is only the head of that Self' said he" (Ch. V. xii. 2), and it condemns the separate meditations in such sentences as, "Had you not come to me, your head would have dropped off" (ibid.). Again, turning back from the separate meditations and following the meditation on the total aspect, the text shows the result pertaining to the whole in the sentence, "He eats food in all the worlds through all beings and through all the souls" (Ch. V. xviii. 1). As for the mention of results individually in respect of meditations on heaven etc., these are to be considered from this point of view as pertaining to the parts of a whole, but getting united in that whole which is the principal factor. Similarly the use of the predicate, "(you) meditate" (by Aśvapati) in relation to each "limb" (of Vaiśvānara) is meant simply as a reiteration of the other's idea (i.e. of the sage he is speaking to), but it is not meant for prescribing a partial meditation. Hence the view advocating the meditation as a whole is more weighty.

Some, however, while establishing here the view that the meditation on the whole is more weighty, argue on the very basis of the term "greater importance" that the meditation on the limbs is also approved by the aphorist. But that is improper. For when a unity of idea is palpable, it is improper to resort to a splitting of that unity (by assuming two meanings for the same passage). Moreover, that would run counter to such deprecating sentences as, "your head would have dropped off" (Ch. V. xii. 2) etc. Furthermore, when the meditation as a whole becomes clear from the conclusion, it is not possible to deny it from the point of view of the opponent. Besides, the statement about "greater importance" in the aphorism may well be justified as meant for showing the greater validity of the entire meditation as compared with the partial meditation.

Topic 33: When Meditations Differ

नाना शब्दादिभेदात् ॥५८॥

(The meditations are) नाना different शब्द-आदि-भेदात् in accordance as terminology etc. differ.

58. The meditations are different when there is a difference in terminology etc.

Opponent: Under the earlier topic it was stated that the meditation on the whole is better in spite of the mention of separate results for meditations on heaven etc. From this the idea crops up that other meditations also, even though occurring in different Upaniṣadic texts, have to be undertaken in a combined form. Moreover, when the entity meditated on is the same, the meditations cannot be cognized as different. Even as the articles and gods (associated with a sacrifice) determine the nature of a sacrifice, so also the entity meditated on determines the nature of the meditation. And although the Upaniṣadic texts differ, the object of meditation is known in the following texts to be the same God alone: "Identified with the mind and having *Prāṇa* as the body" (Ch. III. xiv. 2), "*Ka* (Bliss) is Brahman, *Kha* (Space) is Brahman" (Ch. IV. x. 5), "Having inevitable desire and irresistible will" (Ch. VIII. i. 5), and so on; similarly also in, "*Prāṇa* is but one", "*Prāṇa* is the place of merger" (Ch. IV. iii. 3), "*Prāṇa* is indeed the first-born and the foremost" (Ch. V. i. 1), "*Prāṇa* is the father, and *Prāṇa* the mother" (Ch. VII. xv. 1), and so on, where we gather from the Upaniṣad the oneness of the meditation owing to the oneness of the object of meditation. From this point of view the diversity of the Upaniṣadic texts is not useless, since these texts are concerned with stating the different characteristics (of the same entity involved in a meditation). Hence for the completion of a meditation, all the characteristics prescribed in either one's own branch or other branches with regard to the same object of meditation have to be combined together.

Vedāntin: This being the position, the aphorist holds: "The meditations are different" etc. Even though the object of meditation be the same, still the meditations of this class ought to be different.

Why?

"Because of the difference of terminology etc.", inasmuch as such difference of terminology is met with as "*veda* (knows)", "*upāsīta* (should meditate)", "*sa kratum kurvīta* (He shall make a resolve)" (Ch. III. xiv. 1), and so on. And it was ascertained earlier (in Pūrva-Mīmāṁsā II. ii. 1), that a difference in terminology causes a difference in the rites: "when there is a difference of words (conveying different ideas, e.g. *yajati*, *dadāti*, *juhoti*—sacrifices, gives, pours oblation), the rites differ, since they are accepted as denoting separate actions". From the use of "etc." in the aphorism it follows that attributes etc. are also to be understood as making difference in rites as far as possible.[53]

Opponent: In the case of such words as "*veda*", a mere difference of form is noticed, but there is no difference of meaning like "*yajati* (sacrifices)", etc., since *veda* etc. imply the same mental mood, and since no other meaning is possible.[54] So how can a difference in words lead to a difference in meditations?

Vedāntin: That is no fault, since even though there may be no difference as regards the mental mode implied, still a difference may arise from the things they are linked up with.[55] Though God, who is to be meditated on, is the same, still different and exclusive attributes are taught about Him in different contexts. Similarly even though *Prāṇa*, as an object of meditation, is the same in different contexts, it is to be meditated on in one context as possessed of some attributes, and in another context as possessed of still others. Thus from the fact that the

[53] The meditations are different according to the (1) different characteristics attributed to the object in different contexts, (2) the difference of results, (3) difference of names, or (4) impossibility of combining all the characteristics.

[54] *Vid* may either imply knowledge or meditation; but no injunction about knowledge is possible, and hence *veda* means "meditates".

[55] Sacrifice, gift, pouring oblation, etc. do not differ as meaning acts; yet they have their specific differences. So "*veda*", "*upāsīta*" etc. may not differ as mental moods, and yet may differ for reasons shown in an earlier footnote (53).

injunctions differ in accordance with the chain of things with which an object is linked up, the meditations also come to be known as separate. And it cannot be argued that in such a case, one is the injunction about meditation, while the others are subsidiary injunctions (about attributes); for there is no reason determining such a division. Again, since the attributes are quite numerous in each context, it is not proper to call into service some meditation already known and add to it the different attributes (in the different contexts, for that will lead to a break in the unity of idea). And from the (opponent's) point of view, there is no justification for the repeated mention of such qualities as possession of "inevitable desires" etc., since they are the same. Besides, these cannot be combined under a single idea, since in every context each separate text proceeds like this, "One desirous of such a result shall meditate thus", and "one who desires such another result shall meditate thus", which leave no lacunae to be filled up by borrowing from another context. And unlike the injunction about the meditation on Vaiśvānara as a whole, there is no injunction about meditation as a whole in the cases of "the meditation of Śāṇḍilya" and so on, on the strength of which the meditations occurring in the different contexts could have become subsidiary meditations and could have been thus combined to give rise to a composite idea. But if any such absolute assertion is made that in all cases of the sameness of the object of meditation, the meditation also must be one and the same, then one will be undertaking the impossible task of combining all the characteristics (everywhere). Hence it is well said, "The meditations are different when there is a difference in terminology". Of course it is to be understood that the topic of the unity of idea in the Upaniṣads (III. iii. 1-4), proceeds by assuming that this topic is already in existence.[56]

Topic 34: Alternative Meditations

विकल्पोऽविशिष्टफलत्वात् ॥५९॥

(Any one meditation is) विकल्प: an alternative (for others),

[56] Logically this topic should head this chapter, though it crops up here as a side issue connected with other topics.

अविशिष्ट-फलत्वात् because of the indistinguishability (i.e. sameness) of result.

59. Any one meditation (can be accepted as) an alternative for other meditations, because their result is the same.

Doubt: It having been established that the meditations differ, now it is being considered whether the aspirant has the option to undertake them collectively or alternatively just as he pleases, or it is compulsory to choose only one of these alternatives.

Opponent: Among these alternatives, there is no reason in evidence that can decide in favour of a compulsory combination, since the difference of meditations is an established fact.

Objection: But such rites as Agnihotra, Darśa-Pūrṇamāsa, etc., are seen to be combined regularly, even though they are divergent.

Opponent: That creates no difficulty, since in respect of those rites there is a scriptural prescription about their regular combination; but in respect of these meditations no such scriptural text about regular combination exists. Hence there can be no compulsion about combination. Nor can there be any compulsion about accepting only one from among them; for if a man is qualified for one meditation he is not debarred thereby from another. As a last alternative the meditations can be adopted indiscriminately.

Objection: Since these meditations have the same result, they should logically be considered alternatives to be chosen from. Thus it is noticed that the meditations contained in, "identified with the mind and having *Prāṇa* as the body" (Ch. III. xiv. 2), "Bliss is Brahman, Space is Brahman" (Ch. IV. x. 5), "having unfailing desire, and irresistible resolve" (Ch. VIII. i. 5), and other texts, have the same result consisting in the realization of God.

Opponent: That creates no difficulty, since it is seen in the case of rites leading to heaven that though they bear similar results, yet are undertaken according to the option (of the aspirants).

Vedāntin: Thus the conclusion being that the meditations are to be undertaken indiscriminately (but not collectively or only one out of many), it is being said: Any one of the meditations is individually as good as the others; and no combination is needed.

Why?

Since the result is the same. For the result of these meditations consisting in the direct perception of the object of meditation, is the same and when the perception of the object of meditation, be it God or any other entity, occurs as result of a single meditation, the other meditations become useless. Moreover, the theory of combination will lead to an impossibility of direct perception, since such a combination will lead to distraction of the mind. And the result, viz illumination that is achievable through direct perception, is shown in such Upaniṣadic texts as, "An aspirant who has such a vision (that he is Brahman), and has no doubt, attains Brahman" (Ch. III. xiv. 4), "becoming God (in this life) he attains Godhood (even after death)" (Bṛ. IV. i. 2) etc., as also by Smṛtis in such texts as, "continuously engaged in His thoughts" (Gītā, VIII. 6), and so on.[57] So an aspirant should choose one of the meditations, bearing the same result; and he should continue in it wholeheartedly till he attains the result through the direct perception of the object of meditation.

Topic 35: Meditations Yielding Worldly Results

काम्यास्तु यथाकामं समुच्चीयेरन्न वा पूर्वहेत्वभावात् ॥६०॥

तु But काम्याः the meditations yielding desired (worldly) results (either) समुच्चीयेरन् will be combined वा or न not यथा-कामम् at will, पूर्व-हेतु-अभावात् since the previous reason does not exist.

60. As for the meditations (based on symbols and) undertaken for fulfilment of worldly desires, they may be either

[57] The aphorism deals with *ahaṁ-graha-upāsanā*, meditation based on self-identity with divinity. The opponent can argue that these meditations yield results through *adṛṣṭa* just like rites; and hence direct perception is uncalled for. But the texts quoted show that *ahaṁ-graha-upāsanā* leads to direct perception.

combined or not combined according to one's option, since the previous reason (of sameness of result) does not exist.

The present aphorism is by way of illustrating the opposite of what was stated under, "because their result is the same" (III. iii. 59). In meditations (through symbols) which are undertaken for prosperity etc., as mentioned in such texts as, "One who knows thus that Air is the calf of the directions, does not have to lament for the death of a son" (Ch. III. xv. 2), "He who meditates on names as Brahman, moves about freely at will in all places where names exist" (Ch. VIII. 1. 5), and so on, and which like rites yield their own fruits by being first converted into *adṛṣta* (unseen potential result), there is no expectancy of direct perception. These may be combined or not combined at will, "since the previous reason does not exist", "since the previous reason", viz possession of the same result, "does not exist" here to determine an alternative adoption at will.

Topic 36: Meditations Based on Subsidiaries

अंगेषु यथाश्रयभाव: ॥६१॥

अंगेषु In the cases of (meditations based on) the subsidiaries, यथा-आश्रय-भाव: their position is the same as of their bases.

61. In the cases of the meditations based on the subsidiaries (of rites), their position is the same as of their bases.

Opponent: The doubt arises as to whether the conceptions prescribed in the three Vedas in connection with Udgītha etc., which are the subsidiaries of rites, are to be combined or they are to be undertaken at will. The aphorist says that "their position is the same as those of their bases". As their bases, viz the hymns etc., are applied in groups, so also must be the concepts in a meditation, for the concepts are determined by their bases.

शिष्टेश्च ॥६२॥

62. (The meditations are to be combined), also because they are enjoined (in the Vedas).

Opponent: Just as the bases of the meditations, viz hymns etc., are enjoined in the Vedas, so also are the meditations based on them. Even from the point of view of instruction there is no difference between the accessories of rites and the conceptions based on them.[58] This is the meaning.

समाहारात् ॥६३॥

63. (The meditations are to be combined) because of the (indicatory mark of the) rectification (of one with the help of another).

Opponent: The greatness of the knowledge of the sameness of *Om* and Udgītha is stated in the text, (by virtue of his meditation on the unity of the *Om* of the Ṛg-Veda with the Udgītha of Sāma-Veda) "The priest Udgātā (of the Sāma-Veda) rectifies any defect occurring in (his own) singing of the Udgītha by borrowing from the well-performed act of the priest Hotā (of the Ṛg-Veda)" (Ch. I. v. 5). While stating here that by virtue of the strength of that knowledge the Udgātā rectifies the defects in his own act by borrowing from the good action of the Hotā, the text implies through this indicatory sign that the conception mentioned in one Upaniṣad is to be added to the conceptions found in other Upaniṣads on the basis of a common relationship with the object of meditation spoken of elsewhere.

गुणसाधारण्यश्रुतेश्च ॥६४॥

च And गुण-साधारण्य-श्रुतेः from the Upaniṣadic declaration that (*Om* which is) an accessory of rites is common to all.

64. And from the Upaniṣadic declaration that Om, which is an accessory of the Vedic rites is common to all the Vedas, (it follows that the meditations based on it must co-exist).

Opponent: And although *Om* enters as an attribute, that is to say, though *Om* supplies a basis for the meditation on Udgītha, the Upaniṣad declares it to be common to all the Vedas in, "The

[58] The meditations are to be combined like the accessories, since they are enjoined similarly.

rites enjoined in the three Vedas start with the utterance of *Om*. One chants hymns to gods after the utterance of *Om*; uttering *Om* one praises the gods; by uttering *Om* one sings the Udgītha" (Ch. I. i. 9). From noticing thus that the basis is the same, it can be inferred from this indicatory mark, that the meditations based on this are also the same.

Or the aphorism can be explained thus: If these Udgītha and other things, constituting parts of rites, were not meant for use in all the rites, then the conceptions based on them would not also have occurred together. But as a matter of fact, the statements about application, which cover the accessories as a whole, mention that these Udgītha and other things are common to all the sacrificial acts. Hence from the fact that the bases are common, it follows that the meditations based on them are also to be used collectively.

न वा तत्सहभावाश्रुतेः ॥६५॥

वा Or rather न not; तत्-सहभाव-अश्रुतेः their correlation not having been mentioned in the Upaniṣad.

65. (The meditations are) rather not to be combined, since the Upaniṣads do not declare this.

Vedāntin: The words "rather not" set aside the (above) opposite view. The meditations (based on *Om* etc.) have not the same state (of co-existence) as their bases (B. S. III. iii. 61). Why?

Since their co-existence is not mentioned in the Upaniṣads. For there is no Vedic text showing the co-existence of the meditations, unlike what is shown with regard to the accessories of rites and hymns etc. enjoined in the three Vedas, in such texts as, "taking up the vessel or holding aloft the ladle, the priest chants the hymn, utters the praise, and then he says, 'O Prastotā, you sing the Sāma song, O Hotā, you perform this sacrifice' ", and so on.

Opponent: Their co-existence is gathered from the statement about the application itself.

Vedāntin: We say, no; since the meditations are meant to

subserve the aspirant (and not any rite). The statement about application only leads to a correlation among the Udgītha etc. meant for a sacrifice, whereas the meditations on Udgītha etc., though connected with the accessories of rites, contribute to the aspirant's personal purpose like the milking pot etc., as we said under the aphorism "inasmuch as a separate result belongs to meditations" (III. iii. 42). This is precisely the distinction between the instruction about the accessories of rites and the meditations based on those accessories, that the former are meant for making their contributions to rites, whereas the latter are for subserving the aspirant's purposes (by purification of his mind). The two indicatory marks (in aphorisms 63 and 64) cannot lead to a co-existence of the meditations, since no Upaniṣadic text or logic is found in support. It cannot be that since in every application the bases of the meditations are taken up together, therefore the meditations based on them have also to be known as meant for being undertaken in combination, for the meditations are not applied to those rites. Even though the meditations be determined by their bases, so that they may well cease to exist when the bases do not exist, still they cannot be combined merely because the bases go together. This is so owing to the very reason that there is no Vedic declaration about their combination. Hence these meditations are to be undertaken according to one's desire.

दर्शनाच्च ॥६६॥

66. And (there is no obligation about combination) since the Upaniṣad shows (contrariwise).

Moreover, the Upaniṣad shows that absence of co-existence among the meditations in, "The (priest called) Brahmā who knows thus protects the sacrifice, the sacrificer, and all the priests from all sides" (Ch. IV. xvii. 10). If all the meditations were to be combined, then all the priests would have known everything, so that there would not have been any mention of the protection of all by (the priest) Brahmā, who has that knowledge. Hence the meditations can be undertaken collectively or alternatively just as the aspirant wants.

Section IV

Topic 1: Knowledge not a Subsidiary of Rites

पुरुषार्थोऽतः शब्दादिति बादरायणः ॥१॥

पुरुष-अर्थः The highest human goal (i.e. liberation) अतः is from this (knowledge) शब्दात् on account of Vedic declaration इति thus (says) बादरायणः Bādarāyaṇa.

1. Bādarāyaṇa thinks that liberation results from this (knowledge of the Self), (as presented in the Upaniṣads), because the Vedic texts declare so.

Now then, the question is whether the knowledge of the Self, presented by the Upaniṣads, forms a part of rites etc. through the medium of the man qualified for them, or it leads independently to some human goal (viz liberation). While engaging himself in this discussion, the aphorist starts with the conclusion itself in the aphorism, "Bādarāyaṇa thinks" etc. The teacher Bādarāyaṇa thinks that liberation results independently "from this", from the knowledge of the Self, as imparted by the Upaniṣads.

How is this known? The aphorist says, "because the Vedic texts declare so". Thus the following Upaniṣadic texts, as also others of this class, speak of knowledge alone as the cause of liberation: "The knower of the Self crosses over sorrow" (Ch. VII. i. 3), "He who knows that supreme Brahman becomes Brahman Itself" (Mu. III. ii. 9), "The knower of Brahman attains the Highest" (Tai. II. i. 1), "He knows who has a teacher. For him the delay is only that long as his body does not fall; then he merges in Brahman" (Ch. VI. xiv. 2). Starting with "That which is the Self, free from sins" (Ch. VIII. vii. 1), it is said, "He who realizes the Self after comprehending It from his teacher, attains all the worlds and all the desirable things" (ibid.). Again, starting with, "The Self, my dear, is to be realized" (Bṛ. IV. v. 6), it is said, "This much is (the means of) immortality" (Bṛ. IV. v. 15).

Against this stands up another (i.e. an *opponent*):

शेषत्वात् पुरुषार्थवादो यथाऽन्येष्विति जैमिनिः ॥२॥

शेषत्वात् (The Self) being in subservient relation (to rites etc.), पुरुष-अर्थवादः (The result of knowledge is merely) a glorification of the agent (of rites) यथा as it is अन्येषु in other cases इति this is how जैमिनिः Jaimini (thinks).

2. Jaimini thinks that since the Self holds a subservient position in rites etc., the mention of the result of knowledge is (merely) in glorification of the agent, as is the case elsewhere.

Since the individual Self comes into subservient relationship with religious acts by becoming their performer, the knowledge of the Self, too, must form a part of the rites etc. even as the purification of paddy by sprinkling of water and such other acts become parts of the rites through the objects they are related to. Hence the mention of any result that occurs in the Upaniṣads with regard to this knowledge, whose purpose is ascertained to be this, must be by way of eulogy. This is what the teacher Jaimini thinks. This is like the Vedic mention of results by way of eulogy, as it is found in such texts as, "He whose sacrificial ladle is made of Palāśa wood does not hear any evil", "When a sacrificer applies collyrium to his own eyes, he covers the (evil) eyes of his enemy thereby", "That the (subsidiary rites) Prayāja, Anuyāja, etc. are performed, thereby is created an armour for the sacrificer and the (main) sacrifice, so that the enemy of the sacrificer may be defeated", and so on.

Vedāntin: Since this knowledge of the Self is not spoken of in connection with some other topic (e.g. rites), and since for that very reason, nothing like context etc. is in evidence to justify its application to any rite, how can it be included in a rite?

Opponent: On the strength of the Vedic text about the result (e.g. "The knower of Brahman transcends grief"), it will be included in a rite through the medium of the agent (like the fact of being made of Palāśa getting connected with a rite through the ladle, on the strength of the text).

Vedāntin : This cannot be so, since from that sentence (about result) it does not logically follow that this knowledge of the Self is to be applied to a rite. For things that have not been spoken of in the course of some definite topic can be imagined to be applicable to some rite on the strength of some sentence (stating a result), only if some invariable medium (like a ladle) is in evidence. But an agent is a variable medium, he being common to both ordinary and Vedic acts. Hence the knowledge of the Self cannot be proved to be connected with sacrifices through the medium of such an agent.

Opponent : Not so, since the knowledge that the Self is distinct from the body has no applicability anywhere else but Vedic rites; for the knowledge that the Self is different from the body has no scope in ordinary human acts, since men can engage under all circumstances, (i.e. even when identifying the body with the Self), in acts having perceptible (worldly) results; but they cannot engage in Vedic duties, yielding their results after death, unless they have the knowledge that the Self is different from the body. And thus the knowledge of this difference has an applicability precisely in such a case.

Vedāntin : The Upaniṣadic knowledge of the Self to the effect that it is free from transmigration, which fact becomes obvious from the use of such attributes as "free from sin" (Ch. VIII. vii. 1), and so on, cannot be subservient to any impulsion to activity.

Opponent : Not so, since the instruction is about the realization of the transmigrating Self Itself, as is suggested through the use of such words as "*priya* (lovable)"[1] (Bṛ. IV. v. 6). As for the attributes like "freedom from sin" and so on, they must be meant for eulogy.

Objection : Has it not been established in the various contexts that the transcendental and birthless Brahman is the origin of the world, and that the very same Brahman is taught in the

[1] The Bṛhadāraṇyaka text shows that the Self that is to be realized is the entity for whose enjoyment all things exist, thereby suggesting that there can be no Self which is not an experiencer and hence subject to transmigration.

Upaniṣads as constituting the real nature of the transmigrating soul?

Vedāntin: True, it has been proved; yet for re-affirming this fact the process of objection and refutation, which centres round a discussion of the result, (as to whether it is meant for liberation or for subserving rites), is resorted to on the analogy of driving in a pile (by alternately driving it down and pulling it up so as to make it fixed firmly and deeply in soft ground).

आचारदर्शनात् ॥३॥

आचार-दर्शनात् Because of the revelation of the behaviour.

3. (This is confirmed) on the strength of what is revealed about the behaviour (of the knowers of Brahman).

Opponent: We meet with the Vedic revelation of connection with rites even for the knowers of Brahman in such texts as, "Janaka, emperor of Videha, performed a sacrifice in which gifts were freely distributed" (Bṛ. III. i. 1), "Sirs, I am about to perform a sacrifice" (Ch. V. xi. 5), which occur in other contexts (purporting to deal with the knowledge of Brahman). And this is in line with the behaviour noticed in the cases of Uddālaka and others, where their connection with a householder's life is inferable from their instruction etc. to their sons. If liberation can be achieved through knowledge alone, why should they have undertaken (the householder's) duties involving strenuous effort, for proverbially it is known, "Why should one go to a hill if one has honey at hand?"

तत्-श्रुतेः ॥४॥

तत्-श्रुतेः Since the Upaniṣad declares this.

4. (This is so) because the Upaniṣad declares this.

In the text, "That rite becomes more powerful that is done along with meditation, faith, and secret knowledge" (Ch. I. i. 10), knowledge is heard of as forming a part of some rite; hence knowledge by itself cannot be the cause of liberation.

समन्वारम्भणात् ॥५॥

सम्-अनु-आरम्भणात् Because of following together.

5. (This is so), because both knowledge and work follow the Self (when it transmigrates).

And knowledge cannot be independent, since in the text, "It (i.e. the departing soul) is followed by knowledge, work, (and past experience)" (Bṛ. IV. iv. 2), knowledge and work are seen to act in association in producing the result.

तद्वतो विधानात् ॥६॥

6. (And this is so) because rites are enjoined for one who is possessed of that (knowledge of the Vedas).

The Upaniṣadic texts like the following show that one who is possessed of the knowledge of all the things revealed in the Vedas is qualified for undertaking rites: "One who comes back from his teacher's house after duly reading (i.e. reciting) the Vedas, during the intervals of serving him, and then enters the householder's life and continues the study of the Vedas in a holy place and performs other prescribed duties, attains the world of Brahman" (Ch. VIII. xv. 1). From this also it follows that knowledge cannot produce its result independently.

Objection: In this sentence we find mention of merely the reading (i.e. reciting) of the Vedas in the phrase "after reading", and not of the comprehension of the meaning.

Opponent: That is no defect, since the conclusion arrived at (in the Pūrva-Mīmāṁsā) is that the phrase "reading of the Vedas" includes the idea of comprehension of meaning as well, for the reading has a perceptible result in view.[2]

[2] The injunction, "He shall pound the paddy" has in view the making of rice by removing the husk, for the perceptible result sought for is the making of cakes (for the sacrifice) with the rice. So also the perceptible result of reading is the comprehension of meaning. An imperceptible result comes through *apūrva*—unseen potential result. Thus Brahman becomes known to a student during his study of the Vedas, even though he becomes a householder afterwards.

नियमाच्च ॥७॥

7. *And (this follows) from the restrictive texts.*

From such restrictive injunctions as contained in the texts, "By doing religious acts, indeed, should one wish to live here for a hundred years. For a man, such as you are (who wants to live thus), there is no way other than this, whereby *karma* may not cling to you" (Īś. 2), "That which is known as the Agnihotra is a sacrifice that has to be followed till decrepitude and death, for one gets released from it either through decrepitude or death", it follows that knowledge is a subsidiary of rites.

Vedāntin: Such being the position, the refutation is being stated:

अधिकोपदेशात्तु बादरायणस्यैवं तद्दर्शनात् ॥८॥

तु But अधिक-उपदेशात् because of being taught to be greater बादरायणस्य (the view) of Bādarāyaṇa एवम् stands just as it is तत्-दर्शनात् for so it is revealed.

8. *But Bādarāyaṇa's view stands unshaken because of the instruction that the supreme Self is even greater (than the agent); for so it is revealed (by the Upaniṣads).*

By the word "but" is rebutted the opposite view. The view held out that "the mention of the result of knowledge is in glorification of the agent", "since the Self holds a subservient position in rites" (B. S. III. iv. 2), is not proper.

Why?

On account of something even greater having been taught. Had the transmigrating soul alone, inhabiting the body as the agent and experiencer, been taught in the Upaniṣads as something distinct from the mere body, then the Upaniṣadic mention of result could have been a eulogy as elaborated by the opponent. But over and above (i.e. greater than) the embodied soul, the birthless God, free from such mundane attributes as agentship—the supreme Self, possessed of such attributes as freedom from sin—is taught in the Upaniṣads, as an object to be realized. And His knowledge cannot supply any impulsion for work, on the contrary it uproots all works. This fact will be stated in the aphorism, "Knowledge is independent of rites, since it uproots all worldly distinctions" (III. iv. 16). Hence the opinion of the venerable Bādarāyaṇa, as expressed in, "Liberation results from this knowledge of the Self, because the Vedic texts declare so" (III. iv. 1), remains just as it is, and it cannot be shaken by the fallacious arguments that knowledge is a subsidiary of rites, and so on. Thus it is that the Upaniṣads reveal God, the (supreme) Self, as something over and above the embodied soul, in such texts as, "He who is omniscient in general and all-knowing in detail" (Mu. I. i. 9), "Out of His fear the wind blows, out of fear the sun rises" (Tai. II. viii. 1), "A great terror like an uplifted thunder" (Ka. II. iii. 2), "Under the mighty rule of this Immutable, O Gārgī" (Bṛ. III. viii. 9), "That deliberated, 'let me become many, let me be born diversely.' That created fire" (Ch. VI. ii. 3), and so on.

And it was argued that the transmigrating soul indicated by such terms as "lovable" is again referred to as the object to be known, in such texts as, "but for one's own self, all is loved. The self, my dear, should be realized" (Bṛ. IV. v. 6); "That which breathes through *Prāṇa* is your Self that is within all" (Bṛ. III. iv. 1); starting with "The infinite Being that is seen in the eye" (Ch. VIII. vii. 4), and ending with, "I shall explain this very Being to you again" (Ch. VIII. ix. 3); and so on. But this reference to the transmigrating soul cannot be meant for absolute difference (between the individual Self and God), in the face of the texts occurring in the complementary portions of those passages, and meant for imparting instruction about some super-reality, as for instance the texts, "The Ṛg-Veda, Yajur-Veda,... are the breath of this infinite Being" (Bṛ. II. iv. 10), "That which transcends hunger and thirst, grief, delusion, decay, and death" (Bṛ. III. v. 1), "Just so this placid soul rises up from this body and unites with the supreme Light to get established in its own nature" (Ch. VIII. xii. 3). It is known also from such texts as "That thou art" (Ch. VI. viii. 7), "There is no other witness but this" (Bṛ. III. viii. 11), etc. that in its real nature, the embodied soul is but God Himself, while its state of embodiedness is a creation of limiting adjuncts. All this was elaborately ascertained by us earlier in the appropriate contexts.

तुल्यन्तु दर्शनम् ॥९॥

तु But दर्शनम् the Upaniṣadic declaration तुल्यम् is equally in evidence.

9. But the Upaniṣadic declaration (of conduct) is equally in evidence (proving that knowledge is not subservient to religious acts).

As for the argument that from the Upaniṣadic mention of the conduct of enlightened men it follows that knowledge is subservient to rites (B. S. III. iv. 3), our reply is this: The Upaniṣadic mention of the conduct of enlightened men is equally in evidence to show that knowledge is not subservient to rites. Thus there is the text, "The Kāvaṣeya seers, who had known this very entity, said, 'Why need we study (the Vedas), why need we perform sacrifices?' This is that very entity, having known which, the enlightened of yore ceased to perform the Agnihotra sacrifice" (Kau. II. 5), "Knowing this very Self the Brāhmaṇas renounce the desires for sons, for wealth, and for worlds, and lead a mendicant life" (Bṛ. III. V. 1), and so on. Moreover, it is known that Yājñavalkya and others, who had realized Brahman, did not engage in rites, from such texts as, " 'This much indeed is immortality, my dear,' saying this Yājñavalkya embraced a mendicant's life" (Bṛ. IV. v. 15). Moreover, the indication (about the combination of rites and knowledge) as found in the text, "Venerable sirs, I am about to perform a sacrifice" (Ch. V. xi. 5), relates to the meditation on Vaiśvānara, and it is quite possible to come across a combination with rites in the domain of conceptions regarding the qualified Brahman. But even here, there can be no possibility of the knowledge of Brahman becoming subsidiary to religious acts, for nothing like context etc. is discernible here (to substantiate a contrary view).[3]

[3] The enlightened man may continue performing his usual acts for setting an example to others. But his is no ordinary work, as he lacks the usual ideas of "I and mine".

As for the argument that the Upaniṣads declare this (B. S. III. iv. 4), our reply is:

असार्वत्रिकी ॥१०॥

10. The declaration is not universal.

The text, "whatever one does with knowledge" (Ch. I. i. 10), does not refer to all kinds of knowledge, it being confined to the relevant meditation that forms the topic. And the topic under discussion there is the meditation on Udgītha as contained in, "One shall meditate on the letter *Om* as Udgītha" (Ch. I. i. 1).

And it was said (B. S. III. iv. 5) that the text, "He is followed by knowledge, work, (and past experience)" (Bṛ. IV. iv. 2), which speaks of the pursuit (of the soul by knowledge etc.), is an indication of the subservience of knowledge. That is being refuted:

विभागः शतवत् ॥११॥

विभागः (Knowledge and work) are to be divided शतवत् like a hundred (things).

11. Knowledge and action are to be divided like a hundred things.

A division is to be noted here to the effect that knowledge follows one, and work another. This is like the distribution of a hundred (things). For instance, when somebody says, "Pay a hundred to these two", the hundred is given by dividing it into two moieties, fifty being given to one and fifty to another. Similar is the case here. Moreover, this text about "being followed by" is not spoken of with regard to one who would have liberation, since the conclusion is made with reference to a transmigrating soul in the sentence, "Thus does the man (transmigrate) who has desires" (Bṛ. IV. iv. 6), and since the man hankering for liberation is treated separately in, "But then, as for the man who does not desire" (ibid.). Now, the knowledge that is considered in that text (about "being followed by knowledge and action"—Bṛ. IV. iv. 2), relates to the transmigrating soul and comprises knowledges of both kinds—enjoined and prohibited; for no reason for distinction exists. The action again is considered irrespective of whether it be prescribed or prohibited, the text having taken them (knowledge and action) up just as they obtain elsewhere. From this point of view (that they relate to the transmigrating soul), the text about "being followed" can be justified even without resorting to a division.

It has been stated, "Because rites are enjoined for one who is possessed of the knowledge of the Vedas" (B. S. III. iv. 6); hence comes the reply:

अध्ययनमात्रवतः ॥१२॥

अध्ययन-मात्र-वत: For him who has merely read (i.e. recited) the Vedas.

12. (Engagement in religious actions is prescribed)for him only who has merely recited the Vedas.

Since we hear of "reading" alone in the text, "One who comes back from his teacher's house after duly reading the Vedas" etc. (Ch. VIII. xv. 1), we arrive at the conclusion that the prescription for rites is meant for one who has merely recited the Vedas.

Opponent: In that case a man may not have the necessary qualification for rites owing to his lack of knowledge.

Vedāntin: That defect does not arise. We do not rule out the information about the rites, acquired in the course of the recital, that endows one with the competence for rites. What do we do then? We establish this fact only that since the knowledge of the Self, acquired from the Upaniṣads, is obviously possessed of its own independent purpose, it cannot become a cause for generating competence for rites. And this is to be understood in the same way as when a man qualified for a certain rite has not to depend on the knowledge of some other rite.

Again, it was stated, "And this follows from the restrictive texts" (B. S. III. iv. 7). To this it is replied:

नाविशेषात् ॥१३॥

न Not so अविशेषात् because of the absence of specification.

13. (The restrictive texts) do not apply (to the man of knowledge), since the restriction is made without any specification.

In the restrictive texts like, "By doing *karma*, indeed, should one wish to live here for a hundred years" (Īś. 2) etc. there is no specific mention that these apply to the man of knowledge, since the restriction is made in a general way.

स्तुतयेऽनुमतिर्वा ॥१४॥

वा Or rather अनुमतिः the consent (of action) स्तुतये is for the glorification (of knowledge).

14. Or rather the consent (accorded) for doing religious acts is meant for the glorification of knowledge.

With regard to the text, "By doing *karma* indeed" etc. another independent interpretation can be advanced thus: Even if on the strength of the context this sentence is construed in a way to connect the man of knowledge with "doing *karma*" (as its agent), still it is to be understood that this approval of doing work is accorded only by way of eulogizing knowledge; for it will be stated later, "*Karma* does not cling to you". The idea implied is this: "Even though a man of knowledge may perform work during his whole life, work does not become a cause of blemish, owing to the presence of his knowledge". In this way knowledge is praised.

कामकारेण चैके ॥१५॥

च And एके some (refrain from work) कामकारेण according to their own predilection.

15. Moreover, some refrain from (religious) work according to personal predilection.

Moreover, the Vājasaneyins have a text according to which some enlightened men, who have direct experience of the result of knowledge, take their stand on that experience and declare out of personal predilection that there is no need for them for begetting children and such other acts which are meant for other purposes. That text runs thus: "This is the reason for it: the ancient sages, it is said, did not desire children thinking, 'What shall we achieve through children, we who have attained this Self, this world (i.e. result)?' " (Bṛ. IV. iv. 22). Furthermore, it has been declared by us more than once that unlike the result of work which comes to fruition after some time, the result of knowledge is a matter of direct and immediate experience. For this reason also, knowledge cannot be a subsidiary of rites, nor can it be held that the Upaniṣadic mention of the result of knowledge is unreal (i.e. eulogistic).

उपमर्दं च ॥१६॥

16. Moreover, (from knowledge comes) the destruction (of the whole world).

Moreover, the scriptures declare that the whole world of manifestation, which consists of actions, instruments, and results, bestowing the necessary qualification for work, and which is a creation of ignorance, is destroyed root and branch by knowledge, as stated in, "But when to the knower of Brahman everything has become the Self, then what should one smell and through what?" (Bṛ. II. iv. 14), and so on. But should one build his hope of deriving the requisite competence for rites from the knowledge of the Self as taught in the Upaniṣads, he will be left only with a destruction of all rites. From this also it follows that knowledge is independent of rites.

ऊर्ध्वरेतःसु च शब्दे हि ॥१७॥

च And ऊर्ध्वरेतःसु (knowledge belongs) to those (monks) observing continence हि for शब्दे (they are mentioned) in the Vedas.

17. And knowledge belongs to the monks, for they are met with in the Vedas.

Moreover, knowledge is heard of in connection with the order of life (i.e. *Sannyāsa*, monasticism) in which continence is observed. And knowledge cannot become subsidiary to rites there, since (in that order) rites are absent; for they (the monks) do not have such Vedic rites as Agnihotra etc. It may be argued that there is no such stage of life mentioned in the Vedas as that of the continent people. But that argument also has no basis; for they are mentioned in such Vedic texts as, "Virtue has three divisions. (All these attain the virtuous world, while the one who is fully occupied with Brahman attains immortality)" (Ch. II. xxiii. 1), "And those who follow faith (meditation), austerities, etc. while living in forests" (Ch. V. x. 1), "Those who live in the forest, begging for alms, viz those (forest-dwellers and hermits) who resort to the duties of their respective stages of life as well as to meditation" (Mu. I. ii. 11), "Desiring this world (i.e. the Self) alone, monks renounce their homes" (Bṛ. IV. iv. 22), "One should embrace monasticism even from the stage of Brahmacharya" (Jābāla, 4), and in such other texts, where monasticism is a well-recognized fact in the Upaniṣads and Smṛtis in the case of those people who might have had either entered or not entered earlier the householder's life, as also those who might have had or had not repaid their debts (to gods, manes, and seers). For this reason also knowledge is independent of rites.

Topic 2: Sannyasa Prescribed by Scriptures

परामर्शं जैमिनिरचोदना चापवदति हि ॥१८॥

जैमिनिः Jaimini (thinks) परामर्शं (that to be a mere) allusion (to other stages), अचोदना (it is) no injunction, च and हि because (the scripture) अपवदति condemns (them).

18. Jaimini thinks that to be an allusion to other stages and no injunction; and (this is so) since the scripture condemns them.

Opponent: The texts starting with, "Virtue has three divisions" (Ch. II. xxiii. 1), that were quoted (under the last aphorism) to prove the existence of people belonging to an order (of monks) observing continence, cannot prove that fact, since the teacher Jaimini thinks that the texts are reminiscent of the other stages of life (as distinct from that of the householders'), and they impart no injunction.

Why?

Because nothing, such as a verb in the imperative mood, occurs here to indicate an injunction. Moreover, each of them is noticed to imply something else. In the text, "Virtue has three divisions" etc. (Ch. II. xxiii. 1), for instance, an allusion is made to the stages of life and it is declared that their results are not limitless in the sentences, "The first division consists of sacrifice, study, and offer of wealth; the second division of austerity; and the third of the *Brahmacārin* living in his teacher's house for life and laying down his body there" (ibid.). Then the continuance in Brahman is praised as yielding an infinite result in the sentence, "All these attain the virtuous worlds; but he who is steadfast in Brahman (that is, meditates steadfastly on Brahman with the help of *Om*) gets immortality" (ibid.).

Objection: Even though this be a mere allusion, still as a matter of fact, the stages of life become known from it.

Opponent: True, they become known; but their recognition is derived from the Smṛtis and common usage and not from the Upaniṣads. Hence in a case of conflict with direct Vedic texts, they are to be disregarded or accepted as referring to people who are debarred from rites (e.g. the blind, lame, etc.).

Objection: Is not the householder's life also mentioned along with the continent in, "The first division consists of sacrifice, study, and offer of wealth"? (So the whole passage must be equally authoritative.)

Opponent: Quite so. Still from the fact that the rites like Agnihotra etc. are prescribed for the householder alone, that stage of life exists as a thing well recognized by the Vedas. Hence this allusion to other stages is merely by way of eulogy (of steadfastness in Brahman), and not by way of an injunction. Moreover, the direct Vedic texts denounce any other stage of life: "One who gives up the fire is a destroyer of the valour (i.e. a murderer) of the gods", "Having offered the desirable wealth to the teacher, do not cut off the line of progeny" (Tai. I. xi. 1), "A man without a son has no world in future. All creatures are aware of this", and so on. Thus the texts, "Those who undertake faith (meditation), austerities, etc. while living in forest" (Ch. V. x. 1), "Those who live in the forest . . ., who resort to the duties of their own stages of life as well as to meditation" (Mu. I. ii. 11), impart instruction about the "path of the gods" and not about other stages of life. Moreover, it is doubtful if the other stages of life are prescribed in the texts, "The second division is austerity" (Ch. II. xxiii. 1) etc. Similarly the text, "Desiring this world (i.e. the Self) alone, monks renounce their homes" (Bṛ. IV. iv. 22), is not an injunction for monasticism, it being only a eulogy of the world (of the Self).

Objection: Have not the Jābālas a direct and clear injunction about renunciation in the text, "One should enter into monasticism even from the stage of *Brahmacarya*"?

Vedāntin: Quite so; but it is to be noted that the present discussion is carried on by ignoring this text.

अनुष्ठेयं बादरायणः साम्यश्रुतेः ॥१९॥

बादरायणः Bādarāyaṇa (thinks) (that other stages also are to be) अनुष्ठेयं observed साम्य-श्रुतेः Vedic texts being equally extant.

19. Bādarāyaṇa thinks that the other orders of life are also to be observed, since Vedic texts speak equally of all the stages of life.

The teacher Bādarāyaṇa is of the opinion that the other stages of life are to be resorted to on account of their reference in the Vedas. Since on account of the obligatoriness of the performance of Agnihotra etc., a conflict with monasticism arises, and it is concluded (by the *opponent*) that this other stage of life is to be resorted to by those (blind, lame, and others) who are debarred from Agnihotra etc., therefore Bādarāyaṇa refutes this view under the belief that one has to admit willynilly the other stages of life just as much as the householder's.

Why?

Since the texts speak equally of all the stages; for the text, "Virtue has three divisions" etc. (Ch. II. xxiii. 1), is seen to allude to the other stages of life equally with the householder's. It is to be noted that just as the householder's life, prescribed by other Vedic texts, is alluded to here, so also are the other stages of life. And this is as in the case of the *Nivīta* and ***Prācināvīta*** which though prescribed in a separate injunction are yet understood to be referred to along with *Upavīta*.[4] Hence the pursuit of the other stages of life is as valid as the pursuit of the householder's life. Similarly in the text, "Desiring this world (i.e. the Self) alone the monks renounce home" (Bṛ. IV. iv. 22), renunciation is mentioned along with the study of the Vedas etc.; and in "Those who undertake faith (meditation), austerities, etc. while living in forests" (Ch. V. x. 1), the stage of living in forest is read along with the meditation on the five fires (so that they are equally enjoined).

It was also stated that it is a matter of doubt whether any other stage of life is enjoined in the passage; "The second division is austerity" (Ch. II. xxiii. 1) etc.; that too is nothing damaging, since a reason for a definite conclusion is in evidence. For in the text, "Virtue has three divisions" (ibid.), an assertion is made about the threefold division. Moreover, the multifarious virtuous deeds like sacrifices, which have diverse (injunctions of) origin, cannot be included under the three divisions, unless it be through their association with the stages of life. Of these, one division of virtue is the householder's life indicated by "sacrifices" etc. In the word "*Brahmacārin*" we find a clear reference to an order of life. And by the word "austerity" what division of virtue can be accepted other than that order

[4] The sacred thread held round the neck like a garland is called *Nivīta*; when held from the right shoulder, across the chest and passing under the left arm, it is *Prācināvīta*; the opposite position from the left shoulder to the right gives the *Upavīta*. The sentence, "*Nivīta* is meant for rites performed for men (i.e. guests), *Pracīnāvīta* for rites for the manes; for rites for the gods the *Upavīta* is used", is interpreted to mean that the injunction here is only about the *Upavīta*, the use of the other two being known otherwise. These known uses are referred to here for eulogizing the *Upavīta*.

of life (of the *Vānaprastha*) in which austerity preponderates? On the strength of the indicatory word "forest" occurring in, "those who undertake faith and austerity, etc. while living in forests" (Ch. V. x. 1), an order of life is necessarily to be understood as meant by the words "faith" and "austerity". Hence though the stages of life occur by way of allusion only, they are still to be resorted to.

विधिर्वा धारणवत् ॥२०॥

वा Or rather विधिः an injunction धारण-वत् like holding (the sacrificial fuel).

20. Or rather it is an injunction as in the case of holding the sacrificial fuel.

Or rather it is an injunction about the other orders of life, and not a mere allusion.

Opponent: If an injunction be accepted here, the comprehension of a unity of idea (of the passage) will be debarred. As a matter of fact, however, a unity of idea is obvious, viz that the three divisions of virtue lead to virtuous worlds while the steadfastness in Brahman yields immortality.

Vedāntin: This is true; and yet the apparent unity of idea has to be rejected and injunction accepted on account of the uniqueness of the fact (not heard of before) and the absence of any other injunction. And in the face of a clear comprehension of other stages of life, there is no need to take shelter under a unity of idea by supposing the text to involve an attributive corroboration (or a glorifying eulogy),[5] "As in the case of the holding of the sacrificial fuel". In the text, "He shall approach

[5] *Guṇavāda*, as in, "The sun is the sacrifical stake", which glorifies the stake by saying that it shines like the sun. The opponent interprets the Chāndogya passage under discussion.to mean, "Steadfastness in Brahman, yielding infinite result, is eulogized by decrying the other orders of life as yielding limited results". Thus the passage has, according to him a unity of idea. An *Anuvāda* restates a known fact, as in, "Fire is the remedy for cold". A *Bhūtārthavāda* states something which neither contradicts nor confirms a known fact, as in "Indra holds a thunder in hand". Contradiction leads to *Guṇavāda*, and confirmation to *Anuvāda*.

(the sacrificial altar) by holding the fuel below (the vessel of oblation); for in a case of sacrifice to the gods, the fuel is held above", even though the fact of holding above appears to constitute a single idea along with the fact of holding below, still an injunction is admitted about holding above, since it relates to a unique fact. Thus it is that in the course of determining the subsidiaries (in the Pūrva-Mīmāṁsā) it is said, "But there is an injunction in the matter of holding above, since the fact is unique"[6] (Jai. Sū. III. iv. 15). Similarly, it is inferred that the text alluding to the orders of life is in fact an injunction. Even if this be a mere allusion to the other orders of life, still on the strength of the eulogy (implied in, "All these attain the virtuous worlds, the man steadfast in Brahman attains immortality)", an injunction about "steadfastness in Brahman" has to be admitted. And then it has to be considered as to whether that steadfastness is meant for anyone belonging to any one of the four stages of life or for the monk alone. Now, if by the mention of the stages of life down to *Brahmacarya* (in "Virtue has three divisions" etc.), the monk too becomes alluded to, then it may as well follow that anyone belonging to the four stages of life can be steadfast in Brahman, since all the four stages are mentioned equally and nobody can logically be outside the four. If, however, the monk is not alluded to, then the conclusion will be that the monk alone can be "steadfast in Brahman", he alone having been left out of the enumeration.

Some think that the monk also is alluded to in that text by the term "austerity", implying thereby the *Vaikhānasas* (one of the four classes of forest-dwelling *Vānaprasthas*). But that is improper; for when there is a way out, it is not proper to understand the monk from an attributive word signifying the *Vānaprastha.* It is but proper that just as the *Brahmacārin* and the householder are presented here through their respective

[6] When the ghee placed in the *sruk* is carried to the Āhavanīya fire in a Mahāpitṛ-sacrifice or a Pretāgnihotra, then this injunction is to be followed, "One shall approach by holding the fuel" below that ghee. Hence the text about holding the fuel above may be taken as a mere eulogy of this holding below. But in fact a fresh injunction is admitted about holding above, by breaking the unity of the sentence.

distinctive attributes, so also are the monk and the *Vānaprastha*. And austerity is a distinct feature of the order of *Vānaprasthas*, since the word austerity comes to be applied to it by usage owing to the predominance of the mortification of the body among them. But the monks' attributes consisting of control of senses etc. are not surely referred to by the term austerity. And it is improper that the stages of life, well known to be four in number, should be referred to as three. Moreover, it is noticed that they are mentioned separately thus: "These three become fit for the virtuous worlds, whereas the other one becomes fit for immortality". This reference in a separate way is justifiable only if there is a difference. For it cannot be asserted that Devadatta and Yajñadatta are dull of intellect, while one of them has a bright intellect; but it can well be said that Devadatta and Yajñadatta are both dull of intellect, while Viṣṇumitra has a bright intellect. Hence it is the people in the earlier three stages of life that achieve the virtuous worlds, while the remaining one, viz the monk, attains immortality.

Opponent: How can the term "steadfast in Brahman", used in its derivative sense and possible of application to people in all the stages of life, be confined to the monk alone? Or should you argue that the term is used in its conventional sense to imply a monk, then the conclusion will be that immortality is attained by the mere fact of belonging to a certain order of life (viz monasticism), so that knowledge will become useless.

The (*Vedāntin's*) reply here is being given: The term "steadfastness in Brahman" implies a consummation in Brahman, a total absorption in Brahman, which is the same as the absence of any other preoccupation except that. And that is not possible for people in the other three stages, since the Vedas mention that one incurs sin by giving up the duties of one's own stage of life. But the monk can incur no sin of non-performance of duties owing to his renunciation of all duties. But virtues like control of senses and organs, which characterize him, merely strengthen his steadfastness in Brahman, but do not oppose it. The duty for his order of life consists of steadfastness itself in Brahman, supported by self-control etc., whereas sacrifices etc. are the duties for others; the monk incurs sin by transgressing his own duties, (as much as others do by transgressing theirs). In support of this occur these texts: "Monasticism is Brahmā (Hiraṇyagarbha), because Brahmā is the highest (being), and the highest Entity has become Brahmā. These other austerities are surely inferior; monasticism indeed transcended them"[7] (Nārāyaṇa, 78); "Those to whom the entity presented by the Vedantic knowledge has become fully ascertained, and who endeavour assiduously with the help of the Yoga of monasticism (become free)" (Mu. III. ii. 6), and others. And the Smṛti texts like, "Those who have their intellect absorbed in that, whose life is that, whose Self is that, whose steadfastness is in that, whose consummation is in that (attain liberation)" (Gītā, V. 17), show that a man who is steadfast in Brahman has no duty. Hence the criticism has no scope that since the monk gets immortality from the mere fact of his belonging to an order of life, knowledge becomes useless. Thus it is that even though the other orders of life be merely alluded to (in the text "Virtue has three divisions" etc.—(Ch. II. xxiii. 1), we do gather from it monasticism as well consisting of steadfastness in Brahman.

The teacher introduced this discussion without taking into consideration the text of the Jābāla Upaniṣad which enjoins the other order of life (viz monasticism). But as a matter of fact, direct texts do occur which prescribe the other order of life, "Having finished the life of the *Brahmacārin* (i.e. bachelor student of the Vedas) one shall become a householder; after becoming a householder one shall retire to the forest; after retiring to the forest one shall become a monk. Should it, however, happen otherwise (that is, should dispassion become ripe), one shall become a monk from the stage of *Brahmacarya*, or from that of the householder, or from that of the forest-dweller" (Jā. 4). Moreover, it cannot be argued that this Upaniṣadic text refers to those who are debarred from Vedic rites, because the text speaks in a general way so it cannot be restricted to a certain category, and because a separate prescription is made for the unqualified in the text, "Again (one

[7] Monasticism being equated with the Highest, must itself be the highest; and this monasticism consists in remaining steadfast in Brahman, the meaning of *Om*, by giving up all other activities.

shall renounce) even if one has undertaken a vow or not, one who continues or does not continue to serve his teacher even after the completion of his study, one who has given up the fire after being a widower, or one who has not lighted the fire at all" (ibid.). Moreover, monasticism is meant as a subsidiary of the knowledge of Brahman for its full maturity; and this is shown in the text, "Then the monk who adopts a discoloured robe, shaves his head, desists from accepting wealth, becomes pure, and free from enmity, resorts to begging, becomes fit to attain the state of Brahman" (Jā. 5). Hence is proved the existence of the stages of life for the continent, and hence also is proved the independence of knowledge, it having been enjoined for the continent.

Topic 3: Injunctions for Meditation not Eulogistic

स्तुतिमात्रमुपादानादिति चेन्नापूर्वत्वात् ॥२१॥

स्तुति-मात्रम् Mere praise उपादानात् because of having been accepted (as subsidiaries of ritual acts) इति चेत् if this be the contention न not so, अपूर्वत्वात् because of extraordinariness.

21. If it be contended that texts (about Udgītha etc.) are merely eulogistic, because of having been accepted as subservient to ritual acts, then not so, because of the extraordinariness (of the texts).

Doubt: With regard to the texts, "That *Om*, called Udgītha, is the essence of all essences; it is the highest; it is the symbol for the highest, and the eighth in number" (Ch. I. i. 3), "This (viz the earth) is Ṛk, and fire is Sāma" (Ch. I. vi. 1), "This fire that is lighted up is but this world", "This very Uktha (collection of hymns) is this earth to be sure", the doubt arises: Are these Vedic texts meant for the eulogy of Udgītha etc., or are they for prescribing meditation?

Opponent: When under such a doubt, the reasonable position is that they are meant for eulogy, since the texts are accepted as referring to Udgītha etc. that are subsidiaries of rites; and these are on a par with such sentences as, "This earth itself is the sacrificial ladle (*Juhū*)", "the sun is a tortoise (the form of the altar)", "Heaven is the Āhavanīya fire", and so on, where they are meant for eulogizing the *Juhū* etc.

Vedāntin: The teacher says that it is not reasonable that the purpose of these texts should be merely praise because of the extraordinariness (of their content). And this extraordinariness remains intact only if these sentences are injunctive, whereas they become useless if they are eulogistic. For it has been said in the aphorism, "But since they are in syntactical unity with an injunction, they must be meant for the eulogy of the injunction" (Jai. Sū. I. ii. 7), that a eulogy derives its applicability by becoming an appendage to a text imparting an injunction. As a result, this eulogy of the Udgītha etc., (as contained in the texts cited), that occurs in a different context (i.e. in the Upaniṣads) will become useless since it cannot be tagged on to the Udgītha etc. mentioned in a different context (in the *Karma-kāṇḍa*). But the text, "This earth itself is a *Juhū*", occurs in the very proximity of an injunction. So there is a difference between the present passage and that illustration. Hence the Upaniṣadic texts like the above are meant only as injunctions (of meditation).

भावशब्दाच्च ॥२२॥

22. Moreover, (these must be injunctions) on account of the occurrence of words having an injunctional meaning.

Moreover, words of injunction occur clearly in such texts as, "One should meditate on the Udgītha" (Ch. I. i. 1), "One should meditate on Sāma" (Ch. II. ii. 1), "One should think of oneself as 'I am Uktha' (Tai. Ā. II. i. 2)". These will be set at naught if their only purpose be eulogy. Thus also runs a Smṛti text of those who are adepts in reasoning; "In all the Vedas these (verbal moods) are the invariable signs of injunction, viz 'should do', 'should be done', 'must be done', 'may become', 'should be' ". They make this statement under the belief that the verbal endings like the *liṅ* etc. express injunction. Besides, under every topic a result is mentioned (in the Upaniṣads), such as, "He becomes certainly a fulfiller of desires" (Ch. I. i 7), "For he is able to fulfil desires by singing the Sāma song" (Ch.

I. vii. 9), "All the worlds above and below become available for his enjoyment" (Ch. II. ii. 3), and so on. From this also it follows that the texts about the Udgītha etc. are meant for enjoining meditation.

Topic 4: Upanisadic Stories

पारिप्लवार्था इति चेन्न विशेषितत्वात् ॥२३॥

पारिप्लव-अर्थाः Meant for Pāriplava इति चेत् if this be the contention, न not so विशेषितत्वात् on account of having been specified.

23. If it be argued that they (the Upaniṣadic stories) are meant for the (ritualistic application called) Pāriplava,[8] *(we say) that this is not so, on account of the stories for the Pāriplava having been specified.*

Doubt: There occur some stories in the Upaniṣads as recounted in such texts as the following: "Now Yajñvalkya had two wives Maitreyī and Kātyāyanī" (Bṛ. IV. v. 1), "Pratardana, son of Divodāsa, went to the beloved place of Indra" (Kau. III. 1), "Jānaśruti, the great grandson of Janaśruti, used to distribute gifts with reverence; he gave plentifully; he (had food) cooked for many people" (Ch. IV. i. 1). With regard to these the doubt arises: Are these stories meant for use as a ritualistic act called Pāriplava, or are they for the easy comprehension of the knowledge imparted along with them?

Opponent: These Upaniṣadic stories are meant for Pāriplava, for they are on a par with other stories, and stories are prescribed for use in Pāriplava. From this it would follow that the Upaniṣads do not have knowledge as their main purport, they being meant for application in rites just as much as the *mantras*.

Vedāntin: Not so.

Why?

[8] There is an injunction that in the course of the horse-sacrifice, the priests should tell stories to the sacrificing king and his family and councillors. On the first day is to be related the story of Vaivasvata Manu, on the second of Vaivasvata Yama, and on the third of Varuṇa and Sūrya.

Because certain stories are specified for that (ritualistic) purpose. Thus it is that the topic is raised with the sentence, "The priests shall relate the stories"; and then only a certain number of stories, counting from the one beginning with, "Manu, a descendant of Vivasvān" etc. are specified. Were it the case that all the stories are to be used, just because they are stories, this specification would have been useless. Hence these Upaniṣadic stories are not meant for Pāriplava.

तथा चैकवाक्यतोपबन्धात् ॥२४॥

च And एकवाक्यता-उपबन्धात् because of becoming joined through unity of idea तथा in that way.

24. And because (the stories) become connected (with meditations) through unity of idea in that way, (therefore they are meant for illuminating the proximate knowledge).

Moreover, if the stories are not meant for use in Pāriplava, it is but natural that they should be meant for illuminating the proximate knowledge (meditation), for they are joined to them by way of unity of idea. Thus it is that in the respective contexts they are noticed to be connected with the proximate meditations through unity of ideas, by virtue of the interest they create in the meditations (or knowledge) and the ease of comprehension that they supply. For instance, in the *Maitreyī Brāhmaṇā* (of the Bṛhadāraṇyaka Upaniṣad) the story of Yājñavalkya, Maitreyī, and Kātyāyanī is seen to have a unity of idea with the knowledge contained in the text, "The Self, my dear Maitreyī, is to be realized" etc. (Bṛ. IV. v. 6); in the story of Pratardana also, the unity of idea with the knowledge imparted in, "I am Prāṇa, the Self that is consciousness" etc. (Kau. III. 2), is obvious; and the story starting with, "The great grandson of Janaśruti", is connected with the knowledge imparted in the text, "Air indeed is the place of merger" etc. (Ch. IV. iii. 1). Just as the stories occurring in the ritualistic portion of the Vedas, for instance, "He plucked out his own marrow (or omentum)" etc., are meant for emphasizing the proximate injunctions, so also is the case here. Hence they are not meant for Pāriplava.

Topic 5: Sannyasins Free from Rituals

अतएव चाग्नीन्धनाद्यनपेक्षा ॥२५॥

अत: एव च For that very reason again अग्नि-इन्धन-आदि-अनपेक्षा there is no need of "lighting fire" and so on.

25. For that very reason again, (the Sannyāsin has) no need of "lighting fire", and such other rites.

Since the aphorism, "Bādarāyaṇa thinks that liberation results from this (knowledge), because the Vedic texts declare so" (III. iv. 1), is applicable in this context as well, though it is far removed, therefore, it is being alluded to in this aphorism by saying, "for this very reason". "For this very reason", from the fact that knowledge is the cause of liberation, the ritualistic works like "lighting up a fire" etc., that are enjoined for the different orders of life, are not required by knowledge for producing its own result. Thus the present topic restates the result of the discussion raised under the first topic; and the aphorist does this with a view to adding something more.

Topic 6: Rituals etc. Needed for Knowledge

सर्वापेक्षा च यज्ञादिश्रुतेरश्ववत् ॥२६॥

सर्व-अपेक्षा All (religious actions) are necessary च as well यज्ञ-आदि-श्रुते: on the authority of the Upaniṣad prescribing sacrifices etc. अश्व-वत् This is like the horse.

26. On the strength of the Upaniṣadic sanction of sacrifices etc., all religious activities as well are necessary. This is the same as in the case of a horse (in matters of its adequacy).

The question to be considered now is whether knowledge derives absolutely no benefit from the duties enjoined for the different orders of life, or it does derive some benefit. As to that, since it was concluded under the previous aphorism, "For that very reason the *Sannyāsin* has no need of lighting fire etc.", that knowledge does not at all depend on the performance of the duties of the different stages of life for producing its own result (viz liberation), therefore the answer is being given, "All religious activities are also necessary" etc. As a matter of fact knowledge needs the help of all the duties of the various stages of life, and it is not a fact that there is absolutely no dependence on them (for purification of heart).

Opponent: Is it not contradictory to say that knowledge depends and yet does not depend on other duties?

We (*Vedāntins*) answer that there is no contradiction. For once knowledge has emerged, it does not depend on any other factor for producing its (own) result (viz liberation); but it does depend on others for its own emergence.

Why so?

"On the strength of the Upaniṣadic texts prescribing sacrifice etc." Thus there occurs the text, "The Brāhmaṇas seek to know it through the study of the Vedas, sacrifices, charity, austerity consisting in a dispassionate perception of sense-objects" (Bṛ. IV. iv. 22), which shows the helpfulness of sacrifices etc. to the attainment of knowledge. Moreover, it is understood from their association with "seeking to know" (Bṛ. IV. iv. 22), that they act as a means for the emergence of knowledge. Furthermore, from the text, "Now, again, what is called a sacrifice is really *Brahmacarya*" (Ch. VIII. v. 1), where bachelor-studentship, a means to the acquisition of knowledge, is praised by comparing it with sacrifices etc., it appears that the sacrifices etc. are also a means to it. Again, such Upaniṣadic texts as, "I tell you briefly of that goal which all the Vedas with one voice propound, which all the austerities speak of, and wishing for which people practice *Brahmacarya*; it is this, viz *Om*" (Ka. I. ii. 15), indicate that the duties of the different stages of life are helpful to the acquisition of knowledge. Smṛti texts also support this, for instance, "The duties result in scorching away sins; the supreme goal being knowledge, when sins are scorched by duties, knowledge begins to emerge", and so on.

"As in the case of a horse" is meant for illustrating the adequacy (of sacrifices etc.). As from the standpoint of propriety, a horse is not employed for drawing a plough, but a chariot, similarly the duties of the different stages of life are needed not for the fruition of the result of knowledge, but for the emergence of knowledge itself.

शमदमाद्युपेतः स्यात्तथापि तु तद्विधेस्तदंगतया तेषामवश्यानुष्ठेयत्वात् ॥२७॥

तथा-अपि Still स्यात् one should be शम-दम-आदि-उपेत: endowed with calmness, self-control etc. तु for अवश्य-अनुष्ठेयत्वात् तेषाम् they have to be practised perforce, तत्-विधे: they having been enjoined तत्-अंगतया as subsidiaries of that (knowledge).

27. *(Even though there be no injunction about sacrifices etc.), still one must be endowed with self-control and the like, since these are enjoined as subsidiaries of knowledge; and hence have to be practised as a matter of course.*

Someone may argue that sacrifices etc. cannot properly be the means to knowledge, because no injunction (to that effect) exists, and because the text starting with, "They seek to know through sacrifice", is a mere restatement (of a fact known otherwise), meant for glorifying knowledge, and not as an injunction for sacrifices etc., the meaning implied being this: "So fortunate is knowledge that they seek to attain it through those very sacrifices etc."

We (*Vedāntins*) say: Even if this be so, still a seeker after knowledge must be endowed with control of body and mind and such other virtues; because control of body and mind, etc. are enjoined as means to the acquisition of knowledge in the text, "Therefore he who knows it as such becomes self-controlled, calm, withdrawn into himself, enduring and concentrated, and sees the Self in his own self (body)" (Bṛ. IV. iv. 23), and because it is compulsory to undertake what is prescribed (by the scriptures).

Opponent: Even here there is no injunction but a statement in the present tense implying that one sees by being endowed with self-control etc.

We (*Vedāntins*) answer that it is not so, since the idea of injunction becomes clear from the use of the term "therefore" which alludes to the praise of the subject-matter under discussion, and since the Mādhyandinas use a clear injunction in their reading "should see" (in place of "see"). Hence even though there be no need of sacrifices etc., self-control etc. are needed. As a matter of fact, however, sacrifices etc. are also needed on the strength of the Upaniṣadic text itself that mentions them.

Opponent: Did we not point out that in the text "(they) seek to know through sacrifice" etc. (Bṛ. IV. iv. 22), no injunction is discernible?

Vedāntin: You did say so; still from the uniqueness of the connection, an injunction has to be inferred. For this connection of "seeking to know" with "sacrifices" etc. is not known from any other source, in which case alone it could have occurred here by way of a restatement. And it is by inferring an injunction on the strength of the revelation of an extraordinary fact in such texts as, "Since the sun is toothless, therefore he has a claim to a share of offering that is well crushed", where no injunction is met with, that a discussion about an (implied) injunction is introduced in the Pūrva-Mīmāṁsā by saying, "Crushing for the sun in all cases of 'derivative sacrifices' (based on the Darśa-Pūrṇamāsa) should become obvious" (Jai. Sū. III. iii. 34). Similarly also it has been said herein, "Or rather there is an injunction (in the text) just as it is in the case of holding sacrificial fuel" (B. S. III. iv. 20). And in the Gītā and other Smṛtis it has been stated elaborately that sacrifices etc., when performed without any motive for fruits, become the means for the attainment of knowledge by an aspirant who desires liberation. Hence sacrifices etc. and self-control etc., which are the duties of the respective stages of life, are all but means for the emergence of knowledge. And yet among these, such means as self-control etc., which are connected with knowledge by the clause, "He who knows it as such" (Bṛ. IV. iv. 23), are proximate to knowledge, while the other means, viz sacrifices etc., are external (i.e. remote), they being connected with the "seeking to know" (Bṛ. IV. iv. 22). This is how these are to be distinguished.

Topic 7: Restrictions about Food

सर्वान्नानुमतिश्च प्राणात्यये तद्दर्शनात् ॥२८॥

सर्व-अन्न-अनुमतिः All kinds of food are permitted च only प्राण-अत्यये when life is in danger तत्-दर्शनात् for so it is revealed.

28. All kinds of food are permitted only when life is in danger; for so it is revealed.

Doubt: In the anecdote of *Prāṇa*, as contained in the recension of the Chandogas, the text occurs, "For a man who knows *Prāṇa* thus, nothing becomes uneatable" (Ch. V. ii. 1). The Vājasaneyins also have the text, "He who knows the food of (*Prāṇa*) the vital force to be such, never happens to eat anything that is not food or to accept anything that is not food" (Bṛ. VI. i. 14), the meaning implied being that everything becomes eatable to him. Now, is this permission of everything as food meant as an injunction to be followed as a means to the acquisition of knowledge like self-control etc., or is this a mere declaration by way of eulogy?

Opponent: When under such a doubt, the conclusion to be arrived at is that it is an injunction, for thus alone can this instruction generate a special tendency (to act), (so that it is an extraordinary instruction implying injunction). Thus it becomes a subordinate part of the meditation on *Prāṇa* owing to its proximity to that meditation; and by being such a subordinate part, it indicates the abrogation of the general rule (about food).

Objection: If that be the case, it will set at naught the scriptures making a division between things that can be eaten and not eaten.

Opponent: That is nothing damaging, since this contradiction can be logically reconciled from the standpoints of a general rule and its exception. For instance, the prohibition of animal slaughter is modified by the injunction to kill animals in sacrifices, or the general division of women into those with whom one can have intercourse and those with whom one cannot is modified by the text about not rejecting any woman as contained in, "His vow is that he shall not reject any woman" (Ch. II. xiii. 2), occurring in connection with the Vāmadevya meditation. So also the scriptural division between the eatable and non-eatable can be modified by this text about eating all kinds of food occurring in connection with the meditation on *Prāṇa*.

Vedāntin: To this we say that this is not an injunction permitting the eating of all kinds of food, for no word of injunction is met with here, inasmuch as the present tense is used in the expression, "For him who knows *Prāṇa* thus, nothing becomes uneatable" (Ch. V. ii. 1). And even when no injunction is discernible, one cannot read into it an injunction just out of the temptation of making it a generator of a distinct kind of activity. Besides, it is only after declaring that the range of food for *Prāṇa* extends right down to that of dogs etc., that the declaration is made, "For him who knows *Prāṇa* thus nothing becomes uneatable". It is not possible for anyone with a human body to eat all that is food to dogs etc., though it is possible for one to think that all these are food to the vital force. Hence this is only a eulogy meant to glorify the knowledge of *Prāṇa's* food, and it is not an injunction permitting everything as food. And the fact, that all kinds of food can be permitted when life is in danger is pointed out by the aphorist. The idea expressed is this: It is only when in a great calamity one's life itself is in danger, that all kinds of food are permitted, for such is the declaration of the Upaniṣad. Thus it is that the Upaniṣad shows in the *brāhmaṇa* portion starting with, "When the crops in the country of the Kurus had been destroyed by hail" etc. (Ch. I. x. 1), that the sage Cākrāyaṇa was impelled to eat forbidden food when in straitened circumstances. A sage named Cākrāyaṇa under calamitous conditions, ate some bad black pulses, a portion of which had already been eaten by an elephant driver; but after the food, he rejected the offered drinking water on the plea that the man had already drunk from it. And the sage gave the reason for this, "I would not have survived if I had not eaten these grains; but drinking water I can have at will" (Ch. I. x. 4). Again, the next day, he eats the same stale pulses left over after being eaten by himself and another. By recounting thus the eating of the remnant of somebody else's food, and the remnant as well as insipid food, the Upaniṣad only reveals an eagerness to express the idea that when a question of life and death arises, one can eat even a forbidden thing for preserving life. But from the rejection of the drinking water, it is understood that this must not be done in a normal state even by a man of knowledge. Hence the text, "For him who knows *Prāṇa* thus" etc. (Ch. V. ii. 1), is a eulogy.

अबाधाच्च ॥२९॥

29. And (this should be the interpretation) so that the scriptures (about permissible and forbidden food) may not be contradicted.

And the texts, "when the food is pure, the mind becomes pure" etc. (Ch. VII. xxvi. 2) and others, which make a division between what can be eaten and what not, will remain uncontradicted if such an interpretation is accepted.

अपि च स्मर्यते ॥३०॥

अपि च Moreover स्मर्यते mentioned in the Smṛtis.

30. Moreover, the Smṛtis support this view.

Moreover, the Smṛtis mention that when a calamity befalls, all kinds of food can be eaten indiscriminately by the enlightened and unenlightened alike: "Just as a lotus leaf is not drenched by water, so also a man, who eats food from wherever he gets it when life is in jeopardy, is not affected by sin." So also the Smṛti speaks of the avoidance of prohibited food, as in, "A Brāhmaṇa shall for ever avoid wine. They should pour hot wine into the mouth of a Brāhmaṇa who drinks liquor. The drunkards become worms on account of taking prohibited things".

शब्दश्चातोऽकामकारे ॥३१॥

अतः Hence च also शब्दः scriptural text (occurs) अ-काम-कारे prohibiting licence.

31. Hence also occur the scriptural texts prohibiting licence.

In the *saṁhitā* of the Kaṭhas is found a text which forbids the eating of uneatable food and purports to check activities dependent on licence: "Therefore a Brāhmaṇa should not drink spirituous liquors". And that text becomes all the more logical if the text, "For a man who knows *Prāṇa* thus" etc. (Ch. V. ii. 1), be a eulogy. Hence texts of this kind are eulogies and not injunctions.

Topic 8: Duties of Orders of Life should be Fulfilled

Doubt: It was ascertained under the aphorism, "And there is need for all duties" etc. (III. iv. 26), that the duties of the different stages of life are conducive to knowledge. The question being considered now is whether those duties are to be performed or not performed by a man who simply sticks to his own stage of life without any hankering for liberation and any desire for knowledge.

Opponent: As to that, the text "The Brāhmaṇas seek to know it through the study of the Vedas" etc. (Bṛ. IV. iv. 22), enjoins the duties of the different stages of life as means for the acquisition of knowledge and hence the obligatory duties are not to be performed by one who does not want knowledge but craves for some other result. On the contrary, should these be obligatory for him also, then these duties cannot be conducive to knowledge, since obligatoriness and unobligatoriness cannot meet at the same point.

Vedāntin: In answer to this, the aphorist says:

विहितत्वाच्चाश्रमकर्मापि ॥३२॥

च And (the same time) अपि even आश्रम-कर्म duties of the different orders of life (are to be performed) विहितत्वात् for these have been enjoined.

32. At the same time the duties of the orders of life are to be performed (by one who does not want liberation), since these have been enjoined.

The obligatory duties are to be performed even by one who

simply sticks to an order of life without any craving for liberation, for these are enjoined by such texts as, "One shall perform the Agnihotra sacrifice as long as one lives". And yet from this point of view there can be no such criticism that the very same Vedic text is being overburdened (with too many purposes).[9]

And it was objected that in that case these religious duties will not conduce to knowledge. Hence the answer is being given:

सहकारित्वेन च ॥३३॥

च And सह-कारित्वेन because of being jointly the generators (of knowledge).

33. And (these have to be performed, since these are enjoined as) being jointly the generators of knowledge.

And these must be jointly the generators of knowledge just because these have been enjoined to be so in, "The Brāhmaṇas seek to know it through the study of the Vedas, sacrifices" etc. (Bṛ. IV. iv. 22). That fact was stated in the aphorism, "And there is need for all duties, with due regard to adequacy, as in the case of a horse" (III. iv. 26). Yet it is not to be concluded that this text about the cooperation (*sahakāritva*)[10] of the duties of the stages of life with knowledge refers to the production of the result of knowledge, as in the case of Prayāja etc. (helping in the production of the result of Darśa-Pūrṇamāsa), since knowledge can never be a matter for injunction, and since the result of knowledge cannot be a product. For rites like Darśa-Pūrṇamāsa alone, which can be subjects of injunction, need other cooperating means for producing such results as heaven. But knowledge is not of that kind. Thus it is that the aphorist said, "And for that very reason there is no dependence on such acts as lighting up a sacrificial fire, and so on" (III. iv. 25). Hence the only idea implied in speaking of their helpfulness is that they

[9] For the sentence enjoining obligatory duties is not interpreted to enjoin them as helpful to knowledge, nor is the sentence admitting helpfulness interpreted to mean that all duties are so under all circumstances.

[10] *Sahakāritva* means cooperation. But *Ratnaprabhā* prefers a derivative meaning as given under the aphorism.

are conducive to the emergence of knowledge. Yet there is no scope for apprehending here an opposition arising from their obligatory and occasional association (with the same person), because the association differs although the duties are the same. For different is the obligatory association as it is gathered from the texts about lifelong performance and the like. This does not produce knowledge as its result. Again, occasional is the other kind of association as gathered from the text, "The Brāhmaṇas seek to know it through the study of the Vedas" etc. (Bṛ. IV. iv. 22). This has knowledge as its result. This is just like a sacrificial stake made of Khādira wood which, through its obligatory association with the sacrifice, serves the purposes of the sacrifice, but by occasional association serves the purposes of the sacrificer.[11]

सर्वथाऽपि तु त एवोभयलिङ्गात् ॥३४॥

सर्वथा Considered in every (i.e. either) way, अपि तु however, ते एव the very same (duties are meant) उभय-लिङ्गात् because of the indicatory marks of both kinds.

34. Considered either way, however, the very same religious duties are meant for performance, because of the indicatory marks of both kinds.

"Considered either way"—whether they be the normal duties of the different orders of life or the cooperators in acquiring knowledge, these very same religious acts, viz Agnihotra and the rest, are to be performed.

What does the teacher rule out then by his emphasis in, "the very same duties"?

We say that he rules out the misconception of these being different from the (usual) rites. In the scripture of the Kuṇḍapāyin an Agnihotra, different from the Agnihotra

[11] The stake is to be made according to injunction from Bilva, Khādira, or Palāśa wood to serve the purposes of the sacrifice. This is the general rule. But for a sacrificer who wants valour, the stake must be of Khādira. This is a special rule. The two rules do not contradict each other, but have their special fields.

performed daily, is enjoined in the text, "One performs the Agnihotra sacrifice for a month". Unlike that, these are not different here. This is the idea.

Why?

"On account of the indicatory marks of both kinds", on account of the indicatory marks both in the Vedas and the Smṛtis. As for the Vedic indicatory mark, it occurs in the text, "The Brāhmaṇas seek to know it through the study of the Vedas" etc. (Bṛ. IV. iv. 22), which shows the applicability of the very same sacrifices etc. as they already exist with their forms well determined, but does not prescribe a new extraordinary form for them, as is done by saying "one sacrifices" (i.e. "shall sacrifice"). The indicatory mark in the Smṛti occurs in, "He who performs his bounden duty without leaning to the fruit of action" (Gītā, VI. 1), which shows how the rites, already known as obligatory, become conducive to the rise of knowledge. And such text as, "He who has to his credit these eighty-four sanctifications" etc., which allude to the fact of these Vedic rites being well known as sanctifying, occur in the Smṛtis with the idea of showing that knowledge arises in one who is sanctified by them. Hence this emphasis on non-difference is quite proper. And this presence of the indicatory mark only strengthens the view that the rites are helpful to knowledge.

अनभिभवं च दर्शयति ॥३५॥

च Moreover, (the Vedas) दर्शयति show अनभिभवम् (the fact of) not being overpowered.

35. The Vedas also show that one (equipped with Brahmacarya etc.) is not overpowered.

Moreover, the Vedas show in the texts like, "For that Self does not perish which one attains by *Brahmacarya*" (Ch. VIII. v. 3) etc., that one who is equipped with practices like *Brahmacarya* is not overpowered by the torments like passion. Hence the conclusion is confirmed that sacrifices etc. are not only the duties pertaining to the stages of life, they are also helpful in the rise of knowledge.

Topic 9: Knowledge for People outside Orders

The *doubt* arises as to whether the widowers and others, who do not remain affiliated to any order of life because of their lack of the requisites like wealth and other resources, have any competence for knowledge or not.

Opponent: When under that doubt, the conclusion should be that they have no competence, since it has been emphasized that the duties of the stages of life are helpful to the rise of knowledge, and since these cannot possibly perform any duty prescribed for those stages.

अन्तरा चापि तु तत्-दृष्टेः ॥३६॥

तु As a matter of fact, however, अन्तरा one standing in between two stages (is) अपि also (entitled) तत्-दृष्टेः for such cases are met with.

36. As a matter of fact, a person standing in between two stages is also entitled, such cases being met with (in the Upaniṣads).

Vedāntin: This being the position, the answer is given by saying, "As a matter of fact, a person, standing in between two stages, is also entitled", even one occupying an intermediate stage, owing to being debarred from any one of them, is also entitled to knowledge.

Why?

"Such cases being met with in the Upaniṣads"; for Vedic texts are noticeable which speak of the possession of the knowledge of Brahman by Raikva (Ch. IV. i. iii) Vācaknavī (or Gārgī) (Bṛ. III. vi. 1), and others who were in similar circumstances.

अपि च स्मर्यते ॥३७॥

37. Moreover, the Smṛtis also mention this fact.

Moreover, in the histories it is mentioned that Samvarta and others, who had nothing to do with the duties of the stages of life owing to such habits as remaining naked and so on, were still great Yogins.

Opponent: These are mere indicatory marks found in the Vedas and Smṛtis that have been cited here. But what is the net result derived from them?

Vedāntin: That is being stated:

विशेषानुग्रहश्च ॥३८॥

38. And (in their case) there can be the favour of special factors (like japa etc.).

In the case of those widowers and others also, it is possible for knowledge to be helped by such virtuous acts as repetition of *mantras* (*japa*), fasting, worship of gods, etc., which can be resorted to by men in general, and which do not clash with the fact of one's standing outside any stage of life. In support of this occurs the Smṛti, "A Brāhmaṇa can succeed merely through *japa*. There can be no doubt as regards this. A kind-hearted man is called a Brāhmaṇa irrespective of whether he does anything else or not" (Manu. II. 87), which shows that one can take up prayer even though the performance of the duties of any order of life may not be possible for him. Moreover, it is possible for knowledge to be helped by the virtuous deeds performed in the different stages of life in earlier lives, as is evident from the Smṛti: "The Yogin, gaining perfection through many births, reaches the highest goal" (Gītā, VI. 45), which shows that particular mental impressions acquired in past lives also help knowledge. And since knowledge has a directly perceptible result, the mere absence of any prohibition is enough to qualify an aspirant for liberation to undertake "hearing" etc.[12] Hence nothing stands in the way of the widowers and others also becoming qualified for pursuing knowledge.

अतस्त्वितरज्ज्यायो लिङ्गाच्च ॥३९॥

तु But अतः compared with this इतरत् the other ज्यायः (is) better लिंगात् because of indicatory mark च as well.

[12] An injunction is necessary for unseen results like heaven etc., but not so for the immediately perceptible results like cessation of ignorance.

39. But as compared with this, the other one is better, because of indicatory sign (in the Upaniṣad and Smṛtis) as well.

"But as compared with this", as compared with the fact of continuing in the intermediate stages, "the other one", the other state of belonging to some stage of life, is "better" as a means to the rise of knowledge, because there occurs the indicatory sign in the Upaniṣad in, "Any other knower of Brahman, who has done good deeds and is identified with the supreme Light, also treads this path" (Bṛ IV. iv. 9), as also the indications in the Smṛti, contained in, "A twice-born man shall not stay outside the stages of life even for a day", and "Should one stay outside the stages of life for a year, one should undertake some austerity (as a penance)".

Topic 10: Defection from Monasticism

Doubt: It has been established that there are orders of life for the continent as well. Now the doubt arises as to whether a man belonging to those orders can have any reversion from there or not.

Opponent: One may even fall back out of a desire to perform the earlier virtuous deeds well or owing to passion etc., since no special reason exists for not doing so.

Vedāntin: This being the position, the answer is given:

तद्भूतस्य तु नातद्भावो जैमिनेरपि नियमातद्रूपाभावेभ्यः ॥४०॥

तु But तत्-भूतस्य for one who has become so, न (there can be) no अ-तत्-भाव: reversion from that नियम-अतद्रूप-अभावेभ्यः on account of restriction, absence of text (sanctioning defection), and good precedence. (This is the view) अपि even जैमिने: of Jaimini.

40. But for one who has become so, there can be no reversion from it, on account of restriction, absence of text sanctioning reversion, and absence of good precedence. This is the view of Jaimini as well.

"But for one who has become so", one who has embraced

the life of the continent (*Brahmacārin* or *Sannyāsin*), "there can be no reversion from it," no falling back from it, under any circumstances.

Why?

"On account of restriction, absence of texts about reversion from such a life, and absence of good precedence." Thus the restrictive rule occurring in the following texts shows the absence of reversion: "One who spends his whole life in the teacher's house" (Ch. II. xxiii. 1), "The path indicated by the scripture is that one shall retire to the forest; and the esoteric (purport of the scripture) about it is that one shall not return from there", "Being permitted by the teacher, he shall duly follow one of the four stages of life till the body falls off", and others. And though we meet with sentences speaking of ascension to a higher order, such as, "After finishing the *Brahmacārin's* life, one shall become a householder" (Jā. 4), "One shall embrace monasticism from the *Brahmacārin's* life itself" (ibid.), yet we do not come across sentences sanctioning reversion. Nor do good precedents exist.

As for the argument that there can be a falling back from a desire to perform well the (wonted) earlier duties, that is invalid, since the Smṛti declares, "Better is one's own duty though imperfect, than the duty of another well performed" (Gītā, III. 35). Logic also supports this; for one's own duty is that which has been prescribed (by the scriptures) for one, and not what one can perform well, since duty is determined by scriptural injunction. And there can be no such thing as (exoneration of) defection owing to passion etc., for the scriptural restriction is more authoritative. By saying "(This is the view) of Jaimini as well", the aphorist points out the concurrence of Jaimini and Bādarāyaṇa in this matter, so that our conviction may become all the more strong.

Topic 11: Expiation or Transgression of Celibacy

न चाधिकारिकमपि पतनानुमानात्तदयोगात् ॥४१॥

च And अपि even (that expiation) आधिकारिकम् mentioned in *Adhikāra-Lakṣaṇa* (Jai. Sū. VI.) न (is) not (meant) (for him)

पतन-अनुमानात् since his fall is inferred (from the Smṛti) (to be without remedy). तत्-अयोगात् (and) hence he has no connection with it.

41. And even an expiation is not available for him, since his fall is known from the Smṛti to be irremediable, and he has no connection with it.

Doubt: If a (*Naiṣṭhika*) *Brahmacārin*, wedded to lifelong continence, breaks his vow through some inadvertence, can he or can he not undertake a penance as enjoined in, "A *Brahmacārin*, falling from his vow, shall sacrifice a donkey to Nirṛti"?

The answer (of the *opponent*) is, no. As for expiation mentioned in the chapter dealing with qualification (in the Pūrva-Mīmāṁsā) in the aphorism, "The offering of the animal in the case of a *Brahmacārin* breaking his vow is to be made, as in the *upanayana* sacrifice, in the ordinary fire; for the time for lighting up the Āhavanīya fire (after marriage) is not ripe (in the case of the *Brahmacārin*)" (Jai. Sū. VI. viii. 21), that too cannot apply to the lifelong *Brahmacārin*.

What is the reason?

Since the Smṛti mentions that this fall cannot be set right, "For one who after being established in the norm of the lifelong celibate (*Naiṣṭhika*) falls from it, we cannot imagine any expiation by which that self-immolating man can be purified"; for no remedy is possible for one whose head is cut off. But that expiation is possible for an *upakurvāṇa Brahmacārin* (who would marry after finishing his studies), since that kind of absolute fall is not mentioned in his case.

उपपूर्वमपि त्वेके भावमशनवत्तदुक्तम् ॥४२॥

तु However एके some (consider this) उप-पूर्वम् a minor sign, (and admit) भावम् existence (of expiation), अशन-वत् as in a case of eating (forbidden food); तत्-उक्तम् so it is explained (by Jaimini).

42. Some, however, consider this to be a minor sin and concede expiation as in a case of eating forbidden fooa. So it is explained by Jaimini.

On the contrary, "some", some teachers, think that it is only a minor sin. If a lifelong celibate breaks his vow by misbehaving with a woman other than his teacher's wife for instance, that does not constitute a major sin (*mahāpātaka*), since it has not been counted among such major sins as dishonouring one's teacher's wife. Hence they assert that a lifelong celibate can have expiation just as much as a *upakurvāṇa Brahmacārin*, since they are on the same footing as *Brahmacārins* and breakers of their vow. And this is as in the case of eating prohibited food. Just as a *Brahmacārin*, who breaks his vow by drinking wine or eating meat, can be purified again, so also is the case here. Those who assert that a lifelong celibate who slips can have no expiation cannot produce any text to that effect. But those who assert that he can have an expiation have as their support the text, "A *Brahmacārin* falling from his vow shall sacrifice a donkey to Nirṛti" which is applicable to both classes. Hence the existence of expiation is the more reasonable position. And this is in accord with what has been stated in a chapter of the Pūrva-Mīmāṁsā in the aphorisms, "Should it be maintained that either can be understood as equally applicable" (Jai. Sū. I. iii. 8), (then the answer is that) "the comprehension must be according to what is stated in the scripture, for virtuous deeds are determined by them"[13] (Jai. Sū. I. iii. 9). This being the case, the mention of the absence of expiation in the Smṛti is to be explained as meant for inducing (in the lifelong celibate) an intensity of effort (for keeping his vow). Thus also it is to be kept in mind that expiations are prescribed for the mendicants and the forest-dwellers in such texts as, "Should a forest-dweller break the vow of his order, he shall undertake a penance for twelve days and help in growing grass on the grazing ground", "Should a mendicant break his vow, he shall, just like the Vānaprastha tend the pasture barring the cultivation of Soma

[13] A passage in the Veda speaks of pudding made of *yava*. Now *yava*, generally meaning barley, sometimes means a different kind of grain. Following such popular usage the opponent would have the pudding made of either. But the conclusion, drawn from another Vedic passage, which clearly describes *yava* as meaning barley, is that barley alone is to be used, for that conforms with the scripture.

plants, and he shall undertake the purificatory rites according to the Vedic branch he belongs to".

Topic 12: They are to be Excommunicated

बहिस्तूभयथाऽपि स्मृतेराचाराच्च ॥४३॥

तु But अपि even उभयथा in either case बहिः (they are to be kept) outside (society) स्मृतेः in compliance with Smṛti च and आचारात् good conduct.

43. (Whether their transgression constitutes a major or a minor sin), they are to be kept outside in either case in accordance with Smṛti texts and behaviour of good people.

Whether the lapse of the continent people from their respective orders of life constitutes a minor sin or a major one, in either case they are to be expelled from society by the good people, because of the extreme condemnation shown in such Smṛti texts as, "For one who after being established in the norm of the lifelong celibate, falls from it, we cannot imagine any expiation by which that self-immolating man can be purified", "One shall undertake the Cāndrāyaṇa (expiatory rite) if one happens to touch a Brāhmaṇa fallen from a higher stage of life, excommunicated from his own society, or dead through hanging or by being bitten by some insect". This also follows from the behaviour of the good people. For decent people do not undertake any sacrifice, study, or matrimonial ceremony in association with them.

Topic 13: Meditations Connected with Rites

स्वामिनः फलश्रुतेरित्यात्रेयः ॥४४॥

(The meditations subserving religious acts) स्वामिनः are for (i.e. are to be undertaken by) the sacrificer फलश्रुतेः because the Upaniṣads mention the results, इति thus (says) आत्रेयः Ātreya.

44. The teacher Ātreya thinks that the agentship for medita-

tions belongs to the master of the sacrifice, since the Upaniṣads mention their results.

Doubt: With regard to the meditations connected with the different parts of a sacrifice, the doubt arises as to whether they are to be undertaken by the sacrificer or the priests. What would be the conclusion here?

Ātreya: They are to be undertaken by the sacrificer.

Why?

On account of the mention of results. For the results are stated thus: "Rain pours down for him who having such a knowledge meditates on the five kinds of Sāma as rain; and he can make rain pour down for others also" (Ch. II. iii. 2). Logically a result should go to the master, for the ceremony as a whole (with its parts) is enjoined for him, and the results of such meditations are prescribed for one who is empowered for the main rite. Moreover, from the Upaniṣad it is known that the result of the meditation belongs to the meditators, as stated in, "Rain pours down for him who meditates" (ibid.) etc.

Objection: Is not the priest also seen to derive a result, as stated in, "Whatever objects this chanter, possessed of such knowledge, desires either for himself or for the sacrificer, he secures by chanting" (Bṛ. I. iii. 28)?

Ātreya: No, because the result accrues there to the priest on the strength of the text.[14] Hence the teacher Ātreya is of opinion that the master himself of the rite (i.e. the sacrificer) has to undertake the meditations bearing fruits.

आर्त्विज्यमित्यौडुलोमिस्तस्मै हि परिक्रीयते ॥४५॥

आर्त्विज्यम् It is the priest's duty इति so says औडुलोमिः Auḍulomi हि for तस्मै for that (work), परिक्रीयते (he) is retained.

45. The (teacher) Auḍulomi says that it is the duty of the

[14] That text states an exception to the general rule; it does not override that rule.

priest (to undertake such meditations), for he is retained for that.

The teacher Auḍulomi is of opinion that there is no such rule that the meditations are to be undertaken by the sacrificer. They should be undertaken by the priest.

What is the reason?

For a priest is retained (by the sacrificer) for the performance of the rite together with its parts; and such meditations as on the *Udgītha* are included in that performance, since the competence for the performance of the parts is derived from that for the main rite. Hence the meditations have to be performed by the priests on such analogy as regulation of the milking of a cow (by the priest for one who owns it). It is thus that the Upaniṣad shows in the following text how the meditation is to be undertaken by the Udgātā (priest singing the Sāma), "Baka, son of Dalbha, knew that Udgītha, and he became the Udgātā of the people in the Naimiṣa forest" (Ch. I. ii. 13). As for the assertion that the result is seen in the Upaniṣad to accrue to the sacrificer, that creates no difficulty, since the priests act for others, and the fruits cannot accrue to them unless a text says so explicitly (as an exception).

श्रुतेश्च ॥४६॥

46. And from Vedic texts also (this stands confirmed).

"He said, 'whatever blessing the priests pray for in a sacrifice, they pray for it for the sacrificer alone'" (Śa. B. I. iii. i. 28), "Hence an Udgātā, possessed of this knowledge, will ask, 'What desire shall I fulfil for you by singing?'" (Ch. I. vii. 8-9), such texts show that the result of the meditation undertaken by the priests accrues to the sacrificer. Hence it is concluded that the meditations on things forming parts of a sacrificial act are to be undertaken by the priests.

Topic 14: Injunction about Meditativeness

Doubt: In the Bṛhadāraṇyaka Upaniṣad (III. v. 1) occurs the text, "Therefore the Brāhmaṇa, having known all about scholarship (*pāṇḍitya*), should try to live (*bālyena*, i.e.) upon that strength which comes of knowledge[14]; having known all about this strength as well as scholarship, he becomes meditative (*muni*); having known all about meditativeness and its opposite, he becomes a Brāhmaṇa (knower of Brahman)". The doubt arises here whether meditativeness is enjoined here or not.

Opponent: When under such a predicament, the conclusion to be arrived at is that it is not enjoined, since the injunction ends with, "should try to live upon that strength which comes of knowledge" (ibid.). Beyond that no verbal ending, denoting an injunction, is met with in "he becomes meditative" (ibid.). Hence this is a mere re-statement of a known fact.

Objection: How is it gathered that it is a known fact?

Opponent: Since the terms "meditative" and "scholar" imply knowledge, meditativeness becomes already known in the text, "having known all about scholarship" (ibid.). Moreover, it is obvious that the text, "having known all about meditativeness and its opposite, he becomes a Brāhmaṇa" (ibid.), does not purport to enjoin Brāhmaṇahood, since the term Brāhmaṇa had ocurred even earlier. Hence just as much as "he becomes a Brāhmaṇa" is said by way of praise, so also should the sentence "he becomes meditative" be a praise (of the strength that comes from mediate knowledge), since both have the same form of expression.[15]

Vedāntin: To this we say:

सहकार्यन्तरविधिः पक्षेण तृतीयं तद्वतो विध्यादिवत् ॥४७॥

सहकारि-अन्तर-विधिः An injunction is implied about the other auxiliary (viz meditativeness), (which is) तृतीयम् the third,

[14] *Bālyena* may also mean, "through childlike innocence and purity of heart". Knowledge here means mediate knowledge, which leads to immediate knowledge, enlightenment.

[15] According to the Vedāntin, *pāṇḍitya* (scholarship) implies *śravaṇa* (hearing), *bālya* (strength coming from knowledge) implies *manana*, consisting in eliminating the idea of impossibility with the help of reasoning; and *muni* means one engaged in *nididhyāsana*. The Vedāntin maintains that a man aspiring for liberation must undertake *nididhyāsana*. The opponent denies this.

तत्-वत: for one who is possessed of that (knowledge) पक्षेण in a case of partial application (to knowledge) विधि-आदि-वत् like the main injunction (being applicable to the subsidiary acts).

47. In case of a partial application to knowledge by one possessed of (imperfect) knowledge, an injunction is implied in another auxiliary which is the third; this is like the main injunction being applied to the subsidiary acts.

In the case of meditativeness which leads to enlightenment, an injunction has to be admitted as much as in the cases of the "strength which comes of knowledge" and "scholarship" on account of its uniqueness (of not having been heard elsewhere).

Opponent: Was it not pointed out that meditativeness is already implied by the word scholarship?

Vedāntin: That creates no difficulty, since the term "*muni*" (lit. sage) implies an abundance of knowledge, and it is possible to derive the word in the sense of "one who contemplates". Moreover, such usage is met with as, "Among the *munis* (contemplative sages) I am Vyāsa" (Gītā. X. 37).

Opponent: The word "*muni*" is seen to refer to the highest stage of life (monasticism), as in "the householder's life, life in the teacher's home, life of a *muni*, and life in the forest".

Vedāntin: No, since a different meaning[16] is noticed in such usages as "Vālmiki, the greatest *muni* (sage)". In the text quoted above, the word *muni* can be understood to mean the highest stage, for it is mentioned along with the others, and monasticism alone remains to be mentioned after them, and because this highest stage of life is distinguished by a predominance of knowledge. Hence this "meditativeness" which is a third factor counted along with "strength arising from knowledge" and "scholarship", and consists in an abundance of knowledge, is enjoined here. And the assertion was made that the injunction culminates with "the strength arising from knowledge". Even

[16] *Mauna*, according to the *opponent* means knowledge or monasticism, which are spoken of elsewhere, and so need no fresh injunction. The *Vedāntin* says: It means excellence of knowledge, which is a new idea needing a new injunction.

so we resort to an injunction in the case of meditativeness by construing the sentence to mean, "one should become meditative"; for it is unique. Again, from the fact that meditativeness is spoken of as a thing to be acquired, it follows that an injunction has to be accepted about it as in the cases of "strength" and "scholarship".

By "for one possessed of that", is to be understood, "for the monk, possessed of knowledge".

Opponent: How is it known that the monk possessed of knowledge is meant?

Vedāntin: From the fact that the context deals with him (i.e. his competence) as is obvious from, "knowing this very Self the Brāhmaṇas renounce[17] the desire for sons, for wealth, and for worlds and lead the mendicant's life" (Bṛ. III. v. 1).

Opponent: If one has knowledge, the perfection of that knowledge follows as a matter of course. So what is the need of prescribing meditation?

Vedāntin: It is hence that the aphorist says, "in case of partial application". The idea implied is this: This injunction is made from the point of view of one whose knowledge cannot achieve perfection owing to the dominance of dualistic ideas. "Like subsidiary injunctions based on the main one"—the idea implied is this: As from the (main) injunction like, "one desiring heaven should perform the Darśa-Pūrṇamāsa sacrifice", the subsidiary acts like the lighting of fire etc. are assumed to be prescribed (though no clear injunction is discernible), they being helpful to the main sacrifice, so also it is admitted that meditativeness is prescribed here in this context of knowledge, although injunction cannot play any dominant part here.[18]

Opponent: When monasticism with its characteristic of "strength derived from knowledge" stands there as a stage of

[17] After an intellectual comprehension they renounce for complete enlightenment: A monk alone can be fully meditative.

[18] The *opponent* argues: "When a man has known from the scripture and reasoning that Brahman alone is real and all duality is unreal, the striving for full enlightenment will follow from the aspiration itself of the man, so that an injunction about meditativeness is uncalled for." The *Vedāntin* answers: "The topic here is of monasticism and

life sanctioned by the Vedas, why should the conclusion have been made in the Chāndogya text with the householder as the last as in, "Having finished his studies and embraced the life of the householder, (he attains the world of Brahman)" (Ch. VIII. xv. 1). By concluding thus, the Upaniṣad displays a preference for him.

Vedāntin: Hence the aphorist replies:

कृत्स्नभावात्तु गृहिणोपसंहारः ॥४८॥

तु But कृत्स्न-भावात् on account of its all-inclusiveness उपसंहारः the conclusion (is) गृहिणा with the householder.

48. But the conclusion is made (in the Chāndogya Upaniṣad) with the householder, since he has an all-inclusive life.

The word "but" is used to make a distinction. The distinct feature of the householder is that he has an all-comprehensive life. For the scriptures have prescribed for him many duties of his own stage of life such as sacrifices, which involve great effort, and he has also to practise the virtuous duties of other stages, as far as possible, such as non-injury, control of senses, etc. Hence it involves no contradiction to end with the householder.

मौनवदितरेषामप्युपदेशात् ॥४९॥

उपदेशात् Since there is injunction अपि even इतरेषाम् of the others (i.e. stages of life) मौनवत् like meditativeness.

49. Since there is injunction even about the others, just as much as of meditativeness.

Just as much as the two stages of life, viz meditativeness (i.e. monasticism) and married life, are approved by the Vedas, so

śravaṇa etc. are its complements. The unique fact about all of them here is that they are causes of enlightenment. And this uniqueness calls for an injunction. Although an injunction is unnecessary for one who is already enlightened, it is necessary for one whose knowledge has not matured.

also are the other two, viz life in the forest and life in the teacher's home. For the relevant text was pointed out earlier: "Austerity is the second, and the third is the *Brahmacārin* living in his teacher's home" etc. (Ch. II. xxiii. 1). Thus because the four stages of life are enjoined equally, there is an option of belonging to any one of them singly or to all of them successively. The plural (rather than the dual number) in the term "others (i.e. other stages of life") indicating the two stages of life, occurs because of the variety of their sub-divisions or the multiplicity of their adherents. This is how it is to be understood.

Topic 15: The Childlike State

अनाविष्कुर्वन्नन्वयात् ॥५०॥

(*Bālya*, i.e. the childlike state means behaviour) अनाविष्कुर्वन् without display (of parts), अन्वयात् for so it fits in with the context.

50. (The word 'bālya' in the Bṛhadāraṇyaka means that a man of enlightenment should behave like a child) without displaying his parts, for so it fits in with the context.

Doubt: In the text, "Therefore the Brāhmaṇa, having known all about scholarship (*pāṇḍitya*), should try to live a childlike life (*bālyena*)" (Bṛ. III. v. 1), *bālya* appears as a thing to be followed. Now the word *bālya* is derived from the word *bāla* (child) with the help of a suffix, so that the word means either the state of a child or the conduct of a child. But a child's state, meaning a certain age, cannot be achieved at will. So it may mean either childlike behaviour like answering calls of nature just as they occur or the qualities of guilelessness, freedom from egoism and pride, and the undeveloped state of the organs? This is the doubt. What should be the conclusion then?

Opponent: The meaning of the word *bālya* is more well known in the world as behaving, talking, eating at will, and answering calls of nature just as they occur. Hence it is reasonable to accept this.

Objection: It is not reasonable that he should resort to unrestrained behaviour, as that would lay him open to the charge of degrading himself through such wilful transgression.

Opponent: No, since a monk with enlightenment will remain free from blemish on the strength of scriptural authority, like one in such matters as killing animals (in a sacrifice).

Vedāntin: This being the conclusion, the answer is that it cannot be so, since this text can have some other meaning. For one should not think in terms of overriding an injunction in case one can get something else as the meaning of *bālya* that does not contradict that injunction. Moreover, an auxiliary is prescribed for aiding the main factor. The continuance in knowledge is the main thing here that has to be practised by the monks; and the pursuit of knowledge will cease to be a possibility if childlike behaviour be adopted in its totality. Hence by the term *bālya* is to be understood here some inward state of a child such as having immature functional ability etc. That fact is referred to by the aphorist in, "without any display". That is to say, without showing himself off by parading his wisdom, learning, virtuousness, etc.; he should be free from pride, conceit, etc. like a child who, owing to the immaturity of his senses, does not try to make a display of himself before others. Thus interpreted, the (Upaniṣadic) text reveals a meaning that logically reinforces the main injunction. And thus it has been stated by the authors of the Smṛtis in, "He is a Brāhmaṇa whom nobody recognizes either as an aristocrat or a commoner, either as well-read or not well-read, either as well-behaved or not well-behaved. A man of enlightenment should resort to unostentatious behaviour while following his spiritual practices in secret. He should roam over the earth like a blind man (not attracted by sense-objects), like one benumbed (i.e. without the sense of taste etc.), like one who is dumb (i.e. without active organs)", and "without any outer sign and with unostentatious behaviour" etc.

TOPIC 16: TIME OF FRUITION OF KNOWLEDGE

ऐहिकमप्यप्रस्तुतप्रतिबन्धे तद्दर्शनात् ॥५१॥

(The fruition may be) अपि even ऐहिकम् in this life अप्रस्तुत-

प्रतिबन्धे if there is no obstruction to what (means) is adopted; तत्-दर्शनात् for so it is seen (in the Upaniṣads).

51. The generation of knowledge takes place even in this life if there is no obstruction to the means adopted. For this is what is revealed (by the Upaniṣads).

Doubt: The means of knowledge, both higher and lower, have been ascertained under the aphorisms starting with, "And all religious duties are necessary on the strength of the Upaniṣadic sanction of sacrifice etc." (III. iv. 26). Now the question to be considered is whether the knowledge, resulting from them, emerges in this very life or sometimes even in a later life. What should be the conclusion then?

Opponent: It fructifies here itself.

Objection: What is the reason?

Opponent: Because enlightenment is preceded by "hearing" etc., and nobody engages in "hearing" etc. with the motive, "May enlightenment come to me in the next world". As a fact, however, a man is seen to engage in them with the purpose of having enlightenment emerge in the very same life. Sacrifices etc. also are helpful to the generation of knowledge through the medium of hearing etc., since knowledge is generated by its valid means. Hence the birth of enlightenment must occur in this very life.

Vedāntin: This being the position, our answer is: "The generation of knowledge takes place even in this life if there is no obstruction to the means adopted". The idea implied is this: Knowledge is possible even in this life, provided the means adopted for enlightenment are not obstructed in any way by some other result of past work that fructifies just then. Should it, however, be obstructed, the fruition comes in a subsequent birth. The fructification of a past act occurs from a (suitable) concurrence of space, time, and causation. And there can be no such rule that the very same space, time, and causation that lead to the fruition of one act, also lead to the fruition of some other act, since acts can have opposite results. Moreover, the scriptures stop by stating merely that a particular act has a particular result; they do not enunciate also the peculiar space, time, and causation. As a matter of fact, some supersensuous power manifests itself with regard to some acts owing to the assiduous application of its means, while the power of some other act remains arrested under its influence. It is not a fact that a motive for rise of knowledge either here or hereafter cannot be entertained equally, since the motive, "May I get knowledge either in this life or the next", can be held freely. Even when knowledge emerges from "hearing" etc., it arises only after the impediments wear away. This is why the Upaniṣad shows the inscrutability of the Self in the text, "Of that (Self) which is not available for the mere hearing to many and which many do not understand, the expounder is wonderful and the receiver is wonderful, and wonderful is he who knows under the instruction of an adept" (Ka. I. ii. 7). And when the Upaniṣad says that Vāmadeva realized the state of Brahman even when in his mother's womb (Ai. II. i. 5), it only shows that knowledge may emerge in a succeeding birth as a result of practices gone through in an earlier life; for a child, in the womb itself, cannot possibly undertake any practice that is usually gone through in this world. In the Smṛti also it is seen that, being questioned by Arjuna, "What end does one, failing to gain perfection in Yoga, meet, O Kṛṣṇa?" (Gītā, VI. 37), the Lord Kṛṣṇa says, "For the doer of good, O my son, never comes to grief" (Gītā, VI. 40); then again he speaks of his (i.e. of the fallen Yogin's) attainment of virtuous worlds and birth in virtuous families; and then in the passage beginning with, "There he is equipped with the intelligence acquired in his former body", etc. and ending with, "gaining perfection through many births he reaches the highest goal" (Gītā, VI. 43-45), Śrī Kṛṣṇa reveals the very same fact. Hence the conclusion is confirmed that knowledge arises either in this life or a subsequent one depending on the removal of impediment.

Topic 17: Liberation is Uniform Everywhere

Doubt: In the case of an aspirant for liberation, who adopts the means of knowledge, a rule, applicable to each individually, has been discovered to the effect that a distinction, as to whether the resulting enlightenment will occur in this life or a subsequent one, is created by the relative assiduousness in the pursuit of the practices. Now the doubt arises as to whether there is any such rule applicable to the aspirants individually that a distinction will be created in the resulting liberation as well in conformity with the superiority or the inferiority of the knowledge itself.

Vedāntin: Having that doubt in view the aphorist answers:

एवं मुक्तिफलानियमस्तदवस्थावधृतेस्तदवस्थावधृतेः ॥५२॥

मुक्तिफल-अनियमः There is no rule with regard to the result called liberation **एवम्** of this kind, **तत्-अवस्था-अवधृतेः** because that state has been definitely ascertained (to be the same).

52. There is no rule of this kind with regard to the result called liberation, because that state has been definitely determined (to be the same), because that state has been definitely determined (to be the same).

With regard to liberation, the result of knowledge, there is no such rule. One must not entertain any misconception of any such rule being applicable with individual variation in the matter of the resulting liberation.

Why?

"Because the Upaniṣads have definitely ascertained that state (to be the same)". For in all the Upaniṣads, the state of liberation is determined to be uniform in nature, the state of liberation being nothing but Brahman Itself. And Brahman cannot be of many sorts, since Its characteristic indication is declared to be uniform by such texts as, "neither gross nor minute" (Bṛ. III. viii. 8), "This Self is that which has been described as 'Not so, not so'" (Bṛ. III. ix. 26), "Where one does not see anything else" (Ch. VII. xxiv. 1), "All that is in front is but Brahman, the immortal" (Mu. II. ii. 11), "and all this are the Self" (Bṛ II. iv. 6), "That great birthless Self is undecaying, immortal, undying, fearless, and Brahman (infinite)" (Bṛ. IV. iv. 25), "But when to the knower of Brahman everything has become the Self, then what should one see and through what?" (Bṛ.

IV. v. 15). Moreover, in accordance with some peculiar efficacy belonging to the means of knowledge, they may (possibly) impart some excellence to knowledge itself, which is their result; but they cannot do so to liberation which is the result of knowledge. For we said it more than once that liberation cannot be a product of anything, it being realized through knowledge as a fact eternally present in its own right. For the matter of that, there can be no such thing as superiority, constituted by perfection, even in the case of knowledge, since an inferior knowledge is no knowledge, the superior one alone being so. Hence knowledge can possibly have only such a distinction as having arisen late or promptly. But in liberation there can be no superiority. Again, unlike the differences in the results of *karma*, the result of knowledge can have no difference owing to the absence of any difference in the knowledge itself. For unlike *karma*, knowledge as the means to liberation has no difference. But so far as the meditations on the qualified Brahman are concerned, as for instance in, "He who is identified with the mind and has the subtle body as His body" (Ch. III. xiv. 2), they can be different, owing to addition or elimination of attributes; and hence there can be a difference among their respective results, even as in the case of the results of *karma*. In support of this is noticeable an indicatory mark in the text, "The aspirant becomes just as he meditates on Him." Similar also is the Smṛti text, "There is no such thing as a higher goal for one realizing the absolute Brahman, for they speak of difference only in cases where qualities obtain".

The repetition of "Because that state has been definitely determined (to be the same)" indicates the end of this Part.

Chapter IV

PHALA—RESULT

Section I

Topic 1: Repetition of Meditation etc.

The Third Chapter was mostly occupied with a discussion of the practices connected with the conceptions (*vidyās*) of the qualified Brahman and absolute Brahman. Now this Fourth will be concerned with a discussion about the results, and it will also consider some other matters stemming out of that subject. To start with, however, we shall follow through a few sections, some special considerations regarding the practices themselves.

Doubt: We meet with such Upaniṣadic texts as, "The Self, my dear, should be realized—should be heard of, reflected on, and meditated upon" (Bṛ. IV. v. 6), "Knowing about this (Self) alone, the intelligent aspirant after Brahman should attain intuitive knowledge" (Bṛ. IV. iv. 21), "He is to be searched after, He is to be desired to be known" (Ch. VIII. vii. 1), and so on. The doubt arises with regard to these, whether the mental act is to be undertaken once only, or it is to be repeated. What should be the conclusion?

Opponent: Like the performance of the Prayāja sacrifice etc. the mental act is to be undertaken once only; for the requirement of the scripture is fulfilled by that much alone. Were one to resort to repetition, even though not stated by the Upaniṣad, one would be doing something not envisaged by the scripture.

Doubt: We quoted above the instructions about the repeated mental acts as contained in, "should be heard of, reflected on, and meditated upon" (Bṛ. IV. v. 6), and so on.

Opponent: Even so, one should repeat only as many times as the scripture demands. There should be one hearing, one reflection, and one meditation, and nothing more. There can be no repetition where the instruction is uttered but once with a "He should know" or "He should meditate".

Vedāntin: This being the position, we reply:

आवृत्तिरसकृदुपदेशात् ॥१॥

आवृत्तिः Repetition (is necessary) अ-सकृत् उपदेशात् the instruction having been given more than once.

1. Repetition is necessary, since the Upaniṣads instruct repeatedly.

The mental act is to be repeated.

Why?

Since the instruction is repeated. Such repeated instruction as "should be heard of, reflected on, and meditated upon" indicates a repetition of the mental act.

Opponent: Did we not point out that the repetition should be as many times as the scripture demands and no more?

Vedāntin: No, since these have to culminate in the intuitive realization of Brahman; for hearing etc. fulfil their purpose of producing a (tangible) perceptible result in this case when they culminate in realization through repetition, even as husking etc. culminate in producing rice etc. Besides, by the word *upāsanā* (continuous remembrance, adoration) and *nididhyāsana* (profound meditation) are implied acts involving this aspect of repetition. It is thus that when in this world somebody follows his teacher and others continuously and devotedly, he is referred to by such sentences as, "He adores his teacher", "He adores the king". Similarly by the sentence, "The woman meditates on her husband who is on a sojourn", a woman is referred to who is engaged in thinking of her husband constantly and is anxious about him. The verbs *vid* (lit. to know) and *upās* (lit. to sit near or to meditate) are seen to be used in the Upaniṣads interchangeably. Sometimes the text starts with *vid* and ends with *upās*, as for instance in the context starting with, "I speak of him also as Raikva who knows what Raikva knew (*veda*)" (Ch. IV. i. 4), where it is said later, "O venerable sir, instruct me about the God on whom you meditate (*upāsse*)" (Ch. IV. ii. 2). Sometimes again the start is made with meditation and conclusion with knowledge, as in, "One should meditate on the mind as Brahman" (Ch. III. xviii. 1), and "He who knows thus becomes resplendent in fame, prowess, and the brilliance arising from the Vedic studies" (Ch. III. xviii. 3). Hence repetition has to be resorted to even where the instruction occurs only once, while a repeated instruction indicates repetition as a matter of course.

लिङ्गाच्च ॥२॥

2. *And (this is so) on account of the indicatory mark.*

The indicatory sign also conveys the idea of repetition. Thus it is that after starting with the meditation on the *Udgītha*, the meditation on the *Udgītha* as the sun is decried as productive of a single son. Then in the sentence, "You meditate repeatedly on the *Udgītha* (separately) as the (sun and its) rays" (Ch. I. v. 11), the text prescribes (by the term *paryāvartaya*—meditate repeatedly) the meditation on the multiplicity of the rays for getting many sons. Thereby the text indicates that the repetition of the mental act is assumed as an established fact. Hence from a similarity of this it follows that repetition should be the rule in all cases of mental acts.

The *opponent* says here: Granted that the mental acts that are productive of results may well be repeated when some excellence can be produced in them through the repetition. But what purpose can be served by the repetition where a (single) mental act about the supreme Brahman calls up the supreme Brahman which is eternally pure, intelligent, and free by nature, and which is identical with one's own Self?

Objection: Repetition has to be undertaken, since the realization of the identity of Brahman and the Self does not reasonably result from a single hearing.

Opponent: No, since that will not logically follow even after repetition. If the hearing of such texts as "That thou art" (Ch. VI. viii. 7) once only does not generate the realization of the identity of Brahman and the Self, then how can it be expected that even a repetition of that will produce it? Again it may be argued that a mere sentence cannot produce the direct perception of anything, and hence that sentence, helped by reasoning, will produce the realization of the identity of Brahman and the

Self. But (even so), this reasoning also may well lead to a perception of its object after a single application.

(*Objection*) : It may also be argued that reasoning and the text can only produce a knowledge of the general features of the object, but not so of its special features. From such a declaration as, "I have a pain in the heart", and from such symptoms as the contortion of the body, another person can understand in a general way that there is a pain, but he cannot have a full experience of the pain like the suffering man. Since an intimate knowledge (of this nature) leads to the removal of ignorance, the repetition is needed for that purpose.

Opponent : This cannot be so, since the intimate knowledge cannot possibly arise even if that much is done repeatedly. For a special aspect that cannot be known from the scripture and reasoning at the first instance, cannot be known even after resorting to them a hundred times. So whether it be the intimate knowledge or the general knowledge that is produced by scripture and reasoning, it must be so at the very first application, so that repetition has no place. And there can be no such rule that nobody can have any intimate knowledge at the very first instant, since people who would know have divergent intelligence. Again with regard to a thing of this world, possessing common and peculiar features, there may be scope for repetition inasmuch as a man may understand only one feature at one attempt and others at subsequent attempts, as for instance in reading a long chapter. But it is not reasonable that there should be any need of repetition for comprehending Brahman which is absolute Consciousness without common and peculiar features.

To this we (*Vedāntins*) say: Repetition will be unnecessary for one who can realize the Self as Brahman after hearing "That thou art" once only. But for one who cannot do so, repetition is a necessity. Thus it is noticed in the Chāndogya Upaniṣad that Uddālaka teaches his son, "That thou art, O Śvetaketu" (Ch. VI. viii. 7), and then being requested by his son again and again, "O revered sir, explain to me again" (ibid.), he removes the respective causes of his (Śvetaketu's) misconceptions, and teaches that very fact "That thou art" repeatedly. That very process is referred to by citing the text, "It is to be heard of, reflected on, and meditated upon" (Bṛ. IV. v. 6).

Opponent: Was it not stated that if the text "That thou art", uttered once, cannot bring about a realization of its meaning, then it will not be able to do so even when repeated?

Vedāntin: That difficulty does not arise, for nothing is illogical about facts directly perceived. It is a matter of experience that though the meaning may be vaguely apprehended from a sentence uttered only once, people understand it fully after removing progressively the false ideas standing in the way, through a process of sustained consideration. Again, the text "That thou art" speaks of the identity of the entity denoted by "thou" with the entity denoted by "That". By the word "That" is denoted the Brahman under discussion that is Existence, the Witness, and the cause of the birth etc. of the universe as is well in evidence in such texts as, "Brahman is Truth, Knowledge, and Infinite" (Tai. II. i. 1), "Knowledge, Bliss, Brahman" (Bṛ. III. ix. 28), "This Immutable is never seen, but is the Witness, It is never known, but is the Knower" (Bṛ. III. viii. 11), "Without birth, decrepitude, death", "Neither gross nor minute, neither short nor long" (Bṛ. III. viii. 8), and so on. In these texts, changes like birth etc. that befall all things are denied by the words, "without birth" etc. and the properties of matter like grossness etc. are denied by the words "neither gross" etc. By the words "knowledge" etc. it is stated that Brahman is by nature Consciousness and Effulgence. This object called Brahman, which is denoted by the word "That", which is free from all mundane attributes, and which is by nature Consciousness, is well known to the people who are adepts in the Upaniṣads. Equally well it has been known by them that the inmost Self of the taught (i.e. disciple) is the meaning of the word "thou", which is the seer and the hearer, and which is thought of as the inmost entity inhabiting the sheaths starting from the gross body, and which is then ascertained as Consciousness Itself. That being the case, the sentence "That thou art" cannot produce a direct realization of its own meaning in those people to whom these two entities remain obstructed by ignorance, doubt, and confusion; for the meaning of a sentence is dependent on the meaning of the words (constituting it). Thus it is that for such people it becomes desirable to resort repeatedly to the scriptures and reasoning that lead to a clarification of the concepts. Although the Self to be realized is partless, still many constituents are superimposed on It, such as the body, sense-organs, mind, intellect, perception of objects, etc. That being so, one false constituent may be discarded at one attempt at comprehension, and another at another. In this sense the dawn of a conception in a progressive manner becomes justifiable. But even this is only the penultimate stage of the realization of the Self. Those of sharp intellect on the other hand who have no obstruction like ignorance, doubt, and confusion, with regard to the object to be known can realize the meaning of "That thou art" even from the first utterance, so that a repetition in their case is certainly useless. For the knowledge of the Self emerging once for all is able to remove ignorance, and no progressive development is admitted here.

Opponent: This may be proper if anybody can have this realization thus. As a matter of fact, however, the idea that one is subject to sorrowfulness etc. is strong, so that nobody can realize the absence of sorrowfulness etc.

Vedāntin: No, since the reasonable position is that the self-identification with misery etc. is as unreal as the self-identification with the body etc. For it is a matter of direct experience that when the body is cut or burned, one has such false identification as, "I am being cut", "I am being burnt". Similarly it is seen that when more external objects like sons and friends suffer, one superimposes this suffering on oneself by saying, "I am suffering". The self-identification with misery etc. must be similar, since like the body etc., miserableness etc. are perceived to be separate from consciousness. Besides, this does not persist in deep sleep etc., whereas consciousness is present even in sleep as stated in, "That It does not see in that state is because, although seeing then, It does not see" (Bṛ. IV. iii. 23). Hence the realization of the Self means the realization that "I am the Self which is one and is characterized as consciousness and freedom from all sorrow". A man who realizes the Self thus can have no other duty. Thus it is that the Upaniṣadic text shows the absence of any duty for a knower of the Self in, "What shall we achieve through children, we who have attained this Self, this result?" (Bṛ. IV. iv. 22). The Smṛti also says, "But the man who is devoted to the Self and is satisfied with the Self and content in the Self alone, has no obligatory duty" (Gītā, III. 17). But to one to whom this realization does not come promptly, this very repetition is meant for bringing about the realization. Even there, however, the teacher should not distract him from the understanding of the sentence "That thou art" in order to direct him to mere repetition; for nobody marries his daughter to a bridegroom for killing him. So long as a man acts under direction, he must have such ideas opposed to the ideas of Brahman as, "I am qualified for this, I am the agent of action, and I have to do this". For the man who is dull of intellect and discards the meaning of a sentence just because it is not obvious to him, it is admitted that his mind has to be fixed on the meaning of that sentence through the process of repetition etc. as stated (above). Hence even in the case of the knowledge of the supreme Brahman, a repetition of the instructions, leading to that knowledge, is necessary.

Topic 2: Identity of the Self with Brahman

आत्मेति तूपगच्छन्ति ग्राहयन्ति च ॥३॥

तु But (the Upaniṣads) उपगच्छन्ति acknowledge (Brahman) इति as आत्मा the Self च and ग्राहयन्ति make (others) understand (It as such).

3. But the Upaniṣads acknowledge Brahman as the Self and cause It to be so understood.

The aphorist discusses whether the supreme Self which is possessed of the characteristics as presented in the scriptures is to be realized as identical with oneself or different from oneself.

Opponent: When the word Self is heard of in the Upaniṣads as referring to the innermost Self, why should any such doubt arise?

Doubt: The answer is this: This word "Self" can be taken in its primary sense only if the Self and God be non-different; otherwise it has to be understood in a secondary sense. That is how the aphorist thinks. What should be the conclusion then?

Opponent: It is to be understood as different from 'I' (oneself). For the entity, possessed of such qualities as not being blemished by sin and so on, cannot be understood to be possessed of the opposite qualities; and the entity, possessed of the opposite qualities, cannot be understood to be possessed of the qualities of not being blemished by sin and so on. The entity, possessed of the attributes of being free from sin and so on, is the supreme Lord, while the entity, possessed of the opposite attributes, is the embodied soul. Now, if God becomes identical with the transmigrating soul, God will cease to exist; and as a result, the scriptures will become useless. Similarly if the transmigrating soul becomes God, there will be none to follow the scriptures, which will certainly become useless. This will also contradict such means of proof as common experience.

Objection: Even though there be difference, one has to resort to the idea of identity on the authority of the scriptures, just as one has to think of Viṣṇu in images etc.

Opponent: This may well be so if it pleases you; but then you must not lead us to admit that God is the Self of the transmigrating being in the primary sense.

To this we (*Vedāntins*) say that the supreme Lord is of course to be realized as one's Self. Thus it is that the Jābālas, while speaking of the supreme Lord, present Him as identical with the Self in, "O blessed Deity, I indeed am Thee, and Thou indeed art me, O Deity". Similarly also the other texts like "I am Brahman" (Bṛ. I. iv. 10) are to be understood as postulating the identity of the Self with Brahman. As a matter of fact, the Vedic texts make us understand God as our very Self, as for instance, "This is your Self that is within all" (Bṛ. III. iv. 1), "This is the internal Ruler, your own immortal Self" (Bṛ. III. vii. 3), "That is Truth, that is the Self, and That thou art" (Ch. VI. viii. 7).

As for the argument that on the analogy of an image being Viṣṇu, this is only a meditation with the help of an image (which in this case is "I"), that is improper, since that would amount to a figurative interpretation (of the texts about unity). It is also improper because the syntactical forms of the passages are different. Where the intention is that a symbol should have an idea superimposed on it, a sentence occurs only unilaterally, as for instance, "The mind is Brahman" (Ch. III. xviii. 1), "The sun is Brahman" (Ch. III. xix. 1). But here the Upaniṣad says, "I am Thee, and Thou art me". Hence identity is to be understood from this kind of texts that are dissimilar to those dealing with symbols. Moreover, the dualistic conception is condemned, as in, "While he who worships another God thinking, 'He is one, and I am another', does not know" (Bṛ. I. iv. 10), "He goes from death to death who sees difference as it were in It" (Bṛ. IV. iv. 19), "All ousts one who knows it as different from the Self" (Bṛ. IV. v. 7); and there are many other Upaniṣadic texts of this kind which denounce the dualistic conceptions.

It was argued that the two things of opposite characteristics cannot be identical with each other. That is nothing damaging as the reasonable position is that the opposition in characteristics is unreal.

And it is a false argument that God will cease to be so, because one has to accept scriptural authority and because such a position is not held by us. For we do not admit that the scriptures speak of God Himself as the transmigrating soul.

What do you admit then?

We hold that the scriptures aim at establishing the identity of the transmigrating soul with God Himself by removing from the soul all vestiges of transmigration. From this point of view it becomes affirmed that God is possessed of the characteristics of being untouched by sins etc., and that the opposite characteristics of the soul are unreal.

The criticism is also unfounded that no one will be left over to practise the Vedāntic path and that direct perception etc. will be outraged. For the transmigratory state is conceded before enlightenment, and the activities like perception are confined within that state only, because texts as this, "But when to the knower of Brahman everything has become the Self, then what should one see and through what?" (Bṛ. II. iv. 14), point out the absence of perception etc. in the state of enlightenment.

Opponent: In the absence of perception etc. the Vedas also will cease to exist.

Vedāntin: That is no defect, since that position is admitted by us. For according to the texts starting with, "In this state the father is no father" and ending with "The Vedas are no Vedas" (Bṛ. IV. iii. 22), we do admit the absence of the Vedas themselves in the state of enlightenment.

Opponent: Who is it then that has this unenlightenment?

Vedāntin: We say that it is you yourself who ask thus.

Opponent: Is it not stated by the Upaniṣad that I am God?

Vedāntin: If that is so, you are already an enlightened man, and so nobody has unenlightenment. Hereby is also refuted the criticism of some people who say that the Self becomes associated with a second entity owing to the very presence of nescience, so that non-dualism becomes untenable.[1] Hence one should fix one's mind on the Self which is God.

Topic 3: No Self-identity with Symbols

Doubt: Some meditations based on symbols are presented thus: "One should meditate about the mind as Brahman. This is on the corporeal plane. Then is the meditation on the material plane. One should meditate about space as Brahman" (Ch. III. xviii. 1); similarly, "The sun is Brahman. This is the instruction" (Ch. III. xix. 1), "He who meditates about name as Brahman" (Ch. VII. i. 5). With regard to these meditations with the help of symbols the doubt arises whether self-identification should be resorted to or not even in these cases. What should be the solution here?

Opponent: It is logical that one should identify oneself with those symbols as well (thinking thus: "I am the symbol which is Brahman").

Why?

Because Brahman is familiar in the Upaniṣads as the Self and

[1] Nescience is indeterminate and hence ceases to exist on the rise of enlightenment.

the symbols also are forms of Brahman. Since these symbols are modifications of Brahman and are hence Brahman Itself, therefore it is but reasonable that they should be the Self (of all).

To this we (the *Vedāntins*) say:

न प्रतीके न हि सः ॥४॥

न Not (self-identification) प्रतीके in the symbol हि because सः he (the aspirant) न (does) not (comprehend thus).

4. *(The aspirant is) not to identify (himself) with a symbol, for he cannot understand himself to be so.*

One should not fix the idea of the Self on symbols, because an aspirant cannot think of the separate symbols as himself. The reasoning is hollow that the symbols being forms of Brahman are Brahman Itself, and hence are the same as the Self; for that would lead to the brushing away of all symbols. For it is only when the names etc. are deprived of their transformed states (as names etc.), that one arrives at Brahman which is their essence. But when names etc. as such are done away with, how can they become symbols and how can there be any self-identification? It cannot also be argued that since Brahman is the Self, we can have a meditation involving self-identification wherever an injunction about contemplation on Brahman occurs; for (in meditation) the idea of agentship still remains intact. Brahman is taught to be identical with the individual Self after eliminating all mundane characteristics like agentship etc. from the latter, whereas meditation is prescribed without eliminating these. From this fact also that the aspirant and the symbols are equally limited entities, self-identity (with symbols) is not a possibility; for a *rucaka* and a *svastika*, (which are both different kinds of gold ornaments), cannot be identical. But should the aspirant and the symbols be the same from the point of view of their Brahmanhood, just as much as the two ornaments are from the standpoint of being gold, then we have already showed the difficulty that the symbols will cease to exist (as such). Hence one is not to identify oneself with a symbol.

Topic 4: Superimposition of the Higher on the Lower

With regard to those very instances another *doubt* arises. Should the ideas of the sun etc. be superimposed on Brahman or should the idea of Brahman be superimposed on the sun etc.?

Why should the doubt arise?

Because no reason is discernible for these being placed in apposition (with the same case-endings). Here we find the word Brahman placed in apposition with the words sun etc., the same case-endings being used in the texts, "*Āditye brahma*", "*Prāṇo brahma*", "*Vidyud brahma*", and so on. But this apposition does not quite fit in here on account of the divergent meanings of the words *āditya* (sun), *brahma* (Brahman), etc. For there can be no such apposition (between a cow and a horse) as would be implied in "The cow is horse (i.e. the cow that is a horse)".

Objection: Just as clay and a plate (made of clay) can be placed in apposition (the latter being a modification of the former), so also can be placed Brahman and the sun etc., they being related as the material cause and its modifications.

Doubt: The answer is that it cannot be so, since from such an apposition (meaning identity) with the material cause, the modified thing will lose its individuality, and that will lead to an elimination of symbols, as already pointed out. Moreover, in that case, this will amount to a mere statement about the supreme Self, so that the scope for meditation will be effaced, and the mention in the Upaniṣad of a limited (i.e. selected) number of modifications (of Brahman) will be meaningless. Hence it is a case of superimposing the idea of one thing on another, as in sentences like "The Brāhmaṇa is the Vaiśvānara fire". That being so, the doubt arises as to what is to be looked upon as what.

Opponent: Such being the case, there can be no definite decision, because no scriptural text is in evidence to help a decision. This is how it has to be accepted. Or we can rather decide that the very ideas of the sun etc. are to be superimposed on Brahman; for it is thus that Brahman becomes adored (i.e. meditated upon) by being looked upon as the sun and the rest; and the conclusion of the scripture is that the worship of Brahman is productive of fruits. Hence the sun and the rest are not to be looked upon as Brahman (but rather Brahman is to be looked upon as these).

Vedāntin: This being the conclusion, we say:

ब्रह्मदृष्टिरुत्कर्षात् ।।५।।

(The sun etc. are to have) ब्रह्म-दृष्टिः the idea of Brahman superimposed (on them) उत्कर्षात् because of the (consequent) exaltation.

5. *The sun etc. are to be looked upon as Brahman because of the consequent exaltation.*

The idea of Brahman Itself is to be superimposed on the sun and the rest.

Why?

On account of the exaltation; for thus the sun and the other things will come to be looked upon as raised in status, because of the superimposition on them of an exalted idea. Thus also will be honoured the custom in ordinary life, according to which the inferior one is to be fancied as the higher, as is evident in honouring a king's charioteer as the king himself. For it will not lead to any good result if the king be lowered in estimation by being looked upon as the charioteer. That should be the method of approach here as well, for a contrary approach will lead to evil.

Opponent: No possibility of evil should be apprehended here since there is the sanction of the scripture; and the scriptural views are not to be regulated by common norms.

Vedāntin: To this the answer is that this would be so in a case where the meaning can be ascertained; but when the meaning of the scripture is in doubt, it is nothing unbecoming to take the help of the canons of ordinary life for arriving at a decision. If in accordance with this the scripture is ascertained to mean the superimposition of the exalted status, it is but obvious that one will merely court evil by superimposing the idea of the lower on the higher. Now, because the words sun (*āditya*) etc. occur first, their primary meanings have to be accepted, for that creates no difficulty. And while the intellect remains occupied with these words in their primary senses, the word Brahman makes its appearance in these sentences at a later stage. But since the word Brahman, in its primary sense, cannot stand in apposition with the sun etc., the only remaining conclusion that stands affirmed is that the intention here is to prescribe the superimposition of the idea of Brahman. Besides, from the use of the word *iti* (meaning "as") after Brahman (in *ādityam brahma iti upāsīta*), this very meaning becomes appropriate. Thus it is that the Upaniṣad everywhere uses the word Brahman with an *iti* after it in such sentences as, "*Brahma iti ādeśaḥ*", "*Brahma iti upāśita*", "*Brahma iti upāste*"[2], and so on, while the words *āditya* (sun) etc. are used by themselves. From this it follows that as in the sentence "*Śuktikāṁ rajatam iti pratyeti*—He perceives the nacre as silver", the word *śuktikā* (nacre) denotes the nacre itself, while the word *rajata* (silver) denotes an appearance of silver by a figure of speech, meaning thereby that the man has merely a cognition of silver, though in fact there is no silver, so in the present case we understand that one has to look upon the sun etc. as Brahman. Again by using the accusative case (after *āditya* etc.) in the complementary portion, the Upaniṣad shows that the sun etc. are the objects of the verb "to meditate", as in: "He who having known thus meditates about the sun as Brahman—*sa ya evaṁ vidvān ādityaṁ brahma iti upāste*" (Ch. III. xix. 4), "He who meditates about the organ of speech as Brahman—*yo vācaṁ brahma iti upāste*" (Ch. VII. ii. 2), "He who meditates about resolve as Brahman—*yaḥ saṅkalpaṁ brahma iti upāste*" (Ch. VII. iv. 3).

As for the assertion that the meditation on Brahman Itself is to be preferred here for the sake of acquiring the result, that is untenable, since according to the above reasoning, the sun etc. are themselves known as the objects of meditation. But the result will of course be ordained by Brahman in these cases just as much as in the cases of the service to the guests and so on, for Brahman is the ordainer of everything. This fact was elaborated

[2] "The instruction is, 'It is as Brahman'", "It should be meditated on as Brahman", "He who meditates as Brahman".

under the aphorism, "From Him are the fruits of action, since that is reasonable" (III. ii. 38). The very fact that the idea of Brahman is superimposed on the symbols is a worship of Brahman, just as much as the imagination of the images as Viṣṇu and others is the worship of those deities.

Topic 5: Subordinate Parts of Rites as the Sun etc.

Doubt: Certain meditations occur in connection with the auxiliaries of rites as found in such texts as, "Meditate on the sun, that shines yonder, as *Udgītha*" (Ch. I. iii. 1), "Meditate on the worlds as the fivefold *Sāma*" (Ch. II. ii. 1), "Meditate on speech as the sevenfold *Sāma*" (Ch. II. viii. 1), "This (earth) indeed is *Ṛk*, fire is *Sāma*" (Ch. I vi. 1), and others. With regard to these the doubt arises as to whether the ideas of *Udgītha* etc. are to be superimposed on the sun etc. or the *Udgītha* etc. are to be viewed as the sun etc.

Opponent: The conclusion to be arrived at here is that either of the two things can be done indiscriminately, since nothing occurs there to decide in favour of either of them. No one is understood here as having any special exaltation like Brahman. It is possible to understand that Brahman is more glorified than the sun etc., It being the origin of the whole universe and possessed of the attributes of being free from sin etc. But since the sun, the *Udgītha*, and other things are all equally the modifications of Brahman, nothing can be understood (in those contexts) as elevating any one of them above the rest.

Or it may be that the ideas of the *Udgītha* etc. are ever to be superimposed on the sun etc.

Why?

Because *Udgītha* etc. constitute the rites, and because the rites are well known as meant for yielding results. The sun etc., when meditated on by viewing them as the *Udgītha* etc. will become part and parcel of the rites and will thus produce their results (as a part of the results of the rites themselves). Thus it is that in the text starting with, "This (earth) indeed is *Ṛk*, fire is *Sāma*" (Ch. I. vi. 1), the earth is alluded to by the word *Ṛk*, and fire by the word *Sāma* in, "That *Sāma* is established on this *Ṛk*" (ibid). This becomes consistent if the earth and fire are sought to be looked upon as *Ṛk* and *Sāma*, but not so if *Ṛk* and *Sāma* are intended to be viewed as the earth and fire (respectively). The word king comes to bear a figurative sense when it is applied to his charioteer, but the word charioteer is not thus applied to the king. Moreover, from the sentence, "Meditate on the fivefold *Sāma* (as existing) among the worlds (*lokeṣu*)" (Ch. II. ii. 1), it is obvious that the *Sāma* is to be superimposed on the worlds as they are pointed out to be the locus (by the use of the locative case-ending—in *lokeṣu*—after worlds). The text, "This *Gāyatrī Sāma* is established among the *prāṇas*" (Ch. II. xi. 1) only confirms this view. In such sentences as, "The sun is Brahman—this is the instruction" (Ch. III. xix. 1), the idea of Brahman, coming later, is superimposed on the sun etc. occurring earlier. And in such Upaniṣadic texts as, "The earth is *hiṅkāra*" (Ch. II. ii. 1), the earth etc. occur earlier, while *hiṅkāra* etc. occur later. Hence the ideas of the auxiliaries of the rites are to be superimposed on the sun etc. which are non-auxiliaries.

Vedāntin: To this we reply:

आदित्यादिमतयश्चाङ्ग उपपत्तेः ॥६॥

च And आदित्य-आदि-मतयः the ideas of the sun etc. (are to be superimposed) अङ्गे on the subsidiary part (of rite) उपपत्तेः for that is reasonable.

6. And the ideas of the sun etc. are surely to be superimposed on the subsidiary parts of the rites, for that is reasonably maintainable.

The ideas of the sun etc. are of course to be superimposed on such subsidiaries as *Udgītha* etc.

Why?

On account of reasonableness. For it is but reasonable that when *Udgītha* etc. become sanctified by being looked upon as the sun etc., the rites become more fruitful. This is owing to the proximity of (parts like) *Udgītha*[3] to the unseen poten-

[3] *Udgītha*, sanctified by being looked upon as the sun, leads to a better result, but the sun, looked upon as the former cannot do so; the sun is not a part of the rite.

tial results of the rites. The text, "Whatever is done with knowledge, faith, and meditation becomes more fruitful" (Ch. I. i. 10) shows that knowledge leads to an enhancement of the potency of the rites.

Opponent: This may be so in the cases of those meditations which are calculated to enhance the efficiency of the rites. But what about those meditations that have independent results as mentioned in the texts beginning with, "He who having known this thus, meditates about the worlds as the fivefold *Sāma*" (Ch. II. ii. 3), and others?

Vedāntin: Since these meditations are to be undertaken by those who are already qualified for the relevant rites, it is proper on the analogy of the milking pot[4] to assume even in their case that the result emerges in association with the result of the rite in question. And the sun etc., standing for the results of the rites, are logically more elevated than the *Udgītha* etc. constituting the rites; for the Upaniṣads mention the world of the sun and such other worlds as the results of rites. Besides, the *Udgītha* itself is presented as the thing to be meditated on in the texts, "Meditate on *Udgītha* as the letter *Om*" (Ch. I. i. 1), "Up to this is explained the glory of the letter *Om*" (Ch. I. i. 10). After presenting it thus as the entity to be meditated on, it is enjoined that it should be viewed as the sun etc.

The argument was advanced that when the sun etc. are meditated upon with the ideas of the *Udgītha* etc. superimposed on them, they will become constituents of an act and will thus produce results. That is untenable, because the meditation itself is an act and can reasonably produce a result. Moreover, the *Udgītha* and the rest do not cease to be the auxiliaries of rites even when viewed as the sun and other things. In the portion of the text, "On this *Ṛk* is established this *Sāma*"[5] (Ch. I. vi. 1),

[4] A sacrificer who wants cattle should bring the water in a milking pot when he is already engaged in some specific sacrifice. This getting of cattle is not an independent result, nor the bringing of water an independent act. The act produces its result in association with the result of the main sacrifice. So also here.

[5] The whole passage is: "This (earth) itself is *Ṛk*, fire is *Sāma*; thus on this *Ṛk* is established *Sāma*; therefore they sing the *Sāma* as established on *Ṛk*" (Ch. I. vi. 1).

it is only in a figurative sense that the earth and fire are called *Ṛk* and *Sāma*. In a figurative use a word conveys some sense varying as far as possible between the senses proximate to and remote from its primary sense. Now in that passage ("This indeed is *Ṛk*, fire is *Sāma*" etc.), although the intention is that the *Ṛk* and *Sāma* should be viewed as the earth and fire, still it is definitely understood that (in the portion "On this *Ṛk* is established this *Sāma*") the words *Ṛk* and *Sāma* are used to imply the earth and fire themselves because these latter are connected with *Ṛk* and *Sāma*. This is so understood because the well-known *Ṛk* and *Sāma* are spoken of separately (in "Therefore they sing the *Sāma* as established on *Ṛk*", so that if *Ṛk* and *Sāma* be meant in the earlier portion "On this *Ṛk* is established this *Sāma*", it will involve a repetition), and because the earth and fire occur in their proximity (in the still earlier first portion "This (earth) indeed is *Ṛk*, fire is *Sāma*"). Even the word charioteer cannot be prevented from denoting the king figuratively when by some reason it can come near enough to the king (as for instance, when the king himself drives the chariot). Moreover, the sentence, "This (earth) itself is *Ṛk—iyam eva ṛk*" (Ch. I. vi. 1) indicates from its very construction that the *Ṛk* is to be looked upon as the earth; for if the earth were to be looked upon as the *Ṛk*, the form of the sentence would have been, "*iyam ṛk eva*—the *Ṛk*, itself is this". Besides, the text, "He who having known thus sings *Sāma*" (Ch. I. vii. 7), only concludes a meditation based on an auxiliary, and not one based on the earth. Similarly in the text, "Meditate on the fivefold *Sāma* (as existing) among the words" (Ch. II. ii. 1), though the word world is used in the locative case (*lokeṣu*), still the worlds are to be superimposed on the *Sāma*, since the word *Sāma* is used in the accusative case, thereby indicating that it is the object of meditation. For *Sāma* becomes meditated on as the worlds when the worlds are superimposed on it, while a reversal of this leads to the worlds becoming meditated on as *Sāma*.[6] Hereby (i.e. on the ground that one case-ending alone is to be changed)

[6] The opponent's explanation involves a change in the case-ending of both; ours involves a single change (in *lokeṣu*, but not in *sāma*).

is also explained the text, "This *Gāyatra Sāma* is fixed on the *prāṇas*" (Ch. II. xi. 1), (where *Gāyatra* has the nominative case and *prāṇa* the locative). Where two words are used equally in the accusative case, as in "*Atha khalu amum ādityaṁ saptavidhaṁ sāma upāsīta*—Then meditate on this sevenfold *Sāma* as the sun" (Ch. II. ix. 1), even there the sun is to be superimposed on the *Sāma*, since the topic that is started with is the meditation on *Sāma*, as is evident from, "It is good indeed to meditate on the *Sāma* as a whole" (Ch. II. i. 1), "Here ends the meditation on the fivefold *Sāma*, then starts that on the sevenfold *Sāma*" (Ch. II. viii. 1). And since it is gathered from this very text that the *Sāma* is to be meditated on, the idea of the earth etc. are to be superimposed on *hiṅkāra* etc. even when the construction of the sentence is different, as in "*pṛthivi hiṅkāraḥ*—the earth is *hiṅkāra*" (Ch. II. ii. 1). Hence the conclusion is that the ideas of the sun etc., which are not the auxiliaries of rites, are to be superimposed on the *Udgītha* etc. which are the auxiliaries of rites.

Topic 6: Meditation in a Sitting Posture

आसीनः सम्भवात् ॥७॥

(Mental adoration is to be pursued) आसीनः while in a sitting posture सम्भवात् since (it is) possible (in that way only).

7. *One should adore mentally while having a sitting posture, since it is possible in that way alone.*

The consideration about the requisite posture etc. does not arise with regard to the mental adoration or meditation (*upāsanā*) connected with the auxiliaries of rites, since that is regulated by the rites themselves. Again, this question does not crop up in a context of full enlightenment because knowledge is determined by the reality itself. But with regard to other kinds of *upāsanā* one has to consider whether one should meditate in a sitting, standing, or lying posture just as one likes, or always in a sitting posture.

Opponent: Now since an *upāsanā* is a mental act, the conclusion is that there can be no rule about posture.

Vedāntin: Hence the aphorist says that one should adore (mentally) in a sitting posture alone.

Why?

Since it is possible in that way alone. *Upāsanā* consists in setting up a current of similar thoughts; and that is not possible for one while walking or running, because movement etc. disturb the mind. Even for a standing man, the mind remains busy about keeping the body erect, so that it is not able then to look into subtle things. A man lying on the ground may suddenly fall asleep. But for a sitting man, innumerable troubles of this kind are easy to avoid, so that *upāsanā* becomes possible for him.

ध्यानाच्च ॥८॥

8. And because of (the possibility of) concentration (in that way).

Moreover, the meaning of the term concentration is this, namely the setting up of a continuous stream of similar thoughts. The verb "to concentrate" is applied figuratively to one having his limbs relaxed, gaze fixed, and mind concentrated on a single object, as in such sentences as, "The heron has its mind concentrated", "The woman who has her lover in exile has her mind fixed (on him)". This proceeds easily for one in a sitting posture. Hence also *upāsanā* is to be undertaken by one when seated.

अचलत्वं चापेक्ष्य ॥९॥

च And अपेक्ष्य from the standpoint of अचलत्वम् motionlessness.

9. And (meditativeness is attributed) from the standpoint of motionlessness.

Furthermore, in such sentences as, "The earth is in meditation as it were" (Ch. VII. vi. 1), the assertion of meditation in the cases of the earth etc. is made from the standpoint of motionlessness alone. That also is a sign that *upāsanā* is to be undertaken by a man when seated.

स्मरन्ति च ॥१०॥

10. Moreover, they mention (this) in the Smṛtis.

Moreover, the worthy people mention this in such Smṛti passages as "Having established his seat firmly in a clean place" (Gītā, VI. 11). It is because of this that the sitting postures like *padmāsana* (lotus-seat) are prescribed in the books on Yoga.

Topic 7: No Restriction of Place

यत्रैकाग्रता तत्राविशेषात् ॥११॥

यत्र Wherever एकाग्रता concentration (is possible) तत्र there (one should meditate) अविशेषात् because of the absence of specification.

11. Meditation is to be undertaken wherever the mind gets concentrated, because there is no specification.

The *doubt* arises about the direction, place, and time, as to whether there is any regulation about them or not. Now somebody may think that since in the Vedic rites the directions etc. are noticed to be well determined, the case must be similar here as well.

The answer (of the *Vedāntin*) to such a one is being given. The regulation about direction, place, and time is concerned only with that much regarding them as conduces to meditativeness. One should meditate facing any direction, in any place, at any time that leads to one's concentration of mind easily. Unlike the regulations fixing the eastern direction, forenoon, and a place sloping down to the east, and so on, as met with in the cases of rites, no such specific regulation is mentioned in the Upaniṣads; while the one thing desirable is that one should always have concentration of mind (while engaged in *upāsanā*).

Opponent : Some Upaniṣads prescribe even specific rules as in, "One should concentrate one's mind on the supreme Self by taking shelter in a windless cave or such other places as are level and clean, free from pebbles, fire, and sand, free from noise, remote from busy places like water ponds or public sheds, and at the same time pleasing to the mind but not oppressive to the eyes" (Śv. II. 10).

Vedāntin: True, there are directions like that. But taking for granted these directions, the aphorist advises like a friend that with regard to the details of these matters there is no hard and fast rule. And the phrase "pleasing to the mind" in the above quotation only shows that the place can be anywhere that is conducive to concentration.

Topic 8: Meditation till Death

Doubt: Under the first topic it was established that repetition is to be welcomed in all cases of contemplation. Among them, those contemplations that are meant for complete enlightenment can well be understood to have a limit to their repetition, inasmuch as they end with the object aimed at, as is seen in the process of husking paddy (which stops with producing rice). When the result, consisting in full enlightenment, is achieved, no other effort can be prescribed, since a man goes beyond the domain of scripture when he realizes the oneness of the Self with Brahman. But with regard to those meditations which have in view some fruit of the nature of secular prosperity this doubt arises: Should one stop after revolving the idea in one's mind for a certain time, or should one do so for life? What would be the conclusion then?

Opponent: One should give up the meditation after revolving the idea in one's mind for a certain time, since thereby is fulfilled the requirement of the texts enjoining the practice of repeated meditation.

Vedāntin: This being the position, we say:

आप्रायणात्तत्रापि हि दृष्टम् ॥१२॥

आ-प्रायणात् Up till the moment of death हि for तत्र अपि even then दृष्टम् it is seen (to happen in the scripture).

12. *(Meditation is to be repeated) up till the moment of death, for it is noticed in the scriptures that it is done so even then.*

One shall contemplate on the idea repeatedly till the moment of death, because the acquisition of the unseen potential result of action is dependent on the final contemplation on the idea. For even the fruits of past actions which are destined to produce a result enjoyable in a subsequent birth, arouse at the time of death a pattern of consciousness replete with the thoughts conforming to that, as is known from such Upaniṣadic texts as, "Then the soul has consciousness of the fruits in the form of impressions that it has to experience, and it goes to the next body which is the fruit associated with that consciousness" (Bṛ. IV. iv. 2), "Together with whatever world (i.e. result of action) he had in mind (at the time of death) he enters into *Prāṇa*. *Prāṇa* in combination with *Udāna* and in association with the soul leads him to the world desired by him" (Pr. III. 10). This is so also because of the illustration of grass and a leech (Bṛ. IV. iv. 3). What other pattern of consciousness can these ideas have at the time of death apart from their repetition just as they are? Hence those ideas are to be revolved in the mind till death, which are nothing but a contemplation of that very result which is to be achieved. Thus it is that a Vedic text shows the repetition of the idea at the time of death: "The resolves with which that man departs from this world" (Ś. B. X. vi. 3.1). To this effect occurs the Smṛti passage also: "Remembering whatever object at the end he leaves the body, that alone is reached by him, O son of Kuntī, because of his constant thought of that" (Gītā, VIII. 6), "at the time of death, with the mind unmoving" (Gītā, VIII. 10). And "He shall think of these three at the time of death" (Ch. III. xvii. 6) shows the last duty that remains to be done at the time of death.

Topic 9: Knowledge Destroys all Results of Actions

The topics left over from the Third Chapter are ended. Now arises some consideration regarding the result of the knowledge of Brahman.

The *doubt* crops up as to whether after the acquisition of the knowledge of Brahman, its opposite result, viz sin, is removed or not. What would be the conclusion?

Opponent: Since work is done for some result, it cannot be obliterated without producing its result; for from the Vedas it is gathered that action has the innate power of ensuring its result. If the work should be destroyed even before its fruit is experienced, the Vedas will lose their validity. In the Smṛti also we have, "For the results of work are not destroyed".

Objection: In that case the prescription of expiation becomes useless.

Opponent: That is no defect, because acts of expiation are to be classed with occasional rites[7] like the sacrifice occasioned by one's house being burnt. Moreover, as the acts of expiation are prescribed as a consequence of the commission of some guilt, that may as well conduce to the removal of that guilt. But the knowledge of Brahman is not prescribed in that way.

Objection: Unless it is admitted that the results of past actions are washed away for the knower of Brahman, he will have to experience the results of those actions as a matter of course, so that there will be no liberation.

Opponent: The answer is in the negative, for just like the results of actions, liberation comes out of an adequate combination of place, time, and causation. Hence a man is not absolved of his sins by acquiring the knowledge of Brahman.

Vedāntin: To this we reply:

तदधिगम उत्तरपूर्वाघयोरश्लेषविनाशौ तद्व्यपदेशात् ॥१३॥

तत्-अधिगमे On the realization of that (Brahman), (there occur) अश्लेष-विनाशौ non-attachment and destruction (respectively) उत्तर-पूर्व-अघयोः of the succeeding and earlier sins तत्-व्यपदेशात् because it is declared so.

13. On the realization of That, there occur the non-attachment and destruction of the subsequent and previous sins respectively, because it is declared so.

When That, viz Brahman, becomes realized, then come the non-attachment of subsequent sins and the destruction of the earlier ones.

Why?

[7] So an expiation does not absolve a man of his sins.

"Because it is so declared" (in the scriptures). Thus it is declared in the course of dealing with the knowledge of Brahman that a future sin that might be expected to arise in the usual way does not arise in the case of a man of knowledge: "As water does not stick to a lotus leaf, even so sin does not contaminate a man possessed of this knowledge" (Ch. IV. xiv. 3). So also the destruction of the past accumulated sins is declared in, "Just as the fluffy tip of a reed placed in fire burns away completely, similarly all his sins are burnt away" (V. xxiv. 3). Here occurs another declaration about the destruction of the results of work: "When the Self which is both high and low is realized, the knot of the heart gets untied, all doubts become solved, and all one's actions become dissipated" (Mu. II. ii. 8).

It was argued that on the assumption that the results of works get destroyed even before being experienced, the purport of the scripture will be distorted. But that creates no difficulty; for we do not mean to deny the power of works to produce their results. That remains just as it is. But we assert that this power is arrested by other factors like knowledge etc. The scripture is committed to the existence of the power of work, but not to the existence or non-existence of opposing factors. Besides, the Smṛti texts, "For the results of work are not destroyed", is only a general rule; for the potential result of work does not get destroyed except through experience, inasmuch as it is meant for that. As a matter of fact it is desired that sin should be dissipated by expiation etc. as it is stated in such Vedic and Smṛti texts as, "He gets over all sins", "A performer of the *Aśvamedha* sacrifice, as also a man possessed of this knowledge, gets over the sin of killing a Brāhmaṇa" (Tai. Ā. V. iii. 12.1).

And it was said that the expiatory rites are to be classed with the occasional rites (occasioned by certain circumstances; and hence that they cannot wash away the sins). But that is wrong. Since the expiatory rites are prescribed in connection with certain commissions, they may well have the destruction of the resulting sins as their effect; and hence it is improper to infer some unseen potency for them (as in the case of occasional rites). Again, it was argued that unlike expiatory rites, knowledge is not enjoined for dissipating sins. With regards to this we say: In the case of meditations on the qualified Brahman, such injunctions are surely in evidence. And in the complementary portion of these it is stated that the meditator gets superhuman powers and cessation of sin as his reward. Since there is nothing to show that these two results are not intended to be indicated, it can be ascertained that those meditations lead to the acquisition of divine powers after the eradication of sins. But as regards contemplation on the absolute Brahman, though there be no such prescription, still it can be concluded that the burning away of the results of past *karma* is the effect of the realization that the Self is free from all actions.

By the term non-attachment the aphorist implies that the knower of Brahman has no idea of agentship whatsoever with regard to the actions occurring in future. Although the man of knowledge appeared to have some ownership of the past works on account of false ignorance, still owing to the cessation of false ignorance through the power of knowledge, those works also are washed away. This fact is stated by the term destruction. The knower of Brahman has this realization: "As opposed to the entity known before as possessed of agentship and experiencership by its very nature, I am Brahman which is by nature devoid of agentship and experiencership in all the three periods of time. Even earlier I was never an agent and experiencer, nor am I so at present, nor shall I be so in future." From such a point of view alone can liberation be justified. For on a contrary supposition—if the results of works flowing down from eternity continue unhampered in their course—there can be no liberation. Besides, liberation, unlike the results of work, cannot be produced by a concurrence of place, time, and causation, since that would make it impermanent. It is also unreasonable that the result of knowledge (which is really immediate) should be mediate (as the *opponents*' theory implies). Hence the conclusion is that sin becomes dissipated when Brahman is known.

TOPIC 10: NO REMNANT OF VIRTUE EVEN

Under the previous topic it was ascertained on the authority of the scriptures that when knowledge dawns, it causes the non-attachment and destruction of all potential results of works that are naturally calculated to cause bondage. But a doubt may arise that the virtuous deeds do not come into conflict with the knowledge arising from the scriptures, since they also originate from the same source. Taking this doubt into consideration, the reasoning of the previous topic is being extended here with a view to dispelling it.

इतरस्याप्येवमसंश्लेषः पाते तु ॥१४॥

इतरस्य Of the other (i.e. of virtue) अपि also एवम् in this way असंश्लेषः there is no contact; तु surely (liberation comes) पाते when (the body) falls.

14. In the very same way there is no attachment of the other (i.e. of virtue) as well. Liberation must follow as soon as the body falls.

To the man of knowledge occur the non-attachment and destruction "of the other as well", of virtue also, as of sin itself.

Why?

Since that may put obstacles in the path of the fruition of knowledge; for that (virtue) too is productive of its own result. In the Upaniṣadic texts like, "He conquers both of them" (Bṛ. IV. iv. 22), the destruction of virtue, just as much as of vice, is declared, since the destruction of action consequent on the realization of the Self that is not an agent occurs equally in the cases of both virtuous and vicious acts, and since the Upaniṣad speaks of the destruction of all works without any exception in "and all one's actions become dissipated" (Mu. II. ii. 8). Even where the single word vice is used, the word virtue is also to be understood, because its result is inferior to that of knowledge. Moreover, in the Upaniṣad itself occurs the word vice to convey the idea of virtue as well. Thus in the sentence, "Day and night cannot reach this barrage (which is the Self)" (Ch. VIII. iv. 1), virtue is introduced along with vice; then it is said, "All sins desist from It (the Self)" (ibid.),[8] thereby using the word

[8] The full text is, "Now then, that which is the Self is a barrage that holds apart, so that the worlds may not get mixed up. Day and night

sin (vice) to indicate virtue as well without any distinction. In "*pāte tu*", the word *tu* (lit. but) is used to imply emphasis. The text emphasizes the fact that since virtue and vice, causing bondage, are thus shown to become separated and destroyed by the power of knowledge, liberation must come to the man of enlightenment when his body falls.

Topic 11: Past Accumulated Results are Destroyed

Under the previous topic it was ascertained that virtue and vice are destroyed by knowledge. Now it is being discussed whether that destruction occurs indiscriminately with regard to all the virtues and vices that have begun or have not begun to yield their fruits, or they occur specifically with regard to those virtues and vices that have not begun to yield fruits. Now since in the Upaniṣadic texts like "He conquers both of them" (Bṛ. IV. iv. 22), no specification is met with, the destruction may occur indiscriminately to all. That being the possibility, the aphorist refutes by saying.

अनारब्धकार्ये एव तु पूर्वे तदवधेः ॥१५॥

तु But पूर्वे (the) past (two) अनारब्ध-कार्ये which have not begun to produce results एव alone (are destroyed) तत्-अवधेः for that (death) is set as the limit of waiting for that liberation.

15. But only those past (virtues and vices) get destroyed which have not begun to bear fruit, for death is set as the limit of waiting for liberation.

After the acquisition of knowledge, those virtues and vices that have not begun to yield their fruits and that were accumulated in earlier lives or even in this life before the dawn of knowledge are alone destroyed, but not so are those destroyed whose results have already been partially enjoyed and by which has been begun this present life in which the knowledge of Brahman arises.

cannot reach this barrage, nor old age and death and sorrow, nor virtue and vice. All sins desist from It, since this is the world of Brahman unafflicted by sin."

How is this known?

Because the text, "He lingers so long only as he is not freed from the body; then he becomes free" (Ch. VI. xiv. 2), shows that liberation is put off till the death of the body. Were it not so, the text would not have spoken of any waiting till the death of the body. For one would then attain liberation immediately after the acquisition of knowledge inasmuch as there would be no reason for his continuing in the body after all the works are annihilated by knowledge.

Opponent: If this realization that the Self is not an agent annihilates all results of work by its own intrinsic power, how can it demolish only some leaving behind others? For when the same kind of contact is present between fire and some seeds, it cannot be held that some of the seeds will lose their power of germination while others will not.

Vedāntin: The answer is: It cannot be that knowledge can arise without the help of some residual results of actions that have begun to bear fruit. And when it is granted that knowledge is based on that medium (viz the body produced by the residual results), it is but natural that knowledge has to wait (for its result) till the acquired momentum of that medium exhausts itself out as in the case of a wheel of a potter; for there is nothing to stop it in the intervening period. As for the knowledge of the Self as the non-performer of any act, that destroys the results of works by first sublating false ignorance. This false ignorance, even when sublated, continues for a while owing to past tendencies like the continuance of the vision of two moons.[9] Furthermore, no difference of opinion is possible here as to whether the body is retained (after knowledge) for some time or not by the knowers of Brahman. For when somebody feels in his heart that he has realized Brahman and yet holds the body, how can this be denied by somebody else? This very fact is elaborated in the Upaniṣads and the Smṛtis in the course of determining the characteristics of "the man of steady wisdom" (*sthitaprajña*—Gītā, II. 54). Hence the conclusion is that only

[9] For a man who had suffered from eye-disease, the false idea may persist for some time even after the defect is removed.

those virtues and vices are washed away by knowledge which have not begun to bear fruit.

Topic 12: Agnihotra etc.

अग्निहोत्रादि तु तत्कार्यायैव तद्दर्शनात् ॥१६॥

तु But अग्निहोत्र-आदि *Agnihotra* etc. तत्-कार्याय are conducive to that result एव surely तत्-दर्शनात् for so it is revealed.

16. But Agnihotra etc. conduce to the very same result, for so it is revealed (in the Upaniṣads).

The conclusion arrived at about the non-attachment and destruction of sin in the case of the man of knowledge was extended to the non-attachment and destruction of virtue as well. Lest it be inferred that this extension covers all kinds of virtue, it is being refuted by the aphorism, "But (daily) *Agnihotra* etc". The word "but" refutes the misconception. The obligatory daily duties like *Agnihotra*, enjoined in the Vedas, are meant for that very result. The idea is that their result is the same as that of knowledge.

How can this be so?

From such Upaniṣadic texts as, "The Brāhmaṇas seek to know It through the study of the Vedas, sacrifices, charity, and austerity" (Bṛ. IV. iv. 22).

Opponent: Since knowledge and works produce divergent results, they cannot reasonably have the same result.

Vedāntin: That creates no difficulty; for just as curds and poison, known to produce fever and death respectively, become tasteful and nourishing when mixed with sugar and *mantra*, similarly (religious) work also, when associated with knowledge, may lead to liberation.

Opponent: Since liberation has no beginning, how can it be said to be an effect of work?

Vedāntin: That objection is hollow, since work helps from a distance (i.e. indirectly) in producing the result. As work leads gradually to knowledge, it is said by courtesy to lead to liberation itself. Accordingly, the statement that knowledge and work produce the same result refers to the work that had preceded knowledge, for the knower of Brahman can have no such rite as *Agnihotra* etc. after enlightenment, because as a result of the realization of the unity of the Self with Brahman that cannot be the object of any injunction, the man of enlightenment has walked out of the pale of scriptures. But so far as meditation on the qualified Brahman is concerned, a subsequent performance of *Agnihotra* etc. is possible, since the agentship for such a meditator remains intact. Even so, when these are performed without any motive and hence have no separate result, they can well be associated with meditation.

Opponent: Well then, to what action does this statement about the non-attachment and destruction of the results of works refer to? And to what action does this Vedic assignment (of results to friends, foes, and others) refer to as stated in the following sentence found in a certain branch of the Vedas: "His sons inherit his wealth; the friends acquire the merits; and the foes get the demerits" (Kau. I. 4)?

Hence the aphorist replies:

अतोऽन्याऽपि ह्येकेषामुभयोः ॥१७॥

अतः Apart from these अन्या another action अपि also हि certainly (exists) एकेषाम् according to some people; (the assignment to friends, foes, and others refers to this); उभयोः according to both (Jaimini and Bādarāyaṇa).

17. Besides these, there is also another kind of (good) action with regard to which some people (make the assignment), according to both Jaimini and Bādarāyaṇa.

Apart from these obligatory rites like *Agnihotra* etc. other good works surely exist that are performed with a motive for results. Of these, the appropriation has been indicated by people of a certain (branch of the Vedas) in, "The friends acquire the merits" etc. And by saying, "In the very same way, there are non-attachment and destruction of the others (i.e. virtues) as well" (B. S. IV. i. 14), the non-attachment and destruction of these very works have been ascertained. Thus both the teachers Jaimini and Bādarāyaṇa agree in accepting the view that this kind of works, done with a desire, do not help in the generation of knowledge.

Topic 13: Rites Unaccompanied by Meditation

Doubt : Under the topic just finished it has been well established that when the obligatory duties like *Agnihotra* etc. are done for the purpose of getting liberation by one aspiring for it, they become the cause of exhausting the accumulated sins, and thereby the cause for purifying the mind. Becoming in this way contributory to the realization of Brahman, which leads to liberation, they come to have the same result as the knowledge of Brahman itself. Now these *Agnihotra* etc. may be performed along with meditations that are based on the auxiliaries of rites or without them. For from the following texts we know that *Agnihotra* etc. can be done either separately or along with meditation: "One who possessed of such knowledge makes a sacrifice", "One who possessed of such knowledge pours the oblation", "One who knowing thus chants the hymn", "One who knowing thus sings", "Therefore one should select a man possessed of this knowledge as (the priest called) Brahmā, and not one who is ignorant of this" (Ch. IV. xvii. 10), "With that *Om* both perform rites—the one who knows and the one who does not" (Ch. I. i. 10). Now the point to be considered is whether *Agnihotra* and other rites, not just as they are but as associated with meditation, become the cause of knowledge to an aspirant for liberation and thus come to produce the same result as knowledge, or such rites do so, equally without distinction, either by themselves or in association with knowledge.

Why does this doubt crop up?

Since in the text, "They seek to know it through sacrifice" (Bṛ. IV. iv. 22), the rites like *Agnihotra* are heard of without any reservation as the causes of knowledge, and since *Agnihotra* etc. when associated with meditation are known to acquire a special advantage. What should be the conclusion then?

Opponent : Rites like *Agnihotra* etc. when associated with meditation can alone become helpful to the knowledge of the Self, but not so those that are devoid of meditation. For a man of knowledge is known to have an advantage over the man without knowledge from such Upaniṣadic texts as, "He who knows as above conquers further death the very day he makes that offering" (Bṛ. I. v. 2), and from such Smṛti texts as, "Endowed with which wisdom, O son of Pṛthā, thou shalt break through the bonds of *karma*" (Gītā, II. 39), "Work with desire is verily far inferior to that performed with the mind undisturbed by the thoughts of results, O Dhanañjaya" (Gītā, II. 49).

Vedāntin: This being the position, the aphorist explains:

यदेव विद्ययेति हि ॥१८॥

"यत्-एव Whatever (is done) विद्यया with knowledge"—इति this text हि surely (shows this).

18. The Upaniṣadic text, "whatever is done with knowledge" surely indicates this.

It is true that *Agnihotra* and other rites when associated with meditation are better than the *Agnihotra* etc. not associated with meditation, just as much as a learned Brāhmaṇa is better than a Brāhmaṇa without learning. Even so, *Agnihotra* and other rites are not absolutely useless when they are not associated with meditation.

Why?

Since in the Upaniṣadic text, "They seek to know It through sacrifice" (Bṛ. IV. iv. 22), the rites like *Agnihotra* etc. are heard of without any reservation as the means of knowledge.

Opponent: Since it is known that *Agnihotra* etc. when associated with meditation have a distinct advantage over those without meditation, it is but proper to say that *Agnihotra* etc. when unassociated with meditation are not conducive to knowledge.

Vedāntin: That is not so. It is rather proper to think that since *Agnihotra* etc., when associated with meditation, acquire a certain distinction owing to the presence of meditation, therefore they have just a special efficacy in producing knowledge, while it is not so in the case of mere *Agnihotra* etc. that are not similarly associated; from that, however, one cannot conclude that *Agnihotra* etc., heard of in a general way in the text, "They seek to know through sacrifices", as auxiliaries of knowledge, are not their auxiliaries. For the passage which declares, "Whatever one does along with knowledge, faith, and meditation, becomes more efficacious" (Ch. I. i. 10), speaks of the rites like *Agnihotra* etc. as becoming "more efficacious" in producing their own results when they are associated with their own meditations; it thereby shows that the very same *Agnihotra* etc. have at least some efficacy in producing their results even when not in association with meditation. The efficacy of a rite consists in its being able to fulfil its own purpose. Hence the conclusion is this: The obligatory rites like *Agnihotra* etc., both as associated and unassociated with meditation, that were undertaken either in this life or the previous life before the dawn of knowledge, with a view to attaining liberation by one who hankers after it, become the destroyers as far as possible of the accumulated sins that stand in the way of the realization of Brahman. Thus indirectly they become the cause of the realization of Brahman Itself, so that in collaboration with such proximate causes of enlightenment as hearing, reflection, faith, meditation, devotedness, etc., they come to have the same result as the knowledge of Brahman has.

Topic 14: Experience of the Active Merit and Demerit

भोगेन त्वितरे क्षपयित्वा सम्पद्यते ॥१९॥

तु But क्षपयित्वा exhausting इतरे the other two भोगेन through experiencing (them) सम्पद्यते one merges in Brahman.

19. But the (enlightened) man merges in Brahman after exhausting the other two, (viz merit and demerit that have started fruition), by experiencing (their results in the present life).

It has been said that the virtues and vices that have not begun yielding their results get annihilated through the power of knowledge. But from the texts like, "He has to tarry so long as the body does not fall, and then he merges (in Brahman)" (Ch.

VI. xiv. 2), "Being but Brahman, he is merged in Brahman" (Bṛ. IV. iv. 6), it is known that the other virtues and vices that have already begun to fructify are exhausted through experiencing the results, and then the aspirant becomes Brahman.

Opponent: May it not be that on the analogy of seeing two moons, the dualistic vision will persist even when the body falls just as much as that vision continues as long as the body lasts even after full enlightenment?

Vedāntin: No, since there is no reason for this. That the dualistic vision lasts before the fall of the body is because of the need of exhausting the remaining portion of (the result of active virtue and vice) through experience. But here after death there is no such factor present.

Opponent: May not other outstanding virtues and vices produce newer experiences?

Vedāntin: No, since their seeds are burnt away. For other outstanding results of works can produce a fresh body after the death of the present one only when they have false ignorance to prop them up. But that false ignorance has been burnt away by full enlightenment. Therefore it is but proper that when the effect already produced wears away, liberation comes inevitably to the man of knowledge.

Section II

Topic 1: At Death the Organs Merge in Mind

वाङ्मनसि दर्शनाच्छब्दाच्च ॥१॥

वाक् Speech (merges) मनसि in the mind दर्शनात् because it is so perceived च and शब्दात् from scriptural statement.

1. The (function) of the organ of speech merges in the mind (at the time of death) for so it is seen, and so the Upaniṣads say.

Now before introducing the path of the gods, meant for arriving at the result of the inferior meditations (i.e. on the qualified Brahman), the aphorist first speaks of the order of the departure (from the body) as taught by the scriptures. He will say later that the departure is similar for both the man who has the knowledge[1] (of the qualified Brahman) and the man who has not. Thus occurs the Upaniṣadic text about death, "O amiable one, when this man is about to die, his speech is withdrawn into the mind, the mind into the vital force, the vital force into fire, and fire into the supreme Deity" (Ch. VI. viii. 6).

Doubt: Now the doubt arises as to whether the above passage speaks of the entry into the mind of the organ of speech together with its functions or of the entry of the functions alone.

Opponent: While under this doubt, the conclusion that can be drawn is that the organ of speech itself enters into the mind; for thus would (the proper sense of) the passage be honoured, while otherwise one would have to resort to a figure of speech. Whenever a doubt arises about the literal or figurative meaning of a text, the literal one has to be accepted and not the figurative. Hence the withdrawal here is of the organ of speech itself into the mind.

[1] Although the text speaks of "*vidvān*", Ānandagiri takes it in the sense of a meditator on the qualified Brahman, while *Ratnaprabhā* uses the term "*upāsaka*—meditator" as its synonym.

Vedāntin: This being the position, we say that the functions alone of the organ of speech are withdrawn into the mind.

Opponent: How is this interpretation about the withdrawal of the functions of the organ of speech arrived at when the teacher's (i.e. aphorist's) statement is, "Speech goes into the mind"?

Vedāntin: This is true, but later he will state, "The parts (i.e. the organs of the enlightened man), merged in Brahman, become non-distinct from It on the authority of the scriptures" (IV. ii. 16). Hence it is understood that what is meant here is merely the cessation of the functions (of all in general). If, however, the merger of the organ of speech itself be meant, then since the non-distinction is the same everywhere (for the enlightened and the ignorant), why should the aphorist make a separate mention of it (in the case of the enlightened) by saying, "non-distinct" (in IV. ii. 16)? So the intended meaning here being the cessation of the functions of the organ of speech, the idea conveyed is that the functions of the organ of speech become withdrawn even while the functions of the mind continue.

How can this be so?

Because it is seen to be so. For it is a matter of experience that the power of speech stops earlier even while the power of the mind still continues. Not that the withdrawal of the organ of speech together with its functions into the mind can actually be seen by anybody.

Opponent: On the strength of the Vedic text it can be asserted that what is spoken of here is the merger of the organ of speech into the mind itself.

Vedāntin: The answer is given by saying, no, since that is not its material cause. A thing can merge into what its material cause is, as for instance an earthen plate into earth. But there is no valid proof to show that the organ of speech originates from the mind; whereas the engagement of the functions in activity or their disengagement is seen to be based on something that may not be the material cause. For instance, the activity of fire, which is of the nature of light and heat, (*tejas*) may originate from fuel which is by nature earth, and it may get extinguished in water.

Opponent: On such an interpretation, how will the Upaniṣadic text, "Speech is withdrawn into the mind" (Ch. VI. viii. 6) be reconciled?

Vedāntin: That is why the aphorist says, "and so the Upaniṣads say" (in a figurative sense that is not antagonistic to reason). The idea implied is that the Upaniṣadic text fits in with this interpretation according to which the organ and its functions are understood to be the same in a figurative sense.[2]

अत एव च सर्वाण्यनु ॥२॥

च And अत: एव for the same reason सर्वाणि all (the functions of all the organs) अनु follows (i.e. get merged in the mind).

2. *And for the same reason all the functions of all the organs get merged in the mind.*

In the text, "Therefore one who gets his light extinguished (or heat cooled off) attains rebirth together with the organs that enter into the mind" (Pr. III. 9), we hear of the entry of all the organs without exception into the mind. Since even here, "for the same reason" (as in the foregoing aphorism), viz that just like the organ of speech, the organs of sight etc. are seen to lose their functions even when the mind continues to be active, and since it is not possible that the organs as such can merge in the mind, and since the Upaniṣadic text also fits in thus, therefore the conclusion is that it is in the sense of the cessation of their functions alone that all the organs get withdrawn into the mind. Although there is no exception to this withdrawal of all the organs into the mind, the separate mention of the organ of speech (in the first aphorism) is in accordance with its mention in, "Speech is withdrawn into the mind" (Ch. VI. viii. 6).

Topic 2: Mind Merges in Prana

Doubt: It is well understood that in the text, "Speech is withdrawn into the mind", what is intended to imply is the withdrawal of the functions. Now, as regards the succeeding

[2] The literal sense being impossible, a resort to a figure of speech is quite logical.

text, "The mind into the vital force" (Ch. VI. viii. 6), is it the withdrawal of the functions alone that is meant here as well, or is it the withdrawal of the possessor of the functions?

Opponent : When under such a doubt, the conclusion should be that the withdrawal of the possessor of the functions is meant here, since this view is supported by Upaniṣadic texts and since the vital force can well be the material cause of the mind. Thus we have, "O amiable one, the mind is derived from food (i.e. earth), food is derived from water" (Ch. VI. v. 4), where the scripture mentions the mind as originating from food and food from water. There occurs also the Upaniṣadic text, "And water created food" (Ch. VI. ii. 4). So to say that the mind merges in the vital force is the same as to say that food itself merges in water; for food is mind, and water is the vital force, since a material cause and its transformations are the same.

Vedāntin : This being the position, we say,

तन्मनः प्राण उत्तरात् ॥३॥

तत् That मनः mind (merges) प्राणे in the vital force उत्तरात् as (revealed) in the subsequent (text).

3. That mind merges in the vital force as is revealed in the subsequent text.

From the subsequent portion of the text (cited above) it is to be understood that when this mind merges in the vital force, it does so through (the absorption of) its functions alone together with the functions of the external organs that are withdrawn into it. Thus it is that when a man wants to sleep or is about to die, the activities of the mind are seen to cease even while the function of the vital force, consisting in its vibration (respiration), still persists. Besides, the mind as such cannot merge into the vital force, since that is not its material source.

Opponent : Have we not shown that the vital force is the material cause of the mind?

Vedāntin : That is not valid, for it is not logical that the mind should merge into the vital force in accordance with the above ratiocination. For even so, the mind would have to be absorbed into food (i.e. earth), food into water, and the vital force too into water. But even from such a standpoint no proof can be adduced to show that the mind originates from water transformed into the vital force. Hence the mind as such does not get absorbed into the vital force. It was also shown earlier that the text can fit in even if the merger of the functions is meant, for the functions and the possessor of the functions are figuratively understood to be the same.

TOPIC 3: PRANA MERGES INTO THE SOUL

Doubt: This much has been established that the functions of one entity can be withdrawn into some other entity that is not its material cause, but not so can the entity itself be absorbed. Now with regard to the text, "the vital force into (*tejas*) fire" (Ch. VI. viii. 6), the consideration that arises is whether the function of the vital force is withdrawn into fire, just as the text literally implies, or is it withdrawn into the soul that is the master of this cage formed by the body and sense-organs?

Opponent: As to that, the vital force should get absorbed into fire, since the meaning of a Upaniṣadic text cannot be laid bare to doubts and because it is improper to imagine something not heard of.

Vedāntin: This being the position, the aphorist explains:

सोऽध्यक्षे तदुपगमादिभ्यः ॥४॥

सः That (*Prāṇa*) अध्यक्षे (merges) into the presiding entity (i.e. the Self) तत्-उपगम-आदिभ्यः because of such facts as approaching that.

4. That one (i.e. the vital force) is (known to be) withdrawn into the ruler (i.e. the individual Self) from such facts as approaching that (Self at the time of death).

"That one", the vital force that is being considered, subsists in "the ruler", in the (individual) Self identified with the intellect and having ignorance, past works, and past experiences as Its limiting adjuncts; that is to say, the activities of the vital force remain chiefly concerned with It.

How is this known?

"From such facts as its approaching that Self." For thus it is that another Upaniṣadic passage shows in a general way how all the *prāṇas* (organs) without exception approach the ruler, "All the organs approach the departing man at the time of death when breathing becomes difficult" (Bṛ. IV. iii. 38); and in the text, "When it departs, the vital force follows" (Bṛ. IV. iv. 2), it is specially shown how the vital force, having five functions, follows the ruler; and in the text, "When the vital force departs all the organs (*prāṇas*) follow" (ibid.), it is shown how the other *prāṇas* follow the vital force. Besides, by showing in the text, "Then the Self remains equipped with the organs of knowledge" (ibid.), that the ruler has consciousness inside, it is made clear that the vital force, with the sense-organs merged in it, subsists in that soul.

Opponent: Since the Upaniṣad declares, "The vital force is withdrawn into fire" (Ch. VI. viii. 6), how can an erroneous meaning be asserted by saying that it goes to the ruler?

Vedāntin: That creates no difficulty, since in such activities as leaving the body, the soul plays the dominant part and any special point stated in other Upaniṣads has to be taken into account.

Opponent: How then is the Upaniṣadic text to be explained that the vital force is withdrawn into fire (*tejas*)?

Vedāntin: Hence the aphorist says,

भूतेषु तत्-श्रुतेः ॥५॥

(The soul stays) भूतेषु among the elements तत्-श्रुतेः that being so declared in the Upaniṣads.

5. The soul comes to stay among the elements, it being so declared by the Upaniṣads.

On the authority of the text, "The vital force is withdrawn into fire", it is to be understood that this ruler, associated with the vital force, exists amidst the subtle elements that are associated with fire and constitute the seed of the body.

Opponent: But that text shows the existence of the vital force in fire, and not of the existence of the ruler, accompanied by the vital force, in fire.

Vedāntin: That is no defect, since in the aphorism, "That one is merged in the ruler", it has been pointed out that the ruler also is to be understood as having been mentioned by the Upaniṣad in between the vital force and fire; for one, who having gone from Śrughna to Mathurā, proceeds then to Pāṭaliputra, may well be said to have proceeded from Śrughna to Pātaliputra. Hence the text, "The vital force is withdrawn into fire" is to be understood to mean that it is the ruler (i.e. soul) itself, associated with the vital force, that continues to stay amidst the subtle elements which are the associates of *tejas* (fire).[3]

Opponent: Since fire alone is mentioned in the text, "The vital force is withdrawn into fire", how can it be asserted that the ruler exists amidst the elements which have fire as an associate?

Vedāntin: Hence the aphorist says,

नैकस्मिन् दर्शयतो हि ॥६॥

न Not एकस्मिन् in a single one हि for दर्शयतः both show (otherwise).

6. (The soul does) not (come to stay) amidst a single element, for both (the Upaniṣads and Smṛtis) show otherwise.

It is not a fact that at the time of the soul's desire to attain a new body it exists in the midst of a single element, viz fire, for the gross body is seen to be formed of many elements. The question and answer also reveal this in the passage starting with, "Do you know how water comes to be called man when the fifth oblation is poured?" (Ch. V. iii. 3). That fact was explained under the aphorism, "On account of water being constituted by three elements, the soul goes enveloped by all of them, though

[3] So "fire" actually means the subtle elements, or rather the subtle body, where the soul subsists, as also does *Prāṇa* through its existence in the soul.

water is mentioned because of its preponderance" (B. S. III. i. 2). The Upaniṣadic and Smṛti texts also point to this. The relevant Upaniṣadic text runs thus: "That Self is identified with ... earth, water, air, space, and fire" (Bṛ. IV. iv. 5). The Smṛti text is, "All this in the universe emerges, as of yore, along with the five subtle elements that are indestructible" (Manu, I. 21), and so on.

Opponent: With regard to the time when the soul wants to acquire a new body after the organs of speech etc. are withdrawn, another Upaniṣadic passage starts with the sentence, "Where is the man then?" (Bṛ. III. ii. 13), and then decides that the soul rests on the results of past works (*karma*) in the text, "What they mentioned there was only *karma*, and what they praised there was also only *karma*" (ibid).

Vedāntin: As to that the answer is: The subject dealt with there is the emergence of bondage which is constituted by the senses and sense-objects, called the *grahas* (i.e. perceivers) and *atigrahas* (i.e. impellers of the perceivers—i.e. objects of perception) and which is determined by past works. In this sense it is said that the soul rests on *karma* (work). But the subject dealt with here is the creation of a fresh body from the materials, viz the elements. In this sense it is said that it rests on the elements. Besides, by using the word "praise" in the other text (i.e. Bṛhadāraṇyaka) a mere predominance of *karma* is shown there, and it is not that any other resting place is also negated thereby. Hence there is no contradiction.

Topic 4: Departure of the Enlightened and the Unenlightened

Doubt: Is this departure from the body the same for the enlightened and the unenlightened persons? Or is there any distinction?

Opponent: When under such a doubt, the conclusion that can be arrived at is that this departure has got a distinction, inasmuch as this departure occurs in conjunction with the subtle elements, and it is for rebirth that the elements are resorted to. Moreover, there can be no rebirth for the enlightened man, for the Upaniṣad declares that the man of knowledge attains immortality. Hence this departure is related to the unenlightened man alone.

Objection: Since this discussion occurs in the scripture under the topic of knowledge, this must be about the man of knowledge.

Opponent: No, since this departure is described there as a fact already known (or a matter of natural occurrence) just like sleep etc. Just as even in a context of knowledge, sleep etc., occurring to all creatures, are described in such texts as, "When a man comes to be known as 'He sleeps' " (Ch. VI. viii. 1), "When he comes to be known as 'He wants to eat' " (Ch. VI. viii. 3), "When he comes to be known as 'He wants to drink' " (Ch. VI. viii. 5); and this is done so because this is helpful to the comprehension of the subject being explained but not for describing the man of knowledge as possessed of such distinctions; similarly this departure from the body that is common to men in general is being described in order to establish the fact that the supreme Deity in which the fire of the departing man merges is the Self and that "Thou art That". Besides, this departure is denied in the case of a man of knowledge in, "His organs do not depart" (Bṛ. IV. iv. 6). Therefore this departure is of the unenlightened man alone.

Vedāntin: This being the position, we say.

समाना चासृत्युपक्रमादमृतत्वं चानुपोष्य ॥७॥

च And (the mode of departure is) समाना the same आ-सृति-उपक्रमात् up to the beginning of the path; च and अमृतत्वम् the immortality (is relative) अनुपोष्य without burning ignorance.

7. *And the mode of departure (at the time of death) is the same (for the knower of the qualified Brahman and the ignorant man) up to the beginning of the path (of the gods); and the immortality (that is spoken of) is the one that is attained without burning ignorance.*

It is but proper that the departure as described in such texts as, "Speech is withdrawn into the mind" (Ch. VI. viii. 6), should be "the same for the knower and the ignorant" upto the point where they start for their respective separate paths; for this is spoken of without any distinctive specification. The ignorant man moves on, resting on the subtle elements constituting the seed of the next body and under the impulsion of his past works, for the sake of fresh experiences in a new body. But the man of knowledge pursues the path through the nerve (passing out of the crown of the head[4] and) lighted up by knowledge and leading to liberation. This fact is stated in the aphorism by saying, "Up to the beginning of the path (of the gods)".

Opponent: The enlightened man has to attain immortality, which does not depend on going from one place to another; so how can there be any resort to the elements and the commencement of a path?

Vedāntin: As to that, the answer is that this immortality is relative for the man whose blemishes have not been totally burnt away—for one who wants to attain a relative immortality by virtue of his knowledge of the qualified Brahman without completely burning away his ignorance. In such a case both reliance on the elements and the commencement of a path are possible. For the sense-organs cannot move without something to rest on. Hence there is no fault.

Topic 5: Relative Merger of Fire etc.

Doubt: It has been ascertained in accordance with the context that the meaning of the text, "Fire gets withdrawn into the supreme Deity" (Ch. VI. viii. 6), is that the fire of the dying man, which is under consideration, gets merged in the supreme Deity along with the ruler, the vital force, the assemblage of sense-organs, and the other elements. Now it is being considered what this merger actually is.

Opponent: As to that, the conclusion arrived at is that the merger is absolute and of the thing itself in its entirety; for that is the reasonable position inasmuch as the Deity is its material cause. For it has been established earlier that the

[4] The ignorant move through the other inferior nerves—this is the difference.

supreme Deity is the material cause of all things that are born. Hence this attainment of identity is absolute and complete.

Vedāntin: To this we say.

तदापीतेः संसारव्यपदेशात् ॥८॥

तत् That (group of elements—fire and the rest) (continues) आ-अपीतेः till final release संसार-व्यपदेशात् for there is declaration of the transmigratory state (till then).

8. That group of elements (counting from fire) continues till complete liberation; for there is a declaration of the continuance of the transmigratory state till then.

"That", the group of subtle elements counting from fire that supplies the basis for the organs of hearing etc., "continues till complete liberation", till liberation from the transmigratory state as a result of full enlightenment; for the state of transmigration is described thus (for the ignorant alone): "Some souls enter the womb for acquiring bodies and others follow the motionless in accordance with their (past) works and in conformity with their knowledge" (Ka. II. ii. 7). On a contrary supposition all would become Brahman in an absolute sense, since at the time of death their limiting adjuncts would become extinct. In that case all scriptures of injunction would be useless, as also all scriptures about knowledge. Moreover, the bondage that arises from false ignorance cannot be removed by anything apart from full enlightenment. Accordingly, though Brahman is the material cause, still the merger in Existence (Brahman) at death occurs in such a way as to ensure the continuance of these (organs etc.) in a latent state (so that they can re-emerge) just as it happens during deep sleep and dissolution.

सूक्ष्मं प्रमाणतश्च तथोपलब्धेः ॥९॥

च And सूक्ष्मम् minute प्रमाणतः in (its) size (or measure) तथा such उपलब्धेः being the experience.

9. That fire (as also other elements) is minute in its nature, as also in size, because it is seen to be so.

And that fire along with the other elements, which constitute a habitat for the soul emerging out of its present body, must be subtle in nature and measure. It is thus that we gather from the Upaniṣadic declaration about its going out through the nerves that fire (as also the other elements) is a subtle element. It is possible for it to move through the nerves because of its minuteness in size, and it is unobstructed because of its fineness by nature. It is because of this fact again that it is not perceived by people near by when it departs from the body.

नोपमर्देनातः ॥१०॥

न Not (is the subtle one destroyed) उपमर्देन by the destruction (of the gross body) अतः for this reason.

10. For this (very) reason the subtle body is not destroyed even when the gross one is.

"For this very reason", just because it is subtle, the other body, "the subtle body", "is not destroyed, even when the gross body is destroyed" through cremation etc.

अस्यैव चोपपत्तेरेष ऊष्मा ॥११॥

एषः This ऊष्मा warmth अस्य belongs to this (subtle body) एव to be sure उपपत्तेः for that stands to reason.

11. And this warmth belongs to this subtle body to be sure, for that stands to reason.

The warmth that people feel by touching a living body "belongs to this" one, to the "subtle body, to be sure". Thus it is that when death takes place and the body still persists, heat is not perceived even though the other attributes of the body like form etc. persist; but it is perceived only when the body is alive. Hence it stands to reason that this heat belongs to something other than the well-known gross body. In support of this occurs the Vedic text, "It is warm indeed so long as it lives, and cold when it dies".

Topic 6: No Departure for a Knower of Brahman

प्रतिषेधादिति चेन्न शारीरात् ॥१२॥

(The organs do not depart) प्रतिषेधात् because of the (scriptural) denial इति चेत् if it be argued thus, then न not so; (for the denial means that they do not depart) शारीरात् from the individual soul.

12. If it be contended that the organs of the man of knowledge do not depart from the body because of the denial in the scripture, then (according to the opponent) it is not so, for the denial is about the departure from the individual soul.

From the reservation made under the aphorism, "And the immortality spoken of is one that is attained without burning ignorance" (IV. ii. 7), it is admitted that in the absolute immortality there is an absence of any course to be followed and any departure from the body. Still lest there be any apprehension of departure owing to some reason or other, that is denied through the text, "But the man who does not desire (never transmigrates). Of him who is without desires, who is free from desires, the objects of whose desire have been obtained, and to whom all objects of desire are but the Self—the organs do not depart. Being but Brahman he is merged in Brahman" (Bṛ. IV iv. 6). Now since this denial occurs in the context of the supreme knowledge, the organs of the man who has realized the supreme Brahman have no departure from the body.

The reply (to this by the *opponent*) is: No, since this "denial is concerned with the departure of the organs from the embodied one", and not from the body.

Objection: How is this known (that the organs depart not from the body but from the embodied entity)?

Opponent: Because in the other (*Mādhyandina*) branch the fifth case-ending is used (in *tasmāt*—from him). Since the sixth case-ending (in *tasya*—of him) (in the *Kāṇva* recension) is used to imply relationships in general, it can be delimited to a particular relationship on the strength of the ablative (fifth case-ending) (in *tasmāt*) in the other (*Mādhyandina*) recension. And by the word *tasmāt* (from him) the embodied soul that is qualified for secular prosperity or liberation is referred to, for it is the chief subject (of the context), but not so is the body referred to. The idea implied is this: "From him", from the individual soul, that is about to depart from the body, the organs do not depart; they remain in its company. When the soul departs, it departs from the body along with the organs.

Vedāntin: This being the position, it is being refuted:

स्पष्टो ह्येकेषाम् ॥१३॥

(This is not so) हि because एकेषाम् in the case of the followers of one branch, स्पष्टः (there is) a clear (denial of the soul's departure from the body).

13. This is not so, for in case of the followers of one recension there is a clear denial of the soul's departure.

The assertion was made to the effect that even for the man who knows Brahman there can be such a fact as departure from the body, the denial of departure having been made about the departure (of the organs) from the embodied soul. This is not correct, for the denial of the departure (of the organs) from the body is clearly met with in a particular recension. Thus in the course of answering the question of Ārtabhāga, "When this one (i.e. the body of the liberated man) dies, do the organs then go up from this one, or do they not?" it is stated from the point of view of the departure (from the body). "'No,' replied Yājñavalkya" (Bṛ. III. ii. 11). Then since the misconception might arise that in that case this one does not die because the organs do not depart, the assertion of the merger of the organs is made in, "they merge in this one only" (ibid); and for establishing this fact it is said, "This one swells, this one is inflated, and in that state lies dead" (ibid), where swelling etc. are asserted about something that is referred to by "this one" (*saḥ*) that is under discussion and that forms the basis from which the departure can occur. Such descriptions fit in with the body and not the embodied soul.[5] In conformity with this, the text that has a reading with the fifth case-ending, viz "The organs do not depart from this one, they merge in this one only" (*Mādhyandina* reading), has to be interpreted to mean that though the embodied soul is primarily alluded to by the pronoun (this one), still the denial is concerned with the departure from the body that is figuratively identified with the embodied soul. But in the case of those (of the *Kāṇva* recension) who have the reading ("of this one") with the sixth case-ending, the departure is denied in relation to the man of knowledge, so that the denial in that sentence is concerned with the departure as it is well known (in the world); and what is a well-known fact is the departure from the body and not from the embodied soul, so that the denial comes to mean the denial of the departure (of the organs) from the body. Moreover, the departure of the ignorant man from the body and his course of transmigration are described elaborately in the text, "The soul departs either through the eyes or through the head or through any other part of the body. When it departs, all the organs follow" etc. (Bṛ. IV. iv. 2). That topic of the ignorant man is ended with, "Thus does the man transmigrate who desires" (Bṛ. IV. iv. 6). Then the man of knowledge is mentioned thus, "But the man who does not desire" (ibid). Now, should the (latter) text mean that the departure from the body (in the earlier text) is meant for him as well, then this separate mention becomes incongruous. Hence to make this separate mention purposeful, the text is to be explained to signify the denial of the departure and the following of a course in the case of a man of knowledge, though they are but natural to a man of ignorance. Besides, it is unreasonable that a man who has known Brahman and become identified with the all-pervasive Brahman and has his desires and results of *karma* annihilated should depart or have any course to follow, for there is no rhyme or reason for that. And texts like, "Attains Brahman in this very body" (Bṛ. IV. iv. 7) indicate the absence of departure and paths for him.

[5] Even though the word used is *puruṣa* (man), it means the body; for the soul cannot have swelling etc. that are stated about it by referring to it by the term "this one".

स्मर्यते च ॥१४॥

14. And the Smṛti also says so.

Moreover, the absence of movement and departure is mentioned in the *Mahābhārata*: "Even gods become befooled in the course of finding out the path of one who has become one with the Self of all beings, who has understood all beings truly as the Self, and who has no state to reach."

Opponent: But the Smṛti also mentions a path that the knowers of Brahman tread: "Once upon a time Śuka, son of Vyāsa, became desirous of liberation and proceeded towards the solar orb. When called back by his father who was following him, he responded saying, 'Sir'".

Vedāntin: Not so, for it is to be understood that Śuka reached a particular region through his power of Yoga even while he was in the body, and there he gave it up. For such facts as being seen by all beings are mentioned in that connection, whereas nobody can have any visual perception when a disembodied soul moves on. It is in line with this that in that very context the conclusion is made thus: "But Śuka accelerated his speed to more than that of wind, moved across space exhibiting his own power, and then he became merged in all beings". Hence the knower of Brahman has neither any departure from the body nor any course to follow. We shall state later on as to whom the Upaniṣadic texts about courses refer (IV. iii. 7).

Topic 7: The Organs of the Knower Merge in Brahman

तानि परे तथा ह्याह ॥१५॥

तानि Those (organs) परे (merge) in the supreme Brahman हि because तथा so (the Upaniṣad) आह says.

15. Those organs get merged in the supreme Brahman, for such is the declaration of the Upaniṣad.

And "those organs", called the *prāṇas*, as also the (subtle) elements, of the knower of the supreme Brahman "merge in the supreme" Self.

Why is it so?

Since "such is the declaration of the Upaniṣad" (as in): "So also these sixteen parts (i.e. limbs) of the all-seeing *Puruṣa* (i.e. infinite Being) that have *Puruṣa* as their abode get absorbed on reaching *Puruṣa*" (Pr. VI. 5).

Opponent: Another Upaniṣadic text, speaking about the man of realization, states that the "parts" get merged somewhere other than the supreme Self: "To their sources repair the fifteen parts (constituents of the body)" (Mu. III. ii. 7).

Vedāntin: Not so, for this (Muṇḍaka) text speaks from the phenomenal point of view, and it means that the constituents that are the products of the elements—earth etc.—repair to their own material sources. But the other (Praśna) text states from the standpoint of the man of realization that (in his view) all the constituents get absorbed in the supreme Brahman Itself. Hence there is no defect.

Topic 8: Absolute Absorption of the Constituents

Doubt: Does the merger of the constituents of the body of the man of realization occur wholly as in the case of others, or is some part left out?

Opponent: Since that is a resorption like any other resorption, their potentiality must remain intact.

Vedāntin: To this the aphorist says,

अविभागो वचनात् ॥१६॥

अ-विभाग: Non-distinction (with Brahman results) वचनात् on the authority of scriptural declaration.

16. (Absolute) non-distinction (with Brahman comes about) on the authority of the scriptural declaration.

It is a total unification to be sure.

Why so?

"On the authority of the scriptural declaration". Thus it is that after relating the merger of the constituents, the Upaniṣad says, "When their names and forms are destroyed and they are simply called *Puruṣa*. Such a man of realization is without the constituents and is immortal" (Pr. VI. 5). Besides, the constituents that spring from ignorance can have no remnant after their resorption through knowledge. Accordingly, they must become absolutely unified (with Brahman).

Topic 9: Departure of One who Knows the Qualified Brahman

तदोकोऽग्रज्वलनं तत्प्रकाशितद्वारो विद्यासामर्थ्यात् तच्छेषगत्यनुस्मृति-
योगाच्च हार्दानुगृहीतः शताधिकया ॥१७॥

तत्-ओकः-अग्र-ज्वलनं There occurs an illumination of the top of its (i.e. soul's) abode (viz the heart); तत्-प्रकाशित-द्वारः having the door illumined by that (light), (the soul goes out), विद्या-सामर्थ्यात् owing to the efficacy of knowledge च and तत्-शेष-गति-अनुस्मृति-योगात् owing to the appropriateness of the constant meditation about the way which is a part of that (knowledge), हार्द-अनुगृहीतः under the favour of Him who resides in the heart, शत-अधिकया through that (nerve) which is the hundred and first.

17. *(When the soul of the man who has realized the qualified Brahman is about to depart), there occurs an illumination of the top of the heart. Having that door illumined by that light, the soul, under the favour of Him who resides in the heart, departs through the hundred and first nerve, owing to the efficacy of the knowledge and the appropriateness of the constant thought about the course which is a part of that knowledge.*

Doubt: The incidental consideration of the knowledge of the supreme Brahman is concluded. Now, however, the aphorist pursues the reflections about the inferior knowledge. It has been stated that the process of departure from the body is the same for the man of knowledge (i.e. of one who meditates on the qualified Brahman) and the man of ignorance up to the point where the path of the gods begins. Now is being considered the entry (of the soul) into that course. When the soul, identified with the intellect, that has all its organs counting from the organ of speech withdrawn into itself, is about to leave the body, then the heart becomes its abode, the place of its existence, in accordance with the Upaniṣadic text, "Completely withdrawing these particles of light (i.e. powers of the organs), it comes to the heart" (Bṛ. IV. iv. 1). The illumination of the top of the heart and the departure from such bases as the eye after that top becomes lighted up are mentioned by the Upaniṣad in the passage, "The top of the heart of this one brightens. Through that brightened top the soul departs, either through the eyes or through the head, or through any other part of the body" (Bṛ. IV. iv. 2). Now does this departure occur in the same way both in the cases of the enlightened and the unenlightened, or is there any distinction in the case of the enlightened?

Opponent: When under such a doubt, the conclusion should be that there is no distinction, for the Upaniṣadic text is the same.

Vedāntin: That being the position, the aphorist says that though the top of the heart becomes illumined both for the man of knowledge and the man of ignorance, and though the door is illumined thereby, yet the man of knowledge departs from the region of the head, whereas the others depart from other regions.

Why?

Because of the power of knowledge. Should the man of knowledge also depart from any region indiscriminately just like the others, he will not attain a virtuous world, so that his knowledge will be useless. And this is so "because of the appropriateness of constant thought about the course forming a part of the knowledge". In connection with certain meditations it is enjoined that the soul's path that is associated with the nerve at the top of the head and forms a part of the meditation itself has to be reflected on. And it is reasonable that by virtue of thinking on it he should emerge through that very thing. Therefore the man of knowledge, favoured as he is by Brahman which is meditated on as having Its abode in the heart, becomes unified in thought with Brahman and emerges out of the body through the nerve counted as the one over and above a hundred; but others emerge through other nerves. That is why it is stated in the scripture in connection with the meditation about the heart, "The nerves of the heart are a hundred and one in number. Of them the one passes through the head. Going up through that nerve one gets immortality. Other nerves that have different directions become the causes of death" (Ka. II. iii. 16, Ch. VIII. vi. 6).

Topic 10: The Soul Follows the Rays of the Sun

रश्म्यनुसारी ॥१८॥

रश्मि-अनुसारी By following the rays (of the sun).

18. (The soul of the man of knowledge) proceeds by following the rays of the sun.

Starting with the sentence, "Now then, there is the palace of Brahman in the shape of the tiny lotus of the heart that is within the body; in that exists (Brahman called) the small inner Space" (Ch. VIII. i. 1), a meditation about the heart is enjoined. In the course of describing this meditation, the start is made with, "Now these nerves of the heart" (Ch. VIII. vi. 1), and then a connection is elaborately shown between the nerves (in the heart) and the rays (of the sun) in the passage, "Then when anyone departs from this body thus, he goes up along these rays" (Ch. VIII. vi. 5), and again it is stated, "Going up through that nerve one gets immortality" (Ch. VIII. vi. 6). From this it is known that the soul, while emerging through the hundred and first nerve, goes out along the rays.

Now the *doubt* arises as to whether the soul follows the rays equally, irrespective of the occurrence of the death during the day-time or night, or it does so only when dying in the day-time.

Vedāntin: This being the doubt, the aphorist declares that the soul progresses by the way of the rays irrespective of the time of death, for the Upaniṣad speaks in general terms.

निशि नेति चेन्न सम्बन्धस्य यावद्देहभावित्वात् दर्शयति च ॥१९॥

निशि In the night न there is no (progress along the rays) इति चेत् if it be argued thus, then न not so, यावत्-देह-भावित्वात् since there is a continuance as long as the body lasts सम्बन्धस्य of the relationship (between the nerve and the rays); च also दर्शयति the Upaniṣad reveals this.

19. If it be argued that the soul departing at night can have no progress along the rays, then it is not so, since the connection between the nerve and the rays continues as long as the body lasts; and this is revealed in the Upaniṣad.

Opponent: The nerve and the sun's rays remain connected during the day, so that a man dying in the day may well follow the rays (in his upward course); but that is not possible for a man dying at night because the connection between the nerve and the rays is then snapped.

Vedāntin: Not so, for the connection between the nerve and the rays lasts as long as the body itself, for the nerve and the rays remain in association as long as the embodied state continues; (the connection is not broken by night). This fact is revealed by the Upaniṣad in, "Extending from that solar orb they (the rays) enter into the nerves, and spreading out from the nerves they enter the solar orb" (Ch. VIII. vi. 2). In summer the presence of the rays, even during nights, is perceived from their effect of producing heat etc. If it is difficult to perceive them during the nights in other seasons, it is because they are present in very small measures even as they are in cloudy days during winter. The text, "The sun makes of it a day even at night", reveals this very fact. Were a man, dying at night, to proceed upward even without following the rays, the pursuit of the rays itself would become useless. The Upaniṣad does not mention separately that those who die in the day-time proceed upward by following the rays, while those who die at night do so without depending on the rays. On the contrary if it be supposed that even a man of knowledge cannot proceed upward owing to the offence of his dying at night, then the fruit of knowledge will become uncertain, so that men will have no inducement to it, for one cannot regulate the time of one's death. It cannot be that a soul that has become detached from the body at night, must wait till day dawns; for even when day dawns, its body may not come in contact with the solar rays, it (the body) having been already consigned to fire etc. The text, "In the little time that the mind takes to travel from one object to another, the man of knowledge reaches the sun" (Ch.

VIII. vi. 5), also shows that there is no waiting (for daybreak). Therefore the soul's pursuit of the rays is the same whether it departs at night or in the day.

Topic 11: Soul's Journey During the Sun's Southern Course

अतश्चायनेऽपि दक्षिणे ॥२०॥

अतः च For the same reason अपि even (when dying) दक्षिणे अयने during the southern course of the sun (the soul gets the fruits of knowledge).

20. For the very same reason (the soul gets the result of knowledge) even when departing during the sun's southern course.

Just because of this—because there is no need for waiting, because the result of knowledge is not uncertain, and because the time of death is unpredictable—if a man of knowledge should die during the southward course of the sun, he will get the result of his knowledge all the same. By this aphorism the aphorist demolishes the misconception about the necessity of waiting till the sun starts northward that may arise from the facts that the sanctity of the northern course is well recognized, that Bhīṣma is known to have waited for it, and that the Upaniṣad says, "From the bright fortnight he goes to the six months during which the sun moves northward" (Ch. IV. xv. 5). The well-known sanctity is a fact in relation to the men of ignorance. As for Bhīṣma's waiting for departure during the northern course, it was by way of showing respect to popular sentiment and demonstrating the validity of his father's boon that his death would be at his own command. As for the meaning of the Upaniṣadic text, it will be explained under the aphorism, "These are deities conducting the soul for there are indicatory marks to that effect" (B. S. IV. iii. 4).

Opponent: In the Smṛti the start is made with the verse, "Now I shall tell thee, O thou mightiest of the Bharatas, of the time travelling in which, the *Yogins* return, (and again of that taking which) they do not return" (Gītā, VIII. 23), and then the special times like day, calculated to lead to cessation from rebirth, are defined in the main; so how can a man departing at night or during the southern course of the sun be freed from rebirth?

Vedāntin: As to that, the answer is:

योगिनः प्रति च स्मर्यते स्मार्ते चैते ॥२१॥

च And (these times etc.) स्मर्यते are mentioned in the Smṛti योगिनः प्रति for the *Yogins*; च and एते these two (Sāṁkhya and Yoga paths) are स्मार्ते mentioned in the Smṛti (and not the Vedas).

21. And these times etc. are mentioned in the Smṛti for the Yogins; and these (paths of) Sāṁkhya and Yoga are mentioned in the Smṛtis and not the Vedas.

These limitations of time etc. as leading to the cessation of rebirth are mentioned in the Smṛtis for the *Yogins*. These (paths of *Yoga* and *Sāṁkhya*[6] belong to the Smṛtis and not to the Vedas. Thus owing to a difference of the subject-matters and the special qualifications of the people following them, the fixation of time found in the Smṛtis is not to be applied to the Upaniṣadic context.

Opponent: The paths of the gods and the manes, just as they are presented in the Upaniṣads, can be recognized as recounted in the Smṛtis as well: "Fire, flame, day-time, the bright fortnight, the six months of the northern passage of the sun.... Smoke, night-time, the dark fortnight, the six months of the southern passage of the sun" (Gītā, VIII. 24-25).

Vedāntin: The answer is that since a promise about the time is made thus in the Smṛti, "I shall tell thee of the time" (Gītā, VIII. 23), therefore the aphorist apprehends a contradiction and so shows how that can be resolved. In reality, there will be no contradiction in the Smṛti as well if there too the gods conducting the souls are meant by those terms (as they are in fact in the Upaniṣads).

[6] *Yoga* means the performance of the obligatory daily duties like *Agnihotra* as an offering to God; *Sāṁkhya* means a feeling of not being the agent of any work (vide Gītā). Both these are different from the Upaniṣadic meditation.

Section III

Topic 1: Only One Path to the World of Brahman

Doubt: It was stated that up to the point where the path (of the gods) starts, the order of departure from the body is similar. But the path itself is variously described in the various Upaniṣads. One course starts from the association of the nerves and rays: "Then he rises up along these very rays" (Ch. VIII. vi. 5). Another starts with the flame: "They reach (the deity identified with) the flame, from the flame (to the deity of) the day" (Bṛ. VI. ii. 15). There is another course stated in: "Reaching the path of the gods, he comes to the world of Fire" (Kau. I. 3). Yet another is: "When a man departs from this world, he reaches the air" (Bṛ. V. x. 1). Still another is: "Free from all contaminations they go by the path of the sun to where lives that *Puruṣa*, immortal and undecaying" (Mu. I. ii. 11). Now the doubt arises: Are these paths different from one another, or are they the same one with many features?

Opponent: When in such a predicament, the conclusion to be drawn is that these paths are certainly different on account of their occurring in different contexts and forming the appendages of diverse meditations. Moreover, the categorical assertion in, "Then along these very rays" (Ch. VIII. vi. 5), will be nullified if the flame etc. (of Bṛ. VI. ii. 15) are taken into consideration. Also the text about quickness, contained in, "He reaches the sun as quickly as it takes the mind to move from one object to another" (Ch. VIII. vi. 5), will be compromised. Therefore these paths must be different from one another.

Vedāntin: To this we say,

अर्चिरादिना तत्प्रथितेः ॥१॥

अर्चिः-आदिना Along the path starting from flame (i.e. light) तत्-प्रथितेः that being well known.

1. The soul travels along the path starting from flame, that being well known.

We assert that all who would reach Brahman have to proceed along the path starting from flame.

Why so?

"That being well known," that path being well known to all men of realization. Thus it is that in the text, "And those others as well who meditate with faith upon the *Satya* Brahman in the forest (reach the deity identified with flame)" (Bṛ. VI. ii. 15), occurring in a context dealing with the meditation on the five fires, we hear of the progress along the path starting from flame even in the case of those who practise other kinds of meditation.

Opponent: It may well be that in the case of those meditations where no course is mentioned, this course starting from flame will find its scope. But in the cases where other courses are mentioned, why should one resort to this course starting from flame?

Vedāntin: To this the reply is that this might have been so if these courses were totally disparate. As a matter of fact, however, this course leading to the world of Brahman is the same though possessed of diverse features and indicated in certain places through a few of these characteristics only. This is what we maintain. Since in all the descriptions, the particulars can be recognized as so many aspects of the same path, therefore these can be comprised in a single conception by considering them as inter-related in a successive series of attributes and substantives. Just as in the case of a meditation occurring in different contexts, the different aspects have to be collected into a single whole, similarly the characteristics of the path also have to be integrated. Although the meditations may differ, the path must be the same, since it is recognized that it is an aspect of the same path that is present in a particular case and since the goal to be reached is the same for all. Thus it is that in the different contexts the very same result, viz the attainment of the world of Brahman, is shown in the texts, "They attain perfection and live in those worlds of Brahman for a great many superfine years" (Bṛ. VI. ii. 15), "He lives there (in the world that is free from grief and cold) for eternal years" (Bṛ. V. x. 1), "He attains the same victory (everywhere) and the same pervasiveness that Brahman (Hiraṇyagarbha) has" (Kau. I. 4), "Those who attain this world of Brahman through *Brahmacharya*" (Ch. VIII. iv. 3). As for the contention that the categorical assertion in, "along these very rays", (Ch. VIII. vi. 5), will be stultified if the path starting from flame be accepted, that creates little difficulty, since that text is meant merely to imply the attainment of the rays.[1] For a single word "very" cannot posit the attainment of the rays and also the rejection of the flame. Hence it is to be understood that this text merely emphasizes the connection with the rays. And the text about quickness (Ch. VIII. vi. 5) is not compromised even if the path starts from flame, for what is meant to imply is that in comparison with other goals, Brahman is reached more quickly; and this is just as one might say, "I shall reach here in a trice." Moreover, the text, "They (i.e. the creatures averse to scriptural duties) do not proceed along either of these two paths" (Ch. V. x. 8), which enumerates a third state, shows that apart from the path of the manes there is only another path, viz that of the gods, which is divided into the stages of flame etc. Besides, in the Upaniṣadic texts that speak of the path as starting from flame, the stages in the path are quite a number, whereas they are few in other texts; and it is proper that the fewer should be made to fit in with the greater. It is from such considerations that it has been said, "The soul travels along the path starting from flame, for this is well known."

Topic 2: The Departing Soul Reaches Air after Year

वायुमब्दादविशेषविशेषाभ्याम् ॥२॥

(The soul of the knower of the qualified Brahman reaches) **वायुम्** air **अब्दात्** from the year, **अविशेष-विशेषाभ्याम्** owing to the absence and presence of specification.

2. The soul of the knower of the qualified Brahman goes from the year to air, on account of the absence and presence of specification.

[1] To imply that a man dying even at night proceeds along the rays. Thus it denies only the possible non-attainment of the rays. It cannot also deny the progress through flame etc.

In what definite order, again, should the different presentations of the progress of the soul (along the path of the gods) be linked up in a chain of attributes and substantives? That link is supplied by the teacher acting as a friend. The Kauṣītakins read of their path of the gods thus: "Attaining this path of the gods, he comes to the world of Fire; he comes to the world of Air, (he comes to the world of Varuṇa); he comes to the world of Indra; he comes to the world of Prajāpati (Virāṭ); he comes to the world of Brahmā (Hiraṇyagarbha)" (Kau. I. 3). There the term "world of Fire" is synonymous with flame (of Bṛ. VI. ii. 15), since both indicate burning, so that one need not take any pains for the establishment of an order with regard to these. But since (the deity of) air is not heard of in the path starting from (the deity of) flame (in the Chāndogya), where should it be placed? The answer is being given by saying that in the text, "They reach (the deity of) flame, from flame (the deity of) day, from day (the deity of the) bright fortnight, from the bright fortnight (the deity of) the six months during which the sun moves northward, from the six months to (the deity of the) year, from the year to (the deity of) the sun" (Ch. V. x. 1), they assign the position of air after the year and before the sun.

Why should it be so?

"Owing to the absence and presence of specification". Thus it is that the air that is not very definitely located in the text, "he comes to the world of Air" (Kau. I. 3), is seen to be spoken of definitely in another Upaniṣad, "When a man departs from this world, he reaches air, which makes an opening there for him like the hole of a chariot wheel. He goes upward through that and reaches the sun" (Bṛ. V. x. 1). Since in this text air is specifically placed before the sun, air is to be assigned a position between the year and the sun.

Opponent: Why again, after noticing the specific mention of air after fire (in Kau. I. 3), should not air be placed after flame?

Vedāntin: We claim that there is no such specification.

Opponent: Was not the text quoted, "Attaining this path of the gods, he comes to the world of Fire, he comes to the world of Air, (he comes to the world of Varuṇa)" (Kau. I. 3)?

The *answer* is that here the statement is merely in the form of an enumeration of the things one after the other, there being nothing indicative of any serial order. The objects reached are alone enumerated here by saying that he goes to such and such regions, whereas in the other (Bṛhadāraṇyaka) text it is stated that he proceeds up through an opening as big as the hole of a chariot wheel to reach the sun, so that a sequence is well understood. Hence the statement, "Owing to the absence and presence of specification", is quite reasonable. The Vājasaneyins, however, have this reading, "from the months to the world of the gods; from the world of the gods to the sun" (Bṛ. VI. ii. 15). According to that text, the soul should reach air from the world of the gods, so that the sun may be reached next. But when the aphorist says that the soul reaches air from the year, he has the Chāndogya text in view (V. x. 1). As between the Chāndogya and the Bṛhadāraṇyaka Upaniṣads, one omits the world of the gods, and the other the year. But since both are authoritative, both these have to be added to both; and while doing so, it has to be borne in mind that the year, being connected with the months, has to be placed earlier and the world of the gods later.[2]

Topic 3: The Soul Proceeds from Lightning to Varuna

तडितोऽधि वरुणः सम्बन्धात् ॥३॥

वरुणः Varuṇa तडितः अधि after lightning सम्बन्धात् because of (their) connection (with water).

3. Varuṇa is to be placed after lightning, because of their connection with water (i.e. cloud).

In the text, "He goes from the sun to the moon, from the moon to lightning" (Ch. IV. xv. 5), Varuṇa is to be placed after lightning on the authority of the text, "He comes to the world of Varuṇa" (Kau. I. 3); for lightning and Varuṇa (Rain-god) are related to each other. When long streaks of lightning

[2] So the order is: Months, ,ear, abode of gods, air, sun.

dance within the bowels of the clouds with sharp thundering sounds, then comes down rain, which fact is also noted in the Brāhmaṇa text, "Lightning flashes and thunder roars; it will surely rain" (Ch. VII. xi. 1). It is well known from the Vedas and Smṛtis that Varuṇa is the god of waters. After Varuṇa are to be placed Indra and Prajāpati, because the Kauṣītaki Upaniṣad recites that way and no other position can be found for them. Varuṇa and others have to be relegated towards the end, since they are fresh entrants and have not been assigned any position in the path (in Ch. IV. xv. 5 or Bṛ. VI. ii. 15) starting with flame and ending with lightning.

Topic 4: Guiding Deities

Doubt: With regard to flame etc. the doubt arises as to whether these are marks on the path, or places of experience, or the conductors of the souls moving forward.

Opponent: As to that, the conclusion to be arrived at is that the flame etc. are merely descriptive marks on the path, for by its very nature the instruction is concerned with such landmarks. As it occurs in common experience that when a man wants to go to a village or a town, he is instructed thus: "You should go to such a hill, then to a banian tree, then to a river, and then you will reach the village or town", so also it is said here, "From flame to the day-time, from the day-time to the bright fortnight", and so on. Or it may well be that these are places of experience. It is thus that fire etc. are associated with the word "world", as for instance in, "he comes to the world of Fire" (Kau. I. 3). In common parlance, the word "world" is used with regard to places where the creatures experience (the results of virtues and vices), as for instance, "the world of men, the world of manes, the world of gods" (Bṛ. I. v. 16), and so on. Even so is the Brāhmaṇa text, "They get attached to the worlds of days and nights"[3] (Ś. B. X. ii. 6.8). Hence the flame etc. are not the conducting deities. Besides, these cannot reasonably conduct the souls as they are insentient; for in common

[3] The men of rites and meditations get their results in the worlds figuratively called days, nights, etc.

experience it is the intelligent men, employed by a king, that escort others who have to be guided along inaccessible roads.

Vedāntin: To this we say,

आतिवाहिकास्तल्लिङ्गात् ॥४॥

(These are) आतिवाहिकाः guiding deities तत्-लिङ्गात् because of the indicative mark to that effect.

4. (Flame etc. are) conducting deities, owing to the indicative mark to that effect.

These must reasonably be conducting deities.

Why?

"Owing to indicatory mark to that effect". Thus the text, "From the moon he reaches the deity of lightning. A superhuman (lit. "not belonging to Manu's creation") comes, and he escorts them from there to the world of Brahman" (Ch. IV. xv. 5), reveals this escorting to be an established fact.

Opponent: That sentence cannot go beyond what it actually states.

Vedāntin: Not so, since the attribute (viz superhuman) is meant simply to deny the assumption that this being is human (lit. belongs to Manu's creation) which might arise from an already established fact. The adjective "superhuman" placed before "being" for the sake of ruling out human guides becomes justified if sentient beings are already known as guides in the flame etc. and these are also understood to be within Manu's creation.

Opponent: A mere indicative mark cannot decide thus in the absence of any logic behind it.

Vedāntin: That defect does not arise,

उभयव्यामोहात्तत्सिद्धेः ॥५॥

तत्-सिद्धेः: That being established उभय-व्यामोहात् on account of both (the person and the path) being unconscious.

5. Because that stands established on account of both (the traveller and the path) being then unconscious.

Now those who would pass along the path through flame etc. have their senses and organs bunched up owing to their separation from the bodies, and so they are devoid of independent action. The flame etc. also are not independent, they being insentient. So it can be understood that some deities who are sentient and identify themselves with (and preside over) the flame etc. are engaged in the work of escorting. In common experience too, when people become intoxicated or unconscious and have their senses befuddled, they are led through their paths by others. Besides, the flame etc. being uncertain, cannot be the indicative marks or features of the path; for one dying at night cannot reasonably have an accession of daylight, and it was stated earlier that there can be no waiting for the day. But such a defect does not arise when these have permanence in their identity with the deities. That the deities are mentioned by the words flame etc. can be justified on the ground that they identify themselves with these. And such statements as, "from flame to the day-time" (Ch. IV. xv. 5, V. x. 1,) do not create any difficulty even if the escorting deities are meant, the meaning in that case being, "Through the instrumentality of the deity of flame they reach the deity of the day-time, through the instrumentality of the deity of the day-time they reach the deity of the bright fortnight". In common parlance also people impart instruction about the guides on the way thus: "From here you go to Balavarman, then to Jayasiṁha, thence to Kṛṣṇagupta". Moreover, the statement in the beginning is, "They reach the flame", which merely tells us of coming in contact, but not of any special form of it. At the end, however, comes the statement, "he escorts them to Brahman" (Ch. IV. xv. 6), where a special form of contact as between an escort and the escorted is stated. From this it can be ascertained that the same kind of contact exists in the beginning as well. But owing to the very fact that all the senses then become bunched up, no experience is possible there. As for the word "world" (lit. place of experience), that can well be used even with regard to the beings who simply pass through without getting any experience, inasmuch as these worlds supply (real) experiences to their own residents. Hence a man who reaches the world presided over by the deity of fire is guided along by the god of fire, and the man who reaches the world presided over by the god of air is guided forward by the god of air. This is how the passage is to be construed.

Opponent: On the supposition that the conducting deities are meant, how would that view be valid in the cases of Varuṇa and others? For Varuṇa and others are placed after lightning, and from lightning up till Brahman is reached, a super-human being is mentioned in the Upaniṣad as acting as the escort.

Vedāntin: Hence the aphorist gives the answer:

वैद्युतेनैव ततस्तत्-श्रुतेः ॥६॥

ततः From there (i.e. from lightning) (they are guided) (from above) वैद्युतेन एव by the very same being who comes to lightning तत्-श्रुतेः for so the Upaniṣad says.

6. From there they are guided by the very same being who comes to lightning; for it is of him that the Upaniṣad speaks.

It is to be understood that "from there", after arriving at lightning, they go to the world of Brahman, being led through the worlds of Varuṇa and others, under the guidance of a superhuman being who exists (even) beyond lightning; for that very being is mentioned as the guide in the Upaniṣadic text, "A superhuman being comes and escorts them from there to the world of Brahman" (Ch. IV. xv. 5). As for Varuṇa and others, it is to be understood that they somehow contribute to the task of that superhuman being by either not creating any obstruction or helping positively. Accordingly, it is well said that flame etc. stand for the escorting deities.

TOPIC 5: THE PATH LEADS TO THE CONDITIONED BRAHMAN

कार्यं बादरिरस्य गत्युपपत्तेः ॥७॥

बादरिः Bādari (thinks that the souls are led) कार्यं to the conditioned Brahman गति-उपपत्तेः because of the possibility of becoming the goal अस्य on Its part.

7. *Bādari thinks that the souls are led to the conditioned Brahman, for it (alone) can reasonably be the goal.*

Doubt: With regard to the text, "He escorts them to Brahman" (Ch. IV. xv. 5), the point to be considered is whether this deity escorts them to the inferior, conditioned Brahman or to the superior, unconditioned Brahman Itself.

Why should such a doubt arise?

On account of the use of the word Brahman and the Upaniṣadic mention of progress.

Bādari: As to that, the teacher Bādari thinks that they are led to the inferior, conditioned, and qualified Brahman alone.

Why?

"For It can logically be the goal." For this conditioned Brahman can properly be a goal to be reached, since It has a locus. But with regard to the supreme Brahman there can be no such conceptions as an approacher, a goal, and progress towards It, for the absolute Brahman is omnipresent and is also the inmost Self of the travellers.

विशेषितत्वाच्च ॥८॥

8. *And (the conditioned Brahman must be the goal) owing to the specific mention of this.*

Since in another Upaniṣadic text a specific statement is made thus, "Then a being created from the mind (of Brahman, i.e. Hiraṇyagarbha) comes and conducts them to the worlds of Brahman. They attain perfection and live in these worlds of Brahman for a great many superfine years" (Bṛ. VI. ii. 15), therefore it can be understood that the path is related to the conditioned Brahman only. For it is improper to use the plural number (in "worlds") in the case of the supreme Brahman whereas this plural number quite befits the conditioned Brahman, since there can be such a thing as difference of states in It. Even the Upaniṣadic use of the word "world", constituting a place of experience with its multiple aspects, fits in well with a conditioned entity, whereas in the other case (of the absolute Brahman) the word can be used only in a figurative sense as in such texts, "O Emperor, this is *Brahmaloka* (the world that is Brahman Itself)" (Bṛ. IV. iv. 23). Again, to speak in terms of a container and a thing contained (as in, "In those worlds of Brahman") hardly fits in with the supreme Brahman. Hence this escorting relates to the conditioned Brahman alone.

Opponent: The word Brahman cannot be used even for the conditioned Brahman inasmuch as it was established earlier in the First Chapter that Brahman is the cause of the origin etc. of the whole universe (I. i. 1).

Vedāntin: As to that the answer is:

सामीप्यात्तु तद्व्यपदेशः ॥९॥

तु But तत्-व्यपदेशः: the designation as such सामीप्यात् (is) owing to nearness.

9. But (the conditioned Brahman has) that designation owing to nearness (to the absolute Brahman).

The word "but" is used for removing the objection. Since the inferior Brahman is very close to the supreme Brahman, the use of the word Brahman with regard to the former creates no difficulty. The established practice is that the supreme Brahman Itself is called the inferior Brahman when It is conditioned by the pure adjuncts and is taught as though possessed of the attributes of being identified with the mind and such other features of creation for the sake of meditation by some aspirants under certain circumstances.

Opponent: On the supposition that the aspirants reach the conditioned Brahman, their non-return, as mentioned in the Upaniṣad, becomes untenable; for unless it be in the supreme Brahman there can be no such thing as eternal existence. As a matter of fact, the Upaniṣads show that an aspirant who goes along the path of the gods, does not return: "Those going by this path never return to this human cycle of birth and death" (Ch. IV. xv. 5), "For them there is no return here" (an echo of Bṛ. VI. ii. 15), "Going up through that nerve one attains immortality" (Ka. II. iii. 16, Ch. VIII. vi. 6).

Vedāntin: To this we say,

कार्यात्यये तदध्यक्षेण सहातः परमभिधानात् ॥१०॥

कार्य-अत्यये On the final dissolution of the world (of Brahman), (they) सह together with तत्-अध्यक्षेण the lord of that (world) परम् (attain) the supreme (Entity) अत: beyond that अभिधानात् on the strength of (Upaniṣadic) declaration.

10. On the final dissolution of the world of the conditioned Brahman, they attain, along with the lord of the world, what is higher than this conditioned Brahman, as is known on the strength of the Upaniṣadic declaration.

The idea conveyed is that when the time for the final dissolution of the world of the inferior Brahman is imminent, the aspirants who have acquired full realization there itself attain thereafter, along with Hiraṇyagarbha, the ruler of that world, the supreme state of Viṣṇu which is absolutely pure. This kind of liberation by stages has to be admitted on the strength of the Upaniṣadic texts speaking of non-return etc. For we established earlier that it is incomprehensible that the supreme Brahman should be reached by any process of moving forward.

स्मृतेश्च ॥११॥

11. This is confirmed by Smṛti as well.

The Smṛti also confirms this view: "When the time of final dissolution comes at the close of the life of Hiraṇyagarbha, all of them, with enlightenment already attained, enter into the supreme state along with Hiraṇyagarbha" (*Kūrma-Purāṇa, Pūrva-bhāga*, XII. 269). Hence the conclusion is that the Upaniṣadic mention about the progress (along a path) relates to the conditioned Brahman.

Doubt: What was the objection in the background, in answer to which the conclusion is presented in the aphorisms starting with, "Bādari thinks that they are led to the conditioned Brahman" etc. (IV. iii. 7)?

That objection is now being shown by the aphorisms themselves.

परं जैमिनिर्मुख्यत्वात् ॥१२॥

जैमिनि: Jaimini (thinks that they are led) परम् to the supreme Brahman मुख्यत्वात् that being the primary meaning.

12. Jaimini thinks that they are led to the supreme Brahman, that being the primary meaning (of the word Brahman).

But the teacher Jaimini thinks that in the text, "He escorts them to Brahman" (Ch. IV. xv. 6), what is meant is that he leads them to the supreme Brahman Itself.

Why so?

Since "that is the primary sense"; for the supreme Brahman is the primary meaning of the word "Brahman", the inferior one being its secondary meaning. And as between the primary and secondary meanings, one readily understands the primary one alone.

दर्शनाच्च ॥१३॥

13. And (this is so) because the Upaniṣad reveals (this fact).

And the text, "Going up through that nerve, one gets immortality" (Ka. II. iii. 16, Ch. VIII. vi. 6), shows that immortality is preceded by moving forward; and immortality is logically possible in the supreme Brahman, but not so in the conditioned Brahman, that being subject to destruction. For the Upaniṣadic text runs thus, "Again, that in which one perceives a second entity is limited, it is mortal" (Ch. VII. xxiv. 1). This movement is mentioned in the Kaṭha Upaniṣad in connection with the supreme Brahman; for no other knowledge is presented in that context, the topic of the supreme Brahman alone having been mooted with the text, "that which is different from virtue, different from vice" etc. (Ka. I. ii. 14).

न च कार्ये प्रतिपत्त्यभिसन्धि: ॥१४॥

च Moreover, प्रतिपत्ति-अभिसन्धि: the firm resolution about attainment (is) न not कार्ये with regard to the conditioned Brahman.

14. Moreover, the firm resolution about attainment is not concerned with the conditioned Brahman.

"Moreover, the firm resolution about attainment", expressed in the text, "May I attain the assembly hall in the palace of Prajāpati (lit. Hiraṇyagarbha)" (Ch. VIII. xiv. 1), is not directed towards the conditioned Brahman, for the supreme Brahman, as distinguished from the conditioned Brahman, forms the topic under consideration, as is clear from the preceding text, "He who is known as Space is the manifester of name and form. And Brahman is that in which are included these two" (ibid). This is also evident from the text, "May I become the fame (or glory) of the Brāhmaṇas, (the fame of the Kṣatriyas, the fame of the Vaiśyas)" (ibid), which presents Brahman as the Self of everything; for from the text, "That which is called the great fame has no parallel" (Śv. IV. 19), it is well known that the supreme Brahman alone is called "fame". This arriving at the palace, which must be preceded by movement, is described in connection with the meditation about the heart (*Dahara-Vidyā*) in the text, "There exists the palace of Brahman called Aparājitā (unconquerable), there exists the golden altar made specially by the Lord Himself" (Ch. VIII. v. 3). And since the root *pad* (as contained in *pratipadye*—may I arrive at) conveys the sense of motion, it also shows the necessity of taking the help of some path. So the other (opposite) view that can be held is that the Upaniṣadic texts, which speak of the progress along a path, are connected with the supreme Brahman.

Vedāntin: These two views have been presented by the teacher (Vyāsa) in these (two sets of) aphorisms. Of these the one view is contained in the aphorisms starting with "Bādari thinks...; for It alone can reasonably be the goal" (IV. iii. 7-11); and the other view is presented in the aphorisms beginning with "Jaimini thinks..., that being the primary meaning of the word Brahman" (IV. iii. 12-14). Of these two groups of aphorisms, the group commencing from "...for It alone can reasonably be the goal" can prove the falsity of the other group commencing with "that being the primary meaning", and not vice versa. So the earlier point of view has been explained as the acceptable position, whereas the second one is held by the *opponents* (of Vedānta). There can be none to command that one must stick to the primary sense alone (of the word "Brahman") even when there is no such possibility. Besides, with a view to eulogizing the superior knowledge, it is quite proper even in a context of the superior Brahman, to describe the path connected with the other kind of inferior knowledge, just as it is done in the text, "The other (nerves) that have different directions become the causes of death" (Ch. VIII. vi. 6). As for the text, "May I reach the hall in the palace of Prajāpati" (Ch. VIII. xiv. 1), it involves no contradiction to treat it separately from the earlier sentence so as to mean a resolution for attaining the conditioned Brahman. (From the standpoint of eulogy or meditation) it is quite in order to speak even of the qualified Brahman as being the Self of all, as is done in, "He who is possessed of all activities, possessed of all desires" (Ch. III. xiv. 2, 4). Hence the Upaniṣadic texts about movement are connected with the inferior (qualified) Brahman alone.

In pursuance of the usual practice, however, some would ascribe the earlier aphorisms to the *opponent*, and the latter ones to themselves. In accordance with such an arrangement, they would prove that the texts connected with movement are concerned with the supreme Brahman Itself. But that is improper since Brahman cannot logically be a goal to be attained. The supreme Brahman can never become a goal to be achieved which pervades everything, which is inside everything, which is the Self of all, and whose characteristics have been thus indicated by the Upaniṣads: "All-pervasive like space and eternal", "That which is Brahman, immediate and direct, that is the Self within all" (Bṛ. III. iv. 1), "The Self Itself is all this" (Ch. VII. xxv. 2), "This world is nothing but Brahman the highest" (Mu. II. ii. 11). For one cannot reach where one already is. The well-known fact in the world is that one thing is reached by something else.

Opponent: In ordinary life, a place already reached can still be reached again in terms of change of environment, as for instance, a man already on this earth may still reach it in terms of altered position. Similarly a boy who continues to be the same person may be noticed in terms of change in the period of life to be progressing towards old age occurring to himself. So also Brahman may somehow become a goal to be approached by virtue of Its being equipped with all kinds of power.

Vedāntin: Not so, for all distinctions are ruled out from Brahman in accordance with such Upaniṣadic and Smṛti texts and logic as, "Without parts, without action, calm, free of blemishes, free of taints" (Śv. VI. 19), "It is neither gross nor minute, neither short nor long" (Bṛ. III. viii. 8), "Since He is coextensive with all that is internal and external, and since He is birthless" (Mu. II. i. 2), "That great birthless Self is undecaying, immortal, undying, fearless, and Brahman (i.e. infinite)" (Bṛ. IV. iv. 25), "This is the Self, which has been described as 'Not this', 'Not this' " (Bṛ. III. ix. 26), according to which it cannot be imagined that the supreme Self can have any connection with any distinct time, space, etc., so as to be reached on the analogy of a particular place on the earth or a stage of life. The earth or age can well become the goal to be reached in terms of particular place or time, since they can have distinct localities and periods.

Opponent: Brahman can have different powers since the Upaniṣads show It to be the cause of the origin, continuance, and dissolution of the universe.

Vedāntin: Not so, since the Upaniṣadic texts denying distinctive attributes cannot be interpreted in any other way.

Opponent: In the same way the texts about origin etc. cannot be interpreted otherwise.

Vedāntin: Not so, for their purpose is to establish unity. The scripture that propounds the reality of Brahman, existing alone without a second, and that proves the unreality of all modifications with the help of the illustrations like clay, cannot be meant for establishing the truth of origin etc.

Opponent: Why again should the texts about origin etc. be subservient to the texts denying distinction and not the other way round?

Vedāntin: The answer is that this is so because the texts denying distinction lead to a knowledge which is complete by itself (and leaves behind no more curiosity to be satisfied). For when one has realized that the Self is one, eternal, pure, and so on, one cannot have any more curiosity to be satisfied as a result of the rise in him of the conviction that the highest human goal has been reached, as is known from such Upaniṣadic passages as, "then what sorrow and what delusion can there be for that seer of oneness?" (Īś , 7), "You have attained that which is free from fear, O Janaka" (Bṛ. IV. ii. 4), "The enlightened man is not afraid of anything. Him indeed this remorse does not afflict, 'Why did I not perform good deeds, and why did I perform bad deeds?' " (Tai. II. ix. 1). This is confirmed equally by noticing the contentment of the enlightened ones, and from the condemnation of the pursuit of unreal modifications in, "He who sees as though there is difference here goes from death to death" (Ka. II. i. 10). Accordingly, the texts denying distinctions cannot be understood to be subservient to others. But the texts about origin etc. cannot give rise to any such self-contained knowledge (that allays further curiosity). As a matter of fact, they are seen to aim at something else. Thus it is that (in the Chāndogya Upaniṣad) the start is made with, "O amiable one, know this sprout (that this body is) to have come out of something; for it cannot be without a root" (VI. viii. 3); and then the Upaniṣad says later (in "with the help of that sprout try to find out the root that is Existence" VI. viii. 6) that Existence alone which is the source of the universe has to be known. Similar also is the text, "Crave to know that from which indeed all these creatures originate, by which they are sustained after birth, towards which they advance, and into which they merge. That is Brahman" (Tai. III. i. 1), (where also the reality to be known is Brahman alone). Thus since the texts about creation etc. are meant for imparting the knowledge of oneness, Brahman cannot be possessed of many powers and hence also It cannot reasonably be a goal to be reached. Any travelling towards Brahman is denied in the text, "His organs do not depart. Being but Brahman, he is merged in Brahman" (Bṛ. IV. iv. 6). This fact was explained under the aphorism, "For in the case of the followers of one recension there is a clear denial of the soul's departure" (IV. ii. 13).

On the supposition, again, that there is such a thing as travelling, the travelling soul must be a part or a transformation of Brahman, or something different from it; for travelling is impossible in a case of total unity.

Opponent: Even if it be so, what does it amount to?

Vedāntin: The answer is that if it be a part, then since the whole (Brahman) is a goal ever attained by that part, there can be no such thing as going to Brahman. Moreover, since Brahman is well known to be partless, it is improper to imagine such things in Brahman as a part and a whole. The position is the same even in case the soul be a transformation; for the transformed thing is ever present in the material of which it is a transformation. An earthen pot can never exist unless it be in identity with the earth, for it will cease to exist when it is not so identified. Again, even if the soul be either an effect or a part (of Brahman), then since Brahman, the possessor of such transformations or parts, remains unchanged, there can be no possibility of the soul's entering into the transmigratory state (for the parts of an inert stone cannot move, nor can a frog be confined within it). If the soul be different from Brahman, it must be either atomic or all-pervasive, or of an intermediate size. If it be all-pervasive, there can be no travelling. If it be of a medium size (indeterminate size changing with the body), it will become impermanent. If it be atomic, any feeling of sensation all over the body will be inexplicable. Besides, the views about the atomic and medium sizes were previously refuted (under the aphorism II. iii. 29) in an elaborate way. If the soul be different from the supreme Brahman, such scriptural declarations as, "That thou art" (Ch. VI. viii. 7) will be nullified. This defect is equally in evidence even if the soul be either a transformation or a part.

Opponent: Since the source and its modifications and parts are the same (constituting a single whole), no defect arises from these two points of view.

Vedāntin: Not so, because (in that case) unity in the primary sense becomes impossible. Besides, from all these points of view there arises the predicament of liberation being entirely ruled out, owing to the non-eradication of the notion of the identity of the soul with its transmigratory state. Or even if that identity should cease, the soul will lose its innate nature (by merging in

Brahman), since its identity with Brahman is denied (by the *opponent*).

There are some people who prattle thus: The obligatory and occasional rites are performed for the sake of avoiding evil, the optional and prohibited rites are given up for avoiding heaven and hell, and the results of works which are to be experienced in the present body get exhausted by experiencing them; so that when the present body falls, at the same time that there is nothing to connect the soul with a fresh body, a man who proceeds in this way will achieve liberation consisting in the continuance in his own real natural state even without having realized the unity of the individual Self with Brahman.

This is not correct on account of the absence of any valid evidence; for it is not established by any scripture that a man wanting liberation should act thus. This is a position born out of one's own intellectual cognition only that the transmigratory state is a creation of rites, so that it can cease to exist in the absence of these rites. This, again, is not even a matter for inferential reasoning, inasmuch as the absence of the causes of the transmigratory state is beyond (such) determination. There may be many results of works accumulated in past lives by each creature, which have good or bad fruits in store for them. But since they cannot be experienced simultaneously owing to their results being opposed to one another, some of them which get a suitable opportunity produce this life, while others wait for the adequate space, time, and cause. And since these remaining ones cannot be exhausted by the experiences in the present life, it cannot be asserted that, after the fall of the present body, a man will get freed from the causes calculated to produce fresh bodies, even though he has followed the course of life described earlier (by the *opponent*). That the results of past works persist (even after death) is proved on the authority of such Upaniṣadic and Smṛti texts as, "Those who perform virtuous deeds here (obtain excellent births)" (Ch. V. x. 7), "With the residual results of these".

Opponent: It may well be that the obligatory and occasional duties will eject them (i.e. the residual results).

Vedāntin: That cannot be, because there is no opposition

between them. In a case of opposition alone can something be ejected by something else. But the accumulated virtues of past lives are not antagonistic to the obligatory and occasional duties, since both are equally meant for purification. As for the vices, they may be ejected when they stand in opposition, for they are impure by nature; but that does not prove the absence of the causes of rebirth, since the virtues can well constitute such a cause, and since the vices even are not known to be totally eliminated. Besides, there is no proof to show that the performance of the obligatory and occasional duties produce no other result apart from hindering the emergence of evil; for it is quite possible that a concomitant by-product will come into being, as Āpastamba mentions in his Smṛti, "Just as when a mango tree is planted for its fruits, its shade and sweet aroma are produced as by-products, so also when virtuous deeds are done, other factors come out as by-products". Moreover, until complete enlightenment comes, nobody can make a promise of remaining totally free from the optional and prohibited acts in the period between birth and death, for subtle lapses are noticed in the cases of the most careful men. Maybe all this will be considered a doubtful contingency. Even so, it becomes difficult to be convinced that no cause for rebirth remains. Besides, unless it is admitted that the soul's identity with Brahman is a truism realizable through knowledge, it is idle to expect liberation for a soul which is (believed to be) an agent and an experiencer by nature; for one's nature can never be given up like heat by fire.

Opponent : It may well be that it is an evil for the soul to act as an agent and an experiencer, but not so is the power itself for the action and the experience, so that liberation may come when the expression of the power (in the form of action) is stopped while the latency remains.

Vedāntin : That too is wrong, for so long as the potentiality remains, the manifestation of the power becomes irresistible.

Opponent : In that case it may well be that the power by itself cannot accomplish anything without the aid of other causes, so that even when that power abides (potentially) alone, it cannot run into evil.

Vedāntin : That also is wrong since the other causes (like *adṛṣṭa*—unseen potentiality of past action, as also the potential results) ever remain associated (with the soul) through their association with the latency (of agentship and experience). Hence there can be no hope of liberation so long as a soul persists to be by nature an agent and experiencer when at the same time that its identity with Brahman, realizable through knowledge, does not exist. And the Upaniṣad denies that there can be any other path of liberation except knowledge, "There is no other path to reach the goal" (Śv. III. 8).

Opponent: Even if the soul be non-different from the supreme Brahman, this will only result in the annulment of all human dealings (including the scriptural instruction), for then there can be no application of the means of knowledge like perception etc.

Vedāntin: Not so, for that is possible before enlightenment like the behaviour in a dream before awakening. The scripture also speaks of the use of perception etc. in the case of the unenlightened man in the text, "Because when there is duality, as it were, then one sees something" (Bṛ. II. iv. 14, IV. v. 15); and then it shows the absence of this in the case of an enlightened man, "But when to the knower of Brahman everything has become the Self, then what should one see and through what?" (ibid) etc. Thus since the notion of Brahman as a goal to be reached and such other ideas are eliminated for one who has realized the supreme Brahman, any movement cannot be asserted in his case in any way.

Opponent: Where then can the texts about movement find proper scope?

Vedāntin: The answer is that their scope is limited within the meditations based on attributes. Thus it is that the pursuit of a path is sometimes spoken of in connection with the meditation on the five fires, and sometimes with the meditation on the couch (of Brahman) or on Vaiśvānara. Even where a movement is spoken of in connection with Brahman, as in "*Prāṇa* (lit. vital force) is Brahman, Bliss is Brahman, Space is Brahman" (Ch. IV. x. 4), and "Then the tiny lotus of the heart that exists as a place in this city that this body is" (Ch. VIII. i. 1), there also a movement is possible, because what is meditated on there is but the qualified Brahman Itself, possessed of the attributes of being "the ordainer of the results of works", "the possessor of all true desires", and so on. But nowhere is any movement indicated in connection with the supreme Brahman in the same way as it is denied in, "his organs do not depart" (Bṛ. IV. iv. 6). Since even in passages like, "The knower of Brahman attains the Highest" (Tai. II. i. 1), where the root-meaning of "attainment" implies movement, there is no possibility of reaching anywhere according to the reasons already adduced, therefore it is the very realization of one's own nature that is spoken of as this attainment from the standpoint of erasing out this universe of name and form superimposed through ignorance. And it is to be understood as having been said in the same sense as, "Having been Brahman, he attains Brahman" (Bṛ. IV. iv. 6) and similar texts. Again, even if movement has to be explained in connection with the supreme Brahman, it must be held to have been asserted either by way of inducing the aspirant or for meditation. Now, no inducement can be generated by speaking of movement to one who has realized Brahman, since that is already an accomplished fact for him by his having become established in his own Self, which consummation is brought about by the knowledge of Brahman, and which is directly (and not mediately) self-evident to himself. Moreover, it does not stand to reason that the realization of Brahman, which is not productive of any result, but merely presents liberation as an ever accomplished fact, should depend in any way on the reflection about a course to be followed. Accordingly, movement is possible only in relation to the inferior Brahman. That being so, it is only through a failure to distinguish between the superior Brahman and inferior Brahman that the texts about travelling that refer to the inferior Brahman are ascribed to the superior Brahman.

Opponent: Are there then two Brahmans—one superior and the other inferior?

Vedāntin: Quite so; for we come across such texts as, "This very Brahman, O Satyakāma, that is inferior and superior is but this *Om*" (Pr. V. 2).

Opponent: Which again is the superior Brahman and which the inferior?

Vedāntin: The superior Brahman is spoken of where It is indicated by such terms as "not gross" through a negation of all the distinctions of names, forms, etc. called up by nescience. That very Brahman becomes the inferior Brahman where It is taught as possessed of some distinct name, form, etc. for the sake of meditation, as in such words as, "Identified with the mind, having *prāṇa* (i.e. the subtle body) as his body, and effulgence as his form" (Ch. III. xiv. 2).

Opponent: In that case the texts about non-duality will be compromised.

Vedāntin: Not so, for that objection was met from the point of view of the limiting adjuncts created by name and form which spring up from nescience. The results accruing from that meditation on the qualified Brahman, mentioned in the relevant contexts and consisting in the divine powers over the world and so on as heard of in such texts as, "Should he be desirous of the world of the manes, the manes come to him at his very will" (Ch. VIII. ii. 1), however, are confined within the transmigratory state itself on account of the continuance of ignorance. Since this result is associated with some particular space, any travelling for Its attainment involves no contradiction. Even though the Self is omnipresent, we said earlier under the aphorism, "On account of its having for its essence the qualities of that intellect" (II. iii. 29), that a movement comes to be perceived when the limiting adjuncts like the intellect move, just as much as space appears to be moving when vessels etc. containing it move. Hence the view that stands well established is "Bādari thinks that they are led to the conditioned Brahman" etc. (B. S. IV. iii. 7). And the view contained in, "Jaimini says that the supreme Brahman is attained" etc. (IV. iii. 12), is presented merely as an apparent, alternative view by way of helping the (student's) development of the power of intellect. This is how it is to be understood.

Topic 6: Worship with and without Symbols

Doubt: This is well established that any travelling is concerned with the conditioned Brahman and not with the supreme Brahman. Now the doubt is this: "Does the superhuman being

(Ch. IV. xv. 6) lead to the world of Brahman all aspirants without exception who meditate on the conditioned Brahman, or does he lead only some of them?" What should be the conclusion here?

Opponent: All these knowers of Brahman must reach a goal other than the supreme Brahman; for in the aphorism, "The passage of the soul by the path of the gods is not restricted to certain meditations only; it applies to all" (III. iii. 31), this path is promised equally for all the other meditations.

Vedāntin: To this comes the aphorist's rejoinder:

अप्रतीकालम्बनान्नयतीति बादरायण उभयथाऽदोषात्तत्क्रतुश्च ॥१५॥

(He) नयति leads अ-प्रतीक-आलम्बनात् those who do not depend on symbols इति this is what बादरायण: Bādarāyaṇa (says); अदोषात् there being no contradiction उभयथा on (admitting) this twofold division च and (because of the logic of) तत्-क्रतु: of (becoming) what one resolves.

15. Bādarāyaṇa says that the superhuman being leads to Brahman only those who do not use symbols (in their meditation), since this twofold division involves no contradiction and one becomes what one resolves to be.

The teacher Bādarāyaṇa thinks that leaving out those who meditate with the help of symbols, the superhuman being leads all others, who meditate on the conditioned Brahman, to the world of Brahman Itself. For it involves no contradiction to admit this twofold division, since the reasoning about non-restriction (cited above—B. S. III. iii. 31) is applicable to all meditations that are not based on symbols. A confirming reason for this twofold division is found in "the resolution for that"; for it is but reasonable that one who resolves to be Brahman should get the divine glories of Brahman as it is stated in the text, "one becomes just as one meditates on Him". But one cannot have the belief of being one with Brahman when meditating with the help of symbols, since in such a meditation the symbol predominates.

Opponent: The Upaniṣad mentions that even without any

resolve about Brahman one can reach Brahman, as it is stated in the text, "He leads them to Brahman" (Ch. IV. xv. 5), heard of in connection with the meditation on the five fires (and not on Brahman).

Vedāntin: Let this be so where a direct (specific) declaration to the contrary is met with. But the aphorist thinks that in accordance with the logic of becoming what one wills to be, the general rule is that in the absence of any specific declaration, those meditators who entertain a resolution about Brahman, alone reach Brahman.

विशेषं च दर्शयति ॥१६॥

च And दर्शयति the Upaniṣad reveals विशेषम् a speciality (about results).

16. And the Upaniṣad reveals a speciality about the results (of meditations with symbols).

Besides, the Upaniṣad shows with regard to the meditations based on such symbols as name etc., that the succeeding ones have better results than the preceding ones, in such passages as, "(One who meditates upon name as Brahman) gets freedom of movement as far as name extends" (Ch. VII. i. 5), "The organ of speech is surely greater than name" (Ch. VII. ii. 1), "He gets freedom as far as speech extends" (Ch. VII. ii. 2), "Mind is surely greater than speech" (Ch. VII. iii. 1), and so on. This distinction about results is possible for these meditations as they are dependent on symbols. But if they be based on Brahman, how can there be any gradation in the results, since Brahman is without such differences? Accordingly, the meditations based on the symbols cannot have the same result as the others based on Brahman.

Section IV

Topic 1: Nature of Freedom

Doubt: In the Upaniṣad occurs the text, "Thus indeed does this serene, happy being become manifest (or established) in its own real form (i.e. Self or nature) after having risen from this body and having reached the highest Light" (Ch. VIII. xii. 3). With regard to this the doubt arises, "Does that being become manifest with some adventitious distinction as (it happens) in some region of enjoyment like heaven, or is it established as the Self alone?" What should be the conclusion?

Opponent: That manifestation must be in some fresh form even as in other regions, for liberation too is well known to be a result, and the term "becomes manifest" is synonymous with "is born". If this be a mere establishment in its own form (or nature), then since one's own nature is not eliminated even in the earlier stages (of being under other guises), that nature should have manifested itself even there. Hence the "being" becomes manifest as something distinctive.

Vedāntin: This being the position, we say,

सम्पद्याविर्भावः स्वेनशब्दात् ॥१॥

सम्पद्य Having reached (the highest Light) आविर्भाव: there is manifestation (of the soul) स्वेन-शब्दात् because of the use (in the Upaniṣad) of the term (स्वेन) "in its own (Self)".

1. Having reached the "highest Light", the soul becomes manifest in its own real nature because of the use of the term "in its own" (in the Upaniṣad).

The soul manifests itself just as it really is, but not as possessed of any other quality.

How can this be so?

Because the word "own" occurs in "becomes established in its own real form". Otherwise this specification with the word "own" would have been inappropriate.

Opponent: The word "own" should be interpreted to mean "owned by (itself)".

Vedāntin: No, for that is not under reference here. Had that been meant here, then in whatever form that being would become manifest would certainly be owned by it, so that the use of the word "own" would be useless. But if the meaning "in its Self" be accepted, it serves a purpose inasmuch as it implies that the soul becomes manifest merely in its own form and not in any adventitious form as well.

Opponent: What difference is there between the earlier states and this (final) one, when the non-elimination of the true form is the same in either case?

Vedāntin: Hence comes the reply:

मुक्त: प्रतिज्ञानात् ॥२॥

(The soul is then) मुक्त: free, प्रतिज्ञानात् that being the declaration.

2. The soul then attains liberation, that being the (Upaniṣadic) declaration.

The entity that is spoken of here as becoming manifest in its Self, becomes free from its erstwhile bondage and continues as the pure Self, whereas in the earlier state it "seemed to have become blind" (Ch. VIII. ix. 1), "seemed to be weeping" (Ch. VIII. x. 2), "seemed to have undergone destruction" (Ch. VIII. xi. 1)—so that it was in a condition of being tainted by the three states (of waking, dream, and sleep). This is the difference.

Opponent: How again is it known that the soul becomes free?

Vedāntin: The aphorist answers by saying, "that being the Upaniṣadic declaration". Thus it is that in the text, "I shall explain it to you over again" (Ch. VIII. ix. 3), the promise is made of explaining the Self, free from the defects of the three states, and then it is stated, "The being that is really without any body is not touched by likes and dislikes" (Ch. VIII. xii. 1), and the conclusion is made with, "It becomes established in Its own Self; that is the highest Being" (Ch. VIII. xii. 3). So also at the commencement of the story, the text, "The Self that is beyond sin" etc. (Ch. VIII. vii. 1), makes a declaration about the free soul alone. Liberation comes to be considered as a fruit merely from the point of view of the cessation of bondage, and not from the standpoint of production of any fresh result. Although the term "becomes manifest" is synonymous with "is born", still that is said by way of contrast to the earlier state, just as we would say that a man becomes established in health when his disease leaves him. Hence there is no defect.

आत्मा प्रकरणात् ॥३॥

(The "Light" is) आत्मा the Self, प्रकरणात् because of the context.

3. The Light is the Self as it is obvious from the context.

Opponent: How can the soul be said to be liberated, since the text, "having reached the supreme Light" (Ch. VIII. xii. 3), describes it as within creation itself? For by usage the word light denotes physical light. One who has not turned back from created things cannot become free, since all created things are well known as sources of sorrow.

Vedāntin: That is no defect, since from the context it is obvious that the Self Itself is presented here by the word "light". As the topic of the supreme Self is made the starting point in the sentence, "The Self that is beyond sin, free from all dirt, and free from death" (Ch. VIII. vii. 1), it is not possible to jump to the physical light all of a sudden; for that will be tantamount to discarding the subject-matter under discussion and introducing something foreign to it. The word "light" is seen to be used for the Self as well, as in, "Upon that immortal Light of all lights, the gods meditate" (Bṛ. IV. iv. 16). This was elaborated under the aphorism, "Light is Brahman" (I. iii. 40).

Topic 2: Liberated Soul Inseparable from Brahman

अविभागेन दृष्टत्वात् ॥४॥

(In liberation the soul exists) अविभागेन in a state of inseparableness (from the Self) दृष्टत्वात् for so it is noticed (in the Upaniṣad).

4. In liberation the soul exists in a state of inseparableness from the supreme Self, for so it is noticed in the Upaniṣad.

One would like to know whether the entity which becomes established in its own Self after reaching the highest Light remains separate from the supreme Self or continues in a state of identification. Now when in such an inquisitive mood one might conclude that the being exists separately, because in the text, "He moves about there" (Ch. VIII. xii. 3), speaks of something holding something else in itself; and in the text, "having reached the Light", a subject and an object are separately mentioned. The aphorist explains to such a (doubting) one that the liberated soul remains identified with the supreme Self.

Why so?

Because it is so noticed in the Upaniṣad. Thus it is that texts like, "That thou art" (Ch. VI. viii. 7), "I am Brahman" (Bṛ. I. iv. 10), "Where one does not see anything else" (Ch. VII. xxiv. 1), "But there is no such second thing separate from it which it can see" (Bṛ. IV. iii. 23), etc., reveal the supreme Self as non-separate from the (individual) soul. And in conformity with the logic of becoming what one resolves to be, the result (freedom) should accord with one's (Upaniṣadic) knowledge. The text, "O Gautama, as pure water poured on pure water becomes verily the same, so also becomes the Self of the man of knowledge who is given to deliberation (on the supreme Self)" (Ka. II. i. 15), and other texts which set forth the nature of the liberated soul, as also the illustrations like the river and the sea (Mu. III. ii. 8), reveal only this fact of non-difference. As regards any statement implying difference, that is possible in a secondary sense even in a context of non-difference, as is seen in such texts as, " 'O venerable sir, on what is that Infinity established?' 'On Its own majesty' " (Ch. VII. xxiv. 1), "Delighting in his own Self, disporting in his own Self" (Ch. VII. xxv. 2).

Topic 3: Characteristics of the Liberated Soul

ब्राह्मेण जैमिनिरुपन्यासादिभ्यः ॥५॥

ब्राह्मेण As possessed of the attributes of Brahman जैमिनिः (says) Jaimini उपन्यास-आदिभ्यः on account of the references etc.

5. Jaimini says that from references etc. (in the Upaniṣads) (it is evident that the liberated soul) becomes established in the attributes that Brahman has.

This is well settled now that in the text "in its own form" (Ch. VIII. xii. 3), what is meant is that it becomes established in itself as the Self, and not in any extraneous adventitious form. But now when the desire to know in detail arises, it is being said that "in its own form" means in the form of Brahman that is its own real form and that is possessed of the characteristics beginning with freedom from sin etc. and ending with true desire (Ch. VIII. vii. 1), as also omnipresence and rulership over all. It becomes established in that form which is its own. This is how the teacher Jaimini thinks.

How is this known?

For such a fact is known from the references in the Upaniṣads and other reasons (i.e. fresh information etc.). Thus it is that through the very reference contained in the text beginning with, "This Self that is beyond sin" etc., and ending with, "Having true desires and inevitable will" (ibid.), the Upaniṣad makes us understand that the individual soul is the same as the supreme Self possessing these attributes. Similarly through the (fresh information in the) text, "There he roams about eating, playing, and making merry" (Ch. VIII. xii. 3), as also, "He gets freedom of movement in all the worlds" (Ch. VII. xxv. 2), it presents its form of divine majesty. From this view-point, the statements like, "He is omniscient and ruler of all" etc. become quite logical.

चिति तन्मात्रेण तदात्मकत्वादित्यौडुलोमिः ॥६॥

चिति In consciousness तत्-मात्रेण as that much (i.e. consciousness) only, तत्-आत्मकत्वात् that being its real nature इति this (is (what) औडुलोमिः Auḍulomi (says).

6. Auḍulomi says that the liberated soul becomes established in consciousness as consciousness itself, that being its true nature.

Although the attributes, such as freedom from sin etc., are enumerated as though they are different from one another, still they are based on false concepts arising from dependence on mere words; for all that can be understood there is a mere negation of sin etc. The real nature of the soul, however, is consciousness alone, so that it is proper that the liberated soul should be established in that nature only. And thus only the Upaniṣadic texts like, "Even so, my dear, is the Self without interior and exterior, entire and pure intelligence alone" (Bṛ. IV. v. 13), become duly honoured. Even though "having true desires —*satyakāma*" etc. are spoken of as if they are real attributes belonging intrinsically to some entity in the derivative sense of "he that is possessed of true desire", still such attributes are dependent on association with limiting adjuncts, so that they cannot constitute the true nature of the entity like consciousness; for the Self is denied to have many forms inasmuch as a diversity of forms is denied about Brahman in the aphorism, "Even from difference of place a twofold characteristic cannot be predicated of Brahman" (III. ii. 11). Hence even the declaration about eating etc. (Ch. VIII. xii. 3) is made merely for praise, meaning thereby only an absence of sorrow; and this is just like the phrases, "delighting in his own Self" (Ch. VII. xxv. 2) etc. For any delight, play, or merry-making can never be described as happening in the Self in the primary sense, since all these presuppose the presence of a second entity. Hence the teacher Auḍulomi thinks that the freed soul manifests itself as the Self in which there is no trace of phenomenal existence, which is consciousness itself, which is serene and happy, and which defies all verbal description.

एवमप्युपन्यासात् पूर्वभावादविरोधं बादरायणः ॥७॥

एवम् अपि Even so अविरोधं there is no contradiction पूर्व-भावात् owing to the persistence of the earlier nature उपन्यासात् in accordance with the Upaniṣadic reference बादरायणः (says) Bādarāyaṇa.

7. *Bādarāyaṇa says that even so, there is no contradiction, since the earlier nature exists according to Upaniṣadic reference.*

"Even so", even though it be admitted that the soul manifests itself in its own real nature of pure consciousness, still (its possession of) the earlier form, the divine majesty of (the qualified) Brahman that is known from such reasons as Upaniṣadic reference is not denied from the empirical point of view; and hence there is no contradiction. This is what the teacher Bādarāyaṇa thinks.

Topic 4: Fulfilment of Desire through Will

Doubt: In connection with the meditation based on the heart it is heard from the Upaniṣad, "Should he desire the world of the manes, the manes become associated with him at his mere wish" (Ch. VIII. ii. 1) etc. The doubt here is whether the mere wish is the cause of the appearance of the manes or it is the cause in association with some other factors.

Opponent: As to that, although the Upaniṣad declares, "at his mere wish" still it is proper that in consonance with the affairs of the world, there should be dependence on some other factors. Just as in the world we become associated with our fathers and others as a result of our desire coupled with some other causes like approaching, so also it must be the same in the case of the liberated soul. It is only thus that nothing contrary to common experience has to be imagined. When it is said, "at his mere wish", it is done so from the point of view of the easy availability of the other means that lead to the fulfilment of the desire as it is seen in the case of a king. Moreover, the manes and others who follow the dictates of one's desires will be as unsteady as the other things fancied by the mind, so that they will not be able to provide sufficient enjoyment.

Vedāntin: This being the position, we say,

संकल्पादेव तु तत्-श्रुतेः ॥८॥

तु But संकल्पात् एव from volition alone तत्-श्रुतेः because such is the Upaniṣadic text.

8. (The fathers and others come) as a result of the will alone, because the Upaniṣad says so.

The contact with the fathers and others comes about owing to the will alone.

Why so?

"Because the Upaniṣad says so." For such Upaniṣadic texts as, "the manes become associated with him at his mere wish" (Ch. VIII. ii. 1) will be compromised if other causes have to be relied on. As for the other factors, they may well be there if they come in obedience to his will; but no other means that requires an additional effort, can be admitted, since in that case the volition will remain infructuous till that other factor comes into play. Moreover, in a matter to be known from the Upaniṣad, any general argument based on empirical experience has no application. Besides, the will of a liberated soul is different from any ordinary will, so that through the force of their mere volition these (manes and others) can remain steady for as long as the occasion demands. Hence this occurs through volition alone.

अत एव चानन्याधिपतिः ॥९॥

च And अतः एव for this very reason अनन्य-अधिपतिः without any other lord (to rule over).

9. And for that very reason (a man of knowledge has) no other lord (to rule over him).

"For that very reason", just because his will cannot be infructuous, the man of knowledge is without any ruler, that is to say, none else can rule over him. For even an ordinary man who desires something does not wish that he should be dominated over by somebody else so long as he can avoid that. The Upaniṣadic text also reveals this fact in, "Again, those who leave this world after realizing the Self and these true desires get freedom of movement in all the worlds" (Ch. VIII. i. 6).

TOPIC 5: BODY AFTER REACHING BRAHMA-LOKA

अभावं बादरिराह ह्येवम् ॥१०॥

बादरिः Bādari (asserts) अभावम् the absence (of body and organs) हि because (the Upaniṣad) आह has said एवम् thus.

10. Bādari asserts the absence of body and organs (for one who reaches the Brahma-loka—the world of Brahman), for the Upaniṣad says so.

From the text, "The manes become associated with him at his mere wish" (Ch. VIII. ii. 1) it becomes established that the mind at least exists as the instrument of desire (even after realizing the qualified Brahman). Now it is being examined whether the body and the sense-organs also exist or do not exist for the man who attains divine powers. As to that, the teacher Bādari thinks that the body and senses do not exist for the man of knowledge who becomes thus exalted.

How can this be so?

Because the scriptural passage runs thus: "He becomes delighted by seeing mentally (through these divine mental eyes) these desirable things that exist in the world of Brahman" (Ch. VIII. xii. 5). Were it the case that he roamed about with his mind, as well as body and sense-organs, then the specific mention of "mentally" would not have occurred. Hence there is absence of body and sense-organs after liberation.

भावं जैमिनिर्विकल्पामननात् ॥११॥

जैमिनिः Jaimini (asserts) भावम् the existence (of body and sense-organs) विकल्प-आमननात् since the Upaniṣad speaks of option.

11. Jaimini asserts the existence of body and sense-organs (after the realization of the qualified Brahman), since the Upaniṣad speaks of option.

The teacher Jaimini thinks that like the mind, the body and sense-organs also exist for the liberated man, since in the text, "He remains one, he becomes threefold, fivefold" etc. (Ch. VII.

xxvi. 2) the Upaniṣad mentions that he has the option of changing his state variously. And diversification without a difference of bodies is not easy to accomplish. Although this diversification is read of in the Upaniṣad as a matter of option in the context of the knowledge of the absolute, Infinite (Brahman), still it is presented there (in that context) for the sake of eulogizing the knowledge of the Infinite, just because this divine power does accrue as a matter of fact in the context of the knowledge of the qualified Brahman; and hence this result does actually emerge in connection with the meditation on the qualified Brahman.

द्वादशाहवदुभयविधं बादरायणोऽतः ॥१२॥

अतः Hence बादरायण: Bādarāyaṇa (considers the released soul as) उभय-विधम् of both characteristics द्वादश-अहवत् like the *Dvādaśāha* sacrifice.

12. Hence Bādarāyaṇa considers the released souls to be of both kinds (i.e. with or without bodies and senses) just as it is the case with the Dvādaśāha (twelve-day) sacrifice.

Vedāntin: "Hence", because both these indicatory marks are noticed in the Upaniṣad, therefore the teacher Bādarāyaṇa thinks that it is valid both ways. When a liberated soul wishes to have a body, he gets one; and when he desires to remain without it, he has none; for his will is true and desires are diverse. This is like the sacrifice performed for twelve days (*Dvādaśāha*). Just as a *Dvādaśāha* can be both a *satra* and an *ahīna*[1], because the Vedas present indicatory marks of both, so also is the case here.

तन्वभावे सन्ध्यवदुपपत्तेः ॥१३॥

तनु-अभावे In the absence of a body, (the fulfilment of desires) उपपत्तेः becomes reasonable सन्ध्यवत् as it is in dream.

[1] The same rite *Dvādaśāha* is sometimes spoken of (with the verbs *upayanti*, *āsīram*) as resorted to by many sacrificers, in which case it becomes a *satra*; again it is enjoined (with *yājayet*) that a man desiring progeny should be made to perform the *Dvādaśāha* sacrifice, in which case it becomes an *ahīna*, because of the injunction about the sacrifice itself and the specification of the sacrificer.

13. In the absence of a body, the fulfilment of desires is reasonably possible as in dreams.

In the view that the body, together with the sense-organs, ceases to exist in liberation, the liberated souls can have their desires for manes and others fulfilled (through their minds alone) by merely feeling their presence just as one would have them in a dream. For it can be justified in this way:

भावे जाग्रद्वत् ॥१४॥

भावे When there is existence (of the body etc.), (the fulfilment occurs) जाग्रद्वत् as in the waking state.

14. When the body exists, the fulfilment of the desires is just as in the waking state.

In the view, however, that the body exists, the liberated soul can reasonably have desires for father and others fulfilled by their actual presence just as much as in the waking state.

Topic 6: Entry into Many Bodies

Doubt: In the aphorism, "Jaimini asserts the existence of body and sense-organs, since the Upaniṣad speaks of option" (IV. iv. 11), it has been stated that the liberated soul is possessed of a body. Now when on becoming threefold and so on (Ch. VII. xxvi. 2), many bodies are created, one would like to know whether these bodies are created lifeless like wooden puppets, or they are endowed with animation.

Opponent: When this is asked, one may conclude that since the mind and the soul cannot be separated,[2] and hence they remain (encaged in and) associated with a single body, the other bodies must be lifeless.

Vedāntin: Such being the assertion, the aphorist explains:

[2] The soul, though all-pervading, resides only in one mind that bears the impressions of all past actions. The new minds cannot have these impressions.

प्रदीपवदावेशस्तथा हि दर्शयति ॥१५॥

आवेश: Entry (i.e. animation occurs) प्रदीपवत् like a lamp; हि for तथा so दर्शयति (the scripture) reveals.

15. The released soul can animate different bodies like a lamp, for the scripture shows this to be so.

Just as a single lamp can appear to be many through its power of transformation (i.e. lighting up other lamps from itself), so also the man of knowledge, though one, can through his divine power become many and enter into all the bodies (to animate them).

How can this be so?

Because the scripture shows it thus that one can become many: "He remains one, he becomes threefold, fivefold," etc. (Ch. VII. xxvi. 2). This cannot be possible if the illustration of the wooden puppets be accepted, nor can it be possible if these are understood to be animated by other souls. And bodies without souls can have no movement. As for the argument that since the mind and soul cannot be separated, there is no possibility for the soul to become associated with many bodies, that creates no difficulty. For as he is possessed of inevitable will, he will create bodies equipped with minds that will act in accord with a single mind. When these are created, the same soul can also appear as their separate rulers in conformity with the differences in the limiting adjuncts. This is the process described in the Yoga scriptures as well about the assumption of many bodies by the *Yogins*.

Opponent: How again can it be admitted that a liberated man can have such divine powers as of entering into many bodies, since texts like, "then what should one know and through what? Through what should one know that owing to which all this is known?" (Br̥. IV. v. 15), "But there is not that second thing separated from it which it can know" (Br̥. IV. iii. 30), "It becomes transparent like water—one, the witness, and without a second" (Br̥. IV. iii. 32), and other texts of this kind deny the existence of particularized knowledge?

Vedāntin: Hence comes the answer of the aphorist:

स्वाप्ययसम्पत्त्योरन्यतरापेक्षमाविष्कृतं हि ॥१६॥

अन्यतर-अपेक्षम् From either of the two viewpoints स्व-अप्यय-सम्पत्त्योः of deep sleep and absolute union; हि because आविष्कृतं (this is) made clear (in the Upaniṣad).

16. (The declaration of the absence of particularized knowledge is made) from either of the two points of view, viz deep sleep and absolute union; for this is made clear in the Upaniṣad.

Svāpyaya (lit. merger in oneself) means deep sleep, as is shown in the Upaniṣadic text, "He becomes merged in his Self, and that is why they speak of him thus: 'He is deep asleep' (lit. 'He is in his Self')" (Ch. VI. viii. 1). And *sampatti* (lit. attainment of a state) means liberation, as shown by the Upaniṣadic text, "Having been Brahman, he becomes Brahman" (Bṛ. IV. iv. 6). Having in view either of these two states, it is asserted thus that there is an absence of particularized knowledge. This is said sometimes in relation to the state of deep sleep and sometimes to absolute liberation.

How is this known?

Because this is made clear by the Upaniṣad under a context dealing with that very subject in such sentences as, "The Self comes out as a separate entity from these elements and the separateness is destroyed with them. (After attaining this oneness it has no more particular consciousness)" (Bṛ. II. iv. 12), "But when to the knower of Brahman everything has become the Self" (Bṛ. II. iv. 14), "Where falling asleep he craves no desire and sees no dream" (Bṛ. IV. iii. 19, Mā. 5). But the state in which the divine powers are asserted is a different state like heaven etc., that comes as a result of the maturity of meditation on the qualified Brahman. Hence there is no defect.

Topic 7: Acquisition of Divine Powers

Doubt: Do those people, who attain union with God, while still having minds, acquire unlimited or limited divine powers, as a result of meditation on the qualified Brahman? What should be the conclusion?

Opponent: Their divine power should be without any limitation, as is obvious from the Upaniṣadic texts, "He himself gets independent sovereignty" (Tai. I. vi. 2), "All the gods carry presents to him" (Tai. I. v. 3), "They get freedom of movement in all the worlds" (Ch. VIII. i. 6, VII. xxv. 2).

Vedāntin: To this the aphorist replies:

जगद्व्यापारवर्जं प्रकरणादसन्निहितत्वाच्च ॥१७॥

(The released soul gets all the divine powers) जगत्-व्यापार-वर्जं barring the power of running this universe, (as is known) प्रकर-णात् from the context च and असन्निहितत्वात् from non-contiguity.

17. The released soul gets all the divine powers except that of running the universe (with its creation, continuance, and dissolution), as is known from the context (which deals with God) and from the non-proximity (of the individual soul).

It is proper that barring the power of creation etc. of the universe, the liberated souls should have all the other divine powers like becoming very minute etc. The power, however, of creation etc. of the universe can reasonably belong to God alone who exists eternally.

Why should it be so?

Since God forms the subject-matter of that topic, the others being far from being considered there. For the supreme Lord alone has competence for activities concerning (the creation etc. of) the universe, inasmuch as the fact of creation etc. is taught in connection with Him alone, and the word "eternal" is attributed to Him. The Upaniṣads mention that others get the divine powers of becoming atomic in size etc. as a result of search and hankering for knowing Him. Thus they are remotely placed from the activities connected with creation etc. of the universe. Moreover, from the very fact that the liberated souls are equipped with minds, they cannot have any unanimity, so that someone may at one time want the continuance of the universe and someone else its destruction; in this way they may at times be opposed to one another. If then one should seek a reconciliation by making all other wills dependent on one will only, then that reconciler will perforce arrive at the conclusion that all other wills are dependent on God's will alone.

प्रत्यक्षोपदेशादिति चेन्नाधिकारिकमण्डलस्थोक्तेः ॥१८॥

(The powers of the liberated soul are unlimited) प्रत्यक्ष-उपदेशात् owing to direct scriptural declaration इति चेत् if this be the objection, then न not so, आधिकारिक-मण्डलस्थ-उक्तेः since it is (the attainment) of Him (i.e. God) who appoints others as lords of the spheres and resides in those spheres that is spoken of.

18. If it be held (that the powers of the liberated soul are unlimited) owing to direct scriptural declaration, then it is not so, since it is (the attainment) of Him (i.e. God) who appoints others as lords of the spheres and resides in those spheres that is spoken of (in the Upaniṣad).

The statement was made earlier that from such direct teaching as "He himself gets independent sovereignty" (Tai. I. vi. 2), it is but reasonable to conclude that the liberated souls get unfettered divine powers. That has to be refuted. As to that, it is said that this is nothing damaging, "since it is God, appointing others to their respective spheres and Himself residing in those spheres that is spoken of" (in the Upaniṣad). It is declared that this bestowing of independent sovereignty is at the disposal of God who ordains others to be the rulers of particular spheres and who resides in such special abodes as the orb of the sun. It is because of this that a little later the Upaniṣad says, "He attains the lord of the mind" (Tai. I. vi. 2), which amounts to saying that he attains God who is the lord of all minds and who is ever present there as a pre-existing reality. It is in line with this that the Upaniṣad says still later, "He becomes the ruler of speech, the ruler of eyes, the ruler of ears, the ruler of knowledge" (ibid). Thus in other places also the texts are to be construed as far as possible to mean that their divine powers are attained at the behest of God alone who exists eternally.

विकारावर्ति च तथा हि स्थितिमाह ॥१९॥

च And (there is a form of the supreme Lord which) विकार-

अवर्ति does not abide in the effect, हि because आह (the Upaniṣad) has stated स्थितिम् (His) existence तथा in that manner.

19. And there is another form of the supreme Lord that does not abide in the effect, for so has the Upaniṣad declared.

And it is not a fact that the supreme Lord resides merely in the solar orb etc., within the range of effects (i.e. changeable things); He has also another aspect which is eternally free and transcendental to all changes. Thus it is that the scripture speaks of His existence in two forms in, "His divine majesty spreads that far; the whole universe of all these beings is but a quadrant of His. But *Puruṣa* (the infinite Being) is greater even than that, His three immortal quadrants being established in His own effulgence" (Ch. III. xii. 6), and other passages. It cannot be asserted that this changeless aspect is attained by those who stick to the other (qualified) aspect, for they have no desire for that. Hence it is to be understood that just as with regard to the supreme Lord, possessed of two aspects, one may continue in His qualified aspect possessing limited powers without attaining His unqualified aspect, so also one can exist in His qualified aspect with limited divine powers without acquiring unfettered powers.

दर्शयतश्चैवं प्रत्यक्षानुमाने ॥२०॥

च And प्रत्यक्ष-अनुमाने direct knowledge (i.e. Upaniṣads) and inference (i.e. Smṛti) दर्शयतः show एवं thus.

20. And both the Upaniṣadic and Smṛti texts show thus (that the supreme Light is beyond all changing things).

The Upaniṣadic and Smṛti texts also show that the supreme Light is transcendental to all changes, in such passages as, "There the sun does not shine, neither do the moon and the stars, nor do these flashes of lightning shine. How can this fire? He shining, all these shine; through His lustre are all these variously illumined" (Ka. II. ii. 15, Śv. VI. 14, Mu. II. ii. 10)? "The sun does not illuminate that, nor the moon, nor fire" (Gītā, XV. 6).

Thus it is a well-known fact that the supreme Light is beyond all changing things. This is the idea.

भोगमात्रसाम्यलिंगाच्च ॥२१॥

च Also भोग-मात्र-साम्य-लिंगात् from the indicatory mark (in the Upaniṣads) about the equality of mere experience.

21. Also from the indicatory mark in the Upaniṣads about the equality of experience alone (it is known that the liberated souls do not get unfettered powers).

Here is an additional reason to show that those who hold on to the effect (i.e. the conditioned Brahman) do not get unfettered powers; for from the indicatory marks declaring their difference as contained in the following Upaniṣadic passages, it is clear that all that they have in common with the eternally existing God is an equality of experience only: e.g. "He (i.e. Hiraṇyagarbha) said to him (when he had reached His world), 'The liquid nectar alone is enjoyed by Me, for you also it is the thing to be enjoyed'" (Kau. I. 7), "As all beings adore this Deity, so do they adore him (who knows Him)" (Bṛ. I. v. 20), "Through it he attains (gradual) identity (or equality of body) with the Deity, or lives in the same world with Him" (Bṛ. I. v. 23).

Opponent: From such a point of view the powers will have degrees and so they will be subject to termination. Hence these liberated souls will be liable to returning to this world.

Vedāntin: Hence follows the reply of the venerable teacher Bādarāyaṇa:

अनावृत्तिः शब्दादनावृत्तिः शब्दात् ॥२२॥

अनावृत्तिः There is no return शब्दात् on the authority of scriptures, अनावृत्तिः शब्दात् no return on the authority of scriptures.

22. There is no return for the released souls on the strength of the Upaniṣadic declaration; there is no return for the released souls on the strength of the Upaniṣadic declaration.

Those who proceed along the path of the gods, associated with the nerves and the rays of the sun and divided into the stages of light etc., reach the world of Brahman as described in the scripture thus: In the world of Brahman, existing in the third order of heaven (i.e. *Brahma-loka*) counted from this earth, there exist two seas called *Ara* and *Nya*, where is to be found a lake full of delightful food, where exists a banian tree exuding ambrosia, where is to be seen a city of Brahman called Aparājitā (the unconquered), and where stands a golden palace made by the Lord Himself (Ch. VIII. v. 3). That world is also spoken of variously in the *mantra* and eulogistic (*arthavāda*) portions. After reaching there, they do not return as others do from the world of Moon when deprived of their enjoyment (i.e. having run through their quota of experience).

How is this known?

From such Upaniṣadic passages as, "Going up through that nerve one gets immortality" (Ka. II. iii. 16; Ch. VIII. vi. 6), "They no more return to this world" (Bṛ. VI. ii. 15), "Those who proceed along this path of the gods do not return to this human cycle of birth and death (in Manu's creation)" (Ch. IV. xv. 5), "He reaches the world of Brahman and does not return here" (Ch. VIII. xv. 1). And even though their powers come to an end in time, it was shown how one has no return under the aphorism, "On the final dissolution of the world of the conditioned Brahman, they attain along with the Lord of that world what is higher than that conditioned Brahman" (IV. iii. 10). But non-return stands as an accomplished fact for those from whom the darkness (of ignorance) has been completely removed as a result of their full illumination and who therefore cling to that liberation as their highest goal which exists ever as an already established fact. The non-return of those who take refuge in the qualified Brahman becomes a fact only because they too have that unconditioned Brahman as their ultimate resort. The repetition of the portion, "There is no return on the strength of the Upaniṣadic declaration", shows that the scripture ends here.

INDEX TO SŪTRAS

(Figures indicate Chapter, Section, and Sūtra respectively)

अंशो नानाव्यपदेशात्० II. iii. 43
अकरणत्वाच्च न दोष० II. iv. 11
अक्षरधियां त्ववरोध:० III. iii. 33
अक्षरमम्बरान्तधृते: I. iii. 10
अग्निहोत्रादि तु० IV. i. 16
अग्न्यादिगतिश्रुतेरिति० III. i. 4
अङ्गावबद्धास्तु न० III. iii. 55
अङ्गित्वानुपपत्तेश्च II. ii. 8
अङ्गेषु यथाश्रयभाव: III. iii. 61
अचलत्वं चापेक्ष्य IV. i. 9
अणवश्च II. iv. 7
अणुश्च II. iv. 13
अतएव च नित्यत्वम् I. iii. 29
अतएव च सर्वाण्यनु IV. ii. 2
अतएव चाग्नीन्धनादि० III. iv. 25
अतएव चानन्याधिपति: IV. iv. 9
अतएव चोपमा० III. ii. 18
अतएव न देवता भूतं च I. ii. 27
अतएव प्राण: I. i. 23
अत: प्रबोधोऽस्मात् III. ii. 8
अतश्चायनेऽपि दक्षिणे IV. ii. 20
अतस्त्वितरज्ज्यायो० III. iv. 39
अतिदेशाच्च III. iii. 46
अतोऽनन्तेन तथाहि० III. ii. 26
अतोऽन्यापि ह्येकेषाम् IV. i. 17
अत्ता चराचरग्रहणात् I. ii. 9
अथातो ब्रह्मजिज्ञासा I. i. 1
अदृश्यत्वादिगुणको० I. ii. 21
अदृष्टानियमात् II. iii. 51
अधिकं तु भेदनिर्देशात् II. i. 22
अधिकोपदेशात्तु० III. iv. 8
अधिष्ठानानुपपत्तेश्च II. ii. 39
अध्ययनमात्रवत: III. iv. 12
अनभिभवं च दर्शयति III. iv. 35
अनवस्थितेरसम्भवाच्च० I. ii. 17
अनारब्धकार्ये एव० IV. i. 15
अनाविष्कुर्वन्नन्वयात् III. iv. 50
अनावृत्ति: शब्दाद्० IV. iv. 22
अनियम: सर्वासाम्० III. iii. 31
अनिष्टादिकारिणामपि० III. i. 12
अनुकृतेस्तस्य च I. iii. 22
अनुज्ञापरिहारौ देह० II. iii. 48
अनुपपत्तेस्तु न शारीर: I. ii. 3
अनुबन्धादिभ्य: प्रज्ञा० III. iii. 50
अनुष्ठेयं बादरायण:० III. iv. 19
अनुस्मृतेर्बादरि: I. ii. 30
अनुस्मृतेश्च II. ii. 25
अनेन सर्वगतत्वम्० III. ii. 37
अन्तर उपपत्ते: I. ii. 13
अन्तरा चापि तु तत्-दृष्टे: III. iv. 36
अन्तरा भूतग्रामवत्० III. iii. 35
अन्तरा विज्ञानमनसी० II. iii. 15
अन्तर्याम्यधिदैवतादिषु० I. ii. 18
अन्तवत्त्वमसर्वज्ञता वा II. ii. 41
अन्तस्तद्धर्मोपदेशात् I. i. 20
अन्त्यावस्थितेश्चोभयो० II. ii. 36
अन्यत्राभावाच्च न० II. ii. 5
अन्यथात्वं शब्दादिति० III. iii. 6
अन्यथानुमितौ च० II. ii. 9
अन्यथा भेदानुपपत्तिरिति० III. iii. 36
अन्यभावव्यावृत्तेश्च I. iii. 12
अन्याधिष्ठितेषु पूर्ववत्० III. i. 24
अन्यार्थं तु जैमिनि:० I. iv. 18
अन्यार्थश्च परामर्श: I. iii. 20
अन्वयादिति चेत् स्यात्० III. iii. 17
अपरिग्रहाच्चात्यन्तम्० II. ii. 17

अपि च सप्त	III. i. 15
अपि च स्मर्यते	I. iii. 23
” ”	II. iii. 45
” ”	III. iv. 30
” ”	III. iv. 37
अपि चैवमेके	III. ii. 13
अपि च संराधने प्रत्यक्ष०	III. ii. 24
अपीतौ तत्प्रसंगाद्०	II. i. 8
अप्रतीकालम्बनान्०	IV. iii. 15
अबाधाच्च	III. iv. 29
अभावं बादरिराह ह्येवम्	IV. iv. 10
अभिध्योपदेशाच्च	I. iv. 24
अभिमानिव्यपदेशस्तु०	II. i. 5
अभिव्यक्तेरित्याश्मरथ्यः	I. ii. 29
अभिसन्ध्यादिष्वपि चैवम्	II. iii. 52
अभ्युपगमेऽप्यर्थाभावात्	II. ii. 6
अम्बुवदग्रहणात्तु न०	III. ii. 19
अरूपवदेव हि तत्०	III. ii. 14
अर्चिरादिना तत्प्रथितेः	IV. iii. 1
अर्भकौकस्त्वात्तद्व्यपदेशात्०	I. ii. 7
अल्पश्रुतेरितिचेत्तदुक्तम्	I. iii. 21
अवस्थितिवैशेष्यादिति०	II. iii. 24
अवस्थितेरिति काशकृत्स्नः	I. iv. 22
अविभागेन दृष्टत्वात्	IV. iv. 4
अविभागो वचनात्	IV. ii. 16
अविरोधश्चन्दनवत्	II. iii. 23
अशुद्धमिति चेन्न शब्दात्	III. i. 25
अश्मादिवच्च तदनुपपत्तिः	II. i. 23
अश्रुतत्वादितिचेत्०	III. i. 6
असति प्रतिज्ञोपरोधो०	II. ii. 21
असदिति चेन्न प्रतिषेध०	II. i. 7
असद्व्यपदेशान्नेति चेन्न०	II. i. 17
असन्ततेश्चाव्यतिकरः	II. iii. 49
असम्भवस्तु सतोऽनुपपत्तेः	II. iii. 9
असार्वत्रिकी	III. iv. 10
अस्ति तु	II. iii. 2
अस्मिन्नस्य च तद्योगं शास्ति	I. i. 19
अस्यैव चोपपत्तेरेष ऊष्मा	IV. ii. 11
आकाशस्तल्लिङ्गात्	I. i. 22
आकाशे चाविशेषात्	II. ii. 24
आकाशोऽर्थान्तरत्वादि०	I. iii. 41
आचारदर्शनात्	III. iv. 3
आतिवाहिकास्तल्लिंगात्	IV. iii. 4
आत्मकृतेः परिणामात्	I. iv. 26
आत्मगृहीतिरितरवद्०	III. iii. 16
आत्मनि चैवं विचित्रा०	II. i. 28
आत्मशब्दाच्च	III. iii. 15
आत्मा प्रकरणात्	IV. iv. 3
आत्मेति तूपगच्छन्ति०	IV. i. 3
आदरादलोपः	III. iii. 40
आदित्यादिमतयश्चाङ्ग०	IV. i. 6
आध्यानाय प्रयो०	III. iii. 14
आनन्दमयोऽभ्यासात्	I. i. 12
आनन्दादयः प्रधानस्य०	III. iii. 11
आनर्थक्यमिति चेन्न०	III. i. 10
आनुमानिकमप्येकेषाम्	I. iv. 1
आपः	II. iii. 11
आप्रायणात्तत्रापि हि०	IV. i. 12
आभास एव च	II. iii. 50
आमनन्ति चैनमस्मिन्	I. ii. 32
आर्त्विज्यमित्यौडुलोमि०	III. iv. 45
आवृत्तिरसकृदुपदेशात्	IV. i. 1
आसीनः सम्भवात्	IV. i. 7
आह च तन्मात्रम्	III. ii. 16
इतरपरामर्शात्स इति०	I. iii. 18
इतरव्यपदेशाद्धिताकरण०	II. i. 21
इतरस्याप्येवमसंश्लेषः०	IV. i. 14
इतरेतरप्रत्ययत्वादिति चेन्न	II. ii. 19
इतरे त्वर्थसामान्यात्	III. iii. 13
इतरेषां चानुपलब्धेः	II. i. 2
इयदामननात्	III. iii. 34
ईक्षतिकर्मव्यपदेशात्सः	I. iii. 13
ईक्षतेर्नाशब्दम्	I. i. 5

उत्क्रमिष्यत एवंभावाद्० I. iv. 21
उत्क्रान्तिगत्यागतीनाम् II. iii. 19
उत्तराच्चेदाविर्भूतस्वरूपस्तु I. iii. 19
उत्तरोत्पादे च पूर्वनिरोधात् II. ii. 20
उत्पत्त्यसम्भवात् II. ii. 42
उदासीनानामपि चैवं सिद्धिः II. ii. 27
उपदेशभेदान्नेति चेन्न० I. i. 27
उपपत्तेश्च III. ii. 35
उपपद्यते चाप्युपलभ्यते च II. i. 36
उपपन्नस्तल्लक्षणार्थोपलब्धेः० III. iii. 30
उपपूर्वमपि त्वेके भावम्० III. iv. 42
उपमर्दं च II. iv. 16
उपलब्धिवदनियमः II. iii. 37
उपसंहारदर्शनान्नेति II. i. 24
उपसंहारोऽर्थाभेदाद्० III. iii. 5
उपस्थितेऽतस्तद्व० III. iii. 41
उपादानात् II. iii. 35
उभयथा च दोषात् II. ii. 16
उभयथा च दोषात् II. ii. 23
उभयथापि न कर्मा० II. ii. 12
उभयव्यपदेशात्त्व० III. ii. 27
उभयव्यामोहात्त० IV. iii. 5

ऊर्ध्वरेतःसु च शब्दे हि III. iv. 17

एक आत्मनः शरीरे० III. iii. 53
एतेन मातरिश्वा० II. iii. 8
एतेन योगः प्रत्युक्तः II. i. 3
एतेन शिष्टापरिग्रहा० II. i. 12
एतेन सर्वे व्याख्याता० I. iv. 28
एवं चात्माऽकात्स्न्र्यम्० II. ii. 34
एवं मुक्तिफलास्त्व्यम्० III. iv. 52
एवमप्युपन्यासात् IV. iv. 7

ऐहिकमप्यप्रस्तुत० III. iv. 51

कम्पनात् I. iii. 39
करणवच्चेन्न० II. ii. 40
कर्ता शास्त्रार्थवत्वात्० II. iii. 33
कर्मकर्तृव्यपदेशाच्च I. ii. 4
कल्पनोपदेशाच्च० I. iv. 10
कामकारेण चैके III. iv. 15
कामाच्च नानुमानापेक्षा I. i. 18
कामादीतरत्र० III. iii. 39
काम्यास्तु यथा० III. iii. 60
कारणत्वेन चाका I. iv. 14
कार्यं बादरिरस्य IV. iii. 7
कार्याख्यानादपूर्वम् III. iii. 18
कार्यात्यये तदध्यक्ष्येण० IV. iii. 10
कृतप्रयत्नापेक्षस्तु० II. iii. 42
कृतात्ययेऽनुशयवान् III. i. 8
कृत्स्नभावात्तु० III. iv. 48
कृत्स्नप्रसक्तिर्नि० II. i. 26
क्षणिकत्वाच्च II. ii. 31
क्षत्रियत्वगतेश्चो० I. iii. 35

गतिशब्दाभ्यां० I. iii. 15
गतिसामान्यात् I. i. 10
गतेरर्थवत्त्वमुभय० III. iii. 29
गुणसाधारण्य० III. iii. 64
गुणाद्वा लोकवत् II. iii. 25
गुहां प्रविष्टावा० I. ii. 11
गौणश्चेन्नात्मशब्दात् I. i. 6
गौण्यसम्भवात् II. iii. 3
,, II. iv. 2
चक्षुरादिवत्तु तत्सह० II. iv. 10
चमसवदविशेषात् I. iv. 8
चरणादिति चेन्नोपलक्षण० III. i. 9
चराचरव्यपाश्रयस्तु स्यात्० II. iii. 16
चितितन्मात्रेण तदात्मक० IV. iv. 6

छन्दत उभयाविरोधात् III. iii. 28
छन्दोभिधानान्नेति चेन्न० I. i. 25

जगद्वाचित्वात् I. iv. 16
जगद्व्यापारवर्जं प्रकरणात्० IV. iv. 17

जन्माद्यस्य यतः	I. i. 2
जीवमुख्यप्राणलिङ्गान्नेति०	I. iv. 17
जीवमुख्यप्राणलिंगान्नेति०	I. i. 31
ज्ञेयत्वावचनाच्च	I. iv. 4
ज्ञोऽत एव	II. iii. 18
ज्योतिराद्यधिष्ठानं तु०	II. iv. 14
ज्योतिरुपक्रमात्तु तथा०	I. iv. 9
ज्योतिर्दर्शनात्	I. iii. 40
ज्योतिश्चरणाभिधानात्	I. i. 24
ज्योतिषि भावाच्च	I. iii. 32
ज्योतिषैकेषामसत्यन्ने	I. iv. 13
त इन्द्रियाणि तद्व्यप०	II. iv. 17
तत्-श्रुतेः	III. iv. 4
तडितोऽधि वरुणः०	IV. iii. 3
तत्तु समन्वयात्	I. i. 4
तत्पूर्वकत्वाद्वाचः	II. iv. 4
तत्प्राक्श्रुतेश्च	II. iv. 3
तत्रापि च तद्व्यापाराद्०	III. i. 16
तथा च दर्शयति	II. iii. 27
तथाचैकवाक्यतोपबन्धात्	III. iv. 24
तथाऽन्यप्रतिषेधात्	III. ii. 36
तथा प्राणाः	II. iv. 1
तदधिगम उत्तरपूर्वाघ०	IV. i. 13
तदधीनत्वादर्थवत्	I. iv. 3
तदनन्यत्वमारम्भणशब्दादिभ्यः	II. i. 14
तदन्तरप्रतिपत्तौ रंहति०	III. i. 1
तदभावो नाडीषु०	III. ii. 7
तदभावनिर्धारणे च प्रवृत्तेः	I. iii. 37
तदभिध्यानादेव तु तल्लिङ्गात्सः	II. iii. 13
तदव्यक्तमाह हि	III. ii. 23
तदाऽपीतेः संसारव्यपदेशात्	IV. ii. 8
तदुपर्यपि बादरायणः०	I. iii. 26
तदोकोऽग्रज्वलनं तत्प्रका०	VI. ii. 17
तद्गुणसारत्वात्तु तद्व्यपदेशः०	II. iii. 29
तद्धेतुव्यपदेशाच्च	I. i. 14
तद्भूतस्य तु नातद्भावो०	III. iv. 40
तद्वतो विधानात्	III. iv. 6
तन्निर्धारणानियमस्तद्दृष्टेः०	III. iii. 42
तन्निष्ठस्य मोक्षोपदेशात्	I. i. 7
तन्मनः प्राण उत्तरात्	IV. ii. 3
तन्वभावे संध्यवदुपपत्तेः	IV. iv. 13
तर्काप्रतिष्ठानादप्यन्यथा०	II. i. 11
तस्य च नित्यत्वात्	II. iv. 16
तानि परे तथा ह्याह	IV. ii. 15
तुल्यं तु दर्शनम्	III. iv. 9
तृतीयशब्दावरोधः संशो०	III. i. 21
तेजोऽतस्तथा ह्याह	II. iii. 10
त्रयाणामेव चैवमुपन्यासः०	I. iv. 6
त्र्यात्मकत्वात्तु भुयस्त्वात्	III. i. 2
दर्शनाच्च	III. i. 20
,,	III. ii. 21
,,	III. iii. 48
,,	III. iii. 66
,,	IV. iii. 13
दर्शयतश्चैवं प्रत्यक्षानुमाने	IV. iv. 20
दर्शयति च	III. iii. 4
,,	III. iii. 22
दर्शयति चाथो अपि स्मर्यते	III. ii. 17
दहर उत्तरेभ्यः	I. iii. 14
दृश्यते तु	II. i. 6
देवादिवदपि लोके	II. i. 25
देहयोगाद्वा सोऽपि	III. ii. 6
द्युभ्वाद्यायतनं स्वशब्दात्	I. iii. 1
द्वादशाहवदुभयविधं०	IV. iv. 12
धर्मं जैमिनिरत एव	III. ii. 40
धर्मोपपत्तेश्च	I. iii. 9
धृतेश्च महिम्नोऽस्यास्मि०	I. iii. 16
ध्यानाच्च	IV. i. 8
न कर्माविभागादिति चेन्न०	II. i. 35
न च कर्तुः करणम्	II. ii. 43
न च कार्ये प्रतिपत्त्यभि०	IV. iii. 14
न च पर्यायादप्यविरोधो०	II. ii. 35

न च स्मार्तमतद्धर्माभि०	I. ii. 19
न चाधिकारिकमपि०	III. iv. 41
न तु दृष्टान्तभावात्	II. i. 9
न तृतीये तथोपलब्धेः	III. i. 18
न प्रतीके नहि सः	IV. i. 4
न प्रयोजनवत्त्वात्	II. i. 32
न भावोऽनुपलब्धेः	II. ii. 30
न भेदादिति चेन्न प्रत्येकम्०	III. ii. 12
न वक्तुरात्मोपदेशादिति०	I. i. 29
न वा तत्सहभावाश्रुतेः	III. iii. 65
न वा प्रकरणभेदात्परो०	III. iii. 7
न वायुक्रिये पृथगुपदेशात्	II. iv. 9
न वा विशेषात्	III. iii. 21
न वियदश्रुतेः	II. iii. 1
न विलक्षणत्वादस्य०	II. i. 4
न संख्योपसंग्रहादपि०	I. iv. 11
न सामान्यादप्युपलब्धे०	III. iii. 51
न स्थानतोऽपि परस्यो०	III. ii. 11
नाणुरतत्-श्रुतेरिति चेन्न०	II. iii. 21
नातिचिरेण विशेषात्	III. i. 23
नात्माश्रुतेर्नित्यत्वाच्च०	II. iii. 17
नाना शब्दादिभेदात्	III. iii. 58
नानुमानमतच्छब्दात्	I. iii. 3
नाभाव उपलब्धेः	II. ii. 28
नाविशेषात्	III. iv. 13
नासतोऽदृष्टत्वात्	II. ii. 26
नित्यमेव च भावात्	II. ii. 14
नित्योपलब्ध्यनुपलब्धि०	II. iii. 32
नियमाच्च	III. iv. 7
निर्मातारं चैके पुत्रादयश्च	III. ii. 2
निशि नेति चेन्न सम्बन्धस्य०	IV. ii. 19
नेतरोऽनुपपत्तेः	I. i. 16
नैकस्मिन्दर्शयतो हि	IV. ii. 6
नैकस्मिन्नसम्भवात्	II. ii. 33
नोपमर्देनातः	IV. ii. 10
पंचवृत्तिर्मनोवद्व्यपदिश्यते	II. iv. 12
पटवच्च	II. i. 19
पत्यादिशब्देभ्यः	I. iii. 43
पत्युरसामंजस्यात्	II. ii. 37
पयोम्बुवच्चेत्तत्रापि	II. ii. 3
परं जैमिनिर्मुख्यत्वात्	IV. iii. 12
परमतः सेतून्मानसंबंध०	III. ii. 31
परात्तु तत्-श्रुतेः	II. iii. 41
पराभिध्यानात्तु तिरोहितं०	III. ii. 5
परामर्शं जैमिनिरचोदना०	III. iv. 18
परेण च शब्दस्य ताद्विध्यं०	III. iii. 52
पारिप्लवार्था इति चेन्न०	III. iv. 23
पुंस्त्वादिवत्त्वस्य सतो०	II. iii. 31
पुरुषविद्यायामिव चेतरे०	III. iii. 24
पुरुषार्थोऽतः शब्दादिति०	III. iv. 1
पुरुषाश्मवदितिचेत्तथापि	II. ii. 7
पूर्वं तु बादरायणो हेतु०	III. ii. 41
पूर्ववद्वा	III. ii. 29
पूर्वविकल्पः प्रकरणात्०	III. iii. 45
पृथगुपदेशात्	II. iii. 28
पृथिव्यधिकाररूपशब्दा०	II. iii. 12
प्रकरणाच्च	I. ii. 10
प्रकरणात्	I. iii. 6
प्रकाशवच्चावैयर्थ्यात्	III. ii. 15
प्रकाशादिवच्चावैशेष्यं०	III. ii. 25
प्रकाशादिवन्नैवं परः	II. iii. 46
प्रकाशाश्रयवद्वा तेजस्त्वात्	III. ii. 28
प्रकृतिश्च प्रतिज्ञादृष्टान्त०	I. iv. 23
प्रकृतैतावत्त्वं हि प्रतिषे०	III. ii. 22
प्रतिज्ञासिद्धेर्लिङ्गमाश्मरथ्यः	I. iv. 20
प्रतिज्ञाहानिरव्यतिरेका०	II. iii. 6
प्रतिषेधाच्च	III. ii. 30
प्रतिषेधादिति चेन्न०	IV. ii. 12
प्रतिसंख्याप्रतिसंख्यानि०	II. ii. 22
प्रत्यक्षोपदेशादिति चेन्न०	IV. iv. 18
प्रथमेऽश्रवणादिति चेन्न०	III. i. 5
प्रदानवदेव तदुक्तम्	III. iii. 43
प्रदीपवदावेशस्तथाहि०	IV. iv. 15
प्रदेशादिति चेन्नान्तर्भावात्	II. iii. 53

प्रवृत्तेश्च II. ii. 2
प्रसिद्धेश्च I. iii. 17
प्राणगतेश्च III. i. 3
प्राणभृच्च I. iii. 4
प्राणवता शब्दात् II. iv. 15
प्राणस्तथाऽनुगमात् I. i. 28
प्राणादयो वाक्यशेषात् I. iv. 12
प्रियशिरस्त्वाद्यप्राप्ति॰ III. iii. 12

फलमत उपपत्तेः III. ii. 38

बहिस्तूभयथाऽपि॰ III. iv. 43
बुद्ध्यर्थः पादवत् III. ii. 33
ब्रह्मदृष्टिरुत्कर्षात् IV. i. 5
ब्राह्मेण जैमिनिरुप॰ IV. iv. 5

भाक्तं वा नात्मवित्त्वात्॰ III. i. 7
भावं जैमिनिर्विकल्पा॰ IV. iv. 11
भावं तु बादरायणोऽस्ति I. iii. 33
भावशब्दाच्च III. iv. 22
भावे चोपलब्धेः II. i. 15
भावे जाग्रद्वत् IV. iv. 14
भूतादिपादव्यपदेशोपपत्ते॰ I. i. 26
भूतेषु तत्-श्रुतेः IV. ii. 5
भूमासंप्रसादादध्युपदेशात् I. iii. 8
भूम्नः क्रतुवज्ज्यायस्त्वं॰ III. iii. 57
भेदव्यपदेशाच्च I. i. 17
भेदव्यपदेशाच्चान्यः I. i. 21
भेदव्यपदेशात् I. iii. 5
भेदश्रुतेः II. iv. 18
भेदान्नेति चेन्नैकस्यामपि III. iii. 2
भोक्त्रापत्तेरविभागश्चेत्॰ II. i. 13
भोगमात्रसाम्यलिङ्गाच्च IV. iv. 21
भोगेन त्वितरे क्षपयित्वा॰ IV. i. 19

मध्वादिष्वसम्भवादनधि॰ I. iii. 31
मन्त्रवर्णात् II. iii. 44
मन्त्रादिवद्वाऽविरोधः III. iii. 56
महद्दीर्घवद्वा ह्रस्वपरिम॰ II. ii. 11
महद्वच्च I. iv. 7
मांसादि भौमं यथाशब्द॰ II. iv. 21
मान्त्रवर्णिकमेव च गीयते I. i. 15
मायामात्रं तु कात्स्न्येन॰ III. ii. 3
मुक्तः प्रतिज्ञानात् IV. iv. 2
मुक्तोपसृप्यव्यपदेशात् I. iii. 2
मुग्धेऽर्धसम्पत्तिः परिशे॰ III. ii. 10
मौनवदितरेषामप्युपदशात् III. iv. 49

यत्रैकाग्रता तत्राविशेषात् IV. i. 11
यथा च तक्षोभयथा II. iii. 40
यथा च प्राणादि II. i. 20
यदेव विद्ययेति हि IV. i. 18
यावदधिकारमवस्थिति॰ III. iii. 32
यावदात्मभावित्वाच्च न॰ II. iii. 30
यावद्विकारं तु विभागो॰ II. iii. 7
युक्तेः शब्दान्तराच्च II. i. 18
योगिनः प्रति च स्मर्यते॰ IV. ii. 21
योनिश्च हि गीयते I. iv. 27
योनेः शरीरम् III. i. 27

रचनानुपपत्तेश्च नानुमानम् II. ii. 1
रश्म्यनुसारी IV. ii. 18
रूपादिमत्त्वाच्च विपर्ययो II. ii. 15
रूपोपन्यासाच्च I. ii. 23
रेतःसिग्योगोऽथ III. i. 26

लिङ्गभूयस्त्वात्तद्धि बलीयः III. iii. 44
लिङ्गाच्च IV. i. 2
लोकवत्तुलीलाकैवल्यम् II. i. 33

वदतीति चेन्न प्राज्ञो॰ I. iv. 5
वाक्यान्वयात् I. iv. 19
वाङ्मनसि दर्शनाच्छ॰ IV. ii. 1
वायुमब्दादविशेषविशेषा॰ IV. iii. 2
विकरणत्वान्नेति चेत्तदु॰ II. i. 31
विकल्पोऽविशिष्टफलत्वात् III. iii. 59
विकारावर्ति च तथाहि IV. iv. 19

विकारशब्दान्नेति चेन्न०	I. i. 13
विज्ञानादिभावे वा तद्०	II. ii. 44
विद्याकर्मणोरिति तु०	III. i. 17
विद्यैव तु निर्धारणात्	III. iii. 47
विधिर्वा धारणवत्	III. iv. 20
विपर्ययेण तु क्रमोऽत०	II. iii. 14
विप्रतिषेधाच्च	II. ii. 45
विप्रतिषेधाच्चासमंजसम्	II. ii. 10
विभागः शतवत्	III. iv. 11
विरोधः कर्मणीति चेन्न०	I. iii. 27
विवक्षितगुणोपपत्तेश्च	I. ii. 2
विशेषं च दर्शयति	IV. iii. 16
विशेषणभेदव्यपदेशाभ्यां०	I. ii. 22
विशेषणाच्च	I. ii. 12
विशेषानुग्रहश्च	III. iv. 38
विशेषितत्वाच्च	IV. iii. 8
विहारोपदेशात्	II. iii. 34
विहितत्वाच्चाश्रमकर्मापि	III. iv. 32
वृद्धिह्रासभाक्त्वमन्त०	III. ii. 20
वेधाद्यर्थभेदात्	III. iii. 25
वैद्युतेनैव ततस्तत्-श्रुतेः	IV. iii. 6
वैधर्म्याच्च न स्वप्नादिवत्	II. ii. 29
वैलक्षण्याच्च	II. iv. 19
वैशेष्यात्तु तद्वादस्तद्वादः	II. iv. 22
वैश्वानरः साधारणशब्द०	I. ii. 24
वैषम्यनैर्घृण्ये न सापेक्षत्वात्	II. i. 34
व्यतिरेकस्तद्भावाभावि०	III. iii. 54
व्यतिरेकानवस्थितेश्चान०	II. ii. 4
व्यतिरेको गन्धवत्	II. iii. 26
व्यतिहारो विंशिषन्ति०	III. iii. 37
व्यपदेशाच्च क्रियायां न०	II. iii. 36
व्याप्तेश्च समंजसम्	III. iii. 9
शक्तिविपर्ययात्	II. iii. 38
शब्द इति चेन्नातः प्रभ०	I. iii. 28
शब्दविशेषात्	I. ii. 5
शब्दश्चातोऽकामकारे	III. iv. 31
शब्दाच्च	II. iii. 4
शब्दादिभ्योऽन्तः प्रतिष्ठा०	I. ii. 26
शब्दादेव प्रमितः	I. iii. 24
शमदमाद्युपेतः स्यात्तथापि०	III. iv. 27
शारीरश्चोभयेऽपि हि०	I. ii. 20
शास्त्रदृष्ट्या तूपदेशो०	I. i. 30
शास्त्रयोनित्वात्	I. i. 3
शिष्टेश्च	III. iii. 62
शुगस्य तदनादरश्रवणात्०	I. iii. 34
शेषत्वात्पुरुषार्थवादो०	III. iv. 2
श्रवणाध्ययनार्थप्रतिषेधात्	I. iii. 38
श्रुतत्वाच्च	I. i. 11
श्रुतत्वाच्च	III. ii. 39
श्रुतेश्च	III. iv. 46
श्रुतेस्तु शब्दमूलत्वात्	II. i. 27
श्रुतोपनिषत्कगत्यभिधा०	I. ii. 16
श्रुत्यादिबलीयस्त्वाच्च न	III. iii. 49
श्रेष्ठश्च	II. iv. 8
संज्ञातश्चेत्तदुक्तमस्ति तु०	III. iii. 8
संज्ञामूर्तिक्लृप्तिस्तु त्रिवृत्०	II. iv. 20
संयमने त्वनुभूयेतरेषाम्०	III. i. 13
संस्कारपरामर्शात्तदभावा०	I. iii. 36
स एव तु कर्मानुस्मृति०	III. ii. 9
संकल्पादेव तु तत्-श्रुतेः	IV. iv. 8
सत्त्वाच्चावरस्य	II. i. 16
सन्ध्ये सृष्टिराह हि	III. ii. 1
सप्तगतेर्विशेषितत्वाच्च	II. iv. 5
समन्वारम्भणात्	III. iv. 5
समवायाभ्युपगमाच्च०	II. ii. 13
समाकर्षात्	I. iv. 15
समाध्यभावाच्च	II. iii. 39
समान एवं चाभेदात्	III. iii. 19
समाननामरूपत्वात्०	I. iii. 30
समाना चासृत्युपक्रमाद्०	IV. ii. 7
समाहारात्	III. iii. 63
समुदाय उभयहेतुके०	II. ii. 18
सम्पत्तेरिति जैमिनि०	I. ii. 31
सम्पद्याविर्भावः स्वेन०	IV. iv. 1

सम्बन्धादेवमन्यत्रापि III. iii. 20
सम्बन्धानुपपत्तेश्च II. ii. 38
सम्भृतिद्युव्याप्त्यपि चातः III. iii. 23
सम्भोगप्राप्तिरिति चेन्न I. ii. 8
सर्वत्र प्रसिद्धोपदेशात् I. ii. 1
सर्वथानुपपत्तेश्च II. ii. 32
सर्वथापि त एवोभयलिङ्गात् III. iv. 34
सर्वधर्मोपपत्तेश्च II. i. 37
सर्ववेदान्तप्रत्ययं चोदना० III. iii. 1
सर्वान्नानुमतिश्च प्राणा० III. iv. 28
सर्वापेक्षा च यज्ञादिश्रुते० III. iv. 26
सर्वाभेदादन्यत्रेमे III. iii. 10
सर्वोपेता च तद्दर्शनात् II. i. 30
सहकारित्वेन च III. iv. 33
सहकार्यन्तरविधिः पक्षेण० III. iv. 47
साक्षाच्चोभयाम्नानात् I. iv. 25
साक्षादप्यविरोधं जैमिनिः I. ii. 28
सा च प्रशासनात् I. iii. 11
साभाव्यापत्तिरुपपत्तेः III. i. 22
सामान्यात्तु III. ii. 32
सामीप्यात्तु तद्व्यपदेशः IV. iii. 9
साम्पराये तर्तव्याभावात्० III. iii. 27
सुकृतदुष्कृते एवेति तु० III. i. 11
सुखविशिष्टाभिधानादेव० I. ii. 15
सुषुप्त्युत्क्रान्त्योर्भेदेन I. iii. 42
सूक्ष्मं तु तदर्हत्वात् I. iv. 2
सूक्ष्मं प्रमाणतश्च तथोप० IV. ii. 9
सूचकश्च हि श्रुतेराचक्षते० III. ii. 4
सैव हि सत्यादयः III. iii. 38
सोऽध्यक्षे तदुपगमादिभ्यः IV. ii. 4

स्तुतयेऽनुमतिर्वा III. iv. 14
स्तुतिमात्रमुपादानादिति० III. iv. 21
स्थानविशेषात्प्रकाशादि० III. ii. 34
स्थानादिव्यपदेशाच्च I. ii. 14
स्थित्यदनाभ्यां च I. iii. 7
स्पष्टो ह्येकेषाम् IV. ii. 13
स्मरन्ति च II. iii. 47
" III. i. 14
" IV. i. 10
स्मर्यते च IV. ii. 14
स्मर्यतेऽपि च लोके III. i. 19
स्मर्यमाणमनुमानं स्यादिति I. ii. 25
स्मृतेश्च I. ii. 6
" IV. iii. 11
स्मृत्यनवकाशदोषप्रसङ्ग० II. i. 1
स्याच्चैकस्य ब्रह्मशब्दवत् II. iii. 5
स्वपक्षदोषाच्च II. i. 10
" II. i. 29
स्वशब्दोन्मानाभ्यां च II. iii. 22
स्वात्मना चोत्तरयोः II. iii. 20
स्वाध्यायस्य तथात्वेन० III. iii. 3
स्वाप्ययसम्पत्त्योरन्यतरा० IV. iv. 16
स्वाप्ययात् I. i. 9
स्वामिनः फलश्रुतेरित्यात्रेयः III. iv. 44

हस्तादयस्तु स्थितेऽतो० II. iv. 6
हानौ तूपायनशब्दशेष० III. iii. 26
हृद्यपेक्षया तु मनुष्याधि० I. iii. 25
हेयत्वावचनाच्च I. i. 8